A HISTORY OF LAW IN CANADA

Volume One

Beginnings to 1866

A History of Law in Canada: Beginnings to 1866 is the first of two volumes. It starts at a time just prior to European contact and continues to the 1860s, while volume two will start with Confederation and end at approximately 2000. The history of law includes substantive law, legal institutions, legal actors, and legal culture. The authors assume that since 1500 there have been three legal systems in Canada – the Indigenous, the French, and the English. At all times, these systems have co-existed and interacted, with the relative power and influence of each being more or less dominant in different periods.

The history of law cannot be treated in isolation, and this book examines law as a dynamic process, shaped by and affecting other histories over the long term. The law guided and was guided by economic developments, was influenced and moulded by the nature and trajectory of political ideas and institutions, and variously exacerbated or mediated intercultural exchange and conflict. These themes are apparent in this examination, and through most areas of law including land settlement and tenure, and family, commercial, constitutional, and criminal law.

(Osgoode Society for Canadian Legal History)

PHILIP GIRARD is a professor at Osgoode Hall Law School, York University.

JIM PHILLIPS is a professor in the Faculty of Law at the University of Toronto.

R. BLAKE BROWN is a professor in the Department of History and Atlantic Canada Studies at Saint Mary's University.

PATRONS OF THE SOCIETY

Blake, Cassels & Graydon LLP
Chernos, Flaherty, Svonkin LLP
Hull & Hull LLP
The Law Foundation of Ontario
McCarthy Tétrault LLP
Osler, Hoskin & Harcourt LLP
Paliare Roland Rosenberg Rothstein LLP
Torys LLP
WeirFoulds LLP

The Osgoode Society is supported by a grant from The Law Foundation of Ontario.

The Society also thanks The Law Society of Ontario for its continuing support.

A HISTORY OF LAW IN CANADA

Volume One

Beginnings to 1866

PHILIP GIRARD, JIM PHILLIPS,
AND R. BLAKE BROWN

Published for The Osgoode Society for Canadian Legal History by
University of Toronto Press
Toronto Buffalo London

utorontopress.com
osgoodesociety.ca

Reprinted in paperback 2019

ISBN 978-1-4875-0463-2 (cloth) ISBN 978-1-4875-4746-2 (paper)

Publication cataloguing information is available from Library and Archives Canada.

University of Toronto Press acknowledges the financial assistance to its publishing program of the Canada Council for the Arts and the Ontario Arts Council, an agency of the Government of Ontario.

Funded by the Government of Canada
Financé par le gouvernement du Canada

Contents

PART THREE: THE LONG EIGHTEENTH CENTURY, 1701–1815

Foreword

THE OSGOODE SOCIETY FOR CANADIAN LEGAL HISTORY

This book is a major achievement in Canadian legal history. It is the first of two volumes by three of Canada's leading legal historians, our editor-in-chief, Jim Phillips, our associate editor, Philip Girard, and R. Blake Brown, the author of two previous Osgoode Society publications. This volume presents the history of law in what is now Canada, from the first European contacts with northern North America in the very early sixteenth century to the period immediately before Confederation. The authors examine the roots of Canada's three legal traditions, Indigenous, French, and English. Indigenous people are central to the narrative throughout, including after 1815 when their influence waned as their land base was largely lost in central and eastern Canada. The book is principally a legal history, set against and integrated with the well-known major political, military, social, and economic transformations of the pre-Confederation period. Court systems, the judiciary, and the legal professions for each of the legal traditions at each stage of development are carefully considered. The areas of law covered include criminal, family, constitutional, commercial, land, succession, and civil and criminal procedure. This volume combines new research with a synthesis of the remarkable scholarship on Canadian legal history, so much of it fostered and published by the Osgoode Society over the past thirty-five years.

The purpose of the Osgoode Society for Canadian Legal History is to encourage research and writing in the history of Canadian law. The

Society, which was incorporated in 1979 and is registered as a charity, was founded at the initiative of the Honourable R. Roy McMurtry and officials of the Law Society of Upper Canada. The Society seeks to stimulate the study of Canadian legal history by supporting researchers, collecting oral histories, and publishing collections of essays and monographs. This year's books bring the total published to 107 since 1981, in all fields of legal history – the courts, the judiciary, and the legal profession, the history of crime and punishment, women and law, law and economy, the legal treatment of ethnic minorities, and famous cases and significant trials in all areas of the law.

Current directors of the Osgoode Society for Canadian Legal History are Heidi Bohaker, Bevin Brooksbank, Shantona Chaudhury, David Chernos, Linda Silver Dranoff, Michael Fenrick, Timothy Hill, Ian Hull, Trisha Jackson, Mahmud Jamal, Virginia MacLean, Waleed Malik, Rachel McMillan, Roy McMurtry, Malcolm Mercer, Caroline Mulroney, Dana Peebles, Paul Reinhardt, William Ross, Paul Schabas, Robert Sharpe, Jon Silver, Alex Smith, Lorne Sossin, Mary Stokes, and Michael Tulloch.

The annual report and information about membership may be obtained by writing to the Osgoode Society for Canadian Legal History, Osgoode Hall, 130 Queen Street West, Toronto, Ontario, M5H 2N6. Telephone: 416-947-3321. Email: amanda.campbell@osgoodesociety.ca. Website: www.osgoodesociety.ca.

Robert J. Sharpe
President

Mary Stokes
Director

Acknowledgments

When you spend as long on a book project as we have on this one you incur many and varied debts, material and personal. We should begin by thanking the institutions that funded the research – the Social Sciences and Humanities Research Council of Canada in particular, and also the Law Foundation of Ontario, Osgoode Hall Law School, the Osgoode Society for Canadian Legal History, and the University of Toronto Faculty of Law.

Individually or collectively we presented aspects of this book at a variety of fora, and always received a generous reception and stimulating and helpful critiques. We thank those in attendance at meetings of the Canadian Law and Society Association, the American Society for Legal History, the Australia/New Zealand Legal History Society, the Canadian Legal History conference at the University of Calgary, and the Osgoode Society Legal History Workshop. We also thank the law schools at Queen's, Manitoba, Victoria, and Lakehead Universities, and the Centre for Criminology and Sociolegal Studies at the University of Toronto, for invitations to speak and the attendees there for their helpful comments.

In the summer of 2016 we held a one-day workshop on a draft of this manuscript, and thank all the attendees for taking the time to read the manuscript and improve it greatly. A particular debt of thanks goes to those who travelled to Toronto for that workshop: Constance Backhouse from Ottawa, Lori Chambers from Thunder Bay, Michael Grossberg from Indiana, and Michel Morin from Montreal.

Because two of us are officers of the Osgoode Society for Canadian Legal History other people from the Society had to perform the roles normally played by the Editor-in-Chief and Associate Editor. We are indebted to Justice Robert Sharpe, President of the Society, and Dr Mary Stokes, a director, for shepherding the manuscript through the external review process with aplomb, and for reading and commenting on it themselves. Amanda Campbell, Administrator of the Osgoode Society, was instrumental in making this process run smoothly. We also are most grateful to the two anonymous reviewers for their very perceptive reading of, and detailed comments on, the manuscript.

A number of colleagues read parts of this manuscript in its final stages and provided very useful suggestions. We are grateful to Don Fyson, Douglas Hay, Jacquie Briggs, Carolyn Podruchny, Naiomi Metallic, and, especially, Jeff McNairn for their assistance and encouragement. Lori Chambers deserves special mention here, for she read not parts but the entire manuscript.

Nobody does academic publishing as well as the University of Toronto Press, and we were greatly assisted in getting this book out by Len Husband, Canadian history editor, and Wayne Herrington, associate managing editor. All of us have worked with Len and Wayne before, and again they did a superb job. The copy editor tasked by the Press with doing this book, Ian MacKenzie, was new to us, and excellent in every way. The index was prepared by Dr Justin Irwin, a student at the University of Toronto Faculty of Law.

Philip Girard would like to thank the many research assistants who worked with him on this project, but especially David Sworn, whose efforts in 2017–18 were crucial to getting the manuscript into final form. He also thanks Dalhousie University and York University for sabbatical leaves in 2010–11 and 2017–18 respectively, and the Centre for Criminology and Sociolegal Studies at the University of Toronto which so generously hosted him on both occasions. An Osgoode Hall Law School Research Fellowship in fall 2014 was also much appreciated.

Philip dedicates his contribution to Sheila Zurbrigg, without whose love and assistance this project might not have come to fruition.

Jim Phillips was also fortunate in benefiting from the work of a number of research assistants over the years, with a special thank you due to Dr Justin Irwin for his work in 2017–18. He owes a great debt to colleagues in the Canadian history community for their generous welcome and support over many years, especially Bettina Bradbury, Don Fyson, Allan Greer, and Jeff McNairn. He sees this book as in some ways the collective product of the Canadian legal history community. They know who they are and will appreciate that they are too numerous to list. One institution and two persons, however, must be named. The Osgoode Society and the legal profession of which it is a part have been the mainstay of the discipline for nearly forty years. Blaine Baker was a friend and mentor for decades to all Canadian legal historians, and his untimely death just before this book appeared was the saddest of events. Finally, Dick Risk made the discipline of Canadian legal history what it is and has always been the kindest and most generous of friends.

The biggest thank you goes to Christine Davidson, whose love and support through illness and better times were unconditional and absolute. Jim dedicates his contribution to this volume to her.

PART ONE

Introduction

1

Introduction

Law is a fundamental feature of all human societies. As a product of human imagination and experience, it is bound to vary across time and space. Settler societies such as Canada offer an example of the coexistence – sometimes cooperative, sometimes conflictual, sometimes parallel and autonomous – of two major types of legal orders: Indigenous law, on the one hand, and European law, whether common law or civil law, on the other. The principal characteristics and historical development of each of these will be discussed in the three chapters that follow, but we begin with a few introductory remarks about them. There can be a tendency to regard each of these legal orders as a hard-edged 'system' with a high degree of internal consistency and uniformity. Neither history nor current practice would support such a view. We use the labels 'Indigenous law,' 'common law,' and 'civil law' as broad umbrellas that are meant to embrace the diversity that each displays in space and time. The laws of Indigenous peoples on the Pacific coast were very different from those of the Inuit, just as the coutumes of early modern France varied from one region to another, and English law in one part of the empire might be very different from that in another part. Each of these traditions contains considerable pluralism within itself, though each may be more or less resistant to change or 'outside' influence at different historical periods. We use the terms *legal tradition* or *legal order* to capture this diversity, and generally avoid the word *system*, which is associated with a nineteenth-century, state-centred, and monistic view of what law is or should be.

Nonetheless, for analytical purposes it is necessary to outline some broad features of these traditions. We begin with Indigenous law because its very existence has been contested and problematized over time, and not just in the distant past. In 2005 during the trial phase of an important Aboriginal title case, Professor Hamar Foster was asked in cross-examination by counsel for the Canadian government whether, 'because the Tsilhqot'in were "a pre-literate culture with no central institutions of government," their rules [as to which he had testified on the basis of the documentary record] were more like elevator etiquette than law.'[1] We understand that counsel may sometimes put forth propositions in argument to which they would not subscribe outside the courtroom. Still, this position is striking in the continuity it displays with the views expressed by the earliest European observers. Some of them thought Indigenous peoples had no law at all – Samuel de Champlain offered that the 'sauvages' had 'ni foi, ni loi, ni roi' (without faith or law or authority) – because they did not see any legal institutions with which they were familiar, or any obvious forms of coercive authority. Other early observers came to realize that Indigenous societies were governed by law, called 'jurispractice' by some modern scholars, and 'chthonic law' by others, though we decline to use either of these terms.[2]

While the legal traditions of Indigenous peoples varied considerably across northern America, all shared certain basic characteristics. All relied primarily on oral transmission, featured 'self-complete non-state systems of social ordering'[3] in which community opinion played an important role in securing adherence to accepted norms, and saw law as integrated with all other aspects of life, as opposed to confined to a separate realm. On this latter point, Susan Hill states, 'The Haudenosaunee knowledge base exists as a complete entity, and the various parts of it are interconnected and dependent upon each other in order to understand the whole. When one removes a segment of it, that portion ceases to be what it is within the context of the whole.'[4] Or, as Sarah Noël Morales observes of the Hul'qumi'num (Coast Salish) legal tradition:

> *Snuw'uyulh* is a Hul'qumi'num word that means 'our way of life.' It includes our language, our governance, our culture and traditions, our sacred bathing holes; it also embraces our spirituality and all the teachings. *Snuw'uyulh* helps regulate our relationships and resolve our disputes. It contains standards and practices for judgment and decision-making. It touches on all aspects of life and cannot be separated from our relations to each other, to the natural world or to the spiritual world.[5]

The civil law and common law, meanwhile, relied more heavily on written texts (although oral transmission was by no means unimportant during the early modern period, when literacy was far from universal); saw law as an autonomous field of intellectual endeavour and social practice that could be distinguished from society itself and from religion; and thought of law in large part through various coercive institutions, whether of state, church, or other bodies, that existed to administer, apply, and interpret it. In northern North America, the civil and common law were based on a continuing dialogue between the law of the 'mother country' and the law as it was implemented, adapted, and supplemented in what were originally French and English colonies. Even after the cession of New France to Britain in 1763, and after the legislative independence of Canada pursuant to the Statute of Westminster 1931, French law and English law continued to exert a degree of persuasive influence upon the development of Canadian civil law and common law respectively. After the American Revolution, an emerging republican legal tradition also had some impact upon British North American law, in spite of differing constitutional traditions, while post-Confederation immigrants from non-British and non-French backgrounds sometimes sought to carve out a space for their own legal traditions within Canada.

Legal Pluralism in Empires and Nations

The 'story' of law in the space we call Canada is thus not a simple one. It is characterized by a search for a balance between liberty and order in a context of continuing legal pluralism. We will consider the latter first. For a long time the relationship between common law and civil law was the main focus of legal pluralism in Canada;[6] more recently it has shifted to the study of how the long-suppressed law of Indigenous peoples might be renewed and reconciled with the European-derived legal orders that came to dominate Canada in the twentieth century.[7] The coexistence of three legal traditions on the territory of modern-day Canada represents a major challenge in writing a work of this kind, and may explain why such a study has not appeared before. Modern legal history of the nation tends to take for granted the existence of a unitary national law for each nation state. Indeed, the story of the modern nation state is often one of suppressing competing legal pluralisms, whether of the regional, ethnic, religious, or Indigenous variety. Legal history has thus had some difficulty accommodating multinational heritages and, beyond the European context, the presence of Indigenous peoples and their legal traditions. The standard legal history of Australia, for example, contains only a brief chapter on Indigenous law,[8] though the comparable work for New Zealand is somewhat better in this respect.[9] Lawrence Friedman's *History of American Law* draws a bright line between European-style legal pluralism and Indigenous law. The work addresses the 'civil law fringe,' albeit briefly, but contains just four references to 'Native Americans' in the index and no discussion of Indigenous law.[10] This follows a long tradition, evident in some of the earliest English charters, in which colonial law was seen to have operated on a clean slate in North America.[11]

A moment's reflection will reveal, however, that legal pluralism is quite widespread, even in modern nation states: Spain has its *fueros* (regional customs that coexist with the Spanish *Civil Code*), India recognizes different personal laws for citizens of different faiths, and many countries from Cameroon to Sri Lanka to Vanuatu have multiple colonial heritages as well as maintaining Indigenous legal traditions.[12] The United Kingdom itself embraces two distinct legal traditions, the civil law of Scotland and the common law of England, but these are always treated in distinct literatures, as if Scotland and England were independent nation states. Unlike earlier syntheses of United States legal history, the recent *Cambridge History of Law in America* aims to overcome the anti-pluralist strain in legal history. It includes Indigenous law within its embrace, but this commitment, strongest in the first volume, fades somewhat over the next two, with Indigenous law virtually absent from volume 3 (the twentieth century). The work also has little to say about the history of civil law in America, whether in Louisiana or in the middle and far west.[13]

While legal pluralism is a significant theme in this book, it is important to register some caveats and clarifications about the notion. The first is that the common law and civil law were themselves plural legal regimes in the early modern period, and indeed thereafter.[14] While monarchs may have wished to assert the proposition that all law proceeded ultimately from their authority, both England and France bristled with special jurisdictions that were only tenuously linked to the Crown and exercised an authority based essentially on prescription and custom.[15] Indigenous confederacies such as those of the Haudenosaunee and the Huron-Wendat generally respected the individual traditions of their constituent nations.[16] It is not known whether Indigenous legal traditions borrowed from each other prior to European contact, but they did begin to draw inspiration from colonial law afterwards, as discussed in subsequent chapters. The second observation is that legal pluralism is not always benign. While modern thought tends to privilege pluralism and diversity as desirable social goals, Paul Halliday reminds us that 'plural legal spaces could be as productive of tyrannies … as they were of liberation.… Claims of liberty and other moral goods often needed the sovereign's protection in a plural legal world.'[17] For example, while the preservation of French law in Quebec was generally broadly supported by the francophone population, the seigneurs had the most invested in its continuation because of their desire to maintain the privileged position they occupied under seigneurialism.

Canada's legal pluralism has deep roots and has arguably remained a prominent feature of the juridical landscape in part because of the long history of empire in northern North America. For if nation states tend to suppress competing legal traditions in favour of a uniform national law, empires more often succeed by tolerating them, adapting to them, or building on them – albeit often reluctantly. Empires almost always had to work with a legal status quo: imperial authorities seldom had the resources to eradicate existing legal traditions, whether of a prior Indigenous or European people, or engage in the full juridical assimilation of such populations. It was often much easier to work with existing elites and power structures through techniques of indirect rule than to try to ignore them and start with a tabula rasa.[18] How far pre-existing legal traditions would survive was often determined by demographic and military factors. In seventeenth- and eighteenth-century northern North America, these factors weighed against both the French and the British as colonizers. The French needed Indigenous peoples as economic and military partners for the entire period of their rule. After 1763 the British found they could not impose a foreign legal order on a population of nearly 70,000 Canadiens, while later in the century Indigenous allies became more rather than less important, given the twin threats of revolutionary America and France. Under such conditions it was all imperial authorities could do to manage the legal diversity represented by civil law and Indigenous law, rather than ignore it or attempt to stamp it out. Later attempts to assimilate French-Canadians legally and culturally, most notably after the Union of the Canadas (1840), failed largely because their natural increase outweighed British immigration.

After 1815, however, with relative peace between the United States and the British North American colonies and dramatically increased settlement, the demographic and military balance shifted decisively against Indigenous peoples and in favour of the European populations. By the 1850s 'responsible' colonial governments could begin to contemplate a complete replacement of Indigenous legal traditions with European ones, though such efforts would not be made in earnest until after Confederation. Even then, however, lengthy traditions of accommodation did not disappear overnight, and Indigenous traditions of customary marriage, for example, whether between Indigenous persons or between Indigenous and non-Indigenous persons, continued to be recognized as legally valid by the Canadian state well into the twentieth century.[19] And whether or not Indigenous laws were recognized by the Canadian state, they continued to be transmitted and practised to varying degrees by Indigenous peoples themselves.

Another aspect of this theme of legal pluralism related to empire in northern North America is the phenomenon of the 'long goodbye.' There was no formal break between colonial and postcolonial law, as in nations with a revolutionary tradition. Neither French law (in Quebec) nor English law (outside Quebec) was seen as 'foreign law,' nor was the invocation of either in its 'daughter' jurisdiction seen as an exercise in comparative law. Long after the cession of 1763, France remained an important source of juridical inspiration for Quebec, although its appeal waxed and waned over time.[20] Quebec's version of the civil law was rooted in pre-revolutionary French law, while an English-style judicature gave rise to a common law style of decision-writing, law reporting, and legal literature. These factors, along with the French Revolution, distanced Quebec law from the French parent in the first part of the nineteenth century, although the adoption of the *Civil Code of Lower Canada* in 1866, modelled in part on the *Code Napoléon* of 1804, helped to bridge the gap in some respects. The opacity of French case law prevents it from exerting any influence over modern Quebec jurisprudence, so that any continuing influence results largely from French juristic writing and, to a lesser extent, legislation. While recognizably part of the civilian 'family,' Quebec law has long remained distinctive, and in the wake of the Quiet Revolution of the 1960s looked as much to other civilian jurisdictions in Europe and to common law Canada, as to France for inspiration.[21]

Outside Quebec (and even, on certain matters, within it) English law remained highly influential long after the achievement of responsible government in the 1840s.[22] Indeed, some have argued that the pattern of colonial mimesis became more rather than less pronounced by the end of the nineteenth century, inverting the usual 'colony to nation' narrative.[23] Owing to the legislative supremacy of the imperial Parliament down to the Statute of Westminster 1931 and the judicial supremacy of the Judicial Committee of the Privy Council down to 1949, a variety of formal mechanisms existed for the supervision of Canadian law (including Quebec law) long after the creation of the Dominion of Canada in 1867. Even aside from these mechanisms, however, English-Canadian judges and legislators long saw the English common law as the fount of all wisdom and English legislation as a desirable model for federal and provincial law.[24] While both judges and legislators could and did reject British or English models as unsuitable on occasion, loyalty to English precedent in the courts really began to wane only after the adoption of the *Canadian Charter of Rights and Freedoms* in 1982. Under such conditions, it is sometimes difficult to discern a 'Canadian common law.' With regard to statute law, however, legislatures felt free from the beginning to depart from English norms, as, for example, Nova Scotia did at its first legislative session in 1758 when it substituted partible inheritance for the English rule of primogeniture, New Brunswick in 1791 when it instituted judicial divorce, and Upper Canada when it rejected both England's bankruptcy laws and its poor law in its first reception statute in 1792. It is in the interstices of statute law that the assertion of a distinctive Canadian law can be found.

Indigenous Law in History: Methodological and Theoretical Issues

Turning to Indigenous law, we have had to face the fact that the literatures on the implantation and development of European legal traditions and institutions in Canada are much more extensive than those dealing with Indigenous law itself. Hence our work may appear lopsided in its treatment of the three pillars of Canadian law. It is revealing that amidst the thousands of pages of research commissioned by the Royal Commission on Aboriginal Peoples in the mid-1990s, documenting almost every aspect of historical and contemporary Indigenous culture and Indigenous-settler relations, there is very little on Indigenous legal traditions.[25] While a literature on the subject has emerged since that time, much of it written by Indigenous scholars, it tends to focus on the legal traditions of a particular people.[26] It is thus 'challenging to talk broadly about Indigenous legal traditions without grossly oversimplifying them or resorting to sweeping pan-Indigenous generalities.'[27] There is not at present an overall synthesis of pre-contact Indigenous laws as they existed in northern North America, and indeed some might question the value or even the soundness of such an enterprise. While we do hazard some generalizations about pre-contact Indigenous law in chapter 2, thereafter we rely on case studies of specific Indigenous communities. In particular, there is a need for more studies of how Indigenous law itself changed – for good or ill – under the impact of colonialism.[28]

There are a number of novel methodological issues that arise regarding historical research into Indigenous law. First, there is the challenge of working with a tradition that is primarily oral. Some Indigenous peoples have maintained strong oral traditions over centuries that can be accessed today through the proper protocols, but in other cases the tradition has become attenuated over time through the impact of disease, war, and colonialism.[29] Indigenous laws have sometimes been written down in modern times, but there is also resistance to written law from some who believe that oral transmission through personal contact is the best form of diffusing and internalizing legal knowledge.[30] As expressed by Mariano Aupilaarjuk, an elder from Rankin Inlet, Nunavut, 'The *maligait* [laws] of the Inuit are not on paper. They are inside people's heads and they will not disappear or be torn to pieces.... It is part of a person. It is what makes a person strong.'[31]

This emphasis on orality has led many non-Indigenous scholars to rely on the written accounts of early European explorers and missionaries, especially the French writers of the seventeenth and early eighteenth centuries, and on the work of folklorists and early anthropologists who used interviews and their observation of Indigenous people to try to reconstruct their legal and other traditions. It is clear that this work can be flawed by cultural bias, misunderstanding, or even a desire to misrepresent. However, these writings are sometimes the only contemporary documentary sources that can testify to certain practices at given points of time. We do not believe that historians should forego such sources simply because they were produced by non-Indigenous authors. Rather, historians should treat these as they do any historical record: with a critical approach, attuned to possible sources of bias, triangulated against other sources, including oral tradition, and with as much knowledge as possible about the contemporary context in which both the Indigenous and non-Indigenous actors existed.[32] Historians are accustomed to using documents from 'problematic' sources and 'reading against the grain,' an approach similar to what Indigenous scholars refer to as a 'decolonizing methodology.'[33] This is not to say that we, as non-Indigenous authors, will necessarily be cognizant of all the cultural misunderstandings or biases that European writers might display, and we stand to learn from Indigenous scholars who work with these sources.

In this regard we believe that the approach of Mohawk historian Susan Hill provides an example of how cultural sensitivity to Indigenous history can be reconciled with the document-dependent methods of Western-style historical research and writing. Speaking of the writings of travellers and missionaries, she observes that 'many of these sources need to be reinterpreted in order to get a clearer picture of what was being told, but there is a great deal of useful information to be found in these records … [provided they are] used very carefully and preferably in the context of critical analysis.'[34] In dealing with the work of the Jesuit writer Joseph-François Lafitau, for example, who spent nearly six years with the Mohawk at Kahnawake, she notes, 'His reflections differ strongly from those of his peers…. [H]is attention to culture demonstrated a greater interest and respect for Haudenosaunee beliefs than that exhibited by other Jesuits,' though he 'swung the depiction too far in the other direction' in connection with the role of women; that is, while attentive to the role of women in Haudenosaunee society, he ascribed to them an overwhelming dominance they did not actually possess.[35]

Recently some scholars have sought to supplement what can be gleaned from oral tradition with those forms of material culture used by Indigenous peoples to record important events, cultural knowledge, transactions, and the like: petroglyphs, birch bark scrolls, wampum belts, and doodems (animal drawings used as signatures on treaties). While we are accustomed to wampum belts being used to record important treaties, Lafitau observed that their use was much more general:

> The bank or public treasury consists principally of belts of [wampum] which take the place … of contracts, public acts, and, in some wise, of records, annals and registers. For, since the Indians have not the use of writing and letters, … they supply this lack by making themselves a local record by the words which they give these belts, each of which stands for a particular affair or the appurtenances of an affair which it represents throughout its existence.[36]

The Anishnaabe and other peoples of the northeast represented their teachings pictorially on birch bark scrolls that needed to be recopied periodically because the medium deteriorated.[37] It is not clear to what extent these survive, while wampum belts are often located in museums scattered around the globe and not easily accessible. Eventually these may prove to be rich sources for reconstructing Indigenous laws, but work in this field is only beginning and we have not sought to work with such sources ourselves.[38]

If the most accessible written accounts of Indigenous peoples and their customs often come from European observers rather than Indigenous participants, even these sources diminish over time. During the first century or so after contact, Europeans sought to acquire all the information they could about Indigenous peoples, in order to be able to better understand and adapt to this new environment themselves, and to facilitate trade, proselytization, and eventually domination. As the advance of settlement shunted Indigenous peoples to the margins of settler society, Europeans became less interested in Indigenous ways. By the mid-nineteenth century, in light of the widely predicted extinction of many Indigenous peoples, such interest as remained took on an antiquarian character, though the emerging discipline of anthropology also began to shed some light on Indigenous legal traditions.[39] Meanwhile, some Indigenous peoples began to write down their laws in European languages.[40] At the same time, particularly after the development of the residential school system, the usual ways of passing on knowledge inter-generationally among Indigenous peoples were seriously interrupted. Given the importance of the oral transmission of traditions in Indigenous culture, the suppression of their languages in residential schools – immortalized in Rita Joe's poem 'I Lost My Talk' – was especially disruptive.[41] Much was lost in this respect in the first half of the twentieth century, and even though the recovery and renewal of Indigenous traditions, legal and otherwise, currently proceeds in vigorous fashion, it will be a work in progress for a long time. Should another version of this book appear in ten years' time, it may look quite different from the present one in the presentation of Indigenous law.

Aside from the methodological issues regarding Indigenous law, there is a deeper theoretical, even epistemological, issue. History in the Western tradition is inevitably shaped by Western concepts of time as linear and unidirectional. The year 1787, to pick one at random, will never happen again, and events in that year cannot be 'caused' by events in 1795. Indigenous concepts of time are more circular than linear: as Deborah Doxtator observes, 'In Rotinonhsyonni history, place and space are more important than chronological time.' Moreover, 'In the creation stories, the Rotinonhsyoni world has no beginning or end, only certain repeated patterns about a particular place or centre.'[42] This is not to say that there is no development over time: Haudenosaunee history teaches that there was internecine warfare among the Five Nations for a long period of time, followed by the emergence of the Confederacy and the Great Law of Peace at a particular time, now located around the year 1450.[43] Once again Susan Hill's work is instructive: she is attentive to chronology at a general level, but is more interested in probing for the continuities that underlie the flux of events that make up the surface of the historical record. Our own approach is located within the traditions of Western historiography, which try to balance both continuity and change in its inquiry, but we believe that any history also has to be attentive to place and space, as Doxtator advises.

Liberty and Order

Our second theme, the role of law in the balance between liberty and order, is closely related to the first, given that conflict based on gender, ethnicity, race, and religion, in addition to social class, often pits liberty against order.[44] To European observers, Indigenous societies combined in an almost miraculous way a great respect for personal liberty with a high degree of internal social order and cohesiveness, though this internal order coexisted with extreme violence and sometimes enslavement, as between different Indigenous nations who were not allies. Observers often thought Canadiens and Acadiens also highly valued personal liberty, even though they lived in a relatively ordered society with few representative institutions under the French regime.[45] After the cession of 1763, the British Crown managed to serve simultaneously and somewhat mystically as a guarantor of both liberty and order for British, French, and Indigenous inhabitants. As W.L. Morton claimed, the unifying fiction of the Crown 'allowed a diversity of customs and rights under law in a way that the rational scheme and abstract principles of republican democracy did not.'[46]

The Crown held itself out as the protector of Indigenous peoples (and implicitly, of their laws and way of life) in the Royal Proclamation of 1763, while Indigenous peoples themselves insisted on the reciprocal obligations that comprised their relationship, in which the proclamation was only one element.[47] The Crown also pledged to respect the traditions of French Canadians in the *Quebec Act* of 1774. And while colonial and British authorities treated Black Loyalists very poorly in the eighteenth century, Black people were keen to proclaim their loyalty to the Crown in the nineteenth as a means of asserting their respectability and equal status.

Yet the Crown also represented order. Appointments to courts and most important offices were made by or in the name of the monarch, while criminal acts were a breach of the king's peace. The English civil war of the 1640s–1650s established that the Crown could not rule without Parliament, and after the Glorious Revolution of 1688 it was clear that the supreme authority in the British world was the king-in-Parliament. Unlike the British colonies on the Atlantic seaboard, which mostly predated the Glorious Revolution, the colonies of settlement in northern British America (that is, excluding Rupert's Land and Newfoundland) were established afterwards. Thus, while the earlier colonies, which had received charters directly from the Crown, had some claim to be independent of parliamentary authority, the later British North American colonies from Nova Scotia onwards could never make such an assertion.[48] While the Crown represented order, it did so within a tradition of constitutional monarchy wherein Parliament exercised most effective power.

This temporal distinction in turn had an impact on the legal cultures of these societies, particularly in their conceptualization of rights. The Puritan and other colonists of the early seventeenth century cherished the individual rights that they believed had been secured to them by their charters, and were quick to implement the possibilities for self-government guaranteed therein. The availability of land – once it had been purchased or wrested from the Indigenous inhabitants – helped to create a class of independent farmers among whom the patterns of deference familiar in the Old World rapidly disappeared. In such a climate it was natural to focus on the instrumental quality of law, to view it as a facilitator of individual liberty, and to resist when the Crown, and later Parliament, sought to rein in the freedoms granted under the early charters.

The seventeenth-century charters in Rupert's Land and Newfoundland, to be discussed in chapter 7, related to territories of resource extraction, not to agricultural colonies of settlement. These charters either did not contemplate settler governance at all (Rupert's Land), or where they did, a population large enough for institutions of self-government to arise did not materialize (Newfoundland). The eighteenth-century colonies of British North America, by contrast, had no charters. They were established under governors appointed via the royal prerogative, as in Nova Scotia, St John's Island, New Brunswick, and Cape Breton

Island, where the constitution was contained principally in the governor's commission and instructions; or under parliamentary legislation, as in the *Constitutional Act 1791*, which provided governments for the newly established colonies of Upper and Lower Canada. While British subjects were entitled to certain rights and liberties, among which recourse to 'British justice' (including trial by jury and habeas corpus) was paramount, these rights could be modified by the imperial Parliament or even by the local assembly once representative government was granted in a colony, subject, of course, in the latter case to disallowance in London. The legal calculus of liberty and order, then, did not have to contend with natural law–based ideas of individual rights (though these ideas were not unknown and would make an appearance during the rebellions of 1837–8).[49] For settler populations, the Crown represented, however imperfectly in practice, the harmonization of disparate interests in the name of the public welfare and good government, while for Indigenous peoples it was the link symbolizing the relationship between them and settler polities.

The balance between liberty and order also raises the issue of the impact of law on economic development. Clearly the main drivers of imperial expansion were economic gain and geopolitical dominance. Within northern North America those goals implicated fundamental questions about the relationships among law, order, liberty, and economy, both as between Europeans and Indigenous peoples and within the socially, linguistically, and ethnically diverse peoples of non-Indigenous origin. In the early centuries of European-Indigenous contact, cooperation marked the relationship, for the most part. Equal trading and military relationships, often treaty-based, coexisted with, indeed were sustained by, a balance between liberty and order on both sides.[50] Indigenous law was largely unchanged and unaffected by limited interaction with European governments and settlers. It was in part for the purpose of respecting and maintaining that mutually beneficial relationship that Britain sought through the Royal Proclamation of 1763 to limit the liberty of its own subjects in the interests of a well-ordered relationship with its Indigenous allies.

By the nineteenth century, however, the pursuit of economic gain by a rapidly expanding settler population meant that settlers' economic liberty came to prevail over order, in a process of land acquisition that would not end well for Indigenous peoples. Nothing exemplifies this as clearly as the Janus-faced response of colonial governments from the 1840s to the extra-legal acquisition of land by Europeans. When the land at issue was owned by European individuals or colonial governments, those same governments did what they could to impose a semblance of legal order, even if that involved making the settlers ultimately pay for their land rather than removing them. But when the land at issue was the remnant of what remained to Indigenous people after European acquisition, and new groups of Europeans still wanted even that, colonial governments' responses were weak and ineffective. Squatters on reserve lands were not removed; settlers' 'liberty' to acquire overrode even the limited conception of order that prescribed reserves for Indigenous people.[51]

Conflicts between liberty and order in the economic realm also affected the pursuit of economic gain by settlers themselves and by French or British capital, those conflicts being played out in both public and private law with varying impacts on different groups within the settler population. In New France, the law was rather less solicitous than in France itself of the rights of both settlers and seigneurs when they conflicted with the imperatives of settlement. Thus, where a censitaire (a farmer who held land of a seigneur) did not clear the land within a certain time, it could be reunited to the seigneur's domain, to be re-granted to someone else. Seigneurs who did not see to the clearing of their seigneuries could also see them escheated to the royal domain; neither procedure was permitted in France.[52] Likewise, legal privileges and immunities that existed with regard to land in England – for example, that it could not be seized for debt – were not considered appropriate for British North America, where land was considered a commodity and British creditors might wish to realize on it if their loans were not repaid. In some respects, then, British North America had a more purely liberal economic basis than England itself, where land was more closely tied to a set of non-economic values that stressed community and tradition.[53]

To similar effect, the economic liberty of employers was assumed to be best served by the market, in which the coercive power of the state played a minor role. Yet master and servant law, both that of New France and that imported from England and reinforced by local statutes, was heavily employer-oriented; employees' breaches of the employment contract were criminalized. What role the fact that labour was generally in short supply in British North America played in this disjuncture is unclear, but the more important fact was that while workers' liberty was constrained by the criminal sanction, that of employers was not. Debtor-creditor law, the fulcrum on which much of the economy turned, reflected yet another tension between liberty and order. Its 'backstop' was imprisonment for debt, and many saw this use of a state-supported coercive remedy as a necessary bulwark of an older conception of order based on fundamental moral certainties.[54]

Overview: Historiography and Periodization

While scholarship inserting the history of law in Canada into imperial and transnational frameworks is growing,[55] Canadian work in legal history has tended to deal with one province, one area of law, or the law of one Indigenous people, usually over a restricted time period, while works providing a synthetic overview over longer periods of time are few and far between. In particular, historical studies that address the three pillars of Canadian law together – Indigenous law, common law, and civil law – do not exist.[56] This work aims to fill this gap. The fragmentation and eclecticism of the literature on the history of law in Canada means that we cannot present a traditional historiographical overview.[57] An earlier effort to provide an overview of the history of law in Canada, *Canada's Legal Inheritances*, covers some of the same ground and has been a very useful resource. It includes only one chapter on Indigenous law and one on post-Confederation treaties, however (a reflection of the state of the literature at the time), and is essentially a collection of thematic essays oriented around particular areas of law.[58] While we do not present this work as a 'canon,' we hope that it will help to focus future work in the field by Canadianists and comparative legal historians. We also hope that it will serve as an entry point for anyone – scholars, journalists, legal professionals, members of the public – wishing to know more about the history of law in northern North America. If this book provokes research in legal history of any kind, nothing would please us more.

We are three white males, one of French settler background, one of British settler background, and one a British immigrant. Two of us are close to retirement while one is in mid-career, and all of us are materially comfortable. We recognize that we do not represent, in our own persons, the variety of people who engaged with the law – as creators, interpreters, litigants, and victims – who will appear in the pages to come. Yet that is not unusual in historical writing, which always involves an imaginative leap of some kind into the lives of people and events far removed from the writer's own subjective and temporal experience. There is a great deal of excellent writing on the experience of women, Indigenous peoples, racial, religious and ethnic minorities, workers, and the dispossessed with the law, which will be referred to throughout this work. In this and much else, we stand on the shoulders of those who have come before us.

This work builds on four bodies of literature. The first is an older Canadian literature oriented to consensus and nation-building, one that focused on the development of British-style political and legal institutions, the establishment of the legal professions and the superior court judiciary, the emergence of Canadian constitutional autonomy and the distinctiveness of Quebec civil law.[59] It had little to say about Indigenous law or the place of Indigenous peoples in constitutional arrangements, other than pursuant to the Royal Proclamation 1763. While we may not share the somewhat uncritical and celebratory attitudes of some of these authors, they brought to light a good deal of original research in their chosen areas that can be repurposed for modern use. The second body of scholarship is the 'new legal history' literature that has emerged since the 1960s in Canada. Influenced both by legal realism and critical legal studies in the United States and by the turn to social history in both Europe and America, this literature is more inclined to focus on conflict rather than consensus, to explore the experience of subordinated groups with the law, and to employ archival resources beyond the official correspondence of imperial and colonial officials. Especially since the foundation of the Osgoode Society for Canadian Legal History in 1979, a steady stream of books, now numbering well over one hundred, has appeared, in addition to hundreds of articles; most of this literature could be classified under the rubric of the new legal history.[60] Third, we rely on the international legal history literature, European, American, and Australasian, that has emerged since the 1960s. The *Cambridge History of Law in America* has been an inspiration, as has the *Oxford History of the Laws of England*, currently in progress. In addition, there is now a large literature dealing with the legal dimensions of the British and French Empires, their relationship with Indigenous peoples, and the role of law in settler societies.[61] We cannot claim to be familiar with all of this literature, but we have consulted it where it seemed likely to provide assistance. Finally, we draw on the newer work on Indigenous law referred to earlier, which, while not always framed as historical scholarship, intersects with our project in various ways.

The title of this work reflects its pluralist commitments. We chose to call it *A History of Law in Canada* rather than *A History of Canadian*

Law because the existence of law and legal orders, both Indigenous and European, in the northern part of the continent long predates the creation of the nation state of Canada itself. Moreover, some Indigenous peoples in Canada today would not describe their law as being 'Canadian law.' In this respect our title echoes that of the *Cambridge History of Law in America*, which directs attention to the history of legal traditions that have existed in the geographic space now occupied by the United States, rather than exclusively to the law produced by the nation state known as the United States of America and its constituent units.

Our periodization too reflects an attempt to organize the work in a way that incorporates important transitions in all three legal traditions. Thus it is not a conventional one for Canadian historians, any more than that adopted in the *Cambridge History of Law in America*, which is ambivalent about independence and does not use the Civil War as a major turning point in its structure, is for American historians.[62] Likewise, we do not use 1763 as a turning point, even though it clearly marks important events in our narrative. In volume 1 we use 1701, 1815, and the 1860s as turning points, while volume 2 will use 1914 and 1982 for reasons to be elaborated there.

The next three chapters in this part contain an overview of the laws of Indigenous peoples as they existed in northern North America at the time of contact, and brief sketches of the development of pre-revolutionary French law and of English law down to the time of Blackstone's *Commentaries* in the 1760s. Part 2 then begins at the moment when Indigenous and European peoples and their respective legal orders were beginning to come into contact with one another. Leaving aside the Norse and their early encounters with the Inuit and other Indigenous peoples, these contacts began in the fifteenth century, continued sporadically in the sixteenth, and increased dramatically in the seventeenth, particularly in Mi'kmaki and the St Lawrence valley/ Great Lakes region. The legal institutions of provincial France and a body of law based on the Custom of Paris and Roman law had been implanted in the St Lawrence colony by the end of the seventeenth century (though less solidly in Acadie), largely because the French had adapted their law so as to reduce potential points of friction with Indigenous law. Even when Indigenous people killed settlers, for example, the French accepted reparations and almost never demanded that the perpetrators undergo a trial pursuant to French criminal law. For the most part the French treated Indigenous peoples as allies rather than subjects. Even in the settlements of domiciliés (Indigenous converts to

Christianity) in the St Lawrence valley, the latter chose which aspects of French law they would recognize and deploy for their own purposes, and otherwise followed their own ways. The French regarded this situation as a temporary anomaly and fervently hoped that over the long term they would be able to apply their law fully to Indigenous peoples, but this dream was never realized while New France existed.

While contacts between the English and Indigenous peoples were extensive on the Atlantic seaboard south of the Bay of Fundy in the seventeenth century, the history of the common law in the northern reaches of British America had barely begun. Within the vast watershed of Hudson Bay, inhabited by many Indigenous peoples but claimed by British monarchs as Rupert's Land via the Hudson's Bay Company charter of 1670, by the 1690s only a few Company outposts existed where a form of English law operated among Europeans, and all but one of these had been captured by the French by 1697; otherwise Indigenous law governed. In Newfoundland, the withdrawal of the Beothuk from contact with Europeans after about 1620 meant little interaction between the two groups until considerably later. Meanwhile, the English authorities were highly ambivalent about implanting the common law on an island they preferred to treat as a seasonal fishing station, and introduced only the barest legal infrastructure by means of a variety of charters and orders culminating in King William's Act of 1699.

The Great Peace of Montreal of 1701 marks a key turning point for both Indigenous law and the civil law. This treaty finally put an end to the long rivalry of the French and the Haudenosaunee, but in the context of a much larger settlement adhered to by representatives of some thirty-eight Indigenous peoples stretching from the western Great Lakes to the Atlantic. From the Indigenous point of view it seemed to represent a mutual acceptance of the way of life of the other, including their laws, such that each would continue to develop their respective societies in their own way, as equals. In this way it was similar to the 'two-row wampum' concept that the Haudenosaunee Confederacy used in their relations with the English further south, whereby the societies were seen as developing in parallel and respecting but not interfering with each other. Indeed, just prior to the Great Peace of Montreal, the Confederacy entered into the Treaty of Nanfan with the governor of New York, wherein they renewed the Covenant Chain relationship they had earlier established with the British after the fall of New Netherland in 1664. While the Haudenosaunee who entered the treaty were resident in what would later become the United States, the later re-establishment of the Confederacy at Grand River in Upper Canada after the American Revolution meant that the Covenant Chain relationship travelled with them. The summer of 1701 thus marked a grand constitutional settlement where the Indigenous peoples of northeastern North America agreed to share their space with the British and French as kin, provided each party followed their own laws and respected those of the other.

In the short term this arrangement was beneficial for both parties. The Indigenous peoples had suffered much from war and disease in the later seventeenth century and needed a period of peace and stability to recover their strength. Over the longer term, however, the advantages redounded more to the benefit of the Europeans. Take the French, for example. The civil law and its institutions, created for what was still a very small European population in 1701, would become ever more deeply implanted over the ensuing six decades, providing the legal infrastructure for a settler society that would prove less accommodating to Indigenous interests than had been the case in the seventeenth century. The alliance of the Great Peace provided crucial breathing space for the French society of the St Lawrence valley, increasingly menaced by the expanding English colonies on the eastern seaboard, although the treaty did not require the Indigenous parties to support the French militarily. They would continue to make their own decisions, supporting some French sorties against New England during Queen Anne's War after 1702, for example, but not coming to the aid of Port-Royal when it was besieged and captured by British and New England troops in 1710.[63] And Indigenous inhabitants of the mission villages in Canada continued to carry on the fur trade with English merchants at Albany for decades prior to 1760, when it was prohibited by the law of Canada and, at times, by the law of New York as well.[64]

The long eighteenth century, the subject of part 3, largely represented continuity for the civil law, change for the common law, and mixed signals for Indigenous law. As will be discussed in more detail in the relevant chapter, the impact on the civil law of the cession of Canada to the British in 1763 was much less marked than was traditionally thought. It is now clear that the day-to-day legal affairs of the Canadien population continued virtually unaffected by the high politics of the day, taken in hand by the notaries who served as the crucial link of continuity over the potential rupture of the conquest. To be sure, English criminal law was introduced, but even there, with regard to both personnel and administration of the law there was a much less dramatic shift than has traditionally been portrayed. The creation of an English-style judicature, however, accompanied by English-inspired procedural reforms, the introduction of the profession of advocate, and the creation of an elected assembly undoubtedly set Quebec on the path of becoming a hybrid or 'mixed' jurisdiction.

The century was also notable for the definitive introduction of the common law and of representative institutions of government. While the British at first took little interest in peninsular Nova Scotia, acquired from the French by the Treaty of Utrecht in 1713, with the founding of Halifax in 1749 English law and its institutions were introduced in full force, crowned with the importation of a chief justice for the newly created Supreme Court in 1754. The deportation of most of the Acadians in 1755–8 and the fall of Louisbourg in 1758, after which its inhabitants were repatriated to France, spelled the end of Acadian law in the Maritimes, at least in a formal sense. Meanwhile, the creation of an elected assembly in 1758, the migration soon after of some 8,000 settlers ('planters') from the Atlantic seaboard colonies to take up the lands forfeited by the deported Acadians, and the arrival of 30,000 Loyalists in 1783–5, ensured that the common law would become dominant in a jurisdiction where few Acadians remained. Lands subject to Mi'kmaw law and governance diminished rapidly as colonists exploited farms, fish, forest, and furs, in spite of treaties reached in 1726 and 1760–1 that purported to preserve zones of Mi'kmaw autonomy. The Treaty of Paris 1763 declared the common law to apply in St John's Island, while the Loyalist colonies of New Brunswick (1784) and Upper Canada (1791) followed suit in due course. Even Newfoundland, long the orphan child of the empire, legally speaking, secured its own Supreme Court in 1792.

The situation with regard to Indigenous law in the eighteenth century was mixed. In the far north, in Rupert's Land and in the lands west of the Rocky Mountains, Indigenous law continued as the principal source of law, even as the fur trade led to increasing contacts between Indigenous inhabitants and European traders across the plains, and on the west coast from the 1790s. In some respects the legal position of Indigenous peoples improved, as the Royal Proclamation of 1763 aimed to ensure that consent governed transactions involving Indigenous lands, and contained an implicit promise that Indigenous laws would continue in full vigour on unceded lands. Traditional governance was established on the southern Ontario lands granted to the Six Nations after the American Revolution, in return for their support during the war. But outside Upper Canada, where some semblance of a treaty process for land surrenders was followed, the boundary between 'ceded' and 'unceded' lands remained blurry, resulting in the constant erosion of the Indigenous land base. Colonial governments still valued Indigenous peoples as military allies, however, and relied heavily on them during the War of 1812. The conclusion of that war represented a watershed for Indigenous peoples in British North America. Along with the post-war decline in their political and military value went the rapid advance of settler society in both the English and French portions of British North America. In the west, the Red River colony, established in 1811, represented the first beachhead of settler society on the Great Plains, heralding the enormous changes that would occur later in the century. The growth of Red River also spurred the development of the Métis people, although this identity did not emerge clearly for some decades afterwards.[65]

The period between 1815 and the 1860s, the subject of part 4, represented the consolidation and entrenchment of settler society, legally speaking, a process that began before the achievement of responsible government but was much accelerated by it. Where justices of the peace had often been the principal legal actors in the countryside prior to 1815, thereafter lawyers spread out from colonial capitals to the numerous small towns springing up in the Canadas and the Maritimes, though less so in Newfoundland. The number and frequency of circuits by superior court judges increased dramatically to serve growing hinterland populations, though not in Quebec, where locally based superior court judges became the rule. Court structures began to take on a more familiar organization, with the emergence of modern courts of appeal in the Canadas, composed only of professional judges, being a particularly noteworthy feature.[66]

Yet while pressure on the Indigenous land base increased with the rapid advance of settlement, illustrated especially by the Robinson-Huron and Robinson-Superior Treaties of 1850, colonial governments did not seek to *legislate* major changes in Indigenous societies prior to mid-century. It was only after the achievement of responsible government, and as the imperial government sought to divest itself of responsibility for Indigenous peoples in British North America shortly thereafter, that colonial governments began to legislate aggressively with a view to transforming Indigenous societies along western lines. The preamble to the *Gradual Civilization Act* of 1857, for example, observed that it was

> desirable to encourage the progress of Civilization among the Indian Tribes in this Province, and the gradual removal of all legal distinctions

> between them and Her Majesty's other Canadian Subjects, and to facilitate the acquisition of property and of the rights accompanying it, by such Individual Members of the said Tribes as shall be found to desire such encouragement and to have deserved it.[67]

Such an approach had little patience with Indigenous law, viewing it as a badge of social inferiority and an impediment to the assimilation of native peoples to the superior European way of life.

The responsible government period also witnessed major changes in Quebec law, in particular the abolition of seigneurial tenure in 1854 and the passage of the *Civil Code of Lower Canada* in 1866 and the companion *Code of Civil Procedure* in 1867. Both were attempts to realign Quebec law with the needs of an industrializing and capitalist society, but the goals of the *Civil Code* went beyond the merely economic. The code sought to proclaim Lower Canada's adherence to the modern post-revolutionary version of the civil law, one based on a civil code as a social constitution, even as it incorporated a number of provisions based on English law and on Lower Canada's own distinctive history and experience. While later generations in Quebec would come to see the *Civil Code* as a bastion of French-Canadian culture and values, it was not drafted as a monument to legal purity but rather drew from both civil and common law traditions. It did not, however, afford any recognition to Indigenous law, in spite of contemporary developments in case law that were much more receptive to legal pluralism outside the settler world. Thus, the famous decision of the Quebec superior court in *Connolly v Woolrich* (1867) upheld a marriage between a Montreal trader and a Cree woman in the Athabaska country entered into according to the customary law of the Cree, in a lengthy judgment canvassing authorities from a dazzling array of jurisdictions and legal traditions from biblical times to the present.[68]

Largely free to chart their own destinies after the achievement of responsible government, the provinces of British North America were not slow to seize the opportunity, and legislation was the primary means by which they sought to do so. Codification in the English provinces did not reach the level of sophistication of the *Civil Code of Lower Canada*, but the revised statutes of Nova Scotia (1851) and New Brunswick (1854) and various consolidations of the Province of Canada statutes in 1859 and 1861 were code-like in their organization and aimed at a simple and rational presentation of the law that would be accessible to ordinary citizens. As they entered Confederation, the formal legal orders of the eastern British

North American provinces had matured and would provide models for the emerging western provinces, while those of most Indigenous peoples were under increasing stress. That is one reason why we end this volume with a 'soft boundary' in the 1860s and not with Confederation itself. The very 'maturity' of these colonial states, however, reflected decades, in some cases centuries, of efforts to normalize and legitimate the presence of settler polities on the lands of Indigenous peoples.

Confederation created another layer of government, but it had little to do with the longer-term processes examined here. It did not build colonial court structures, reform the law and practice of colonial criminal justice, see the increasing acceptance of the corporate form or the rejection of old forms of insolvency law based on imprisonment of the debtor, deal with problems of squatting and imperfect land titles, or influence many other aspects of legal development. Confederation was as much a beginning as an end. It was the beginning for a new political entity, made possible the creation of a national supreme court in 1875 (itself still subject to further appeal to the Judicial Committee of the Privy Council), and shifted some powers from colonial legislatures, such as those relating to the content, though not the administration, of criminal law. But while post-Confederation developments built on the experience of the previous fifty years, 1867 in itself brought few substantive changes to laws, legal institutions, and legal practices. In perhaps only one area did Confederation bring about large legal change, and that was in the position of Indigenous peoples. Yet even the *Indian Act* built, to some extent, on developments that had started in the Province of Canada in the late 1850s and 1860s.

2

Roots: Indigenous Legal Traditions

Each of the three legal traditions in what is now Canada has a long genealogy. That of Indigenous law is part of the original peopling of the Americas. Civil law and common law are imported traditions with a long history in Europe, some 2,500 years for the former and 1,500 years for the latter. From the time of their continuous contact in North America about 1500 CE (that is, ignoring earlier contacts with the Norse), these traditions have interacted in a variety of ways. Some have been positive, some negative, but each tradition has always sought to retain its own autonomy and integrity, even if its adherents decided, or were forced, to adopt new ways.[1] The purpose of this and the following two chapters is to provide an overview of the development and principal characteristics of each of these traditions before they met each other in North America. Later chapters will refer back to a variety of institutions, concepts, and practices that are introduced here.

Indigenous Legal Traditions: Basic Features

Indigenous peoples have inhabited the Americas for at least fifteen thousand years, and possibly much longer.[2] Approaching the history of the Americas from the Indigenous point of view means not only extending one's temporal horizon, but also reversing one's spatial orientation. Whereas Europeans arrived via the Atlantic and gradually spread west, the dominant view is that Indigenous peoples arrived from the northwest and spread south and east. For millennia, the Pacific coast of North and South America was the most highly populated and wealthiest region of the Americas. What is believed to be the oldest human habitation in North America was found at Hatzic (Mission), British Columbia, where remains of an ancient dwelling built by the ancestors of the Sto:lo people have been dated to some 6,000 years ago; carbon dating of other material at the site shows human activity up to 9,000 years ago.[3]

Indigenous law is thus much older than either the common law or the civil law. As Patrick Glenn observes, it is 'the oldest of traditions; its chain of *traditio* is as long as the history of humanity.'[4] Human development over such long periods of time is bound to lead to diversity: by the sixteenth century the Americas as a whole had some 2,000 different societies, speaking 2,200 languages. At that time some fifty-eight founding peoples occupied northern North America, all of whom had ways of life governed by their respective legal traditions.[5] In spite of this diversity, three basic features united the legal traditions of these peoples. The first – and this is perhaps the most fundamental difference from modern European law – is simply that law was mixed in with everything else, or as Glenn states more colourfully: 'Law is thus not command, or decision, and can be found only in the bran-tub of information which guides all forms of action' in Indigenous societies.[6] Richard Overstall makes similar observations about the Gitxsan legal order: 'It is beneath the surface, felt as much as known, and uncomfortable with abstract questions.'[7] Law in the Indigenous world view was not an autonomous or semi-autonomous realm of human endeavour or thought, separate from religion, hunting, agriculture, food preparation, family life, or entertainment. This may lead one to question the very existence of Indigenous law, but such scepticism presupposes a non-Indigenous point of view wherein law is very much a matter of self-conscious perception and action.

Even early European observers, who at first doubted whether Indigenous peoples were governed by law, came to accept that the regularity and predictability of their behaviour in a wide variety of social contexts could indeed be viewed as a type of law.[8] Or, as John Borrows has stated, 'Indigenous legal traditions are best viewed through the lens of customary law.'[9] Joseph-François Lafitau, a Jesuit priest who lived among the Mohawk at Kahnawake for nearly six years in the early eighteenth century (1712–17), strongly criticized the contrary view held by some of his contemporaries: 'I have seen, with extreme distress, … that [most of] those who have written of the customs of primitive peoples, have depicted them to us as ... people without law, social control or any form of government; in a word, as people who have scarcely anything except the appearance of men.'[10] By contrast, he praised the way in which individual liberty and social order were balanced in Mohawk society, where 'there is found a mutual adaptation of chiefs and members of society and a hierarchy such as could be desired in the best regulated state.'[11] For a Frenchman of the eighteenth century this was the highest possible compliment he could bestow, and it would not be wrong to discern in it a veiled critique of his own society, one made much more explicitly by the Baron de Lahontan in his writings.[12]

The second major characteristic of Indigenous legal traditions is that they assumed and sought to perpetuate a sustainable relationship between human beings and the natural world. The need of Indigenous peoples to understand the earth – its animal and vegetable life, minerals, terrain, waters, and climate – was fundamental to their survival. As Susan Hill observes, the Mohawk word for *earth* translates as 'She-to-us-mother provides-[for our]-needs,' and this name, 'along with the history of how that name came into being, explains Haudenosaunee land philosophy. Everything a person could possibly need to know is there.'[13] There had to be a mechanism to transmit this knowledge once obtained. And each society had to be sufficiently organized to draw on the labour of its members to exploit the earth's resources sustainably and assure the group's continuation. The first principle of this social organization was the maintenance of harmony and social cohesion. This goal is not necessarily inconsistent with a ranked society, provided all members 'know their place' and accept it, but it tends to favour more inclusive, participatory forms of governance, as noted by Lafitau among the Mohawk. Without the effective transmission of ecological and sociocultural knowledge and a high degree of social cohesion, the fine line between survival and extinction, especially in the challenging climatic environments of northern North America, could easily be crossed. And what was true for intra-group relations also extended to neighbouring polities at times. In Haudenosaunee tradition, it was the need to overcome constant warring among various nations of the north-east that led to the Great Law of Peace and the emergence of the Five Nations Confederacy as the vehicle for maintaining that peace.[14] Similarly, the Huron-Wendat Confederacy appeared in the Georgian Bay region, and the Wabanaki Confederacy on the East Coast.

Orality is the third important feature of Indigenous legal traditions. While artefacts such as wampum belts and birchbark scrolls were used to record important events and agreements, and some features of the natural environment can be 'read' as law, most Indigenous legal tradition has been transmitted orally and is reliant on human memory.[15] Much flows from this. As it is easier to remember stories than lists of abstract rules, 'law' is often contained in origin stories of a people or found interstitially in the oral histories of a particular lineage, such as the adaawk of Gitxsan clans. According to Richard Overstall, 'a lineage's adaawk describe[s] its ancient migrations, its encounters with the power in the land, its defence of its territories, and major events in its history, such as natural disasters, epidemics, war, meeting new peoples, the establishment of trade alliances, and major shifts in political power.'[16]

Oratory was cultivated to a high degree in Indigenous society. Once European observers had learned the local languages, they were much impressed with the rhetorical abilities of Indigenous speakers. Charles Huault de Montmagny, an early governor of New France, 'compared the orations of Montagnais [Innu] speakers at a council meeting to those of Roman senators in the Forum.'[17] Lafitau made similar observations but also noted that only a few skilled orators, who were selected purely on merit with no reference to lineage, could be found in any given community. Their role was to communicate decisions made by the council to the entire community, thus 'bearing the news authoritatively in the name of the entire village and nation.'[18] Oratory was also important in other contexts, such as the giving of presents to the family of an injured or murdered person in atonement for the act causing such harm; entire days might be spent in the proffering of these gifts and the explanation of how they were meant to assuage the harm done.[19]

Among the Inuit, oratory was also highly prized and formed the basis of a highly popular form of dispute resolution: the song duel. For all interpersonal disputes except murder, the parties could be obliged to settle it by this means. It involved each party making up a satirical song loosely based on the incident in question in which the foibles of the adversary were stressed. The community decided the winner on the basis of whose song was thought to be more entertaining and effective in skewering the opponent, after which the parties were expected to make up. The ritual was not meant to be a determination of 'rights' but a restorative practice that released tension and re-established a communal equilibrium.[20]

The dominance of orality and the governance structure of most Indigenous societies also had an impact on modes of dispute resolution, with regard to both broad policy questions and more individualized conflicts. All important matters had to be discussed openly, though after consultation some final council deliberations could occur in secret, at least among the Mohawk.[21] Councils of elders consulted broadly before making decisions, and their authority usually rested on understanding 'public opinion,' while that of chiefs rested on the power of persuasion. Lafitau observed,

> In general, we may say that they are more patient than we in examining all the consequences and results of a matter. They listen to one another more quietly, show more deference and courtesy than we toward people who express opinions opposed to theirs, not knowing what it is to cut a speaker off short, still less to dispute heatedly: they have more coolness, less passion, at least to all appearances, and bear themselves with more zeal for the public welfare.[22]

Even if there is some idealization in this description, such processes would have operated to prevent many disputes from arising by providing opportunities for people to have input into important decisions that needed to be made.[23] In some Indigenous societies, notably the Haudenosaunee, women formed councils of matriarchs who met separately and provided their opinions to elders on important questions.[24]

Indigenous Law: Process and Content

Given the existence of nearly sixty First Nations in northern North America when European contact intensified around 1500, it is not possible to catalogue all the variations that existed among different legal traditions. No single tradition can be held up as perfectly representative of all the others, but in this account Mohawk law will be used as illustrative, supplemented by examples drawn from other Indigenous legal traditions. Although groups of Mohawk migrated from their heartland in what is now upper New York state to the Montreal area in the seventeenth century and, along with members of other nations of the Confederacy, to what became southern Ontario as Loyalists in the eighteenth, they maintained their traditions largely intact in spite of these moves. Also the conversion of many of them to Christianity, Catholicism at Kahnawake and Protestantism on the Grand River, does not seem to have had a significant impact on their legal traditions. What the anthropologist Lewis Morgan described as Haudenosaunee practices in mid-nineteenth-century New York state were almost identical to those described at Kahnawake by Joseph-François Lafitau (whose work he did not know) nearly 150 years earlier.[25]

Of all the early commentators, Lafitau (1681–1746) was the most attuned to issues of Indigenous law and practice. His accounts have been relied upon by both Indigenous and non-Indigenous scholars, though always with care and critical distance. He was taught the Mohawk language by Jesuits who had mastered it, seems to have been trusted by the people of Kahnawake, and was familiar with existing accounts of the Indigenous peoples of North America. He lived among the Mohawk for a period long enough to provide some authority to his observations and was present when the entire settlement moved in 1716 for the third time to the site it occupies today. We should not assume that he, or any other European observer, necessarily had unfettered access to knowledge of all the laws governing the Kahnawake community. While he observed a good deal, Indigenous knowledge-keepers did not always wish to share everything about themselves with outsiders and may have held back information on certain matters. And it is possible too that certain matters were 'hiding in plain sight' – that he did not always understand the significance of the acts he witnessed.

Although the Mohawk were nominally Catholic, Lafitau's account displayed a lack of interest in any such influence. Often referred to as the 'father of modern anthropology,' he tried to shed his own cultural presuppositions in order to undertake a scientific study of Indigenous customs. He might have been surprised by the role of women in public life, for example, but he reported on the topic at length and without criticism, though he may have gone to the opposite extreme of overestimating women's influence.[26] Nor did he offer adverse comment when noting that elderly people who were 'helpless' might be dispatched in order to husband community resources, though he must have found the practice shocking. While he separated 'religion' from 'law' and thus downplayed the infusion of spiritual and supernatural beliefs in Indigenous law, his behavioural approach yielded an early form of comparative legal ethnography.

Lafitau was less interested in the process of dispute resolution in Indigenous society than the substance of their traditions. He noted that the council of elders could decide disputes between individuals or family groupings after hearing the parties, or delegate resolution to an arbitrator, but he and other Europeans were struck by the infrequency of interpersonal disputes:

> Their little disputes are soon settled by arbitration but, I must do them the justice of saying that their quarrels are rare. When they do occur, they come to an end shortly, [being settled] either by reason, to which they yield as soon as it is made clear to them, or through deference to the per-

> sons who intervene to settle them; or, they even prefer to yield their rights willingly rather than to be obstinate at the wrong time, especially when they have to do with people who wish to win through sheer arrogance.[27]

In part, the implied contrast between European litigiousness and Indigenous harmony depended on very different distributions of property and resources in these two societies. Individual property, a money economy, and a highly unequal distribution of resources all contributed to a very disputatious and turbulent society in early modern Europe, while more egalitarian (if not always entirely 'communal') access to resources meant that such disputes were far less likely in Indigenous settings.[28] A strong emphasis on the need for social cohesion may at times have discouraged individuals from bringing forward legitimate grievances, as hinted at by Lafitau in the above passage. It is possible that such repressed resentment may have occasionally resulted in private violence where other recourses seemed unavailable. But similar consequences could also ensue in Europe from imperfect access to justice, whether from financial or other causes.

Living in societies where 'law' and 'way of life' were inseparable, Indigenous peoples themselves did not distinguish between different areas of 'substantive law.' Lafitau, however, keen to explain Indigenous ways to his European audience in terms they would understand, observed that

> the affairs treated in the Council of the Indians are of almost the same nature as those which our jurisprudence and politics in Europe comprise. There are purely civil matters, regulatory and criminal, and other matters which are properly affairs of state, such as making war or peace, sending or receiving ambassadors, contracting new alliances or strengthening old ones.[29]

For Lafitau, Indigenous law could be described using the European categories of private law, public law (regulatory and criminal law), and international law. His discussion of the political system of the Mohawk could be seen as a study of constitutional law, though he did not use the term. The 'purely civil matters' discussed by Lafitau were primarily those related to marriage and the family; he was the first European to work out, from actual observation, the rules of Haudenosaunee kinship and exogamy, rules that would be independently 'discovered' by Lewis Morgan in the nineteenth century. Nonetheless, marriage and kinship were hardly 'purely civil matters' from the Mohawk point of view – they were foundational to Indigenous society. Meanwhile, Lafitau had surprisingly little to say about property and gift, which are very important concepts in Indigenous law, and almost nothing to say about the law of obligations (contracts between individuals and redress for harms); the latter omission is more justifiable as Indigenous law is not overly concerned with such matters, though it is certainly concerned with social duties. For criminal law Lafitau relied considerably on the works of earlier authors, supplemented by his own observations. We will use these categories to provide a brief overview of the content of Indigenous law across northern North America, while conceding that they are used for heuristic purposes and do not always have a strong resonance within the Indigenous world view.

Constitutional law among Indigenous peoples is rather broader than that familiar in non-Indigenous societies, where it describes the relationship of different governmental institutions to each other and governs the relationship of individuals and the state. Indigenous peoples understood themselves to have duties and relationships with the non-human world of plants, animals, and minerals, and with the spirit world, as well as with other human beings. Thus constitutional law is nothing more or less than a law of right behaviour, but one that is agreed on collectively. In the Anishnaabe language, for example, the term for constitutional law, *chi-inaakonige*, translates roughly as deciding important things in a certain way, or agreeing on important matters.[30] These decision-making processes may lead to a political structure to guide right behaviour within the group and right relations with other groups. In some cases, as with the Inuit, spread out in small groups across a vast territory, such structures may be elementary or non-existent. In others, such as the Haudenosaunee, they may be complex and effective, and may endure over centuries, as with the Great Law of Peace and the Five Nations Confederacy. Most Indigenous societies fell somewhere in between on this governance spectrum, but even at its most elaborately structured, as with the Confederacy, Indigenous constitutionalism always abjured a concentration of power, avoided coercion, and tried to maximize respectful human agency within the limits required for group survival.[31]

Marriage and kinship were fundamental to Indigenous society and permeated all aspects of their law. For the Secwépemc (Shuswap) people of the interior of British Columbia, '*Ḱwséltkten* (being relatives) is what bonds the Secwépemc as a people and bonds us to our allies and friends in neighbouring nations.'[32] Already we see how difficult it is to separate 'constitutional law' from 'family law' or 'international law.' Bonds could be created by blood, marriage, adoption, or treaty, but the concept of marriage could extend beyond the union of human persons. As was stated for the trial court in *Delgamuukw* by a Gitxsan elder,

> The ownership of territory is a marriage of the Chief and the land. Each Chief has an ancestor who encountered and acknowledged the life of the land. From such encounters came power. The land, the plants, the animals and the people all have spirit – they must all be shown respect. That is the basis of our law.[33]

This marriage obliged the chief and all his successors to ensure that the laws were followed on the group's territory. Doing so renewed the power that arose upon the initial marriage of the chief and the land and maintained his authority and status, while failure to do so would have the opposite effect. Similarly, as James Sakej Henderson observes, 'the Mikmaq do not regard their territories as "natural." Instead, they view [them] as created by interactions between their ancestors and the ancestors of other life forms or species.'[34]

Referring to the Haudenosaunee, Deborah Doxtator observed that marriage 'was as much an alliance between two different clans, as it was between two individuals.'[35] In Indigenous societies, where one's status and identity were often determined by membership in a particular clan, a complex set of rules often discouraged intra-clan unions and encouraged extra-clan marriage. Among the Gitxsan, each person is born into a House, which itself is part of one of four clans: Frog, Eagle, Wolf, or Fireweed. Marriage with another member of the same clan is proscribed.[36] The Haida had only two exogamic clans, Ravens and Eagles; thus Ravens could only marry Eagles and vice versa.[37] Even on the west coast, however, such rules were not universal. The Nuxalk of Bella Coola practised endogamy until at least the mid-twentieth century, believing that children born of such unions 'would come into this world provided by both parents with common relatives, so that the child would be, as they express it, "[h]eld close and supported by a close circle of ancestors."'[38]

The rules on exogamy no doubt emerged from an imperative to maintain a wider gene pool, but they also played a role in creating alliances and subduing conflict between different clans and nations. The Five Nations Confederacy took this idea to its highest peak of development by using clan and nation as the warp and weft of their governance structure. The five founding nations of the Confederacy were the Mohawk, Seneca, Onondaga, Cayuga, and Oneida. Each had a number of clans, divided into moieties that represented elder/younger and father/mother polarities. The clans were not identical in each nation, but there was considerable overlap, creating clan-based bonds across the nations that reinforced the Confederacy itself. At the moment of founding, which is estimated to have occurred around 1450, fifty sachemships or royaner positions were created.[39] These were not distributed equally among the five nations, but decisions were made only by consensus, and each nation had a veto.[40]

The Gitxsan also had similar practices, though they did not recognize an overarching council or central power. Nonetheless the relations between lineages created strong horizontal bonds, such that 'the whole society is covered with a cloak of authority.'[41] These alliances based on marriage, kinship, and clan identity seem to have been much more stable than similar practices in early modern Europe, where marriage alliances among royal houses often led to more conflict, possibly because each territorial enlargement achieved by a royal marriage seemed to threaten neighbouring states.[42] And these European alliances involved only the rulers of the states in question, while marriage laws in Indigenous society distributed their effects through the entire populace.

The relationship between family law and citizenship was also a close one. Adoption was widely practised in Indigenous society and served a variety of purposes. It might be used strategically: if a man wanted to marry a woman of his own clan where that was forbidden, he might arrange for her to be adopted by another clan so that the marriage could proceed.[43] More commonly, those captured in war were adopted into the host society in order to replace those lost to battle and disease. The integration process might be violent, involving the ritual torture of adult captives in order to strip them of their former identities and ready them to be accepted into their new family, or it might be gentle, especially if they were children. And the status of captives once 'adopted' varied considerably. Some were accepted virtually as full citizens of their new community, while others, although not slaves, bore a stigma that might continue into the next generation.[44]

Yet other captives might be treated as slaves and traded for goods or given as gifts to seal an alliance. A traffic in slaves existed in the midwest and the upper Great Lakes, but their fate rested on the customs of the group to whom they were traded or given, and their status was usually not indelible.[45] Among some northwest coast chiefdoms, however, the status of slavery was heritable.[46] In a sense this was the obverse of the focus on kinship: groups to whom one was not related might be treated as inferior or indeed as non-persons. The rich animal and vegetable resources of the west coast enabled the creation of complex societies that witnessed a degree of stratification and hierarchy unique among Indigenous peoples in northern North America, and more like the civilizations of Central and South America. Among the Nuu-chah-nuulth and Kwakwaka'wakw, for example, while the main distinction was between freemen and slaves, among freemen there was a fine-grained status hierarchy from the highest-ranking individual to the lowest, based largely on inherited wealth. Relations of blood and marriage helped to unite these societies, however, in spite of the existence of inequality.[47] The status of slave in these chiefdoms was permanent and hereditary, intermarriage with free people was forbidden, and masters held the power of life and death over their slaves. Wars were fought between chiefdoms to obtain slaves, as well as for plunder and revenge, the Haida in particular being much feared in this respect.[48]

After the arrival of Europeans, they too might be captured and incorporated into Indigenous society. One of the most famous adoptee-captives was Eunice Gannenstenhawi Williams (1696–1785), who was captured in the raid on Deerfield, Massachusetts, in 1704 during the hostilities known as Queen Anne's War. Aged seven, she was marched to Montreal along with about a hundred other captives, including her siblings and parents. Her mother was killed along the way when she could not keep up. Eunice was given to a Mohawk woman at Kahnawake who wanted her to replace a daughter who had died in a smallpox epidemic. She was catechized in the Catholic faith, learned French and Mohawk and lost English, and later married a young Mohawk man with whom she would have three children. While her father and siblings were ransomed and returned to Massachusetts, her adoptive family refused to give her up, the Jesuits reporting that 'they would as soon part with their hearts as the child.' Once acculturated, she too refused to leave, although she visited her homeland later in life, communicating via an interpreter on these occasions.[49]

Kinship was also used to structure relations with other groups, whether Indigenous or European. Trade relations and peace could exist only among kin groups; such relationships invariably involved the two groups recognizing each other as brothers, or as fathers and children.[50] Trade was not perceived only, or even primarily, in economic terms – it involved intimate relationships of trust that could be conducted only with those who were virtual kin.

Family law (in the narrow Western sense) was the domain that presented perhaps the greatest contrast with European practices. The relative sexual freedom of youth in many societies, the existence of polygamy, the tolerance of the sexuality of 'two-spirited' people among some Indigenous groups, the ease of divorce, the absence of paternal authority, and the great freedom afforded children were all startling at best and shocking at worst to Europeans. They would not have believed that all these features, excepting polygamy, would come to characterize their own societies centuries later. Meanwhile, Indigenous people were shocked by the seemingly despotic authority of parents and the widespread corporal punishment of children.[51] Family law was an illustration of the great value placed on personal liberty in Indigenous societies. The maximum amount of personal freedom was permitted, consistent with the imperative of reproducing the society in question.

This summary may give the impression that Indigenous society was a paradise for women, but it needs to be stressed that even if the position of Indigenous women was in some respects better than that of their European sisters, they did not experience perfect gender equality. Where polygamy was practised (while common, it was not universal in Indigenous culture), the 'first wife' often enjoyed privileges not possessed by later 'subordinate' wives, whose children might also be seen as inferior in status to those of the first wife.[52] The sexual division of labour practised in all Indigenous societies could also leave to women the often tedious work of agriculture, grinding corn, preparing and preserving meat or fish, fetching water, and preparing hides for clothing or tents, while men devoted themselves to the more exciting and prestigious, albeit more dangerous, work of the hunt and warfare. Female political agency varied considerably across different peoples, who were not all as enlightened as the Haudenosaunee in this respect. Among the more stratified societies of the west coast, honour killings were not unknown: a high-ranking woman whose sexual behaviour was thought to be too free and a source of familial shame might be killed by her relatives.[53]

On the positive side, child care responsibilities were lightened by the fact that they were shared by the whole village or encampment. Disciplining children was seldom required because they were expected to learn by example and internalized self-control from an early age. A married woman also had more options than her European sister if the relationship with her husband went sour. Some societies were matrilocal, such that the husband joined his wife's people upon marriage. Thus if things did not go smoothly she would not find herself among strangers and would be supported by her own family if need be. There was no religious or other stigma attached to ending a relationship. Child custody generally followed the mother rather than the father, though this was not always the case on the west coast.[54]

Turning from family law to criminal law, redress for harms was a matter for the families of the victims and the perpetrator, although in the case of serious crimes the harm done to the community itself by the disruption of its harmony also had to be acknowledged. In modern parlance, the entire focus of the process was restorative rather than retributive: restoring the right relationship between the two affected families, and between the perpetrator and his or her community. Referring to legal traditions common to Pacific coast Indigenous peoples, Hamar Foster observes that 'causation, collective responsibility and compensation are fundamental, rather than fault, individual responsibility, and punishment.'[55] Murder or inflicting serious physical harm on another member of one's own community was rare, as was rape, according to seventeenth- and eighteenth-century observers.[56] When such acts occurred they had either to be atoned for via the giving of presents to the victim's family, or a blood feud could result between the two families. There were strong societal pressures to resolve such matters by composition rather than ongoing feuds, which could disrupt the community for long periods of time. And the heavy burden that could be imposed by the giving of presents was a strong disincentive to commit harmful acts in the first place: not only would responsibility for acquiring the presents fall upon the offender's kin, but such acts also brought shame upon one's entire family.

Each society had a kind of criminal code, containing understandings about how many presents of what nature were required to make reparations for particular harms. Gender, lineage, age, and status (slave or free) of the victim, and sometimes of the perpetrator, could influence the nature of the reparation or direct that no reparations were necessary. Among the Inuit a headman whose mentally unstable brother had killed another member of the community in turn killed the offender to general approval.[57] Lafitau likewise reported that it was permitted to kill someone of one's own lineage if he brought extreme dishonour on the family by odious actions; whereas killing someone of another lineage called for sixty presents to be given to the family of the deceased.[58] Unjustified slaying of a male member of one's own lineage required thirty presents, but forty for a female, partly because it was shameful to kill someone of the weaker sex, and partly because of their valuable reproductive capacity.[59] It was also traditionally permitted to put to death aged members of one's own lineage who were too great a burden on the community. Lafitau reported that this practice was less commonly encountered in recent times; this was possibly due to the influence of Christianity at Kahnawake, though interestingly he did not make this connection.[60]

In the harsh environment inhabited by the Inuit, 'helpless' elderly people were also put to death, or committed suicide, a practice that was documented into the 1930s.[61] Infanticide, mostly of females, was also not considered unlawful well into the twentieth century and was not necessarily connected to male domination. A Netsilik woman, Nalungiaq, informed Danish anthropologist Knud Rasmussen that 'parents often consider that they cannot "afford" to waste several years nursing a girl.... If my daughter Quertilik had a girl child I would strangle it at once. If I did not, I think I would be a bad mother.'[62]

Relatives of the victim might judge the presents offered as insufficient. In that case the murderer might be delivered to the victim's family to be held as a captive or even slave, though he or she would not be killed for fear of starting up a vendetta. In some cases the family would come to adopt and love the murderer almost as they loved the deceased person, considering the former as a replacement for the latter.[63] In spite of the primacy given to reparations to victims and their families in what we might call the criminal process, reparations did not suffice in two situations involving threats to the entire community: deaths allegedly caused by shamans or by sorcery, and acts involving betrayal of one's people to a rival group. Very few examples of the latter are recorded among the annals of the missionaries, but accounts of the former are frequent.[64] Among some Indigenous peoples, shamans were thought to have special abilities to communicate with the spirit world and to use these powers for good or ill. While their aid was sought for a variety of problems, they were also much feared. Thus when a shaman was believed to have caused a death through 'bad medicine,' he or she could be summarily slain by a community member without any consequences. Similarly, among the Ojibwe (Anishnaabe) and the Cree (Nehiyaw) the transformation of a band member into a wendigo (wetiko) required defensive action. The wendigo was a spirit creature believed to be driven by insatiable greed and prone to cannibalism; thus, a person possessed by such a spirit posed a grave threat to the community and had to be removed, by slaying if necessary. These beliefs have been seen as a means of enforcing taboos against cannibalism and all forms of selfish behaviour during times of famine.[65]

With regard to property, some European observers thought Indigenous peoples practised a form of primitive communism with regard to the exploitation of land and resources, but they came to realize that a complex blend of familial and communal claims coexisted in many societies. Lafitau, for example, noted that even though Mohawk land at Kahnawake looked like one big field to the untrained eye, it was not: each family had set limits, even though no fences separated their plots. Sir William Johnson, speaking more generally about Indigenous peoples of the northeast, made a similar observation:

> That it is a difficult matter to discover a true owner of any Lands amongst Indians is a gross error.... Each nation is perfectly well acquainted with their exact original bounds, the same is again divided with due proportions for each Tribe, and afterwards subdivided with shares to each family, with all [of] which they are most particularly acquainted, neither do they ever infringe upon one another, or invade their neighbour's hunting grounds.[66]

Rights over land (as opposed to 'in' land) nonetheless varied according to geography, climate, and culture. The Mi'kmaq, who did not practise agriculture in the early modern period, had a more communal approach to resources, but even so 'certain families ... had "rights" to use certain animals, plants, materials and access sites (hunting and fishing traps) because of their particular relationship.'[67]

One aspect of Indigenous property often missed by European observers was the emphasis on what we might call intellectual property, while acknowledging the inadequacy of the word *property* to describe the 'bundle of rights' recognized in various cultural practices and artefacts. The rights to perform particular songs, dances, and rites, and to use certain crests, names, designs, and headdresses, were and are highly valued in Indigenous society. Their transfer and use are governed by complex ceremonial protocols, generally based on an idea of stewardship rather than individual ownership.[68]

The Indigenous world view was and is premised on ideas of existence as cyclical and of the interconnectedness of all things, as opposed to linear ideas of time or straightforward notions of cause and effect. As Deborah Doxtator observes, in the Haudensoaunee world view, 'the world has no real beginning or end, only certain repeated patterns about a particular place or centre.'[69] And the experience of Indigenous law over the last five hundred years has itself gone through a cycle of life, near-death through colonial oppression, and rebirth. Modern Canadian legal systems and legal thought based on European models are turning increasingly to ideas of restorative justice, ideas that formed the foundation of Indigenous legal orders for thousands of years. Modern Canadian social practices and legal doctrines relating to the family are much more similar to traditional practices among First Nations peoples than to those of early modern Europe. Modern environmental law is only beginning to absorb the lessons that Indigenous people could teach regarding the web of ecological relationships that include humanity within them. And it is not just with regard to 'content' that Indigenous law should be examined. Indigenous law had its own legal theory and methods, even if not expressly articulated as such, first brought to light for a non-Indigenous audience by Llewellyn and Adamson-Hoebel in their classic work *The Cheyenne Way* (1941). These have been further elucidated by contemporary scholars such as John Borrows, Gordon Christie, Hadley Friedland, and Val Napoleon.[70] In turn, Indigenous law has not stood still and should not be frozen in a pre-contact past. It has adapted to new conditions of life and will continue to offer its resources to all who need them.

3

Roots: French Legal Traditions

French law today is invariably associated with the idea of codification represented by the *Code Napoléon* of 1804. However, codification was not a traditional part of French law, and the law received in New France was conceived of very differently from what developed in the wake of the French Revolution. Pre-revolutionary French law represented a synthesis of Roman law and the customary law of the various regions of France, one in which case law and doctrine (in the sense of learned juristic writing) played an important role. To appreciate this synthesis, we need first to return to the period before the emergence of Rome.

The Roman Legacy

European societies of ca 3,000 years ago were not so different from those in pre-contact North America. We might say that they were chthonic: transmission of information was primarily oral, and people were governed by the cycle of the seasons and the rhythms of the natural world. No clear distinction could be made between 'law' and 'way of life.'[1] By 2,500 years ago, however, we have in the Twelve Tables (450 BCE) of the early Roman republic evidence of written law, seen as necessary in a society of some material and social complexity. We know it was divided between patricians and plebeians, because table 11 forbade their intermarriage. Extensive provisions relating to theft, private property, the power of husbands over wives and children, and succession attest to material prosperity, if also to inequality in the distribution of wealth. References to courts, trials, civil procedure, and judge-like officials (judex, magistrate, praetor, arbiter) suggest a somewhat structured legal order, although all of these officials were laypersons and not professionals.[2]

From the founding of the Roman kingdom in the eighth century BCE, through the republic (527–509 BCE) and the empire (27 BCE to 476 CE), Rome lasted well over a thousand years. Yet what has come down to us as Roman law is primarily a product of the 'classical period' of the first three centuries of the empire. It is contained not in case law as such, but in the collected writings of the classical jurists. More precisely, it is contained in their *responsa*, the advice they gave when asked about specific legal problems. The jurists were not lawyers as such. They were men of high birth, often occupying seats in the Senate or holding administrative offices under the emperor, who took a particular interest in the law. For them, studying it, clarifying it, and giving advice on it was considered a high public calling. There was no career path as such; those who took an interest attached themselves to the great jurists of their own day and learned from them. The advice they gave was written down, but they also wrote free-standing commentaries on various legal topics and on imperial legislation. In its entirety the law of Rome was known as the *jus civile*, derived from the Latin *civitas*, the collective noun for all the *cives*, or citizens of Rome. The civil law was the glue that bound the *civitas* together.

In the early fifth century the Goths invaded western Europe from the north, attacked Rome, and began founding kingdoms in France, Italy, and elsewhere, marking the 'fall' of the western Roman Empire. The eastern Roman Empire (also known as Byzantium), with its capital at Constantinople, survived for another millennium. The Byzantine Emperor Justinian managed to reunify the two halves of the empire briefly during his reign (527–65 CE), but the effort did not long survive his death. His most enduring legacy lay not in the realm of politics but law. In 527 he commissioned a compendium of the legislation of prior emperors in which all repetitive and spent provisions were to be eliminated, a sort of Revised Statutes of Rome. The version completed in 534 is known as the *Code* or *Codex* of Justinian. In 530 Justinian appointed a commission headed by the jurist Tribonian to digest the opinions of the classical jurists (that is, those writing before 300 CE) into a single restatement of Roman law. These opinions amounted to a massive repertoire of learning that ran to over 1,500 volumes. The commission was to omit all that was no longer relevant and decide between contradictory opinions where authors disagreed, selecting the 'best' view. In this work, known as the *Digest*, the passages selected as representing 'the law' are identified with their respective authors.[3] Tribonian was also charged with updating an introduction to Roman law known as the *Institutes* of Gaius, based on lectures the latter gave to law students, probably at Beirut, in 160–1 CE.[4] Both these works were completed in 533 and together with the *Codex* are known as the *Corpus Juris Civilis*. The entire package, running to over a million words in Latin, was proclaimed to be the sole source of law, and commentaries on it were forbidden. While arranged in recognizable legal categories, the sheer length of the *Digest* prevents it from being a code in the modern sense. It would, however, prove to be a priceless vehicle for the transmission of the sophisticated legal learning of antiquity to the medieval, and ultimately the modern, world.[5]

The Emergence of the French Customs

With the decline of the Roman imperium in the west, the *Corpus Juris* was soon lost; an entire copy of the *Digest* would surface only over five hundred years later, leading to a revival of Roman law across medieval Europe, while it would be 1816 before a complete copy of the *Institutes* was discovered in the cathedral library of Verona. After Justinian's death Roman law continued to exert some influence in the south of France, which came to be known as the pays de droit écrit. In the northern two-thirds of what is modern-day France – the pays de coutumes – local customs developed to regulate the main concerns of an agricultural society: succession, property (both peasant and seigneurial), gifts, and matrimonial regimes. Meanwhile, canon law governed marriage itself and the status of children (legitimate or illegitimate).[6] The customs did not deal with criminal law or what we would call public law, nor, other than incidentally, with the law of obligations (delict or contract). They were oral and held in the collective memory of the community. In cases where the content of a particular custom was disputed, a royal ordonnance of 1270 established the enquête par turbe, or group inquest, as the normal way to resolve it. This involved summoning several local people (later set at ten) to testify as to their understanding of the custom in the situation at issue. Provided they were unanimous in their verdict, it would be taken as conclusive. Such a process made sense in a society with low literacy, and the role of 'local elders' displays some affinity with processes used in Indigenous societies to clarify the law. The enquête par turbe also shows that the core of private law was considered to be produced by, and belong to, the people, not to the state. This was also demonstrated by the fact that when some of the customs began to be written down in the second half of the thirteenth century, they were set down in the vernacular, not in Latin.

As part of the monarchy's attempt to superintend all aspects of law and justice, the king ordered in the late Middle Ages that all the customs be written down. A first effort, via the Ordonnance de Montil-les-tours (1454) was not very successful because it required the king to approve the final product before it could be promulgated, a top-down approach that inspired suspicion and resistance. In 1498 Louis XII changed the process so as to remove the royal veto. The king would name two or three experts in local law to prepare a draft that would then be presented to the provincial estates-general, the political body containing representatives of the clergy, the nobles, and commoners. If a majority of each estate approved the draft articles, they would be registered by the local parlement (high court) and enter into effect immediately. If there were disagreements, the parlement itself had to decide on the final version. Local variants within the custom of a given region could also be recognized. By the time of the French Revolution, sixty-five customs and over three hundred local variants had been recognized. Among these the Custom of Paris, approved in 1510 and revised in 1580, was the most prestigious and the one eventually recognized as authoritative in New France.[7]

Thus, even as the territory governed by the French monarchy expanded to approximately its modern boundaries by the end of the Thirty Years' War in 1648, and even as the monarchy sought to centralize power in the seventeenth and eighteenth centuries, the French kings never aimed to unify private law. In fact, they pledged to uphold the customs and privileges of the various regions under the Crown. Louis XIV issued several ordinances in the seventeenth century that were 'the first indications of a centrally directed, national law on the continent,'[8] but these dealt primarily with civil and criminal procedure and with commercial and maritime law, all matters outside the purview of the customs.

The ostensible aim of reducing the customs to writing was to eliminate uncertainty, but it has been argued that the process effectively fossilized the law as of the date of redaction and prevented the subtle evolution and adaptation that oral tradition permits.[9] In many ways the customs were already antique when they were written down, appropriate to an early medieval agricultural society but not to the increasingly commercial society of the early modern period. A possible way of 'modernizing' them would have been by judicial interpretation, but that was difficult for reasons we shall examine shortly. Nonetheless, one should not equate the writing down of the customs with the end of innovation and flexibility. They were written in sufficiently terse language and contained enough silences and ambiguities that, with the advice of notaries, individuals and families could adapt them to new situations and desires, and clearly did so in New France.[10]

For areas of law not governed by the customs, a high degree of legal pluralism prevailed. Commercial law was dealt with by arbitrators at trade fairs or by consular courts in the cities, both of which applied primarily mercantile custom and featured lay decision-makers. Canon law governed marriage, tithes, and the legal status of ecclesiastics. Contracts between non-mercantile parties and non-contractual liability – for accidental harms, trespass by persons or animals, defamation, and so on – were dealt with by Roman law as set out in the *Digest* of Justinian and the various commentaries and glosses upon it. Maritime law was developed collectively by the Mediterranean nations and found in the so-called Rolls of Oléron and the compendium known as the *Consolato del Mare*.

The substantive criminal law of the ancien régime was found in a variety of sources: local customs, natural law, court decisions, and doctrinal writings. The royal injunction to reduce customs to writing did not apply to criminal law, leaving an important role for jurists in rationalizing the law. They generally classified crimes as against the state and religion, persons, or property, but there was often variation in the definitional details of particular crimes in different regions of the country.[11] The most serious crimes called for capital punishment or various forms of bodily mutilation, always carried out in public in order to impress on observers the terrible fate that awaited those who should transgress against the laws of God and king.

Institutional Development

Unlike England, where the Norman Conquest of 1066 produced the legal fiction that all land in the kingdom was owned mediately or immediately by the king, when Hugh Capet founded the Capetian dynasty in 987 the French monarchy could claim only a modest domain around Paris, known as Île-de-France. Its territorial reach would expand only gradually over the centuries through marriage, succession, war, and purchase. Thus in many areas acquired by the French Crown there were already functioning judicial institutions that formed part of the feudal order established after the break-up of the Roman Empire. Much of the French countryside was governed by the seigneurial system, in which a local notable or ecclesiastical body held the domaine éminent (overarching title) to much of the land and administered justice to the local inhabitants, known as censitaires, who were nonetheless considered owners of their plots and not tenants. Seigneurs generally assumed authority to administer basse and moyenne justice (low and middle justice), while some could also administer haute justice (high justice); the former involved small debt claims, moyenne justice dealt with a number of civil matters and minor criminal matters, while haute justice gave the authority to adjudicate serious crimes and impose bodily penalties up to and including the death penalty.

As the French monarchy consolidated its power, it took more of an interest in asserting its authority over the seigneurial courts. This was accomplished via the theory that all justice flowed ultimately from the king, the corollary being that jurisdiction exercised by bodies other than royal courts had been 'conceded' at some point in the past but was nonetheless subject to royal supervision and might be resumed at any point. This supervision might undermine or shore up seigneurial jurisdiction. Thus a judicial hierarchy whereby appeals would go to the royal courts was established, and seigneurs would be gradually deprived of the power of haute justice. However, other initiatives actually aimed to regularize and professionalize seigneurial justice. Unlike England, where the lord of the manor served as judge in his own court until such courts were abolished, in France from 1493 the seigneur was required to name a judge, a procureur fiscal, and a registrar; to provide a jail (with jailer); and to designate a set place where the court would be held. The procureur fiscal was an official who could serve as prosecutor and look after both seigneurial interests and the wider public interest – in effect a sort of local attorney general. In 1680 Louis XIV required that all seigneurial judges hold a law degree, an obligation never extended to New France. Although the jurisdiction of seigneurial courts declined over time, they endured down to the Revolution and remained popular as small claims courts for local inhabitants, given their low fees and ease of access.[12] Seigneurial justice would be the principal form of European justice in New France for its first half-century, until the establishment of royal courts, and it survived, though it did not exactly thrive, until the English takeover in 1760.

The thirteenth century saw the regular creation of royal courts, notably the prévôté (provost's court) and the bailliage (bailiwick) or sénéchaussée (seneschalcy), the latter term being more in use in the south and west of France. These courts became an important instrument by which the French Crown extended its authority and built up the French state. The bailli or sénéchal became an intermediate appellate judge, hearing appeals from the prévôté or the seigneurial courts, but subject to appeal in turn to the local parlement. The royal courts also took over much of the jurisdiction of the ecclesiastical courts and asserted an appellate authority over them. Initially a lay person, from the fourteenth century the bailli/sénéchal had become a professional judge. In their early incarnation, the judges in these courts presided more than decided; the judge often sat with assessors, and the enquête par turbe or other similar process would be relied upon when the content of local custom was disputed. Over time, the increased presence of lawyers and the waning interest of lay people to participate in these activities led to the disappearance of the popular element and the professionalization of the royal courts.[13]

The most important royal court was the parlement, the highest appellate court in the realm. The Parlement of Paris emerged out of the king's council or *curia regis* in the mid-thirteenth century. It met in the Palais de la Cité, the king's principal palace, on Île de la Cité in the heart of Paris, and would remain there down to the abolition of the parlements by the Revolution in 1790.[14] When courts later returned to the site, the building was renamed the Palais de Justice and, much restored and renovated in the later nineteenth century, it remains the nerve centre of the judicial system of France today. We will see this association between an impressive seat of royal power and the administration of justice again in the English context. This can be contrasted with the venues used by Indigenous peoples for deliberations about justice, which were either quite ordinary, thus emphasizing the openness and accessibility of justice, or sacred natural sites where wisdom was thought to reside.[15]

The Parlement of Paris soon had a very large number of judges, between 80 and 180. It required these numbers because it in effect treated appeals as trials de novo, requiring the re-establishment of all facts proved at trial. In doing so it followed canonist procedure, which involved examiners going out to interrogate witnesses wherever they lived, recording the answers in writing, and then delivering the whole back to Paris. Either the judges had to travel to the litigants, as in England, or the witnesses' testimony had to be carried back to the judges, and in France the latter path was chosen. Additional parlements were created to serve areas newly acquired by the French Crown, beginning with Toulouse in 1443, such that by 1789 there were thirteen of them. Initially labelled as a 'cour souveraine' (sovereign court) in its jurisdiction, a royal edict of 1665 changed the title of these courts to 'cour supérieure' as the Crown attempted to retain all manifestations of sovereignty for itself. Each was the highest court within its geographic jurisdiction, and there was no 'supreme court of France' that coordinated the decisions of the various parlements. Their decisions could, nonetheless, be questioned in the supreme tribunal of the land: the king's council, or conseil d'état. Its role was one of review for error of law, not appeal; if it invalidated a decision, the case would be remitted to the parlement for rehearing, keeping in mind that its prior decision had been quashed. This was the beginning of the process known as cassation, found today in France's highest court, the Cour de cassation.[16]

In New France, the Conseil souverain created at Quebec in 1663 was a North American parlement with a different name. Although its members were at first appointed by the governor, in 1675 a new edict provided that its members would be appointed for life directly by the king, bringing it more in line with the parlements of France. In two important respects it differed, however. Where judges of the Parlement of Paris all had degrees in Roman or canon law by the fifteenth century, no legal qualifications were required of members of the Conseil souverain in New France. And the office itself could not be bought and sold in New France as it could in old France, on which more shortly.

Much of the above-noted institutional development arose in the thirteenth century in the wake of important changes in the law of proof. Early medieval trials throughout Europe often involved trial by ordeal (fire, water, or battle), which assumed that divine intervention would aid the person who was in the right.

> A piece of iron was put into a fire and then in the party's hand; the hand was bound, and inspected a few days later: if the burn had festered, God was taken to have decided against the party. The ordeal of cold water required the party to be trussed and lowered into a pond; if he sank, the water was deemed to have 'received him' with God's blessing, and so he was quickly fished out.[17]

In 1215 the Lateran Council forbade the participation of priests in ordeals, which led to a decline in recourse to them, though it would be

1258 before Louis XII definitively outlawed trial by battle. Justice would be returned henceforth to human agency, requiring improvements to judicial infrastructure and expanding the domain of legal thought.

To return to the parlements, while they eventually gave rise to a functioning system of case law, it was in spite of the obligation of secrecy imposed on their judges. An ordonnance of 1344 forbade them from disclosing the reasons motivating their decisions or the facts underlying them, and similar strictures remained in place down to the Revolution. It is thought that the close relations between the Parlement of Paris and the king's council that still existed in this early period provided the basis for this concern over the preservation of secrecy.[18] In any case, this naturally made it very difficult for lawyers to understand what kinds of reasoning were authoritative. Moreover, it appears that the vigorous questioning that went on between bench and bar in English courts had no counterpart in France, nor was there any body like the inns of court where bench and bar could mingle informally and 'talk shop.'[19] Judges of the parlements discussed legal matters intensely with each other, but not with anyone else. In Dawson's evocative phrase, the French system 'walled off the judges of the Parlements in a private and protected world of their own.'[20]

In spite of these inauspicious conditions for the development of a doctrine of precedent, it is clear that the parlements kept records of their own decisions and consulted them frequently, demonstrating a desire to maintain a consistent jurisprudence. Eventually advocates attached to the Parlement of Paris made their own collections of precedents, which provided accounts of trials they had attended and included extensive reference to the facts and to the advocates' arguments. From these it is possible to see that advocates did cite previous decisions of the parlement, along with Roman law, canon law, the provisions of local customs, the Bible, well-regarded legal authors, and classical writers, with no clear sense of hierarchy or rationalization. Even though the reasons of the court were unknown, legal authors would try to deduce what they must have been from their knowledge of the facts and the bare decision of the court.[21] It should be noted here with regard to the interpretation of the written customs, that what had become important was the precedent declaring what the custom was (or was not), and not the actual decision of the local elders gathered in the enquête par turbe. Interpretation of the customs thus shifted away from community memory and reliance on local elders to professionalized bodies that carried on their own increasingly technical discourses.

The parlements were invested with authority beyond the judicial. In the absence of any body exercising legislative authority beyond the king himself, the parlements exercised a fairly broad regulatory authority, one that grew during the chaos of the Hundred Years' War (ca 1350–1450). They acted in effect as municipal governments, regulating everything from prostitutes' attire to the price of bread to prison conditions, and also intervened in the affairs of the universities located within their jurisdiction. These rule-making powers were exercised by what were referred to as arrêts de règlement – general rules for future conduct as opposed to decisions between parties in litigation. The Conseil souverain at Quebec likewise assumed such powers, the first comprehensive exercise of which was manifested in the 'Règlements généraux de police' of 11 May 1676.[22]

Much of the time the French Crown was content to allow the parlements to enact this kind of interstitial legislation, the authority for which was in theory delegated from the Crown itself. But as there was no clear limitation between the subjects on which the parlements might legislate and those reserved for royal decree, conflict was bound to occur. From the fourteenth century royal legislation was required to be registered with the Parlement of Paris before it was effective, and thereafter with the new parlements as they arose. The parlements regarded themselves as the guardians of local law and did not take kindly to royal legislation that might alter it. Thus they might make critical observations on royal legislation, known as remonstrances (remontrances in French) with a view to seeking alterations before registering the edict or ordonnance in question. The king in turn did not appreciate these critiques, and matters could escalate from there. Ultimately the king could force registration against the will of a parlement if he or his delegate appeared personally pursuant to a ritual known as the lit de justice (bed of justice), a reference to the canopy that had to be carried at such times. Increasingly in the eighteenth century these struggles centred not on private law but on new measures of taxation (which the parlements resisted) or administrative reforms.[23] Even as the parlementaires safeguarded their own interests, they cast themselves as representatives of 'the nation' standing up to arbitrary royal authority. Louis XV became so frustrated with their obstructionism that he abolished the parlements in 1771, but his successor Louis XVI restored them in 1774.

Registration by the Conseil souverain became an issue in New France as well, as will be seen, but the controversy there was framed in legal rather than political terms. Most of the key ordonnances of Louis XIV were never registered by the Conseil souverain, for reasons that are unknown but were not likely meant to display any resistance to the authority of the Crown. With regard to the 1667 ordonnance on civil procedure, the Conseil made some suggestions for change that could be analogized to the remonstrances made by the parlements in France, some of which were accepted by the king and others of which were not. In fact the ordonnances of Louis XIV, although mostly unregistered, were for the most part applied faithfully in New France. It was only much later, under the British regime, that the lack of registration came to be seen as a potential obstacle to a given ordinance being in force locally.[24]

The Crown's power over the parlements was fatally impaired by the practice of the sale of offices, which was chronic and ubiquitous under the ancien régime. Judgeships in the parlements were royal appointments, but by 1500 these were effectively lifetime positions made during good behaviour, a status that would not be achieved definitively in England until 1701. By the sixteenth century an impecunious Crown was selling fantastic numbers of offices, including judgeships, for immediate cash, even though the salaries would become a permanent drain on the treasury. Sale of office was not unknown in England, but it did not occur on such a scale and was often engaged in more as an aspect of the patronage system than to raise funds. In 1604 an edict of Henry IV permitted purchasers of an office to pay the Crown an annual tax in return for acquiring full power of disposal by sale or will, failing which it would descend to the holder's intestate heirs. This enabled the parlements to become self-perpetuating oligarchies, especially when appointment was conceded to bring with it noble status, and hence an exemption from most taxes. Judges were also permitted to exact fees from litigants, which encouraged them to spin out litigation and enhanced their unpopularity in the public mind. It is not surprising that parlementaires were targeted during the French Revolution, with the rates of execution rising as high as 50 per cent for the Parlement of Toulouse, as compared to 14 per cent at Paris and 20 per cent at Bordeaux.[25]

The parlements played such a prominent role in the political life of the ancien régime because there were no independent representative bodies, such as the English Parliament, that did not depend on the king's will. The only body that might have played this role was the estates-general. In the Middle Ages the king consulted with large assemblies of subjects divided into the three recognized orders or estates of medieval society: clergy, nobles, and commoners. Such an assembly might be convoked at the provincial level, or nationwide, for consultation on matters of great importance. Initially members of the first two estates were invited personally, whereas cities elected their representatives and rural areas were not represented at all. As of 1484, all three orders elected their representatives, and any subject, rural or urban, who paid the principal royal tax, the taille, was entitled to vote. Single women and widows also voted in these elections.[26] The weakness of this body was that it was called only at the king's pleasure. After meeting occasionally in the sixteenth century, the estates-general were not called after 1614 until the eve of the French Revolution. This hiatus in turn enabled the parlements to assume a pseudo-representative role for which they had not been designed.

Legal Education, the Legal Professions, and the Role of Doctrine

The discovery of a complete copy of the *Corpus Juris Civilis* in Italy in the late eleventh century electrified medieval jurists and led to a revival of interest in Roman law. Students began to arrive at Bologna in 1088 to study the newly discovered texts, hired professors to guide them, and thereby created the first European university. The predecessor of the University of Paris emerged about 1150 and was recognized by the king in 1200, to be followed by a number of other French universities where either Roman law or canon law or both were taught. Oxford University would be created in 1167 for similar reasons. When the struggles between the papacy and the Holy Roman emperor over their respective legal jurisdictions had been settled by the Concordat of Worms in 1122, the relative realms of secular and ecclesiastical law were separated more distinctly.[27] Afterwards, the church rapidly developed its own canon law and a system of courts with layers of appeal reaching up to the pope himself, a form of institutional development that was widely imitated within the nascent monarchies of western Europe. The church issued its own legislation in the form of papal decretals, and writing on the canon law flourished until there was a sufficient mass of literature calling for something like Justinian's *Digest* to make sense of it all. This was undertaken by the twelfth-century canon lawyer known as Gratian, in a work known as the *Decretum*. This work in addition to five others became known collectively as the *Corpus Juris Canonici*, in conscious imitation of the *Corpus Juris Civilis*. The former served as the basis for canon law studies, the latter for civil law studies in the universities.

Lawyers emerged more or less contemporaneously with the Parlement of Paris in the mid-thirteenth century. The existence of a high court seemed naturally to call forth a class of pleaders to argue cases before it, and early on the distinction between avocats and procureurs, roughly equivalent to barristers and solicitors in England, was established. In theory the parlements had disciplinary authority over avocats practising within their jurisdiction, but they never used it to declare any formal qualification process. It was rather the monarch who did so; an edict of Philip VI in 1344 required that avocats serve an apprenticeship, or stage, of unspecified length with an admitted avocat, while Charles VIII in 1490 required five years of university study prior to admission.

Later edicts set the stage at two years, to be served after university studies, but it seems clear that the practical training of the stage was by far the more important part of professional qualification, for two reasons. First, the law of the customs, the main law encountered in practice in much of France, was not taught in the universities until 1679, just as the common law was not taught in English universities until Blackstone gave his lectures in the 1750s. Second, law teaching in the universities declined from the fifteenth century onwards: degrees were sold, and many complaints were heard about professors pocketing students' fees but delegating the lecturing to novices. Such abuses prompted the Parlement of Paris to repeatedly scold the law schools within its jurisdiction, but to little effect. Students found legal education 'largely pointless' and 'a minor inconvenience.'[28] Thus the would-be avocat was counselled to watch his principal, attend court, and listen, to read juristic works covering those topics not taught in the universities, and even to spend some time working for a procureur or notary in order to understand the nuts and bolts of the law. While the distinction between avocats and procureurs – the former conducting oral pleading and the latter experts in procedure who filed the written documents necessary for litigation – was well established, the division of labour gave rise to many conflicts and was not resolved until the two professions came to an agreement in the mid-seventeenth century, confirmed by an edict of Louis XIV in 1693.[29]

The third legal profession in France was that of notary, with an ancient history going back to Roman times. The continental notary is not to be confused with the notary public in the English tradition. The latter is principally a verifier of the signatures on documents; he or she does not draft or retain them. On the continent, the notary was considered to hold a form of public office, granted either by the king or by a seigneur. Parties relied on notaries to draft documents for them, typically contracts, property dispositions, or wills, which, when done in the proper form and signed by the notary as well as the parties, were considered authentic; thus, in civil law tradition, there was no need for the 'probate' of a will, for example. Notaries kept registers of all documents they drafted, and these served as official repositories before the creation of state registry offices. Their information monopoly made them a centre of interest for the French state, which regulated both their fees and their education. An ordonnance of Francis I in 1535 required that aspiring notaries pass an examination administered by four judges of the parlement in the region where they proposed to begin practice. Societies of notaries in each city tended to make further rules regarding admission that would be approved by the relevant parlement, and these usually involved some period of apprenticeship.[30]

One was not prohibited from cumulating the offices of notary, advocate, and procureur, though engaging in litigation on behalf of parties for whom one had drafted documents as a notary was prohibited. Other non-legal offices or occupations might, and often were, cumulated with that of notary, especially in rural areas. In addition to their role in preparing marriage contracts and property dispositions for families, notaries played an important role in employment law, drafting the apprenticeship contracts that were required in almost all trades and occupations, and preparing commercial contracts. Of the three historic legal professions in France, only the notary would emerge as a recognized profession in New France. Some persons, notaries and non-notaries, assumed the functions of avocat and procureur, but these activities always existed in a kind of legal grey zone in New France. Aside from regulating the fees of notaries, however, the colonial state took a rather hands-off approach, leaving notaries to organize their own education and training.[31]

It was members of the practising profession, mainly avocats, rather than university professors, who moved into the vacuum created by the opaque decision-making process of the parlements. They were interested in law at a fairly granular level, as most lawyers are, but in order to give a comprehensive account of French law they felt compelled to blend Roman law and the law of the customs. Some even referred to the resulting synthesis as a 'common law of France.' In this France was distinct from the German states, where the received Roman law itself was thought to be the common law, and from England, where local customs were synthesized by royal judges into a unified national common law. As John Dawson has observed, 'France did not have what the "common law" gave to Germany – a large body of widely accepted and well-known rules to which most lawyers would habitually recur. French law was more a kaleidoscope, presenting different views to different observers, than it was a structure with a firm foundation that called for the talents of an architect.' Or, as the author Claude de Ferrière observed wistfully in 1685, 'il y a peu de veritez dans la Jurisprudence, qui soient incontestables.'[32]

Doctrinal writers made important contributions to the law, but given the 'kaleidoscopic' nature of French law, there could never be a 'canon' that would command universal respect. Charles Dumoulin (1500–66) freely rejected doctrines he felt were not in accordance with contemporary French needs and was not afraid to suggest innovations. His views were cited to the court and had a great influence on the revised Custom of Paris that appeared in 1580. Some doctrinal writers, such as François Bourjon, tried to compare the different customs and synthesize a 'common core' of customary concepts.[33] Claude de Ferrière, an author much cited in New France both before and after 1760, tried to synthesize the views of all the commentators on the Custom of Paris in a three-volume work first published between 1685 and 1692, and running to many editions over the next century. In the preface to this work he found fault with the work of all previous authors on the topic, either because they committed errors of interpretation or were now out of date. De Ferrière paints a portrait of a law that was constantly changing and therefore responsive to social change, but also dauntingly complex. Such complexity tended to reproduce itself exponentially, such that the sheer volume of legal literature by the eighteenth century was truly enormous. The best-known of all the pre-revolutionary authors, Robert Pothier (1699–1772), managed to synthesize much of the existing law in an accessible style that achieved comprehensiveness while avoiding excessive detail. Both a judge and a law professor, he also wrote texts in areas of the law that previous authors had largely avoided, such as the law of obligations and the law of partnership. Codifiers in both France and Lower Canada would rely greatly on him to guide them through the labyrinth of pre-1789 law.

The Constitution

The French monarchy claimed for itself supreme legislative, executive, and judicial power. By the early modern period, around 1500, the theory had developed that all bodies exercising any of these powers did so as delegates of the king and subject to his ultimate superintendence. Thus even though the parlements exercised extensive and important judicial authority, their decisions were subject to review by the king and his council, as noted above. The parlements were suffered to exercise a certain regulatory authority, but the principal source of legislation was the king himself. He generally resorted to one of three forms: the ordonnance (ordinance), the édit (edict), or the arrêt (decree).[34] The *ordonnance* dealt with large subjects in a programmatic way, such as the Ordonnance sur le commerce (1673) or the Ordonnance criminelle (1670). The *edict* dealt with a more particular problem, such as the status of Protestants in the realm (Edict of Nantes 1598). The *decree* did not come from the king personally, but from the king's council (Conseil du Roi). As royal absolutism became more entrenched in France, there were too many matters for the king to attend to personally; he was assisted in governing the realm by a council composed of nobles, clergy, and legal professionals, who could issue decrees in his name on certain matters. We have noted already the absence of representative bodies possessing legislative power: the estates-general and their provincial counterparts played only a consultative role in the elaboration of legislation, the final decision resting with the monarch.

There was thus little law that one could qualify as properly constitutional. The most imperative related to the monarchy itself: the monarch had to be a male (established in 1316), and to be descended through the male line (1328). The king had to be of legitimate birth and could not himself change the rules relating to the succession. Thus Louis XIV's purported legitimation of some of his illegitimate children could not bring them into the line of succession. Even the Catholicism of the king seems to have been a convention rather than a constitutional requirement as such. On the death of Henry III without issue in 1589, the Protestantism of Henry of Navarre did not prevent his succession as Henry IV; his later abjuration of Protestantism in 1593 ('Paris is well worth a Mass') was a practical concession aimed at quelling opposition to the rule of a non-Catholic.

The place of religion in the French constitution caused much tumult in the sixteenth century, giving rise to a lengthy civil war. In 1598 the politico-religious settlement ending that conflict was embodied in the Edict of Nantes, promulgated by Henry IV. It recognized liberty of conscience and most civil rights for Protestants but did not grant them equality with Catholics. The Edict of Nantes remained uneasily in force for nearly a century before its revocation by Louis XIV in the Edict of

Fontainebleau of 1685. The Sun King believed that national unity could be maintained only with unity of religion and was prepared to go to any lengths to ensure religious orthodoxy throughout the realm. About a quarter of the Huguenots (French Protestants) fled the kingdom, while those remaining either converted or pretended to do so while practising their faith in secret.

The struggles over religion in France inevitably had an impact in the colonies. Some of the early colonizers of Acadia were Protestant, such as Pierre Dugua de Monts, but in 1627 the Company of One Hundred Associates was directed to settle only Roman Catholics in the colony of Canada. In spite of the disabilities imposed on non-Catholics, a small number of resident Huguenot merchants carried on business in Canada. They were unofficially tolerated because of the economic benefits they afforded, possibly controlling a majority of the trade between France and Canada during the last twenty years of the French regime.[35] The only known Jew to arrive in Canada under the French, however, was expelled after a year. Esther Brandeau, originally from Bayonne, led a colourful life, having lived as a male for some years and arriving in Quebec disguised as a ship's boy. The intendant Gilles Hocquart had her returned to France when he could not get her to convert, a decision made easier by the king's offer to pay her transportation expenses.[36]

Although not perhaps a 'fundamental law' of France, the law relating to personal status should be noted as having constitutional significance. Unlike England, which certainly witnessed large social distinctions between classes but formalized them in law only episodically, the three orders of French society each possessed a distinct legal status. This translated into special privileges and immunities for the clergy and the nobles. These could be sumptuary, such as the ability to carry a sword for the nobility; honorific, entitling the holder to places of precedence on various special occasions; fiscal, such as the exemption from direct taxation; or juridical, such as the privilege of nobles to be judged only in the royal courts. Special status could impose constraints as well: nobles who practised a manual trade or engaged in commerce without licence of the king, for example, could lose their noble status, referred to as dérogeance (derogation). There was a long debate about whether being a notary was consistent with the status of 'gentleman,' resolved eventually in the affirmative.[37] The distinctions due to noble status were not of great moment in New France for there was a paucity of nobles and no taxes from which they might be exempted, but the clergy always aimed to maintain their privileges, particularly that of levying the tithe on their parishioners.

France took a bifurcated approach to slavery: legal in the colonies, where it was regulated by the *Code Noir* of 1685 (applicable only to the West Indies, however, and not to New France), its status in France itself was much contested. Tradition held that slaves became free the moment they set foot in France, but encountered resistance by slave-owners who wished to use slaves purchased in the Caribbean as domestic servants in France. Edicts of 1716 and 1738 permitted this on certain conditions but were never registered in the Parlement of Paris, which released hundreds of slaves who applied for their freedom in the eighteenth century.[38] As will be seen, Indigenous slavery would be more commonly encountered in New France than Black slavery, and both would be governed by local customary law.

The legacy of French law in the St Lawrence colony, and ultimately to modern Quebec and Canada, was profound; it continued so in Nova Scotia as well until the deportation of the Acadians effectively obliterated it. The governmental structure of the French regime was swept away by the cession of Canada to the British in 1763, but much of its law and legal culture remained, as did the seigneurial system, shorn only of its justice functions, and the profession of notary. Central to the identity of French Canadians was the Custom of Paris, which guided so much of family life and the transmission of property. Also important was the heritage from Roman law, which would become more visible in years to come. In France both were the subject of an immense and learned literature that sought, somewhat futilely, to pin down the 'kaleidoscopic' character of pre-revolutionary French law. If this variety would ultimately prove frustrating to Lower Canadian observers, both French and English, by the second quarter of the nineteenth century, it would also provide rich resources for the codifiers who laboured to produce the 1866 *Civil Code of Lower Canada*.

4

Roots: British Legal Traditions

Should we refer to an 'English' or 'British' legal tradition? Largely for the reasons given by Bora Laskin in his book *The British Tradition in Canadian Law*, we have adopted the latter course.[1] It is of course true that most of the law transferred to the British colonies was English law, in the sense that it derived from the English common law and English statutes prior to 1707. After the union of England and Scotland in that year, even though the two jurisdictions retained their own laws and systems of judicature, it became increasingly common to speak of British law, British justice, and the British throne, while the Parliament at Westminster became the British Parliament. The House of Lords became the final court of appeal for all of Britain and Ireland in the eighteenth century, while imperial authority was wielded in the name of a British Empire in which Scots played a highly important role, in Canada in particular.[2]

The Anglo-Saxon Legacy

Long before the arrival of the Anglo-Saxons and the Normans, Britain was inhabited by Celtic peoples, the original 'Britons.' They left no written records, and their legal practices are likely to have been inseparable from their druidic religion. The Celts inhabited Britain when the Romans colonized it from 43 CE, but when the latter departed four hundred years later, they left no impact on Celtic legal tradition. Subsequent invasions by the Teutonic Angles and Saxons pushed the Celts to the fringes of Britain, to Cornwall, Wales, and Scotland, creating the geographic space that would come to be known as England. The Anglo-Saxons had written laws, the first known text written in Old English being a collection of laws associated with King Aethelberht I of Kent dating from the early 600s CE. These laws are not a code as such but are thought to be a compendium of pre-existing oral customs, committed to writing following the example of the Romans. The content, however, bears no Roman influence; the provisions set out the amounts payable to compensate victims for various types of physical injuries and property damage, in an effort to pre-empt blood feuds and private revenge.[3]

The Anglo-Saxons founded a number of kingdoms after the departure of the Romans, but by the late ninth century Alfred the Great (d. 899 CE) had managed to unify them under his rule against a common enemy, the invading Danes. He too is known for his written laws, which display a much greater Christian influence than those of Aethelberht. The Danes eventually united all of England under the rule of King Cnut (1016–35).[4] Many Old Norse words entered English at this time, including the word *law* itself, from the Norse *log* or *lag*, meaning 'something laid down.' Written law was still highly exceptional, however, and this period is important more for the creation of institutions than for the growth of substantive law.

By the time of Cnut, England was already divided into shires, or counties, some thirty-five in number, which have mostly retained their ancient boundaries down to the present. Twice yearly these shires held an assembly, or shire-moot, at which important regional affairs would be discussed, attended by the bishop and the ealdorman (earl), who was the king's commander in the shire.[5] Justice in both spiritual and secular matters might also be dispensed at these meetings, which thus functioned as county courts. The shires themselves were divided into units called hundreds, which held their own assemblies monthly to carry on judicial and administrative business. Shire and hundred were autonomous bodies, however, with no appeal or connection between them. The monarch appointed a reeve in each shire – a shire-reeve, hence sheriff – to make sure that law was administered properly in the shire-moot, order maintained, and taxes properly levied. This law was local customary law, or 'folk-right,' not any uniform law common to the entire realm. Civil matters were often disposed of by reliance on the number and quality of persons who could be gathered to make oaths in support of either the plaintiff or defendant in a cause. Criminal matters would be dealt with by the ordeal of fire or water. Alongside the shire-moot, there were also courts held by the lords of local manors, in which the lord himself presided and applied local custom.[6]

Institutional Development after 1066 and the Emergence of the Common Law

The Norman Conquest of 1066 forever altered the course of English law, but it took some time for this to become evident. The Normans did not bring with them any body of law ready to be imposed and allowed the Anglo-Saxons to keep their laws. They brought a new and more forceful brand of military feudalism that featured William the Conqueror as the supreme feudal overlord, a regime implemented by taking over the lands of the Anglo-Saxon nobility via execution, forfeiture, or marriage. This would have important consequences for the land law but did not have any immediate impact on the administration of justice.

The idea that the king was the ultimate source of earthly justice within his realm was a common one in medieval Europe, but the Normans early on made clear their desire to link the justice function with impressive displays of royal authority and power. Thus William II ordered the construction of Westminster Palace on the site of a smaller structure built by King Cnut. Completed by 1099, it was the largest hall in Europe, 240 feet (eighty metres) by 68 feet (twenty-one metres). It survives to this day, along with the incomparable hammer-beam roof constructed in the 1390s to replace the original. Large enough to host royal events and functions of all kinds, and in effect the antechamber to both houses of Parliament, Westminster Hall would come to house the four main royal courts for some seven centuries: King's Bench, Common Pleas (initially known as the Common Bench), Exchequer, and Chancery.

These courts grew out of the *curia regis* or king's council between the twelfth and fourteenth centuries, just as the Parlement of Paris had in France, but they functioned very differently. For one thing they were much smaller: even in the eighteenth century each of the common law courts had only four judges, while the chancellor sat alone in chancery. The English courts could make do with such small numbers because they relied on oral testimony and the jury, unlike the canonist process employed in France that required all testimony to be written down. They also had, at least at first, a severely limited jurisdiction, dealing mainly with cases that impinged in some way on royal interests. Perhaps the greatest difference from the French parlements, however, is that the English courts based at Westminster were national courts that early on began to develop a law common to the whole realm, unlike the situation in France where regional customs remained sacrosanct.

How did this happen? As noted above, the early Normans did not interfere directly with the local customs applied in the old county courts. For the first century or so of their rule they named royal justices to visit the countryside and preside in these courts, but the decisions in individual cases were actually made collectively by the local notables present. Such decisions were ostensibly based on local custom, but local power relations likely also factored into these determinations. Then, under Henry II (ruled 1154–89) the instructions to the itinerant justices changed. From the later 1170s they make clear that the justices are actually to decide the cases, not just preside over local decision-making. They might still have chosen to apply local custom but were not required to. And given that a fairly small group of men sat at Westminster to hear litigation and also travelled to the counties, their tendency was to synthesize local customs into a uniform product: the common law of the royal courts.[7] Already by the late twelfth century, the treatise known as Glanvill dealt only with the law applied in the royal courts, outlining how to gain access to them and what procedures applied once you got there.[8]

'Custom' thus became something distinct from the common law, a local exception that was suffered to remain intact; in Kent, for example, land descended not according to the common law's rule of primogeniture, but according to the custom of gavelkind, which directed equal division among the sons of the deceased. Married women could not carry out legal acts without their husband's authorization under the common law, but according to the custom of London (and some other centres) they could run small businesses on their own. Local customs continued to be observed in matters not governed by the common law. Only causes where the amount in question was forty shillings or more – a considerable sum in medieval times – were cognizable in the royal courts; thus county courts retained jurisdiction over smaller claims, and the local law of contracts and torts might not reflect the common law.[9] But, as in France, the royal courts eventually asserted powers of review over the decisions of 'inferior' courts, which provided a vehicle for the common law to 'trickle down' to them as well.

Still, one should not exaggerate the reach of the common law in early modern England. It coexisted and competed with a variety of other types of law in a context of high legal pluralism: manorial law, urban law, and guild law (these bodies often asserting law-making powers acquired by long usage), ecclesiastical law, equity, civil law (used in the Court of Admiralty), and mercantile law. All of these bodies of law were administered by distinct courts that were mostly not created by the state but had grown up organically. Most litigation in England in the eighteenth century occurred in these courts, and while borough courts increasingly applied common law process, courts of request were staffed by lay commissioners 'using broad equitable powers.'[10] The colonies would receive a 'stripped-down' version of this legal pluralism, one in which the common law coexisted with equity and with the civil law doctrines used in admiralty courts.

The English legal system was also linguistically plural, using different combinations of French, English, and Latin over time.[11] The Norman Conquest did not result in any immediate change: Latin remained the language of record for statutes, court verdicts, and pleading. Legal treatises were also written in Latin but shifted to law French about 1260. Curiously, French did not become the language of oral debate in court until about the same time, a century after it was no longer widely spoken as a result of intermarriage between the Normans and the native Anglo-Saxons. It is thought that the rise of French as the language of international diplomacy and learning in the thirteenth century may have influenced its adoption among English pleaders and judges. Not until the later seventeenth century was English widely adopted by legal authors. Parliamentary statutes were drafted in either Latin or French but increasingly in English from the fifteenth century. Not until 1731 were Latin and law French finally dethroned as languages of record in the courts and elsewhere in the legal system, though both have left their imprint on legal English.[12]

To return to the royal courts, they possessed two other features that permitted them to function with such a small complement of judges. The first was the jury, which spared the judges from much fact-finding and allowed them to concentrate on the law, and the second was the writ system, which rigorously limited access to the royal courts to certain kinds of cases. The jury came to be a regular part of English trial process after the Lateran Council prohibited priestly participation in ordeals in 1215, but in its initial form the jury did not hear evidence from witnesses. Jurors were chosen because they already possessed knowledge of the facts, in particular the reputations of the parties.[13] By the end of the fourteenth century, however, the jury was expected to hear and weigh evidence from witnesses, in addition to using their own knowledge. All that was required in a jury trial was to ensure that the jury was asked the right questions and instructed properly on the applicable law. The jury system thus entailed a rigorous separation of facts and law that was not present in the French legal process.[14] At first those presiding at jury trials might be any royally appointed commissioner, including lay persons, but after 1340 they had to be either judges of the Common Pleas or King's Bench, or serjeants at law, the most senior lawyers from whom new judges would be appointed.[15] More will be said shortly about the relationship between jury trials in the counties and at Westminster, a key element in the centralization of royal justice. First, however, we need to consider the procedures by which access to the royal courts could be obtained.

The use of writs in the royal courts ensured that only certain types of litigation, especially cases dealing with lands held in free tenures, would be heard there, and only the most serious crimes. In the county courts, or even in the early days of royal itinerant justice, complaints could be made orally, allowing for maximum flexibility. Once the courts of Common Pleas and King's Bench became established, however, it was necessary to purchase a royal writ from the king's chancery to initiate the suit. These writs were addressed to the sheriff and required him to convey an order to defendants – typically to appear in court on a certain day to answer a particular kind of complaint, or have judgment found against them. Different writs came to be issued for different kinds of legal claims and soon came to have precedential value. The chancery clerks would not issue a novel writ if the complaint fit within an existing one, and by the end of Henry II's reign in 1189 there were already about thirty original writs.[16]

The issuing of new writs came to be seen as problematic, and the Provisions of Oxford 1258 prohibited the chancellor from issuing new writs without the consent of the king's council. This effectively froze the existing law in place, requiring all litigants to pigeonhole their claim within the ambit of an existing writ. Each writ laid out a particularized procedural road map and mode of proof for the action associated with it, and one could not 'mix and match.' Lawyers came to refer to these as the 'forms of action,' while the entire legal framework is known as the formulary system. The jurist Sir Anthony Fitzherbert confirmed in his 1534 *Natura Brevium* that writs were the 'fundamentals on which the whole law depends.'[17] Indeed, most legal literature for many centuries would be organized around the forms of action, which encouraged a laser-like focus on the law of remedies and procedure and stunted any broader conceptual thinking about substantive law or 'rights.'

Attempts to freeze the law seldom work. A variety of expedients were used to enable the law to respond to new situations. One was the 'action on the case,' a residual type of writ that allowed new causes of action to be smuggled into the law, eventually giving birth to claims in negligence and breach of contract. Another was the use of legal fictions, through which old doctrines could be repurposed. Thus, the action in ejectment, initially created to permit wrongfully evicted lessees to regain possession, was later used by freeholders to try questions of title, the plaintiff being permitted to bring an action in the name of a fictitious wrongfully dispossessed lessee.[18] Legislation creating new law was always possible in theory but seldom resorted to in fact. The most significant response to the common law's tendency to stasis was the creation of the Court of Chancery and, eventually, the body of law known as equity.

The chancery was a department of state headed by the chancellor, and we have already noted its important role in the administration of justice.[19] Claimants who had lost after pursuing their common law remedies in the ordinary way often asserted, probably justifiably, that justice had not been done because of the negligence or corruption of officials or judges. In such cases they would petition the chancellor to alter the result. This was not an appeal as such, nor did it involve any assertion that the law itself was unjust or needed to be changed. Rather, it was a plea for an improper legal decision to be varied or suspended as a matter of 'conscience' or 'equity.' The chancellor proved receptive to such pleas, and soon a 'Court of Chancery' emerged; it began to grant relief in certain types of cases with such regularity that a body of law known as equity, existing in parallel to the common law, came into being. This was quite unlike the civil law or Indigenous law, where 'equity' in the sense of individualized considerations of fairness was always part and parcel of the ordinary law. Two other unique features of chancery deserve to be noted. First, it used canonist procedure, where questions were put to witnesses and the answers written down by court officials, rather than the oral testimony known to the common law. And second, it used the English language in its written process. In fact, according to linguists, the 'genealogy of modern Standard English goes back to Chancery, not to Chaucer.'[20]

Equity was never as all-encompassing as the common law, however, being confined to certain areas of property law and to obligations involving trust and confidence. The trust device, the fiduciary relationship, and the doctrine of unconscionability, all important concepts in modern law, derive from equitable doctrines. Chancery also created new remedies, notably the injunction and the ability to 'discover' documents – that is, to have them provided to the opposing party before trial – that did not exist at common law. For centuries, until jurisdiction over both the common law and equity were vested in the new High Court of Judicature created in England in 1875, common law and equity were administered in parallel, pursuant to a system characterized by a delicate and intricate institutional balance. Chancery courts and equitable doctrines would be imported into the colonial context outside Quebec, where they became embedded in local legal cultures.

We now return to the institutional context for the spread of royal justice across the realm. If at first royal justice 'piggybacked' on the old county courts, eventually the royal judges were authorized to hold court independently in the countryside. The process came to be known as the *nisi prius* system and would be faithfully transported to the colonies. Juries would be summoned to appear at Westminster (or in North America, the colonial capital) on a certain day 'unless before then (*nisi prius*) the king's justices should have come into the county.'[21] No one expected the jurors to go to Westminster, as there were two circuits in each county each year, later known as the assizes; Magna Carta made the biannual assize mandatory in 1215. If novel points of law came up while the judges were on circuit, they would adjourn the case until all the judges could discuss the matter back at Westminster.

With regard to criminal business, the assize conscripted the hundreds in each county. Formerly decision-making bodies in their own right, they were now responsible only for investigating crimes and presenting them to the assize judges; gradually they turned into the grand jury, which scrutinized indictments to determine whether they should proceed to trial or not. In the former case a 'true bill' was found, in the latter, the indictment would be marked *ignoramus* (we do not know).[22] Another innovation in the prosecution of crime was the appointment of justices of the peace. Initially knights of the shire were appointed to keep the peace, but in the fourteenth century these officials were given judicial functions. Each county would have a 'commission of the peace' drawn up from time to time, naming local notables to the office. They were to inquire into many types of crime and had power to arrest suspects, commit them to jail, and require anyone to give a surety for keeping the peace. Their 'sessions of the peace,' at which two constituted a quorum, came to be held four times a year, hence 'quarter sessions.' They also handled various administrative duties in the county and poor relief. Although unsalaried, the justices could charge fees to litigants for their services and were later given a minor civil jurisdiction.[23] They, much more than the superior court judges, would be the workhorses of the justice system in the colonies of British North America, their cheapness and flexibility proving irresistible to colonial governments.

With the spread of the assize system and the sessions of the peace, the old county and hundred courts declined to the point of irrelevance. Justice, formerly meted out locally according to local custom, was now more centralized as a royal function, although part of a complex matrix featuring both central and local elements. Administered by royal appointees, either itinerant judges or resident justices of the peace, justice was nonetheless carried out in the counties, using local fact-finders in the form of the jury. The system allowed for considerable information flow in both directions and discouraged the royal judges from becoming too isolated from the populace, as tended to happen with judges in the French parlements. It also began to develop, from 1195, a judicial archive, the plea rolls, in which the records of all judgments could be found, though these as yet contained only the final decision, not any reasons for judgment.[24]

As in France, lawyers were dissatisfied with bare decisions and wanted to understand the reasoning that underlay them. The real 'action' lay in the oral interchanges between bench and bar; by the 1250s, and continuously from the 1290s, reporters were capturing these as best they could and recording them in a form that came to be known as the yearbooks. These reports were not in any way official and were composed for centuries by anonymous hands under unclear circumstances. They do not contain 'briefs' of the cases before the court, nor were they meant to set down the 'rule' that a given case stood for. The parties might not even be named, key facts were often omitted, and arguments in similar cases sometimes conflated. The yearbooks are best viewed as repertoires of legal thinking, principles, and argument that lawyers needed to be familiar with. They capture the common law as a process of specialized intellectual debate rather than a set of dry precedents.[25]

Precedents were indeed rising in importance, but they were not determinative or conclusory in the way they would, much later, become. Starting in the sixteenth century, the anonymous yearbooks turned into nominative reports, written by identified authors such as Dyer and Spelman, but most of them still leave a lot to be desired compared to modern-day reports. Thus, as Dawson has pointed out, there was something of a chicken-and-egg problem: a rigorous doctrine of precedent requires accurate case-law reporting, but the demand for accurate case-law reporting presupposes a doctrine of precedent.[26] Certainly a single precedent of no matter what level of court was not considered binding; individual decisions might always be wrong. The process by which the judicial decision became isolated as a source of law, distinct from the 'common learning' of bench and bar, was lengthy and very gradual, emerging no earlier than the seventeenth century. By that point the distinction between *obiter dicta* – passing remarks not germane to the legal issue to be decided – and the actual reasons for decision had been articulated. And the growth of legal literature, discussed below, also contributed to the idea that judicial decisions were actually law in themselves, as opposed to mere evidence of it. But it was still late in the nineteenth century before the idea of *binding* precedent became settled.[27] Until then, precedent in the English context was not very different from the French idea of jurisprudence constante: only a consistent string of decisions on the same point could be considered to have created 'settled law.' Thus, English law at the time of the creation of the northern colonies was not considered to derive exclusively from case law and legislation. The common law itself was a mishmash of principles, maxims, legal fictions, and rules derived from judicial decisions, supplemented by equity – an unwieldy body of law to be sure, but one that contained a capacity for growth and adaptation in the new settler societies of North America.

While the common law courts at Westminster exercised a review jurisdiction over inferior courts, there was no real appeal from the common law courts themselves. At first Parliament, and then only the House of Lords, would hear petitions to overturn such decisions, but it very rarely accepted them until the seventeenth century. After the *Act of Union* 1707 the House of Lords became the final court of appeal for Scotland as well, except in criminal matters, where the Scottish High Court of Justiciary remained the court of last resort. The Lords' appellate jurisdiction gradually became more regular, but the decisions had little impact for some time for two reasons. First, the House would not allow their reasons to be reported until the late eighteenth century,[28] and second, lay lords were permitted to vote, sometimes outvoting the 'law lords' who were legal professionals; not until 1844 was a convention established that lay peers did not vote.[29]

An appellate body of more direct significance to the colonies was the monarch's Privy Council. While Parliament gradually wrested control of the English domestic courts from the Crown, those in the colonies remained a matter for the royal prerogative. Thus from an early date petitions against the decisions of overseas courts, beginning with those of the Channel Islands, went to the Privy Council. When ad hoc committees proved unequal to the task, it was given to the Board of Trade in 1679, and then to an appeals committee of that body in 1696. Within a century this body too was found wanting: by 1783 some 1,500 appeals to it were launched from thirty-five different jurisdictions.[30] The loss of the Thirteen Colonies took the pressure off for a while, but the dramatic growth of the second empire, in particular the growth of appeals from India, renewed it. As a result, the Judicial Committee of the Privy Council in more or less its modern form was created by statute in 1833.[31] In 1876 its membership was restricted to the law lords, those members of the House of Lords who carried out its judicial functions.

Legal Education, the Legal Professions, and the Role of Doctrine

As in France, the emergence of royal courts seems to have created a demand for personnel specializing in the preparation and pleading of cases before them. A precondition for anything of this kind is the recognition that A can represent B who is not actually present in court and take action on their behalf. It is thought that the first such representatives were the business agents of landowners, such as their stewards or bailiffs, who handled all their affairs and, by extension, their legal affairs. But such agents did not possess any special legal expertise, and litigants soon wanted to engage persons with some knowledge of the courts and the law to defend or advance their interests in particular cases. In addition, once the writ system came into use, the royal judges themselves wanted pleaders before them who were familiar with this increasingly technical system. By the thirteenth century the core functions of the two modern professions recognized in England – oral pleading and the preparation of documents needed for litigation – had become the specialty of two occupational groups, serjeants and attorneys, the ancestors of barristers and solicitors. The division of labour between them was not strictly enforced and would not be for some time, but already the calling of oral pleader was considered more prestigious than that of the documentarist. The former needed to know the learned law in order to be able to debate with the judges, while the latter needed only a mechanical understanding of its processes.[32]

On the continent, the reception of Roman law and the spread of canon law led to the association of legal studies with the university. The reception of Roman law in England was more muted; hence, the continental pattern was replicated in England only with regard to those courts where civil law was dominant, the ecclesiastical and admiralty courts. The oral pleaders, called advocates, who appeared there had to have a doctorate in civil law from Oxford or Cambridge, while those who performed the solicitorial function were called proctors. These professions would retain their independent existence until the courts upon which they depended were abolished in the mid-nineteenth century.[33] They had no counterpart in the colonies, however. Ecclesiastical courts on the English model were not created in the northern colonies in any case, and any duly qualified lawyer could appear before local courts of admiralty.

The professionals who practised in the common law courts, the seat of the vast majority of legal business in the realm, formed their own career path, independent of both the universities and the church. Common lawyers learned their profession by attending at court, apprenticing themselves to senior practitioners, and following exercises at the inns of court. The origin of the inns is shrouded in mystery, but they began as shared living accommodation for younger legal apprentices and clerks in which, by the fourteenth century, an educational regime of some rigour was being conducted.[34] The four inns of court – Inner Temple, Middle Temple, Gray's Inn, and Lincoln's Inn – were collectively sometimes referred to as the third university of England, though this analogy can be misleading in that there was no set curriculum, nor career professors.[35] The lectures, known as 'readings,' were not frequent: twice a year a barrister of at least ten years' standing would give a series of lectures on a particular statute. Upon completing this task he became a bencher of the inn in question; collectively the benchers governed the inn and also took the role of judge at the moots that were a constant feature of the educational regime. Most days after the midday meal a short problem would be set, to be mooted by a pair of students and commented on by a panel of benchers.[36]

After seven or eight years of participation in the social and educational routines of his inn, a candidate would ask to be called to the bar. By 1590 the royal courts recognized such barristers as having a monopoly on pleading before them. The devotion of the inns to their educational mandate waned considerably in the early modern period, and such activities virtually ceased after the disruptions of the English civil war in the 1640s and 1650s.[37] Nonetheless, residence at an inn for the set period continued to be the passport to the degree of barrister. After the Glorious Revolution of 1688 the English state left barristers to their own devices and never intervened by legislation or otherwise in their affairs.[38] The royal judges were sometimes said to have a visitorial jurisdiction over the inns, but this appears to be inaccurate. Only judges who were alumni of a particular inn seem to have been involved in any discipline involving its members; they exercised this power by way of arbitration until the judges of the common law courts began to accept appeals from the benchers in the 1780s.[39]

The situation with attorneys was rather different, as they handled clients' money (and indeed acted as clients' bankers before the rise of commercial banking) and thus were in a position to do more harm than barristers.[40] This situation inspired regulatory legislation to reduce abuses by and within the profession. Attorneys were eventually excluded from the inns of court as part of the growing separation of the two professions, which would end in the nineteenth century with the complete withdrawal of barristers from contact with clients, leaving attorneys as the intermediary. The training of the latter was exclusively by apprenticeship, and they were subject to discipline by the courts in which they practised. For centuries seen as somewhat disreputable and prone to sharp practice, by the eighteenth century the reputation of attorneys was on the ascendant. In 1729 they formed a voluntary society, the Society of Gentlemen Practisers in the Courts of Law and Equity, to enhance their public image and maintain standards of behaviour. It was the ancestor of the Incorporated Law Society (1826) and hence of today's Law Society of England and Wales. The colonial legal profession in North America outside Quebec derived formally from the attorney rather than the barrister, but in practice the colonial attorney would unite the functions of both English legal professions.

The role of the universities in producing either common lawyers or common law doctrine was virtually nil, though barristers were increasingly expected to have spent some time in general (non-law) studies at Oxford or Cambridge before entering the inns of court. It was lawyers and judges who produced the literature of the law. They understood law almost entirely in procedural and jurisdictional terms, and hence organized their doctrinal writing in this way. Studies of the forms of action proliferated, as did alphabetically organized 'abridgments' or digests of legal topics, and legal dictionaries. Giles Jacob's *New Law Dictionary*, first published in 1729, was one of the first law-books referred to in the common law colonies of British North America, being cited to the county court at Halifax in 1751.[41] Not until William Blackstone, a rather unsuccessful barrister with a doctorate in civil law, gave a series of lectures on the common law at Oxford between 1753 and 1766 did the study of English law enter the halls of academe.

These lectures became the basis of his *Commentaries on the Laws of England*, the four volumes of which appeared between 1765 and 1769. Organized around the themes of private rights and wrongs and public rights and wrongs, Blackstone's work was the first to break with the traditional organization of English legal writing around the writ system and to point toward, if he did not fully articulate, a common law oriented around substantive rights rather than remedies and procedure. Written in an elegant and accessible style far removed from the dry and technical presentation of most legal authors, the *Commentaries* became the 'go-to' text for generations of aspiring lawyers in North America. As Blackstone's biographer concludes, 'Although mounting criticism tempered an initial highly favourable reception, Blackstone's *Commentaries* would become the most celebrated, widely circulated, and influential law book ever published in the English language.'[42]

The Constitution

There are two, interrelated ways to approach the growth of constitutional law. The first is to examine relations between the Crown and the bodies that emerged from the *curia regis*: Parliament and the courts. This is largely an institutional story in which the autonomy of these bodies as against the Crown was eventually secured by law or convention. The second is to consider the rights of the subject vis-à-vis the state, in particular the right to be free from arbitrary detention or punishment, to express oneself freely, to demand due process of law (normally trial by jury) and equality before the law, and so on. We begin with the institutional story and then turn to the subject of individual rights.

In the early medieval period no clear distinction was made between adjudication and legislation. When the monarch with the aid of his council decided a dispute, the result might be considered binding only on the parties, or it might be considered to lay down a rule guiding future conduct, similar to a statute. Even a document that appears legislative in form may amount to no more than a restatement of the common law, as opposed to the adoption of some new measure of 'policy.' Until Tudor times, statutes were most often adopted as the response to a petition from dissatisfied subjects, and their exact wording was not considered terribly important. This in turn encouraged medieval judges to be rather freewheeling in their interpretation of them.[43]

When deciding upon important petitions, it became the monarch's practice to seek advice from assemblies of subjects. As in France, the main 'estates' of the realm, the lords and commoners, met separately. Yet in the thirteenth century there was no rule that either had to be consulted at all before legislation was promulgated. Magna Carta was issued in the name of the king alone in 1215 and was arguably not a statute but more in the nature of a royal proclamation. Later legislation sometimes mentioned, as did the statute *Quia Emptores* (1290), that it was passed 'at the instance of the great men of the realm,' but this was not invariable.[44]

Yet, unlike in France, where the calling of the estates-general remained a matter of royal discretion and their concurrence unnecessary for the promulgation of legislation, the summoning of representatives of the lords and commons became a regular part of English governance, and thus of the constitution. During the reign of Edward III (1327–77), the meetings of the commons began to take on a more institutional form, and its members asserted a right to participate in government. In 1340 Edward agreed that no taxation should be imposed without their consent. Finally, 'in 1407, Henry IV recognized that the proper legislative procedure was for the lords and commons to debate propositions as separate houses, and only when they were both agreed should the matter be submitted to the king for his assent.'[45] From this moment, parliamentary legislation was thus the product of the king-in-Parliament, to which the separate assent of both houses of Parliament and the monarch was necessary. Even though the scope of the royal prerogative was still vast, the achievement of constitutional monarchy in England arguably dates from this time. The monarch retained a veto over legislation until the reign of Queen Anne (1702–14), after which it became a convention that the monarch would not veto a bill that had been duly passed by both houses of Parliament. The bill regarding the Scottish militia that she refused to sign in 1708 was the last ever vetoed by a British monarch.[46]

The use of statutes as deliberate instruments of policy may be dated to the Tudors. Henry VIII (ruled 1509–47) and his Parliaments passed some 677 statutes, more than had been passed in the previous three hundred years together. It was via statute that the break with the church of Rome was implemented, conveyancing transformed (the Statute of

Uses 1535), the willing of freehold land permitted (Statute of Wills 1540), and various state interventions in the economy effected. Much more attention was devoted to drafting statutes, which were now given extensive preambles aimed at discouraging judges from interpreting them too freely.[47] Tudor and Stuart monarchs were not great fans of the independence of the judiciary in any case. Their theory was that judges, as royal appointees, should not be quick to decide against the interests of the Crown. Or, as former Lord Chancellor Francis Bacon put it in 1625, the judges should remember that 'Solomon's throne was supported by lions on both sides: let them be lions, but yet lions under the throne, being circumspect that they do not check or oppose any points of sovereignty.'[48] Numerous judges were dismissed by the Stuarts in the seventeenth century, the most notorious example being that of the chief justice of King's Bench, Edward Coke, by James I in 1616, when he refused the king's request to delay the hearing of a lawsuit implicating royal interests.

If the Stuarts did not value judicial independence, or the doctrine that kings were subject to the law, they did not respect the role of Parliament in the constitution either. When king of Scotland, James VI (James I of England from 1603) had expressed the view in his *Trew Law of Free Monarchies* (1598) that he could legislate without Parliament and could suspend the law at will. The monarch was accountable only to God, not to any earthly authority. His son Charles I took this to its logical conclusion by not calling Parliament for eleven years (1629–40), an action that, though not illegal, helped to turn much of the country against the king. The ensuing civil war led to the abolition of the House of Lords, the execution of Charles in 1649, and the proclamation of a republic under a council of state (later a protectorate under Oliver Cromwell). It also unleashed a movement for law reform advocating the fusion of law and equity, the establishment of small claims courts and of an appellate hierarchy, abolition of the forms of action, primogeniture, and imprisonment for debt, a mass of criminal law and prison reforms, and the introduction of an income tax – all of them reforms that would not come to pass for two centuries and more.[49]

The restoration of Charles II did not completely resolve the issues that had divided the country during the civil war, and they returned in full force on the accession of his brother James II in 1685. While James's Catholicism played a central role in resistance to his rule, his dismissal of no fewer than fourteen judges in under four years and his claim to be able to suspend the law in particular cases also inspired discontent.

His deposition in 1688, the acceptance of the Crown by William of Orange and Mary, and their agreement to abide by the Bill of Rights 1689, led to the final confirmation that sovereignty resided in the king-in-Parliament. The Bill of Rights made a number of assertions regarding the 'true, ancient and indubitable rights and liberties of the people of this kingdom' that mostly restated older understandings. Among other provisions, it stated that the monarch had no power to dispense with or suspend the law; parliamentary consent was needed for taxation; 'excessive bail ought not to be required, nor excessive fines imposed, nor cruel and unusual punishments inflicted'; all subjects had the right to petition the monarch without penalty; and Protestants could bear arms 'suitable to their conditions and as allowed by law.' The Bill of Rights also declared that Parliaments should be held 'frequently,' a pious hope given concrete form by the *Triennial Act* of 1694, which required general elections every three years until the *Septennial Act* of 1716 extended the maximum life of a Parliament to seven years.[50]

Another consequence of the Glorious Revolution was the *Act of Settlement* 1701, which, in addition to securing the Protestant succession, finally ensured that all superior court judges would be appointed during good behaviour – effectively a guarantee of life tenure barring serious corruption or criminal conviction.[51] This provision did not apply to colonial judges, who continued to be appointed at pleasure until, starting with Upper Canada in 1834, the northern colonies began to legislate good behaviour appointments for their own judges.[52] The Revolution of 1688 would be seen nonetheless by British North American colonists as the critical event of their own constitutional inheritance, confirming the rule of law and defeat of arbitrary royal authority.[53] The sovereignty of the Crown-in-Parliament became the defining feature of the constitutions of the British North American colonies as far as the settler population was concerned, although how it related to pre-existing Indigenous sovereignty was left an open question. One of the Revolution's key episodes, the defeat of James II by William III at the Battle of the Boyne in Ireland on 12 July 1690, would long resonate in a more disturbing way in North America, as an inspiration for militant Protestants to exult in the crushing of Catholicism.

This institutional story concludes with the observation that the separation of powers, increasingly seen as the anchor of constitutional government by eighteenth-century theorists, continued to make little headway in Britain. The office of Lord Chancellor long combined legislative, executive, and judicial powers, while the House of Lords functioned in both legislative and judicial capacities. These practices were exported to British North America, where controversy over the judicial presence on legislative and/or executive councils would, in due course, become linked to the campaign for 'responsible government' in the mid-nineteenth century.[54]

Turning to the protection of individual rights, it is often thought that the story begins with Magna Carta, the 'great charter' that a group of rebellious barons obliged King John to sign at Runnymede in 1215. This argument is based on clause 29 of the version of Magna Carta issued in 1225 by Henry III, which reads as follows in English translation (the charter having been drafted in Latin):

> No free person shall be taken or imprisoned, or disseised of any free tenement or of his liberties or free customs, or outlawed, or exiled, or in any way destroyed, nor shall we go against him or send against him, except by the lawful judgment of his peers or by the law of the land; to no one shall we sell, to no one deny or delay, right or justice.[55]

The main purpose of the charter was backward as opposed to forward looking: the barons aimed to have the king swear to observe existing customs and preserve their existing privileges. It applied only to free persons, at a time when many in England existed in a state of unfreedom known as villeinage status. Villeins were not slaves or even serfs but were bound to remain on the manor of their lords, could be prevented from leaving by force, and could thus be lawfully imprisoned by their lords in appropriate cases pursuant to 'the law of the land.' The status was heritable, though freedom could be obtained in a number of ways. Villeinage status effectively died out by the end of the sixteenth century, however, thus potentially enlarging the scope of Magna Carta to include the entire English population.

What exactly was included within the scope of rights protected by clause 29 was not clear for a long time. A statute of 1354 reworded part of the clause to read 'no man ... shall be put out from land or tenement or arrested, imprisoned or disinherited or put to death without being brought to answer by due process of law,' thus adding that hallowed phrase to our law.[56] This revision broadened the scope of the clause by making clear that it applied not just to the king, but to any person who might detain another illegally. Magna Carta itself provided no remedies for breach of the duties mentioned therein, however, leaving its impact unclear. In succeeding centuries it all but disappeared from the law courts and from the 'common learning' of the inns of court, where it was thought to be mostly obsolete and certainly not treated as any kind of fundamental law. It may have survived, but only dimly, in the popular imagination.

Only in the later sixteenth century was there a revival of interest in Magna Carta as it became linked with habeas corpus and trial by jury, providing the remedial apparatus that had long been lacking. In the second half of the sixteenth century the courts had developed the writ of habeas corpus into 'the most expansive remedy of the common law, available whenever a person was detained anywhere in the king's dominions, without any restrictions.'[57] This occurred without reference to Magna Carta, but once the writ's purview was established, lawyers were not slow to make the linkage. The reason anyone could be called upon to justify the detention of another was found in clause 29: no one, including the monarch, was above the law, and only an independent judiciary could decide whether the reason for detention was within the law. Magna Carta declared the principle, habeas corpus provided the remedy. Clause 29 also came to be linked with trial by jury and provided the basis for challenging arbitrary action regarding the deprivation of liberty or property, often via the writ of prohibition. In the power struggles of the early seventeenth century, Magna Carta took on a constitutional significance it had lacked almost since its appearance. Its open text came to be seen as the source of some of the most important guarantees of lawful treatment by both state and private actors, an anchor of constitutional government itself, and the basis of a popular concept of 'British justice' that was widespread in British North America down to the Second World War.[58]

This heritage of personal liberty could nonetheless coexist with its opposite for long periods of time, and the heritage of legal coercion was most pronounced where labour was concerned. The Crown prerogative to impress ordinary men for service overseas in the military or the navy – a severe restraint on liberty and often a threat to life itself – was not considered inconsistent with Magna Carta or remediable by habeas corpus. The *Recruiting Act* 1756 permitted impressment only of those who did not 'follow or exercise any lawful calling or employment,' allowing those who fell outside its purview to challenge their enlistment by habeas corpus; but those who fell within the statute had no remedy.[59] African slavery existed for centuries pursuant to customary law in the colonies, and when the status of African slaves brought into England itself was tested by habeas corpus in the 1770s, the most that the courts would say was that such slaves could not be forced to leave against their will.[60] Master and servant law, codified in the *Statute of Artificers* 1562 and exported to a hundred colonies in one form or another, for centuries subjected workers to criminal penalties, including imprisonment and sometimes corporal punishment, for breach of their terms of employment. All of this was part of 'the law of the land,' administered as 'low law' by justices of the peace in a summary way with no written record and very little recourse to superior courts.[61] The unemployed or marginally employed could be jailed or whipped under vagrancy statutes both in England and colonial jurisdictions, while the poor law or analogous provisions permitted local authorities to bind out minors and sometimes adults as apprentices or servants against their will.[62] And for a long time after Blackstone uneasily conceded it in the 1750s, the power of husbands to restrain the liberty of their wives, at least for 'gross misbehaviour,' was accepted.[63]

Thus the heritage of liberty under English law was not unalloyed. The Glorious Revolution may have restrained the power of the Crown, but it opened up another potential source of tyranny: the supremacy of Parliament itself. Prior to the *Reform Act* of 1832, when Parliament was rendered somewhat more representative, it was the embodiment of class rule. The courts were reasonably effective at protecting the liberty of white propertied Protestant males who already enjoyed many societal advantages, but the experience of less favoured groups was highly unpredictable.

The British legal heritage is everywhere evident in modern Canada: in court structures, the legal profession, legal thought and vocabulary, trial process, penal institutions, and substantive law. Once celebrated as evidence of the British connection so highly valued by large parts of the settler population, these features of the legal order have now been so thoroughly Canadianized that their British roots are either no longer evident or not emphasized. This work attempts to walk a middle road between these two extremes. Uncritical celebration of the British legal heritage overlooks many of its flaws, such as its biases with regard to class, race, and gender, but ignoring that heritage, with all its flaws, leads to incomplete and inaccurate historical understanding. It may also lead to undervaluing resources in the common law tradition that could be put to effective use today. The protection of individual liberty was for a long time highly selective in Britain itself, and this ambiguous heritage formed the basis of the colonial constitutions of British North America. Once implanted, however, notions of liberty under law could be expanded to other groups in an effort to create a more inclusive society: a process of struggle that will occupy a good part of the second volume of this work. But liberty as freedom from all restraint was not a part of the British tradition, just as it was not part of French or Indigenous legal traditions. Liberty needed to be balanced with order in the British parliamentary tradition; the Canadian experience demanded that it incorporate pluralism, creating a distinctive legal and constitutional tradition that will be explored in this volume and the next.

PART TWO

European Chartered Enterprise, New France, and the Encounter with Indigenous Law, 1500–1701

5

Early Contacts, Early Charters

In July and August 1701 some 1,300 delegates, representing dozens of Indigenous peoples from the Atlantic to the headwaters of the Mississippi, arrived in Montreal for an enormous peace conference. In numbers they equalled half the entire European population of the island.[1] As the delegates arrived the calumet was smoked, while dancing and feasting created an atmosphere of goodwill. A gift-giving ceremony between Governor Louis-Hector de Callière and the chiefs occurred on 25 July, after which the gates of the town were opened so that the delegates might enter and trade as they wished. Even though an epidemic that struck the town killed the great Huron-Petun chief Kondiaronk on 2 August, the treaty was concluded and ratified by all present. The spectacle of his funeral and burial in Notre Dame church on 3 August (Kondiaronk was nominally Christian) may even have assisted in the ratification of the accord at the final grand assembly on 4 August. A large area had been cleared near the river, and a hall built in which the final speeches would be made. All the 'quality' of the town came out to witness the event: among the two or three thousand present, 'Native chiefs "wearing their long robes of pelts," with painted faces and feathered head-dresses, rubbed shoulders with stiff, bewigged officers in uniform and elegant ladies in their most beautiful finery.'[2] Callière's opening speech was replete with Indigenous references – burying instruments of war in a pit, providing broth to all in a common pot, and smoking the calumet – while he had prepared a wampum collar for each of the Indigenous leaders. When his speech was translated by the five interpreters present, it was greeted with cheers of approval by the delegates. Afterwards, each orator representing his nation held his wampum collar as he addressed the gathering, while some had adopted elements of French dress in order to symbolize the welcoming of the French into this great alliance. An enormous feast and bonfire closed out the day, while more gift-giving followed on subsequent days. As witness Claude-Charles Bacqueville de la Potherie observed,

> The marks of esteem and friendship we had shown until then to all our allies would have made little impression on their minds if we had not at the same time done something more real and more effective, to acknowledge all the good services they had rendered to us. We therefore planned to give them the presents that had been prepared in the storehouses of the King.[3]

The French had well understood the links between gift-giving, trade, and peace that were so crucial in Indigenous societies.

The text of the agreement reached by the parties was not a treaty in the European sense. Rather, it was a transcription of the orations delivered by Callière and the Indigenous representatives at the peace conference. While the existence of a written document was in accordance with European traditions, its attempt to record the oral agreement of the parties – the only real agreement in the view of the Indigenous parties – was not. The pictographs by which each leader 'signed' for his respective people represented assent to the conclusions of the oral discussions, not a decision to be bound by written terms.[4] Such an agreement, from the Indigenous point of view, represented the beginning of a relationship of kinship, not the finalization of a 'deal.' It had taken many decades, but French attempts to enter into the legal and diplomatic world of their Indigenous hosts had finally succeeded: the understandings contained in the 1701 accord would last until the end of the French regime itself.

A little earlier that summer, a somewhat similar gathering had taken place in Albany, on the border of Mohawk territory and lands claimed by the English colony of New York. Representatives of the Five Nations of the Haudenosaunee Confederacy, Mohawk, Seneca, Onondaga, Oneida, and Cayuga, met with Lieutenant Governor John

Nanfan. They both wished to renew a long-standing relationship that had its origins as far back as the Five Nations' first treaty with the Dutch in 1613, where the idea of kaswentha (guswentha), or two-row wampum, was first adopted between European and Indigenous peoples in the northeast. The idea symbolized by the parallel rows of wampum beads, that each people would look after its own affairs but cooperate in trade and other matters, was a huge step forward in intercultural relations. When the Dutch surrendered New Netherland to the English in 1664, the latter continued the relationship the Dutch had established with the Confederacy; in 1677 the parties renewed their relationship in the form of the covenant chain, which espoused ideas similar to those of the kaswentha. Thereafter, peace councils were held at Albany almost annually. The 1701 Nanfan Treaty, as it came to be known, referred to the 'firm league and covenant chain [made] with these Christians that first came to settle Albany on this river which covenant chain hath been yearly renewed and kept bright and clear by all the Governours.'[5] With the treaty the Confederacy sought protection for their hunting grounds as far west as 'Quadoge' (Chicago), which they asserted were being intruded upon by the French and by Indigenous nations to the west. The English, meanwhile, were seeking an alliance, or at least neutrality on the part of the Confederacy, in what was expected to be a renewal of war with France.[6] While the written terms of the treaty purported to surrender and 'quitclaim' a huge area of land to the English, the understanding of both sides was that the Confederacy was not giving up land but seeking protection and alliance.[7]

These negotiations in Montreal and Albany in the summer of 1701 show both the English and French entering the world of Indigenous diplomacy, while the Indigenous peoples were prepared to adapt their own practices to some extent to deal with the Europeans. The result was a body of intercultural law that would govern relations between Europeans, represented by the English (later British) and French Crowns, and Indigenous peoples, represented by their own leaders. The covenant chain, although entered into when the Five (later Six) Nations lived in what would later become the United States, would continue to govern the relationship between them and the British Crown when the Confederacy was re-established after the American Revolution at the Grand River settlement in Upper Canada. It would also be extended to other Indigenous peoples in the wake of the Seven Years' War.[8]

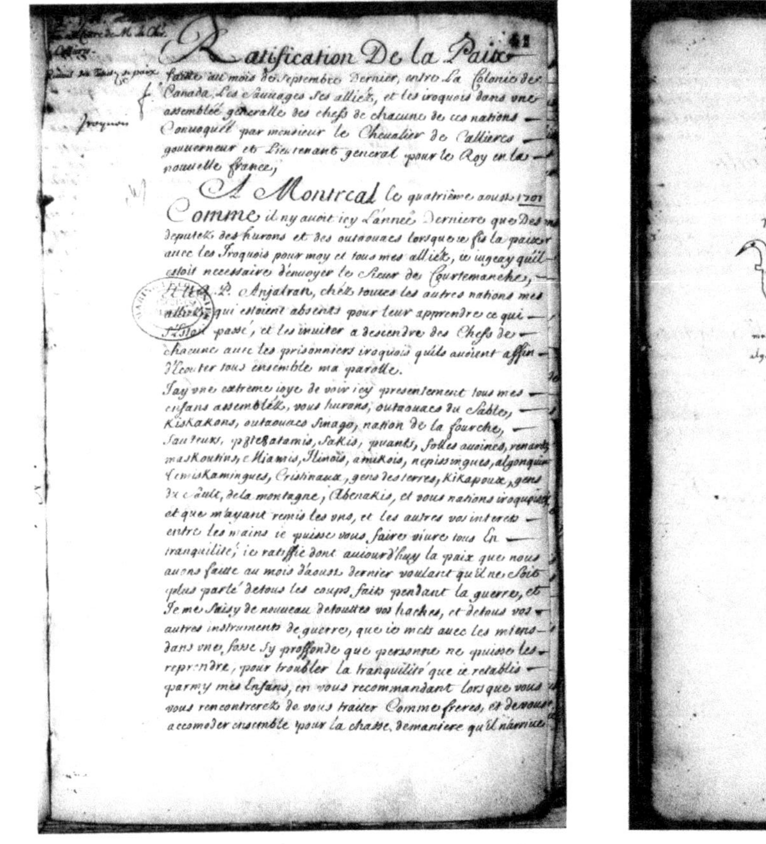

Ratification De la Paix
faitte au mois de septembre dernier, entre La Colonie de Canada, Les Sauvages Ses alliez, et les iroquois dans une assemblée generalle des chefs de chacune de ces nations Convoquée par monsieur le Chevalier de Callieres gouverneur et Lieutenant general pour le Roy en la nouvelle france;

A Montreal le quatrième aoust 1701

Comme il ny avoit icy L'année Derniere que Des deputez des hurons et des outaouacs lorsque ie fis la paix avec les Iroquois pour moy et tous mes alliez, ie iugeay qu'il estoit necessaire d'envoyer le Sieur de Courtemanche, et le R. P. Anjalran, chés toutes les autres nations mes alliez qui estoient absents pour leur apprendre ce qui s'estoit passé, et les inviter a descendre des Chefs de chacune avec les prisonniers iroquois qu'ils avoient affin d'Ecouter tous ensemble ma parolle.

J'ay une extreme ioye de voir icy presentement tous mes enfans assemblez, vous hurons, outaouacs du Sable, Kiskakons, outaouacs Sinago, nation de la fourche, Sauteurs, poutouatamis, Sakis, puants, folles avoines, renards, masKoutins, Miamis, Ilinois, amikois, nepissingues, algonquins, temiskamingues, Cristinaux, gens des terres, KiKapoux, gens du Sault, de la montagne, Abenakis, et vous nations iroquoises, et que m'ayant remis les uns, et les autres vos interests entre les mains ie puisse vous faire vivre tous En tranquilité; ie ratiffie dont aujourd'huy la paix que nous avons faitte au mois d'aoust dernier voulant qu'il ne soit plus parlé de tous les coups faits pendant la guerre, et Je me Saisy de nouveau de toutes vos haches, et de tous vos autres instruments de guerre, que ie mets avec les miens dans une fosse sy proffonde que personne ne puisse les reprendre, pour troubler la tranquilité que ie retablis parmy mes Enfans, en vous recommandant lorsque vous vous rencontrerez de vous traiter Comme freres, et de vous accomoder ensemble pour la chasse, de maniere qu'il n'arrive

Treaty signed at Montreal, 4 August 1701, by Governor Louis-Hector de Callière and representatives of thirty-eight or thirty-nine Indigenous nations. The latter signed by pictographs, or doodems, rendered on this copy by a French scribe. The text recorded the speeches of the parties, not the numbered clauses of a 'deal.'

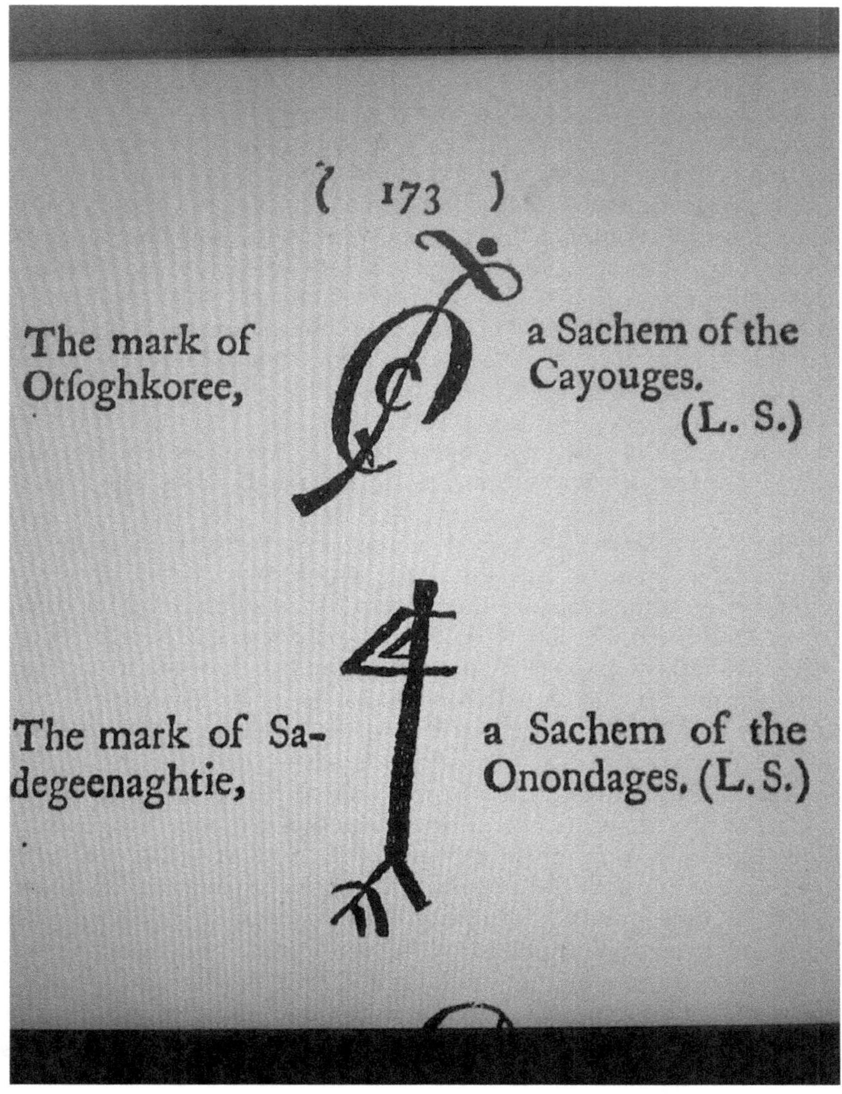

Thomas Pownall, former governor of Massachusetts, included the text and signatures of the Nanfan Treaty of 1701 in his book *The Administration of the Colonies* (1765). Note the care taken to reproduce the doodems of the sachems. 'L.S.' refers to locus sigilli, or 'the place of the seal,' indicating that the British equated Indigenous doodems with the seals used to authenticate deeds and important documents in English legal usage.

It was the rich resources of fish and marine mammals off the east coast of North America that initially enticed Europeans to cross the Atlantic in the early modern period. Interest in furs would come later. The Basques, French, Spanish, and Portuguese all fished and whaled off the east coast throughout the sixteenth century and probably had started doing so in the previous century.[9] When Jacques Cartier sailed through the Strait of Belle Isle between Newfoundland and Labrador in 1534 and met another French ship from La Rochelle, he noted the event in his account of the voyage without surprise, suggesting that the French presence was already well established.[10] The resources of the sea could be harvested without any kind of formal colonization, but this is not to say that 'law' was absent even at this early period: in order to maintain order in the coves of Newfoundland that ships from various European countries used as bases during the fishing season, a custom early developed that the captain of the first ship in a given harbour was authorized to resolve disputes among later arrivals.[11]

The fish trade was enormously valuable: by the later sixteenth century, it exceeded in value Spain's trade with its American colonies and would remain for centuries much more valuable than the fur trade. Unlike the fur trade, however, the cod fishery could be prosecuted without Indigenous participation; as a result there was little contact between the Beothuk and European fishers in the seventeenth century. By the mid-seventeenth century, the catch off Newfoundland was about 200,000 tonnes a season, as much as was taken in the early twentieth century.[12] In spite of the value of the industry, it was not cod or whales as such that encouraged European monarchs to become interested in asserting their sovereignty in this part of the world, but the promise of mineral wealth such as had been found in South and Central America, and the idea that a northwest passage to China might be found through North America. Jacques Cartier's voyages between 1534 and 1543 on behalf of the French Crown were so motivated, as were John and Sebastian Cabot's between 1497 and 1508, and Martin Frobisher's voyages between 1576 and 1578 on behalf of the English Crown.

As soon as the European monarchies began to take an interest in establishing some kind of official presence in North America – and both Cartier's and Frobisher's voyages were state-supported – they were concerned to legitimate their actions and claims through legal instruments. Typically they used letters patent, which could be used to create companies or proprietorships, but a variety of other instruments such as commissions were also deployed.

The purposes of those instruments were multiple: first and foremost, establishing claims prior to those of other European powers; second, framing relations with Indigenous peoples for purposes of governance, trade, and evangelization; and third, setting up structures of authority and justice for the eventual settlement of Europeans. These goals were articulated even in the earliest known French commission relating to North America, that of Jean la Roque, Sieur de Roberval, in 1541.[13] But it would be wrong to see this emerging law of colonization simply as an instrument for dealing with other states and with native peoples. Subjects of the European monarchies sought to use the law for their own domestic purposes and to gain economic, political, and honorific advantages against fellow subjects. Monopolies on trade with Indigenous peoples were especially sought after and were a useful carrot for monarchs to use to encourage investment by their subjects in colonial ventures. In turn, monarchs used their authority over colonies to shore up and enhance their own power at home as well as abroad.[14] Colonization abroad and state formation at home were intertwined processes.

The French and English had come rather late to the colonization enterprise. In 1493, following the first voyage of Columbus, Pope Alexander VI had purported to grant to the Crown of Spain the rights to 'such islands and lands ... as you have discovered or are about to discover' in a zone west of a meridian 100 leagues west of the Azores.[15] The following year in the Treaty of Tordesillas, Spain and Portugal arrogated to themselves the power to divide up the Americas without any further approval by the pope. France never accepted this position and argued first, that the papacy's authority was spiritual, not temporal; and second, even if it possessed temporal authority, it was bound by the fundamental principle, known to any lawyer, of *nemo dat quod non habet*: one cannot give away what one does not own. Furthermore, neither the French nor the English Crowns accepted the theory that discovery was sufficient to make a legal claim to a new territory binding on any other nation; only discovery followed up by actual occupation would do. Both England and France were generally respectful of the claims of other European monarchs and careful in their commissions and charters to limit their own claims to lands not yet possessed by other sovereigns. Thus in Roberval's commission Francis I went out of his way to state that he had no desire to invade the lands of 'any prince or power allied to us, and especially those of our most dear and beloved brothers the Emperor [Charles V] and the King of Portugal,'[16] while Humphrey Gilbert's letters patent of 1578 enjoined him to 'search out ... barbarous lands, countries and territories not actually possessed of any Christian prince or people' and to 'inhabit or remain there.'[17] Both John Dee, who accepted the validity of the papal bull of 1493, and Richard Hakluyt the Elder, who did not, insisted that discovery gave rise to only a potential claim that had to be perfected by taking possession of the lands in question.[18]

All European nations looked to Roman law to provide the supranational framework within which their claims to extra-European territory could be asserted and defended. Just as Latin was the lingua franca of educated early modern Europeans, so Roman law was their common legal language. The nascent law of nations was considered to be based on Roman law and natural law, as well as on the actual practice and emerging customs of nations. Settlement of new territories was considered to fall under a monarch's absolute (or extraordinary) prerogatives, which were informed, even in England, by Roman law.[19] As Sir Edward Coke observed, 'The common law meddles with nothing that is done beyond the seas.'[20]

The French initiatives of the early sixteenth century in northern North America were not followed up for over half a century as France became embroiled in the wars of religion, in which between two and four million people died.[21] Elsewhere, short-lived French colonies in Brazil (1555–60) and Florida (1562–5) were wiped out by their Spanish and Portuguese rivals – demonstrating, incidentally, the wisdom of not encroaching on territories claimed by other monarchs.[22] When the wars of religion ended with the ascension of Henry IV to the throne and the promulgation of the Edict of Nantes in 1598, granting civil rights to Protestants and tolerance to their religion, the colonial enterprise started up again immediately. The Marquis de la Roche was granted a commission to establish a colony on Sable Island in 1598, and Pierre de Chauvin de Tonnetuit was granted a commission with exclusive trading privileges in 'New France' in 1599 with the obligation of establishing fifty settlers annually.[23] Neither of these colonies survived, but the commission granted by Henry IV to de Monts to Acadia in 1603 would have longer-lasting results, even though the company he formed had failed by 1607.[24]

One key lesson the French retained from their sixteenth-century failures had been learned in Brazil. There, they sent young French men to live with the native inhabitants, the Tupinambá, in order to learn their language, customs, and way of life. This resulted in fruitful relations with the local population, and continued access to the dyewood sought by the French.[25] In Acadia and Canada, the French would repeat this strategy with various Indigenous peoples, learning not only how to survive in the harsh climate but also how to conduct trade, war, and diplomacy in accordance with Indigenous expectations. This strategy would bear fruit a century after French settlement began, with the Great Peace of Montreal of 1701, with which this chapter opened. It was this achievement and its promise of peace that allowed the small and struggling colony to put down deeper roots in the eighteenth century, and along with them, the civil law.

The early charters and commissions issued by monarchs were addressed as much to fellow European sovereigns as they were to their own subjects. They were legal performances used to stake claims to portions of the American continent before an international audience. Often considered as constituting mere 'paper empires,' recently they have been taken more seriously.[26] In particular, 'there is little [in the charters] to show that the French Crown viewed North America as *terra nullius*, vacant land appropriable by discovery or token occupation.' De Monts's 1603 commission, which was used as a model for Champlain's of 1612 and 1625, directed him to make alliances and/or treaties of peace and friendship with Indigenous peoples, suggesting that they possessed international juridical capacity of some kind. War against them was authorized, but only if efforts at peaceful interaction failed.[27] The commission purported to authorize De Monts to make grants of land to French subjects without the permission of the Indigenous inhabitants, but this has to be read against the injunction to maintain good relations with them. We return to this question in chapter 8, after reviewing the legal structures put in place by the colonial powers, as these would also have a role to play in the legal characterization of the European–Indigenous relationship. Those of the French, whose colonization efforts in northern North America were much more advanced than those of the English in the seventeenth century, will be considered first, followed by a brief account of the more tentative English presence in Rupert's Land and Newfoundland.

6

Law and Governance in the French Possessions: Public Law and the Growth of Institutions

The establishment of small settlements at Port-Royal (1605) and Quebec (1608) was followed later in the seventeenth century by others at Plaisance (Placentia, Newfoundland) and Louisiana, and by fortified trading posts in the Pays d'en haut (the Upper Great Lakes) and the Mississippi valley. All these settlements and forts were known collectively as New France. 'Canada' referred to the St Lawrence colony with its headquarters at Quebec, and its inhabitants were called Canadiens by the French and later the English. The territory now known as Nova Scotia was called Acadie by the French from an early date, but the label Acadien/Acadian for its European settlers was an eighteenth-century development. French settler law in the areas claimed as part of northern New France was shaped by three main factors in the seventeenth century: security concerns with regard to the Haudenosaunee, the Dutch, and the English; low immigration and slow population growth, which exacerbated the security situation but allowed imported institutions to be established with a minimum of resistance; and the French state's desire to establish an ordered, deferential, and Catholic society (ideally including native converts) modelled on that found in the French countryside.

The alliance of the French with the Innu, Algonquin, Etchemin, and Huron-Wendat emerged early on, and almost fortuitously. When the naval captain François Pont-Gravé visited Tadoussac in 1600, where fur-trading with the Innu and other nations had been established for some time, he persuaded the Innu elders to let him take two young men 'of rank' back to France. There they learned the language, were exposed to French life, met King Henry IV and many of the nobility, and were treated well by their own account. When Pont-Gravé returned to Tadoussac in 1603 with Samuel de Champlain in tow as an observer, they brought with them the young Innu men. The party happened to arrive just as a gathering of about 1,000 Innu, Algonquin, and others were celebrating a victory over their mortal enemies, the Haudenosaunee. The French were welcomed and given a place of honour at the tabagie, or tobacco-feast, that was being held to mark the event. When one of the Innu ambassadors spoke to the gathering about his experiences in France, Champlain noted that the audience listened 'with the greatest possible silence.' The Innu chief Anadabijou proposed an alliance with the French, which all present agreed upon. The welcoming of the French into a kinship relationship confirmed that they too would be enemies of the Haudenosaunee, or Five Nations Confederacy.[1]

The alliance of the Dutch with the Five Nations, continued with the English after their taking of New Netherland in 1664, was a potent threat to the French colony. An English expedition under the Kirke brothers managed to capture Quebec in 1629, but it was returned to France in 1632 by the Treaty of St-Germain-en-Laye. The French remained at war with the Haudenosaunee on and off for the entire century until the Great Peace of 1701, deepening their dependence on their Indigenous allies. Meanwhile, their English rivals would also pose an existential threat by the end of the century. After taking Acadie's capital Port-Royal in a bloodless attack in 1690, New England troops under Sir William Phips sought to take Quebec; they were repulsed, with the outcome determined by the decisions of the Europeans' Indigenous allies. First, the Abenaki warned the French of the attackers' approach, without which they would have been taken completely by surprise. Then the Haudenosaunee warriors refused to fight when they realized that some of the English soldiers had smallpox, throwing Phips's offensive strategy into disarray.[2]

In Acadie the situation was the obverse of that in the St Lawrence valley. There, the French were allied with the Mi'kmaq, the Wulstukwiuk (Maliseet), and the Wabanaki Confederacy but subject to constant attack by other Europeans.[3] The colony was raided by a New England expedition in 1613, settled briefly by Scots (1629–32), embroiled in a civil war between rival leaders in the 1640s, captured by the English in 1654 (returned to France by the Treaty of Breda 1667, though the handover did not take place until 1670), and captured again in 1690 (returned to France by the Treaty of Ryswick 1697). This chronic instability, along with little in-migration and low population growth, prevented the development of something resembling the more sophisticated legal infrastructure that emerged in Canada during the same period.

By 1700 the population of Acadie amounted to 1,000 Europeans in addition to some 2,000 Mi'kmaq and 1,000 Wulstukwiuk, while that of the St Lawrence valley was approximately 14,000 Europeans as well as some 2,000 Indigenous inhabitants.[4] Both were dwarfed by the rapidly growing English colonies on the Atlantic seaboard, which harboured some 250,000 persons by the beginning of the eighteenth century. This demographic imbalance meant that native alliances were crucial to the future of New France, and these in turn required an understanding of Indigenous languages, customs, and legal orders.

From Seigneurial Fief to Royal Colony: Institutional Development

In Acadie and Canada, the French king's commissions continued for some time to be modelled on Roberval's of 1541. These granted very extensive powers to a lieutenant or viceroy to deal with native peoples, preferably by peaceful means but if not, by war; to appoint such officers of 'justice et police' as might be necessary; with the advice of 'gens prudens & capables' to make laws (provided these were not repugnant to the laws of France); to occupy such lands as the viceroy wished; and to grant lands to others. Such were, for example, the principal powers contained in Pierre Du Gua de Monts's commission of 1603, which he was to exercise over the lands found between 40 and 46 degrees of latitude.[5] De Monts made use of these powers to grant the lands around Port-Royal to his fellow colonizer Jean de Biencourt de Poutrincourt et de St-Just during their voyage in 1604. This grant of a seigneury was confirmed by Henry IV in 1606, and in 1614 Poutrincourt deeded his interest to his son Charles de Biencourt de Poutrincourt et de St-Just; the grant was superseded by others until the king was finally forced to declare the true owners of the seigneury, along with the ownership of others in Acadie, in 1703.[6]

Henry IV was a great supporter of colonial initiatives, but his assassination by a Catholic fanatic in 1610 led to a seven-year long regency during the minority of his son Louis XIII. It was not until Cardinal Richelieu became the king's chief minister in 1624 that French colonial policy found more direction, although all colonial efforts at this time remained very much works in progress, with many errors and setbacks. Richelieu was the prime mover behind the Company of New France (CNF), or Company of One Hundred Associates, to which the king purported to cede an enormous area stretching from the Arctic Circle to Florida as a seigneury in 1627. In return for this immense tract the company was granted a perpetual monopoly on the fur trade in the area and a fifteen-year trade monopoly. It was also required to provide settlement services: 4,000 settlers over fifteen years, in addition to support for a religious establishment that would help convert the Indigenous inhabitants.[7]

Company rule was a form of indirect rule, by which the king delegated his powers of governance, including the administration of justice, to the company. Unlike the state-subsidized efforts of the sixteenth century, those of the early seventeenth century in both England and France involved no substantial financial commitment from the monarch. The CNF in turn granted seigneuries to individuals or ecclesiastical bodies, who were entitled to create seigneurial courts within their domains. Thus the religious organization responsible for the founding of Montreal, the Société de Notre Dame, exercised seigneurial justice there from 1647 until it transferred the seigneury to the Sulpicians in 1663, who in turn exercised seigneurial justice until 1693. While as of 1636 a governor with a royal commission effectively held all powers military and civil in Canada, including the power, in theory at least, to pass final judgment in all civil and criminal matters, the predominance of seigneurial justice was hard to overcome. In 1651 Governor Jean de Lauson created a seneschal's court, or senechaussée (a level of royal court), that was to be superior to the seigneurial jurisdictions, but without success: it remained the court only for Quebec itself and any surrounding areas that did not have an existing seigneurial court. The court ceased to function in the wake of the transformation of governance in Canada in 1663.[8]

In that year the CNF surrendered its rights to the French Crown, which meant that Canada came under the direct control of Louis XIV. Although a new company, the Company of the West Indies (Compagnie des Indes Occidentales) (CWI) was created in 1664 and governance of Canada vested in it, this company in turn was dismantled in 1674 and Canada was returned to royal government once again. For the most part, the institutions created during the period of first royal government (1663–4), especially the Conseil souverain, survived after the CWI was created. Moreover, the king's appointment of an intendant in 1665 with extensive powers overlapping those of the governor and the CWI meant that royal authority continued to have a strong presence. In fact the king overrode the CWI's charter powers in several key areas, and it receded in importance well before its formal disappearance.[9]

The Conseil souverain was initially composed of the governor general, the vicar apostolic (elevated to the position of bishop in 1674), the king's attorney, and five councillors appointed by the governor, assisted by a clerk of the court.[10] From 1675, when the number of councillors was increased to seven (now including the intendant, who was to preside over it), they were appointed by the king for life; the initial three ex officio members were increased by one with the addition of the intendant.[11] Modelled on the provincial parlements of France, it initially held both administrative and judicial powers, although it tended to focus mostly on its appellate functions after 1700. The Conseil souverain functioned as the supreme court for all the colonies of New France, hearing appeals from seigneurial courts and lower royal courts. It had the power to register royal edicts and ordinances, which in theory, though not always in practice, was required to make them effective in the colony. In addition, it could issue regulatory rulings ('arrêts de règlement') in areas not covered by royal law. For example, the Conseil issued the comprehensive 'Règlements généraux de police' of 11 May 1676, dealing with a wide variety of matters from the regulation of trade, to fire prevention, to road maintenance and the disciplining of servants.[12] The Conseil souverain was renamed Conseil supérieur in 1703, at which time the number of councillors was raised to twelve. It remained a key institution throughout the remainder of the French regime.

Acadie escaped the CWI interlude because at the time of the company's creation the Atlantic colony was under the nominal control of the English. From 1670, when the French formally resumed control, until the end of the French regime in peninsular Acadie in 1713, the colony would be subject to the governor general at Quebec and decisions of its courts and officials subject to appeal to the Conseil souverain. In practice, however, the governor of Acadie was allowed to report directly to France because the St Lawrence was frozen for nearly half of each year.[13]

A system of royal courts gradually took shape after the establishment of royal government in 1663, and these also remained in place until the end of the French regime. Their geographic jurisdiction followed the division of Canada into three administrative areas, each with its own governor: Quebec, Trois-Rivières, and Montreal. The Prévôté de Québec was formally created by royal edict in 1677, although in fact it continued a court created by the CWI in 1666. The royal court at Trois-Rivières was also created in 1677 and likewise continued a court set up in 1667 by the CWI. Royal jurisdiction in Montreal did not arrive until 1693, as the Sulpicians exercised jurisdiction as seigneurs of the island until then. The only change made to these arrangements before the end of the French regime was the creation of an admiralty court at Quebec in 1717, to hear disputes about maritime trade formerly heard by the Prévôté and to decide on prizes during wartime. In addition to these courts, a diocesan officiality was created in 1660 by the vicar apostolic and formally recognized by the king in 1684. It was the court of first instance for canon law matters, and civil or criminal cases where an ecclesiastic was involved, and appeals from it, like those from the admiralty court, went directly to the Conseil souverain.[14]

The royally appointed judge in each of the three jurisdictions was called the lieutenant civil et criminel. He was assisted by a deputy judge (except at Trois-Rivières) and a variety of judicial auxiliaries (auxiliaires de justice). These comprised a king's attorney (procureur du roi), a registrar (greffier), bailiffs (huissiers), and notaries. The king's attorney looked after royal interests, undertook prosecutions, and was supposed to ensure procedural regularity at all times. Notaries assisted the court and sometimes represented litigants, as did bailiffs. In France this would have been the province of an avocat (barrister), but the profession was never formally established in New France, ostensibly because its members encouraged litigiousness among the inhabitants.[15] The most burdened justice official was the registrar, who had to maintain the judicial archives, make a summary of each case as it went on, and arrange for copies of deceased notaries' records to be stored with him. The post of bailiff was only part-time, and there were six royal bailiffs in the region of Quebec alone, who often competed for work.[16]

In criminal matters, the royal courts of Canada were assisted by the marshalcy, or maréchaussée. This institution, headed by a provost (prévôt) and modelled on the French original, was created by royal edict of 9 May 1677 'to seek out and punish criminals.'[17] As soon as a royal judge was presented by an individual or the king's attorney with knowledge of the commission of a crime, he would so inform the provost of the marshalcy, who would then attempt to find the criminal and bring him or her before the court. Criminal procedure was inquisitorial and laid down in the Great Ordinance of 1670, which, although never registered by the Conseil souverain, was scrupulously followed throughout the French regime.[18]

The royal courts had concurrent jurisdiction with the seigneurial courts in those localities where the latter existed and also heard appeals from them. This issue will be explored more fully below, but it appears that in the rural seigneuries close to Quebec, habitants preferred to use the local seigneurial court rather than the Prévôté. The town of Quebec, with only 20 per cent of the population of the area under the jurisdiction of the Prévôté, furnished 75 per cent of the latter's clientele, with no appreciable change over time during the French regime. Thus its caseload was surprisingly commercial and 'urban' for an overwhelmingly rural society. Criminal law made up a minuscule proportion of its caseload, between 1 and 3.5 per cent.[19]

Royal courts such as the Prévôté had a broad range of functions beyond the purely judicial. Its officers, the king's attorney and the bailiffs, had the duty of enforcing local regulations and made weekly tours of inspection checking for infractions. The prices of basic commodities were set, for example, and only farmers, not middlemen, were allowed to sell their produce in town. The royal courts also ensured that the laws were publicized: new ordinances were read out in the hearing room, posted in the public square, and read out after Sunday mass by a court official or local notary. Nor were the royal courts' justice functions limited to litigation. Various private documents such as marriage contracts and contracts of gift were read publicly and then registered in what was called the register of insinuations. The royal courts played an important supervisory role in the administration and transmission of family property on marriage and death, especially with regard to the property of minors. Some of these functions were transferred to notaries over time, but all records of deceased notaries or those leaving practice had to be left with the clerk of the royal court so that they would be available to interested parties in future. Until 1698 these records were often kept by the clerks of the seigneurial courts, but an ordinance of that year required them to be left only with the royal courts.[20]

Studies of the cost of litigation are rare as a result of gaps in documentation. Dickinson's study of the rates and costs of litigation in the Prévôté de Québec found that costs were lower in Canada than in France, mainly because most matters were concluded rather more quickly in the colony, but also because fewer litigants employed (and thus had to pay) lawyers or others to represent them. Responsibility for the costs of civil litigation was the same in England: the loser paid most of the costs of the winning party. While the costs of litigation did not put it out of reach of the majority of the population, they were nonetheless a burden, and hence a possible disincentive, for the poorer half of the population.[21]

No account of the courts would be complete without reference to what is called in French l'infrajudiciaire, or alternate dispute resolution. Both in France and New France, the state welcomed efforts to resolve disputes outside of court. In Canada, notarial records reveal that settlements arrived at with the assistance of third parties were fairly common at all levels of society, particularly in family and commercial disputes, although the affluent and urban residents were over-represented in this activity.[22] When arbitration was court-directed, it related more to the evaluation of items in dispute than questions of law.[23]

By the end of the seventeenth century there was a coherent and relatively straightforward judicial system in place in Canada – certainly a much simpler one than in France, where multiple overlapping jurisdictions created a highly complex legal order. Another improvement over the French system was the fact that offices were not venal: judicial and other offices could not be legally bought and sold as they could in France. The Canadian system was characterized by checks and balances. Not only was there a structure of appeal, but each court level had a general supervisory jurisdiction over the one below. Thus the royal courts could inspect the registers of the seigneurial courts and could hear complaints about their judges. The intendant had an overarching jurisdiction allowing him to intervene at any court level and bring up a case for his personal decision (a process known as évocation), especially one directly involving the king's interests. Different intendants used this power to varying degrees – Jacques Raudot (1705–11) claimed to have decided some 2,000 cases personally in just over a year, but he was unusual.[24] The Conseil souverain also had a procureur général du roi, who played a role similar to that of the procureur du roi at the royal courts, but in addition functioned as a sort of deputy minister of justice for the colony of Canada.[25]

The courts, both seigneurial and royal, were key elements in the creation of a settler society in the St Lawrence valley, and not only as a forum for resolving disputes. Their role in conserving documents relating to land and wealth transfers, marriage and guardianship made them key repositories of information for both state and subject, creating a paper trail that ensured the generational transfer of wealth and naturalized the continued presence of the European newcomers in these alien territories. The courts' symbolic role as sources of justice and as one face of the colonial state was also important. The administration of justice was a principal function of old regime societies: handled well, it was a source of stability and shored up monarchical power, but handled poorly, it could have the opposite effect. Louis XIV himself recognized this soon after embarking on his personal reign in 1661; in secret instructions to Louis Gaudais-Dupont, who had been deputed to report on the state of the colony, the king's minister advised that

> up to the present there has been in that colony no regular system of justice the authority of which was universally recognized, and through the weakness of character of those who were charged with rendering justice, the judgments which were pronounced were generally unexecuted. Therefore His Majesty resolved some time ago to create a Sovereign Council in the said country.[26]

A functioning justice system identified with the king could contribute to the legitimacy of the colonial state under a regime where there were restricted opportunities for popular input.[27]

In Acadie the state of judicial and overall administration was much more rudimentary, given its small population and constant swapping between empires. Seigneurial concessions virtually always accorded haute, moyenne, and basse justice to the seigneurs, but the small numbers of settlers would have made it uneconomical to hold a seigneurial court, and there is little evidence of the exercise of seigneurial justice. In two instances where important matters arose, one of sedition and one involving an allegation of witchcraft, the local seigneur declined jurisdiction, sending the accused in the first case to La Rochelle in France for trial, and in the other referring the matter to the Prévôté de Québec for decision.[28] To the extent that royal justice was available in Acadie, the habitants seem to have had recourse to it rather than seigneurial courts.[29]

There was no body in Acadie similar to the Conseil souverain. After the French resumed control in 1670, a lieutenant civil et criminel (royal judge) was appointed, but he was enjoined by the king to urge the inhabitants to seek arbitration rather than to decide cases pursuant to formal process. Given that the incumbents of this office had no formal legal training, that no courthouse is known to have existed under the French regime, and that there is no evidence that a single law book existed in Acadie during that period, this may have been wise counsel.

No records survive to illuminate the way in which this officer exercised his judicial functions, but there are suggestions that local dispute-resolution techniques developed organically to supplement or fill gaps in the official organs of justice. In 1692 Governor Villebon approved an initiative from the inhabitants of Minas whereby three men chosen by the inhabitants of the area would decide their disputes, especially those relating to land. In 1704 the king approved a locally generated plan to have three assessors sit with the lieutenant civil et criminel in criminal cases, so as to enhance the legitimacy of the result; this plan is known to have been followed in subsequent years.[30]

Turning from the judiciary to the legislative and executive branches of government, the story is rather different. Where, generally speaking, the royal courts at least presented a rational and coherent face, other law-making and enforcing bodies did not. In the towns, for example, as many as six different bodies could create by-laws: the seigneurial judge, the local governor, the intendant or his delegate, the town major, the governor of New France, and the Conseil souverain.[31] Each tried to guard its privileges and jurisdiction, resulting in frequent friction and confusion. In particular the relationship between the governor and the intendant was often fraught. In theory, after 1665 the governor was to deal with military and diplomatic matters, while the intendant dealt with finance, administration, and public welfare. The inextricability of war and finance needs no elaboration.

The bishop was also a source of law in his own right in an almost exclusively Catholic society. His ability to direct the actions of parish priests through pastoral letters, or mandements, in effect gave him law-making power among the faithful, backed up by the power of excommunication where necessary. For example, he effectively created a licensing scheme for midwives by requiring parish priests to conduct an examination of all candidates to ensure that they were faithful Catholics; the priest also had to administer an oath to them by which they swore to perform their duties diligently. Midwives often had to baptize sickly infants in the absence of a priest, and the church wanted to ensure that only trustworthy and pious women were able to carry out this important task. When a midwife died, the priest was to call on the 'most virtuous and honest women of the parish' to nominate her successor.[32] In 1683 Bishop de Laval circulated a pastoral letter responding to a particularly boisterous 'charivary' that had, in his view, disturbed the peace of the capital and displayed disrespect towards a newly married (though in popular eyes, mismatched) couple. He had called upon the secular authorities to help repress the 'disorder' and in his letter enjoined priests to make their parishioners aware that all participants in such activities risked excommunication. This is not to say that the bishop's injunctions were always followed, but the same could be said of any law.[33]

In addition to all these local sources of law, the king of course remained the supreme source of law, and he often issued laws that were applicable to both new and old France, or sometimes just to New France.[34] In theory, royal ordinances needed to be registered with the Conseil souverain at Quebec, in the way that they were registered with the parlements of France, before they were effective in New France, but it is clear that the practice was otherwise. It was only long after the end of the French regime that the argument equating non-registration with non-enforceability was made with any vigour.[35]

It is easy to issue laws, much harder to have them implemented and enforced. Where the king's laws could be enforced directly by the courts, they were generally observed scrupulously, as with the Ordonnance criminelle. Where they required action by officials or the expenditure of money by individuals, it was often a different story. An arrêt of 1686 applicable to New France required all seigneurs to construct flour mills on their lands if they had not already done so; if they did not, anyone could construct a mill and invade the seigneurial monopoly. While the arrêt was registered by the Conseil souverain at Quebec soon after its promulgation, it was not actually publicized at Montreal, Quebec, and Trois-Rivières until 1707.[36] In 1702 the lieutenant civil et criminel of Acadie reported that there was not a single French miller there, although an English miller had apparently set up shop. It was not until 1710, just before the fall of Acadie, that the Conseil souverain directed the ordinance to be registered at Port Royal.[37] The challenges of geography and communication meant that the 'command and control' model aspired to by the French state did not always translate well to New France. Communications with the mother country were impossible during the half of each year that the St Lawrence remained frozen, while much of the fur trade was carried on in the Pays d'en haut, far from the centres of Quebec and Montreal. In addition, the decision early on to attempt colonization by means of the seigneurial system meant that the power of the colonial state remained somewhat diffuse, although the resulting legal pluralism could have its advantages for the inhabitants. Against this must be weighed the fact that conditions were somewhat more propitious for the unfolding of absolutism in Canada than in France itself, where a tangle of ancient jurisdictions and institutions and a variety of vested interests could impede the centralizing plans of the monarchy.[38]

Seigneurial Law

Louise Dechêne, the great historian of Canada under the French regime, said it best: 'Before everything else, there was the seigneury.'[39] More recently, Allan Greer has echoed the sentiment: 'In land tenure terms, it would be the presence of seigneuries that defined the legal geography of the colony of Canada within the larger imperial space known as New France.'[40] The seigneury granted by Louis XIII to the Company of New France in 1627 purported to stretch from Florida to the Arctic Circle. The geographic ambition was overweening, but in fact the seigneury was the basic instrument of colonization virtually everywhere in New France, from Plaisance in the east to the Ottawa valley in the west, from Acadie to the St Lawrence valley.[41] From 1627 until the end of the French regime, virtually all land was granted to a seigneur, lay or ecclesiastic, who in turn granted portions of it to censitaires. In France some land was held outside of a seigneury, in a free tenure called franc alleu roturier, similar to socage tenure in the common law, but this tenure was almost never encountered in New France.[42] Land could be held directly from the king in a seigneurie directe, in what were called censives du roi, as was some land around Quebec and Trois-Rivières. The new settlement founded at Détroit in 1701 was also set up this way, but this was still a seigneurial tenure, not a 'free' one.[43] The institution of the seigneury not only survived the fall of Acadie and the conquest of New France mostly intact but flourished in the St Lawrence valley for nearly a century after 1760, until the abolition of the seigneurial regime in 1854. Even afterwards, the seigneurs remained figures of some importance in Quebec society,[44] and the compensation due to them and their heirs for the expropriation of their dues was not finally paid off until the 1970s. Seigneurial claims in some sense thus survived well into the period of the Quiet Revolution.[45]

By the early modern period the seigneury in France itself had long outgrown its origins in medieval feudalism, when its functions were primarily military and political. Medieval feudalism was based on a bargain: access to land and protection in return for loyalty and military assistance. As the central state grew more powerful and created professional armies, regional militaries were less needed and indeed came to be seen as a threat. The early days of New France coincided with the Fronde (1648–53): a civil war instigated by some of the chief nobles during the minority of Louix XIV aimed at defending their ancient privileges and autonomy. Louis's forces triumphed, leading to the consolidation of absolutism in France.[46] By the seventeenth century, then, most seigneurs in France were essentially rentiers who did not live on their estates but managed them through agents who collected the various seigneurial dues. Shorn of their military roles, they nonetheless played an important function in local governance in administering justice. In France seigneurs were expected to maintain and staff courts for the carrying out of basse, moyenne, and haute justice, but in New France the low population density often led seigneurs to neglect their justice functions. Basse justice involved petty civil claims worth less than sixty sols.[47] Moyenne justice involved a variety of civil matters, both contentious and non-contentious, relating to seigneurial dues, succession and the family, and minor criminal infractions where the fine was less than sixty sols. Haute justice was the right to adjudicate all crimes and to pronounce any sentence up to and including the death penalty, although the latter had to be confirmed by the king or his representative. The ability to administer haute justice was highly prestigious, and not all seigneurial concessions granted it, either in France or in New France. Royal courts heard claims outside seigneurial jurisdiction and entertained appeals from seigneurial courts.

The seigneury granted to the Company of New France (CNF) took up the old idea of the feudal bargain, but, in return for an immense tract of land, it assumed the obligation to settle 4,000 settlers in twenty years and to assist in the conversion of Indigenous peoples.[48] It in turn granted seigneuries to individuals or religious orders to assist in carrying on the work of settlement and evangelization. The individuals so favoured were, at first, major investors, influential figures with ties to the French court, or military officers, especially after the arrival of the Carignan-Salières regiment in 1665, which was sent to defend the colony from the Haudenosaunee. Over time, however, seigneuries were granted to a wider variety of grantees, including even some illiterate habitants. Some – and this illustrates the protean and adaptable nature of the seigneurial institution – were granted directly by the French Crown to an Indigenous community or to a religious order for the benefit of an Indigenous community. The sole example of the former is the seigneury of Sillery, near Quebec City, granted to 'Chrétien sauvages' in 1651, with the Jesuits named as their 'tutors.'[49] The latter included the royal concession of Sault-Saint-Louis, or Kahnawake, to the Jesuits on behalf of the Mohawks in 1680. Some Indigenous groups took title from an existing seigneur rather than from the Crown, as occurred in 1700 when the seigneurs of St-François granted part of their domain to the Abenakis and Sokokis; the community would come to be known as Odanak.[50] The exact legal nature of these transactions would be called into question in later centuries as colonial authorities sought to establish more control over Indigenous people and lands.[51]

The land granted to a seigneur was called a fief (the word shares the same derivation as the English fee simple), which was a form of noble property. Both persons and property in ancien régime France fell into two categories: noble and roturier (non-noble). A seigneury remained noble property even if its owner did not belong to the nobility, and conversely, the mere acquisition of a seigneury did not ennoble the owner. The legal significance of this was, inter alia, that succession to fiefs followed rules different from those of non-noble property. Seigneuries descended according to a modified form of primogeniture, to be discussed later, while censives (lands granted to the habitants, who were also known as censitaires) were considered non-noble and descended according to the principle of partible inheritance, whereby the male and female children of a landholder shared equally.[52]

Another feature of the fief was that it could be sub-infeudated: the seigneur could create an arrière-fief, or sub-fief, by which a portion of the fief (to a maximum of two-thirds of the area of the fief, according to article 51 of the Custom of Paris) could be given to a person who would in turn become a seigneur over that portion, with the right to grant land to his or her own censitaires. In theory this process could continue indefinitely, such that the holder of the sub-fief could create a sub-sub-fief, and so on. By 1700 there were seventy arrière-fiefs in Canada spread over some twenty-six seigneuries; often these were held by children of the 'head' seigneur.[53]

While most accounts emphasize the relationship between seigneur and censitaire, it is important to recall that the seigneury also created a relationship between the seigneur and the state. When a new seigneury was conceded, or when an existing seigneury was transferred through sale or descent, the new seigneur had two important acts to perform. The first was the ritual of 'foi et hommage,' to be performed in principle within forty days of taking possession, whereby the seigneur would kneel before the state's representative and pledge loyalty to him. Within forty days of this ritual, the seigneur was supposed to prepare the 'aveu et dénombrement' of the seigneury, a kind of mini-census. This was a cadastral description of the lands comprised in the seigneury, with an account of its population and improvements. The seventeenth-century documents are fairly rudimentary, but in the 1720s Louis XV ordered more detailed returns, down to the level of the individual censitaire and the amount of cens et rentes payable by each.[54] Almost all seigneurs eventually complied, and, taken collectively, these formed the papier-terrier of Canada, a kind of colonial Domesday Book.[55] Unfortunately, given its less settled conditions, no similar document seems to have survived for Acadie.

The seigneur–state relationship was also expressed in the droit de quint. Where a seigneury did not descend by inheritance, but was transferred, the purchaser had to pay one-fifth of its value to the king or the colonial administration. This was aimed at discouraging the acquisition of seigneuries by the non-elite. Finally, mines and minerals in the seigneury were generally reserved for the king, although in some concessions the king settled for a percentage of the profit to be derived from mines of gold, silver, and copper; after 1672, oak trees, which were needed by the royal navy, were also reserved to the king.

The seigneury presented a highly attractive package of attributes as a vehicle of colonization. It was familiar to all concerned, it put land in the hands of those willing to work it at little or no charge, and it provided incentives to settle colonists (even if most seigneurs were not as active in this respect as they might have been).[56] It also offered a structure of authority and order, sometimes including seigneurial courts, that commanded deference in a society where the demographics initially favoured those who laboured rather than those who inherited wealth. In the seventeenth century in particular, the relative paucity of settlers introduced a certain equilibrium into the seigneurial equation. As the population grew and land became scarcer, the balance shifted more in favour of the seigneurs as the seigneury became more 'envahissante' (invasive) in the words of Louise Dechêne.[57]

While the seigneury can be understood from a variety of perspectives – geographic, economic, social – the law was the crucial element that structured the seigneury and tied its different elements together. Both seigneur and censitaire were understood to have legal rights and obligations, defined by the Custom of Paris, royal legislation, local edicts and ordinances, and local custom. In addition, while much of the content of this legal relationship was mandated by law, the contract of concession could vary or add to these rights and obligations in certain respects. These rights were enforceable in the seigneurial courts and the royal courts, while the intendant exercised a general supervisory jurisdiction over the administration of the seigneury. As with any legal order, rights were sometimes abused, obligations sometimes shirked, and redress not always available for a variety of reasons.[58]

It is important to understand what the seigneury was not: it was not a formal unit of political administration. In both France and New France, the parish was the basic unit of ecclesiastical and political administration. Each parish had an assembly, to which all heads of household, in theory, belonged. These assemblies dealt with a variety of local administrative issues and annually elected a delegate, or syndic, who represented the parish to the outside world and in dealings with the local seigneur(s). The boundaries of parish and seigneury might coincide but did not necessarily do so. In Canada the role of the parish assemblies was gradually taken over by the captain of the militia, who was appointed by the colonial government, but in Acadie the assemblies retained their traditional role, and the British relied on them as intermediaries after the conquest in 1710.[59] The parish assembly, where it existed, should not be confused with the vestry (fabrique), another parish body that dealt exclusively with the temporal affairs of the church itself, such as maintenance, purchase of supplies, collection of pew rents, and the like. The vestry remained an important local body in Canada, even though the parish assembly declined. The functions of the parish were spiritual, political, and administrative, rather than legal, hence it is not considered at length in this work.[60] The seigneury, by contrast, bristled with law, and the rights and obligations contained in the seigneur–censitaire relationship made it the primary legal relationship, aside from marriage, in the lives of virtually all inhabitants of New France.

Likewise, it is important to understand what a censitaire was not. A censitaire was not a serf or unfree in any way. He or she had no restrictions on mobility and did not need the consent of the seigneur to marry. Nor was the censitaire a tenant: the censitaire 'owned' the censive conceded by the seigneur, though it remained subject to the seigneur's overarching rights, known as the domaine direct. The seigneur was obliged to grant lands to censitaires free of charge in order to promote colonization. The censitaire's two main obligations were to 'tenir feu et lieu' – that is, to occupy the land and make it arable – and to pay two forms of annual dues, known as cens and rentes. Censitaires could sell or lease the land without the seigneur's consent; it was inheritable and could be willed insofar as the Custom of Paris permitted it. Only in two situations would the censive revert to the seigneur's demesne: if the censitaire died without heirs and with no will (called the right of deshérence, or escheat); or if the censitaire abandoned the property for a certain period of time.[61]

The cens was typically a very low amount: when the seigneur Alexandre Le Borgne conceded a censive at Minas in Acadie to brothers Pierre and Mathieu Martin in 1679, the cens was expressed to be one penny, to be paid on 1 January each year.[62] In Canada, the day for payment of the cens was typically 11 November, the feast of St Martin, a date just after the harvest. The cens represented an acknowledgment of social hierarchy: even where the seigneur was not of noble blood, the seigneury itself conferred a certain status or dignity on its holder. Imprescriptible and perpetual, the cens could never be extinguished by non-payment or be 'bought out' by the censitaire.

The cens itself was not 'rent,' but contracts of concession invariably referred to 'cens et rentes.' In the above concession, for example, the rentes payable to seigneur Le Borgne were 'one capon and one bushel of wheat' to be delivered annually to the lord's house in Port Royal on the same day that the cens was payable.[63] The rentes were indeed rent, although still levied at a relatively low rate, and were not strictly speaking seigneurial. In the practice of New France, the two were often stated as a single amount and tended to be thought of as a single levy, even though the two components were juridically distinct. While the cens could not be raised, in theory the rentes could reflect market values and could rise over time as new concessions were granted in a given seigneury. However, resistance by the habitants and occasional intervention by the colonial state combined to prevent pure market forces from operating in this regard.[64]

The other major tax due to the seigneur was casual and irregular rather than annual. If the censitaire transferred the land otherwise than by gratuitous title, a tax known as 'lods et ventes,' amounting to one-twelfth of the value of the land, had to be paid to the seigneur by the purchaser. The Sulpicians on the island of Montreal derived as much as a quarter of their seigneurial revenues from the lods et ventes.[65] A related right known as the droit de retrait, or right of first refusal, could also be exercised on the sale of a censive, but only if it was specified in the initial contract of concession. After a sale the purchaser could be compelled to convey the land back to the seigneur at the purchase price, at the latter's request.[66]

Seigneurial monopolies led to additional levies that added to the censitaire's burden. In France seigneurs held monopolies on various elements of local infrastructure: bread ovens, wine presses, and flour mills. In Canada only the last were commonly encountered, and even they were scarce, given the small and scattered population. In theory the seigneur had an obligation to build such a mill and the censitaires had to use it, paying in return one-fourteenth of all grain brought to the mill. The repeated ordinances of the king and the Conseil souverain mandating the construction of such mills on pain of losing the monopoly suggests that seigneurs were slow to erect them, especially in the seventeenth century. Given that thirty families would be required to break even on the estimated 500-pound investment, this is not surprising. A census in 1725 showed that fewer than one-third of all seigneuries in Canada possessed flour mills.[67]

Commercial fishing with nets or weirs was subject to a seigneurial monopoly, fishing for personal consumption being permitted by French law, but the seigneurial monopoly was abolished in 1710. Censitaires could hunt on cleared land or within a one-league radius, but were not to hunt on the seigneur's own demesne without permission. Seigneurs frequently complained to the intendant about such illicit hunting, however, but not where the hunters were Indigenous; they did not believe they had a right to stop the latter from hunting or fishing.[68] The head seigneur had the right to control the foreshore, regardless of who owned the land next to it, and in the 1640s the CNF began parcelling out and renting parts of the foreshore near Quebec City to those who wished to exploit the eel fishery, a major source of food for the Innu. When Governor D'Ailleboust sought to prevent them from fishing altogether, the Jesuits went over his head to the regent of France, Anne of Austria, and he was dismissed.[69]

Last but definitely not least in this catalogue of rights and duties, came the seigneur's honorific rights. These gave the seigneur precedence in various ecclesiastical matters: the right to the front pew, without pew rent, on the (honourable) right side of the local church; the right to receive communion first; to be mentioned first in prayers for the intentions of the parish; to march at the head of any religious procession immediately after the priest; and, finally, to be buried in the church under the seigneurial pew. The existence of these rights conveyed the uncomfortable idea that there might be a hierarchy in heaven just as there was on earth, and their interpretation could give rise to heated disputes that required intervention from the highest authorities in the colony.[70]

In addition to the mandatory rights and obligations that accompanied the seigneurial relationship, various obligations and privileges might be included in the contract of concession. Corvée, or labour obligations, for example, were not a set part of the seigneurial relationship but might be included in the contract of concession. These were generally not extravagant: two or three days' labour annually might be required on the seigneur's demesne, or access to a communal pasture set aside by the seigneur might be conditional on a day's labour spent maintaining the pasture; sometimes the censitaire could pay a set sum instead of labouring. As of 1716, the intendant forbade stipulations for corvée in future contracts of concession.[71]

In early modern law, legal jurisdiction often accompanied land, and the seigneurial system was no exception, as noted above. Like the seigneurial monopoly on flour mills, the right to administer justice entailed investing in infrastructure – primarily intellectual rather than physical in this case – before one could reap any rewards. If a seigneur wished to establish a court, he or she had to pay a judge (bailli), clerk (greffe), bailiff (huissier) and notary, provide a space where the court could be held, and possibly even construct a prison. As in the case of mills, economies of scale encouraged the larger seigneurs to maintain courts, while the smaller ones could not afford to do so. It has been estimated that about a quarter of the rural population had access to seigneurial courts, which were more likely to be created by religious orders who held large seigneuries in and around Quebec and Montreal.[72] The Jesuits, for example, were granted their seigneury at Notre-Dame-des-Anges near Quebec in 1626, even before the creation of the CNF.[73] They had created a seigneurial court by 1664 at the latest, and it continued to function until the abolition of seigneurial justice by the British after 1760. In Montreal, the Société de Notre Dame exercised seigneurial justice from 1647 to 1663, followed by the Sulpicians from 1667 to 1693, when their right to exercise haute and moyenne justice on the island was abolished. Pursuant to an arrangement with the nearby seigneurs of Saint-Ignace, Lépinay, and Orsainville, the Jesuits' court at Notre-Dame-des-Anges administered justice for their seigneuries as well. The acquisition by the Jesuits of more seigneuries in the area – Sillery, Saint-Gabriel, and Bélair – only enhanced the economies of scale. All levels of haute, moyenne, and basse justice were administered: in 1695, for example, Jean Denis was found guilty of murder by the seigneurial court at Notre-Dame-des-Anges and hanged. In the eighteenth century the colonial administration would begin to transfer haute justice from some seigneuries to its own courts, but the process was piecemeal; some seigneurs, such as the Séminaire de Québec, retained their rights of haute justice down to the end of the French regime.[74]

Even though the exercise of haute justice was highly prestigious for the holder, the main business by far of the seigneurial courts was civil. In the seventeenth century their caseload involved mainly the recovery of debts and wages and disputes over the delivery or quality of goods, along with matters relating to property and seigneurial rights. Non-contentious issues included the fixing of the value of the community of property on the death of a spouse, supervising the work of tutors appointed to look after the interests of children who had lost a parent, and approving inventories of the property of deceased persons prior to distribution. Seigneurs pursued their censitaires, and censitaires sued each other, but typically the latter chose to make claims against their own seigneurs before the intendant, or the Conseil souverain, where they sometimes achieved success. Sieur Duchesnay, for example, was required by the intendant to reverse the reunion of a censive to his demesne, which he had done because of the alleged abandonment of the premises by the censitaire.[75]

The seigneurial courts had concurrent jurisdiction with the royal courts established at Montreal, Quebec, and Trois-Rivières in most matters, but their geographic proximity and lower costs probably made them more attractive than the royal courts in many instances. Costs at the Jesuits' court at Notre-Dame-des-Anges were one-third lower than at the Prévôté de Québec, and a seigneurial notary (also called a procureur fiscal), pursuant to a royal edict of 1678, could charge only half the fees of a royal notary, or procureur royal. In Acadie the small size of the settlements probably discouraged the establishment of seigneurial courts, and no records have been found illustrating the exercise of seigneurial justice.[76]

While the seigneury was not a formal unit of political administration, the seigneurial court did play a certain role in colonial administration in addition to its adjudicative functions, in at least two respects. It registered and publicized ordinances of higher bodies such as the Conseil souverain, the Prévôté de Québec, and the intendants, thus creating a link between the colonial government and the habitant: the important ordinance of 7 April 1686 fixing the price of bread, for example, was registered by the seigneurial court of Notre-Dame-des-Anges. Moreover, the seigneurial notary was supposed to enforce these ordinances and to prosecute offenders before the seigneurial court. In addition, the seigneurial court might issue its own ordinances relating to local matters, such as the use and repair of roads or fixing the price of local ferries.[77] The seigneurial courts' administrative functions were thus similar to those of sessions courts and grand juries in common law jurisdictions, though perhaps carried out in a less systematic way.[78]

Notaries

Champlain's aversion to the legal profession is well known: in 1618 he wrote that he wanted justice rendered without the 'chicaneries et procédures' of old France, 'sans qu'il soit besoing de procureur ny avocat' (without the need of either attorneys or lawyers).[79] His anti-lawyer sentiment was common in the early modern period, but it should be noted that notaries are not included in his critique. The French legal order could manage without avocats, but it could not easily do without notaries, who were required to record land concessions, employment contracts, debt obligations, and important documents at major points in the life cycle: marriage and death. Champlain's family found this out after his death in 1635, when his will was challenged in France because it was not prepared by a recognized notary.[80]

No advocates were ever formally commissioned in New France, but contrary to assertions often made, they were never formally prohibited.[81] Meanwhile, hundreds of notaries were commissioned over the duration of the French regime, even if only one was named in Canada prior to the assumption of royal control in 1663.[82] As in so many other areas of early colonial life, necessity was its own law: priests, court clerks, governors' secretaries, and literate laymen recorded marriage contracts and other important transactions, which were accepted as legitimate in the colony (even if they might not have been in France). This was especially the case in Acadie, where, after the appointment of the first known notary about 1651, there were long periods, such as 1685–1700, when the colony had no notaries at all.[83]

The first official notary appointed in Canada was Guillaume Audouart dit Saint-Germain, named in 1649. Fortunately, he collected as many of the early documents drafted by unofficial notaries as he could find and preserved them in his own registry, or greffe; it survives, containing entries for some 1,067 transactions, or 'minutes.' Although he held other offices, he seems to have struggled to earn a living: when he returned to France in 1663, his house in Quebec was seized by creditors.[84] During these years, some seigneurs also began to appoint seigneurial notaries to work within the limits of their concessions.

Upon the assumption of royal control of Canada in 1663, the Conseil souverain was given the power to appoint notaries, and did so; however, the power quickly gravitated, with the Conseil's acquiescence, to the intendant. Soon the intendant was even naming the seigneurial notaries, with the seigneurs retaining only a right of nomination, but the king did not give up his prerogative to commission notaries directly; he did so on four occasions: three in the seventeenth century and once in the eighteenth.[85] The courts had some role in disciplining notaries, concurrently with the intendant, but played no role in their admission to the profession.

The early notaries were obviously self-taught, as there were no established notaries from whom they could learn, but this continued to be the norm: a tradition of apprenticeship never developed during the French regime. In France itself, a five-year apprenticeship was required in Paris but nowhere else; in the countryside the main requirement for entry was passing an exam administered by other notaries.[86] In the English tradition, the courts and later Parliament developed rules requiring apprenticeship of a certain length with an established solicitor or attorney, followed by an examination before the judges, before a candidate would be recognized as qualified. But with the appointment of notaries a seigneurial, then royal, privilege in New France, neither apprenticeship nor examination was required. Nor do the notaries of New France ever seem to have established a society to promote their interests and improve their profession. The challenges of distance and communication probably rendered such a move impractical, but the dependence of notaries on the favour of the intendant might also have discouraged notaries from formally associating, lest such activities be seen as potentially subversive. As was appropriate in a society built on absolutist principles, the colonial state discouraged the creation of guilds and similar bodies that might constitute competing sources of authority.

Throughout the French regime a number of royal and local edicts and ordinances would regulate the notarial profession's fees and conduct, often in minute detail. This attention is not surprising. In a largely illiterate society, notarial records provided a precious anchor and counterweight to the fallibility of human memory, and an aid to governance. The colonial state relied increasingly on the written records generated by notaries to facilitate orderly settlement and the transmission of wealth. The regulatory gaze of the colonial state in turn helped to solidify and legitimate the profession and enhance its status; nonetheless, the colonial state seemed to regard notaries in a utilitarian light and remained mostly uninterested in their formal education. This was in contrast to surveyors, who had to pass an examination administered by the surveyor general, a post already established in the mid-seventeenth century.[87]

A young man wishing to become a notary first petitioned the intendant, proclaiming his good character, literacy, and legal knowledge (though the last was bound to be rudimentary and was not tested in any event). He was supposed to be of the age of majority, twenty-five in New France, but in practice minority was no bar to becoming a notary; commissions were often granted with the proviso that a relative of the candidate would be a surety for him until he came of age. For example, Pierre Duquet de la Chesnaye of Quebec, the first native-born notary, was commissioned as a royal notary at the age of twenty in 1663.[88] It is not clear whether women were formally barred from the notariat, but in any case none became notaries in New France. The intendant issued a commission if he thought it advisable, but before entering into practice the candidate first had to undergo the 'information de vie et de moeurs,' a prerequisite common to many offices in New France. This was a character inquiry that also required the candidate's parish priest to testify that he was a practising Roman Catholic. The applicant then proceeded to take the oath of office and could practise within the geographic limits specified in his commission. Royal notaries were entitled to practise anywhere in their district (Quebec, Montreal, or Trois-Rivières), or sometimes anywhere in the colony, while seigneurial notaries could practise only in one or more seigneuries.[89]

How did an aspiring notary acquire the necessary knowledge? Early notaries purchased the greffes of their predecessors, gaining a ready source of precedents. In addition there were published texts and formularies, the best known of which was Claude de Ferrière's *La science parfaite des notaires*, published first in 1682 but running to many editions. The legal knowledge required was not all that extensive or arcane: the notary's work under the French regime comprised a relatively small number of legal operations repeated frequently with small variations. Over 80 per cent of the work of rural notary Guillaume Barette, who practised at La Prairie between 1709 and 1744, for example, involved land concessions, marriage contracts, and succession.[90] Many documents in notarial greffes from the French regime are relatively short and written in plain language, quite unlike the lengthy and arcane writings that were part of conveyancing under English law.[91]

The life of a notary under the French regime was not an easy one, especially in the seventeenth century. The tariff for various services set by the king in 1678 was half that recommended by the Conseil souverain, and seigneurial notaries were entitled to charge only half the fee allowed to royal notaries for the same service.[92] A much-awaited revision in 1749 barely changed the tariffs.[93] Geography and low population density compounded the problem of low fees. Outside the three nascent urban settlements, a population thinly scattered over a large area needed the services of a notary at various points in their lives. This led early on to an oversupply of notaries: by 1681 a population of some 10,000 was served by two dozen notaries, twelve royal ones in the three main settlements and twelve in the rural seigneuries, or one notary for every 416 people.[94] Given the poverty of the population and their intermittent need for notarial services, this was a very unfavourable ratio. Unlike in Paris and in many continental jurisdictions, where the number of notaries in a given area was fixed, no set number of notaries was ever established in New France. The problem of oversupply obtained only in some areas, however; many rural settlements lacked a notary within a reasonable distance and were obliged to rely on priests or officials in seigneurial courts to draft necessary documents. Curiously, it was not until the eighteenth century that formal legislation was forthcoming permitting priests to receive wills, for example, when the problem must have been most acute in the earlier period.[95]

While a certain stratification was becoming evident later in the seventeenth century – some notaries in the two main urban centres were generally able to attract a wealthier clientele with a need for more varied services – few notaries could make a living exclusively from their practices.[96] This was the case even in the much more densely populated rural areas of France, where notaries were permitted to cumulate certain other offices such as court clerk and bailiff with their notarial work. Outside of Paris, notaries could act as advocates in cases where they had not drafted documents for the parties.[97] This cumulation of offices was probably even more frequent in New France than in the mother country, and it was common for notaries to engage in commerce or to continue practising their former professions, especially that of land surveyor; rural notaries sometimes engaged in agriculture.[98]

As noted earlier, no commissions for advocates were ever issued in New France. This left room for a variety of persons to hold themselves out as representatives of litigants.[99] Some twenty-one practiciens have been identified in the period prior to 1702, three of whom later became notaries. Practiciens guided clients through the litigation process, appeared for them in court, and charged a fee for it. Indeed, part of the attraction of providing the service was that it was not subject to the low notarial tariff of 1678. The fact that advocacy fell into a grey zone also meant that women were not excluded from it. While it is unlikely that any Canadienne Portia pleaded for fees, a number of married women represented their husbands in the seigneurial courts and even before the Conseil supérieur.[100] Thus, after a shaky start, Canada was reasonably well supplied with legal professionals by the beginning of the eighteenth century, even if many of them were self-taught and their occupational boundaries were more fluid than those found in old France.

Civil Procedure

In contrast to modern notions of the separation of powers as between the executive, legislative, and judicial branches, French law saw the administration of justice as part and parcel of royal authority. The monarch was considered the highest temporal judge, just as God was the ultimate judge over all, and all justice was considered to derive ultimately from the king. The interest of the monarch in the administration of justice did not stop with the creation of courts, but extended also to the details of their procedure. The Grande Ordonnance on civil procedure of 1667, known also as the *Code Louis* or *Code civil*, was an attempt by Louis XIV to ensure a uniformity of legal process across the realm. While not a comprehensive code in the modern civil law sense, it did abolish many anachronistic doctrines and practices, and prefigured the codes of the nineteenth century. It also aimed to make justice more accessible to the king's subjects by expanding and clarifying the reach of summary process. The latter was in principle conducted without lawyers and accomplished quickly at one court sitting, in order to minimize costs. The code was not a procedural manual narrowly understood but also included provisions on matters such as judicial ethics, setting out detailed rules on when judges were required to recuse themselves from sitting on particular cases (title 24).

The opening words of the *Code Louis* encapsulated the role of justice in French legal and political thought, declaring that 'la justice est le plus solide fondement de la durée des États, [qui] assure le repos des familles et le bonheur des peuples' (justice is the firmest guarantee of the longevity of states, ensuring the peace of families and the happiness of peoples). This justice was seen as unitary, such that article 7 of title 1 prohibited judges from interpreting the law: if they ran into difficulties implementing a clause of the ordonnance, they were to refer the matter to the king to learn the royal intention. In practice, however, the provincial parlements in France continued to exercise some interpretive power.[101]

As soon as the first royal court, the Prévôté of Quebec, was established in 1677, Louis XIV's government wanted the ordinance to be extended to New France but understood that it might require some local adaptation. Thus its registration by the Conseil souverain in 1678 was preceded by an explanatory note stating that the king had requested the intendant Duchesneau on behalf of the Conseil souverain to scrutinize the terms of the code and to submit for royal approval any suggestions for alteration that might be thought apposite.[102] The note catalogued the challenges faced by colonial society that might require such changes: 'the poverty of the inhabitants, the state of the country, the difficulty of travelling in all seasons, the lack of experience of most of the judges, and the inadequacy of bailiffs.' The note's author also asserted that the inhabitants often began lawsuits 'thoughtlessly and without having sought the advice of counsel,' though he went on to observe somewhat contradictorily that 'there were no avocats, procureurs, or practiciens, it being to the advantage of the colony to exclude them.'[103]

These problems of geography, poverty, illiteracy, and lack of qualified legal personnel informed the changes to the ordinance desired by the Conseil. Many of the changes requested related to lowering the amount of the fines set for certain offences against the administration of justice, or leaving them to the discretion of the court. Thus, for witnesses who failed to show up at the appointed time, the ordonnance imposed a fine of ten livres; the Conseil suggested three. Other changes proposed were longer deadlines for appeals and various procedural steps, given the geography of New France and the difficulty of transportation. And in cases where parties were required to appoint procureurs (attorneys) in France, as before the highest courts, the Conseil affirmed that parties could appear in person, even before the Conseil itself.

In summary matters, regulated in title 17, article 16 declared that higher courts could not raise defences not considered in the courts below. The Conseil, 'because of the lack of expertise on the part of trial judges,' wished to be able to do so. This was one of the matters where the king did not accept the Conseil's suggestion and insisted on the terms of the ordinance being respected. Another related to the Conseil's desire to be able to bring up any matter before itself, even if it should have gone initially to a lower court, 'since the Conseil administers justice without charge.' Higher courts in France were severely restricted from doing this by title 6, article 2 of the ordonnance, and the king insisted on its being observed in New France as well. However, the intendant himself possessed this power in any case.

Finally, the royal government insisted on the institution of a clear appeal process. Appeals from seigneurial courts within the district of Quebec were to go to the Prévôté, and thence to the Conseil souverain, not directly to the Conseil, and as soon as royal courts were established in the other two districts, the same process was to be followed. While the royal government was prepared to accept some flexibility in fines and timelines, it wanted the system of justice in the colony to follow that of the mother country in its essentials. In the end the king approved many of the changes requested by the Conseil by an edict of June 1679.[104]

In theory the 1667 ordinance was applicable in Acadie, returned to the French Crown by the Treaty of Breda in that year, but almost nothing is known of the manner in which civil justice was administered there under the French regime. As noted earlier, various modes of informal dispute resolution were encouraged by the Crown, and these are likely to have generated their own procedural practices. Hence what follows relates exclusively to Canada rather than New France as a whole.

Summary justice, which provided for a simpler and more expeditious procedure, ideally without the participation of lawyers, covered a broad variety of common claims. All personal causes of under 200 livres were included, as well as 'affaires de police' (regulatory matters) of whatever value, disputes over wages up to 1,000 livres, the purchase of foodstuffs, sales in markets or ports, trespassing animals, and various other matters. The common element in these was not low monetary value, but the urgency of the matter: perishable goods were involved, or a defendant might sail away out of the court's reach, or a low-paid worker needed to recover wages immediately to purchase necessaries. In all these cases plaintiffs could plead in person but could hire a practicien if they wished. Such cases were to be disposed of at the hearing itself without formality.[105]

They began by the plaintiff serving an 'adjournement' on his adversary by means of a bailiff. It had to explain the gist of the complaint and attach any relevant documents. The date of appearance before the court would be specified. The parties would then both go in person or appear by a representative. The judge would himself question them, look at the documents, and give a judgment that would be registered by the registrar. The defendant was permitted two defaults before judgment was rendered, but parties sometimes reached settlements before the first appearance, or after the first default. Most of the cases heard by the royal courts followed this summary process.

Non-summary cases normally began with a petition (requête) addressed to the judge. This contained a summary of the claim, extracts of any relevant documents and the relief claimed. The judge would then decide if this disclosed a cause of action and, if so, would allow the party to bring the defendant before him. The preparation of the petition often required a practicien (for the illiterate plaintiff), usually either a bailiff or a notary, whereas the adjournement was a standard form that could be obtained from the bailiff. Once the judge certified that the case could proceed, a bailiff took this 'exploit' to the home of the defendant; it contained the date he or she should appear and the nature of the cause, allowing the preparation of a defence.[106]

Several avenues were open after such a case began. If it seemed capable of being settled, it could be referred to arbitrators chosen by the court and accepted by the parties. If the evidence of experts was required, they would be called upon at a later session. Sometimes testimony by witnesses was necessary and a later date would have to be set for them to be heard. Witnesses had to be paid, as did experts, and cases involving them might extend over several sessions, with a concomitant increase in costs. Third parties who feared their interests might be harmed might also apply to join ongoing litigation – French law was relatively generous in this respect – but once again this led to delay and additional expense. Costs usually followed the event, though if a dispute arose without bad faith on either side, the court might make each party bear his or her own costs.[107]

Judicial remedies were minutely regulated by the Ordonnance of 1667 and included pre- and post-judgment seizures of property (saisies), renting out land for a period sufficient to satisfy the debts, the taking of accounts, and of course damages. Seizures were the most difficult part of the bailiff's work because they might lead to spirited resistance, or what was known as a 'rébellion à justice.' For example, when a bailiff delivered an adverse decision to tavern-keeper Pierre Marchand and his wife, she ripped up the document while he hit the bailiff over the head. They had to pay twenty livres damages to the bailiff and a fine of ten livres, as well as some forty-three livres in costs.[108]

It was difficult to tell how long a trial would last in non-summary proceedings, but the Prévôté seems to have delivered speedy justice in most cases, and its legitimacy was accepted by the parties – even if those executing court decisions sometimes ran into resistance.[109] A major difference with France in this respect was that judicial offices were not bought and sold in New France; local judges did not have the same incentive to spin out procedures and gain extra fees in order to pay off the purchase price of their judgeships.

The legitimacy and 'user-friendly' nature of the courts is illustrated indirectly by the frequency with which the inhabitants resorted to them. From the later 1660s to about 1675, at the time of the highest immigration to Canada, the rates of litigation in the Prévôté de Québec rose as high as 175 cases per 1,000 inhabitants, one of the highest rates recorded in seventeenth- and eighteenth-century North America, and this does not even include cases in the seigneurial court of Notre-Dame-des-Anges, which had concurrent jurisdiction with the Prévôté in some matters and drew away much of the latter's rural clientele. The rates of litigation in the Prévôté dropped steadily after 1675, dipping to 45 per 1,000 inhabitants by the end of the century, and as low as 20 by the end of the French regime. Arguably, the large influx of strangers in the 1660s led to a breakdown in trust and a turn to impersonal institutions such as the courts to resolve disputes, before the establishment of social, familial, and economic ties among the new immigrants broke down mutual suspicion and resulted in decreased recourse to the courts.[110] These patterns suggest that the courts played an important role in the social integration of immigrants in this new society, and that the almost obsessive interest of the French Crown in recreating the judicial institutions of the mother country was not unrewarded.

Criminal Procedure

The criminal law in any society is always used to uphold a particular vision of order. In New France that vision centred on a hierarchical Catholic society, where each knew his or her place. Criminal matters did not take up a lot of time in the courts, but the most serious crimes provided occasions for spectacular public punishments that emphasized the perpetrator's transgressions against the laws of both God and king. In France the lower orders were thought to be undisciplined, ignorant, and constantly on the edge of rebellion. Thus they needed to be managed harshly to maintain order. Such drastic measures were not required in New France, where, aside from mutinies at Louisbourg in 1744 and 1750, no serious challenges to the state had to be contained. The chronic shortage of labour, especially in the seventeenth century, also moderated the administration of the criminal law, a theme particularly evident in the differing treatment of troublesome servants in New France and the mother country.[111]

The substantive criminal law of the ancien régime was found in a variety of sources, as noted in chapter 3. Where the centralizing forces of Louis XIV's state chose to make a mark was in the domain of criminal procedure, which was codified in the Grande Ordonnance of 1670. Although never registered in the colony, it was well known and punctiliously applied. Criminal matters, especially those involving capital punishment or severe penalties (peines afflictives), were treated with procedural fairness as understood within the French inquisitorial process and defined in the ordinance, and subject to serious appellate review such as would not be found in the common law for centuries. Thus, every capital sentence and those imposing peines afflictives were subject to automatic review by the Conseil souverain at Quebec after 1663, although some occasionally escaped this scrutiny.[112] Moreover, the king's attorney could appeal sentences he thought too light, a process known as an appeal *a minima*.

This commitment to procedural rigour was evident from the very beginning of the colony, in the trial of Jean Duval and others for conspiracy to kill Samuel de Champlain in 1608. The plan was discovered when one of the conspirators had a change of heart and informed on his comrades.[113] Champlain had the plotters arrested and confined, and promised a pardon to those who divulged all they knew. First he took written depositions from informants; their testimony was read back to them and signed. Then the accused were brought in and confronted with the evidence of their accusers. They 'confessed that they had acted wickedly, and deserved punishment, unless mercy should be shown them.... Duval was unable to say anything, except that he deserved death; and that everything contained in the depositions was true.' After hearing these exchanges, Champlain, Pont-Gravé, 'the Captain of the ship, the surgeon, master, mate, and other seamen ... decided that it would be sufficient to put to death Duval as the first mover of the conspiracy, and also to serve as an example to those who remained, to behave properly in the future in doing their duty.' Duval was duly hanged, and 'his head placed on the end of a pike and set up in the highest spot in our fort.' Three other conspirators were also convicted but sent back to France with copies of the proceedings for confirmation of their sentences; they were eventually pardoned by Henry IV.[114]

All these steps – taking down evidence in writing, verifying the witnesses' statements, confronting the accused with the same, requiring a confession and providing for the judge to be assisted by assessors rather than a jury – were well-entrenched aspects of French criminal process as eventually re-codified in 1670. The only departure, unavoidable under the circumstances, was that Champlain in effect played the role of king's attorney (prosecutor) as well as judge. The emphasis on exemplary public punishment was also part of French criminal law, while the lenity displayed by Champlain in his treatment of the co-conspirators would be more characteristic of the administration of criminal justice in New France than in old France.

French and English criminal process are often contrasted, but they were marked by both similarities and differences. French criminal process was characterized by much more public intervention than contemporary English practice, which depended largely on private prosecution by the victim or his or her family. It was thus more highly professionalized, as public prosecutors were legally trained. French criminal process took place largely in private, while the English system, reliant on the jury, was mostly public. Yet the English criminal trial before the appearance of lawyers in them in the later eighteenth century was, like the French, largely inquisitorial, with the judge and jury aggressively examining witnesses and defendants making their defence as best they could.[115]

A French criminal proceeding typically began with a complaint (plainte) made in secret by a citizen, after which the king's attorney generally took over the prosecution at state expense. In cases of assaults or slanders, victims could be civil parties to the proceeding, otherwise not.[116] On the basis of the complaint, the king's attorney would file a petition with the royal judge (lieutenant civil et criminel) in that jurisdiction, who would in turn advise the complainant of when and where the first part of the hearing (séance des informations) would take place. This was like a preliminary inquiry, where the judge, on hearing the testimony of the witnesses, had to determine whether a crime had been committed. The witnesses were heard in secret and separately, without even the king's attorney present, because of a concern that they might withhold or falsify their testimony out of fear of or deference to the accused, or his or her supporters. Witnesses were paid for their attendance in order to encourage their participation. The court clerk wrote down all the testimony and read it back to the witnesses before inviting them to sign. On the basis of these statements and the seriousness of the crime, the king's attorney would then ask the judge either to order the accused to be taken into custody, or simply to appear before the court at a certain time.

Once again it was up to the judge to interrogate the accused in secret, and alone: he or she was not permitted to have a lawyer or anyone else present. On reviewing the written results of the interrogation, the king's attorney might ask the judge for one of two outcomes. In the case of less serious offences, such as slander or minor assaults, he might request a definite sentence, often a fine, or ask that the matter be converted into a civil proceeding where the victim could seek damages. With more serious crimes where a corporal or infamous punishment might be warranted, the king's attorney would ask that the matter be dealt with according to extraordinary process (règlement à l'extraordinaire). No one was to be convicted of a serious crime without the opportunity to test the statements of the witnesses, a process known as récolement. This required first that the testimony of the witnesses be read back to them by the clerk in the presence of the judge, after which they would be asked whether they wanted to add or subtract anything. Then the matter would proceed to 'confrontation' – the first time that the accused was presented with the basis of the charges against him or her. The witnesses' testimony would be read out and they would be asked whether it related to the person before them (the accused). The accused was then asked if he or she wanted to dispute any part of the testimony, and any objections were written down.

After reading these statements, the king's attorney might be prepared to present his final conclusions (conclusions définitives) to the judge, asking for either an acquittal or a guilty verdict and a particular sentence. However, he might not be ready to present his final conclusions, believing that some matters, such as a potential defence, should be inquired into further; or noting in a capital case that the accused's admission was lacking. In such cases, the accused might be permitted to adduce further evidence – for example, to substantiate an alibi. Should a confession or full proof (the eyewitness testimony of two intelligent and trustworthy persons) be lacking in a capital case, however, the judge might be asked to permit the accused to be put to 'la question' – a rarely used form of judicially sanctioned torture that was administered only if first permitted by the Conseil souverain. Only three such cases are known in the eighteenth century, out of nearly 1,000 criminal cases brought before the royal courts of Canada, and a few from the seventeenth, out of just under 500 cases brought before the royal courts in the second half of the century.[117] In France, too, its use declined dramatically in the eighteenth century, such that its abolition by the king in 1780 merely confirmed existing practice.[118]

Administering la question required the accused to sit upon a bench, while four planks of oak (brodequins) were tied very tightly to his legs below the knee. Wedges were then inserted between the shin and the plank and hammered in. The judge first conducted the interrogation without torture. If the accused did not confess, the torture, which could last a maximum of one and one-half hours, began. An accused who did confess during torture had to confirm afterwards, without torture, what was said during torture. An accused who denied his confession afterwards could still be convicted if the judge found the evidence pointed strongly to guilt, and could thus ignore the denial. An accused who did not confess during torture might still be found guilty but could not be sentenced to death, and torture was not to be repeated. Those who did not confess after la question might even be acquitted, as was François Judieth dit Rencontre, charged with the capital crime of bestiality in 1697.[119]

The ordinance of 1670 (title 25, article 10) required that the judge sit with two assessors in all cases where a capital sentence or peine afflictive was a possible outcome. In the royal courts this was generally done, but during the period when Montreal was a seigneurial jurisdiction the judge almost always sat alone.[120] The role of assessors was somewhat similar to that of the jury, although they did not decide on guilt but only on sentence. Each provided a written opinion on every case, and in case of disagreement, title 25, article 12 of the 1670 ordinance required imposition of the more moderate penalty. The ordinance was silent on standards of proof, giving large discretion to the judge, but the presence of multiple decision-makers presumably provided some kind of protection against arbitrary fact-finding. Acquittals were by no means unknown: while there are no figures for the seventeenth century, in the next century about 20 per cent of all criminal cases resulted in acquittals or were dismissed for lack of evidence. But the court also had other options: a provisional acquittal, which required the accused to stay in prison for a certain period while further evidence was gathered; or a provisional verdict of guilt, which allowed the accused to go free but on a sort of probation after swearing to appear before the court if asked.[121]

The intertwining of secular and ecclesiastical authority in New France was evident in the imposition of criminal penalties. The least serious penalties were the reprimand (blâme), the admonition (admonestation) – a warning that a serious penalty would be exacted if the accused engaged in such conduct again – and the fine (amende). Fines were often directed to be paid to the poor of a parish or to charitable institutions such as the Hôtel-Dieu of Montreal or Quebec, hospitals that cared for the poor as well as the better-off.

Theft or sexual offences other than rape usually resulted in the public infliction of corporal penalties, such as whipping, often accompanied by branding with a fleur-de-lys in the shoulder or cheek, or confinement in an iron collar (carcan) attached to a post in a public place for a period of time. The latter was often used to discipline servants who had left their masters without permission. Thus, when Marin Varin was found to have quit the service of the Sieur de Tilly, a member of the Conseil souverain, he was sentenced to stand in the carcan for two hours on 3 June 1673 with a sign on his chest reading INDENTURED SERVANT WHO LEFT THE SERVICE OF HIS MASTER. For a second such offence by a servant, the Conseil specified a punishment of beating with sticks and branding.[122] Banishment, temporary or perpetual, either from the colony or from the particular district, was another option, as was a sentence to service in the king's galleys. Women could not be sentenced to the galleys but might be confined to the Hôpital-général, a hospital for the poor.

The most serious offences – murder, rape, treason – called for the most spectacular punishments, as part of what Peter Moogk has called 'the liturgy of humiliation, pain, and death.'[123] Thus when Jaques Bertault and his wife Gilette Baune were convicted in 1672 of poisoning their son-in-law, the husband of their daughter Isabelle, a truly exemplary punishment awaited them. All three were first to perform the amende honorable, a ritual form of penance whereby they would be 'brought before the door of the parish church of this city [Quebec], a noose around their necks, holding a burning torch, ... naked except for a [long white] shirt, and there on their knees demand forgiveness of God and the king for the crimes they have committed.' The judge of the seigneurial court, in which the trial was held, ordered that Jaques Bertault be secured to a cross of St Andrew in the main square of the upper town, where his right arm would be broken by an iron bar, and the rest of his limbs broken after he had been strangled. His body would then be exposed on a wheel at the highest point in the city, Cap-aux-Diamants, 'to serve as an example.' Gilette Baune would be hanged, and while Isabelle would be required to watch the execution of her parents with a noose around her neck, her own life would be spared in light of her age (she was thirteen, having been married to the deceased the previous year against her will). In addition, the three convicts would be jointly liable for a fine of 100 livres payable to the local seigneur. On appeal, the Conseil souverain varied the sentence slightly, ordering that Bertault be strangled before any of his limbs were broken; it also substituted a fine of 60 livres, half to be paid to the Récollet fathers for masses to be said for the repose of the soul of the deceased victim. The rest of the convicts' goods were to be forfeit to the king, but as an act of grace it was ordered that they be turned over to the now orphaned minor children of Bertault and Baune.[124]

A variation on the amende honorable required that the accused be beaten with sticks at various points after performing penance at the church door, though it is not clear whether these were administered solely by officers of the court, or whether bystanders were expected to join in. In any case, such events were by no means rare in the colonial capital in the 1670s and must have had a great impact, given that it was no more than a small town, growing from 547 inhabitants in 1666 to 1,345 in 1681. In 1671 the Conseil souverain spared the life of Jean Bourgeois, who had been sentenced to death for the rape of a girl aged six or seven, substituting perpetual banishment but requiring that he perform the amende honorable, be 'beaten with sticks at the main intersections of the upper and lower town, and thereafter be branded in the cheek with a fleur-de-lys.'[125] In the same year Françoise du Verger was hanged and her body exposed on a gibbet at Cap-aux-Diamants after she was convicted of murdering her newborn infant after having tried to abort it three times.[126] In 1672 the execution of the parents of Isabelle Bertault, discussed earlier, must have convulsed the town. The next year three men were convicted of disturbing divine service, threatening the police magistrate, speaking words of rebellion, and writing insulting letters to two of the councillors of the Conseil souverain. They were required to perform the amende honorable by begging forgiveness at the door of the homes of the three officials and given relatively light fines, but warned that they would suffer the death penalty for a second offence.[127] In 1675 Jean Dubauc was required to perform the amende honorable and to be beaten ten times with sticks at the door of the governor's residence and at each of the main intersections of the town, for having returned to Quebec after having been previously banished from the town for a number of thefts. This time he was banished for life from the colony, consigned to prison until the next ship parted for France.[128]

In 1677 Simon du Verger, who had escaped from jail pending trial for an unspecified crime, was hanged in effigy in the lower town when he could not be found.[129] Through these rituals and punishments, an ideology of majesty and terror, justice and mercy, typical of old regime societies, was mobilized in order to maintain order and deference.

Again typical of old regime societies, prisons were not generally sites of punishment but rather places where an accused could be held pending trial or banishment to France, though occasionally imprisonment was ordered when a convict could not pay a fine. Prisoners were kept chained at the ankles to prevent escape and permitted only brief exercise each day. The climate posed a particular challenge: firewood was not permitted to prisoners, as it was feared they would use it to burn down the building. During periods of extreme cold prisoners might simply be released, but it was still the case, as Governor Jacques-René de Brisay de Denonville observed in 1686, that 'in winter the prisoners are frozen and it has happened that some have had to have their feet cut off as a result [of frostbite].'[130]

If punishments recalled Catholic doctrine, crimes against religion itself, known as lèse-majesté divine, seem to have been prosecuted with decreasing rigour over time. Even in 1670, when Louis de Gaboury of Île d'Orléans was initially sentenced to perform the amende honorable and to be exposed in the iron collar for three hours for having eaten meat in Lent without the church's permission, the Conseil souverain remitted these parts of his sentence and let him off with a warning and a fine.[131] And while some fourteen prosecutions for blasphemy can be found in the seventeenth century, only one has come to light in the eighteenth.[132] Given the prevalence and tenacity of folkloric beliefs in witchcraft among the settler population, it is perhaps surprising that aside from a few early cases, prosecutions for witchcraft were virtually unknown in the colony. The contrast with Massachusetts, where twenty people (fourteen of them women) were executed after the notorious witch trials of 1692–3, is striking. Key demographic differences from old France and New England, such as the extended pattern of settlement and the relative absence of vulnerable older widows, may explain this state of affairs.[133]

As noted earlier, serious penalties were subject to automatic review by the Conseil souverain at state expense.[134] As the Conseil sat only at Quebec, appeals on lesser matters were infrequent, discouraged by distance and expense if they arose outside the capital. The procedure before the Conseil souverain was a combination of judicial review and sentence appeal. Both the Conseil and the king's attorney reviewed the written documentation to ensure that all procedures in the ordinance had been correctly followed. If not, a new trial could be ordered. If all was procedurally correct, the king's attorney went on to interrogate the accused and to report to the Conseil his conclusions as to whether the sentence was appropriate. The councillors also interrogated the accused, after which one councillor would write a report and the others indicated their agreement or disagreement. Judgment was rendered by a plurality of votes; the most severe penalty had to pass by a majority of two votes, so a division always benefited the accused. In theory the accused could appeal to the Conseil d'État privé of the king in France, but in practice only one example has been discovered, and the result is not known. Pardons from the king were not much more frequent, and the half-dozen known cases all involved death by duel or accidental homicide.[135]

The administration of the criminal law in early Canada reflected a commitment to procedural regularity and a semi-professional administration that was not necessarily to be expected in a small and struggling colony. In spite of occasional spectacular punishments meant to instil fear and deference to king and church, in some respects the criminal law was administered less harshly than in France itself. Differing demographics probably explain much of this difference. While most inhabitants of New France were poor, the colony did not possess the desperate masses of impoverished peasants who regularly starved during the subsistence crises of ancien régime France, and whose food riots were much feared by the authorities. Access to land, higher wages, and easily available game and fish meant that the overall security and health status of the habitant population was superior to their French counterparts; the average caloric intake of seventeenth-century Canadiens was twice that of their French counterparts in the next century, for example, and the survival rate of their children almost twice as high.[136] Poverty was not equated with disorder in the same way as in France. There, thieving servants might be executed, for example, but this did not happen in New France. And as will be seen below, Indigenous offenders – largely for strategic reasons – were virtually exempt from the criminal law.

7

Law and Governance in the English Possessions

The colonies that comprised New France were treated as a unity by the metropole and endowed with legal and governmental structures as similar as possible to those in provincial France. The earliest English possessions in northern North America, Newfoundland and Rupert's Land (discounting the brief English takeover of Quebec in 1629–32 and the English and Scottish interludes in Acadia prior to 1710) were both devoted to the extraction of a sole resource but differed in other ways, and their legal infrastructures (or lack of them) reflected these differences. In this they demonstrated the unsystematic but flexible nature of seventeenth-century English colonizing. While an imperial law, perhaps even an imperial 'constitution,' was emerging to regulate the relations between the colonies and the metropolis, the English did not think of themselves as having an 'empire' until some time in the next century. The term *plantations* was the one most used when the English spoke of their overseas possessions. There was no assumption that each plantation should have the same legal institutions or infrastructure, allowing for a certain amount of experimentation and innovation.[1]

Newfoundland: From Company to Proprietorship to Anti-Colony

After failed attempts at 'Meta Incognita' (Baffin Island) under Martin Frobisher (1578), Newfoundland under Humphrey Gilbert (1583), and Roanoke, North Carolina (1587), the last effort sponsored by Gilbert's half-brother Sir Walter Ralegh, English colonization ventures were interrupted by the long war with Spain, which ended only in 1604 with the Treaty of London. Efforts resumed shortly thereafter with the founding of Jamestown, Virginia, in 1607. Unlike his kinswoman Elizabeth I, who had invested significant amounts in the Baffin Island venture, James I was prepared to charter companies for the exploitation of Newfoundland but not to provide significant state backing. A succession of companies in the decade of the 1610s failed as the result of insufficient capitalization before a different expedient was tried in the patent to Sir George Calvert in 1623. But some context about the nature of the Newfoundland fishery is necessary to understand the course of events.

There were two ways of preserving Newfoundland's cod in the days before refrigeration: the wet cure and the dry cure. Those practising the former fished on the Grand Banks and heavily salted their catch on board ship, needing shore access only for fresh water. The dry cure was based on an inshore fishery, where the catch was dried on wooden flakes on land. The French carried on both, the latter using the western shore of the Avalon Peninsula – eventually known as the colony of Plaisance – and the Great Northern Peninsula of Newfoundland.[2] The English carried on only an inshore fishery, initially using the east coast of the Avalon Peninsula.[3] The competition among the hundreds of ships arriving in May for convenient spaces on the 'English shore' had been dealt with by a tradition that the captain of the first ship to arrive in a particular harbour became the 'fishing admiral' for the season, with power to adjudicate disputes over access to shore sites by those ships arriving subsequently. This tradition was ancient and referred to as such in the 1634 Western Charter that formalized it, the charter itself being a document issued by the Privy Council in the name of the Crown, which aimed to affirm the privileges of west country fishermen to use the shore of Newfoundland to prosecute the migratory fishery.[4] The jurisdiction of the fishing admirals was limited only by the requirement that in cases of murder or theft of over forty shillings, the accused and two witnesses be transported to England for trial in any English county.[5]

The fishery did not depend on Indigenous labour, and after some initial contacts the Beothuk did not engage in the fur trade with the Europeans. They saw no need to do so because they were able to take nails and other iron goods left by the migratory fishers in their huts and fishing flakes when the latter left the island in the fall. The Beothuk reasonably assumed such goods were abandoned and were able to replenish their supplies each year. As a result there was little contact between Europeans and the Beothuk during the seventeenth century, but the absence of a fur trade to foster good relations between the two groups would have terrible consequences for the Beothuk later on.[6]

Merchants from the western counties of England controlled the migratory fishery and saw the foundation of permanent settlements as unwelcome competition. Tensions between those for and against settlement marked the Newfoundland experience throughout the seventeenth and eighteenth centuries. The Crown was called upon to mediate these disputes and did not always pursue a consistent policy in doing so. In this the experience of Newfoundland was similar to that of early New France, where the interests of merchants from the western ports of France aligned more with trade than settlement, and royal authority often vacillated between favouring one or the other.[7]

In 1623 Sir George Calvert (later Lord Baltimore), the former secretary of state to James I, received letters patent to most of the Avalon peninsula. In spite of clauses in his charter reserving their customary liberties to those who 'at this present or hereafter shall trade or voiag to the partes aforesaid for ffishing,' those in the migratory fishery complained that the planters were keeping the best fishing spots for themselves and purporting to exercise a jurisdiction over the fishers that the charter did not give them; the Privy Council agreed, affirming their ancient liberties in the 1634 Western Charter.

Calvert's patent conveyed the land to be held as tenant-in-chief of the king in a feudal tenure known as knight's service, and in addition gave him palatine jurisdiction over the colony of Avalon. This authority, exercised only by the bishop of Durham and a few others in England, was the highest power that could be granted to a subject. It involved in essence a delegation of law-making powers (subject to a repugnancy clause and to the approbation of an assembly of freeholders), including the power to appoint judges, magistrates, and officials of all kinds, and to execute the laws up to and including the power of capital punishment. In the plenitude of powers given, it was similar to the early commissions given to French colonizers such as De Monts.

Calvert had a large manor house built for himself, his family, and retinue at Ferryland harbour, the foundations of which still survive.[8] He spent the winter of 1628–9 there and, after observing that winter did not lift until May, left to pursue his colonizing initiatives in the gentler climate of Chesapeake Bay. Although Calvert left an agent in charge, this did not prevent a subsequent adventurer, Sir David Kirke, from securing letters patent for 'that whole continent Island and Region aforesaid, commonly knowne by the name of Newfoundland' in 1637. Calvert had died in 1632, and Kirke's patent recited that Cecil Lord Baltimore 'his [Calvert's] Sonne and heir apparent, [had] deserted the said Province and Plantation.'

Kirke was made the 'right Lord and Proprietor of Newfoundland,' which was granted to him in knight's service, and for which he was to provide to His Majesty and his heirs 'two white horses whensoever ... [we] shall happen to enter into the said Island' and a fifth of any gold and silver found thereon. He was also granted extensive law-making and adjudicative powers similar to Calvert's, although not palatine authority. The patent specifically prohibited him from exercising any authority over the migrant fishers and forbade the 'inhabitants' from taking up the best fishing places in advance of the arrival of the migrant ships. It even prohibited the inhabitants from settling or erecting any structures within six miles of the seashore, a provision that would have rendered a settled fishery impossible to prosecute. The restriction was never observed and was removed and restored via amendments to the Western Charter several times in the seventeenth century.[9]

Kirke ousted Lord Baltimore's agents from the manor house in 1639 and had forts built along the English shore at St John's and Bay de Verde. He is known to have exercised a manorial jurisdiction around the settlement at Ferryland in the mid-seventeenth century, although unfortunately the records have not survived. In this he played a role very similar to that of the seigneur in early New France. Political and commercial conflicts ensured that Newfoundland's legal and political evolution moved in a very different direction, however. As a royalist, Kirke was targeted during the English civil war and brought to England in 1651 to face charges before the Council of State; he died there in jail in 1654.[10] After the Restoration, Cecil Lord Baltimore managed to get his father's patent restored by Charles II but never resided in Newfoundland and exercised no justice functions; at most, his agents may have managed to collect rents for a time. Kirke's widow and sons remained at Ferryland, but in view of the uncertainty over the validity of the various patents, it is not clear what, if any, authority they were able to exercise in the latter half of the century. No governor was appointed, probably as a result of opposition from west country interests, in spite of the constant threat of war with France.

Nothing in any of the earlier patents introduced the common law as such. Rather, the patentees, as delegates of the king, were allowed to make such laws as they wished, subject to the repugnancy clause. In Kirke's patent these laws were declared to 'extend not to the Right or Interest of any persons whatsoever in their Freehold Estates, or by Meanes whereof any of their Goods or Chattells may be destroyed, engaged, burthened or taken away from them,' providing some protection for the inhabitants. In addition those who should 'resort thither' were said to 'have and Possess all other Liberties Franchises, and Priviledges of this Kingdome, and them use and enjoy as our Naturall Liege People, borne or to be borne within England, without any impediment.' They had rights as English subjects, but their rights against each other were not necessarily to be determined by the common law. As there were no counties, there could be no sheriff; nor, as juries were composed of the freeholders of a county, could there be trial by jury. Justices of the peace would not be appointed until 1729. In the wake of the uncertainty over the jurisdiction of the Kirkes, no familiar structures or personnel of English governance or judicature emerged to take up the slack. A vernacular legal order loosely based on the common law and the settlers' own legal culture must have emerged, but the records by which it could be reconstructed have not yet been discovered.

Population growth was slow: the eastern shore had fewer than 2,000 inhabitants in 1679. The uncertainty about the source of legitimate authority at Ferryland reflected the little plantation's vulnerability to metropolitan manoeuvrings. Even though the migratory and the settled fishery were in fact complementary and interdependent, at times the strength of one faction of west country merchants opposed to settlement was such that they almost succeeded in having the settlers removed altogether. In 1675 the Privy Council instructed the naval commodore Sir John Berry to remove all permanent inhabitants of Newfoundland. On arrival, Berry formed the view that this was neither just nor practical, and ignored his orders; the edict was later rescinded.[11] This did not stop the idea of removal from being seriously mooted until the 1720s, when the British government finally decided to endow the island with a minimal year-round governmental infrastructure.[12]

French victories during the war of the League of Augsburg (1689–97) resulted in the capture of Ferryland in 1696 and the removal of all its inhabitants to England, but they were allowed to return the next year after the signing of the Treaty of Ryswick. This near-death experience for English Newfoundland evidently prompted some consideration of its future by the authorities, but King William's Act of 1699 reflected the same tensions that had afflicted Newfoundland throughout the century.

It forbade overwintering, thereby seeming to deny that the island was or could be a colony of settlement; yet it 'grandfathered' those who had resided there prior to 1685, and those who had arrived since if they pursued non-fishery occupations. Such persons were allowed to keep the lands they occupied, though the nature of their interests could be based only on possession, not on the 'estates' known to the common law of real property.[13] The fishing admirals were to keep their powers to allocate fishing stations and settle local disputes, although their decisions were now to be subject to appeal to the captain in charge of the naval station. Serious crimes were to be tried by a court of oyer and terminer in any English county, as before. There were various prohibitions, such as those forbidding the sale of alcohol, enjoining Sunday observance, and preventing unnecessary destruction of trees, but no penalties were specified. The combination of seasonal rule by the fishing admirals with naval oversight is thought to have emerged by the 1680s, with King William's Act thus formalizing an earlier practice.[14]

If the experience of Newfoundland after the Kirke era was one of 'settlement without governance,' this does not mean that it was entirely lawless. Just as the habitants of early Acadie or Canada were familiar with the local customs of their provinces of origin in France, so the inhabitants of Newfoundland were familiar with the customs of their own manors and some of the basic liberties of English subjects.[15] (The Irish did not arrive in Newfoundland in significant numbers until later in the eighteenth century.) Those who sailed to Newfoundland were familiar with the authority of the captain while on board; the authority of the fishing admiral and the naval officer may have seemed simply an extension of a familiar kind of hierarchy. The authority of the church was not, however, available to fill the gap in state-sanctioned legal structures: missionary clergy showed up only episodically in the seventeenth century, and there were no parishes or vestries.

The example of Newfoundland illustrates the variability of colonial law and models of governance in the British world, and the strong priority accorded to fostering commerce. The desire for statutory protection for free trade by those investing in the Newfoundland fishery largely drove King William's Act, which was not meant to set up a 'government' that could be paid for only by a tax on the fishery – one stoutly resisted by the fishing trade's financial backers. The Act was not a failure, as so many have termed it, because it actually aimed to forestall the emergence of a local government; hence the fishing industry was eventually able to free-ride on the Royal Navy for the provision of some basic services relating to the maintenance of order and the administration of justice.[16] Contrary to the top-down legal order of New France, or at least Canada, Newfoundland's inhabitants were in a sense invited to create their own legal order, leading to a preference for local and customary solutions to many problems.[17]

Rupert's Land: The Emergence of a Company-State

The themes of colonial variability and the fostering of commerce are also present in the history of the colony of Rupert's Land. By the 1660s the English (thanks largely to the efforts of Pierre-Esprit Radisson) had realized that the watershed of Hudson Bay contained an untapped wealth of furs. The Hudson's Bay Company (HBC) charter of 1670 provided a way of pursuing a potentially valuable commercial endeavour while positioning the English Crown to resist the incursions of the French in the area. Although it says nothing about settlement, the charter purported to grant to 'the governor and Company of Adventurers of England trading into Hudson's Bay' all the territory draining into Hudson Bay in free and common socage and to make them the 'absolute Lordes and Proprietors of the same Territory lymittes and places aforesaid,' echoing the language of Kirke's Newfoundland patent of 1637.[18] This extravagant language was mainly to ward off European competitors, however. The HBC's governors in England and their local agents at the Bay understood the necessity of seeking the consent of the Indigenous inhabitants before building any forts, and following Indigenous laws in order to establish trading relations. The company advised the governor of Port Nelson to 'make such contracts with the Natives for the River in and above Port Nelson as may in future times ascertain to us a right and property therein & the Sole Liberty of trade & Comerce there, and to make Leagues of friendship and peaceable Cohabitation with such Ceremonies as you shall find to bee most Sacred and Obligatory amongst them.'[19]

The main advantage sought by the incorporators and granted to them by the Crown was the 'sole Trade and Commerce' of the territories in question, that is, a monopoly over the fur trade. A colony of settlement was never really contemplated. The most that could be said is that the governor and his 'committee' (the name given to the company's board of directors) hoped that the forts could undertake enough agriculture to be self-sufficient in food, given the high cost of transporting provisions to the Bay. But they did not contemplate exports and soon reconciled themselves to the fact that even a modest self-sufficiency was unrealizable, given the harsh climatic conditions.[20] The adoption in 1684 of a policy forbidding any company official or employee from bringing a British-born wife or children to Rupert's Land demonstrates that settlement in the ordinary sense was not envisaged. And unlike some other HBC policies, this one was rigorously observed: until 1830, when Governor George Simpson brought his British wife Frances to live at Red River, no HBC man would breach this policy.[21] Moreover, HBC employees were prohibited from remaining in Rupert's Land when their contracts ended – hardly the way to create a settlement colony.

While the Privy Council vacillated about the status of Newfoundland as a colony of settlement, the HBC had no doubts: it would be devoted entirely to commerce. For the first century of its existence it showed no interest in exploring the interior of the vast territory granted to it. A half-dozen fortified trading posts on the shores of Hudson Bay were sufficient to exploit the region's furs in a profitable manner, allowing the company to economize on personnel, defence, and supplies. The English hold on the area was very tenuous during the first forty years of the company's existence: the French captured most of the forts at one time or another, before France finally gave up its claims in the Treaty of Utrecht in 1713. The company never had to make use of the power granted in its charter to 'make peace or Warre with any Prince or People whatsoever that are not Christians': wars with a rival Christian nation were the main threat.

The law-making powers granted to the governor of the HBC were not nearly as extensive as those granted in other patents and charters of the seventeenth century, mainly because the headquarters of the company remained in London, and it was thus subject to English law; but some authority had to be delegated to the Bayside governors. The company's governors could 'make ordyne and constitute such and soe many reasonable Lawes Constitucions Orders and Ordinances as to them ... shall seeme necessary and convenient for the good Government of the said Company and of all Governors of [the forts, etc. in Rupert's Land],' subject to a repugnancy clause, but these were more like corporate bylaws. The governors of the forts or factories whom the company might appoint were to have the power 'to judge all persons belonging to the said Governor and Company or that shall live under them in all Causes whether Civil or Criminall according to the Lawes of this Kingdome and to execute Justice accordingly'; this clause was the basis of the later understanding that English law was received into Rupert's Land as of

1670. With the possible exception of the 'home guard Indians,' however, small groups who eventually settled near the forts, the above clause was understood to extend only to Europeans. Indigenous people did not live 'under' the HBC but rather maintained their own laws and systems of governance. Unlike areas further south, European diseases took a long time to penetrate the north, and major epidemics did not arise until later in the eighteenth century.

While the local governors were to have the power to try their own employees for 'any crime or misdemeanor,' those who could not be tried locally for whatever reason were to be 'transmitt[ed] ... into this Kingdome of England for trial and punishment.' Unlike the Newfoundland patents, the HBC's charter contained no reference to any law-making role for an assembly of freeholders, for the good reason that there were not expected to be any freeholders. No Europeans could enter Rupert's Land without licence from the HBC, and its own employees had to leave at the end of their terms.

As in Newfoundland, the church had no role in Rupert's Land. No clergy ministered to the Europeans, and the HBC had no interest in 'civilizing' the Indigenous people with whom it traded, hence no missionaries were permitted. Not until much later did the company take an interest in educating the children produced by unions between its men and Indigenous women; until then it was forbidden to teach Indigenous persons to read or write. The absence of clergy also meant that these unions could not be regularized under English law. The governor and committee in London wished to discourage the French practice of métissage, as they believed the mixing of the two peoples would be detrimental to trade, although governors and senior officials of the forts flouted this policy, and the company came to accept unofficially that 'ties with Native women were key to establishing good trading relations.'[22] Some of these unions were fleeting, but others were long-term committed relationships that followed the Indigenous custom of mariage à la façon du pays.

Although the common law was arguably received into Rupert's Land in 1670, the only relevant parts of it were the law of master and servant and some parts of the criminal law, as will be seen in the next part. Given the frequent state of state of war that existed between English and French at this time, however (1689–97, 1702–13), military law was the most important legal tool available to the Bayside governors as they sought to maintain discipline and punish incipient mutinies among their employees. Men found guilty by the governor of serious insubordination tinged with sedition in the 1690s were typically flogged publicly and sent home to England on the next available ship.

But threats from the French without and seditious employees within were in some ways not as serious as threats to the validity of the charter itself. Just as the charters of the eastern seaboard colonies proved vulnerable in light of the political turmoil surrounding the Glorious Revolution of 1688, so did that of the HBC.[23] The actions of Charles II in granting the charter came to be viewed as extravagant and possibly illegal a generation later. In 1690, sensitive to the growing power of Parliament, the governor and committee sought as a precautionary measure to have the charter confirmed by legislation. They initially proposed an act that would be effective for fourteen years, but it ran into some resistance; in the end the *Act for Confirming to the Governor and Company Trading to Hudson's Bay Their Privileges and Trade* was limited to seven years.[24] When it came up for renewal in 1697, the proposed Act did not pass, but this did not amount to a 'nullification' of the charter, as some have asserted. The charter had been a creature of the prerogative, and so it remained. The Act had provided an additional patina of authority, but its non-renewal did not undermine the validity of the original HBC charter. The 1707 *Act for the Encouragement of the Trade to America* provided expressly that nothing in it should 'any ways extend, or be construed to take away or prejudice any of the Estates, Rights, or Privileges of or belonging to the Governor and Company of Adventurers of England trading into Hudson's Bay,' a saving clause that would have been unnecessary if the company's charter had been voided in 1697.[25] Looking forward, the charter that seemed the most vulnerable of all the early English charters outlasted them all, even that of the fabled East India Company, and formed the basis of the transfer of 'underlying title' to the immense Hudson Bay watershed to Canada in 1869.

8

The Interface of European and Indigenous Law

In spite of demographic crises due to war and disease, Indigenous peoples controlled northern North America down to 1701 (and beyond), except for a few small European enclaves. Relations between the two groups were driven at least as much by Indigenous desires and perspectives as by European ones. Even in Newfoundland, the Beothuk withdrew from contact with Europeans after about 1620, largely as a result of their own agency, not because they were driven away from their traditional haunts. On the mainland, Europeans occupied their settlements at the sufferance of their hosts, who tolerated them for two reasons. First, the newcomers possessed goods, such as copper kettles, guns, knives, axes, and blankets, that made life easier: already by the early 1600s, the Innu near Quebec had adopted some Western dress and were using the sturdy French longboats that were safer than canoes for navigating the broad St Lawrence.[1] Second, the Europeans' weapons made them useful allies in the Indigenous nations' own wars. Relatively feeble immigration and low population growth in the seventeenth century meant that the French could not hope to defeat militarily all the Indigenous peoples they encountered as they ventured west through the Great Lakes and south through the Mississippi valley. Alliance was the only option.

The French were also assisted in their colonization endeavours by two rather fortuitous factors. In Acadie the Mi'kmaq were the only Indigenous people inhabiting peninsular Nova Scotia, Île Royale, and

Île St-Jean. The French thus avoided being drawn into local wars, and the Acadian coastal settlements were so small in the seventeenth century that there was little competition for resources.[2] Meanwhile, the colony of Canada, heartland of the French agricultural frontier, while not 'empty' of Indigenous people, was no longer home to the St Lawrence Iroquoian agriculturalists.[3] The Indigenous population of the St Lawrence valley declined from an estimated 14,000 at the time of Cartier's visits in the 1530s to about 4,000 by 1600 and to about 2,000 by 1650. The reasons for the pre-1600 decline are still debated, but it meant that 'the French ... did not encounter a large, well-established, sedentary local native population when they settled the St Lawrence Valley early in the seventeenth century.'[4] Nonetheless, the Mohawks of northern New York 'seem to have considered the lower St Lawrence as part of their security zone' and attacked the Innu and other Indigenous groups who tried to use it, as well as the French. The establishment of Montreal was considered a 'special provocation.'[5] The fact that the French felt entitled to settle in these areas and to grant lands to settlers without explicit consent of the prior inhabitants did not mean that they denied Indigenous territorial claims. As seen in chapter 6, even on settled land the French did not believe they had a right to control Indigenous hunting or fishing. The French were perfectly aware that different Indigenous groups claimed and controlled specific territories and did not subscribe to any theory of *terra nullius*.[6] For this reason lands were rarely granted if occupied by Indigenous people. Thus when some seigneuries were conceded around Lake Champlain on lands occupied by Mohawks, upon complaint by the latter to the governor the grants were revoked before the grantees could take them up.[7] This was very different from the situation in the New England and Chesapeake colonies, where wars between the settlers and the Indigenous population – themselves engaged in agriculture – broke out almost immediately and continued throughout the seventeenth century.

The St Lawrence colony was engaged in wars with the Haudenosaunee throughout the seventeenth century, but these did not result from direct conflict over settlement as such. Rather, they resulted from the French having inserted themselves into a system of alliances that had arisen as a result of long-standing pre-contact rivalry between the Haudenosaunee, based in what is now New York, and the peoples to the north and west, the Innu, Huron-Wendat, and Algonquin. The main principle on which Indigenous society was organized was kinship, by blood, marriage, or clan identity, the last often based on fictive descent from a non-human ancestor.[8] Those with whom one did not share kinship were by definition strangers and enemies, and thus legitimate objects of attack.

Two basic kin groups emerged around the St Lawrence–Great Lakes basin after the arrival of Europeans: the French-Wendat-Algonquin alliance, which included most of the Great Lakes peoples, and the Haudenosaunee-Dutch (later English) alliance known as the Covenant Chain, based in New Netherland/New York. Both the French and the Dutch were recognized as brothers by their respective Indigenous allies, though in the case of France the metaphor shifted later in the seventeenth century to one of father-child relations, with the French governor recognized by some Indigenous peoples as Onontio, or father-figure. This development was not necessarily as paternalistic as it may appear, given that the Indigenous concept of fatherhood was based on generosity and forgiveness, not on authority and discipline; fathers were understood to mediate solutions to conflicts, not to impose them. Nor did the fatherhood metaphor imply a lack of autonomy or surrender of sovereignty from the Indigenous point of view, although Europeans may have sometimes interpreted this differently.[9]

The interaction of natives and newcomers in the context of attempted European settlement in northeastern America after 1600 gave rise to many questions for the legal orders of both groups. Both recognized a distinction between 'domestic law' applicable to one's own nation or people, and a 'law of nations' that governed interactions with outside polities. Each side had to decide how the respective 'other' fit within their own laws and practices governing such external relations. Did emerging European notions of sovereignty apply in North America? Could the French be inserted in Indigenous confederacies? Related questions arose around subjecthood: Were Indigenous persons subjects of European monarchs? (The converse was not argued, because Indigenous law had no concept of subjecthood as such.) And how would the 'domestic law' of the two groups interact once the Europeans began to erect their own legal, political, and judicial institutions?

European authors had been discussing the legal status of Indigenous peoples since the 'discovery' of the Americas in the 1490s. By the seventeenth century, they had mostly accepted that such peoples possessed a kind of international legal personality.[10] Indigenous groups were recognized as entities with a sufficient political organization for treaties to be agreed with them, and their chiefs were greeted in the capitals of New France as ambassadors. However, there were always some qualifications in this regard. The treaties entered into with native peoples did not follow the protocols that European monarchs followed with each other. Rather, relations between the French and their Indigenous allies, and between the English and Haudenosaunee via the covenant chain, were governed by a body of intercultural law that evolved between them, rather than by the law of nations as such.[11] This can be seen most clearly in the Great Peace of 1701, which poured Indigenous content into the form of a treaty document familiar to Europeans. The Indigenous peoples did not see themselves as surrendering any sovereignty in their agreements with the authorities of New France, even if the French text sometimes stated it expressly, as in the peace treaties with the Haudenosaunee of 1665–7. Moreover, even if there is sometimes an element of subordination expressed in these treaties, European authors such as Bodin and Grotius stated that forming an alliance whereby one monarch agrees to bring another under his protection does not imply a surrender of sovereignty by the latter.[12]

On the related topic of subjecthood, French thinking on this topic underwent a change over the course of the seventeenth century. At first the issue was tied to conversion. Indigenous persons who converted to Christianity were considered to have recognized in some way the authority of the monarch and therefore were to be considered subjects. The 1627 charter of the Company of New France declared in article 17 that those Indigenous individuals who embraced Christianity would be considered 'naturels françois,' French subjects. Within Indigenous societies, however, Christian converts posed a serious challenge (just as religious diversity did in Europe in the early modern period). For peoples whose decision-making was based on consensus, the converts' attempts to remake their own societies along Christian lines led to deep divisions. The Innu leader Etinechkaouat explained to the Jesuits his reason for not converting: 'I will tell you frankly that I was afraid my people would look upon me as a Frenchman, hence I did not wish to give up the customs of my nation to embrace those of yours.'[13] Thus, as the Jesuits tried to convert the Wendat people in the 1630s and 1640s, 'the antagonism between converts and traditionalists … shook the foundations of Huron society.'[14] In Mohawk society too, the appearance of Christianity exacerbated factionalism.[15]

Many of the converts, styled 'domiciliés' in French, thus left their ancestral lands and formed communities near Montreal, Quebec, and Trois-Rivières, partly for their own protection, and partly to be closer to Christian institutions.[16] The Huron-Wendat negotiated the conditions of their settlement with French authorities after their decision to abandon Huronia/Wendaké in the wake of military defeat at the hands of the Haudenosaunee in 1649, eventually establishing themselves at Jeune-Lorette after a number of moves. Many Christian Mohawks migrated north to the Montreal area after the French and Haudenosaunee made (a short-lived) peace in 1667, also moving a number of times before settling at Kahnawake (Sault-St-Louis).[17] Among the migrants was Kateri Tekakwitha (1656–80), who would become (in 2012) the first Indigenous North American canonized by the Roman Catholic Church.[18] After the conflict known as Metacom's War (also known as King Philip's War) in New England in the 1670s, a number of Abenakis also sought refuge in the St Lawrence valley, forming another mission village at Odanak (St-François).

The restructuring of authority in New France after 1663 led to a rethinking of the policy of automatic subjecthood for Christianized Indigenous people. The Crown assumed direct authority for the governance and administration of the colony, at first acting through its agent, the new Company of the West Indies, created in 1664. Its charter postponed subjecthood for one generation, declaring that only the children of Christian converts would be subjects of the king.[19] After the annulment of its charter in 1674, no formal text ever sought to clarify the status of the inhabitants of the mission villages or other Christian converts.[20]

Even during the period when Christian converts were formally declared to be subjects, however, they denied that they were subject to the laws of New France. In spite of the appearance of subjugation of the mission communities, they remained autonomous allies, with much greater autonomy than the 'praying towns' of New England or the *congregaciónes* of Mexico.[21] Their members were not subject to conscription into the militia, for example, but made their own decisions about which French military expeditions they wished to assist. While French subjects were forbidden, often on pain of death, from trading with the English, inhabitants of the mission villages were not prevented from doing so. With regard to the criminal law, even where Indigenous persons killed Europeans, the offender's law usually prevailed. Indigenous traditions required that the offender and his family provide presents to the victim's family to atone for the killing. Wendat tradition, for example, required that thirty presents be paid for the murder of a man, and forty for a woman.[22] In 1627 an Innu killed two Frenchmen, and Champlain demanded that the murderer be turned over to the French. A year later the accused was brought to the French but was released after a period of imprisonment, without even an official pardon or, apparently, any presents being provided by the murderer's family or village.[23] By 1648 the French had grasped the nature of local traditions and mostly accepted presents as reparations when settlers were killed by Indigenous people.

The issue of penalties for rape arose in 1664, soon after the establishment of the Conseil souverain, when an Algonquin, Robert Hache, was accused of raping a married woman, Marthe Hubert, of Île d'Orléans. He was arrested, imprisoned, escaped, and recaptured. Feeling its way, the Conseil first convoked a meeting of the inhabitants to determine 's'il est apropos d' assujettir les sauvages aux loix françoises.'[24] The result of this consultation is not recorded, but the next month the Conseil met with six chiefs, including Noel Tek8erimat, chief of the Algonquins of Quebec. He observed through an interpreter that for a long time his people had had friendly relations with the French, but they did not know that rape was punishable by death, only murder. They did not want Hache's wrong to imperil 'une amitié si ancienne' and were willing to observe French law in this regard in the future, but asked that Hache be spared. The Conseil agreed, concluding that 'in order to avoid future disorders, with the consent of the [six chiefs] it is ordered that the said Savages will be subject to the penalties imposed by the laws and ordinances of France for murder and rape,' penalties that the chiefs agreed to publicize among their people.[25] The careful wording makes clear that the Conseil did not seek to impose French law on the Algonquins; rather, the chiefs agreed on behalf of their people to observe it with regard to these two crimes, in order to continue their good relations with the French. Even so, only two executions of Indigenous persons convicted of murdering a European are known to have been carried out in Montreal during the entire French regime. More usual was the case of the Wendat Nicolas Tonobl8an, who was found guilty of the attempted murder of a missionary in 1684. Fined 100 livres and banished from the Montreal district, he was back in the town of Montreal four years later.[26]

With regard to theft and other offences, colonial criminal justice, normally so punctilious in its observance of the ordinance of 1670, was virtually suspended for Indigenous accused, whether Christian or not. Virtually all Indigenous accused brought before the royal court at Montreal under the French regime, accused of crimes ranging from disorderly conduct to murder, allegedly broke the law while intoxicated. The entire focus of the court process was to identify the liquor suppliers;

once that was accomplished the accused would be released and the supplier would be put on trial for breaking the law against supplying natives with alcohol.[27] Thus, on 11 May 1664 the Conseil ordered the imprisonment of two 'sauvages,' Ta8iskaron and Anaka8abemat, for drunkenness; they were to be released upon identifying their supplier. The next day they named 'le Sieur Rouvray soldat' and were released.[28] The penalty for supplying Indigenous persons with alcohol had been 300 livres for a first offence, and whipping for a second, but in 1664 the Conseil souverain observed that in light of widespread violation of the law, the penalties would be made even more severe. Past offences were forgiven, but for the following year, no one was allowed to possess alcohol even in their own home without the consent of the governor, and in future contraventions of the law would be met with confiscation of the offender's goods and banishment.[29] It is doubtful if these draconian penalties were exacted frequently, but they indicate the degree of frustration experienced by the authorities in trying to resolve the intractable problem posed by the easy availability of alcohol to Indigenous persons.

Paris, for its part, understood the strategic reasons underlying the leniency of the criminal law vis-à-vis Indigenous people. When Governor Vaudreuil questioned it, he received the following reply from the king in 1714:

> As regards the Indians' claim that we cannot put them in prison without their consent and that they are absolutely not subject to the laws of the country. The matter is very delicate and has to be approached cautiously … [W]e can hope to subject them to laws, but we have to do it slowly, prudently, and with caution. One has to start to subject them to military justice and then, step by step, they will be subjected to the same justice as the French inhabitants.[30]

A few years earlier, the intendant Jacques Raudot opined that the process of legal acculturation would take 'several centuries.'[31] His prediction was more accurate than the king's. Converting Indigenous people to French mores remained little more than a fond hope until the end of the French regime. If anything, it was the legal order of Canada that adapted to Indigenous ways, rather than the reverse. The presence of the mission settlements was crucial to the security of the St Lawrence colony, before 1701 with regard to the Haudenosaunee threat, and afterwards with regard to the British colonies. Alienating them through a heavy-handed application of French law was simply too great a risk to take.

Even as the missionaries sought to 'civilize' Indigenous peoples through evangelization, they were never able to succeed completely in getting Christian converts, much less non-converts, to abandon their way of life and traditional laws. In some respects, such as the enforcement of monogamy and ideas of Christian marriage, the missionaries had success with converts. But in general Indigenous people chose which aspects of French life and law they wished to emulate, or not, and the colonial administration could do little about it. In chapter 17 we will see that inhabitants of the mission communities did partially integrate into the colonial legal order, just as they integrated into its religious life, in a variety of ways, but always through their own choices. This is not surprising, as these settlements were close to the major centres of settler population, and their economies were somewhat integrated. The French military's purchase of canoes and snowshoes from the Huron-Wendat at Quebec brought considerable income to their community, for example.[32] Beyond the areas of French settlement, Indigenous peoples had less reason to adopt French ways.

If, in the case of criminal law, the French reluctantly accepted Indigenous traditions for strategic reasons, with regard to the law of war, peace, and diplomacy, they quickly adopted Indigenous protocols to further their own geopolitical and economic goals. After the dispersal of the Huron-Wendat in 1648–50, the French looked for allies further west to rebuild their trade network and developed alliances in the Pays d'en haut with the Odawas, Ojibwas, Potawatomis, Miamis, Illinois, Mascoutens, Kickapoos, Nipissings, Winnebagos, and Sauks. In the east they were allied to the Wabanaki Confederacy, which included Penobscots, Mi'kmaq, Wulstukwiuk, and Passamaquoddys. They could not have done so without mastering Indigenous languages and, to some extent at least, understanding their allies' mental, spiritual, and juridical world view. They came to appreciate the significance of gift-giving and kinship, the importance of eloquence, dance and chanting, the rituals of sweet-grass and tobacco, the need to allow every leader to have his say, and the subtleties of the proper speaking order and seating arrangements.

This century-long learning process came to fruition in the Great Peace of 1701 with which this part began, an accord that finally brought about a lasting rapprochement between the French and the Haudenosaunee, as well as embracing thirty-seven other Indigenous peoples.

The peace accords reached periodically in the preceding decades were short-lived, leaving the colony constantly under threat. The end of the North American extension of the war of the League of Augsburg in 1697 provided an opening for peace with the Five Nations Confederacy. With the French and English at peace, the English tried to argue that the Haudenosaunee, as their supposed subjects, had to be at peace with the French too. The Haudenosaunee were anxious to show that they were not subjects of the English and wanted to negotiate a separate peace with the French to demonstrate it. The French seized this opportunity and held successful negotiations with the Haudenosaunee in the summer of 1700, which led to the grand conference of 1701.

As noted in the prologue to this part, the negotiations and rituals were held in accordance with Indigenous tradition, and the treaty itself represented a marked departure from earlier efforts. The 1665–7 treaties with the Haudenosaunee, for example, had followed the forms of European treaties with numbered clauses indicating the principal points of agreement. The 1701 text was, rather, a transcription of the orations delivered by Callière and the Indigenous representatives at the peace conference. It thus represented a living relationship meant to be elaborated upon and renewed in the future, rather than simply a means of settling past disputes. The Haudenosaunee also renewed their covenant chain with the English in the same year, thus confirming their own sovereignty and establishing in effect a neutral buffer state between New York and Canada. The French colony, with its 14,000 European inhabitants, had bought itself, and the civil law, another half-century of existence on a continent studded with British colonies containing some 250,000 inhabitants.[33] Without understanding and adapting to Indigenous legal and political traditions, it would never have been able to achieve this result.

Another area where the logic of the French system of alliances led to the incorporation of Indigenous concepts into French law was that of Indigenous slavery.[34] The inhabitants of the upper Great Lakes such as the Sioux, Cree, and Ojibwe often enslaved members of enemy tribes captured in war, not as a labour source but more for political and cultural reasons. Slaves were ritually degraded to strip them of their former identities and partially assimilated into the host nation. Female captives might be taken as second or third wives but remained vulnerable to abuse, as they had no kin to protect them. Their children might be recognized as full members of the host nation, but the initial captives retained a certain stigma throughout their lives. They were given servile work to do, such as fetching water or preparing animal skins by picking fleas from them, and might be given away to allied nations as tokens of friendship. The Algonquins, Innu, Wendat, and Haudenosaunee of the lower Great Lakes and the St Lawrence valley with whom the French had initially interacted did not practise slavery in this sense or use captives as symbolic gifts. Their practice was to assimilate captives into their own kinship group via a form of adoption rather than giving them away.

After achieving peace with the Haudenosaunee in 1667, the French were able to rapidly expand their alliances throughout the Pays d'en Haut. As a result, they found themselves being offered slaves by potential allies. In 1678, for example, Daniel Greysolon Dulhut received three slaves from the Odawas, which they saw as effecting a symbolic unification of their two peoples.[35] The gift of a slave could even assuage the murder of a French trader committed by members of the Sauk nation: Governor General Louis-Hector de Callière pardoned the offenders after accepting a 'small slave' as compensation.[36] As these exchanges became more common, canny fur traders began to turn these 'gifts' into a commodity, and a market in Indigenous slaves developed in Montreal. Their presence is increasingly visible in the public records of Montreal and Quebec from the 1690s.[37]

At first these sales were conducted in a legal grey zone. French law had long insisted, in the context of African slavery, on a distinction between the act of enslavement and the purchase of a slave. The former was a matter for the law of nations, as part of the law of just war, while the latter – the legal status of an already enslaved individual – could be regulated by national laws. The French developed a legal fiction that all African slaves were purchased from sovereign nations in Africa who had acquired them in just wars, regardless of their actual origins; thereafter, such slaves could be legitimately bought and sold in the colonies without breaking French law.[38] Likewise, in North America it was important for legal purposes for French traders to show that they were not actually enslaving Indigenous persons but rather purchasing individuals already enslaved by others. Thus developed the fiction that all Indigenous slaves were from the Pawnee nation (Panis in French), who inhabited the area around the Missouri River and who had been enslaved by neighbouring rivals. While some slaves were indeed Pawnees, many were not; the denomination Panis came to be used for any Indigenous slave.

In spite of the beginnings of a trade in Indigenous slaves, their use mainly in household settings did little to alleviate the perennial shortage of agricultural workers in New France. Thus, the king, urged on by the attorney general of New France, François Ruette d'Auteuil, settled on a new source of labour: African slaves. In 1688 Louis XIV authorized their importation into New France, but only a handful of African slaves appear in the records over the next twenty years.[39] More would arrive in the eighteenth century, but Indigenous slaves would outnumber them by a ratio of at least 9:1 until the 1740s. The Great Peace of 1701 greatly expanded the system of Native alliances but also resulted in a steadily enhanced flow of Indigenous slaves to the Montreal market.

9

French Private Law

The French Customs

Private law in France was not unified at the national level until the *Code Napoléon* of 1804. Until the Revolution it consisted principally of collections of customs followed in a particular region or province, as noted in part 1.[1] Immigration during the early decades of French settlement came mostly from western and central France, not from Paris. The settlers would thus have been familiar with the customs of their own regions and not necessarily that of Paris. Indeed, there is some evidence that customs from the west of France continued to be observed in both Acadie and Canada, even after the Custom of Paris was declared in 1664 to be the only authoritative one in the colony.[2]

It is important to realize that the customs were not codes in the nineteenth-century sense. They did not purport to be comprehensive statements of the law, even within the fields that they covered expressly, nor was their content equivalent to that of modern statutory law. The articles of the customs are often expressed in terse language, more akin to statements of principle than detailed regulations. For reasons noted in part 1, case law was not a useful means of resolving interpretive difficulties. The meaning of provisions of the custom was expanded on by learned commentators, but they were not always in agreement, leaving parties and their advisers considerable flexibility in ordering their affairs. The customs were thus more facilitative than regulatory in many respects.[3]

The Custom of Paris comprised 362 articles in sixteen titles, of which one-quarter dealt with seigneurial law, and another 30 were found to be unsuited to New France and not applied.[4] The rest dealt with property, succession, family law, the execution of judgments, and recovery of debts. The custom had virtually nothing to say about contract in general or delict (tort). These matters were regulated by the uncodified law (droit commun) and given shape by treatise writers in the eighteenth century, who often looked to Roman law for inspiration. The custom did not treat criminal law, nor did it treat marriage itself, which was a matter of canon law supplemented by royal ordinances. Both the custom and the droit commun were motivated by several basic principles: protection of the vulnerable, family solidarity, and the maintenance of ancestral lands within the lineage. If the custom in general was infused with a patriarchal ethos, conferring extensive powers on husbands and fathers over their wives and children, it also limited the powers of both parents and spouses in the interests of family solidarity and continuity, as will be detailed below. The provisions of the custom on family law in particular were extraordinarily long-lived: set down in 1580 in France (although based on an earlier version of 1510), they would survive into the *Civil Code of Lower Canada* of 1866, and thereafter with only minor reforms until the 1960s. Thus, while this chapter is meant to deal with the civil law as it existed in the sixteenth and seventeenth centuries, some examples from the eighteenth century will be used from time to time, as there was no change in the provisions of the custom itself.

While the Custom of Paris did not deal directly with personal status, a brief account of the topic is in order before discussing the custom in more detail. French law formally distinguished three classes of persons: nobles, ecclesiastics, and roturiers (commoners), while colonial law added a fourth: the slave. Indigenous slavery has already been considered: it was governed by a local customary law that evolved in Canada as a result of interactions with Indigenous allies. African slaves in Canada were also governed by a locally developed customary law, but as very few such slaves were present there prior to 1701, it is discussed in chapter 11.

Nobles benefited from a variety of privileges in France, including exemption from various state taxes. The latter was not such an issue in New France because taxes did not exist in the same form. In New France, noble status was more a matter of social than legal recognition. Most noble families in North America came from France itself, although the king did ennoble eleven individuals in New France in the seventeenth century as a means of encouraging colonization; the practice was not repeated in the eighteenth century.[5]

The status of ecclesiastics comprised both privileges and, in certain cases, disabilities. The property of ecclesiastics benefited from certain exemptions from seizure, and they were spared various public duties, such as militia service and the obligation to house troops. Parish clergy were permitted to collect the tithe from their parishioners, set in 1667 at one-twenty-sixth of certain kinds of produce, half the rate that applied in France.[6] Those who belonged to regular religious orders were subject to civil death. As a result they lost all civil rights, including the capacity to contract and to inherit property; their legal personality was subsumed in that of their order, which in turn assumed the obligation to support them. Such persons could, however, still testify in court. The solemn vows required to join an order were subject to certain conditions and formalities in order to ensure that they represented the candidate's free and genuine choice: a minimum age (twenty-one for men, eighteen for women), a written attestation witnessed by the superior and two witnesses, and the lapse of a year between entering the order and taking one's vows. In default of any of these, candidates could renounce their vows within five years and resume their legal personality. Secular clergy, such as parish priests, did not suffer civil death.[7]

The Law of Marriage and the Family

Pressure from church and society combined to ensure that the vast majority of families were founded on matrimony. Marriage was indissoluble under the law of both state and church, although canon law permitted annulments in certain cases. The conditions for a valid marriage were governed mainly by the canon law of the Catholic Church, supplemented by royal edicts over the centuries, while the civil effects of marriage were determined by the relevant custom. While the general principles of canon law were similar throughout the Catholic world, bishops were allowed a certain discretion to tailor a local version in their own dioceses. This task was taken up by the second bishop of Quebec, Jean-Baptiste de Saint-Vallier, whose *Rituel du diocèse de Québec* was published in Paris in 1703. A delicate dance had long gone on between church and state over the legal regulation of marriage, with the church seeking to ensure the independent and uncoerced consent of the parties to the union, while the state was more concerned to uphold parental authority to influence the conjugal choices of their children, often for reasons connected to property.

The Council of Trent (1545–63) accepted the medieval theory of the sacrament – that the parties married themselves – and required the presence of a priest only as a witness. The French state, however, at least after a royal declaration of 1639, took the position that the parish priest actually married the parties for purposes of state law and was not a mere witness. Between 1598 and 1685 Protestant clergy could celebrate valid marriages, but the revocation of the Edict of Nantes in the latter year outlawed Protestantism in France and its colonies, making such marriages invalid. In theory, mixed marriages were possible, prior to a royal ordinance of 1680 that foreshadowed the revocation of the Edict of Nantes; it forbade such marriages in the future, declaring them null and void and any children born of them illegitimate.[8]

The canon law of the Catholic Church recognized no fewer than fourteen impediments to marriage.[9] In general the state accepted the canon law's prescriptions regarding the validity or otherwise of a marriage, but with regard to the role of the parents of the affianced there was a significant disparity between canon and state law. For the church, marriage was purely consensual and no parental consent was required. Even though the age of majority for most civil purposes was twenty-five, parties could marry as young as twelve for females and fourteen for males under canon law. Parents had other views, which found their way into the 1556 edict on clandestine marriages, a royal law that aimed to undercut the canon law on marriage indirectly. The edict, which remained in force throughout the French regime, required parental consent (in effect, paternal consent if the father was alive) to the marriage of their offspring, for women until the age of twenty-five and for men until the age of thirty. Marriages entered into without parental consent remained valid according to both canon law and civil law. But the lack of consent permitted the parents to disinherit the disobedient child, an act that, as will be seen, was not generally allowed under the law of succession.[10] Thus Marie-Catherine Peuvret, seigneuresse of Beauport after the death of her husband, disinherited her eldest surviving son Antoine in 1737 when he planned to marry the daughter of one of the censitaires on her estate – a potentially disastrous mésalliance from the maternal point of view. Two months later, when he announced his plans to marry Marie Françoise Chartier de Lotbinière, daughter of an old seigneurial family – a marriage to which Peuvret heartily consented – she revoked her earlier will. In fact, her son was thirty-three at the time and the act of disinheritance could probably have been challenged; but Antoine clearly preferred to take no chances and conformed to his mother's wishes.[11]

In Canada the relatively high age of parental permission to marry was a potential obstacle to the rapid peopling of the colony so desired by the French state. An arrêt applicable only to Canada (Acadie being under English control at the time) adopted by the king's council in 1670 aimed to lower the age of marriage through a package of carrots and sticks. The carrot was a one-time 20-pound gift to men who married before their twentieth birthday and women who married by their sixteenth birthday. The stick was a penalty to be imposed on fathers whose children were not married by these ages, though the penalty was not specified and was left to the Conseil souverain. A further pronatalist measure was the promise of a pension of 300 pounds to fathers who had ten living children, none of whom were priests or had entered religious orders, and 400 pounds to those with twelve such living children. It is not clear whether any of these measures were actually implemented or if implemented had any effect. The age of women at first marriage in Canada in the seventeenth century was nineteen, lower than the twenty-two of metropolitan France, but the average age for men was twenty-eight, a year higher than in the metropole. The birth rate and infant survival rate was higher in New France, but likely because of a better diet and more favourable socio-economic conditions, not because of state policies.[12]

Given the small pool of potential marriage partners, especially in Acadie, the question of consanguinity was the potential impediment most often encountered in New France. However, papal dispensations appear to have been regularly obtained through the offices of the bishop, or in Acadie, through local clergy who exercised an authority delegated by him.[13] Once a valid marriage had been entered into, the Custom of Paris prescribed in some detail its effects upon the personal rights of the parties, and on their property and that of their children, both during life and after death. It provided considerable scope for tailoring these rights and obligations, however, and the vast majority of couples in Canada (though probably not in Acadie), even the relatively disadvantaged, entered into notarized marriage contracts prior to their marriage.[14] Why they did this in greater numbers than in France has not been satisfactorily explained. While separation of property between spouses was theoretically possible, it was almost never contracted for under the French regime, and the 'default' regime of community property governed the lives of virtually all married couples.

Marriage had a major impact on the civil rights of the parties, but especially those of the wife, who experienced a virtual suspension of her legal personality during marriage. The law will be set out here, but comparisons with the common law and larger conclusions with respect to the status of women in the seventeenth and eighteenth centuries will be made in the conclusion to part 3. As a single woman or a widow, a woman possessed the same legal capacity as a man under the private law. On her wedding day, even if married in separation of property, she came under the marital authority of her husband and thereby lost her contractual capacity, her ability to deal with any pre-marital assets on her own, and her ability to appear in court without the authorization of her husband. She could make a will without her husband's consent, but freedom of testation was severely restricted under French law in any case.

While the Custom of Paris went into some detail regarding the effects of marriage on the property of spouses, it was less forthcoming on the personal effects of marriage. These arose from a mixture of Roman law and the droit commun, elaborated on in the writings of French jurists. The latter were not always in accord, and no local author digested this body of law before François Joseph Cugnet did so in 1775.[15] Unfortunately he too followed the tendency of the Custom of Paris to emphasize property over personal relations, such that it has been necessary to draw on a later work as well in order to secure a local account of these principles.[16] Such sources are less than ideal as an account of the law as it existed under the French regime, but with regard to basic principles they are no doubt accurate.

Marriage was described by legal writers of the day as a partnership, but it was of a peculiar kind, given the imbalance of power in the relationship. The essential bargain of marriage was one in which the wife gained her husband's 'protection' in return for her obedience and a surrender of formal control to him over virtually all the economic aspects of married life. The husband was the head of the family, and the wife was obliged to join him wherever he decided to establish the familial residence; she also acquired his domicile if hers was different at the time of marriage. Should the wife leave the husband without legitimate cause (and 'mere' adultery on his part did not constitute such cause), he could oblige her to return and also had an action against any third parties who might be harbouring her, even her own parents.[17] The husband was obliged to receive the wife, and should he exclude her without grave cause (for example, her adultery), or abuse her physically, such an act authorized her to seek what was later known as separation from bed and board, or séparation d'habitation in the language of the day. Such requests were rare; only twenty-eight are known from the entire period of the French regime.[18] Probably requests for separation from bed and board were made before the officialité (the ecclesiastical tribunal) as well as the royal courts, but the records of the former have disappeared. Even the church recognized that although the marriage bond could not be broken, the law allowed married persons to live separate and apart where grave cause was established, but only after a judicial decision.[19] Where physical abuse was alleged, however, the standard to be proved was very high. The husband was thought to possess a right of 'moderate correction' over his wife, analogous to that he possessed over his children and servants, and might plead that any physical abuse was only an exercise of that right and 'deserved' by her.[20]

While community of property was by far the preferred matrimonial regime for couples in New France, separation of property could be adopted by marriage contract. Separation from bed and board also brought with it separation of property, but in neither case did this translate to economic independence for the wife. A woman married under separation of property was still subject to the marital authority of her husband and could not alienate even her own inherited property without his consent or act as a litigant other than in matters dealing with the simple administration (as opposed to transfer) of her property. The idea that only the male was capable of making rational economic decisions was deeply ingrained. Thus, according to Claude de Ferrière, a separated woman 'cannot be made guardian of her property without [her husband's] permission because it is a man's job [une charge virile], and for a woman to do it would be unseemly.'[21] Voluntary separation of spouses on mutual consent was not authorized by law, but such agreements were entered into before notaries.[22]

The economic disempowerment of married women created its own contradictions and inconveniences, especially in a society where husbands might be away from home for long periods of time. Thus, a number of escape routes evolved. The droit commun permitted the wife to exercise a customary implicit agency for household necessaries, albeit one that could be revoked by the husband on notice to creditors.[23] Des Rivières Beaubien stated that the wife could acquire food and clothing for herself, her husband, children, and her parents, without express authorization from the husband, though earlier French authors did not go this far.[24] The creation of a formal agency, or procuration, whereby a wife could represent her husband in court and in various legal acts, appears to have been relatively common under the French regime. The fact that wives as opposed to third parties were most often chosen for this task suggests that the household partnership model contemplated by the law had some basis in social fact.[25] Another way for married women to elude some of the restrictions of the husband's marital authority was through asserting the status of a marchande publique. Articles 234–6 of the Custom of Paris regulated this status, which permitted a married woman to 'trade separate and apart from her husband,' in which case she could 'bind herself without her husband respecting the acts and expenses of her trade.' The custom was silent on how this status began and whether married women traders could take legal actions in their own name connected to their business. At least at a later period, Quebec jurists asserted that while the husband's requisite consent to such a business could be implicit, a marchande publique could not be a party to litigation connected to her separate business without her husband being party to the action.[26]

The marital authority of husbands had its counterpart in the father's paternal power over his minor children, a power that endured until the child married, reached the age of majority (twenty-five under French law), or became emancipated from parental control below that age.[27] While both parents were alive, such authority was to be legally exercised only by the father, unless he was absent or incapable. The father possessed a right of moderate physical correction over his minor children, but the excesses of paternal authority in old regime France were not permitted in New France. In France, fathers could prevail upon state authority to grant lettres de cachet permitting them to imprison their disobedient children. No such power existed in New France. Observers from France were surprised at the minimal extent of parental control over their children compared to the mother country, a situation they attributed to the earlier opportunities for economic independence that existed in North America – though as seen in the examples of Marie-Catherine Peuvret and Mme Hertel de Rouville above, parents' legal control over their children's marriages could still be highly potent.[28]

In spite of the relative freedom of children in North America, familial obligations could extend beyond one generation. The support obligation of parents for their minor children could extend to them in adulthood if they were in need, and even to their grandchildren, but only if the parents of those grandchildren could not support them. Likewise, adults could be obliged to support their own parents in need, as well as their grandparents if the children of the latter could not do so. With regard to the support of parents, this could take the form of a pension, or of bringing the parents to live with their adult children.[29] As will be seen shortly, however, parents in rural society did not usually rely on the general law but on securing a contractual obligation of support from a child, normally a son, at the time of conveying all or part of the family landholding to him during their own lifetimes.

The Law of Family Property: Matrimonial Regimes and Succession

Turning to property matters, married couples could choose from three different matrimonial regimes: separation of property, community of property, or simple exclusion of community.[30] The last was a somewhat anomalous regime that did not create a community of property but, unlike separate property, left the right to collect and manage all income from both parties' property with the husband. It did not feature as a significant part of the legal landscape until the nineteenth century and will not be further considered in this part. Community of property was the default regime for those who married with no marriage contract. The vast majority of Canadiens prior to 1760 were governed by this regime, either as the default or because they adopted a tailored version of it by marriage contract. The basic idea was simple: property acquired by the joint efforts of the spouses during marriage was accumulated in a notional economic entity called the community, which would be shared equally on the death of the first spouse. Half would go to the surviving spouse, and half to the heirs of the deceased spouse – his or her children, if any, otherwise, to the closest blood relatives of the deceased. Complexity arose because the law distinguished between property that came to one of the spouses from their own family, which did not fall into the community, and everything else. The former – land owned before marriage or inherited during marriage – was called private property (propres). The rest – the moveables and conquêts (immoveables acquired by purchase during marriage) were community assets. Most income arising during marriage, including income produced by private property, also entered into the community.

While the wife's entitlement to half the community assets was an important post-mortem guarantee for her, should she survive her husband, and a recognition of the partnership theory of marriage espoused by French law, the husband had the sole legal power over the community while the marriage lasted. The Custom of Paris in article 225 went so far as to declare him the 'seigneur' of the moveables and conquêts acquired during marriage – the implication being that the wife was a mere censitaire in the household. The husband could dispose of his private property independently, but the wife required his authorization (or that of the court) to dispose of hers. Alienation of community property required the consent of both spouses, but acts of 'administration,' such as leasing out or repairing property, lay solely within the husband's authority. With regard to the private property of the wife, he could not dispose of it or mortgage it without her consent, but he could lease out 'city' property for six years or 'country' property for nine years on his own.[31] In fact, in all but the wealthier families, many spouses had no private property of any value at the time of their marriage, such that most property fell into the community. Or the parties sometimes specified in their marriage contract that what would otherwise be private property would be treated as a community asset.[32] The custom gave spouses great flexibility in defining the community, on a spectrum from a 'maximalist' community encompassing all the property however acquired of both spouses, to a 'minimalist' community little different from separation of property. Whatever its content, upon the death of either spouse, half the community assets went to the surviving spouse, and the other half was shared among the children, who also inherited the private property subject to any dower interest of the widow. If any or all of the children were minors, the surviving spouse also enjoyed a usufruct (that is, a right to enjoy the income for her lifetime) over their shares in the community property inherited from the deceased spouse. This provision was to enable her to fulfil her support obligation to the children of the marriage.

In addition to her half of the community assets, the widow was also entitled to dower, of which there were two forms: préfix and customary. The latter entitled her to a usufruct in half of the husband's private property; the former to a set amount stated in the marriage contract, which she took out of the husband's share of the community on his death, ahead of any creditors, in lieu of any claim against his private property. The marriage contract could allow her the choice between these, as was common in Canada. An additional advantage afforded the widow was her right to claim her customary dower ahead of any creditors of her husband's estate; to do so she had to renounce her right to her share of the community, but could take from it free and clear any assets she had contributed to it. Spouses were not entitled to make gifts to each other during their lifetimes or by will, in order to preserve adequate assets for their children or blood relatives. Exceptionally, they could provide that the survivor should enjoy a usufruct in all the community property, but this provision, known as a don mutuel (mutual gift), had to be specified in the marriage contract and was operative only where the couple had no children.[33]

In addition to securing a spouse's private property for his or her bloodline, the Custom of Paris featured other provisions aimed at maintaining family lands within the lineage. Where an individual sold inherited property to a third party, the vendor's closest blood relative (typically a parent or sibling) had a pre-emptive right to buy back the property at the same price the purchaser had paid, within a year and a day of the sale. This retrait lignager, or right of lineal redemption, in effect allowed property to be reclaimed for the lineage, and its existence was meant to discourage sales to outsiders.[34]

Likewise, the principles of succession law restricted freedom of testation in the interests of the family. Here the characterization of the property as noble or roturier (non-noble) was essential. Noble property that formed part of a 'fief de dignité,' such as a duchy, barony, etc. – of which there were few in New France – descended to the eldest son subject to his duty to pay an indemnity to his siblings. Ordinary seigneuries descended according to a modified law of primogeniture. If the deceased left two children, the son (or elder brother) took two-thirds of the seigneury, including the manor house, and the other sibling one-third. If there were more than two children, the eldest son took half as well as the manor house, and the other children shared the remaining half. If the deceased was survived only by daughters, however, they shared equally.[35]

With regard to non-noble property, all children of the deceased shared equally, subject to the rights of the widow or widower if any, if there was no will. In order to safeguard this equality, all *inter vivos* gifts or advances made on a child's share during the deceased's lifetime had to be accounted for. Testamentary freedom was also restricted in order to prevent undue favouritism among children. A parent was prevented from willing away more than one-fifth of his or her private property, leaving the 'réserve des quatre-quints' to be divided equally among the children. As few habitants had much private property, however, this was not a significant constraint for most people. An additional restriction on freedom of testation, the légitime, was also found in the Custom of Paris. This provision applied to all the property of the deceased and aimed to ensure that all his or her children received a minimum share of the estate. The parent could not leave a child a share worth less than half of what the child would have received if the deceased's assets had been divided equally among all the children. The value of the estate for these purposes, however, would be calculated to include all legacies and gifts *inter vivos* made by the deceased, minus their debts and funeral expenses. How much of a constraint this actually imposed on the parental generation is debated. Louise Dechêne asserts that it was not applied at all in the seventeenth century,[36] while Jean-Philippe Garneau notes that it was relatively easy to avoid, as opposed to not applied, at least in the eighteenth century. Not until a royal ordinance of 1731 was a remedy provided for those who felt their rights pursuant to the légitime had not been respected, while a child who had received a large gift *inter vivos* could renounce the succession and keep the gift, even if it meant his or her siblings were short-changed.[37] This was another example of the way in which the seemingly strict provisions of the Custom of Paris could be softened or even evaded.

Two limited inroads on the principle of equal division were permitted. The first, as noted earlier, arose where a minor child who flouted parental wishes with regard to a marriage partner could be disinherited. The second was permitted by the institution known as the fiduciary substitution. A substitution allowed a wealth holder to gift an asset to a donee, called the grevé, who was to hold it with the obligation of transmitting it to another party, called the appelé or substitué, on the death of the grevé. The asset thus became inalienable, indivisible, and immune from creditors during the lifetime of the grevé, who in effect possessed a special type of life interest. Parents who were upset with their children for legitimate reasons were permitted to leave them less than they would normally be entitled to by means of the fiduciary substitution. Thus, the parents of Marie Brazeau, scandalized by her behaviour, created a substitution over what would have been her share of their property in 1695, pursuant to which she would be the grevée; she would thus receive only the income from the property for her lifetime, while the ownership would be transferred to her children upon her death. Marie had emigrated from France in 1681 with her husband, by whom she had three children, but he departed for France in 1688, never to return. Marie ran a tavern from her home in order to survive; she eventually had three children outside marriage by two different men, incurring her parents' wrath, though she would later marry again and have six more legitimate children.[38]

The case of Marie Brazeau was exceptional. In practice, most parents arranged their affairs prior to death with the goal of transferring their landholding intact to one of their children, while either providing monetary payments to their other children to enable them to acquire land of their own, or ensuring that the favoured heir was responsible for doing so. The child who received the principal landholding was usually required to agree to support his (the obligation fell almost invariably upon sons) parents until death, with this duty often expressed in very specific language. There has been some debate over who was disadvantaged by the traditional modification of the principle of equal division: the heir who was burdened with the obligation of paying off numerous siblings? Or the siblings who, as sometimes happened, might have to defer receiving their share of the parental property until many years after the latters' deaths?[39] In either case, the Custom of Paris, with its principled commitment to sibling equality, ironically provided sufficient flexibility for families to tailor their succession plans such that their landed property could be passed on intact to a single heir.

Succession under French law followed the Roman idea that the heirs continued the personality of the deceased, unless they accepted the succession under benefit of inventory. Ordinary acceptance without an inventory meant that the heirs were fully responsible for the debts of the deceased, even if these exceeded the amount of property coming to them from the succession. Where minor heirs were concerned, it was prudent to accept the succession only under benefit of inventory; concurrently, the accounting regarding the dissolution of the community of property would be conducted in order to determine what property would be included in the deceased's, and hence the children's, share.

While much of the law of succession was dealt with in the Custom of Paris, the mechanism for protecting the interests of minor children – the institution of tutorship – was not, being part of the Roman law. When the death of a spouse led to the dissolution of the community, the surviving parent normally sought the nomination of a tutor and subrogate-tutor, who were to look after the interests of minor heirs, especially by assisting the notary in the preparation of the inventory. Upon the death of one spouse the survivor would ask the court, normally the seigneurial court, to convoke a meeting of a family council, a group of the minor's relatives and 'friends' in the early modern sense: those adults who took an interest in the child's future well-being. A minimum of seven persons was required, all male by tradition. They would almost invariably choose the surviving parent as the tutor, but their main function was to select the subrogate-tutor, or légitime contradicteur, who would typically be an uncle or cousin. The légitime contradicteur was to act as a sort of devil's advocate. The tutor-parent was normally in a conflict of interest position regarding the characterization of property as either community or private property; as a surviving spouse, his or her interest was to have an asset considered part of the marital community, while the child would benefit from having the asset characterized as private property. Hence the role of the subrogate-tutor was to ensure that the accounting was conducted fairly for both the surviving parent and the children. An additional safeguard was that the value of the property in the inventory was to be attested to either by a bailiff of the court or by two older inhabitants of the neighbourhood. The court had to confirm the naming of the tutor and subrogate-tutor, and also confirm the inventory once it was concluded. The tutor and subrogate-tutor were then responsible for looking after the property of the minor heirs until they reached the age of majority at twenty-five.[40]

The law governing marriage, family, property, and succession was of long standing and well known. Its strength also derived from its congruence with the Catholic values espoused in New France. Although some 10 per cent of brides in Canada may have been pregnant at their nuptials, illegitimacy as such was rare. In Acadie in the first half of the eighteenth century it has been estimated at 0.6 per cent, in Canada at 0.8 per cent in the seventeenth century.[41] Marriage contracts were very common and demonstrated an awareness of the facilitative nature of law in achieving life goals and estate planning. The law's concern with sibling equality and protecting the interests of minor heirs and widows was broadly shared. Parents nonetheless used the law's flexibility to achieve a delicate balance among their goals of passing on their landholding intact to one heir, providing for a fair distribution of their resources to their other children, and ensuring some security for themselves in their own old age.

It is more difficult to judge the impact of the law on wives. The law subordinated the interests of both husband and wife to those of the family and lineage writ large, but unevenly; it gave the husband disproportionate power over his wife and children and made him, at least formally, the sole decision-maker in all major decisions affecting the family. It may be that husbands regularly implemented decisions reached jointly by the spouses, but such arrangements will always remain a closed book to the researcher; legal records tend to record only conflict, not harmony. The law gave the wife few legal tools to contest the despotic power vested in the husband and father in those cases where he abused it. If husbands exercised their ample powers responsibly, it may well have been because of the perceived cost to their reputation incurred by behaving otherwise in the tightly knit communities of New France, where few matrimonial problems remained private for long.[42]

The Law of Obligations

As noted earlier, the law of obligations – contract and delict – was not dealt with in the Custom of Paris (other than marriage contracts), was found in a variety of sources, and did not possess the conceptual unity of modern law. It was very much a law of contracts and delicts, plural in each case. Two kinds of labour contracts will be briefly examined here, those of the engagés or indentured labourers, and the apprenticeship contracts of artisans. Both were normally entered into in notarial form, providing a ready-made database for historians. The indentured labourer was a key figure in the economic development of Canada in the mid-seventeenth century.[43] This person, usually male, was hired in France for a set number of years, normally three to five, to labour in the colony.[44] An unskilled labourer, he would be employed mostly in the heavy work of clearing the land for a religious community or large landowner. Few smallholders could afford the cost of such labour. The master had to agree to pay for the sea voyage, which was treated as an advance on the engagé's wages, and advances for laundry, medicine, alcohol, and other expenses meant that the engagé often ended his contract with little or no savings. Some were entitled to a plot of land at the end of their service, but it too would have to be cleared before it became productive.

The law was not kind to indentured labourers. An engagé was 'a man obliged to go wherever and do whatever his master commanded like a slave during the time of his indentureship,' reported Governor Frontenac in 1681.[45] The slavery metaphor was not inapt as engagés were often leased out daily or monthly during the course of their apprenticeship, or the balance of their term might be sold to a third party: their contracts were treated as a form of assignable property, from which middlemen could profit handsomely by linking supply and demand. Engagés could not marry during the term of their indenture, nor move anywhere without the consent of their master. Severe penalties awaited those caught transporting engagés without such permission, enticing them away from their masters, or harbouring them. The master's certification that the engagé had completed his term served as a passport, as he or she was now free to move about the colony or leave it without anyone's permission. Desertion by engagés was a substantial risk for masters, and the penalties for it, set out in arrêts of the Conseil souverain in 1663, 1673, and 1679, were severe. In 1665 the Conseil souverain sentenced three deserters as follows: one was to be hanged unless he agreed to become the hangman for the colony; one was to be whipped, and the third had his contract extended by two years; the record is unfortunately silent on any justification for the wide disparity in these punishments.[46]

These unequal contracts – with criminal penalties for employee breaches but only civil consequences for employer breaches – were a familiar feature of early modern European societies, which saw strict labour discipline as fundamental to the maintenance of social order. Their heyday in New France lasted only a generation. By the 1680s the population had increased sufficiently that locally produced labour was available to satisfy much of the demand. Smallholders could now rely on family labour, and while indentured labourers still arrived in New France, it was occasionally rather than in the numbers seen at mid-century.

Skilled workers, or those apprenticed to them, were in a much better position than unskilled labourers, who were barely distinguishable from vagrants and criminals. And apprentices in particular were in a better position in New France than in the mother country, where powerful guild organizations controlled entry and resulted in lengthy apprenticeships on terms favourable to masters. Guilds did not exist in New France, and no certificate of competence was required to ply one's trade, saving only surgeons. Freedom of contract was given free rein here, and it worked mainly to the advantage of the apprentice. A study of over 600 apprentice contracts under the French regime showed a median length of three years, as opposed to five or six in Paris, with few apprentices paying a fee to their masters (unlike France), and masters sometimes paying their apprentices in addition to providing shelter and food. Apprentices were in theory subject to the same penalties for desertion as engagés, but given their conditions of work, had much less reason to do so.[47]

The law of non-contractual civil liability was a hodgepodge of distinct actions protecting a variety of interests. Some grew out of the *Lex*

Aquilia, a Roman law of the third century BC providing for redress for certain kinds of harms to property. The jurists of the ancien droit developed and adapted the Roman law, but they were not interested in theory or system-building, being content to resolve practical problems.[48] The Romans recognized three degrees of fault, or *culpa*, but neither they nor their French successors developed a general theory of fault; such would await the *Code Napoléon* in 1804. Not surprisingly, given the role of honour under the ancien régime, actions in defamation were common, and French law was receptive to protecting a variety of sentimental harms under the heading of 'injure' or moral injury.[49]

10

The Early Modern Legacy

Law was an important tool of the European monarchies as they sought to extend their sovereignty over parts of the extra-European world. It could be used to stake out claims against rival states, to authorize the setting up and governance of new polities, and to develop relations with the Indigenous inhabitants. But Indigenous peoples, even those who converted to Christianity, insisted on observing their own laws and denied that they were subject to those of the intruders unless they freely chose to adopt them. During the early years of contact, European and Indigenous legal orders confronted each other in northeastern North America, except on the island of Newfoundland, where there was little contact between the Beothuk and the Europeans. By the end of the seventeenth century, in spite of much devastation from war, disease, and displacement in the Great Lakes and St Lawrence valley, Indigenous legal orders remained more or less intact, if under some strain, in northeastern North America, but vigorous in the north and northwest. The most significant legal achievement of this early period was the development of a body of intercultural law, embodied in the Great Peace of Montreal and the Covenant Chain, that was meant to enable European and Indigenous peoples to live together in a mutually beneficial way and to afford each society relative autonomy in governing its own people. This is not to deny that some forms of dispossession had already begun, but it does show the willingness of both sides to reach a modus vivendi.

The resource base and demographics of northern North America differed considerably from those of the English colonies along the Atlantic coast south of the Bay of Fundy, and these differences shaped the way in which law could be used, created, and implemented in these new societies. In the more southerly colonies, European agriculturalists confronted Indigenous agriculturalists, resulting in frequent wars. While the settlers and Indigenous peoples in New England and the more southerly colonies made tactical alliances and treaties with each other from time to time, the relentless tide of settlement meant that cooperation between the two groups was not likely to last. Already in the seventeenth century native peoples were subjected to Puritan justice and present as litigants in Massachusetts courts.[1] The letters patent granted to establish new colonies from the 1620s often ignored the presence of Indigenous peoples altogether, as if the land were already vacant. Immigration and rapid population growth gave the settlers the upper hand militarily and allowed them to pursue their own course without assistance from Britain. The New England settlers' victories in Metacom's War (1675–8) shifted the balance of power decisively in their favour, effectively opening up large areas for settlement.

The letters patent that created corporations or proprietary governments normally required the calling of an assembly of elected representatives. The first assembly of this kind met at Jamestown, Virginia, in July 1619, but even after Charles I revoked the company's charter in 1625, the governor and assembly continued to function as a law-making body, eventually forcing the Crown to recognize its legitimacy. In New England too, as Mary Sarah Bilder argues, 'sectarian corporate governance practices and lawmaking authority surpassed the legal limits of the corporate form.'[2] As for proprietary colonies such as Pennsylvania and Maryland, the assembly that was supposed to advise the proprietary had typically, by the end of the seventeenth century, become the real authority and relegated the proprietary to the role of a figurehead.

The same legal instruments were used in the English colonies in northern North America, Newfoundland and Rupert's Land, but produced very different results in both relations with native peoples and settler governance. In Newfoundland, early interactions with the Beothuk resulted in their withdrawal from European contact; in fact the Beothuk seem to have been the only North American Indigenous group not to pursue an ongoing trade relationship with Europeans. In Rupert's Land the HBC charter provided war-making powers to the company if necessary, but relations with the Indigenous peoples were relatively harmonious. Without access to land as a source of conflict, the relationship focused almost entirely on trade; even the intimate relationships that developed between Indigenous women and European men were shaped to some extent by their perceived advantages in the trading relationship. Trade was conducted according to protocols mixing both Indigenous and European practices, with gift-giving playing an important role.

Governance in these two possessions evolved very differently from that in the more southerly British colonies. Early experiments with proprietary government in Newfoundland petered out, with no assembly ever being called as a result of slow population growth. Thereafter, doubts about whether Newfoundland should even be a colony of settlement prevented it from being endowed with formal institutions of governance, even as a vernacular legal order evolved with the participation of the fishing admirals and the navy. In Rupert's Land too, without permanent settlement there was no need for institutions of settler governance or elaborate provisions about law-making authority; nor was the full panoply of the common law needed. The English law of master and servant and military law would suffice to govern the small European population for the foreseeable future.

Low immigration and slow population growth in New France shaped the colonial state's relationship with native peoples, leaving the colony of Canada in a state of insecurity until the Great Peace of Montreal. Peace was achieved not after a devastating war (although the Haudenosaunee had been weakened by epidemics and by wars with other Indigenous nations and the French) but as a result of negotiations conducted according to Indigenous traditions. The French would have liked to transform Indigenous people into loyal subjects but even in the mission communities could not impose the French legal order upon them, even for cases of serious crime.

In Canada, the charter of the Company of New France, in spite of its unrealistic geographic ambition, set the parameters of settler landholding for the next two hundred years and more through the vehicle of seigneurialism. After 1660 or so, the realities of settlement in Canada – enabled by the arrival of many more women – required a more complete legal framework than was necessary in either Newfoundland or Rupert's Land. The French introduced laws, such as the Custom of Paris, and institutions such as the parish, that were familiar to the population. Bodies such as the parish assembly provided a form of settler input, but representative government as such was not prized by the authorities in old France or New France. In the era of French absolutism, authority was supposed to flow from the top down, and colonial innovation was not encouraged, though it was tolerated at times. Through a dizzying array of ordinances, edicts, and decrees, the French state and the colonial administration at Quebec sought to shape New France into an ordered, productive, deferential, and Christian society. Even if these were sometimes ignored at the local level and spottily enforced, they accustomed the inhabitants to an active and somewhat intrusive state, especially in the towns. In rural society, the institution of the seigneury, although not formally part of the state apparatus, functioned as a rudimentary municipal government. Moreover, a workable court structure involving both seigneurial and royal justice was put in place in Canada, if not to the same extent in Acadie. A notable gap in this replication of the legal structures of provincial France was the absence of advocates – suspected of fomenting opposition to the government and driving up legal costs – and the low level of support provided for the notarial profession. Notaries were essential to the working of French law, but the profession was left essentially to pull itself up by its own bootstraps; after some initial struggles, however, it had achieved some coherence and stability by 1701 and would begin to flourish in the eighteenth century. The appearance of the self-made advocates called practiciens spoke to the growth of a demand for legal representation in litigation.

All of these measures represented a considerable investment in legal infrastructure in a relatively impoverished society surrounded by sometimes hostile Indigenous and European neighbours, with a mere 14,000 European inhabitants in the St Lawrence colony by the century's end, and another 1,500 at most in Acadie. They reflected the confidence of the French state in the law as a critical tool of colonialism and of ensuring loyalty to the king, as well as an important means of assuring its settler population that familiar ways of life would be reproduced in the new environment. Thus, the second most significant achievement of the seventeenth century, legally speaking, was the successful transplantation and adaptation to local circumstances of the backbone of the civil law, that dealing with marriage, family, property, and succession. While providing opportunities for capital accumulation, the civil law was also concerned to establish a complex balance among competing goals: to uphold the authority of husbands over wives and parents (mostly fathers) over children, while also aiming at the equality of siblings (of both genders) and the protection of the interests of widows and minor children.

While the civil law of early New France was meant to replicate that of the mother country, in some ways it was already establishing a distinct identity. The absence of trained advocates and of professional judges on the Conseil souverain meant that justice had a more 'popular' flavour. The fact that judgeships and official positions were not bought and sold also helped legitimize the judicial apparatus. The seigneurial system was flexible enough to incorporate the idea of Indigenous seigneurs, while French law in general had to accommodate the Indigenous presence in a variety of ways, especially with regard to the criminal law. The opportunities for children to establish their economic independence at an earlier age than in France helped temper the rigour of ancien régime paternal authority and provided for a somewhat more supple family law. While the law was recognizably French, there were many aspects that would have surprised a visitor from France.

By 1701 the civil law had put down deep roots in New France. It would take the deportation of the Acadians and the inhabitants of Louisbourg to uproot it from Nova Scotia, while its survival in Canada would depend on decisions made in the wake of the British conquest.

PART THREE

The Long Eighteenth Century, 1701–1815

11

Constitutional Law in the Long Eighteenth Century

The Politico-Military Context

The contours of the law in northern North America during the long eighteenth century were shaped by three sets of overlapping political struggles: conflicts between native peoples and Europeans, imperial wars between the British and French, and the civil war within British America known as the American Revolution. The year 1815 marks the true conclusion of the latter two struggles, which in turn exercised a significant influence on the nature of European-Indigenous relations. Although the Treaty of Paris 1763 marked the formal cession of most of France's North American possessions to Britain, and the Treaty of Paris 1783 marked the formal end of the war between Britain and the former Thirteen Colonies, each of these conflicts featured a second act. While the French monarchy showed little interest in retaking its erstwhile possessions in North America – and even committed itself to not doing so in the 1778 treaty by which it recognized the United States – the French Revolution and the rise of Napoleon gave rise to British fears that a newly energized and militarized France would try to reconquer Canada. These fears put strains on relations between English and French in Lower Canada, with repercussions for the law.[1]

Meanwhile, Britain hoped that the volatile new American republic would splinter, causing some or all of its parts to rejoin the empire. Long-festering grievances between Britain and the United States, only some of which were resolved by the Jay Treaty of 1794, led to a renewal of conflict between them.[2] It was not until 1815, which marked both the end of the Napoleonic wars and the Treaty of Ghent concluding the War of 1812, that the political future of most of northern North America could be said to have been settled. In fact, most of the terms of the Treaty of Ghent related to the drawing of the international border from the western end of Lake Superior to the Atlantic, a matter that had been left somewhat imprecise in 1783. Two subsequent treaties, the Rush-Bagot Treaty of 1817 and the Anglo-American Convention of 1818, demilitarized the Great Lakes and established the forty-ninth parallel as the international boundary from the Lake of the Woods to the Rockies, while providing for joint administration of the territory beyond the Rockies. Known as the Oregon Country to the Americans, the territory was known to the British as New Caledonia in the north and the Columbia District in the south, these names being those used by the Hudson's Bay Company (HBC) to denote fur-trading districts pursuant to its licence to trade in the area.

With that political settlement, the legal geography of British North America east of the Rockies was confirmed: mainly civil law in Quebec, existing under a British constitution; mainly British-derived law elsewhere, with an uncertain frontier demarcating the line between settled areas subject mostly to European law, and those lands where Indigenous law continued in force. The Royal Proclamation 1763 contained an implicit promise that Indigenous law would continue unimpaired in those territories currently inhabited by Indigenous peoples and unceded by them. Thus, in the north and on the western plains, outside the nascent Red River settlement (1811) and some Hudson's Bay Company outposts, Indigenous law governed. On the northwest Pacific coast British claims were bolstered by the Nootka Conventions of 1790–4, in which Spain ceded its rights, but these arrangements did not displace the Indigenous peoples as the true governors of the territory west of the Rocky Mountains. In eastern Canada, however, particularly after the arrival of the loyalists in the 1780s, Indigenous law came under increasing pressure in two ways. Increased competition for land meant that the territory subject to Indigenous law was gradually diminishing. But even where the land base was relatively secure, Indigenous law was being challenged from within, as the colonial courts provided a forum for Indigenous actors to contest traditional laws and dispute resolution processes with which they did not agree.

The eighteenth century was the great century of constitution-making, a process propelled by war and revolution. The very meaning of the term changed, becoming more precise, more 'legal,' and more oriented to the rights of 'citizens' rather than the duties of 'subjects' to monarchical rulers. Earlier understandings of the term 'constitution' were more fluid, embracing a range of legal instruments (statutes, royal proclamations, charters such as Magna Carta) as well as a broad range of customary practices and shared beliefs: traditionally, in England the term 'constitution' was almost synonymous with 'way of life.'[3] Under the influence of the American and French revolutions, a constitution came to be equated with a particular document setting out the governmental institutions of a nation and declaring the rights possessed by its citizens. Even Britain, with its famously 'unwritten' constitution, participated in this trend, as the development of a burgeoning cult of Magna Carta in the last quarter of the eighteenth century demonstrated.[4] The *Constitutional Act* of 1791 was further evidence of this turn to foundational documents, providing written constitutions and new institutions of government for the new colony of Upper Canada and the newly reorganized colony of Lower Canada.[5] The inhabitants of British North America would continue to be 'subjects' of the king in legal-constitutional theory, but in practice began to behave as 'citizens' as the legacy of the eighteenth-century revolutions made itself felt.

The Great Peace of 1701 removed the threat of war between Canada or Acadie and the Indigenous peoples of northeastern North America, but the outbreak of the War of the Spanish Succession in Europe in 1702 (known in North America as Queen Anne's War) meant that the English and French colonies in America were soon at war with each other. From Canada's point of view, the wisdom of securing peace with Indigenous peoples, especially the Haudenosaunee, was proved during this war. The 1701 settlement, along with the renewal of the Covenant Chain between the Haudenosaunee and the British in that year ensured that they remained largely neutral, thus impeding English attacks via New York. After the easy conquest of Port Royal in 1710 (renamed Annapolis Royal), both New England and the British government were anxious to conquer Quebec and thus take all of Canada.[6] In 1711 a large British fleet sailed from Boston with this goal but encountered disaster when several vessels ran aground in the St Lawrence with great loss of life, causing the mission to be abandoned.[7]

France thus maintained Canada during the negotiations leading up to the Treaty of Utrecht 1713 but gave up other possessions: its Newfoundland colony (Plaisance), peninsular Acadia 'with its ancient boundaries,' and its claims to the territory draining into Hudson Bay. Along with fishing rights on the north shore of Newfoundland, it retained all the islands in the Gulf of St Lawrence and began erecting a major fortress at Louisbourg on Île Royale (Cape Breton Island) almost immediately after the peace. The French inhabitants of Plaisance, transplanted there, became its first settlers. Louisbourg emerged as a thriving community, its economy based on the lucrative fish trade and buoyed by France's expenditures on defence.

The Treaty of Utrecht left a number of important issues unresolved. Some, such as the definition of the 'ancient boundaries' of Acadia, eventually became irrelevant after the Seven Years' War.[8] Others, such as the legal status of the Acadians and the nature of the rights of the Indigenous peoples over the ceded territory, gave rise to grave difficulties. The treaty contained no reference to Acadia's original inhabitants, leading the Abenaki allies of the Mi'kmaq to observe angrily, 'The French never said anything to us about it and wee wonder how they would give it away without asking us, God having first placed us there and They having nothing to do to give it away.'[9] The Mi'kmaq and their allies thus resisted British control, harassing the garrison at Annapolis Royal and interfering with New England shipping and fishing. At the conclusion of a regional war between the British and the Wabanaki Confederacy of Maine (1722–5), the Mi'kmaq signed a separate treaty with the British at Annapolis Royal in 1726.[10] This treaty is the ancestor of the better-known treaties of 1760–1, discussed below.

Aside from the tense relations between British and Mi'kmaq in Nova Scotia, peace reigned east of the Great Lakes in the three decades after 1713. When that peace was shattered in 1744, it was once again European events – the War of the Austrian Succession – that triggered North American hostilities. The first casualty was Louisbourg, captured by New Englanders in 1745, after which its inhabitants were deported to France. It was restored to France by the Treaty of Aix-la-Chapelle in 1748 (in return for the restoration of Madras to Britain), and its people allowed to return, before being captured a second time in 1758 during the Seven Years' War.[11] Once again Louisbourg's entire population was sent back to France, but this time there would be no return. The British were thus able to ignore French law when Cape Breton was merged with Nova Scotia post-1763.

This war proved to be only a prelude to the wider conflict that came to be known as the Seven Years' War, a struggle many historians have labelled as the first global war.[12] This time, hostilities erupted in North America earlier (1754) than in Europe (1756), triggered by Anglo/French/Haudenosaunee conflict over the future of the Ohio valley. Immediately after the peace treaty of 1748 the British had founded Halifax as a counterweight to Louisbourg and had begun to settle Nova Scotia with British, Irish, and German Protestants; Halifax with its large, ice-free, and easily defensible port would become a crucially important naval base in the ensuing war. An early casualty of the growing Anglo-French conflict were the Acadians, deported from Nova Scotia in 1755 when Governor Lawrence believed he could not be certain of their loyalty in case of war (war having not yet been formally declared between Britain and France). Many Acadians had previously removed to Île St-Jean, but they too were deported in 1758. The recapture of Louisbourg (1758), the fall of Quebec (1759), and the capitulation of Montreal (1760) led to France's cession of its northern territories to Britain in the Treaty of Paris 1763, leaving it with rights to dry fish on the northwest coast of Newfoundland, and the islands of St Pierre and Miquelon as a demilitarized base for its fishery. Meanwhile, Louisiana was ceded to Spain in the same year by the Treaty of Fontainebleau.

The European population of Canada, some 60,000 to 70,000 people, could not be dealt with *à l'acadienne*: deporting such a large population was logistically impossible with the resources the British had at their disposal. Accommodating such large numbers of French Catholic subjects within the empire would pose enormous political, social, and legal challenges. The fate of the former French territory between the Alleghenies and the Mississippi, an area inhabited mostly by Indigenous peoples, also raised important questions. After 1760 the British altered key aspects of French policy regarding the Indigenous population. The British commander-in-chief, General Jeffrey Amherst, stopped the practice of giving presents to maintain their alliance and restricted the supply of gunpowder provided to them, believing they no longer posed a military threat to Europeans. Indigenous discontent fuelled a broad resistance movement known as Pontiac's War, which erupted in the spring of 1763 in the lower Great Lakes and resulted in the capture of several forts and the deaths of hundreds of British soldiers and settlers, as well as unknown numbers of Indigenous warriors.[13]

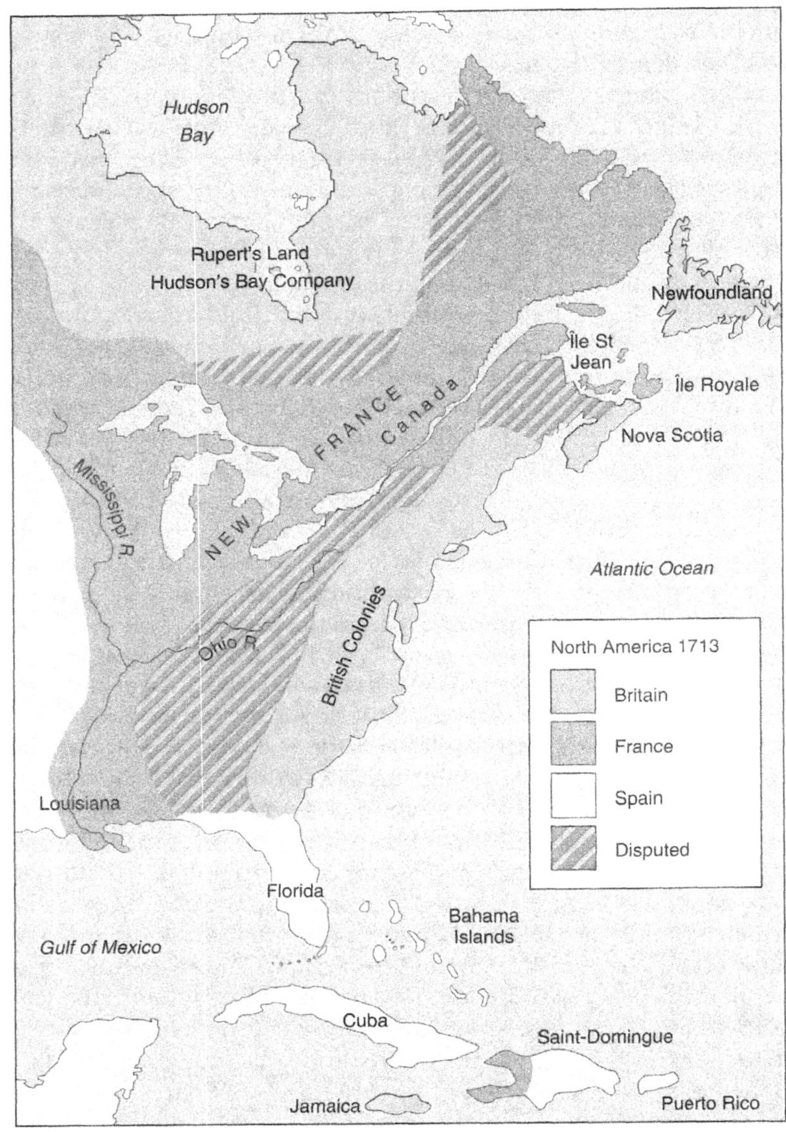

North America, 1713, showing spheres of influence of European powers after the Treaty of Utrecht. Indigenous peoples in fact controlled most of the territory shown, but were not party to the treaty.

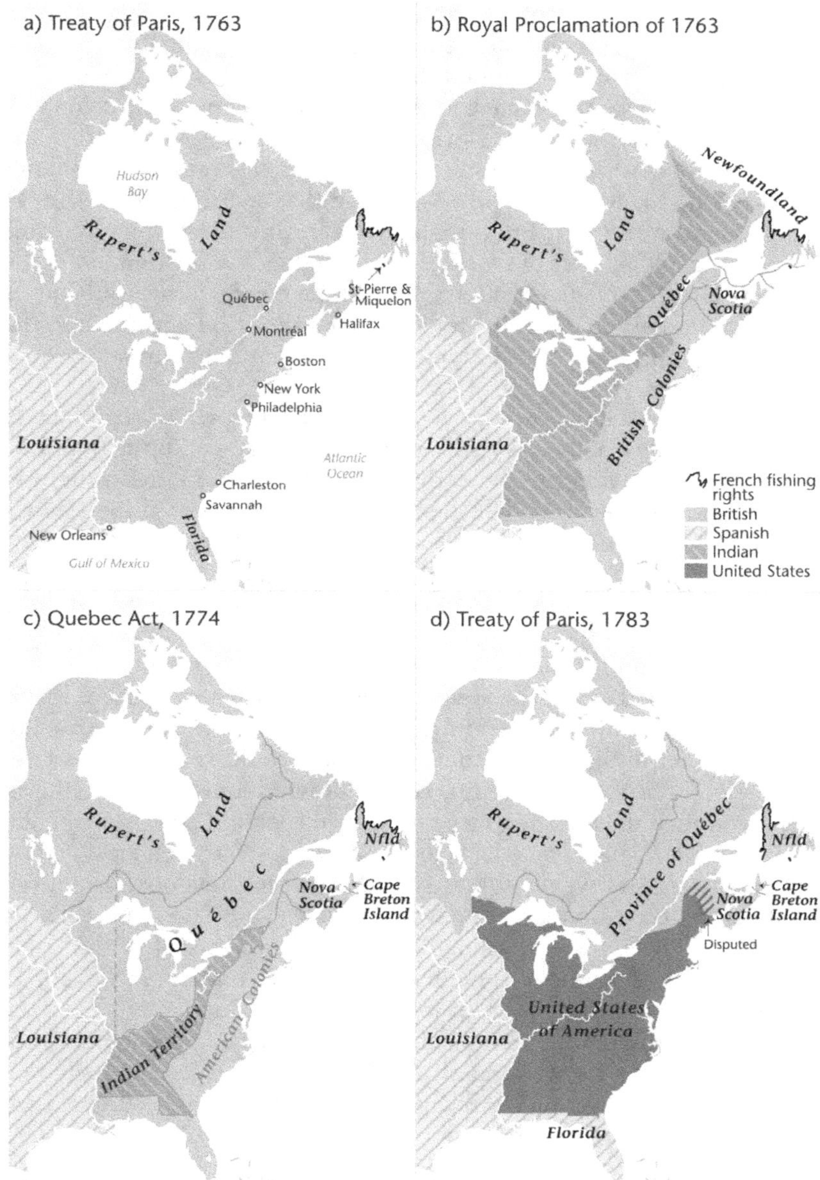

War and revolution led to a rapidly changing geopolitical map of North America in the generation after 1763.

The British government attempted to address the twin challenges of Canadien governance and Indigenous resistance with the Royal Proclamation of 1763, issued some months after the conclusion of the Treaty of Paris. The proclamation created governments for four new colonies – Quebec, East Florida, West Florida, and Grenada – and redrew the boundaries of existing British colonies: jurisdiction over Labrador, Anticosti, and the Magdalen Islands was given to Newfoundland, while St John's Island and Cape Breton Island were annexed to Nova Scotia. The 'Benefit of the Laws of Our Realm of England' was extended to the new colonies. Their governors were to create courts to hear all causes 'according to Law and Equity, and as near as may be agreeable to the Laws of England,' and to call representative assemblies similar to those existing in the royal colonies of America.[14]

While the proclamation was in preparation before the eruption of Pontiac's War, it nonetheless responded to the climate of Indigenous discontent already evident in the early 1760s. The proclamation sought to preserve the area between the Alleghenies and the Mississippi as a protectorate for Indigenous peoples, free of European settlement for the time being, but did not attach it to any of the new civil governments in North America. The motivations of the British in this regard were not entirely benign: they feared that if settlers pushed into the interior they would be obliged to manufacture their own goods, instead of relying on British goods transported along rivers flowing into the Atlantic. William Knox, future undersecretary of state for the colonies, put forward the argument for creating an Indigenous 'buffer zone' that would not only win over native peoples but serve to confine Britain's own colonists; indeed, this in effect continued the French policy of trying to contain British settler colonies to the Atlantic watershed.[15] Without endowing the territory with any civil governance, however, it was very difficult to prevent settlers from violating the 'proclamation line,' which they began to do almost immediately. Nonetheless, the proclamation, which has been called 'the single most important document in the history of treaty-making in Canada,'[16] outlined protocols that continued to inform Crown-Indigenous relations for centuries: Indigenous lands were not to be sold to private individuals, but only to the Crown; and any such sales were to be conducted 'at some publick Meeting or Assembly of the said Indians to be held for that Purpose' convoked by the governor of the colony in question. Sir William Johnson, appointed superintendent of Indians for the Northern Department in 1756, followed these provisions in negotiating the Treaty of Niagara in the summer of 1764, which will be elaborated on below.

The Quebec Act 1774 responded to the inadequacies and ambiguities of the royal proclamation on both the French-Canadian and the Indigenous questions. On the latter point, it belatedly extended the boundaries of Quebec into much of the territory the proclamation had sought to reserve for native peoples, the better to protect the area from rampant settlement;[17] it also annexed to Quebec the territories given to Newfoundland in 1763, although protection of the Labrador fishery was to remain the responsibility of the commander-in-chief in Newfoundland. On the former point, the Act confirmed that in all matters pertaining to property and civil rights, the French civil law would govern in the colony. It also confirmed the free exercise of the Roman Catholic religion by the king's 'new subjects,' subject to the king's supremacy, allowed the continued collection of tithes by the Catholic Church, and provided a new oath for (potentially Catholic) office-holders that did not include the traditional anti-Catholic elements. It revoked the provisions of the royal proclamation relating to the government of Quebec, thus backtracking on the promise of representative government made in 1763. Instead, a new 'conciliar' form of government with an appointed legislative council was created to assist the governor, one to which some Canadiens would be appointed. Given the growing instability in the Atlantic seaboard colonies, Britain was inclined to reproduce the more authoritarian elements of the old French constitution than to spread the 'blessings of liberty' to its new subjects, leading to a variety of battles over the limits of executive authority, the place of trial by jury, and the availability of habeas corpus. While the proclamation, 'so far as the same relates to the said Province of Quebec' was revoked by the *Quebec Act*, it does not appear that the provisions relating to dealings with Indigenous peoples were intended to be revoked within the limits of the new province of Quebec, and the new instructions to Governor Carleton assumed that they would continue in force.[18]

The precise role of the Quebec Act in the lead-up to the American Revolution is still debated by historians, but it was certainly regarded with alarm by those in the Thirteen Colonies who were questioning the authority of Parliament to tax them and alter their established governments, as the Massachusetts Government Act of 1774 purported to do.[19] The American revolutionaries sought to include the northern colonies in their movement and occupied Montreal in the winter of 1775–6 but were defeated at Quebec and did not subsequently renew their efforts. A 1776 uprising sympathetic to the revolution in Nova Scotia was easily put down by the British.[20] In 1778, in an effort to stem revolutionary sentiment, Parliament passed a declaratory act providing that the proceeds of any tax levied in the colony would be spent in the colony for local purposes.[21] The measure proved to be too little and too late to influence the Thirteen Colonies, but the statute would continue to anchor imperial policy in the second empire. A half-century later, Nova Scotia treatise-writer Beamish Murdoch would still refer to it as the 'celebrated statute' of 1778, and its provisions would be incorporated into the *Constitutional Act* of 1791.[22]

The success of the American Revolution was confirmed in the Treaty of Paris 1783, by which the British recognized the existence of the United States as 'free, sovereign and independent states.' The boundary between the British colonies and the United States was established between Lake Superior and the Atlantic and now became an international boundary. Some 60,000 loyalists and 15,000 slaves left the new United States, many of whom found refuge in the northern British colonies.[23] The influx led to the creation of two new colonies to accommodate them: New Brunswick and Cape Breton Island were both split off from Nova Scotia in 1784; St John's Island had been separated from Nova Scotia and given its own government in 1769. All the Maritime colonies were given the usual apparatus of settler governance under a British governor or lieutenant governor, but as the result of the slow growth of population in Cape Breton no assembly was called there before the island was re-annexed to Nova Scotia in 1820.

The arrival of the loyalists in Quebec once again put the constitutional issue in the forefront. The British merchants clamoured for an assembly, albeit one in which only they would have the franchise. The Canadiens would support an assembly only if they too possessed the franchise, while the imperial authorities wanted an assembly so that the colony could tax itself to pay for its own administration. A different form of pressure came from the loyalists who settled west of the present-day Quebec/Ontario boundary, where there were few French inhabitants. They wished to be subject to English law and desired to be separated from Quebec. Debate ensued in London as to whether this was a wise policy: retaining a single province would have the advantage, from the imperial point of view, of achieving a quicker assimilation of the French-Canadians in light of the influx of loyalists and expected British immigration. In the end, however, the path of lesser resistance was chosen: less conflict would be engendered, thought Home Secretary William Wyndham Grenville, drafter of the 1791 Act, if the two groups were given separate provinces, even if this left the British merchants in Lower Canada in a somewhat anomalous position.

The old province of Quebec thus was divided by Order in Council, following which the *Constitutional Act 1791* provided for a bicameral representative assembly for Quebec, renamed Lower Canada, and for the newly created Upper Canada. In each colony the Act established an appointive upper house, the legislative council, in which councillors were to hold their seats for life. In the new elective assemblies elections were to be held every four years. Patents of nobility might be issued to which could be attached a hereditary right to be summoned to the legislative council, but this provision remained a dead letter. The Act also directed that reserves for the support of Protestant clergy be set aside in each province from ungranted lands, and confirmed the continued applicability of the Declaratory Act of 1778 on the deployment of local tax revenues.

The Legal Contexts

The British takeover of peninsular Acadia in 1713, of Canada in 1763, and the emergence of the American republic after the Revolution all posed a basic constitutional law issue: subjecthood. With regard to the Acadians, article XIV of the Treaty of Utrecht stated that those who did not depart within a year after its ratification, but were 'willing to remain there, and to be subject to the kingdom of Great Britain,' would have freedom of religion 'so far as the laws of Great Britain do allow.' Did 'subject *to* the kingdom of Great Britain' mean that the Acadians became subjects *of* the king? This ambiguity later played a role in the sequence of events leading to the deportation of the Acadians. It was never clearly stated that the Acadians had the rights of British subjects and therefore had to be dealt with as such, while the British labels for them, either simply 'the French,' or 'the French neutrals,' suggested a shadowy second-class status. By 1763 a more robust concept of British subjecthood had emerged, such that there was no question but that the Canadiens 'became subjects of the King,' in the words of Jeremy Amherst. The description of them as 'new subjects,' as opposed to the 'old subjects' – British and American immigrants after 1760 – was merely a label of convenience, not an indicator of any lesser constitutional status, an approach confirmed by King's Bench in *Campbell v Hall* in 1774.[24]

With regard to the subjecthood of Indigenous peoples, article XV of the Treaty of Utrecht stated that the native peoples were to have freedom of movement across any colonial boundaries, 'without any molestation or hinderance,' but it was 'to be exactly and distinctly settled by commissaries, who are, and who ought to be accounted the subjects and friends of Britain or of France.' This article assumed that all Indigenous peoples were subjects of one monarch or the other, but they did not regard themselves in this way. British attempts to treat the Mi'kmaq as subjects were violently resisted by the latter, as will be discussed below, and whatever the British may have said among themselves, they tended to leave the question of subjecthood in suspense during the eighteenth century in their dealings with Indigenous peoples. The latter saw the treaties engaged in with the British as affirmations of their independence and value as allies.

After the American Revolution, the effect of the emergence of a new American nationality raised particularly acute issues in Upper Canada, to which many 'late loyalists' resorted from 1790 onwards; by 1815 as much as half the land in the province may have been owned by American immigrants. Their status was unclear, however. John Beverley Robinson thought that all those born under the Crown pre-1783, along with their children, were still British subjects, but this would have meant that almost all Americans were still British subjects. An imperial act of 1740 had set out a procedure by which 'foreigners' could become naturalized, but this process had generally not been followed in Upper Canada with regard to the American immigrants. If these Americans were considered aliens, they would run afoul of the common law disability of alienage regarding landholding, putting many titles in the province in jeopardy. The problem lay uneasily dormant until the War of 1812 brought it to light; its resolution is discussed in chapter 30.[25]

Turning from subjecthood to constitutional law in general, the main theme, especially after the consolidation of British control post-1763, was the development of a two-track constitution, one governing settlers' relations with each other and with the imperial government, and the other governing relations between Indigenous peoples and settlers, but mediated through the imperial Crown. These will be dealt with in turn, taking as a point of departure a 1721 report of the Board of Trade to the king, which conducted a review of the North American empire along both of these axes.

Taking the settler constitution first, the main problem identified by the board was how to rectify what were seen as the errors of the previous century in delegating too much authority to the colonists themselves. The board observed that some of the proprietary and chartered governments had shown 'too great an inclination to be independent of their mother Kingdom, & have carried on a trade destructive to that of Great Britain.' It would be better

> if they were all of them under your Majestys immediate government, & were by proper laws compelled to follow the proper commands sent them by your Majesty; & it hath ever been the wisdom, not only of Great Britain, but likewise of all other states to secure, by all possible means, the entire, absolute and immediate dependency of their colonies.

As for the older Atlantic seaboard colonies, they should all be 'reassumed to the Crown, either by purchase, agreement, or otherwise.'[26] The board refrained from noting that an earlier attempt in this direction, the resumption of the charters and the creation of the Dominion of New England, had ended in a revolt by the New England colonists, the deposition of Governor Edmund Andros in 1689, and a return to the status quo.[27] The Atlantic colonies' defence of what they perceived as their chartered rights would continue to follow a collision course with imperial attempts to create an 'entire, absolute, and immediate dependency' in its overseas plantations.

With regard to new acquisitions, observed the board, the powers of the governor should be enhanced, and it should be made clear that he reported to the Crown and not to the colonists themselves. The king was urged to create the position of captain general for all the colonies 'from Nova Scotia to South Carolina,' who would be paid directly by the Crown, to whom all the governors would report and who would be attended by two councillors from each colony in a quasi-federal structure.[28] This structure would then enable the Crown to tax and levy military support in the colonies. These plans were not fully implemented, but later attempts at imposing direct taxes on the colonies would help to trigger the American Revolution.

The board did not spell out how the 'command and control' model it envisaged could be squared with the established practice that white settler colonies were effectively self-governing, with the right to expect a representative assembly, trial by jury, habeas corpus, and a judicature capable of applying English law. This was not such a problem in Nova Scotia prior to 1749 or Quebec after 1760, where the vast majority of the inhabitants were not British and did not have such expectations. But the dilemma had to be faced when Nova Scotia was refounded as an English settler colony with the establishment of Halifax, and its constitution pointed to the way forward.[29] The 'new' Nova Scotia had no charter (the 1621 charter granted to Sir William Alexander being conveniently ignored), nor was it granted to a grand proprietor. It had what we term a 'hip-pocket constitution,' one that could be carried by a new governor, figuratively speaking, in his hip pocket when he went off to begin administering a colony. Such a constitution was described by John Stewart, Prince Edward Island's first historian:

> The Commission or patent under the great seal of Great-Britain granted to our first governor, ... forms the constitution of the Island, and the instructions received therewith, are explanatory of the patent and regulate the governor's conduct in almost all the common routine of public business incident to his situation. The instructions are pretty voluminous, they are changeable at the king's pleasure, and additional instructions are sent as circumstances may require.[30]

Such a constitution flowed from the royal prerogative but was very different from the royal charters upon which the early governments of most of the original Thirteen Colonies were based, which delegated many of the Crown's powers to proprietors and/or local assemblies. The charter was the bedrock of local autonomy for the earlier colonies and ferociously defended by them; the hip-pocket constitution, by contrast, was meant to keep local autonomy within clear limits and to ensure that the Crown was much more present in the legal and governmental orders of the newer colonies, in accordance with the theme sounded in the Board of Trade's 1721 report. Insofar as these new British North American constitutions recognized 'rights' in the people of the colony, such recognition was implicit, grounded in references to the adoption of the common law and to the creation of courts and institutions, such as assemblies, that would protect the rights recognized by English law. At some level, however, all such rights were provisional in that they existed under the aegis of the prerogative. What the Crown gave, the Crown might take away. Not until *Campbell v Hall* in 1774 was it decided that where the Crown had granted a representative assembly to a colony, it could no longer legislate via the prerogative for that colony.[31]

Thus, the entire government – assembly, courts, and executive – lay in embryo in the instructions Governor Edward Cornwallis brought with him to Chebucto Harbour in 1749. He would be paid by the imperial government, not dependent on the whim of the local assembly, as many governors were in the Thirteen Colonies. Likewise, when the first chief justice of the province, Jonathan Belcher, was appointed in 1754, he held a royal commission and enjoyed a salary paid by London, insulating him from local pressures.[32] Most other important posts were also held pursuant to Crown appointment. In a further attempt to bolster the gubernatorial position, most governors and lieutenant governors of Upper and Lower Canada, and all those of the Maritime colonies except one prior to 1848, were military men, accustomed to command and to deference.[33] The continuing presence of British troops in the northern colonies meant that there was in effect a 'standing army' in the midst of civilian society, a situation very different from that in the American states after the revolution.

The Nova Scotia pattern would be followed in the Maritime settler colonies created out of 'greater Nova Scotia' later in the century: Prince Edward Island, so named in 1798 after George III's son Edward, Duke of Kent; New Brunswick; and Cape Breton (both created in 1784). However, in the wake of the American Revolution, a new type of constitution was adopted for the Canadas, when Upper Canada was separated from Lower Canada in 1791. Unlike the prerogative-based constitutions of the Maritimes, the constitutions of the Canadas were established by an imperial act passed by the Parliament at Westminster. While formally an amendment to the *Quebec Act* entitled *An Act to Repeal Certain Parts of an Act, Passed in the 14th Year of His Majesty's Reign, Entitled, An Act for Making More Effectual Provision for the Government of the Province of Quebec in North America, and to Make Further Provision for the Government of the Said Province*, the statute came to be known, appropriately, as the *Constitutional Act*. The first lieutenant governor of Upper Canada, John Graves Simcoe, went so far as to call it the 'Magna Charta [of Upper Canada], under which that colony will immediately be admitted to all the privileges that Englishmen enjoy.'[34]

While the 1791 Act did not contain a broad declaration of rights in the manner of the French and American constitutions, it did set out in a clear and public way how the two societies of Upper and Lower Canada would be governed. Under its pseudo-aristocratic overlay, it improved upon the democratic element of the constitution, the assembly, compared to both the Maritimes and the older Atlantic seaboard colonies.[35] The Act provided for quadrennial elections, where the frequency of elections in the Maritimes was left entirely to the governor's discretion (Nova Scotia's 'Long Parliament, for example, sat from 1770 to 1784). The assembly was empowered to create new constituencies and to deal with the franchise, matters strictly reserved for the royal prerogative in the older colonies. A new oath of loyalty to the monarch allowed Catholics to vote and to sit in the legislature in both Canadas. While Nova Scotia had extended the franchise to Catholics in 1789, they could not sit in the legislature there or in the other Maritime colonies until much later and could not vote in New Brunswick until 1810 or Prince Edward Island until 1830. In general the 1791 Act went into great detail about the nature of the institutions to be created, unlike the constitutions of the Maritime colonies, which provided only broad outlines and left much to the governor's discretion. This shift in form, from governors' instructions to an imperial statute that could be considered as analogous to a foundational charter, was clearly a product of the changed environment after 1783.[36] If the colonies of New Brunswick and Cape Breton Island could be erected on the basis of old-style governors' instructions in the immediate post-revolutionary period, such was no longer the case even a few years later, when the British government had had time to absorb the lessons of the Revolution.

The Act of 1791 was also drafted in a more 'constitutional' manner than the hip-pocket constitutions. The royal instructions to governors were a series of commands addressed only to the governor himself, and indeed the governor did not need to reveal them to anyone, even to his council; only the commission itself was a public document. The Act of 1791 is drafted in a declaratory manner and addressed to all inhabitants of the territory in question, not just the governor. It speaks directly to a people, not simply to an imperial civil servant. It encourages readers to believe that they are participants in the enterprise, perhaps even parties to a compact, who possess a right to see government carried on in the way described in the Act. Even before the American Revolution, imperial civil servants such as William Knox, undersecretary of state for the colonies, had seen the defects of the hip-pocket constitutions and argued in favour of giving all the colonies statutory constitutions, arguing that only these could provide the necessary assurance of stability, publicity, and transparency so lacking in prerogative-based instruments.[37]

The British statesmen who drafted the Act had the advantage of doing so during the 'pause' between the American and French revolutions.[38] If the former helped focus the mind on what lessons there might be for the empire, the latter had not yet made all talk of reform seem synonymous with sedition. William Wyndham Grenville, acknowledged as the main drafter of the Act, could afford to take the long view. In discussing an earlier version of the bill in 1789, he made some revealing comments to

Lord Dorchester, the governor of Quebec. Grenville began by stating a classic imperial point of view: the main thing to be considered was 'by what means, the connection, & dependence of Canada, on this Country, may be so preserved, & cultivated, as to be render'd most beneficial to Great Britain, during its continuance, & most permanent in its duration.' Given 'the late events in America,' was the proposed bill, with its commitment to representative institutions, 'not inconsistent with the existence of a dependant Government'? Grenville turned philosophical:

> It may perhaps, be justly doubted, whether any form of Administration which could now be established, would prevent the separation of so great, & distant a dominion, after it should have arrived at a certain point of extension, & improvement. But the real question now to be decided is, what system is best calculated to remove this event to a distant period & to render the connection, in the interval, advantageous to the Mother Country without oppression or injury to the Colony?[39]

To paraphrase: the separation of populous white settler colonies is probably inevitable; the best we can do is try to keep such colonies in the fold for as long as we can by making the connection mutually palatable. And the way to do that is to give them a free constitution. As Edmund Burke said in the debate on the bill, Britain should give a free constitution to Canada 'because the people of Canada should have nothing to envy in the constitution of a country so near to their own [the United States].'[40]

The whole tenor of the debate on the 1791 *Constitutional Act* supports the view that it was not intended as a counter-revolutionary document, but rather one in tune with emerging Anglo-American ideas of constitutionalism. Certainly the British sought to restore the famous 'balance' of the three orders of monarchy, aristocracy, and democracy that they believed had been insufficiently present in the constitutions of the Thirteen Colonies and endowed each colony with an unelected upper house filled with life appointees – the ancestor of the modern Canadian Senate. But the democratic component of the constitution was reasonably robust. The franchise upon which members of the assembly would be elected was relatively broad, there being no overt restrictions of race, religion, or even gender, and a property qualification in line with that in many U.S. states, only three of which permitted universal white male suffrage by 1800.[41] Most Indigenous persons were excluded, not by race, but because they did not hold individual property; those who did, such as the Hurons at Lorette and the Mohawk at Kahnawake, voted.[42] The unavailability of early voting records makes it difficult to know if free Blacks voted from the outset, but by the 1820s they were voting in Montreal.[43] In Upper Canada the common law was considered to hold women ineligible to vote, but in Lower Canada the civil law did not contain such a formal disqualification. Women who met the property qualification did in fact vote over the next fifty years, in small but not insignificant numbers, with little contemporary comment.[44]

Perhaps one of the most important spurs to inclusivity in the Act was contained in an omission: the Act did not say anything about the language of government or of debate in the assembly. The proceedings of the legislative council created under the *Quebec Act* took place in both languages. While this de facto bilingualism was not elevated to the status of a right in the Act of 1791, the absence of any declaration that English was to be the only official language led to an assumption that English and French would both be allowed in the new legislature. The government itself fostered this assumption. At the opening of the first assembly, Lieutenant Governor Alured Clarke invited the members first in English and then in French to elect a speaker as the first order of business and made available to them a bilingual version of a summary of the rules by which the House of Commons governed itself. While some members fought for English to be the only official language, and others for French to have primacy, in the end both the assembly and the legislative council worked out a set of rules that amounted to a pragmatic recognition of bilingualism.[45] While the Act arguably followed previous practice in not declaring which language(s) would be official, its implicit endorsement of a functional bilingualism was critical for members of the assembly to be able to carry out their democratic responsibilities in the Lower Canadian context.

The 1791 constitution did not constitute a complete code. It was meant to be read against a backdrop where traditional rights and liberties were implicit rather than expressly declared. By 1791 both habeas corpus and trial by jury had been restored in Quebec after various flip-flops.[46] The complete package was one undergirded by the post-1688 concept of modern liberty, where individual rights to life, liberty, and property were to be respected, but where the legislature retained the ultimate authority to decide upon conflicts between rights or to limit rights for compelling reasons of public policy, subject of course to the ultimate power of disallowance in London.

The British aimed to remedy the 'weak governor' model of the seventeenth century, under which governors were often paid by the assembly and had little room for independent action, with a 'strong governor' model in the northern colonies. In the latter, the governor would be paid by the Crown, accountable to it, and also command the military. This model would in turn give rise to its own problems, as the colonists resisted the 'entire, absolute, and immediate dependency' envisaged by the mother country. But this shift left a legacy of strong executive authority that continues as a hallmark of the Canadian constitutional experience, especially in times of perceived threats to the security of the state, from the deportation of the Acadians, to the 'reign of terror' of Governor Craig in Lower Canada in the early nineteenth century, to the Winnipeg General Strike of 1919 and the FLQ crisis of 1970.[47] The ability to mobilize the state in times of crisis, however, did not translate into the power to initiate and implement a legislative program. As will be seen in the next part, the 'strong governor' model worked negatively rather than positively, more as a restraint on the popular will than as a means of implementing a government program. The lack of direct connection between the governor and the assembly meant that each could effectively veto the plans of the other, to their mutual detriment.

These constitutions, even those we have termed hip-pocket constitutions, were based fundamentally on the notion of the liberty of the subject (understood mainly as the adult, white male, propertied, and preferably Protestant subject). But the liberty of the seventeenth-century English colonists on the Atlantic seaboard and that of the northern colonies in the eighteenth century were differently conceived. The earlier liberty, what Michel Ducharme has termed 'classical liberty,' emphasized popular sovereignty and direct participation by an equal and virtuous citizenry. This concept underlay the Cromwellian revolution, the American and eventually the French; in the American case, the basis for these ideas can be traced back to the experience of the chartered colonies. The northern colonies of settlement (that is, excluding Rupert's Land and Newfoundland, which were considered 'commercial' possessions) were founded post-1688, by which time the 'modern liberty' of the Glorious Revolution had become the foundation of the British constitution. This was liberty exercised within the parameters of the 'mixed and balanced' constitution of king, lords, and commons, represented by the king-in-Parliament, liberty that emphasized the representation of interests rather than individuals. In this conception, authority flowed downwards from the king-in-Parliament, rather than upwards from the people.[48] The post-1688 founding of the British North American colonies also meant that they 'could not claim a constitutional autonomy from Parliament and an allegiance to the Crown alone in the way the people in the older colonies did.'[49] In short, liberty was an important value in the northern colonies, but it was not conceived as an inherent attribute of individuals; rather it existed within a given institutional context and might be abridged for sufficiently compelling reasons.[50]

The constitutions of the northern colonies were not a perfect reflection of the king-in-Parliament model, however. First of all, the monarch was present only through a viceroy, a governor or lieutenant governor, and thus a more abstract figure in the colonies than in Britain itself.[51] Second, the upper branch of the colonial legislatures, in the absence of a hereditary nobility and a powerful church establishment, could not play the same role as the House of Lords. And third, the assemblies themselves were denied a co-ordinate status with the 'mother of Parliaments' at Westminster. While the imperial authorities generally did afford a fairly wide latitude to the colonies in the exercise of their legislative powers, Acts could be reserved by the governor for the king's pleasure, or disallowed in London after passage. And Westminster reserved the right to legislate for the colonies in a variety of areas, from the trade regulations contained in the Navigation Acts, to the disposition of natural resources,[52] to basic creditor-debtor law.[53] These limitations were somewhat balanced by the fact that the colonial electorate was broader than in Britain itself, land being more widely distributed; the gap between the governors and the governed was also less extreme than in the mother country. The barring of elective municipal government until the mid-nineteenth century[54] – an attempt to avoid the 'excessive' democracy of New England town meetings – suppressed participation in local politics but further enhanced the role of provincial assemblies as the true vox populi.

Although a formal separation of powers was not part of the British constitution of the era, the courts had a potentially important role to play in the constitutional struggles of the era, such as the limits of freedom of the press, the availability of habeas corpus, and the enforceability of slavery. The results were decidedly mixed, with the courts tending to afford a wide latitude to the executive to imprison without trial and to adopt very broad interpretations of sedition and treason.[55] These trends were most pronounced in Quebec, especially during the American Revolution and in the aftermath of the French. Printer Fleury Mesplet and lawyer-editor Valentin Jautard were imprisoned for over three years (1779–82) after they criticized some judicial rulings, while Pierre Du Calvet was tried by a jury and acquitted for a similar offence in 1780, then imprisoned for three years without trial for allegedly seditious activities. Charles Hay was suspected of being in touch with the American rebels and similarly imprisoned. Habeas corpus was sought in the courts unsuccessfully on several occasions on behalf of all these detainees. In the 1797 treason trial of David McLane, an American spy in Quebec acting on behalf of revolutionary France, not only was the law stretched unpardonably by Chief Justice William Osgoode, but he acted virtually as a co-prosecutor in the case, and two informants were each rewarded with a township of land with his approval. He sentenced McLane to be hanged by the neck, cut down and disembowelled while still alive, beheaded, drawn and quartered – the prescribed punishment for treason under English law. In fact McLane died quickly on the scaffold, and the rest of the sentence was not carried out. As an American McLane was a convenient target for this display of state power; his death would overawe the populace but not arouse disaffection as the execution of a Canadien might have done.[56]

In the matter of judicial tenure, once again the colonial constitution did not mirror the British: colonial judges were commissioned at pleasure and did not benefit from the independence guaranteed to English judges in the *Act of Settlement 1701*.[57] An imperial statute of 1784 set out a process for disciplining colonial judges, and some during the period found themselves subject to recall, discipline, or impeachment when they upset influential parties in the colonies or in London.[58] The only two cases in which colonial *assemblies* sought to impeach judges were unsuccessful. The Nova Scotia assembly's charges of incompetence and partiality against James Brenton and Isaac Deschamps in 1790 before the Committee of the Privy Council on Trade and Plantations were found not to be proven, while its successor body similarly rejected complaints of unconstitutional and oppressive behaviour by judges Jonathan Sewell and James Monk of Quebec in 1814–15.[59] Suspensions or dismissals by colonial *governors* were not uncommon, however, early examples being Peter Livius (dismissed by Governor Carleton as chief justice of Quebec in 1779 in a dispute over the availability of habeas corpus); Caesar Colclough (suspended from the Supreme Court of Prince Edward Island in 1812 and sent to Newfoundland), Thomas Tremlett (formerly chief justice of the Supreme Court of Newfoundland but sent to replace Colclough in 1813 and dismissed in 1824), and Robert Thorpe (suspended from the Court of King's Bench of Upper Canada in 1807 and sent to the bench in Sierra Leone, from which he was dismissed in 1815).[60]

From the British point of view, the divergences between the 'colonial' and 'home' versions of the constitution were a necessary aspect of colonialism. While the colonies were an extension of the mother country, they were also meant to serve the latter's economic and political goals. From the perspective of British North Americans, however, these divergences were an unfortunate reminder of their inferior status. Settlers might be grateful for the economic and military support provided by Britain, by the haven and compensation provided for loyalists after the American Revolution, and for the relatively broad capacity for self-rule afforded by the granting of representative government. But they became increasingly restive under a system in which the governor was accountable for the exercise of his extensive powers not primarily to the settlers themselves as represented in their assemblies, but to the imperial government and to cliques of local advisers with transatlantic patronage connections. The almost constant wars between the 1740s and 1815 meant that critiques of governmental policies and power always risked being labelled as sedition rather than simple dissent; but with the return of peace in 1815 and steady population growth, the reform of the colonial constitutions would become a more urgent and more feasible goal of British North American settler societies.

The second major theme in the development of the northern colonies' constitutions was the place of Indigenous peoples. Once again the Board of Trade's report of 1721 provides a convenient point of departure. Taking the long view, the board stressed the 'need for cultivating a good understanding with the Native Indians.' Surprisingly, perhaps, it lauded the French approach and urged emulating it, observing,

> Herein at all times hath consisted the main support of our French neighbours who are so truly sensible of what consequence it is to any European nation, settling in America, to gain the natives to their interest; that they have spared no pains, nor cost, nor artifice to attain this desirable end; wherein it must be allowed, they have succeeded, to the great prejudice of your Majesty's subjects in those parts, having debauched ... some parts of the five nations bordering upon New York from their Ancient league & dependence on the Crown of Great Britain.[61]

This strategy of alliance was fortified by the activities of missionaries, giving presents to native leaders, and 'encouragement given for intermarriages between the french and natives; whereby their Empire may in time be peopled, without draining france of its inhabitants.' So impressed was the board with this strategy that 'in the draught of Instructions for the Governor of Nova Scotia, we took the liberty of proposing to your Majesty that proper encouragement should be given to such of your Majesty's subjects as should intermarry with the native Indians; and we conceive it might be for your Majesty's service that the said Instructions should be extended to all other British Colonies.'[62]

The board admitted that heretofore presents had not been given as 'regularly or seasonably' as was desirable, though no concrete change was proposed. But then the board revealed its secret weapon:

> There is however one other method left for gaining the goodwill of these Indians, which providence has put into our hands, and wherein the french could not possibly rival us, if we made a right use of our advantage, & that is, the furnishing of them, at honest & reasonable prices, with the several European commodities, they may have occasion for, but even this particular, from the unreasonable avarice of our Indian traders, & the want of proper regulations, has turned to our detriment, and instead of gaining us friends, has very probably created us many enemies.[63]

Trade was the key to expanding inland, and monopolies had to be prevented, so that trade was free and no single person or group of persons could engross it. There was nothing the board could do, however, about the monopoly over trade in Rupert's Land already granted to the Hudson's Bay Company in 1670, and their report did not refer to it. Moreover, the board did not understand the linkage between trade and all other areas of life that was characteristic of Indigenous law. The provision of trade articles at reasonable prices was not a panacea for British-Indigenous relations unless accompanied by other indicia of a full relationship, something Britain's representatives in North America generally understood better than those in London. The board seems to have had no inkling about the Covenant Chain and would probably not have known what to make of it.

In conclusion, the board urged that the governors of colonial America should endeavour to make 'treaties and alliances of friendship with as many Indian nations as they can; [and] all the Indian Nations ... should, if possible, be reconciled to each other,' again implicitly following the lead of the French in the Great Peace of 1701. And if forts needed to be erected, they should be built 'by permission of the Indian proprietors.'

Thus, the board supported the plan of the governor of New York to raise a fort at Niagara 'by the consent & assistance of the Senecas, one of the Five Indian Nations dependent on your Majesty, to whom the soil belongs.'[64] The defeat of the French in 1760 led to a flurry of actions by the British imperial government to secure the allegiance of Indigenous peoples in the former French territories. The Articles of Capitulation of Montreal stated, 'The savages or Indian allies of his most Christian Majesty, shall be maintained in the lands they inhabit, if they chuse to remain there; they shall not be molested on any pretence whatsoever, for having carried arms, and served his most Christian Majesty; they shall have, as well as the French, liberty of religion, and shall keep their missionaries.' Although somewhat ambiguous, this suggested a continuity of approach from the French regime. William Johnson met with representatives of Haudenosaunee nations at Montreal in 1760 in order to renew the Covenant Chain and to promise that they would 'enjoy the same Priviledges they did under the French Govemt.'[65] A year later, he met at his home Johnson Hall with the Six Nations and with representatives of the western nations, the Huron, Odawa, Ojibwe, and Potowatomi, where the last were invited to join the Covenant Chain relationship.[66] The superintendent position, it is important to note, was an imperial commission enabling Johnson to represent the Crown directly in its relationship with Indigenous peoples, and not through the agency of colonial governments. Johnson was strongly opposed to General Jeffrey Amherst's policies of stopping presents to Indigenous allies, which helped foment Pontiac's War and which Johnson knew would be regarded as a breach of the Covenant Chain. Amherst's recall in 1763 ensured that Johnson's expertise in 'forest diplomacy' would be given full rein thereafter.

From the British point of view, the Royal Proclamation of 1763 was a unilateral declaration emanating from the royal prerogative, directing how relations with native peoples were to be carried on in future in North America. From the Indigenous point of view, however, the proclamation was presented and understood as another element in a long-standing and evolving bilateral relationship.[67] William Johnson visited the Algonquin and Nipissings at Oswegatchie, New York, in the winter of 1764, gave them a copy of the proclamation, explained its provisions, and urged them to invite the Western nations, who were part of a loose Great Lakes confederacy, to attend the gathering he had planned for the summer of 1764. Some 2,000 representatives of twenty-four First Nations from eastern North America met in a treaty council that July. Through Johnson's efforts, the British sought to replicate the Great Peace of 1701 and replace the French in the web of native alliances. They succeeded to the extent that all nations present were admitted to the Covenant Chain previously established between the British and the Haudenosaunee. It is clear that the promises contained in the royal proclamation were presented as an incentive to the Indigenous parties to enter the treaty. William Johnson observed at the end of the ten-day meeting, 'We have frequently met to renew and Strengthen our Engagements and you have made so many Promises of your Friendship and Attachment to the English that there now only remains for us to exchange the great Belt of the Covenant Chain that we may not forget our mutual Engagements.'[68]

While the land area ceded by the treaty was not large – a strip four miles wide on the west side of the Niagara River – it was highly strategic, and the process served as a model for treaties covering much larger areas after the arrival of the loyalists in what would become Upper Canada. Nonetheless, the Niagara Treaty was not primarily about land. As Mark Walters has observed, 'The Covenant Chain ... contemplates not a right to do this or that practice or activity; it is, rather, a comprehensive constitutional relationship that seeks *right* in its broadest sense.'[69] The treaty council at Niagara aimed to renew a relationship that had become frayed by the turbulence of the Seven Years' War, the bad decisions made by General Amherst and others, and the exclusion of Indigenous peoples from the negotiations leading to the Treaty of Paris. Applicable to a vast area of northeastern North America, it was meant to guarantee, via the 'great [wampum] Belt of the Covenant Chain,' the fundamental principle of the kaswentha: that Europeans and Indigenous parties would respect each other's ways, including their laws and internal governance. The one partial exception contemplated by Johnson was his intention to seek a commitment by the Indigenous parties to surrender 'such of their people as may be guilty of Robbery or Murder, that they may be tried according to the English laws.'[70] Whether this was actually agreed to at Niagara is not certain, but even if it was, it clearly represents a limited exception to the general principle that the laws of the Indigenous parties would be respected.[71]

The royal proclamation was hastily put together. It was meant to be merely a prologue to a parliamentary statute that would reiterate its main points and put the management of Indian affairs in North America under a unified imperial direction that would allow little room for the intervention of colonial governments.[72] This plan, based to a

Portrait by Edward Chatfield of Nicolas Vincent Tsawenhohi, chief of the Hurons of Lorette, with the wampum belt he presented to King George IV of England in 1825. The origin of the belt is uncertain, but it was meant to support the chief's petition to the Crown regarding lands granted to the Hurons by the French King, of which they had been dispossessed.

considerable extent on the suggestions of William Johnson, would have given a statutory basis to the Department of Indian Affairs, and while instituting free entry into the trade with Indigenous peoples (subject to posting a bond for good behaviour), would have regulated it so as to prevent fraud and abuse. Adopted in Britain in July 1764, even as the great treaty council was meeting at Niagara, its weak point was financing. How would the required administrative personnel be paid for? Given the adverse colonial reaction to the *Stamp Act*, passed in March 1765, further attempts to raise revenue in the colonies to finance imperial plans and projects were put on hold. As conflict with the colonies loomed, relations with Indigenous peoples shifted into a different register for the next generation.

Thus constitutional matters in British North America followed a two-track policy, with an 'Indigenous constitution' and a 'settler constitution' existing in parallel. Indigenous affairs were dealt with under the royal prerogative, through the superintendents of Indian Affairs or through treaties and administrative actions carried out by or under the aegis of colonial governors. The Indigenous constitution featured a body of intercultural law, based principally in the kaswentha, that aimed to permit Indigenous peoples and settlers to coexist peacefully and to exercise jurisdiction over their own kind. Such an arrangement necessarily presupposed the continuity of Indigenous law itself, but as a legal order recognized by imperial common law as part of imperial legal pluralism, not as a sovereign legal enclave – what has been termed a theory of 'inclusive' legal continuity. On this view, in this respect, the emergent legal position in the United States differed, where 'native people remained aliens and native law remained part of an alien legal system unconnected to the American (or British) system' – a theory of 'exclusive' legal continuity.[73]

The settler constitution was based on the royal prerogative in the older Atlantic colonies, but in the Canadas it was based on statute from the time of the *Quebec Act* and later developed in the *Constitutional Act 1791*. While these constitutions eventually revealed their own weaknesses in settler-imperial relations, they were more transparent and stable than the prerogative-based measures that governed the relations of the imperial and colonial governments with Indigenous peoples. While Indigenous peoples regarded their relationship with the British Crown as based on certain fixed principles, on the British side the commitments made pursuant to the Covenant Chain and other treaties were always in flux, subject to shifting governmental priorities, settler pressures, and geopolitical calculations. Instructions to colonial governors about how to deal with Indigenous peoples and their lands could change from year to year, and while Indigenous people might petition the imperial Crown for perceived breaches of treaty obligations, there was no real system of accountability or clear mode of redress in such cases.

The flashpoint of discord between Indigenous people and settlers usually came down to land. The land rights of Indigenous peoples would be proclaimed rhetorically but acted on only fitfully in the colonies of British North America. Thus, in spite of the guarantees contained in the royal proclamation, a variety of local and imperial considerations, rather than any overarching theory or legal doctrine, determined the course of action in a given colony at a given time. In some the Crown's representatives entered into a treaty with a particular Indigenous group acknowledging their title and providing compensation for land surrendered (for example, the Mississaugas of southern Upper Canada); in others Indigenous title was acknowledged by a treaty containing no mechanism for surrender or compensation, but no clear boundary was established between areas where Europeans could settle and where they could not (the Mi'kmaq and Wulstukwiuk of the Maritimes); elsewhere the authorities did not enter treaties or formally acknowledge Indigenous title but acted to impede European settlement in certain areas inhabited by Indigenous peoples (Quebec). Governors did not generally inquire into precedents from other colonies when dealing with their own Indigenous inhabitants, and while the Board of Trade provided a measure of supervision, its powers to enforce uniformity were limited, as governors were granted plenary power to enter treaties with Indigenous peoples; such treaties did not have to be ratified by the Crown, as did treaties with European nations. This variety of experience requires that disputes over Indigenous land be dealt with on a colony-by-colony basis, as will be undertaken below.

Slavery, Race, and the Constitution

The great irony of the eighteenth century is the coexistence of a constitutional discourse based on liberty with the widespread practice of slavery. Under the French regime and the British, on land and sea, in the civilian and military spheres, and serving Catholic and Protestant clergy, Black and Indigenous slaves (also known as Panis) were part of everyday life in northern North America, even if their absolute numbers were not large.[74] They toiled for Jean-Pierre Roma at his estate in eastern Île St-Jean, served as status symbols ('footmen') for governors general of New France such as the Marquis de Beauharnois de la Boische, who had twenty-seven of them, worked for voyageurs in the fur trade in the pays d'en haut, and performed all manner of domestic tasks for urban mercantile families from Halifax to Detroit. They displayed personal courage and loyalty to their owners as well as violent resistance to their enslaved status. A slave named Georges Sauzy saved the life of his wounded master, Captain Pierre Morpain, during the first siege of Louisbourg in 1745, an act of heroism for which he received his freedom.[75] The Black slave Marie-Joseph-Angélique was convicted of burning down her mistress's house and much of Montreal along with it in 1734, an act for which she suffered judicial torture and hanging.[76] The Panis soldier known as Charles was transported to Martinique as a slave as his punishment for taking part in a mutiny at Fort Niagara in 1729.[77] In Upper Canada, Chloe Cooley's fierce, though ultimately unsuccessful, attempts to resist her master's attempts to sell her to a buyer in New York played a role in the passage of Upper Canada's 1793 law for the gradual abolition of slavery in that colony.[78]

The numbers of the enslaved rose from a handful of Black slaves and a few dozen Indigenous slaves in the French colonies in 1700 out of a population of some 14,000 settlers to 304 in British Quebec according to a census of 1784, in a population of some 113,000.[79] With the arrival of the loyalists the number of slaves in British North America rose considerably, mostly in the English-speaking colonies. In Upper Canada, there were reported to be some 300 slaves, predominantly Black but including some Panis, in the Niagara District alone in 1791.[80] In the Maritime colonies, the number of Black slaves increased from around 100, most of whom accompanied the first Planter migration in 1759–60, to over 1,200, mostly brought by their Loyalist masters after 1783.[81] Yet by the end of the first decade of the nineteenth century, and earlier in Lower Canada, slavery as a legal institution had virtually died out, well before its formal abolition in the empire by the imperial Act of 1833. Panis slavery seems to have left no legacy in the treatment of Indigenous peoples distinct from the general impact of colonialism itself on them, such that it was rapidly forgotten after its demise. It was otherwise with Black slavery: the racist attitudes associated with it continued to haunt the lives of free Black persons for many generations by shaping the administration and application of laws that appeared race-neutral on their face.

There were some differences between the law of slavery in New France and in the British colonies, but in both places it originated in local custom rather than statutory enactment or imperial edict.[82] The *Code Noir* of 1685 was meant for the Caribbean islands, while another *Code Noir* was promulgated for Louisiana in 1724. No such code was ever established for Canada, for two reasons. In 1685 there were virtually no Black slaves in Canada, and later, when slaves entered the colony in greater numbers, they were primarily Indigenous rather than Black. When colonial administrators in Canada thought about slavery, it was primarily the Panis whom they had in mind. Over the whole period of slavery in Canada/Quebec, from 1608 to approximately 1800, just under two-thirds of the slaves in the jurisdiction were Panis, while the remainder were Black.[83]

Domestic regulations on slavery began with Intendant Raudot's 1709 ordinance confirming its legality: 'All Panis and Negroes who have been and shall hereafter be bought, belong in full ownership to those who purchased them as slaves.'[84] Raudot's fond hope was that the Panis could be to Canada what Blacks were to the Caribbean islands, supplying the agricultural labour so needed in the under-populated colony. To achieve this, legal confirmation that slaves were indeed property was required to reassure potential owners, because slaves themselves seem to have become familiar with the trope that 'there are no slaves in France.'[85] The preamble to the ordinance stated that slaves 'almost always leave their masters on the pretext that there are no slaves in France, which is not always true with respect to its colonies.'[86]

While the ordinance itself did not distinguish between Panis and Black slaves, they did come to be treated differently in some respects. Raudot ruled in 1710 that Panis slaves could not be transported as slaves to the Caribbean, as once outside Canada they became free, a recognition of the localized basis of this kind of slavery.[87] However, the colonial state itself did this from time to time, as noted earlier with regard to the mutinous Panis Charles, and this may have encouraged private owners to do the same. It was also useful for masters to be able to threaten slaves with transportation to the more abusive slave societies of the Caribbean. A rumour of being sold to the Caribbean led to an ultimately unsuccessful escape by Marie-Joseph-Angélique from her mistress a few months before her incendiary act.[88] And as will be seen, the one freedom suit known to have been initiated by a Panis under the French regime was triggered by the master's decision to ship the woman in question to the Caribbean for sale.

The customary basis of Panis slavery was troubling to the bureaucratic mind, and Intendant Hocquart requested the issuance of a formal edict on the subject from Louis XV, who declined to do so. The king advised that the judges of Canada should continue to apply customary practice with regard to Panis slaves, and left it to the discretion of the intendant to determine the formalities for emancipation.[89] In 1736 Hocquart issued an ordinance requiring emancipation of slaves to be done by formal act before a notary, and the act to be registered with the nearest royal court.[90] The king gave no formal rationale for his decision, but it was probably based on the need to maintain the native alliance system upon which French power in America rested. It was one thing to participate in a slave trade initiated by the Indigenous peoples themselves; it was another to erect a formal legal apparatus around Indigenous slavery, which might convey the wrong message to native allies.

The customary basis of Panis slavery was thus a strength and a weakness from the European point of view. It was a strength because the flexibility of custom allowed the French to adapt this Indigenous practice to their own needs. The result was a law of slavery that permitted a certain degree of legal capacity to Panis slaves, avoiding the paradoxes and inconveniences of an absolute doctrine of chattel slavery. They could be required to appear in court, could witness certain legal acts, and in criminal trials they were generally accorded the same rights as French subjects.[91] In addition, their 'paths to freedom' were easier in a society where the vast majority of native people were free. Consider André Rapin dit Skaianis, traded as a child at Montreal in 1686 to André Rapin dit Lamusette. Skaianis lived with his master until the age of eighteen, when the latter died, freeing his 'adoptive son' by will. Skaianis began to farm on his own and in 1706 married a Canadien widow.[92] Such flexibility encouraged Panis slaves to think of their status as impermanent. Thus, when attitudes towards slavery in general began to change in the late eighteenth century, Panis slavery declined rapidly.

The only known formal challenge to slavery was the 1740 freedom suit of the Panis slave Marie-Marguerite Radisson dite Duplessis before the courts of Canada. Born on the western plains about 1715, Marguerite was enslaved by the Iowa nation, given to the French in 1726 and brought to Montreal; there she bore a child in 1728 who was baptised and died shortly thereafter. In 1740 she came into the hands of Marc-Antoine Huard Dormicourt, a Martinique sugar plantation owner who had commercial interests in the port of Quebec. For reasons unknown, he had her imprisoned. With the aid of a priest who guaranteed any legal costs she might be obliged to pay, and an unlicensed legal practitioner, she launched a suit in the Prévôté de Québec based on two arguments: that as a faithful Roman Catholic she was a subject of the king and could not be enslaved; and that she was the illegitimate daughter of one of her former owners.[93] Neither of these arguments succeeded at first instance, or in the ensuing appeal to the Conseil supérieur, but they demonstrate nonetheless the germ of a 'rights consciousness' that would emerge more forcefully some fifty years later.[94]

The fall of New France did not bring about any change in the status of slaves resident in the colony. In the negotiations between Governor Vaudreuil-Cavagnial and General Amherst after the fall of Montreal, the former made a request:

> The Negroes and Panis of both sexes shall remain in their quality of slaves in the possession of the French and Canadians to whom they belong; they shall be at liberty to keep them in their service in the colony or to sell them; and they may also continue to bring them up in the Roman Religion.[95]

Governor Amherst granted this request, 'except those who shall have been made prisoners,' and such became article 47 of the Capitulations of Montreal. Thus, as with so many other features of post-conquest transitional law, the operative rule was one of continuity: the rules of the French regime remained in force until changed by the new government. The main change post-1760 was not legal but demographic: the importation of many more Black slaves into the province by the loyalists, changing the composition of the slave population from primarily Panis to a more mixed population.[96]

For a quarter-century after 1760, virtually no discussion of the status of slavery appeared in the public sphere. Then, suddenly, the 1780s and 1790s witnessed a flurry of activity. Acting chief justice and legislative councillor Adam Mabane gave notice in 1785 that he would introduce an ordinance abolishing slavery, and in 1787 the council debated his proposal to ban the importation of slaves and emancipate after five years all those who were in the province.[97] The ordinance failed, but the idea of abolition was furthered by the *Quebec Gazette*, which began to publish anti-slavery verse and stories of atrocities connected to slavery.[98] Bills proposing the gradual abolition of slavery appeared in the new assembly of Lower Canada in 1793, and again in 1800, 1801, and 1803, but these were actually aimed at postponing abolition rather than the reverse. None passed, and the anti-slavery initiative passed to the courts. In 1794 the court of quarter sessions at Montreal declared that 'slavery was not known by the Laws of England' and would not allow an American suitor to recover his slave who had allegedly escaped from New York.[99] In 1798 James Monk, chief justice of the Montreal Court of King's Bench, in three separate suits released runaway slaves whom their masters sought to reclaim.[100] His reasoning is available only indirectly, and it is not clear whether he was making a broad declaration against the legality of slavery, or merely demanding that the alleged owner meet a high evidentiary bar to prove ownership, the preferred judicial tactic in Nova Scotia, Monk's former home.[101] This caused sufficient alarm among slave-owners that a number of them petitioned the Legislative Assembly in 1799 advocating the continued recognition of slavery, using as their first argument Raudot's ordinance of 1709. They alleged that as a result of Monk's decisions, 'the Negroes in the city and district of Montreal threatened a general revolt,' although they may have exaggerated this possibility out of self-interest.[102]

It appears the petitioners were already too late. The last known sale of a slave from Lower Canada occurred when Marguerite Boucher de Boucherville sold her nine-year-old Black slave Thomas to Joseph Campeau of Detroit for twenty-five pounds in 1799, while the last known advertisement for the sale of a slave appeared in the *Montreal Gazette* on 29 January 1798.[103] As in the other colonies, the unwillingness of some courts to uphold slavery in the 1790s led to uncertainty and to a rapid decline in the market for slaves after 1800. The relatively small numbers of slaves in British North America meant that the institution could be judicially undermined without a severe backlash by erstwhile slave-owners or loud demands for compensation.

As in Lower Canada, slavery in Nova Scotia and New Brunswick rested on a customary foundation, while in St John's Island and Upper Canada it had a statutory basis. New Brunswick had no legislation on the subject, while a reference to 'Negro slaves' in a 1762 Nova Scotia statute was considered, according to Chief Justice Sampson Salter Blowers, 'as merely a description of a Class of people existing in the province, and not as a recognition of the Law of Slavery.'[104] In both these provinces, slave-holding interests proposed legislation that would have legalized slavery under the guise of regulating it, but all such attempts failed. The legislature of St John's Island, however, passed *An Act Declaring that Baptism of SLAVES Shall Not Exempt Them from BONDAGE*, which further specified that people of African descent 'who now are on this Island, or may hereafter be imported or brought therein (being Slaves) shall continue such, unless freed by his, her, or their respective owners.'[105] The 1781 Act was arguably a response to the 1778 Scottish decision *Knight v Wedderburn*,[106] which declared that Christian baptism set a slave free.[107]

Lawsuits in the 1790s and 1800s aimed at freeing individual slaves by habeas corpus or impugning the legality of slavery as an institution were generally unsuccessful in Prince Edward Island and New Brunswick, though majority sentiment in New Brunswick by 1800 was thought to be anti-slavery. In Nova Scotia, some cases in the 1780s saw the successful re-enslavement of Blacks who were likely free, but by the 1790s, under the chief justiceships of Sir Thomas Strange (1789–97) and Sampson Salter Blowers (1797–1830), slave-owners' claims generally failed. The preferred judicial strategy, according to Blowers, was 'to wear out the claim gradually, than to throw so much property as it is called into the air at once.'[108] They did this by finding against owners on evidentiary grounds rather than making bold declarations that slavery was illegal. In New Brunswick, where the judges were more resolutely pro-slavery, advertisements for slave sales can be found as late as 1816, almost twenty years after the last one in Lower Canada.[109] A customary foundation for slavery did not mean a weak one if the judges were determined to uphold the institution.

Many loyalists in Upper Canada's establishment owned slaves, putting them at odds with the abolitionist views of the colony's first lieutenant governor, John Graves Simcoe. They compromised on a 1793 Act providing for gradual emancipation, but it was a double-edged sword.[110] The law has sometimes been lauded as the first slave emancipation statute passed in the British Empire. In declaring that no slaves could be imported into the colony, it did make Upper Canada a magnet for freedom-seeking slaves from other jurisdictions. But in confirming the lifelong slave status of all those slaves currently in the colony, as well as that of all children born thereafter to slave mothers, up to age twenty-five, it provided only for very gradual abolition. Under this dispensation, slavery would have continued to exist in Upper Canada into the 1860s. In one sense the legislation was quite bold, however. In 1790 the British Parliament had passed a law allowing U.S. citizens who moved to British colonies to bring their slaves with them with the governor's permission. The 1793 law in effect nullified the imperial law by removing the governor's power to do so. Such action was arguably unconstitutional, but Simcoe was a willing participant in this end-run around Westminster.[111]

RAN away from her Master JOHN ROCK, on Monday the 18th Day of August last; a Negroe Girl named *Thursday*, about four and an half feet high, broad sett, with a Lump above her Right Eye: Had on when she run away a red Cloth Petticoat, a red Baize Bed Gown, and a red Ribbon about her Head. Whosoever may harbour said Negroe Girl, or encourage her to stay away from her said Master, may depend on being prosecuted according as the Law shall direct. And whosoever may be so kind to take her up and send her home to her said Master, shall be paid all Costs and Charges, together with TWO DOLLARS Reward for their Trouble.

JOHN ROCK.

HALIFAX, Sept. 1st, 1772.

Ad appearing in the *Nova Scotia Gazette*, 1 September 1772. Note the threat of legal action against those harbouring Thursday or abetting her escape. Such ads were common in British North America until about 1800.

The legislation was derived from similar statutes in Pennsylvania, Connecticut, and Rhode Island and was a mirror image of the situation across the border in Michigan. There, the Northwest Ordinance had declared that slavery did not exist, but the status of slaves present in the territory when the ordinance was passed in 1787 was 'grandfathered.' Even as such slaves sought freedom in Upper Canada after 1796, when Detroit was returned to the Americans, those in Upper Canada also sought freedom by crossing the Detroit River. Thus, in 1807 an unnamed slave of attorney James Woods of Sandwich and her four-year-old son found freedom in Detroit by rowing across the river with the help of friends on the American side. Their freedom was guaranteed by court decisions of 1806 and 1807 in the newly established Michigan Territory (1805) that fugitive slaves did not have to be surrendered to their Upper Canadian owners, a position then followed by the Upper Canadian authorities with respect to American fugitive slaves.[112]

After Simcoe left the province, a bill permitting the importation of slaves to Upper Canada passed the lower house in 1798 but was defeated in the legislative council. Nonetheless, perhaps because of its legislative recognition, slavery seems to have continued in vigour at least a decade longer in Upper Canada than Lower Canada. Examples can be found of slave sales in 1806, and in 1811 Provincial Secretary William Jarvis charged one of his slaves with burglary and horse-stealing.[113] The proximity of the international border provided an ever-present escape route, however: in 1807 the 'Proprietors of Slaves in the Western District of the Province of Upper Canada' petitioned Lieutenant Governor Francis Gore for redress for the constant losses they suffered in this regard, but to no avail.[114]

The one place where slavery was not moribund by the early nineteenth century was the west coast. Long after it had died out in the eastern colonies, NWC and HBC traders encountered a deeply entrenched culture of Indigenous slavery, which was practised everywhere from the Aleutian Islands to northern California. Certain nations were prominent in slave-trading, such as the Tsimshian and the Haida. In 1845 two British lieutenants estimated that some 5,100 slaves inhabited the territories west of the Rockies.[115] The HBC does not seem to have participated actively in the slave trade – Chief Factor James Douglas, later governor of British Columbia, quipped that the company had finally encountered 'a description of property that we cannot compete in.'[116] Nonetheless, some company officials purchased slaves, and others entered HBC forts as slaves owned by Indigenous women who married traders. The HBC and the Royal Navy tried to suppress slavery by discouraging the intertribal warfare in which the institution was based and achieved some success in this regard.[117] Slavery on the west coast was not eradicated by law – the imperial Act of 1833 did not 'extend its influence to these remote shores,' a trader observed in 1838.[118] Rather, it died a slow death as a result of the far-reaching changes in Indigenous society that followed European contact.

The British North American colonies of the late eighteenth century may have been remote outposts of empire, but they participated in the international debate over the legality of slavery that shook the Atlantic world along with the American and French Revolutions. The customary basis of slavery in three of the colonies provided judges possessed of anti-slavery views a ready means of undermining the institution if they wished to do so. Given the contradictory precedents within English case law and in Scottish jurisprudence – Chief Justice Blowers stated in 1800 that he thought *Knight v Wedderburn* stood 'on Better reason' than the English authorities on the subject – it was possible to choose the more liberal path without contradicting a statute. But the example of New Brunswick, whose loyalist judges rigorously upheld slavery, shows that there was a good deal of contingency in the sudden appearance of judicial activism in Nova Scotia and Lower Canada in the 1790s. The personal views of the judges in question made all the difference, but those views were likely shaped in part by their knowledge that the undermining of slavery would not lead to economic upheaval in the British North American context.

Free Black persons were present along with slaves in British North America, and their presence raises somewhat different legal issues.[119] Nearly 2,700 free Blacks along with over 300 slaves were evacuated from New York to Nova Scotia in 1783, their identities recorded in the *Book of Negroes*, which has achieved literary and media fame in recent years.[120] Along with free Blacks who came from other places, it is estimated that as many as 5,000 may have come to the Maritimes, of whom at least 3,550 came to Nova Scotia.[121] Some had already possessed free status, while others were former slaves who had responded to the Dunmore Proclamation of 1775 or the Phillipsburg Proclamation of 1779. The first promised freedom to those slaves who left their masters and enlisted in the British forces, while the latter required only escape to British lines, not enlistment.[122] Outside the Maritimes the free Black presence was smaller and is harder to document, but it is clear that Blacks both slave and free were present in all the colonies except possibly Newfoundland.

Even in Nova Scotia, the numbers of free Blacks fluctuated considerably. Just under 1,200, unhappy with conditions in the province, left for Sierra Leone in 1792, while some 2,000 more arrived in the wake of the War of 1812, attracted by the same promises of freedom that motivated their predecessors in the 1780s.[123]

The Black loyalists sought freedom, but they also expected equality under the law and the full rights of British subjects. The British authorities of the day seem to have genuinely believed that, aside from slavery (a rather large exception), English law did not make distinctions among free people on the basis of race, and in the abstract they were mostly correct. Rare were the instances of formal discrimination, such as Shelburne magistrates' prohibition of 'Negro Dances, and Negro Frolicks in this Town,' or the decision of New Brunswick Governor Thomas Carleton to exclude Blacks from the franchise in the first provincial election – a highly ironic act, given the efforts of his brother Guy in protecting free Blacks and evacuating them from New York.[124] But in virtually every case where Blacks needed or came into contact with government action, and in all too many court proceedings, Blacks encountered discrimination in the application of laws or policies that appeared neutral on the surface. Insofar as these actions contributed to Black impoverishment and economic dependence, these results seemed only to confirm white stereotypes that equated Blacks with cheap labour and lack of initiative, members of a group who could never aspire to positions above the bottom of the social hierarchy.

The plight of the Black loyalists of Nova Scotia has been documented in some detail because their relatively large numbers generated a good deal of documentation in legal and other sources. Some of their leaders, such as David George and Boston King, left eloquent though surprisingly mild accounts of their experiences.[125] The arrival of 30,000 loyalists in Nova Scotia overwhelmed the meagre bureaucratic resources of the colony, leaving many in both the white and Black communities frustrated by delays in the allocation of food, supplies, and land. But, as James StG Walker observes, among a population for whom privation and physical suffering was common, 'for Black Nova Scotians as a group, the threat was greater and more frequently realised than for any others.'[126] Where land was concerned, in comparison with white families, Black loyalists received less per household, often much less, were assigned lands of poorer quality, received them later, and often did not get formal grants. Only a third received any land at all, and that was almost invariably in segregated settlements, inconveniently located. One of the most egregious examples occurred in Annapolis County, where Black loyalists were to get town lots in a settlement called Brindley Town near Digby as well as farmland in the surrounding area. Twice the Black settlers were moved from farmlands they had been assigned, and after six years no grant was forthcoming to the lands that were finally selected for them. At a time when white loyalists in Annapolis were receiving grants of between 100 and 400 acres each in addition to their town plots, 76 Black loyalists received an acre each in Brindley Town and no other land at all.[127] Those in the fortunate one-third who eventually were assigned land tended to get about fifty acres each.

Mostly unable to procure a subsistence from small plots with little potential for agriculture, Blacks turned to labour. Here they competed with disbanded soldiers and other disadvantaged whites who were also desperate for work. The ensuing competition drove down wages, creating tensions that led to the first 'race riot' in what is now Canada. On 29 July 1784 Simeon Perkins recorded in his diary that 'an Extraordinary mob or Riot has happened at Shelburne. Some thousands of People Assembled with Clubs and Drove the Negroes out of the Town.'[128] They were pursued to Birchtown, the nearby Black settlement, where some twenty houses were burned down, and repeated intrusions continued for up to a month.[129]

Such actions did not bode well for the impartiality of the local magistracy, and the records of the Shelburne General and Special Sessions are rife with examples of discriminatory treatment of Blacks. Patterns of punishment were highly racially skewed, with Black defendants in criminal and labour discipline cases often receiving onerous corporal punishment while whites convicted of similar offences got off with a fine. Dianna, convicted for two petty larcenies, was 'sentenced to 200 lashes at the cart's tail on Saturday at noon for the first offence; 150 lashes at the cart's tail the following Saturday for the second offence.' George was sentenced to receive 199 lashes for an act of petty larceny. Patty Brown's conviction for stealing a gown merited ten lashes and banishment from the community.[130] In the ten years after the settlement of Shelburne, no white person received more than ten lashes for any offence, and none was banished.[131] Conversely, where Blacks were victims of violence at the hands of their employers, they could expect little protection. In 1801 Samuel Andrews and his two sons went on trial for the murder of their Black servant Jude, whom Samuel had accused of theft. The coroners' jury brought in a verdict of murder based on the marks of violence on her body, as well as witness testimony, but the all-white jury acquitted the men.[132]

Thomas Peters, a Black loyalist leader, poured out his complaints about Nova Scotia in a petition to Lord Grenville in 1790. Free Blacks 'ha[d] already been reduced to Slavery without being able to attain any Redress from the King's courts.' One man had 'los[t] his Life by the Beating and Ill Treatment of his Master and another who fled the like cruelty was inhumanly shot and maimed.'[133] In short, they were 'entirely deprived of the privileges of British subjects, particularly trial by jury.'[134] Faced with little economic security and a marked lack of protection under the law, many were attracted by the prospect of a return to Africa. About one-third of the free Black population of Shelburne departed for Sierra Leone in 1792. For those who remained, the legacy of broken promises, unequal treatment, and residential segregation would continue for generations.

In the other colonies, where the numbers of free Blacks were much smaller, the situation seems to have been less dire, though never exactly beneficent. In Lower Canada they certainly faced discrimination in various ways: Blacks who met the low property qualification were excluded from jury service by tradition, not law, and they were excluded from all court-related offices except that of hangman. They seem not to have been excluded from voting, however, as noted earlier. On the basis of a detailed study of cases involving both Blacks and whites, the principal historian of Black Montreal concludes that 'the criminal justice system of the day, resolutely white, did not betray racial bias in its handling of cases involving blacks, whether they were the accused or the accusers.'[135] At most one Black person was executed for crime in the city between 1760 and 1815, while punishments were nothing like as severe as in Nova Scotia, nor were they out of line with what white convicts experienced.[136] In part this was likely due to demographic and economic factors. Only 1,000 Blacks are estimated to have lived in Montreal over the whole period 1760–1840, while non-European defendants (that is, both Blacks and Indigenous persons) were found in only 1 per cent of quarter sessions cases for the district of Montreal between 1780 and 1835.[137] It is likely that African-Canadians in Montreal found more economic opportunities than those in the rural or small-town Maritimes and thus fell afoul of the criminal law only rarely. Their small numbers made them less threatening, providing fewer targets for racist diatribe and little competition with white workers.

The experience of Upper Canada probably fell between the extremes of Nova Scotia and Lower Canada. It had a larger Black population than Lower Canada, but the numbers were still small enough that it is difficult to generalize about their experience during this early period. Certainly matters did not start well from the perspective of African-Canadians. The crime resulting in the first execution in Upper Canada was a theft by a Black slave in Detroit in 1791, just before the creation of the province in December. Tried by Chief Justice William Dummer Powell in the Court of Common Pleas in October 1792, Josiah Cutten was sentenced to death and hanged.[138] Yet, as noted earlier, William Jarvis charged his own slaves with theft, rather than punish them himself, as slave-owners were entitled to do in the United States.

The treatment of slaves and free Blacks was not uniform across the colonies, varying according to the attitudes of those in power, especially judges, as well as broader social attitudes; these in turn depended a good deal on the numbers, economic position, and general situation of the Black population in a given colony. In spite of the variations in treatment of slaves and free Blacks across the different colonies, it seems clear that post-1760, those Blacks who had most need of legal protection – the slaves and free Blacks of the Maritimes – were afforded it least, while those whose position was a little more secure, in Lower Canada, could expect fairer treatment when they came in contact with the legal system, voluntarily or involuntarily.

12

New France/Quebec/Lower Canada: Political Institutions, Courts, and Relations with Indigenous Peoples

New France before 1760

The constitution of the colony of Canada experienced some modest evolution prior to the British conquest, but aside from the addition of an admiralty court in 1717, the institutional structure established in the seventeenth century remained intact. Some change was spurred by the efforts of the French monarchy to centralize power in the colony in the hands of the intendant, in line with developments in France itself. The Conseil souverain was renamed the Conseil supérieur in 1703, for example, reflecting a change in its role and functions. It gradually ceased to exercise its broader administrative and executive powers, which gravitated to the intendant and the governor, and restricted its activities principally to those of an appellate court. This did not happen all at once in 1703: it was not until 1726 that Louis XV directed the Conseil to devote itself exclusively to its judicial duties, which included a supervisory jurisdiction over the lower courts and the right to regulate their procedure.[1] The Conseil could be quite assertive in obliging lower courts, whether royal or seigneurial, to follow the procedures laid down in the great ordinances of 1667 and 1670; on occasion it even ordered costs against judges who had employed unjust procedures.[2] Thus, while there was no concept of independence of the judiciary as such under the French constitution, there was a strong commitment to the provision of justice according to law, and to the public accountability of the lower courts at least.

The cession of mainland Acadia and Plaisance to Britain in 1713 enhanced French interest in its remaining possessions in the Gulf of St Lawrence, Île Royale, and Île St-Jean. The French state showed considerable flexibility when creating the new settlement at Louisbourg and in effect refounding the colony of Île Royale after 1713. Louisbourg was an emanation of the French state in the same way that Halifax would be when summoned into existence by the British state in 1749. Both centres were established immediately after a peace treaty, demonstrating that each side regarded their rivalry as far from over. Imperial subsidization gave each state a free hand to shape the constitution of the new colony in ways meant to serve imperial interests. Louisbourg was created as the maritime guardian of France's Laurentian colony, but it also became a thriving commercial colony focused on the fishery. Its constitution reflected these twin concerns, and the formal influence of the church was correspondingly reduced.

While Île Royale's constitution was certainly recognizable as that of a French colony, with its governor and commissaire-ordonnateur (similar to the intendant at Quebec) at its apex and its own Conseil supérieur, in other respects the island's constitution was quite distinctive. No seigneuries were created on Île Royale for, as Louis XIV's minister stated in 1714, '[His Majesty] does not wish there to be any seigneur other than himself on this island.'[3] The settlement was thus a seigneurie directe, with the lands held immediately of the king. There were no seigneurial courts, only royal courts, although the Conseil supérieur had to serve as both trial court and appellate court until 1734, when the population had increased to the point where a separate bailliage court could be created as a court of first instance.

Although Louisbourg fell within the jurisdiction of the bishop of Quebec, he had no representative on the Conseil supérieur, nor did he ever visit the colony. No tithe was ever paid by the inhabitants of Louisbourg, nor did they ever tax themselves to build a parish church, preferring to use the garrison chapel. All priestly salaries were paid by the royal treasury, further reducing the independent influence of the church.

Île St-Jean occupied a shadowy position in New France. In theory a French possession in the seventeenth century, it became a 'dependency' of Louisbourg after the latter's establishment. Louis XIV and XV made several large grants of territory to noblemen conditional on their planting settlers – the same technique the British would use in 1767 – but then, unlike the British, revoked them when the conditions were not met. Some Acadians moved there after the cession of Acadie to the British, followed by some French migrants in the 1720s.[4] In 1731 a large grant in the east of the island was made to the Compagnie de l'est de l'Isle St-Jean, controlled by Jean-Pierre Roma and others, in franc alleu noble (a non-seigneurial tenure), free from all royal dues.[5] As in previous grants, justice was reserved to the king to be administered by a sub-delegate from Louisbourg, but any serious crimes were sent to Louisbourg for trial. In one such case in 1721, where a woman was accused of being complicit in the murder of her husband, the commissaire-ordonnateur at Louisbourg sent the case on to Bordeaux for review, fearing that errors had been made in the trial.[6] Even in its remote and marginal possessions, the French state tried to ensure that justice was administered correctly.

Quebec/Lower Canada after 1760

The Capitulations of Montreal sketched out the broad outlines of the new constitution of Quebec. The Canadiens would become subjects of the king and would retain full freedom of religion. A request that the British government continue to enforce the payment of tithes to the Roman Catholic Church was referred to the king's pleasure. Seigneurs, censitaires, and religious communities would remain undisturbed in the peaceful possession of their property, which included any Black or Panis slaves they might own.[7] It was also agreed that the 'Indian allies of his most Christian Majesty shall be maintained in the Lands they inhabit, if they chuse to remain there.'

But one key issue was left unsettled: to the request that 'the French and Canadians shall continue to be governed according to the custom of Paris and the laws and usages established for this country,' General Amherst replied with the seeming non sequitur that 'they become subjects of the king.' Aside from the imposition of English criminal law, however, it appears that the Custom of Paris was in fact applied by the tribunals operating during the period of military rule that lasted until the formation of a civil government in April 1764.[8] This maintenance of the civil law did not extend to the continuation of the seigneurial courts. While they were never expressly abolished, possibly because the right to administer justice was considered a form of property, the 'expropriation' of which might have called for compensation, it was assumed that they could and would not survive the change of regime.[9]

The problem of 'which law' became more acute after the erection of civil courts based on the English model pursuant to the judicature ordinance of September 1764, which also included the possibility of trial by jury for both civil and criminal matters, a process unknown under the French regime. Moreover, the royal proclamation directed that all causes should be judged 'according to Law and Equity, and as near as may be agreeable to the Laws of England,' effective as of 10 August 1764. These measures were meant to implement imperial plans in the wake of the conquest to assimilate the Canadiens, culturally and legally, by all possible means. Governor James Murray was instructed to establish the Anglican Church and to open English schools, and the royal proclamation confidently directed the governors of the new polities created by it 'to summon and call General Assemblies ... in such Manner and Form as is used and directed in those Colonies and Provinces in America which are under our immediate Government.' Murray, his successor Guy Carleton, and William Hey, the chief justice of the King's Bench, were sceptical about London's plans, pointing out the 'impossibility of abrogating at once the Laws of a Country well cultivated and long settled, and substituting others in their stead, [given that] the Manners and Habits and Sentiments of a people are so intimately connected with the Laws and the established form of things.'[10] In any case, the parties to litigation in the new courts and their counsel – mostly notaries from the French regime functioning as advocates – relied largely upon the Custom of Paris and local usages in their pleading.[11] Meanwhile, Murray essentially disregarded his instructions in permitting the appointment as court personnel of Canadiens who had held similar positions under the French regime but who would have been excluded by a rigorous application of the *Test Act* oaths. It was also decided that notaries did not have to take the oaths, a crucial step permitting the main repositories of the law of the former regime to continue in practice – at a time when Catholics were not permitted to become attorneys or barristers in England or Ireland.[12]

Thus, the *Quebec Act* of 1774, which directed that 'in all Matters of Controversy, relative to Property and Civil Rights, Resort shall be had to the Laws of Canada, as the Rule for the Decision of the same,' can be seen as a measure of continuity with past practice, rather than a 'restoration' of the civil law.[13] It also gave statutory foundation to the Catholic Church's power to collect tithes, which had already been recognized in practice, though it specified that tithes paid by Protestants were to be used for the support of Protestant clergy.[14] In other respects, however, the Act did innovate. It provided a new form of oath of allegiance that could be taken by Canadiens, shorn of the anti-Catholic elements that accompanied such oaths in Britain, thus opening the way for Canadiens to take up the full range of public positions. A number of Catholic seigneurs joined the council, and two francophone Catholics were named judges immediately after the coming into force of the Act, though one, René-Ovide Hertel de Rouville, was extremely unpopular and the other, prominent notary Jean-Claude Panet, did not live long. The 1776 commission of the peace featured a number of prominent Canadiens, who made up a strong majority in subsequent commissions in most areas of the province until the 1810s, when concerns about their loyalty during the Napoleonic Wars led to a resurgence of appointments from the British population.[15] The key offices of attorney and solicitor general, however, remained an anglophone preserve down to 1840 with only one exception: Louis-Charles Foucher, who served as solicitor general from 1795 to 1804.

The Act declared that the calling of an assembly was 'inexpedient' for the moment and created a new legislative council of between seventeen and twenty-three members to assist the governor in passing ordinances for the 'peace, welfare and good government' of the colony; pointedly, the council had no power to tax the inhabitants, other than permitting towns or districts to tax themselves for local improvements. Finally, it instituted freedom of willing for all property whether held under French tenure or not, a major departure from French traditions of forced heirship. The innovation was effected clumsily, raising many legal questions that required an amending Act in 1801, though even then questions remained that were not settled until codification in 1866.[16]

It was in the area of religion that London's early plans for assimilation were most dramatically reversed. The Treaty of Paris had confirmed Amherst's promise of freedom of religion in somewhat ambiguous terms: the king agreed 'that his new Roman Catholic subjects may profess the worship of their religion according to the rites of the Romish church, as far as the laws of Great Britain permit.' Those laws imposed many restrictions on the activities of priests and on the rights of individual Catholics. But rather than seek to enforce them, Murray went in the opposite direction, forming an alliance with the church and permitting the appointment of a de facto Roman Catholic bishop of Quebec; this action arguably contravened British law, which, in the words of Lord Egremont, Secretary of State for the Southern Department, 'prohibit[ed] absolutely all Popish Hierarchy in any of the Dominions belonging to the Crown.'[17]

Murray's choice, Jean-Olivier Briand, who had been vicar general at the time of the conquest, was advised to proceed quietly to France to be consecrated, and then return to Quebec. Although Pope Clement XIII recognized Briand as the bishop of Quebec, in the colony itself he had to be content with the title of 'superintendent of the Catholic Church in Canada.' Murray's action fulfilled the spirit if not the letter of the treaty's guarantee, as without a bishop to ordain new priests, the Catholic Church in Quebec was destined to wither away. Briand, for his part, proved to be a stout defender of the new regime; he advised his priests that prayers should be said for the sovereign during mass and issued a pastoral letter during the American invasion ordering the faithful to support the government and repulse the invader. The colonial government also cooperated with the religious orders, except for the Jesuits, who were expelled from the capital but permitted to keep their seigneuries for the time being. When the order was disbanded by the pope in 1773, the number of Jesuits went into decline until the last died in 1800, after which their lands were declared forfeit to the Crown.[18]

The *Quebec Act* was an example of the imperial technique, evident elsewhere in the empire, of co-opting local elites to assist in the furtherance of British rule. By confirming the applicability of the Custom of Paris, the *Quebec Act* largely satisfied the seigneurial elite. The main group dissatisfied with the Act were the British merchants, who were aghast at the lack of provision for habeas corpus, trial by jury in civil matters (the Act backtracked on the recognition of civil juries provided in the 1764 ordinance), and an elected assembly. All three would eventually be granted, however, in 1784, 1785, and 1791 respectively. Canadiens were not necessarily opposed to an assembly but were unwilling to agitate for one until it was clear that they would have the vote in it. Owing to bilingual coverage of current controversies in France, Britain and America in the 1760s and 1770s in the *Quebec Gazette*, literate francophones were able to educate themselves to some extent about the nature of the British constitution and to begin to demand that the rights allegedly secured by it be respected.[19]

The court system under the British underwent numerous revisions in the first half century of British rule, consequent upon the three major constitutional reorderings of the period: the establishment of civil government in 1764, the *Quebec Act* of 1774, and the *Constitutional Act* of 1791.[20] The judicature ordinance of 1764 attempted to establish an

English-style system, with a superior court, the Court of King's Bench, granted province-wide jurisdiction in all civil and criminal matters, and an 'inferior' court, the Court of Common Pleas, with jurisdiction over civil claims below 10 pounds. While the former was to judge according to English law and any provincial ordinances, the latter was to decide according to 'equity in taking account of English law.' The latter court was expected to be the main resort of the Canadiens, and the reference to 'equity' seems to have been an invitation to its judges to take account of French laws and customs, which indeed they did. The Court of King's Bench had a single legally trained judge, who held set terms at Quebec and terms as needed at Montreal; its first chief justice, William Hey, was an English barrister not fluent in French who was obliged to work with an interpreter. Initially a single Court of Common Pleas was created, but in 1770 two independent courts were established at Quebec and Montreal. Their judges were not legally trained, but most were bilingual. A Court of Appeals composed of the governor in council was added in 1773, to hear appeals in civil matters over 10 pounds sterling – a much lower limit than in the English colonies – and appeals from it to the king in council could be had in matters over 500 pounds.

The ordinance of 1764 also introduced the jury into Quebec, for both civil and criminal matters. The old English usage of the jury *de medietate linguae*, whereby a non-English speaker could request a jury in which half the members spoke his or her language, was pressed into service in this new context, while a supplementary ordinance of 1766 clarified its application: juries adjudicating disputes between 'old subjects' would comprise only English-speakers; between 'new subjects,' only French-speakers; and mixed cases would be heard before a mixed jury. Canadiens participated in the new system until juries were discontinued by the *Quebec Act*; they were then reinstituted a decade later.[21] Alongside the jury, an existing institution – arbitration – came to be used much more frequently after 1764 than it had been during the French regime. Whether court-ordered or initiated by the parties themselves (often with a notary as arbitrator), it played a significant role in dispute resolution in the decades after 1764.

The *Quebec Act* abolished the existing courts, then recreated them with reshuffled jurisdictions. The Court of King's Bench was re-established with exclusively criminal jurisdiction, and its civil jurisdiction was given to the reborn Court of Common Pleas. The judges of the latter now had a discretion to hold circuits in their districts, a concession to long-standing complaints about inaccessibility. More far-reaching changes occurred after the *Constitutional Act* of 1791. In 1794 the Court of Common Pleas was abolished and its jurisdiction transferred to the Court of King's Bench, which now possessed all original criminal jurisdiction above the level of the quarter sessions, and all civil jurisdiction, divided between 'superior terms' for matters of over ten pounds, and 'inferior terms' for causes involving lesser amounts. Quebec and Montreal each had its own Court of King's Bench, presided over by a chief justice and three puisne judges. Trois-Rivières also had its own Court of King's Bench, but the sole resident judge there was assisted by judges from either Quebec or Montreal. The King's Bench judges took over the circuits formerly carried out by the judges of Common Pleas, holding annual circuits in each county within their district. The appellate authority of the governor in council remained a constant. With minor changes, the structure of the higher courts remained stable for nearly half a century, until a major restructuring in 1841.[22]

It was at the level of low law that the greatest change took place, at least initially: the 1764 ordinance established the English institution of justice of the peace, unsalaried, untrained magistrates with mainly criminal jurisdiction (their minor civil jurisdiction was abolished in 1770) who replaced the professional judges of the royal jurisdictions of Quebec and Montreal under the French regime. Every three months, benches of three magistrates held quarter sessions at Quebec and Montreal, while petty sessions (known as weekly sessions of the peace) were held every week, and additional special sessions could be held if business warranted. In contrast to England and other colonial jurisdictions, however, where quarter sessions were held at the county level, those in Quebec were held only in the major centres. Even after the creation of judicial districts in the Gaspé (1788) and Trois-Rivières (1790), the size of each of these four districts was enormous. Single justices in the countryside could and did dispense summary justice, but not on any significant scale until the early nineteenth century. In its urban bias and relative inaccessibility, the British regime of criminal justice continued the pattern of its predecessor. Eventually, as a result of increased caseloads and heightened concerns over security in the later years of the Napoleonic Wars, it also reinstituted the professionalization of the French regime. In 1810 Ross Cuthbert was appointed chairman of quarter sessions and inspector of police at Quebec at a salary of 500 pounds sterling. In the same year Jean-Marie Mondelet and Thomas McCord were named joint police magistrates of Montreal, at 250 pounds each, while Thomas Coffin was named to a similar position at Trois-Rivières a year later.[23]

Through trial and error, the government at Quebec established a court structure featuring notable continuities with the French regime, while remaining adaptable enough to respond to new demands of both the French and English population. The continued use of the French language and the naming of some Canadiens as judges, justices of the peace, and court officials, together with the ability of 'new subjects' to serve on juries and to have recourse to arbitration by members of their own community, offered some reassurance to the majority population. Older views declaring that Canadiens boycotted the new English tribunals have been significantly revised by recent scholarship, as will be elaborated on below.[24] For all its shortcomings, the administration of justice in the half-century after the fall of Quebec seems to have presented enough elements of familiarity to permit the juridical acculturation of the Canadien population to the unfamiliar ways of 'British justice,' while also obliging the British population to adapt to Canadien ways in some respects.

Relations with Indigenous Peoples

The situation in Quebec with regard to Indigenous peoples was complex. The Gaspé and the northeast part of the province had been inhabited by the Mi'kmaq and the Innu since time immemorial, as had the Ottawa valley by the Algonquins. However, there were also the mission communities of mostly Christianized Mohawk, Abenaki, and Huron-Wendat who, around the time of the conquest or perhaps before, came together in a loose alliance known as the Seven Fires.[25] The British had negotiated with each of these communities prior to the fall of Montreal, with a view to incorporating them into the Covenant Chain alliance. In spite of their historic ties to the French, the mission communities were prepared to deal with the British in light of their promises that matters would continue as they had been: in essence, that their autonomy would be respected. The transition was accomplished with relatively little difficulty, largely because the British had officials such as William Johnson on the ground who understood the desires and protocols of Indigenous peoples; such was the not the case in Nova Scotia, as will be seen in the next chapter.[26] With regard to the Indigenous populations outside the mission communities, Governor James Murray's instructions required that he observe the provisions of the Royal Proclamation 1763, and on this basis settlers' requests for land in the traditional territories of the Mi'kmaq and Innu were denied in the later 1760s.[27]

However, the government did not believe that the proclamation applied to the Mohawk, Abenaki, and Huron-Wendat in the mission communities. They were considered to have rights only to the lands the French had accorded them, even though some at least arguably had earlier connections with the territory. The Treaty of Oswegatchie, concluded with representatives of the Seven Fires on 30 August 1760, at least as later interpreted by the British, also followed this logic, although the Indigenous parties interpreted it as guaranteeing a broader set of territorial claims.[28]

The *Quebec Act* abrogated the provisions of the royal proclamation relating to civil government within the newly enlarged territory of Quebec but did not refer to native peoples in any way. It does not seem, however, that any change was intended to the legal necessity of securing their consent with regard to dealings in their ancestral lands. This view is confirmed by Governor Carleton's 1775 instructions, which ordered him to forbid settlement in the interior country beyond the limits of existing trading posts, and then in 1786 extended the ban to the entire province:

> 31. You are not to allow any Settlements to be made beyond the Boundaries ascertained to the different Posts among the Indian Nations *within the Limits of Our Province of Quebec in Alliance with Us*, as such Settlements may tend to disgust those Savages, excite their Enmity and perhaps finally destroy the Peltry-Trade which ought to be cherished & encouraged by every Means in your Power.[29]

The process for negotiating with native peoples over land was not laid down explicitly in Carleton's instructions. Article 32 of his 1775 instructions, however, referred to an addendum dealing mainly with the regulation of the fur trade, which nonetheless contained two important clauses relating to land. Section 42 required 'that proper Measures be taken, with the Consent and Concurrence of the Indians, to ascertain and define the precise and exact Boundary and Limits of the Lands, which it may be proper to reserve to them, and where no Settlement whatever shall be allowed'; while section 43 largely tracked the provisions of the Royal Proclamation with regard to land cessions.

Whether these protocols were followed or not depended very much on a calculus weighing strategic imperatives and local pressures. Thus, when it was necessary to settle Loyalists in what would become the new colony of Upper Canada, the government at Quebec rapidly negotiated treaties with the Mississaugas, who inhabited the area between modern-day Toronto and Lake Erie. Conversely, it did not ratify a treaty negotiated in 1786 by the lieutenant governor of the Gaspé and the Mi'kmaq by which the latter would have reserved some land in the Restigouche valley and ceded other lands. In this instance the executive council sought the counsel of François-Xavier Cugnet, an official under the French regime who had become the 'French secretary' (official translator) for the British in 1768 and was commissioned as an advocate by them in 1777. Cugnet advised the executive council that they could do what they wanted as the French had always done so, allocating lands 'with a perfect disregard of any supposed prior title in the Indians.'[30] As noted in chapter 8, this was not an accurate portrayal of the French position.

While there was evidence to support Cugnet's position in legal theory, in practice the French position did not differ substantially from the historic British tradition of voluntary cession and compensation (a practice that could itself be highly problematic, rife with fraud and unethical dealing).[31] It could not have been otherwise in a context where the French relied so heavily on their Indigenous allies. In the end, even though the Gaspé treaty was not ratified, the executive council still decided to give presents to the Mi'kmaq. The government at Quebec did not seek to rely on the supposed French legal position as a universal rule but from the late 1780s became less inclined to negotiate with native peoples east of the Ottawa River. When Carleton, named Lord Dorchester in 1786, became governor general of Upper and Lower Canada in 1791, his commission revoked the instructions provided under earlier mandates. Article 32 was not reproduced in his new instructions of 1791, and the 'addendum' containing the clauses relating to the negotiation of land surrenders with native peoples was neither included nor referred to. However, these provisions were not included in the instructions to Dorchester regarding Upper Canada either (he held separate commissions for each colony), and yet treaty negotiations with native peoples continued to be carried out there, in line with the process laid down in the royal proclamation. It would not be until the 1830s that the government at Quebec devised a new juridical justification for the dispossession of Aboriginal peoples in the province.

13

The British Colonies of Settlement: Political Institutions, Courts, and Relations with Indigenous Peoples

Nova Scotia, New Brunswick, and Prince Edward Island

The cession of Acadia to the British in the Treaty of Utrecht led to a constitutional anomaly. In theory a population of some thousands of Acadians and Mi'kmaq were to be subject to the English government at Annapolis Royal, comprising at most a few hundred soldiers and a minuscule civilian population. There were not even enough civilians (that is, white propertied males) to constitute the council of twelve appointed by Governor Richard Philipps in 1720, and some had to be military men. Philipps's 1719 instructions stated that until he was able to call an assembly, he was to follow those given to the governor of Virginia in 1715, but the two colonies were very different. The Virginia instructions guaranteed fundamental rights such as habeas corpus, speedy trial, jury trial, and the limitation of martial law, but they presupposed an English-speaking population aware of such rights and able to invoke them. The absence of a sufficient number of freeholders meant there could be no assembly (one would not be called until 1758), nor even a proper jury constituted. This in turn meant that no one could be tried for felony. Thus, even when it was fairly clear that a number of Acadians had committed treason by giving aid to French troops attempting to retake the colony during the War of the Austrian Succession, the most the governor could do was declare their lands forfeit.[1]

There were always two views on the future of the Acadians under a British dispensation. Thomas Caulfeild, the lieutenant governor of Annapolis Royal, observed that 'their numbers are considerable and in case they quit us will onlie strengthen our enemys when occasion serves by so much. And though wee may not receive much benefit from them, yett theire children in process of time will be brought to our Constitution.'[2] The Board of Trade was of the opposite view, urging the king in 1721 that 'it is absolutely necessary for your Majesty's service, that these French inhabitants should be removed; for it is not to be expected, that they will ever become good subjects of Your Majesty, & there is all the reason in the world to apprehend, that, upon any rupture between the two Crowns, they may openly declare in favour of France.'[3] Whether the Acadians could be 'brought to our Constitution' depended on the energy, good will, and resources of the government at Annapolis Royal. The first two were not lacking, but the third always was: British control of the territory would remain largely a fiction until the founding of Halifax in 1749. Without the military might to enforce Acadian agreement to take an unconditional oath of allegiance, Governor Philipps was satisfied with a compromise negotiated in 1730. In return for swearing to be 'completely loyal' to 'King George [as] the Sovereign Lord of Nova Scotia and Acadia,' the Acadians were exempted 'from the war against the French and Indians' and promised 'never to take up arms in the event of war against the kingdom of England and its government.'[4] While this result led to a generation of peace, a conditional oath was of dubious legal validity and paved the way for grave difficulties when the security environment shifted in the 1750s.

Philipps commissioned three justices of the peace in 1721 – the first ever named in what is now Canada – and the council constituted itself a Court of Judicature in the same year.[5] The council was the main instrument of government, combining executive, legislative, and judicial functions. Its judicial practice most resembled that of the long-abolished Court of Star Chamber, proceeding as it did upon petition, complaint, or information. It legislated by general orders, in a manner similar to the old Conseil souverain at Quebec. At virtually every point, however, the council had to work within an Acadian framework rather than creating new institutions, presaging the post-1760 adaptations in Quebec. Thus, Acadian notable Prudent Robichaud was named a justice of the peace in 1729, although as a Roman Catholic he should have been forbidden from holding public office; the government also enforced the collection of tithes by the Catholic Church. The institution of notary was left in place, with the council appointing one for each of the main settlements, though Robichaud often acted as attorney in fact for litigants before the council and served as an authoritative source on Acadian custom. Far from abolishing the seigneurial system, the English affirmed it, purchasing the rights of one of the main seigneurs and declaring another forfeit to the Crown when the incumbent died without heirs in 1724.[6] The council wanted to institute a policy of regranting all holdings and allowing no new ones without grant; but grants presupposed surveyors, and one did not arrive until 1732; even after his arrival, little was accomplished.[7]

Perhaps the most significant institution maintained and even enhanced by the new colonial government was the system of deputies that had evolved under the French. The naming of local leaders (sometimes by election, sometimes by a more diffuse process) to negotiate with central authorities was an established feature of life in the provinces of France, and one replicated in Acadia. Philipps rapidly expanded the number of deputies from the six named in 1720 to twenty-four, elected annually.[8] In the absence of an assembly they remained the principal channel of communication between the Acadian communities and government and seem to have played a role in negotiating with the Mi'kmaq as well. The deputies were charged with the endless negotiations over the new oath of allegiance the British wanted the Acadians to take after 1749.

The council probably did the best it could with the limited resources available, and in general it showed a commitment to *audi alteram partem* in its judicial work and to working within the rule of law as it was understood at the time. But when under threat, the regime unquestionably exceeded even the limits of military law on one occasion. During the hostilities with the Mi'kmaq during the 1720s, several Mi'kmaq hostages were held at the fortress of Annapolis Royal. An attack on the fortress led to the killing of a sergeant and a civilian by the Mi'kmaq. As exemplary retribution, a Mi'kmaq hostage was shot and scalped on the spot where the sergeant was killed. Writing in the next century, lawyer-historian Beamish Murdoch called the murder 'a blot on the fair fame of our people,' there being 'no way in which it can on any grounds be justified.'[9]

The hostilities of the 1750s also led to the deportation of the Acadians, which is often seen as a single event but in fact unfolded over the period 1755–63, during which time some 10,000 individuals of the total population of 14,000 Acadians (70 per cent) were removed from their homeland; the rest fled to Canada or went into hiding.[10] Between 6,000 and 7,000 were sent to the British colonies from Massachusetts to Georgia during the first deportations in August and September 1755. A further 3,100 were deported from Île St-Jean to France after the fall of Louisbourg, but about half of them died en route from disease and shipwreck. British soldiers continued to hunt down and imprison those, mostly unarmed, who were in hiding on the mainland, as well as those who had fled up the St John River or to the coast of what would become northeast New Brunswick. Even Prudent Robichaud, the senior Acadian deputy, friend of the British and long-time justice of the peace, by then in his later eighties, was meant to be sent to North Carolina. His ship was commandeered by its deportee passengers and redirected to the St John River, where it was run aground and burned. The mutineers hoped to attain Quebec by land, but the elderly Robichaud did not survive the rigours of the trip.[11]

The status of the Acadian deportation in law is not entirely settled. Certainly under international law, then in its infancy, there was no impediment to the British acting as they did, such that modern discussion of the deportation in terms of genocide or crimes against humanity is, legally speaking, anachronistic. Under domestic law, European monarchs claimed the ability to move their own populations around at will for strategic reasons: several times the deportation of the entire population of Newfoundland was seriously entertained as a matter of imperial policy. The French too used loyalty oaths and deportation (or forced relocation) as tools against the Acadians. In 1746 the French sent a massive fleet under the duc d'Enville (Anville) to recapture Acadia. In the event of success, he was instructed that 'if there are those whose loyalty cannot be counted on, he will send them from the colony, either to old England or to one of its Colonies,' while even those whose loyalty was not in doubt would have to take 'the oath of loyalty to H[is] M[ajesty].'[12] Bad weather and sickness led to the failure of the expedition, but had it succeeded, the Acadians might have found themselves in much the same situation as they did in 1755. In 1750 the French forced some hundreds of Acadians settled at Beaubassin on the east side of the Missaguash (Mésagouèche) River on the Chignecto peninsula to move to the west side, when it was anticipated that the boundary dispute between the English and French in the region was about to be settled, leaving Beaubassin on the 'wrong' side from the French point of view. To prevent any backsliding and to frustrate the British, the Mi'kmaq then burned the entire vacated settlement at the behest of the French authorities. The next year, the governor general of New France, the marquis de la Jonquière, ordered that all Acadians in the Chignecto area who within eight days 'have not taken the oath of fidelity and are not incorporated within the Militia companies which we have created, will be declared rebels to the orders of the King and as such expelled from the lands which they hold.'[13] Neither of these events occurred during wartime, demonstrating that such coercive tools were considered part of the normal repertoire of governance.[14]

The government at Halifax did not wish to portray the deportation of the Acadians as 'business as usual,' however. Rather it sought to justify the action as a penalty legitimately exacted from them for their failure to take the unconditional oath of allegiance. Whether not only deportation but the forfeiture of lands of thousands of subjects was a valid penalty under British law for failure to take the oath may be doubted. Clearly those Acadians who did not take up the Treaty of Utrecht's offer to remove themselves with their moveable property within a year of the treaty's signing were British subjects and hence amenable to British law. There were, admittedly, a number of English and British statutes requiring Catholics to take oaths of allegiance; upon failure to do so, various penalties could be exacted. Governor Lawrence hoped to be able to portray his proposed action as legal and asked the newly appointed chief justice, Jonathan Belcher, for a legal opinion on the validity of the deportation – indeed, this was Belcher's first assignment after his swearing-in in October 1754. His opinion misstates the provisions of the Treaty of Utrecht, relies almost entirely on policy, and cites little law, concluding that 'the French inhabitants may be removed from the Province' for reasons of 'the highest necessity which is *Lex temporis*.'[15] The only statute adverted to in his opinion was the *Security of the Sovereign Act 1714*, which was cited for the proposition that 'persons who are declared recusants if they refuse on a summons to take the Oaths ... can never after such refusal be permitted to take them.'[16] The statute in fact says the opposite, that where anyone convicted as a 'popish recusant' under the statute for refusing to take the oaths 'shall at any Time thereafter take and subscribe the oaths, [such persons] shall be and are hereby, from such Time discharged from such Conviction.'[17]

While section 10 of the Act did authorize any two justices of the peace or any person specially appointed for that purpose to tender the oaths to 'any Person ... whatsoever, whom they shall ... suspect to be dangerous or disaffected to His Majesty or his Government,' the refusal of such a person to take the oath led to a variety of steps that had to be taken before he or she would be considered a 'popish recusant convict.'[18] Even assuming Lawrence was a 'person specially appointed' to tender the oaths, none of the due process required by the Act was observed following the deputies' refusal to take the oath, nor could their refusal collectively engage the guilt of the entire Acadian people, especially women and children.[19] In their zeal to 'seize the moment,' Lawrence and his council were content with a fig leaf of legal justification and proceeded on the basis of raison d'état.

While the Acadian built environment was left essentially intact on Île St-Jean, in Nova Scotia all houses and outbuildings were burned, to signal to the former inhabitants that they should not contemplate returning. These extreme measures amounted to the obliteration of Acadian law along with the disappearance of the Acadians themselves, such that the legal techniques of British colonization, long suspended under the Annapolis Royal regime, could be deployed in earnest: the familiar apparatus of counties, freeholders, justices of the peace, courts applying the common law, lawyers, and juries appeared rapidly in the decade after 1749. Governor Charles Lawrence delayed calling an assembly as long as he could, but upon its establishment in 1758 one of the first laws it passed declared Acadian titles forfeit, opening the way for their lands to be regranted to New England planters in free and common socage.[20]

Pursuant to his instructions, Cornwallis created an inferior court of common pleas staffed with lay judges to handle civil causes at first instance. Appeals could be had from it to the general court, which comprised the governor and his council. The general court also possessed all criminal jurisdiction, including capital cases. But the absence of legal professionals was keenly felt by the colonial government, which persuaded the Board of Trade to appoint Jonathan Belcher, a Massachusetts-born, Irish-trained barrister, as chief justice of the Supreme Court of Nova Scotia in 1754. This court replaced the General Court from that date. It heard all serious criminal cases from which no appeal existed, although application for a royal pardon was possible, and also heard appeals in civil matters from the Inferior Court of Common Pleas. Misdemeanours would be heard by justices of the peace in quarter sessions, where they also heard some minor felonies such as petty larceny.

A decade later two 'assistant judges,' neither legally trained, were named to the Supreme Court. The assembly, which advocated the enlargement of the Supreme Court and paid for the new judges, was motivated by both utilitarian and 'constitutional' concerns. Having three judges would allow the court to sit outside Halifax, bringing justice to the people more conveniently, while the decisions of a court dealing with 'all matters concerning the life, reputation and ... property' of the people 'should not depend solely upon the opinion and judgment of any one man, however capable and upright.'[21] In fact, the court did not begin to go on circuit until 1774, and when it did the change was motivated largely by awareness of the turbulence sweeping the Thirteen Colonies. The solicitor general of the province, James Monk, worried that the inferior courts of common pleas in the counties were becoming theatres for provocative orations on 'Equity, Liberty and Constitutional Justice.' The appearance of the Supreme Court in the county towns would counter this tendency: its judges, men of 'knowledge, Wisdom and attachment to the Crown, [displayed] a degree of dignity and Authority that would overawe, punish and prevent any tumultary meeting' while the court's presence would 'keep the Clamorous and disaffected in quietude, duty, and subordination.'[22]

The separation of powers was not a strong feature of either the British or the colonial constitutions. Chief justices automatically presided over the council, and the assistant judges were often named as councillors; some judges even served as members of the House of Assembly while sitting on the bench, a practice that did not stop until 1834.[23] The judges were key players in colonial governance and administration, expected to provide advice to government, assist in drafting legislation, undertake commissions of inquiry, and use their tact and authority to help resolve the many political disputes that erupted in a fractious colonial society. As newly arrived Chief Justice Robert Thorpe of Prince Edward Island observed in 1803, 'My situation is critical. I have much to do with the Law, the Politics, and the internal arrangement of the Island, with the views, the interest, and the parties; I have much to say and much to detect and prevent: all must be done without any insinuation or partiality.' As noted in chapter 11, Thorpe's unfortunate failure to act on these reflections resulted in his dismissal from the bench of Upper Canada a few years later. Eventually the cumulation of roles provoked some reaction. When Chief Justice Belcher served as administrator of the province for three years in the early 1760s in the absence of the lieutenant governor, London felt that a line had been crossed and prohibited the two offices from being held by the same person in future. This did not apply elsewhere, however, and it was not until the 1820s that the same prohibition was imposed on New Brunswick.[24]

If the judges did 'political' work, the executive also continued to do judicial work, even after the erection of a supreme court. The lieutenant governor and council sat as a Court of Marriage and Divorce in all three Maritime provinces, authorized by statutes of 1758 (Nova Scotia), 1791 (New Brunswick), and 1833 (Prince Edward Island). The same body also sat (except in Prince Edward Island) as a Court of Escheats and Forfeitures, deciding whether Crown grants should be revoked for failure to fulfil a condition. The lieutenant governor in all three provinces sat as chancellor, usually assisted by some of the judges of the Supreme Court. He was also titular head of the probate court, and appointed surrogates in the counties to deal with routine matters of succession to property on death. While the lieutenant governor held the title of vice-admiral, he did not personally exercise the jurisdiction. It was sometimes held by a judge of the Supreme Court, or by a senior lawyer in New Brunswick, but on occasion a judgeship in vice-admiralty was created directly by the Crown, as with the appointment of Dr Alexander Croke to the Nova Scotia vice admiralty court in 1801.[25] The court exercised jurisdiction over seamen's wages, suits arising from maritime collisions, salvage, and murder at sea, although offences arising from alleged acts of piracy were tried by a special court established in each colony under an imperial statute of 1700, upon which the governor or lieutenant governor, councillors, and Supreme Court judges sat.[26] The court also possessed a prize jurisdiction enabling it to order the sale and distribution of the proceeds of ships and their cargo captured during wartime. The fees generated by this process during the American Revolutionary War and the War of 1812 were extremely lucrative for the judge and the court's main official, the advocate general, who prosecuted the claims. In Nova Scotia, where Attorney General Richard John Uniacke Sr held this office, the emoluments enabled him to acquire an 11,000-acre estate and to build there his stately family seat, Mount Uniacke.[27]

The lieutenant governor in council sat as a court of error, hearing appeals from the Supreme Court, but these were rare. Most 'appeals' from trial decisions of the Supreme Court were heard by the court itself. Several times in the year all the judges would meet in the capital to hear appeals from inferior courts and to consider disputed points that had come up before them while sitting as trial judges on circuit.[28] This was referred to as the court sitting *en banc* or *in banco* – that is, as a full bench. Although technically reconsiderations, these were functionally appeals, but the trial judge was not prohibited from participating in the collective reconsideration of his own decision until early in the twentieth century. And not until the mid-twentieth century would a separate 'appellate division' with distinct judges be created to replace the *en banc* process.

The plethora of superior courts dealt with only a small fraction of all the criminal and civil litigation carried on in a given year. A great deal more was dealt with by justices of the peace, whether sitting in a panel in their civil capacity on the inferior court of common pleas, or in general sessions of the peace to deal with all but the most serious criminal matters.[29] JPs out of court also wielded criminal and civil judicial power. Infractions of local regulations were prosecuted before JPs sitting singly or in pairs, sometimes called petty sessions, and those same JPs had jurisdiction over small debts. The justices were also the mainstay of local government, as they were in England. Institutionally they shared this role with the quarter sessions, but in personnel the two institutions were synonymous, because the judges who presided at the latter were the JPs of the area. Sitting as the judges of the quarter sessions, JPs determined what local taxes should be raised and what the money should be spent on. Typical substantial expenditures were local jails and court houses. The sessions also made regulations for jails, markets, and many other things. Out of sessions, JPs carried on much of the administrative work of the county, the principal division of local government. The details of exactly which functions they performed varied slightly from colony to colony because those functions were often designated by local statutes, but in general outline they did the same kinds of things in all colonies. They appointed local officials, inspected jails and courthouses, granted tavern licences, appointed a wide range of local officials, administered oaths to those chosen for local offices, and so on. One particular task, relief of the poor, was confided in Nova Scotia and New Brunswick to overseers of the poor pursuant to legislation modelled on England's Elizabethan poor law.[30] Finally in this wide-ranging litany of powers and duties, as discussed in chapter 16, JPs were central to the pretrial processes where more serious crimes were alleged. They took depositions from complainants, issued arrest warrants, examined and took depositions from those brought in accused of a crime, and committed them to jail to await their trial.

A key official in the administration of justice in all colonies of settlement was the sheriff. In England the position was one of some prestige, reflected in the title 'high sheriff' and the fact that it was a royal appointment. The process of selection and the duties of the sheriff in Nova Scotia were almost identical to those in England, and the other colonies generally followed this pattern. The chief justice compiled a list each year of three individuals qualified to serve by being resident in the county and of sufficient stature, from which the governor chose one. In England the judges also made the list, the king choosing. The term of office was one year, refusal of the appointment brought a fine of fifty pounds, and appointees had to give security for their performance. The duties of the office were multitudinous: the sheriff played an active role in the enforcement of civil judgments, the regulation of elections, and the superintendence of all local regulations. In criminal matters he was responsible for keeping the peace, organizing the pursuit and arrest of offenders, keeping them in custody before trial, attending and maintaining order in the Courts, summoning juries, and last but not least, carrying out the sentence of the Court, be that the collection of a fine, incarceration, or the infliction of corporal or capital punishment.[31] So vast were the sheriff's duties that he often hired deputies to assist him. As with so many other functions in colonial society, however, society was keen to impose duties but not to pay for their performance. The position of sheriff was unsalaried, and although a fairly lucrative table of fees was provided by legislation, there was little prospect of recovering fees from those caught up in the criminal justice part of the sheriff's job.

A wrinkle in the Nova Scotian situation took some time to sort out before conformity with the English model was achieved, and led to grievances that featured in the province's response to the American Revolution. Governor Hopson's 1752 instructions authorized him to appoint a sheriff for Halifax, but he appointed a provost marshal instead. This title was associated with the military police but was sometimes used in a civilian context where the military had extensive roles to play, as in early Halifax. As counties were erected, the provost marshal would sometimes appoint deputies to act for him, but there were no county sheriffs as such. By the 1770s this lack of local services and accountability had given rise to widespread complaints. When the governor responded that his instructions did not permit him to name sheriffs, the assembly responded by passing a law in 1778 to authorize him to do so.[32] Normally the Crown might have resisted this attempt to interfere with the royal prerogative, but given the revolutionary context it was probably felt that it was better to concede the point. The appointment of county sheriffs did not guarantee local accountability; however, the best the assembly could do in this regard was to pass an amendment in 1783 specifying that a sheriff's second term could be vetoed by a majority vote of the county JPs.[33]

The tumultuous events of the 1770s provided Nova Scotians with an opportunity to voice critiques of their Constitution, even as they decided to stay within the empire. An address to the king and both houses of Parliament drafted by the House of Assembly in 1775 acknowledged the supremacy of Parliament (which the southern colonies were unwilling to do), but deplored the concentration of power and cumulation of roles in Nova Scotia's own Constitution. The lieutenant governor and chief justice should never be natives of the colony, the address urged, and judges' commissions should be 'during good behaviour,' as they were in England. Government officials should be prevented from interfering in elections, which should be triennial and fixed by law. This demand occurred during the tenure of Nova Scotia's notorious 'Long Parliament,' when no election was called between 1770 and 1784. Local officials should be accountable locally: too many officials were based in Halifax and acted through deputies in the counties. As just noted, the assembly wanted the office of provost marshal abolished and each county to have its own sheriff; likewise with the registrar of deeds. The prerogative courts also came in for some criticism. Equity cases should be heard by the Supreme Court judges and a jury. And the Court of Vice Admiralty should be composed of the lieutenant governor, council, and Supreme Court justices.[34]

Even as the assemblymen of Nova Scotia expressed a willingness to remain under the British Constitution, they demonstrated their expectation that its content would be negotiated with them and that the rights they understood they possessed would be respected. These rights were not 'natural' or 'inherent': they flowed from the particular history of the British people and might be abridged, given the supremacy of Parliament. But that did not mean these men saw themselves as powerless. They were willing to shoulder their fair share of burdens for the greater good but expected to be able to negotiate their content.

This attitude was most evident in the battles over naval impressment that began during the Seven Years' War and endured until the end of the War of 1812. When Governor Charles Lawrence advertised in New England in 1758–9 for settlers to come to the vacated Acadian lands, he sparked interest in Connecticut, Massachusetts, and Rhode Island. Their delegates negotiated the conditions of the move, a key demand being an exemption from impressment for ten years. The exemption was granted but had expired by the time of the American Revolution, when the impressment issue flared up again. In 1775 the assembly asked, unsuccessfully, for a complete ban on impressment, but Vice

Admiral Samuel Graves agreed to exempt all Nova Scotian 'residents.' Press gangs nonetheless tried to claim transients who could not prove local 'residency,' causing popular unrest 'attended with Quarrels and Bloodshed and the loss of Life.'[35]

When the demand for sailors rose again during the wars against revolutionary France, the colonial government, backed up by the courts, managed to insulate Nova Scotians almost entirely from impressment. The naval authorities agreed not to press on land without approval of the council, which granted permission about once a year between 1793 and 1805, and only under strict conditions, including magisterial supervision. When these conditions were not respected in 1805, a riot ensued in Halifax in which one person was killed. No more warrants permitting impressment were issued until the War of 1812, and then only two. In effect, 'popular resistance combined with merchant hostility and government resolve to ban press gangs from Halifax for most of the Napoleonic Wars.'[36] The story was much the same in Lower Canada, where an informal policy spared French Canadians from impressment; while in Newfoundland, where civilians attacked and killed a naval officer in 1794 and released the two men he had impressed, pressing on shore was thereafter prohibited. There is perhaps no better example of the limits to imperial power in a 'negotiated empire' endowed with the institutions of settler societies.

St John's Island, while following the Nova Scotia model of a constitution contained in the governor's instructions when it was separated from the mainland colony in 1769, differed from all other British possessions in North America as a result of its pattern of landholding. The imperial government, having deported most of the Acadians and ignoring the Mi'kmaq, decided to divide up the island among a select group of landowners and delegate to them the task of finding British settlers, similar to the 'undertaker' system used in Ulster in the previous century. The island was surveyed into sixty-seven lots of 20,000 acres each. One was reserved for the Crown, and the remaining sixty-six were distributed by lottery in 1767, three to the officers of a storied Scottish regiment, and the rest to ninety-eight individuals comprising 'high-ranking colonial administrators and military officers, members of Parliament, intimates of the establishment, merchants, and entrepreneurs.'[37] Each proprietor would be obliged to find one Protestant settler for every 200 acres within ten years, and pay quit rents to the Crown to fund the colony's administration. Proprietorial resistance to paying the quit rents led to an impoverished administration and the necessity of a £3,000 annual parliamentary grant starting in 1777.[38]

The island's small size also necessitated other adjustments. The whole island constituted a single county, and the Supreme Court consisted of a single paid judge from the appointment of John Duport (1770–4) until 1848, although at times a second unsalaried judge also served. The small population rendered unnecessary a lower civil court, such as the inferior court of common pleas in the mainland colonies. Nor were there general sessions of the peace for lesser criminal offences, although justices of the peace did have jurisdiction over petty breaches of the peace and over debts under five pounds. A local observer, reflecting on consequences of these arrangements, complained in 1820,

> We see the Chief Justice ... now trying a murder, then an appeal from an eighteen-penny summons, now the right to a Township, or a ship, now a slap in the face, now engaged with a mandamus, now reading the Lumber Act, now partitioning a proprietor's estate, now choosing a constable.[39]

In spite of the seemingly obvious need for the occupant of such a position to possess a wide knowledge of the common law, for most of the period from 1769 to 1824 the chief justice was either not trained in English law or not legally trained at all. This made the governor's role as chancellor even more crucial, leading to continuing upheaval and accusations of partisanship and improper behaviour. Not until a former New Brunswick Supreme Court judge was appointed as chief justice in 1828 did the island finally enter a calmer period in its judicial affairs.[40]

The arrival of the Loyalists in 1783–4 led to a further dismemberment of 'greater Nova Scotia,' as two new provinces were carved out of it in 1784: Cape Breton Island and New Brunswick. The nascent Loyalist colony of New Ireland, occupying an area in what is now Maine between the Penobscot and St Croix Rivers, was ceded to the new republic in 1783.[41] Many of its inhabitants migrated to the British side of the St Croix, while some 10,000 Loyalists from New York arrived to settle the valley of the St John River and the future city of Saint John. Both the Loyalists themselves and the authorities in London, for their own reasons, agreed that the establishment of a separate colony was called for.[42] The imperial government would have preferred to give New Brunswick the kind of constitution it envisaged for New Ireland, where a land-owning aristocracy would have been the dominant force in government, but a virtual revolt by less-favoured Loyalists caused this plan to be shelved;

it would be partially resurrected for the Canadas in 1791.[43] Both Cape Breton and New Brunswick would receive standard governor's commission-and-instructions constitutions.

New Brunswick had a 'mushroom'-type governmental and judicial establishment: unlike in other colonies, which started off with a small legislature and perhaps a sole superior court judge, the colonial authorities seem to have believed in the axiom 'If you build it they will come.' In this case 'they' took their time in arriving. The Supreme Court of New Brunswick started off with four judges, Chief Justice George Duncan Ludlow having been a judge on the Supreme Court of New York; a fifth would not be added for seven decades, until 1854. The legislature began with twenty-six members, and it took another forty years before any more seats needed to be added. The size of the Supreme Court seemed even more top-heavy after a statute of 1802 gave jurisdiction in civil claims of up to twenty pounds to the inferior court of common pleas, while allowing a single JP to adjudicate claims of up to five pounds, limits said to encompass 95 per cent of all litigation.[44]

Both the optimism with which the province began and its demographic stagnation after 1790 owed much to British policy. In 1783, after flirting with the idea of free trade, the British government decided to maintain the *Navigation Act* system, ensuring that the trade with the British possessions in the West Indies would need to be carried in British vessels. The Maritime colonies were well placed to service these needs and did so for generations.[45] This good news was followed by very bad news indeed. In 1790 London instructed its British North American governors to refrain from further free grants of land and did not lift this fiat until 1807. This policy, which arrived 'like a bolt from the blue,' was influenced by the U.S. example of charging a dollar an acre for lands granted in the western territories. Dorchester refused to apply it in Canada, and in Nova Scotia most of the good lands had already been granted.[46] In New Brunswick, where the instruction was followed, the prohibition created a disincentive to invest in clearing land when title could not be guaranteed, leading to widespread squatting, outmigration, and economic decline until the rise of the timber trade during the Napoleonic Wars.

Aside from the courts, religion was seen as the second major bulwark of social order, with Protestantism, preferably Anglicanism, seen as a valuable proxy for loyalty. These views translated into legal advantages for Anglicans, disabilities for Catholics and those of other faiths, and some disadvantages for dissenting Protestants,[47] although the last were guaranteed full liberty of conscience and worship by Governor Lawrence's proclamation of 1759. Thus the Anglican Church was established at the first session of the Nova Scotia Assembly in 1758, while another law obliged Catholic priests to leave the colony; following the English penal laws, Catholics were forbidden to take property except by Crown grant and forfeited to the Crown any property they might inherit. By executive decree, Catholics were forbidden from exercising the franchise. As more Catholics arrived in the province, these disabilities were removed without undue struggle: a 1783 statute removed disabilities on landholding and inheritance and permitted the return of priests, while the franchise was extended to Catholics in Nova Scotia's first electoral law in 1789. New Brunswick inherited the 1783 law when it became a separate colony, and Prince Edward Island passed a similar statute in 1786, but the franchise was more jealously guarded. New Brunswick waited until 1810 to follow Nova Scotia's lead, while Prince Edward Island, with by far the largest Catholic population, had to be forced by the imperial government to extend the franchise to Catholics in 1829 upon the adoption of Catholic relief in Britain. In all three colonies, admission to the bar and to membership in the assembly was precluded by the necessity of taking anti-Catholic oaths until laws altering the oaths were passed in 1830.[48]

The legal establishment of Anglicanism in the Maritimes did not always carry the desired impact, because of the relatively low numbers of Anglicans compared to those of other denominations. Even the creation of the first bishopric in British North America with the appointment of Charles Inglis as bishop of Nova Scotia in 1787 did not greatly alter this situation.[49] The Committee for Trade and Plantations was careful to deprive the office of the temporal powers associated with bishops in England, restricting the bishop's duties to ordination and supervision of the clergy and confirmation of the laity. Thus matters such as the granting of marriage licences and probate of wills were reserved for the lieutenant governor. Insofar as the privileges afforded Anglicans caused resentment among members of other denominations, Bishop Inglis found establishment 'rather injurious than serviceable to the Church.'[50] In practice, some Anglican privileges were ignored or invasions thereof condoned or even aided by the governor and local assemblies: non-Anglican ministers and Catholic priests were suffered to conduct marriages, dissenting congregations sometimes secured glebe lands, and individual non-Anglican clergy occasionally received governmental stipends. When the Nova Scotia Assembly was asked to provide financial assistance to Anglican clergy in 1811, however, it refused unanimously.[51] Religious diversity in British North America ensured that the exclusionary nature of a state church would not long be tolerated in more than a nominal fashion.

Relations with the Mi'kmaq and the Wulstukwiuk, who inhabited the St John River valley that would become part of New Brunswick as of 1784, remained difficult over the eighteenth century, in spite of a number of treaties signed between them and the British. After the Treaty of Utrecht, the British expected the Mi'kmaq to behave like a subject people, tried to treat them as a single entity when they formed a collection of seven regional groupings, and had no officials who could serve as intermediaries or knew anything about Mi'kmaw traditions.[52] The Mi'kmaq had expressed a willingness to treat with the British, but the Board of Trade provided no guidance to the government at Annapolis Royal; nor were any presents forthcoming from Britain to cement a new relationship until 1722, by which point hostilities had broken out. Ultimately a treaty was signed in Boston in 1725 with all four Indigenous groups inhabiting the Bay of Fundy area: the Abenaki, Passamaquoddy, Wulstukwiuk and Mi'kmaq; the Mi'kmaq adhered to it separately in 1726 after a meeting at Annapolis Royal.[53]

The treaty should have completed the unfinished business of the Treaty of Utrecht, which had ignored the existence of the native peoples of the region, but it gave rise to its own difficulties: there were crucial ambiguities in the English wording, and the understandings conveyed orally to the Mi'kmaq did not necessarily coincide with the written terms. Article 2 said that the Mi'kmaq signatories recognized King George's 'Jurisdiction and Dominion' over Nova Scotia as its 'Rightfull Possessor,' and made their 'Submission to His said Majesty in as Ample a Manner as wee have formerly done to the Most Christian King of France.' Article 3 obliged them not to molest the British 'in their Settlements already made or Lawfully to be made,' while the British in turn agreed that the 'Indians shall not be molested in their persons, Hunting, Fishing and Planting Grounds nor any other their Lawfull Occasions.' Article 6 specified that in disputes 'between the English and the Indians no private revenge shall be taken, but Application shall be made for redress according to His Majesty's Laws,' leaving Mi'kmaw law to govern intra-communal matters.[54]

The treaty appeared to be a mixture of British law, Mi'kmaw law, and British (mis)understandings of the customary law governing French-Mi'kmaq relations, but it left crucial questions of authority and territory unclear. The British understood the 'submission' language to constitute recognition of a hierarchical, subject relationship between the monarch and the Mi'kmaq, but their relationship with the king of France had been one of alliance, not submission. As noted in the previous part of this volume, by the 1670s the French had stopped insisting that even Christianized Amerindians were 'subjects'; the king's paternal role as 'Onontio' was not understood in political terms. The thrust of the agreement was that the British would recognize the Mi'kmaq as 'a political and legal entity that existed independently of the colonial and imperial order.'[55]

On the surface, the provisions regarding territory looked reasonably clear: the Mi'kmaq would not molest the British or Acadians in their 'settlements,' while the British would respect the 'Hunting, Fishing and Planting Grounds' of the Mi'kmaq, suggesting a recognition of Mi'kmaw land tenure outside areas of European settlement. But the treaty did not provide any way of determining how this fluid frontier could be determined; in particular, what was meant by settlements 'Lawfully to be made' remained unclear – 'lawful' according to whose law? Did the Mi'kmaq have to consent, or at least be consulted, before new settlements were made?

So long as no new British settlers were forthcoming, the treaty's lack of clarity on territory posed no major problem. But from 1749 on, matters took a different turn. New settlements at Halifax and Lunenburg were established without notice to the Mi'kmaq, even though there was an existing Mi'kmaw settlement, Mirligueche, at the latter site. Violent resistance ensued, resulting in the killing of some settlers, followed by British rewards for the killing or making prisoners of Mi'kmaq, including the notorious proclamation of Governor Edward Cornwallis offering 'ten guineas for each Indian, living or dead, or his scalp.'[56] Cornwallis proposed to 'root [the Mi'kmaq] out of the [Halifax] peninsula decisively and forever,' but the Board of Trade dissuaded him from doing so.[57] A 1752 treaty, which recapitulated the 1726 treaty and added some new clauses, was ratified only by Mi'kmaw communities at Shubenacadie, Cape Sable, and La Hève. In the final phase of the French-English struggles in the Seven Years' War, the Mi'kmaq supported the French at Louisbourg and Fort Beauséjour and engaged in all-out war with the British.

After the fall of Louisbourg and Quebec, the colonial government entered into another round of treaty-making with the Wulstukwiuk, Passamaquoddy, and Mi'kmaq peoples in an effort to make the province safe for European settlers. Even with the loss of their ally France, the Indigenous peoples were still considered enough of a threat that the colonial government negotiated with them rather than imposing terms as on a defeated enemy, returning to the 1726 treaty as a framework for their relationship. A 1760 treaty with the Wulstukwiuk contained the 1726 treaty word for word, but those entered into with nine Mi'kmaq communities in 1760–1 did not. Nonetheless, in their first six clauses they dealt with the same issues as the 1726 treaty in the same order and should probably be understood as incorporating it. However, the British commitment to respect Mi'kmaq hunting grounds was undercut by a small but critical change in wording. Whereas the 1726 treaty referred to British settlements 'Lawfully to be made,' the 1760 treaty obliged the Mi'kmaq and Wulstukwiuk not to 'molest any of His Majesty's Subjects or their dependants in their settlements as already made, *or to be hereafter made*.' In effect, this gave a blank cheque to the colonial government to create settlements wherever it wanted. Already in 1768 the Mi'kmaq were complaining about settlements outside the traditional Acadian territories, suggesting they saw this as a violation of the treaty relationship.[58] While the Nova Scotia government acted in accordance with the Royal Proclamation of 1763 at least some of the time, the government of New Brunswick seemed not to know of it. Large tracts of land were allocated in theory to certain Indigenous groups in the Loyalist colony, but only one resulted in written documentation, a licence of occupation for the Eel Ground Reserve in 1789; the size of the others was cut down by 90 per cent as the settlement frontier advanced.[59]

As in Quebec, the absence of any clear line of demarcation between Indigenous and European zones permitted constant encroachment on Mi'kmaw hunting and fishing territories. With the arrival of the Loyalists in 1783, the Mi'kmaq faced serious competition for land and sustenance: in 1794 they lamented in a petition to Lieutenant Governor John Wentworth that there was nowhere to hunt any more.[60] Indeed, the exports of furs from Nova Scotia increased dramatically after 1783, suggesting widespread hunting and trapping by some Loyalists.[61] Thomas Chandler Haliburton reported that the latter engaged in an extraordinary slaughter of moose 'merely for their hides,' an activity that imperilled one of the principal food sources of the Mi'kmaq and led to stringent regulations in the nineteenth century. The environmental degradation unleashed by the Loyalists was already recognized in 1794, when the assembly was obliged to pass an Act creating a closed season for partridges and blue-winged ducks. This Act, like one in 1816 aimed at protecting snipes and woodcocks, excluded 'any Indian, or other poor settler' who killed a bird for their own use during the season, implicitly recognizing the extent to which competition from settlers had jeopardized the Mi'kmaw way of life.[62] The inauguration of a system of reserved lands in 1820 was a belated attempt to address this dire situation but, as with the Black Loyalists two generations earlier, the lands reserved were small in area and of poor quality for agriculture.[63]

Upper Canada

The end of the Revolutionary War saw the old province of Quebec shorn of its territory south of the Great Lakes, but it still contained the vast triangle of land between Montreal, Georgian Bay, and Detroit, the homeland of Anishnaabe, Odawa, Nipissing, Mississauga, and other native peoples. This western extension of Quebec bore a strong physical resemblance to the original Laurentian colony, with European settlement eventually occupying a narrow strip of land along the upper St Lawrence and the shores of Lake Ontario and Lake Erie. As some 6,000 Loyalists relocated to this area after 1783, they encountered civil law institutions such as seigneurial tenure with which they were not enamoured and almost immediately began to petition the authorities for the adoption of familiar English-style laws and institutions.

First, however, treaties had to be negotiated with the existing Indigenous inhabitants; and second, the particular issue of finding land for the Crown's loyal Haudenosaunee allies who did not wish to remain in the new republic had to be addressed. In a burst of treaty-making activity in 1783–4, the British entered into treaties with the Mississauga covering most of the expanse from the confluence of the Ottawa and St Lawrence Rivers west to the Niagara Peninsula and Long Point on Lake Erie. Further treaties with them and other peoples followed in the 1780s and 1790s, and in 1805–6, extending the area in question to Lake St Clair and also covering a tract north of Lake Simcoe. Most of these treaties dealt with an area only two or three townships inland from the water and would be followed by later treaties dealing with the interior in 1818–20. They mostly followed the procedures laid down in the Royal Proclamation of 1763, but produced results that seem highly one-sided to modern eyes, an imbalance explained by three factors: need, misunderstanding, and population decline. The Mississauga had become dependent on European trade goods and were attracted by British promises of presents in perpetuity. Moreover, they understood themselves as sharing or renting their lands, as opposed to ceding them forever, in return for these 'gifts.' Finally, their reduced population meant they had lost considerable bargaining power and military might.[64] Great stretches of land were given up for trade goods and one-time money payments, often with no land reserved and no hunting rights over ceded land expressly mentioned in the documents.

By the mid-1790s the new settlers were threatening the former inhabitants with trespass and desecrating grave sites, leading the Mississauga to realize the implications of their dealings with the British. Their discontent came to a head in 1796 with the murder of Wabakinine, head chief of all the Credit River Mississauga, and a strong ally of the British. The chief was injured in an alcohol-fuelled melee with some soldiers who were seeking sex with his sister, and he soon died of his injuries. The soldier who had killed Wabakinine was charged but released for lack of evidence, leading the Mississauga to consider declaring war to get satisfaction. They sought out the aid of the Six Nations, but the threat of a general Indigenous uprising was averted, much to the relief of the authorities in the poorly defended capital at York.[65]

The treaties themselves are a curious amalgam of Indigenous protocols and English conveyancing practice. Negotiator Captain W.R. Crawford reported to Governor Haldimand in 1783 that at the conclusion of negotiations with the Mississauga 'a large one [wampum belt] was Delivered to the other Chiefs concerned in the Sale, with the usual ceremonys to be kept in the nation [as] a memorial to their Children that they may know what their Fathers had done at this Time.'[66] A 1784 treaty covering part of the Niagara Peninsula was stated to be entered into by Wabakinine and nine other named individuals described as 'Sachems and War Chiefs and Principal Women of the Messissague [*sic*] Indian Nation,' expressly recognizing the important political role of matriarchs in some Indigenous cultures. Yet the treaties were drafted in legal language appropriate to the grant of a cottage in the Cotswolds: they recited that the Mississauga leaders 'did grant, bargain, sell, alien, release and confirm unto His said Majesty His Heirs and Successors' the tract in question, 'to have and to hold unto our Sovereign Lord the King, His Heirs and Successors forever.'[67] In 1790 the chiefs of the 'Ottawa, Chippawa, Pottawotamy and Huron Indians [*sic*] Nations of Detroit' were said to grant to the Crown a tract of land near Lake St Clair with 'all and singular the appurtenances ... belonging or in anywise appertaining, and the reversion and reversions, remainder and remainders, rents and services of the said premises, and all the estate, right, title and interest, property, claim or demand whatsoever of us the said Chiefs.'[68] The Amerindian peoples not having any concepts analogous to those found in the common law of real property, the use of this boilerplate language from English conveyancing practice leads inevitably to questions about how well these treaties reflected the intentions of the Indigenous adherents.

The influx into the lower Great Lakes included not just European Loyalists but also the Haudenosaunee who had fought alongside the British in the Revolutionary War and retreated to British territory thereafter. They were not represented at the Treaty of Paris negotiations, with predictable results. Just as the French had purported to cede Mi'kmaq territory to the British in the Treaty of Utrecht, the British purported to surrender their homeland in the former colony of New York to the new republic. Allan Maclean, superintendent of Indian affairs at Niagara, advised the governor of Quebec of the disbelief of the Six Nations: 'The Indians ... told me they never could believe that our King could pretend to Cede to America What was not his own to give, or that the Americans would accept from Him, What he had no right to grant.'[69] The Haudenosaunee had been promised compensation in case they suffered losses in the war, and regarded a grant of territory to them as the British fulfilling their part of the bargain. While the British probably regarded this promise as growing out of the immediate concerns of the 1770s, the Haudenosaunee likely saw it as part of the Covenant Chain going back to the Treaty of Albany in 1664, renewed in 1701.[70] The compensation took the form of the so-called Haldimand Tract, a substantial area along the Grand River where about 2,000 refugees settled in the mid-1780s. These included members of the 'dependent nations' of Tuteloes, Nanticokes, and Delawares, as well as the Six Nations; the former participated in the proceedings of the re-established confederacy council through their 'hosts,' the Oneida and Cayuga.[71]

It was not entirely clear whether the Mississauga had a claim to the Grand River area, but out of an excess of caution Haldimand entered into a treaty with them in order to provide 'clear title' to the Haudenosaunee. The land was fertile and promising, and the Crown's Indigenous allies were initially treated much better than the Black Loyalists of Nova Scotia, who were allotted substandard land and left with little assistance in the resettlement process. However, it soon transpired that the title of the Haudenosaunee was anything but 'clear.' The first problem related to the extent of the territory conceded: Haldimand's October 1784 proclamation allotted lands 'Six Miles deep from each Side of the [Grand] River beginning at Lake Erie, & extending in that Proportion to the Head of the said River, which them & their Posterity are to enjoy for ever.' A subsequent survey showed the grant as covering only the lower two-thirds of the Grand River valley, and that is all that John Graves Simcoe was prepared to confirm in 1793. Yet, when the Mississauga later surrendered their claims to the upper third to the Crown, the lands were granted to white squatters rather than to the Six Nations.[72]

A more intractable problem was the nature of the interest in the Grand River lands created by the Haldimand Proclamation. The Haudenosaunee assumed that they possessed a freely marketable interest, as they had had in New York, where they regularly leased and sold parcels of land with council approval but without the intervention of the Crown. Through their main interlocutor, Joseph Brant, they also asserted the same right of disposition as non-Indigenous Loyalists. Various technical arguments would be made against the validity of the Haldimand Proclamation under common law doctrines later in the nineteenth century. More immediately, Simcoe denied that the council could lease or alienate any lands without the intervention of the Crown, a matter they found frustrating, insulting, and contrary to their own laws. Further problems arose from squatting by settlers, and conveyances by individual Haudenosaunee to settlers not approved by the Confederacy Council; the latter lacked effective enforcement mechanisms to deal with recalcitrant settlers, relying on the often unreliable Department of Indian Affairs to do so. It could try to 'name and shame' individual Haudenosaunee who sold land to settlers, but once the transaction was completed it was very difficult to eject a settler in possession.

Well before the division of the Canadas in 1791 and the establishment of a new colonial assembly and government at Newark in Niagara (the capital moved to York, later renamed Toronto, in 1796), the courts were the institution most immediately needed by the new population. Colonial assemblies sat at most for a few weeks a year, while travel to and from the capital was difficult before the construction of adequate roads. The courts were the most visible emanation of the colonial state and the most crucial institution for the functioning of the local economy. They needed to be decentralized and accessible to the people. Not surprisingly, as the area was at first under the jurisdiction of Quebec, the Quebec pattern of courts was followed.[73]

Four districts were established in 1788, later renamed the Eastern, Midland, Home, and Western Districts, travelling westward from Montreal to Detroit, each endowed with a court of quarter sessions and a court of common pleas. The former was responsible for local government and criminal matters, while the latter had unlimited civil jurisdiction. All the judges were laymen except for the Western District, where a salaried professional, Loyalist William Dummer Powell, was appointed. Three judges were appointed to the common pleas in each district; one was to preside over a summary court for small claims of ten pounds or less, while at least two were to be present for larger claims. Provision was made for each court to make circuits within its district, but at least within the Midland district this did not happen, making the court less accessible than it might have been. The common pleas courts did, however, use a simplified English procedure, met weekly, and kept costs low. Appeals to the provincial executive in matters over ten pounds were in theory available if one wanted to travel to Quebec before 1792, or Newark as of 1793; but such appeals were impractical and almost never pursued. These courts were staffed mostly by North American–born mercantile men, familiar with local mores.[74]

Great change lay in store when the new government of Upper Canada, headed by Lieutenant Governor John Graves Simcoe, arrived in 1792. Simcoe, his friend Chief Justice William Osgoode, and other British officials disliked the decentralized Quebec system and wanted to replace it with a centralized court structure headed by salaried professionals. They got their wish with the *Judicature Act* of 1794, drafted by Osgoode, which abolished the courts of common pleas and replaced them with a two-tier edifice: district courts with jurisdiction in claims between 40 shillings and 15 pounds in value, and a new superior Court of King's Bench at York, staffed with three salaried judges appointed from the ranks of English barristers, with jurisdiction in civil cases over 15 pounds and in serious criminal cases. These it heard during its annual assize in the capital of each district. Appeals in matters over 100 pounds were heard by a 'court of appeal' which was in reality the executive council, presided over by either the lieutenant governor or the chief justice; an independent court of appeal composed exclusively of professional judges would not be created until 1849. A further appeal to the king in council was possible in cases above 500 pounds.

These heights of the judicial superstructure were rarely reached. As in the Maritimes, most judicial work took place in the district courts, composed of the justices of the peace of each of the four districts, who sat in quarter sessions for the hearing of criminal trials and carrying out their administrative duties, and also heard civil cases quarterly prior to holding the general sessions of the peace. At the bottom of the court hierarchy were the courts of requests, with jurisdiction over small claims of up to 40 shillings. These were the courts closest to the people and attracting the largest volume of litigation. The justices of the district presided as commissioners over these courts; in sessions they could create divisions within each district in which a court of requests could be held, and in this way could be responsive to the ebbs and flows of population rather than remaining confined to predetermined boundaries. This flexibility on paper was not always matched in reality: justices sometimes did not show up at the appointed times or places, given the inconvenience of travel and the slight remuneration. Nonetheless, the courts of requests were emblematic of the efforts of the colonial administration to provide access to justice to even the humblest households.[75] Access to poor relief was a different matter. For reasons still unclear, Upper Canada's reception statute specifically forbade the introduction of the English poor laws, although various measures official and unofficial were gradually developed to fulfil this lacuna.[76]

The naming of English judges with English predilections and loyalties to the highest court in Upper Canada led to a variety of conflicts with North American–born lawyers, who were used to local adaptations of English law and not keen to have the entire panoply of English institutions and practices introduced. These interactions had a marked impact on the shaping of the colony's institutions and legal culture, as seen by contrasting the respective experiences of Upper Canada and New Brunswick. Both were founded as Loyalist colonies in the wake of the American Revolution, and one might therefore have expected their legal institutions and cultures to be similar. Broadly speaking, they certainly were, but the English presence left its mark in Upper Canada in a much stronger way than in New Brunswick. In large part this was due to the continued presence of English appointees on the bench of Upper Canada, as opposed to the appointment of North Americans in New Brunswick and in the Maritimes more generally. It would be nearly twenty-five years before Upper Canada would have its first Loyalist chief justice (William Dummer Powell, in 1816), while all the judges in New Brunswick were Loyalists from the outset. So too were all of the governor's advisers, to whom the first lieutenant governor, Thomas Carleton, usually deferred. In Nova Scotia, too, Belcher was North American, albeit British-trained, and so were the assistant judges. While his successors as chief justice over the next two decades were English or Irish, the Loyalist Sampson Salter Blowers assumed the post in 1797, and thereafter all the judges were 'locals.'[77] At a time when chief justices presided over a colony's legislative council and often drafted important legislation, their influence on a fledgling colonial legal order could be profound. Thus, in matters related to the legal profession, divorce, equity courts, and procedure, among others, New Brunswick in particular and the Maritimes in general leaned more to colonial American traditions than to English ways. In spite of the shared founding moment between Upper Canada and New Brunswick, the latter's legal culture would remain part of a Maritime legal culture influenced by New England, rather than being brought within Upper Canada's more English-inflected orbit.

14

The British Commercial Territories: Newfoundland and Rupert's Land

Justice beyond the Settlement Frontier: The Challenge of Remoteness

While fish and furs have long been considered together by economic historians as part of the 'staples thesis' of Canadian history, in legal and political history the two territories producing these commodities have traditionally been treated in isolation from one another.[1] It will be useful to consider first the ways in which Newfoundland and Rupert's Land posed similar challenges of law and governance before examining each of them separately. In both these territories the exploitation of a single resource, fish or furs respectively, drove European interest in the area. In both, settlement was long discouraged, albeit eventually tolerated, and small European populations were widely scattered over a large land mass. In both, the nature of the resource determined the nature of the relations between Europeans and Indigenous peoples – mutual isolation in the case of Newfoundland, where Indigenous partners were not required to exploit the fishery, long cooperation in Rupert's Land, where Indigenous participation was crucial to the fur trade. And in both societies seventeenth-century legal choices about the economic parameters within which each of these resources would be exploited directed their development over the following century and beyond. Newfoundland was shaped by the demands of British mercantile adventurers for free trade, safeguarded by King William's Act of 1699, while Rupert's

Land was subject to the Hudson's Bay Company's (HBC) monopoly on trade granted in its 1670 charter.

In spite of this difference in economic orientation, locals and imperial policymakers in both jurisdictions faced a similar challenge in the administration of justice: overcoming distance. How to maintain order and provide some semblance of a legal infrastructure among the thinly populated and widely scattered outports of Newfoundland? How to maintain the rule of law among Europeans in Rupert's Land, where communications with London occurred only once a year, and the HBC governors were effectively subject to no outside authority? The foundational documents of both possessions remained essentially unaltered, even as the face of both societies changed considerably over the course of the eighteenth century.[2] This fact meant that usage, self-help, and informal modes of ordering became ever more important.

Neither Newfoundland nor Rupert's Land was officially a colony of settlement in the eighteenth century; their status remained somewhat vague, defined more by what they were not than what they were. When the Board of Trade reviewed the current situation in each North American 'plantation' for King George I in 1721, it did not include Newfoundland or Rupert's Land, 'neither of them being a Colony under civil government, or lying contiguous to your Majesty's other Plantations on the continent.'[3] Even in 1789, Home Secretary William Grenville could declare that 'Newfoundland is in no respect a British colony and is never so considered by our laws.'[4] In spite of this imperial ambivalence and various proposals to deport the entire population, by the end of the eighteenth century Newfoundland had become home to a settled population of a size that could not be ignored. Natural increase was long held back by the absence of women: not until after 1790 would women represent more than 14 per cent of the European population, and unlike Rupert's Land, there was no intermarriage between Europeans and the sparse and declining Indigenous population.[5] Immigration created a permanent population of about 12,000 by 1783, a figure that would triple by 1815. Growth was triggered by the imperial wars of the second half of the eighteenth century, which drove the demand for fish as never before, even as they made the migratory fishery more difficult to prosecute. By the end of the century the migratory fishery was virtually extinct, the long dominance of the west country merchants in decline, and the demand for adequate legal institutions to service a settled population on the rise.[6]

In Rupert's Land, settlement long remained anathema to the HBC as incompatible with its principal business, the fur trade. The company had neither the desire nor the means to alter the Indigenous way of life, which resulted in a steady flow of furs to its trading posts and remarkably little conflict between the two groups over long periods of time. Nonetheless, by the early nineteenth century, the HBC had decided to create an agricultural settlement within its own territory. In 1811 it granted to a Scottish peer, Lord Alexander Selkirk, an enormous tract of land (some 300,000 square kilometres) centred on the forks of the Red and the Assiniboine Rivers as the basis for the new district of Assiniboia. The company had decided that such a venture was required as a place of retirement for officers who had spent long periods in its service, as a source of agricultural produce, and also as a bastion against possible American expansionism, while Selkirk was concerned to settle some of the victims of the Highland clearances. Selkirk's concession was more like those of the eighteenth-century Prince Edward Island proprietors than the semi-feudal magnates of the previous century in Newfoundland. The grant conveyed land only, not jurisdiction.[7] Those in the new colony were considered to 'live under' the HBC, in the words of its charter, and were subject to such institutions of judicature as it should set up, while the 'governors' of Assiniboia were company, not royal appointees. The establishment and development of these institutions is more properly treated in the next part of this volume.

In Newfoundland new institutions for the administration of justice in the island's far-flung settlements emerged under the aegis of the royal prerogative long before Parliament authorized the creation of a supreme court in 1791–2. These achieved a measure of success in meeting the challenge of distance, abandoning the idea that transportation to England for trial was an adequate response to local problems of order. In 1729 justices of the peace were appointed for the first time, and they were permanent residents, not seasonal visitors. By 1751 it was accepted that felons could be tried locally and capital punishment administered even without prior approval in London. Meanwhile the Royal Navy began conducting a kind of marine circuit, visiting the outport communities in order to administer justice.

Such an expedient might have been desirable in Rupert's Land, except that the HBC itself did not wish to surrender any of its authority to an outside body. As it was, the HBC charter was not adequate to the task of maintaining order, once the intense rivalry with other fur trading companies reached its apogee in the late eighteenth and early nineteenth centuries. Prior to the fall of Quebec, the HBC's main competition came from its French counterpart, the Compagnie des Indes. Where the HBC occupied only tidewater forts and required Indigenous hunters to bring their furs to them, the voyageurs of the Compagnie des Indes travelled deep into the northern river systems to conduct trade. These techniques secured them a greater part of the fur trade than the HBC while the French regime lasted, but relations between the two companies were nonetheless relatively cordial.[8] After 1760, new Montreal-based companies run by Scots took up where the Compagnie des Indes had left off. The Northwest Company traded in areas beyond the Hudson Bay watershed, in the 'Indian territories' draining into the Pacific and Arctic Oceans, which were beyond the jurisdiction of any British or colonial court. It established posts in the Athabasca watershed, starting with Fort Chipewyan in 1788, in the upper Fraser River valley in 1805–7, in the lower Columbia River valley in the 1810s, and it purchased John Jacob Astor's Pacific Fur Company in 1813. The NWC also challenged the HBC monopoly directly by building trading posts and doing business within Rupert's Land. In response, the HBC began establishing inland posts, beginning with Cumberland House on the Saskatchewan River in 1774; by 1821 it had opened some 240 more.

It was doubtful whether the HBC charter permitted the company to create its own judicature to bring charges against interlopers who threatened its monopoly (clearly, such individuals did not 'live under' the HBC); but even if such power existed, the company did not exercise it. The HBC's directors in London, always conscious of the threat of parliamentary revocation of their charter, were anxious to conduct their business within the four corners of the law, though their Bayside officials could be more cavalier. The directors consulted the law officers of the Crown and London's most eminent counsel on numerous occasions for advice on the interpretation of the HBC charter. While that advice consistently stated that the grant of the soil in the charter was legally sound, opinions were divided, and mostly negative, on the validity of the trade monopoly.[9] It was, paradoxically, the directors' deference to law that drove much of the conflict in Rupert's Land. The directors were reluctant to pursue legal action against interlopers because they feared the company's monopoly would be challenged and invalidated. So long as no court had so ruled, the company had at least a colour of right to assert its monopoly as best it could. Competitors took advantage of this hesitancy, with the result that extra-legal tactics of violence and intimidation became the means to resolve commercial disputes.

Various expedients, to be examined below, were tried, but proved ineffective. Only the merger of the HBC with the Northwest Company in 1821 finally removed the main source of conflict and opened a less turbulent period in the history of Rupert's Land, as new institutions of justice emerged in Assiniboia, albeit still under the aegis of the HBC. Meanwhile the 1825 Royal Charter of Justice in Newfoundland refounded the Supreme Court and spelled out its authority in a way similar to that vested in the superior courts of the other British North American colonies.

Newfoundland

In 1708 the historian John Oldmixon observed casually that in Newfoundland 'there's no need of much Law, for the Inhabitants have not much Land and no Money.'[10] The premise was correct, but the conclusion did not necessarily flow. Observers constantly pointed out the need for institutions to maintain order and resolve disputes, and in the absence of imperial initiative a vernacular legal infrastructure gradually developed.[11] The fishing admiral system, described in the previous part of this volume, along with appeals to the naval commander as instituted by King William's Act, continued as the official judicial apparatus of Newfoundland, but its flaws were many. The admirals' jurisdiction extended only to the fishery, they had none of the powers of a JP, and had no authority over crimes. Those committing felonies, including theft over forty shillings, were to be transported with two witnesses at private expense to England for trial in any county, but the Act did not provide any legal process by which this could be accomplished. A prominent merchant, William Keen, apprehended a suspected murderer in 1720 and another suspected felon in 1728 and sent them with the requisite witnesses to England at his own expense, pointing out to the British government his lack of legal authority and pleading for 'such power and instructions as may keep us from being destroyed.'[12]

Even the limited powers of the fishing admirals were not available during the winter season, when they were absent. And when present, they did not always exercise their jurisdiction, with the result that the commanders of visiting warships tended to act as front-line dispute-settlement officers. As George Larkin, an English lawyer sent out in 1701 to report on colonial policy, observed, 'It hath been customary for the commander in chief upon complaints to send his Lieutenant to the several harbours and coves to decide all differences and disputes that happen betwixt commanders of merchant ships and the inhabitants and planters and betwixt them and their servants.'[13] On a number of occasions in the 1710s the naval commodore held such courts at St John's every two weeks in the fall; he also convoked public meetings of the principal inhabitants of St John's at which various regulations were made 'for better discipline and good order of the people.'[14] In effect, a customary legislature under the aegis of the navy evolved to supply the institutional lacuna in King William's Act.

Unfortunately, naval ships were seldom present for more than the months between August and November. The winter could be a time of disorder, when violence between masters and servants often broke out. In response, the leading men of St John's took matters into their own hands after the departure of the ships in 1723. Fifty-one of them (out of ninety-three 'masters' present in the town) signed a declaration invoking John Locke's *Second Treatise on Government*, whereby they covenanted to 'enter into an Association and embody ourselves into a Community for the mutual Preservation of His Majesty's peace and the PROTECTION OF US AND OURS during the winter, that is until the arrival of the British Fishing Ship in this harbour.'[15] To this end they elected three of their number to hold court; over the winter it dealt with cases of assault and theft, settled property disputes, and disciplined refractory servants. The authors of the document declared that their actions were in no way meant to challenge the king's authority; but with that authority unexercised for so long, they felt obliged to act.

This unusual event, along with other petitions and William Keen's actions, may have finally provoked the Board of Trade into providing for a year-round judicature. In 1728 it recommended that the naval commodore serve as governor during his residence at St John's and be empowered to appoint JPs to hold quarter sessions.[16] Captain Henry Osborne was duly named governor in 1729 and appointed sixteen justices of the peace and thirteen constables in six districts from Placentia to Bonavista; Newfoundland would continue to have 'districts' rather than counties. The office of governor would remain only a seasonal one until 1818, but the officials he appointed would be year-round residents and exercise their authority in all seasons.

That authority did not go unchallenged. King William's Act remained in force until 1824, and the fishing admirals were not keen to see their powers superseded. They sometimes contested the authority of the JPs, alleging that it was grounded in the royal prerogative and could not prevail over their own, based on the Act of 1699. The populace also resisted this new source of authority on occasion, threatening magistrates who made unpopular decisions. William Keen, one of the first magistrates appointed in 1729, was himself murdered in 1754, although in the course of a robbery and not, apparently, as a direct result of his magisterial actions.[17]

More layers of legality were gradually added – a vice admiralty court was created at St John's in 1736 – but the most important changes were carried out by the reforming governor, Captain George Brydges Rodney, appointed in 1749. He solidified the navy's hold over the administration of justice in Newfoundland by creating his own 'governor's court' at St John's, at which he presided personally over both civil and criminal suits, and by appointing surrogates (naval officers) to travel to the island outports. Such forays had happened since the 1680s at least, but on an ad hoc basis; under Rodney the process was formalized, in effect creating a circuit court. This shift marked the end of the independent power of the fishing admirals, who now on occasion sat with the naval officers when they held court, as did the JPs. Although the jurisdiction of the surrogates and the JPs in sessions overlapped, they cooperated with few problems, the sessions tending to come into its own during the winter season when the navy was less active.

Rodney also persuaded the secretary of state to end the system whereby felons had to be transported to England for trial. In 1750 his successor was authorized by Order in Council to hold a court of oyer and terminer for the trial of capital crimes, provided it sat only once a year during the governor's residence, and convicted felons were not to be executed without prior approval of the British government. The next year, even that restriction was lifted. Although the commission was granted to persons without legal training (usually to some of the JPs), the forms of British justice were observed, with a grand jury of twenty-four scrutinizing the indictments and a petit jury of twelve deciding on guilt or innocence. All suspects and witnesses were brought to St John's for trial during the September assizes. The surrogate courts also took on the role of local government along with the magistrates, approving proposals for taxes for local improvements or the support of the poor put forward by ad hoc assemblies of resident notables; the latter functioned as a kind of informal grand jury.

All of these reforms arguably contravened King William's Act, which was mostly re-enacted in Palliser's Act of 1775, but no challenge was taken until 1787 to the legality of these prerogative-based measures. Although naval justice was often criticized by later observers and some historians as arbitrary, more recently it has come to be seen as effective and suitable for the conditions then prevailing on the island. As Jerry Bannister has argued, it provided an authoritative and reliable presence, even in distant outports, administered justice impartially, and kept adequate records, and its costs were absorbed by the navy itself and not levied on the inhabitants.[18] All of this was achieved without recourse to personnel with formal legal training, save that naval officers themselves were conversant at least with the code of the Royal Navy and the customary law administered on board ship to maintain order and deal with infractions.

The edifice of vernacular Newfoundland justice, based as it was on customary practices and creative avoidance of the foundational statutes of 1699 and 1775, was shaken to its foundations when challenged in 1787. In that year Richard Hutchings, a merchant resident in Devonshire, had sued to recover a debt in Ferryland. The civil magistrates ruled against him, as did the naval surrogate. Back in Exeter, Hutchings successfully challenged the authority of the surrogate. Although the reasons for decision are not available, the basis for the ruling was likely the fact that according to King William's Act, naval surrogates could hear appeals only from the fishing admirals, not from magistrates.[19]

With the administration of civil justice potentially in disarray (though the authority of the magistrates themselves was not challenged), the creation of a statutorily authorized court was at last seriously mooted by the British authorities. A *Judicature Act* was passed in 1791 creating a 'Court of Civil Jurisdiction,' and John Reeves, a barrister of the Middle Temple and member of the Royal Society, was named as its chief judge. The Act was to remain in force for a year only, but in 1792 Parliament accepted Reeves's recommendation that a full-fledged Supreme Court, with plenary civil and criminal jurisdiction, be created. The king was to appoint its chief justice (Reeves was the first incumbent), and the governor, with the advice of the chief justice, could institute surrogate courts for civil matters in different parts of the island, thereby insulating Governor Rodney's innovation from further attack. In criminal matters the court was to follow English law, while in civil cases English law 'as far as the same can be applied to suits and complaints' arising in Newfoundland was to be the rule for decision.[20]

There are many parallels between the careers of Reeves and his near-exact contemporary, Chief Justice William Osgoode of Upper and later Lower Canada. Both came from undistinguished parentage, read law and became barristers, were highly conservative in politics and exuberant supporters of the monarchy, became accomplished writers (though Reeves's output left a much greater mark than Osgoode's), spent relatively little time in their judicial posts in British North America before returning to Britain (Osgoode a decade, Reeves only two seasons), and died wealthy bachelors. Their careers illustrate the way in which, for those of obscure social origins, a legal career coupled with the right political ideas could lead to highly prestigious posts in the empire, if not at home.[21]

The 1792 Act too was to be in force for only one year but was renewed annually until 1809, when it was made permanent. In some ways it spoke to continuity – given its formal recognition of the surrogate courts, the influence of the Royal Navy continued much as before, although some civilians began to be appointed as surrogates. But in other ways it represented a break with the past; it recognized only four courts for the trial of civil claims, 'any law, custom or usage to the contrary notwithstanding': the Supreme Court itself, the Court of Vice Admiralty, the surrogate courts, and two justices sitting together. Gone was the governor's court, gone the fishing admirals. The JPs exercised a summary jurisdiction over claims under forty shillings in tort or contract, including claims for seamen's wages, which were taken from their traditional home, the Court of Vice Admiralty. When the chief justice of the Supreme Court was required to reside on the island year-round in 1798, it appeared that the impact of the death of the migratory fishery had finally been absorbed in Whitehall. Although not an agricultural colony, Newfoundland was now effectively recognized as a colony of settlement whose residents deserved a basic level of legal and judicial infrastructure, even if the establishment of the formal institutions of representative government had to await the eve of Victoria's reign.[22]

Rupert's Land

France's abandonment of its territorial claims to Rupert's Land in 1713 did not mean that it withdrew from its trading activities there. The Compagnie des Indes continued to expand its trade networks with Indigenous peoples until the fall of Quebec, but the commercial rivalry between it and the HBC led to remarkably little conflict. Even the European wars of the mid-eighteenth century had little impact in Rupert's Land; the two large trading companies, understanding that war between them was bad for business, worked out a policy of de facto neutrality.[23]

Unlike Newfoundland, where authority was highly dispersed and, at least before Rodney's reforms, it was never quite clear who was in charge, the HBC Charter vested overall legislative authority in the governor and company in London, who were empowered 'to make ordyne and constitute such and soe many reasonable Lawes Constitucions Orders and Ordinances as ... shall seeme necessary and convenient for the good Government of the said Company,' provided they were 'reasonable and not contrary or repugnant but as neare as may bee agreeable to the Lawes Statutes of Customes of this our Realme.' Judicial power resided in the Bayside governors, who were granted the

> power to judge all persons belonging to the said Governor and Company, or that shall live under them in all Causes whether Civil or Criminall, according to the Lawes of this Kingdome and to execute Justice accordingly. And in case [of crimes] where Judicature cannot be executed for want of a Governor and Councill there then in such case itt shall and may bee lawfull for the chiefe Factor of that place and his Councill to transmitt the party, together with the offence to such other Plantacion Factory or Fort where there shall bee a Governor and Councill, where Justice may bee executed or into this Kingdome of England as shall be thought most convenient.[24]

These provisions were somewhat misleading in that they applied only to the company's servants who inhabited its forts and trading posts, and possibly the 'home guard Indians' settled nearby; they did not apply to the vast realm of Rupert's Land that remained under the control of the Algonquian, Athapaskan, and Montagnais-speaking peoples of the Hudson and James Bay watershed, and subject to their laws.

The powers bestowed by the charter were adequate for dealing with the company's servants, who were subject to an amalgam of company regulations, the common law of master and servant, and the customary code of discipline used at sea.[25] Violence, excessive drunkenness, and insubordination might all be expected during the long winters in the all-male environment of the company's subarctic posts. Such infractions were not dealt with through any formal process for the most part but, like Royal Navy discipline, through immediate physical punishment. Thus when two men at Eastmain Fort refused to follow orders in 1738, Governor Isbister recorded that he 'gave each of them two or three Cuffs with My hand as for a small Fault not according to their

Deserving.'[26] Such punishments were an accepted, and even expected, part of the law of master and servant in the eighteenth century. But unlike in Newfoundland, where servants could take action against their masters for abusive behaviour before JPs (after 1729) and sometimes succeeded, the servants of the HBC had no such option.[27]

Alleged acts of private trading, theft, or more serious offences were heard before a post council where the governor acted as prosecutor, judge, and jury, but punishments were seldom severe. Joseph Robson, a stone mason in the HBC's service in the 1730s and 1740s, reported that in cases that would have been subject to capital punishment in England, 'the governor only whips [the offender], and afterwards sends him home to be prosecuted by the company: but from a mistaken lenity, ... they proceed no farther than a quiet dismission from their service.'[28] Of course, no governor would have wanted to administer capital punishment without a jury verdict, and no court in England was likely to administer the death penalty for an offence committed in the plantations. Exacting unduly harsh penalties in the small, intimate atmosphere of a company fort would have undermined the loyalty and deference on which HBC governors depended, although some undoubtedly tended to be more disciplinarian while others were more paternalistic. Each fort was an insular community with its own moral economy, which a governor ignored at his peril.[29]

HBC regulations initially forbade Indigenous women from entering the forts, but this prohibition was not strictly enforced. Governors and officers of the HBC regarded the taking of a local wife as a perquisite of their position and soon came to realize that such unions could also lead to improved commercial relations by drawing the Europeans into a broad network of local kinship. The offering of wives or daughters to other men as a way of forming bonds of alliance with strangers was part of Cree tradition, a custom to which the British eventually adapted. As HBC trader Andrew Graham observed in the late eighteenth century, the Cree 'frequently lend their wives to other men for a night, week, month, or year; and will sometimes make an exchange for several years. And afterwards the women return to their former husbands, taking with them all the children they have born by the other man.'[30] Such exchanges had to be strictly consensual, however, and a failure to observe the protocols surrounding them could lead to retaliatory action. Officers might also have more than one Indigenous 'wife,' following Cree custom whereby leading men were expected to practise polygyny.[31]

Whether ordinary servants of the company were permitted to form relationships with local women depended on the indulgence of the particular governor, but over the course of the eighteenth century such unions became more widely tolerated and recognized among all social classes in fur trade society. The daughters of mixed marriages became especially valued as traders' wives, while many of the sons became HBC servants. The progeny of unions between mainly Scottish men and Indigenous women led to the creation of an English-speaking branch of the Métis people, in addition to the French-speaking Métis who had arisen from the French fur trade in the upper Great Lakes. While some of these relationships began and ended casually, some occurred according to the 'custom of the country' and were later found to produce effects under European law.[32]

With few exceptions, the HBC did not seek to assert jurisdiction over native peoples. One exception was the 'home guard Indians,' those families who chose to live permanently near a given fort and assisted with tasks ranging from translation to procuring game to defence. In return, the company assumed welfare obligations towards them, assisting the old and infirm and providing sustenance when food was in short supply. Even 'upland Indians,' who lived inland and whose relationship with the HBC posts was limited to trade, might come there for food during lean years. Unlike elsewhere in the empire, such assistance was provided on a 'secular' basis, without a corresponding effort at evangelization. In general the HBC did not seek to change the Indigenous way of life and allowed no missionaries to enter Rupert's Land until the 1820s, after the founding of Assiniboia.[33]

On the rare occasion when the company sought to bring Indigenous persons to justice, the offence was a form of insurrection that the company could not ignore. Thus, when credible rumours reached Moose Factory in June 1759, at the height of the Seven Years' War, that one Esquawenoe, an 'upland Indian,' was planning in league with the French to destroy the station, he was seized and imprisoned. He hanged himself in his cell days later, sparing the HBC the need to conduct a trial. An earlier example arose at Henley House on the Albany River, erected in 1743 as the HBC's first inland post.[34] Its master, William Lamb, kept two Indigenous women as his companions, one the daughter and one the daughter-in-law of Wappisis (also known as Woudbee), the captain of the home guard Cree at Albany Fort. When Wappisis and his two sons visited Henley House and were denied provisions, they considered this action a violation of the compact by which they had provided their womenfolk to the traders. Wappisis and his two sons killed Lamb and four servants of the HBC, and took over the post with all its trade goods. When Cree informers revealed the truth to Governor Isbister, he had the three men seized and tried before a post council consisting of all the chief officers and men at Albany Fort. The council sentenced them to be 'hanged until they are dead, dead, dead for a terour to all the Savage Natives from ever being guilty of the like barbarity in future,' a sentence duly carried out on 21 June 1755.[35] Such examples are virtually unique during the long period of HBC rule in Rupert's Land.

Ironically, it was the disappearance of the French threat after 1760 that led to the most prolonged period of instability in Rupert's Land, one that demonstrated the inadequacy of the judicature provisions under the HBC charter. For however functional post councils may have been for dealing with internal problems of order, they were not designed to deal with outsiders who did not recognize the company's authority. Thus the rivalry between the new trading companies based in Montreal and the HBC by definition spilled into the extra-legal domain. The imperial government, much as it wished to let the locals resolve these problems themselves, feared that the increasing violence threatened the existence of the fur trade itself and stepped in with a number of measures designed to curb it.

The first expedient adopted was to issue special commissions under the *Quebec Act* to authorize the trial of cases from the 'Indian country' (Rupert's Land and beyond) in Lower Canada, but the law officers of the Crown advised in 1788 that the *Quebec Act* provided insufficient authority for such commissions.[36] The legal vacuum thus created became painfully evident in 1802, when one James King was killed in Rupert's Land in a dispute over some furs. King was an employee of the Northwest Company, while Joseph Lamothe, the alleged murderer, was a clerk of the XY Company, a rival company also based in Montreal. The HBC was thus not involved in this proceeding, other than through the happenstance that the killing occurred in its territory. Lamothe, who might well have had a good claim to self-defence, travelled to Montreal to give himself up. He was indicted by a grand jury, but Attorney General Jonathan Sewell advised that the Quebec courts had no jurisdiction to try a crime that had allegedly occurred in Rupert's Land.[37]

The outcry following this sequence of events led the imperial Parliament to adopt the *Canada Jurisdiction Act, 1803*.[38] It authorized the governor of Canada to appoint justices of the peace for the Indian territories with the power to commit persons 'guilty of any Crime or Offence' for trial in Canada. As in Newfoundland, the appearance of such magistrates marked an important milestone in the evolution of a local judicature. The Act also authorized 'any Person or persons whatever to apprehend and take before [a territorial justice], or to apprehend and convey … to the province of Lower Canada, any Person or Persons guilty of any Crime or Offence, there to be delivered into safe Custody for the Purpose of being dealt with according to Law.' Any resulting trials could be held either in Upper or Lower Canada, whichever was more convenient. It seems clear that the 1803 Act was aimed mainly at providing a means to remedy violence between Montreal-based companies in the fur trade country by providing them with access to a jury trial by their peers in Montreal; thus it was irrelevant to the HBC. However, events soon caused it to be turned against the HBC, much to its chagrin.

The cure administered by the 1803 Act proved to be much worse than the disease. The NWC and the XY Company merged in 1804, ending their rivalry, but the newly merged company and the HBC both secured the appointment of some of their representatives as justices of the peace under the 1803 Act. Both sides abused these powers in an effort to gain commercial advantages against one another. The founding of Assiniboia in 1811, seen by the NWC as a plot by the HBC to block its westward expansion, only exacerbated matters. NWC men responded to a perceived provocation by the first governor of Assiniboia, Miles Macdonell, by using their powers under the 1803 Act to spirit him away to Montreal in 1814, then intimidating the settlers and causing them to flee.[39]

Matters escalated when the new governor, Robert Semple, seized the NWC's Fort Gibraltar near the Red River settlement. This move led to a battle at Seven Oaks between Semple and his settlers on the one hand and a party of Métis allied with the NWC on the other, in which Semple and some twenty settlers were killed, as well as one Métis. This debacle finally compelled the governor of Canada, Sir John Coape Sherbrooke, to act. He appointed William Coltman, a member of the executive council of Lower Canada, to conduct an inquiry into the causes of lawlessness in Assiniboia. The commission's report, issued in 1818, was relatively even-handed, placing more of the blame on the NWC but not exonerating the HBC or Lord Selkirk.[40] Some of these disasters could have been averted had the company acted on a detailed proposal to erect its own judicial system and legal code, drafted at the time of the grant to Selkirk, but it would not pursue this avenue for some decades.[41]

All of the proceedings and counter-proceedings proved only that the violent rivalry between the two companies could not be resolved by trials conducted 1,500 or more kilometres from the sites of conflict, or by placing the levers of the legal system in the hands of the parties themselves. By 1820 both companies were in financial difficulty and agreed to merge under the name of the Hudson's Bay Company in 1821. This time Parliament chose to cut through the jurisdictional tangle that had created so many difficulties in Rupert's Land. The 1821 *Act Regulating the Fur Trade* declared that the *Canada Jurisdiction Act* applied to Rupert's Land as well as the Indian Territories, although it expressly affirmed the company's charter jurisdiction to administer justice in the former. The Act also empowered the Crown to appoint trial judges to decide civil and criminal trials in both Rupert's Land and the Indian Territories.[42] But no such judges were appointed, and now that the fur trade violence had largely ceased, the imperial government was content to leave the administration of justice to the organs created by the HBC itself in Assiniboia – where it remained until the creation of the province of Manitoba in 1870 after the surrender of Rupert's Land to Canada. Not only that, but the statute gave the newly merged company an exclusive licence to trade west of the Rockies, where the North West Company had established a presence following its overland expeditions to the Pacific in 1793, 1805, and 1807. After all the vicissitudes of the previous two decades, the HBC had at last secured the parliamentary sanction it had been seeking back in the 1690s.

15

The Legal Professions

The eighteenth century began with no more than a few dozen notaries in Canada, a handful in Acadia, and no legal professionals in Newfoundland or Rupert's Land.[1] The end of the century saw little change in this respect in the latter two jurisdictions, but in Lower Canada and the English colonies of settlement, by 1815 the legal professions had laid a solid foundation for their dramatic growth in the nineteenth century. They achieved this by setting out distinctive entry requirements and developing mechanisms for self-governance, either with state aid or by voluntary activity. Entry by apprenticeship of a set length followed by some kind of examination was required for notaries and advocates by ordinance in Quebec in 1785, and for barristers and attorneys, by legislation in Upper Canada in 1797 or rules of court in the Maritime provinces.[2] Although these legal professionals came from a variety of backgrounds – locally born Canadiens, imports from France and the continent, English, Scottish, and Irish immigrants, Loyalists, and others – they began to develop a certain esprit de corps in each colony. In Quebec a voluntary society, the Communauté des avocats, appeared by 1779, while a Forensick Society was established by articling students in Saint John, New Brunswick, in the 1790s. Growth in population and economic expansion, together with the colonial state's increasing need for documentation and record-keeping as a means of maintaining order, fostered a modest demand for lawyers, although most sought out some governmental office to supplement the unpredictable earnings that could be gleaned from private practice.

Given its political and legal upheavals, it was the province of Quebec that experienced the most significant changes over the long eighteenth century. As noted in the previous chapter, while advocates as such did not exist in New France, some notaries pleaded informally in court, while others known as praticiens also did so even though not formally commissioned as notaries. Demand for such services grew impressively over the course of the French regime, such that by the 1750s, over half of the parties in court for civil matters, and almost all merchants, were represented by a notary or praticien of some kind.[3] The colonial state also began to display greater interest in the records of notaries, upon which the validity of marriage contracts, land grants, and all manner of obligations rested. The tradition in France was for the notary's records to pass to his family, but this proved unsatisfactory in Canada. At the request of Attorney General Mathieu Collet, the king issued a declaration in 1717 requiring all notaries to keep their files in chronological order and providing for annual inspections by officials of the royal and seigneurial courts. It further decreed that upon the death of a notary, his minute-books would be transferred to the registry of the nearest royal or seigneurial court. Finally, a process was put in place for recovering, inventorying, and storing the records of deceased notaries.[4]

The inventory eventually revealed an alarming number of errors in notarial acts, resulting in an unprecedented examination by Collet's successor, Louis-Guillaume Verrier (formerly an advocate in the Parlement of Paris), of all the records of deceased notaries in the Quebec district. The task took him some two years (1730–1) and required the checking of thousands of documents. While most notaries had an error rate of less than 2 per cent, two displayed rates of over 20 per cent. This threat to 'les biens et la tranquillité du peuple' could not be ignored: the governor, the intendant, and Verrier together drafted three declarations, which they forwarded to the king. In 1733 the government of Louis XV duly followed their advice and formally issued the declarations, the first validating the prior defective instruments, the second setting out a detailed code of conduct for notaries, and the third establishing a process for the validation of marriage contracts in those areas where no notaries existed.[5] Such a searching inquisition of the notarial profession would not occur again, but nothing could better illustrate the unique role of the notary, poised on the cusp of public and private, both state agent and professional adviser. The responsiveness of the French imperial government to colonial needs in this instance also demonstrates that the concept of a 'negotiated empire' was not unique to the British.

Verrier himself then undertook to provide a course of lectures in law free of charge, thereby becoming the father of legal education in Quebec, and indeed in North America north of Mexico.[6] Argou's *Institution au droit français* (1710) served as the basis for the course, after which students read the civil and criminal ordinances of the colony. The lectures began in 1733, increased from one to two per week in 1739, and continued for some twenty years, but no law school as such was established, and the number of students remained very small. Verrier's efforts were somewhat similar to those of Blackstone at Oxford in the 1750s, their courses aimed not at preparing students for the practice of law, but rather at providing members of the elite with an overview of the legal order. Indeed, one of Verrier's students in the 1750s, Jacques Imbert, was already a royal notary when he took the course. Verrier's students were of two kinds: the first comprised high officials and members of the Conseil supérieur who required some knowledge of law in connection with their duties. The second comprised ambitious younger men from elite families who sought advancement in colonial government. The king let it be known that in appointments to the Conseil preference would be given to those who had taken Verrier's course; such a 'graduate' could expect to be named as an 'assessor' or probationary councillor, followed in due course by a regular appointment to the Conseil. As with Blackstone, following Verrier's death in 1758 there would be a hiatus of nearly a century before any organized university instruction in law was again available in the province.

As the economy became somewhat more diversified in the eighteenth century, notaries undertook more managerial and business-oriented tasks beyond the strictly legal sphere, much as English attorneys did at the time, and they also accumulated governmental and/or seigneurial offices of various kinds. They were inspired to do so by necessity, as the 1749 revision of the notaries' original fee tariff of 1678 reflected barely any improvement. The colonial state may have regarded notaries' work as a public service, but notaries themselves had other ideas. In spite of a shaky start and ongoing challenges, the status of the notarial profession rose steadily over the course of the French regime. In rural settlements, the notary was considered to rank immediately after the parish priest, the seigneur, and the militia officers. He played a crucial mediating role between the habitant and the authority of state and church, reading out royal edicts and proclamations after Sunday mass. The populace might ask him to chair a meeting to discuss an issue of local controversy, and he was expected to preside over the elections of syndics to represent the local parish assembly.[7] Even if a notary's income was low in the early years, his status might attract a propertied bride, and – especially if he practised in Quebec or Montreal – he might eventually secure higher positions in the judicial or colonial administration. A notary of very humble origins might see his daughter marry a seigneur, and his sons become seigneurs in their own right. The supposed poverty of the notary has probably been exaggerated, as notaries' own marriage contracts in the district of Quebec reveal that many were able to provide comfortably for their widows and socialized within elite circles.[8]

The transition to British government from 1760 only enhanced the position of notaries in provincial society. As the only repository of local legal knowledge in the colony, British officials had every incentive to use them as intermediaries in their dealings with the Canadien population. Almost immediately the governor began to commission new notaries, just as the intendant had done, and recommission old ones. After some hesitation, it was decided that notaries did not have to take the oaths required by the *Test Act*, such that there was nothing to prevent Catholic notaries from continuing to practise their profession. This was a critical concession, given that Catholics could not be admitted to practise law in England until 1791 or in Ireland until 1792. In fact, many notaries carried on without awaiting new commissions from the governor. And while some British notaries were commissioned – the first being Thomas Gage, the military governor of Montreal, in 1762 – British merchants tended to use experienced Canadien notaries, who presumably had a surer grasp of local law and procedure.[9]

With the return to civilian rule, the British also introduced the profession of advocate as part of the judicature reforms of 1764. For a generation there was no prohibition on notaries also holding commissions as advocates, and in Quebec and Montreal 'virtually all the notaries pleaded in court.'[10] In reality this was simply an official ratification of what had gone on for decades unofficially under the French regime. With regard to their traditional tasks, notaries carried on as if the Custom of Paris had not been affected by the Royal Proclamation of 1763, without any discernible protest from the colonial government. When Charles Louis Tarieu de Lanaudière and Geneviève-Élisabeth de La Corne signed their marriage contract in 1769, establishing French-style community of property and purporting to oust all other customs or laws, it was witnessed by John Fraser, judge of the Court of Common Pleas, and Daniel Robertson, a justice of the peace.[11]

The requirements for entry to the notariat were never standardized under the French regime, and the intendant retained the power to commission an applicant with no previous exposure to the profession. The British governor followed the same policy, even after the recognition of advocates in 1764. When Governor Haldimand commissioned a failed businessman from France, Alexandre Dumas, as a notary in 1783 and an advocate in 1784, the nascent Communauté des avocats protested strongly, as did Attorney General James Monk. The incident seems to have triggered the landmark ordinance of 1785, which for the first time standardized entry to both professions (a five-year apprenticeship) and required an examination by senior practitioners of the relevant profession under judicial supervision. The Act also forbade the cumulation of the professions for the future, giving all who held both commissions a year to choose one of them.[12] In addition, it forbade legal professionals from acting as land surveyors, thus providing a harder occupational edge to both professions.

In most respects, however, the British continued French practices regarding the notariat, directing that the rules of French law would govern the validity of notarial Acts and maintaining in the 1785 ordinance the provisions regarding inspection of notarial registers. In some ways the post-cession period was a golden age for notaries: the British enlarged the districts within which notaries could practise and did not increase their number (though those dying or retiring were replaced), even though the population doubled in the generation after 1760. In 1760 there were forty-three active notaries; in 1781, forty-two.[13]

Both legal professions attracted entrants from British and French (as well as Swiss and German) backgrounds, and they became a key site for the development of a common juridical language and culture drawing on elements of both legal traditions: a 'culture de l'amalgame' in the words of Jean-Philippe Garneau. This project was assisted by a developing tradition of having English articling clerks spend part of their time with a French advocate and vice versa. Moreover, about 20 per cent of the time an advocate represented a client from the 'other' linguistic community, though this was more frequently the case for francophone advocates than anglophones. And about a third of the time, an advocate would be faced by one from the 'other' linguistic community in court. Canadien notaries often had anglophone clients, and vice versa.[14] The constant mixing of languages in legal proceedings horrified purist legal observers from Europe such as Alexis de Tocqueville but was a workable solution to the situation in which both linguistic groups found themselves.[15] Members of the Indigenous mission villages also sought out the help of notaries and advocates, as will be seen in chapter 17.

The profession of advocate itself was not a reproduction of the French profession of that name, but a mix of French and colonial American elements. Advocates in France were much like English barristers, who restricted themselves to court pleading and did not meet with clients or concern themselves with the paperwork leading up to a trial. The Quebec advocate retained the court side of the work but also performed the tasks that in England were normally performed by an attorney (in the common law courts) or a solicitor (in chancery), that is, the preparation of the documentary side of litigation from the initial meeting with the client down to the actual appearance in court. In colonial America there were no barristers as such, and attorneys performed all the work that barristers did in England as well as the ordinary tasks of attorneys. A Quebec advocate was in essence a colonial American attorney, except that he was prohibited from performing the tasks that fell within the purview of the notarial profession.

Prior to the separation of Upper and Lower Canada in 1791 and for some time thereafter, the ordinance of 1785 governed the legal professions in both jurisdictions. The 1794 *Judicature Act* of Upper Canada suspended its provisions for the training of lawyers, however, and authorized Lieutenant Governor Simcoe to license a maximum of sixteen British subjects 'as he shall deem from their probity, education and condition of life best qualified to act as Advocates and Attorneys, in the conduct of all legal proceedings in this Province.'[16] In 1797 the legislature of Upper Canada repealed the 1785 ordinance in an Act relating to the legal profession that was unique in the British Empire at the time. The *Act for the Better Regulating the Practice of the Law* stated that those lawyers currently practising in the province should form themselves into a society to be called the Law Society of Upper Canada, 'as well for the establishing of order amongst themselves as for the purpose of securing to the province and the profession a learned and honorable body, to assist their fellow subjects as occasion may require, and to support and maintain the constitution of the said province.'[17] In future, to practice as a barrister in any of the courts of the province required admission to the society as a student at law and maintaining that status for five years while conforming to the rules and regulations that the society was authorized to promulgate. Admission to practise as an attorney or solicitor would require only three years as a student at law, but it was expected that most students at law would obtain both qualifications in due course. Whereas in England, barristers had to be called to the bar of an inn of court to be recognized as pleaders in the courts, in Upper Canada the Law Society was given that role, as well as the power to govern and educate attorneys. After an initial period of torpor it took up that challenge with some vigour, devoting considerable time and resources to the education of future lawyers.[18]

The Maritime provinces had early on adopted the colonial American model of entry to the legal profession, involving an apprenticeship of some length prior to an oral examination by the judges. In Nova Scotia (1799) and Prince Edward Island (1808) a rule of court set the period at four years.[19] In New Brunswick the early lawyers formed the cream of the Loyalist bar in New York and New England; they followed their own traditions of a five-year apprenticeship until a rule of court formalized the practice in 1823.[20] The colonial state provided official recognition to the bar in Nova Scotia by an innovative Act of 1811, which upgraded the requirements for entry but also provided a mechanism for bestowing the prestigious title of barrister on local lawyers.[21] Apprenticeships would henceforth be five years, to be followed by an examination by the judges, proof of good character, and the taking of the attorney's oath before admission. There was no minimum age for starting the apprenticeship, but no attorney could be called before reaching the age of majority. Graduates of King's College, Windsor, and barristers already called in England or Ireland could be called as barristers as well as attorneys immediately upon completing these steps. Non-graduates had to spend a further year attending three terms of the Supreme Court, upon which they too were entitled to be called as barristers.

The long period of (in principle) unpaid apprenticeship ensured that only men subsidized by well-off families could aspire to the bar or the notariat during this early period. Notaries were frequently to be found in the Lower Canadian countryside, but advocates located mainly in Quebec and Montreal, while in the English colonies too, lawyers tended to remain close to the capital in the hope of picking up some governmental patronage. Immigration and population growth after 1815 would alter this geographic pattern dramatically, as earning a living from private practice outside the colonial capitals became a realistic option for many. Through statute and voluntary associations lawyers were already staking their claim as a specialized professional group entitled to a position of leadership in colonial society. In spite of widespread anti-lawyer sentiment, they would make good on this claim in the following century, based on the utility of the services they provided, their role as community leaders, and their participation in political life at every level. In Lower Canada, lawyers in the Assemblée took on the role of defenders of French-Canadian interests and traditions against a government seen as dominated by British interests. One of them, Pierre-Stanislas Bédard, imprisoned under Governor Craig in 1810–11 for allegedly seditious activities, is seen as 'the first person in the British Empire to formulate in a coherent manner the theory of ministerial responsibility.'[22] In this he presaged the crucial role that lawyers in all the colonies would play in the movement to reform the colonial constitutions in the 1830s and 1840s.

16

Criminal Law and Criminal Justice

Criminal law is the legal domain that most centrally involved the coercive power of the state, often manifested in physical violence, to enforce norms regarding both interpersonal behaviour and political loyalty, and differential distributions of property. Its study has always been of particular importance in colonial legal history, because it was through criminal justice that fledgling colonial states most visibly exerted their authority over subject populations and, equally visibly, exerted that authority through the legitimating power of law. At the same time, criminal justice, like all other aspects of colonial legal history, was not simply planted in new colonies; it was also adapted to new conditions, sometimes directly through overt changes in law or institutions, more often indirectly, through changes in practice and procedure.

Much of what we know about Canadian criminal justice history has concerned the offences defined as warranting serious punishment and the legal system that apprehended, prosecuted, and punished those who committed such offences. Such offences were prosecuted not just in the highest courts of the colonies, but also in inferior bodies called sessions courts (sometimes quarter sessions, sometimes courts of session or other variants). There was also a 'low law' of criminal justice history, one concerned with minor breaches of the peace, infractions against local regulations, and the like. This low law was very important historically, for it affected more people in their everyday lives than high law. But what one historian has aptly named 'everyday criminal justice'[1] was different from high law. Breaches of market regulations, refusal to perform statute labour, selling liquor without a licence, and the like did not involve the threat of physical punishment of the body or the death penalty, and it did not engage politicians and others in debates about the meaning and legitimacy of the criminal law. This section is thus concerned mostly with the more serious offences, prosecuted in superior courts and at sessions. It examines the introduction of laws defining such offences and prescribing punishments, and how colonial systems of law enforcement – policing, prosecution, and trial – operated.[2]

English Criminal Law in the Eighteenth Century

The English system of criminal justice was introduced into all Canadian colonies founded or acquired from mid-century. Not only did this mean the substantive law of crimes and punishments, but all aspects of criminal procedure and law enforcement. For the English in the eighteenth century, the central pillars of criminal justice, such as trial by jury and private prosecution, were key elements of the constitution, features that distinguished English public law from its continental counterparts, and thus it was unthinkable that an English colony would not have English criminal law. The most notable example of this attitude was Quebec, which prior to its acquisition by Britain had a long-established and relatively efficient system of French criminal justice. Although the arrangements eventually settled on for the new colony included retention of the Catholic Church and the French civil law, there was no compromise on the criminal law.[3]

Eighteenth-century English criminal law divided offences into two broad categories, felonies and misdemeanours, with the former, the more serious category, encompassing everything from petit larceny (theft of goods worth less than a shilling) to murder and treason.[4] At common law all felonies except for petit larceny were capital offences, but from the medieval period it was possible to plead 'benefit of clergy' on any first offence, and an offender so convicted would not be executed but be branded on the thumb. Benefit of clergy derived from the medieval need to determine whether clerical offenders should be dealt with by secular or ecclesiastical tribunals. It was originally available only to those in holy orders, but over time eligibility was widened in stages: the literate as well as those ordained, then those who could recite a standard passage of scripture whether they could read it or not, and finally women as well as men. By 1706 anybody could claim their 'clergy.'

In contrast to this expansion of personal eligibility for the defence, many common law offences were removed from clergy, and particular statutory offences were created 'without benefit of clergy,' to use the standard formula of legislation. The earliest offences to be removed from clergy were those considered most serious – murder, rape, burglary, robbery, etc. But the large-scale reliance of the system on the supposed deterrent effect of capital punishment, and the lack of effective secondary punishments, meant a constant expansion in the late seventeenth and eighteenth centuries of non-clergyable felonies. In the eighteenth century 'whether an offence was within clergy or had been removed from its privileges ... [was] the most significant determinant of the way it was ... treated by the courts.'[5] Most of these new non-clergyable offences were species of theft – theft of particular kinds of property, or theft from particular places, or theft committed in particular circumstances – although some were offences against the person, essentially forms of assault that did not lead to the death of the victim but were nonetheless seen as serious threats to the peace. Examples of the former are thefts from churches, horse theft, or theft by picking pockets. Among the offences against the person made capital by removing them from clergy were stabbing and maliciously shooting at someone. By the end of the eighteenth century this piecemeal but constant process of removing offences from clergy culminated in some 200 capital offences on the statute book, four times greater than the number in the late seventeenth century.[6] The most notable offences never removed from clergy were grand larceny (theft of goods worth one shilling and up) and manslaughter.

The pre-nineteenth-century English criminal law thus relied heavily on punishment of the body. Execution, the terror of the gallows, was its centrepiece, designed to deter crime by exaction of the ultimate penalty for those who were caught and convicted. The gallows were augmented by other non-capital physical punishments, especially public whipping, the standard punishment for petit larceny and many misdemeanours, and by the pillory. Imprisonment was meted out to minor offenders and involved short terms of months only in the county gaol or house of correction. As in France and Quebec, gaols were in fact used much more to hold those awaiting trial for serious felonies than as punishment. The principal secondary punishment available from the late seventeenth century on was transportation to the American colonies; an important milestone in its history was the 1718 *Transportation Act*, which began a system of state payment to contractors that greatly increased the numbers of those actually transported. Transportation to America stopped, of course, with the onset of revolution, but transportation assumed an even larger role a decade and a half later with the establishment of penal colonies in Australia.

Had the criminal law been administered as strictly as the 'law on the books' made possible, it would have taken many thousands of lives and potentially lost its legitimacy. In practice, relatively few of those indicted for a capital offence ended up on the gallows. Prosecutors could choose not to charge with the capital offence by undervaluing goods stolen or by omitting the circumstances that made the theft capital. Jurors had a similar discretion and used it frequently, either acquitting or convicting of a lesser, non-capital offence, even if the evidence showed otherwise. And although there were no criminal appeals, even those who were capitally convicted could petition for a royal pardon and if successful either go free or suffer some lesser punishment. Terror was thus mitigated by mercy in a delicate balance in which pardon decisions took into account not just the individual circumstances of particular offenders but also the political consequences of extending mercy. The result was that through the second half of the eighteenth century the numbers of those executed fluctuated from year to year but overall stayed constant, despite the population increase and the rapidly growing number of capital offences. Moreover, the vast majority of those executed for property offences were convicted of offences that had long been capital, such as robbery and burglary; the 'new' property offences of the second half of the eighteenth century played a relatively minor role in the execution statistics.

The Reception of English Criminal Law in British North America

This English criminal law was introduced into the British North American colonies in the half century after 1750. Nova Scotia received all of English law with the founding of Halifax in 1749, although a few years later a counterfeiting case raised doubts about whether every single English statutory enactment was applicable.[7] The court of oyer and terminer established in St John's, Newfoundland, in 1750 applied all of English criminal law and procedure.[8] Quebec received English criminal law after the conquest and the formal cession of the colony to Britain. Prince Edward Island was made a colony separate from Nova Scotia in 1769 and received English criminal law as of that date. New

Brunswick's reception history generally is somewhat tortuous, but for our purposes it is clear that as of the early 1790s the vast majority of English criminal law applied in the new colony.[9] The only significant changes to English law were local statutes raising the petit/grand larceny distinction to twenty shillings and permitting courts to punish those who received benefit of clergy by imposing a fine or whipping, the 'punishment of burning in the hand' being often 'disregarded or ineffectual.'[10] Upper Canada initially had English criminal law as of its introduction into Quebec, of which it was a part until 1791.[11] In 1800 the colony amended that, formally declaring the law to be the English criminal law as of 17 September 1792, the date the first Upper Canadian assembly met.[12] The same statute made some minor amendments to English law: it allowed judges to dispense with burning on the hand for those who received benefit of clergy, and it substituted banishment for offences where English law prescribed transportation.[13]

The 'reception' of English criminal law was not merely a technical legal reception of common law and statutes relating to criminal punishment. The colonies received all of English criminal procedure as well, so that the everyday practice and operation of the criminal courts mirrored English process. Moreover, reception included the ideological reception of the theory of criminal justice. English criminal law had constitutional significance, from the place of the jury as a marker of English liberty to the royal pardon as exemplary of monarchical power. Hence one of the first statutes passed by the newly established Upper Canadian assembly in 1792 was one introducing trial by jury.[14] Criminal law was also seen as indispensable to social and economic order by its use of the terror of state power. In defending the use of capital punishment in a 1768 burglary case, for example, Nova Scotia Chief Justice Jonathan Belcher refuted the recently published Beccarian theory of proportionality in his sentencing speech, asserting that 'the measure of all penalties is not the proportion between crimes and punishment,' but rather 'the grand end of government is the measure by securing obedience to necessary laws.'[15]

The only colony in which the introduction of English criminal law represented a real change from the past was Quebec.[16] After more than a century of French criminal justice, Quebec's criminal law was changed to English law by the Royal Proclamation of 1763. The commission and instructions given to the first governor after the Peace of Paris laid down that Governor Murray was to establish courts to hear 'all causes, as well Criminal as Civil, ... as near as may be agreeable to the Laws of England.'[17] This decision was confirmed in the *Quebec Act* of 1774, which confidently asserted that 'the Certainty and Lenity of the Criminal Law of England' were benefits 'sensibly felt by the inhabitants.' Chief Justice William Hey of Quebec had uttered similar sentiments before the House of Commons the same year, insisting that Canadiens were 'perfectly satisfied' with English criminal law and indeed that he 'cannot conceive them so stupid as to wish for the French law.'[18] In fact the introduction of the English criminal law as of 1774 meant that many more offences were formally punishable by death than under French law.

In two of the colonies a local code was legislated that ameliorated the severity of the received law. In 1758 the first Nova Scotia Assembly passed a *Treason and Felonies Act*, a compilation of English statutory provisions that removed from clergy only fourteen offences.[19] This left a broader range of clergyable offences in Nova Scotia than in England. Thus after 1760 nobody was sentenced capitally for an offence removed from clergy by English statutes but not included in the 1758 local Act. The other colony to ameliorate English law by local legislation was Prince Edward Island, which largely imitated Nova Scotia's 1758 statute in 1792.[20] These two Maritime colonies were exceptional; none of the others passed similar general legislation. It also bears noting that both Nova Scotia and Quebec/Lower Canada passed local legislation adding capital offences in the later eighteenth and early nineteenth centuries.[21]

Punishment in Practice

British North America may have largely replicated the English Bloody Code, but in practice the death penalty was used sparingly, even more so than in England. The figures are more reliable for some colonies than for others, and it must be borne in mind both that executions started at varying dates, from 1749 in Nova Scotia to 1792 in Upper Canada, and that populations also differed dramatically. But even allowing for time and population differences, the statistics show a sparing use of the rope. Only five persons were hanged in Prince Edward Island before 1815; of these, two were convicted of murder, one of rape, and two of property offences.[22] Probably the number for New Brunswick before 1815 was just as small, certainly fewer than ten,[23] and that for Upper Canada not much larger. There were seventeen civilian executions in Upper Canada between 1792 and 1815, an average of almost one a year, but this figure is inflated as a measure of criminal punishment because eight of them were executions for treason in 1814, the hanged men fighting on the American side in the War of 1812. Of the nine people executed other than for treason, six had been convicted of murder, and one each of burglary, forgery, and arson.[24] Newfoundland witnessed just twelve executions in the forty years after 1750.[25]

There were, not surprisingly, rather more executions in the much older colonies of Nova Scotia and Quebec/Lower Canada, the latter being the most populous British North American colony. Nova Scotia saw at least fifty-three hangings in the sixty-six years between 1749 and 1815, twenty-three for murder, twenty-seven for property offences, and three for rape. This might appear as if the death sentence was commonly employed for property offenders, but in fact the pardon rate was much higher for capital property offences – around two-thirds of those sentenced were pardoned – than for murder, with only sixteen of thirty-nine condemned persons pardoned.[26] To the west there were forty-six executions in the colony of Quebec between 1760 and 1790, and fifteen when the jurisdiction was named Lower Canada, between 1791 and 1815. At sixty-one over fifty-five years this was slightly more than in Nova Scotia in absolute terms – fifty-three in sixty-six years – but given the much higher population of Lower Canada, Nova Scotia saw a higher rate of execution per capita.

Few people were hanged, in part because many capital statutes 'on the books' were simply not enforced. In particular, capital property offences that were larceny made capital by the circumstances of the theft were rarely prosecuted as capital crimes and even more rarely led to capital convictions. The vast majority of capital property offences for which capital convictions were secured were the two that were considered more serious and had been capital under English law since the sixteenth century – burglary and robbery. The most important factor in keeping executions low, however, was the extensive use of the power to pardon. In all colonies local governors could not pardon those convicted of murder or treason; such cases had to be referred to London. But even decisions in those cases were effectively made locally, for the colonial executive's recommendation was invariably followed. Indeed the local government really did have the power of life and death. It could recommend a pardon, and London invariably agreed, or it could go ahead with the execution without having to refer that decision. Local authorities kept the numbers executed low. In Nova Scotia before 1815 over half of those sentenced to death were pardoned (67 of 121, or

55 per cent).[27] The pardon rate was even higher in Upper Canada. As noted above, there were seventeen civilian executions between 1792 and 1815, but only nine of these were sentenced to death for crimes other than treason arising out of the War of 1812. Those nine represented just 26 per cent of those sentenced to death in the same period for offences other than treason (thirty-five), and thus the pardon rate was 74 per cent.[28] It was a very similar 71 per cent in Newfoundland.[29] Lower Canadian authorities were equally merciful, although as everywhere the pardon rate fluctuated over time. In the late 1770s and 1780s authorities pardoned just over half of those sentenced to death, but the rate was much higher before ca 1775 and after 1790, meaning that overall it was over 70 per cent in this period.[30] No figures are available for the other colonies, but anecdotal evidence shows the pardon being freely used. As with the total number of executions, Nova Scotia had the harshest system, pardoning a smaller percentage than other colonies.

Although pardon documents worded in formulaic terms do not provide us with the real reason why colonial executives pardoned a particular individual, they exercised their discretion for reasons similar to those operating in England. Women and young persons were pardoned at a much higher rate than others. For the rest of the offender pool the nature of the offence – murder vs property offences – mattered a good deal, as did the seriousness of the crime – was it a planned and deliberate murder for gain or the result of a spur-of-the-moment altercation? Other factors that played a role included whether the offender was otherwise of good character, and whether the crime rate generally was high enough to merit an example to others of the consequences of breaking the law. In addition to all of these considerations, patronage and influence played a role. Whom convicts could enlist to petition on their behalf could be crucial; indeed things could hardly be otherwise in societies where the patronage of social and political betters determined many things. In Nova Scotia being able to have senior military officers command the ear of the lieutenant governor was unquestionably an advantage to the many soldiers and sailors convicted in the Halifax Supreme Court, and it seems possible that the slightly lower rate of pardon in Quebec in the 1770s and 1780s was the product of the English governors being more willing to hang French Canadians.[31] Having said all this, the result of very few pardon petitions was inevitable or preordained. The attitude of particular colonial governors at particular times must have mattered, and chance probably played some role in decisions that will always remain formally opaque to the historian.[32]

For convicts who did not merit the gallows, the range of lesser sentences mirrored those that dominated English law. They included the pillory, which was rarely used, as it was a sentence reserved for ignominious offences, such as perjury and non-capital coining, which revealed deception, and assault with intent to commit rape or sodomy, which marked a person as deviant and dangerous.[33] Despite its being rarely used, it was a punishment much feared by those who were threatened with it, for a variety of reasons. Sometimes it could be accompanied by physical mutilation. Christopher Moore, for example, convicted of counterfeiting dollars at the Halifax Quarter Sessions in 1770, was sentenced 'to stand in the pillory one hour with one of his ears nailed thereto.'[34] Moore escaped a worse fate because of uncertainty about whether the ear should be removed first; a statute of 1758 was ambiguous on the point, but one of 1774 made it clear that removal was indeed the prescribed punishment.[35] More importantly, it was a shaming punishment. Pillories were set up in market squares, and pillory times were invariably set for market days. On occasion the crowd showed its wrath by pelting the convict with dirt and offal, but even without that the shame could be intensely felt and feared. One John Harris was convicted of assault with intent to commit a rape at the Shelburne, Nova Scotia, sessions court in 1786, and sentenced to stand in the pillory for an hour. He petitioned the lieutenant governor for clemency, acknowledging his guilt and expressing his contrition, and also insisting that the pillory sentence 'will inevitably drive him out of the settlement since he can never afterwards look his fellow citizens in the face, or mix again in that society before which he hath been made so public an example of disgrace.'[36] In England crowds could go very far indeed, stripping an offender of his clothes, pelting him with stones, and flagellating the unfortunate man, at times treating him so severely as to cause death.[37] But there is no evidence of such extreme measures in British North America. Indeed there is evidence that in Lower Canada at least it was an unpopular punishment, with crowds occasionally trying to prevent a person being pilloried or destroying the pillory.[38]

Perhaps the most innovative punishment recorded in this period was also a public shaming. Peter, Marquess de Conty and Gravina, a Sicilian nobleman whose use of the Nova Scotia Court of Chancery will be examined later, was convicted in 1758 by the Halifax Supreme Court of an assault with intent to rape one Jane Gleason, a nine-year old resident of the orphan house. He was sentenced to three months in gaol and a £30 fine, and also 'to walk in Custody of the Sheriff and Constables between the Hours of Eleven and Twelve ... from the North to the South Side of the Parade and from thence to the Gaol having a paper fixed on his Brest with his crime thereon inscribed.' He paid the fine and did the time, but pleaded for relief from the walk. The talk of the town was that the less-than-noble lord had actually succeeded with the rape and given the girl venereal disease, and presumably he wanted to be spared the apparently innocuous walk because he feared the public shame or perhaps did not trust his escort to protect him from popular anger. For whatever reason, Lieutenant Governor Charles Lawrence granted him his wish.[39]

So far we have dealt with the punishments that were overwhelmingly used by superior courts for what were considered the more serious offences. The superior and sessions courts also employed a range of punishments for a variety of lesser offences. The most prevalent was public whipping, carried out in very visible locations like market squares and parade grounds. It was used in all colonies as the standard punishment for petit larceny, for men and women alike. Thus Jane Tolmy, convicted of petit larceny in Halifax in 1774, was sentenced to be publicly whipped twenty-five times. She escaped the scourging not simply because of her gender but because she turned out to be pregnant.[40] Whipping was also employed for a few other offences; Stephen Adams and Thomas Keep were so sentenced by the Halifax General Court in 1751 for spreading 'false news' and 'scandalous lies' in 1751.[41] By the late eighteenth century those convicted of grand larceny and given benefit of clergy were also increasingly likely to be whipped rather than burned in the hand, which came to be seen as an ineffectual punishment. When William Hawkins was found guilty of grand larceny at York in 1798, for example, he was sentenced to be whipped in the market square.[42] In all the examples given here the sentences were handed down by superior courts. But simple larceny was also prosecuted at sessions courts, which had the same power to impose physical punishment. The Montreal Quarter Sessions used that power with a vengeance in 1811, sentencing Jean-Baptiste Mathieu to thirty-nine lashes in the marketplace.[43] The surrogate and sessions courts of Newfoundland also readily employed the lash to punish and discourage pilfering in the seasonal fishery.[44]

Fines were another weapon in the lower courts' arsenal, frequently employed to punish those convicted of assault, which was the principal offence prosecuted at sessions.[45] Fines were also given for a range of other infractions – disorderly house prosecutions, breaches of local regulations, such as those involving liquor licences, and the like. Some 60 per cent of people convicted at the Montreal Quarter Sessions before 1800, for example, were fined, and fines were routinely meted out at the Halifax Quarter Sessions and those of various Upper Canadian districts.[46]

Perhaps the biggest difference between English and colonial patterns in punishment practices during the second half of the eighteenth century was the larger role played by transportation in the former jurisdiction. The reason is simple and obvious – prior to the American Revolution convicts were transported from Britain to the American colonies, not from one colony to another.[47] Indeed there were suggestions and even unsuccessful attempts before 1776 to make at least one of the future British North American colonies, Nova Scotia, a convict destination,[48] and this idea was revived again after the Revolutionary War when Britain was searching for penal alternatives before finally settling on Australia.[49] The only British North American possession that transported offenders to the American colonies before 1775 was Newfoundland, not itself a colony.[50] In place of transportation all British North American colonies employed banishment, largely as a condition of pardon and largely following a capital conviction, although persons could be pardoned and then banished as a condition of that pardon when their offence was not a capital one. As early as 1754 John Hoffman, leader of the discontented German settlers at Lunenburg, Nova Scotia, was released from prison after a year, provided he gave security 'in a considerable sum' to 'depart the province and not to return.'[51] In 1789 one Godfrey Hogg was found guilty at the Halifax Supreme Court of 'felony' (probably grand larceny) and sentenced to three months in prison, after which he was 'to transport himself out of the province.'[52] But such examples were rare. Banishment was used much more often for capital convicts pardoned, with exile being the condition of pardon. Perhaps the largest single 'mass banishment' was that ordered for the seven men spared from hanging following the 1814 treason trials in Ancaster, Upper Canada; they were sent to the United States.[53]

In some cases the convicts were kept in custody until, in the words of one Nova Scotia pardon, he could leave 'by the first Opportunity which shall be notified to him,' which turned out be a Virginia-bound ship.[54] In the late eighteenth century three Blacks, two slaves and a free woman, were put on a ship in Prince Edward Island bound for the Caribbean.[55] Yet on other occasions people were not removed but required to effect their own departure from the jurisdiction, with no stipulation of where they should go. Given the length of time granted to find a passage and the difficulty of arranging one from a prison cell, it is unlikely that they were incarcerated in the meantime.[56] Contributing to the variety of ways in which conditions of pardon could be used to govern the behaviour of convicts, on occasion executive authorities would impose a requirement that the convicted person join the armed forces. In 1781, for example, one Roger Cain was convicted of rape in Halifax and pardoned 'on consideration of his entering the navy and serving during the rebellion.'[57]

To this point we have discussed banishment as a condition of pardon, but in Upper Canada it was also a prescribed sentencing option in itself. Upper Canada received all of English criminal law as of 17 September 1792, which meant that it received some English transportation statutes as a penal option. But, as the 1800 statute stated, English laws regarding transportation were either 'inapplicable to this province, or cannot be carried into execution without great and manifest inconvenience.' The statute went on to substitute banishment for transportation wherever English law would have provided for the latter. Banishment was intended to be simply a direct substitute for transportation. It was to be imposed 'for and during the same number of years, or term, for which ... [the convict] would be liable by law to be transported.'[58] The power to banish was used on nineteen occasions by Upper Canadian courts before 1815.[59] Banishment was meted out for a wide variety of offences, wider probably than the statute's limitation of it to 'any crime, for which ... [a person] was liable by law to be transported.' Most of those banished had committed simple larceny, grand or petit, a relatively minor property crime. One Allan Gould, for example, was convicted of 'stealing ... to the amount of 1 pound, 6 shillings' at the Midland District Assizes in September 1803 and was sentenced 'to be banished out of the province for seven years, and within four days to depart.' This last injunction was in line with the 1800 statute, which specified that no banishment should start less than two days after sentencing, nor more than eight. But some banished offenders had been charged and convicted of more serious, sometimes capital, crimes, such as murder, forgery, and horse-stealing, and been found guilty of a lesser offence.

The range of penal options included the one that became dominant in the nineteenth century – imprisonment. But prisons were not used for the punishment of serious crimes in the eighteenth century. In all colonies jails were built, but they were very different from later penitentiaries, in three principal ways. First, they were the responsibility of local, not central government, as shown by the prevalence of statutes authorizing the magistrates in sessions to tax local inhabitants for the purpose.[60] Second, they were used as punishment for only a limited number of offenders and for those serving short sentences. In the thirty-five years between 1765 and 1800, for example, only 8 per cent of those sentenced by the Montreal Court of Quarter Sessions were given a prison sentence.[61] Finally, gaols were used for multiple purposes, holding those committed for trial, those convicted and given a short sentence, those being held between conviction and execution, and imprisoned debtors. Gaols were often makeshift structures, especially in the early years of each colony, and some could be found in converted private homes. They were frequently insecure and as frequently unsuitable for housing people in the winter months.[62]

Bringing an Offender to Court: Policing and Prosecution

Just as English criminal law was transplanted with some modifications to the British North American colonies, so too were the principal features of the English system of policing and prosecution. The word prosecution is used here to mean the pretrial process, from investigation of an alleged crime to pretrial procedures up to the formal accusation; a later section deals with prosecution in court as part of the trial. In the second half of the eighteenth century this pretrial process was dominated largely by private initiative, usually that of the victim of crime, rather than being orchestrated by a police force, although the state did provide some resources to assist victims of crime. These resources consisted principally of justices of the peace (JPs) and the constables who operated under their authority. JPs performed a large number of administrative and quasi-judicial tasks. Sitting as judges at sessions they made local regulations and adjudicated minor criminal cases. Sitting either alone or in groups of two or three they heard regulatory infractions and exercised a small civil jurisdiction. Most importantly for current purposes, they oversaw the investigation of offences and the apprehension and bringing to court of suspected offenders.[63]

In this last area JPs in the English colonies were assisted by constables, untrained amateurs appointed by their communities to carry out the constables' duties as part of their civic responsibility. They were paid by fees rather than regular salaries (as were the JPs themselves) and were largely reactive rather than being at the forefront of the investigation of crime and the apprehension of criminals.[64] In all colonies provision was made early for the appointment of constables by local authorities. One of the first orders of the first governor of Halifax, Edward Cornwallis, was to divide the town into eight wards and to order the inhabitants to select sixteen constables annually, who were to patrol the city day and night. This system soon gave way to the English model whereby constables were chosen by the JPs in sessions, on the recommendation of grand juries.[65] Most other colonies followed the English model,[66] but Quebec had a different structure.[67] A bailiff and two sub-bailiffs were selected for each parish by a system combining householder voting with central government selection, a continuation of the French system.[68] Constables were introduced only in 1787 to augment the bailiff system.

Constables were a key part of the law enforcement system, even though their roles were limited and they effectively worked as adjuncts to JPs and crime victims. The case of Hugh Cameron, suspected of stealing some money from his temporary employer William Lavers, in Halifax in 1798, illustrates how the system of investigation and apprehension typically worked.[69] When Lavers, a King's County tailor and smallholder, journeyed to Halifax in March to sell some beef at Timothy Noonan's stall, he took on Cameron, a journeyman butcher, to help him. When he went for his lunch between two and three o'clock in the afternoon, Lavers left Cameron in charge of the meat and a small money bag. When he returned the money bag was missing, but Cameron denied any knowledge of it. Lavers inquired among those in the vicinity whether they had seen anything but received no information other than that Cameron was a 'bad character.' Lavers took his complaint to JP Michael Head, a surgeon and a leading citizen of Halifax,[70] who took down his deposition and issued a warrant to Constable Michael Leonard to search out and arrest Cameron. Assisted by soldier James Anderton, who was deputed by Head for the occasion to help him, Leonard found some coins secreted in Cameron's stockings. No money bag was found, and the coins did not add up to what Lavers thought he had lost, but Cameron, when taken before JP Head, 'acknowledged before me to his having taken the bag and money found upon him, and to his having thrown away the bag.' He also claimed he was drunk, whereupon he was remanded to the county gaol. Lavers signed a recognizance to return and prosecute, and Cameron was tried and convicted at the next sitting of the Supreme Court in Easter Term (April) 1798. His offence was grand larceny, a clergyable felony, and he asked for and received benefit of clergy. Cameron was perhaps lucky to be fined ten pounds rather than be branded, although he had to stay in gaol until the fine was paid, and there is no knowing how long that would have taken.

Four features of this account merit stressing. First, the initial investigation was carried out by the victim. Second, when Lavers required state help, he enlisted the services of a JP, not a police force in the modern sense. It was the JP who questioned the suspect, took down his statement, and deputed a constable and invested him with the legal power to search. It was also the JP who committed Cameron to the county gaol for trial. The Marian bail laws of the 1550s, in force in all the colonies, required JPs to take down the written depositions of the victim and witnesses and to examine the accused and reduce his or her statement to writing.[71] They also stipulated that bail was not to be granted in felonies; it was limited to minor assaults, misdemeanours, and the like, with the result that the vast majority of accused persons who were tried in a superior court, and many at sessions courts, were held in custody.

Third, while a constable was involved, he did nothing on his own initiative. He did what he was told and conducted the search but did not 'investigate' the matter at all. In this case he was assisted by a soldier, a not uncommon procedure in colonial cities with garrisons. Michael Leonard, the constable in this case, was a shopkeeper doing a period of service as a constable, selected by the freeholders of his parish and remunerated by fees.[72] Presumably in connection with his duties Leonard got into trouble the same year, prosecuted for assault by fellow shopkeeper Andrew Reynolds. The jury found him guilty, but he was fined only one shilling by an obviously sympathetic bench.[73] Fourth, although we have no account of the trial, evidence from other trials strongly suggests that the victim Lavers's presence and evidence was indispensable to the prosecution. As we will shortly see, the presentation of the case in court was the preserve of a public prosecutor. But the prosecutor needed the victim to testify about the circumstances. Hence Head not only took down Lavers's evidence, he also followed standard practice and issued him a recognizance to appear in court and prosecute, on pain of a fine. If the victim did not adhere to the recognizance, the case might be carried over, but it equally might be abandoned. In another case in 1798, in Trinity term, one Frederick Charles was discharged without a trial because the victim/prosecutor did not appear.[74]

For a long time historians deprecated the office of constable and the efforts of people like Michael Leonard, stressing the amateurism and inefficiency of the system and those who operated it, compared to the 'modern' police forces of the nineteenth century. But drawing such a sharp and simple contrast distorts the reality of what was happening. The eighteenth-century system was not like the one that emerged in the 1820s and 1830s, but it was nonetheless a more complex and effective policing system than it was once thought to be.[75] Three developments in particular were significant, one pertaining only to Quebec/Lower Canada, the other two to the other colonies. In Quebec, while parish bailiffs were in theory the principal law enforcement officers, some of the actual work was done in the rural areas by militia captains. More importantly, in both rural and urban areas, the major players were 'a small group of generally long-serving justice professionals who acted both for the civil and criminal courts.' They were the creation of, and employees of, the JPs who issued court orders and the sheriffs formally responsible for carrying them out. Hence there emerged a cadre of men, paid to carry out law enforcement duties and experienced at the tasks they had to perform.[76]

In Lower Canada and elsewhere, change also took place under the surface of a traditional system. In Montreal and Quebec after 1787, and in Halifax throughout this period, constables were increasingly experienced men who performed the duties year after year. This transition was brought about by those chosen by the community deciding not to serve personally but rather engaging substitutes to do so, and paying them. If a substitute was contracted in this way by a number of different men over a number of years, he was in effect a paid professional. He made a living from serving the justice system and presumably became better at it over time. Of the 561 men who served as constables in Montreal between 1787 and 1820, for example, only 132 – about a quarter – actually served in person; 429, or 76 per cent of them, 'served' through substitutes.[77] The substitute system also operated in Halifax, although we do not have as detailed an account of it. Extant constable lists of those actually attending court sessions from the 1790s show many names reappearing year after year, which would not have happened in a system of annual election. And the use of substitution is clearly, if ironically, exampled by the case of Henry Rand, a constable whose 'improper and indecent behaviour' was complained of by JP Henry Wood in 1794. The quarter sessions ordered that Rand 'be discharged from the office of constable, never to serve again in that or any other public office whatever' and also that 'he pay Mr Charles Prescott the sum he received from him to serve in that office.'[78]

A further significant development, which took place in Halifax at the end of this period and a little later elsewhere,[79] was the emergence of 'police offices' – places where JPs would meet regularly to dispense civil and criminal justice at the minor level, be consistently available for other law enforcement tasks, and be supported by full-time paid constables. The Halifax 'police office' proper was founded in 1815, at the conclusion of the Napoleonic Wars, a period of considerable disorder and heightened criminal activity in the city. It had a predecessor in a 'rotation court' established from 1792, so-called because all JPs were required to attend in turns in the courthouse.[80] Although they were denied jurisdiction to sentence anyone to prison, they were to question anyone apprehended and brought before them and commit them to gaol for trial at the next meeting of the appropriate court. The 1815 Act went much further. It formally established a police office consisting of three full-time salaried constables superintended by a salaried police magistrate who would attend at the office every day. While the police magistrate adjudicated minor criminal offences, he was also to 'perform and execute, each and every act, matter and thing, appertaining to the said office of a Justice of a Peace, necessary for the apprehension, committal, conviction, and punishment of criminal offenders, and for carrying into effect the Laws now in force for the preservation of peace and good order.'[81] The new police office was a response to an assembly committee report on the policing of Halifax,[82] and the same statute that authorized the police magistrate appointment also established a new prison, the Bridewell.

The Criminal Courts: Pretrial Procedures

As already noted, the vast majority of defendants apprehended on evidence of their having committed a serious crime were committed to the custody of the county jail to await their trial at the next meeting of the court. The wait could be a long one. Most superior courts based in colonial capitals met four terms a year, following the English calendar of Hilary, Easter, Trinity, and Michaelmas terms, and a defendant apprehended just after one term ended would have to wait two or three months for trial at the next term. When the courts met in England, much theatricality accompanied them, designed to impress all and sundry with the power of the law and the royal authority it represented. Attempts were often made to reproduce this in British North America, with assize sermons, processions from church to courthouse, judges dressed in scarlet robes, and the public reading of commissions.[83] In New Brunswick the judges were met by the sheriff and 'constables carrying staves of office embellished with a gold crown.'[84] But the effect was often somewhat less than impressive in the unpaved streets of some colonial capitals with their makeshift courthouses. It was even less majestic on circuit, with judges arriving on horseback rather than carriages, after having travelled many wearying hours on poor roads, which were often just cart tracks. Worse still, the travel delays caused by weather sometimes meant they would not arrive at all on the appointed days.[85]

When the court did meet to conduct criminal business, the first item on the agenda was the convening of the grand jury, a body of men of indeterminate number. It required a minimum of twelve to find an indictment, and by mid-century the general rule was that twenty-three ought to be called to serve, even if fewer than that actually attended.[86] There was no formal property qualification for grand jury service, the only requirement being that 'honest and legal men' be summoned. But in practice grand jurors were men occupying the higher ranks of colonial society – leading merchants, large landowners, JPs, and the like. Grand juries also played a role in local government, reporting on the need for better gaols or road repairs and the like, and thus it was important that the 'better sort' served. Grand jurors in Nova Scotia were chosen for the year, so that they served at four court sessions, while those in Quebec/Lower Canada served for three successive court sessions. Elsewhere they were chosen for the term, but grand jurors everywhere were men experienced in the criminal process, for it was not unusual for them to be called in more than one year.[87]

The grand jury was first charged by the presiding judge, in a speech that combined instruction in the basics of the criminal law with commentary on the political situation and the need to use the law to ensure loyalty to the Crown and its servants. The grand jurymen were then presented with indictments drawn up by the clerk of the Crown, who worked from jailers' lists of those in custody and depositions taken by JPs, and, as we shall see, was often assisted in the process of framing an indictment by one of the Crown law officers. The grand jury heard only the evidence from the prosecution in support of each indictment,[88] and if a majority of them, and at least twelve members, thought there was a prima facie case to go to trial, they would sign the indictment as a 'true bill.' If they thought the evidence insufficient, it would be signed 'ignoramus,' and the defendant would be freed. Perhaps not surprisingly, grand juries indicted most of those brought before them – 90 per cent in Halifax prior to 1815, for example.[89] For those with true bills found against them, arraignment and pleading followed, usually on a later day. Almost all defendants pleaded not guilty; indeed those who attempted to plead guilty were actively discouraged from doing so. This aspect of the trial process, like many others, was influenced by the law of punishments. The trial of those charged with capital offences was as much about finding reasons not to hang those found guilty as it was to determine guilt. A guilty plea meant no trial and no evidence which might persuade a judge to recommend or support an application for a pardon.

Before trials could take place trial juries had to be selected. In every colony there was a property qualification for jury service, not a high one but enough to exclude labourers and domestic servants and the like. Trial jurors tended to be men of lower socio-economic status than grand jurors – small traders, artisans, shopkeepers, and their ilk.[90] Jury lists were drawn up by the sheriff (provost-marshal in Nova Scotia prior to 1778), and a number of names, usually thirty-six, were selected from those lists just before the start of each term, and those chosen summoned to attend court. There were always absentees when the court met, sometimes because men were genuinely away from the colony, and sometimes because people resented losing time from their occupations. Absentee jurors were supposed to be fined, but rarely were. Jurymen who did show up were then selected into panels of twelve, with each panel hearing multiple cases in a day and sitting for multiple days, with only minor changes. Trial jurors therefore, like grand jurors, were men who became experienced at the task in hand. With all the preliminaries over, the trial itself would come on. Before discussing how the trial process operated in British North America, however, it is necessary to briefly describe the English trial inherited by the colonies.

The Criminal Trial

The English criminal trial underwent a drawn-out but profound transformation from the middle of the eighteenth century, a transformation that was not completed until well into the second half of the nineteenth.[91] In circa 1750 the trial was still very much what one historian has termed the 'accusation trial,' a short, sharp contest between the person harmed by the crime, or members of his or her family, and the defendant. Lawyers played a role in the process on very few occasions. Few victims of crime could afford to hire a prosecuting attorney, and there was no state system of Crown counsel. The vast majority of prosecutions were private, conducted by the victim or his or her family.

Defendants also laboured under disadvantages: they were incompetent to testify under oath,[92] there was no right to defence counsel except for those faced with a charge of treason, and when defence counsel did appear it was by permission of the trial judge. Even when defence counsel was present, their roles were circumscribed. They were always able to address the court on matters of law, and in addition most judges by mid-century also allowed them to cross-examine prosecution witnesses on behalf of their clients. But under no circumstances could lawyers address the jury. When all the evidence was in, and perhaps with the possibility of a death sentence to follow any guilty verdict, it was the accused who had to plead with the triers of fact, to make an argument as to why the evidence did not merit conviction. When complaints were voiced about this procedure, the standard answer was that defendants did not need lawyers, in part because the judge was there to ensure fairness, even to be, in a well-worn phrase, 'counsel for the prisoner.' This myth endured well into the nineteenth century, despite much evidence that judges could at times pursue convictions with remarkable tenacity.

Largely because of the absence of lawyers on either side, eighteenth-century trials were often very short affairs, normally lasting well under an hour from beginning to end. There were no opening statements: the prosecutor, usually the victim or a member of his or her family, simply told the story he or she had come to court to give, and this was sometimes, but not always, followed by other prosecution witnesses. The judge could interrupt with questions, as could the accused. The same process would then occur with the defence case, the accused trying to refute the prosecution evidence, provide some alternative explanation, or, very often, to convince the jury that he or she was of good character and thus either unlikely to have committed the crime alleged or not the kind of person who deserved to be hanged. This was a difficult task, not simply because the accused was rarely experienced in conducting a case but also because he or she had no knowledge beforehand of the precise nature of the evidence. Nor was the accused easily able to get supporting witnesses organized, for he or she had languished in jail since being committed. The defences offered were therefore generally poor efforts. The principal player in the trial was the judge. The judge was 'very much in charge' and 'very active' He led witnesses through their testimony and examined and cross-examined and thus had an 'immense influence on the way the jury received the evidence and the impression it made on them.' He was 'the dominant figure.'[93]

Not surprisingly, given this description, trials did not take long. Some lasted only a few minutes, occasionally two or three hours, but the average trial time in the mid-eighteenth century was half an hour. Trial time included jury deliberation and verdict, a process that could also be very rapid. Only infrequently did jurors leave the courtroom to deliberate; usually they conferred among themselves in the presence of prosecutor and accused before announcing their verdict. In fact one historian has cogently argued that when juries did not retire they could not really have been deliberating but acquiescing in the result suggested by the foreman, especially if he was a juror with considerable experience in the criminal courts.[94] When they did retire it was not for long; a murder case could take as much as twenty minutes' discussion, but rarely more than that.

Although the rules governing trials did not change in the second half of the eighteenth century, two significant and related modifications of trial practice occurred. First was the increased presence of defence lawyers. From mid-century their presence at trials slowly increased, probably in response to the increasing numbers of prosecuting counsel. By around 1800, it has been estimated, somewhere between a quarter and a third of defendants had the assistance of counsel.[95] The second development was derived from the first. Once lawyers started to play a larger role in trials, the nature of the process slowly and subtly changed. Although the restrictions on lawyers' roles remained, they came in practice to be able to test the prosecution evidence more effectively than defendants themselves could, pointing out inconsistencies, questioning motives and recollections. Slowly the trial shifted towards being more of an adversarial process, less wholly the 'accusation trial.'

Perhaps the most important changes wrought by the lawyers, however, were legal developments, most notably the solidification of the onus of proof. It is often assumed that the need to prove guilt beyond a reasonable doubt has been a pillar of English procedure for centuries. But as late as the mid-eighteenth century it was not a leading principle of the everyday work of the courts, even if some version of it was to be found in treatises. The leading historian of the eighteenth century trial concludes that while the prosecution needed to prove its case, and while the requirements of doing that were more onerous in capital cases than others, the defendant was not in some favoured position as far as presumptions went. The prevailing assumption at mid-century 'was not that he [the accused] was innocent until the case against him was proved beyond a reasonable doubt, but that if he were innocent he ought to be able to demonstrate it for the jury by the quality and character of his reply to the prosecutor's evidence.' In practical terms there was an onus on the defendant to assert and demonstrate his or her innocence. This changed with the increased use of defence lawyers. They were able to slowly persuade the judges to adopt and articulate the beyond-a-reasonable-doubt standard as an 'active principle' by the 1780s, and from the turn of the nineteenth century confident expressions of it were voiced by all participants in the trial.[96] This change was accompanied by other developments in the rules of evidence. Hearsay evidence and confessions were treated with suspicion from mid-century, and accomplice evidence was often the subject of doubting attacks if uncorroborated. The people casting such aspersions and issuing warnings were the lawyers, and this development contributed to the further evolution of the trial into an increasingly adversarial one.

In general the criminal trial operated in much the same way in the British North American colonies as it did in Britain. Judges played a prominent role, the evidence was produced in the same order, trial jurors were experienced men, except in Upper Canada, where, uniquely, a new panel was sworn for every case, and the accused persons had spent their pretrial time in custody.[97] But in two very significant respect trials in British North America were different. First, in one colony, Quebec/Lower Canada, the criminal process represented a profound change from what had gone on before the conquest under French procedure. Public trials, prosecutions that could be brought forward by anyone, and trial by jury were all features that marked large differences from the French regime. Indeed the fact that Quebec was under military occupation until 1764, and that trials were held by court martial, was a further innovation to both the francophone and anglophone populations. The attitudes of the Canadiens to the new criminal law, and the adaptations they made to it, are themes that run throughout what follows.[98] Second, in the higher courts of all colonies a Crown prosecutor, usually the attorney general himself, always conducted the prosecution, and Crown prosecutors were also often present in the much less serious cases prosecuted at quarter sessions. There were other differences also from the English trial, some of which resulted from the presence of prosecuting lawyers. Before turning to other aspects of the trial, therefore, the ubiquitous presence of Crown counsel in the superior courts, and their occasional appearances in quarter sessions, the major colonial departure from English practice, deserves more detailed examination.

The practice began at mid-century, in the General Court of Nova Scotia and its successor, the NSSC, and the attorney general's role began at the commencement of criminal proceedings, with the preparation and presentation of indictments to the grand jury.[99] It was the attorney general who oversaw the drawing up of these indictments, presented the evidence supporting them to the grand jury, and then conducted the prosecution when each individual went to trial. This was the practice in the capital and generally when, after 1774, the court went on circuit to other communities or held trials outside Halifax on special commission, with either the attorney general or solicitor general travelling with the court. If on occasion neither law officer did so, some other lawyer did, or one was drawn from the local bar to conduct the prosecution. Thus when George and James Boutelier were tried for murder in the relatively inaccessible town of Lunenburg, Nova Scotia, in 1791, they were prosecuted by James Stewart, who travelled from Halifax to do so. Stewart later became solicitor general and later still a Supreme Court judge, but when he conducted this prosecution he had served only four years at the bar.[100] When Walter Lee was tried at Guysborough, Nova Scotia, in 1812 for murder by a special commission of oyer and terminer, the remoteness of the location, and perhaps the fact that this was the only case tried on the commission, meant that no law officer or other lawyer had travelled with the judge from Halifax. The deputy clerk of the Crown for the county conducted the prosecution, bringing forward and eliciting testimony from five witnesses.[101] In Halifax the law officers of the Crown also prosecuted some cases at quarter sessions, although this was unusual within British North America.[102]

This is not to say that there was no place for the victim in the process. If the victim did not appear, cases were dismissed or held over, because whether or not the victim was the prosecutor in court, his or her presence was vital to the prosecution case. Crown counsel's role was limited to using materials gathered by others to frame indictments and to presenting the case in court. He did not gather the evidence, question potential witnesses, summon them to court, or generally organize the case before trial. As discussed above, those were tasks performed in part by JPs and in part by the victim. In this regard prosecution was a hybrid of the public and private. Moreover, from the limited evidence available it seems there were occasional examples of victims or their families presenting the cases in the superior courts. But this was not the invariable practice as it was in England.

The attorney general of Quebec played a similar role in that colony to that of Nova Scotia from the 1760s.[103] When the Loyalist colonies of New Brunswick and Upper Canada were founded in the 1780s and early 1790s, Crown law officers again took on all the prosecutorial work. Public prosecution was a feature of colonial governance for a number of reasons. In part the motive was simply financial. Crown law officers saw this as a way to enhance their low official salaries.[104] By the 1810s, for example, prosecutions produced three-quarters of the Upper Canadian attorney general's revenue.[105] But this does not by itself explain the departure from English practice. In newly established colonies the criminal law was an important tool of social control, and government support for prosecution – in personnel and in financing – was an indication of the importance attached to this practice. The importance attached to professional prosecution in Upper Canada is suggested, ironically, in an early nineteenth-century dispute over the always contentious issue of whether the attorney general had the right to monopolize prosecutions. In the early 1810s there was a factional dispute among the elite, during which the lieutenant governor tried to make Attorney General Firth take the less-remunerative (western) of the two circuits. Firth protested, calling prosecution work 'the first, highest and most important Branch of the official Duty of the Attorney-General.' But the executive council disagreed, arguing that there was no need for a Crown law officer to prosecute 'unless matters especially regarding the King's interest are there to be agitated.' The council argued that the practice of the attorney general conducting prosecutions was a local expedient from the days when no one else was qualified; by now others could do the job, and this idea of delegating the task to somebody else received support from one of the King's Bench judges, who proposed that a system of king's counsels be set up for various districts. Tellingly, the dispute was over who should get the job and the fees; nobody suggested that prosecution should be left in private hands.[106]

Defence lawyers also appeared in colonial superior courts, in increasing numbers as the eighteenth century wore on. This was a radical innovation in Quebec, for defence lawyers had never appeared in New France. Indeed advocates as such did not exist in the colony, although bailiffs and notaries did assist parties in civil proceedings.[107] We do not know exactly how often defendants had counsel, but the number seems to have varied from place to place. In the Montreal Court of King's Bench in the early nineteenth century their presence is 'very evident' in the notebooks of Chief Justice James Reid, while a study of the Upper Canadian assizes calls their presence 'routine.'[108] In the NSSC in the 1780s and 1790s defence lawyers probably appeared in 25–30 per cent of the trials, roughly the same as in England, but in the NBSC at Fredericton no more than 10 per cent of defendants had legal representation.[109] In all jurisdictions lawyers were more likely to appear for persons facing capital charges. When Daniel Disney, a British army officer, was tried for burglary in 1767 in Quebec, he had three British lawyers to help him.[110] Similarly, Elizabeth Borlee, tried for arson in Fredericton in 1813, was represented by Charles Peters, who was rumoured to have the most lucrative practice of any at the local bar. Peters also secured an acquittal two years later for two men charged with the capital offence of forgery.[111] Unfortunately we know nothing about whether this work was performed pro bono or remunerated. It was unlikely that criminal defence work paid much, if at all, since many defendants were poor and there was no system for paying defence lawyers out of the public purse. Especially in the early years of settlement of a colony, the 'defence bar' was a very small one, no more so than in Quebec, where in the years immediately after the conquest lawyers were required to perform tasks entirely alien to them. Indeed the tendency for the Quebec criminal bar to consist largely of anglophones persisted until at least the 1820s.[112] The small size of colonial bars everywhere meant that defendants who did want a lawyer had little choice about who represented them, although that also meant that they got experienced men. The afore-mentioned Charles Peters was one of just three men noted as defending in the Supreme Court at Fredericton in the early nineteenth century.[113] In one colony only, Nova Scotia, defence lawyers also made occasional appearances in the quarter sessions in the 1790s, defending people accused of assault, regrating, and petit larceny.[114]

The formal rules governing defence lawyers' participation were the same as in England, and the practice of the judges was to allow them to participate, argue points of law, and cross-examine witnesses, but in no circumstances to make speeches to the jury.[115] Hence when the trial of Walter Lee for murder at Guysborough, Nova Scotia, in 1811 ended, he was on his own in addressing the jury, in giving a speech for his life. He was less than persuasive needing, in the words of the presiding judge, 'repeated pauses for recollection and to recover from the distress he appeared to be in.'[116] Before this climatic moment arrived, defence lawyers shared the questioning of witnesses with the judges. Surviving judges' trial notebooks, such as those of Isaac Deschamps of the NSSC and James Reid of the Montreal Court of King's Bench, show lawyers as actively and persistently cross-examining prosecution witnesses.[117]

The differences and similarities between Britain and British North America over the presence of lawyers in the criminal trial resulted in subtle differences between the nature of the process at home and across the Atlantic. The colonial trial was less the 'accusation trial' than it was in England, and it was more adversarial and slightly more drawn out. Whereas the Old Bailey could get through anywhere from a dozen to two dozen cases a day, the NSSC in Halifax only twice tried ten people a day in the second half of the eighteenth century. On more than half of its trial days in the same period it only heard one case, and it heard three or fewer cases on three-quarters of its trial days. Similarly, in New Brunswick, in nineteen terms between 1802 and 1815 in which the Supreme Court conducted criminal trials – in some terms there were none – the average number of trials per term was just over two.[118] In early Upper Canada the superior courts often took a day for a trial.[119] The slower pace of trial was to a large extent the result of having fewer defendants to try, but the invariable presence of prosecuting counsel must also have played a role.

Yet the time it took to conduct trials was likely the only major difference between colonial and English criminal process.[120] The other features of the English process that make it seem so foreign to modern eyes were present in the colonies. While the trial was partly 'adversary,' most witnesses gave their evidence as a narrative, even if one prompted by a few general questions from Crown counsel. Defendants were expected to tell their side of the story in response. Jurors sat for multiple cases in a term and reappeared in court in subsequent terms.[121] Juries did not take long to give their verdicts and often did not leave the courtroom to deliberate. Judges were consistently interventionist and often directory. On both sides of the Atlantic the 'beyond a reasonable doubt' principle emerged only in the early nineteenth century. Tellingly, the familiar phrase was never mentioned by the prosecutor in explaining the law about the standard of proof to the jury in the Bouteliers' 1791 case, discussed earlier, nor by Chief Justice Strange, presiding after recently arriving from England. Stewart did say that he was 'happy' to remind the jurors 'of an ancient maxim, well-known to the humanity of the English law, that "it is better that ninety-nine guilty men should escape than one innocent man suffer."' But on the onus of proof he and Strange used a variety of formulations other than 'beyond a reasonable doubt': they needed the evidence to be strongly against the accused, a 'mild presumption of guilt' would not suffice, and the Bouteliers should be acquitted if there was the 'smallest doubt' about guilt.'[122]

The similarities between colonial and English criminal procedure were also present in the one colony in which English procedure was an alien imposition to most inhabitants – Quebec/Lower Canada. Although there was much about the new system that was culturally unfamiliar to the Canadiens, such as trial by jury and a process open to all, and although some in the colony resented the loss of the control that their elite status had given them in the old system,[123] on the whole the Canadiens adapted to the new system, learned how to work it, and saw it as no less – and no more – legitimate than what had gone before. Principal among the innovations in trial process that responded to the new political reality was the use of juries *de medietate*, juries composed of half Canadiens and half British-descended subjects; they were introduced for civil trials by an ordinance of 1766 and then became a feature of criminal trials by convention.[124] So common was the phenomenon that it became 'ingrained in the legal culture of Quebec' as a kind of customary right.[125] Also of great significance was the fact that not only were defence counsel allowed to practise in the criminal courts, but that local lawyers learned how to operate in this new context.

Most notably among this catalogue of similarities to the English trial in the same period, the trial was often a contest in which the character of the accused and the nature of the prescribed punishment mattered. With not much evidence presented, the former often determined the outcome in jurors' minds, while those same jurymen could have the decision they gave influenced by whether they believed the person should face hanging, even if he or she had likely committed the crime. Hence, as in England, acquittal rates were, by modern standards, quite high. About a third of all defendants in the Halifax Supreme Court were acquitted in the second half of the eighteenth century, and fully 61 per cent of those charged capitally were either acquitted altogether or found guilty only of a lesser, non-capital offence.[126] The acquittal rate was much the same in Quebec/Lower Canada, meaning that it was much higher than it had been under the French system.[127] Rates were slightly different at the Upper Canadian assizes, with more people acquitted (40 per cent) but fewer found guilty of a lesser charge (6 per cent), meaning that the convicted as charged rate (53 per cent) was higher than elsewhere.[128] The outright acquittal rate was highest in the New Brunswick Supreme

Court at Fredericton in the early nineteenth century – 63 per cent.[129] While there were therefore some differences across the colonies, partially accounted for by the small numbers in some places, overall the eighteenth- and early nineteenth-century system did not convict nearly as many people as modern trials do.

17

Indigenous Law

The contours of Indigenous law in the long eighteenth century varied significantly according to the geography of settlement and Indigenous demographics. In those areas untouched by settlement, such as the north and west, Indigenous law continued to be the dominant legal tradition.[1] From the Great Lakes east, Indigenous law encountered common law or civil law in many areas. Given that Indigenous traditions were mainly oral and that the colonial courts were seldom used by Indigenous people during this period, it is difficult to trace the impact of this encounter on Indigenous law. There are some areas, however, where the content of Indigenous law and its interaction with colonial European law can be reconstructed in some detail: the mission communities in the St Lawrence valley, and the Six Nations settlement at Grand River in Upper Canada. Recent work has focused on three of the former communities: the Huron-Wendat of Wendaké (Jeune-Lorette) near Quebec City, the Mohawk of Kahnawake (Sault-Saint-Louis) near Montreal, and the Abenaki of Odanak (St François), near Trois-Rivières.[2] Grand River will play a lesser role here because the migration of the Six Nations to Upper Canada occurred only towards the end of the period covered in this chapter, but it will become more prominent in chapter 23.

The experiences of these four communities were not identical to those of all Indigenous peoples, and indeed were quite distinctive in many respects. Nonetheless, they prefigured conflicts that would arise more widely in the nineteenth century with the spread of settlement, while providing evidence of integration into the colonial legal order. They will be used as case studies in this chapter, with the caution that their experience cannot be generalized easily. Historians have struggled to find metaphors or models to describe the interaction of Indigenous and European societies and their legal orders: middle ground,[3] common ground,[4] shared space.[5] We believe it is premature to adopt any of these models as a generalization, and indeed it is not surprising that each of the above arose from the study of a specific geographic space: respectively, the Upper Great Lakes, Montreal, and Jeune-Lorette. Deborah Doxtator's reminder that place and space are more important than time in the Indigenous world view is apposite here.[6] We would add that place and space should not be understood purely in their topographical sense but must include reference to their inhabitants as well. The Huron-Wendat of Jeune-Lorette, for example, made decisions about how to structure their interactions with others in the highly seigneurialized space near Quebec City, that were different from those they made when hunting in territories on the north shore of the St Lawrence, which they shared with Algonquins and other Indigenous peoples. They could be highly integrated with the colonial legal order in some spaces and act independently of it in others.

Scholars have tended to privilege colonial court archives to trace the interaction of Indigenous and settler law. Certainly much can be derived from these records, though litigation did not always pit Indigenous people against Europeans directly, but sometimes involved disagreement within Indigenous communities over whether their law should change to accommodate new opportunities, technologies, and patterns of life. Conflicts did erupt over land use and management, over the use of traditional methods of dispute resolution versus those of settler society, and over how far Indigenous law would be receptive to European notions of economic liberty, and these will be examined in this chapter. If you look only at records of conflict, however, that is all you will see. Recent work by historians of Quebec has begun to exploit notarial records as a resource for the study of the legal experiences of Indigenous peoples. These form the paper trail of facilitative law, where parties enter into contracts and property dispositions to achieve goals that are important to them. Notarial greffes present a rather different picture of Indigenous legal behaviour, one that portrays them as integrated in some respects into the colonial legal order and using it to advance their own purposes. Integration should not be equated with assimilation, however, as Indigenous people clearly remained committed to their own traditions and ways of life while at the same time using elements of the colonial legal order strategically.

We will begin with Kahnawake, as it was one of the first Indigenous communities to face the problems arising from the interaction of Indigenous and settler law for a number of reasons. The emphasis here will be mainly on conflict. We then turn to the issue of the mission communities' engagement with the seigneurial system and with the settler legal order more generally, drawing on examples from Kahnawake, Jeune-Lorette, and Odanak. Here the emphasis will be on cooperation and Indigenous agency. Finally, we will try to balance these two perspectives.

With a population between 1,000 and 2,000 in the eighteenth and nineteenth centuries, Kahnawake became the largest Indigenous community in New France and remains so in Quebec today.[7] After 1760 it was considered by the British and by other Indigenous communities in Quebec as the lead partner in the Seven Fires (Sept Feux), a loose confederation of all the mission settlements in Quebec, and the primary interlocutor with the colonial government.[8] The proximity of Kahnawake to Montreal meant that it was close to colonial courts, unlike many other Indigenous communities located further from European settlements. This proximity also provided possibilities for more diverse economic opportunities than in other places, holding out possibilities of individual enrichment that were difficult to reconcile with traditional communal norms. Over the course of the eighteenth century residents supplemented their traditional agriculture with European practices, growing grains and potatoes as well as their customary crops, and raising domestic animals. The men of Kahnawake largely adopted Western dress, and by the end of the century most families no longer lived in longhouses but in individual dwellings similar to those occupied by French habitants. A parallel evolution had occurred in the Mohawk valley homeland in New York state, and these patterns were also found in the Grand River territory in Upper Canada on which the Six Nations settled after the American Revolution.[9]

One cannot assume that this visual evidence of the adoption of some European ways necessarily reflects an adoption of underlying values, or a straightforward process of assimilation. The teachings of the Seneca prophet Handsome Lake, derived from visions he experienced in 1799–1804, demonstrate this. While his Good Message, or Karihwiyo, preached the legitimacy of European agriculture, stock-raising, and house construction as consonant with Haudenosaunee traditions, it also strongly affirmed many traditional beliefs and practices, giving rise to what would later be called the longhouse religion; this cultural development would influence Kahnawake and the Six Nations settlement in Upper Canada, providing competition for the Christian churches that were also well established in those communities.[10] Accommodation had its limits, however, and regular interaction with European society would eventually put pressure on the maintenance of Haudenosaunee customary law.

Kahnawake grew out of the decision of members of a variety of Indigenous nations to resettle near the French in the wake of the 1667 peace reached between the latter and the Haudenosaunee. The Mohawks became the dominant cultural group after some 200 of them arrived from the Mohawk valley in 1673–4.[11] Those who came to Kahnawake did so for a variety of reasons: the desire of some converts to be closer to a Christian community, flight from war, and the possibility of exploring new trade opportunities.[12] As noted in chapter 8, in 1680 the French Crown granted the seigneury of Sault Saint-Louis, some 40,000 acres (over 16,000 hectares), to the Jesuits to hold for the benefit of the Mohawks.[13] At first the settlement moved every generation or so, in accordance with Haudenosaunee agricultural practice. The last move occurred in 1716, to what would become the community's permanent home, although some fifty families moved one hundred kilometres upstream in 1750 to found the community of Akwesasne.[14]

The Jesuit missionary Joseph-François Lafitau who resided at Kahnawake for nearly six years (1712–17) left a detailed and perceptive account of many of the customs and traditions of the Mohawk, or Iroquois as he called them.[15] While Kahnawake was outside the Five Nations Confederacy, its traditions demonstrated significant continuity with those in the Mohawk heartland over a long period of time. As noted in part 1 of this volume, Lafitau adopted a universalist and humanist perspective rather than one centred on assumptions of racial or cultural superiority.[16] He provided a wide-ranging account of the institutions of governance and dispute resolution, marriage and family law, criminal law, and property law. Like many Europeans, Lafitau was impressed with the way that Mohawk society combined active government with a strong respect for individual liberty.

> The chiefs' authority properly extends over the people of their clan whom they consider their children. They usually call them their nephews. They rarely use a term corresponding to that of subject. Although they have a real authority which some know how to use, they still affect to give so

> much respect to liberty that one would say to see them, that they are all equal. [The chiefs] have neither distinctive mark, nor crown ... to differentiate them from the common people. Their power does not appear to have any trace of absolutism. It seems that they have no means of coercion to common obedience in case or resistance. They are obeyed, however, and command with authority; their commands, given as requests, and the obedience paid them, appear entirely free. This freedom serves to hold the chiefs in check. It engages them to command nothing which might cause trouble and be followed by a refusal.... Good order is kept by this means.[17]

Authority was widely dispersed in Kahnawake society, which featured a variety of checks and balances. Lafitau's account is generally in accord with the Great Law of Peace as recounted by Indigenous sources and scholars. The Great Law 'sanctioned a set of leaders for each of [the forty-nine] clan families including a Royaner, Yakoyaner (Clan Mother), a Runner or assistant (sometimes referred to as a subchief or deputy), and a male and female "Faithkeeper."'[18] Kahnawake had representatives of only seven clans – four Mohawk and three from the Ononadaga and Oneida – but otherwise followed the pattern.[19]

Lafitau was correct to observe that women played a key role in Kahnawake's matriarchal society:

> In each clan, each individual and distinct matrilineage has one person who acts as representative for it. The women choose them and are often in this position themselves. Their duty is to watch more immediately over the nation's interest; to keep an eye on the funds or public treasury; to provide for its conservation and watch over the use which should be made of it.[20]

However, his later description of Mohawk society as a 'gynocracy' where men were 'mere pawns in a female-dominated Haudenosaunee world,' a view that became very influential among later scholars, has been justly criticized as excessive.[21] Coming from a society where women exercised no political power, and where authority was equated with domination over others, it would have been difficult for Lafitau to conceive of men and women sharing power in any governance structure, as they did in Haudenosaunee society.

The authority of the Rotiyanehson related mainly to what we might call 'executive' matters. 'Policy' issues, dealings with outside bodies, and dispute resolution required decisions of the council of elders, or senate as Lafitau sometimes calls it.[22] With regard to policy matters, before the council was convoked, women and men deliberated separately. The women did so first, advising the chiefs of their views. The chiefs then deliberated and provided their opinions to the council, in which the role of any given chief was relatively unimportant unless he also happened to be a respected elder.

It is not entirely clear whether the council itself dealt with dispute resolution (except for grave offences, when it might order the death of the offender), or whether it appointed third parties to do so. Lafitau recorded that 'their little disputes are soon settled by arbitration but, I must do them the justice of saying that their quarrels are rare,' and he noted that parties often preferred to concede a point rather than push matters to a confrontation.[23] The fact that such an orderly society could get along without specialized officers of dispute settlement was a marvel. 'By good fortune for them, they knew neither code of law, nor digest, nor lawyers, nor attorneys, nor constables: if, along with that, they did not have their shamans who are very bad doctors, would they not be the most fortunate people in the world?'[24] Lafitau here displayed the anti-lawyer sentiment common to early modern Europeans, imagining a world without lawyers as a kind of paradise. He perhaps did not recognize that the wide diffusion of 'legal knowledge' within Haudenosaunee society, along with a more egalitarian distribution of resources, played a role in minimizing intra-societal conflict.

With regard to land use and management, Lafitau observed that the Kahnawake Mohawk knew both communal and individual, or at least familial, property. Under the superintendence of the women, the community grew corn, beans, and squash, though they would later also cultivate grains and potatoes, introduced to them by Europeans.[25] While their cleared unfenced fields might look like a single communal space to the casual observer, each family had its own space, which it knew very well, even though all women helped each other with routine agricultural labour. Sir William Johnson also attested to these practices among the New York Mohawk in the 1760s, suggesting that they had been faithfully transferred to Kahnawake.[26] Lewis Morgan in the mid-nineteenth century stated, 'No individual could obtain the absolute title to land, as that was vested by the laws of the Iroquois in all the people; but he could reduce unoccupied lands to cultivation, to any extent he pleased; and so long as he continued to use them, his right to their enjoyment was protected and secured.'[27] Some versions of the Great Law refer to women as 'proprietors' or 'owners' of the land, but these terms need to be understood in the context of Haudenosaunee property concepts.

Cleared land was indeed female-oriented space, but the role of women was more analogous to that of stewards than 'owners' under European law. As Susan Hill notes, in Haudenosaunee languages the word for ownership 'denotes a connection with something and a responsibility to it.'[28] The fact that women had a special relationship to the clearings does not mean that men had no claim or interest in them; they just had fewer responsibilities.

Lafitau had little to say about inheritance. Under traditional Mohawk practice, when the community moved to a new locale, all use rights or claims to the former territory were abandoned, such that inheritance would have been limited mostly to movable property, or to intangibles such as names, songs, and the like. Even when inheritance was permitted, however, Mohawk law did not allow an individual to amass more land or assets than he or she could use, and prohibited sale for speculative purposes. At Grand River this issue sometimes came up in the context of mixed marriages. Thus in 1809 the council wrote to the superintendent general of Indian affairs with regard to land that 'was given to a John Huff [a settler] for the good of his family who are of a Delaware mother.' On learning that he planned to sell the land, they requested that the purchasers be expelled and 'his family left in peaceable possession,' as council had forbidden such sales.[29] Council was prepared to let the land descend to Huff's children, as it would provide support for them as Haudenosaunee citizens, but regarded a sale by Huff to outsiders as impermissible. Attempts to treat property as capital, including moves by some citizens of Kahnawake to exploit resources with hired labour, created tensions within the community in the late eighteenth century, leading residents to resort to colonial courts for the first time to resolve internal disputes.

Some early signs of trouble came in 1771. A delegation of '22 Indians Deptys from the Village of Caghanawaga' complained to the son-in-law of Sir William Johnson, the British superintendent of Indian Affairs, that 'two Indian Families there have expressed an Intention to bring some French Families and Settle them on the Lands reserved for their common use, the ill consequences of which ... they have fully enlarged upon.'[30] This complaint was not about Europeans squatting on Indigenous lands, a common complaint then and later. It was about some inhabitants of Kahnawake inviting French families to settle among them, perhaps by purporting to sell land to them. A small group of inhabitants of Kahnawake were clearly trying to evade seeking the approval of council, which would be required before any land could be alienated to outsiders, pushing community leaders to seek back-up from British colonial officials.[31] While this particular conflict does not appear to have ended up in court, a quarter-century later both 'modernizers' and 'traditionalists' at Kahnawake would begin to bring their internal disputes to the courts of Lower Canada.

Many of those conflicts centred upon two people: Thomas Arakwente and his wife Sagosinnagete, also known as Agathe. Between 1760 and 1820 only twenty-seven cases in Quebec courts between Indigenous parties relating to matters on their lands have been found. Almost all arose in Kahnawake, and half of these (thirteen) involved Arakwente or his spouse.[32] For the Irish traveller Isaac Weld, Arakwente's reputation had preceded him: this member of the 'Cachenonaga nation ... was [said to be] a very rich man ... and had a most excellent house in which ... he lived as well as a seignior.'[33] Weld reported that Arakwente was fluent in French as well as his mother tongue and also spoke English passably; he discovered later that the Mohawk 'was not a man respected among the Indians in general, who think much more of a chief that is a good warrior and hunter, and retains the habits of his nation, than of one that becomes a trader, and assimilates his manners to those of the whites.'[34] Daniel Rueck's catalogue of his activities shows how likely it was that he would come into conflict with Kahnawake's communal traditions: he 'ran an inn that sold liquor legally to non-Natives and illegally to his fellow Mohawks. He was also a fur trader, land-holder, speculator, and money-lender, and held a lucrative ferry license' for the river crossing between Lachine and Kahnawake.[35] In modern parlance, Arakwente was an entrepreneur in a community that had not had to deal with such a phenomenon before.

Arakwente's initial attempts to use the courts to settle disputes related to land at Kahnawake were not successful.[36] In 1796 he sued a chief who had caused to be torn down a fence with which Arakwente had enclosed a piece of land. Both parties agreed that Mohawk custom allowed anyone to assert title to unoccupied land that they had possessed for a year. The Court of King's Bench heard evidence from Mohawk witnesses on this custom, and some also testified that it was customary for the chiefs to decide any such disputes; the defendant argued that as he had acted on behalf of the chiefs, his action could not be impugned. While the court found for the defendant, it is not clear which argument prevailed.[37] The case is interesting not only because of the court's upholding and enforcing of Mohawk customary law, but also because of the identity of the parties' counsel. Arakwente was represented by Arthur Davidson, a prominent Montreal advocate who would join the Montreal Court of King's Bench in 1800. The chief's counsel was Louis-Charles Foucher, named solicitor general the previous year and elected to the assembly in 1796; he too would join the Montreal Court of King's Bench, in 1812.[38] In 1799 when Arakwente's hired labourers were cutting wood on the seigneury with a view to selling it to outsiders, the chiefs again intervened. This time he alleged that Mohawk customary law authorized his actions. Certainly an individual had a right to cut wood on the seigneury as required for personal heating, cooking, and building, but there was no customary right to cut wood for outside sale. Arakwente brought suit in the Montreal Court of King's Bench but withdrew it before a decision was reached.

Matters soon escalated to threats, personal violence, and attempted expulsion of one or both Arakwentes from Kahnawake. Here, where personal safety and mobility were concerned, they were more successful in seeking the protection of the courts. Sagosinnagete sued one of the chiefs who had caused her to be expelled from church in 1799, and he had to enter into a bond to keep the peace. Her husband achieved the same result in that year when he complained that two residents of Kahnawake, a father and son, had made death threats against him. In 1806, when Arakwente again complained of threats of violence and a bailiff from the Court of King's Bench attempted to arrest the defendant, a crowd of fifty people prevented him from doing so, shouting that they 'n'avaient rien à voir avec la loi de Montréal' (they had nothing to do with the law of Montreal). Later that year a large crowd, at the council's direction, seized Arakwente and physically expelled him from Kahnawake, warning him that he risked death if he returned, because he would not 'renounce the law of this country [that is, European law], nor give up his business.'[39] Arakwente was able to use the courts again to secure his return to Kahnawake, and the chiefs were fined thirty pounds. While the reasons of the court are not available, it appears that British criminal law was held to prevail over Mohawk custom, assuming the validity of Arakwente's expulsion under that custom. While one can understand the desire of colonial courts to redress acts of personal violence, depriving the government of Kahnawake of the authority to enforce its decisions regarding expulsion of inhabitants believed to be a fundamental threat to the community's well-being was a serious blow to the integrity of customary law and authority, and indeed to the community itself. The chiefs had seen this coming much earlier: when Arakwente began his first action in 1796, they asked Governor Carleton that

Mohawk not be allowed to use the colonial courts to resolve disputes internal to Kahnawake. He referred the matter to Attorney General John Sewell, who advised that any person living under the protection of the British Crown had the right to seek assistance and protection from the courts.[40]

Arakwente did not remain a solitary dissenter in his desire to redraw the limits of Mohawk customary law in favour of more economic liberty; some dissident chiefs joined him, although it appears a large majority of the community favoured the maintenance of traditional ways. It may have been these disagreements that led the chiefs to write down their fundamental laws for the first time in a European language and format. The 'Règlements établis par les chefs du Sault Saint-Louis, Feb. 26, 1801' (hereafter referred to as the '1801 code') are of interest from a number of perspectives.[41] The preamble declares that they were adopted by a meeting of the chiefs who met for this purpose in the council house on the day in question, but they were recorded in French by a notary, presumably in order to give the document more weight with regard to external authorities. Twenty-one rules were proposed, of which all but one were noted as accepted. While in the main the twenty rules reflect traditional communal principles regarding residence, social behaviour, and land use and management, they also show acceptance of European legal ideas and practices at various points. Whether these features truly convey the conclusions of the Mohawk chiefs or represent a conscious or unconscious translation of Mohawk concepts by the notary into a legal vocabulary more familiar to him cannot be known.

The 1801 document began with a declaration that the seigneury was the 'propriété de la Nation Iroquoise dudit village' common to all the members of the Nation, and therefore that it was not permitted to subdivide, sell, or transfer any part of it in any manner. However, subsequent articles make it clear that the entire seigneury was not held purely as communal property but that, in accordance with Mohawk law, some private property was recognized. Article 3 stated that no one could 'posséder ni distribuer' more land than he could clear personally, while article 6 declared that where cleared land was abandoned by its 'proprietor,' it could be worked by anyone else who took possession of it. Interestingly, no minimum length of time was stated to establish this claim, in contrast to the 1796 Arakwente dispute, where the custom was said to require one year's possession of vacant land to establish title. The existence of individual property – based on possession, as the rules contain no express mention of inheritance – was also assumed in other places, such as article 9, subjecting to a penalty anyone damaging or taking down the fence of another, or article 10, requiring all owners of pigs to put them in pens in the spring, lest they damage the crops of any proprietor, who was then authorized to kill the offending animal without compensation to its owner.

Article 5 forbade any owner of lands or sugar-bush from 'selling or ceding' (vendre ni céder) such lands without the permission of the council. Depending on how frequently the council was prepared to grant such permission, an active land market could have arisen, and *céder* is a more inclusive word than *vendre*, such that it might have included the possibility of inheritance, lease, or gift. On the topic of cutting and selling wood, which had attracted such attention in the disputes with Arakwente, article 4 was categorical: no proprietor could cut wood on his own property for sale to outsiders. All wood was reserved exclusively for those living on the seigneury.

So far, the 1801 code reflects primarily the traditional layering of communal and individual property rights characteristic of Mohawk society, but the extent of the rights of 'owners' (propriétaires) to deal with their plots is left somewhat unclear – perhaps intentionally. Meanwhile, frequent references to fences and to domestic animals suggest that the adoption of some European agricultural practices had obliged the residents of Kahnawake to adapt their law to deal with problems arising from these innovations. Significantly, too, gender was nowhere mentioned. While in traditional Mohawk society women controlled agricultural plots, it seems that by the end of the eighteenth century men were asserting a form of 'ownership' of such lands. If the actions of Arakwente are any indication, men were more likely than women to want to commercialize lands on the seigneury.

A final trait to note in the code of 1801 is the frequency with which the penalty for infractions is specified as an amount of money to be split between the informer and the property owner in question, or given to the church. Thus, someone who milks a cow (article 12) or takes a canoe not belonging to them (article 15) will be liable to pay a fine of forty sols, of which half will go to the informer and half to the owner of the cow or the canoe. Anyone who pastures his horse outside the common pasture will be subject to a fine of one Spanish dollar, to be paid to the parish church for the repose of the souls of the deceased of Kahnawake (article 15). This kind of provision, which aimed to provide some financial incentive to individuals to bring misdeeds to light for prosecution, was common in both English and French law and represents another example of intercultural borrowing by the people of Kahnawake.

In 1804 the chiefs went to a different notary and adopted a different set of laws. While the introductory articles are the same, the rest feature notable differences with the code of 1801. In particular the 1804 document shows the council acting almost like a municipal council, enacting 'règlements' related to local public order and sanitation. Disturbing the peace, holding gatherings before or after mass, refusing to bury dead animals, conducting horse races in the village – all are constructed as offences with the chiefs given the power to impose fines for breaches.[42] Clearly the troubles with the Arakwentes had inspired reflection among the chiefs about the extent of their authority more generally, although the most dramatic confrontation with Thomas lay in the future. The chiefs gave a special procuration to Guillaume Chevalier de Lorimier to request the assembly that it enact these laws, but for unknown reasons it appears this was never done. The 1801 code was declared by the chiefs to be 'revoked' in a notarial document of 1808. No such revocation of the 1804 code has been found, and its ultimate fate is unclear.[43]

Given the timing of its adoption so soon after the conflicts involving the Arakwente family, these codes may have been intended to constitute a reaffirmation of traditional customary law while conceding limited adaptations to it arising from new agricultural practices, a more settled society, and increasing intercourse with residents of the growing urban centre of Montreal nearby. They may have been directed primarily at the members of Kahnawake itself, restating their law and implicitly encouraging them to resolve disputes internally using traditional processes, as the code contains no reference to colonial courts. Some have seen the codes as an assertion of the power of the chiefs over their people at a time when their authority was beginning to be questioned.[44] Another interpretation might suggest that the primary motivation related to external, not internal, audiences. The idea of codification may not have arisen from the chiefs themselves, but from their lawyers: they may have suggested that the best way for the chiefs to defend their practices in colonial courts, should it come to that, would be to have some account of them written down. The statement in article 1 of the 1801 code that the chiefs could delegate their authority 'by notarial act approved in a full council called for that purpose' suggests that they were concerned to be able to prove facts to outside authorities, as such formality would have been unnecessary for an internal audience.

These two motivations, internal and external, are not mutually exclusive, but both are no more than educated guesses. Both the adoption of the code and its revocation are useful in illustrating the state of flux in which Indigenous law found itself at Kahnawake at the turn of the nineteenth century. The codes represent a reasonably faithful restatement of traditional Mohawk law, but they also contain some perhaps purposeful ambiguity about individual property rights that could be exploited by members of the community later on. The revocation of the 1801 code would have done nothing to erase that ambiguity. There is also a more coercive element to the 1804 code, which seems to mimic the colonial legal order in its remedial repertoire more than Indigenous customary law. The biggest threat to the coherence of Kahnawake's law related to a factor beyond the purview of code or council: the fact that residents of Kahnawake could make an 'end run' around traditional law and chiefly authority by appealing to colonial courts. If, down to 1815, the latter on occasion upheld traditional law, such would not always be the case thereafter.

Analysing the interaction of Indigenous peoples and the seigneurial system presents intercultural legal relations in a less confrontational light.[45] As noted in chapter 6, grants of seigneuries were made in the seventeenth century either directly to some Indigenous communities, or to a religious order on their behalf. Some of these were not, in strict law, seigneuries, because they were not created using the traditional formula of a grant 'en fief et seigneurie.' However, they came to be treated as seigneuries by the colonial states, both French and British, by their Indigenous populations, and by the Canadien censitaires who lived on them. The Jesuits at Kahnawake granted a large number of censives to Canadiens during the French regime, from whom seigneurial dues were collected; but the Mohawk community was in some sense also treated as the seigneur because the Kahnawakehro:non did not pay seigneurial dues in the areas they occupied. At Odanak, the Abenaki chiefs directly granted censives to Canadiens from whom they collected seigneurial dues, without the interposition of any religious order.

The Huron-Wendat at Jeune-Lorette were obliged to interact most closely with the colonial legal regime because they lived next to the capital of New France and were surrounded on every side by Canadien neighbours.[46] Early on, they migrated out of the seigneury of Sillery and after various movements settled in 1697 at Jeune-Lorette in the Jesuit-owned seigneury of St Gabriel.[47] The village site was quite small, and in 1742 the Jesuits made some 1,600 square arpents of land available to the

Huron-Wendat a few kilometres away. They were not charged seigneurial dues on this land or in their village, but throughout the eighteenth century individual Huron-Wendat of Jeune-Lorette acquired censives in neighbouring seigneuries, for which they did pay seigneurial dues. Their patterns of use could be quite different from Canadiens, however. While a few individuals acquired scattered plots, more commonly several Huron-Wendat would acquire neighbouring plots individually but farm them collectively. For these transactions they regularly made use of notaries, and the chiefs sometimes hired notaries and surveyors even for transactions within Jeune-Lorette itself. The Huron-Wendat thus used the colonial legal order for their own purposes.

When outside the gaze of the colonial state, however, the Huron-Wendat acted differently. They hunted on the north shore of the St Lawrence, the area called the domaine du roi by the French, where settlement by Europeans was forbidden during the French regime. Here, they managed the territory cooperatively with other Indigenous peoples such as the Algonquin who also regarded it as their hunting grounds (a practice provided for in the Great Peace of 1701).[48] Differing spaces called for different legal regimes, according to whether the 'other' was European or Indigenous, and the Huron-Wendat seem to have moved with relative ease between these different worlds. They also, like many Indigenous peoples, regularly incorporated outsiders into their communities: captives from New England and from enemy Indigenous nations, Canadien spouses (women and men), and Canadien babies abandoned at Jeune-Lorette by their unwed mothers. The last practice seems to have been sufficiently common that a colonial ordinance of 1717 banned it, but likely to little effect.[49] Just as they incorporated Canadien babies into their community, it might be better to say that the Huron-Wendat integrated French practices into their legal order, than to say that they integrated into the colonial legal order.

The change of legal regime after the conquest produced more continuity than change. At Kahnawake the Mohawk seized the opportunity to throw off the tutorship of the Jesuits. The Mohawk had become concerned about the increased presence of French settlers on their land, especially after the conquest when the Jesuits dramatically accelerated the pace of their concessions to Canadiens. A formal complaint by the chiefs of Kahnawake to the governor of Montreal, Thomas Gage, resulted in a quasi-judicial hearing by him, held during the period of military rule after the capitulation of the city and before the establishment of civil courts. In March 1762 he rendered a decision negating the rights of the Jesuits and awarding the 'seigneury' to the Mohawk, though he ruled that underlying title resided in the Crown, and the governor should appoint someone to collect rents and dues owing to the inhabitants of Kahnawake. Concessions made by the Jesuits prior to the capitulation of Montreal were confirmed, but those made thereafter were annulled.[50] The chiefs rapidly made use of their newly affirmed rights, granting lands to third parties, arranging for the construction of a mill and leasing land for the same, and making contracts directly with external bodies in the 1770s.[51] In effect, they acted as seigneurs in their own right. While the first receiver, the notary Pierre Panet de Méru, was named by the governor in 1765, his appointment was also authorized by the principal chiefs of Kahnawake by notarized act. When the governor did not appoint a new receiver after the death of the incumbent in 1813, the chiefs named their own agent and granted censives in their own name for a time without hindrance from the colonial authorities. Matters evolved in similar fashion at Odanak, although there the Abenakis had always been able to appoint their own 'procureur' to look after their interests and take legal actions on their behalf.

This de facto juridical capacity of Indigenous collectivities to acquire rights in land recognized by the civil law and to act as seigneurs was not seriously questioned under either the French regime or for many years under the British. The same legal fluidity was evident in Upper Canada, where no one at the time questioned the ability of the Six Nations to be legally capable grantees of Governor Haldimand's grant of the lands at Grand River. A 1795 decision in which the status of the Abenakis' 'seigneury' at Odanak was contested was a portent of things to come. There the argument was made that 'the said Indians as a nation are incapable of acquiring and holding Real property according to the Laws of this province,' but the Court of King's Bench at Trois-Rivières managed to decide the case on another ground, and the Abenakis' status as seigneurs was left intact.[52] The turning point was an 1820 decision of the Montreal Court of King's Bench in which it rejected an action begun by the agent of the Mohawk at Kahnawake where the exercise of seigneurial rights was at issue. The reasoning of the court is not available, but it was interpreted as establishing not merely that Indigenous communities could not exercise seigneurial rights, but that they were legally incapable more generally; that is, they did not possess legal personality.[53] This decision came to be seen as applicable to all the mission communities (and perhaps beyond), and the conclusion was independently arrived at by Upper Canadian courts as well after 1820. The negative consequences for self-rule and thus for the integrity of Indigenous law can easily be imagined and will be considered in chapter 23.

In the seventeenth century the French adapted their laws to Indigenous ways in many respects, as seen in chapter 8. In the eighteenth century the tide began to flow the other way, as Indigenous peoples adapted to successive colonial legal regimes in Quebec, and to the British regime in the other colonies. There has been little about Nova Scotia in this chapter because the strategy of the Mi'kmaq seems to have been avoidance of the British colonial order, which they mistrusted. They addressed petitions to the colonial government complaining of settler encroachments and treaty violations, but these tell us little about Mi'kmaw law itself. Oral tradition suggests the continuance of traditional law over those areas still controlled by the Mi'kmaq. In view of these 'two solitudes,' there is little room to discuss the adaptation of Mi'kmaw law or any strategic use of British law.

In the St Lawrence valley, avoidance was not a possible strategy for mission communities located in the seigneurial zone close to Canadien settlements. Inserting Indigenous participants into the seigneurial system required creative adaptation on both sides, but the process may not have been as difficult for the Indigenous participants as has been thought. The overlapping sets of rights in seigneurial property were not so different from the use-rights recognized in Indigenous settlements, especially those in which agriculture was practised. There, the chiefs retained a general supervisory authority over land use and transfer, somewhat analogous to the domaine éminent of seigneurs vis-à-vis their censitaires, though the authority of the chiefs was more extensive than that of seigneurs. Once some lands within Indigenous 'seigneuries' were transferred to Canadiens, complex sets of property rights existed side-by-side: in the village itself, in the plots surrounding the village possessed and worked by Indigenous families, and in the censives occupied by Canadiens. While not unusual in the eighteenth century, this combination would come to be seen as unstable in the nineteenth, as the push by settler states to make all property conform to a liberal model of absolute individual property coincided with the desires of some Indigenous individuals for more economic liberty than contemplated by their customary law. Here the role of colonial courts would come to the fore. The direct intervention of the colonial state in the affairs of Indigenous communities would occur mainly in the second half of the nineteenth century, but the incremental and indirect role of colonial courts in undermining Indigenous law was already underway by 1800 in places like Kahnawake.

Members of the mission settlements seem to have had little difficulty in using those elements of the civil law tradition that they found advantageous, and notaries played a key role in this process of 'translation.' Both chiefs and individuals regularly sought out the services of notaries to record land and other transactions. Indeed, there is evidence that the Huron-Wendat at Jeune-Lorette had higher rates of literacy than their Canadien neighbours by the 1790s.[54] Whether they invoked community of property or civil law succession rules within their own families has not been investigated for this period. But if so, it was because they chose to do so (possibly in some cases as a result of intermarriage), as no attempts were made to impose such laws on them. In any case, the family-oriented provisions of the civil law of succession were more in tune with Indigenous laws regarding family support than common law traditions of testamentary freedom. This legal syncretism, once again, should not be seen as equivalent to assimilation. The mission communities insisted on their distinct identity and the maintenance of their culture and languages, while those among them challenging aspects of customary law were a distinct minority.

One other legal development during this period deserves to be noted here. That is the resort of some chiefs to seeking backup for their authority by the colonial state. Traditional modes of dispute resolution focused on the achievement of consensus, not coercion. Colonial courts provided an avenue for the expression of dissent that circumvented traditional forms of authority and dispute resolution. Whether on the advice of their lawyers or on their own initiative, chiefs began to take proactive steps to insulate their authority from attack. The adoption of the 'codes' of 1801 and 1804 at Kahnawake, and the request that they be 'enacted' by the assembly, should probably be seen in this light. This was a slippery slope, however, and one that risked creating a dynamic where the chiefs could be seen as the ruling body of the community, distinct from its members, rather than the trustees of community authority. These developments will be further explored in chapter 23.

18

Private Law: The Civil Law

The Civil Law to 1760: Canada, Acadia, Louisbourg

The imperial conflicts of the eighteenth century greatly affected the footprint of the civil law in northern North America. The Great Peace of 1701 allowed the civil law to persist and even to flourish in its North American heartland in the St Lawrence valley. But fate intervened as well. Had Quebec been captured in 1711 by Admiral Walker and kept by the British after the Treaty of Utrecht, there is no guarantee that the civil law would have endured. The failure of Walker's expedition gave the French colony another half-century of breathing space, during which time the population increased rapidly and the civil law became ever more entrenched. Its main outlines were sketched in part 2 and need not be repeated here, as there were no alterations to the Custom of Paris during the decades prior to the conquest. The main change during this period was the increase in settled territory subject to the civil law, an expansion driven by the increase in the European population from about 14,000 at the beginning of the century to between 60,000 and 70,000 by 1760.

New seigneuries were created to accommodate the growing European population, and the seigneury remained the socio-legal environment within which most Canadiens lived, though the parish also served as an important locus of religious and social life, with some role in state administration. Authority over the creation of parishes had caused some friction between the bishop and the intendant, and in 1721 the attorney general, Mathieu Collet, took steps to end it. He conducted an extensive survey of all eighty-two existing parishes, created a plan setting out their boundaries, and secured the agreement of the bishop, governor, and intendant. Their joint ruling was approved by Versailles in an edict of 1722.[1]

The seigneurs had an effective monopoly on the distribution of new land for settlement, but as some seigneuries became populous and competition for good land developed, they were tempted to raise rents or demand additional services of the censitaires. Seigneurs, for their part, complained that some censitaires took concessions but did not develop the land. In order to facilitate settlement, the French state intervened by means of the Edicts of Marly in 1711. These royal edicts, applicable only in New France, obliged seigneurs to grant unconceded lands free of charge at existing rentals and on the traditional terms. If the seigneur refused to do so, the intendant could do so in the king's name. Conversely, the censitaire was obliged to tenir feu et lieu, that is, to live on the concession and develop it, on pain of losing it. While the edicts mostly confirmed the existing local ordinances on the subject, their authoritative source was meant to impress on Canadiens the king's desire to foster settlement and suppress abuses on both sides of the seigneurial relationship. If the king wished to shore up seigneuralism as a settlement device, however, he and the colonial administration sought to reduce the seigneurs' justice functions by removing haute and moyenne justice from a number of seigneuries and transferring them to the royal courts.[2]

Other royal ordinances on matters relating to property law, applicable to both France and its colonies, were promulgated prior to 1760: on wills (1735), gifts (1737), and fiduciary substitutions (1747). These were considered declaratory of the old law, however, and their content was already part of the law of Canada prior to their promulgation, as noted in the examples of fiduciary substitutions given in part 2. The Custom of Paris as applied in New France and explicated by French doctrinal writers such as de Ferrière, the canon law on marriage, the great seventeenth-century ordinances, and the droit commun in various areas falling outside the custom thus remained the basis of the private law in the constituent parts of New France down to 1760, and in many respects, beyond. The Conseil supérieur rendered many decisions applying the custom and the droit commun in individual cases, but in the absence of law reporting these were not widely known. Pierre-Georges Roy prepared a summary of its decisions for the period 1717–60, which alone ran to seven volumes; he estimated that reproducing the full text would have taken twenty to twenty-five volumes of some 1,100 pages each.[3] The output of the Conseil supérieur contained a good deal of regulatory minutiae and decisions in non-contentious business as well as decisions in appellate litigation, and its decisions in the latter, like those of its counterparts in France, were not reasoned in the modern sense.

In the absence of any global analysis of this daunting amount of material, it is hard to say whether the law of Canada took on an identity distinct from that of France itself in the decades prior to the conquest. The French-trained jurist Louis-Guillaume Verrier, who tried heroically to raise the standard of legal education in New France, thought so. He tried to instil in his students the idea that colonial law was distinct from French law, especially as regarded the regulatory law of the colonial state. But he was frustrated in his desire to see his views diffused more widely by the absence of a printing press. Fearful that the circulation of printed documents could lead to subversion, the French state forbade the importation of a printing press into New France. This inhibited the development of a legal literature (although the small size of the potential market would also have done so), while at the same time preventing the easy diffusion of the colonial state's own laws and decrees. In 1758, as in 1658, the main way of publicizing decrees was to have them read publicly after Sunday mass in each parish by the court clerk, a local notary, or the captain of the militia, who would then affix a written copy to the church door.[4] Aside from a few highly educated figures such as Verrier, it seems doubtful whether Canadiens perceived their law as developing an identity distinct from that of France.

Where the first half of the eighteenth century saw the maturation of the civil law in Canada, in Acadia it was consigned to an uncertain future after the colony's cession to Britain in 1713. In some respects the situation in Acadia, where the English council at Annapolis Royal tried to resolve disputes between Acadians according to their own legal traditions, presaged that in Canada after 1760. The English even appointed notaries in the main districts of Acadia to assist the population with their legal needs. But in other respects their situations differed markedly. Law in Acadia remained largely an oral phenomenon: unlike in Canada, where some large and sophisticated law libraries were being built up, no law libraries, or any books on French law, are known to have existed in Acadia before the Deportation. Again unlike Canada, Acadia could not benefit, after 1713, from the arrival of legally trained

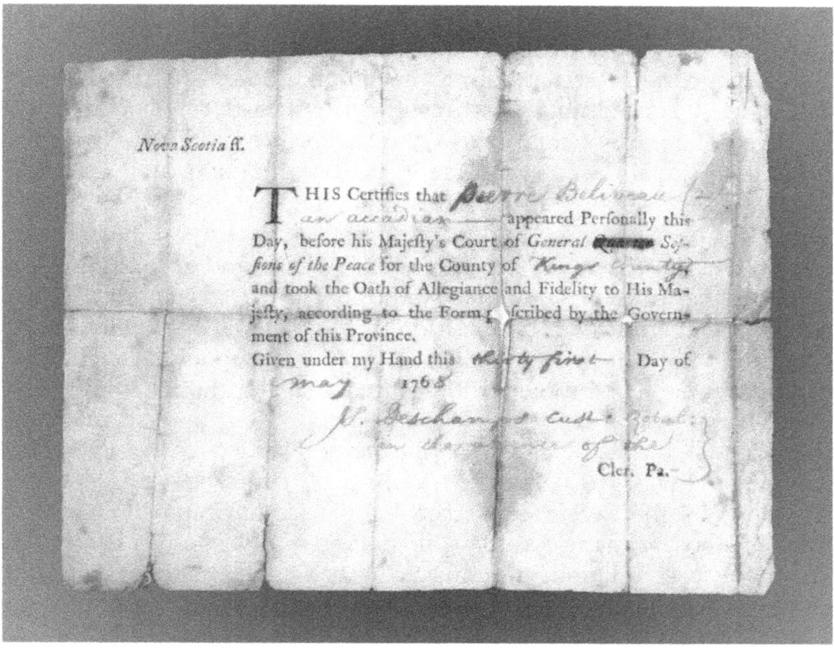

Nova Scotia ss.

THIS Certifies that Pierre Belimeau [illegible] an acadian —— appeared Personally this Day, before his Majesty's Court of *General* [illegible] *Sessions of the Peace* for the County of Kings County and took the Oath of Allegiance and Fidelity to His Majesty, according to the Form prescribed by the Government of this Province.

Given under my Hand this thirty first Day of may 1768

J. Deschamps Cust. Rotul:
[illegible] of the
Cler. Pa.

Having deported the Acadians in 1755–58, the British allowed them to return to the northern colonies after 1763. Those returning had to make an oath of allegiance.

French jurists such as Collet or Verrier, who occasionally turned up in Quebec to serve in the colonial administration.

The cession of Acadia 'with its ancient boundaries' in the Peace of Utrecht in 1713 did not at first result in any drastic legal change. The British maintained a small garrison at the former Port Royal (renamed Annapolis Royal after its capture in 1710) but did not open the territory to settlement, leaving most of it to be governed by default by Mi'kmaw law. The governor and his council did not seek to impose English law, except to a limited extent in the criminal sphere, and allowed the Acadian population to observe their traditional laws and customs. All that would change after the deportation of the Nova Scotian Acadians in 1755 and those on Île St-Jean in 1758. As in Louisbourg, the civil law would be largely uprooted with its people, even though some thousands of Acadians managed to evade deportation both in mainland Nova Scotia and on Île St-Jean, while many returned to the region after an amnesty was proclaimed by the British government of Quebec in 1764. By 1800 there were some 8,000 Acadians living in peninsular Nova Scotia, almost as many as in 1755. In their own communities, along with their language, religion, and musical heritage, they maintained a form of their own legal culture, based on local traditions of dispute resolution. In 1798 the French missionary Abbé Sigogne, assigned to minister to the Acadians in Digby and Yarmouth counties in Nova Scotia, drafted a set of 'Regulations' – in essence, a sort of Judicature Act – for his flock, specifying in great detail how disputes among them were to be resolved, and how they were to conduct themselves in disputes with strangers to their community.[5] The emphasis throughout was on the need to display Christian charity, and inimical to the assertion of rights or the invocation of adversarial procedures other than as a last resort in the face of flagrant injustice.

The Civil Law after 1760: The Emergence of a Mixed Legal Tradition

By 1760 four or five generations of Canadiens had lived under a French-derived legal order. It was familiar to them and affected all important aspects of their lives. It is not surprising that they would struggle to retain it after the transfer of sovereignty accomplished formally by the Treaty of Paris 1763. The *Quebec Act*, however, was only the first step in the preservation of French law in the province. It stated that 'in all Matters of Controversy, relative to Property and Civil Rights, Resort shall be had to the Laws of Canada, as the Rule for the Decision of the same; and all Causes that shall hereafter be instituted in any of the Courts of Justice ... shall, with respect to such Property and Rights, be determined agreeably to the said Laws and Customs of Canada, until they shall be varied or altered by any Ordinances' to be passed subsequently.[6] The 'Laws of Canada' were not frozen in time: they could be varied by ordinances passed by the legislative council, or by the legislative assembly after its establishment.

In general, the debate over the content of the laws of Canada was characterized by more acrimony than the creation of new courts and the introduction of innovations such as the jury or habeas corpus. With regard to such measures, the Canadien population seems to have accepted that the conqueror could create new institutions for the adjudication of rights. When it came to the actual content of the laws, however, the demands of some parts of the British population for far-reaching changes to unfamiliar laws ran up against Canadien attachment to those same laws. This is not to say that all British inhabitants were convinced of the need for wide-ranging reform or that Canadiens were uniformly opposed to all reform. Neither side was monolithic: Canadien merchants, habitants, seigneurs, and clergy did not always think alike; nor did British officials, merchants, and artisans always share the same views.[7] Canadien and British merchants made common cause on a number of law reform issues in the 1780s, best illustrated by the 1785 joint petition to the Crown of Canadien and British merchants, drafted in English but translated into French and circulated in the countryside as a pamphlet entitled *Aux citoyens et habitants des villes et des campagnes de la province de Québec*. It called for an elected assembly and the adoption of English commercial law, as England was the 'greatest commercial kingdom in the world'; the Custom of Paris, meanwhile, 'was never made for the protection and encouragement of commerce.'[8] In fact the introduction of English commercial law had already begun with an ordinance of 1777 that permitted legal interest to a maximum of 6 per cent, introduced imprisonment for debt (which existed only in exceptional situations under French law), and replaced the strict French evidentiary rules for commercial debts with the less formal English ones.[9] Unlike English law, however, where imprisonment for debt was available to any creditor, in Quebec it was restricted to commercial debts between merchants, and debts owed by consumers to merchants for goods sold; and it could occur only if execution against the debtor's land and movables had already been found insufficient to satisfy the debt.[10]

It is not clear exactly which 'commercial laws' the authors of the 1785 pamphlet had in mind. The biggest complaint of the British mercantile community, one that would endure well into the nineteenth century and become entangled with the demand for registry offices for land and the abolition of customary dower, regarded the existence of 'secret hypothecs,' or security interests, under French law. There were many instances where the immovables of a debtor could be subject to the claims of prior creditors without these being necessarily obvious to later ones.[11] Formal notarized debt obligations imported such hypothecs, as did court judgments and customary dower. Such creditors could demand the sale and preferential payment of their debt not only with regard to any immovables possessed by the debtor at the time of the obligation, but any subsequently acquired. Certainly the francophone authors of the 1785 pamphlet supported customary dower and presumably the 'secret hypothec' that went with it; but the specifics of their demands are less important than their receptivity to the idea that some provisions at least of English commercial law could be profitably grafted on to traditional Canadien law. This openness, and the bourgeois alliance itself, would soon come under severe strain.

The very idea of a 'mixed' legal system towards which both British and French were groping after 1763 received a setback in 1786 in the decision of Chief Justice William Smith, a former chief justice of New York, in *Gray v Grant*. In it, he interpreted the *Quebec Act* to say that suits between 'old subjects' would be determined by English law alone, while those between Canadiens would continue to be governed by their own law. This harked back to the system of 'personality of laws' of early medieval Europe, before the emergence of territorial nation states. While some British subjects seemed to assume that this had always been the case, many are known to have employed Canadien notaries for their legal business and hence to have accepted the applicability of Canadien law. Fortunately the decision gained little traction in either Quebec or London, where the law officers of the Crown deprecated it, and it seems to have been quietly forgotten after Smith's death in 1793.[12]

A much greater strain on the bourgeois alliance occurred as a result of the French Revolution and the almost constant state of Anglo-French hostilities between 1793 and 1815. Ethnic lines became much sharper, and many in the British elite came to suspect all Canadiens of disloyalty. Demands for legal reform from the British side came to be seen as aggressive and menacing to national survival by the Canadiens, who tended to rally around traditional institutions and laws. After the election of the first assembly in 1792, for example, all attempts to reform or abolish seigneurial tenure were resisted by Canadien members, some of whom might have been receptive to such measures a decade earlier.[13]

In the assembly the weight of numbers ensured that no laws could be passed without Canadien consent. The courts, however, were another matter. While all judges after 1791 were legally trained, most were anglophone, and some did not hide their views that anglicization of Canadien law would be for the best. In some ways it is hard to blame them. Mastering Canadien law was not an easy task, even though the government had in the early years put considerable effort into understanding what the traditional laws of the colony were, as they also did in their possessions in India. In doing so they relied on the services of François-Joseph Cugnet, the Quebec-born son of a long line of Parisian jurists.[14] Although not a notary, Cugnet had taken the two-year course of lectures given by Louis-Guillaume Verrier, had access to his father's extensive law library, and was acknowledged to possess a superior knowledge of the Custom of Paris and French law in general. The government at Quebec named him French secretary and official translator for the governor and the legislative council in 1768, making him effectively the senior adviser on local law; in 1777 he would be commissioned as an advocate. Before the enactment of the *Quebec Act*, Cugnet was so exercised by the possibility of English law being imposed that he wrote directly to William Blackstone in July 1773, seeking to enlist his aid in preventing this result.[15] He cited the passage in the *Commentaries* where Blackstone states that the inhabitants of a conquered country preserve their laws until the king actually changes them, and called upon Blackstone to urge the king and Parliament not to do so, as the Canadiens were committed to their existing civil laws, although they did not object to the imposition of English criminal law. Blackstone, who had by this point been appointed a judge, transmitted Cugnet's appeal to the attorney general.

Governor Carleton requested that Cugnet prepare a description of local law, which he did in a 1768 unpublished text entitled 'Coutumes et usages anciens de la province de Québec.' François Masères, the bilingual Huguenot attorney general of the province, and Chief Justice William Hey asked Cugnet to present his work to them, which he gladly did. Their reactions were not encouraging and presaged much of the difficulty that would plague the mixed jurisdiction of Quebec in the ensuing decades. Masères reported to a London correspondent, 'I remember we were above four hours understanding the five first pages

Advancement eluded François-Joseph Cugnet (1720–1789) under the French regime, but he succeeded brilliantly under the British. He was named French secretary to the governor and council of Quebec in 1768 and authored the first treatises on the civil law as applied in Quebec.

of it, though we had Mr Cugnet at our elbow all the time to explain it to us. In short, it was like a lecture upon a chapter of Justinian's Institutes.'[16] Hey, for his part, doubted that any judge trained only in English law would be up to the task of learning Canadien law:

> It would require great Abilities, uncommon Industry, Length of Time, and a perfect acquaintance with the French Language to attain such a Knowledge of the Canadian Laws considered as a compleat system of Jurisprudence, as would enable them to execute their office with any degree of sufficiency.[17]

Governor Carleton, undaunted, called upon various clerics and seigneurs to prepare a text containing an abbreviated account of French customary law to complement Cugnet's work. Published by the British government in 1772–3, in the absence of authorial attribution it became known as the *Extrait des Messieurs* and achieved a quasi-official status, given the circumstances of its publication. After the passage of the *Quebec Act* assured the survival of French customary law, Cugnet went on to publish three treatises and a collection of legal documents from the French regime in 1775.[18] For those fluent in French, there was at least a basic doctrinal corpus on Canadien law to assist those who wished to understand and apply it.

Most judges of the period trained in the common law, with some notable exceptions, seem not to have been inclined to learn the civil law in depth, though the extent of their anglicization of Canadien law has not been studied extensively. In one area, however, their success was clear: civil procedure. The *Quebec Act* provision declaring that 'all Causes that shall hereafter be instituted in any of the Courts of Justice … shall … be determined agreeably to the said Laws and Customs of' Canada could be interpreted to include adjectival law, including the ordinance of 1667, as well as substantive law in its embrace. However, already in 1777, an ordinance regulating procedure in the courts introduced the writ system, the practice of using *viva voce* evidence in open court, imprisonment for debt, and English evidentiary rules in commercial matters, while the jury was definitively reinstated in 1785 for commercial disputes and actions seeking to establish liability for personal injuries.[19] While not completely overturning the pre-1760 procedural system, these changes were made without any attempt to integrate them into the pre-existing law. In 1801 the passage of a seemingly innocuous law permitted judges of all court levels in the province to make rules of procedure in their courts. In 1809 and 1811 respectively, this authority was taken up with gusto by Chief Justice Jonathan Sewell of the King's Bench at Quebec and Chief Justice James Monk of the Court of King's Bench at Montreal. Each adopted a veritable code of civil procedure for his court – that created for Quebec ran to some 180 pages – encompassing all stages of a proceeding from initiation to execution of judgments.[20]

Some of the changes were highly controversial within the Canadien bar, especially those calling for higher deposits to cover future court actions and introducing the English law of contempt of court. Their main complaint, however, was that the judges were using the powers in the 1801 statute to adopt a far-reaching reform that was more appropriately in the domain of the legislature – a somewhat difficult argument to make, given the wide authority granted by the Act itself. These complaints were probably secondary to those of political involvement by the two judges, which motivated the (ultimately unsuccessful) impeachment of the judges before the Privy Council in 1814.[21] In the end, it took codification in 1867 to bring more coherence to procedural law in Quebec.[22]

Two other potential flashpoints of legal conflict deserve to be noted: land tenure and the language of court proceedings. Debates over land tenure raised multiple issues: whether seigneurial tenure should be abolished or reformed; whether the Edicts of Marly were still enforceable after 1763; and whether English or French law applied to Crown grants in free and common socage, which were used liberally in the Eastern Townships of the province along the U.S. border. On all of these matters the Canadien position was largely upheld, although on some of them the differences between seigneur and censitaire were just as important as ethnic divides. On the first issue, all attempts at legislative reform of the seigneurial system were rebuffed by the Canadien party in the assembly, in part a casualty of the hardening of positions brought on by the Revolutionary and Napoleonic Wars. On the second, class was more important than ethnicity in the outcome. After 1760 many seigneuries were bought by British merchants and officials; but whether British or French, the seigneurs began to assume that with the disappearance of the office of intendant, the Edicts of Marly could no longer be enforced. This was flagged as a problem as early as the late 1760s by Carleton and Hey. By the 1790s, wrote Attorney General James Monk, 'the Censitaires hold lands, in many parts of the Province, at rents and services, exorbitant, in comparison to what they were granted at in 1711 … and at double and treble the rents.' However, the unrest generated by such exactions took on a different colouring in the new security environment following the execution of Louis XVI in 1793. Reporting on his 1794 *Judicature Act* to Lord Dundas, Monk explained why it gave the Court of King's Bench the authority formerly possessed by the intendant to enforce the Edicts of Marly: 'The Rents and Services of the Seigniors, forms that ground of complaint by the Peasants, which the Enemies of His Majestys Government, do not fail to … foment to the utmost, as the best means of detaching His Majestys Subjects from their Loyalty, to acquiesce in, or wish, or aid a Revolution!'[23] It is not clear to what extent the courts used the enforcement powers granted in the statute of 1794, although in 1811 a judgment of Justice James Reid of the Montreal Court of King's Bench resoundingly confirmed the Edicts of Marly as part of Quebec law.[24]

The issue of the (in)applicability of French law on socage lands was in some ways the most perplexing of all those related to land tenure. Section 9 of the *Quebec Act* stated that 'nothing in this Act contained shall … be construed to extend, to any Lands that have been granted by His Majesty, … His Heirs and Successors, to be holden in free and common Soccage.' Initially the government had continued to grant lands in seigneurial tenure but acceded to the demands of the Loyalists for socage lands in the Eastern Townships, which did not form part of any seigneury. Were such lands subject to the English law of property or to French law with respect to issues of dower, inheritance, and security interests? The *Constitutional Act* of 1791 further muddied the waters when it confirmed the power of the Crown to grant lands in socage tenure, 'but subject nevertheless to such Alterations, with respect to the Nature and Consequences of such Tenure of Free and Common Soccage, as may be established.' This implied that English law had indeed applied to socage lands but that the new legislature could make 'Alterations' to this state of affairs as it saw fit. None were made until the 1820s, but local practice seems to have assumed the applicability of French law from the outset, contradicting the assumption of the 1791 Act. Not until an Act of 1857 declared definitively that all incidents of land held in free and common socage should be those recognized by French law was the matter finally settled.[25]

The language issue was not as problematic in eighteenth-century Quebec as might be expected.[26] For the most part the British authorities knew they had to communicate in French to their 'new subjects' if they wished to be understood. Ordinances were published in both languages, and court proceedings and everyday government administration were functionally bilingual. The *Quebec Gazette*, which contained government notices as well as ordinary news items, was almost entirely bilingual. Criminal court records were kept mainly in English, but the main civil court, the Court of Common Pleas, kept dual registers in English and French and produced many of its documents in both languages. Ordinances of 1777 and 1785 stated that writs must be in the language of the defendant. There were often complaints about unilingual anglophone judges in the higher courts, but these courts heard only a small proportion of the entire caseload in a given year. In 1801, however, the assembly passed a law repealing the relevant provisions of the earlier ordinances regarding pleading. It is not known why this measure was not resisted by the Canadien members, unless they were unaware of its true intent. The Act did not specifically mention language at all and did not state that all pleadings had to be in English. After repealing the parts of the earlier ordinances dealing with the language of writs, the Act went on to state that every person having a civil claim could 'sue out and as of right ... obtain ... a Writ or Summons against the party or parties Defendant,' without more.[27] By not restricting the language of such 'Writ or Summons' the section implied that it could be drafted in the language preferred by the plaintiff, but this may not have been clear to all readers. The problem remained only a potential one, however, as existing practice seems to have continued until 1825, when, as will be noted in the next part of this volume, the issue came forcefully to public attention.

Much of the legal historiography on the post-conquest period has viewed matters through the lens of ethnic, and sometimes class, conflict, based implicitly or explicitly on the thesis of a 'rupture' with the past, confirmed in law by the supposed substitution of English law for French law contained in the Royal Proclamation of 1763. This conflictual interpretation became entrenched after one particularly influential study of the decade 1764–74 by André Morel. This study purported to find that Canadiens had engaged in a 'boycottage' of the new Court of Common Pleas with regard to their most intimate concerns – marriage, family, and succession – although they had recourse to it in other matters. Morel hypothesized that, as a form of 'résistance passive,' the Canadiens now turned to private arbitration to deal with such matters, though he had no actual evidence of such arbitrations.[28]

More recently, with the digitization of virtually all surviving notarial records down to 1785 in the Parchemin database, scholars have been able to approach the issue of which law prevailed during the crucial decade 1764–74 from a more 'bottom-up' perspective, based on the actual practices of the Canadien population. What they have found accords, ironically enough, with the observations of Chief Justice Hey and Governor Carleton in 1769, cited by Morel in support of his own thesis:

> They have regulated their private economy, and conducted themselves in the same manner, they would have done, if that Ordinance [the ordinance of 1764 establishing the new courts] had not been made. Their Marriage Contracts, their Guardianships, and Disposition of Minor Estates, their distributions of personal property in case of intestacy, are all modelled according to the Custom of Paris.[29]

Both in the Court of Common Pleas and in the practice of notaries, the Custom of Paris and the droit commun in matters of family law, succession and obligations were overwhelmingly the sources of law relied upon prior to the *Quebec Act*. It is hard to see how it could have been otherwise, as the notaries and practiciens knew no English law. Where Morel erred was in treating this phenomenon as a politically motivated 'boycott' of English tribunals. Rather, it was simply a manifestation of legal continuity. In the family matters highlighted by Morel, the role played by the courts under the French regime was mostly administrative, confirming and registering transactions accomplished by the parties with the assistance of their notaries; seldom were the courts required to decide actual conflicts. The notary had always been the front-line legal officer for all matters relating to marriage and succession, and his role in this regard was only enhanced after 1763, with the blessing of the new government.

Take, for example, the issue of tutorships, required when one parent died leaving minor children. As noted earlier, under the French regime there were three steps to this process: first the surviving parent (or other relative if the children were now orphaned) had to request the seigneurial court to convoke a family council, who would elect the tutor and subrogate-tutor. The election often took place at home, though it had to be confirmed by the seigneurial judge, who always rubber-stamped it. In areas far from a seigneurial court, the judge might name a priest or notary to preside over the election. The next step was the preparation of the inventory, which took place in the deceased's home, under the supervision of the notary. Finally, the inventory had to be formally approved by the seigneurial court, in the presence of the tutor and subrogate-tutor.

A study of these processes pre- and post-conquest in the seigneury of Beauport, owned by the Séminaire du Québec, revealed that there was almost no change over the period. Even after Murray's order of 1760 suspended the activities of the seigneurial courts, the government was at pains to appoint various officials to preside over the election of tutors and the closure of inventories. Soon after its creation in 1764, the Court of Common Pleas established a 'division des prérogatives,' which in effect carried on the role of the seigneurial court in matters of succession. In 1768 Guillaume Guillimin, a former judge in Admiralty under the French regime, was named to this post; residing in Quebec, his practice was to authorize a local notary to preside over the election of tutors, though he sometimes required the family members to appear before him in the city. Upon his death in 1771, a British judge, Thomas Dunn, took over the role and maintained the same procedure. The inhabitants of Beauport did not hesitate to bring their successoral affairs, even in times of conflict, before Dunn. Post-1764 the role of the notary became even more important than it had been under the French regime, as he came to fill in for the now defunct seigneurial judge in various legal processes. Only the formal closure of the inventory had to be done invariably before the judge at Quebec. Far from boycotting the new courts, the inhabitants carried on as before and were only too glad to take advantage of the opportunities afforded by the new government to do so.[30]

With regard to arbitration, an increase in recourse to arbitration has been found post-conquest, as hypothesized by Morel, but not for the reasons he advanced. Arbitration was not unknown under the French regime and was indeed encouraged by the state as a process complementary to, not in conflict with, the work of the established courts. It continued as such under the British, both in the form of court-ordered arbitration and extra-judicial arbitration – arbitration agreed to by the parties without the commencement of legal action. Arbitral awards can be found in all fields, not just in matters of family and succession, with notaries typically acting as the arbitrators. Arbitration was a familiar part of the dispute-resolution repertoire of Canadiens, and it remained so after 1760. Seen over the *longue durée*, once again the picture appears as one of continuity rather than disruption, of the preservation of Canadien law rather than its marginalization.[31]

The fate of the private law in the first half-century after the conquest is thus not easy to summarize. There was confusion among both

European groups about the impact of the conquest itself, of the royal proclamation, and of the *Quebec Act* on the pre-existing law. Likewise, individuals and groups of British and French descent and the government itself tried to use this uncertainty strategically to advance their own interests and positions, both materially and symbolically. The British government had the constitutional power to alter the pre-existing law and did so in a number of well-known ways: replacing much of the civil procedure of the old regime with English forms, first in a piecemeal way with the introduction of the civil jury and the reforms of 1777, then in a more holistic way pursuant to the powers granted to the courts in 1801 to regulate their own process; instituting freedom of willing in 1774 and clarifying the impact of that change on the pre-existing law in 1801; granting some lands in socage rather than seigneurial tenure; introducing imprisonment for debt, altering some of the evidentiary rules in commercial matters and abolishing the customary process used for bankruptcy; and reducing the age of majority from twenty-five to twenty-one.[32]

Yet in the end this catalogue of change, while not trivial, represents the minimum amount of reform that might have been expected in a jurisdiction where the authorities faced both pressure for change and pressure to retain the status quo. The government at Quebec was caught between several conflicting policy goals after the conquest with regard to the survival or otherwise of Canadien law: to anglicize their 'new subjects' as thoroughly as possible, to keep their loyalty in a turbulent world by not unduly upsetting their traditional arrangements as to law and religion, to make the new colony more profitable by enacting legal reforms seen as facilitating economic development, and to create a legal environment familiar enough to attract, or at least not discourage, British immigration.

After 1791 there were two conceivable modes of further anglicizing the law: by legislation, with the consent of the Canadien representatives, or by the courts, without it. The first route rapidly came to an impasse. The second was pursued largely through the continuing appointment of English-trained judges, some with little knowledge of the civil law, to the top positions in the court hierarchy. If they had been fully committed to the project of the *Quebec Act*, the British might have appointed men with some knowledge of Scots law, well versed in the principles of civil law, to these positions. They did not, but their project of undermining the civil law through naming judges uncommitted to it nonetheless did not fully succeed. The most startling example of attempted

Anglicization, *Gray v Grant*, which denied the applicability of the civil law to dealings between 'old subjects,' was doubted by the law officers in London and gained no traction locally. While no detailed study of the influence of English common law upon the case law prior to the rebellions has been made, one author has opined that 'la jurisprudence publiée n'offre pas le portrait d'une invasion par la common law.'[33]

Whether by design or not, the legal changes instituted in the half-century after 1763 enabled the British population to work around key elements of French law strategically if they wished, while permitting the Canadien population to retain the core of the Custom of Paris and related traditions. The latter itself provided sufficient flexibility that it could be used to institute separate property between spouses, for example, while the freedom of willing instituted by the *Quebec Act* could be used to avoid the custom's insistence on partible inheritance. Customary dower, often a target of the British community, was not that different from the English law of dower, which likewise attached to all realty a man might acquire while married and might survive to plague a purchaser if not barred by the wife in a sale by the husband. Where in England jointure had evolved as a substitute for dower, so in Canada stipulated dower (douaire préfix) served a similar function. Commercial law remained something of a battleground, but because it existed outside the Custom of Paris and was largely a matter of practice, it could be gradually altered by the practices of the British mercantile community if these were seen as beneficial by their Canadien counterparts, without the need for formal amendment. And in some instances, Canadiens could avoid new doctrines they disliked or felt were unnecessary, such as imprisonment for debt, simply by not using them.[34]

The previous focus on the high-profile quarrels among legal elites and political figures has given a misleading impression of how the 'mix' in Quebec's legal system actually unfolded. Much of it occurred in the everyday actions of litigants and lawyers trying to navigate the post-1764 system.[35] The evolution of the legal professions was critical in this regard. The introduction of 'avocats' in the 1764 *Judicature Act* and its opening to Canadiens proved a crucial step. Even as the judges became more English over time, the avocats became more Canadien: by 1805 eleven of the seventeen avocats pleading before the Court of King's Bench at Quebec were Canadien. Becoming an avocat often led to a seat in the assembly as well, providing an important platform for those concerned to preserve traditional laws and customs. After the introduction of apprenticeship in the 1785 ordinance, aspiring lawyers, regardless of ethnic background, had to master Canadien law. And many aspiring lawyers felt the need to have exposure to both languages and both legal traditions: about a quarter of all British apprentices spent some time with a French principal, and vice versa. Clienteles did not divide along strictly ethnic lines: British clients made up about a quarter of the clientele of Canadien avocats down to 1805, although the converse was about half as common (13 per cent). Court proceedings were conducted in both languages as required.[36] Thus, in spite of the increasing political strains between English and French elites in the wake of the French revolution, the metissage of Quebec's legal system continued at the ground level, even if the legislative avenue was increasingly blocked.

Nonetheless, the impact of the French Revolution was significant. In England it allowed the government to portray any attempt at reforming the common law or Parliament itself as potentially revolutionary and hence undesirable. In Quebec the revolution tended to throw the Canadiens on the defensive and to sap any desire to reform their own laws, when interest in such reform had been manifest in some quarters in the 1780s. The legal turmoil engendered by the French Revolution meant that developments in French law were no longer a suitable guide for Canadiens to follow. Pre-revolutionary doctrinal writers remained authoritative in Quebec, but they had no successors in France, especially after the adoption of the *Code civil* (*Code Napoléon*) in 1804, which purported to abolish all pre-existing law. The small production of local legal literature focused on elucidating the pre-conquest law rather than critically analysing it with a view to reform. The traditional sources of Quebec law became increasingly fragmented and out of date, while an increasing stream of domestic legislation responded to specific problems but provided no overall coordinating authority. It would take the rebellions of 1837–8 to begin the modernization and systematization of Quebec law that would ultimately lead to codification.

19

Private Law: The Common Law

Unlike the seventeenth century, when the common law served as only a loose guide for the development of local laws, by the eighteenth century the Crown was asserting more forcefully that settler polities were to be governed by the common law. Thus the Royal Proclamation of 1763 not only gave governors and assemblies the power to adopt such laws 'as may be agreeable to the Laws of England,' but stated that 'until such Assemblies can be called as aforesaid, all Persons Inhabiting in or resorting to our Said Colonies may confide in our Royal Protection for the Enjoyment of the Benefit of the Laws of our Realm of England.' These 'Laws' would in principle include the common law and English and British statutes. Nonetheless, Blackstone was somewhat cautious in describing what parts of the English legal inheritance accompanied the settlers to new plantations; he opined that they brought with them

> only so much of the English law as is applicable to their own situation and the condition of an infant colony; such, for instance, as the general rules of inheritance, and of protection from personal injuries. The artificial refinements and distinctions incident to the property of a great commercial people, the laws of police and revenue (such especially as are enforced by penalties), the mode of maintenance for the established clergy, the jurisdiction of spiritual courts, and a multitude of other provisions, are neither necessary nor convenient for them, and therefore are not in force.[1]

This rendering left much room for uncertainty, as noted by Prince Edward Island historian John Stewart. In his 1806 history of the Island, after citing Blackstone, Stewart observed that

> the colonies are understood to take the common law, and all the Statute Law of England antecedent to their establishment, which may be applicable to their situation and circumstances, but this must be understood with many, and very considerable restrictions … [W]hat is admissible, and what shall be rejected, has hitherto, been left to the discretion of their respective courts, and on this head it may easily be believed opinions will differ much; it is therefore to be wished, that a more certain mode of determining the length to which it is to be carried may be devised.[2]

The distinction between common law (long established custom and judge-made law) and statute law was critical. Common law, in the words of Chief Justice Francis Forbes of Newfoundland, was treated as 'a common fund, from which the Colony may draw as often and as largely as its exigencies may require,' but statute law was another matter.[3] Were all statutes passed by the British Parliament in force prior to a given colony's establishment in effect there? Or only those that were 'suitable' to its circumstances? And when did new British statutes cease to become, automatically, part of the colony's law?

The 'more certain mode' desired by Stewart was adopted in Upper Canada, where the very first statute adopted by the new legislature was one specifying the date of reception. The Act stated, 'In all matters of controversy relative to property and civil rights, resort shall be had to the laws of England as they stood on the 15th day of October, 1792, as the rule for the decision of the same.'[4] A statute of 1800 specified 17 September 1792 as the date for reception of English criminal law into the province.[5] This was understood to mean that no ordinary statute passed in the United Kingdom after the dates in question would become the law of Upper Canada; should Upper Canada wish to adopt such a law, its own legislature had the power to do so.[6] As for a statute passed prior to 1792, judges would have to determine whether it was 'suitable' for reception into the colony.

The remaining colonies did not enact such legislation, leaving considerable scope for confusion but also judicial creativity. In spite of the assumption by twentieth-century writers that each province has a 'reception date' after which newly enacted British statutes would not become part of provincial law, the historical record reveals that in the

Maritime provinces at least, the practice was considerably more fluid.[7] Disputes over the reception date flared into a constitutional crisis in New Brunswick in the 1790s, while debates over reception in Nova Scotia and Prince Edward Island continued well into the nineteenth century and may be said to lack a definitive conclusion even today.[8]

In New Brunswick the governor and council early on adopted 1660 as the reception date in that colony. The theory was that from the time of the Restoration, English statutes began to reference many of the plantations by name if the statute was meant to extend to them, such that no statute after that date should be deemed to apply to a given colony unless it was specifically named. In reporting on this matter to the imperial government, Solicitor General Ward Chipman observed that such a date ensured that 'the stability of the Province will be guarded from a spirit of innovation,' revealing that the motivation was more political than legal.[9] In 1795 and 1796 the Opposition party in the assembly expressed discontent with the government's position, stating that many were desirous of 'enjoying the benefit of all the laws of England and Acts of the British Parliament applicable to their colonial situation down to as late a period as the fundamental principles of constitutional Law will admit.'[10] Thus bills were drafted that would have moved the reception date up to 1750 (which the proponents mistakenly assumed to be the date of the foundation of Halifax) in one case, or 1758 in another. As with many other reform measures of the day, the Loyalist government saw these as attempts to subvert all authority and opposed them strenuously; both died in the legislative council. The 1660 theory was never advanced in any other British North American colony, but the date was adopted by the New Brunswick courts and continues to be applied by them.[11]

The New Brunswick position at least had the merit of certainty, subject to the question of 'suitability' of pre-1660 statutes in the local context. In Nova Scotia there were many disputes over the reception of particular statutes in the 1750s, illustrating a variety of views. The lay judges of the Inferior Court of Common Pleas expressed the view that 1621, the date of the charter by which King James (as king of Scotland) granted Nova Scotia to Sir William Alexander was the effective reception date for statutes. For his part, Chief Justice Jonathan Belcher believed that all the criminal laws of England passed 'antecedent to the Plantation and Settlement of the Province' (1749) were in force; accordingly, in 1756 he sentenced to death a man convicted of counterfeiting Spanish dollars, which were then legal tender in the colony, contrary to a statute of 1553.[12] Seeking confirmation from the law officers of the Crown in London as to the correctness of his approach, he was disappointed to be told he was wrong as to the statute's applicability. According to them, the view that 'inhabitants of the Colonies carry with them the Statute Laws of this Realm is not true as a general Proposition, but depends upon Circumstances, the Effect of their Charter, Usage, and Acts of their Legislature; and it would be both inconvenient and dangerous to take it in so large an extent.'[13] Nova Scotia had no charter nor, yet, a legislature, but in mentioning 'Usage' the law officers put their finger on a simple and flexible test, one that turned responsibility for reception questions back to the locals: statutes generally relied on and thought to be in force, were in force; those that were not, were not. In a young colony, custom and usage were in a fluid state, but in North America a generation or less could suffice to legitimate a particular practice. Conversely, a 'usage' test would weed out the sudden applicability of obscure English statutes, especially criminal ones, not previously acted on or thought to be in force in the colony. Given the potential reception of hundreds if not thousands of early English statutes, copies of most of which would not even have been available in the colonies, a presumption of non-reception had much to commend it. In practice, each colony acted early on to re-enact those statutes felt to be most needed in the local context.[14]

We turn now from the question of reception of law to the content of the law received. Our discussion will focus on substantive law, even though a distinction between substantive and procedural law was not well established in the common law until later in the nineteenth century – indeed, even the term *civil procedure* was unfamiliar until much later, lawyers typically speaking of 'pleading' or 'practice.'[15] The common law's long love affair with the writ as an organizing category of legal thought and practice retarded the emergence of substantive law in the modern sense, as will be seen particularly in the discussion below of contract and tort.

In settler societies as in the mother country, property law, family law, and the law of inheritance were the cornerstones of social order and social reproduction. In its detailed attention to the regulation of marriage and its virtual proscribing of divorce, family law was aimed not at maximizing the happiness or personal fulfilment of family members but at providing a stable and enduring framework for the raising of children and the inculcation of dominant social values. Property law described what resources could be commodified and mobilized for the economic support of individuals and families, and how they could be used, transferred, or employed as collateral. Inheritance law linked the two, facilitating the transfer of assets between the generations and the accumulation of capital.

Roughly 80 per cent of the land in eighteenth-century England was held by about 2 per cent of the population, mainly aristocrats and landed gentry.[16] Land was intimately associated with lineage, family honour, and political identity. Historically all land in England had been held in various forms of feudal tenure, but the *Tenures Abolition Act 1660* essentially abolished these and provided that all future grants, including those in the colonies, were to be made in free and common socage.[17] This tenure was burdened with no onerous incidents, although the Crown could and did require the payment of small annual quitrents on some lands granted in the colonies to support the costs of local administration. It might also demand a symbolic rent in recognition of its authority, as in the 1670 grant of Rupert's Land to the Hudson's Bay Company, which Charles II directed was

> To be holden of Us, Our Heirs and Successors, as of Our Manor of East Greenwich in our County of Kent, in free and common Soccage, and not in Capite or by Knight's Service; Yeilding [*sic*] and paying yearly to Us, Our Heirs and Successors, for the same, two Elks and two black Beavers, whensoever, and as often as We, Our Heirs and Successors, shall happen to enter into the said Countries, Territories and Regions hereby granted.[18]

Holding land in a free tenure was seen as a cornerstone of liberty and thus carried important ideological value for British settlers, though the justice of securing such liberty at the expense of that of the Indigenous peoples was seldom questioned. Even the levying of small quitrents became a hot political issue in some colonies, while an important element in the Loyalist demand for a colony separate from Quebec was the desire to escape from seigneurial tenure, associated with dependency and submission.[19] Even within Quebec, as noted in the previous chapter, land grants to Loyalists in the Eastern Townships were often made in free and common socage, not in seigneurial tenure.

The basic building block of the law of real property was the freehold estate. All rights to possess land, but not movable property, existed as a type of estate, the estate being the bundle of rights and obligations interposed between the holder and the land itself. The fee simple was the largest estate known to the law, being functionally equivalent to ownership. The fee tail was a modified form of fee simple, to be discussed shortly, while the life estate endured only for the life of the holder. Leasehold interests were also considered to be estates by this time but were not considered estates of freehold, the key distinction being that only freehold estates carried the franchise at common law (though nineteenth-century legislation would later grant the vote to tenants); in fact they represented a hybrid of property and contract doctrines. All of these estates could exist in 'absolute' form, or they could have various kinds of conditions attached, such as the common provision that a widow's life estate should cease if she remarried. The power to make estates conditional provided considerable flexibility to wealth-holders, while also allowing them to exert a good deal of control over the life choices of the objects of their bounty. Estates could also exist in either of two forms of co-tenancy: joint tenancy, where the survivor took all, and tenancy in common, where no survivorship operated and the share of a deceased co-tenant would descend to his or her estate.[20]

Like the notion of 'free' tenure, these concepts were invested with considerable ideological significance. Holding a fee simple in a free tenure came to represent the acme of liberty, embodied in the Jeffersonian ideal of the virtuous yeoman farmer who embodied economic and political independence – an ideal that also resonated in the settler colonies to the north. Meanwhile, tenancy was traditionally associated with dependency because of the obligation to pay rent and the insecurity of leasehold tenure. However, North America displayed significant geographic variation in the position of tenants. In Prince Edward Island and upstate New York, as in Ireland, a powerful landlord class existed alongside a more or less permanent tenantry, giving rise to discontent, resistance, and ultimately political reform.

In Upper Canada, however, tenancy existed without landlordism, even if one-quarter to one-half of all farming households were tenants at any given point prior to about 1850. Opportunities to take out long leases at low rents on the Crown and clergy reserves were a boon to newly arrived settlers when the system became operational in 1803. Many small and medium-sized farmers themselves rented out their land to others at times, for a variety of reasons. And even large landlords were relatively lenient in the collection of arrears of rent, preferring not to alienate tenants who assisted with the clearance and improvement of the land. The ability of tenants to sell their improvements, recognized on a customary basis if not always strictly at law, and to will, mortgage, and sell their leases to others, created a thriving market in leases and ensured that the work of improvement was compensated.[21] Detailed work on the history of tenancy in Nova Scotia and New Brunswick is lacking, but their experience probably fell somewhere between the oppressive landlordism of Prince Edward Island and the more varied and instrumental possibilities associated with tenancy in Upper Canada.

Some early legal challenges in the distribution of the land resource deserve to be noted, although they illustrate that the attraction of the fee simple ultimately prevailed over local peculiarities. In Newfoundland, where settlement was long discouraged, albeit acquiesced in, the full panoply of the law of real property was not considered to have been imported.[22] King William's Act of 1699 reserved land in Newfoundland for the fishery but directed that those who had built fishing rooms before 1685 were not to be interfered with, while article VII guaranteed that those who had built fishing rooms since then on land not previously occupied 'may peaceably and quietly enjoy the same to his or their own Use.'[23] As Chief Justice Francis Forbes would note in an 1819 decision, 'The statute of William does not define the quantity or quality of estates, but it fully recognizes the right of quiet possession, which supposes property of some kind.'[24] More colourfully, he observed in the previous year that 'possession peaceably acquired and used in the fishery are the best title-deeds that can be produced in Newfoundland.'[25] Titles based on possession and custom thus remained the norm in Newfoundland, but insofar as such interests could be sold, leased, inherited, or seized for debt, they became functionally similar to the fee simple. A United Kingdom statute of 1811 provided support for this view by allowing some buildings in St John's formerly used by the migratory fishery to be leased as private property 'in like Manner as any other Portions of Land in *Newfoundland* may be.'[26]

Elsewhere, fee simple estates were certainly recognized but, as noted in chapter 13, in 1790 London instructed its British North American governors to refrain from further free grants of land, a policy that caused particular hardship in New Brunswick and Cape Breton. Not until 1807 was the British fiat lifted; thus most of the land was held not by fee simple title but pursuant to Crown leases or licences of occupation. Nonetheless, as Lieutenant Governor Sir James Kempt observed in reporting to London on the matter in 1825, holders of such licences were given to understand that

> all Persons who actually settled, should receive a Grant, whenever the disability was removed; upon the Faith of this Assurance settlements were made and the Lessees and Occupants consider themselves to be possessed of a Fee Simple, and Lands thus situate are conveyed and devised as a Fee Simple Estate, and are universally considered as such in the Island.[27]

Aside from providing an instance of the 'honour of the Crown' in operation, this example, like that of Newfoundland, illustrates the power of custom and social expectation in the moulding of the law.

In Upper Canada it was the commencement of settlement under seigneurial tenure that caused difficulties. The Loyalists were initially granted only certificates of location prior to 1792, in order to avoid a formal grant under seigneurial tenure, with the expectation that socage tenure would soon be instituted. Within a few years some of the original grantees died and others purported to convey their 'holdings' informally, as the granting of formal patents by government did not commence until 1795. The British law officers proposed a formal and complex process for regularizing the titles, one that did not appeal to the government at York. After the anglophile Lieutenant Governor John Graves Simcoe departed in 1796, Chief Justice Elmsley proposed a commission to address the claims of the heirs, devisees, and assignees of the original grantees; it would sit locally all over the province and accept evidence that would not have been admissible in court. Ignoring the British plan, the assembly passed an act in 1797 setting up the Heir and Devisee Commission along the lines proposed by Elmsley; the Act was renewed in 1805 and went a long way towards sorting out the title problems of landholders large and small throughout the colony.[28]

In New Brunswick it was not the abstract nature of a title-holder's interest that posed problems; rather, how to map a fee simple on to the shifting topography of the St John River basin and its islands was the issue. Powerful spring floods, combined with an unpredictable flood cycle, destroyed fences and improvements and constantly altered the contours of the river's banks, posing a challenge to the common law's assumption that every acre of the earth's surface could be easily demarcated by static boundaries and allocated to an individual owner. As riverine proprietors acquired knowledge of the river's habits, through a combination of legislation and local regulation via the quarter sessions the common law was adapted to create workable solutions. The legislature essentially delegated the power to manage these troublesome lands to the local level, where the most expertise about local ecology resided; different management techniques relying on a combination of private property and common field pasturing could therefore be used at different points along the river's course.[29]

Over the centuries the basic scheme of the common law of real property had been amplified and made more flexible by equitable doctrines developed by the Court of Chancery, particularly with respect to mortgages and trusts. When land was mortgaged, the borrower transferred legal title to the lender as security for the repayment of the loan. If the loan was not paid by the agreed date, the lender could retain the land as well as all the monies paid to date, but the Court of Chancery gradually recognized an interest in the borrower called an equity of redemption. This allowed the borrower to redeem the land for a certain period of years, even after the initial date had passed, by paying the arrears with interest. In cases where the borrower had little prospect of ever redeeming, chancery would permit a lender to apply for a writ of foreclosure by which the borrower's right to redeem would be forever cut off.

Trusts also relied upon this distinction between legal and equitable title; by this device a trustee could be invested with legal title to property (land or movables) with the obligation to invest and administer it on behalf of named beneficiaries, who were said to hold equitable title in the property. Although this equitable title was not recognized in the courts of common law, it became a powerful interest virtually equivalent to legal title and vigorously protected by chancery courts. Trusts for the benefit of widows and minor children became a prominent feature in English testamentary provision among the elite. They also became the dominant mode of business organization for over a century after the creation of corporations was forbidden by a 1720 statute in the wake of the financial scandal known as the South Sea Bubble.

The needs of the landed classes shaped the common law of real property. While in theory England possessed a liberal land law by the eighteenth century, one in which land and other property could in principle be alienated without restriction *inter vivos* and willed freely on death, free alienation was in fact a threat to landed families wishing to preserve their estates indefinitely for future generations. Thus various legal devices evolved by which the landed could seek to ensure that their heirs did not alienate the family patrimony but rather acted as stewards of it. Primary among these devices was the fee tail, or entail, which permitted a grantor to leave land to 'A and the heirs of his body' or even to 'A and the heirs male [or female] of his body.' Entailed land could descend only to the direct descendants of the first tenant in tail (A in the example), thus ensuring that the land would remain in the family. In *Pride and Prejudice* (1813), for example, Mrs Bennet is frustrated by the fact that the land where her family lives is held by her husband in tail male, meaning that on his death a male cousin of his will inherit it, not the couple's five daughters. As an alternative to the entail, landowners could leave property to their heirs with the condition that it never be sold out of the family, or not be mortgaged for a certain period. They could also direct their heirs' marriage and spiritual choices by providing they were to lose property by marrying a named person, or gain it by converting to a particular religion. Such clauses were regularly upheld by the courts on both sides of the Atlantic in the eighteenth and nineteenth centuries, before being more rigorously scrutinized in the twentieth.[30]

The development of the equity of redemption also advantaged the landed classes, who were often in debt and obliged to pledge all or part of their lands as collateral to guarantee repayment. By delaying almost indefinitely the time at which a loan needed to be finally repaid, the equity of redemption ensured that aristocratic families would lose their land to creditors only in the most extreme circumstances. In the case of ordinary debts not secured by mortgage, landowners benefited from a partial immunity from seizure.[31] While in ordinary cases of unpaid debts, the sheriff could seize and sell most forms of the debtor's property to repay the creditor, land in England benefited from an immunity: title to land could not be seized and sold, only a portion of the rents could be claimed by the creditor. While this privilege applied to all landowners, not just the elite, the landed classes benefited disproportionately from it.

A final example of the influence of the landed classes relates to the registration of deeds. When a demand arose in eighteenth-century England for a registry of deeds to facilitate the workings of the land market by providing public information about the state of land titles, the landed classes opposed it strenuously. Secrecy about their land transactions was important to the aristocracy, who remained suspicious of the land market in any case. Only limited experiments were tried, with the result that establishment of title registration legislation awaited the nineteenth century, and the practice did not become common until the twentieth.[32]

The land resource in North America was viewed differently than in England, leading to important divergences in the applicable law. While the basic doctrine of estates in land was received intact, many of the features of land law driven by landed interests did not survive the Atlantic crossing. In the mother country much land was traditionally associated with particular families, and free alienation was a privilege of dubious value. In America, land meant investment, not tradition and lineage. America was land rich and capital poor; hence money might be borrowed from metropolitan sources to purchase or improve land in North America. If the debt was not paid, no particular indulgence was extended to the borrower. An imperial statute of 1732 subjected land in America to seizure for debts in the same way as chattels, contrary to English law.[33] Mortgage law in Upper Canada and the Maritimes also became much more creditor-oriented than English law, displaying little of the tenderness afforded to landed debtors in England. Finally, deed registration was not nearly as threatening in British North America as in England, such that registries of deeds regularly sprang up alongside the county courthouses established in the colonies of settlement, providing a publicly accessible means of ascertaining the state of title to any given property.[34] They also served, whether consciously or not, to confirm settlers in the view that they, rather than Indigenous inhabitants, were the 'true' owners of the land.

The controversy over the reception of the 1732 statute in early Upper Canada illustrated the contrast between English and North American attitudes regarding the land resource. In 1799 the Court of King's Bench decided by a majority that the statute applied: land could be seized and sold for debt. The dissenting judge, Henry Allcock, was an English appointee concerned to uphold the common law as it existed in England wherever possible. With a change in judges, by 1802 Allcock's view was in the majority. In spite of a local act of 1801 regulating the right of seizure, the King's Bench continued to resist the applicability of the 1732 Act until a decision of the king in council in 1809 finally confirmed that land in the colony could be sold at execution.[35]

Yet if there was change, there was also continuity. Chancery courts were established in all the colonies of settlement, albeit tardily in Upper Canada, while the Supreme Court of Newfoundland precociously exercised both common law and equitable jurisdiction in the early nineteenth century.[36] Much of the business in chancery courts dealt with the foreclosure of mortgages and was expeditiously accomplished, but some of their proceedings could rival the fictional *Jarndyce v Jarndyce* for length and complexity.[37] The complex law of conditional estates used by the landed classes in England to tie up land was also invoked by British North American farmers in their own efforts to ensure that their hard-earned land would remain in the hands of their descendants for as long as the law allowed. Conveyancing followed English models, albeit using somewhat simplified precedents, but the statutory monopoly over conveyancing granted to English solicitors in 1804 was not reproduced in British North America, and deeds, wills, and mortgages were often drafted by untrained justices of the peace.[38] And landholding was still required to exercise the franchise, albeit with less stringent requirements in some British North American jurisdictions than in England.

Property law and family law were intimately linked, but asking what 'family law' applied in the English colonies is to ask an anachronistic question. It did not emerge as a discrete legal field until the mid-nineteenth century, and even then it was referred to as the law of domestic relations, which included the head of household's authority over servants as well as family members. Family law in the modern sense emerged only after the Second World War, the first English text with that title appearing only in 1953, the first in Canada only in 1984.[39] The phrase will nonetheless be used here to indicate the body of law dealing with spousal and parent-child relations.

British North America inherited a family law that was, on the surface at least, strongly oriented to preserving the power of men as fathers, husbands, and heads of household. In eighteenth-century England marriage led to the suspension of the wife's legal personality. A wife lost her status as a *feme sole*, whose legal status was almost identical to that of a male, and became a *feme covert*, unable to contract, make a will, run a business, control property she may have owned prior to marriage, or take legal action in her own name in the common law courts.[40] Her personal property (goods and chattels), with the exception of her paraphernalia (jewels and clothes appropriate to her station in life), became the husband's absolutely on marriage. She retained title to any realty she owned, but the husband alone was legally empowered to administer it and receive any profits from it during their joint lives. In neither case was the husband obliged to account to the wife for his administration.

In return the husband was obliged to support his wife and the children of the marriage, although the level of support he provided was not justiciable; he also became liable for the torts of the wife and for her premarital debts. If a wife survived her husband, her independent legal personality revived and she recovered control of her own property. A widow's economic situation could be perilous, however; she was not an heir of her husband and, aside from any testamentary provision he may have made for her, was entitled only to her dower right, being a life interest in one-third of his realty. A husband, by contrast, was entitled to a life estate in all the realty left by his late wife, known as an estate by the curtesy, provided a child had been born alive of the marriage.[41]

The legal nature of marriage in England was intimately tied to Anglican doctrine, which had continued Catholic ideas about the indissolubility of marriage. Divorce was very rare, obtainable only by Act of Parliament beginning in the late seventeenth century. Available for only one cause (adultery), it was also biased against women: men could petition for divorce on the basis of adultery alone, women only if their husband's adultery was aggravated by another offence such as bigamy or incest.[42] Judicial separation was available only from the ecclesiastical courts for grave cause, but private separation agreements were valid where spouses had decided to live apart.

The husband could not, however, by separation agreement or any other contract divest himself of his sole right to legal custody of any children of the marriage, and by the *Tenures Abolition Act 1660* he had the sole right to appoint a guardian for them by deed or will, ignoring the mother if he so chose.[43] As Blackstone stated, the father was the guardian of the child 'by nature,' while the mother was entitled to 'no power but only reverence and respect.'[44] This paternal power could be forfeited only for the most extreme reasons, such as serious physical abuse of the child or squandering its property, bankruptcy, or leaving the realm.

The illegitimate child, meanwhile, was *filius nullius*, the child of no one, with no rights of maintenance or succession vis-à-vis either parent. Such children were sometimes recognized and provided for by will, and in rare cases could be legitimated by private Act of Parliament, but legal adoption would not be available until much later in either England or British North America. Nor did the law make it easy to remove the stain of illegitimacy: unlike the civil law, which allowed the retrospective legitimation of children by the subsequent marriage of their parents, the English common law provided no such escape route until amended by the *Legitimacy Act 1926*.[45]

Even in England, this highly patriarchal legal infrastructure proved unsuitable in some respects. Fathers did not wish to see their daughters' property squandered by improvident sons-in-law; husbands sometimes relied on their wives' contributions to the family economy. Thus various 'workarounds' favouring female agency evolved: equity afforded the propertied the means to preserve a married woman's financial autonomy by allowing assets to be conveyed to trustees to her 'separate use.' Income produced from such assets could not be claimed by the husband, and the wife could dispose of it as she liked; she could also deal with assets held to her separate use without her husband's consent. Another expedient, attractive to middle- and lower-class women, was the doctrine of the *feme sole* trader. By custom in certain areas, including the city of London, married women were permitted to carry on business as if they were single; they could contract on their own credit, pursue legal actions relating to their businesses in their own names, and any profits they earned would be insulated from their husbands' creditors. These measures related to property, however; the 'core' of family law, relating to the preservation of marriage and the favouring of legitimate offspring, remained intact, even as the ideal of companionate marriage became more popular and theological works justifying divorce by writers such as Milton emerged.

The British North American colonies by and large remained faithful to the English inheritance, departing from it in some respects as a result of New England influence in the Maritimes, but on the whole not following the move to a more 'republican' law of the family that emerged after the American Revolution. The dominant trend in post-revolutionary family law was the replacement of the traditional family, conceived as an organic unit presided over by a patriarchal male, with a vision of the family as a collection of individuals each of whom had 'rights' that demanded respect.[46] Indeed, it is in family law, and in particular in the resistance to liberalizing divorce law, that some of the most enduring differences between the law and legal culture of the Canadian colonies and that of the United States can be found, differences that would endure until after the Second World War. These differences cannot be attributed simply to 'illiberal' attitudes in largely Roman Catholic Quebec; on the issue of the dominance of a familial interest over the 'rights' or 'interests' of its members, Protestants and Catholics in British North America were largely united. This divergence ultimately rested on foundational constitutional ideas. In British North American society, the authority of God the Father in the spiritual realm, of the royal father in the national realm, and of the natural father in the familial realm all inexorably reflected and reinforced one another. The dethroning of the king in the American colonies generated a reconfiguration of authority not just in the political realm but in that of the family – the 'little commonwealth' – as well.

The theological objections to divorce were much less important to the dissenting Protestants of New England, where divorce emerged in various modes (governor and council, legislative, judicial) soon after settlement. Massachusetts and Connecticut in particular were leaders in this regard, granting some 800 divorces between them in the second half of the eighteenth century.[47] Members of the early assemblies of Nova Scotia and New Brunswick were familiar with this experience, and both adopted legislation constituting the governor and council as a court of marriage and divorce. Nova Scotia's first assembly in 1758 passed an Act authorizing divorce on very broad grounds, including even desertion; it was disallowed by London, but an Act of 1761 permitting divorce on narrower grounds, including adultery, cruelty, impotence, and consanguinity, was upheld.[48] New Brunswick's Act of 1791 did not include cruelty in this list but added 'frigidity.'[49] The preamble to the latter Act articulated the widely held view that it was 'necessary … to the keeping up of a decent and regular society, that the Matrimonial union be settled and limited by certain rules and restraints'; it was copied almost verbatim by Prince Edward Island in 1833.[50] In the Canadas, meanwhile, a combination of Roman Catholic opposition to divorce and the strength of the English patriarchal inheritance restrained access to divorce until well after 1815.[51]

The divorce Acts of the Maritime provinces went far beyond what was permissible in England at the time. Imperial policymakers came to be very much concerned about the possible emergence of 'divorce havens' in the empire via which English couples might escape the rigidity of domestic law. In 1773 the Board of Trade circulated to many colonies in North America and the Caribbean, including Nova Scotia, St John's Island, and Quebec, an additional instruction to all governors forbidding them from assenting to any bills 'for the divorce of persons joined together in holy marriage' (that is, individual Acts of divorce, as were permitted in England).[52] The approval of the 1761 and 1791 Acts can be attributed only to a less rigorous process for review of colonial legislation in the eighteenth century than would exist later on, especially after the appointment of James Stephen Jr as legal counsel to the Colonial Office in 1813.

The surface gender neutrality of the Maritime divorce Acts and the inclusion of cruelty as a cause of divorce in Nova Scotia did not, however, lead to enormous changes in practice. Women and men petitioned in approximately equal numbers, but divorce remained extremely rare, adultery remained by far the most common cause advanced for seeking divorce, and the standard for cruelty was set very high, requiring extreme physical violence or the threat thereof. The courts gave only formulaic reasons for granting divorces and none for refusing them; hence we have little evidence on which to probe judicial attitudes. One fact stands out, however: in Nova Scotia at least, absence of children and a relatively short period of cohabitation were the factors most strongly associated with successful petitions.[53] While the Maritime model of divorce appears relatively liberal compared to England's, all the British North American colonies nonetheless upheld a strongly patriarchal view of marriage and the family, one that shored up and legitimated male power in all but the most extreme cases.

The legal fiction of coverture played a major role in colonial family life as in England, as illustrated by the career of Halifax businesswoman Jane Wallace. Widow of affluent Halifax merchant Andrew Wallace, she carried on his business after his death in 1780 in order to support herself and their four sons and appears in the court records suing for various debts. She then married an impecunious Protestant minister and carried on the business but disappeared from the records, while he pursued 'his' debtors in court. After his death in the 1790s she re-emerged as an active litigant in her own right.[54] Exceptions to coverture were known and acted upon, however. The Nova Scotia Supreme Court recognized the doctrine of *feme sole* trader in the 1750s and 1760s.[55] As for the use of trusts, when Elizabeth Watson married an Italian nobleman, the marquis de Conty and Gravina, in London in 1746 she took care to convey her assets to trustees to her separate use prior to the marriage and to secure her prospective husband's consent to this arrangement. She followed her husband to Halifax in 1752 and carried on business on her own account, though whether based on her 'separate' assets or as a *feme sole* trader is not clear. A dispute arose over her will, signed hours before she died in childbirth in August 1753, leaving all her assets to her infant daughter. The marquis alleged that the will was invalid as made without his consent. His consent was not required with regard to a will of Elizabeth's separate property, but the Court of Chancery found in his favour nonetheless, because she had brought only a copy of her trust deed with her, and not a duplicate original containing his actual signature. With the trust deed unenforceable on evidentiary grounds, he could assert his common law rights to all her personal property.[56]

Sometimes married women tried to use coverture as a shield. In 1789 when Halifax trader Timothy Sullivan sued Frances Storey for a debt of sixteen pounds for goods sold to her, she pleaded coverture, having been married to William Storey in New York in 1782. William had left for England earlier in the year, and Frances appears to have carried on business on her own account.[57] The Nova Scotia Supreme Court found her liable for the debt on the basis that she was a *feme sole* trader, but after a number of English decisions narrowed the exceptions to coverture in the early 1800s, British North America, with the possible exception of Newfoundland, seems to have fallen in line; no references to *feme sole* traders have been found after 1800.[58]

The law of child custody too reflected the father's position as head of the family. When Elizabeth de Conty's executors sought to follow her last wishes by confiding her infant daughter to a friend, the marquis filed a bill of complaint in chancery alleging that their actions would 'Alienate the filial Duty and Affection of your Orator's said Daughter from her Father to Whom by the Law Divine and Human your Orator and no one else ought to have the care and guardianship.' The court found for the marquis, although the child's early death rendered the matter moot.[59] Paternal rights would remain paramount in British North America until well into the nineteenth century and beyond, with change always a result of legislation.[60] In the United States, however, the judiciary began to make inroads on paternal authority as early as 1809, when a South Carolina court ruled in favour of a mother separated from her husband, who was living openly in adultery; further inroads on the common law followed quickly.[61] U.S. law also began to address the position of illegitimate children much earlier than in England or British North America; Virginia passed a statute in 1785 allowing children to be legitimated by the subsequent marriage of their parents, while other states improved the status and rights of the illegitimate child in various ways in the early nineteenth century.[62] By contrast, the law on legitimation by subsequent marriage was not altered in Ontario until 1921.[63]

Children born to unmarried mothers not cohabiting with the fathers of such children were a cause of great concern in colonial society. They represented both a negative moral example and potential paupers who had, reluctantly, to be supported. In Nova Scotia and New Brunswick, where the Elizabethan poor law was in effect, overseers of the poor were required to tax ratepayers of the local parish in order to provide for the child's support. In practice a vigorous effort was made to find and fix legal liability on the putative father in order to keep taxes low. If the parents of such children died or could not be found, or impoverished children of married parents became orphaned, the overseers of the poor had the authority to bind out the children as apprentices or domestic servants once they reached the age of twelve or thirteen. Those employing them then became responsible for their shelter, food, and clothing.[64]

In Upper Canada, where the poor law was not received, the magistrates at quarter sessions nonetheless administered an ad hoc poor relief system, though one with many gaps and inadequacies. In the absence of legislation, Upper Canadian magistrates took upon themselves the authority to order putative fathers to pay support for their illegitimate children, sometimes to the mother, sometimes to church officials.[65] In 1799 an Act was passed authorizing magistrates to bind out poor children as apprentices, until age eighteen for females and twenty-one for males, thus adopting an important element of the English poor law rejected seven years earlier.[66] This accomplished several goals at once: alleviating the chronic labour shortage in colonial society, ensuring that young people would be properly socialized through work, and minimizing the burden of pauperism on local taxpayers. Those who had reached the age of fourteen had to consent to such placements, however, and complaints by such adolescents were not unknown. Just before the passage of the 1799 Act, the Midland District magistrates in quarter sessions at Kingston upheld the complaint of one James Cannon that he be discharged from his master, because the latter treated the boy 'rather as a domestic drudge than in learning his trade [as a hatter], and further because he [was not] provided with sufficient food.'[67]

Family relationships also played a large role in the law of inheritance. By the eighteenth century, English law recognized virtually complete testamentary freedom, subject only to the law of dower and curtesy, referred to earlier. The default rules for inheritance where the deceased died intestate (left no will) were also important, however, especially for married women, who were, in general, not allowed to make wills.[68] English law had long distinguished between interests in land (real property) and interests in movables (personal property) with regard to succession and various other matters such as exigibility for debt. If a decedent died intestate, interests in land descended according to the rules of primogeniture, by which the eldest son of the deceased inherited all the land, subject only to any dower or curtesy interest of the deceased's widow or widower. If the deceased left no son or issue of a son, the daughters shared the real property equally in a form of joint tenancy called co-parcenary. Movables descended according to a scheme set out in the *Statute of Distributions 1670*, pursuant to which the widow took one-third absolutely, and the surviving children (along with the issue of any children who had predeceased the intestate) shared the remaining two-thirds equally, without regard to gender or birth order.[69] Rules for married women dying intestate were not needed, because their personal property, with few exceptions, had already passed to their husbands absolutely on marriage.

Primogeniture was justified by the desire of England's aristocracy to pass on their landed estates intact from one generation to the next. While eldest sons benefited disproportionately from this practice, daughters and younger sons were not generally disinherited: typically the heir would be required to pay capital sums to his siblings and might have to mortgage the land to do so. The aristocratic ethos was much less prevalent in North America, where most parents sought to provide for all their children, though daughters were often less favoured than sons. This model, labelled 'family capitalism' by some historians, recognized the economic unity of the family as a productive unit in societies where land was more widely held than in Europe.[70] Thus many of the New England colonies abolished primogeniture in favour of equal division among the children of the intestate. Puritan Massachusetts adopted a scheme based on a biblical prescription (Deuteronomy 22:17) entitling the eldest son to a double share of the estate of his deceased parent. That scheme proved attractive to the legislators sitting in the first session of Nova Scotia's assembly, who adopted it in 1758; Prince Edward Island followed in 1781 and New Brunswick in 1786.[71] In Newfoundland, equal division of land on intestacy without the eldest son's double share was the rule, although this was driven by local custom and the distinctive characterization of interests in land there as based on possession rather than freehold estates. In Upper Canada, meanwhile, primogeniture prevailed until the mid-nineteenth century.[72]

Probate proceedings could be very lengthy and complicated, especially if the deceased had been involved in business, yet many fairly affluent people died without wills during the early colonial period and seem to have devoted little thought to what we now call estate planning.[73] Among those who left wills, the scheme adopted by farmer Andrew White, who died in Granville Township, Nova Scotia, in 1787, was fairly common. He left his farm to his widow for life 'as Long as She Stays at home and takes Care of the Family and Remains my Widow.' The farm itself was to be divided among his sons after her death or remarriage, while his five daughters were to be given small sums of money when they came of age. None of the sons was to sell or mortgage the property 'to any stranger, or to any other person out of the Family.'[74]

For those, like White, who left a modest to middling estate, the principle of perceived future need, rather than abstract equality or dynastic ambition, governed testamentary directions.

Clauses depriving widows of their life interests on remarriage generally aimed not to punish but to free up assets for the heirs on the assumption that the second husband would provide for his new wife. Daughters were typically left less than sons, on the basis of the same principle – that they could rely on future husbands for their support. These assumptions could turn out to be horribly wrong: the widow's second husband could turn out to be abusive or a spendthrift; a daughter might not marry or be widowed early and have to depend on the charity of family or community. But in allocating scarce resources, most testators could not afford to consider worst-case scenarios; they based their decisions on what was likely to happen, not what might happen, and hoped that family members would pitch in to assist each other should disaster strike. Even where wills exist, however, they provide an incomplete picture of the transmission of familial assets, as parents often transferred some assets to adult children during their own lifetimes.[75]

The law of dower also illustrated the tensions involved in allocating scarce resources. Dower represented the trade-off between the claims of the widow and the next generation.[76] It was not generous: the widow would be entitled to a life interest in only one-third of her late husband's realty. But it could not be overridden by will and could be asserted ahead of the claims of creditors. Thus even where a husband died bankrupt, as long as he left realty, the widow could assert her claim. Dower also had an impact while the spouses were alive: it had to be barred every time a husband sought to convey realty during marriage, otherwise his widow could assert her right against the purchaser. This safeguard gave the wife a notional say at least in the family economy. Some of the English colonies' earliest statutes dealt with the assignment of dower and with the procedure for a married woman to be 'separately examined' by a justice of the peace prior to her signing away her dower, in order to ensure that her consent was genuine. Dower itself was usually assigned by lay commissioners from the community, who were to mark off physically the widow's one-third interest in a manner that was fair to her and the heirs. In England the long-term trend was for dower to be replaced by jointure, a substitute permitted by law as long as contained in a marriage contract, prior to dower's virtual abolition in 1833; in British North America, however, dower was amplified rather than restricted and remained a core aspect of financial provision for widows into the twentieth century.[77]

Dower was a minimum entitlement, and some men allowed their wives considerably more, such as a life estate in all their lands. Others sought to make the inheritance of sons conditional on supporting their mother, as did David Bent, who left his wife Mary 'two cows, his household furniture and one room in the house,' and ordered that two of his sons were to 'Provide for her meat, drink, clothing and all things needful for her both in sickness and in health' in his 1796 will.[78] Such provisions mirrored those of Quebec parents, who typically inserted them in *inter vivos* conveyances to the child who was to take over the family farm. Not all widows lived quietly in their assigned room, however: Eleanor Parsons and her son had broken the window in her room 'by Sending Brick Batts or Stone at Each other' in 1783, much to the disgust of her late husband's executor.[79]

While the law of property, family relations, and inheritance can be discussed in terms bearing some relation to modern legal conceptions, it is difficult to do the same with the law of obligations. Tort law was barely developed; it dealt mainly with assaults, defamation, and injuries to personal property, while the substantive law of contract beloved of modern commentators did not exist. Blackstone barely discussed contract and did not regard it as a free-standing legal category. The first treatise on the subject, *An Essay upon the Law of Contracts and Agreements* by J.J. Powell, did not appear until 1790.[80]

Yet contract suits, in which plaintiffs attempted to enforce promises to pay, were notionally the subject of the vast majority of civil suits filed in early colonial courts and constituted the cornerstone of the local economy. There were chronic shortages of cash in early British North America, resulting in extensive networks of credit covering virtually all classes in society, from the tavern owner keeping an account of a client's drinks over some months, to a wealthy merchant purchasing supplies from Britain on credit. Eventually, however, accounts had to be settled: the tavern owner might learn that the client was about to leave town; or the British supplier might hear rumours of the merchant's financial difficulties. Creditors might be pressed by their own suppliers, from whom they had purchased on credit, causing them in turn to seek payment from their customers. There were few disputes about the formation or interpretation of contracts; rather, the defendant might deny the purchase of the goods or services in question, or admit liability but state that a lesser amount was owed, either because he had already made partial payment that was not credited, or because the goods were not of the stated quality.

What civil suits lack in substantive law analysis, they make up for in providing ample opportunity to observe the civil procedure of the early colonial courts. Much civil litigation was begun not in the Supreme Court of the colony but in the intermediate courts – the inferior courts of common pleas in Nova Scotia and New Brunswick, and the district courts (after 1794) in Upper Canada. Many claims were also made before JPs, singly or in pairs, who had authority over small debts in their civil capacity, but their summary hearings were not required to be recorded; hence it is difficult to determine directly the quantity of such claims. However, the business of the three levels of court could be visually represented as a pyramid, with a relatively small number of claims in the Supreme Court at the apex, a moderate number in the middle before the intermediate courts, and the highest numbers at the bottom before the JPs.

The intermediate courts were staffed by unsalaried, mostly lay justices of the peace who were remunerated by fees. If the justices were untrained in law, however, most litigation was handled by lawyers, at least on the plaintiff side, as was also the case in Canada under the French regime in the eighteenth century. The Inferior Court of Common Pleas in Halifax (ICCP) was a very busy court indeed during its earliest years (1750–66), the number of new actions started in it each year ranging between 23 and 155 per 1,000 population (compared to 14 per 1,000 today in Nova Scotia). Such rates were higher than any other contemporary jurisdiction in England or British or French America studied to date, though they approached the high rates seen at Quebec in the 1660s.[81] Scholars such as James Muir and John Dickinson have argued that these rates should not be seen as markers of social pathology but rather as a sign of the accessibility of the courts, the regularity of their process, and thus the confidence reposed in them by the population. In a society dependent upon a web of credit relations, where most people were both creditors and debtors, 'going to law' to crystallize and realize upon debts was not an unfamiliar or intimidating experience. Rather, in many instances it was simply part of doing business.

Over three-quarters of the more than 4,300 actions commenced in the ICCP during these years were for debt. The debt might be 'on account' or 'by note.' Account debts were those where the creditor had extended credit over multiple transactions, often over a series of years, but now wanted the debtor to 'settle up.' Debts by note were simpler. Regardless of the source of the debt, the creditor could ask the debtor to sign a promissory note requiring him or her to pay to the creditor or assignee a certain amount of money by a certain day. These notes could and did circulate as currency. Other common suits were based on wages or payment for work done.

The procedure required that a writ of summons be served by the provost marshal (the predecessor of the sheriff) on the defendant, demanding that he or she pay the amount in question or appear in court for trial on a set day. It was required to state the form of action (debt, trespass on the case, etc.). The writ itself was formulaic, but a declaration could be attached setting out the factual history on which the plaintiff relied; this put the defendant on notice about the specifics of the case to be met. A variant of the writ of summons included an attachment, requiring the provost marshal to 'attach' some of the defendant's property as security, to take bail in cash, or to imprison the defendant. Unless the defendant paid cash, attachment did not involve any transfer of property: the defendant could still use the land or goods until trial. Even attaching the body of the defendant involved the threat of imprisonment rather than actual imprisonment in most cases. Attachment required written proof of the debt, however, and hence was not available as a matter of course.

The most significant aspect of civil procedure in early Halifax and Upper Canada was the adaptation of the English writ system by the intermediate courts to be much simpler and more flexible. Under English practice, as noted in chapter 4, every type of claim had its own specific writ (debt, trespass, trover, ejectment, etc); commencing an action with the improper writ was fatal, though one could recommence it in the proper way, provided no limitation period had intervened. The number of writs was historically fixed, leaving novel claims without redress, but by the mid-fourteenth century a new writ of 'trespass on the case' was permitted in which the plaintiff could explain the facts in question and why they should be considered a legal wrong. Trespass on the case functioned as a kind of residual writ, and in Halifax this was taken to its logical conclusion: trespass on the case became the default writ, used even where another writ would have been more appropriate. Eighty-five per cent of all actions in the ICCP were brought 'on the case,' and defendants' counsel did not object even where another writ might have been the 'correct' one. In effect, trespass on the case permitted the court to proceed directly to the substance of the dispute without it getting short-circuited for procedural reasons. A similar evolution characterized the district courts of Upper Canada after 1794.[82]

It should not be assumed that with this procedural flexibility, all actions went to trial. In fact, over two-thirds of all actions begun in the ICCP did not. In this it was unlike the NSSC, where almost 90 per cent of actions ended by trial, usually by jury, or arbitration. Defendants had many choices about how to proceed when summonsed. They could default or confess to the claim, as half did, withdraw the action (13 per cent), go to a jury trial (18 per cent), or agree to arbitration (11 per cent), though in Upper Canada arbitration was used much less frequently. Defendants might also plead abatement, i.e., that the plaintiff's claim should be dismissed because it contained an error in pleading or disclosed no valid claim in law, similar to a modern motion to strike. However, early on the ICCP judges sought restrictions on abatement, so that no court process 'shall be abated [or] arrested ... for any kind of circumstantial or clerical Error or mistakes nor thro the defect and want of form only, Provided all the Essential and Substantiall matters thereof be plainly sett forth therein necessary to proceed upon the merits of the case'; their petition was accepted and the new rule promulgated by the governor in council in late 1752.[83] In a court where none of the judges had legal training, this 'substance not form' approach had much to commend it.

Jurors and arbitrators had important roles to play in the unfolding of civil justice. In theory, men of varying levels of wealth could sit on the jury, but in practice the trial jury tended to be the preserve of artisans rather than merchants; coopers, blacksmiths, carpenters, and small retailers all sat regularly on juries. The other distinctive feature about jurors in the early colonial period was the extent to which they were repeat players. Many jurors sat on a number of cases in one term and also sat across many terms. Peter Mackey, the most active juror in Halifax during this period, served on fifty-three juries over thirteen years.[84] The jury process was expeditious, even if it carried extra costs: charges to the jury were simple, and the jurors did not even leave the courtroom to deliberate but came to their verdict, in civil as in criminal cases, on the spot.

While there were no formal qualifications for arbitrators, in fact they were drawn from a more select group than jurors. Most were commercial men of some substance and also repeat players. They shared with jurors the fact that both groups also tended to have considerable experience before the court as litigators. Arbitration awards were made into judgments, and execution could proceed thereon as with judgments of the inferior court.

Only 1 per cent of arbitration awards were appealed, suggesting this was a dispute resolution mechanism with a high degree of legitimacy. While some 17 per cent of jury awards from the ICCP were appealed, this does not necessarily represent dissatisfaction with the jury as such; more likely, some litigants simply sought 'another kick at the can' with a different jury. Any matter over five pounds could be appealed, and the procedure for requesting an appeal was simple. Appeals to the Supreme Court took the form of trials *de novo* before a new jury at this time, so that the appellant got a fresh look at his or her case and was not restricted to finding errors in the judgment *a quo*. The ease of appeal probably contributed to its relatively frequent use.

The relative informality of process in the ICCP did not apply, or at least not to the same degree, in the Supreme Court. The latter had no original civil jurisdiction in the first decade after its founding. After being given concurrent original jurisdiction with the ICCP in 1764 the Supreme Court was obliged to formulate rules for civil process, and in 1767 it ordered that 'all original Actions and proceedings thereon ... be as near as may be conformable to the proceedings in the Courts of Westminster Hall in England.'[85] As far as can be determined, this meant that the traditional common law writ system applied. One might have thought that where litigants had a choice, the more informal process of the ICCP would have been preferable, but in fact the civil caseload of the Supreme Court grew rapidly. Ease of process was clearly not the only factor driving litigants' choice of venue. Some feared the 'Partiality, Prejudice and Ignorance' of the ICCP judges, while after 1774, when the Supreme Court began to go on circuit, litigants could access it locally without having to attend at Halifax. And this is not to say that process in the Supreme Court adopted practices identical to the English. Evidence from a later period, to be considered in the next part of this volume, suggests that even in the Supreme Court, civil process could be more user-friendly than in England, even though the writ system was retained in its essentials. Even in Upper Canada, where most judges appointed from England loyally tried to maintain English procedures, the general trend was towards the adoption of a simpler and more expeditious civil procedure, suited to the needs of early colonial society. For example, where at first all papers relating to superior court actions anywhere in the colony had to be filed at York, a 1797 statute set up regional offices at which all written process prior to judgment could be filed.[86]

The relative efficiency of court process in personal actions (legal conflicts relating to land were often a different story) was not necessarily a panacea in a society characterized by high economic inequality, as it tended to the advantage of the more economically secure classes of the population. And experienced commercial men could use the law to harass competitors or ex-partners to the point of economic ruin.[87] But similar observations might be made about the law today. The main point is that the courts were a much more integral part of economic and social life in early colonial society than they would later become. The extensive involvement of juries, arbitrators, and lay judges in the legal process seems to have inspired a familiarity with and confidence in the work of the courts, attested to by high rates of litigation. The crowds who attended court days in the county shire-towns of early British North America came partly for entertainment and social interaction, but mostly they came because they needed the services of the courts to carry on business, had to respond to claims made against them, or were required to serve as jurors. As the most important service provided by the colonial state, the courts were well worth their attention.

20

The Early Modern Legacy

The long eighteenth century saw both continuity and change in the law in northern North America, but as of 1815 legal pluralism was still the dominant feature of the landscape. After the long period of relative peace between Europeans and Indigenous peoples in the Great Lakes and St Lawrence valley ushered in by the grand settlement of 1701, enormous political, legal, and social change occurred due to war, revolution, and large-scale migration in the second half of the century. The territory subject to the common law increased enormously by 1815 while that subject to the civil law shrank, but the latter still held sway over the important St Lawrence valley heartland, anchored by the *Quebec Act 1774* and confirmed in the *Constitutional Act 1791*.

From the Great Lakes east, the fate of Indigenous law was mixed. In the Maritime provinces, the steady advance of the European settlement frontier after the arrival of the Loyalists, whether by Crown grant or squatting, presaged a pattern that would become all too familiar in central and western Canada. The colonial states showed little inclination to interfere with the law of the Mi'kmaq or Wulstukwiuk within the territories occupied by them, however. The strongholds of Indigenous law remained relatively stable in Lower Canada, with Kahnawake retaining its place as the Indigenous 'capital,' although some difficulties arising from the interface of Indigenous and settler law were beginning to be felt there. Large swathes of territory were given up by treaty in Upper Canada, but the migration of the Six Nations from their New York homeland to the Grand River settlement provided a counterweight to the narrative of territorial loss and declining influence of Indigenous law. Grand River became the largest and wealthiest Indigenous community in the Canadas. The reconstitution of the Confederacy Council was a highly significant event, providing the opportunity for the continuation of the Great Law that formed the basis of Haudenosaunee law, governance, and tradition; today the Grand River settlement is still considered 'the strongest repository of traditional Haudenosaunee knowledge.'[1] Finally, west and north of the Great Lakes, Indigenous law governed and European fur traders accommodated themselves to it. Everywhere interaction between Indigenous people and the colonial criminal justice system was rare or non-existent.

The arrangements of 1701 that provided for the coexistence of Indigenous and European peoples evolved in varying ways after mid-century in different parts of the northeast. In Nova Scotia, where the Mi'kmaq were most exposed to British-French rivalries, the intercultural law embodied in the Indigenous constitution was most unstable. After the founding of Halifax in 1749, Edward Cornwallis and his successors took a much more aggressive and unilateral stance on both the Acadians and the Mi'kmaq, building new settlements without consulting the latter. The governors began to interpret the word *law* in earlier treaties, as in 'settlements lawfully to be made,' to refer only to British law. Forced by Mi'kmaq resistance (and pleas by the Board of Trade to avoid expensive wars with Indigenous peoples) to enter into the treaties of 1760–1, the British goal was to ensure that settlement could proceed unimpeded rather than to ensure the continuation of a mutually respectful relationship for the future. This was not the way the Mi'kmaq understood these treaties, but it would be over two centuries before they would be able to argue their interpretation in Canadian courts.[2]

The Royal Proclamation 1763, when interpreted along with the Treaty of Niagara and the Covenant Chain, was more aligned with the 1701 accords. It spawned a treaty tradition in Upper Canada that would be renewed in the West in the post-Confederation era, although there remain many questions about the circumstances under which those treaties were negotiated and the extent to which the written text reflects Indigenous understandings – questions that will be addressed in a future volume. In Lower Canada a more 'ambivalent system' evolved in a jurisdiction with a complex history of Indigenous-European interactions featuring both 'imported' mission communities and historic

Indigenous populations in the east and north. Inhabitants of the mission communities made more use of the settler legal system than occurred elsewhere in British North America, consulting notaries for many types of transactions and enforcing their rights as seigneurs. This strategic use of the settler legal system did not detract from their determination to follow their own laws in their own communities, a stance not questioned by the colonial state.

If the seventeenth century was the century of the reception of French law, the eighteenth saw the reception of English law in the northern colonies of North America. The common law received at that time was, on the whole, a more coherent body of law than that received by the early American colonies. Although in practice still oriented around procedure and remedies, Blackstone's *Commentaries* showed in the 1760s that the common law could be understood as a comprehensive body of substantive law. Admittedly he had to almost ignore the presence of equity to make this claim, but this was probably a price worth paying in order to establish his new approach. Indeed, Upper Canada in a sense proved him right by coping without equity or a chancery court for over four decades after its founding.

Much of the substantive law Blackstone wrote about, however, was not as important in the early colonial period as the modes of organizing people and space that the common law provided. These were all on display during the founding of Halifax and replicated later in other colonies: the establishment of counties or their equivalent (districts in Newfoundland, civil parishes in Quebec); provision for grand and petit juries; and the appointment of justices of the peace and sheriffs (or a provost marshal). While the surveying and mapping of counties did give rise to some expense, juries, JPs, and sheriffs came at no cost to the state. The early British colonies could manage without lawyers and often without professional judges for considerable periods of time, but even when professional judges arrived they were often taken up with ceremonial roles and advising the executive, more than with actual judicial work. The first task of Chief Justice Jonathan Belcher in Nova Scotia, as we saw, was advising Governor Lawrence on how the Acadians might be legally deported. Chief Justice William Osgoode was rather more interested in drafting legislation and helping the executive develop policy than he was in the routine work of judging.[3]

The actions of juries and JPs appeared to give a self-administering, self-executing, 'bottom-up' capacity to the law, but these activities were still carried out under the aegis of the Crown. What Jack P. Greene has correctly observed in the context of the seventeenth-century British American chartered colonies – that 'the earliest settlers did not so much bring authority with them across the Atlantic as a licence to create their own authorities' – was not true, or at least not as true, of the eighteenth-century British North American colonies.[4] The Crown was understood to be the umbrella under which all powers and authorities were exercised, whether through the governor's commission and instructions in the Atlantic possessions, or pursuant to the *Constitutional Act 1791*. 'Pure' self-help was not condoned, and this may explain why a vigilante tradition never evolved in British North America. Thus, when the 'masters' of St John's, Newfoundland, gathered in 1723 to create their own court to maintain order in the absence of any British officials during the winter months, they felt the need to proclaim that they were not challenging royal authority but only acting out of necessity in the public interest.

In contrast to the traditional understanding of the British Constitution as 'unwritten,' the *Constitutional Act 1791*, influenced to some extent by the new American Constitution, provided the Canadas with a written constitution. It was an important advance over the 'hip-pocket' constitutions granted to the Maritime provinces and, eventually, Newfoundland. Often overlooked as part of the 'constitutional moment' of the late eighteenth century, it was the building block upon which the *British North America Act 1867* would eventually be based. While traditional accounts have stressed the backward-looking nature of some provisions of the 1791 Act, our interpretation emphasizes the ways in which it looked forward, by strengthening the representative element of the Constitution, the assembly, in its provisions regarding the franchise, the timing of elections, and the creation of new constituencies.

The maintenance of the civil law in Lower Canada, albeit as part of a 'mixed' tradition post-1760, was given an enormous boost by the creation of an assembly in which Canadiens would have a majority of the seats. At a time when most judgeships and official positions went to anglophones, the assembly was the central instrument of Canadien legal nationalism and the principal institutional guarantor of the maintenance of the French language. Lower Canada's unique legal tradition was also shaped by the creation of the profession of advocate in 1785, joining the established notarial profession. Both professions, in their clientele, personnel, educational patterns, and professional activities created a culture de l'amalgame in which the English and French languages and laws met, mingled, and cooperated, no matter how tense inter-ethnic relations might become in the assembly.

Contemporaries lauded the British Constitution for its protection and advancement of liberty, but whose liberty and what kinds of liberty remained contested. By 1792 parliamentary institutions on a fairly broad, albeit mostly male franchise, existed everywhere in the British North American colonies of settlement except Cape Breton. In spite of developing conflicts between upper and lower houses, and their abbreviated meeting times, colonial assemblies were quite active in the field of legislation. Britain took a largely hands-off attitude and did not frequently exercise its power of disallowance. A full complement of superior and inferior courts, along with specialized tribunals such as admiralty courts and courts of marriage and divorce in the Maritimes, existed by 1815. Outside Lower Canada, superior courts were beginning to conduct circuits that created a more accessible justice system and allowed for a two-way flow of information between colonial capitals and their hinterlands. The record of the courts on issues of constitutional significance was mixed, with some evidence of 'Baconian' tendencies among the Canadian judiciary in cases where high state interests were involved. The record of the courts on racial equality before the law was also mixed, with the local courts in Nova Scotia displaying obvious bias against free Black persons; in other colonies such bias seems to have been attenuated or at least less blatant.

On one issue, however, the courts in some colonies took more leadership: slavery. By 1815 a few theoretical slaves may have existed in British North America, but the institution was for all intents and purposes dead, undermined by court decisions that made it virtually impossible for slave-owners to reclaim their slaves. While the abolition of slavery did not guarantee racial equality, it nonetheless represented a significant constitutional commitment on a continent where the 'peculiar institution' was well entrenched.

It is difficult to generalize about women, liberty, and law over the long eighteenth century. Indigenous women saw some reduction in liberty as the territory of their people shrank in some parts of British North America after 1749, though their political role was expressly recognized in some of the eighteenth-century treaties. For the most part, in 1815 Indigenous women lived in spaces governed by their own laws, which usually accorded them some degree of political participation. In fur trade society, however, women who were partnered with European men sometimes inhabited an amphibious zone where both sets of laws might apply.

Under the common law, women were denied political agency, while in marriage their legal identity was suspended by the operation of the law relating to coverture. Even as widows they could be subject to 'patriarchy beyond the grave' if their husbands made testamentary gifts conditional, and husbands were free to appoint anyone by will as guardian of their minor children. Such loopholes as had once existed seemed to be closing: the doctrine of *feme sole* trader, for example, was arguably part of the law of Nova Scotia until the 1790s, but by 1815, following English precedent, it seems to have disappeared in British North America. Trusts for the separate use of married women were not much employed in British North America, while Upper Canada had no Court of Chancery where they could be enforced if they did exist. Property acquired during the marriage was normally acquired in the husband's name, leaving the wife no claim should the parties separate, and no guaranteed claim on death other than her dower right. Married couples may have acted in a more egalitarian fashion than the law contemplated, but all depended on the attitude of the husband, to whom the law delegated all marital authority.

The civil law, particularly the regime of community of property, provided somewhat more economic security for married women but deprived them of any formal power to manage that property during marriage, like their sisters in common law jurisdictions. Even their own separate property could not be alienated without the husband's consent. Customary dower was more generous than under the common law and could not be barred. Provision for the marchande publique was made in the Custom of Paris and continued as a recognized institution. Married women's liberty was extended by the *Quebec Act*'s provision instituting freedom of testation; ironically, married women could make wills without their husband's authorization in Quebec when they could not do so under the common law, unless they had separate property under a trust. This was not, however, a liberty most Canadiennes valued very highly, as most succession planning traditionally took place at the time of marriage. Fathers exercised paternal authority over minor children, although in the rare cases of judicial separation, the successful woman was normally entitled to custody. And on the husband's death, the widow was virtually always named tutor to any minor children. Women in Lower Canada were not denied the vote, though they did not exercise it frequently. Individual women of high rank could exercise considerable local authority as, for example, did the seigneuresse Marie-Catherine Peuvret. Settler married women, whether in Lower Canada or outside, lived under conditions of patriarchy, but the 'customary patriarchy' of the civil law may have been somewhat of an improvement over the 'liberal patriarchy' familiar in British society.[5]

PART FOUR

British North America, 1815–1860s

21

Law in British North America, 1815–1866: Introduction

By 1815 what is now eastern and central Canada was firmly part of British North America; the Anglo-French struggle for North America was over, as was the internecine conflict among the British. Six colonies with settled constitutions emerged from the latter,[1] colonies no longer dependent for their survival on maintaining military alliances and productive economic relationships with Indigenous peoples. Armed conflict with Indigenous inhabitants would occur again, but not until the second half of the nineteenth century and not in eastern or central Canada. In the interim, between 1815 and the 1860s, Indigenous law governed most Indigenous peoples living within British colonies in the central and eastern regions, and an even larger percentage of those living west of Ontario, the only exceptions being some in the Red River colony and some, after 1850, in the new Pacific colonies. European law had little day-to-day effect on the lives of Indigenous people, although it did profoundly affect their economic conditions, by either sanctioning the loss of Indigenous land to the Crown or proving ineffective when it was acquired by private parties.

The legal geography of British North America was settled in broad outline, but within the region much changed in law and legal institutions by the mid-1860s. A number of large processes that marked these years were intimately connected to and often facilitated by law and legal institutions. European immigration and natural increase brought very substantial population growth; the Canadas increased by some

600 per cent, from approximately 430,000 to over 2.6 million, while the Maritime colonies and Newfoundland almost quadrupled, from some 213,000 to 840,000. The European population west of Upper Canada was a little over 20,000 by the mid-1860s.[2] The result was that the proportion of the population made up by Indigenous people dropped dramatically in the east, from 8 to 10 per cent in some areas to 1 or 2 per cent in most places, although they remained a substantial majority in the west. Economies became increasingly diversified and self-sufficient, as subsistence agriculture was joined by the export-oriented lumber and wheat trades. Transportation networks to improve internal communications and for defence and to facilitate the export trades expanded, canals in the 1820s and 1830s and railways in the 1840s and, especially, the 1850s. Immigration and economic growth brought political changes as well. The collection of government institutions that broadly made up the state grew in influence, complexity, and maturity, and everywhere the balance of power within the existing constitutional framework tilted towards the more democratic elements. The power of elected assemblies suffered a setback with the rebellions, but it was short-lived, and civil unrest and repression was followed little more than a decade later by responsible government, a major constitutional landmark.

While these developments occurred at different times and with varying intensity in different places, they all involved the law and legal institutions and legal actors in one of two ways. First, sometimes those institutions and actors were an integral part of larger processes. To take but one example, both the development of state institutions and the democratization of decision-making were marked by changes in the composition, status, and role of the higher judiciary. High court judges ceased to be imported from outside and ceased also to be active participants in executive and legislative processes. The second way in which law was crucial to other developments was less direct but equally important – the law facilitated them. The settlement of tens of thousands of Europeans on Upper Canadian land once occupied by Indigenous peoples was a process driven by economics and politics but effected and legitimized by law. To similar effect, much, though by no means all, colonial economic and transportation infrastructure – canals, railways, bridges, harbours, banks, municipal services – was built by corporations, a relatively new legal form. 'Railway law' and 'corporate law' both emerged as new legal categories and new areas of professional specialty by the 1860s.

The 1860s have been chosen as an appropriate, although of course imperfect and approximate, dividing date for the history of law in Canada. Not only was it marked by Confederation, in addition, by then all the colonies but one had achieved responsible government, albeit by evolutions within the existing constitutional structure rather than revolutionary change. Similarly, all colonies had legal systems that, while based on English models, were adapted to local circumstances and were dominated at every level by personnel who made their life permanently in the colony. All had also created a distinctive local body of statute law, covering everything from which criminal offences were capital to bounties for killing wild animals, and a system of local governance. There remained, of course, many differences among the colonies. What law applied and how it was used in particular places at particular times for particular activities was an always complex question, and the history of law in this period cannot be reduced to any simple and overriding theme or formula. In using, making, and remaking their legal world, British North Americans drew on a variety of legal heritages – Indigenous, British, and French – and also showed themselves willing to innovate in response to environmental and social conditions and to adopt influences and models from their southern neighbours, especially but by no means only in the legal rules governing economic activity, in the legal institutions charged with urban policing, and those that remade the world of criminal punishment.

Having stressed variety and complexity, there are perhaps two very broad themes that run through and unite the following account of the years before 1867. Constitutional continuity may have been ever present, but so too was reform – change whose object was the modernization and rationalization, as contemporaries understood those terms, of legal systems and ideas. The 'Age of Reform' is a term often used by Canadian historians to describe the 1830s and 1840s, and it also infuses the history of law in this period. It was employed to describe changes in substantive criminal law, procedure, and punishment, new court structures aimed at making civil justice more accessible, efforts to make legal knowledge more available, and the doing away with judges on governing councils. Reform also animated vigorous but unsuccessful or partially successful campaigns to do away with 'archaisms' as varied as imprisonment for debt and courts of chancery. A second omnipresent theme is what can best be termed state-formation,[3] a combination of building infrastructure and institutions, and of founding and developing bureaucracies, which profoundly affected areas as diverse as local and municipal government, the establishment of police forces and penitentiaries, and the use of business corporations to build economic infrastructure, including fledgling transportation networks.

The following ten chapters organize this period into broad themes rather than treat the whole chronologically. Chapter 22 analyses the various court systems and the judges who staffed them, looking, among other things, at the growth of a home-grown judiciary, the expansion of circuit systems, the increasing professionalism of lower court judges, and demands for more accessibility in practice and procedure. Chapter 23 follows with an examination of the sources of law – common, civil, statutory, and Indigenous. It reveals that Canadian substantive law mixed together its English and French inheritance with innovations to reflect local conditions and sometimes borrowed from the United States. Much of this substantive law was necessarily statutory, a response both to the inherent unwillingness of many judges to alter the common or civil law and to popular demands for more accessible law. Indigenous law, examined in chapter 24, was still largely independent of settler law but could hardly be entirely unaffected by it, while Indigenous society was often assailed by incursions of settler law.

Chapter 25 analyses the development of the legal professions – notaries, advocates, solicitors, and barristers – of British North America, on many levels. Lawyers of course appear throughout this volume, but while they were an integral part of the operation of law and legal institutions in all fields, their own internal organization merits separate treatment. The chapter examines in turn the rules for entry and governance, lawyering as a business, legal education, legal literature, and law reporting. Chapters 26 through 29 deal with what is often termed public law – constitutional developments and criminal justice. Chapter 26 combines analysis of two constitutions – that governing the relationships between Indigenous people and European settler governments, and that which ordered the internal affairs of the latter, the 'old colonial system' of representative government and the legal reaction to the armed revolts against that form of government that broke out in the Canadas in the late 1830s. Chapter 27 continues the constitutional story, the centrepiece of which was the achievement of responsible government in the late 1840s. Responsible government was arguably the major constitutional development of the nineteenth century. Confederation, dealt with in volume 2 of this history, was obviously highly significant, but Confederation divided up subjects of legislative authority and executive power between two levels of government; the principle that at each of those levels authority ultimately resided in the elected representatives of the people had been established nearly two decades earlier. The responsible government period also coincided with major developments in the social, legal, and political relationships among settler and Indigenous societies, and with the expansion of British settlement in the west. By the late 1840s various colonies were turning to law to reach into previously effectively independent Indigenous communities in an effort to remake those societies, to eliminate traditional cultures and ways of life. This was a process firmly and irrevocably institutionalized by the post-Confederation passage of the *Indian Act*, but it was one that began some decades before that.

Chapters 28 and 29 analyse all aspects of criminal justice. The former begins with the substantive law and contemporary practice of physical punishments, and follows with an analysis and how and why the old regime of punishing the body was replaced by a system of criminal sanctions that relied principally on imprisonment. Many historians have described these developments as the emergence of the modern system of criminal justice. That system is also said to encompass another topic examined in chapter 28, policing. The nineteenth century also witnessed profound changes in the nature of the criminal trial, which increasingly became an adversarial process dominated by lawyers and is examined in some detail in chapter 29.

Chapter 30 is devoted to land law and policy. While traditionally land, and more generally all forms of property law, are said to be private, not public, law, this chapter reveals that term as something of a misnomer. There were numerous major controversies about land law and policy in the nineteenth century, all of which involved political, social, economic, and cultural considerations that involved communities and were thus public. Should aliens be allowed to hold freehold land and therefore vote? Was the system of seigneurial tenure in Lower Canada an essentially anti-modern and anti-developmental way of organizing rights in land? Were tenants and squatters, those who actually worked the land and contributed thereby to the common welfare, entitled to own the land by dint of their labour? By what right were Indigenous peoples dispossessed of their land? Even when English law permitted and facilitated such dispossession, why did the state not do more to protect the remaining land rights of the original inhabitants of the colonies? To what extent did law itself make land an easily marketable commodity, or did the law reflect and reinforce social and moral obligations to family and community? All of these questions are dealt with in chapter 30, which touches in different ways on every region of British North America.

Historians of law have long been concerned with the extent to which societies have shaped the law to organize economic life and promote economic development, the subject of chapters 31 and 32. Law in this context refers as much, if not more, to statute law as to the common law. Chapter 31 beings with an examination of the extent to which judges, who made and applied the common law, did so with the goal of facilitating economic development. It then briefly examines the ever-increasing ways in which local statute law shaped and facilitated economic activity. The most substantial section of this chapter deals with how many hundreds of statutes contributed to the exponential growth of the rise of the business corporation as a legal form for organizing business enterprise. Corporations were a vital, if by no means the sole, mechanism used to build the transportation networks and other infrastructure that transformed the economy from one overwhelmingly localized and reliant on subsistence agriculture to one supplying distant markets and producing a wider variety of goods and services. A second chapter on law and economy, chapter 32, deals with debtor-creditor law, crucial to a credit-based exchange economy. Here the law was shaped by old and new values that clashed and coexisted. In the eighteenth and early nineteenth centuries the principal legal remedy for the creditor against a debtor who did not pay was imprisonment until he or she did so. Imprisonment for debt even became available in Quebec/Lower Canada after 1777, in contrast to the regime of New France and early Quebec. Imprisonment for debt remained available throughout this period and beyond, but its use diminished over time. It was always controversial, because whether a debtor should be made to pay by the use or threat of imprisonment, or have his or her debts forgiven in some way, was as a much a moral as a practical economic question.

Legal systems, like societies, invariably work better for some groups than others, and this part concludes with chapters 33 and 34, on the various ways in which those without power had their subordinate status reinforced by law. It examines the laws governing working people in their relationships with employers, the links between the formal equality under the law enjoyed by British North America's Black population and the myriad ways in which formal equality did not translate into substantive common citizenship with white counterparts, and, in a wide-ranging analysis, the subordinate legal status of half the population – women.

22

Court Systems and Judicial Personnel

Courts and judges are an integral part of the history of law. Between 1815 and the 1860s the number of superior court judges in British North America (BNA) increased substantially, those appointed to judgeships were largely home-grown, and some, if by no means all, came to enjoy the same security of tenure as English judges. In the same period, court systems were diversified and made somewhat more accessible to the populations they served. Diversification came about through, at the elite level, the addition of chancery courts and, lower down the system, the growth of intermediate levels of court. Accessibility was enhanced by the development of circuit systems to take the highest courts out of colonial capitals, granting limited civil jurisdiction to lower courts, and simplified procedures in all courts. Accessibility always had a substantial financial component; going to court was a strain on the ordinary person's resources.

The story told in this chapter is neither simple nor linear. Considerable regional variation marked the history of the courts, and the developments described here drew on the inherited British tradition, the influence of American models, and the felt unique needs of BNA societies. The story is also further complicated by temporal variations. Nothing illustrates more the complexity of court history than the account below of the courts of chancery. As we saw in the previous part, such courts operated in the Maritime colonies in the eighteenth century with the governors acting as chancellors. In the nineteenth century they were professionalized in Nova Scotia and New Brunswick with the establishment of equity judgeships in the 1820s and 1830s, and then abolished as separate courts in the 1850s. Abolition in these two colonies came only a decade and a half after Upper Canada established a chancery court for the first time.

The organization of this chapter reflects these regional and temporal variations and at the same time presents much of the story around discrete themes that transcend region. The first five sections all deal with the superior court judiciary.[1] They look in turn at the origins and professional formation of the judges, the emergence of a separation of powers between the judicial branch of government and the executive and legislative branches, the appointment and removal process, judicial remuneration, and the growth of circuit systems bringing the highest level of civil and criminal justice to colonial hinterlands. The next two sections examine developments in courts other than the highest common law courts, looking at chancery courts and at the oft-changing relationship between superior and lower courts, especially in the area of civil justice. The final two sections deal with institutional and procedural innovation, the principal elements of which were the introduction of professional appeal courts in the Canadas, and procedural reform in all common law colonies.

It bears emphasis that this chapter is not a straightforward history of internal technical adjustment and inevitable 'modernization.' Many of the developments outlined here were controversial, and many were connected to broader social, economic, and particularly political developments. Some of these controversies emanated from within the judiciary and the legal profession, but most were driven by people outside the system. Examples include the robust debate about a separation of powers in the 1820 and 1830s and popular dissatisfaction with chancery courts in the Maritimes in the late 1840s and 1850s. The history of courts and judges is thus always a part of broader histories of the period.

The Development of a British North American Judiciary

Newly established colonies invariably relied on imported personnel to fill the highest positions in newly created institutions, and, as we saw in part 3, BNA superior court judges were no exception. This had changed for Nova Scotia and New Brunswick before 1815, and the one glaring exception to local appointments showed that judges being 'parachuted' into colonies could be bitterly resented. When twenty-nine-year-old

James Carter was appointed to the NBSC directly from England in 1834, drawing on the political influence of his cousin John Bonham Carter, a storm of protest followed. Attorney General Charles Peters, whom many had expected to be named, chaired a meeting of the bar that passed a resolution of 'deep regret' at the appointment, one that 'tend[ed] to degrade' the local profession and would have 'a pernicious effect' on the colony. London could hardly rescind the appointment, but it effectively promised not to do the same thing again.[2]

In the Canadas after 1815 local legal professions became well enough established to demand that their members fill the major judicial offices. Upper Canada still received the occasional import after 1815 – John Walpole Willis of King's Bench in 1827, and the first vice chancellor, Robert Sympson Jameson a decade later, having arrived in Upper Canada as the attorney general just four years before. But Willis and Jameson were the last of their kind.[3] All judges appointed from the 1840s were local, either born in the colony or immigrants who lived there most of their lives. By that time the bar had grown sufficiently numerous and sophisticated – and politically well-connected – to ensure preferment for locals. The chief justice for much of our period, from 1829 to 1862, was John Beverley Robinson, who was born in Lower Canada of Loyalist stock, taken to Upper Canada a year later, and lived the rest of his life and enjoyed his entire legal career in Upper Canada.[4]

A similar story can be told with regard to Lower Canada. For thirty years from 1808 the chief justice of the colony was Jonathan Sewell, whose origins have been discussed in part 3. The other principal judges were all local men, although the dominance of the Lower Canadian judiciary by anglophones meant that many francophone leaders did not exactly see them as such. Three of the famous 92 Resolutions of 1834, effectively a nationalist manifesto, were very critical of the judges for their lack of knowledge of both the French language and the civil law.[5] Typical of these judges was Sir James Monk, chief justice of the Montreal District King's Bench. A Nova Scotian, he had studied law in England, obtained the solicitor generalship of Nova Scotia through the influence of Lord Hillsborough, and after a somewhat chequered career there and in Quebec was made attorney general of Lower Canada in 1792. A year later he became Montreal chief justice and held the post until 1825.[6] Sewell's and Monk's successors were also anglophones, and no francophone judge had a chief justiceship until after the rebellion crisis; Joseph-Rémi Vallierès de Saint-Réal was made chief justice of the Montreal district in 1842. Louis-Hippolyte La Fontaine was the first francophone chief justice of the colony, appointed in 1854. Francophones were better represented as puisne judges of King's/Queen's Bench and the Superior Court (founded in 1849), but they were still a minority.

The biggest linguistic controversy involving the anglophone judges of Lower Canada was that provoked by Justice Edward Bowen's dismissal of several actions at Kamouraska in 1825 because the writs of summons were drafted in French – even though both parties were francophone.[7] At this time pleadings were typically drafted in the language of the defendant, another example of the pragmatic bilingualism that characterized the legal order under the 1791 constitution. Augustin-Norbert Morin, destined for great things but then a young law student, took Bowen to task in a widely circulated pamphlet in which he argued that both legal and policy reasons supported the previous practice. In guaranteeing the continuation of French laws under the *Quebec Act*, Parliament must be supposed to have afforded a protected status to the language in which those laws were expressed, while the need to provide English documentation would entail extra expense and impair access to justice for large parts of the population. It turned out that only in the district of Quebec did Bowen's move have some support: in Montreal and Trois-Rivières the older practice had continued. A committee of the assembly set up to investigate disagreed with Bowen's position. Even though no legislation resulted, it seems that the older practice was reinstated, as the issue died down thereafter. It nonetheless signalled the continuing pressure for assimilation found in important segments of the anglophone community.

Judges may have been overwhelmingly home-grown, but appointments were made by the Crown, and before the 1830s in particular that meant that a candidate needed influence in London. When the aging Sampson Salter Blowers was known to be contemplating retirement as chief justice of Nova Scotia in the later 1820s, various rivals lobbied their English connections, by post and in person, to get the job that eventually went to Brenton Halliburton. That appointment in turn created a vacancy for a puisne judge, and William Hill, reported Simon Bradstreet Robie, 'has gone to England in pursuit of it.'[8] The importance of the Colonial Office was similarly laid bare in 1828–9 after John Willis had been suspended by Upper Canada's Lieutenant Governor Colborne from King's Bench. Colborne named Christopher Hagerman to replace him, but the appointment was not confirmed by London, who gave the job instead to John Macaulay. As Chief Justice Robinson presciently noted some years earlier, Hagerman lacked 'interest.'[9]

Superior court judges in the less populous colonies of PEI and Newfoundland, and those of the Quarterly Court of Assiniboia and the new colonies of Vancouver Island and British Columbia, tended initially to be outsiders. PEI's eighteenth-century judges had all been imports, and the practice continued well into the nineteenth, the island even importing a non-lawyer in 1813, Thomas Tremlett, who held office until 1824. With the PEI Supreme Court's two unpaid and non-professional assistant judges, Tremlett was a member of a triumvirate of equals. Such was the difficulty of finding a properly qualified person that his replacement in 1824 was Samuel G.W. Archibald, Nova Scotia's solicitor general, who made only occasional visits to the island to hold court. Archibald's successor, Edward Jarvis, of Loyalist parentage from New Brunswick and a lawyer, became a 'local' through his twenty-four years as chief justice, from 1828 to 1852, and his successor, Robert Hodgson, was born and lived all his life on the island.[10] Newfoundland's chief justices in the first half of the nineteenth century were also all imports; one of them, Henry John Boulton, appointed in 1833, was from Upper Canada. The first locally born chief justice was Hugh William Hoyles, appointed in 1865 after a long and successful career in local politics.[11]

Further west, the Quarterly Court of Assiniboia was presided over by the first recorder of Rupert's Land, Adam Thom, the ultimate outsider – a recent Scottish immigrant to Lower Canada and a pronounced francophobe. A few years later, when British colonies were established on the Pacific coast, David Cameron was appointed as Vancouver Island's first chief justice in 1853, four years after the colony's founding. A Scottish trader who had lived in Demerara (later British Guyana) since the 1820s, he was something of a throwback to earlier patterns in the Maritimes. He had no legal training, but he was married to the sister of the colony's governor, James Douglas. Cameron was often vilified, both personally and because of his lack of legal knowledge. A House of Commons committee on the HBC was told that 'before he can decide upon a case, he has to refer to his books even in the most common case.' He nonetheless hung onto his job until 1865, when he was replaced by English barrister Joseph Needham. Mainland British Columbia fared better: its first chief justice, and its only judge before Confederation, was an English chancery barrister. To some iconic and to others the scourge of Indigenous defendants, Matthew Baillie Begbie rode his circuits in the interior on horseback.[12] The chief justices of early PEI and Newfoundland, and those of the Pacific colonies, tended to conform to standard patterns in the nineteenth-century empire. Often imports, they lived in places with small settler populations frequently marked by factions and long-standing personal and professional animosities.[13]

Separation of Powers, Appointment and Removal of Judges, and Judicial Remuneration

During the 1820s and 1830s elected assemblies often found themselves embroiled in disputes with unelected councils and with lieutenant governors. A common element in these disputes was the separation of powers. Before the 1830s judges were heavily involved in the political administration of all colonies in the empire. In New Brunswick, which until the early 1830s had a single unitary council exercising both executive and legislative power, every single Supreme Court judge was a councillor as well, almost all of them elevated to that body when appointed to the bench. Nova Scotia also had a unitary council, and between 1815 and 1830 four of its six Supreme Court judges were also councillors.

The Canadas had a different structure of government under the 1791 *Constitutional Act*, and judges served on both the legislative and executive councils. William Dummer Powell was a member of the Upper Canada executive council while a judge, and when he was made chief justice in 1816 he switched to being the Speaker of the legislative council. His successors as chief justice, Sir William Campbell and John Beverley Robinson, held that post as well as the presidency of the executive council. It was less common for puisne judges to be on a council than in the Maritimes, and the same was true in Lower Canada. But the lower colony had its share of very prominent judge-politicians. All the chief justices of Quebec down to 1830 were on both councils. Chief Justice of the Montreal District King's Bench James Monk was also on both councils, although his successor from 1825, James Reid, was not. A few puisne judges also held council appointments. James Kerr, on the Quebec District Court of King's Bench from 1809 to 1833, was put on the executive council in 1812 and the legislative council in 1823. Olivier Perrault of the same court was a legislative councillor from 1818 until 1827. In 1830 there were four judges on the legislative council, out of twenty-three, and two of the nine executive councillors were judges.[14]

Removing the judges from councils was one of the principal goals of the reformers in both Canadas from the mid-1820s, and in the 1830s the issue also animated Nova Scotian politicians. Objections were much more than formal, for many colonial judges were ardent tories who did indeed take an active role in politics. Sewell, for example, promoted American immigration and, for a time, union with Upper Canada. He was described by Governor General Lord Dalhousie in 1820 as 'my confidential adviser in the ... administration of the Government, I turn to him on all occasions of difficulty.' In part this was because Sewell, for all his toryism, had an extensive knowledge of the civil law and was fluent in French.[15] Brenton Halliburton of Nova Scotia, a Supreme Court judge from 1807 and chief justice from 1833, was a notorious tory; reform leader Joseph Howe condemned his appointment as chief justice because he had 'mingled much and warmly in politics' and was 'the head of a party exclusive in its views and violent in its measures.'[16]

The judges' presence on councils was initially defended, locally and in London, on the grounds that judges were both the best available advisers in general and particularly useful in drafting local legislation. As James Stephen, legal adviser to the Colonial Office, told a House of Commons committee on the Canadas in 1828, the judges were necessary members 'from the want of other competent persons,' and while it might be better not to have them there in an ideal world, their 'superiority of knowledge, talents, and other accomplishments' justified their presence. Tory Nova Scotia lawyer and at the time of writing soon to be Supreme Court judge William Blowers Bliss agreed with Stephen, noting, 'In theory it seems well enough that the Judges should not belong to' the council, but that 'in practice ... they are its best members,' and were necessary 'to read, to watch, and to amend or reject' the foolish laws passed in the assembly. But the argument for a separation of powers drew on emerging British constitutional principles and thus ultimately largely prevailed. The 1828 Commons committee concluded forcefully that 'it is not desirable that Judges should hold seats in the Executive Council.'[17]

The committee was equivocal about legislative councils. Although it insisted that generally judges 'had better not be involved in ... political business' and thus should largely be excluded from that body as well, it was prepared to make an exception for the chief justice, 'whose presence on particular occasions might be necessary.'[18] The committee's views found favour with the government, so that in 1830 London ordered a substantial separation of powers. In the Canadas all judges were to be excluded from executive councils and all, with the exception of the chief justice, were to absent themselves from legislative councils; they could not be removed from the latter because appointments were for life. Robinson stayed as Speaker of the legislative council until

1838, when he was temporarily replaced by King's Bench puisne judge Jonas Jones, in contravention of London's 1830 edict. After the union the speakership went to chancery judge Robert Sympson Jameson, until 1843 when a local statute finally barred all judges from both Upper and Lower Canada from both councils.[19] In the Maritimes all judges, except the Chief Justices, were taken off the unitary councils in line with the 1830 instruction.

Despite London's intervention, the issue of judges on councils did not disappear. In the Canadas the chief justices' continued membership of the legislative councils agitated reformers until the rebellions. The Lower Canadian assembly passed legislation to remove the chief justice in 1831, 1832, and 1833, to no avail. In Newfoundland and the Maritime colonies unitary councils meant that the chief justices' retention on the council also meant membership on the executive. In Newfoundland the presence of Chief Justice Henry John Boulton on the council was a constant source of friction with the assembly in the 1830s. After Boulton was dismissed in 1838 following an assembly request to London motivated by his political partisanship, no future chief justice sat on the council.[20] As early as 1833 the problem was resolved in New Brunswick, the council being split into two and the chief justice not appointed to the executive council. But this did not occur in Nova Scotia until 1838, and Halliburton's continued active involvement in politics until then was one of the most controversial political issues of the 1830s, especially as he was directly implicated in another controversy, the collection of fees from litigants by the judges, discussed in more detail below. Suffice it to say here that the assembly passed a series of bills abolishing fees, all of which failed in the council, those defeats laying bare the incongruity of judges being involved in politics. Howe did not mince his words: 'When Bills abolishing the illegal exaction of One Thousand Pounds per annum taken by the Judges in the shape of fees, are year after year burked in the other end of the Building, by a Body over which presides a gentleman largely interested in that exaction, is it unfair to attribute to him some agency in their destruction, or to wish that he had not been placed in a situation where his public duty interferes so much with his private interests?'[21]

These various movements towards a separation of powers coexisted with the continuing political involvements of judges in politics. Chief Justice Robinson was not a councillor, but he drafted the principal post-rebellion legislation passed in 1838.[22] Judges sat on the Special Council that ruled Lower Canada from 1838 to 1840. Most notably, when new colonies were formed on the Pacific coast in the 1850s, judges, in the absence of anybody else legally trained, acted as throwbacks to an earlier age. Chief Justice Begbie of British Columbia drafted most of that colony's early legislation and was also on Governor Douglas's executive council. David Cameron was similarly on the Vancouver Island Council in the 1850s and acted as legislative draftsman.[23]

All British North American superior court judges were formally appointed by the Crown, in the early decades by the Crown in London and more latterly by the local Crown representative. With responsible government the appointment became in effect, though not in form, a local appointment.[24] When it came to removal of judges, however, this period saw real differences among colonies.[25] In 1815 superior court judges, like all other prerogative appointments, held their appointments 'at pleasure,' meaning that they could be dismissed by the Crown, at will, if they incurred the displeasure of the executive, although a judge so treated could appeal to the Privy Council in London. At pleasure appointment was an anachronism in Britain itself, done away with by the 1701 *Act of Settlement*, but it was considered necessary by London to ensure that colonial judges were compliant to government wishes. Campaigns for fully independent judges – tenure on 'good behaviour' – were staples of the reform movements in both Canadas in the early 1830s, especially driven in Upper Canada by the governor's dismissal of Willis in 1828. London conceded the constitutional principle but demanded in return that the colonies pay for their own judges and guarantee their salaries: judges would not be allowed to escape servitude to the Crown and instead be financially dependent on assemblies. Good behaviour appointment came first to Upper Canada in 1834, and then to Lower Canada in 1843 and Nova Scotia in 1848. Arbitrary dismissal was replaced by a joint address of assemblies and legislative councils to the lieutenant governor. As discussed below, Upper Canadian district/county court judges also had good behaviour tenure, principally from 1857, although a different method of removal was prescribed for them.

The strangest debate over judicial tenure occurred in Nova Scotia, where the issue riled the judges, not to demand good behaviour appointments, but to unsuccessfully oppose them, for they feared any involvement of the elected branch in judicial dismissal. One of the first acts of the first Nova Scotia administration to come to power after responsible government was to extend good behaviour appointments to that colony's judges, in 1848. This brought forth an animated opposition from conservatives and the judges themselves, because they feared the corollary of good behaviour appointments, removal in exceptional circumstances by assemblies. If judges could no longer be dismissed without cause, some mechanism needed to be legislated for dismissal if there was sufficient cause. The Nova Scotia Act replicated the British system of charges brought by the lower house and tried in the upper, the Legislative Council, but despite this congruence with England the judges railed against it. They feared, they said, that judges would be treated unfairly by their political opponents, voted out of office for no good reason. The claim was without local historical foundation and couched in what Lieutenant Governor Harvey himself described as 'hysterical' language, and it failed. But the incident reveals that to the end some elements in colonial society preferred autocratic monarchical government to a modern liberal state.

The issue never animated politicians or judges in the other Maritime colonies, although for some unexplained reason the New Brunswick master of the rolls, a post created in 1838, had good behaviour tenure under the local statute, something none of the Supreme Court judges enjoyed until Confederation.[26] The judges of the New Brunswick county courts, created in a statute passed on 17 June 1867, just two weeks before the new dominion officially came into existence, also had good behaviour tenure while their superiors did not![27] British Columbia's and Prince Edward Island's judges were also 'at pleasure' until those colonies joined Confederation in 1871 and 1873 respectively. So too were Newfoundland's judges until the later nineteenth century.

Levels of judicial remuneration varied quite substantially across the colonies. The chief justice of Upper Canada received £1,500 sterling in the 1830s, while his Nova Scotian and New Brunswick counterparts were paid £850 and £900 sterling. When two superior courts of common law were created in 1849 in Upper Canada, the chief justice of each actually received less than the chief justice of Upper Canada had in the 1830s, £1,250 sterling. Much less well paid in most colonies were puisne judges holding judgeships established by local statute. The two judges added to the Upper Canada Court of King's Bench in 1837 got £1,000, in local currency, not sterling, worth 10 per cent less, while their Nova Scotia equivalents received only £600 local currency, 75 per cent of sterling. Upper Canada's superior court puisne judges were still getting £1,000 in the 1850s, but that was sterling.[28] More important than the varied levels of colonial salaries, however, is the fact that judicial remuneration was not infrequently a heated political issue, as illustrated by three controversies, two in the 1830s and one in the early 1850s.

In Upper Canada in the 1830s reformers complained that high salaries made judges subservient to government, and that even more so did discretionary pensions. There was no established pension system, but many judges were given one by colonial executives. This was sometimes done as an inducement to retire, but reformers saw the discretionary nature of pensions in a more sinister vein, as an incentive for sitting judges to be quiescent to government. In this they shared the concerns of English critics about a Baconian judiciary long after the *Act of Settlement*.[29] As soon as they had won the battle for good behaviour tenure, reformers turned their guns on the pension system. A substantial part of the work of the assembly's Committee of Grievances in 1835 was taken up with this issue, many witnesses being asked the leading question: 'How can a bench of judges, dependent on the Colonial Office for their customary retiring pensions, ... act impartially between the parties in cases where a collision may arise between the Legislative and Executive departments in this colony?' Such concerns were muted after the rebellion, and in 1849 the judges of both Queen's Bench and common pleas were given the presumption of a still discretionary pension; not until the eve of Confederation, in 1866, did the Province of Canada inaugurate pensions for all judges as of right. No other colony did so; many judges received pensions, but by virtue of individual statutes or executive acts. When Augustus Wallet Desbarres and James Simms, the assistant judges of the Newfoundland Supreme Court, retired in 1858 'being no longer able, from age and bodily infirmities,' to discharge their duties, they were granted pensions of £275 sterling. When the chief justice retired a few years later he too was given a pension by legislation, a rather more generous one of half his salary.[30]

In Nova Scotia in particular, judicial remuneration was a very contentious political issue in the 1830s and 1840s.[31] To some degree the problem was simply salaries that were too high, resentment at them boiling over when the judges asked for a raise. Many assemblymen reminded them that they were already very well paid, compared to the vast majority of residents, and told them to accept their good fortune, not to yield to 'the cravings of rank and luxury.' A more profound challenge to judicial remuneration came from the fact that, as noted above, the judges received a salary supplement in the form of fees paid by litigants. Reformers thought it indecorous that well-paid judges should be able to fleece ordinary people in this way, but worse to reformers was that they believed there was no legal basis for fee collection. Fees were 'Exactions made upon the most distressed part' of the community. Fee opponents were able to stop their collection from litigants, but at the cost of a salary supplement paid for by government. The fee debate involved some of the harshest words used in any colony against superior court judges. New Brunswick Supreme Court judges also received fees until the early 1850s, without the matter ever being a subject of much rancour.

New Brunswick was the site of a third major controversy around judicial remuneration in the early 1850s. An economic downturn led to widespread demands for retrenchment in government spending, including judges' salaries. In 1849 salaries were reduced for future judges, but not for incumbents, and London approved the measure. But it would not sanction an 1850 attempt to extend the reductions to incumbents or a bill the same year to abolish judicial fees without compensation. London was adamant that this was an attack on judicial independence, Colonial Secretary Grey telling Lieutenant Governor Head that for judges to be truly independent 'their Salaries shall be fixed by permanent appropriation, not provided for by annual votes.' New Brunswick's experience was a lesson learned by the Newfoundland assembly when it too enacted retrenchment in salaries in 1855. The reductions, to £800 for the chief justice and £650 for puisne judges, applied only to anybody appointed in future.[32]

Circuit Systems: Bringing the Centre to the Hinterland

The highest court in each colony sat regularly in its major city in formal term times based on the English court calendar. Between terms they also became itinerant courts, and these circuit or assize systems were continually expanded throughout this period. The one place colony-wide circuits did not operate was Lower Canada, where the superior courts were organized into the principal districts of Montreal and Quebec, and the lesser ones of Trois-Rivières and St Francis. Judges did circuits within, not between, these districts.[33]

In Upper Canada circuits were referred to by the English name of assizes. In the 1820s there were two, the eastern and the western, which, after 1822, the judges travelled twice a year.[34] A judge of the court went out each time armed with a Commission of Assize and Nisi Prius, to try civil cases, and one of Oyer and Terminer and General Gaol Delivery, for criminal cases. Over time more and more towns were added, often following local requests to be included on the assize itinerary, since a visit of the King's Bench judge brought status and money into the town.[35] As the assize system expanded the time spent on travel, and the caseload, steadily increased. Christopher Hagerman did ten or so such journeys annually between 1840 and 1846, holding court almost fifty times in various towns.[36] Upper Canadian judges presided at assizes solo, unlike those in Nova Scotia, and they sat solo in civil cases but in criminal cases were joined on the bench by associate judges drawn from the local magistracy. Such men were there to display their connections to the grandees from the capital; they did not have to make any legal decisions, because the results in criminal trials were determined by juries.

The expansion of Nova Scotia's system aptly illustrates the way in which circuits in every colony were added with the spread of settlement. In 1815 the court visited just seven locations, mostly twice a year, and by the time of a major reorganization of 1841 it was going to sixteen towns, all of them twice annually, in the spring and the fall, and by mid-century another town had been added.[37] Circuit visits were not lengthy affairs, the court staying at a locale no more than a few days before moving on. Circuits were also an integral part of the court systems of New Brunswick, British Columbia, PEI, and Newfoundland, although in the latter two instances circuits did not begin until well after the establishment of the respective Supreme Courts.[38] As noted above, Matthew Baillie Begbie of mainland British Columbia was well known for circuit riding on horseback, although most of the time he probably had little choice about his method of transportation. The Newfoundland Supreme Court became itinerant after its reorganization of 1824 which added two judges to the court. Each did an annual circuit by sea to the north and south of St John's, not going to the west coast because that was the 'French shore.' Even remote Labrador was served for a few years, but that circuit was suspended in the early 1830s. The Newfoundland circuit, for obvious reasons, was likely the most expensive in British North America.[39]

In both Nova Scotia and New Brunswick circuits generated considerable controversy. In Nova Scotia it was because politicians wanted to get their money's worth by having two judges travel each circuit, while the judges themselves disliked the work and connived to evade the two-judge statutory requirement. In addition, as in other colonies, there were local disputes, not simply about whether the circuit should go to a particular area, but also where in that area it should hold court. In New

Brunswick there were frequent disputes between the judges, assembly, and government over circuit expenses.[40] Circuits generated much less controversy in the 1850s and 1860s, in part because judges in many colonies travelled by the rapidly increasing rail network. Judges arrived much more reliably and had less to complain about. When there was occasionally a problem, it made headlines. Upper Canada Judge Joseph Curran Morrison did so, when he was briefly thrown off the train from Coburg to Toronto for refusing to leave the sleeping car, where his ticket did not entitle him to travel. He sat there because there were no other seats available, but the conductor was unimpressed with his legal argument that his ticket entitled him to a seat, and when Morrison would not budge he was physically ejected by a group of railway officials. Other passengers persuaded the conductor to let Morrison back on the train, and he stood the rest of the way. He apparently threatened legal action but thought better of it.[41]

The visit of a superior court judge to a small town was an important event in the community, bringing visiting dignitaries to town and causing many locals to leave their homes to act as jurors, witnesses, and litigants, or simply to engage in business and gossip. At the same time, having to attend court, especially as jurors, could be bitterly resented by those with more pressing occupations, especially when weather and travelling conditions delayed the judge(s), as they often did. Before the advent of railways some judges also resented some of their circuit itineraries greatly, especially those with rigorous travel over inadequate roads and less than ideal accommodations along the way. D'Arcy Boulton of Upper Canada's Queen's Bench was not the only judge to find that circuit travel took a heavy toll on his health. Ironically, for much of this period, given the colony's almost complete lack of roads, the Newfoundland judges had relatively easy travel, coasting 'in style' in a government ship from community to community. It was only a pleasant cruise, of course, if one did not suffer severely from sea-sickness, as Chief Justice John Gervais Bourne did.[42]

Chancery Courts

The superior courts possessed a very broad jurisdiction, both civil and criminal, but not a complete one, for they shared judicial authority with a small number of specialized courts. There were Courts of Vice Admiralty in Halifax, Quebec City, Saint John, and St John's, which had jurisdiction over vessels taken as prizes at sea, as well as salvage, disputes between masters and crew of vessels, and of major crimes – murder and piracy – committed on the high seas. When Admiralty sat as essentially a criminal court it was originally staffed by lay judges – politicians and naval officers – but over time the practice grew of superior court judges presiding. In some colonies a Court of Escheats operated, comprising the lieutenant governor and his council, to deal with cases involving land grantees who had failed to fulfil the conditions of their grants and thus forfeited the land. In the Maritime colonies Courts of Marriage and Divorce operated. Initially the lieutenant governors presided, but in the nineteenth century these courts invariably comprised superior court judges.[43]

Far and away the most important of these 'specialized' courts were Courts of Chancery. In 1815 the Maritime colonies' lieutenant governors formally exercised the powers of the chancellor and thus presided over chancery, while in Newfoundland the Supreme Court, in the form of Chief Justice Francis Forbes, simply assumed equitable jurisdiction, granting specific performance of contracts and recognizing the equity of redemption. When the island's Supreme Court was reconstituted under a royal charter in 1824 it was given the jurisdiction of the common law courts of Westminster Hall and of the 'High Court of Chancery,' making it and New South Wales the first British jurisdictions to combine law and equity. In doing so it was formally different from other colonies, but not practically so, because the vast majority of the courts' work in the Maritimes was done by the Supreme Court judges as masters in chancery.[44] Foreclosure suits dominated the dockets. In Nova Scotia almost 80 per cent of equity cases were foreclosure actions in 1821–45. The staple of the English Court of Chancery, trusts, occupied only a minuscule portion of the court's work. After foreclosure the major business of the court was to act as a kind of informal appeal from the Supreme Court by way of injunction applications. The chancery court in New Brunswick operated in much the same way, with a predominance of foreclosure suits, as did the court in Upper Canada once it was established. Between 1845 and 1851, for example, they made up 216 of the 246, or 88 per cent, of the cases heard in that jurisdiction.[45]

In 1826, 1838, and 1848 respectively, Nova Scotia, New Brunswick, and PEI created separate equity courts, establishing a judgeship called the master of the rolls (MR), the name given to the chancellor's principal deputy in England.[46] Although these initiatives emanated from the lieutenant governors, the reasons given were slightly different. Sir James Kempt of Nova Scotia adverted to his own lack of competence and to the fact that what legal assistance he had came from common law lawyers. Although he made little of it, the court's caseload had grown quite substantially in the early 1820s and this no doubt was also a factor. When Sir John Harvey addressed the New Brunswick Assembly in 1838 he also discussed the incongruity of the same judges deciding both law and equity when the two systems were supposed to be distinct – based 'upon principles and ... administered in modes widely differing from each other.' He seems not to have worried that he himself knew little, suggesting that, unlike Kempt, he actually took no active role as chancellor. A New Brunswick assembly committee agreed with Harvey, calling the two jurisdictions 'incompatible' and also asserting that the Supreme Court's common law caseload was so great that its judges could not do the equity work with dispatch.[47]

Although both New Brunswick and Nova Scotia established the new court, it was a controversial measure in the latter, opposed by those who saw it as an unnecessary burden on the public purse and a plum patronage post. Lawyer William Young, who thought it disrespectful to oppose the lieutenant governor outright and argued for a temporary, not a permanent, position, complained that it would only add to the 'heavy expence [of] the Judicial establishment.' The critique was apt. As discussed below, Nova Scotia had just created four new judgeships to head up the lower courts and also had five men on the Supreme Court bench. Moreover, the first MR was Simon Bradstreet Robie, until then solicitor general and a councillor, and a former Speaker of the assembly, and the appointment seemed a perfect example of the official class creating a job for itself. In subsequent decades attacks on the various MRs, and on the institution of chancery, became a staple of the burgeoning reform movement. Howe castigated Robie in 1832 as someone who 'year after year pocketed the public money, for keeping up a body of costly and dangerous absurdities.' While there is evidence that the Nova Scotia court resolved its cases reasonably quickly, it was an expensive venue, costs being considerably higher than elsewhere, and could not escape the perception of being plagued with delays.[48]

Neither Maritime chancery court was long lived. In 1854 and 1855 respectively New Brunswick and Nova Scotia abolished the court and merged common law and equity in the Supreme Court. New Brunswick's abolition, Canada's first, was a relatively uncontroversial affair, with criticism of the court low key. It was carried out on the recommendation of a commission on statute revision and equity, which concluded that the current system gave too much power to one man, especially given that the jurisdiction of the court was defined by the idea of conscience, which 'must afford a pretty extensive latitude of interpretation.' From the judgments of this one man the only appeals were to the chancellor, the lieutenant governor, and then to the Privy Council in England. It had become untenable, 'as our Province advances in population and prosperity ... that the people will submit to be deprived of their property by the decision of a single judge.' As a result the commission recommended, and the Assembly uncontroversially enacted, the abolition of the court and of the post of MR, with the incumbent moving to the Supreme Court bench. Henceforth any single judge of the Supreme Court could hear an equity case, with an appeal to all five judges.[49]

Much more heat was generated by abolition in Nova Scotia. Expense, delay, obscurantism, and an easy workload compared to that of the Supreme Court were all regularly trotted out as reasons to reform or abolish the court, although some of these complaints, particularly regarding delay, were not justified. The last person to hold the post of MR, Alexander Stewart, was also widely detested for his toryism and haughty manner. The legal establishment defended the court largely by insisting that equity expertise was required and not even the Supreme Court judges possessed that. But its critics easily won the day, adverting constantly to what one newspaper called the 'misery and ruin to families' caused by the court; the same editorial trumpeted that abolition was a measure 'vastly more important and beneficial in every respect' than any other recently passed. Long before an abolition bill passed the assembly, the debate was not so much about abolition as about what should be done with Stewart – transfer him to the Supreme Court as New Brunswick had done, or pension him off. Under pressure from London the government offered him a place on the Supreme Court but, typically arrogant, he declined it because he was not also offered seniority dating back to his appointment as MR. He took a pension instead. By then also some American states, notably New York and Ohio, had abolished separate courts of equity. Nova Scotia's statute effected a more radical change than New Brunswick's, which was simply the creation of an equity side to the Supreme Court. It made changes to procedure that mirrored those enacted in England three years previously, notably the elimination of taking evidence solely by deposition and the simplification of pleading.[50]

Upper Canada's experience with chancery was a study in contrast with the Maritime colonies. The conclusion that Upper Canadian authorities had come to in the 1790s, that no equity jurisdiction existed, remained the accepted wisdom until 1837, when a chancery court was finally established – only a decade and a half before its equivalent was abolished in the Maritimes. Key to both the objections to a chancery court through the first three decades of the nineteenth century, and to the eventual creation of one, was the mortgage question. For decades creditors were able to use a variety of local practices to make good on the land security given by mortgagors, in part because there was no court to enforce the equity of redemption. The lack of chancery thus favoured creditors. But when the tide turned, and both courts and assembly moved to supporting the idea that there was an equity of redemption, creditor advocates, especially Chief Justice Robinson, favoured creating a court so that foreclosure would become available. The new court was presided over by a newly created judgeship, the vice chancellor of Upper Canada, with the post going to Attorney General Robert Sympson Jameson.[51]

Almost from its inception Upper Canada's chancery court came under attack.[52] As elsewhere, the perception was that it was an elite, expensive, inaccessible, and tardy tribunal. It took just three years after the court's founding for the assembly to demand an account of the court's work. The figures supplied by the registrar must have pleased those who thought the court did not give good value. Of the 223 suits started in 1840–1, fewer than half, 102, had been completed. The registrar was careful to point out that of the incomplete cases some were still in progress, and 'a considerable part' had been settled, although he did not know how many (prompting the question of how he knew that many had been settled). An almost inevitable demand arose among some younger lawyers and radical lay politicians for abolition of chancery and transfer of its jurisdiction to Queen's Bench, to achieve greater speed and reduce costs. When abolition was discussed in the assembly, the court was always saved by the votes of the Lower Canadian members, who toed the government line on this issue. As early as 1841 a commission comprising chancery lawyers and senior judges, chaired by Robinson, was struck, but it recommended no immediate change in the short term, preferring to study and mirror English developments. Indeed for elite lawyers, expense and exclusivity, far from being a problem, were necessary checks on frivolous litigation by unscrupulous people wanting to get their claws on others' land. The commissioners saw some value in reducing costs, but it had to be done without making chancery 'that kind of cheap tribunal, that parties may be tempted by the facility of access, to abuse its purposes.'[53]

Much of the criticism aimed at the court centred on Chancellor Jameson. After the Union he moved his court to Kingston, the capital, because he was also Speaker of the legislative council; he thereby infuriated the Toronto legal establishment as much as the ordinary litigant. He was considered lazy and inefficient, although in his defence some pointed out that the court was inadequately staffed by support personnel. Critiques of the court were muted by the 1849 system reforms, discussed below, which increased chancery to three judges and created a Court of Error and Appeal to which dissatisfied chancery litigants could go. Although radicals never stopped their sporadic attacks on the court, the 1849 changes, and the elevation of William Hume Blake to chancellor in 1850, made the court cheaper and more efficient and accessible. The *Globe* could state in 1850, 'No man can be found to defend the Court of Chancery as it formerly existed,' but more recently 'not a complaint is heard' for 'the costs are cut down' and 'the delays greatly shortened.'[54] Matters were improved further by the devolution of a degree of equitable power to county court judges in 1856, and by having the court go on circuit from 1857.[55] Procedural reforms, begun in the early 1850s and continuing piecemeal over the next decade and a half, also helped. The traditional reliance on detailed written pleadings was reduced, and shorter pleadings supplemented by *viva voce* evidence became increasingly common.

The Rise of Inferior Tribunals

The colonies' superior courts in 1815 had a small cadre of elite, legally trained judges (except for Thomas Tremlett), operating from the colonial capitals. In the 1860s this system was still essentially in place, but there had occurred considerable expansion and various reorganizations of the superior and lower courts, and the latter had become more numerous and more important. These developments were not simply the result of administrative rationalization and a concern for economy, but were also driven by political and ideological considerations, some of which cut in contradictory directions.

The superior court system experienced only modest growth in the absolute numbers of judges before Confederation, and a considerable decline in per capita numbers. The number of superior court judges grew from twenty-two in 1815 to fifty-three by the mid-1860s. The expansion came partly from the creation of chancery courts, partly from the addition of the Pacific colonies, but mostly from a substantial expansion of personnel in the Canadas, especially in Lower Canada after a reorganization of the Superior Court in 1857, which increased that bench from ten to eighteen.[56] But this expansion overall was a decrease in per capita numbers. There was one superior court judge for every 38,000 European inhabitants in 1815, and one for every 65,000 by the mid-1860s.

Concentrating only on superior court judges does not tell the whole story of judicial numbers. In every colony there was a hierarchy of courts and judges. At the top of the pyramid were the superior courts with inherent jurisdiction over almost all matters, civil and criminal. The only areas with which they could not deal were the preserve of the specialized courts discussed above, and a few others, such as Trinity House in Montreal and Quebec City or the Marine Court of Enquiry, established in Newfoundland in 1866 to investigate accidents at sea.[57] At the lowest end of the hierarchy were JPs, who, as discussed in part 3, sat either singly or in pairs, to adjudicate minor civil cases, overwhelmingly small debts (except in Upper Canada, as noted below), and enforce a wide range of regulatory prohibitions. JPs did not need to be legally trained, and very rarely were, and were remunerated by fees collected from users of their services, not salaries.[58]

Between superior courts and JPs operated a range of courts created by colonial assemblies with jurisdiction, either civil or criminal, that was intermediate. The exception was Prince Edward Island, as we saw in part 3. The only such intermediate courts that were not founded by local legislation because they were part of the English inheritance were Courts of Quarter Sessions, sometimes called Courts of Sessions. They had important local government functions, discussed in more detail in chapter 26, but their importance for current purposes is that they dealt with criminal cases one rung down from the superior courts. They were staffed by lay, unsalaried JPs, sat with juries, operated only in one county (district in Upper Canada until 1848), and tried mostly common or garden assaults or relatively minor larcenies.

When we examine the lower levels of civil justice we find much less consistency across the colonies. Lower civil courts went by a variety of names and had different histories in different colonies, and their heterogeneity makes them difficult to categorize. But three general points can be made about them before we provide some examples. First, although they all began as entirely lay courts, the tendency over time was for the highest inferior tribunal to become more professionalized, presided over by judges required to have legal training and remunerated at least in part by salaries, not solely by fees. Second, proposals to expand the jurisdiction of lower courts, including JPs sitting alone or in pairs, were made frequently and engendered often heated debate between advocates of cheap, locally based, and speedy justice and those who preferred what they saw as the higher quality of adjudication meted out in superior courts. The most obvious way to ensure that more cases would go to the latter was to limit the jurisdiction of lower courts. Third, discussions over these two issues – professionalism and expanded lower court jurisdiction – were at times combined in proposals to advance both ends – to give a lower court an expanded jurisdiction and to staff it, at least in part, with professionals.

Upper Canada provides a good illustration of these points. In 1815 high-value civil cases were the preserve of King's Bench, below which operated two distinct tribunals, the Courts of Request and the District Courts.[59] The former, originally established in 1792, were empowered to hear cases of a value up to five pounds, an increase of three pounds from the original forty-shilling limit. They, and their successors from 1841, the Division Courts, performed in Upper Canada effectively the same small claims function that JPs did elsewhere. The District Courts, one per district and established in 1794, had a more expansive jurisdiction, up to forty pounds in a simple debt case. Both courts had lay judges, invariably JPs, remunerated by fees, but the fees were higher in District Court. The jurisdiction of the Courts of Requests was expanded in 1833 to ten pounds, but numerous proposals had been made before then to raise the jurisdictional limits of each court, and they all failed in the assembly or the legislative council. Equally unsuccessful proposals had been made by different interest groups to require some degree of professional legal training for District Court judges. In 1830, for example, an assembly select committee report argued that if District judges were required to be legally trained and were salaried, the salary would 'induce persons of talent and experience to accept the Office.' The committee saw nothing incompatible between professionalism and economy, for the fees paid to District Court judges were 'much out of proportion to the labour required,' and a fixed salary would make for cheaper law.'[60] The same assembly battles continued after 1833, and although the monetary limit was not raised, major changes were made in 1841, which represented a victory for the advocates of professionalism. The Courts of Request were renamed Division Courts, districts were divided into divisions each with its Division Court, and the Division Courts were henceforth to be presided over by District Court judges, who travelled from town to town within their district for this purpose. Most importantly, the District Court judges were now to be paid by salary and required to be barristers. In essence they were to supervise the operations of the local lay worthies in the Division Courts, who now had to sit with a lawyer. The salaries of District Court judges fluctuated, depending on the caseload, but they could not be less than £150.[61]

Debates over the 1841 bill reveal the battle lines. Those opposed to the changes objected to the intrusion of outsiders, albeit men from the same district, into local affairs. William Hamilton Merritt, a moderate conservative, a St Catharines and Niagara-based merchant, land speculator, and entrepreneur, best known for his promotion of the Welland Canal, vigorously defended the soon-to-be-abolished Courts of Request. 'In his part of the country,' he said, 'the Courts of Request ... [were] universally approved of.... It was called the poor man's court.' Merritt very much approved also of the fact that neighbours decided neighbours' cases, local knowledge being a desirable incident of cheap and easy access to the courts. Attorney General William Henry Draper took the opposite position, attacking lay judges for lack of legal competence and for their presumption that they knew best:

> In some cases the Commissioners [the proper term for Court of Request judges] had acted in the very teeth of the Statute; sometimes in opposition to every principle of justice; sometimes taking on themselves to decide points which Courts of a higher jurisdiction would hesitate to decide upon. They constituted themselves a sort of general court for legislation, and not for the administration of the law.[62]

The shift in 1841 to legal professionals continued to be condemned in some quarters, especially the radical Clear Grit faction, who lamented the loss of local autonomy and highly localized justice, but to no avail. Indeed in 1845, emblematic of their higher status, District Court judges were also given good behaviour tenure, although that arrangement lasted just one year. In 1849 the District Courts were renamed County Courts, when the districts of Upper Canada were abolished and their monetary jurisdiction was raised to £100. Somewhat confusingly, just four years later new districts were established in the more remote areas not within any existing county, and the principal judges for each new district were called District Court judges. They had the same powers and were required to have the same qualifications as County Court judges. Between 1850 and Confederation the monetary jurisdiction of both Division and County Courts was raised further, to £100 and £200 respectively.[63]

Upper Canada's District/County Court judges were made professional in the same year, 1841, that Nova Scotia's equivalent judgeships were abolished, an indication of the complexity and variety of the history of British North America's intermediate judgeships. As explained in chapter 13, below the level of the Supreme Court in both New Brunswick and Nova Scotia there operated county-based Inferior Courts of Common Pleas (ICCP, civil) and Courts of Quarter Sessions, staffed by lay judges. In Nova Scotia the ICCPs had a jurisdiction in debt cases essentially equivalent to the Supreme Court, while in New Brunswick their jurisdiction was also substantial, including most cases of contract and debt. After Cape Breton had been re-annexed to mainland Nova Scotia in 1820, and partly because the NSSC judges were strongly averse to travelling there any more than absolutely necessary, the assembly established the post of chief justice of common pleas and president of quarter sessions throughout the island. The man chosen, John Joseph Marshall, presided at all meetings of both courts in all the Cape Breton counties. In 1824 a similar system was created on the mainland, which for the purpose was divided into three divisions. Depending on one's point of view, the 1823–4 measures were either a step forward in the professionalization of the lower courts, or a measure designed to foist four additional judgeships, drawn from elite members of the legal profession, on the public purse.[64] The divisional chief justice system was controversial from the start, and there was never a consensus on whether it should remain. The demand for economies in the justice system led to its demise in 1841, although some critics also complained that the ICCPs were not professional enough, despite being led by lawyers, and therefore the law was different in one part of the colony from another. The ICCPs were abolished, their civil caseload transferred to the Supreme Court, and the sessions were left as the local government body only, with no criminal jurisdiction. The divisional chief judges were pensioned off, and an additional judge added to the Supreme Court to handle the increased workload.[65] New Brunswick also had county-based ICCPs, but never instituted a requirement that any of the judges be legal professionals. The ICCPs stayed until 1867, being abolished and replaced by county courts, as noted above just two weeks before the new dominion came into being.[66] The province presumably created county courts at that point because section 96 of the *British North America Act*, which was about to be in force, required the federal government to pay the salaries of all 'superior, district and county courts.' Lower Canada also established a system of intermediate judges. As of 1849 the principal court below the Superior Court was called the circuit court and staffed by paid legal professionals. Circuit courts operated within the main judicial districts and had an extensive civil jurisdiction of up to fifty pounds ($200 at Confederation).[67]

This category of 'middle tier' judgeships created in the first half of the nineteenth century includes stipendiary police magistrates sitting in city courts and exercising some of the jurisdiction previously given to sessions courts. Stipendiary magistrates were sometimes required to be lawyers and were paid a salary. Quebec and Montreal were the first cities to provide for a salaried police magistrate, in 1810, and in 1815 Halifax followed the lead. The stipendiary magistrate system, often referred to as police courts, was expanded over the decades; at various times Toronto, Montreal, Saint John, Charlottetown, Kingston, St John's, and Halifax all adopted it.[68] A major landmark in their development in Upper Canada was the 1849 *Municipal Act*, which provided that on the request of any incorporated municipality the central government would appoint a stipendiary magistrate to be paid for by the locality.[69] Similar legislation was passed fifteen years later in Nova Scotia, with county quarter sessions being given the power to appoint a stipendiary for a district or districts.[70] One sui generis stipendiary magistrate was Adam Thom, the recorder of Rupert's Land, the first judge of the Red River colony. A Lower Canadian lawyer first appointed in 1839, he has received mixed reviews from historians for his work. Though legally capable, he was nonetheless impaired in his objectivity by being an employee of the Hudson's Bay Company and by being opposed to French-Canadian influence and interests.[71]

Stipendiary magistrates' courts operated in some places in conjunction with another purely urban innovation, mayor's courts. Saint John had the first of these, as discussed in the previous part, and Toronto also got one in 1834, when its name was changed from York. The mayor presided, assisted by one or more of the aldermen. The court had the jurisdiction of a Court of Quarter Sessions, and much the same structure – quarterly meetings, a grand jury, petit jurors, and a jurisdiction limited to criminal cases. Halifax also got a mayor's court on its incorporation, in 1841, with a different jurisdiction, handling both minor civil and criminal cases.[72] Montreal's mayor's court followed a few years later, in 1845, with any three city councillors presiding. It lasted only until 1851, when it was abolished and its jurisdiction assumed by the Montreal Recorder's Court, presided over by a salaried professional.[73] Of course, these courts were not staffed by genuine elected judges, because those presiding had been elected as city officials, not as judges. But they do provide a rare example of the elective principle having some role to play in choosing who should preside in a court.

Along with the creation of new courts, a constant theme in civil justice administration in this period was whether inferior courts should enjoy an expanded jurisdiction. We have seen above that this issue was continually raised in Upper Canada, and it was very much a live one elsewhere. In Nova Scotia, for example, in 1815 two JPs had jurisdiction in cases worth up to five pounds, and it was also possible to have small debt cases tried summarily, without a jury, in one of the higher courts. In 1837 the limit was raised to ten pounds and remained at that level thereafter. From 1817 the colony also allowed for the creation of commissioners courts to exercise two JPs' jurisdiction and raised the limit to ten pounds. The statute was permissive, not mandatory, and was taken up avidly in the capital, on Cape Breton Island, and in various other locations. Initially only a temporary measure, it was frequently renewed. Whether litigants went to JPs or to higher courts using summary jurisdiction they could employ a quicker and cheaper process than would otherwise be the case in the Supreme Court or ICCP; such courts and procedures, said one contemporary legal author, 'combine cheapness with despatch.'[74]

Lower Canada also introduced a system of small claims courts, called commissioners' courts. Temporarily established in 1807, they were made permanent in 1821 by a statute that allowed the governor to appoint commissioners in any parish or township (excepting the counties of Montreal and Quebec and the town and parish of Three Rivers) for the hearing of small causes – debts or contract breaches involving amounts up to four pounds, three shillings. The legislation was extensively revised in 1843, most notably in providing that if at least 100 landowners in 'any Parish, Township or extra-Parochial place' petitioned for such a court one would be established. The same three urban centres were excluded, and the monetary limit raised to six pounds, three shillings. Access to justice was front and centre in the legislation. The commissioners were to decide according to the rights of the parties but also according to 'equity and good conscience'; anyone aged fourteen could sue in the court for wages, awards could be paid in monthly or weekly instalments, and oral testimony could be used in all cases, even those where writing was ordinarily required. Many communities took up the opportunity to request one of these courts, including, as discussed in chapter 24 below, the Mohawks at Kahnawake. Regrettably no records of these courts have survived.[75]

In all colonies these issues of small claims and summary jurisdiction could engender passionate debate and not a little controversy, with the legal profession and its allies in the colonial elite against other interests, both rural and urban. Proponents of an increased role for small claims courts stressed that they gave quicker and cheaper justice, and this critique became part of a sustained 'anti-lawyer culture' that was very strong in the Maritimes.[76] Lawyers, or at least the cost of lawyers, were a frequent subject of complaint. Anti-lawyer sentiment perhaps reached its height in the 1840s, and a decade or so later, in both Upper Canada and Nova Scotia, legislation was introduced to end lawyers' monopolies in pleading in the superior courts. But the attempt failed in the former, and while it passed in the latter it was little used and short-lived. To some extent earning the opprobrium they received, from the 1820s to the 1840s lawyers invariably opposed bills that increased or maintained JPs' jurisdiction, bills that generally were brought forward by rural and urban commercial members. The latter grouping also supported increasing the number of cases that could be heard summarily in the higher courts. In 1832, for example, the Nova Scotia Assembly passed a 'Cheap Law' bill that raised the monetary jurisdiction for which one did not need a jury trial from twenty to fifty pounds. The Act was in force for only a year, and when reintroduced in 1833 it passed the assembly but was lost in the council, in which elite lawyers were influential. The legal profession stoutly opposed it, while farmer/reformers Charles Roach and John Homer acted as its principal sponsors.[77]

New Superior Courts and Professional Courts of Appeal in the Canadas

The court systems of the Maritime colonies were radically altered in the 1850s by the abolition of the chancery courts, but underwent no other institutional changes of note, while Upper Canada's chancery court survived, but its common law courts were substantially reorganized in 1849, as were Lower Canada's superior courts. In Lower Canada a new court was established, the Superior Court, which took the civil jurisdiction of Queen's Bench and most of its judges and its organization into three major districts: Montreal, Quebec, and Trois Rivières, and four minor ones. Queen's Bench remained, with jurisdiction over all major criminal cases. The new Superior Court had a chief justice and nine puisne judges, Queen's Bench a chief justice and three puisne judges. The number of puisne judges on the Superior Court was increased to seventeen in 1857, the consequence of population increases and, more importantly, of the fact that the judiciary was decentralized and new districts, nineteen in all, were created to match a revamped municipal government system. The 1857 reorganization also saw the abolition of the position of circuit judge, but not the circuit court itself, which was henceforth staffed by a superior court judge.[78]

Upper Canada underwent a similar major change, with a new Court of Common Pleas created with concurrent jurisdiction with Queen's Bench. Each had three judges, whereas Queen's Bench had had five before the reorganization. Part of the purpose was to reduce the dominance of the chief justice of Queen's Bench, Robinson. In the same year the chancery court was expanded from one to three judges, for reasons discussed in a previous section. Although legislators assumed that the two common law courts would attract the same number of litigants, Queen's Bench had far more cases, a fact usually attributed to the reputation of Robinson. The solution was further legislation setting up just one person as the clerk for both courts and requiring him to assign cases alternately to each court in batches of twelve.[79]

More notably, the new arrangements for Upper Canada included the establishment of the colony's first appellate tribunal separate from the governor and council. A professional appeal court was a major plank of the reformers. The principal sponsor of the measure was Solicitor General William Hume Blake, for whom an appeal court was a deeply political commitment, a rejection of the 'despotic' power, effectively with no appeal, that the Court of Queen's Bench had wielded. 'Give us the Court of Appeal,' he had told Robert Baldwin in 1845, 'and you do more to liberalize the people and the bar than can well be conceived.'[80] The Court of Error and Appeal, to give it its full name, was to be presided over by the chief justice of Queen's Bench who would sit with any two other judges of Queen's Bench, common pleas, or chancery. When Blake made the portentous pronouncement cited above, Lower Canada already had an appeal court separate from the governor and council, although only since 1844. Thomas Cushing Aylwin, solicitor general, played a role similar to that of Blake in Upper Canada in pushing for the court. All Queen's Bench judges were members of the court, and any four could preside at any of its three annual terms. This appeal court lasted only until 1849, when it was replaced in the judicial reorganization of that year by the Court of Queen's Bench, Appeal Side.[81]

Upper Canada's court system remained largely the same from 1849 until Confederation, although some details were altered. In 1857 retired judges of the superior courts were made eligible for appointment to the Court of Error and Appeal. The same year County Court judges were given good behaviour tenure, which they had briefly previously enjoyed in the mid-1840s. The same statute provided that petitions for removal of these judges were to be heard by a Court of Impeachment, made up of the three presiding judges in the superior courts of common law and equity. Hence Upper Canada had two methods of removal for judges with good behaviour, this one and that provided by the 1834 Act for King's Bench judges.

Procedural Reform

The 1850s and early 1860s were notable for developments in practice and procedure. The common law colonies will be discussed in this section, Lower Canada in the following chapter. Writing in the 1820s about the procedures followed in the highest courts in the Maritime colonies, one observer succinctly noted of Nova Scotia, 'The Supreme Court of Judicature is modelled after the [English] Court of King's Bench, the practice of which is strictly adhered to, both in criminal and civil matters.'[82] What that meant is that civil litigation in the early nineteenth century was organized according to the traditional English writ system, discussed above in chapter 19. The evidence from commentators like McGregor, from the relatively few studies that have been carried out for British North America, and from contemporary law books, is that the writ system continued to operate fully in the colonies' high courts. Beamish Murdoch devoted some twenty-five pages to the forms of action in his account of Nova Scotian law written in the early 1830s, noting that in the common law 'forms were early invented to distinguish one kind of complaint from another, and parties have been ever obliged to take a form of complaint (or action) corresponding with the facts of their case.'[83] The writ system meant that procedure combined 'complexity, abstraction and confusion,' but it endured because judges and lawyers had learned the procedures and imbibed them so thoroughly that they had become 'a way of thinking' about the law.[84]

The intricacies of pleading were not always appreciated, even by lawyers. William Blowers Bliss, soon to become a judge of the NSSC, complained in 1831 of 'poxy decisions and pleas and other such pleasant writing,' which was so 'irksome' that 'I always hated it most heartily.'[85] Bliss was surely not alone. Cases about pleading comprised the largest single category of reported cases from Upper Canada during the union period.[86] Bliss wrote at a time when English legislators began reforming pleading. In 1832 the *Uniformity of Process Act* abolished all the old personal writs and substituted for them one writ, the writ of summons. However, the forms of action were effectively maintained, because the plaintiff had still to insert into the summons mention of one of the forms of action. Even more sweeping change came with the *Common Law Procedure Act* of 1852, which did away with the requirement to state the old form of action.[87]

No British North American colony passed a statute equivalent to the 1832 English Act, but from the 1830s to the 1850s the practice and procedures of superior courts were contentious issues everywhere. There was general agreement that some reform was necessary, but no certainty over whether the judges should effect the necessary changes by amending rules of court or whether legislatures should do the job. The result was incremental change by the former until the 1850s. One can date legislative intervention from law reform commissions established in both Nova Scotia and New Brunswick in the early to mid-1830s with a mandate to advise on, among other things, the rules of practice and procedure.[88] The Nova Scotia commission was able to report that recent judicial reforms had effectively done their work, new rules having been made by the judges 'to reduce the expense of suits, by abridging the common forms of written Pleadings.' The afore-mentioned William Blowers Bliss, from 1834 on the NSSC, asked his English barrister brother to send him 'any good treatise or book of practice under the late new [English] rules of Court.' Bliss was never much interested in the law in his private correspondence, but he thoroughly approved of the modern trend towards simplified procedure. 'I believe the law itself has nearly had its day,' he opined, adding that 'the humbug of the thing is wearing away though a good deal still remains to be changed.' In particular, the law 'may still be more simplified than has been attempted.'[89] A similar development took place in Upper Canada, an 1837 statute citing the need to reduce the 'expense of suits' by 'having the pleadings therein ... in some respects altered.' The King's Bench judges were instructed to make rules to make process cheaper and quicker.[90]

Assemblymen, not judges, kept up the pressure for reform of procedure, by legislation requiring superior court judges to amend the rules of their courts. To use Nova Scotia as an example, in 1841, when that colony's county-based ICCPs were abolished, litigants who preferred the simpler process employed in those courts lost the option of taking their cases there. The assembly, in the same statute that abolished the ICCPs, demanded that rules of court should be revised to 'simplify the proceedings in suits ..., and to prevent delay, and lessen the expense of such proceedings.' The judges were to present the new rules in the next session of the assembly; indeed, suggesting some distrust of the co-operativeness of the bench, the statute insisted that they be presented 'within the first four days' of the session.[91] The following year the UCQB judges submitted their new rules to the assembly, rules 'for simplifying the proceedings ... and rendering the same less expensive to the suitors.'[92]

Not all opinion in every colony saw the answer as imitating what the English were doing, even though there was general agreement that reducing time and cost was desirable. The early 1840s also saw 'commissioners of judicial inquiry' appointed in New Brunswick with a mandate that included considering whether 'the new Rules of Pleading in Civil Actions, at present in force in England,' should be introduced into that colony. The commissioners' conclusions were somewhat equivocal on the principal question, which was whether a defendant should be required always to plead the 'general issue,' allowed, that is, to offer a general denial with few particulars, or whether the defendant should have to plead specially, and made much of the differences in litigation rates (apparently higher in New Brunswick than in England) and of the fact that England had a split profession, which led to higher costs. They suggested a compromise between the two systems: introduce special pleas in some cases but retain the general issue. The report is notable for its detailed knowledge of English practice and its insistence that local conditions should be taken into account when recommending change in the colony. 'Admitting the extent of the evil [costly and imprecise pleadings] in England, and the necessity of applying some remedy to it there,' they cautioned legislators to proceed with care, 'to consider whether in fact any great injustice has proceeded from the existing practice.'[93]

The caution of the New Brunswick commissioners aside, the demand for more simplification in pleading was consistently kept up through the 1840s and 1850s. Late in the former decade the Nova Scotia Assembly declared in a statute that 'many of the Rules of Practice in the Supreme Court' had 'become obsolete' and that it was 'expedient to revise the same, and to introduce other Rules suited to our own Legislation, and to the circumstances of the country.' The statute abolished all existing rules, laid out eighty-three new ones, and required the judges to make more 'as near as may be conformable to the proceedings and practice of the Superior Courts of Common Law in England.' The eighty-three rules shortened declarations of bills of exchange and promissory notes, specified that unimportant errors in pleading should not lead to delays, did away with various technical objections to pleadings, and limited the number of lawyers who could speak on motions.[94] The purpose was obviously to reduce the time and cost of lawsuits.

Incremental reform became wholesale change in the 1850s, any remaining reluctance by the judges being overcome by the fact that the British Parliament passed the 1852 *Common Law Procedure Act*, discussed above. With change in the air in the homeland, Nova Scotia created another law reform commission in the early 1850s to investigate practice and pleading in the NSSC, which reported in March 1852 and led in turn to an 1853 statute that, while not identical to the English Act, replicated its principal provisions. It stated succinctly in section 1 that 'all personal actions shall be commenced by writ of summons or replevin,' and then laid down in section 2 that 'it shall not be necessary to mention any form of action in the writ or other proceedings.' Standard forms of writs were legislated in the appendices to the statute.[95] The change was enthusiastically welcomed; one newspaper deprecated the profession's adherence to 'antiquated legal forms and technicalities' and called the 1853 statute 'one of the most important and popular measures' passed 'for sometime.'[96]

Very similar pleading reforms were passed contemporaneously in New Brunswick in 1854 and Upper Canada in 1856.[97] Most of the latter statute was a literal reproduction of sections of the English Act of 1852, although the section numbering was different. The 1856 Act followed a series of attacks on the court system, especially by the Clear Grit party, whose views were exemplified in one newspaper's assertion that 'hitherto ... a host of useless forms peculiar to the legal tribe has been used to make law a profitable mystery'; the same newspaper insisted that anybody who reformed procedure 'so as to make justice simple, cheap and accessible to the poorest in the land will deserve an enduring monument to his memory.'[98] But in the end it was lawyers who shepherded through procedural reform, probably as a way to assuage radical critics who wanted chancery abolished, conciliation courts established, and other reforms designed to reduce the status of the superior courts. The ultimate architect of procedural reform was Conservative Attorney General John A. Macdonald. New Brunswick's adoption of the English Act, and thus its abolition of the forms of action, similarly came from the work of elite lawyers, the reports of commissioners to revise the colonial statutes discussed in detail in the next chapter. Those reports showed that its law reformers had thrown away much of the caution their predecessors had displayed a decade before. They contrasted the rapid improvement 'according to the requirements of modern civilization' in 'everything social, industrial and political' in the province of recent years, a stark contrast to the practices of the courts, which 'retain too many features of a barbarous age, and too much of its ancient gothic character.' What was needed were 'radical reforms … the abolition of so much that is technical.' The 'present practice of the law appears to delight in technicalities,' which were 'a disgrace to the jurisprudence of an enlightened people.' The commissioners recommended the abolition of all 'forms of action' other than contract, tort, replevin, and ejectment. Every action should be commenced by one standard summons.[99] The last colony to enact these procedural reforms was Newfoundland, which did not do so until 1864.[100]

23

Sources of Law and Law Reform

The law applicable in the BNA colonies was a combination of inherited European traditions and locally made law. The former comprised both French and English law, and in some respects the English part of that law, the common law supplemented by statutes in force in the colonies, drew both on the English common law as it was derived from English court decisions and an 'English' common law that was an adaptation forged by American courts. The second of these principal branches of law, locally made, consisted of Indigenous laws, which applied to Indigenous communities only, and the statute law of the colonies. Depending on their location, the time period, and the degree of adaptation to European law, Indigenous communities were governed not only by Indigenous law but sometimes also by European law, French or English, and colonial statutes. Indigenous law is dealt with principally in the next chapter. It continued through the British North American period to be the law governing most Indigenous inhabitants from Upper Canada and eastwards, and practically all of them to the west of Upper Canada to the Pacific coast. The same was wholly true for residents of the Pacific region until ca 1850, and largely true from then until Confederation.

This chapter begins with an examination of the sources of law used by courts in common law colonies, asking to what extent they saw themselves obliged to follow English precedents and, conversely, to what extent they felt able to draw on American sources and/or to fashion a distinctive local common law. Because it is concerned with sources of law it does not, except inferentially, examine the substantive content of the common law. That topic has been covered in part 3 and will be further examined in a number of the chapters that follow in this part. This review of the common law is followed by two sections on the civil law of Lower Canada, one a general review of its sources and the other on the making of the new codes of 1866–7. The civil law did change significantly in this period, necessarily adjusting to the presence and influence of the common law, to large-scale changes in Lower Canada's society and economy, and to the increasing popularity of liberal ideas about property and societal organization in the wake of the rebellions.

The last section of this chapter examines statute law. The 'statutory product' of colonial assemblies was considerable, particularly after the late 1840s in the province of Canada. But all colonies in all periods produced a good deal of statutory law, especially given the short time for which colonial assemblies sat, in the first three decades of the century. Colonial assemblymen took the inherited traditions, French and English, and moulded them to the conditions of their own societies. In part, therefore, statutory law was both a cause and a reflection of the building of distinct new societies and was an inward-looking process. At the same time, it was a response to the ever-increasing intensity of relationships among colonies, metropole, and the North American world, both Indigenous and European, in which the colonies were situated. Our section on statutes also examines the extent to which codification and law reform movements – the two invariably go together in legal historical accounts – became part of the British North American legal landscape at mid-century. Law reform in this chapter means large changes to the overall structure and content of the law, not changes to particular legal doctrines or court structures or the like, which are also dealt with in subsequent chapters on discrete areas of law. Codification featured largely in the history of Lower Canadian law, and with the new *Civil Code of Lower Canada* (CCLC) of 1866 and the new *Code of Civil Procedure* (CCP) of 1867 came substantive change to the content of the law. But elements of codification and accompanying law reform were more a feature of developments in common law British North America than traditional accounts of legal history have shown, even if still not as significant a part of the legal landscape as in Lower Canada.

Sources of Law in Common Law Jurisdictions

In 1835, shortly after becoming chief justice, Brenton Halliburton of the NSSC stated clearly his belief in an imperial judicial hierarchy. American decisions were often informative and instructive, but empire and the British connection on which it rested mattered more: 'We are not bound to defer to them [American court decisions] as we might to the decisions at Westminster,' he said. Halliburton's statement suggests that Canadian courts in this period were wholly deferential to the English legal hierarchy. Another chief justice, John Beverley Robinson, stated to similar effect in 1842 that 'our adherence to the principles of the English common law is a duty imposed upon us by written law.' Robinson's contemporary, future chief justice of Canada William Buell Richards but a puisne judge of the UCCP in the 1850s, was equally dogmatic: 'We are bound by the authority of the cases decided in England, and until the law is entitled differently, we must carry it out in the mode indicated by those decisions.' In 1848 the NBSC decided *Smith v Hill*, a case about a promissory note on which English and American law were different. The English case was 'decisive upon the point raised in this case, and must govern this Court.'[1]

A caveat is necessary before we examine the extent to which these statements reflect the everyday approach of the British North American superior courts to the sources of law that bound them. The resources on which to base such an analysis are limited, especially for the years before ca 1850, because law reporting was slow to develop, particularly outside Upper Canada. An analysis of legal doctrine as applied by the NSSC in the first half of the nineteenth century, for example, must rest on only volume 1 of the *Nova Scotia Reports*, which reported cases decided between 1835 and 1851 and was not published until 1855. The very fact that law reports were the principal source of law makes the common law colonies very different from Lower Canada, discussed below, where the civil law relied on a complex variety of sources; and from Indigenous law, where oral tradition remained the principal source of law.[2]

This limitation aside, two principal points can be made. First, a constant theme running through the reported cases from all colonies is that the courts were bound by English authority. All case reports contain much citation of it, more so than cases from any other jurisdiction, including the colony itself. This insistence on the use of English cases was most marked in Upper Canada, particularly in the decisions of Robinson, who was, with James B. Macaulay, the most prolific judgment writer of the period.[3] Robinson and Macaulay exemplify the depth of English legal culture among the elite of Upper Canada. Robinson consistently cited English law as authoritative and rarely acknowledged that local conditions might render specific doctrines inapplicable. Judges in the Maritime colonies often enunciated the same insistence on deference to imperial leadership in law, testified to by the quotations above and by other judges in the 1850s, who referred to Lord Mansfield as the 'very highest authority' and to English judges generally as 'the sages who preside in Westminster Hall.'[4] The second theme that emerges from reported cases is that, despite their many invocations of English authority, all courts drew on two other sources – their own prior judgments and American decisions. Cases from domestic courts were cited increasingly over time, in part because local bodies of statute law occupied more and more fields, in part because cases involved local rules of court, and, most importantly, in part because courts had over time a body of common law jurisprudence to draw upon. This last tendency was most pronounced in Newfoundland, which at times referred to 'the custom of Newfoundland' as reason to both not use English cases and to cite its own prior decisions.[5] Almost never cited by any court were decisions of another British North American court.

More importantly, in all jurisdictions judges not infrequently made reference to American cases, even when they also cited English ones and sometimes without necessarily naming them. It was not uncommon for a judgment to refer generally to 'the American decisions.' There were distinct regional differences in the use of American decisions. In the Upper Canada common law courts it was quite rare, although, as we shall see in volume 2, it was greater than it would be in the later decades of the century. The Upper Canada Chancery, especially Chancellor William Hume Blake, was more willing to cite American cases. In the Maritime colonies the use of American authority – both judicial decisions and treatises – was more pronounced. Law reporter David Kerr, in his preface to the third volume of the *New Brunswick Reports*, noted both that English laws were often 'awkward in their application' to New Brunswick, and that when English law did not meet the colony's needs, 'the United States decisions are heard with approbation.' The compiler of the second volume of the *Nova Scotia Reports* was also confident that 'American decisions are ... frequently employed with effect to influence the decisions of our Provincial courts.' This tendency increased over time; by 1867 Chief Justice William Young of Nova Scotia treated English and American cases as equally influential in declaring that his court 'must look' at both 'to ascertain the principles they have established.'[6] Not surprisingly, given the different history of relations and exchange between regions of British North America and the United States, the NSSC and the NBSC referred mostly to Massachusetts law, and Upper Canadian courts preferred to reference New York.

Kerr's reference to English cases being 'awkward in their application' suggests why American decisions were employed. American courts dealt with social and material contexts that were different from those of England and more similar to what pertained in northern North America. *Lawrence and Hill v McDowall*, decided by the NBSC in 1838, illustrates the point well. At issue was whether an agreement between adjoining landowners about the boundary was a conveyance, and the court stated that it had 'not found any English authority directly bearing upon this point.' But there was one from the U.S. Supreme Court 'in which it was expressly held that an agreement with regard to a boundary did not import a conveyance of title.' Chipman J. was at pains to make it clear that 'I quote this case, not as an authority which governs my judgment, but as showing the opinion of a learned court in a foreign country on the point in hand.'[7]

American law was looked to because, judges like Chipman often argued, the American experience with an issue was more pertinent than England's. Even the anglophile Halliburton thought American decisions useful because of the similar context. 'We derive great satisfaction and advantage from the views taken by the able lawyers who sit on many of the benches in [the United States],' he noted, because those views were given in relation to 'transactions so similar to those which frequently occur in this.'[8] The particularities of the jurisdiction's economy, geography, history, settlement, and landholding patterns rendered some English precedents unsuitable. In the Maritimes, cases about land – roads, surveys, and boundaries – were especially prone to this kind of treatment. Lemuel Wilmot of the NBSC, in an 1851 boundary case, pointed out what a stark contrast there was between England, where 'from the value of land and the denseness of the population, the boundaries of districts, honors and manors, are generally … well defined and known,' and New Brunswick, where 'boundaries and lines are frequently unknown.'[9] To similar effect, in *McLean v Jacobs*, a Nova Scotia case involving a survey found to be erroneous after sixteen years' adherence by neighbouring landowners, Halliburton declined to follow the English rule of reliance on surveys, because 'in this country' that could create mischievous results. He concurred with William Hill, who ruled that the parties were bound by their long acquiescence and that strict conformity to the English rule was not required 'in a country like ours where deeds are often written by ignorant and unlettered persons,' and where 'lines are often ... not traced and run with the nicest accuracy.' It was necessary in such cases to 'keep our eyes steadily fixed on possession.'[10] As we will see below in chapter 30, surveys were often non-existent or very poorly done in the Maritimes, causing much uncertainty about titles.

To similar effect were the judgments of the NBSC in the 1826 case of *The King v Good* and the 1842 case of *Doe on the demise of Des Barres v White*. In the former Good had purchased land and fenced in an area that had been previously used as a road between lots. The attorney general contended that 'the same principle would apply here as obtains in *England*; that a road used by the public for a length of time, should be considered as dedicated to the public, and as a highway.' The court held otherwise, that only roads established by statute or with public money were public roads. It would be 'highly pernicious' in New Brunswick, and 'a barrier to the establishment of new settlements,' insisted Ward Chipman Senior, if 'a man [who] permits his fellow settlers to use a pathway over his land until regular roads are laid out and opened,... should be presumed to have dedicated this pathway to the public, and it should be deemed a public highway.' Chipman was well aware that 'in *England*, the dedication of roads to the public was a presumption of fact, arising from the ... circumstances.' But 'it by no means followed that the same presumptions would arise ... [on] facts under a totally different state of circumstances here.' In *Des Barres* the problem was not an inappropriate precedent but the lack of any prior case from England; a case on an aspect of adverse possession doctrine 'could not be looked for in any of the Courts of Westminster.' But it was nonetheless 'satisfactory' to find that 'the question has frequently been discussed in the Courts of the United States.' Those courts displayed 'great unanimity' on the question, and although the American cases were not 'binding authority,' they were nonetheless 'intrinsically entitled to the highest respect' because they involved 'principles of law' that 'are applied to a state of things similar to our own, by Judges of high character, learning, and experience.'[11]

American decisions were not only useful when they involved land, they also came from a country of a more commercial bent than England. Halliburton's colleague William Blowers Bliss thought that his court could 'with advantage' read American cases on marine insurance, as they came from 'a great commercial country' where that area of law was 'continually ... discussed and decided.' To similar effect Ward Chipman Senior relied on 'the authorities in the United States, from whence we derive this particular clause in our marine [insurance] policies.'[12] Case reports therefore show us that Maritime courts fashioned a distinctive common law in this period, a blend of English and American decisions moulded to fit the distinctiveness of colonial conditions without departing from what the judges saw as their constitutional duty to follow Westminster Hall.

Upper Canada provides less evidence of this attention to local circumstances, and most of what there is comes from Chancellor Blake, not Robinson. In *Hook v McQueen* Blake insisted that 'rules deducible from English authorities cannot be applied, without considerable modification, to a country where the habits of society and the condition of property are so widely varied.' Even Robinson conceded this point at times. He stated in 1844, 'In any doubtful question before us, it will always be an advantage to know' how American judges have handled the question. In part this was because they were 'men of great ability and research.' But even more importantly, their opinions were 'especially desirable when the point happens to be a novel one, arising out of transactions and circumstances unusual in England and with which people in America are more familiar.' To similar effect a few years later in *Bank of Montreal v Delatre*, Robinson stated, 'It is always advisable and useful on questions of [mercantile contracts]' to examine American cases, because 'American courts have generally gone before those in England ... in moulding the principles of common law to suit supposed exigencies.' Despite these words, however, in the end Robinson found that the English cases did provide an answer in the *Bank of Montreal* case, and he relied on them.[13]

Overall the contrast between Blake and Robinson deepened over time and was perhaps most evident in decisions of the Court of Error and Appeal, on which both judges sat. Blake had argued in an 1845 pamphlet that English institutions had to be adapted to local conditions. Moreover, perhaps as a result of Blake's influence as chancellor or perhaps simply because Upper Canada's equity judges had a more expansive and innovative view, other Chancery judges were similarly often dubious about English decisions. Vice Chancellor Spragge opined in an 1864 case that 'we are of course bound by English decision,' but he went on to say that there was 'much force in the reasoning' that the

English rule in the case – a general principle of contract interpretation – was not the ideal solution, and therefore 'the doctrine of the English courts upon that point should not be carried further than it had already gone.' Another Chancery judge, Philip VanKoughnet, similarly stated that 'the statute law of this Province' and his judicial oath made him follow the English courts, but he thought that the opposite view, which the Court of Error and Appeal had adopted, 'may probably be the more just one.'[14]

If we look beyond reported cases at other sources, the picture becomes more complicated for Upper Canada. There is evidence of a broader legal culture, of a willingness to find the law in a range of sources beyond England. Upper Canada's law libraries contained a great deal of material from outside England – American law reports, treatises by Kent and Story, digests, European treatises and codes. The principal historian of this phenomenon has argued that Upper Canada had a 'well-developed and subtle legal supra-nationalism, or at least pan-Americanism,' and indeed that 'legal pantheism' is also a fitting description.[15] This argument stands very much in opposition to those who depict Upper Canadian judges as devoted followers of only the English legal tradition, although 'judges' is perhaps the wrong word anyway when so much of what we know is from Robinson. The long-serving chief justice may not have been as generally influential as he seems at first sight, especially in the Union period. Another leading lawyer in the 1850s, Oliver Mowat, was certainly a continentalist when it came to the sources of central Canadian law. He was adamant that 'in Canada we must find advantage and interest in examining [American] decisions,' because 'our local circumstances are more nearly like those of the people of the United States.'[16] Lower Canadian judges' libraries also contained much more than English common law or French civil law, including a good deal of American material.

It is difficult to draw conclusions from all this. Lawyers and legal authors, often engaged not just in private practice but also in public policy debates about the law, especially in the Union period, may well have had views that differed from a representative of the highly conservative elite that had ruled Upper Canada in the 1820s and 1830s, of whom Robinson was the exemplar. Robinson was a much older man than his fellow elite lawyers who argued before him or proposed law reform measures in the Union period. He did not retire from Queen's Bench until 1862, when he was seventy-one and had been on the court for thirty-three years, and it would not be surprising if he was out of touch with contemporary trends. It may seem remarkable that there would have been such a disconnect between Robinson and so many other lawyers, but as we will see later in this chapter, elite lawyers pursued legal change through legislation, so if they were unhappy with Robinson they effectively bypassed him. And elite lawyers were not all lawyers. Everyday practitioners may well have shared, or at least been content with, the bench's anglophilia.

Not surprisingly Maritime sources other than case reports also make the case for a distinctive British North American law. The most comprehensive analysis of the law of a single jurisdiction, Halifax lawyer Beamish Murdoch's four-volume *Epitome of the Law of Nova Scotia*, published in 1832–3, had much to say about the particularities of Nova Scotian law.[17] Murdoch insisted that the 'common and statute law of England are not, as a whole, suited to our situation as a colony.' He went on to argue that local law was not just different from but better than English, shorn of artificial distinctions and unjust rules derived from English social structures and class distinctions. Murdoch stressed the many ways in which local statute law superseded English law, largely English private law. But he went further. When he did discuss the common law he, like many of the Supreme Court judges in their reported decisions, made numerous references to American authority. The reports of the statute revision commissioners of the 1850s, discussed elsewhere in this chapter, also openly acknowledged American influence.

Sources of Law: The Civil Law

The issue of sources of law in Lower Canada was rather more complex than elsewhere in British North America. By the second quarter of the nineteenth century, the full impact of its polyjurality was beginning to be felt. An anonymous writer in 1846 expressed a common view when lamenting that 'there is perhaps no country in the world subject to more legal rules, drawn from such diverse systems of law.'[18] Those who would be entrusted with codification of the civil law (in essence, the private law) in the 1850s would identify fourteen different sources of law that, in theory, had to be consulted – and this catalogue did not include any form of Indigenous law.[19] Aside from the Custom of Paris itself, there was legislation from both the French and British regimes (although much of this was regulatory or criminal in nature and thus did not directly affect the civil law), judicial decisions from the Conseil supérieur and the courts of the British regime, and juristic writings on the Custom of Paris and on the ancien droit of pre-revolutionary France. In addition, Lower Canadian courts referred at times to English, Scottish, and American precedents, treating them as possessing persuasive authority if no directly applicable provision of local law could be found. One legal author, Nicolas-Benjamin Doucet, also included Indigenous law among the legal sources applicable in Lower Canada but was not equal to the task of elaborating upon it.[20]

Doctrinal writers, courts, and the legislature were all potential ways of bringing some order to this varied legal landscape. It was not so much the variety of sources as the lack of a mechanism for coordinating or harmonizing them that created problems. For various reasons, none of these three actors was able to play the role of coordinator. Taking doctrinal writing first, Quebec jurists had traditionally relied on a steady flow of learned commentary from French authors on the Custom of Paris and the ancien droit. The Revolution, and the *Code Napoléon* of 1804, changed that irrevocably. Claude de Ferrière's commentary on the Custom of Paris was treated as highly authoritative in Quebec, but its last edition appeared in 1788, the French code's abrogation of pre-revolutionary law having made further commentary on the Custom superfluous.[21] Even though the *Code Napoléon* reiterated some parts of the Custom, post-1804 French commentators interpreted those provisions in the context of the new codification of which they were now a part. French booksellers responded by trying to unload their now worthless back stock of treatises on the ancien droit in Lower Canada.[22]

The French now recognized three temporal divisions in their law: the ancien droit or old law (pre-1789); the droit intérimaire or interim law, the law of the revolutionary period itself (1789–1804); and the droit nouveau or new law (post-1804). The droit nouveau, built on the anti-clerical and anti-feudal legacy of the Revolution, manifested an ethos very different from that animating the law in Lower Canada. Thus, new French doctrinal writing was no longer a reliable guide to the interpretation of local civil law. Locally produced legal literature began to appear, but no single author was able to take on the herculean task of synthesizing the varied and complex corpus that now existed. Doctrinal writers could not agree even on the fundamentals of Lower Canadian law: while Henry Des Rivières Beaubien devoted a good part of his *Traité sur les lois civiles* (1832–3) to seigneurial law, Nicolas-Benjamin Doucet, writing in 1841, ignored it entirely, predicting – accurately – that the seigneurial system was on the way out. University law faculties, begun at McGill in 1848 and Laval in 1854, were still very small undertakings whose professors would not be in a position to produce much scholarship until later in the century.

If Lower Canada produced no Pothier or Blackstone, two other potential means of bringing order to the legal landscape existed: the courts and the legislature. There were a number of reasons why it was unrealistic to expect the courts to take a major role in clarifying the law. First, the doctrine of precedent was not yet carved in stone in either English law or in Lower Canada. In French law the central idea was that of jurisprudence constante – the notion that while a single decision on a point of law was not authoritative, if a series of decisions all went the same way, the result should normally be followed. By the 1860s in Lower Canada some judges, of both French and English background, supported the emerging idea in the common law that a single precedent was binding. But the idea of jurisprudence constante still had its adherents too, and the question was not yet settled.[23] Judicial decisions were seen primarily as contributing to a continuing conversation about the law, not as settling for all time the legal issues discussed in them. This is not in itself an unhealthy approach to legal interpretation, but it works best where the fundamentals of a legal tradition are settled, which was not always the case prior to codification.

Second, even had the judges taken a more assertive role, their decisions were not widely circulated. As noted in the section on law reporting in a later chapter, regular publication of judicial decisions did not begin in earnest until 1851, with the result that our knowledge of the work of the courts in the first half of the century will always be incomplete. Judges were not required to give reasons for their decisions until 1843, and even thereafter many decisions were accompanied by only brief and conclusory reasoning.[24] Third, where judicial decisions were known, they did not always inspire confidence. Some judges were openly francophobic, and James Kerr of King's Bench did not help matters by confessing in 1831 that he 'did not know what the law of Lower Canada might be.' Patriote Elzéar Bédard complained that the English judges 'did not understand our language, nor could know our modes of proceeding – they introduced a strange mixture of English and French practices, which has brought confusion and uncertainty into every Court.'[25] The perception by francophones that the largely anglophone judiciary prior to 1850 disliked or ignored laws of French origin was widespread enough to feature as a major grievance in the 92 Resolutions of the Patriotes in 1834.

This perception was not always accurate. While some anglophone judges treated the civil law cavalierly, others did not, and the views of individual judges also changed over time. Jonathan Sewell, for example, became very proficient in both the French language and the civil law after moving to Quebec from New Brunswick in 1789. His published decisions demonstrate great facility with the civil law, supported as they are by references to a wide range of French sources.[26] In 1824 he chose the legal history of France as his topic for the first paper given before the Quebec Literary and Historical Society, remarking that the old French law was 'built on the soundest foundations of natural and universal Justice, approved by experience, and ... admired by those who know it best.'[27] On a trip to Paris two years later he bought six hundred books on French law for the Advocates' Library at Quebec. Judges of both ethnic backgrounds at times rejected English authorities or rules proferred to them by counsel, preferring to rely on French sources.[28] Especially after the rebellions, anglophone jurists seem to have come increasingly to the defence of the civil law. By the 1860s, jurist François-Maximilien Bibaud could praise 'the leading English advocates of Montreal [who] love our French laws and constantly quote their concise maxims,' and lament that 'the others seem to desire only imported laws.'[29]

The remaining avenue for reforming and clarifying the law, the legislature, was blocked because of the near-constant state of legislative deadlock between the upper and lower houses in the two decades leading up to the rebellions. While the Special Council of 1838–41 achieved some particular legal reforms in the creation of registry offices and the rationalization of security interests, and took the initial steps towards dismantling the seigneurial system, it could not begin to address the overall problem of the multiplicity of sources of Lower Canadian law, nor was it expected to. If the local legislature could or would not act, it was sometimes tempting after 1804 for Quebec judges to assume that provisions of the *Code Napoléon* on a particular topic were declaratory of the ancien droit, thus providing a new legislative foundation for the old law. But this interpretive move had to be handled with care, and the Lower Canadian appellate court sometimes overturned the decisions of trial judges who had too quickly assumed that an article of the 1804 code could stand in for local law.[30]

After the rebellions jurists of both British and French background turned their attention to the problem of rationalizing the sources of Quebec law. Two solutions rapidly came to the fore: university legal education and codification, which developed in tandem during the two decades prior to Confederation. University legal education, considered in chapter 25, became a reality earlier, because it could get off the ground through private initiative, the actions of a few 'movers and shakers' with links to the universities; thus McGill and Laval could be pioneers in the field in 1848 and 1854 respectively. Codification required money, legislative action, and a broader base of support within the legal community, if not the population at large.

Most notably sounding the alarm about the state of Lower Canadian law, an article of 1846 in a new legal journal deplored the 'babel légale' then prevailing in Lower Canada, rehearsing familiar complaints but proclaiming a relatively new solution – codification.[31] Codification would not only solve the problem of conflicting and outmoded rules deriving from two or more legal traditions, it would allow Lower Canada to follow the path of modern civilization traced by others. The central idea of modern law was liberty, particularly economic liberty, freeing property from outmoded legal restraints to allow its unhindered circulation. Thus the vestiges of feudalism inherent in the seigneurial system needed to be abolished, and seigneurial dues forcibly converted into 'rentes foncières,' based on the historic value of the seigneurs' claims, not on the unjustified encroachments and excessive amounts demanded by them in more recent times. The commercial law of Lower Canada, vacillating between French and English law, also needed to be settled, and here the author had no hesitation in advocating that the province's commercial code be assimilated to that prevailing in the United States, Britain, and Upper Canada – Lower Canada's principal trading partners. The law of succession, matrimonial regimes, and family property also needed to be reformed, though the author was less forthcoming about the content of these changes, except to query whether freedom of testation had perhaps gone too far and needed to be restrained.

Such a task was enormous, but the author pointed to the models of France (1804) and Louisiana (1808 and 1825) as showing that it could be done. It was important, however, to entrust the work to a commission of jurists removed from the hurly-burly of politics, who could complete their work in an atmosphere free of partisan considerations. Moreover, those entrusted with the work should keep in mind 'the future of all British America, of which Lower Canada ought to be the centre, and envisage a system that would suit all the populations who will one day form a vast empire, by giving them uniform institutions that will meld them into a single people, distinct from the neighbouring nation.'[32] The confidence of the author, coming only a few years after the trauma of the rebellions and suspension of the constitution, is remarkable. For him, codification was not a process focused narrowly on preserving and renewing French-Canadian traditions: it was an instrument that could make all British North Americans into 'un seul et même peuple' (though it is unlikely he had Indigenous peoples in mind). Indeed, his title refers to the codification of the 'lois du Canada,' not to those of 'Bas-Canada.' This view adumbrates one that would appear during the Confederation debates two decades later, the idea that being 'Canadian' was a political identity transcending ethnic and religious differences.[33] The author followed through on this idea by emphasizing that any codification of Lower Canadian law must be bilingual. So much of existing law was a closed book to the British-descended population because it was available only in French; one could not expect loyalty to a set of laws that were unknown or misunderstood.

Within the brief compass of five pages, the author predicted with uncanny accuracy all the major legal changes that would be consummated over the next twenty years. The seigneurial system was abolished in the manner indicated. Codification of the laws of Lower Canada would be entrusted to a commission of three jurists, who would have almost total autonomy in their work before submitting it to the legislature. The code would be bilingual and suffused with the spirt of economic liberalism desired by the author, indeed ardently so, except for the provisions dealing with the family. This dichotomy was itself portended in the author's expression of discomfort with complete freedom of testation: while it would be upheld in the *CCLC*, the author's disquiet with allowing liberalism to run amok in intra-familial relations was strongly reflected in the code's upholding of ancien régime traditions of marital and paternal authority. The only prediction by the author that did not come to pass was the code's adoption by other parts of British North America. Interest in such a move, expressed in the 1850s in some quarters in Upper Canada, ultimately waned.[34]

Before examining the process of codification itself, it should be noted that one of the problems it was designed to address – the multiplicity of sources of Lower Canadian law – has sometimes been overstated and might have been addressed in other ways. The legal professions' own traditions – the 'culture de l'amalgame' addressed in part 3 – were bicultural in both language and legal tradition. Unlike the British judges decried by the Patriotes, British notaries and advocates could not afford to disdain or ignore French legal sources. Clientele, apprenticeship, litigation, and legal literature all crossed linguistic and legal-cultural lines. Lawyers needed to work daily with the 'other' tradition and with lawyers and clients of the 'other' cultural background. Indeed, as seen in the next chapter, some worked with Indigenous communities to help them restate and defend their own laws. For years lawyers had found ways through the babel légale decried by publicists and would have continued to do so had codification not intervened. The movement by civic-minded lawyers to publish their own translations of important texts, such as Doucet's unofficial translation of the Custom of Paris into English and Jacques Crémazie's work on the criminal law in French, was a step in the direction of both public legal education and cross-cultural education for lawyers.[35] So too was the insistence of the statutory consolidation commissioners of 1845, discussed below, that an accessible translation of all statutes would make anglophones more knowledgeable about all of Lower Canada's statute law. Partial codification of particular areas of law, such as commercial law or family law, could have been undertaken without tackling all of the private law at once. With the rise of university legal education, doctrinal writing might have substituted for codification in some domains of law. While the availability of the French and Louisiana codes was a powerful stimulus to codification, not all civil law jurisdictions succumbed: Scotland, for example, never codified its law. As will be seen in volume 2 of this work, codification gave rise to its own problems, and in that context it is useful to remember that it was not inevitable. Once a code in the civilian style is adopted, however, it is virtually impossible to 'uncodify' and return to the legal status *quo ante*. All future legal reforms have to take the code as their starting point.

Sources of Law: The *Civil Code of Lower Canada*

A code in the civilian tradition is much different from a mere statutory consolidation. The latter includes in one statute all or most of the provisions relating to a particular area of law, but is enacted mainly for ease of reference and does not adhere to any particular philosophy or any set principles of statutory drafting. A civil code has higher goals. It is more comprehensive, including within it the fundamental principles of all three areas of private law: persons, property, and obligations. It is meant to be read as a unity: provisions in any area of law can be used to interpret those elsewhere in the code. It puts a premium on clarity and economy of expression, explaining terms of art and avoiding both over-generalization and excessive qualification and detail. It is addressed to the people it is meant to govern in language intelligible to them, not just to lawyers or specialists. Other, more detailed statutes in the field, such as those governing lessor and lessee, are expected to build on the concepts and principles set out in the civil code. It anchors the private law philosophically and culturally and thus functions as a sort of social constitution.[36] The *Civil Code of Lower Canada* (*CCLC*) was meant to be a beginning, not an end in itself. It was not conceived in a spirit of legal positivism, as a mere catalogue of rules, however much it may have been interpreted that way in later years. It was meant to provide a conceptual vocabulary and a set of basic principles for the private law, but not to forbid recourse to sources outside itself or to usurp the judicial function. As Charles Dewey Day stated in the conclusion to the codifiers' First Report:

> Every code of laws, however complete, necessarily presupposes the obligation of certain primary and fundamental principles which must underlie and sustain all positive legislation; and no care or foresight can secure such comprehensiveness and precision as to render unnecessary processes of reasoning and inference based upon these, and upon the experience and knowledge which lie outside of the expressed law.[37]

Day was cautioning readers about what could and could not be expected of codification. They should not expect to find the last word on a given topic in the code. Every legislative enactment, even one that aims at comprehensiveness, exists in a dialogue with unwritten law and must be interpreted in light of the accumulated 'experience and knowledge' of the society in which it exists. Although 'the formal process of codification in Quebec proceeded almost without reference to the theoretical and practical concerns voiced in the European debates' between Anton Thibaut and Carl Friedrich von Savigny over the value of codification, it attempted some reconciliation of their views.[38] A code may be a practical necessity in some circumstances, as Thibaut argued, but it should be interpreted with due regard for the history and *Volksgeist* of the people in question, as suggested by the ideas of von Savigny, who opposed codification.

The Act of 1857 entrusting the task of drafting the two codes to three jurists specified that they were to follow the plan of the *Code Napoléon* and to contain 'the like amount of detail upon each subject.'[39] In one important respect, however, the Act directed the codifiers to depart from the French path. Instead of following the lead of the French *Code de commerce* of 1807, they were to include all provisions on commercial law within the *CCLC*. Where French commercial law was conceived as an autonomous legal domain distinct from the civil law itself, applicable to traders and to commercial transactions and often dealt with in special courts, such courts had not been created in New France, and after 1763 commercial law had been influenced by the common law in various respects. As it turned out, most of book 4 on commercial law, dealing with bills of exchange and cheques, was redundant within a year when the subject matter was assigned to federal jurisdiction under the *British North America Act*. Other provisions dealing with commercial transactions, such as specifying shorter limitation periods for commercial as opposed to non-commercial dealings, were integrated within the civil code at the appropriate point.

With the French model available since 1804, why did it take so long for Lower Canada to follow in its path? As in France itself, codification was strongly affected by the political environment, and it was not propitious for such a significant reform until the 1850s. Prior to the rebellions, codification was unlikely, not only because of legislative impasse, but also because of differing views on codification within the French-Canadian population. While some social conservatives favoured codification as important for the education of immigrants, the Patriote party feared that any codification might replace Lower Canada's French customary law with English law. By the 1840s the latter outcome was less likely, but there was still another obstacle: the seigneurial system. Codification on the continent was associated with the revolutionary tradition, hence with an anti-feudalist ethos that made it impossible to consider including seigneurial law within any future civil code. Thus no movement towards codification was likely until the abolition of the seigneurial system in 1854, discussed below in chapter 30, and the complementary Act of 1857 proclaiming that non-seigneurial lands in the Eastern Townships would henceforth be held in the free tenure known as franc-alleu roturier and subject in all respects to the incidents of the civil law of property.[40] The legal definition of interests in land would now be ostensibly uniform in all areas of the colony, a prelude to the universalist aspirations of a civil code. The silence of the code on Indigenous interests in property, whether in the lands occupied by the communities known as the Seven Fires or in those occupied by Indigenous peoples elsewhere in Lower Canada, spoke volumes about the code as a project of, by, and for settlers. In all respects, the code addressed itself to a

European-descended population, a feature that could only have further delegitimated and marginalized anything related to Indigenous law.

With the issue of settler property finally disposed of, the lawyer-statesmen of Lower Canada could turn their minds to the next big law reform challenge. If the impetus for the code was the trinity of technical problems related to the diversity of sources, lack of translation of basic texts, and unavailability of legislative or doctrinal synthesis, the enactment of the *CCLC* also provided a golden opportunity to re-engineer the substance of Lower Canadian law in a manner more in tune with the tenets of Victorian liberalism. The codal enterprise may not have been 'political' in the sense of riven with ethnic or partisan tensions, but it was very much a creature of the political economy of the period, impressed as it was with doctrines of improvement, free will, and progress. The technical and linguistic aspects of codification will be considered first, followed by an analysis of the major areas of continuity and change in the code.[41]

With the appointment of George-Étienne Cartier as attorney-general in 1856, codification gained not just a powerful advocate but one with the political ability to set it in motion. The Act that he shepherded through the legislature provided that the commissioners' drafts were to distinguish clearly between setting out the law 'actually in force,' with authorities in support, and any revisions they thought advisable. They were to report from time to time to the governor, and their reports were to be sent to the judges for comment. The Act was somewhat laconic, a mere eighteen sections long, yet it set in motion the most important change in the colony's law since the *Quebec Act*.[42]

The success of the Act would depend on those chosen as commissioners. Cartier wanted Louis-Hippolyte La Fontaine, chief justice of Lower Canada and first co-premier under responsible government, to chair the commission. In failing health, he declined. Three judges were appointed – Charles Dewey Day, Augustin-Norbert Morin, and René-Édouard Caron – and released from all their judicial duties for the duration of the work; Caron would serve as president. All had had extensive practices as advocates, while Day and Morin were connected to the beginnings of legal education, at McGill and Laval respectively. All possessed political experience. Day had sat on the Special Council and Morin in the assembly, while Caron had been mayor of Quebec City as well as a legislative councillor. The three were carefully chosen to represent different shades of political opinion. Day had long supported a legislative union of the Canadas and presided at the trials of some of the Patriotes after the rebellions. Morin had drafted the 92 Resolutions in 1834, had been actively involved on the side of the Patriotes as a young lawyer and was briefly imprisoned in 1839. Caron was a moderate nationalist who had opposed both Papineau and the Union of 1841. They were assisted by two secretaries, whose linguistic abilities the Act specified in detail: one was to be 'a person whose mother tongue is English but who is well versed in the French language, and the other a person whose mother tongue is French but who is well versed in the English language.' The men chosen – Thomas K. Ramsay and Joseph-Ubalde Beaudry – amply satisfied these requirements. Ramsay was dismissed for partisan reasons in 1862 and replaced by Thomas McCord, while upon Morin's death in 1865 Beaudry replaced him as a commissioner and in that capacity was largely responsible for the drafting of the *Code of Civil Procedure*; Louis-Siméon Morin replaced Beaudry as French-language secretary. The Act imposed no linguistic requirements on the judges, but all seem to have been at least functionally bilingual.

The linguistic question was taken very seriously by the commissioners: even the minutes of their 206 meetings over five years (1859–64) were written bilingually.[43] In this respect the bilingual Louisiana codes were of assistance in developing civilian terminology in English. While Day drafted portions of the code in English and the other two judges in French, there were extensive discussions among the judges and secretaries regarding the translations, resulting at times in adjustments to the original as well as to the translation. Both versions of the code were effectively originals and equally authoritative.[44] Article 2615 was designed to solve problems of interpretation where the two versions did not seem identical. If the provision related to existing law, 'that version shall prevail which is most consistent with the provisions of the existing law on which the article is founded'; in the case of new law, the version 'most consistent with the intention of the article and the ordinary rules of interpretation' was to govern.

Article 2615 provides a window on another question, that of the status of the law prior to the code. Unlike the *Code Napoléon*, the *CCLC* did not contain a provision abrogating all previous law. Such a provision was appropriate for post-revolutionary France, but not for mid-century Lower Canada, where the legal heritage of New France was a link to the past valued by the French-Canadian population. The same choice, to preserve any prior law not inconsistent with the code itself, would be made later in the century by the drafters of the *Criminal Code* of 1892. This reluctance to cut the umbilical cord to metropolitan law, to emphasize continuity, is thus an important characteristic of the European legal traditions in Canada, a gesture of transatlantic solidarity that served, unwittingly or not, to legitimate the settlement project in North America.

The legislative direction to the codifiers that they had not only to state the existing law but also to provide the sources on which it was based made their task a herculean one. Nonetheless, they worked steadily and methodically and got through an enormous amount of research. They issued seven reports on various areas of the law to be codified, as well as a supplemental volume containing corrections, totalling over 1,500 pages of text. While their reports contain, by one account, references to some 350 different sources of law, in fact they drew predominantly on two sources: the Custom of Paris, and the work of French doctrinal writers of the seventeenth and eighteenth centuries. With regard to the former, Ramsay established that only 198 of the 362 provisions in the French version of 1580 were still in force in Lower Canada, and of these, 50 had been affected by local legislation, leaving 148 as 'existing law.'[45] The extent to which the commissioners drew on Roman law was 'non negligeable,' but it was deployed primarily in a rhetorical fashion.[46] The law distilled by the commissioners was thus neither primarily statutory nor found in judicial decisions: it was a learned law, the *opinio juris* of an era long vanished in France itself but prolonged in Lower Canada by historical circumstance.

The commissioners conducted their work free of interference from the legislature or the government, with the one exception of Ramsay's dismissal. They received relatively little response from the judges who were sent their reports, nor did the bar, the notariat, the young law faculties, or the nascent legal press comment on the reports as they were issued.[47] The government did not go out of its way to circulate the reports, but if it had the lay public would probably have expressed little interest. All in all, there appeared to be a consensus on the new *CCLC* when it passed through the legislature in 1865, to be proclaimed in force as of 1 August 1866. This consensus was likely based on the perception that production of the code was largely a technical exercise, aimed at conservation of existing law rather than change.

To some extent this perception was correct. The commissioners recommended changes to the law in only 10 per cent of the articles drafted by them, virtually all of which were accepted by the legislature, but this number is misleading. Assessing the changes wrought by the code entails viewing them in the context of a variety of other legal changes enacted in Lower Canada in this period.[48] All of these made the legal infrastructure more amenable to capitalist relations in the economy, commodifying all forms of property by rendering it both more fungible and more secure, and orienting contract law around hypothetically equal contracting parties: among these changes, some discussed elsewhere in this part of the volume, were the abolition of seigneurial tenure, the creation of registry offices, the abolition of 'secret hypothecs' and the partial abolition of customary dower by the Special Council,[49] the uniformization of settler interests in land across all areas of the province, the abolition of penalties for usury, and the adoption of bankruptcy laws.

The code elevated the role of the will and formal equality in contract law, illustrating the famous shift 'from status to contract.' Master and servant law, for example, was formerly more of a status relationship, one of 'domestic dependency,' wherein the master assumed some responsibility for the servant's well-being.[50] Neither the Custom of Paris nor the ancien droit had much to say about employment law; work in the professions or trades was regulated by guild practices, while the supply of unskilled labour was regulated largely by local custom. In practice the employment relationship was in a state of flux with the beginnings of industrial production in the 1840s and 1850s, with the contractual elements of the master–servant relationship on the ascendant. The codal provisions on employment, called 'Of the Lease and Hire of Services' in the *CCLC*, confirmed this trend, leaving the parties to bargain 'freely' over the content of the relationship. The five articles in question (1667–71) contained virtually no regulation beyond stating that the employment relationship could not be perpetual, and that it would end with the death of the employee or his or her incapacity arising without fault, or in some cases by the death of the employer. No protections were provided for vulnerable parties except for those relevant to contract law as a whole, and these dealt mainly with situations of impaired consent in the formation of contracts, such as duress, drunkenness, mental illness, and the like (articles 991–1000).

The one protection provided at least theoretically under the old law, the concept of lesion, was retained in the code for minors only. Lesion came from the Roman law and was expanded in the ancien droit, largely under the influence of Christian morality and Aquinian notions of 'just price.' It provided that a contract could be avoided where there was a gross disparity between the prestations of the parties – in essence, where there was substantive unfairness. It is a good example of how 'equity' was upheld as part of the civil law, rather than administered in a separate court as in common law jurisdictions. While lesion tended to be raised mostly in transactions for the sale of immovables at gross undervalue, in theory it was available in any type of contract, including labour contracts, providing the inequality was present at the outset and not the result of supervening factors. The *Code Napoléon* restricted lesion to the sale of immovables and partition of estates, while the Lower Canadian codifiers abolished it completely for those of the age of majority (article 1012).[51]

If the move from 'status to contract' was a popular one with the codifiers in the realm of the economy, it was not so in the realm of the family. There, the powers of husbands and fathers under the Custom of Paris were confirmed and in some cases enhanced, while the situation of married women in particular underwent something of a decline. The *Code Napoléon* also, for the most part, refused to enact liberal reforms in the area of family law, but the Lower Canadian commissioners declined to follow the French code's lead, even in those few areas where it broke with the old law. They refused even to consider adding divorce or adoption to the code, for example, in spite of their presence in the French code of 1804, and provided no explanation for their reluctance. Article 174 of the *CCLC* succinctly expressed the views of the codifiers on gender and marriage: 'A husband owes protection to his wife; a wife obedience to her husband.' The new code did not repeat the maxim from article 225 of the Custom of Paris that the husband was 'maître et Seigneur' in marriage, but that phrase nonetheless reflected perfectly the thinking of the codifiers on the legal nature of the marital relationship. As Brian Young has noted, there was no particular division along religious lines among the codifiers on attitudes to gender; the Protestant Charles Dewey Day was just as keen to uphold marital authority as his Catholic colleagues.[52]

The new code, with its expansive embrace of freedom to contract, nonetheless denied this important right to wives, maintaining the law as it stood in the Custom of Paris and confirming the second-class status of married women in the eyes of the law. Only in a few carefully delineated situations were exceptions made to the principle of the wife's incapacity to contract, and these mostly followed the old law. A wife having obtained a decree of separation from bed and board necessarily could contract independently because the husband's marital authority over her was terminated. Under any matrimonial regime, wives could not as a rule bind themselves or alienate or accept property independently of their husbands, even in exigent situations where, for example, the husband was in jail or absent from the jurisdiction (articles 179, 1297), but if a husband refused consent a judge could provide the necessary authorization. Women married under separation of property could contract alone, however, regarding the administration of their property; for example, if a wife separate as to property owned a house, she could contract on her own with someone to repair the roof, even though she could not sell the house without her husband's written authorization (article 177). The doctrine of marchande publique, or *feme sole* trader, allowed married women who carried on a trade or business to contract without the consent of their husbands, but only for matters connected with their business; like other wives, they could not commence any legal proceedings without their husbands joining the action or giving authorization (though, again, a judge could give the necessary authorization where a husband declined). The only exception here was in favour of wives separate as to property, who could sue alone relating to acts of administration of their property; thus, in the earlier example, if the wife hired a workman to repair the roof and he did a bad job, she could sue him without her husband's authorization. Women married under community of property needed the consent of their husbands, express or implied, to enter into a trade or business, but article 179 was unclear whether women married under separate property also needed such authorization. A new exception to wifely incapacity referred to in article 177 of the code had been enacted for the benefit of a bank: in 1862 a statute extending the powers of the City and District Savings Bank of Montreal permitted anyone, 'whether such person ... be qualified by law to enter into ordinary contracts or not,' to deposit up to $2,000 in a savings account without the intervention of any other person, 'any law, usage or custom to the contrary notwithstanding.'[53]

With regard to marital property, the code of 1866 maintained the protections that women married under community of property had previously enjoyed, but it did not adopt the new restraint on the power of the husband as administrator that had been added to the French code in article 1422. That article stated as new law that a husband could not alienate assets of the community by gratuitous title – could not give away assets of the marital community, as he could under the Custom of Paris. The codifiers refused to adopt this modification, which had the potential effect of negating some of the benefits of the community property regime (article 1292).[54] One of the few areas in which a wife could carry out a juridical act without her husband's consent was in the making of a will, but this was really a by-product of the adoption of testamentary freedom in the *Quebec Act* and not any particular concession to married women.

The legal concept of paternal authority over children of the marriage was also carried over from the Custom of Paris, but here the codifiers of Lower Canada parted company with the authors of the French code in almost every way, agreeing only on maintaining the old law that the husband alone exercised paternal authority during marriage.[55] The *CCLC* did not follow two significant innovations in the French code. The latter provided for a near-despotic disciplinary power, allowing a father to order the detention of his minor children for certain periods of time, even without providing reasons in some cases. It also conferred on parents a right of usufruct over any property their children might possess, until the age of eighteen or the child's emancipation. The *CCLC* allowed parents only a right of correction over their children, to be exercised in a reasonable and moderate fashion, and gave parents no interest in or power over property possessed by minor children; such authority could be exercised only in the context of a tutorship validly conferred.[56] These provisions, which recognized the social reality that children in Lower Canada often achieved financial independence at a much earlier age than in France, served only to emphasize the relative autonomy of children, when contrasted with the continuing legal dependence of wives.

While some adherents of ultramontanism in Lower Canada criticized the code for not going far enough in promoting Catholic values in the domain of marriage and the family, and even appealed to Rome in this respect, these critics were, to use the Quebec expression, showing themselves to be 'plus catholique que le pape.' Even the papal delegate charged with hearing them out recognized that the civil code had to govern a religiously mixed population, and concluded that it was 'a good code for a Catholic nation.' There would be no papal intervention in any further debates on the subject.[57]

The *Code of Civil Procedure* was enacted the year after the *Civil Code*, but was proclaimed into force only just prior to Confederation on 28 June 1867.[58] From the beginning it had always been overshadowed by the efforts devoted to its more prestigious elder sibling – where the *Civil Code* had seven reports devoted to it, the *Code of Civil Procedure* had to be content with one.[59] And yet in some ways the need for codification of civil procedure was even more urgent than that of the civil law itself. Much of the uncertainty centred on the status of Louis XIV's ordinance of 1667, discussed in chapter 6. It had set out a rational system of civil procedure that was well understood down to the end of the French regime. Changes made by the British through ordinances of 1777, 1785, and 1787 simply introduced new elements such as jury trials and writs without attempting to reconcile them with the 1667 ordinance, but without abolishing it either.[60] In fact, it was not abolished until the enactment of the 1965 *Code of Civil Procedure*.[61]

And yet it is clear that at least parts of the 1667 ordinance were perceived to be in force down to 1867. In 1855, for example, Lower Canadian legislation expressly abolished the rules on recusal contained in the 1667 ordinance and substituted new, less stringent ones. The 1667 rules on recusal required the judge to step aside if he or his spouse shared a great-great-grandparent with any of the parties, which must have led to much anxious genealogical inquiry. Recusal did not have to take place if all parties consented in writing, but the ordinance did not say what would happen if the relationship were discovered only after judgment. The English rules on recusal for reasons of family relationship were virtually non-existent, but the new rules adopted in Lower Canada struck a balance between these two extremes, requiring recusal only where the judge was a first cousin or closer relation of any of the parties.[62] The statute itself adopted the technique that had bedevilled the field ever since 1760: it did not refer to the 1667 ordinance at all, being content to state, in effect, 'this rule needs to be changed, and here is the new one.'[63]

The ordinance of 1787 and Acts of 1794 and 1801 all gave judges of the superior courts the power to make their own rules. They took up the task with gusto, Chief Justice Sewell producing over 300 pages of rules in 1809 for the Quebec Court of King's Bench, while his counterpart James Monk at Montreal did the same in 1811.[64] Unlike local statutes after 1792, which were always translated into French, these never were, at least in any published version, nor was the ordinance of 1667 ever translated into English.[65] Sewell's and Monk's published rules, while providing minute guidance in some areas, once again did not expressly deal with the ordinance of 1667. They referred the reader to the practice of the courts of Westminster Hall for matters dealing with the prerogative writs of *certiorari*, prohibition, *mandamus*, *quo warranto*, and habeas corpus, none of which had been introduced into the province by legislation except for the last, by the ordinance of 1785. Nor were the judges' rule books intended as complete codes: there was nothing in them about the jury *de medietate*, for example.

It was lawyers who had to make this unwieldy system work, and they must have done so, though only detailed archival work will demonstrate how this was accomplished. Their treatise-writing efforts were devoted mainly to the civil law rather than procedure, and what they did write on procedure was confusing and unhelpful. Nicolas-Benjamin Doucet devoted about ten pages to procedure in his *Fundamental Laws of Canada*, but the content was presented as bald propositions of law, mostly copied from the *Extrait des Messieurs* commissioned by the British government seventy years earlier.[66] It is not clear what guidance this could have provided for lawyers or the law students whom Doucet identified as part of his target audience.

As in so many other fields, the legislature became much more active with regard to civil procedure starting in 1843, but the proliferation of legislation after that date, including the 1849 Act restructuring the court system, did not pursue any coherent or consistent plan. Ideally the new *Code of Civil Procedure* would have provided some overall scheme for reconciling or harmonizing the disparate procedural elements derived from the French and English traditions, but it was generally agreed by commentators then and now that it failed in this task. Essentially the codifiers retreated to presenting the law as it existed, with all its inconsistencies, rather than taking it in hand. Commentator Gonsalve Doutre called it a compilation rather than a codification, the insufficiencies of which made him long for the days prior to the code when lawyers could follow their own instincts: 'Custom,' he observed, 'is always more flexible and accommodating than a written text.' He complained that it had been prepared 'with less maturity than the Civil Code, [was] very confused in several parts and positively contradictory in others.'[67] In fairness to the codifiers, they had a more difficult task than with the *Civil Code*, where the *Code Napoléon* provided a clear model. The French *Code of Civil Procedure* of 1806 followed a very different system, and the court structures of the two jurisdictions had diverged considerably since 1760, making it unsuitable as a model. In the end, the code of 1867 had nothing like the longevity of the *CCLC*: only three decades later it was entirely replaced by a new *Code of Civil Procedure*.[68]

With the enactment of the two codes, Lower Canada had tamed, to some extent at least, its luxuriant polyjurality. It had not cut off recourse to the ancien droit entirely, however, and with the rise of law reporting across British North America, jurists in what would soon become the province of Quebec would be exposed more and more to the common law as applied in neighbouring provinces. With the creation of a federal state in 1867, they would also be exposed to a deluge of legislation drafted in a common law style far removed from the economy of the *Civil Code*. Over time, this seeming assault by the common law would give rise to a more defensive attitude among civilian jurists, one centred on maintaining the 'purity' and integrity of the civil law. Such an attitude contrasts with that displayed during the codification process, where the commissioners were not afraid to canvass a wide variety of sources, including the common law, as they drafted the new codes.

This section will close with a judicial decision that represents in some ways the apogee of Lower Canadian polyjurality in the precodification period. Although Justice Samuel Cornwallis Monk handed down his decision in *Connolly v Woolrich* just a week after Confederation, it dealt with the validity of a marriage that had allegedly taken place between two teenagers in 1803 at Rivière-aux-rats in what is now northern Manitoba.[69] Monk found the territory to be outside the Hudson's Bay watershed and thus in 'Indian territory,' though he concluded that his decision would have been the same had the marriage taken place within HBC territory. Both areas were governed by the Cree who had inhabited it for millennia. The relationship between William Connolly, a seventeen-year-old North West Company trader from Montreal newly arrived in the area, and Suzanne Pas-de-nom, fifteen-year-old daughter of a local Cree chief, was not unusual in fur trade country.[70] As Connolly had told his nephew Thomas Cushing Aylwin, who by the time of the court proceedings was a colleague of Justice Monk on the Superior Court, in order to get ahead in the trade 'he had to get a woman whom he would have to buy from her father; that he had got a chief who had great interest among the Indians, that this man had sold the mother of the plaintiff to the late William Connolly.'[71] The evidence established that William and Suzanne had married according to the custom of the country, cohabited for twenty-eight years and had six children together, and that Connolly introduced her everywhere as his wife and gave her and the children his name. During this time they lived in many places in the northwest, including New Caledonia (later British Columbia). In 1831 Connolly returned with Suzanne and their children to Montreal, whereupon he repudiated Suzanne as his wife and married his second cousin Julia Woolrich in a Catholic ceremony; they would go on to have two children. Suzanne did not thrive in Montreal and returned to the Red River settlement with some of her children, where she was supported by Connolly in the convent of the Grey Nuns at St-Boniface.

Connolly died in 1848 and willed most of his extensive property to Julia, though she continued to provide some support to Suzanne. Upon Suzanne's death in 1862, her eldest child, John, now a member of the bar of Montreal, sought his share of the community of property that he alleged had existed between her and his father. His action demanded that Julia surrender his share of his mother's estate out of the assets she held. He succeeded before Justice Monk at trial, and in two subsequent appeals, to the Court of Revision and the Court of Appeal, in the latter court by a majority of four to one. A further appeal to the Privy Council by Julia's heirs, she having died in 1865, was settled out of court. While John's siblings had not joined him in the lawsuit, they likely claimed their share after his success. His sister, Lady Amelia Douglas, married to Sir James Douglas, the governor of British Columbia, expected that her share – effectively one-twelfth of her late father's estate – might be as much as $50,000.[72]

Justice Monk gave a full-throated endorsement of the validity of Cree law in general in the relevant territory, and of Cree marriage law in particular. Neither the fact that Cree marriage was potentially polygamous nor that it could be dissolved informally were barriers to his finding that the couple had a valid marriage that produced legal effects in Lower Canada. While Connolly might have been able to dissolve his marriage while in Cree territory, once he brought Suzanne back to Montreal he was subject to the local law, which did not recognize divorce. Thus his marriage to Julia was absolutely null, and their children illegitimate. What matrimonial property regime governed his first marriage depended on his domicile, which Monk found to be Lower Canada. In spite of Connolly's long residence in the north, he had always planned to return to Lower Canada when his fortune was made, and his peripatetic existence as a trader meant that it was impossible to say where he might have acquired another domicile. Thus the default law of his domicile of origin, community of property, applied, and John Connolly was within his rights to claim his portion of his mother's half share of the community assets that should have devolved to her upon William Connolly's death.

Monk's 70-page virtuoso judgment ranged over common law, civil law, Indigenous law, international law, and canon law, citing some seventy sources, including works of general history and ethnology, as well as references to witnesses' testimony to establish points of Cree law. The five Court of Appeal judges wrote another 150 pages of erudite prose.[73] The determination of the judges to follow where the law led them, even though the application of Indigenous law resulted in the disruption and stigmatization (via illegitimacy) of an elite settler family, is striking and not what might be expected from a mid-Victorian settler court. Arguably it was the judges' ease in navigating the babel légale of the Lower Canadian legal world that enabled them to regard Cree law as a valid source of law that had as much claim as European law to be enforced. Such an attitude would face resistance later in the century with the emergence of a more hard-edged and statist legal positivism, but the approach to Indigenous marriage laws in *Connolly v Woolrich* anchored the federal government's approach to the recognition of such marriages for decades to come.[74]

Statutes: Making and Remaking Local Laws and Societies

Statutory law increasingly shaped both the law itself and the social and economic world in which colonists lived. We cannot provide a detailed account of all the statutes passed, but some general points about their collective focus should be noted. A great deal of the legislation of the later eighteenth and early nineteenth centuries was enacted to put in place the basic institutions of government and social order – to establish local courts and determine where and when they met, to build local jails, to guard against the dangers of fire in wooden cities. Another large category of legislation regulated the economy – establishing seasons for exploitation of the creatures that inhabited the waters and the woods, prohibiting the destruction of dikes and riverbanks, regulating the export of fish and lumber, and barring 'ignorant and unskilful persons from the practice of Physic and Surgery.' These examples are all taken from one colony, New Brunswick, in one year, 1816.[75] If we fast forward a decade and a half to Lower Canada, we find many of the same subjects covered, and also that it was felt necessary to toughen laws preventing people ignoring or damaging fences, to set currency conversion rates, to establish quarantine facilities for immigrants arriving with a variety of contagious conditions, and to improve navigation on the St Lawrence.[76] Taken collectively these statutes meant that British North American colonies were regulated societies, not jurisdictions in which laissez-faire swept all before it.[77]

Yet another collection of statutes, beginning in the 1820s and continuing on past mid-century, empowered both governments and private individuals to participate in the development of infrastructure projects and other forms of economic activity. Legislation directed at governments in this regard generally authorized the raising of money for public works, while that which concerned individuals might grant them a franchise or a patent, or, as we shall see in detail in chapter 31 below, allow them to pool their capital and/or raise money from others through the corporate form. As a leading legal historian perceptively pointed out some forty years ago, 'The common law was extensive, but it was not all of the law about the economy,' and one of the principal purposes of legislation was 'the establishment of supplemental terms to facilitate the working of the market.'[78]

By the 1830s the colonies had developed sufficient confidence to also engage in substantial exercises in law reform, including the remaking of the criminal law, discussed below in chapter 28. These reform efforts encompassed court systems and procedure, the protection of family property from the vicissitudes of the economic cycle, also discussed elsewhere, and many other topics. Perhaps in no other jurisdiction was the belief that legislation could and should remake the social and economic structure stronger than in Lower Canada. The *CCLC* represented a very substantial reorientation of the civil law to embody liberal values. It was by no means the only legislation of the Union period to move in this direction – a land registration system, the abolition of seigneurial tenure, and bankruptcy laws all did so. Not all of the initiatives of the Union period were unique to Lower Canada, but enough of them pertained to that colony, and had such far-reaching implications, that one historian has persuasively argued, ironically in an article devoted to a failed legislative initiative, that those responsible for this legislative output, very many of whom were lawyers, were engaging in 'strategic Benthamism.'[79] The enthusiasm for legislative change quickened in the 1850s, not just in Lower Canada but also in the upper colony and the Maritimes.

In the rest of this chapter we chart the changes that were made from the early nineteenth century to the 1850s and 1860s in how statutes were organized and presented. Two themes are dominant, each of which is broadly referable to different periods. The first is that of statutory consolidation. All colonies published annual volumes of statutes, a compilation of all the statutes passed in a given year, from the establishment of their legislative assemblies onwards. But over time, reliance on these annual statute volumes proved unsatisfactory, and various ways of consolidating the statute book were carried out. The second theme can variously be labelled statutory revision, codification, or law reform, all of which entailed more or less ambitious attempts to do more than just consolidate the statutes, but to change the law and to make it more comprehensible and accessible to more people, lay as well as professional. As we have seen, Lower Canada revised and codified both the civil law and civil procedure in 1866–7, and this section deals with cognate attempts to do something similar in the other colonies.

Consolidation of the statute book took place from the very early nineteenth century until the 1840s. It generally involved collecting together the extant statutes, originally published in annual volumes, into one volume. Left out of the consolidated volume was the text of statutes that had been repealed or had expired. Most such volumes included, however, the titles of such acts. Consolidations still arranged the statutes chronologically, not by any thematic ordering scheme. The first such consolidation in nineteenth-century British North America was published in Nova Scotia in 1805. Known at the time and since as Uniacke's statutes after Attorney General Richard John Uniacke Sr, under whose authority they were published, or as volume 1 of the statutes, it ran to over 600 pages. It included the titles of all statutes passed since 1758, but only the text of those still in force was reproduced.[80] Volume 1 was followed by three further similar consolidations in the early nineteenth century at roughly ten-year intervals, in 1816, 1826, and 1835.[81] Similar consolidations were published for Upper Canada in 1818 and again in 1831, for New Brunswick in 1838, and for Prince Edward Island in 1834 and again in 1844.[82] Updated consolidations were published for the island in the 1850s and 1860s.[83] Newfoundland was exceptional among eastern colonies for not producing any consolidations at all before the 1870s, even though its first statutes date from 1833, the year after the establishment of a legislative assembly. Similarly British Columbia produced annual statutes once an assembly was established for Vancouver Island in the late 1850s, and ordinances for the mainland, but no consolidations in the pre-Confederation period.[84]

Consolidation *simpliciter* was an exercise limited in ambition. The principal purpose was to provide in one volume all statutes passed in a given period. Some were paid for by assemblies, indicating that consolidating the statutes was seen as a public service to users of the law, principally but not exclusively lawyers and judges, while others were privately funded ventures.[85] The advantage they gave was that of having physical access to a complete set of statutes in one place, and this advantage was frequently touted in advertisements for consolidations, or in their prefaces, as well as being an argument used to persuade colonial assemblies to fund them. The more significant features of these consolidations were what they lacked. None of these consolidations rewrote any of the statutes, nor did they organize them other than in the chronological order in which they had been passed. They were not arranged by common subject matter or revised in language to make them more accessible. Thus they retained the full text of statutes that in later years were partially amended. Marginal editorial annotations referring the reader to amending statutes did at least make it easier to know the current law than searching for any amendments.

The 1840s and 1850s saw the emergence of a more ambitious approach to the statute book, driven by values and objectives that went beyond mere convenience. Those values were reflective of, and part of, a multi-jurisdictional movement that encompassed Britain and the United States.[86] In the early to mid-nineteenth-century common law world, lawyers, judges, politicians, and social reformers advocated for change both in particular areas of the law and in the structure of the legal system as a whole. Historians have attached various labels to this movement, each of which captures at least part of it. It has generally been called law reform, reflecting the fact that it invariably involved suggestions that particular parts of the common law did not reflect modern social values. The common law was often depicted as 'archaic' or 'feudal,' sometimes in movements for reform of particular legal regimes and sometimes with reference to the entire body of the common law. Many of these campaigns for reform of particular legal regimes are discussed elsewhere in this part, including the changes to court procedures and the partial fusion of law and equity, both discussed in chapter 22. Others that will be later examined include the movement to reduce and eliminate physical punishments in the criminal law, and the campaigns against imprisonment for debt.

These particular campaigns will not be dealt with further here. Yet it bears emphasis that they were not isolated movements but part of a general demand for change in the law. This does not mean that law reform was simply made up of a number of particularized campaigns. Law reform was also a general movement, encompassing attacks on special interests, especially on lawyers and judges. Ordinary non-professional people ought to be able to both understand and use the law, and even practise it, without guild training or membership. People should know the law, be able to understand how to assert their rights, and the law and the legal system should be accessible to a broad swathe of the population. In both Britain and the United States these ideas, sometimes referred to as Benthamite utilitarianism, contributed to a demand for codification, a term that is often associated with law reform and was the principal methodology to effect it. The archaic common law should be systematically reformed by the enactment of codes, which would render it into ordinary language shorn of 'archaisms' and technical terms, organize it rationally, and make it easily comprehensible and widely accessible. Codification would also result in cheaper and more accessible court structures and procedures, which heretofore had made law the preserve of a trained professional elite and also made it slow, expensive, and inefficient.

The codification and law reform movements had considerable success in the United States, rather less so in Britain. They have not been much studied for British North America, although it is clear from limited evidence that such movements existed and at times produced fundamental change.[87] British North American colonies other than Lower Canada did not produce a law reform and codification movement on the scale that was manifest in many American states. But such ideas were in the air, more so in some jurisdictions than others, and the movement had some partial success.

The earliest evidence of a law reform movement in British North America was the establishment of a law reform commission by the Nova Scotia Assembly in 1832. This commission's work on the courts has been discussed in the previous chapter, but it had a broader mandate, to look at 'revising and consolidating the Laws of the Province.' Yet breadth was married to vagueness. Apart from specifically being told to 'report what alteration and amendments' should be made to the criminal law, it was also tersely and generally asked to report on 'how and in what manner it may be proper and advisable to revise, alter and consolidate … the Laws and Statutes of the Province.' The commission was staffed by elite lawyers and seems to have consulted only the judges and the legal profession. It offered only the most modest of reform proposals. Although a general tidying up of the statute book would be useful, it was the commissioners' 'decided conviction' that 'hasty and extensive changes in jurisprudence are more to be feared than sought for.' Typical was their approach to insolvent debtor laws, discussed in chapter 32 below. The eight statutes on the subject 'could easily be reduced into one,' but there was no suggestion that the content of that law should be changed. They would have made a small improvement to accessibility – reducing the statute book from 1,559 pages to fewer than a thousand – but done nothing to alter the substance of the law.[88]

This modest nod to reform was followed in the next decades by statutory consolidations in the Canadas. Upper Canada's two volumes, published in 1843, went further than earlier consolidations, leaving out entirely repealed statutes, but did little else. The eminent judges and lawyers who were the commissioners for revising the statutes described their task as being to 'present the Statute Law of Upper Canada as it stood at the time of the Union…, having expunged all such parts as had been repealed,… [and] carefully revising the whole.' Whatever they meant by using the word 'revising,' they did not do any, they said, because it would have been 'useless labour' unless accompanied by 'a Legislative revision of the whole of … [the] Statute Law.'[89] Lower Canada's statutory revision came out two years later, in 1845.[90] It was arguably the first example of something more than mere consolidation in British North America, for it organized the statutes into ten categories, which were called 'classes,' rather than listing them by year of initial passage. The three commissioners responsible were all lawyers and 'flatter themselves that the publication will have the effect of reducing the statutes and ordinances of Lower Canada into order, and of enabling any person … at once to find the statute law in force on any subject.' Hence accessibility was one of their goals, but it was not to be achieved by changing the substance of the law but by translation: 'It seems very desirable that some means should be adopted for making the civil law of Lower Canada accessible to the English portion of the population,' they declaimed, adding that they believed 'that the prejudice entertained by many to the civil law … arises solely from their want of means of obtaining that general knowledge of its provisions, which it is desirable to place within the reach of every man with regard to the law in which he is bound, but which, under existing circumstances, it is impossible for any inhabitant of Lower Canada to acquire, unless he be intimately acquainted with the French language.'[91] The 1845 statutes were not law reform, but they were a step forward from the pure consolidations that had dominated the field.

In the 1850s a significantly different product emerged in the Maritime colonies – Nova Scotia and New Brunswick's *Revised Statutes* of 1851 and 1854 respectively. The former were the first of their kind in common law British North America, and both jurisdictions were clearly influenced to some extent by reform currents. In 1849, just after the attainment of responsible government, a Nova Scotia assembly committee was struck 'to enquire into the expediency of codifying or consolidating the Laws of this Province, in whole or in part.'[92] This is the first mention in British North America of the use of the word *codify*. The committee – future Supreme Court of Canada judge William A. Henry and lawyers William Young, John Clarke Hall, and James Fraser, as well as non-lawyer Herbert Huntington, a leading light in the new liberal government – resolved that it was 'indispensable ... that the Statutes of this Province should be amended and improved, so as to render the same more intelligible.' Here there was much more than consolidation; amendment, improvement, and accessibility to all were stressed. The following year another assembly committee recommended that the statutes be consolidated, republished in one volume, and, most importantly, to some extent rewritten. There should be a wholesale repeal of all existing statutes and their replacement by new ones. All inapplicable or redundant statutes should be left out, inconsistencies in style and language should be eliminated, and a radical reordering achieved by arranging the remaining statutes by themes, not just by a simple chronology. The *Revised Statutes of Massachusetts* would be used as a model.[93]

The *Revised Statutes of Nova Scotia*, 1851, was the first publication of its kind in British North America. The statute book was reduced to a single 600-page Act, divided into four parts and 160 chapters. Many chapters were written in simpler language than the original statute, and the commissioners praised the codifications that had already taken place in the United States. Yet although the 1851 revision was clearly much more than the mere consolidations that had preceded it, we must be cautious about calling it a codification and seeing it as a wholesale acceptance of law reform ideas. The commissioners insisted that they had made statute law more intelligible and logically ordered, had given the statute book 'order and system,' and eliminated verbiage. But beyond that they did not believe that they had been given a mandate to change the substance of local law.

Nova Scotia's lead in publishing *Revised Statutes* was followed by New Brunswick, in 1854, which went somewhat further. As we have seen, it included the abolition of the Court of Chancery, but it went well beyond that. The 1852 statute providing for the revision, presumably inspired at least in part by Nova Scotia's example, expressed the belief that 'it would greatly facilitate the administration of justice' and 'reduce the expense thereof' if the local statutes were 'revised and properly arranged.' It authorized the appointment of commissioners who should 'consolidate, simplify in their language, revise, and arrange in one uniform code,' all statutes. The commissioners were explicitly told to recommend 'such alterations and amendments' as they thought necessary and, true to the standard tenets of law reform, accessibility was stressed. Again we see 'code' used in the legislation, and the commissioners – William Boyd Kinnear, the solicitor general, and leading lawyers and politicians James Watson Chandler and Charles Fisher – called their work a codification. Their revision contained a large number of new Acts as well as extensive revisions of some existing ones, 'stript of the verbiage of endless expletives and repetitions' and recast in clearer language, so that almost all statutes were much shorter than they had been. The statute book was divided into four parts after the Massachusetts code, and with the parts further divided into titles. All existing statutes were 'examined and compared with great care and labour' and extensively shortened, and the first report provided many examples of areas in which the statute book had been not only 'cleaned' up but also significantly revised.[94]

The reform tide, if tide it was, was short-lived. Subsequent editions of *Revised Statutes* in Nova Scotia in 1859 and 1864 were in no degree law reform exercises.[95] Nor did the law reform and codification movements have more than a minimal influence in the Canadas where three consolidations were produced in 1859 and 1861. Two of them reproduced statutes applicable only to one or the other of the Canadas, the third statutes with application throughout the colony. Hence the court systems of Upper and Lower Canada were in the regional volumes, while the criminal law, which had long since been harmonized, was in the general volume. The most striking thing about this way of organizing the consolidations, as illustrated by these examples, was that it was very similar to the division of powers in the 1867 *British North America Act*. The consolidations would certainly have made the law more accessible, obviating the need to wade through statutes dealing with a different jurisdiction, and the fact that the statutes were organized under titles rather than chronologically would also have helped.[96] The province of Canada certainly had its codification advocates, men such as William Badgley of Montreal, who had earlier drafted a criminal code that was never passed. But the commissioners went out of their way to define the difference between consolidation and codification, and to eschew the latter. They had been careful 'not to infringe upon the true spirit and meaning of the existing law,' and to 'succinctly consolidate,' doing so 'without affecting the import and meaning of the original' in every case.[97]

24

Indigenous Law in British North America

The half-century after 1815 brought several challenges to the maintenance of Indigenous law, though these varied considerably across the northern land mass. In the Hudson Bay watershed and the far west, the HBC generally conformed to Indigenous laws. The Salish nations, for example, were able to oblige HBC traders to conform to their own resource harvesting and criminal law regimes. From the Salish point of view, the traders were not kin (*kw'seltksen* in the Secwépemc language) but guests (*sexlitemc*). Guests were 'considered to be at the mercy of their hosts' and were in some sense 'pitiful' because they had no rights in the hosts' territory; still, as long as they conformed to local laws, they were tolerated and treated in a spirit of reciprocity.[1] The gold rush of 1858 and the departure of Governor James Douglas in 1864 would mark a turning point in settler-Indigenous relations in what was now known as British Columbia, as the violence at Bute Inlet in the latter year demonstrated.[2] As discussed in chapter 27 below, Douglas entered treaties with Indigenous peoples on Vancouver Island and always argued against group punishment where Indigenous people committed violence against settlers, 'on the principle that it [was] unjust to hold *tribes* responsible for the acts of *individuals*.'[3] The deterioration in settler-Indigenous relations that occurred after his departure is more properly treated in volume 2 of this work.

In the Prairie West, a new body of law was emerging along with a new people: the Métis. While both anglophone and francophone Métis came to live in and around the Red River settlement, the nascent justice system established there under HBC auspices did not generally take account of what went on beyond the walls of Upper Fort Garry. The Cree, the Saulteaux, and the Métis were free to follow their own laws or create their own traditions. This was confirmed in an 1845 trial in which the recorder of the General Quarterly Court of Assiniboia recognized 'the separate but subordinate nationality of the aboriginal tribes in its fullest extent, [such that] without violating our laws, [they could] carry fire and sword into the territory of a hostile tribe.'[4] The HBC appointed Métis leader Cuthbert Grant as 'warden of the plains' in 1828 to prevent trade carried out against its monopoly, but his numerous roles in both Métis and settler society illustrate the hybrid nature of law and authority in Assiniboia. Grant called himself 'chief of the Halfbreeds' and was regularly named captain of the annual buffalo hunt by the Métis. Yet he was also made a justice of the peace by the Council of Assiniboia in 1835, named to the council in 1839, and sat on the General Quarterly Court after its establishment in 1835. The Métis adopted a semi-sedentary way of life, planting crops in the spring and then leaving them to the care of women and elderly men while able-bodied men followed the buffalo hunt. The hunt had its own rules, but the Métis, along with their allies the Saulteaux, had to defend their territory and laws from their long-time rivals the Sioux, with whom they had violent encounters in 1844 and 1851.[5]

In both of these the Métis prevailed, but their rivalry led to the only official execution ordered by the General Quarterly Court.[6] In 1845 a Saulteau, Capenesseweet, killed a Sioux who was visiting Red River, in plain view of several witnesses. This occurred just outside the fort walls, and a resident Saulteau bystander was also killed by accident. The event came at a time of high tension: the Sioux had come to formalize a peace accord ending their recent hostilities, one negotiated for the Métis by Cuthbert Grant. The Council of Assiniboia considered the options in advance of the trial, including the issue of the court's jurisdiction. One option was to turn the offender over to the Sioux to administer justice to him, which likely would have involved torture and a lingering death. Another was to set him free, on the ground that Saulteau law did not regard murder in the same way as European law. Both these possibilities were rejected, the latter likely because the Sioux would have attacked the settlement had Capenesseweet been released. The court that tried him sat as a bench of seven, including Cuthbert Grant, presided over by its sole legally trained member, Adam Thom;

the jury was more than half Métis. Capenesseweet argued that he was acting on the orders of his chief, but the court rejected this defence on the ground that even if valid with regard to the Sioux victim, it could not excuse the death of the Saulteau. The governor had advised the jury in advance that should they convict, there was no possibility of mercy, and so it was: Capenesseweet was hanged on 6 September 1845. Underneath the forms of British justice, a hybrid legal order was emerging based on the significant participation of Métis and an awareness (if not always a sophisticated understanding) of the Indigenous laws that obtained in the vast territories surrounding the Red River settlement.

In the eastern part of the continent, where the settler population grew rapidly and a transportation revolution was soon underway, different challenges arose. We will examine how Indigenous leaders responded to this changing environment principally through a consideration of the experiences of Kahnawake and Odanak in Lower Canada and the Six Nations settlement at Grand River in Upper Canada. The latter was the largest and wealthiest Indigenous community in Upper Canada, while Kahnawake was the 'capital' of the Seven Fires communities in Lower Canada. Their proximity to large settler populations meant that they were on the front lines of change. Some of the challenges faced by these communities related to technological change. A railway was built through Kahnawake in 1852, while the Six Nations had to deal with the dams, towpaths, and other facilities built by the Grand River Navigation Company on their lands in the 1830s and 1840s. European immigration put increasing pressure on the land resource, as did population growth in Indigenous communities themselves, testing the limits of traditional modes of resource management. This demographic imbalance was particularly evident in Lower Canada, where the total population increased from 335,000 in 1814 to 1.1 million in 1861, while a census of 1835 counted just 3,028 Indigenous individuals in the Seven Fires communities. While this may represent some under-counting, and while there are no reliable figures for the other Indigenous inhabitants outside the Seven Fires, such as the Innu and Mi'kmaq, it is clear that the population imbalance was extreme.[7]

Elsewhere in this part of the volume, the issues of loss of power due to a declining land base, encroachment on what remained by settlers, and the 'civilizing mission' that gathered steam from the 1840s, are addressed in detail. Here the emphasis is on the way that Indigenous communities tried to maintain and enforce their traditional laws in response to these situations, or adapt them to new realities. There can be an assumption that the settler wave swept all before it, including Indigenous laws, but the Haudenosaunee and Abenaki communities considered here displayed a strong commitment to their traditional ways in the face of very difficult odds. This is not to say that members of these communities were always united in their views on how to respond to their changing environment. Especially at Grand River, Christians and followers of the longhouse religion often diverged in their views; their differences were not confined to religion but disclosed deep philosophical disagreements on many matters.[8] Small minorities at Grand River, Kahnawake, and Odanak resisted the restraints of customary law on their ability to commercialize communal resources such as timber, posing a significant problem for Indigenous leaders. And across the Canadas and elsewhere, the political reform movement of the 1830s and 1840s in settler society spilled over into Indigenous communities, causing some members to consider whether electing their leaders would lead to a more effective and accountable form of governance than traditional practices. Similar movements occurred in the United States as well at this time, where one part of the Seneca nation, for example, emerged with a written republican constitution in 1848, in which elected councillors replaced life-term clan chiefs. Traditionalists who did not agree with this change settled at Tonawanda, New York, where they continue to follow customary patterns of leadership selection.[9]

Prior to about 1840, the colonial state was content that Indigenous people should govern themselves for the most part.[10] Thereafter, Victorian liberalism began to permeate all aspects of settler-Indigenous relations. Lord Elgin, governor general of Canada, perhaps summed it up best. When residents of Kahnawake expressed concerns regarding the disruptions attendant upon the construction of the railway, he observed, 'No one, whether white man or Indian, is allowed to stand in the way of improvements.'[11] The equation of 'improvement' and 'progress' with industrial capitalism, private property, freedom of contract, 'separate spheres' for men and women, patriarchal family relations, and liberal individualism only highlighted the ways in which the values and way of life of Indigenous people seemed out of step with the settler society that surrounded them. Indigenous traditional law, formerly seen as an aspect of imperial legal pluralism, was now devalued as cumbersome, inefficient, and an obstacle to 'progress.' Moreover, some aspects of settler ideologies proved popular with dissident minorities in Indigenous communities, as we saw in the previous part of this volume, leading to internal conflicts that eventually arrived in colonial courts. Chiefs at Kahnawake, Odanak, and Grand River were often fighting battles on multiple fronts, seeking to preserve and enforce customary norms in the face of resistance by government Indian agents, Catholic or Protestant clergy, encroaching settlers and transportation companies, and some of their own people. They were not opposed to all change but wanted to be able to manage it on behalf of their communities in accordance with their traditional laws.

One way in which they sought to do so was by codifying their own laws, sometimes updating them in the process by adopting aspects of settler legal culture.[12] In a previous chapter we noted the code of written 'Règlements' adopted by the chiefs of Kahnawake in 1801 and 'revoked' by them in 1808, and the code of 1804. Attempts to codify traditional laws appeared more frequently after 1815, with written constitutions adopted by the Credit River Mississauga (1830), the Mud Lake Mississauga (1845), the Wyandot (Wendat) of Huron reserve near Amherstburg (1843 and 1846), and the Abenaki of Odanak (1856).[13] The Wyandot stated that they decided 'to declare and to explain in writing, the general powers & authority which they understand the Chiefs ought to possess' but remained silent on the rules governing the selection of chiefs. The chiefs were to have legislative authority over matters affecting the whole people, and judicial authority to resolve disputes between individuals regarding their separate allotments. They were to act 'conscientiously and impartially' and to base their judgments on 'the justice of the case.' While these constitutions appear to reflect Western ideas of rule of law, separation of powers, and the protection of individual rights, these concepts were not unknown to Indigenous law, and their authors no doubt chose to adopt a language that would be understood by a settler readership. Also, much was left unsaid in these constitutions, implicitly referring the reader to oral customary law. The influence of missionaries has been seen as a possible reason for the adoption of these constitutions, but it seems at least as likely that the nations themselves sought legal advice, as they did when the Kahnewakehro:non adopted their 'Règlements' in 1801 and 1804.

What follows will focus largely on conflicts implicating Indigenous law that arose in the three communities. The emphasis on conflict is a function of the sources and the geographic location of the chosen sites. In areas further removed from settler populations, traditional laws may have been more easily maintained, although it may also be that other kinds of conflict, over hunting and fishing rights, for example, featured more prominently.[14] Three problem areas will be examined, though all were interrelated. The first concerns the scope and nature of traditional governance in an era of increasing activity by the colonial state at both the provincial and municipal level, and of challenges to the legitimacy of chiefly authority from within Indigenous communities. Second is the legal agency of Indigenous nations in light of the growing influence of the corporate form in settler legal culture. Finally, a cluster of issues related to land use and ownership, which sometimes intersected with issues of Indigenous identity or citizenship in the community, will be examined.

Indigenous Governance in an Age of Settler Political Reform

Kahnawake was governed by a council of eighteen members, one chief with life tenure and two subchiefs named by each of six clans.[15] The process by which clans chose their chiefs is not entirely clear but involved the participation of clan matriarchs; the candidate also had to be approved by existing members of the council. After a new chief was chosen, the name was forwarded to the colonial authorities for 'approval,' but the chiefs treated this as a mere formality and saw the internal decision as conclusive. Only the six (later seven) clan chiefs could represent the community vis-à-vis the outside world. As the 'capital' of the Seven Fires alliance, whenever the grand chiefs at Kahnawake died, representatives of the other Seven Fires communities would arrive to participate in traditional Haudenosaunee condolence ceremonies prior to the selection of a new chief.[16]

The Abenaki, an Algonquian people, did not have a clan structure. Odanak was governed by a council of about a dozen deputy chiefs who generally held their positions for life and chose a grand chief from among themselves. The tradition in the early nineteenth century was that they also chose the replacements for those who died or were removed. However, a certain democratization occurred in the middle decades of the century: in 1838 all the 'warriors' of the community voted to choose the four new chiefs required to replace two deceased chiefs and two who were removed for cause. By 1856 it appears that all adult males of the community were entitled to vote when a new chief was required. It is not possible to discern whether women also voted or otherwise played a role in council renewal.[17]

The Six Nations at Grand River had a more elaborate governance process, given its multinational nature. The settlement pattern there initially followed national loyalties. Each nation selected the lands it wanted, and each of its clans then occupied lands within that tract. Within each clan's space, villages emerged, each with their own chiefs who helped settle any local disputes about land. Thus, there were three levels of authority: village, nation, and Confederacy Council. For some time, most matters could be dealt with either at the village level or by the national council of the Seneca, the Mohawk, etc. The Confederacy Council was re-established in 1785 but dealt only with matters that affected more than one nation or that involved negotiations with parties outside the community.[18]

As will be seen below, in 1847 a new settlement plan saw all the nations move to a compact, single site within the original Haldimand Grant. After this, the national councils were discouraged from meeting individually, and the Confederacy Council emerged as the principal governing body. It was composed of fifty chiefs or royaner, allocated among the constituent nations according to a traditional formula, but the council could and did add 'pine tree chiefs' from time to time, men who were thought to possess particular skills or knowledge that would assist in the task of governance. Deputy chiefs and war chiefs were also included, such that the actual size of council might rise as high as seventy-six. The role of the 'extra' chiefs was virtually equal to those of the hereditary chiefs, and 'personal ability, not official status, became the basis for influence and respect in the council.'[19]

Within the council there was a well-established process for discussing issues based on the Great Law. The Onondaga welcomed everyone and presided over meetings. The Mohawk and Seneca, the 'older brothers' or 'uncles,' considered any matter first, then on making a decision 'passed it across the fire' to the Cayuga and Oneida, the 'younger brothers' or 'nephews' who reviewed it with the chiefs of the dependent nations.[20] If they were all agreed, the Onondaga considered it, and if they also agreed, the matter was resolved. If there was disagreement, the matter would be sent back for reconsideration until agreement was reached or the matter was dropped.[21] The official language of the council was Mohawk; discussions were held in that language, but the minutes were translated into English. The traditional role of women in decision-making continued, though the written records documenting it are few. One testament to their ongoing influence was the practice of council to use words of condolence to mark the passing of clan mothers as well as royaner.[22] It is likely, however, that their political role declined somewhat with the growing masculinization of the public sphere in settler society.

Across the Canadas, the middle decades of the century saw challenges from within Indigenous communities to traditional means of choosing leaders, generally led by younger members of the community who had more formal education than their elders. At Red River, the Métis, along with many in the settler population, chafed under the rule of the unelected Council of Assiniboia and petitioned for representative government in 1851.[23] A movement for elective governance at Grand River to replace the clan chiefs arose in the 1860s but was fairly easily repulsed. There, young reformers were upset at the role of the Confederacy Council in the investment of community funds in the Grand River Navigation Company, which went bankrupt in 1861 – a somewhat unfair charge, given that the council did not know of or consent to the arrangement.[24] The reformers wanted a more accountable leadership, but the Indian Department opposed any change, on the paternalistic basis that the Six Nations were not 'experienced' enough to handle electoral politics.[25]

At Kahnawake there had been rumblings of discontent for some time with the system of life-tenured chiefs. These erupted in 1852 when twenty-six deputy chiefs addressed a petition to the government of Lower Canada complaining that the grand chiefs 'ruled like veritable despots.'[26] A two-person commission appointed by the government cleared the chiefs of allegations of mismanaging funds but suggested that a new governance system be adopted, modelled on the new municipal corporations that had emerged after 1840. The grand chief would be elected on a one-year mandate, similar to mayors, while the members of council would be elected on two-year terms. A few months later a portion of the Kahnawake community, of uncertain size, petitioned the government to accept the recommendations, declaring they were in favour of adopting 'the method used by the whole province, among the Whites.' In 1854 the four youngest grand chiefs resigned and also asked the province to impose the elective model. They went ahead and organized an election for new chiefs, apparently on a basis of adult male suffrage, but in the result the new chiefs were also life tenured, as no change under either Haudenosaunee law or colonial law had occurred to alter the status quo. Two years later the chiefs of Kahnawake, Odanak, and Kanesetake, claiming to speak for the Seven Fires, petitioned the government to pass a law requiring that every five years there should be 'a general election of grand Chiefs for each Tribe.'[27] Such changes would not occur until after Confederation, however, with the adoption of the *Indian Act*.

It is of some interest that the chiefs at Kahnawake, unlike those at Odanak, sought to change their nation's fundamental laws by a provincial law rather than pursuant to their own internal processes. This may reflect deep divisions within the community that made it difficult to invoke traditional approaches to achieving consensus. Or it may reflect a decline in the legitimacy of the chiefs themselves as they struggled to deal with the many challenges, internal and external, that arose in the rapidly changing socio-political, economic, and technological environment of the 1840s and 1850s. Afterwards, the appearance of municipal corporations, school boards, railways, and party politics, the abolition of the seigneurial system in Lower Canada, and a more activist colonial state all impinged on Indigenous communities and put their leadership on the defensive.

Over time the engagement of the chiefs at Kahnawake with the colonial state altered. In 1820 they successfully resisted the idea that a justice of the peace should be appointed for the seigneury, presumably on the basis that such a figure would undermine their own authority.[28] Yet by 1848 they were requesting the establishment of a small claims court on their territory, pursuant to legislation of 1843 that allowed parish proprietors to petition the government to establish one. When their first petition to Lord Elgin was met with the reply that 100 signatures were needed to trigger the process, they duly found the required signatories within a few months. The government complied with their request and appointed the chiefs' preferred candidate, the Indian agent Édouard Narcisse de Lorimier, as commissioner, but unfortunately the court has left no records.[29] Some have interpreted this and other actions in which the chiefs cooperated with the colonial state as attempts to shore up their own position vis-à-vis their people.[30] Yet they were caught in a vicious circle, faced with problems of 'progress' at the very point that their own scope for independent action was being undermined by colonial courts and legislation. It is not surprising that they would attempt to make a Faustian bargain with the very entity, the colonial state, that was the source of many of their problems.[31]

Legal Personality and Indigenous Agency

One of the biggest changes affecting the powers and legitimacy of chiefs during this period arose from a new attitude by colonial courts toward the juridical status of Indigenous chiefs and their nations. As seen in chapter 17, eighteenth-century colonial governments dealt with

Indigenous communities on the basis that their chiefs had the juridical capacity to bind their people not only for purposes of Indigenous law but also within the settler legal order. They were capable grantors and grantees under both civil law and common law, and were treated, in effect, as a sui generis type of body corporate. In Upper Canada no one raised any objections to Haldimand's Grant to the Six Nations in 1785 on the basis that the latter did not possess legal personality.[32] In Lower Canada no one questioned that the band councils of mission communities could act as seigneurs, in a way similar to ecclesiastical bodies.

The first indication of a change in position by jurists occurred in the 1820 decision of the Montreal Court of King's Bench noted in chapter 17, where the legal capacity of the chiefs at Kahnawake to administer the seigneury was denied. The result was illustrative of a growing trend to view corporate status as flowing only from royal charter or legislative Act, and not from prescriptive right, past practice, or the recognition of other legal orders. The Sulpicians of Montreal encountered similar difficulties; although the order was recognized by the king of France prior to 1760 as possessing a form of legal personality, the British did not accept this as equivalent to corporate status, and much legal uncertainty resulted. The matter was not resolved until an ordinance of the Special Council in 1840 formally endowed the order with corporate status.[33]

The impact of the 1820 decision regarding Kahnawake was soon felt elsewhere. When the Huron-Wendat of Jeune-Lorette petitioned the assembly of Lower Canada in 1823 to recover their seigneury at Sillery, they were advised that they had a right to it but could not take any legal action to enforce it in court because they lacked legal personality.[34] They would have to depend on the grace of the government, which was not forthcoming. The Abenaki at Odanak continued to appoint a 'procureur' or 'syndic' to represent them in court until 1842, when a judge doubted their legal capacity to do so. Only a legally recognized corporate entity, he observed, could name an agent to act for it.[35]

It may have been this case that spawned an 1847 'Bill pour incorporer les diverses Tribus Sauvages du Bas-Canada,' which passed the assembly but was rejected by the legislative council. Speaking for the Seven Fires, the chiefs at Kahnawake opposed it, possibly because it would have resulted in the incorporation of the nation as a whole, leaving their own role in the direction of the corporation uncertain.[36] By 1856 the Seven Fires were themselves requesting incorporation, but of the chiefs as opposed to the nation. Their request was not granted, but Lower

Canada had created in its 1850 *Act for the Better Protection of the Lands and Property of Indians* the position of commissioner of Indian Lands and endowed it with legal personality.[37] The role of this official in trying to halt illicit woodcutting at Kahnawake will be discussed below.

The issue of legal personality also came up in Upper Canada and was decided in the same way without reference to the situation in Lower Canada, suggesting that broad legal-intellectual trends were at play.[38] The argument was made first in 1835 in *Doe ex dem. Jackson v Wilkes*, in which a settler in possession of a small parcel of land within the Haldimand Grant sought to defend his title against a direct grantee from the Crown. The defendant could not show a clear chain of title from the Six Nations, but even assuming he could, Chief Justice Robinson concluded that they had no title to give: the instrument conveying the Haldimand Grant was a nullity because it had only the governor's military seal attached to it and not the great seal of the province of Quebec. Title thus remained in the Crown, which had validly conveyed it to the plaintiff. According to the court the Six Nations were licencees who held the Grand River lands at the pleasure of the Crown, though as Robinson said in the next case to be considered, the invalid Haldimand deed was 'well understood and intended to be a declaration of the government that it would abstain from granting these lands to others, and would reserve them to be occupied by the Indians of the Six Nations.'[39] This conclusion alone, while disappointing for the Six Nations, would not have affected other Indigenous lands in the province, which did not depend on a Crown grant but on long possession for their validity.

It was a claim that Robinson addressed in *obiter* in *Jackson* that was more alarming and of wider import because it struck at the ability of all Indigenous communities to be recognized actors in the colonial legal order. This was the argument that the grant failed because it did not specify a capable grantee. Chief Justice Robinson would have decided this point in the plaintiff's favour as well if necessary, holding that a grant to 'the Mohawk Nation and such other of the Six Nations Indians as wish to settle on the lands described' did not describe a capable grantee, the Six Nations not being a body corporate recognized by English law.[40]

Obiter in 1835, the lack of legal personality argument became the *ratio* in *Doe d. Sheldon v Ramsay* in 1851, another Robinson decision and 'arguably his most important Indian law opinion.'[41] The plaintiff asserted title derived from the commissioners of forfeited estates, who had seized under an 1819 statute of Upper Canada the property of Benajah Mallory, convicted of treason for his role in the War of 1812.[42] Among his property was a 999-year lease of some of the Grand River lands, granted to him in 1805 by Joseph Brant as agent of the Six Nations. The court held that the Six Nations had no legal personality sufficient to appoint an agent, hence Mallory had no title for the commissioners to seize and none to convey to the plaintiff. Nor was there any issue of Haudenosaunee law to be considered: 'We cannot recognize any peculiar law of real property applying to the Indians – the common law is not part savage and part civilized.'[43]

Perhaps realizing that the logical consequence of this decision was the invalidation of any treaty between the Crown and an Indigenous nation, Justice Burns was prepared to confine the court's decision to matters of property alienation. 'The government perhaps in transactions with a tribe may recognize the acts of those known to be the principal chiefs as being the acts of the whole body; but that is a very different matter from calling upon a court of justice to give effect to the alienation of lands.'[44] Even so confined, the decision disempowered the governments of Indigenous polities from engaging in ordinary transactions with the settler world, forcing them to act through agents appointed by the government on their behalf and fostering the idea that they existed in a state of wardship. This did not necessarily have an impact on Indigenous law as applied on Indigenous territory, but it did potentially undermine traditional leadership by reducing the chiefs' powers of independent action. It is no coincidence that no reported cases in the nineteenth century involve the Six Nations or any other Indigenous nation as parties, and that virtually all issues involving Indigenous lands were litigated between settlers with rival chains of title.[45]

In one instance, ironically, the intrusive actions of the colonial state actually enhanced the organs of traditional government, in this case the Confederacy Council at Grand River. As the village of Brantford emerged on lands that had been leased or sold to settlers, the government of Upper Canada wished to separate it clearly from the Six Nations lands, get the various nations to live together on a more 'compact' site, and sell 'surplus' lands with the proceeds to be invested for their benefit. There was disagreement among the chiefs over the merits of the plan, but when it was ultimately adopted in 1847, the fact that all the nations lived in close proximity to each other strengthened the role of the Confederacy Council both within the Grand River settlement and as the interlocutor of the Six Nations with the settler world.[46] It seems to have taken some time, however, for the council to take on the dispute settlement role that the councils of the individual nations had formerly exercised.[47]

Named acting attorney general of Upper Canada at the age of 21, John Beverley Robinson (1791–1863) was appointed chief justice of the Court of King's Bench in 1829 and held the post until his death. Unreceptive to Indigenous law, he observed that 'the common law is not part savage and part civilized.'

Land Use and Citizenship

All the communities considered in this chapter looked to Indigenous law to resolve issues relating to the balance between individual and communal property, to the regulation of communal property, and to entitlement to access property on what were coming to be called Indian 'reserves.'[48] At Grand River, for example, the newly consolidated tract was divided into 100-acre allotments in 1847, each in the name of a family head. Such action did not mean that these plots were automatically treated as private property as understood by settlers. According to Haudenosaunee tradition, 'rights' in these lots were linked to responsibilities: to one's parents, children, and spouse, and to the community as a whole. Lots could be inherited or sold to other members of the Six Nations, but not to outsiders. When a lot-holder died without heirs, the land reverted to the Six Nations, though it might then be auctioned off and the funds placed in the community's trust account. Over the years council developed a variety of policies aimed at preventing exploitation and sustaining the community's natural resources for the benefit of present and future generations.[49] Both at Grand River and at Kahnawake, traditional modes of land use strongly inflected with communal values continued to be practised. At Kahnawake, the communal pasture was fenced, but the lots of individual families were not.[50]

Regulation of timber continued to be a flashpoint of conflict in many Indigenous communities, however, with some individuals violently resisting attempts by chiefs or council to restrict their ability to sell wood outside the community. In 1856 an emissary of the chiefs at Kahnawake was nearly killed when he remonstrated with a number of men who had allegedly cut thousands of cords of wood illegally. When the wrongdoers refused to comply with the chiefs' demands, the entire community rose up against them and destroyed the huts that served as their base. The Indian agent on this occasion strongly supported the maintenance of customary governance of the woods, observing that fifteen or twenty men were trying to arrogate to themselves resources that belonged to 1,300 or 1,400 people.[51] At Grand River the council established forest wardens to protect timber, but one of them was nearly beaten to death in 1865 when carrying out his duties.[52] At Odanak, the council appointed agents to pursue those who cut communal wood without permission and take legal action, but these efforts were sidetracked by the 1842 court decision noted earlier that doubted the Abenaki council's legal capacity to do so. The commissioner of

Indian lands had some success in pursuing actions in the superior court in the 1850s against those cutting wood illegally at Kahnawake, but his remedial repertoire was anaemic under the 1850 *Act for the Better Protection of the Land and Property of Indians*; no fines or penalties were provided for transgressors, and in most cases only the return of the wood was ordered.[53] Moreover, the commissioner was accountable to the government, not the chiefs, further diminishing their authority.

Entitlement to allotments by those of mixed European-Indigenous ancestry also posed a difficult problem. It was particularly acute at Kahnawake, where settlers, both French and English, had long lived and intermarried with the Indigenous inhabitants. More than once in the 1830s the chiefs demanded that the government remove all white people from Kahnawake, not because of their race as such but as the result of a perception that they were not prepared to follow the traditional laws and set a bad example for Indigenous youth. In theory whites needed a licence from the superintendent to remain at Kahnawake, but the department seldom expelled them once settled there. In 1830 it was reported that there were 280 settlers and their families at Kahnawake, which would have represented a significant portion of the population, but the line between 'settler' and 'Indigenous' was not always easy to draw.[54] Some settlers were, in the opinion of the resident priest, Joseph Marcoux, 'sauvagifiés' – culturally similar to the Kahnawakehro:non.[55] Conflicts over this issue were temporarily resolved by an agreement in 1840 that all children of an Indigenous mother would be considered Indigenous, regardless of the father's identity.

This was the traditional approach to membership under Haudenosaunee law, but it widened the pool of persons eligible to use Kahnawake land at time when the good land in the seigneury was mostly filled up. Traditional law allowed any member of the community to clear and work land as needed, but resentment grew that the children of Europeans competed for space with those of full Indigenous ancestry. The fecundity of settler families could be truly remarkable, intensifying the problem. Gervase Macomber was a young man from Massachusetts who at the age of sixteen attached himself to Thomas Arakwente of Kahnawake, who is featured in chapter 17. Young Macomber learned French and Mohawk, converted to Catholicism, and later became a government interpreter. He helped Arakwente with his various business activities, began some of his own, and married Arakwente's daughter

Charlotte. She died young after they had three children together, and Macomber went on to marry twice more, both times to non-Indigenous women, producing twenty-three more children while he lived at Kahnawake.[56]

Issues of land, community identity, and chiefly authority were all inextricably connected, and all posed challenges for Indigenous law. The inclusion of a definition of 'Indian' in the Lower Canadian Act of 1850 was a challenge to the power of the chiefs and ultimately the community to determine its own membership, and strongly resisted at Kahnawake and in the other Seven Fires communities. The Act adopted an expansive definition of membership, including not just those of 'Indian blood, reputed to belong to the particular Body or Tribe of Indians interested in such lands,' but anyone married to such a person, and their descendants.[57] In their joint petition of 1856, the chiefs reversed their 1840 position on how membership should descend in mixed-race families:[58]

> 3 An Indian if lawfully married to a white woman his wife becometh an Indian and her Children reputed to belong to the particular Tribe or Body of Indians. But if male of the Children as above mentioned should marry to a white woman the Children issue of such marriages lose all rights of Indians.
>
> 4 An Indian woman who is lawfully married to a white man loses all her Indian rights [and, presumably, so would their children].

This might be seen as a form of gender discrimination, but some Indigenous scholars have seen the move as a desperate attempt at 'protecting the community from a possible take-over by non-Indian men,' given that marriages between non-Indigenous men and Indigenous women were much more common than the converse.[59] Whatever the interpretation placed on it, such a dramatic shift does prove that Haudenosaunee traditions could be adapted to respond to new situations for which there was no historical precedent.

A final land issue related to the building of transportation infrastructure and other facilities on Indigenous territories. 'Canal fever' in the 1830s, the railway revolution in the 1840s and 1850s, and demands by settlers for a more extensive road network put pressure on Indigenous communities occupying lands suitable for these purposes. Where formerly the colonial state negotiated the location of roads, schools, and the like with the chiefs if access to their land was required, it now began to give powers of expropriation to transportation companies, reducing the ability of Indigenous communities to stop or reshape these initiatives. The Six Nations were the first to experience this new regime.[60] With the opening of the Erie Canal in 1825, Upper Canadian businessmen sought to redirect cargo – which could now easily reach New York – by constructing the Welland Canal, enable access to the St Lawrence and the Atlantic, and thus keep the commerce within Canada. In 1829 a dam was constructed at the mouth of the Grand River to raise the water level in the Welland River through connecting waterways, and future works were contemplated to make the shallow Grand River a transportation corridor. The Grand River Navigation Company, incorporated by Act of the legislature in 1832, was given the power to 'appropriate such land and land covered by water as may be necessary' for the company's purposes and specifically authorized to enter upon lands 'of or belonging to the King ... or to the Six Nations of Indians residing thereon.' If the parties could not agree on a price for any lands taken, a panel of arbitrators would make a final decision on the value of the property. Where Six Nations lands were involved, the chief officer of the Indian Department was to appoint one of the three arbitrators, and any award was to be paid to that official 'to the use of the said Indians.'[61] The business side of this tragic saga is dealt with in chapter 32, which shows that it was common to give corporations expropriation power; here it is sufficient to note that the Six Nations lands were flooded on occasion, crops ruined, and traditional use patterns disrupted by the works carried out by the company. With expropriation at the ready, the colonial state now had a tool that could override Indigenous land law at will, and undermine the authority of the chiefs into the bargain.

Kahnawake had a similar experience, occupying a site on the south bank of the St Lawrence that made it ideal for a railway terminus and trans-shipment point for cargo going to and from Montreal. A railway line from Plattsburgh, New York, was duly built through the seigneury in 1852, although the opening of the Victoria Bridge in 1859 made it less competitive and it was eventually abandoned. As Taiaiake Alfred has observed, 'With the construction of the rail line, Kahnawake was pulled from its position as an isolated community on the periphery of North American industrial society and thrust directly into the new reality of the 19th century.'[62] The Lake St Louis and Province Line Railway Company (LSLPL) was incorporated by Act of the legislature of Lower Canada in 1847 and featured provisions regarding expropriation and arbitration similar to those in the Grand River Navigation Company's 1832 statute. Neither the 1847 Act nor an 1850 Act authorizing the merger of the LSLPL Railway with the Montreal and Lachine Railway referred specifically to lands occupied by the Mohawks, but an 1852 Act dealing with the merged entity did so. It authorized the taking of lands at the 'Indian village of Caughnawaga' but stated that 'if any land belonging to, or in the possession of, any tribe of Indians in the Province shall be required,' the chief officer of the Indian Department was to name an arbitrator and the award was to be paid to him, following the pattern set in the Grand River Act.[63]

In at least two respects the Kahnawake experience differed from Grand River, however. The phrase referring to land 'belonging to ... any tribe of Indians,' without reference to the Crown holding such land in trust, was different from the formulation in the Upper Canadian Act and shows the state of flux in legal conceptions of such property rights. Even though the Gage decision of 1762 had clearly stated that the Crown possessed underlying title to Kahnawake, there was no reference to it in this Act, implying outright ownership by the Mohawks.[64] Also there is some suggestion that the chiefs at Kahnawake may have come to an agreement about the sale price for the lands taken, rather than forcing the matter to arbitration, as happened at Grand River. If so, this may have been another factor undermining their authority and provoking the 1852 petition of the deputy chiefs who accused them of 'despotism.'[65]

Several events in the 1860s illustrate the cross-currents running through this period with regard to the integrity of Indigenous law. In Lower Canada, the Seven Fires alliance dissolved in about 1860 for reasons that are not clear.[66] While always a fairly loose association, it nonetheless provided some bargaining power for this set of small Indigenous communities in their dealings with the colonial authorities. They made a strong response to the new legislative incursions of the early 1850s into traditional governance, but a decade later the association faded from the scene. At Kahnawake the chiefs were so discouraged by the constant intrusions of the colonial state, the railway, and the spillover effects of the explosive growth of Montreal that they held a referendum in 1863 on whether the reserve should be sold, with the community using the funds to move elsewhere. The proposal gained majority support, but the Indian Department would not pay the desired amount and the community stayed put.[67]

Meanwhile, the Confederacy Council at Grand River had gained considerable strength after the consolidation of the national settlements in 1847. It instituted a mainly patrilineal system of landholding and established stricter controls over land use, although its efforts to conserve the timber resource met with little success. Challenges to its composition by younger dissidents influenced by settler democracy did not secure widespread support. And in 1865, when the new council house at Ohsweken had its grand opening, it was marked with a recitation of the Great Law. As a group of settler men were planning the new confederation known as the Dominion of Canada (without any Indigenous input), the leaders of the Six Nations were reaffirming their dedication to their four-hundred-year-old Confederacy.[68]

25

The Legal Professions

A variety of people dealt with the law every day – JPs, constables, other lay legal workers such as conveyancers, and, of course, lawyers. In the long run the drive towards professionalization helped the last-named do better in this competitive process than others. This chapter first examines entry requirements and professional governance, both areas in which British North America developed a unique hybrid legal culture, distinct from that of both Britain and the United States. The second looks at legal practice itself – where were lawyers located, what kind of work did they do, whom did they do it for, and how successful were they? That section paints a picture of professions increasingly tied to the business world, facilitators of corporate and commercial activity. In the third section we deal in detail with a topic partially covered in the first – legal education – examining the advent of university-based legal education. Universities began to play a role in lawyers' preparation before Confederation, but apart from in Lower Canada it was a minor role indeed. The fourth section examines locally produced legal literature, and here again Lower Canada was to the fore, especially before the 1850s. Finally, we analyse law reporting, which was not a feature of any colony other than Upper Canada until the 1850s. For all that advocates for it in the legal profession argued that it was a public service and ought to be paid for by the state, it was essentially a private operation for much of this period, because most people saw it as something that principally benefited the legal profession.

Entry and Governance

As of 1815, the bar and the notarial profession had taken only the first steps in their quest for autonomy, respectability, and influence in colonial society. While Lower Canadian notaries practised in many rural settlements and small towns as well as in urban centres, early colonial lawyers were found mainly in the capitals or the larger towns such as Montreal and Saint John. Often connected to the governing, mercantile, military, or ecclesiastical elites through birth or marriage, lawyers preferred to remain in the capital, where there was some chance of picking up a governmental office or patronage appointment that could supplement the very uncertain rewards to be gained from private practice. In Upper Canada the Law Society was statutorily empowered to govern the nascent profession and to compel membership, but elsewhere legislative intervention did not provide such autonomy, leaving the legal professions to be regulated mostly by the courts and by their own informal practices. While some lawyers held important positions, their status often derived as much from their family or social connections as from their professional identity. Prior to 1815 lawyers were relatively few and somewhat less important in the legal hierarchy than JPs. Eighteenth-century almanacks listed JPs immediately after the superior court judges and did not provide a listing of lawyers at all.[1]

All of this would change in the next few decades, as British North American governments turned increasingly to formal law, especially legislation, as a means of societal control and organization, and lawyers became the ubiquitous 'fixers' and brokers of colonial society. The bar and the notarial profession became much more active in pursuing the four goals identified by one leading historian of the profession as characteristic of lawyers' collective action: controlling entrance to the profession by specifying the necessary educational and/or practical attainments; defending a particular area of work and preventing others from doing it; regulating each other's behaviour; and protecting and enhancing corporate honour and status.[2] Both New Brunswick and Nova Scotia formed Barristers' Societies in 1825, albeit as voluntary associations rather than statutory bodies, while Lower Canada's notaries followed Upper Canada's lead by securing a statutory monopoly on membership and governance in 1847, and Lower Canada's advocates followed in 1849. During the space of a generation or so, the bar moved from defining its status as class-related (keeping out the riff-raff) to basing its claims to respectability on educational attainments, professional merit, and economic utility, following in this respect the broader current of political reform and the demand for 'careers open to talents' in colonial society. This trend was most evident in Upper Canada, where the Law Society disclaimed authority over attorneys in 1822 in an effort to reserve for barristers alone the prestige they were afforded in England. Young lawyer William Draper lamented in 1830 that 'the moral character of the profession is lowered by the combination [of barrister and attorney], for ... I am somewhat disposed to think that there is much in the business of an Attorney which ... is foreign to that high tone of feeling which cannot be too much cultivated at the bar.'[3] In 1857, however, the Law Society began to reclaim this authority, realizing that its earlier action had weakened what was, largely for economic reasons, a single profession in North America, as well as depriving it of any control over the number of entrants enabled to practise law.[4]

Legislation in 1846 allowed the New Brunswick Barristers' Society to incorporate and made it, though still a voluntary society, the gatekeeper to the legal profession, while all law societies and the Lower Canadian notariat established entrance exams for would-be articling students during this period, as well as exit exams, and some also administered intermediate exams.[5] The logical outcome of this process – though not necessarily the only one, as the Upper Canadian experience would show – was the establishment of university legal education, but when established it would function in tandem with apprenticeship, rather than replacing it, as it did in the United States. Indeed, the contrast in this regard with both the United States and England was stark. From the 1820s, apprenticeship was being abolished in the United States as an anti-democratic barrier to entry to the legal profession, with only nine of thirty-nine states retaining it in any form by 1860. This in turn led to the dismantling of all bar associations but one, that of Philadelphia, leaving the governance of the legal profession to the courts and the market, but mostly to the individual lawyer's own conscience.[6] Lawyers had no organized voice until bar associations began to reconstitute themselves after the Civil War. In England, meanwhile, barristers were loosely governed by the inns of court, while solicitors had formed the Incorporated Law Society as a voluntary association in 1825. Both strongly resisted the move to university legal education, while the older universities showed little interest in offering it. The two professions spent most of their time skirmishing with each other and resisted all claims to democratic accountability via legislation, thus finding themselves increasingly out of step with public opinion.[7] British North American lawyers would draw on the experience of both jurisdictions in developing their hybrid professional culture.

The return of peace in 1815 led to a large influx of candidates to the bar and the notariat in British North America, as young men sought out opportunities beyond the agricultural pursuits of their ancestors. In Lower Canada in particular, the six collèges classiques that existed by 1833 were churning out well-educated young men by the hundreds; they could boast an enrolment of a thousand students across the province in 1834, many of whom would enter the legal professions. In New Brunswick the profession in the 1840s and 1850s was more 'crowded' than at any other period in the nineteenth century, and in Nova Scotia and Upper Canada it was much the same.[8] This growth had political as well as economic consequences, but these played out differently in different colonies. All provinces would converge to the governance model of the Law Society of Upper Canada by the early twentieth century and agreed, except for Ontario, that university legal education was a good thing, but this convergence was by no means a foregone conclusion during the first half of the nineteenth century.

The extremes were represented by Upper and Lower Canada. In Upper Canada the watchwords were continuity and incremental change, summed up in the chapter title of a major work on the nineteenth-century professions: 'The Placid Progress of the Law.'[9] Debates there were over the requirements for entry to the profession, but these were usually carried out under the aegis of the Law Society, which was secure in its statutory powers, its mandate to speak for the entire profession, and its strong connections to the governing elite. Generally speaking the society maintained a good working relationship with the legislature and could obtain passage of any legislation it desired. In Lower Canada, by contrast, the desire of the legal professions to attain the kind of corporate organization and autonomy possessed by lawyers in Upper Canada since 1797 ran up against strong governmental resistance and became tangled with the quest for responsible government.[10] The mainly British clique around the governor and in the legislative council were all too aware of the leadership exercised in the assembly by francophone lawyers, especially the advocate Louis-Joseph Papineau, elected speaker of the assembly in 1815 and head of the Parti Patriote in 1826. The province's rulers feared that any further enhancement of the professions' autonomy would make them even more effective centres of opposition to the government.

The government's fears were proven correct during the 'affaire des commissions' in 1830. Lower Canadian practice was unique in British North America in providing that commissions as advocates or notaries were granted by the governor as opposed to the courts or the Law Society, as in Upper Canada. On the death of George IV in 1830, the government took the view that such commissions were held at pleasure and had to be renewed on the death of the sovereign according to a statute of Queen Anne's reign. The proposed fee, three guineas, was a substantial sum but only served as a focus for the real issue, which was the independence of the professions. Outraged, the assembly contested the legality of this move and demanded the removal of Attorney General James Stuart based on this and other grievances. The governor's suspension of Stuart was upheld in London and he was dismissed from his post, though he later rehabilitated himself and was named chief justice of Quebec in 1838.[11] The assembly's success in this controversy did not, however, lessen conflict. In the 1830s and 1840s the bar and the notariat made multiple unsuccessful attempts to obtain corporate status, an issue connected to the struggle for patronage. The reservation of most official legal and administrative positions for anglophones was particularly resented in light of the large numbers of underemployed francophone legal professionals. Eventually these tensions boiled over: it was no coincidence that at least eighteen notaries could be found among the revolutionary leaders of 1837–8, or that three notaries and a notary's apprentice (but no advocates) were hanged in the wake of the rebellions.[12]

It took the advent of responsible government before incorporation of the professions was finally allowed to occur: the notaries achieved it just before, in 1847, the bar immediately after, in 1849.[13] In both cases the tripartite division of the colony, going back to the French regime, was respected. There would be three distinct boards ('chambres') of notaries, one each for Montreal, Quebec, and Trois-Rivières (including the district of St-François); boards proliferated thereafter until 1870 when a province-wide chambre des notaires was created. The 1849 Act created only one barreau for the province, but there would be three sections, one for each of the three districts, each with its own bâtonnier and executive; the general council of the barreau itself would be composed of the executives of the three sections, who would in turn elect the barreau's executive from among themselves. This decentralization of authority, also seen in the organization of the courts, was one of the most enduring differences between the two Canadas.

The experience of the Maritimes lay somewhere between these two extremes, featuring a weak echo of the more dramatic events occurring in the bar south of the border. The Barristers' Societies survived but did not thrive: members drifted away in the 1830s and 1840s, while recruitment to the bar plummeted in the 1850s. Populist legislatures in the United States, even though often well stocked with lawyers, manifested a mostly hostile attitude to the 'privileges' of the bar, and similar attitudes appeared in the Maritimes after responsible government. The New Brunswick Assembly reduced the length of apprenticeship by a year in 1863 without even consulting the Barristers' Society, then in 1867 slashed by seven-eighths the admission fee the society proposed to collect from aspiring attorneys, reduced from two years to one the time an attorney had to wait to be called as a barrister, and forced the society to recognize LLB degrees from Harvard or elsewhere as entitling the holder to a year's reduction in the articling period. Nova Scotia formally removed the lawyers' monopoly on pleading before the superior courts for reward in 1850, though it restored it in 1864; in the latter year Nova Scotia abolished the year's wait between admission as an attorney and call as a barrister. When compared to the United States, however, these measures hardly constituted an assault on the bar: at Confederation a three- or four-year apprenticeship was still required in the Maritimes, and in principle the apprentice could neither be paid nor accept outside employment, though this rule was not rigorously enforced. As of 1860 the Nova Scotia legal profession at least was experiencing a kind of renewal: the Barristers' Society, having achieved incorporation in 1858 after failing in 1844, gave itself a new constitution in 1860 and began to play a more assertive and dynamic role in professional and provincial life.[14]

Beyond the Maritimes and the Canadas, the issues were very different as the legal profession was still in its formative stages. In British Columbia all the early lawyers were English imports, but they were obliged to conform to North American ways. An 1858 order of the Supreme Court permitted barristers to act as attorneys and vice versa, while an 1863 order permitted lawyers from elsewhere in British North America to be called to the local bar. In 1869 thirteen lawyers, including both barristers and attorneys, met at Victoria to 'constitute themselves' into a society called the Law Society of British Columbia, following the pattern by now well established in the east.[15] In Assiniboia and in Newfoundland prior to 1825, in the absence of qualified lawyers the role of informal pleaders resembled that played by the practiciens of New

France. In the former settlement, the only qualified lawyers prior to 1870 were the recorders of Rupert's Land, who were not precluded from carrying on a private practice but obviously could not plead before their own courts. The recorders permitted 'agents' to act for the parties to litigation; over time, a cadre of these attorneys-in-fact came to specialize in this service and to charge for it. Their abilities were not necessarily inferior: in a prosecution for an attempted abortion in 1863, two such agents appeared on each side and 'conducted themselves in the courtroom much as modern barristers would.'[16]

In Newfoundland, too, informal pleaders proliferated. The governor lamented in 1820 that 'any person may come into Court and plead as attorney for another, whatever may be his profession or character, as regular attorneys have hitherto been unknown in this island,' adding that these pleaders were 'mostly bankrupt merchants, having never had any education for the profession of the law.'[17] The profession was put on a formal basis by the Royal Charter of Justice of 1825, which empowered the newly enlarged Supreme Court to admit qualified barristers or solicitors from the British Isles to the bar of Newfoundland, as well as those who had served a five-year clerkship under a local barrister. All so admitted would be authorized 'to act as well in the character of barristers and advocates, as of proctors, attorneys and solicitors,' thus conforming to the North American norm of a unified profession. For the first time the legal profession was given a monopoly on representing clients in court, except that the court retained a discretion to admit 'fit and proper,' albeit unqualified, persons to plead in a given locale if sufficient numbers of qualified lawyers were unavailable.[18] In 1834 one of the first Acts of the newly created legislature permitted the incorporation of the Law Society of Newfoundland, with power to regulate entrance to and the conduct of the profession, but no power to compel membership. The Act, drafted by the conservative Chief Justice Henry John Boulton, reiterated the requirements set out in 1825. It was seen by some as a controversial attempt to exclude the Irish and locals without establishment connections.[19]

While there were by definition no restrictions on who could perform as informal pleaders, it is unlikely that any were women or non-Caucasian. As for the bar and the notariat, their cultural and gender makeup reflected the prevailing view that only white males possessed the leadership capacities necessary to join these professions. The category of white male itself became more diverse over time, as Catholics, the Irish, and some economically disadvantaged men joined the professions, but multiethnic immigration on any scale would occur only towards the end of the century, and domestic Black communities remained very small. The first group to break into the fraternity of white Christian lawyers were the Jews of Lower Canada. Aaron Ezekiel Hart, the first Jew to be called to the bar in British North America (1824), would be joined by 1837 by no fewer than seven members of his extended family, all third-generation Canadian Jews. While they supported the government at the time of the rebellions, Hart's cousin Aaron Philip Hart 'distinguished himself as one of the most ardent defenders of Patriotes' rights.' The only Indigenous person known to be called to the bar before Confederation was Solomon White, the son of a Wyandot chief and a French-Canadian mother, who was born on the Huron Reserve near Amherstburg, Ontario. Called to the bar in 1865, he had a successful legal, business, and political career thereafter – he was the first Indigenous legislator at Queen's Park – but it would be many decades before he had any successor. The only Black lawyer was Robert Sutherland, born in Jamaica to a Scottish father and Black mother, and sent by his parents to Queen's University. Upon graduating in 1852 he was the first university graduate of colour in Canada and went on to become the first Black lawyer in 1855. He practised for over twenty years in small Ontario centres before his death in 1878 – and left his entire estate to his alma mater, saving it from bankruptcy or absorption by the University of Toronto.[20]

The impulse to collective, and preferably state-ratified, action by the British North American legal professions resulted in a very different trajectory for professional governance than that found in the United States, one attributable to a difference in fundamental constitutional ideas between the two jurisdictions. The state was not an enemy in British North America, it was an ally. It was an instrument for getting things done. Responsible government was a way of ensuring that the things that got done were those that served domestic, not just imperial purposes. That difference insulated British North America from two American innovations of the period: free entry to the legal profession and an elective judiciary.[21] When one turns to day-to-day lawyering and law office organization, however, the influence of American ideas and practices is much more evident.

The Business of Lawyering

The rapid influx into the profession in the quarter-century before 1850 inspired changes to the location and nature of legal practice, although not to its form or organization, which remained resolutely small-scale until late in the nineteenth century.[22] Not all the new recruits could be accommodated in the few urban centres, nor could most expect to secure government patronage. Hence a migration into many small towns, right up to the settlement frontier, proceeded apace. These new lawyers had to provide a variety of services to a wide clientele in a competitive environment if they were to survive. They became active in community endeavours and business enterprises of all kinds because, as Harry King of Windsor, Nova Scotia, observed to his fiancée in 1830, 'The more we are before the public the more we become known, and the more we are known, the more likely we are to succeed in our profession.'[23] Even travelling the circuit with the Supreme Court, made easier with the advent of railways, was as much a means of advertising oneself as it was a moneymaker.

It was in Montreal, the unrivalled British North American centre of commercial and industrial growth in the middle decades of the nineteenth century, where the future relationship of Canadian lawyers to business enterprise was most evident. Several law offices worked closely with corporations in the booming fields of transportation, manufacturing, banking, and resource-extraction.[24] They provided business counsel as much as legal advice, sat on corporate boards of companies they advised, and often took company shares in payment for their services, thus becoming part owners of their clients. Their legal advice was important, especially in the polyglot legal environment of pre-codification Lower Canada, where the flipside of legal uncertainty was the availability of great flexibility. Law offices such as that of John Abbott, long-serving (but part-time) dean of McGill University's Faculty of Law (1855–76), director on many corporate boards, and future prime minister of Canada, took advantage of this flexibility to generate extensive contractual and other precedents to guide their clients' enterprises, which these offices then shared with each other. British North American lawyers' involvement with business mirrored the American experience much more than the English; work on solicitors' involvement in railway law in the United Kingdom, for example, reveals that railway companies resented their dependence on solicitors' advice and found them, with some justification, a constant impediment in the pursuit of their commercial goals.[25]

If this immersion in the world of business bristled with potential conflicts of interest, it did not seem to worry most lawyers of the period. As in the United States, resolution of such conflicts was thought to be a matter for the individual lawyer's conscience, not a reason to adopt or police ethical rules. Resistance to this laissez-faire attitude did surface in Lower Canada, however, largely as a result of efforts by the energetic young lawyer Gonzalve Doutre.[26] Reacting to the crush of new entrants to the bar post-1850, Doutre proposed measures to raise standards in order to tighten up admissions and ensure that the conduct of advocates was above reproach. His ideas formed the basis of a total revision of the bar's 1849 constitutive Act in 1866, and two years later he persuaded the general council of the barreau to adopt a set of stringent ethical guidelines based almost entirely on a French work relating to the duties of advocates in that country.[27]

French advocates of the day prized their independence and were concerned above all to remain 'above the fray,' to avoid fraternizing with clients, and to forsake any work that might be considered incompatible with this high calling. They maintained a list of 'incompatibilités,' which for most of the nineteenth century included journalism, teaching (including university law teaching), business agent, any commercial or salaried employment, and company directorships. French advocates were even more particular than English barristers in this respect, since the latter did not frown on accepting directorships as long as the barrister did not also advise the company.[28] Doutre's guidelines duly reproduced these restrictions, stating that 'l'avocat ne doit se livrer à aucun emploi, fonction, charge, métier, négoce, courtage, etc., etc.,' and further, that they should not advertise or solicit clients in any way. While there was certainly work to be done to make advocates more aware of ethical problems, these strictures were entirely unsuited to the way the profession had developed in Lower Canada over the previous half-century and more. It is hard to believe that the barreau itself expected they would be followed, and if anything Lower Canadian advocates became more rather than less involved in business affairs after Confederation.

One form of 'incompatibility' did trouble Victorian lawyers, at least when it initially appeared. Large railway companies generated so much legal work that the idea of securing in-house counsel arose. Among these was Aemilius Irving, who joined the Great Western Railway in Hamilton as its second in-house counsel in 1855; this was slightly later than in the United States, but ahead of England, where the idea was pioneered in 1861. The idea of a salaried lawyer was shocking to mid-century ideas of independent professionalism, leading the *Upper Canada Law Journal* to call Irving's action 'a studied insult to the profession.'[29] But before long the profession had accommodated itself to this new arrangement and such criticism disappeared, providing more proof, if any were needed, that Doutre's rarefied concept of the lawyer's role was not reflected in practice.

The size of law firms prior to the very end of the nineteenth century remained small. Abbott's office, for example, never had more than three lawyers and two apprentices at any given time, and the vast majority of lawyers both within and outside urban centres practised as sole practitioners. Even though these firms were small, their internal organization was often unstructured, bordering on chaotic, with 'management' of the firm delegated to a hapless articling student. The irony was that these firms 'may not have cared about organizing themselves. But they and their contemporaries were clearly good at, and committed to, the promulgation of legal knowledge.'[30]

The Emergence of University Legal Education

This desire to synthesize, systematize, deepen, and promulgate legal knowledge would become linked to the goal of providing a more structured preparation for aspiring lawyers than could be provided through apprenticeship alone. Thus arose two major intellectual developments of the period: the development of university education in law, and the production, on a rather impressive scale for a collection of relatively small jurisdictions, of local legal literature. Both were connected to the movement to reform and codify colonial law discussed in the preceding chapter, itself given impetus by the transition to responsible government.

The rise of university education in law as preparation for professional practice was a North American phenomenon. On the continent, Roman law and canon law had long been taught in the universities, but their study was connected to history, theology, and philosophy, not to legal practice. Roman law had long been taught in the English universities, but it was connected to the practice of law only in the ecclesiastical and admiralty courts, where a doctorate in civil law was required. Only in 1679 did Louis XIV order French universities to begin teaching 'national' law (mainly the customs of the various regions of France). Canon law was no longer taught in the English universities after the Reformation, nor was common law until the nineteenth century, except for Blackstone's brief stint in the 1750s. Even when national law began to be taught in France after 1679, or the common law in English universities after 1800, there was no connection with professional entry, which remained solely under the control of professional bodies. It was the implosion of professional governance in the United States under the assault of Jacksonian democracy, and the consequent demise of apprenticeship, that caused some American universities to step into the resulting vacuum by providing a legal education expressly designed to ease professional entry. No professional entities now existed to oppose such a move, and the ultimate test of the success of this endeavour would be judged by the market. Would aspiring lawyers pay for such an education or not?[31]

In both the United States and Canada, there was initially enthusiasm for such a form of education, followed by a decade or two of waning interest before the enterprise took off again. But even in the United States, until the significant reforms engineered by Christopher Columbus Langdell after his appointment as dean of Harvard Law School in 1870, university legal education was a shoestring enterprise. Harvard itself had only two full-time professors until 1855, when a third was added, and they taught virtually all the courses. After the heroic age of Joseph Story, when the law school had a total enrolment of some 150 students, the numbers settled back to about 100 in the 1850s and 1860s, even though the sole admission standard was English literacy, and the degree took only two years, sometimes less.[32] Jeremiah Travis of rural New Brunswick, with no prior university experience, managed to secure his Harvard LLB in sixteen months in 1865–6.[33] At other law schools, in both the United States and Canada, there would be at most one full-time professor, and all other instruction would be provided by lawyers or judges teaching part-time, with classes often given in law offices rather than on campus. University legal education in North America was everywhere a bootstrap operation in its early decades.

A law course was started at the University of King's College in Toronto in 1842, but the first professor of common and civil law, William Hume Blake, resigned in 1847. The faculty was abolished in 1853 pursuant to an agreement whereby the Law Society itself would provide a course of lectures, at which attendance would be mandatory. Thereafter the Law Society insisted on students following its own program and refused to award any credit for university legal education, effectively eliminating any incentive for local universities to offer it. Thus, the five men awarded the LLB in 1863 by Queen's University in Kingston were the first and last graduates of the program, which closed in 1864 in light of the Law Society's refusal to recognize it. In this Upper Canada was an outlier, but the Law Society's own educational efforts were substantial and not significantly different from those at the nascent law faculties elsewhere in North America.[34]

A more welcoming attitude to university legal education was manifested in Lower Canada, where the 1849 Act incorporating the bar not only contemplated that university legal education would soon be established but positively encouraged it: the normal apprenticeship of five years was reduced to four for those with a university degree, and to three for those who had also followed 'a regular and complete Course of Law in any incorporated College or Seminary.' Pursuant to the Act of 1847, aspiring notaries had to henceforth follow a five-year course of classical study before entering the profession and then complete four years of apprenticeship. While the chambers of notaries lobbied the provincial law faculties to provide instruction appropriate for notaries, they did not succeed until the very end of the nineteenth century.[35]

A university course in law was established at McGill University in 1848; it would be followed by one at the Jesuits' Collège Ste-Marie in Montreal (1851) under the superintendence of the flamboyant and indefatigable François-Maximilien Bibaud, and another at Université Laval in Quebec City in 1854. McGill required the student to follow three terms in arts (one year) and six terms (two years) in law in order to obtain the BCL degree. It was established under trying circumstances: when the Parliament buildings in Montreal were burned down in the Rebellion Losses riots in 1849, McGill's principal fled to Toronto, and it was not clear who was in charge of the university for the next four years. For the twenty-two men who enrolled in 1848, perhaps it was for the best that they paid their fees of two pounds per term directly to the sole professor, William Badgley, just as law students did in medieval Bologna and went to his office for classes. But in the end only five graduated with the BCL degree in 1850.[36]

Things improved a little in 1853, when law was made a separate faculty at McGill, of which Badgley was made (part-time) dean. He was assisted by two professors, John Abbott and Frederick William Torrance, and two lecturers, Toussaint-Antoine-Rodolphe Laflamme and Pierre-Richard Lafrenaye, who were in turn promoted to professorships in 1855; all were part-time appointments. Abbott himself received a BCL in 1854 and was thus Canada's first prime minister to possess a university law degree, as well as being Canada's first native-born prime minister.[37] In 1855 Badgley was named to the superior court of Quebec, obliging him to move to that city just in time to join the newly established Faculty of Law at Laval, and vacating the McGill deanship for his erstwhile law partner John Abbott. The dean of the Laval faculty, part-time of course, was Augustin-Norbert Morin, who was on the side of the Patriotes during the rebellions but was now co-premier of the province of Canada. Elevated to the superior court in 1855, Morin continued as dean until his death in 1865. He apparently did not give many lectures but was no doubt absorbed in his work as one of the commissioners charged with creating a civil code for Lower Canada, a post to which he was appointed in 1859. Badgley did not do much teaching either, leading the rector of Laval to lament, 'Nos juges c'est bon pour l'honneur, il en faudrait d'autres pour le travail.'[38] The 'others' who did most of the teaching were Jacques Crémazie, a legal author of some renown, brother of the famous Quebec poet Octave Crémazie, and Morin's successor as dean; and Auguste-Eugène Aubry, holder of the chair in Roman Law, who had been imported from France in 1857, only to resign in 1865.

The curriculum at the new law schools was evidence of Lower Canada's hybrid legal culture. At McGill it covered Justinian's *Institutes*, the first and second titles of the *Coutume de Paris* as set out in the *Commentaire de Ferrière* (in twelve volumes), the *Traité des obligations* by Robert-Joseph Pothier, and volume four of Blackstone's *Commentaries* (on criminal law). The next year, public and constitutional law, international law, and a course 'On the Origin and History of the Laws of France, England and Lower Canada' were added. The early program at Laval focused on civil law and Roman law, with criminal law, commercial law, and maritime law added later. Roman law was taught as a historical subject, rather than as part of the living law of Lower Canada, an approach much criticized by Bibaud, given that much of the law of obligations in the colony derived directly from Roman law rather than the Custom of Paris. Laval's approach aimed to instil a love of erudition, history, and culture, however – qualities deemed necessary for the formation of an elite – and was not oriented exclusively to the transmission of the precepts of positive law. In keeping with this mandate, students were also required to attend public lectures given by the faculty of arts on philosophy, history, and literature.

The courses at Laval were timed to enable students to pursue their law degree and serve their apprenticeship concurrently, an arrangement authorized by an 1853 amendment to the 1849 Act incorporating the barreau.[39] Students typically attended a one-hour lecture at 8 a.m., proceeded to their offices, then returned to the faculty for lectures at 3:30 and 4:30, while the lectures in arts might occupy two evenings a week. In spite of this attempt to accommodate the needs of articling students and their principals, the law schools struggled to attract and retain students. At Laval, only thirty-six candidates received law degrees in the decade 1856–65, while only thirty-three men received McGill BCL degrees between 1850 and 1860.[40] Bibaud's rival law school at the Collège Ste-Marie was initially more successful. He could boast in 1863 that eighty-six men had graduated in the previous dozen years, but the school was forced to close in 1867 when legislation of the previous year required that law degrees be conferred only by institutions affiliated with universities, which the Collège Ste-Marie was not.[41]

Meanwhile, dozens of would-be lawyers from the Maritimes were attending the newly established law faculties in the United States in the 1850s and 1860s, pending the creation of their own in the later nineteenth century.[42] University legal education would not be a prerequisite to legal practice in Canada until the mid-twentieth century, but it supplemented the sometimes haphazard exposure to legal fundamentals offered by apprenticeship, provided a certain cachet, and may have assisted some lawyers to distinguish themselves from competitors. The latter were not just other lawyers, but also lay legal workers such as JPs who provided a variety of solicitorial legal services, conveyancing and will drafting in particular. University legal education also helped the legal profession in North America to re-establish its ancient reputation as a learned profession, as opposed to a mere trade to be learned through apprenticeship. It bears repeating, however, that much of what lawyers did in the nineteenth century required business acumen as much as legal prowess, for which the university provided little preparation.[43]

Legal Literature

British North American lawyers did not wait for the establishment of universities to begin producing legal literature. In fact, the middle decades of the nineteenth century were something of a golden age for locally produced legal literature, as they were for Canadian literature in general, in spite of the problems associated with a small market. Some of these works were subsidized by colonial governments in light of their public utility, such as the first original JP manual in British North America, John George Marshall's *The Justice of the Peace and County and Township Officer in the Province of Nova Scotia* (1837); the Nova Scotia Assembly voted £289 to cover its printing costs and £50 to Marshall for his work.[44] In other cases, such as Beamish Murdoch's four-volume

Epitome of the Laws of Nova-Scotia, the economic risks of publication were undertaken by the author and his idealistic publisher, Joseph Howe.[45]

Lower Canada, as the oldest jurisdiction and the one most in need of jurisprudential synthesis in light of its hybrid legal culture, was the most prolific producer of legal literature, but writers in other colonies contributed also. The legal treatise had not yet achieved the hegemony it would enjoy later in the century, such that this early literature was somewhat heterogeneous in form. Some were institutional works that followed the format of metropolitan texts: thus, Henry Des Rivières Beaubien's three-volume *Traité sur les lois civiles du Bas-Canada* (1832–3) used the format of the *Code Napoléon* to organize the laws of Lower Canada, while Beamish Murdoch's contemporaneous treatise on the law of Nova Scotia was offered 'in humble imitation of the Commentaries of Blackstone.'[46] Whereas Beaubien's work aimed mainly to present local law without commentary in the interest of clarification, Murdoch was more critical and interventionist: when comparing English law to colonial law, for example, he asserted that Nova Scotian law was 'freed from many [laws] that have formed the subject of constant objection in the mother country.' The game and tithe laws were unknown, while the 'comparative simplicity of our legal forms, in conveyancing and in law suits, would astonish an English practitioner.'

JP manuals and similar works were also a favoured form of local literature, complementing synthetic works such as those of Des Rivières Beaubien and Murdoch with what were essentially instructional manuals for dealing with law at a more granular level, aimed principally at readers with no legal training.[47] The beginnings of university legal education required new forms of legal literature, more critical and reflective in nature. Thus François-Maximilien Bibaud's 1859 *Commentaires sur les lois du Bas-Canada*, prepared mainly for his students, has been called 'the only original, systematic exposition of the law in Canada East to be published before the codification of the civil law in the 1860s.'[48]

In Lower Canada, an additional motive for producing legal literature was the need for accounts of legal topics derived from French law in English and vice versa. This practice had already begun with Joseph-François Perrault's translation of parts of Burn's JP manual in 1789.[49] In 1827 the physician Jacques Labrie took it upon himself to compose an elementary work on the British constitution in French, while in 1842 the first major French-language work on the criminal law appeared.[50] Its author, Jacques Crémazie, observed that as it was 'impossible de trouver dans la langue française, une expression correspondante aux mots techniques ou autres usités en Angleterre,' he had left many English terms untranslated. Thus, such linguistically hybrid titles as 'Forme de l'indictment' and 'Manslaughter volontaire' could be found, along with others, such as 'Stabbing (action de poignarder)' where Crémazie did insert a translation. He assured his readers, however, that where he had used English words, this nomenclature was 'invariablement suivie dans les tribunaux du pays, [et] est plus ou moins familière à tout le monde.'

In the other direction, Nicolas Benjamin Doucet, though francophone, published his *Fundamental Principles of the Laws of Canada as They Existed under the Natives, as They Were Changed under the French Kings, and as They Were Modified and Altered under the Domination of England*, which included the first bilingual version of the Custom of Paris. This was not its only novel feature, as it claimed to include some account of 'the general government, religious, military, civil and criminal, laws of the natives, particularly of the Hurons and Iroquois Indians, at the time the interior of the country was discovered by Cartier.' While Doucet's account was more a sketch of the general history of their societies than an account of Huron or Iroquois law, it would remain almost unique in Canadian legal literature for over a century in treating Indigenous law as one of the three legal traditions contributing to Canadian law. The work was said to be 'compiled with the view of assisting Law Students, in directing them in the course of their studies,' but it must have been both daunting and confusing for any prospective lawyer.[51] The first volume of over 200 pages started with a hurried overview of the personnel and sources of law and its general categories, then shifted abruptly into the history of the world from biblical times down to the end of the Roman Empire, before shifting again to Anglo-Saxon England to follow the highlights of English law down to the time of the *Quebec Act*. A brief history of French law appeared in volume 2 along with Doucet's account of Indigenous law, but most of the volume dealt with the content of the 'civil code.' While this part seems to follow the plan of the *Code Napoléon*, it is not clear if the provisions set out are meant to represent existing law or some ideal codification. The most valuable part of the work was undoubtedly its translation of the Custom of Paris. In spite of the work's many unsatisfactory features, the fact that Doucet was able to produce a book of nearly 500 pages while being probably Lower Canada's busiest notary in the first half of the nineteenth century must occasion some admiration; he is said to have generated some 30,000 notarial instruments in the course of his fifty-one-year career (1804–55).

The attainment of representative government in Newfoundland seems to have inspired E.M. Archibald to publish an overview of the colony's legal order in an 1847 work that combined a reproduction of some of the most important constitutional documents with copious explanatory notes.[52] In the 1850s and 1860s there began to appear utilitarian texts restricted to a particular area of law, often providing the text of relevant cases, statutes, and rules of court in addition to authorial commentary. The rejuvenation of the equitable jurisdiction in Upper Canada at mid-century provided the impetus for a number of these works.[53]

Early British North American legal journals tried to appeal to the broadest possible readership by offering an omnium gatherum of practical tips, reports of new cases, notes on new legislation, historical accounts of particular areas of law, short biographies of legal personnel, and legal gossip, along with occasional glances at these topics in related jurisdictions such as Britain, France, and the United States. In Lower Canada, journal articles appeared in either French or English, elsewhere only in English. The first such initiative, the *Revue de législation et de jurisprudence*, appeared in Montreal in 1845 but ceased publication in 1848. Attention then shifted to case reporting in Quebec, and a journal did not appear again until 1869, with the appearance of *La Revue légale*.[54] It combined case reports with learned articles and lasted well into the twentieth century. The *Upper Canada Law Journal*, which commenced in 1855, also enjoyed a long life. After a decade it recommenced with a new series, changed its name to the *Canada Law Journal* after Confederation, and continued publication until 1922, when the *Canadian Bar Review* began.

Legal literature of the period reflected the characteristics of British North American legal culture in general. While closely attuned to developments in the relevant legal metropolis, whether Britain or France, and increasingly to those in the United States, its authors adapted metropolitan law for local use. Commercial success in small jurisdictions meant appealing to the broadest audience possible, and works of immediate relevance to practice were thus favoured over those that were more speculative, theoretical, or reflective. At a time when the national boundaries of law were not as sharply defined as they would later become, domestic works also had to compete with metropolitan works by authors of international stature, such as James Kent's *Commentaries on American Law*, that seemed more authoritative than the efforts of local authors.

No account of legal literature would be complete without noting the role played by newspapers and pamphlets. Trial accounts, mostly of sensational criminal trials, were a feature in every colony and some are employed to illustrate the trial process in chapter 29 below. Newspapers also used their pages to reproduce grand jury charges, as well as for the reporting of judicial decisions. Indeed, as noted in the section below, the earliest law reports for PEI were published in newspapers. Pamphlets and newspapers were not 'legal literature' in the sense used generally in this section, but they were literature about the law and its operation, and they demonstrate legal literacy of some degree in the everyday citizen.

Law Reporting

Law reporting, the dissemination of the work of the courts on points of law, was slow to develop in British North America compared to both Britain and the United States. In 1843 a two-person select committee of the Nova Scotia assembly, both lawyers, argued that the colony should financially support a proposal to publish the Supreme Court's reports. It would, they said, be 'of great public advantage' if the Supreme Court's decisions could be 'preserved and rendered accessible to the public, as well as to the Profession.' Issues 'deeply affecting the rights and properties of the people' arose constantly in the court, but 'judgments solemnly delivered' soon lost their effect for 'want of … publicity.'[55] For all the concern expressed, however, no reports were published in Nova Scotia until more than a decade later, even though Upper Canada and New Brunswick had published reports from the 1820s and 1830s.[56]

In all the British North American colonies, those in the game early and latecomers,[57] law reporting was seen as an enterprise that overwhelmingly benefited the legal profession and one for which the profession should foot the bill. Pious pronouncements might be made about making decisions 'accessible to the public, as well as to the Profession,' but law reporting never attained the status of a public service. As we have seen in chapter 23, the movement for law reform did bring with it a conviction that statute law should be rendered accessible through public funds, but nobody was persuaded that the same was generally true for court decisions. Public subsidies were provided in some colonies, but the amounts were small and temporary, and as a result law reporting was inconsistent. In most colonies the bar was too small to sustain the enterprise. Newspapers carried many reports of cases, but the degree of public appetite for them can be gauged from the fact that they were overwhelmingly reports of the evidence tendered at trials, mostly criminal but occasionally civil, and not detailed reproductions of legal reasoning from the bench. Newspaper accounts were supplemented by the occasional pamphlet about a case, but again these were trial reports and generally about sensational criminal cases.[58]

The earliest law reports from a British North American court in this period were *Taylor's Reports*, from Upper Canada, which for four years in the 1820s published decisions of King's Bench. The colony thus reproduced the pattern of English law reports in the period – nominative and devoted to a particular court. Thomas Taylor was an official appointee under statute, but that same statute also provided that the Law Society was to pay his salary, which it did by levying its members.[59] The successor to *Taylor's Reports* was *Draper's King's Bench Reports*, published between 1828 and 1831.[60] Law reporting then lapsed, and in 1840 government got out of the law reporting business and gave the responsibility to the profession.[61] The Law Society appointed reporters, who were accountable to it, and salaries continued to be paid by the levy on the profession. Further legislation in the 1840s created new reporters for other courts, and in the same decade the Law Society established rules about the duties of reporters.[62] The *King's Bench Reports* were augmented by a slew of new report series in the 1840s, including the *Error and Appeal Reports*, from 1846, and *Grant's Upper Canada Chancery Reports*, from 1849. The leading figure in this expansion of reporting was Alexander Grant. Although his name is associated principally with the *Chancery Reports*, he also produced the *Error and Appeal Reports*, and the *Upper Canada Chambers Reports*.[63]

Elsewhere, two selections of Newfoundland Supreme Court cases, mostly decided by Chief Justice Sir Francis Forbes, were published in the late 1820s,[64] and very slim volumes of Lower Canadian cases were put together by George Pyke in 1811 and by George Okill Stuart in 1834.[65] There was a more sustained initiative in New Brunswick, where law reporting began in 1836, with reports produced by George Berton 'under the active aegis of the Chief Justice,' Ward Chipman.[66] Berton was a young lawyer with excellent family connections;[67] with Chief Justice Chipman's assistance he also published a consolidation of the statute law in 1838, discussed in chapter 23. Berton's reports were based on notes taken of select Supreme Court decisions, appeared first in the *Royal Gazette*, and were subsequently issued in pamphlet form. In 1837 he was appointed provincial law reporter pursuant to legislation of the previous year. The statute succinctly recounted that it was 'an object of great importance to obtain correct reports of the decisions of the Supreme Court.' Once appointed, Berton republished his earlier pamphlets, and in 1839 he collected his reports into a one-volume consolidation, covering cases decided between 1835 and 1839. He issued it at 'heavy pecuniary expense' to himself, although there was a small legislative subsidy.[68] The volume contained summaries of counsel's arguments, and even exchanges with the bench.

Berton died in 1840 at the young age of thirty-two, and his successor, David Kerr, another young lawyer, took over and published volumes 3–5 of the *New Brunswick Reports*, covering cases from 1839. In volume 3 he made it clear that law reporting would need continued financial support from the legislature. Perhaps for this reason the preface to the volume contained eight pages on why law reports were important, not just to the profession but also to the general public. Law reports would maintain consistency among courts at different levels and would act as a check on what the bar could argue and individual members of the bench decide. They would also provide a written record of legal rights and liberties. Most interestingly, and with reference to the sources of law discussed in chapter 23, he also argued that New Brunswick courts had already changed English law in some respects to suit local needs and on occasions had seen American authorities 'as more applicable in point of locality than any English authorities.'[69] These decisions in particular needed to be preserved; they represented a 'local and qualified' law, which 'form a written and exact precedent for all subsequent cases of the like nature, by reasoning of their locality.' Perhaps as the result of Kerr's arguments, the New Brunswick Assembly did provide some financial support in the 1840s.[70] Kerr resigned in 1849 and a successor produced a further six volumes, covering 1848–66.

Lower Canada and Nova Scotia came to law reporting rather later. Lower Canada adopted the Upper Canadian technique of taxing the profession to pay for law reporting but in a statute of 1850 widened the levy to include judges, sheriffs, and court clerks. This measure enabled the creation of the *Lower Canada Reports*, which began publishing the next year.[71] There were complaints that the reports were not authoritative because the judges did not have the opportunity to proofread them, while the Montreal bar protested that decisions of the courts of the Quebec City district were unduly featured. Thus, a group of a dozen Montreal lawyers led by T.K. Ramsay, mostly the cross-cultural group associated with the McGill Law Faculty, initiated a new series in 1857 called the *Lower Canada Jurist*. This one was purely a product of private enterprise, the publisher having 'most liberally exonerated the Editors from any personal liability consequent upon the undertaking.'[72] The series must have been profitable to some extent, as it lasted until 1891, while the *Lower Canada Reports* ceased publication in 1867 with the disappearance of the body providing its subsidy, the province of Canada.

Although lawyer and future NSSC judge Thomas Chandler Haliburton insisted in the 1820s that it was a service that 'most unquestionably deserves to be borne by the public purse,'[73] it took until 1853 to produce the first volume of the *Nova Scotia Reports*. Prior to that, lawyers clearly knew about some Supreme Court cases and perhaps passed around manuscript decisions, as they clearly did in Lower Canada. Beamish Murdoch's *Epitome*, for example, published in 1833–4, contains reasonably lengthy extracts from NSSC decisions in his footnotes.[74] The first formal request to the assembly for a grant for the purpose dates from 1843, and for more than a decade there was jockeying and lobbying over both the right to produce reports and over a public subsidy.[75]

By the mid-1850s the tide had turned, and a five-person assembly committee, all lawyers, recommended the grant without condition and argued that the lack of law reports had long been a disadvantage, particularly to people in rural districts, 'and has actually led to an increase in litigation, and consequent pecuniary loss.'[76] The first law reports for Nova Scotia were finally published in 1853, the first volume reporting cases between 1834 and 1851; volume 2 covered 1853–5. In the preface to volume 1 reporter Alexander James observed that the availability of reported decisions from England, the United States, New Brunswick, and the Canadas was not good enough, 'because a very large proportion of the cases which arise in this country are founded on our local statutes, or arise out of our own peculiar institutions and circumstances,' and to understand these the decisions of 'foreign tribunals' were of limited use. After he resigned his post in 1856,[77] the assembly resolved to pay for the publication of Supreme Court decisions in one or more Halifax newspapers.[78] The annual grant for reporting decisions was renewed in the later 1850s, although never without debate and divisions.[79] The work of reporting carried on, but the series still totalled only seven volumes by Confederation.

26

Constitutional Developments I: European-Indigenous Relations, the Old Colonial System, and the Rebellions, 1815–ca 1839

Constitutional change invariably comes about in two ways, distinct but related. It can occur incrementally, not necessarily epitomized by some dramatic landmark moment. Or it can be caused by, or crystallized in, such an event. Between 1815 and the 1840s both kinds of constitutional change took place within British North America, involving both major elements of the constitution as it existed at the close of the Napoleonic Wars. One element of the constitution was the relationship between Britain and the Indigenous peoples of the region. That relationship changed profoundly by mid-century, as military and economic developments rendered Indigenous peoples increasingly irrelevant to colonial governments. As the title of the chapter dealing with the period from the 1790s to the 1830 in the leading account of Indigenous-white relations puts it, these years were ones in which Indigenous people went 'from alliance to irrelevance.'[1] There were landmarks charting this decline, both visible and invisible. In Upper Canada those landmarks were the many treaties made with Indigenous groups, which saw them lose much of their land base and thus also much of their ability to act independently of local governments and of Britain. In the Maritime colonies, Lower Canada, and to the west the landmarks were silences, the absence of treaties. Both processes led to the same result – ever-diminishing independence for Indigenous peoples and ultimately, by the 1840s, the beginnings of colonial governments' legislative interventions in their lives.

The other element of the constitution involved the relationships between the British – London and the men London sent to govern the colonies – and the people who lived in the colonies. Here too there was incremental change, alterations in how the constitution worked in practice, in the period down to the late 1830s. The development of this settler constitution was also marked by, and to some extent impelled by, a major landmark – the rebellion crisis of 1837–8 in the Canadas. The rebellions are justly among the most written about episodes in Canadian history. But for the purposes of this volume their significance resides not only in the drama of armed rebellion, but in two other aspects of the constitutional history of this period. First, armed rebellion was the culmination in the Canadas of longer-term demands for fundamental constitutional change, demands that were also voiced, although obviously in non-bellicose accents, in other colonies as well. Among the changes asked for, reforms to the legal system were front and centre. In particular the question of superior court judges' direct involvement in colonial governance and politics engendered fierce debate. Second, the rebellions were highly significant for the reaction they generated. Civil liberties were abridged, and the state acted in significant respects outside legal constraints. Yet violent repression was also tempered by more pragmatic policies driven by restraint and mercy.

There were also two 'jurisdictional' changes in this period. The first, the abolition of the independent colony of Cape Breton Island in 1820 and its annexation to Nova Scotia, was not significant and will not be further discussed. The second, the founding of the Red River settlement in the early nineteenth century, is an important part of the constitutional history of this period. It ultimately led to the addition of Manitoba to the Confederation pact in 1870.

Indigenous Peoples, Treaties, and the Constitution in Eastern British North America

The outstanding feature of the post-1815 period of European-Indigenous relations was that the fluidity and pluralism that had been the hallmark of the interaction between colonial law and Indigenous peoples gave way to the view that European law was supreme, even though it was rarely applied to Indigenous peoples' everyday lives.[2] This development took place alongside other alterations in the military, political, and economic relationships between natives and newcomers, events that both determined legal changes and were frequently facilitated by them. The shift in the balance of power was exemplified by the fact that the Covenant Chain no longer featured in the colonial or British discourse, although it was still seen as important by Indigenous peoples.[3] The most immediate manifestation of changed circumstances was that although the Treaty of Ghent, which followed the War of 1812, referred to Indigenous peoples as 'Indian tribes or nations,' it did not establish an independent state for them, even though Britain proposed one.[4] In the longer term Britain's need for military alliances ended, and with it went, in a slow erosion, Indigenous independence. As a recent pan-imperial study of indigenous sovereignty has put it,

> As the settler-state consolidated its sense of self, it tended increasingly to see and treat aboriginal peoples as part of and entirely subject to its own sovereignty rather than as separate polities. If the [earlier] history of sovereignty ... represented a period when the common law was disposed towards a pluralistic model, its orientation through the nineteenth century tended strongly in the other direction'[5]

Along with this shift in the military-political balance went a decline in the fur trade, a decline made worse for Indigenous suppliers by the violent competition between, and then consolidation of, the North West Company and the HBC. The new entity had a monopoly after the 1821 merger, which drove down prices and imperilled the livelihoods of many Indigenous inhabitants. Finally, peace in Europe and in North America meant large-scale British emigration to the colonies, creating increased demand for land and the spread of European settlement to more and more previously remote areas of each colony. Upper Canada's settler population increased five-fold between 1815 and 1840, from 95,000 to over 450,000, Lower Canada's almost doubled, from 335,000 to approximately 650,000, while that of all of British North America increased from 750,000 in the early 1820s to about 1.6 million by the early 1840s. Much of this influx settled on the land, a process that, for the settlers, required 'removal of the Indian from the path of agricultural settlement.'[6]

This land acquisition by Europeans, and its corollary, the dispossession of Indigenous peoples, was both cause and result of the fundamental change in the constitutional relationship between Britain and Indigenous nations. The very fact that after 1815 Indigenous peoples were increasingly moved off their traditional lands and confined to reserves and/or to marginal land on the fringes of European settlement accentuated Indigenous peoples' loss of power and influence. In turn that loss also meant that by the 1840s colonial governments began to treat Indigenous peoples as subjects, insisting that European law, judge-made and statutory, applied to the original inhabitants of the land, even if this theory was rarely put into practice in regard to the purely internal affairs of Indigenous people before mid-century. The new theory did not really 'bite' until after Confederation with the various *Indian Acts*, but its roots went back to the 1820s and 1830s. Symbolic of this change in orientation was that 'Indian policy' in each colony from 1830 was removed from military control and given to civilian officials. Both the Canadas created an Indian Department, although policy towards Indigenous peoples remained formally with London until 1860. But the effect of these changes was that the role of 'Indian' officials changed, from managing a crucial set of alliances based on treaty obligations to overseeing an increasingly problem-ridden relationship.

The dispossession of Indigenous peoples involved different processes in different places. The principal general distinction was that between Upper Canada and all other colonies and regions. For the most part, Indigenous land was alienated in Upper Canada by more or less formal land surrenders, as had been done in the period between the end of the Revolutionary War and 1815.[7] Some of the agreements by which land was alienated embodied a surrender of Indigenous title, a reservation of land to the Indigenous nation, annuity payments, and a guarantee of continued hunting and fishing rights. Other lands were surrendered by purchase, with no land reserved out of the purchase, and no hunting and fishing rights exempted. Three key aspects of the Upper Canadian land agreements bear emphasis. First, they effectively acknowledged an Indigenous title; if there was no title, no interest to surrender, there would have been no need to make these agreements. Second, they were surrenders to the Crown, not the colony, and the officials who negotiated them, and those who administered policy in their immediate aftermath, were responsible to the Crown, not the colonial legislatures. Third, and perhaps most importantly, these agreements were seen by the Indigenous peoples as part of a much longer process of treaty-making between equals. As Governor Lord Dalhousie acknowledged in 1827, Indigenous peoples 'have their treaties, their peace and war agreements, constantly in their minds.' They demanded that the treaty terms be respected, that they receive 'their presents established by long custom.' Dalhousie warned that if the Crown did not live up to the terms of the treaties, 'they would do themselves justice to their own satisfaction, and we would soon find them most formidable enemies.'[8] Dalhousie was wrong. He was writing at a time that, in hindsight, we can see as the beginning of the period that relations with Indigenous people mattered less and less to London and the colonies.

Between 1815 and 1840 land surrenders in Upper Canada, eleven of them involving tracts of at least 250,000 acres, or approximately 390 square miles, alienated almost all the arable land in southern Upper Canada not previously taken.[9] Six of these were concluded between 1815 and 1822 and saw about 7.6 million acres alienated to the Crown.[10] The post-1815 surrenders were of substantially larger acreages than in the late eighteenth and early nineteenth centuries, and this caused a change in policy from lump sum payments to annuities. Lump sum payments were too heavy a drain on the British treasury, and the change to annuities also enabled the Crown to shift the costs to the colonists – the annuities were paid from revenue derived from the sale of Crown lands, freed up by the surrenders, to European settlers. Annuities were also probably seen by some Indigenous leaders as acceptable because they resembled the presents traditionally given by the Crown as indications of alliance and friendship. Other major alienations occurred in 1827 and 1836 and involved over 37 million acres.[11] Treaty-making in Upper Canada was marked by what one historian has labelled the Crown's 'legal fastidiousness,' a policy of securing legal title to the land to be then granted to settlers.[12] Yet it was not only the Crown, but also Indigenous nations, who insisted on both formal agreements for reserved lands and on the protection of hunting and fishing rights. Without reserves, land-hungry settlers encroached on unceded lands, and/or interfered with traditional Indigenous uses of the land. Treaty-making in the second quarter of the nineteenth century was thus at one and the same time exemplary of Indigenous peoples' loss of power and deteriorating relations with white settlers and their governments, and of their desire to make the best deals they could.

Indigenous dispossession elsewhere stood in marked contrast to Upper Canada. In Lower Canada, as we saw in chapter 12, Britain both inherited arrangements made by the government of New France and made agreements of their own after 1760, particularly in the 1780s and 1790s with the arrival of Loyalists in the Eastern Townships. As a result, in 1815 Indigenous groups lived on lands reserved for their use. No new surrenders were negotiated in the post-1815 period, because Lower Canadian officials did not recognize Indigenous title to the land.[13] There thus occurred the 'compartmentalization' of Indigenous land policy between the Canadas: 'land-cession treaties became the dominant approach west of the Ottawa River, and unilateral appropriation in the east.'[14] The Lower Canadian approach was followed in the Maritime colonies, where the eighteenth-century treaties had not included land cessions. European settlers simply moved onto the land, with or without land grants from the Crown, establishing farms and/or harvesting timber and other resources, and pushed the Indigenous people into areas the settlers did not want.[15]

In Nova Scotia and New Brunswick reserves were created unilaterally by colonial governments. Fifteen small reserves were established in New Brunswick by 1838, totalling only approximately 61,000 acres and supporting only 935 people. In Nova Scotia Lieutenant Governor Dalhousie established a reserve system in 1820, which replaced the licences of occupation given to some Indigenous people. Ten reserves were set up, one in each county, none of more than 1,000 acres, and six more were added in Cape Breton in the early 1830s. The Maritime reserves were uniformly too small to meet peoples' needs and located on poor land; Indigenous people were in this sense treated similarly to the Black Loyalists who came to the colony. Even this paltry allocation was more than was given in Prince Edward Island, where all the land had been granted to proprietors in 1767. The only reserve was Lennox Island off the northwest coast, where the owner allowed the Indigenous inhabitants to live unmolested. For many decades local and British humanitarian organizations tried to have the Mi'kmaq granted title to the 1,400 acres of Lennox Island, but this was not achieved until 1870. The reserve system stayed the same until Confederation. Altogether reserves totalled less than 0.5 per cent of the land in all three Maritime colonies. With practically the whole of their land base taken from them, the constitutional relationship between Indigenous peoples and Britain in the Maritimes was utterly transformed from what it had been in the eighteenth century.

Moving from the macro level of relations between Indigenous peoples and imperial and colonial British governments, to the micro question of the everyday application of English or French law to people once allies and now increasingly subjects, three questions arise.[16] Did colonial administrators believe that Indigenous people were within colonial jurisdiction in all matters? Did Indigenous peoples themselves believe they were within that jurisdiction? And, whatever the theoretical legalities, how did the governance of Indigenous peoples work at a practical level? To the first question the answer is unclear, at least in Upper Canada, until at least the 1820s. The 1822 prosecution of Shawanakiskie for the murder of an Indigenous woman in Amherstburg, Upper Canada, produced considerable correspondence within Upper Canada and between the colony and London over whether the colonial courts had jurisdiction. Jurisdiction, at least in the minds of some lawyers and judges, was fluid and turned on where an offence took place. If it happened in an area settled by Europeans, colonial law applied. If it happened well away from European settlement, but within the boundaries of Upper Canada, it probably did not. If it happened on reserves close to European settlements, the matter was unclear. Some jurists believed that customary law remained in force to deal with inter se disputes among Indigenous people, particularly in non-criminal law matters that did not affect the public peace.[17] By the 1830s, however, there was no question in European minds that their law applied when the public peace was threatened by serious crime. When Tom Williams, a Mi'kmaw resident of Prince Edward Island, killed another Mi'kmaq, he was convicted and sentenced to death in the island Supreme Court. Yet we might question whether the law fully applied in practice, even if jurisdiction was asserted. Trial judge Chief Justice Jarvis combined chauvinism and cultural relativism in reporting that Williams was motivated by the 'savage virtue of revenge.' Lieutenant Governor Gilroy accepted Jarvis's recommendation that Williams not be hanged, noting that he had followed the 'well-known custom of requiring blood for blood,' but at the same time being certain that the Mi'kmaw 'should not be led to believe that they might indulge with impunity in the savage practice of revenge.' Williams was banished from the island.[18]

The answer to the second question, that of how Indigenous peoples viewed their legal status within the colonies and the relevance of English law to them, is uncertain, but we can say that outside of the European settlements of any size Indigenous peoples regulated their internal affairs and frequently ignored local by-laws over such matters as the taking of fish and the lighting of fires in the woods, and also set up temporary camps on land granted to settlers.[19] The third question is much easier to answer: for all the efforts of imperial and local politicians and missionary groups, Indigenous bands, whether on reserves or living on diminishing areas of non-reserve land, were effectively still self-governing at mid-century, and probably later, controlling their use of the land and their internal social relations. As we will see in the next chapter, British and colonial governments did seek to remake

Indigenous communities through education, religious teaching, and encouragements to abandon traditional life ways and become agriculturalists, but they had little or no interest in interfering in the internal affairs of those communities, who therefore lived according to existing systems of law. Nova Scotia historian, fiction writer, and judge Thomas Chandler Haliburton noted, for example, that the Mi'kmaq 'never litigate or are in any way impleaded. They have a code of traditionary and customary laws among themselves.'[20] John Beverley Robinson noted much the same thing in the late 1850s, stating in *R v McCormick* that unceded Indian lands in Canada West were not, and never had been, 'under the actual supervision and charge of its [the Crown's] officers.'[21]

The Settler Constitution: Executives, Councils, and Assemblies[22]

All colonies in 1815 except Newfoundland and Cape Breton had the same tripartite structure of government, modelled on the British constitutional division among king, Lords, and Commons. The royal representative and head of the local executive government was the lieutenant governor of each colony; the only 'governor' was the governor general of Lower Canada, superior to the lieutenant governors of the other colonies. Lieutenant governors of all colonies, the vast majority of whom in this period were military men,[23] were after 1824 appointed for a maximum six-year term and took their instructions from London. Their powers were largely negative – they could refuse assent to legislation, as could London. They superintended the work of officials like the provincial secretary or provincial treasurer, men who were not required to be, and rarely were, members of the assembly. These officials had effective security of tenure in their offices, which were considered a form of property that could not be taken away without good cause and with compensation.

Within the colony the lieutenant governor governed with the assistance of a council of appointed advisers. In the Canadas this advisory body was the executive council, distinct from the legislative council, the upper house of the legislature. Legislative councillors were appointed for life under the 1791 *Constitutional Act*. Executive councillors served at the pleasure of the lieutenant governors, but many did so for very long tenures. In the Maritimes there were unitary councils, bodies doubling as executive and legislative councils until split into two in 1832 in New Brunswick and 1838 in Nova Scotia and Prince Edward Island.

Maritime councillors were not life tenured. Whether the intermediate body between lieutenant governor and assembly was a legislative council or a unitary council, all legislation had to be approved by it as well as by the assembly, just as British legislation went through both Lords and Commons.

The equivalents of the Commons in every colony were the colonial assemblies, made up of members elected on a broad, but by no means universal, franchise. The only exceptions were Newfoundland, which officially became a colony only in 1824 and did not have an elected assembly until 1832, and Cape Breton Island, which did not have an assembly during its forty-year history as a separate colony. Newfoundland saw a protracted and complicated struggle for an assembly, which was somewhat the obverse of events in eighteenth-century Lower Canada. The Irish Catholic inhabitants wanted one, but the island's commercial elite did not, at least until they saw that it could be in their economic interest. The leading account of the campaign for representative government places legal issues at the forefront; it was the system of surrogate courts and naval punishments that attracted the ire of reformers. Their first victory came with the official establishment of the island as a colony under Colonial Office, not Admiralty, control in 1824, and a newly reconstituted Supreme Court shortly afterwards. Once that dam was broken, the reform campaign harnessed a newly vigorous local press, gathered momentum by deprecating local taxation without representation, and appealed to the new reformist constitutional ideas coming increasingly to the fore in Britain itself.

The electoral franchise everywhere was broad enough to include most adult non-Indigenous males but varied from colony to colony.[24] There were no legislated racial restrictions; Indigenous people continued to be excluded because they mostly did not own individual property. Before the 1850s electors everywhere needed to be freeholders, although the required value of that freehold varied. In Nova Scotia and the Canadas it was forty shillings in annual rental value, the same as the traditional and long-standing English qualification, and that enabled more or less all male heads of households to vote. Nova Scotia also gave the vote to people who owned a dwelling house and the land on which it stood or 100 acres of land of which five acres were cultivated. In New Brunswick the qualification was somewhat higher and differently calculated – twenty-five pounds freehold in actual value for residents and fifty pounds for non-residents. This was not as restrictive as it sounds, because initial land grants given between 1784 and 1790 were large enough to enfranchise all heads of families. Qualifications to sit in the assemblies varied. In some colonies – Nova Scotia and Lower Canada – the qualification was the same as for voting, while in others – New Brunswick and Upper Canada – it was higher.

As noted in part 3 of this volume, women occasionally voted. The common law prohibited women from doing so, but some voted in the nineteenth century. They voted in the 1830 New Brunswick assembly election, in Nova Scotia in 1840,[25] and in Halton, Upper Canada, in 1844. The civil law did not have the same prohibition, and women continued to be able to vote in Lower Canada until the right was taken away from all women in Canada by statute in 1849. Even before the statutory removal of the right, women were discouraged from exercising the franchise, especially by the Patriotes. 'The vote,' notes a leading historian of Lower Canadian women, 'became a gendered right ... deemed suitable for those in control of their selves, their passions, and their property.'[26]

The English constitutional inheritance included a variety of limitations on voting and office-holding applicable to Catholics.[27] Voting restrictions had been removed by 1815 in all colonies except PEI, as discussed in the previous part, and the process was completed in 1830. That year Colonial Secretary Murray ordered that the English *Roman Catholic Relief Act* of 1829 be adopted in all colonies, and London backed this up by refusing assent to a PEI statute limiting the franchise to Protestants. Islanders' obduracy had a lot to do with the contentious politics of landlordism, discussed below in chapter 30. Tenants were overwhelmingly Catholic, and to have extended them the franchise would have increased the political support for the escheat movement.[28]

Turning to office-holding, as we have seen, restrictions on Catholics were done away with in the Canadas in the late eighteenth century, and in 1817 the toleration that was the hallmark of policy in Lower Canada was extended to Bishop Joseph-Octave Plessis of Montreal being named to the legislative council.[29] But such restrictions still formally applied in the Maritimes until they too were removed by the imperial and emancipation Acts, although before then Nova Scotia had fashioned a compromise. When in 1820 Cape Breton was annexed to mainland Nova Scotia one of the two men returned for Cape Breton in the assembly election of that year was the wealthy and powerful Irish merchant Lawrence Kavanagh. He refused to take the oath against transubstantiation when he appeared for admission early in 1822. Although Lieutenant Governor Sir James Kempt and Colonial Secretary Lord Bathurst were prepared to see him admitted without the oath, members from Protestant counties objected. Lieutenant governor and council nonetheless supported his admission, and ultimately an assembly vote in his favour passed twenty-one to fifteen. The resolution admitting him also stated that in future Catholics could take their seats 'without making the declaration against Popery and Transubstantiation.'[30] This was a crucial distinction. Kavanagh did not have to take the oaths of abjuration and supremacy, repudiating Catholic doctrine on transubstantiation and acknowledging the monarch as the head of the Church of England, only to swear allegiance to the Crown. The compromise acknowledged that Catholics could be loyal while still holding beliefs in essential matters of their faith.

Newfoundland did not have a representative assembly until 1832, after Catholic emancipation, but exclusion of Catholics from political office was an issue from 1825, when an executive council was established. It initially consisted of the Supreme Court judges and the local military commander, Lieutenant Colonel Thomas Burke, a Catholic. Burke swore the oath of allegiance but refused the other oaths. Governor Sir Thomas Cochrane was prepared to accept this, but the other councillors doubted the legality of doing so, and Burke was not seated. Governor Cochrane then nominated two other Catholics, but London baulked because Cochrane's commission contained the state oaths and required him to administer them to others. London dallied in preparing a new commission, with Catholic emancipation on the horizon, and indeed the passage of the Act of 1829 precipitated much rejoicing among Newfoundland's large Catholic population. It was premature. Late in 1829 the Supreme Court ruled that the various statutes imposing disabilities on Catholics had never been received in Newfoundland, and thus the Catholic emancipation statute did not apply. But the terms of Cochrane's commission still did! Not until 1832 was a new commission issued which both established a representative assembly and removed the offensive oaths. Oddly, Cochrane did not then go ahead with a council appointment; no Catholic sat on the council until 1840.

Other religious disabilities did not affect the franchise or legislative office-holding, but they were part of the constitutional framework and thus merit mention here. Catholics could be JPs in the Canadas, and whether or not it was strictly legal they were also JPs in areas of Nova Scotia that were predominantly Catholic.[31] They could also join the legal profession in the Canadas. But in the Maritimes taking the anti-Catholic oaths was a prerequisite to joining the bar until the emancipation legislation of 1830, making those colonies more restrictive than England, which had admitted Catholics in 1791.[32] Under English law Catholics could not hold commissions in the armed forces, including the militia. Catholic emancipation changed all of that. In the words of the PEI relief statute, Catholics could henceforth 'hold, exercise and enjoy all civil and military offices, ... and ... exercise any other ... civil right.' For each office they had to swear an oath of loyalty to the crown, but were not required to deny a fundamental tenet of their religion.

Removing the legal disabilities on Catholics made it possible for them to participate more widely in politics, society, and the economy, but it did not end religious antipathy and strife. Religious riots were not uncommon, often precipitated by the militant Orange Order. Sectarianism was an ever-present feature of life in the region. The Province of Canada Assembly declared in an 1851 statute that 'the recognition of legal equality among all Religious Denominations is an admitted principle of colonial legislation,' and that it was 'desirable that the same should receive the sanction of direct Legislative Authority, recognizing and declaring the same as a fundamental principle of our civil polity.' By mid-century these statements were correct. But the same statute perhaps went a little too far in further stating 'that the Free exercise and enjoyment of Religious Profession and Worship, without Discrimination or Preference' was 'allowed to all her Majesty's subjects.'[33] The formal law stated a principle of religious equality rather than mere toleration, but social practice meant that that principle was not always observed in practice. Nor was any legal equality given to Indigenous religions.

Civil rights were also extended to a variety of groups outside the Christian mainstream. An 1831 Lower Canadian statute extended all civil rights and privileges to Jews in the colony; also in Lower Canada, seven years earlier Aaron Ezekiel Hart had become the first Jew called to a colonial bar.[34] Upper Canadian legislation of 1833 appeared at first glance to also grant civil rights to Jews. The statute's title stated that it was 'unnecessary to receive the Sacrament of the Lord's Supper as a qualification for offices,' but the text itself referred to 'the Sacrament of the Lord's Supper, according to the Rites or Usage of the Church of England.'[35] Thus arguably only non-Anglican Christians were included, not Jews. Other groups suffered some disabilities because they objected to the swearing of oaths. Quakers' allegiance was never doubted, but their belief that oath swearing was wrong meant that they suffered some disabilities. As we saw in part 3, legislation enabled Quakers to affirm and thereby vote before 1815, but not until 1829 did Upper Canada permit them, and others who would not swear on the Bible, to give evidence in court by affirming.[36] There was, of course, no protection at all for Indigenous religious beliefs; indeed Christianizing Indigenous people, extirpating their religious beliefs, was a central component of the 'civilization' policy discussed in the next chapter.

Some civil liberties were also denied to non-citizens. As discussed in earlier chapters, aliens could not hold freehold title to land. That in turn meant they could not vote or sit in assemblies or take any post for which freehold land ownership was a prerequisite. As detailed in chapter 30, this was really a major issue only in Upper Canada, with its large 'American' population, and the problem was solved there by a statute that confirmed alien-derived titles to land and thus allowed current owners to vote and sit in the assembly. The general prohibition on aliens owning land was not lifted until mid-century, but aliens did benefit from earlier legislation that made it easier to be naturalized and, in a few cases, from individual private Acts of naturalization.[37]

Turning from a description of institutions to an analysis of their operation, the large difference between the English and colonial settler constitutions prior to the 1840s was that colonial executives were not responsible to colonial legislatures. Lieutenant governors, their councillors, and government department heads could collectively govern without being able to command a majority in the assembly. They could not change local statute law or raise local taxes without assemblymen agreeing, of course, but the everyday business of government could be carried on. The executive, more so in the Canadas than in the Maritimes, had its own sources of revenue, principally imperial customs revenues. The lack of dependence of the executive on the legislature did not mean that the two branches of government could not work together, and both sides tried to make that happen, to a greater or lesser extent in different colonies. Many assemblymen saw that their role was to support the royal authority, to work with the executive. While keen to further the interests of their constituents, they were not 'party' men but independent gentlemen, typified perhaps by Beamish Murdoch, sometime member for Halifax, who 'was a steadfast proponent of traditional British ideas about the mixed and balanced constitution, and the necessity of independent thought and action rather than submission to party as the best way of serving the public good.'[38] On the other side of the equation most lieutenant governors knew their administrations would not flourish unless they worked with the assembly, on most issues most of the time. As one historian has astutely noted, 'The initiative in colonial government lay in the hands of the colonists and the Assemblies,' and over time through the 1820s and 1830s 'the constitutional balance of power was shifting from the executive to the Assemblies.'[39]

This shift was a general but an uneven one, varying from time to time and place to place. There was more cooperation than conflict between assemblies and executives in the Canadas and Nova Scotia in the 1820s than in the 1830s, and more generally in the 1830s in the Maritimes, especially in New Brunswick and Prince Edward Island, than in the Canadas. Similarly, party politics, by which is meant politics organized, at least to some degree, around ideological differences, emerged at different times in different places. One can talk of a party system in the Lower Canadian assembly by the early 1820s, where politics was marked by a religious, linguistic, and cultural divide. Conversely, a party system was still only emerging in New Brunswick in the late 1840s. In between were Upper Canada, closer to Lower Canada without the linguistic divide, but where divisions did lead to a short-lived and wholly ineffective armed rebellion in 1837. Prince Edward Island also had somewhat of a party system in the 1830s, in the form of the escheat movement discussed in chapter 30 on land law, and one can date the rise of party in Nova Scotia from the emergence of its reform movement in the mid-1830s.

It must be stressed that, with the obvious and notable exception of the people who resorted to armed rebellion in the Canadas in the late 1830s, those who opposed the power of colonial executives were not republicans. They did not wish to see the colonies leave the empire and live under a constitution that derived its ultimate authority from the people. They wanted something more similar to the mixed and balanced English constitution, one in which the three constituent elements of king, Lords, and Commons all played a role.[40] Even as late as 1834, in Lower Canada, the colony with the most forceful party opposing the governing elite, the 92 Resolutions warned of the danger of severing the ties with Britain, but they did not threaten to do so.[41] It is also worth emphasis that although the opposition Patriotes were mostly French-Canadian, many anglophone assemblymen supported the resolutions. When the Patriotes and other opposition groups in other colonies complained about the large issue of the structure of the constitution, as opposed to smaller particular issues of disagreement, their concerns invariably were couched in terms of the malfunctioning in the colonies of the constitution. As Joseph Howe of Nova Scotia put it, 'In England one vote of the peoples' representatives turns out a ministry and a new one comes in ... Here we may record five hundred votes against our ministry and yet they sit unmoved.'[42] There is some irony in the fact that colonists evoked a British constitution of responsible government that was still in itself evolving, as if it were fully settled. But Howe and his counterparts in other colonies certainly understood that the British constitution did not operate in the same way as colonial ones.

The constitutional politics of the 1820s and 1830s operated on two levels. Taking up most of the time in assemblies and popular discussions were a series of smaller particular issues that frequently led to clashes between executives and assemblies, and between legislative councils and assemblies, and sometimes between executives and legislative councils. At a more macro level was the general structure of the constitution, which was occasionally debated in relation to these particular disputes. The root problem for reformers was that the constitution prevented them from requiring the executive to do what the assembly wanted. Lord Durham's famous report following the rebellions also identified generalized conflict between executives and assemblies as a fundamental and endemic problem. 'The natural state of government in all these [British North American] colonies,' he insisted, 'is that of collision between the representative body' and the executive. In all the colonies 'the administration of public affairs is habitually confided to those who do not co-operate harmoniously with the popular branch of the legislature.'[43] This did not formally change until the late 1840s, but demands for such a change – responsible government of some sort – were occasionally voiced from the mid-1830s.

In the meantime Howe and other reformers – Robert Baldwin and Marshall Spring Bidwell in Upper Canada and Louis-Joseph Papineau in Lower Canada – advocated policies that reflected their interests and those of their constituents, policies therefore favourable to the less wealthy members of colonial society, to rural interests, to non-dominant religious groups, to those who paid taxes rather than those who subsisted on them. It is not possible, in the space available, to chart the history of these disputes in detail for each colony. But certain issues arose in this period in all colonies that were in themselves about the constitutional structure and reflected the growing frustration of some assemblymen with non-responsible government. One was the composition of the upper house of the legislature, and in the Maritime colonies this issue was also linked to its structure: the fact that that legislative body was also the lieutenant governor's executive council. In all colonies prior to the late 1830s the upper houses comprised office-holders and non-official members of the colonial elites, although the elites were differently named and slightly differently constituted from colony to colony. In Upper Canada it was called the Family Compact, in Lower Canada the Chateau clique. No similarly evocative names developed for the governing cliques in the Maritime colonies. In all colonies these elites comprised the same kinds of men – office-holders, often including the law officers of the Crown, judges, leading and wealthy merchants, and the Anglican hierarchy. In Lower Canada the francophone population was represented by some wealthy seigneurs, but the legislative council was overall an 'English' body. Membership of the upper houses was thus distinctly different from the lower ones, peopled by successful farmers, professionals, and small-scale businessmen, people prominent in their local communities as JPs or militia leaders but not necessarily with colony-wide connections or ambitions.

The Nova Scotia Council of Twelve provides a good example of who councillors were. In 1830 it comprised four judges: Chief Justice Sampson Salter Blowers, Justices Brenton Halliburton and James Stewart of the NSSC, and Simon Bradstreet Robie, master of the rolls. Four members were office-holders: Michael Wallace, leading merchant, provincial treasurer since 1797, and five times administrator of the colony in the absence of various lieutenant governors; Charles Morris Junior, surveyor general and son of a man who had been both surveyor general and a Supreme Court judge; Thomas N. Jeffery, the collector of customs; Hibbert Newton Binney, collector of impost and excise; and Attorney General Richard Uniacke, until his death in October, and Acting Attorney General Samuel George William Archibald from then on. Two others were leading merchants: Enos Collins, son-in-law of Halliburton and rumoured to be the wealthiest man in British North America, and Charles Ramage Prescott, a retired merchant. Membership was completed by the Anglican bishop of Nova Scotia, John Inglis. Judge Stewart died late in the year, and in November he was replaced by shipping magnate and entrepreneur Samuel Cunard. Five members had close family connections with other members, and five were partners in the same bank. It was a government, said Joseph Howe, 'like an ancient Egyptian mummy, wrapped up in narrow and antique prejudices.'

Throughout British North America in the 1830s emerging groups of assemblymen, invariably dubbed reformers by historians and contemporaries alike, demanded more broadly based legislative councils. In the Maritimes this demand went hand-in-hand with one for the separation of the council into legislative and executive bodies. This reform was achieved in 1832 in New Brunswick and in 1838 in Nova Scotia and Prince Edward Island. In Nova Scotia, London responded to the demands of a vigorous and effective reform group, led by Howe, which had achieved a majority in the late 1836 election, twenty-six of forty-four seats. As of January 1838 the council was divided into two bodies, with nineteen members on the legislative council. Four of the nineteen had been assemblymen immediately before being elevated, two associated with the reform cause.

The mid-to-late 1830s also saw the beginnings of demands for change in the composition of executive councils. In all colonies a few assemblymen were added to those councils, but Britain fell short of extending this reform to responsible government. The British attitude was neatly summarized in a dispatch by Lord John Russell, colonial secretary, written in 1839, after the rebellions. Russell made it clear that executive councillors and other officials who headed government departments were to be selected and dismissed by the governor on the basis of politics – did they command the support of a majority of assemblymen? But he made it equally clear that this was preferred policy, not constitutional imperative. Full responsible government, the need for ministers to have the confidence of the assembly, would not arrive until the late 1840s.

Another set of constitutional issues common to most colonial reform movements concerned the higher judiciary's role in politics. Demands for the separation of the judiciary from the executive and legislative branches of government were common, as discussed in chapter 22. The issue of judges on councils provides an excellent example of reformers' tendency to voice their complaints in British constitutional language, not republican rhetoric. Denis-Benjamin Viger, for example, a lower Canadian reformer, told a British House of Commons committee in 1828 that it was not in accord with the British constitution for judges to be 'in the morning at court, in the afternoon at the executive council, and at the same day at the Legislative Council, making the laws, ordering their execution, and then judging upon those very laws.'[44] Another issue previously discussed, judicial independence, also involved reform demands being couched as an appeal to British constitutional principles, not republican ones. An Upper Canadian assembly committee made the point bluntly and effectively in an 1829 address to the Crown. After 'rejoicing' at 'the unparalleled happiness of the people of England' at the fact that they had independent and impartial judges, it pointed out that 'as a portion of Your Majesty's free and glorious empire, we also are equally interested and entitled to have justice administered amongst us by independent judges.'[45]

Colonial constitutional struggles also involved public finance. Assemblies had the power to tax, but every colonial government could function at least to some extent independently of the assembly, because they had an independent source of finance, the casual and territorial revenues of the Crown.[46] The amounts collected varied widely from colony to colony. Money came into the executives' coffers everywhere from the land granting system, which remained out of the control of the assemblies until the 1840s; licences to cut timber; fees from surveying and from issuing licences to occupy or fee simple grants; and, after an 1827–31 change in policy, land sales. All such revenue went to the Crown, not to the assembly. In Nova Scotia, which collected money from these sources, the principal source of Crown revenue was actually the rent and royalties payable by the General Mining Association, which operated the coal mines of Cape Breton and Pictou County.

In every colony reformers wanted the assembly to get its hands on these revenues to augment the funds it could raise by local taxation to spend on internal development schemes – roads, bridges, and the like. But there was a complication, one that had an impact on all legal systems. In the eighteenth and early nineteenth centuries the British government had provided an annual parliamentary grant to support the colonies, and this paid the salaries of colonial officials, including many, but not all, superior court judges. When in the mid-to-late 1820s Britain embarked on a policy of retrenchment in colonial spending, reducing and then eliminating the parliamentary grant, it shifted the salaries of judges and colonial officials for which it was responsible to the casual and territorial revenues. When assemblies demanded these revenues be put at its disposal, London responded by conditioning its acceptance of that demand on a guarantee that the local assemblies would continue to pay official salaries, including judicial ones. The issue was a constitutional one: if colonial assemblies could withhold the salaries of the judges, or if those salaries were subject to annual votes of the assembly, they could not be seen as truly independent.

Thus London wanted assemblies to guarantee salaries by a civil list. The 1830s saw intense negotiations over the size of the civil list, that is, the number of people to be included, and the salaries paid, in every colony, but there was a resolution of the question only in Upper Canada (1831) and New Brunswick (1837). The Lower Canadian assembly never agreed to wording sufficient, in London's view, to guarantee payment, and the civil list question was resolved there only after the province of Canada was formed in 1841. Nova Scotia was a very late holdout; the civil list question was not settled until 1849, and the cause of the delay was the argument over judges' fees, discussed in chapter 22. The assembly would not agree to pay the higher salaries given by London in 1838 to compensate the judges for fees foregone, fees that the assembly continued to insist, until 1849, had been illegally collected. Partly for this reason Chief Justice Halliburton's salary was consistently in arrears in the 1840s. In addition, London had put his salary on the casual and territorial revenues, but those revenues plummeted when the rent and royalties paid by the General Mining Association drastically declined from new competition from Pennsylvania. Halliburton plaintively pleaded with Queen Victoria for redress, reminding her that 'I am your Servant and not theirs' (the coal operators), and that as 'my job in the Court is to make people live up to their obligations' it was incongruous for him to be 'reduced in ... old age to the humiliating condition of being compelled to announce to his creditors that he is unable to fulfill his own obligations to them.'[47]

There were many other issues involved in the ongoing disputes between colonial assemblies and executives. Some, such as the allocation of money for roads and other infrastructure, public support for the leading dissenting school in Nova Scotia, the Pictou Academy, arguments about the enforcement of timber licensing rules in New Brunswick, and resentment at the one-seventh of the land set aside in Upper Canada for the support of the established church did not directly engage the law and the legal system. But many of the political controversies did involve such questions, and although they are discussed in other chapters they are worth noting here, for they demonstrate how intimately the law and the legal system were central to social, economic, and political disputes, and thus ultimately to constitutional dissatisfaction. They included, in Upper Canada, the 'alien question,' discussed in chapter 30 on land law, which contributed to the growing belief that the colonial constitution was dysfunctional. In both the Canadas complaints were voiced about the administration of justice by the law officers of the Crown and the judiciary. The best known of these, although by no means the only one, was the failure of Attorney General Robinson to prosecute the offenders after a gang of tory bully-boys had destroyed William Lyon Mackenzie's printing press in 1826.[48] In the criminal law and justice area, reformers tended to favour a reduction in capital and corporal punishment and an expansion of the rights of felony defendants to full representation by counsel. The same politicians favoured good behaviour appointments for judges, while conservatives opposed the principle. Reformers in Nova Scotia argued against the creation of more judgeships to be paid for out of public funds, and similarly minded assemblymen everywhere tended to favour the expansion of the civil jurisdiction of lower, less expensive courts. Examples could be multiplied, but the point is made by these. By the late 1830s substantial elements in the legislatures of the Canadas, Nova Scotia, Prince Edward Island, and, to a lesser extent New Brunswick, had pushed for and achieved changes in policies and in doing so had altered their colonial constitutions.

Rebellion and Repression in the Canadas

The struggles between colonial executives and assemblies were deeper and more divisive in the Canadas, especially in Lower Canada, than in the Maritimes, and led, as is well known, to armed rebellion. Much has been written about the rebellion crisis of the late 1830s.[49] There is not space here to summarize the descent into rebellion; suffice it to say that in Lower Canada the disputes among the assembly, the legislative council, and the executive came to involve not just policy differences, but French-Canadian identity and nationalism, which in turn pushed the opposition into increasingly radical stances. This development began as early as 1822 with an attempt by the English party to have the House of Commons legislate a union of the Canadas, one that would have made English the only official language and, after fifteen years, banned the use of French in the assembly. This episode was key to moving the opposition Patriote party in the assembly, led by lawyer Louis-Joseph Papineau, to increasingly strong critiques of the government, and by the 1830s to advocate not simply reforms in the English-derived constitution but a more democratic constitution altogether, one based on popular sovereignty and republican principles. The Patriotes demanded, among other things, an elected legislative council; the famous 92 Resolutions passed by the assembly in 1834 proposed popular control of all organs of government through elections.

Descent into rebellion in both Canadas followed an essentially complete breakdown of the constitution. Measures passed by the assembly were routinely voted down by the legislative council. When the British Parliament rejected all reformers' demands in 1837, mass protest meetings were held in Lower Canada and Patriotes constructed armed camps outside of Montreal consisting of some 3,500 men. By then also

William Lyon Mackenzie was organizing extra-parliamentary gatherings to put pressure on the Upper Canadian administration. The rebellions themselves were initially short-lived and ineffective. British forces, supported by the Mohawk, perhaps the last occasion that Indigenous peoples' military support as independent forces was utilized, easily defeated the Lower Canadian rebels once fighting broke out in November 1837. Dozens fled to the United States, an untold number died in retributive shootings, and hundreds were arrested. British regulars even more rapidly and comprehensively sent packing the motley crew who advanced on Toronto under Mackenzie in December 1837. Also easily defeated was the western Ontario rising under Dr Charles Duncombe in the same month. Mackenzie, Duncombe, and others fled to the United States, and with that the initial phase of rebellion was effectively over. But in both Canadas hostilities continued. In Upper Canada sporadic invasions were launched from the United States by small bands throughout 1838. These invasions were carried out by Upper Canadians who had decamped after Mackenzie's failure, and their American supporters and the invaders were often joined by persons domiciled in Upper Canada. A more serious threat was posed by Lower Canadian Patriotes in exile, who raised money, bought arms, and established secret societies within the colony – the Frères Chasseurs. Under the leadership of Robert Nelson and Dr Cyril-Hector-Octave Côté a declaration of independence encompassing a democratic constitution based on universal male suffrage was drafted. Plans for coordinated internal insurrections and invasions from outside were laid, and some 13,000 men joined the fight. For all this, the second rebellion in November 1838 took only a week to crush.

There were many similarities in the legal response of the authorities to the rebellions between the Canadas, but there were also large differences.[50] Most Upper Canadian rebels were tried in the Court of King's Bench, and few by court martial. Conversely all the Lower Canadians who were tried went before courts martial. More Upper Canadians were tried in one forum or another than Lower Canadians, despite the more sustained threat in the lower colony. Three Upper Canadians were executed following the initial rebellion in late 1837, while no Lower Canadians were; exemplary hangings in the lower colony had to await the second rebellion. These differences make it appropriate to discuss the legal responses to the two insurrections separately.

The Upper Canadian rebels had clearly committed treason, and the initial legal response to the rebellion was to strengthen the state's power by the passage of three statutes in January 1838. The new legislation suspended habeas corpus and allowed jurors to be selected from out of the district. Most important and controversial, the *Lawless Aggressions Act* provided that Americans and their Upper Canadian supporters could be tried either by courts martial or in King's Bench.[51] Chief Justice Robinson admitted that it was of 'questionable propriety' to treat foreigners the same as British subjects, but justified the legislation by two rationales. It would 'deter the people of Canada from uniting themselves to ... foreign invaders, by subjecting them to court martial,' while at the same time it would deter Americans from invading 'if they were placed upon the same footing in resort to trial and punishment, as the rebels.'[52] Two months later, in March 1838, five more statutes were passed, the most important of which provided for escapees to be convicted, and their property confiscated, in their absence, and allowed the government to issue conditional pardons to those who confessed their guilt. To that point the lieutenant governor could only pardon people convicted of offences other than murder or treason; in these two cases the local authorities could only reprieve and recommend a pardon to London. The Act encouraged guilty pleas without a guarantee of pardon. Another of the five statutes gave JPs power to disperse meetings, arrest those present, and seize any weapons found.[53] This second set of legislative initiatives was motivated by the fact that so many had fled to the United States and were threatening further invasions, along with American supporters.

Chief Justice Robinson was the principal drafter of all this legislation, and he also oversaw prosecution strategies, a prime example of what reformers in both Canadas complained about through the 1830s – the combination of executive, legislative, and judicial power in one person. Formal legal processes against those in custody began at the spring assizes held at both Toronto and Hamilton in March and April 1838. While some trials were underway, and other prisoners were awaiting trial, the executive and Robinson engaged in extensive discussions about how to handle the more than 100 cases. The executive's choices were limited by Colonial Secretary Glenelg's admonition to show as much leniency as possible. To the fore in these discussions was a report authored by Vice Chancellor Jameson, on behalf of himself and two other 'commissioners' appointed 'to Inquire into Charges of Treason and Felony.'[54] The commissioners produced reports on 119 people who had either been tried and convicted, were awaiting trial at Toronto, or had confessed and petitioned for a pardon. Sixty-five were recommended for a penitentiary sentence, thirty-two for transportation for a term of years, and twenty-two, 'those whose guilt is the highest and for whose character the least can be hoped,' were recommended for execution or transportation for life. These recommendations were substantially endorsed by the two judges who had presided over the Toronto trials, Robinson and Jonas Jones. Thus legal and political considerations went hand-in-hand and were co-ordinated, with an eye to the delicate balance of retribution and preservation of the political status quo.

Ultimately only twelve trials were conducted at the Toronto Assizes from the nearly 150 people on the court calendar when the assize opened.[55] Half a dozen had their indictments turned back by the grand jury, and the vast majority of the rest petitioned for and were granted pardons without trial. Five men were acquitted, five were sentenced to death but had those sentences commuted to transportation (four) or banishment, and just two men, Samuel Lount and Peter Matthews, were hanged in the courtyard of the Toronto jail on 12 April 1838. These proceedings thus represent a contradiction. On the one hand were mass arrests, pardoning legislation that persuaded men to confess without a guarantee that pardons would be granted, the chief justice effectively directing executive policy on prosecution and presiding at trials with evident bias, and packed juries. On the other hand most of those who confessed were pardoned, juries did acquit, and only two men were hanged. For all the procedural infelicities and manipulations of the law, the process was successful as an ideological exercise proceeding, in the words of two historians, 'from bloody retribution to merciful forgiveness.' Two men were hanged because somebody had to hang. Both were leaders of the rebellion, and Lount, a successful storekeeper and blacksmith, had briefly served as a member of the assembly. But more important than the leading roles they had played in the rebellion was the fact that they were the most prominent men actually in custody, Mackenzie and many others having decamped to the United States. They were tried first precisely because Attorney General Hagerman and Robinson had already identified them as the best candidates for execution.

Other trials were held through 1838, in Kingston, Hamilton, Niagara, and London, in response to invasions from the United States supported by local residents.[56] The Hamilton proceedings were all at assizes, elsewhere there was a mix of regular King's Bench trials and courts martial, the latter instituted only from the fall of 1838 in response to continued conflicts on the American border. All were marked by procedural irregularities and biased judges and jurors and flimsy evidence, and high numbers of failed indictments and acquittals resulted. Only one man, James Morreau, was executed at Niagara, and seventeen others, mostly Americans tried under the *Lawless Aggressions Act*, were executed following the Kingston and London courts martial, but the majority of those found guilty were transported, most of them Americans. The executive and the judiciary again worked together to moderate the severity of the law lest it work counterproductively. King's Bench Judge Levius Sherwood was to the fore in advocating the judicious selection of a limited number of examples. He argued against what he called 'frequent exhibitions' of state killing in case they both created sympathy for rebels and made British law the same as American, where majoritarian sentiments were supposedly untempered by law.[57]

The most lawless act was undoubtedly Colonel John Prince's summary execution of five American invaders, captured after the Battle of Windsor in December 1838.[58] Prince was a successful English barrister who had emigrated to the Windsor area in 1833 and became a leading citizen, JP, and assembly member. He was also reclusive and paranoid and became disillusioned with what he thought was the weak response of the colony's leaders to American 'outrages.' When he got the opportunity as commander of the local militia, he ordered the extrajudicial executions. The incident sparked a heated debate in the colony, with many stridently supporting him, and although there was a court of inquiry he was exonerated. In addition to Prince's extra-legal Act, more blood was spilled by the state after the Toronto trials than before, likely because the leniency that had marked those initial proceedings had not had the effect the authorities hoped for, of damping further cross-border raids and eliminating local support for them.

Lower Canadian authorities took a different approach from the outset, declaring martial law in December 1837 and suspending habeas corpus, while Britain replaced the assembly and the legislative council with the Special Council. But there were no trials, and by the time the new governor general, Lord Durham, arrived on 27 May 1838, more than 150 prisoners were in jail and the Special Council had passed five security-related ordinances – continuing the suspension of habeas corpus, legitimizing the searching of private homes for arms, and outlawing secret societies. Most significantly, one of the ordinances permitted the pardoning of anybody 'concerned in the late insurrection.'[59] Durham's initial response was driven by an unwillingness to see anybody hang, a policy, as noted above, encouraged by London. He issued a blanket amnesty to the people in jail, except for those involved in the murder of Patriote turned government informer Joseph Armand *dit* Chartrand whose evidence had led to many arrests in late 1837.[60]

Durham also sent eight self-confessed rebel leaders to Bermuda for four years on condition of execution if they returned. There was no local legislation to permit this; an 1835 Lower Canadian statute sanctioned transportation to Australia via England, and only for people convicted.[61] Durham rushed through a local ordinance permitting transportation to Bermuda, but it said nothing about what was to happen to the eight once there.[62] It was effectively banishment rather than transportation, a fact immediately obvious from the conditions they enjoyed en route on a naval ship. Not being under restraint they travelled like modern-day cruise passengers, unshackled, completely free to move around the ship and socialize with the officers, well fed and enjoying ample quantities of wine. Further problems for Durham arose when they arrived. The governor of Bermuda, Stephen Chapman, initially refused to allow them to land, and although he soon relented he could not treat them as he did convicts, and instead placed them on their 'parole of honour,' restricting them to one area of the island. Serious objections were raised in London to Durham's action. The law officers opined that he had no power to banish without trial, nor to order them to be executed if they returned. Parliament overturned the Bermuda Ordinance, and Governor Chapman freed the men after a fourteen-week stay. The irony of the whole episode is that Durham thought he had acted with restraint and expediency, even if not legally. There were no mass trials, most Patriotes were given amnesty and released, and the small number he thought had been ringleaders were banished. His actions with regard to those eight, which have rightly been termed an arbitrary use of power,[63] might plausibly be said to have nevertheless been not just merciful but generous. They foundered on the reef of legality.

The government's response to the second rebellion in Lower Canada was markedly different. When that rebellion broke out there had been only one legal proceeding arising out of the first rebellion, the September 1838 trial of four men accused of the murder of Chartrand. All were acquitted. Counsel for the accused, Patriote assemblyman Charles-Elzéar Mondelet, argued that the region where the killing had occurred was one where all legal authority had broken down, a 'state of nature' subsisted, and the Patriote leaders were the de facto government and their orders lawful. He also insisted that oppressed people were justified in rebelling. Presiding Chief Justice of the Montreal Court of Queen's Bench James Reid directed a verdict of guilty, to no avail, and the acquittals convinced many in the government, including Durham, that French-Canadian jurors would never convict people charged with rebellion-related activity.[64] As a result, when proceedings were taken against some of those involved in the second Lower Canadian rebellion, they were by court martial, a non-jury tribunal.

The general court martial at Montreal took place from November 1838 to May 1839. One hundred and six prisoners were tried in groups, fourteen trials in all, and ninety-nine people were convicted of treason and sentenced to death. Twelve were executed and fifty-eight transported. All of the transportees were pardoned between 1844 and 1848, and most returned to Lower Canada.

The court martial trials, in one author's succinct summary, 'fell well below common law and statutory standards of procedure and evidence.'[65] There were no juries, fact and law being decided by a panel of military officers, with advice on the latter provided by the prosecutors. Some of the 'judges' had taken part in the fighting. All the accused were charged with 'levying war' against the queen and/or with 'compassing Her Majesty's death,' both elements in the statutory definition of treason, and eleven were additionally charged with murder.

A court martial, rather than King's Bench, could be used because martial law had been declared. To perhaps over-simplify what that means, English law by the nineteenth century held that martial law could be invoked only by Parliament, not through the prerogative, and could be used only inside Britain in a period of war within the realm. A period of war was defined as a time when the common law courts had ceased to function.[66] But that was within Britain and was not the practice in the colonies, where the royal prerogative could be and was used to declare martial law, and compliant local legislatures invariably validated 'any measure deemed necessary' to quell rebellion or serious disorder. Martial law was proclaimed in early December 1837, and despite the local law officers' doubts about its propriety because the insurrection was over, not suspended until April 1838. When news of the second rebellion reached Quebec City in early November, Governor Colborne immediately declared martial law again, and in the days that followed the Special Council confirmed this and passed ten other ordinances suspending the usual workings of criminal procedure.[67] The Chartrand trial convinced the authorities not to use juries with francophones, but less drastic alternatives were proposed but rejected – moving the trials to the Eastern Townships, England, or another colony, or creating a non-jury court staffed with judges and lawyers. Colborne considered none of these alternatives – 'he wanted a tribunal where nothing could go wrong.'[68]

Fifteen military officers presided, two legally trained judge advocates and a third military officer prosecuted, and most defendants were represented by leading defence lawyers Lewis Drummond, an Irish Catholic, and Aaron Hart, a Jew. As in Upper Canada most of the rebellion leaders had escaped to the United States, so those on trial were from the second or lower ranks of insurgents. Colborne was right – nothing did go wrong from the prosecution's point of view. Not only were the court martial 'judges' men who had fought the rebels, the prosecution won 90 per cent of motions about procedure and evidence, those accused never received lists of witnesses against them, and only a few days' notice of the indictment. Defence counsel could not examine or cross-examine witnesses, only two years after, as discussed below in chapter 29, criminal defendants charged with a capital offence had been given the right to make full answer and defence through lawyers. Those tried had to defend themselves, an especially difficult job for unilingual francophones. Overall it has been estimated that there were twenty-five miscarriages of justice, combining convictions of the innocent with convictions based on flimsy evidence. Whether it was, as one historian has called it, 'the worst abuse of the rule of law in Canadian history' is a matter for comparative judgment, but it was certainly a deeply flawed episode, marked by bias and procedural irregularities.

27

Constitutional Developments II: The Act of Union, Responsible Government, and the Origins of Acculturation Policy, ca 1840–1866

Britain's solution to the rebellion crises was to unite the Canadas, the new constitution comprising one governor general, assembly, and legislative council for the new province of Canada (hereafter Canada), legislated by the *Act of Union* of 1840, like its 1791 predecessor, a statute of the U.K. Parliament. One of the most important aspects of the policy that underlay the Union was assimilation of the French-Canadians, to be achieved over time by a package of measures, including a specific provision of the *Act of Union* making English the only official language of legislation. The anglicization policy proved unworkable and ineffective. Of more lasting effect were two other aspects of the new constitution. Membership of the assembly was restricted by a high property qualification and also favoured the interests of Upper Canada by giving it the same number of seats as the former lower colony (forty-two), despite the latter having a considerably larger population and, as importantly, making it very difficult to alter the seat allocation between the two regions.

Constitutional change of a different sort also emerged in the 1840s in all the British North American colonies – responsible government. The rebellion crisis, and the rise of reform movements elsewhere, especially in Nova Scotia, brought Britain to an acceptance that a form of government in the colonies in which the executive was responsible to the legislature was inevitable, an acceptance that became a reality in 1848–50. Responsible government was a highly significant constitutional change, as significant as Confederation. Confederation united, over a six-year period between 1867 and 1873, colonies that mostly already had the form of government in which power resided ultimately in elected assemblies, assemblies from which executives were chosen and to which executives were responsible. Only the North-West Territories did not enjoy that form of government in the dominion that emerged from the Confederation settlement.

In its turn the responsible government period saw further changes, all but one occurring in eastern and central Canada. The power to appoint and remove judges shifted to the colonies from London, the franchise was extended, municipal government became the predominant form of local government, especially in Upper Canada, and the legislative council of Canada was made partially elective. Most importantly, responsible government gave the colonies much more influence over policy towards Indigenous peoples, and local governments began to legislate policies aimed at their acculturation, policies that would take greater hold after Confederation but had substantial roots in the later 1840s and 1850s.

The final major constitutional development of the immediate pre-Confederation period was the establishment of settler colonies in the Pacific west. The colony of Vancouver Island was founded in 1849, and that of mainland British Columbia in 1858. In 1865 the two colonies were united, and British Columbia entered Confederation in 1871. As important as the creation and growth of settler colonies, the two decades before 1871 witnessed the erosion and ultimately the destruction of Indigenous independence on the Pacific coast, through a combination of Indigenous dispossession, mirroring what had occurred in the east immediately after 1815, devastating diseases, and armed force. This constitutional review does not include the District of Assiniboia, where major change would have to wait until the acquisition of the region by the new Dominion in 1870 and the consequent conflict with the Métis, matters treated in volume 2 of this work.

The Settler Constitution after the Rebellions: The Union of the Canadas and Responsible Government

Following the suppression of the rebellions, the home government needed to address the related issues of the causes of dissatisfaction and the remaking of the constitution. Lord Durham was made governor general and given a mandate to report on both issues for all of British

North America, not just Canada. Durham's principal proposals are well known, other ideas of his less so, because they were not put into effect. For the long term he advocated a British North American federation, in which the French Canadians would be in a minority. In the short term he proposed a legislative union of the Canadas – a single bicameral legislature with the assembly elected on a representation by population basis, and thus one in which the French would be a minority, the overall balance tilted against them by the residents of the Eastern Townships. Durham also wanted the newly united colony divided into several large administrative units, a kind of quasi-federation, which, he hoped, the other colonies would join and thus achieve his British North American federation. This proposal was not adopted. Durham was an assimilationist when it came to French Canada, writing that 'in any plan, which may be adopted for the future management of Lower Canada, the first object ought to be that of making it an English Province.' But he was also a pragmatist, seeing linguistic assimilation as something that would happen organically over time, and arguing that 'while the people continue to use the French language, their Government should take no such means to force the English language upon them as would, in fact, deprive the great mass of the community of the protection of the laws.'[1]

Britain quickly accepted the union idea, but its implementation was delayed by protests from Upper Canada and by unrelated political problems for the home government. The *Act of Union*[2] was not passed by Parliament until July 1840, with the union taking effect at the beginning of 1841. It was not a long document, sixty-two sections, and operated principally to repeal the 1791 Act and unite the two colonies. To placate the Upper Canadians, and the conservatives in London, the Act gave both sections the same number of seats and distributed the Lower Canadian seats in the assembly to give more representation to the Eastern Townships than their largely anglophone population merited. All existing laws of the Canadas remained in force for the section for which they had been passed. The Act established one assembly and one legislative council for the united colony, the latter to be appointed and to comprise at least twenty men. Assembly elections were to be held at least every four years, as under the 1791 constitution. Among the more important clauses for the future settler constitution of British North America was section 58, which gave the executive the sole power to originate money bills. This made it possible for the executive council to be a genuine executive government, proposing legislation and the raising of taxes to pay for it; the assembly could do the former alone, not the latter.

The *Act of Union* said nothing more about the relationship of the legislature to the executive, although the *Durham Report* had dealt with it at length. Durham believed in a version of responsible government, seeing it as a way of strengthening colonial executives. If the governor was required to appoint to his executive council men who could command a majority in the assembly, then that assembly would no longer be able, as a practical matter, to act independently of the executive. Much has been written about exactly what Durham proposed, because he not only did not define the phrase 'responsible government,' he did not even use it. He talked at one point of 'the true principle of representative government' as being the 'entrusting [of the management of public affairs] to the persons who have the confidence of the representative body.' Hence he defined properly functioning representative government as tantamount to responsible government. At another point he wondered rhetorically 'how any English statesmen could have imagined that representative and irresponsible government could be successfully combined.'[3] Durham was clearer when he turned to practicalities, arguing that the colonies needed 'no invention of a new constitutional theory'; all that was required was to 'follow out consistently the principles of the British constitution,' which meant that the Crown 'has to carry on the Government in unison with a representative body ... [and] consent to carry it on by means of those in whom that representative body has confidence.' But Durham was not listened to. British politicians took the same pragmatic and gradualist approach, not endorsing responsible government but supporting a more representative government, as they had been doing since the early to mid-1830s when a policy of having some assemblymen on the executive councils was implemented.

As importantly, the British government also departed from Durham on language policy. Section 41 of the Act provided that all 'Writs and public Instruments whatsoever relating to the ... Legislative Council and Legislative Assembly,... and all Journals, Entries, and written or printed Proceedings shall be in the English Language only.' This forced official unilingualism was somewhat tempered by a provision allowing the translation of those documents and by the fact that nothing prohibited the use of French in assembly debates. Section 41 was a clear statement of intent but had little effect. The first Union assembly chose Austin Cuvillier, a French Canadian, as speaker, passed legislation specifically providing for the translation of statutes into French, and adopted Rules of Procedure permitting motions in both languages.[4] By 1844 the governor general had reverted to the pre-1840 practice of having a clerk of the legislative council read a French translation of the Speech from the Throne after he had read it in English, and in everyday life French was spoken and taught as it had been before the union. Section 41 was nonetheless very much resented by French Canadians, especially reform luminary Louis-Hippolyte La Fontaine and fellow reformer Thomas Cushing Aylwin, who campaigned for its repeal for almost a decade. La Fontaine and Cushing were adroit in exploiting various issues to keep a focus on section 41. A key moment was the unanimous support given to a motion requesting repeal in 1845, put forward by Louis-Joseph Papineau, then a member of the executive council in the MacNab-Morin ministry. That support made it inevitable that the imperial Parliament would acquiesce, although it took another three years for it to do so. After the Baldwin-La Fontaine ministry came to power in 1847, London finally gave up its pointless pursuit of unilingualism and repealed section 41 in 1848. A year later the Canada assembly revised and consolidated the local election laws, specifically and symbolically providing that election writs were to be proclaimed in both languages in Lower Canada.[5]

Another significant difference between the constitutions of 1791 and 1841 was the enhanced property qualification for assembly members. Although the 1791 *Constitutional Act* had contained no such stricture, from 1818 Upper Canadian members needed £80 in unencumbered freehold land, and in the later 1830s there were serious discussions about introducing a property qualification in Lower Canada.[6] Article 28 of the *Act of Union* went much further, providing that a member needed to be 'legally or equitably seised as of Freehold ... of Lands or Tenements held in Free and Common Socage, or ... of Lands or Tenements held in Fief or in Roture, ... of the Value of £500 sterling.' This provision was vigorously and successfully campaigned for by Montreal's anglophone merchants, who saw it as a way of reducing the influence of radical and republican elements among the francophone population. Although the £500 qualification was much lower than the anglophone merchant lobby wanted, it did cause a few, albeit minor, difficulties for some. Augustin-Norbert Morin was electable in 1841 only because supporters assisted him to qualify. But he did run and was elected, and reformers and Patriotes secured a majority in the first assembly, meaning that the qualification did not significantly affect election outcomes. Opposition to it nonetheless lingered and occasionally was manifested in political debate, through the 1840s and 1850s.[7]

French Canadians may have been relatively quiescent about the property qualification because they were far more concerned about another aspect of the *Act of Union*. Article 26 required that any legislation to modify the number of representatives in the assembly had to be supported by two-thirds of the votes on both second and third readings in both the assembly and the legislative council. The provision was designed to make it almost impossible to legislate representation by population, which would have given Lower Canada, with its population of some 650,000, more seats than Upper Canada, with its 450,000 people. This restrictive provision was much resented by French-Canadian politicians in the 1840s, who tried on a number of occasions to alter the number of representatives but were never able to achieve the two-thirds majority. Over time, inequalities between ridings caused by population changes were added to the representation problem. The number of seats for each section was raised from forty-two to sixty-five in 1853, but there was no lasting solution to inequities. From the later 1850s, with the Upper Canadian population having outstripped the Lower, the shoe was on the other foot, and George Brown's Reform party increasingly advocated representation by population. The two-thirds provision prevented any resolution to the problem before Confederation.

Responsible government was the principal underlying constitutional issue of the 1840s. It ran as a thread through all the particular and local questions of that decade.[8] Reformers everywhere lobbied for the executive councils to be led, if not entirely composed of, men drawn from the assembly and who could command a majority in that body. The Colonial Office did not concede this point formally until the late 1840s, but as early as 1839 it had largely and effectively accepted that it would inevitably happen at some point. In this respect two pronouncements that year by Colonial Secretary Lord John Russell were highly significant. In a dispatch sent in October he rejected the principle of responsible government while at the same time accepting that it should normally be acted on in practice. In a circular letter written the same month to all British North American governors he made it clear that officials in charge of government departments should henceforth be appointed and dismissed for political reasons, rather than holding their posts effectively for life and being compensated if they were removed.[9] In his 1839 pronouncements Russell effectively declared that responsible government in all but name would henceforth be the new constitutional policy, and the name itself could come later.

It came in the late 1840s. The political history of the 1840s is too well known to require repeating here and relevant to Canada's legal history largely because a decade of gradual change in practice culminated in the profound constitutional transition to responsible government proper. Governors worked with politicians in order to increasingly ensure, in the words of Charles Poulett Thomson, later Baron Sydenham, governor of Canada, that local matters would be administered 'in accordance with the wishes of the Legislature.'[10] Governors worked with party leaders and were often identified with particular parties at election time. They chose executive councillors who had the support of an assembly majority. Some executive councillors and heads of government departments did not hold seats in assemblies, but enough did, including always the leader of the administration, to move the colonies closer to a true system of responsible government. As early as 1841 Canada had cabinet government, a system in which all heads of department were political appointees. But it did not yet have full responsible government; in the 1840s a coalition of Conservative and Reform ministers held office, mostly working with, but sometimes in conflict with, the governor. Similar change came to Nova Scotia, and more slowly to New Brunswick and Prince Edward Island,[11] but generally the 1840s were a decade in which the constitution moved slowly but inexorably towards full responsible government, with little resistance from London. It is a misnomer to describe the 1840s as the decade in which British North Americans 'struggled' for responsible government. They rather pushed against an open door.

The years 1847 and 1848 proved to be decisive in this transition, with Nova Scotia playing a leading role. After Lieutenant Governor Campbell had been dismissed and the Reformers had won another majority in the 1840 election, Howe joined the executive council in a coalition with Conservative leader James W. Johnston. It did not work well, and in 1843 Lieutenant Governor Lord Falkland dissolved the assembly and, as he had hoped, found himself with a Conservative majority after the election. Howe and the two other Reform councillors resigned shortly afterwards when Falkland added other Conservatives to the council. For some four years they worked for a return of Reform to power and for responsible government, and got what they wanted in 1847–8. Falkland completed his six-year term in 1847 and was succeeded by Sir John Harvey, who thought he could damp down local dissatisfactions by forming a new coalition. But Reformers would not cooperate and instead demanded a dissolution and an election. They won the August 1847 election and, when the assembly met in January 1848, it voted no confidence in the Conservatives, who all left the executive council. Harvey asked the Liberal (formerly Reform) leader James Boyle Uniacke to form an administration. It was the first 'responsible government election' in British North America; the government lost and resigned, and another party, the winners, formed a government. The reformers' refusal to join a coalition and their election victory were both the result of a hardening of party loyalties and the consequent effective establishment of a two-party system, in the assembly and in the various constituencies.

The events in Nova Scotia coincided with a change in British policy. With the Whigs in power after an election in 1846, the new colonial secretary, Earl Grey, Durham's son-in-law, penned a famous dispatch in which he stated that 'the nature of the constitution established in Nova Scotia renders it necessary that the Government should be carried on by an Executive Council supported by a majority of the Assembly,'[12] that is, by a party. In 1848 also New Brunswick, where politics were the least ideological, adopted responsible government, less because of pressure from reform-minded assemblymen, although there was some, than from the fact that Grey's policy was seen as applicable to that colony as well. In fact New Brunswick's status was equivocal for some years, because the lieutenant governor still on occasion acted independently of the executive in the early 1850s, and not until the Liberals won an election and formed a government in 1854 can true responsible government be said to have arrived.[13]

The year 1848 also brought responsible government to Canada. A new governor, Lord Elgin, arrived with instructions not to interfere in politics and to support the principle that ministers should be responsible to the assembly. When the group led by Baldwin and La Fontaine won the election of that year they formed a ministry strong enough to withstand the opposition, both locally and in Britain, to the Rebellion Losses Bill of the following year. Perhaps the most controversial measure of the Union period, the bill compensated Lower Canadians for losses incurred during the rebellions, including participants in the events of that period and exempting only those convicted of treason.[14] Significantly Elgin resisted pressure from conservatives to oppose the measure, because it had been introduced by his ministry. The bill led to riots in Montreal, the burning of the Parliament buildings, and, more significantly, a vigorous debate in the British Parliament, where opponents argued for royal assent to be refused. The bill was, thundered Lord Brougham, a betrayal of loyal anglophones and an example of 'responsible government carried to an absurd, ridiculous and also to a needless extent.'[15] Brougham's motion to intervene went down to a narrow defeat in the Lords, a critical vote in cementing the principle that neither the local governor nor London would intervene in a decision made by a colonial administration with the support of a majority in the colonial assembly where no broader imperial interests were involved. Grey made the point clearly and succinctly in a consequent letter to Sir Allan MacNab, leader of the Conservatives. If his party did not like what had happened, MacNab was told, 'he ought to look to the elections to restore the majority of his party.'[16]

In only two colonies was responsible government not conceded in 1848 – PEI and Newfoundland. The PEI assembly had no substantial reform faction through the 1840s, but even a conservative-controlled assembly demanded an executive that had the confidence of the assembly by 1846. Two years later a new reform grouping emerged and added its voice to the demand, even more so when reformers won a majority in the 1850 election. But responsible government was delayed for two reasons. One was that there was no civil list, with some of the costs of government still being provided by parliamentary grant, including the salary of the chief justice. This was resolved in 1850. The other, more serious problem was the land issue, discussed in detail in chapter 30 below, which made London wary of ceding responsible government when it might result in local measures depriving the many large absentee landowners of their property rights. The landowners had an effective lobby in London, and in the end Britain's agreement to responsible government was conditional. Lieutenant Governor Sir Alexander Bannerman was told to 'impress upon the Legislature, the necessity of abstaining from the introduction … of any provisions which may infringe on the rights of property.'[17] London thus took a position different from the one it had taken over the rebellion losses bill; there were limits to internal self-government where there was a broader imperial interest – the security of property in the settler dominions once settler governments were 'let loose.'

The last eastern colony to receive responsible government was Newfoundland.[18] From the establishment of an assembly in 1832, politics on the island tended to pit the commercial elite, based in St John's and largely Protestant, against a Catholic-dominated reform grouping drawing support from the outports. The latter generally had a majority in the assembly, which brought that body into political-religious conflicts with the council. In the 1830s fuel was added to the fire of conflict by the attitudes and actions, in court and in council, of Chief Justice Boulton. He used his judicial powers against his political opponents with ruthless severity, sufficient to have London agree to an assembly request for his removal in 1838. With the constitution entirely dysfunctional in the early 1840s, London altered it in 1842 by an arrangement unique in British North America: the legislative council was abolished and the assembly made into a 'blended' legislature, with fifteen elected representatives and ten members nominated by the Crown. At the same time, in an effort to make the elected representatives more 'respectable,' a modest property qualification for the franchise was introduced. The change achieved little, merely exacerbating the problem that beset the constitutions of all colonies, executive power resting with the governor's council but without the means to legislate because the council did not comprise men who could command a majority in the legislature. Reversion in 1848 to the original 1832 constitution did not change that. The reformers, armed with a solid majority from the 1848 election, launched a determined campaign for responsible government which the conservatives countered largely by invoking fears of a Catholic despotism. The campaign bore fruit in 1854–5 when London ordered that the governor abide by responsible government principles.

The Settler Constitutions and Responsible Government

The advent of responsible government meant that colonial governments now enjoyed the power to make all patronage appointments, including judicial appointments. Judicial appointments thus remained patronage-based, but the patronage power was now part of the currency of party politics. It was a lesson that the Nova Scotia Liberals learned in a negative fashion early in 1848, when Supreme Court Judge Lewis Morris Wilkins Senior died. The assembly had not yet met, the old executive council remained in office, and they insisted that the appointment go to Solicitor General Edwin Murray Dodd, a Tory and, frankly, not much of a lawyer. As we have seen and will see again in the second volume of this book, politicians in all colonies and in the new federal government after 1867 used the appointment process to reward political friends, not always enhancing the quality of judges. The most glaring example of the use of patronage before Confederation occurred in Nova Scotia. Chief Justice Brenton Halliburton retired from the bench in 1860, having been on the Supreme Court since 1807 and chief justice since 1833. Premier William Young decided that the best person to replace him was – Premier William Young. A few years later, when they were back in power following the 1863 election, the Conservatives took their revenge, appointing their long-time leader and sitting MLA James William Johnston to the next vacancy.[19] Party patronage operated also at other levels of the legal system. In 1849 the Nova Scotia Liberals, for example, left well over 100 sitting JPs off the commission of the peace and appointed some 300 new ones.

Responsible government also coincided with, and to some extent caused, changes to the franchise.[20] The qualifications for voting stayed largely the same through the 1840s. In 1849, for example, the consolidated election statute for Canada gave the vote to male subjects of twenty-one years old holding seigneurial or freehold tenure with forty shillings annual rental value in the counties, or possessing a dwelling house and lot with an annual value of ten pounds sterling, or being an urban tenant resident for twelve months in the same place who paid an annual rent of ten pounds sterling on a dwelling house. In the 1850s, however, all colonies witnessed demands for, and resistance to, a broadening of the franchise. As the most recent historian of the franchise has noted, arguments over the vote were about the meaning of citizenship and who could participate in the political life of the community, and the changes legislated in this period were the product of often fierce debate and embodied considerable variation. There was variation not just between colonies but within them, as municipal franchises did not necessarily match that for the assembly. The result was 'multiple layers of inclusion and exclusion.'

The various changes to the franchise in this period cannot all be detailed here, but large trends should be noted. The most significant development was a move away from determining who could vote by freehold ownership to basing that determination, in whole or in part, on assessments, done for tax purposes, of a person's worth in both real and personal property. Nova Scotia, for example, enfranchised those who paid county or poor assessment rates as well as forty-shilling freeholders in 1851, while also for the first time specifically excluding women, and extended this to near manhood suffrage in 1854. But the franchise still excluded 'Indians' and the poorest elements of settler society, people 'who shall have received aid as a pauper under any poor law…, or aid as poor persons from any grant of public money.' Wrongly dubbed 'universal suffrage' by contemporaries, Nova Scotia's franchise was nonetheless the most inclusive in British North America. In 1863, however, a quarter of the population was disenfranchised by a new property qualification, introduced to exclude an influx of poor Irish Catholics.[21]

Prince Edward Island also had effectively manhood suffrage from 1853, the vote being given to all men of twenty years or older who were liable to perform statute labour or had a forty-shilling freehold.[22] Making statute labour – the requirement that every able-bodied man work on road repairs for a few days in the summer – the basis for the franchise was a unique qualification, one that both responded to the island's leasehold system of land occupation, discussed in chapter 30, and to gendered ideals of manly citizenship. In 1855 the New Brunswick franchise was also changed, from the law in place since 1795. It was converted from freehold ownership to one based on assessment of the value of all property owned. The story of how this came about is somewhat tangled, but its most significant result was to enfranchise the respectable urban middling class, merchants and professionals.

An assessment franchise was also attempted to be introduced in Canada in the 1850s, a jurisdiction that operated with five different electoral regimes between 1849 and 1867. The clear grits and the *Parti Rouge,* the radicals, advocated universal male suffrage, and when Francis Hincks was forced to bring them into his ministry in 1851 their influence resulted in an 1853 statute extending the franchise to all male subjects twenty-one years or older who had land worth fifty pounds actual value or five pounds in annual value. However, this franchise required the preparation of registers, which was delayed by the twists and turns of electoral politics until 1858. As of that year the franchise was based on assessment, giving the vote to all male subjects twenty-one and older who possessed 'as owner, tenant or occupant real property' to various assessment values, depending on whether the property was within or outside a municipality for municipal assessment purposes.[23] All the franchise legislation discussed here specified that voters had to be male as well as holders of the requisite property qualification.[24]

The 1840s and 1850s also saw changes to the structure of local government, especially in the Canadas, where developments were closely linked to the coming of responsible government.[25] The local government systems described in part 3 of this volume remained largely unchanged everywhere through the first three decades of the nineteenth century, JPs and quarter sessions continuing as the 'governors' of most urban and rural areas, albeit also operating with subordinate institutions such as the township and parish in Upper and Lower Canada respectively. The principal exceptions were incorporated cities: Saint John, which had been incorporated in 1785 and was governed thereafter by an elected common council, Montreal, and Toronto (incorporated in 1833 and 1834 respectively). Montreal's charter expired in 1836 but was renewed in 1840, with the mayor being directly elected from 1852. Other urban centres in both Canadas were similarly made corporations by special Act in the 1830s and 1840s, although there was no standard form for these. Some simply incorporated boards of police, others involved full-fledged city charters.

While elective municipal government was only a subordinate feature of the system before the 1840s, it was one often lobbied for by reform elements in all colonies, who criticized both the undemocratic nature of local government – rule by appointed magistrates – and its inefficiency and, at times, corruption. One of the better-known incidents in this campaign was the 1835 libel trial of Nova Scotia's leading reformer, Joseph Howe, for statements attacking the integrity of the city's leading JPs. In 1841 Halifax was incorporated and imbued with an entirely new governance structure, an elected council and mayor. Yet otherwise the Nova Scotia local government system remained essentially the same until the 1870s. Permissive legislation in the mid-1850s allowed counties and townships to incorporate, but very few took up the opportunity, principally from a fear of increased taxes.[26]

The most sweeping change to local government came in Upper Canada, where the dominant role of JPs and quarter sessions ended in 1841. In that year elected district councils were established, although they were formally subject to considerable central government control.[27] The governor appointed the council head, the warden, the district clerk, and the district treasurer, and could disallow any council by-law. These and other provisions were inserted at the insistence of Governor Sydenham and objected to strongly by reformers like Baldwin. As it turned out they had little effect in practice; district clerks, for example, were invariably 'chosen' by appointing the person with the most votes among district councillors. But while this aspect of Sydenham's scheme may not have worked out in practice, other objectives of the legislation were met. The councils dealt with a host of local matters that previously took up the time of the assembly, they allowed communities to tax themselves for their own projects, and they provided a 'training ground in representative government' for many men. Ultimately the district council system proved unable to satisfy the demands for more responsive and localized local government. The districts were too large and the district seats too remote both physically and psychologically from most people, and the taxation needed to support a not truly representative system was resented. The demand for local autonomy in the Canadas only increased in the mid-to-late 1840s, with numerous Acts to divide various districts into smaller units.

The culmination of the agitation for reform was the *Municipal Corporations Act* of 1849.[28] It abolished the old districts, replacing them with counties as the basic administrative unit, and established a comprehensive scheme of compulsory municipal incorporation throughout the colony, rural and urban areas alike.[29] Its purpose was to provide, 'by one general law, for the erection of Municipal Corporations, and the Establishment of Regulations of Police, in and for the several Counties, Cities, Towns, Townships and Villages in Upper Canada.' The Act was the first of its kind in the Anglo-Canadian world. That it was passed more or less contemporarily with the coming of responsible government was no coincidence. It did for local government what responsible government did for the central branch. Both enhanced the power of the liberal-minded middle classes and further reduced that of the old tories, who had been supported by patronage appointments. The *Municipal Act* has been seen by most historians as the triumph of a democracy and local autonomy, and those same historians have seen the two as inextricably intertwined. Recent work, however, has caused us to modify this view to some extent, arguing that both statutes and the courts limited local autonomy from the 1850s onwards to a significant extent.

The demands for local autonomy and democratic decision-making also affected Indigenous governance, as discussed in chapter 24.[30] Reformers within the Six Nations launched a movement for an elected council at Grand River in the late 1850s, a campaign that gathered momentum after the bankruptcy of the Grand River Navigation Company in 1861. Isaac Powless, a young Mohawk, proposed dissolution of the Confederacy Council of hereditary chiefs and the institution of an elected municipal government under the aegis of the Indian Department. The proposal did not gain widespread support in the community, most inhabitants accepting that the traditional means of accountability – that chiefs were aware of 'public opinion' and sought to conform to it – was suitable and sufficient. But it is noteworthy that the corporate fiasco seems to have spurred some local band members to want to imitate European forms of governance. As we will see in the next volume, elected councils did come later, not by choice but imposed by the *Indian Acts*.

The final development to the settler constitution that deserves mention was the introduction of the elective principle to the upper house of Canada, the legislative council, in 1856. The scheme, enacted by legislation in both London and Kingston, was that twelve of the forty-eight legislative councillors were to be elected every two years for an eight-year term.[31] By 1862 all councillors were to be elected. Canada was a pioneer among English-speaking jurisdictions in moving to an elected upper house; both the United States (federal) and Australia did not do so until the second decade of the twentieth century. The change was in large measure an indirect product of responsible government. That change made executive councillors responsible to the legislature and also gave them the power to appoint legislative councillors, formerly the preserve of the governor. Legislative councillors effectively lost any role they had played as 'independent' voices; they became party men. Reform leader George Brown stated this explanation clearly in 1865. 'Before Responsible Government was introduced into this country, while the old oligarchical system existed, the Upper House continuously and systematically was at war with the popular branch, and threw out every measure of a liberal tendency,' he noted. After responsible government was achieved, the complaint, Brown said, then became that the upper house 'had too faithfully reflected the popular will,' that is, that it felt obliged to bow to the dictates of the elected politicians.[32] Brown thus attributed the demand for elections to a conservative reaction to responsible government, a desire to revert in some respects to the old colonial system, by making legislative councillors to some degree independent of the party in power.

Somewhat ironically, the movement for an elected council brought together conservative ideas with radical ones, people who favoured greater democratization in all political institutions also supporting it. The differences among the supporters of election resulted in an inconsistent approach to the franchise and to qualifications for members. The new legislative council was chosen from the same franchise as the assembly, but those standing for office had to be worth £2,000 of unencumbered real estate. This was a 'gargantuan' restriction, one that excluded all but the richest men in the colony. Every other colonial assembly approved the principle of an elected council after 1856, but the only other colony to legislate the change was Prince Edward Island, in 1863. The island's move to election was, again, a response to democratization, especially the very broad franchise legislated in 1853,

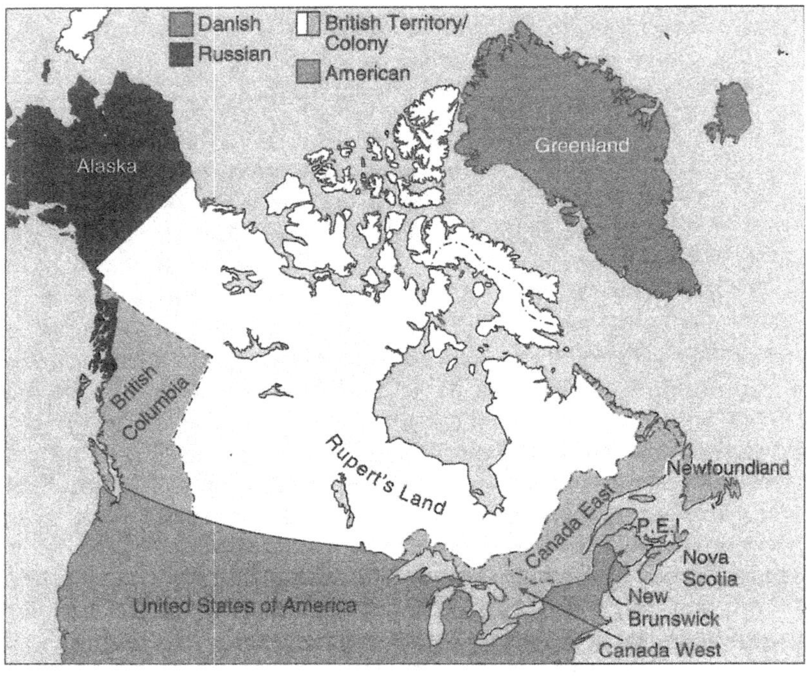

British North America on the eve of Confederation.

and, more particularly, to the tenants' rights movement of the period, discussed in chapter 30 below. As in Canada, it was also supported by radical tenants' rights leaders who saw it as a way of promoting popular sovereignty. Also as in Canada, there was much debate over the franchise and property qualifications for councillors. The franchise was set at £100 of freehold or leasehold real estate, much higher than that for the assembly, while eligibility to sit in the council was set at £500, much lower than in Canada.[33]

Indigenous Peoples and the 'Civilizing Mission'

The 1840s and 1850s saw the further decline of the Indigenous land base, especially in Upper Canada. Two treaties were signed in 1850, named after William Robinson, brother of the colony's chief justice. The Robinson-Superior Treaty was a 16,700 square mile (10.688 million acre) alienation between Lake Superior and Sault Ste Marie. The Robinson-Huron Treaty of 1850 ceded 35,700 square miles (22.848 million acres) from the north shore of Lake Huron to Penetanguishene. The Robinson treaties also involved the establishment of reserves, annuity payments, and guarantees of continued hunting and fishing rights, and became the standard format on which later treaty-making on the prairies was based. A further treaty of 1862 involved the purchase of much of the land reserved on Manitoulin Island following the 1836 Bond-Head treaty.[34]

Treaty-making at mid-century was at one and the same time exemplary of Indigenous peoples' loss of power and deteriorating relations with white settlers and their governments, and of their desire to make the best deals they could. In the late 1840s the Crown Lands Department had issued mining licences on unceded land, and Chief Shingwaukonse, of Garden River, near Sault Ste Marie, made it clear to Governor General Lord Elgin that he expected royalties: 'I want always to live and plant at Garden River and as my people are poor to derive a share of what is found on my lands.' It took a violent confrontation with miners in 1849, and the occupation of one of the mining camps by Indigenous people, for treaty negotiations to be opened, negotiations that were made difficult for the government by the chiefs' determination to extract the best possible bargain.[35]

Newly responsible colonial governments also increasingly used law and other policy instruments to try to change Indigenous societies, economies, and cultures. This acculturation project is often associated with the late nineteenth century, but it had its beginnings in this period. Indeed its roots can be traced to the 1820s and 1830s, to what one historian has dubbed the beginnings of a new-found 'civilizing mission,' a policy of 'directed cultural change.'[36] The civilizing mission was all of this, but it was not the first such attempt. The policy recalled French attempts to create mission villages in the seventeenth century, discussed above in part 2, although such villages always remained more autonomous than the French would have liked. Under the reborn nineteenth-century version, Indigenous people were to convert to Christianity and adopt Western modes of life. They should be farmers, not hunters, sedentary not mobile. Their children should go not just to churches but also to schools where basic literacy in English or French and in Western religious and economic values could be taught. These ideas about how to treat the non-white subject peoples of the empire originated in Britain itself and were proposed and propagated by evangelical Protestant organizations based there, notably the Aborigines Protection Society, founded in 1837. They were led by the same interests – the evangelical middle class – who were able to bring about the abolition of slavery in the empire in 1833. The civilizing impulse was by no means confined to North America; it applied, to a greater or lesser extent, to colonies in South Africa, the Antipodes, and throughout Asia, and came to be highly influential even in the most populous part of the empire, the ever-expanding Indian empire. The notion that Britain had the responsibility of 'civilizing' its imperial charges extended even to the Hudson's Bay Company, which in 1839 reversed its long-held policy against missionaries and began to work with them.

Although much of the work of the civilizing mission in British North America was undertaken by churches and related organizations, governments gradually became involved as well; we saw in chapter 24 the state intervened in Indigenous economies, for example. As the British Colonial Secretary Sir George Murray aptly put it in 1830, Britain and its colonies had ceased being interested in 'the advantages which might be derived' from Indigenous 'friendship in time of war,' and the emphasis should henceforth be on 'reclaiming them from a state of barbarism, and of introducing amongst them the industrious and peaceful habits of civilized life.'[37] The new policy contained an inherent contradiction, which would only deepen over time; 'civilization' was rooted in a humanitarianism that sought to improve the lives of subject peoples but was also crucially and consistently underpinned by a disrespect for Indigenous cultures, laws, and autonomy. We will see in chapter 30 that governments were also ineffective in protecting even the land rights that settler law gave Indigenous peoples.

The principal practical results of the new approach were insistence that Indigenous people adapt to a settled agricultural economy, and, in Upper Canada particularly, the provision of schools in or near reserves. The former, but not the latter, was present in an earlier approach to the Indigenous 'problem,' Upper Canada's Lieutenant Governor Francis Bond-Head's 1836 relocation of as many Indigenous people as possible to Manitoulin Island, where they were to live entirely separate from settler influences. The treaty that Bond-Head made with the Ottawa and Chippewa nations clearly stated what he saw as the cause of the Indigenous peoples' problem, loss of their land base, and equally clearly insisted that the winds of change were blowing with inevitability. The 'unavoidable increase of white population' and 'the progress of cultivation' had had the 'natural effect of impoverishing your hunting grounds,' the treaty pronounced. Indigenous people could keep their lands only if they 'cultivated' them,' but as they had not, 'your Great Father, who has hitherto protected you, has now great difficulty in securing it for you from the whites.'[38] The allusion to improving the land refers to the principal argument that was used to justify aboriginal dispossession – the lack of such 'improvement.'

Bond-Head's relocation and isolation policy was rejected by London in the early 1840s under the prompting of missionary groups and following a Commons select committee, and the 'civilization' project was reaffirmed for the Canadas after a commission appointed by Sir Charles Bagot, briefly governor of Canada in 1842–3, reported.[39] The Bagot Commission was charged with investigating the operations of the Indian Department and the condition of its charges. It found a lack of progress in agriculture and education, inept administration of band funds, and excessive use of liquor. It also found, perhaps not surprisingly, European squatters on reserve lands and the improper recording of land transactions. The Bagot Commission thus highlighted a major flaw in the new civilizing policy. British-based lobby groups could propose it, and even win the support of the London government, but most individual colonials were hostile to it, and colonial administrations, if not also hostile, were indifferent to abuses on the ground, unwilling to anger the European population when its interests clashed with Indigenous ones.

The Bagot Commission proposed, among other things, an administrative reorganization of the Indian Department, which resulted in the dismissal of Samuel Peters Jarvis, previously chief superintendent for Upper Canada, who was thought to have mismanaged department funds. Whether he did or not, he was involved in the Grand River Navigation Company fiasco, discussed elsewhere in this volume. His replacement, James Macaulay Higginson, put into effect most of the Bagot Commission's recommendations, which collectively represented a reaffirmation of the 'civilization' project. Civilized people, said the Bagot report, 'are more regular in their habits, dress more like white people,… attend public worship regularly … their moral habits are materially improved.' Perhaps most notably the commission recommended the building of 'as many manual labour or Industrial schools' as possible. These first residential schools were intended to have far-reaching effects: 'living in boarding schools off reserve, and away from the influence of community and parents,' young Indigenous people would 'imperceptibly acquire the manners, habits and customs of civilized life.' There was one notable exception to the widespread acceptance of Bagot's recommendations. He proposed an additional mark of 'civilization' – individual land ownership, 100 acres per family. This would further Europeanize Indigenous people and enable the Crown to give up the presents it still provided, while protecting reserve lands from European intrusion, as the land could be sold only within the community. But Higginson believed this could not be done without Indigenous peoples' consent – evidence of the continued acceptance of an Indigenous title. The proposal was not generally implemented, because bands would not agree to it, but it was put into effect when in 1847 the Grand River settlements were consolidated on a more 'compact' site.

The civilization policy was reinforced by successor commissions to Bagot. One of these, the Pennefather Commission of 1856–8, was the first to devote considerable effort to enumerating the prevalence of mixed ancestry people in the colony and assessing whether such status made Indigenous people more likely to adopt 'civilization.'[40] As previously discussed, almost a decade earlier Lower Canadian legislation had provided the first legal definition of an 'Indian'; it was thus by 1850 considered necessary to know to whom racially targeted policies were to be applied. Henceforth 'Indian' meant 'all persons of Indian blood, reputed to belong to' a 'particular body or Tribe of Indians,' and 'interested in' Indian land, and their descendants, marriage partners if they resided with an Indian, offspring, and adoptees living on reserved land. It also included 'all persons residing among such Indians, whose parents on either side were or are Indians of such Body or Tribe, or entitled to be considered as such.' Legislation in pursuit of the civilization policy also included provisions making barter transactions for liquor illegal, and exempting property given to Indigenous people for the 'encouragement of agriculture' from seizure for their debts.[41]

The civilization policy was most firmly reflected in the major statute on Indigenous people of the Union period, the *Gradual Civilization Act* of 1857, applicable throughout Canada.[42] Its preamble clearly and succinctly stated the overall policy goal and the principal method of achieving it: 'It is desirable to encourage the progress of Civilization among the Indian Tribes in this Province, and the gradual removal of all legal distinctions between them and Her Majesty's other Canadian Subjects, and to facilitate the acquisition of Property, and the rights accompanying it' by individuals. The Act, among other things, laid out procedures for determining both who was an 'Indian' and how some Indigenous people could be no longer considered people apart but instead be enfranchised like a white person. To qualify a person had to be male, over twenty-one, 'able to speak readily either the English or French language,' of 'sober and industrious habits,' debt free, and 'sufficiently intelligent to be capable of managing his own affairs.' If he met such criteria and applied, he would be placed on probation for three years. If he continued to meet the requirements during that period, he would be enfranchised, a term that in this context meant much more than having the vote. Once enfranchised he was entitled to fifty acres of reserve land for individual use and a portion of any money paid annually to the band. His wife and children would also be enfranchised, 'and shall not be deemed members of his former tribe.' Absolute ownership of the land allotted would be delayed one generation; the newly enfranchised person was given only a life estate, but his descendants would receive a fee simple when they inherited. Very few Indigenous people took up the opportunity provided, most not wanting to so comprehensively lose connection to their people and culture. 'Gradual' civilization was only for the community as a whole under the Act, for individuals changing to European ways was anything but a gradual process. The *Gradual Civilisation Act* was the only legislation to establish a process for enfranchisement, although Nova Scotia's Indian commissioner lobbied for a similar provision in the 1850s.[43]

The 'civilization' policy was influential in all British North American colonies, and law was one of the tools deployed to achieve its goals. Nova Scotia's *Act for the Instruction and Permanent Settlement of the Indians* of 1842,[44] for example, established the position of commissioner of Indian affairs and provided for allotting plots of reserve land to individuals, the assisted purchase of agricultural implements, and the building of churches, schools, and a residence for each chief. The commissioner could also enter into partnerships with 'charitable institutions' to provide education. Inevitably that meant religious institutions, and thus the links between church and state in the provision of residential schools dates back to the 1840s. The principal policies laid down in the 1842 Act were reaffirmed in future legislation, most notably an 1859 statute that sought to expand residential schooling in partnership principally with religious organizations. The Indian commissioner was empowered to 'make arrangements with the trustees or teachers of any schools ... for the board and tuition of Indian children.'[45] New Brunswick's legislation, which as we will see in chapter 30 was concerned mostly with freeing up reserve land for white settlement, also provided for money to be used to purchase 'implements of husbandry and domestic animals,' and for the assignment to individual band members of lots initially to be guaranteed by 'Location Tickets' and then converted to 'absolute Grants' after a ten-year period of residence and improvement of the land. Thus lands reserved for Indians were to be reserved only for 'civilized' ones.[46]

In 1853 Nova Scotia's Indian Commissioner James McLeod asserted that the Indigenous people under his charge 'are becoming more alive to the importance of cultivating the soil, and less disposed to their original roving practices.'[47] It was a not uncommon claim across the colonies, but it was often accompanied by reports stating the opposite and lamenting the lack of change. There were many like George Brown who approved of 'civilization' but doubted that it could be effected because of Indigenous resistance. Speaking in the debate over the *Gradual Civilisation Act* Brown lamented that most Indigenous inhabitants lacked 'ambition' or 'the desire of gaining wealth' and a thirst for 'progress.'[48] In this assessment Brown combined cultural chauvinism with realism. Although 'civilization' was a widely adopted policy, it brought few changes to Indigenous societies. Indigenous peoples proved substantially resilient, continuing to live their lives in the accustomed way. Settler intervention in Indigenous societies must therefore, on its own terms, be considered a failure. Colonial legislatures were parsimonious about providing funds for bureaucrats – there was only one paid employee in the Indian Department for Lower Canada in 1858, the superintendent – for reserve improvements, agricultural instruction, and education. Those same legislatures voted sums for 'relief' on particular occasions, or to help in building churches and schools, but would not spend significant amounts of money.[49] Taking the long view, of course, many now see any attempt at acculturation as bad policy, so to say that the pre-Confederation version of the civilizing mission failed is hardly a criticism. Much more sustained, deeper, and more destructive policies would come in the 1870s and 1880s, a matter to which we will devote considerable space in volume 2 of this history.

Settlement and Colonization in the West

An account of constitutional change prior to the 1860s would not be complete without discussion of two other regions of North America that later became part of Canada and, during this period, saw their constitutional status change, albeit in rather different ways. The area west of Upper Canada and east of the Rockies was, as discussed earlier, nominally British, although until Confederation the British presence there was essentially limited to the fur trade operated by the Hudson's Bay Company (HBC).[50] After the absorption of the Northwest Company by the HBC in 1821, the Red River colony was consolidated as British territory administered by the HBC as the District of Assiniboia. Its European population reached almost 5,000 by about 1840, over 6,500 by the mid-1850s, and over 12,000 by the time Canada bought the HBC lands in 1870.

There were a variety of challenges made to the legality of the HBC's charter, its monopoly, and its governing authority, some of which have been detailed earlier. The HBC survived these challenges, although following the prosecution of a Métis fur trader, Pierre Sayer, for illegal trade in 1849 it stopped trying to enforce its monopoly of the trade in furs.[51] It was the Métis who led the charge against the monopoly, and the Métis also who complained about their lack of representation on the Council of Assiniboia, the legislative body for the district. In fact their leader was on the council, and Métis also sat on juries. There was thus some non-European representation in governing bodies, providing a measure of support for Red River's most recent historian to argue that 'the legal and governmental infrastructure' – the constitution – which functioned until the early 1870s, was 'fundamentally sound, if rudimentary.'[52] Executive authority resided in the governor, who was appointed by the HBC Board in London, not by the Crown, and legislative in the governor and his appointed council, a system similar to the conciliar government created under the *Quebec Act* in 1774.[53] Thus the region did not even have representative government. The council passed regulations on a considerable variety of matters, although as in many other parts of British North America those regulations did not extend to or affect any aspect of Indigenous peoples' self-governance.[54] They dealt with, inter alia, trespassing animals, fire safety, and minor offences. The constitutional history of the Red River colony is to some extent unique, but it nonetheless exemplifies the dual nature of British North American constitutions in this period – involving European-Indigenous relations and governing the European population alone.

The other western region to acquire new constitutional arrangements in this period was what is now British Columbia.[55] There had been a British presence in the region from the 1820s in the form of the HBC, but not British sovereignty as against other nations of European origin until the conclusion of the Oregon Boundary Treaty in 1846. Vancouver Island formally became a British colony in 1849, but although there was a British governor, Richard Blanshard, the real power lay with the Pacific region's chief factor for the HBC, James Douglas, a mixed-race man of 'Scotch-West Indian' origins who was married to the daughter of a European fur trader and a Cree mother.[56] The island was granted in fee simple to the company, subject to a right in the Crown to repurchase it when the HBC's trading licence expired in 1859. Most of the Europeans there were company employees, despite the fact that it was a condition of the land grant that the HBC promote settlement. Those non-HBC settlers who did arrive in the early years bitterly resented the paternalistic and, to their minds, illegitimate governance of the island.

No assembly was initially created, and Blanshard governed, to the extent that he did, through a single advisory council. He resigned and left in 1851, and Douglas succeeded him as governor. There was still no legislature to share power with governor and council until 1856, and until then governor and council ruled by ordinance.[57] The only legislation affecting the colony until then was a permissive British statute allowing the governor to make laws and establish a court system. It was, the province's principal legal historian has noted, 'a bizarre and antiquated constitution.' It was criticized as such in a petition by fifteen independent settlers who protested Blanshard's replacement with Douglas. 'We and we alone represent the interests of the Island as a free and independent British Colony,' they declaimed, pointing out that 'impartial decisions cannot be expected from a Governor who is not only a member of the Company sharing in its profits, but is also ... their Chief Agent.'[58] The constitution remained 'bizarre and antiquated,' even after the assembly was established, for the franchise qualification was set very high – £300 freehold. Douglas was no fan of representative government and established the assembly only when told by the Colonial Office that common law required colonies of settlement to have one. His scepticism about the new arrangements is reflected in his report to London that 'our early attempts at legislation will make a sorry figure,' but having an assembly at all 'will have the effect you contemplate, of removing all doubts as to the validity of our local enactments.'[59] Vancouver Island became a Crown colony proper in 1859, when the ten years expired and the Crown exercised its right to a re-conveyance. In 1864 its council, which included Chief Justice Joseph Needham in a harkening back to the role played by the senior judiciary of the eastern colonies prior to the 1830s, was divided into executive and legislative branches, a complicated governing apparatus for a colony of about 4,000 people.

Vancouver Island's Indigenous-European constitution was much like it had been in eighteenth-century eastern Canada – the coexistence of equals. Indigenous law governed Indigenous societies inter se, making then de facto independent, although the Indigenous population declined substantially from European diseases. Between 1850 and 1854 Douglas concluded fourteen treaties with the Indigenous inhabitants, in which land in and around Victoria – Saanich, Sooke, Nanaimo, and Port Hardy – was exchanged for cash. Just 930 square kilometres was involved, with the amounts specified in eleven of the treaties totalling £553-6s-8d. The Indigenous signatories also received reserved hunting and fishing rights over the ceded land. At that point it seemed as if the Indigenous peoples of the west coast would be treated similarly to those in Upper Canada in the late eighteenth and early nineteenth centuries – as effectively equal partners and with their rights to their land acknowledged by a treaty-making process. Certainly the Indigenous inhabitants themselves believed that distinct Indigenous nations had their own territories and that the treaties were peace and friendship agreements. Reflective of the fact that the Indigenous people did not believe they were selling the land in the Douglas treaties, those agreements had none of the solemnity and formality of the ones made in central Canada only two or three decades before, or the ones made on the prairies in the 1870s. As importantly, while Douglas may have thought he was acquiring land, the most important thing about the treaty-making process was that it stopped in 1854. No colonial government in British Columbia made any further treaties.[60]

In 1858 a second Pacific colony was established, called British Columbia and comprising the mainland of the province that still bears that

Know all men, We the Chiefs and People of the Family of Chilcowitch, who have signed our names and made our marks to this Deed on the Thirtieth day of April one thousand, eight hundred and fifty do consent to surrender Entirely and for ever to James Douglas the Agent of the Hudsons Bay Company in Vancouvers Island that is to say, for the Governor Deputy Governor and Committee of the same the whole of the lands situate and lying between the Sandy Bay east of Clover Point at the termination of the Whengwhung line to Point Gonzales, and thence north to a line of equal extent passing through the north side of Minies Plain. The Condition of or understanding of this Sale is this, that our village sites and Enclosed Fields are to be kept for our own use, for the use of our Children, and for those who may follow after us, and the lands shall be properly surveyed hereafter; it is understood however that the land itself, with these small exceptions becomes the Entire property of the White people for Ever; it is also understood that we are at liberty to hunt over the unoccupied lands, and to carry on our fisheries as formerly.

We have received as payment Thirty pounds Sterling

In token

The Douglas Treaties of the 1850s covered small areas of Vancouver Island and were framed as land sales. This one is known as the Chilcowitch treaty. Note the cheap lined paper, and the use of the 'x' instead of pictograph signatures. (Image I-68330/I-68331 courtesy of the Royal BC Museum and Archives.)

whereof we have signed our names and made our marks at Fort Victoria on the Thirtieth day of April One Thousand eight hundred and fifty

Ponelfagales

1 Qua sun ×
2 Sa-malth ×
3 Ty-la-cha ×
4 Sa-chee-'um ×
5 Colamptan ×
6 Selquoymitchtan ×
7 Ky ah keshin ×
8 Chy-yea hus ×
9 Ich pay mult ×
10 Yellan ×
11 Qwate sââlus ×
12 Supy ilh ×

Done in the presence of
Alfred Robson Benson M.R.C.S.L.
Joseph William McKay
Fort Victoria
30 April 1850

name. James Douglas was appointed governor, provided he sever all connection with the HBC, and he initially enjoyed limitless power, with untrammelled legislative as well as executive authority, granted by an Act of the British Parliament.[61] Not only was there no assembly, Douglas did not even have an executive council. This unusual constitutional arrangement was the product of the circumstances that had caused Britain to establish the new colony in the first place – a gold rush that brought an influx of largely American fortune seekers and a real risk of American annexation. Twenty-five thousand people arrived in 1858, a great many of them from the California gold fields. Douglas used his powers to legislate on a variety of matters – a land-granting scheme, customs duties, and mining regulations among them. He exercised power alone until 1864, when Britain established a legislative council for the mainland, consisting of two-thirds appointed and one-third elected members. Douglas retired in 1864, and in 1866 the two colonies were united, under the name of British Columbia but with the capital at Victoria.

The assertion of British sovereignty in 1846 had very little effect on the Indigenous population, but the coming of European settlers in successive gold rushes in the late 1850s and early 1860s brought profound change to the European-Indigenous constitution, just as it had in eastern Canada decades earlier. Settlers were granted land in fee simple, Indigenous peoples were confined to small reserves unilaterally laid out by the government, Indigenous populations were substantially reduced by disease, and the full force of English criminal law, often supported by military measures, was used against Indigenous people who resisted. The most notable event in this regard was the Tsilhqot'in war of 1864, after which the Indigenous leaders were tried and executed, in proceedings that have been variously described as criminal justice, martial law, or the state murder of defeated enemies.[62] By far the most enduring legal event of these years was a non-event – the European failure to recognize an Indigenous title and thus to accept that treaties had to be made to extinguish the Indigenous interest in the land. Some Europeans, in Victoria and in London, believed this was wrong, but the colonial government was not persuaded. As we will see in the next volume, successor provincial governments took the same view until forced to change their thinking by the Supreme Court of Canada in the later twentieth century.

28

Criminal Justice I: Criminal Law, Punishment, and Policing

Criminal justice systems throughout the English-speaking world underwent profound transformations in the first half of the nineteenth century. Although many of the significant changes discussed here had their origins in an earlier period, the pace of change quickened measurably after 1815, and the decades prior to 1860, especially the 1830s and 1840s, saw permanent and far-reaching developments. This chapter examines three major transformations, principally in relation to the more serious offences: the removal from the statute book of most capital offences and the substantial reduction, both in law and practice, of the use of most corporal punishments; the rise of imprisonment as the dominant mode of punishment for serious crimes; and the consolidation of law enforcement in the hands of increasingly professional police forces, especially in urban areas. This chapter is not a history of crime as such, although the prevalence of prosecuted crime is discussed at times as an influential force on the development of criminal justice ideas, institutions, and practices. Nor does this chapter discuss prosecution and trial; that is dealt with in the next chapter.

The causes of the developments summarized here were frequently related. The colonies in many instances followed the English lead in changes to criminal law, punishment, and policing. But more than imitation influenced change. A common argument was that reform would make criminal justice more rational, more humane, more 'modern.' Thus criminal justice was affected in many of its aspects by a strong sense that

that most Victorian of values, progress, required reform. Moreover, critics of the inherited eighteenth-century system complained that it was not only out of line with the spirit of the times, it was also ineffective – it did not carry out well one of the criminal law's principal functions, the deterrence and reduction of crime.

The Age of Reform: The Demise of Capital and Corporal Punishment

As we saw in chapter 16, the 'Bloody Code' was inherited from England in all British North American colonies and substantially modified by local statutes only in Nova Scotia and PEI. While dissatisfaction with the ancien régime criminal law resulted in a few legislated changes in the 1820s, mostly in Lower Canada,[1] penal reform on a large scale occurred in what is often called the 'age of reform' in British North America, the 1830s and early 1840s. Legal change occurred in two stages. In the first, between 1829 and 1837, four of the colonies passed legislation that greatly reduced the number of offences for which capital punishment was the prescribed sanction. New Brunswick took the lead in 1829 and 1831, reducing capital offences to nine,[2] Upper Canada followed shortly afterwards in 1833, leaving ten offences capital,[3] and Prince Edward Island enacted its reforming statute in 1836, leaving the colony with eleven capital offences.[4] A year later Newfoundland passed a reform statute quite different from those of the other colonies. Rather than list what offences remained capital, it simply noted that English criminal law had undergone 'very considerable revisions and improvements' in recent years, and the colony wanted its law to be congruent. Thus the criminal law of Newfoundland was declared to be the English criminal law as of 20 June 1837. The extremely short, three-section statute, followed with what can only be termed a prospective reception. All future criminal law revisions enacted by the mother of Parliaments would become the law of Newfoundland one year after they had been passed. The result was that very few offences remained capital.[5]

In the second stage of reform Nova Scotia reduced its capital offences to eight, in 1841,[6] and the same year the criminal law of Canada was consolidated, leaving just ten capital offences.[7] Many offences that had been capital in Lower Canada through the 1830s were thus changed to non-capital. The 1841 statutes, unlike their predecessors of the 1830s, did more than simply reduce the number of capital offences; they also altered the definitions of some capital property offences to make them capital only if they involved significant harm to the person. In the 1830s New Brunswick, Upper Canada, and Prince Edward Island, for example, all retained the death penalty for burglary and robbery as defined by the common law, which meant that it applied broadly, at least in theory, to those who broke and entered at night and those who stole from the person with violence or the threat of it. But the 1841 statutes defined robbery as capital only if it was accompanied by stabbing, cutting, or wounding, and burglary only if was also joined with such actions or with assault with intent to murder. Thus although robbery and burglary remained 'capital,' the definition of 'capital' was changed. There were also redefinitions of when arson was capital. The 1830s reforms had left it as capital only if it involved a dwelling house, and in 1841 this was changed in the Canadas to occupied dwelling house, while in Nova Scotia arson was capital only as part of the offence of causing death by setting fire to or otherwise destroying a ship. As Nova Scotia Attorney General James Boyle Uniacke stated a decade later during a debate about capital punishment, the 'very essence' of why some crimes remained capital was that they involved 'the intention to do bodily injury.'[8]

The new emphasis on harm to the person was also reflected in the fact that two offences capital in Upper Canada from 1833 – rescuing from prison a person convicted of murder, and refusing to disperse after the reading of the *Riot Act* – were left out of the 1841 consolidation, and two offences were added that had not been there in 1833 – putting out a false light, or taking any other action, to cause a shipwreck, and attempted murder by poison or by stabbing, cutting, or wounding. From 1841 Canada had ten capital offences, the same as Upper Canada in 1833, but it was a different ten, with purely property crime no longer capital. Nova Scotia went one further, removing sodomy, an offence that reflected moral outrage rather than physical harm to participants, from the capital lists completely. New Brunswick, which had been the first colony to limit the total number of capital offences, enacted similar limitations of robbery, burglary, and arson as the Canadas had the following year, in 1842, and in 1849 consolidated its criminal law, making it practically identical to that of Canada.[9] The number of capital offences remained more or less the same in Canada until 1865, when all crimes other than treason, murder, and rape were made non-capital. PEI enacted further reductions in 1861, removing the death penalty for robbery and rape, and Nova Scotia's first statutory revision of 1851 reduced capital offences to just murder and treason. The new colonies created in the Pacific northwest before Confederation received English law. The *English Law Ordinance* of 1858 established the reception date as 19 November 1858, and the date was confirmed by a later *English Law Ordinance* of 1866. Thus only murder, treason, arson in the royal dockyards, and piracy with violence were capital offences in pre-Confederation British Columbia.[10]

In addition to the reduction in the number of capital offences, corporal punishment was also largely eliminated in the early decades of the nineteenth century. Although only occasionally used after 1815, benefit of clergy was everywhere abolished in the criminal law reform statutes of the 1830s and early 1840s, and with it the branding that had been its hallmark. The pillory was still used in all colonies in the 1820s and 1830s but was substantially done away with a decade afterwards, at different times in different colonies.[11] The Upper Canadian legislation of 1833, for example, retained it for male offenders only who were convicted of forgery or impersonation, but the Canada consolidating legislation of 1841 entirely abolished it, as did Nova Scotia in the same year and New Brunswick in 1842.[12] PEI retained the pillory for a few offences, notably attempted rape or buggery, in 1836, and never expressly abolished it before Confederation.

Whipping, the principal corporal punishment of the eighteenth century, was also largely eliminated as a punishment option for courts. The 1833 Upper Canadian legislation retained it, like the pillory, for male offenders only who were convicted of forgery or impersonation, but it disappeared from the statute book in the 1841 consolidation. It was specifically abolished in 1841 in Nova Scotia. New Brunswick and PEI retained it in the 1830s as discretionary additional punishment on those sentenced to prison for any offence. It was not mentioned in the New Brunswick consolidation of 1849, but an 1836 PEI provision allowing whipping as an additional punishment stayed in force until Confederation, and indeed was augmented in 1861 when the death penalty was removed as the punishment for robbery and rape. Instead males convicted of either offence were liable to be imprisoned for a maximum of twenty-one years and to be 'once, twice or thrice publicly or privately whipped' if the judge before whom they were convicted thought it 'fit.'[13] From 1837 Newfoundland had provided for whipping when English law did but widened the applicability of the lash in 1863 when it was made a discretionary additional punishment of any male who was proved to be a second offender or who damaged the prison or attacked a prison guard.[14] PEI and Newfoundland thus share the perhaps dubious distinction of being the only British North American colonies to still use judicially ordered corporal punishment at Confederation. It should be noted, however, that whipping maintained a substantial but much less visible role in the penal landscape everywhere, for it was regularly used to enforce prison discipline into the twentieth century.

Before all these legal changes were enacted, punishment of the body was used less and less. We do not have a complete picture of the prevalence of capital punishment in British North America, but civilian executions between 1815 and mid-century probably numbered around fifty in Upper Canada, while in Lower Canada there were sixty-seven between 1815 and 1867. In the colonies with smaller populations, executions were even fewer, even allowing for the population difference. Between 1816 and 1860 only six people were executed in Nova Scotia following trials in the Supreme Court sitting in Halifax, and a further eleven following trials conducted outside the capital. Prince Edward Island saw only two executions in this period, Assiniboia just one, and New Brunswick five. The vast majority of those executed were men.[15]

In addition to this overall low rate of execution, two other points are significant. First, the rate of execution everywhere declined over time, a decline that began before the reform of the capital statute book and was not correlated with the legal changes discussed above. The most dramatic such decline occurred in Lower Canada, where no civilian offender was executed between 1840 and 1853; the rash of executions that followed the rebellion of 1837–8 was the probable immediate cause for this, but the colony also had an active abolition movement in the 1840s, a force powerful enough to persuade the authorities to pardon all capitally sentenced offenders for a decade and a half. Executions also declined over time in Nova Scotia. Of the six people executed following convictions in the Halifax Supreme Court, five went to the gallows in 1821 or earlier, but only one thereafter, and outside Halifax eight executions took place before 1838 and only three between then and Confederation. Second, overwhelmingly these were executions for murder, not property or other offences. The rebellions aside, nobody was hanged for an offence other than murder in Lower Canada after 1829, and in Nova Scotia the last man to hang for a property offence was John Lee, convicted in 1834 of a violent highway robbery just outside Halifax. Nobody was hanged for an offence other than murder outside Halifax after 1815.[16]

The glaring exception to this pattern in the pre-Confederation period was the west coast, where capital punishment was one of the tools employed to cow the large Indigenous population.[17] Thirty-two Indigenous people were sentenced to death in British Columbia between 1860 and 1869, of whom twenty-five, a remarkably high percentage, were actually executed. The comparable numbers for non-Indigenous people were two executed out of eighteen sentenced. Five of those Indigenous people were executed in 1864 following the deadly clashes between members of the Tshilhqot'in nation and Europeans driving a road through their territory, an incident that was a criminal act to Europeans but warfare to the Tshilhqot'in. Yet executions of Indigenous people were a two-edged sword. While some Europeans had no difficulty in depicting them as 'savages' fit only for harsh measures, others wondered whether it was right to judge Indigenous peoples by European law, not their own, and also asked who the true 'savages' were.

Executions were rare in the east for a variety of reasons. The relatively low level of serious crime was one cause, but this is only a small piece of the explanation.[18] Whether to prosecute, convict, and ultimately to hang an offender involved many discretionary decisions by a variety of people – victims, law enforcement authorities, prosecutors, juries, judges, and governors. Capital offences on the books were simply not charged as such, but as some lesser offence; crime either went unreported or was partially reported, omitting circumstances that might lead to a capital charge; when potentially capital cases were brought to court, grand juries sometimes refused to indict for the full offence; when an indictment was found, petit juries either acquitted or found the person guilty of a lesser offence. Finally, even if an accused person was found guilty and sentenced to death, he or she (it was overwhelmingly he) often escaped the gallows through the pardon system. There were 216 people sentenced to death in Upper Canada between 1791 and 1841, for example, but fewer than 50 were actually executed. As noted above, 6 people were executed in Halifax between 1816 and 1860, but 24 were pardoned, while outside Halifax the comparable figures were 11 and 23.[19] Decisions on commutation following convictions for murder and treason were formally taken in London, but the recommendations of the local executive were always accepted.[20]

Those pardoned were imprisoned, especially after the establishment of penitentiaries in the 1830s and 1840s, or banished, or, very occasionally, transported to a penal colony. The history of the use of banishment and transportation, both forms of exile for offenders, in British North America is a complicated one and involves both exile as a condition of pardon and its use as a court-ordered sentencing option. The former is dealt with here, because exile was an integral part of the pardon system, the latter later in this chapter. As in the eighteenth and early nineteenth centuries, banishment, generally for life, was a common fate meted out to those pardoned. A typical case was that of Daniel Conway, convicted in 1821 at Sydney, Cape Breton, of the shooting and wounding of John Dunfee, pardoned, and then, as a condition of that pardon, ordered to 'depart from the Province without delay and never return.' Similarly, when John Hinds was convicted of burglary at Pictou, Nova Scotia, in 1826 his death sentence was commuted 'on condition of his leaving the Province,' and the local magistrates were instructed to give him the pardon only when 'they have satisfied themselves of his intention to quit the country.'[21] Banishment was the standard additional punishment for anybody convicted of a capital offence and pardoned in all colonies until the 1840s; as we saw in a previous chapter, Mi'kmaq Tom Williams was banished from PEI in 1839 as a condition of pardon. Banishment was still practised on rare occasions right up until Confederation.[22] We do not know how many of those banished were, like Williams, Indigenous, but the admittedly incomplete research on the question shows that no Indigenous person was executed in Upper Canada prior to 1860, and very few, if any, in other colonies.[23]

The use of banishment for pardoned offenders represented a major difference between British and British North American criminal justice, as the former generally employed transportation to the Antipodes. Transportation was different from banishment in two significant ways – it involved an offender being taken to a penal colony rather than being ordered to remove himself or herself from the jurisdiction, and it involved further incarceration and forced labour once transported. Transportation to the Antipodes from British North America was very rarely used for civilian convicts, because the logistics made it very difficult and expensive and because until the 1820s neither imperial nor colonial statute law gave local authorities the power to order it. The legal situation changed in the early to mid-1820s, when British legislation made it permissible to send a pardoned offender to a penal colony in Australia directly or via Britain, and in the 1830s both Canadas passed local legislation permitting transportation. It was used sparingly; the best-known transportees in this period were the Upper and Lower Canadian rebels of 1837–8. In addition, for a decade or so, 1825–35, a very small number of pardoned offenders were sent from Nova Scotia and the Canadas, principally from Lower Canada, to incarceration and labour on public works in Bermuda, a much closer location, but Britain declared the practice unlawful in 1835.[24]

The early decades of the nineteenth century also saw a reduction in the use of corporal punishment before the legislative changes detailed above took effect, so that legal change in this area was also a case of the law on the books being made congruent to the law in practice. In the 1815–33 period, for example, an average of nine people a year were sentenced to a public whipping as well as time in the Quebec gaol, for larceny and prostitution-related offences, but from 1834 the practice stopped. In Upper Canada nobody was sentenced at the assizes to whipping alone after 1815, although an average of seven to eight people a year were sentenced to a jail term and to be whipped while inside before 1825, with that number falling to two a year (and no women) from 1826 to 1835. The last two men whipped in Hamilton, Upper Canada, for larceny, received their punishment in 1834. Quarter sessions judges were also reluctant to order whippings. In 1825 Robert Bailey was sentenced to thirty-nine lashes for stealing a watch by the Halifax Quarter Sessions, but such punishment was rare by that date. Only in Newfoundland, which until the mid-1820s had a court system and punishment practices operated by the British navy, was whipping still a significant feature of the penal landscape in the early nineteenth century.[25]

Dissatisfaction with Physical Punishments

The legal changes described above were the product of multiple causes. The reduction in capital offences was in part the result of the gap between theory and practice. Although few suggested that capital punishment was not a deterrent,[26] many thought its sparing use compared to its availability on the books made the criminal law an object of ridicule and reduced its deterrent value. John George Marshall, legal author and Nova Scotian judge, noted in 1837 that it was not 'imagined by anyone' that the ultimate sanction would be meted out except in a very few cases, and he was one of many who complained that because the prescribed penalty was rarely applied, the law lost its deterrent effect and was brought into disrepute. A select committee of the Upper Canadian House of Assembly made the same point in 1831: 'Even when juries find a verdict of guilty, and judges pronounce sentence of death in any case of less atrocity than murder, the person administering the government will not allow the law to be carried into execution.' But if more people were hanged, 'it is very probable that in such cases juries would cease to convict, and judges to sentence, so that the law as practised at present amounts very nearly to an act of indemnity for all minor offences.' John Beverley Robinson made the same point in a different way, with the familiar adage that 'it is the *certainty*, more than the *severity* of punishment, which deters offenders.' A decade later Nova Scotia's attorney general, Samuel G.W. Archibald, was more blunt, arguing that the 'severity' that currently marked the colony's statute book resulted in the law being often 'inoperative' and trials 'solemn farces in which the prescribed end was never intended to be carried into effect.'[27] Similar sentiments were expressed in Lower Canada; as noted above, that colony had an active abolition movement in the 1840s.

Thus men at all levels of society who played a role in the criminal law came to see the system as incoherent and thus dangerously inefficient. This helps to explain why criminal law reform received support from both assemblies and legislative councils in all colonies; it was not a contentious political issue. Even after reform, the law on the books was not in accord with the law in action. Given how few executions there were, and how overwhelmingly they followed conviction for murder rather than some other offence, the question is less why so many offences were removed from the statute book as why so many were retained? Most people agreed with the idea that in cases of murder 'the act [of capital punishment] needs no further vindication than the atrocity of the crime.' The criminal law was 'as wise and merciful' as possible, said Nova Scotia's attorney general at mid-century, at the same time 'giving that security to life which is necessary for the preservation of social order.'[28] But beyond this agreement about murder, we do not know why the death penalty was retained on the books for other crimes, because the issue was hardly ever discussed.

The answer to this conundrum may lie in another, oft-cited reason for reform – the need to bring colonial law into line with that of England. While only Newfoundland simply adopted English criminal law reforms, past and present, for many in other colonies it was significant that England itself greatly reduced the number of capital crimes in the early decades of the new century.[29] Colonists were well aware of this development, and many advocated following it. A significant indication of the powerful pull of English law was that they rarely cited another example, the new republic to the south, even though many American states substantially reduced capital punishment after the revolution.[30] The United States provided inspiration for other kinds of law reform, but England was the model to be followed for substantive criminal law. Once the epitome of harshness, it became the poster child for ameliorative reform. In New Brunswick, for example, Ward Chipman Junior, a judge of the Supreme Court and a drafter of the 1831 legislation, referenced Britain's reform legislation and advocated the same for the colony. In presenting the 1831 reform legislation to the assembly, lawyer and moderate reformer Edward Barron Chandler stated that the principal bill was simply a copy of Prime Minister Peel's 'admirable act' for England and 'contained nothing to increase criminal punishments, but rather to mitigate them in many instances.' A decade later, in his closing speech to the assembly in 1842, the year that that body further reduced capital offences, Lieutenant Governor Colebrooke noted that the changes made were 'evidence of the spirit by which you have desired to assimilate' local law to English law and asserted that 'in pursuing this course and securing to the people the full benefits of the British Constitution, you will afford the most effectual guarantee for their freedom and happiness.'[31]

The felt need to follow the mother country was part of the Nova Scotian and PEI debates as well, despite the fact that these two colonies had been decades ahead of Britain in enacting milder codes. Congruence with England was therefore the aim, not substantive change. Commenting favourably on recent English reforms, for example, the *Novascotian* noted, 'The number of capital penalties has been largely diminished' and 'a more mild and *suitable* form of punishment' legislated. William Young, a luminary in the reform movement of the 1830s, argued, 'All that required to be done here was, to follow in the footsteps of those legal sages in the old Country.' When it recommended capital punishment reduction in 1840, Nova Scotia's legislative council committee on the subject was instructed 'to reduce the criminal laws into a system as near that of England as circumstances admit.'[32] And congruence generally was achieved. By 1841 only eight offences were capital in England, approximately the same number as in the British North American jurisdictions.

The principal motivation for legislative reform was that capital and corporal punishments were seen as cruel, out of step with the age, a 'barbarous practice,' and, especially in the case of executions, highly disproportionate to the offence. Physical punishments were the product of 'those days of darkness and superstition' and wholly incompatible with 'the liberal accomplishments and acquirements of the age.' Such humanitarian arguments can be found in the many newspaper reports of executions, in legislative debates, in commentaries, and in official correspondence. Upper Canada King's Bench Judge Jonas Jones believed that executions were too common and, as a result, ineffective as deterrents because they produced criticism of the law itself: 'Frequent exhibitions of the last pangs of expiring nature have a tendency to counteract the end of punishment.' The preamble to the 1833 Upper Canadian *Reform Act* put it simply: 'It does not seem to be indispensable, for the security and well-being of society, that death should follow conviction for other than a small number of offences.' The aforementioned John George Marshall, while proud of the fact that executions were few, nonetheless complained in 1837 that the number of offences still capital in Nova Scotia meant that 'the severity of the Punishment [was] disproportionate to the offence' in many cases.[33] Much the same concerns about brutality also led to the abolition of the traditional additional pain formerly ordered to be inflicted on those convicted of treason.[34]

This humanitarianism involved more than concern for those who suffered physical punishments. Contemporaries also worried about the emotional effect of such brutalizing punishments on the individuals who carried them out and on those who viewed them. As historians of other jurisdictions have argued, a broader cultural shift lay behind, and was partially responsible for, the increasing rejection of physical punishments. Changing sentiments that eschewed violence, especially gratuitous state-imposed violence, what some have called a 'civilizing' process, meant that punishments of the body became 'increasingly out of step with the cultural and social forces of the day.' Reform was thus derived at least in part from concern not just for the objects of physical violence, those executed or flogged, but also for those on the other side of the penal divide. In March 1839, for example, the *Colonial Pearl* of Halifax ran a long article, 'Fifteen Reasons against Death Punishments,' which included 'brutalisation' and the 'alienation of correct human feelings.' The spectacle of an execution 'offends and disgusts the good,' the writer asserted. Criminal justice officials agreed. When John Lee was to be hanged for highway robbery in Halifax in 1834 the sheriff asked for military aid 'to keep order on so distressing an occasion.' It was a memorable occasion indeed; the case was recounted sixteen years later in an assembly debate over the further amelioration of capital punishment.[35] Sentiments of increasing disquiet about physical punishments also undercut the traditional rationale of capital punishment – exemplary displays of state power and the terror of the law.

Often included in accounts of the reform of physical punishments is the rise of imprisonment. We have not emphasized that here, because the reductions in the use of physical punishments and the search for penal reform were largely parallel processes, not simply cause and effect. Prison reform is thus better considered as a process in its own right, part of a decades-long search for alternatives to physical punishments, and is discussed below. We do not suggest that the rise of new forms of prison and the elimination of physical punishments were unrelated. But the state of a colony's carceral institutions affected how long the new prison sentences were, not the simple fact that capital and corporal punishments were reduced in law and practice.[36]

Despite the concerns over the spectacle of executions, they remained public events throughout this period. The dozen Patriotes who paid for their treason with their lives were dispatched in three batches on three market days from gallows erected in front of the Montreal gaol, while a similar fate met Peter Matthews and Samuel Lount, the two Upper Canadian rebels hanged in the courtyard of the Toronto gaol. An execution in 1830 in the London district of Upper Canada saw 3,000 people come to London, population 300, to watch the hanging of Cornelius Burley, who had killed a local constable. Lower Canadian executions invariably attracted large crowds, which included many women, whose presence was often condemned in the press. Yet public executions could also turn people against the law. The year before substantial abolition in Nova Scotia, the colony's leading newspaper deprecated them as a 'disgraceful and demoralizing custom,' one that 'familiarizes men, and women too, to rude jests, acclamations, and a host of ribald misdemeanours in connection with that most awful scene, a fellow creature paying the extreme penalty.'[37] In fact there was an inconsistent approach to the location of executions, which was determined by the structure of the court system more than by a clear sense of which community was to be deterred. In Lower Canada all but one were carried out in either Montreal or Quebec City, because accused persons from around the colony were brought to one of these cities, or Trois Rivières, for trial. Conversely in other colonies, where the highest court performed circuits to local communities, people were tried and went to the gallows in or near the community in which they had committed their crime. Dr William King of Cobourg, Upper Canada, for example, was executed in that town in 1859.[38]

The Search for Penal Reform and the Rise of the Penitentiary

In the first two decades after 1815 the range of non-capital criminal punishments remained the same as it had been earlier – corporal punishments, fines, imprisonment, and, in Upper Canada, banishment. Of these, imprisonment was used more and more over time. In Upper Canada, for example, sentences of imprisonment were handed out to 75 per cent of those convicted at the assizes between 1816 and 1825, and the number rose to 81 per cent between 1826 and the opening of Kingston in 1835; from 1835 virtually all convicted serious offenders were committed there. In Nova Scotia the same transition was marked by an 1816 statute that allowed the courts to impose lengthy prison sentences rather than fines or corporal punishment, and transformed sentencing practices. In the first full year after its enactment, twenty-three people were given prison sentences by the Supreme Court, the longest being three years, and nine more by the quarter sessions. In 1829 the Halifax prison, the Bridewell, had forty-four convicted inmates, 'a larger number than has been known at any former period,' and in the 1830s nearly all those convicted in the Supreme Court were sent there. Lower Canadian prison populations also increased dramatically; in 1815 there were about a hundred people a year convicted and sentenced to prison in the Quebec City jail, and this number had more than doubled by the mid-1830s. In all of British North America's major cities, much of the increase in jail populations was made up of short-term public order offenders, as large-scale immigration brought social unrest and disorder, and middle-class city officials reacted by using the jails more than before. But some of the increase resulted from the use of imprisonment rather than corporal punishment for more serious offences.[39]

Only Upper Canada and Newfoundland had another alternative to both corporal punishment and imprisonment – banishment imposed by a court as a sentence, as opposed to its deployment as a pardon condition. We know little about the practice in the latter jurisdiction; it was sanctioned by a local statute of 1834 that gave courts the discretion to substitute banishment for transportation or 'any Infamous or Corporal Punishment.' Banishment could be for life or a term of years, and no destination was specified. The one thing we do know about exile from Newfoundland was that in some cases ships' captains took people to PEI. That produced a reaction from islanders, in the form of a local statute banning the practice, which it was asserted had the effect of 'letting loose upon society, persons of infamous characters,' and worse, and more fundamentally, 'to a certain extent, making this colony a Convict Colony.' The same Newfoundland statute also contained the only locally legislated use of whipping; if a man (women were specifically exempted) was apprehended after returning from banishment he could, at the discretion of the court, be 'once, twice or thrice publicly or privately whipped' and then banished for life. Banishment continued to be used for decades, as attested by local legislation of 1865 precipitated by England abandoning transportation in the 1860s. This meant that nobody could be sentenced to an offence punishable by transportation in Newfoundland, which in turn removed the basis for banishment in the 1834 Act. The local legislature declared that it was 'expedient to continue the Punishment of Banishment' in certain cases, but no criteria at all were specified beyond conviction for a non-capital felony.[40]

As noted in chapter 16, the Upper Canadian courts were given the power in 1800 to sentence individuals to banishment, and between 1815 and 1839 135 people were banished, only 4 of them after 1835. The vast majority of the sentences were handed down at assizes although 6 such banishments followed convictions at the Home (Toronto) and Midland District (Kingston) Quarter Sessions. Banishment was meted out for a wide variety of offences, wider than the statute's limitation of it to 'any crime, for which ... [a person] was liable by law to be transported.' Most of those banished had committed simple larceny, grand or petit, a relatively minor property crime. One George Young, for example, was convicted of grand larceny at Hamilton in 1828 and was 'sentenced to leave His Majesty's Dominions for the term of seven years, and to depart ... within four days.' But some banished offenders had been charged with more serious, sometimes capital, crimes – murder, forgery, and horse-stealing – and been found guilty of a lesser offence.[41]

For all the prevalence of its use in Upper Canada, banishment still played second fiddle to imprisonment, and the prison came to dominate in all colonies. The story of the prison in British North America has three connected elements. First, as we have seen, there was a rise in the use of imprisonment. Second, there was a parallel and corollary process of reform of the institutions – mostly the county jails – to which the increasing number of people incarcerated were sent. Third, particularly from the 1830s, new ideas about the purpose and design of prisons took hold, a development that most notably culminated in the construction of penitentiaries in Kingston and Halifax.

The people sentenced to prison before this last development were confined mostly in local jails. These held debtors, prisoners awaiting trial, those sentenced to death and awaiting their fate, those suffering from mental illness, and a few people serving short prison sentences. In every colony the jails were seen as inadequate by the early nineteenth century. They were uniformly castigated as poorly constructed, too small, often insecure, and unable to adequately segregate criminal offenders from debtors, men from women, the insane from other people, or young from old. In the Quebec jail, prison reformers complained, 'pre-trial prisoners and convicted prisoners were generally mixed together in the same wards, as were young and old, first-timers and those who were back for the umpteenth time, and those in for serious offences such as murder with those in for quasi-civil offences.' In addition, it was 'the only prison in the District for the Detention of Debtors.' Those confined effectively regulated themselves and were subject to poor diets and miserable living conditions.[42]

Everywhere proposals were made for prison reform, which encompassed both the construction of new institutions and new regulation of existing ones. The Montreal and Quebec City jails, opened in 1811 and 1812 respectively, were based on the ideas of English penal reformer John Howard and divided into wards, so that prisoners could be classified. In 1829 female prisoners in Quebec City were moved out of their ward and into a separate building, the first separate female prison in British North America. Also in 1829 comprehensive rules and regulations for Quebec's jail were promulgated, among other things banning loitering, liquor, and loud talking. Reform notions driven by the new ideas of prison discipline reached far. In the 1830s PEI legislation made hard labour an optional condition of imprisonment for anybody sentenced, and prescribed the separation of male and female prisoners, of those held in pretrial custody from the convicted, and of criminals and debtors. Classification according to offence and age was mandated, visitors were limited, alcoholic drinks were banned, attendance at religious services was made compulsory, and magistrates were named as overseers and inspectors. In Newfoundland any conviction that in England brought imprisonment at hard labour could do the same on the island, the labour to be performed in a jail or on the public streets, or both, and during the hours of labour the convict was to wear 'an iron clog, or other shackle.'[43]

Not only were new regulations introduced, new institutions were established in some cities, a notable example of which was the Halifax Bridewell, built in 1818, which instituted a regime reflecting emerging ideas about imprisonment. Prisoners were separated according to the reason for incarceration, liquor use was curtailed, hard labour was imposed on many inmates, and religious instruction was provided. The Bridewell's physical condition deteriorated in the 1830s because of disputes over financing between the assembly, dominated by members from outside Halifax, and the city's grand jury. But what matters is not the success of the institution but the attempt to reform and modernize imprisonment.[44]

The disparate movements for penal reform in British North America bore fruit in the 1830s most dramatically in Upper Canada, with the construction of Kingston Penitentiary, opened in 1835. The story of Kingston's founding is well known; no development in Canadian criminal justice history has been the subject of more extensive study.[45] The idea of a penitentiary in Upper Canada was first publicly mooted in the assembly in 1826, and within a few short years legislation had been passed (1833) and the building opened (1835). There was some opposition, notably from labour groups concerned about competition from prison manufactures, but there was much broad agreement among reformers and the governing elite about the need for the new institution. Many supported it as necessary to provide punishment for a wide range of offences, given the ineffectiveness and/or increasing illegitimacy of existing sanctions and jails. But for some penitentiary advocates it was to be more than an effective form of secondary punishment, it would also have an overtly reformative purpose, remaking convicts' characters through prayer, reflection, discipline, and labour. The idea that criminal punishment should do more than punish and deter, that it should also rehabilitate, was a new and important departure from the ancien régime. Kingston Penitentiary represented not simply a preference for incarceration over punishment of the body, but also increasing support for the idea of a new form of punishment designed to change the essential character of the convicted criminal. He or she was to be separated from malign influences, isolated as much as possible from other convicts, and inured to wholesome habits by industry, reflection, and prayer.

In contrast to criminal law reform, which as we have seen was modelled on English examples, prison reform drew largely on developments in the United States, where the early decades of the nineteenth century witnessed the embrace of imprisonment as the dominant sanction. Along with their expansion went a radical rethinking of the purpose of prisons and their design and management. The rise of the penitentiary also made prisons reformatory and disciplinary institutions, not just places of incarceration. In the United Kingdom imprisonment also became the dominant form of imprisonment, although for some decades the penitentiary shared the leading role of alternative to execution with transportation to Australian penal colonies, and as a result penitentiary development was a little slower and less intense than it was across the Atlantic.[46]

The need for an effective form of secondary punishment, and the interest of some in rehabilitation, meant that there was little debate in Upper Canada about whether the colony would build a penitentiary. But there was much controversy about the design and function of the new institution. Should it be fundamentally punitive, or should it also seek to rehabilitate, and if it did the latter, which type of penitentiary regime was best? Upper Canadians put much effort into investigating penitentiary design, mostly American models. They were confronted with two different ones, which in the 1820s and 1830s engendered fierce debate among American penal reformers. The 'silent system,' which housed convicts separately but allowed them to eat and work together under a regime of enforced silence, was the one employed by the prisons at Auburn and Sing Sing in New York state. Its rival, employed in the flagship Eastern Penitentiary in Philadelphia, was the 'separate system,' in which convicts were kept continually in solitary confinement, living and working alone in their cells. Kingston was built on the Auburn model, as exemplified by the regulations for the prisoners' conduct. They were 'to labour diligently and preserve unbroken silence,' not to 'exchange looks, wink, laugh, nod or gesticulate to each other.' Yet the optimism of reformers was soon to be first undermined and then destroyed by revelations that the maintenance of such a regime of submission was impossible without recourse to the lash, and a commission headed by George Brown of the *Globe* that investigated the penitentiary in 1848 found use of the whip and other physical discipline to be endemic. It also found, in a telling phrase, that the hopes of prison reformers were not met: 'The Reformation of Convicts is unknown' it bluntly stated.[47]

Other colonies had their penitentiary movements within a decade of Kingston's opening. The New Brunswick Assembly legislated in the late 1830s for a new house of correction for Saint John, which initially became the Saint John Penitentiary and was later renamed the Provincial Penitentiary, with a design modelled on Auburn and regulations stressing labour, silence, and moral reformation. The penitentiary was opened in 1842 and became the colony's principal prison. The new penal philosophy was also clearly articulated in Nova Scotia, where an assembly committee in 1838 argued for a prison reflecting the 'meliorating influence of Science and Christianity,' one that was 'humane,' dedicated to 'correcting but not destroying the guilty.' The *Penitentiary Act* of 1840 also proclaimed that in the new institution 'the punishment of Criminals ought to be applied with a view to their reformation and restoration to Society.' A year later Attorney General Uniacke, in introducing the legislation to repeal many capital offences, asserted that 'repentance and reformation should be the main objects in the treatment of prisoners, that in nearly every case imprisonment might supersede death as a punishment.' The Halifax Penitentiary was completed in 1844.[48] Lower Canada was alone among the major colonies in not constructing a penitentiary by name, although the new jails in Montreal and Quebec City were not dissimilar reforming institutions. There were proposals made for a Lower Canadian penitentiary as there were elsewhere, but the rebellions intervened, and after the union Canada made Kingston the penitentiary for the whole colony. In 1843 it was made possible for one institution to serve both jurisdictions by reserving penitentiaries for convicts with sentences of two years or more.[49] Newfoundland legislated the building of a penitentiary in 1851, the enabling statute stressing both punishment and the reformation of offenders. It was not completed until 1859, and its regime emphasized silence and hard labour. Like others in the Atlantic region, the Colonial Penitentiary, as it was named, was a rather more modest enterprise than Kingston or American prisons, in size, cost, and inmate numbers. At the same time these new institutions bore witness to the pervasive influence of the 'modern' age values of reformation linked to punishment.[50]

Policing

As we saw in chapter 16, the traditional image of pre-modern constables as bungling and ignorant amateurs is no longer tenable. By 1815 the practice of paying substitutes to perform constables' duties in urban centres meant that increasingly the men who fulfilled that role were experienced. Similarly, JPs in the towns did much less of their work in their parlours, but operated regularly out of police offices manned in rotation by salaried JPs who were served by salaried constables, or their effective equivalent, as support staff. We cannot call these urban constables a 'police force' in 1815, but by 1850 that term is appropriate; by then British North American urban centres had developed uniformed, salaried, and permanent police forces. They were under the immediate control of a police chief (who did not always go by that name) and the indirect control of elected city officials. Such institutions were the product of the revolution in municipal government that saw cities governed by elected officials rather than appointed JPs, a transition that, Saint John aside, began in the 1830s and 1840s. But before incorporation policing, using that term broadly and including all those who carried out law enforcement functions, whatever their names, was performed by a highly heterogeneous group of people. Variation in form and function were the hallmarks of policing, making it difficult to generalize.[51]

We can broadly identify three different groups of people performing policing functions before the 1840s.[52] First, there were constables, or their equivalents, who were largely reactive, acting when called on by victims or JPs to assist. They acted in rural and urban areas, appointed annually by the quarter sessions, except in Saint John, where constables were elected pursuant to the city charter. In many towns they operated in a less ad hoc fashion than in the countryside, in part because the practice of substitution meant that constables were experienced men, although they were unsalaried, remunerated by fees, not uniformed, and not governed by any set of purpose-made regulations. More importantly as a harbinger of change to come, some cities had police offices, established both before and after 1815, locales where JPs attended each day to receive complaints and also had constables attached. While they too were reactive, they tended to be different from regular constables in being appointed without term and salaried. Those in Quebec City were also armed with swords and guns. These police office constables have been called Canada's first real 'police force.' They operated in many cities, and the emergence of these cadres of full-time constables meant that in Montreal and Quebec City the system of substitution was abolished in the 1820s. Salaried and full-time police were established everywhere in the years before 1850, including St John's, where by the 1830s a 'high constable,' paid eighty pounds a year, had charge of six salaried ordinary constables. Constables were also appointed in the Red River colony, their number set at fifteen by the 1851 Laws of Assiniboia.[53]

The second group of police in many cities was the night watch. Night watches were generally not permanent bodies. In Halifax, for example, they were ad hoc responses to incidents of unrest and disorder and usually lasted only for weeks or months after the crisis that spurred their establishment. In Lower Canada and Saint John, in contrast, they were permanent institutions.[54] Night watches patrolled, not just reacted, and in British North America's wooden cities they were concerned not just with crime and unrest but also with watching for fires. They were often staffed by the middle classes with property to protect.[55] In garrison towns policing was also effectively performed by a third force, regular military patrols, and by the garrison in general, which would be called on by civic authorities to quell larger-scale disturbances. Not infrequently, of course, substantial disturbances were actually caused by soldiers, making the presence of a garrison always a mixed blessing for urban order.

Municipal incorporation brought major change at the institutional and organizational levels of policing, and to the police function. Police departments were set up, directly consequent upon or soon following incorporation in Toronto (1834), Halifax and Kingston (1841), Hamilton (between 1847 and 1853), Fredericton (1848), and Charlottetown (1855).[56] Saint John got its police force in 1849, decades after it had been incorporated, with a uniformed and armed force of twenty or so under the control of the newly established stipendiary police magistrate. Lower Canada was a special case, as so often it was. Political and social unrest in the immediate pre-rebellion period led government not to renew the cities' charters in 1836, and policing was left in the control of JPs and in the hands, often, of the military. Both major cities received new charters in 1840, and a municipally controlled police force was established in each in 1843. Halifax provides a good example of the changes that incorporation brought. The 1841 statute setting up the new corporation established the position of city marshal and provided for a nine-person salaried force.[57] Three of these positions were the constables who had been permanently attached to the police office since 1815, and six were new. They were provided with a rather gaudy uniform, in which they patrolled the city streets daily, and governed by a set of police force regulations. The force grew to forty strong by Confederation.

The emerging urban police forces were focused not only on crime. Middle-class concerns about urban order intensified with the waves of immigration from the 1820s on. The new police were as much involved with imposing middle-class standards of order and morality as they were simply with crime control.[58] This emphasis became increasingly marked in the decades after 1860, but it originated in this period. The 1840s also saw the new urban police forces frequently confronted with the disorder, including rioting, brought by increasing ethnic and religious conflict. The rebellion losses riots of 1849 in Montreal are the best known of these outbursts, but large-scale street disorders occurred in most major cities and often exposed the inadequacies of fledgling police forces. In Saint John in 1840, for example, the city grand jury castigated the police following a major religious street conflict as 'lamentably inefficient either for the preservation of good order or the prevention of crime.'[59]

The challenges to social order caused by (often religious) riots, and the new emphasis on the need for the police to be symbols of discipline and morality, revealed a problem with the placing of police forces under the control of elected municipal officials.[60] This innovation, an American tradition not a British one, meant that patronage dominated appointments to police forces, and that, in turn, made enforcing discipline and standards difficult. The Toronto force was exemplary of this problem. The tory elite dominated city council in its early years, the tories' strong arm was the Orange Order, and the main 'qualification' for appointment to the force was membership in the order. The price to be paid was that the police force was implicated in the electoral religious violence that marred urban politics in the 1840s. The police either stood by as their co-religionists violently disrupted reform meetings or actively participated in the violence. An 1841 assembly inquiry into the conduct of the police in Toronto during the election of that year concluded that the force had acted partially for political ends, had been 'employed as political instruments in behalf of those to whom the corporation ... [is] friendly,' and called for a force 'remote from ... and independent of local bias or interference.' This did not happen until 1858, when a provincially appointed board assumed control of the force, and in the interim the legitimacy and effectiveness of the police were impaired. Control of urban police forces was wrested from city councils in other places: as we have seen, the new Saint John force was placed under the city stipendiary magistrate in 1849.

It bears emphasis that everything said here concerns urban policing. In the English colonies rural policing was carried out by JPs and constables and was often criticized as ineffective because of the expense and distances involved. A notorious murder would arouse the locality and men would turn out to hunt down an alleged killer, but the community and its constables were often unable and/or unwilling to deal with more routine matters.[61] In Lower Canada the local militia captains were supposed to execute arrest and search warrants, but they rarely did so for the same reasons, and these tasks were more often undertaken, in rural areas within reach of the cities, by urban constables. In more remote regions JPs engaged those whom they could find willing to do the job, usually bailiffs attached to the district courts. The only fully professional force of rural police in British North America in this period was created as a result of the rebellions in Lower Canada. In 1838 a short-lived rural constabulary was formed, armed, mounted, and patterned on the newly formed Irish constabulary.[62]

There was also an international dimension to law enforcement. The long border with the United States meant that suspected criminals often sought to evade apprehension by crossing that border, in both directions. Prior to 1842 there was no international treaty governing extradition between the United States and Britain, but formal and 'informal' extradition, the latter meaning kidnapping, took place, regularly if not frequently, and was deemed not just acceptable but a duty that civilized states owed each other. The duty, insisted numerous commentators, was rooted in customary international law and was bolstered by the need for reciprocity. As Sir John Colborne, administrator of Lower Canada, said in March 1839 when requesting the governor of Vermont to send someone back for trial, doing so would be 'an act which the reciprocity in such conjunctures long subsisting between this province and the State of Vermont would seem to demand.'[63] There was no case decided by the Upper Canadian courts about whether the local executive actually did have the power to order extradition until 1832, and that produced an equivocal result. Extradition was nonetheless approved of by most people and all colonial governments, and any legal uncertainty over it was resolved by the Webster-Ashburton Treaty of 1842, which provided for the extradition by both parties of persons accused of murder, attempted murder, piracy, robbery, arson, forgery, and utterance of a forged paper. As we will see in a later chapter, extradition cases involving fugitive slaves caused a number of controversies.

29

Criminal Justice II: The Criminal Trial

In the nineteenth century the criminal trial evolved into a contest dominated by lawyers on both sides, a process that had begun before 1815 and accelerated once having a defence lawyer became a right of the accused in the 1830s and early 1840s. This chapter begins with a short overview of the trial process, emphasizing the respective roles of grand and trial juries and judges. Included in this overview is an examination of legislation to simplify criminal procedure, making it less technical and rule bound. Subsequent sections analyse in detail the role played by lawyers for each side. There was some change from the pre-1815 world in who conducted the prosecution, especially in Upper Canada, which was the only jurisdiction in this period to move to a system of state-employed specialist prosecutors. The principal development discussed here, however, was in the part played by defence counsel. In the 1830s and 1840s felony defendants received the right to have counsel and, more importantly, the right to have lawyers speak directly to the jury on their behalf. The more prominent role for defence lawyers meant that the essential nature of the criminal process changed. Defendants played a diminishing role as the trial became increasingly a contest dominated by lawyers. In chapter 16 we saw how, during the second half of the eighteenth century, the English criminal trial and its British North American counterpart moved from 'confrontational,' a short sharp contest between prosecutor and defendant, to one somewhat more 'adversarial.' While it took many decades before what one historian has called 'full-fledged adversarial process' was the hallmark of the criminal courts,[1] aspects of the modern trial were well established in this period.

This chapter is principally about how trials for the more serious crimes were conducted in the colonies' high courts. Trials at the lower levels of the justice system, at the quarter sessions or before stipendiary magistrates, are discussed only briefly. We therefore analyse the legal process as it affected only a minority of defendants, but it was the minority who had the most at stake, men and women charged with the most serious crimes and facing the most serious consequences, including capital punishment.

The Criminal Process: Judges, Juries, and Procedure

The essential structure of the trial described in chapter 16 did not change in this period. The grand jury continued to perform the same function that it had, and grand jurors continued to be generally men of higher socio-economic status than either trial jurors or the vast majority of those who stood accused before them. They were substantial merchants and landowners, middle-class professionals and their ilk.[2] The grand jury's function in Lower Canada was to some extent taken over by JPs, who were given powers to conduct something like the modern preliminary inquiry in 1851, but the full-fledged development of the preliminary inquiry came after Confederation.[3] Trial jurors continued to be of middling socio-economic status, always required to own some property, but little enough to make tradesmen, small farmers, and the like qualified. Even Blacks made an occasional appearance.[4] Controversies over trial juries did occasionally arise in British North America, not over issues of class composition, but over religion and politics. The sheriffs who chose which qualified jurors would serve were not infrequently accused of 'jury packing,' making sure in cases with political overtones that government supporters dominated juries, or in ordinary criminal and civil cases that Catholics were excluded. Accusations of jury packing led to reform of the methods of jury selection in both Upper Canada and Nova Scotia at mid-century.[5] Jury membership was also skewed at times by another factor – the unwillingness of some to serve. Jury duty could be resented as an interference with the ability to make a living, especially by those engaged in seasonal work. For some, participating in an institution of great constitutional significance, therefore, was a decidedly mixed blessing.[6]

Jurors behaved much the same way in the nineteenth century as they had in the eighteenth, interrupting the proceedings with questions. In the 1859 trial of George Preeper in Halifax for manslaughter a juror, presumably distrustful of witness John Kenty, interrupted him when he mentioned that he had 'been in prison all summer' to ask, 'What was you in prison for?' He received the unhelpful and unlikely reply that Kenty did not know. Juries usually reached verdicts quickly, sometimes without retiring, but more often leaving the room for short periods. As late as 1856 a Hamilton jury did not retire before convicting railway worker Dennis Sullivan of murder. Juries could at times, however, remain in discussion for a long time. Joey Metzler was tried for arson and insurance fraud at Halifax in 1842, the trial itself took two full days, and the jury then stayed out for twenty-four hours – a fact that a newspaper reported in italics – before acquitting him. At times juries offered opinions that went beyond a simple verdict. At the conclusion of the 1852 Montreal trial for manslaughter of Thomas Burke, a former soldier employed as night watchman on a ship who had fired at an intruder who later died from his wound, the jurors gave their verdict as 'Not guilty, but the Jury is of the opinion that the deceased died from the bad usage and neglect of the Doctors in the Hospital.' On other occasions juries delivered verdicts against the evidence for political reasons. Riot prosecutions against some of those who prevented fugitive slave Solomon Moseby from being returned to the United States, for example, led to acquittals, despite overwhelming evidence of participation. One local official told the lieutenant governor that the jury 'had its own definite sense of what justice constituted' and was willing 'to defy the governing elite of the province' to ensure that that vision of justice prevailed.'[7]

Juries were important and powerful, but they were not always treated in practice as the sole arbiters of guilt or innocence. Judges used commentary on the evidence and explicit directions as methods of 'jury control' in a period when there were no criminal appeals, a topic discussed below. One of the most notorious examples was provided by Christopher Hagerman, who presided over the 1828 Hamilton trial of Michael Vincent for the murder of his wife. Hagerman told the jury that 'the deceased had been murdered by the prisoner' and that 'he had no difficulty in saying such was his opinion.' Hagerman was much criticized in the reform press for this statement, suggesting that some people at least thought there should be limits on the judge's role. A decade and a half later the defence lawyer for George Hiscox, on trial for murder, strongly objected to trial judge Brenton Halliburton telling the jury that 'he thought the Evidence fully sustained the ... Indictment.' Counsel moved in arrest of judgment, arguing on the motion that Halliburton's words were 'more positive than they should have been and that the case should have been left more open to the Jury than it was,' but the judges unanimously ruled against him. Cobourg jurors likely paid heed to Judge Robert Burns, whose 1859 jury charge in the case of Dr William King strongly implied guilt. He was convicted by a jury that also recommended mercy, and Burns made clear that while he would pass on that recommendation, he would not add to it, believing it not justified by the evidence.[8]

That judges were activist did not mean that they always got their way. An unnamed NSSC judge presiding over the 1818 prosecution of Alexander Ramsey for inciting two apprentices to rob their master, 'addressed the jury in a very forcible and expressive manner, commenting with strong feelings of abhorrence, on the enormity and heinousness of the offence, which he considered was proved beyond the shadow of a doubt.... He had no doubt the jury would coincide with him in opinion, that the Prisoner was guilty.' They did, 'after a few moments consultation.' But although Ward Chipman of the NBSC similarly told the jury in the trial of Saint John publisher John Hooper for criminal libel that 'his opinion clearly and decidedly was, that the defendants were guilty of maliciously composing and publishing a libel as charged,' the jury was unable to reach a verdict. In the 1859 Preeper case, Lewis Morris Wilkins of the NSSC had fine words to say about the court remaining a 'sanctuary pure and undefiled,' a 'temple of justice' in which political partisanship' should play no role. But he turned this into a virtual demand for a conviction in a case that involved religious-based electoral violence:

> Your verdict will exercise a powerful influence upon the social happiness of the people of this Province, for it will decide whether peace and order, which are essential to the free elections of representatives in the General Assembly, shall be maintained by the fixed institutions and laws of the land alone, or whether electors, at future elections, may form armed combinations for their protection from apprehended violence, or for the free delivery of their votes.

Wilkins did not stop there. His review of the evidence convinced him that the defence claim of an 'organized systematic attempt to prevent polling at the hustings ... is contradicted by the evidence.' That evidence, *'in any view of the facts in proof,* constrain you to find him guilty.' The jury did not; they acquitted Preeper after forty-five minutes.[9]

Judges' interventions could go the other way. When the evidence did not support the charge, some judges told the jury just that. Brenton Halliburton's review of the evidence in the 1829 murder trial of James Burns 'concluded by stating that in his view the crime amounted to manslaughter, but nothing more,' and the jury agreed. The year before, Lewis Morris Wilkins had advised Crown counsel, once the prosecution case was closed, to abandon an indictment for robbery and go only for larceny. Halliburton was also forceful in telling the jury to acquit two people accused of petit treason in 1830; there was 'no evidence sufficient to convict' one of them, charged as an accessory, and in the case of the other, the alleged principal, the chain of evidence linking her to the poison used was 'defective.' In the Burke case discussed above, Sir James Stuart told the jury 'that no case had been made out against the prisoner, as no identity had been proved.'[10]

That there was no clear and consistent understanding of what judges should say is revealed by the fact that some kept their opinions quiet, even if they disagreed with jury verdicts. After holding the assizes at Hamilton in 1825, William Campbell complained to the lieutenant governor about the large number of acquittals contrary to the evidence. Some were the result of unjustifiable causes 'not infrequent in small communities.' Campbell was making a somewhat oblique reference to juries' willingness to employ more than the evidence presented at trial, but also to use local knowledge to decide whether to convict friends and neighbours. Others not connected to the legal system also observed this attitude. Following an acquittal at Kingston in 1835, an editorial in the *Upper Canada Herald* disagreed with the verdict but went on to note that 'as the jury were mostly from the part of the country in which both parties reside, it is not unlikely they know more about the matter than appeared in open court.'[11]

Judges were interventionist in part because with one exception there were no appeals in felony cases and they had to use other methods to try to control the jury's discretion. The common law gave judges a power of review for error, but this was essentially useless because it was limited to errors on the face of the record, and there was no record in criminal trials, only a verdict. In England a trial judge could reserve a case for the consideration of all twelve judges of Westminster Hall, or after 1848 for the Court of Crown Cases Reserved, but this was wholly a matter for the presiding judge, not something the defendant could request, was again limited to error on the record, and was little used. Many English commentators criticized the lack of an ability to appeal in the nineteenth century, but there was no right of appeal granted until 1907.[12] The situation in the British North American colonies was similar. Upper Canada's Court of Error and Appeal had a criminal jurisdiction, but that was limited to 'all matters which may lawfully be brought before it.' In other words, its criminal law review powers were limited to 'error.' There was no appeal against an unreasonable jury verdict. Appeals were available from summary convictions before magistrates, but not from jury trials in the superior courts. Near identical legislation was passed in other colonies. Only in Upper Canada, from 1857, could those convicted of a serious offence appeal the verdict 'upon any point of law or question of fact.' Not until 1892 was a broader right of appeal made generally available.[13]

Judges could also influence jury decisions by their rulings on evidence. We know little about the general development of evidence law in British North America, but historians have charted some aspects of it, particularly the law relating to the prosecution of rape and that relating to Indigenous testimony. With regard to the former, Upper Canadian judges insisted that a complainant ought to be able to show physical resistance, sometimes considerable physical resistance, to establish her lack of consent. In an 1855 case Queen's Bench Judge William Draper, on appeal, held against a complainant on a different point; consent obtained by fraud made the defendant not criminally liable. A decade later Judge Hagarty of the same court held that it was possible for an insane woman to consent. Judges were also not averse to referring to the possibility of false complaints or to the use of reputation evidence against the accuser.[14]

Non-Christian Indigenous persons were not generally allowed to testify, not because of their ethnicity but because, not believing in a God who would punish them for perjury, they could not swear an oath. Although there were instances where they were allowed to swear, despite judges' doubts that the oath meant to them what it was supposed to mean – Chief Justice Begbie of British Columbia was the exemplar of this practice – it was more common to not allow the oath to be administered and thus not to receive Indigenous testimony. The landmark 1860 ruling of Chief Justice Robinson in *R v Pah-Mah-Gay* changed this. Robinson accepted that the defendant's nation had no equivalent to the oath ceremony, and that an oath on the Bible had no meaning to him. But 'he believed in a Good Spirit or Supreme Being, and in a future state of rewards or punishments,' and thus his sworn testimony could be admitted. That he held or kissed the Bible when sworn 'at least did no harm'; what mattered was that he had invoked a 'Supreme Being.'[15]

All trials, involving Indigenous defendants or not, were subject to the long-standing rule that a person with an interest in the outcome could not give sworn testimony as a result. In legal language this meant that defendants were not competent witnesses, because their evidence was likely to be tainted by their interest. They could give unsworn testimony, but that was considered less reliable. Although this rule was often criticized, and although it was substantially modified in 1841 in Upper Canada, that modification did not extent to parties to a proceeding, covering only those with some other interest. This prohibition was not lifted until 1893.[16]

In two areas in particular the nineteenth-century trial was different from the eighteenth. First, by at least the 1820s the presumption of innocence and the reasonable doubt standard were firmly established and frequently adverted to, even if the latter phrase itself was not always employed. Ward Chipman of the NBSC, for example, referred in 1831 to the need for 'full and undoubted proof of guilt.' Andrew Stuart, solicitor general of Lower Canada, opened his murder case against Isaac and James Jones in 1835 by using the precise phrase, telling the jury that 'if there existed a reasonable doubt, ... the prisoners were entitled to the benefit of that doubt.' And he went on to give the standard reason: 'It was better, according to the humane principles of the Criminal Law, that ninety-nine guilty persons should escape, than that one innocent man should suffer.'[17]

Second, beginning in the 1840s, and part of the broader law reform movement discussed elsewhere, piecemeal changes ate away at what was seen as the excessive technicality of criminal procedure, which was often depicted as an obstacle to truth finding and justice. This trend was present in all colonies, and we will use Upper Canada as the example. The first statute to abolish some technicalities of criminal procedure was passed in 1841, a response to the felt need 'to relax in some instances the technical strictness of criminal proceedings, so as to insure the punishment of the guilty, without depriving the accused of any just means of defence.' A later statute on forgery trials sought to ensure that 'justice should not be defeated by clerical or verbal inaccuracies in the proceedings.' It removed the need for production of a facsimile of the allegedly forged document; it was necessary only to provide a description of it in a manner that could sustain the indictment. The major such statute was the 1849 *Act for the Removal of Defects in the Administration of Criminal Justice*, the purpose of which was to 'further relax' the 'technical strictness of criminal proceedings.' Among other things it permitted the amendment of indictments during trial and allowed them to contain facially inconsistent charges, leaving it to the jury to decide which offence had been committed.[18] A series of other statutory reforms in the later 1840s and 1850s were reflected in the *Act respecting Criminal Procedure* in the *Consolidated Statutes* of 1859. The form of indictments was simplified, samples provided, and defences based on errors largely eliminated.[19]

Prosecution by Counsel for the Crown

Public prosecution was ubiquitous in British North America before 1815 and remained the norm throughout the nineteenth century, although the identity of the prosecutors changed to some extent, particularly in Upper Canada. Crown counsel prosecuted in all cases in all the high courts, and in this regard the British North American colonies took a very different path from that of England and one much closer to that of the United States. In the home country the vast majority of prosecutions, at both the assizes and the quarter sessions, until near the end of the nineteenth century, were privately conducted.[20]

Four principal points can be made about the conduct of public prosecution in this period. First, when courts sat in term times in colonial capitals, most prosecutions were carried on personally by the attorney general or, less often, by the solicitor general, right up to Confederation. Claims were made in both Upper Canada and New Brunswick in the early nineteenth century that the attorney general had a right to monopolize all prosecutions, but although this right was denied by governments it was accepted that in practice the law officers could handle what cases they wanted.[21] The attorney general was invariably the prosecutor in high-profile and/or politically important cases, such as those arising out of the rebellions; Attorney General Christopher Hagerman and Solicitor General William Henry Draper were the prosecutors in the trials that followed the 1837 Upper Canadian rebellion, in Toronto and other locations.[22] But the attorney general's role went well beyond such exceptional events. In 1821 John Beverley Robinson described his duties as including 'conducting all criminal prosecutions on behalf of the crown,' and in 1831 Lieutenant Governor Sir John Colborne similarly stated that 'the Attorney General conducts all criminal prosecutions on behalf of the Crown.' In fact Robinson, a linchpin of the colonial executive, prosecuted only in the Home District at York. His successor Henry John Boulton was similarly active as a prosecutor in York/Toronto in the 1830s.[23]

The law officers in other colonies were equally familiar figures in the higher criminal courts. Lower Canadian attorneys and solicitors general prosecuted from the 1820s until at least the 1840s. Solicitor General Andrew Stuart and Attorney General Charles Ogden not surprisingly oversaw the court martial trials of participants in the second Lower Canadian rebellion of 1838, but the law officers were active in numerous other trials as well.[24] Thomas Wetmore and Charles Peters, New Brunswick attorneys general for more than thirty years between them, were very frequently in court at Fredericton up to the 1840s, as was George Frederick Street, solicitor general, in the 1850s, Attorney General Lemuel Wilmot being busy in the assembly and in jockeying for a place on the Supreme Court bench. One of his successors, Charles Fisher, was more prominent, and in one high-profile case in Fredericton, a murder trial with multiple victims and multiple defendants tried in 1857, both the law officers conducted the prosecution.[25] Fisher was government leader in the late 1850s and apparently spent so much time personally conducting Crown prosecutions that his political colleagues forced him out of government.[26] In Nova Scotia also the attorneys general retained control over prosecution in the capital until after mid-century. In 1844 all the cases tried in the Supreme Court at Halifax were prosecuted by Attorney General James W. Johnston. In 1850 all thirteen cases that went to trial in Easter and Michaelmas Terms were prosecuted by his successor as attorney general, James Boyle Uniacke, and as late as 1859 Johnston, again the attorney general, was an active prosecutor.[27] The same was true for Prince Edward Island; in 1844 it was Attorney General Robert Hodgson who prosecuted William Hiscox in the Supreme Court for killing a member of the volunteers who were assisting a local JP to enforce the law against the illegal traffic in oysters.[28] There were exceptions to this pattern caused by the individual circumstances of attorneys general. Richard John Uniacke, attorney general of Nova Scotia from 1815 until his death in 1830, frequently appeared in court in Halifax as a prosecutor before about 1820, but rarely thereafter. By then in his late sixties he lived most of the time at his country estate of Mount Uniacke, some twenty-five miles outside Halifax, and came to town only to attend council meetings and to do some office work.[29]

A second feature of public prosecution was that when the courts went on circuit in Upper Canada and the Maritimes, it was generally not the attorney general who prosecuted, but the solicitor general or Crown counsel appointed for that purpose. In 1825, for example, the Upper Canadian circuit work was done by Solicitor General Henry John Boulton (western circuit, London, Gore, and Niagara Assizes) and by local lawyer and future King's Bench judge Jonas Jones (eastern circuit). In the 1830s Solicitor General William Draper worked the Upper Canada circuits, while other prosecutions in that and later decades were increasingly conducted by Crown counsel, not law officers.[30] In Nova Scotia leading Halifax lawyers such as Archibald, William H.O. Haliburton, and Lewis Morris Wilkins travelled with the court on some circuits, while local lawyers – Nathaniel White in Shelburne and John Thomas Hill in Guysborough, for example – conducted prosecutions when the court reached their towns.[31] When Andrew Ruff was tried for murder in Truro, Nova Scotia, in 1844, the prosecutor was James Grey, a leading Halifax lawyer.[32] Regular prosecutors were given the KC (QC after 1837) designation in Nova Scotia as early as 1817, although no QCs were appointed in New Brunswick or Upper Canada until 1838.[33] New Brunswick's Thomas Wetmore was something of an exception among attorneys general. He was a very successful lawyer whose extensive private practice necessitated his going on circuit with the court, and he conducted almost all circuit Crown prosecutions personally.[34]

The third notable feature of public prosecution in this period was that in the early 1840s the system in the Canadas diverged from that of the Maritime colonies. The union of 1841 and the rise of Cabinet government meant that henceforth the attorneys general for each section of Canada were too busy with their political and administrative responsibilities to spend time in court, and also contributing to this change was the increase in population. The changes of the union period are nicely described in an 1844 report of a committee of the executive council. It noted that for prosecutions in Upper Canada to be conducted by the law officers had become 'quite impossible.' As a result, 'Queen's Counsel must unavoidably be employed' in most places.[35] The law officers still made occasional appearances in courts in the Canadas in the 1840s and 1850s, more so the solicitor general and more so in Lower Canada, where La Fontaine was co-leader of the Baldwin-La Fontaine government and attorney general. Hence Solicitor General Pierre-Joseph-Olivier Chauveau prosecuted in the Thomas Burke trial already discussed.[36] But the work was increasingly done by Queen's Counsel. Those who did so included Henry John Boulton, who was dismissed by London from the post of Newfoundland chief justice in 1838. He returned to Upper Canada, became a QC in 1842, and went back to private practice, including Crown counsel work. In 1846 he was the prosecutor at the trials of the Markham gang, a notorious criminal organization that operated throughout southern Ontario and was given its name by the press from the location where many arrests brought about its downfall.[37]

Upper Canada was the only jurisdiction in this period to move from an ad hoc system of public prosecutors to one featuring regular salaried county attorneys, in 1857. To understand why we need to bear in mind that 'public prosecution' in the nineteenth century generally meant only prosecution in the courtroom, it did not mean case preparation, evidence gathering, and organizing witnesses. When the attorney general selected men to prosecute, they turned up with no advance knowledge of the cases and had to reply largely on the depositions taken by JPs. Nobody would have done any follow-up inquiries, and witnesses might not even have been summoned. From this patchy background the Crown counsel had to prepare an indictment for the grand jury and conduct the case if that body found a true bill. Add to this the fact that the men sent out as Crown counsel were not always best suited for the work; patronage influenced the selection process. The *Globe* succinctly, if unkindly, referred to this system as one in which 'half-fledged legal deputies' were sent out to assize towns 'to bungle the criminal business for a few days.'[38]

Pressure for reform saw various ideas floated before an 1850 select committee of the assembly.[39] The principal advocate for a system of public prosecutors was Sir James Gowan, founding editor of the *Upper Canada Law Journal* and a close confidante of Attorney General John A. Macdonald.[40] It was Gowan who drafted what became the *County Attorneys Act* of 1857, modelled on the system of public prosecution that operated in Scotland.[41] County attorneys were to be appointed (not elected, as some proposed) throughout the colony, lawyers of three years' standing, and resident in the county. They were to do all the prosecution work at the assizes, unless the attorney general made a special appointment of another lawyer. We have ample evidence that the government did do just this, for high-profile cases where the resident county attorney might be connected with a party. In 1859 one Alexander Galt prosecuted Doctor William King at Cobourg for the murder of his wife, for example, the local Crown attorney assisting.[42] Crown attorneys were remunerated by fees and could continue in private practice as well, although this did not include doing any defence work. This ban also applied to the prosecutor's partners and was a change from the previous system; ad hoc Crown counsel could also take on defence work. The county attorneys' duties as laid out in the Act reflected the problems with the old system. Their job was to obtain all the papers generated by the JPs and the coroners in relation to a criminal prosecution, and to then make further investigations if necessary. Private prosecution could still be carried on at the quarter sessions, although it was considered unlikely that this would happen much, given that a private prosecutor would have to do the job himself or hire counsel with his own money, whereas the public prosecutor was paid by the state. However, in an allusion to the problems of malicious prosecution, the county attorney was to watch over private prosecutions at quarter sessions and take over the case 'where a particular act or omission presents more of the features of a private injury than a public offence,' or where 'justice towards the accused seems to demand his interposition.'[43]

The *County Attorneys Act* was unique in British North America; no other colony created such a system until Manitoba in 1875. It was also a blend of American and Scottish ideas – the very idea of a local public attorney – with English ones – it retained the right of private prosecution at quarter sessions and rejected the idea of electing prosecutors. The system attracted some controversy in the decades following its establishment but stayed in place after Confederation.[44]

Our final point about Crown prosecution concerns the role of prosecuting counsel. When Crown prosecutors appeared in court, they invariably talked about themselves as independent and impartial representatives of the Crown. Since their earliest appearances in seventeenth-century English courts, Crown counsels' role was not supposed to be that of implacable pursuers of convictions, but as persons who presented credible evidence to the jury about the circumstances of a crime, as fully and fairly as possible. Often referred to in both historical and contemporary accounts as a 'minister of justice,' a Crown counsel was supposed to ensure that trials were conducted fairly to all – the accused, victims of crime, and the public. Some prosecutors seem only to have paid lip service to this impressive-sounding code. Henry John Boulton told the jurors in cases involving the Markham Gang in 1846 that he was 'sorry' that it was 'a duty for him to prosecute.' But he quickly went on to say that 'the interests of society, and the peace and security of their fellow-countrymen, rendered it imperative that, if they were guilty the law should be vindicated, and an example set that would deter others.'[45]

Other prosecuting counsel talked the right talk, and some seem to have walked the walk. New Brunswick Attorney General Wetmore did so emphatically in an 1828 sedition trial, telling the jury that 'it was the great principle of our Laws ... that every person is presumed innocent until proved guilty.' Another example of an even-handed prosecutor was Nova Scotia's leading lawyer of the 1820s and 1830s, sometime Solicitor General Samuel G.W. Archibald. In prosecuting James Burns for murder in 1829, he opened the case with 'clearness and perspicuity' before a packed courtroom. He said that murder was a 'high crime' but was careful to remind the court that 'it was for the jury to decide upon his innocence or guilt.' He reinforced that point by noting that testimony would show 'some little discrepancy in the evidence, which it would be the duty of the Jury, if possible, to reconcile.' He told the jury that they would hear that Burns had gone upstairs, changed his clothes, and come down with a knife in his hand, which 'appeared very strong evidence of' a premeditated desire to kill his victim. But Burns could always refute such an impression, and he, Archibald, 'would sincerely rejoice if it should appear that in giving the fatal wound he was acting in self defence.' He concluded that if self-defence was made out, 'it would be the duty of the Jury to acquit him, and if there was a reasonable doubt upon their minds, it ought to be given to the prisoner.' Prince Edward Island's solicitor general, James Peters, was even more emphatic, almost poetic, about the prosecutor's role in 1844: 'The humanity of the British law,' he told the jury, 'enjoined upon its advocates to consider themselves as counsel for the accused, as well as for the Crown.' Thus sympathy for the prisoner 'glowed with equal warmth in the breasts of the advocates of the Crown' as anyone, and if the prisoner was acquitted he would 'hail' the verdict 'with joy not surpassed by any in the vast concourse by which he was surrounded.'[46]

Defence Counsel before the Mid-1830s

Before the mid-1830s the law regarding defence counsel was as it had been in the eighteenth century. Felony defendants had no right to be represented by counsel, but judges always let them into the trial on request, with the only limit to their roles being that they could not address the jury. The better-off could afford lawyers and frequently did so. When George Frederick Street, son of a member of the council and himself a lawyer trained at the inns of court, was tried for his role in a fatal duel in Fredericton in 1822, he had a defence lawyer who engaged in 'a few Law points respecting Duelling.' Even had Street been less well-connected he would have been represented, because he was charged with a capital offence. In capital cases judges delayed proceedings and appointed a lawyer to represent the defendant. A few examples, selected from many, will suffice. When a young Indigenous servant girl, Angelique Pilotte, was tried for murder of her infant at Niagara-on-the-Lake in 1817, Justice William Campbell appointed Bartholomew Beardsley as her counsel. Rufus Fawcett, tried for the murder of his father in Westmoreland County, New Brunswick, in 1830, similarly had counsel appointed for him. Jeremiah Ryan of Montreal lived in a boarding house in Montreal but was defended by a Mr Grant when tried for the murder of Mary MacDonald in 1822. Sometimes these defendants were served by elite lawyers who saw their ethical responsibilities as providing such representation. James Burns was not a wealthy man, but when he went on trial in the NSSC for murder in 1829, he was defended by Lawrence O'Connor Doyle and William Bliss, both leading Halifax barristers. Michael O'Sullivan and Charles Mondelet of Montreal, both prominent lawyers and politicians, were among the Lower Canadian lawyers whose names feature in capital trial accounts.[47] In Upper Canada from the 1830s the government paid lawyers to travel the circuits and provide counsel to defendants.[48]

It is less easy to establish how many defendants charged with a non-capital crime were represented. The leading study of Upper Canada's criminal justice system finds that defence lawyers' presence was 'routine'; in ten cases heard at the 1823 Niagara District Assizes, for example, all defendants were represented.[49] Newspaper reports show that many defendants charged with lesser offences were represented, and it is likely that defence lawyers played some role in most cases in the higher courts for most of this period. But they were not ubiquitous. Moise Plante, for example, an illiterate labourer tried for larceny at Quebec City in 1856, was 'not assisted by Counsel, not having the means to pay for the services of any professional adviser.'[50] Cases where no lawyers are mentioned generally involved people who were unlikely to be able to afford them – private soldiers, common labourers, Blacks – and it makes sense to conclude that defence representation in non-capital cases remained dependent on the ability to pay. In one term of the Halifax Supreme Court in 1819, for example, three trials were held. In the first two, two Black men were quickly convicted, with no legal assistance. In the third the defendant, a merchant captain, was defended in a much longer trial by Charles Fairbanks. Some thirty years later two men charged with shopbreaking and another on trial for rape had no counsel.[51]

We must also bear in mind that when the bar found a volunteer or the court assigned a lawyer, those chosen were frequently drafted in at the very last moment and had no real time to prepare the case. This was true of many of the examples given above. It was also true for Neil Macpherson, Malcolm McMullan, and James Lyons, indicted for burglary and robbery, capital crimes, at Sydney, Cape Breton, in 1837. As they were arraigned and asked to plead, one Mr Smith rose 'and craved the indulgence of the Court, as he had just been engaged on behalf of the prisoners.' Nobody objected to that, but Prosecutor Edmund Murray Dodd, a leading local lawyer and the assembly member for Sydney Township, objected to Smith's request for some time to speak with his clients. Smith cited the precedent of the 1836 English *Prisoners' Counsel Act*, discussed below, not law in Nova Scotia, in support of his request, for it represented the 'humane' principle that defendants should be given every advantage. He bolstered his argument with the fact that not only were the prisoners entirely inexperienced with criminal procedure, they were 'almost ignorant of the English language.' They were presumably Gaelic speakers, and presiding judge Marshall gave Smith time – until the start of the following day.[52]

Defence lawyers, whatever little time they had to prepare, could make a difference. They cross-examined prosecution witnesses, bringing out factors favourable to the accused, and inconsistencies and uncertainties in testimony. When James Burns was tried for murder in Halifax in 1829, for example, his counsel, Lawrence Doyle, was able to elicit from the prosecution's medical expert both that the wound that killed the victim Robert Barry might have been inflicted during a struggle, rather than deliberately, for 'the place where the wound appeared was very soft.' More damagingly to the prosecution case, co-counsel Bliss induced the victim's daughter to admit that Barry seemed to have been intent on starting a fight and that he was generally of a violent temper.[53] Lawyers could also raise legal objections. At *La Minerve* publisher Ludger Duvernay's trial for libel in Montreal in 1836, his lawyer, Cherrier, raised a series of points about the definition of the offence, which were ultimately rejected by the court.[54] On Elizabeth Dunmore's 1830 trial for murdering her husband, unusually prosecuted as petit treason, defence counsel William Sawers made a formal objection to the fact that the only evidence for Dunmore being married to the victim Charles Dunmore was given by her father; he wanted more formal proof of the marriage, but was overruled. Later he reverted to non-legal arguments and was able to get Dunmore's father, Alexander Grant, who had been called for the prosecution, to admit that he had never seen the couple quarrel and that Elizabeth had done 'all she could' for Charles when he became sick, and she 'appeared very sorry' and 'cried' as her husband lay dying from some sort of poison. Counsel elicited similar testimony of marital harmony from other witnesses, and a suggestion of bad blood between a prosecution witness and one of the accused from another prosecution witness. After the doctor had given medical evidence he underwent 'a rigid cross examination.'[55]

Defence counsel thus employed a range of techniques to weaken or gainsay the prosecution evidence. These included putting the victim on trial in sexual assault cases. When Pierre Mackay was tried for rape in Quebec City in 1841 his lawyer, Thomas Aylwin, established that the complainant was a prostitute and then led her into damning lies, even if they were irrelevant to the issue at stake. He asked her where she had slept the previous night, and she responded that it was in a house 'down the street.' He immediately asked if it had been in the gaol, and when she admitted the fact asked her, 'Why did you tell me that you slept in a house down the street?' 'I said so because I did not know that you knew I was in gaol,' she replied, eliciting laughter from the spectators. Aylwin followed this with 'Oh: Then if you had known I was aware of your being in a gaol, you would have told the truth and not a lie?' She admitted this, and Aylwin followed up by asking her why she had been in jail. She answered robbery, and then under further questioning acknowledged that she had been 'committed as a prostitute.' Her evasions were likely the result of a conviction that she would not be believed if she admitted to being a sex worker, and she was unfortunately proved right in this, for after her final admission the prosecuting QC indicated that he wanted to abandon his case, and the jury was directed to acquit.[56]

Something similar likely occurred at Andrew Heffernan's trial for rape in Halifax in 1842. Even without a lawyer Heffernan was acquitted without the jury retiring, presumably because he had been able to assail his alleged victim's reputation. Non-European women had a double disadvantage. Edward Brown, accused in 1847 of raping Sally Newall, an 'Indian girl,' was acquitted by a jury which also did not retire. The prosecution was able to provide two supporting witnesses, but they too were Indigenous, and the jury easily preferred to believe Brown and his six witnesses.[57]

Not all lawyers were effective. When Thomas Berrigan was arraigned in 1845 for horse stealing, Chief Justice Halliburton asked Samuel Leonard Shannon to represent him, even though the charge was no longer a capital one. Shannon asked a few questions of the only prosecution witness and then gave up and told Halliburton that 'the case was so plain that he should not attempt to address the Jury.' Halliburton agreed, and being one of those judges discussed above who were prepared to give their own opinions, told the jury 'the testimony was so strong, and uninvalidated by any conflicting evidence' that they 'could of course have no doubt of the Prisoner's guilt.'[58]

Whether or not a defendant was represented by counsel, before the mid-1830s he or she had to speak to the jury in a closing speech. Some defendants were able to do so very effectively. Publishers Joseph Howe of Halifax and John Hooper of Saint John both spoke to the jury in their 1830s criminal libel trials, and both avoided conviction.[59] Defendants lower down the class structure and without much formal education could also offer effective defences, like Mrs Jakes of Saint John, tried in 1834 for setting fire to the house of Mr Sloot, whose wife had discharged her from her job. The circumstantial evidence was strong against her, and she had an obvious motive, but she offered an effective defence in a half-hour speech to the jury. She 'commented upon the evidence with much judgement, and noted an important discrepancy in the testimony delivered by one of the witnesses between a previous examination and on that day.' She also attacked the logic of the prosecution theory: 'If I wished to set the house on fire, why was I the first to discover it?' 'If I had any intention I had many previous opportunities: Mr and Mrs Sloot were absent for a fortnight before.' The jury acquitted her.[60]

Some defendants made effective speeches because they had assistance in preparation. John Kelly, a sergeant in the 52nd Regiment garrisoning Halifax in 1830, was fortunate in this regard. When invited to address the jury he explained that he 'was but little used to speaking in public,' and so he would read to the jury 'some remarks' he had prepared. He proceeded to read a lengthy statement, which it is of course possible that he had written but which reads much more like the work of someone a good deal more educated than an NCO. Presumably an officer of his regiment was responsible, or even a lawyer engaged by the officer corps. Kelly said he was 'unfortunate' to stand in court 'charged with a crime that is revolting to human nature' but was also confident that he was being tried 'by a learned and honourable Court' and a jury 'discreet, unbiased and humane.' He had the 'consolation that springs from a consciousness of being innocent of the malice that constitutes murder.' There was much more in the same vein, and Kelly also attested to his own good character; even though a soldier he was not 'a stranger to those feelings of affection that form the bonds of social life.' Kelly's speech did not avail. Brenton

Halliburton had no doubt, 'from the Evidence,' that the jury 'must find the Prisoner guilty,' although of course the decision was 'in your hands.' After an hour of deliberation the jury did find him guilty.[61]

Kelly's case was unusual. It was far more common for defendants to say they had been drunk and could remember nothing of the circumstances that had put them in the dock, or that a stranger had given them an article that turned out to have been stolen, or that they had no idea how stolen property had gotten under the floorboards of their room. Aaron Butler was found guilty of larceny at Halifax in 1825, his rather unlikely defence being that articles in his possession had all been found by him 'by mere good luck, on the street'; he 'made it a practice to walk about very early in the morning, and sometimes picked up one little thing or another, but all in an honest way.' Some accuseds, like Rufus Fawcett, tried in Westmoreland County, New Brunswick, for the murder of his father in 1832, said nothing at all. Guilty verdicts were invariable and swift in such cases, but there were exceptions, including Fawcett, whom the jury acquitted.

The Prisoners' Counsel Acts and Their Effect

From the 1820s reformers in England and British North America lobbied for two changes in the law relating to defence counsel. One was for felony defendants to have the right to be represented; this was not a particularly significant change because it would merely put practice into law. The other more significant campaign was for the removal of any limitations on the role of counsel, the principal effect of which would be that defence lawyers could address juries after the evidence was in. In England these two changes came with the passage of the *Prisoners Counsel Act* of 1836.[62] In all British North American colonies these same reforms were effected at roughly the same time – between 1835–6 (the Canadas and Prince Edward Island) and 1840–1 (New Brunswick and Nova Scotia). The Nova Scotia statute was initially a temporary Act of two years, made permanent in 1844. The New Brunswick and Nova Scotia Acts did more than confer the right to counsel; they also provided defendants with the right to see copies of depositions and of the examinations of witnesses who would appear against them. The Lower Canadian statute was unusual, limiting the right to counsel to capital cases; the right was extended to all those tried in Lower Canada when the criminal law of the Canadas was consolidated in 1841.[63]

Legislation granting a right to counsel was first introduced in the Upper and Lower Canadian assemblies in the early to mid-1820s, was consistently reintroduced in subsequent years, and as consistently turned back by the legislative councils. Leading the charge in Upper Canada was Marshall Spring Bidwell, an American immigrant, and most of the principals in the campaign were also of American origin, men who drew on their experience to the south where the sixth amendment to the constitution gave defendants the right to counsel in federal prosecutions. The matter was first discussed in the Maritimes in the 1830s, and, again reform bills were defeated in the council. In all colonies senior legal figures, the law officers of the Crown and the superior court judges, opposed a change in the law.[64]

Speaking in the assembly, Bidwell argued that the lack of a right to counsel was an anomaly in English law, 'repugnant to the general spirit of our laws, and to that tender and considerate regard to the rights of the accused by which they were so gloriously distinguished.' The *Montreal Gazette* took the same view, arguing that it was wrong 'to deny to a prisoner accused of felony the same advantages that are allowed to him who is charged with a misdemeanour.' More than anomalous, the law was unfair to those accused of felonies, and changing it 'would savor much of humanity and equity.' For advocates on both sides, the major concern was whether defence counsel should be allowed to address juries on their clients' behalf. As the Nova Scotia statute put it, it was only 'just and reasonable' that accused persons be able to make 'their full answer and defence.' Acting alone at the crucial moment, an unrepresented accused person could not make a full defence. A correspondent to Halifax's *Novascotian* called it a 'disgrace' that both in Britain and the colony prisoners on trial were engaged in an 'unequal' contest, one that they waged 'against ... fearful odds' while being 'under all the disadvantages of terror, ignorance and inexperience.' The situation was exacerbated by the fact that those accused of a misdemeanour had counsel to assist them, while a person accused of a capital crime 'is cast upon his own resources and must rely on his own feeble and unpractised powers.' This was a 'flagrant injustice' and an 'absurdity.'[65]

The opponents of granting the full right to counsel made three principal arguments. One was simply that English law did not confer the right, and neither should an English colony. This argument, a staple of John Beverley Robinson's resistance, lost its force after the English Act was passed. More substantive was the opponents' second argument, made, inter alia, by nine members of the Lower Canadian legislative council who dissented when a bill finally passed that body in 1835. They insisted that granting the right to counsel would be 'prejudicial instead of beneficial to persons accused.' The councillors were adverting to the argument that the judge played the role of 'prisoner's friend.' Another element of the prejudice that would be suffered by accused persons was that if the accused did have a lawyer speak to the jury on his or her behalf, then the prosecution would become more aggressive, abandoning its 'minister of justice' role and instead pursuing convictions implacably. Robinson used this argument frequently. The prosecutor 'had a simple duty to perform in submitting to the Court and Jury a plain statement of the facts.' Crown counsel would stick to this limited role so long as defence counsel were not more involved. But were they allowed to speak to the jury, in reply prosecutors might be forced 'to take a course less favorable to accused persons,' in the process making 'strong appeals to the feelings of the jury' lest the administration of justice be skewed. Two years later he asked rhetorically, 'Was he when a man's life was at stake, to bring down upon him the weight of professional ingenuity, and to address himself to the feelings and passions of a jury, when the trembling prisoner was not allowed to make his defence by counsel?' Obviously not; in such cases 'he felt it right to do no more than make a plain statement of the facts, such as might enable the Jury to understand the bearing and connection of the evidence.'[66]

The third and principal argument of opponents to the reform bills was that the right to counsel was not just unnecessary but harmful to the efficacy of the trial process. It was unnecessary because counsel for those accused were in practice allowed to cross-examine prosecution witnesses and present their own and argue points of law. It was harmful because it was an opportunity for eloquent obfuscation. The best way to get at the truth was to allow the jury to make up its mind on the evidence and on the demeanour of the accused. The best-known statement of this position, frequently cited, appears in Hawkins's *Pleas of the Crown*: 'Every one of common understanding may as properly speak to a Matter of Fact, as if he were the best lawyer,' and it therefore required 'no manner of Skill to make a plain and honest Defence.' Not only was the 'artless and ingenuous behavior of one whose Conscience acquits him' effective, it was the best way to get at the truth, was 'more moving and convincing than the highest Eloquence of Persons speaking in a Cause not their own.' A correspondent to the *Novascotian*, echoing Hawkins, argued that all lawyers' speeches were 'appeals to the passions or prejudices of a Jury,' exercises in 'forensic ingenuity.' The wisdom of centuries was that a trial by jury should be a trial based on 'evidence and not eloquence.'[67]

In England and British North America the trial was gradually transformed by defence lawyers' larger role. Henceforth they increasingly behaved like James Boyle Uniacke, formerly the attorney general of Nova

Scotia but out of office in 1845 when he defended a client 'very forcibly.'[68] We see Uniacke at work in the trial of Peter Kirby, for highway robbery, in 1846, casting scorn on inconsistences in the prosecution case. The victim, Christopher Mosher, had been drunk and had variously identified the thing in his assailant's hand as 'like a pistol, but it might have been a stone, or a piece of wood, or a thing of tobacco.' He also noted that Mosher testified to seeing only one man approach him; it was another witness who said there were two and that Kirby was one of them. He followed this with a blistering attack on J.S. Clarke, clerk of police, for offering inducements to confess while confining Kirby, a boy, 'with felons in a dungeon' and telling him that his life was at stake, which it was not. The confession was 'extorted by fear and hope,' 'wrung from him under appalling fear, touching the tenderest emotions of the heart, a fear of bringing his family into disgrace.' This was all strong stuff, but it did not much move the jury, who found Kirby guilty. The Kirby trial thus illustrates both a new feature of the trial process and juries continuing to rely on their own intuitions and impressions. More successful than Uniacke was J.P. Wetmore of Fredericton, who acted for Margaret Mahony when Mahony was tried for the murder of her infant child. Wetmore 'did everything which ingenuity could do to extricate her from the terrible situation in which she was placed,' and she was found not guilty. To similar effect Thomas Aylwin of Montreal 'addressed the Jury with much force and eloquence' when defending Josephine Tache accused of attempting to murder her husband in 1841, 'dilating with effect on the avowed character of the principal [prosecution] witness whose wholly unsupported testimony was brought forward to convict a lady of irreproachable character of the most atrocious crimes.'[69]

Having a right to be represented, and having the representative able to speak to the jury, still did not help, of course, those who could not afford a lawyer or for some other reason did not have one. Many such defendants had as little to offer as Henry Clarke, a Black man tried in Halifax in 1842 of the attempted rape of a white woman. The only witness to the alleged event was the victim herself, although others testified to her distress and to the consistent story she told. Nobody defended Clarke, whose defence was that 'he was drunk at the time, and did not know what he was doing.' The jury did not need to retire to find him guilty. Nor did the jury retire to convict railway worker Dennis Sullivan of Hamilton of murder in 1856. He had a lawyer who seems to have offered no defence other than to say that he would leave his client, who did not testify, 'to the merciful considerations of the jury.'[70]

Defence counsel could argue points of law, as they always had done. A particularly effective defence of this kind was offered by PEI lawyer

Charles Binns in 1844, counsel for William Hiscox on trial for his life for the murder of George Tanton. Tanton was one of the men pressed into service by a local JP to apprehend Hiscox for allegedly breaching oyster fishery regulations. Binns employed familiar tactics, seeking to establish that Hiscox was of good character and did not know his gun was loaded, which might have reduced the offence to manslaughter. But Binns's principal concern was to establish the illegality of the attempted search and seizure, because the warrant had both been improperly obtained and then altered. It worked, and Hiscox was found guilty only of manslaughter, much to the displeasure of Chief Justice Jarvis, who presided at the trial.[71]

The changes in the criminal trial discussed here had considerably more effect on the high courts than on lower tribunals, which dealt with cases involving small larcenies, assaults, or minor transgressions of local regulations.[72] The JPs who presided in sessions courts were not legally trained and relied on JP manuals that told them the relevant common law and local statutes. But urban stipendiary magistrates, legally trained, were not much bound by technicality and formality either. In both town and country, prosecution was often, although not always, private, or conducted by the police, not lawyers; defence counsel appeared but not in every case and less so at the lowest levels; trials remained mostly confrontational, involved few witnesses, and were rapidly disposed of. In the Upper Canada Quarter Sessions in the 1820s and 1830s, for example, it was not unusual to process a dozen cases a day.[73] There was some change over time, especially in urban centres where there were more lawyers available. There was thus a marked contrast between the Newcastle District Quarter Sessions, where of nearly 700 cases prosecuted in the Upper Canadian period only three definitely involved lawyers, and the Halifax Mayor's Court in 1860, where three young men accused of assault after the taverns closed had a lawyer to defend them.[74] Class also had an unsurprising impact on lawyer participation. Nova Scotia's queen's printer, John Crosskill, appeared at quarter sessions in Halifax in 1845 charged with assault and battery on Joseph Dodson. Crosskill was represented by well-known Halifax barrister Alexander Primrose, although he chose to address the jury himself – unsuccessfully.[75] Most defendants in lower courts did not have lawyers, and the one detailed study we have of the operation of such a tribunal, the Toronto Police Court, paints a picture of a noisy, fetid, chaotic room in which cases were disposed of very rapidly and often reported on in the newspapers as a kind of amusing diversion for their readers.[76]

30

Land Law and Policy: Titles, Tenure, Squatters, Indigenous Dispossession, and the Rights and Obligations of Ownership

In 1815 all British North American colonies were firmly established political entities and essentially rural societies. Land was far and away the most important economic resource, and most colonies had established procedures for land granting and the confirmation and registration of interests in land. But land granting and settlement was not a simple or tidy process, and the eighteenth century bequeathed a variety of land administration problems to its successor, while at the same time the nineteenth threw up new challenges.[1] The first five sections of this chapter deal with issues of land policy and administration: clergy reserves and alien status in Upper Canada; competing French and English land law and the dismantling of seigneurial tenure in Lower Canada; the escheat movement in PEI, which arose in the 1830s and fought a decades-long battle against landlordism on the island; the problem of squatters in all colonies, especially in Nova Scotia and New Brunswick; and the confirmation of land titles based solely on possession in Newfoundland. Central to all these controversies was the question of title to land. In Upper Canada the problem was who could have a fee simple title by law. In Lower Canada the issues were what kind of title, French or English, should be the norm, and whether the civil law should adopt a more liberal approach to land law with the reform of seigneurial tenure. In the Maritimes and Newfoundland it was the need to deal with those who were without formal titles or who had 'imperfect' ones but occupied and developed the land nonetheless. On PEI there was no doubt about who had fee simple title and who did not; the controversy centred rather on the fact that too few people owned fee simples, while too many rented from those who did.

The sixth section of this chapter looks at Indigenous peoples' continued dispossession from their land, via the reduction of reserves by European incursions, whether those reserves were created by agreement or unilaterally. In this area title to land counted for little in large parts of British North America when it was Indigenous title. This section also includes an examination of the European debate over Indigenous dispossession, for not everybody in the settler community believed that the emasculation of Indigenous communities' land rights was valid.

The final section shifts focus from land settlement policy to substantive land law. As any student of the Canadian common law of real property knows, individuals do not own the land itself, but an estate in the land. Ownership of an estate brings with it a set of rights to both use and alienate the land, and obligations to others. This set of rights and obligations has never been an immutable bundle. Throughout the history of the common law it has changed from time to time and place to place, and this was certainly true of British North America in the early to mid-nineteenth centuries. This last section deals only with the common law. Developments in the area of land law and family property in the civil law are dealt with in chapter 34, below.

Upper Canada: Clergy Reserves and Aliens' Titles

Three principal issues dominated land law and policy in Upper Canada. Through the first half of the century the work of the Heir and Devisee Commission, discussed in the previous part, continued, investigating and generally confirming claims to title from settlers who had been granted certificates of occupation, and performed the necessary settlement conditions, but had never taken the final step of taking out a patent for their land. This increasingly meant confirming the titles not of original settlers but of those who had bought or inherited from them or taken title indirectly through them. It also meant in some cases confirming titles of squatters, for the eighteenth-century legacy of shifting policies and confusing record-keeping was long lived. The Heir and Devisee Commission continued its work for decades, until it was formally abolished in 1911.[2] In the three-year period 1835–7, for example, the commission dealt with 590 claims. These statistics were collected by an assembly considering abolition of the commission now that the work could be done by the newly created Court of Chancery. But this proposal was not carried through, suggesting that the relative informality of proceedings and the willingness of the commissioners, who often included the common law judges, to employ equitable principles that favoured those in actual possession, made the institution popular. In cases where squatters had a long tenure and had improved the land, the commissioners did not hesitate to confirm their title.

The clergy reserves was another issue that caused controversy in Upper Canada, not because title to the land was unclear but because occupants had leasehold title. The *Constitutional Act* required one-seventh of all Crown land in the Canadas to be set aside for support of the Protestant clergy, support provided by leasing out the land. Clergy reserves were 200-acre lots interspersed with other lots in a checkerboard fashion. Through the first half of the nineteenth century there was a chorus of complaints about them. Too few people took them up, and thus progress generally was hindered by a lack of contiguous development. They were resented as associated with the Anglican hierarchy and the Family Compact. In 1817 the assembly dubbed the clergy reserves 'insurmountable obstacles' and demanded that they be sold. But this was stoutly resisted by Bishop John Strachan and the Family Compact. The 1828 Canada Committee of the House of Commons made the same complaint that had been voiced a decade earlier by the assembly: the clergy reserves 'retard more than any other circumstance the improvement of the colony, lying as they do in detached portions of each township, and intervening between the occupation of actual settlers, who have no means of cutting roads through the woods and morasses, which thus separate them from their neighbours.' Recent scholarship has shown that the campaign against the clergy reserves was driven as much, if not more, by the ideology that yeoman freeholding was always preferably to tenancy, which was associated with Old World aristocracy, and that tenants were not the victims of an oppressive system. Leases were long, rents were low, and those administering the system very tolerant of arrears. A clergy reserve lease was in fact 'the best deal around' for tenants, but the critique endured and was also directed at other landlords such as the Canada Company and individual speculators.[3]

The assembly passed legislation to sell the reserves in 1840, but it was disallowed in London. The following year the British Parliament legislated on the matter, but only to distribute the revenues (unevenly) between the two established churches and other Protestant denominations. After responsible government control of the reserves was given to the newly formed Crown Lands Department, but not until the 1850s were the reserves in both the Canadas 'secularized,' with the revenues going to municipal governments.[4]

The major land title issue in Upper Canada was the status of landholding by aliens.[5] In chapter 11 we noted the problems of citizenship faced by American immigrants who had come to British North America sometime after the end of the Revolutionary War, and the influx continued after ca 1815. The land title controversy arose out of British dissatisfaction with this continued immigration of Americans, dissatisfaction fuelled in part by a new policy of encouraging immigration from Britain. In 1816 Britain sought to tighten up on American immigration by banning the granting of land to any new arrivals from the south and instructed the Upper Canadian authorities to dispossess Americans who had moved north after the War of 1812. The policy was based on a common law rule that aliens could not hold freehold land in British territory.[6] The British policy was widely objected to in Upper Canada, and the authorities there cautioned against, and persuaded London not to attempt, the dispossession of relatively new settlers.

But if the short-term crisis was easily dealt with, the implications of the alien question for land titles were potentially very much more serious and wide-ranging. The issue arose of whether the Americans who had come to Upper Canada after 1783 lost their British status and thus civil and political rights by virtue of the treaty. If they were in fact foreigners, then their land titles were invalid at common law. The consequences of such a drastic undercutting of security of title were very substantial, for by ca 1815 some 75 per cent of the colony's population were Americans who had come after the initial Loyalist influx. Not only were the titles of people now potentially aliens at risk, so was any person's title that had been derived from an alien at some point in the past. Also at issue was political power, for the franchise and the right to sit in the assembly depended on being a freeholder. Thus although the alien question heated up in the 1820s largely in connection with civil and political rights other than title to land, involving an ever-broadening dispute between elite and non-elite interests, the land question always lurked in the background. Moreover, although nobody was dispossessed, the policy of not making any new land grants to American immigrants remained and was the subject of much heated contention in the 1820s and 1830s. Many in the colony, especially those who held large tracts of land and hoped to sell it off to immigrants, argued that the policy depressed the land market and limited population growth.

The Upper Canadian authorities successfully pressed London to act or to allow local legislation to deal with the problem. The 1828 *Naturalisation Act* confirmed all titles to land held by or derived through people who might have been aliens before that date, but the Act did nothing for newcomers, who continued to immigrate from the United States, especially to the western districts of the colony. Some bought land, some just squatted. Yet again the Colonial Office advised local authorities to enforce the rule against aliens being freeholders by seizing the property of one or two of them for the Crown, but yet again local authorities did not enforce the policy. In the 1830s the land title issue for Americans did not go away, but it never generated the same heat as it had in the previous decade, for two reasons. First, as discussed in more detail later in this chapter, London shifted its policy from land grants to land sales in the mid- to late 1820s, making Upper Canada less desirable than the American midwest, at the same time that it moved to encouraging immigration from Britain. Second, once the 1828 legislation had passed, there was no issue of taking away long-established rights. In the late 1830s there were legislative attempts to extend the *Naturalisation Act*, most notably in 1837 and 1838 when bills passed the assembly giving aliens the right to hold land if they were residents and held no more than 1,000 acres. The legislative council rejected it, seeing it as essentially a measure designed to attract Americans and their capital. The issue became moribund from the late 1830s, when the rebellion discredited the pro-American party. Responsible government ultimately brought a solution; from 1849 aliens were allowed to hold land.[7]

Lower Canada: Competing Land Law Systems and Seigneuralism

The major land title issue in Lower Canada involved seigneurial tenure, which came under increasing attack in the nineteenth century and was effectively abolished in 1854. But there were other land law controversies beyond the existence of the seigneurial system; principal among them was the question of which law applied to land transactions in the area where the dominant form of land tenure was not the seigneurial system but free and common socage – the Eastern Townships. As we saw in chapter 18, uncertainty resulted over which law relating to real property transactions applied in the area, French or English. The uncertainty did not derive from a lack of clarity in the applicable statutes, which clearly implied that it should be English law.[8] Rather, the problem was that the local practice of settlers, notaries, and courts was the opposite. Imperial legislation of 1825, the *Canada Tenures Act*, and a local statute of 1829 attempted to resolve the issue but only muddied the waters further. Not until 1857 did the legislature finally settle the issue by declaring that all incidents of land held in free and common socage should be those recognized by French law.[9]

Another significant issue in Lower Canadian land law was the registration of interests in land.[10] The Custom of Paris contained numerous customary rights and obligations, including a dower right, which allowed a widow to use half of her husband's land after his death (it was only a third in the common law), subject to a tacit hypothec or mortgage to secure the dower right. This was in addition to any rights she might have arising from any community of property that existed with her late husband. Dower was controversial in the early decades of the nineteenth century for both economic and cultural reasons. Proponents of a liberal individualistic approach to land as a commodity saw dower as an incumbrance on freedom of property disposition, a prime example of the presumed anti-commercialism of the Custom of Paris. The fact that most of those proponents were anglophone meant that the debate also took on nationalistic overtones, francophone supporters of dower stressing its enlightened, as they saw it, protection of women and families. In the mid- to late 1830s there was something of a rapprochement between middle class and professional Patriotes and the anglophone community on this issue, with increasing numbers of the former coming to support freedom and transparency in property transactions, which in turn meant both the reform of customary dower (the dower right, which automatically vested in any married woman unless precluded by contract), and some mechanism for registering interests in land so that potential purchasers would always know what incumbrances went with the land they wanted to buy.

The twists and turn of the politics of the immediate pre- and post-rebellion periods meant that a land registration system was not established until the rule of the Special Council, in 1841.[11] The registry ordinance laid the groundwork for an extensive system of registry offices throughout the colony, restricted the dower right acquired by prenuptial contract by limiting it to the land the husband owned at the time of his death, and gave married women a new right to agree to bar their dower in any of their husbands' lands subject to it. Most importantly, it also specified that dower promised in a marriage contract would not take precedence over other claims to a man's estate unless it had been registered. The ordinance did not abolish customary dower, but it did make it subordinate to all other registered claims. For proponents of greater freedom of alienation, registration was key. One simply had to search the register to know whether this particular 'incumbrance' existed to thwart, delay, or make more expensive any plans the purchaser of land might have for it. The registry ordinance was not just about class relations and a capitalist land market; it also affected gender relations, for it reduced the rights of some widows by altering their expectations of what they would have for their support.

The same tension between tradition and modernism marked the debates over the principal land law issue of this period, that of whether the seigneurial system, which applied everywhere except the Eastern Townships, should be reformed.[12] Lower Canada's anglophones had long favoured reform, seeing seigneurial tenure as antithetical to the emerging liberal value of individual freedom. Liberalism required land law to contain as few restrictions as possible on the use and alienation of land, to be unfettered by traditional and what were depicted as 'feudal' dues, rights, and duties. These included the fact that seigneurs enjoyed a monopoly over the use of waterways for mill construction, greatly hampering the development of mill sites. Similarly disliked was the fact that censitaires were required to grind grain for household consumption at the seigneur's mill and pay a tithe for the privilege.

The debates over seigneuralism were intimately linked before the rebellions with the rise of the increasingly aggressive nationalist movement of the 1820s and 1830s. The middle-class professionals who led that movement may have been modernist in their demands for political reforms, but they viewed the seigneurial system as a linchpin of Canadien culture and social structure. Papineau, for example, himself a seigneur,[13] saw the system as egalitarian, one that supported a community of small farmers in which all held some property, the essence of the Canadien nation. The first legislative attempt to reduce the hold of the seigneurial system was the 1825 *Canada Tenures Act*, which permitted voluntary commutation of seigneurial tenure into freehold, provided the seigneurs and censitaires agreed. No incentives were offered, so very few commutations took place. But the significance of the Act is best measured by the reaction it engendered. Papineau saw it as an affront to the Canadien nation, and the assembly condemned it in 1826 as both the introduction of alien laws and a violation of its independence in domestic matters. Through the 1830s the Patriotes condemned the Act and resisted any suggestion of reform. Eight sections of the famous 92 Resolutions of 1834, for example, were devoted to the *Canada Tenures Act* and demands for its repeal, while an 1836 *Report* from the Assembly Standing Committee on Lands and Seigniorial Rights recommended the status quo.[14]

The tide changed dramatically after the rebellions. The *Durham Report* condemned the system and the censitaires as 'backward,' and the main reason why Lower Canada lagged behind the upper colony in economic development. More importantly, the new generation of francophone leaders, lawyers, and other middle-class professionals, no longer saw the seigneurial system as a crucial part of francophone identity. They thus made common cause with the anglophone merchant and professional classes; as one author has put it, 'Quebec's liberal professions supplanted an agrarian vision with a commercial vision in the 1840s.'[15] Reform party leader Louis-Hippolyte La Fontaine typified this shift; he had differed from other francophone leaders before 1837 in wanting an end to the system, and from ca 1840 he departed further from the nationalism of Papineau and made common cause with anglophones. Even more importantly, La Fontaine and other francophone leaders such as George-Étienne Cartier were firm believers in the legal ideology of a liberal approach to contract and property, and in the 1840s the debates turned more on legal ideologies than on nationalist rhetoric. Freehold tenure would liberate enterprise. No one believed this more fervently than Cartier, who saw freehold as not only good for the economic development of Canada but also as necessary to satisfy the demands of the rural population of Lower Canada who might otherwise be attracted to dangerous socialistic doctrines.[16]

Liberalism also required that there be compensation for seigneurs, a natural concomitant of viewing seigneuralism more as a system of property law than as social structure. Hence when La Fontaine introduced two key resolutions about the system in 1850 he stressed both that ending seigneuralism was a key aim of public policy and that it was necessary to ensure 'that all the interests concerned are protected and equitably adjusted,' that a conversion to freehold tenure could be properly achieved only 'by securing a fair indemnity to all parties whose just rights it will affect.'[17] Seigneurs were to be compensated, just as slaveholders in the Caribbean had been a decade earlier and just as large estate holders in PEI were to be later.

A major landmark on the road to abolition was the *Report* of the 1843 seigneurial commission.[18] Comprising two long-standing and prominent opponents of seigneuralism – notary and legal scholar Nicolas-Benjamin Doucet, and John McCord, scion of an elite anglophone family – and of moderate nationalist George Vanfelson, the commissioners played a 'pivotal ideological role.' They recognized the usefulness of the system in its origins, as one that enabled many to exploit their little piece of land, but insisted that it was now an impediment to progress. They especially deprecated the position of the rural censitaire, who 'toils through existence without the hope of relief, and transmits to his posterity a worthless inheritance. Under the operation of such a tenure, his right of property may become a mere delusion; as a moral being he is degraded, and his position is one of perpetual dependence.' The commissioners nonetheless insisted that an 'equitable' method of commutation – the inclusion of fair compensation – should be found.[19]

The formal abolition of the system, the triumph of modernist liberal values, came about in 1854. *The Seigniorial Act* of that year provided for the conversion of all feudal and seigneurial tenure into that of franc-alleu roturier, the civil law equivalent of free and common socage.[20] It abolished all seigneurial dues and charges, to be replaced by a rente constituée or constituted rent. This was calculated as the old 'cens et rentes' in addition to an amount determined to represent the annual value of the other rights held by the seigneur. The rights held by seigneurs and censitaires were henceforth to be determined by a special seigniorial court, comprising the judges of Queen's Bench and the superior court, sitting *en banc*. Constituted rents could be redeemed upon payment of a capital sum to the seigneur, normally seventeen times the annual value.[21]

The formal change in tenure accomplished by the ending of seigneuralism was a profound development in the legal history of French Canada. At a stroke of the legislative pen a system that had endured since the early seventeenth century, and survived the conquest, was done away with. Former censitaires now became owners of their parcels, while seigneurs became owners of the unceded lands in their seigneuries. And yet there was a definite sleight of hand involved in the 'abolition.' According to section 5 of the Act, the constituted rent was 'payable to the Seignior yearly, at the time and place where the *cens et rentes* on such land are now payable.' Thus the obligations of the 'owner' continued very much as before, with only two alterations: dues formerly payable partly in kind were now converted to cash amounts; and, as noted above, the constituted rent could be redeemed. If not redeemed, however – and as will be seen in volume 2, most were not – the 'owner' was liable to pay the constituted rent indefinitely. The Act even specified that the old terminology was to be maintained: 'The words "Seignior" and "censitaire" shall apply to the owner of any *rente constituée* created under this Act, and the person charged with, respectively.' There was only one advantage to the former censitaire over the long term: the constituted rent was fixed forever, with no provision for indexation, so that it would diminish over time with inflation. Abolition was very much reform from above, not the result of agitation emanating from censitaires. Both anglophone and francophone political and business elites could agree that the main objective was the compensation of the seigneurs and not the 'liberation' of an oppressed peasantry, as the initial reform discourse had seemed to suggest. The constituted rents remained a burden on thousands of new 'freehold' landowners for many generations. Their story will be taken up again, in the second volume of this history.

Prince Edward Island: Landlordism

People who were tenants also eventually become freeholders in Prince Edward Island, albeit through a process drawn out over a longer time, more contentious, and much more the result of a grassroots campaign.[22] The origins of the island 'land question' have been described in part 3 of this volume. Suffice it to say here that despite the fact that proprietors failed to meet their settlement conditions and that many fell behind with their quit rent payments, escheats were rare. Some proprietors sold off their land rather than be saddled with the quit rent obligation, so that by the 1830s, at which time the island's population had grown to some 30,000, about one-third of the estates had changed hands, and some 20 per cent of island land was in the hands of small farmer-owners. But otherwise the few residents and rather more new settlers who came in either rented from the descendants of the original large proprietors, or simply squatted. Tenancy was a significant feature of land occupation in all colonies, but generally it was a relatively benign form of tenancy, not the oppressive landlordism that marked the island's economic and social structure.[23]

The 1830s saw a sustained and popular campaign against landlordism, known as the escheat movement after its demand that large estates be taken back from grantees who had failed to fulfil the terms of their original grants. Its leaders envisaged an 'egalitarian society of small, independent freeholders,' and pursued two parallel policy goals to that end – a tax on 'wilderness' (undeveloped) lands, and the escheat of the least-developed of the proprietorial grants coupled with their redistribution to incoming settlers. The more radical critics of landlordism advocated a wholesale escheat of estates, but this never won a majority position.[24] Nonetheless even the mainstream escheat leaders espoused some version of what one historian has termed 'producer ideology' – that 'those who invest the capital and labour necessary to transform the wilderness into well-ordered communities are entitled to keep the product of their investment.'[25]

The escheat movement had considerable success locally, consistently winning majorities in assembly elections from the early 1830s to 1842. In 1832 sixteen of the eighteen members of the assembly petitioned the lieutenant governor to establish a Court of Escheat, and in the same year legislation passed the assembly to that effect.[26] Escheat advocates also had sympathetic supporters in the Colonial Office, but proposals for far-reaching reform never won favour in London, where the absentee proprietors' lobby had much influence and used it vigorously to rally support for another powerful legal ideology, the defence of private property. That defence also garnered local adherents, and an alternative proposal for a land tax was supported by the island's commercial class and passed both local houses. After 1837 and the Canadian rebellions rural radicalism came to seem like disloyalty, so that even the *Durham Report*, which roundly blamed large proprietors for failing to fulfil the conditions of their grants, shrank from advocating escheat, preferring a tax to encourage sales.

After losing momentum through the 1840s the land reform movement gained new impetus after responsible government was achieved in 1851, but the proprietors used their influence in London to discourage radical reform – responsible government had its limits. The best that could be achieved was the 1853 *Land Purchase Act*, which gave the island government the authority to buy land from large proprietors and sell it to tenant occupiers, if the proprietors would sell.[27] But only one major sale was made under the legislation, and the stalemate continued until 1860, when Britain agreed to pay for a commission of inquiry. The three-person commission, despite including a representative of the proprietors, unanimously condemned the initial sale of the island almost a century before and the proprietorial system that had resulted, and recommended that London provide £100,000 to enable the purchase of more land. In the alternative the commissioners recommended compulsory sale at a price to be negotiated or, failing such negotiations, arbitrated.[28]

The resulting stalemate saw tenant groups turn to political organization and rent resistance. A tenant league operated in the mid-1860s, organizing mass protests and rent strikes, as well as physical resistance to evictions and attempts to distrain for unpaid rent. The league had remarkably wide support, numbering perhaps 11,000 members out of a population of 80–90,000. With no regular forces stationed on the island, and with the militia useless because of widespread sympathy for the league, military aid to the civil power was brought in from Halifax. The full force of the criminal law – substantial terms of imprisonment for assault convictions – was also employed against some tenant leaguers. Proprietors were thus able to continue to resist the demands that had been made against them since the 1830s, but those demands never went away, and the issue was finally resolved after Prince Edward Island had joined Confederation in 1873. The *Land Purchase Act* of 1874 required sale of estates of over 500 acres to the government at prices to be determined by a land commission, for resale to the actual occupiers. The proprietors' compensation, paid in part by the federal government, was to be determined by a tripartite tribunal.[29]

After the commission set prices for ten estates, several proprietors appealed to the island's Supreme Court, which ignored a strongly worded privative clause and unanimously set aside the awards. The government appealed to the newly created Supreme Court of Canada, which in its very first reported judgment ruled that the legislation was constitutional and that the awards were valid exercises of the statutory power of the commissioners.[30] Although most of his judgment dealt with technical and procedural questions, Canada's first chief justice, Sir William Buell Richards of Ontario, adverted to the great significance and longevity of the island's history of land tenure and noted that he was not dealing with 'ordinary legislation' but with 'the settling of an important question of great moment to the community,' a question that was 'in principle like the abolition of the Seigniorial tenure in Lower Canada, and the settling of the land question in Ireland.' 'The great object of the statute,' he declared, was 'to convert the leasehold tenure into freehold estates, a matter of very great importance, and one which, if not settled, would be likely to affect the peace as well as the prosperity of the province.' He also saw the right of property as something that must at times yield to the demands of community – 'the public good' – although he tempered this by noting with approval that the legislation was 'based on the principle of compensation to individuals when their property is taken from them.'

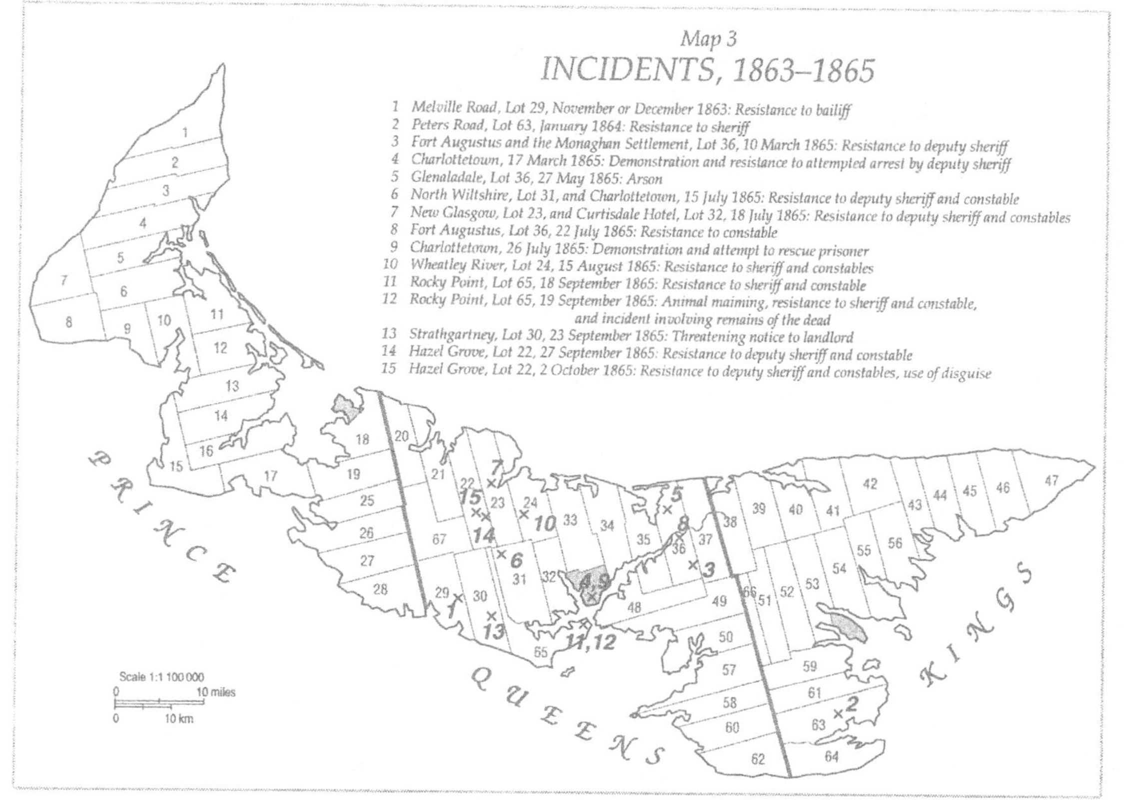

The division of Prince Edward Island into 67 large lots in 1767 and the emergence of a tenant class would inspire resistance in the nineteenth century, clearly shown on this map.

Land Titles and Squatters in Nova Scotia and New Brunswick

European settlers squatting on land they did not own even by European law was rather more prevalent in British North America than popular views – and some academic perspectives – of the process of colonization would suggest. Historians of colonial settlement in general have assumed a sharp dichotomy between the 'orderly' development of the region, including Indigenous dispossession by treaty, compared to the land rushes that characterized the United States, South Africa, or Australia in the nineteenth century.[31] Yet surprisingly large numbers of European immigrants did not have a title of any kind, they simply occupied and used land. In Newfoundland, as we saw in part 3 and as further discussed later in this chapter, almost all titles emanated from possession rather than Crown grant, and this caused no real problem. Elsewhere the presence of squatters created difficulties for colonial governments of how to balance lack of legal entitlement with the fact of occupation. This section deals with squatting in two Maritime colonies, New Brunswick and, especially, Nova Scotia. While squatting did occur in other regions,[32] relative to the population as a whole and relative to the land available it was a much less significant feature of land settlement history than it was in these two Maritime colonies.

The principal causes of squatting in the Maritimes were twofold, and they both derived, at different times, from British policies, including the moratorium on granting freehold land discussed in part 3. Settlers, some Loyalists and some not, still went to Nova Scotia, New Brunswick, and Cape Breton Island after 1790, but without receiving fee simple titles. Some leased Crown land, some occupied it under certificates of location, a Crown licence, and others simply squatted. Squatting was most prevalent on Cape Breton Island; by the time the moratorium was lifted for that area, ten years after the other colonies, in 1817, considerable numbers of immigrants had arrived from the western Highlands and Hebridean islands of Scotland, driven by deteriorating economic conditions at home.[33] There were some 10,000 Europeans settled on the island by the time it was reannexed to Nova Scotia in 1820. According to an 1821 report by the surveyor general of Nova Scotia, these settlers had taken up some 685,000 acres, but only 229,220 acres, or 33 per cent, was held in fee simple. A further 113,600 acres (16 per cent) was occupied pursuant to Crown leases or tickets of location. That left fully 342,820 acres, half of the land in use, occupied by people who were squatters, with no title of any kind.[34] The squatters were present in all regions but were particularly prevalent in Cape Breton County, south and east of Sydney, occupying some 100,000 acres in the valley of the River Mira, an area known as the Mire Grant. This land had been granted to Loyalists in 1787, not much settled, and large parts of it were later escheated in the early nineteenth century. Substantial tracts of the cancelled grants were then occupied by Scots and others as squatters.[35]

The moratorium on granting freehold land was the origin of large-scale squatting on Cape Breton, but the cause of its substantial increase was another imperial policy, the change from free land granting to land sales in 1827.[36] The policy change was inspired by the ideas of a lobby group in Britain known as the colonial reformers, who looked to partially recreate the British class-based social structure of a small group of landowners and a substantial pool of tenants and labourers. It was also intended to raise revenues for colonial governments, for Britain in the 1820s was also implementing a policy of retrenchment in colonial spending, discussed in various chapters above. But there was a large flaw in the scheme. To raise money from land sales, people had to buy land, and to buy land people had to have money. From the late 1820s Nova Scotia generally, and Cape Breton particularly, were subject to a 'perfect storm' of this change in British policy and the large-scale immigration of more impoverished Scottish settlers, fleeing the economic disaster that was the Highland Clearances. The clearances had been going on since the middle of the eighteenth century but intensified from the 1820s, and the socio-economic effects were exacerbated by cholera and famine. Displaced Scots went to many locations in British North America, and the scale of the emigration to Cape Breton was such that by mid-century the island's European population was some 55,000 people, a more than fivefold increase from 1820, of whom two-thirds were Scots. Very few of these immigrants had any money to buy land, and so most of the new arrivals simply squatted. They squatted on ungranted Crown land and on land nominally owned by absentee proprietors. Many squatted on the less productive 'back lands' away from the coasts. In the late 1830s about half the population of the island had no title to the land they occupied and were in a distinctly disadvantaged position compared to those who arrived earlier and had the better land. A 'tide of Emigration' had recently swept into the colony, an 1842 assembly committee noted, and 'nearly all' of those who had come 'have squatted upon Lands to which they have no Title.'[37] The land sales policy was a disaster for the local government. Not only were revenues paltry, the commissioners of Crown lands, one for the mainland and one for Cape Breton until the two offices were combined in 1847, took most of the money paid in the 1840s as their remuneration.[38]

Contemporaries knew what the causes of squatting were and devoted much effort to getting local control of land granting policy and ending, or at least altering the details of, the land sales policy. They achieved the former in stages but were never able to effect the latter before the late 1840s because London would not give the colony control of land policy unless it agreed to retain sales and not revert to free grants. This issue was ultimately resolved by responsible government, which brought with it local responsibility for land granting. From the late 1830s through the 1850s the colony also devoted considerable legislative and administrative resources to trying to regularize the legal problems caused by British policy going back to the moratorium. The land occupied pursuant to the original licences did not pose long-term problems because the occupiers, and others, thought they did have good title, and a market in land operated as if they did. As Lieutenant Governor Sir James Kempt told London in 1825, holders of Crown licences had been given to understand that 'all Persons who actually settled, should receive a grant, whenever the disability [the moratorium] was removed,' and that 'upon the Faith of this assurance' settlers 'consider themselves to be possessed of a Fee Simple, and Lands ... are conveyed and devised as a Fee Simple Estate, and are universally considered as such in the Island.'[39] A process was put in place for those with Crown leases or licences to convert to fee simple title, but not everybody took the time or was willing to spend the fees necessary to do so. After the failure of these attempts to regularize the position administratively, two short statutes of 1850 fixed the problem legislatively. The first declared that anything done by the government of the independent colony between 1784 and 1820 that had to do with 'the Descent, Distribution, and Conveyance of Real and Personal Estate' was valid. The other stated that anybody who had gone into possession under a Crown lease, or had derived title from such a person, 'shall respectively have, hold, and enjoy all such Lands and Tenements in Fee Simple.'[40]

The much more numerous squatters were in a different position, and legislators found them harder to deal with. They were torn between sympathy for impoverished refugees struggling to make a life in the New World and a concern not to reward those who had simply taken unoccupied land. The preamble to an 1840 statute, the first local legislation on the subject of Crown lands, captured this dilemma. 'Numerous settlers ... have gone into possession of Lands belonging to the Crown, and have built on, and otherwise largely improved the same,' and it was 'just and proper that such persons should be able to acquire title to the Lands so occupied and improved by them.'[41] Some people, including Charles Buller, one of Lord Durham's staff who published a study of Crown lands policy, attributed any progress made in agricultural development in Nova Scotia to squatters, achieved in spite of, not because of, government policy. He received support in this view from Lieutenant Governor Falkland, who told London that 'the feeling was very strong throughout the community that a settler, however poor, is a benefit to the province.'[42] This feeling was shared by the judges of the Supreme Court. In the only reported case from this period involving a squatter, the court preferred his claim to that of a rival who asserted an original paper title more than thirty years old. 'What class of persons is better entitled to the favor of the Legislature and of the Courts, than the men who transform a rude country into smiling habitations, and fit it for the use and enjoyment of man,' it rhetorically asked.[43]

On the other hand, policymakers believed squatters should not be so well rewarded for evading the law relating to land occupation; they should pay something, albeit retroactively. Hence a solution like the Heir and Devisee Commissions used earlier in Upper Canada was not contemplated; the principal problem was not uncertain titles but the complete lack of anything other than possession to ground title. Moreover, the problem was not just one between the Crown and squatters, for some squatters were on land granted to, but not occupied by, others. And the situation on Cape Breton in particular was further complicated by non-existent or poor surveying, which made it difficult to know if a person was squatting on Crown land or an unoccupied land grant made to another. The reports of various Crown land commissioners from the 1840s to the 1860s are replete with references to a 'universal trespass upon the Crown property in Cape Breton' and a widespread 'system of plunder' of Crown land. An 1859 report put the amount of land on the island occupied by squatters at 500–600,000 acres, more than half of the million or so acres of ungranted Crown land. The same reports also constantly adverted to inadequate surveys as the principal impediment to actually settling titles when policies were put in place to do so. The 1858 Crown land commissioner's report, for example, noted that in Victoria County the surveyors' task was frustrated by 'a collision of claims' everywhere, and attempts to mediate boundaries were met with 'the most violent opposition' from squatters.[44]

A series of statutes sought to regularize the legal position of squatters, but the first legislative efforts between 1839 and 1843, designed to deal with the Mire Grant area, failed to grasp the nettle of deciding between the claims of those in physical occupation and those whose claims came through a late eighteenth-century grantee.[45] The 1850 Act, noted above, giving Crown lessees a title turned out to cause 'extreme hardship,' because some lessees had left and their heirs at law used the statute to eject squatters who had occupied and improved the land.[46] A turning point was an 1854 statute applying only to Cape Breton, which authorized free grants to people in 'undisputed' possession who applied for them, provided they paid only the necessary fees.[47] Many took up the offer, but not all could do so, and those who could not were subject to the same policy as squatters throughout the colony – they were given a right of pre-emption at a low price, with compensation for improvements already made and payment to be made in instalments. This policy cleared many titles, but it was slow going, in part because of the surveying problems already alluded to. People could apply for fee simple patents, and the Crown Land Department could grant the patent, but exactly where were the boundaries? Large-scale surveys had to be completed before individual titles could be fully settled. The process was also slowed by squatters realizing that if they paid the first instalment on their land they would never be ejected. Officials became frustrated at the arrears in instalment payments, and in 1866 this frustration culminated in further legislation barring the issuance of grants until the purchase money had been paid in full.[48]

Squatting occurred in New Brunswick also, although it was a much less significant issue than in Nova Scotia.[49] It derived, as in Nova Scotia, from the freehold grant moratorium of the late eighteenth and early nineteenth centuries, and the immigration of impoverished Scots and Irish and disbanded soldiers in the first two decades of the nineteenth. They arrived while the free grants policy was still in effect but did not even pay the fees required for getting free grants and simply squatted on both Crown land and the estates of absentee owners. Squatters in New Brunswick never engaged public concern and public policy to any great extent prior to the 1830s, because the timber trade was far and away the colony's economic mainstay. When New Brunswick officials complained of trespassers, they were far more likely to be referring to those who trespassed on Crown or private lands to cut timber without a licence.

Squatting became an issue of public concern and policy only in the late 1830s, an offshoot of the discussions that led to the settling of a civil list, and when the problem was aired a division emerged within the colony over how much sympathy they merited. Lieutenant Governor Sir Archibald Campbell calculated that in late 1836 there were some 1,500 heads of families located on 'waste' land of the Crown, a total of some 9,000 people. Some were there 'under the plea of old Minutes of Council,' that is, tickets of location, while others occupied land 'from ignorance or misapprehension of titles which they procured from others who took original possession.' Campbell himself was sympathetic to their situation. He acknowledged that they were trespassers, but they were also 'British subjects and actual settlers in a state of poverty' whose 'exertions are contributing largely to the improvement of the Province.' Hence he had stopped prosecutions of trespassers, 'tempering justice with mercy' in the name of 'humanity.' He believed that the majority were keen to settle matters with government and were using their best efforts to find the money to pay for their land.[50]

But perhaps surprisingly to him he encountered strong opposition from assemblymen to his proposal to be 'humane' to squatters. A series of assembly resolutions cast doubt on his numbers and in any event insisted that the squatters' plight was not the assembly's problem. The lieutenant governor's approach to the squatters was defeated twenty-four to three, and ultimately all the assembly would do was promise to treat the squatters 'humanely,' whatever that meant. It turned out that assemblymen were more sympathetic in the following decade. By then the numbers were larger. An estimate from Commissioner of Crown Lands Thomas Baillie put the number of squatters *simpliciter* at 1,600 heads of families occupying 160,000 acres of Crown lands, about the same as before, but to this Baillie added another 2,176 people occupying over 250,000 acres who were valid initial occupants but liable to eviction – they had bought land on an instalment plan and paid little or nothing over the years.[51] By now assemblymen were rather more sympathetic, perhaps because these people were seen as victims of the land sales policy, no more popular in New Brunswick than it was in Nova Scotia, and perhaps because, as discussed in the following section, government was faced with hundreds of people squatting on land reserved for Indigenous people, and the assembly did not wish to displace those settlers. If squatters on Indigenous reserves were seen as deserving productive improvers, so too should squatting on Crown lands be regularized.

Whatever the reason, assemblymen talked of the squatters very differently from the way they had six years earlier. Now they were 'worthy persons' who 'have been compelled by necessity to seek a living on vacant lots of land,' and by 'unremitting labour, industry and perseverance, have scarcely procured a bare subsistence for themselves and their families.' The 'industrious poor squatter' deserved 'mercy.' With responsible government the impediment to a local solution, London's insistence that titles could only be sold, not granted, was removed, and the colony was able to fashion its own land policy to deal with squatters and arrears together. An 1849 statute made it possible to grant land in return for labour on the public roads. Two years later Lieutenant Governor Head was pleased to report that the legislation was 'working well' and resulting in 'increased settlement of the country and increased security on the part of occupiers.'[52] New Brunswick's squatting problem, never as serious as that of Nova Scotia, was thus dispensed with and titles largely regularized, albeit in some cases at the expense of Indigenous communities, as discussed later in this chapter.

Newfoundland: The Formalization of Possessory Title

Newfoundland's long and unconventional history of European settlement and land law has been discussed in previous parts. In this period the local Supreme Court gave legal recognition to title based on de facto possession, and the legislature created in 1832 took measures to regularize land titles.[53] The former was principally the work of Francis Forbes: Bermuda-born and raised, and trained in law at Lincoln's Inn, he was made chief justice of Newfoundland at the age of thirty-two. Shortly after arriving he issued two judgments affirming the land rights of residents despite their lack of a grant from the Crown. In one he colourfully remarked that 'possession peaceably acquired and used in the fishery are the best title-deeds that can be produced in Newfoundland.'[54] The significance of Forbes's judgment in this case and others was his willingness to recognize local custom as the principal source of local law. The recognition of title from possession was strengthened by Forbes's judicial reception of English limitations statutes, which gave an occupier title against the Crown after sixty years of undisturbed possession. The effect of this was to validate the titles of people who could not relate their occupation to land reserved for the fishery. In doing so Forbes 'had … given effect to the customary practices of the people of the island over their landholdings,' and he reinforced this position later by holding that adverse possession law applied also to land used for the fishery. There had been considerable legal confusion derived from 'customary practices,' but Forbes resolved that confusion by 'blend[ing] them into formal law.'

Another customary adaptation concerned not title but inheritance. In *Williams v Williams*, an 1818 intra-family dispute over a house in St John's, the mother had died intestate. Real property descended by primogeniture under English law, but Forbes agreed with the defendants that English law on inheritance had never been received, and that real property had always been considered by local custom as chattels real.[55] That custom, which divided personal property equally among heirs-at-law, was the applicable law. Forbes confirmed that 'possession quietly obtained and continued employment in the Fishery' gave a customary title, and also that custom determined inheritance: 'Fishing plantations have passed from holder to holder, and from father to children, without deed or testament, or any solemnity, beyond the fact of delivery, or leaving in possession.' This method of organizing inheritance 'appears to have grown out of those common exigencies which are the best interpreters of positive laws, and in their absence, become laws themselves.' The Colonial Office approved of Forbes's innovation.

Once a legislature had been established in Newfoundland, in 1832, that body set about converting custom into statute law. The first such measure was the *Chattels Real Act* of 1834, which declared that 'the Law of Primogeniture, as it affects Real Estate, is inapplicable to the condition and circumstances of the People in this Island.' The Act worked effectively in later decades, although problems did arise in cases of people who had died intestate before 1834. Some anglophile judges took the ahistorical position that English land law rules had been in force before 1834, a triumph of abstract and uninformed reception theory over the reality of practice. Three years later the legislature altered the land registration statute passed by the British Parliament in 1824 to permit interests in land to be registered many years after they had been transferred, formally or informally, on the basis of an affidavit signed by one person who attested that he or she had been a witness to the transaction. Nothing from the grantor was required. In 1844 the first Crown land Act passed in the colony established the terms for future Crown grants of 'ungranted and unoccupied crown lands,' meaning that ungranted but occupied Crown land could not be granted to new buyers. Instead squatters, including persons who had once been tenants, were given a right of pre-emption, at a lower price than usually charged or free, depending on the degree of improvement. Many people took up the offer, which required them to have their boundaries properly surveyed.[56] By the 1840s, therefore, much of the customary land law and practices of the island had been made the formal law.

Indigenous Peoples' Continued Dispossession

We saw in chapter 26 that a central cause of the decline in Indigenous peoples' status within British North America's constitutional order was the loss of their land base. In this section that account is augmented by examining the continued and illegal, even by European law, incursions onto the limited land resource that had been reserved to Indigenous people, the consequent decline in Indigenous populations that resulted from further loss of their traditional lands, and the legislative and administrative attempts to respond to and prevent further loss of land. Such attempts were generally strong on rhetoric and light on effectiveness. Before the loss of reserve land is detailed, another event of this period should be noted – the demise of the Beothuk people of Newfoundland. No Indigenous group suffered more than the Beothuks from disruption to traditional patterns, disruption that did not come from being settled on reserves, since there were none, or from European occupation of Beothuk territory. Rather the Beothuk had their access to the main source of livelihood, the salmon fishery, drastically reduced by European incursions into their territory and the consequent competition for the resource. The last known Beothuk died in St John's in 1829.[57]

Everywhere else in British North America there were consistent complaints throughout this period from Indigenous people and others aware of their ever-worsening plight about intrusions on and loss of reserve land, a process that continued to Confederation. In New Brunswick, for example, of the approximately 60,000 acres set aside for reserves in 1838, a quarter, some 15,000 acres, was occupied by Europeans by the mid-1840s. Some was in the hands of squatters, some occupied pursuant to illegal land purchases, made for trifling sums or liquor or gunpowder and done in violation of the royal proclamation.[58] Many lots were then sold and resold, making it even more difficult for governments mindful to repair the damage to do so. The largest impediment to protection of New Brunswick reserves, however, was the colonial state, which thought the land would be used better by Europeans who were more deserving. Nothing is more revealing of that policy than the title of the first New Brunswick legislation about reserves in 1844 – *An Act to Regulate the Management and Disposal of the Indian reserves.*[59] Its preamble expressed very clearly the operative philosophy of the legislation. There had been 'extensive tracts of valuable land reserved for the Indians,' but these produced only deleterious effects. They 'tend[ed] greatly to retard the settlement of the Country' and were in 'a neglected state,' not of much benefit 'to the people for whose use they were reserved.' The statute laid down a process for selling the land or leasing it out. Reserves were to be surveyed to establish what land was good but currently unproductive, and such parts of reserves, or indeed whole reserves, should then be 'leased or sold to the highest bidder by Public Auction.' Fifty acres per Indigenous family were to be reserved, after which no impediments were to be placed in the way of a sell-off. The money raised was to be used for welfare and to advance the 'civilisation' policy, the antithesis of reserve protection. The statute did refer to prevention of trespass as one of the commissioner's duties but laid little stress on it. Over 10,000 acres of previously reserve land were alienated under this legislation, often over the protests of the Indigenous groups. The Act was minimally altered in the revised statutes of 1854, with the only substantive change being compensation for squatters on reserves – when reserve land was sold, regard should be had for any improvements made 'by the person in possession, whether he has bought it or leased it from the Indians,' so that the trespasser received 'a just remuneration for such improvements.'[60]

In Nova Scotia a similar shrinking of reserves occurred as Europeans moved onto the land. Officials took an apparently harder line than in New Brunswick. The colony's major statute on Indigenous people, passed in 1842, made the new Indian Commissioner Joseph Howe's first duty the protection of reserve land from 'encroachment and alienation.' Persuasion should first be attempted, which included government funded compensation for improvements, but if this did not work legal action would ensue.[61] Howe's initial report identified some 22,000 acres of poor quality reserve land – some of it 'sterile and completely valueless' – on which lived perhaps 1,300 Indigenous people. He emphasized the need for further reserve creation and protection of what existed, but his interest was short-lived, and his successors did little.[62] There is ample evidence, moreover, that defiant squatters could successfully resist expulsion, especially on Cape Breton Island where, as we have seen, squatting was rampant everywhere. In the mid-1840s Cape Breton Crown Lands Commissioner H.W. Crawley complained, among other things, about some Scots who had settled on reserve land at Wagamatkook. They were 'warned ahead of time not to trespass,' and three times the sheriff had tried to eject them, but they had defied the officials and were still there.[63] Five years later Crawley pointed out that the problem was that non-official Europeans supported squatters and cared not a whit for Indigenous rights. It was 'vain to seek a verdict from any jury in this Island against the trespassers on the reserves,' nor would 'a gentleman of the Bar be found willing and effectually to advocate the cause of the Indians, inasmuch as he would thereby injure his own prospects, by damaging his popularity.'[64] Legislation after 1842 always instructed the Indian commissioner to act, including taking trespassers to the Supreme Court, but commissioners' reports like the above showed that their efforts were ineffective.[65]

Perhaps recognizing the difficulty of protecting reserves, legislation in the early 1850s allowed for the creation of new ones, but none were established. Indeed in the late 1850s and 1860s legislation permitted the government to 'compromise' with squatters who had made improvements or give them other land if they would move. Compromise clearly meant giving their occupation legal sanction, for the statute also permitted the Indigenous people to alienate their land with the lieutenant governor's permission. On the eve of Confederation a tougher approach was manifested in legislation. The government could still 'compromise' with squatters, but any entry after the passage of the legislation 'shall disqualify the person so entering from receiving from the crown a grant of the lands so entered upon.' This provision, however, clearly shows that previous legislation had not dissuaded squatters. Indeed it likely indicates that the possibility of 'compromise,' of having their illegal possession ripen into title, encouraged intrusions.[66]

Substantial encroachments on reserves also occurred in Canada, even though Upper Canadian reserves had been established by treaties. Encroachments occurred in two ways: Europeans bought portions of reserve land in illegal transactions that were often simply ignored by governments and the courts, while other settlers squatted on reserve land and defied the authorities to remove them. Reserves in Upper Canada were 'overrun' with squatters' by the late 1830s, with some 20 per cent of the Indigenous land in the Grand River valley occupied by a white settler population as large as that of the Indigenous people.[67] Resort to the courts was often unavailing. In an 1835 case, *Doe ex d Jackson v Wilkes*, concerning encroachments on the Grand River reserve, the court held that Haldimand's 1795 grant of the reserve made the Six Nations mere tenants at will, and thus unable to eject squatters.[68]

Matters improved a little after government decided to consolidate the Six Nations in one continuous tract, near Brantford, in the early 1840s. Inevitably squatters moved onto the new reserve, but by 1853 they had all been evicted. It was a costly process, in time, in money the Indigenous people were required to pay the squatters for improvement, and in risk to life and limb when some squatters defended their possession with firearms.[69] It was not just individuals who trespassed. The Sulpician order encroached on Mohawk reserves in Lower Canada.[70]

Legislation from the late 1830s sought to prevent or limit squatting on reserves. An Upper Canadian statute of 1839 provided for the removal of squatters on both Crown land and Indigenous reserves, and a later statute of 1850 renewed the ban on squatting and also laid down a punishment (a £200 fine plus imprisonment) for any person who attempted to lease or buy lands from First Nations.[71] In Lower Canada legislation was also passed, initially by the special council in 1840, to prohibit white settler encroachment, and this policy was confirmed in 1850 in legislation that also provided for the appointment of a commissioner to supervise the leasing of reserve lands and the collection of rents from leases.[72] Further Acts in 1851 set out limits on the right to acquire 'immoveable property' allocated to Indigenous people and provided for the creation of new reserves, totalling some 230,000 acres. These lands were supposed to represent compensation for Indigenous lands taken or despoiled in earlier decades but for various reasons did not achieve the intended goal.[73] The considerable body of legislation applicable in both Canadas did not stop squatting which, as in the Maritimes, was consistently discussed in reports presented to the assembly in the 1850s and 1860s. Nor did it prevent squatters from strenuously resisting any attempts that were made to remove them, as they did in the Maritimes.[74] There was a deep irony here. Among the squatters on reserve land in all colonies were individuals who had been displaced from their traditional lands in Britain, most especially through the Highland Clearances. This was a phenomenon in other settler colonies, such as New South Wales, and a classic example of the historical amnesia that often afflicted and still afflicts settler communities.

Indigenous dispossession rarely provoked a serious debate among colonial politicians, with Lower Canada the only exception. There were substantial communities of Indigenous people living in the St Lawrence valley on land reserved for them under the French regime, although the legal consequences of those transactions were vigorously debated in the eighteenth and nineteenth centuries.[75] When newcomers demanded land, Indigenous groups protested incursions on territory they had long occupied, and while governments denied the protests, they did not do so by claiming that the Crown had acquired the territory from New France and that any Indigenous right had been extinguished thereby. Instead they developed the argument that Indigenous people had been compensated for loss of territory, albeit without any treaties, by the creation of reserves, particularly that at Akewsasne, and the giving of presents. Hence when the Nipissing and Algonquin peoples protested incursions of their hunting grounds in the 1830s, a committee of Lower Canada's executive council concluded both that the Indigenous claim was legitimate and that the Indigenous people had been compensated for its loss. It was a just and good policy, the committee insisted, to reserve for the two groups 'a sufficient Tract of Land ... in the Rear of the present Range of Townships on the Ottawa River' and to take measures to encourage them to settle there and adopt a sedentary lifestyle.[76] This theory received further approval from an assembly inquiry in 1847 and lay behind an 1850 statute for Lower Canada that recognized that there were areas set aside for Indigenous use and gave authority over them to the commissioner of Crown lands.[77]

Colonial governments' efforts to protect reserves in all colonies were unsuccessful essentially because, while they accepted that in theory, as local representatives of the Crown, they had a duty towards the Indigenous inhabitants, the stark truth was that carrying out that duty meant displacing Europeans. That required resources and the willingness to overcome white resistance – the resistance of the squatters themselves and of many among the European population who did not believe the Indigenous people deserved rights protection. Squatters consistently refused to give up the land, even if ordered off. As a petition to Queen Victoria from the Mi'kmaq had put it in 1842, 'There seems to be a right and wrong with the white man which Indians cannot comprehend.' The 'wrong' referred to was that many people believed that squatters were good for society, especially when they squatted on Indigenous land rather than the lands of the Crown. A province of Canada assembly committee captured this view perfectly in 1847 when it said that nobody had been able to protect Indian reserves and invoked as both explanation of and justification for this fact the notion that European agricultural use gave settlers a higher moral claim to land. There were 'natural laws of society to which even Governments must bend.'[78]

There was also a basic contradiction between the civilization policy, discussed in chapter 27, and reserve protection. The civilization policy looked to change Indigenous people into English-speaking, Christian, sedentary, peasant farmers living together in small communities. Leaving Indigenous people enough land to hunt and fish and maintain traditional cultures, which vigorous reserve protection would have achieved at least partially, cut against this aim. The result, time and time again, in Upper Canada and the Maritimes, was that investigations would reveal and deprecate the presence of squatters on reserve land, and discuss both the difficulties of removing squatters and the fact that it was good for the colony that squatters had cleared and developed the land. The suggested solution would be that squatters' presence should be legitimated by selling them the land, with the proceeds going to 'Indian welfare.' Welfare meant both a degree of poor relief, which would not have been so necessary had reserves not been shrunk, and infrastructure and programs to advance the civilization mission – schools, churches, agricultural implements and seed, and educational programs. By the eve of Confederation Indigenous peoples were very much worse off than they had been in 1815: no longer valued military allies, no longer important cogs in colonial economies, and no longer living largely unmolested in traditional territories. The tide of white settlement and encroachment had swept over them. Settler law was generally of little assistance in stemming this tide.

The one area that saw extensive reserve creation in this period was the Pacific coast, but this was not a policy to safeguard Indigenous rights – exactly the opposite.[79] As discussed above, the British Columbia colonial governors refused to recognize Indigenous title after the early 1850s and in 1859 established a land granting system for Europeans. Thereafter the government pursued a policy of unilateral reserve creation, allocating minimal acreages. In 1866 dispossession was compounded by a change in the law on pre-emption, which previously had permitted anyone to pre-empt 160 acres of Crown land on the coast or 320 acres in the interior. Henceforth no Indigenous person could do so without the executive's permission. Very few such permissions were ever granted. When British Columbia entered Confederation in 1871 clause 13 of the Terms of Union provided that the new province was to convey land to the federal government for the use of Indigenous inhabitants, with the latter when allocating the land pursuing a policy 'as liberal as that hitherto pursued by the British Columbia government.' The leading historian of the British Columbia Indigenous land question succinctly notes that that phrase, from the beginning, 'provoked a certain amount of mirthless laughter.' British Columbia's Indigenous inhabitants were in fact treated very similarly to those of the Maritime colonies some decades previously. The story of the 'BC Indian land question' will be dealt with extensively in volume 2 of this history.

We conclude this section with a brief examination of contemporary criticism of Indigenous dispossession and marginalization from European residents of the Maritime colonies.[80] Only a dozen or so writers in the nineteenth century raised the issue of its lawfulness. Anglican missionary and school teacher Walter Bromley of Nova Scotia was one of the most vocal critics, penning a number of pamphlets on the subject and stressing not just the moral wrong of dispossession but also its illegality: 'What authority have we to become the general possessors of the Indian territory, to the total exclusion of its original possessors,' he rhetorically demanded. Bromley also castigated his countrymen, who 'thought it no greater sin to shoot an Indian than a Bear or a Carraboo.'[81] Abraham Gesner, doctor and geologist and one of Nova Scotia's Indian commissioners, wrote of the 'treachery, injustice and cruelty with which these simple aborigines were treated.' Another Nova Scotian, Baptist missionary Silas Rand, wrote in equally strong terms and was one of the very few to advocate, in 1855, restitution and reparation. Among the principal New Brunswick critics were lawyer and businessman Moses Perley, the first Indian commissioner, and novelist Douglas Huyghue, who wrote of the 'lawless appropriation of their hunting grounds' and called dispossession an 'injustice and crime.'[82] Huyghue et al. were refuted by Beamish Murdoch, who insisted that Britain had taken 'possession of an uncultivated soil which was before filled with wild animals and hunters almost as wild.' In such circumstances the notion of an original aboriginal title was absurd: 'It might with almost as much justice be said that the land belonged to the bears and wild cats, the moose or the cariboo, ... as to the thin and scattered tribes of men, who were alternately destroying each other or attacking the beasts of the forest.' Murdoch had a change of mind on this question in the 1860s, but by that time his views had provided succour to those who denied Indigenous title for some three decades.[83]

The Rights and Obligations of Land Ownership

The common law of land rights and obligations has long embodied a tension between maintaining aristocratic traditions and family relationships, which required rules discouraging alienation outside the family and class, and a more individualistic economic approach, which saw land in liberal terms as a commodity like any other. In the eighteenth and nineteenth centuries English land law reflected a delicate balance between these two visions. Across the Atlantic, as the previous part has shown, the eighteenth-century American colonies of settlement altered their land law as courts and legislatures looked to shape the law in tune with the developing liberal economic framework and rejection of aristocracy. The same was broadly true of British North America before 1815, and thus land law in British North America was to some extent distinctive from that of the mother country, evolving in a more 'robustly liberal' direction than it did in England.[84] Examples of this kind of change in British North America included making land seizable for debt, abolishing primogeniture for intestate succession in the Maritime colonies, making it easier to bar an entail, and the creation of registry offices to make conveyancing more efficient.

Through the nineteenth century this trend continued in many areas of land law. As we have seen above, in Lower Canada a province-wide system of registry offices was created in 1841, and the seigneurial system, with its perceived anti-modern duties and obligations, was abolished a little over a decade later. With responsible government Nova Scotia and New Brunswick barred the creation of new entails, and the former jurisdiction completed the transformation of intestacy law by abolishing the eldest son's double share in 1842. New Brunswick followed suit in 1858 and PEI in 1873.[85] Mortgage law in both Upper Canada and the Maritime colonies was more oriented to creditors' interests than the law in England, making land more a commodity than a protected resource for a landed class.[86]

This transformation to a liberal, individualistic land law, however, did not continue in linear fashion through the nineteenth century. In two areas – primogeniture in Upper Canada and dower rights everywhere – British North American land law continued to reflect family and community values – what one author refers to as the values of 'embedded liberalism.'[87] In contrast to all other common law jurisdictions in the United States and British North America, primogeniture was not abolished in Upper Canada until the early 1850s, despite its being an often highly controversial subject of debate. Eighteen bills to abolish it were introduced between 1820 and 1851, but only eight passed the assembly and were then lost in the legislative council. Reformers tended to support the measures, but there was never a simple and consistent reform-conservative split. Defenders of primogeniture adverted to the conjoined issues of British traditionalism and Upper Canadian identity. In 1821, for example, Tory Christopher Hagerman argued that to abolish primogeniture would 'be departing from everything venerable, noble, and honorable; Democracy was, like a serpent, twisting round us by degrees, it should be crushed in the first instance, for if the bill passed,' it would leave the British Constitution 'but a mere shadow.' A quarter century later the member for Leeds and Upper Canada's leading Orangeman, Ogle Gowan, depicted equal partibility as essentially French and 'un-English,' while John A. Macdonald insisted to similar effect that the reform was 'anti-British and anti-Monarchical.' To this appeal to tradition were joined other arguments: that primogeniture encouraged enterprise in younger sons and prevented the breaking up of agricultural holdings into small, arguably too small, units, with too many landowners becoming peasant farmers.[88]

Those on the other side of the debate rejected the same Englishness. Lawyer, entrepreneur, and son of a dissolute member of the English middle class, John Prince emigrated to Upper Canada when almost forty and had no time for a gentry class sustained by primogeniture; he insisted in 1845 that he 'knew no greater curse to a country like Canada than a large landed aristocracy.' Ultimately men like Prince won the debate, their victory a triumph for liberal ideas and for the power of democratic values and public opinion over entrenched privilege. The Baldwins exemplified changing times on this issue. William Warren Baldwin, an 1820s reformer, had joined Hagerman in supporting primogeniture, but his son Robert lived in a different world. An economic liberal and a pragmatist, he was not persuaded by appeals to tradition, recognizing that the climate of public opinion was increasingly in favour of abolition, and it was his joint ministry with La Fontaine that legislated the abolition of both primogeniture and seigneuralism.

Another area in which British North American land law diverged from England was dower.[89] In 1833 the English *Dower Act* permitted husbands to bar dower simply by stating in a conveyance, deed, or will, that it would not exist. The wife's consent was no longer needed. Although the 1833 Act seemed to expand the dower right by extending it to equitable estates, this was effectively irrelevant, because by removing the need for a wife's consent to barring dower, it virtually abolished dower rights. The intent was to simplify conveyancing and make land more marketable. In no British North American colony was the equivalent of the English 1833 reform enacted, leaving widows in a stronger position than in England and the law supportive of family obligations that took precedence over an entirely market-driven approach. Thus, far from colonial law being entirely derivative of English law, here we see a decision not to adopt changes made in England. An 1834 Upper

Canadian statute did extend dower to equitable estates as the English Act had done the year before, but left in place the need for the wife's consent when barring dower. Indeed dower was made more powerful in the second half of the century and was not abolished until the widespread reform of married women's property in the 1970s.

Dower may not have been substantially reformed to fit the needs of increasingly commercial societies, but it was still controversial in Upper Canada. Many bills about dower were introduced before 1841, and the few that became law made it easier to bar dower but did not go so far as to remove the need for a wife's consent. Other bills strengthened dower rights, including an 1826 measure introduced by reformer John Rolph that was supportive of dowagers' rights. After the Union the nature of the debate changed, and there were numerous attempts not to reform but to abolish dower, starting in the late 1840s.[90] Proponents of abolition argued that it clouded titles and thus acted as a drag on the land market. They also pointed out that it did this while providing no benefit at all to widows in the case of unimproved lands, which yielded no produce. Widows were therefore entitled to one-third of nothing. At times this was extended to a more general critique that dower was inadequate. 'Of what use is the third part of 100 acres without a house upon it, to a widow without means,' asked one writer. She could not sell, till, or eat it – 'the widow asks for bread, but the law gives her a stone.' The writer may have had a point, but he did not offer any alternative. Those who defended dower argued that it did protect widows and families from the economic disaster consequent on abusive or improvident deceased husbands; heirs could not sell their land because people would not buy encumbered land, and land was still for many the principal asset. It could be used to provide for widows, a cost that would otherwise be thrust upon the public purse. The *Upper Canada Law Journal*, for example, argued in 1857 that dower was equitable because it provided 'for the support of a widow out of the lands of her deceased husband.'[91]

The debates on dower perfectly illustrate the dual and sometimes inconsistent nature of land law in British North America. Modernizers in Upper Canada and elsewhere followed the lead of the liberal forces who were behind the abolition of seigneurial tenure in Lower Canada; they wanted land law to reflect the fact that land was very much a commodity and a resource that could be exploited for economic development. Opponents likely saw land in many of the same ways, but they also viewed it, or at least that part of it that included dower rights, as a necessary economic support for families.

31

Law and the Economy I: Common Law, Statutes, and the Emergence of the Corporation

The first half of the nineteenth century saw considerable variation in the rates of economic development in the different regions of British North America. There is an extensive literature charting and explaining those variations, one that cannot be reviewed here. But in a number of areas the economic history of the period engages with the legal history, and this and the subsequent chapter examines each of them. First, we are interested in the ways in which the courts did – or did not – seek to facilitate economic development through their moulding of private law doctrines, especially in the areas that most directly affected the economy – the law of property, the law of commercial relations of exchange, what we now call contract, and the law of liability for injuries, what we now call tort or delict. The section immediately below, which discusses these, does not attempt to provide a detailed examination of legal doctrine in these areas, but rather to examine judicial attitudes about the extent to which the needs of economic development ought to shape their general approach to private law.

Second, this period saw a great deal of legislation in all regions of British North America passed to supplement the working of the market and the common law. Indeed a full examination of the relationship between law and economic development must pay more attention to statutes that changed, expanded on, or facilitated judge-made law than to the common or civil law themselves. Third, in no area were statutes more important and prevalent than in the rise to dominance in this period of what would become the principal legal institution by which modern economies are organized – the corporation. This chapter examines the rise of the corporation for various commercial purposes, and the development of rules governing their operation. Corporations in this period were largely the product of individual private Acts of incorporation. The history of law here must necessarily be linked to that of moral standards, especially as regards one aspect of corporate law – limited liability. Limited liability shielded those who invested in and ran corporations from personal responsibility for the corporation's debts. In a debate over a province of Canada bill that would facilitate the creation of corporations, Robert Baldwin clearly and succinctly expressed the dilemma he felt. It was, he said, 'very desirable to facilitate the incorporation of companies.' Yet it was also more than desirable, it was 'imperative' to ensure 'that injuries were not done to individuals, by relieving parties of a proper responsibility for debts.'[1] This chapter does not examine the law of debtor and creditor; that is treated separately in chapter 32.

Judges, Private Law, and the Economy

The law that regulated day-to-day economic activity in most parts of British North America was the common law of contracts and property. Contract law determined, among other things, how bargains for the supply of goods and services were made, how the terms of those bargains were to be interpreted, and what remedies were applicable when a contract was breached. Property law allocated rights in things to people and determined the limits of an owner's right to use property. The common law of torts had a less obvious and less direct impact on the economy in this period, but it did affect economic activity because it drew a line designating when activities that resulted in harm to others were compensable, and when they were not. The historical literature on the relationship between law and the economy in British North America is not at all as fully developed as we would like it to be. In particular, studies of the law of civil responsibility in pre-Confederation Lower Canada are rare, such that this section will consider only the common law colonies.

Canadian legal historians have paid rather less attention to the links between the common law and the economy than has been given to it by historians in Britain and the United States.[2] Studies of those jurisdictions have shown that, although there were clearly differences between them in both the degree and timing of the process, the common law in the nineteenth century came more to reflect the doctrines of liberal, laissez-faire economics than it had in the previous century. With a few exceptions we do not know enough about British North America to chart a similar trajectory, but it is reasonable to assume that there was one. The question addressed here is whether British North American judges saw it as their role to promote liberal, pro-development values. Even answering that question is made difficult by the fact that we lack detailed studies of the development of particular common or civil law doctrines, other than for Upper Canada in the Union period. Such studies are in any event difficult to conduct because the sources – principally reported cases – are very limited. The notable exception to this picture is the work of Richard Risk, written in the 1970s and looking at Upper Canada only. Other authors have added here and there to his findings and slightly modified his conclusions, but no major study of the subject has displaced his work, and it is therefore appropriate to begin with it. That also means, as noted in chapter 23, highlighting the influence of Upper Canada's dominant judicial figure of the pre-Confederation period, John Beverley Robinson.[3]

Two large conclusions emerge from Risk's detailed and comprehensive studies. The first is that superior court judges, like many others in Upper Canadian society, believed that economic progress, especially resource development and the building of infrastructure, were both necessary and desirable. The second is that Upper Canada's judges were not generally instrumentalist, did not see themselves as conscious innovators. They were not willing, nor did they think they were able, for constitutional reasons discussed in chapter 23, to amend received English common law rules to promote economic development and the interests of entrepreneurs. Judges had 'little or no power or responsibility for change and creativity.'[4] The tory anglophilia that marked Robinson's and others' work when deciding what the appropriate sources of law were was thus reflected in their choices about the content of that law. Like English judges of the period, the Upper Canadian bench approved of economic development but did not see fostering it as their responsibility.

Robinson exemplifies both of these general points. He was himself a promoter of, and investor in, development schemes, a land speculator, a bank director, and a writer on economic policy. He believed in material progress but thought that it should be 'controlled and gradual, and achieved through effort, not speculation.' The judgments of Robinson and others frequently displayed an understanding of how the economy operated and businessmen thought. In a judgment on whether a commission as well as interest could be claimed on a loan to a lumberman, for example, he stated that 'we have abundant reason to know that such arrangements are not unusual in carrying on the lumber business.' Other judges shared his knowledge of commerce and showed it in their judgments. Common Pleas Judge Sir John Hagarty insisted that 'it would be contrary to the well-established course of merchantile dealing' to allow a factor to set off a debt owed him by his principal against the principal's claim on him, adding that such an action would 'destroy confidence in sales such as the one before us, which are of almost daily occurrence.'[5]

Robinson thought that certainty in the law best promoted economic development. 'It is of much importance that the law should be duly administered on settled principles in regard to commercial transactions,' he stated in *Bank of Upper Canada v Smith*, a sentiment often repeated.[6] He similarly held that that producers, not middlemen, were responsible when products did not match the descriptions on which buyers relied. In so doing he prevented litigation based on the facts of particular cases. He took a limited view of when parol evidence could be used to alter the terms of clearly worded contracts. On some issues certainty was promoted concurrently with the facilitation of economic activity. For example, Robinson followed developments in English law by limiting recovery for breach of contract to what was in the contemplation of the parties. Linked to the need for certainty was an underlying and ubiquitous belief in freedom of contract. The job of the courts was to uphold and enforce the bargains that individuals made. Thus the grounds for not enforcing a contract were limited to fraud, misrepresentation, and illegality, all narrowly defined. Similarly, as noted above, parol evidence could be used only to resolve ambiguities, not to change clear written terms. Robinson also followed English law in a series of cases about whether a contract with a corporation could be enforced by or against the corporation without the corporation having made the promise using its corporate seal. A long line of English cases had established that the seal was necessary, a number of American authorities held that it was not. Robinson never doubted that the English cases should be followed and often justified the content of his decisions solely on the need to follow English precedent. On this issue as in others, Robinson's attitudes were shared by other Upper Canadian judges. William Buell Richards, for example, a judge of common pleas and a future chief justice of the Dominion of Canada, took the same view as Robinson on corporate seals, on the ground that he was bound by English authority.[7] This attitude was also manifested in the deference given to English law in cases involving negotiable instruments and security for debt.

Robinson similarly exemplified the second general conclusion noted above, a lack of innovation. Although one historian has detected a pro-corporation bias in his judgments, the bulk of the evidence suggests otherwise. He was critical of corporations at times, and interpreted the defence of statutory authority narrowly when corporations used the powers granted to them by the legislature to expropriate land.[8] In doing so he was following English law, and not the overtly pro-business decisions of American courts. He never questioned the legitimacy of corporations but insisted that they act only within the limits of the powers delegated to them. In this respect Robinson followed the same line that he took in what we now call tort law, cases involving liability for damage caused to others. He believed that compensation should be paid when the damage was caused deliberately or by negligence; he did not, like some American judges of the period, amend the rules to shield enterprise from liability. The only clear case in which he denied the applicability of English law concerned the Elizabethan Statute of Apprentices, and that concerned the reception of an old statute, not of the contemporary common law.[9]

To this point the discussion has been limited to Upper Canada's courts of common law. If we widen our focus to the Court of Chancery and to the courts in other common law jurisdictions we find a subtly different picture. The dominant Upper Canadian chancery judge, William Hume Blake, who presided as chancellor from 1850 to 1862, was prepared to adapt chancery doctrines to local conditions much more than Robinson would do. In *Hook v McQueen*, for example, Blake stated that 'rules deducible from English authorities' regarding delay in making payments under an agreement to buy land, 'cannot be applied, without considerable modification, to a country where the habits of society and the condition of property are so widely different.'[10] We cannot say whether Blake took this view because he was an equity judge, and thus thought himself more able to be creative, or because he was a mid-nineteenth-century liberal rather than the tory that Robinson was, or because many of Blake's decisions dealt with land, and land settlement had such a different history and raised very different questions in British North America from those in England. It may indeed have been a combination of all three, and evidence can be adduced to support each argument. In *Attorney-General v McLaughlin* Blake said that it was the duty of the English courts of equity 'to modify their rules and practice to meet the growing wants of society,' and this was equally true for Upper Canadian courts; judges must 'render those rules effectual for the ends of justice in our social condition, differing as it does in many respects so widely from that of England.'[11] In this one sentence he viewed equity as distinctive from the common law, and Upper Canada similarly so from England. In other cases Blake, different from Robinson, a large landowner, held that the law of waste – the doctrine governing damage to the land by a tenant – should favour tenants who cleared the land and used it productively thereafter. Here the values being promoted were those of liberal economic progress and Upper Canadian distinctiveness.[12]

The Blake-Robinson difference was perhaps most notable on the issue of the kind of evidence needed to allow an apparent grantor to show that a conveyance in form was intended to be a mortgage in substance; that the 'grantor' was actually a mortgagor. The grantor/mortgagor was invariably the person who actually worked the land, and the court finding a mortgage enabled that person to retain possession while the equity of redemption was paid off. Treating what was in form a conveyance as one in substance gave an advantage to the land speculator. In a series of cases Blake was satisfied to find a mortgage if the evidence was simply convincing, while Robinson applied a more stringent standard.[13] To similar effect Blake favoured active users of land in decisions about specific performance. In *O'Keefe v Taylor* he awarded a purchaser of land specific performance despite the purchaser's delay in making payments, which Blake attributed to the vendor's unreasonable delay in demanding the payments. The purchaser was one of the 'multitudes by whom a country is being peopled,' people 'by whose enterprise and labour the wastes of this vast province are rendered subservient to the purposes of civilization.' In such circumstances land titles that depended on equity's forbearance 'should not be shaken by ... doctrines, which, however suited to other states of society, have no application in our present social condition.' Those doctrines were recent and English and perhaps appropriate to England, but were they to be applied in Upper Canada they would 'produce great evil and injustice.'[14] Overall this last quotation probably explains much of Blake's variance from Robinson. He wanted a local law fostering local development projects and was able to use the pulpit of the chancery to achieve this.

Judges in the Maritime colonies have not received the attention of their Upper Canadian counterparts. A review of the Nova Scotia and New Brunswick *Reports* suggests that they were prepared to adapt the received common law and to use it as an overt tool of economic development to a greater extent than Upper Canadian judges. This was the case because economic development in the region for much of this period meant successful settlement and exploitation of the land resource. In turn the radically different land settlement patterns and land use practices from those of England in the first half of the nineteenth century necessitated innovation in common law rules in response. To take an example from one area of land law, English rules on landlord and tenant law applied a strict approach to waste, which meant that tenants could cut timber only for their own fencing and firewood needs. American courts took a different view, for a country where timber was plentiful and cutting timber, if done 'reasonably,' was improving the land, not wasting its resources. Nova Scotia and New Brunswick courts took the same approach as American ones, allowing cutting when it was done to enable cultivation, although one New Brunswick case insisted that this did not allow a tenant to 'range over the whole piece of land, [determining] what trees may be fit for logs and timber.'[15]

Maritime courts also adverted to patterns of settlement and the legal rules needed to support development of land to enhance the rights given to those who used land productively, even if they had possessed it adversely. In the 1841 case of *Lessees of Lawson v Whitman* the NSSC ruled that an adverse possessor of land having colour of title to a larger area than he actually possessed did not have to clear and occupy that larger area to establish title to it. In so holding it actively rejected English law and preferred the American, thereby favouring at the same time 'active' over 'passive' users of land.[16] The willingness to depart from the formalities of English law was also evident in boundary cases. In *McLean v Jacobs* Brenton Halliburton succinctly asserted that conforming to doctrines that insisted on strict conformity with deeds 'in this country ... would be attended with the most mischievous results.' Hill J. was more expansive. It was certainly possible to insist that lines on a survey always overruled the local reality, but 'in a country like ours where deeds are often written by ignorant and unlettered persons, where lines are often, from various causes, not traced and run with the nicest accuracy, we must and ought to keep our eyes steadily fixed on possession, and especially if for a long period and that too by the consent and agreement ... of all parties concerned.'[17]

The NSSC was similarly unwilling to eject grantees in possession, even those who had not fulfilled the conditions of their grant.[18]

The needs of agricultural settlers also prevailed over English rules in *The King v Good*, a New Brunswick case.[19] Good had bought land and fenced in an area that had previously been used as a road between lots. The New Brunswick attorney general argued for following the English rule that 'a road used by the public for a length of time, should be considered as dedicated to the public, and as a highway.' The NBSC disagreed, holding that only roads established by statute or with public money were public roads: 'It would be highly pernicious, if in this country, in the progress of new settlements, where a man permits his fellow settlers to use a pathway over his land until regular roads are laid out and opened, he should be presumed to have dedicated this pathway to the public, and it should be deemed a public highway.' Chipman J. drew a direct contrast between local and English conditions: 'With regard to cases in England, the dedication of roads to the public was a presumption of fact, arising from the state of circumstances as existing there, and it by no means followed that the same presumptions would arise from the same naked facts under a totally different state of circumstances here.'

We must be careful not to make too much of these differences between the Maritimes and central Canada. As we saw in chapter 23, Maritime superior court judges generally considered themselves bound to follow the courts of Westminster Hall, just as Robinson and his confrères did. In addition, a much larger percentage of the reported cases from the Maritimes involved land settlement, an area both vital to economic development and notoriously confused, as we saw in chapter 30. Moreover, even though both colonies had separate equity courts, the Supreme Courts in both freely discussed equitable principles along with common law ones. And Upper Canadian judges were also attuned to the need to adapt the law to smooth the settlement process. Robinson, for example, developed the doctrine of 'title by estoppel' whereby a grantor was unable to deny the deed; this made nugatory the all too prevalent practice of conveying land twice, before and after a person had obtained letters patent. The grantor was estopped from carrying the second conveyance into effect, and title thus confirmed in the first grantee, who was generally the person who had actually settled and developed the land.[20] These many caveats aside, the differences between Upper Canada and the Maritimes were present, in details and in emphases. The assumption often made, that British North American judges were blindly neutral to instrumentalist considerations, was truer for Upper Canada than for the Maritime colonies. It is an assumption even less valid for the Newfoundland judiciary, who, as we saw in chapter 30, freely adopted custom as a local common law when security of land titles originally acquired by possession was at issue. Indeed Newfoundland was the colony whose judges were the most prepared to adapt English law to local conditions in support of the economy. As we saw in the previous chapter, Newfoundland land law was unique in a number of respects, and the same judicial innovation marked significant aspects of commercial law. Fishermen were exempted from executions against their property until the end of the fishing season, a rule based on custom. Similarly, if a contract called for the 'usual credit,' again custom dictated that this meant no payments were due until the end of the season. Distress was not available to landlords against property used in the fishery.[21] Men like Robinson acted one way in Upper Canada, but his was but one of many approaches discernible when reviewing all of British North America.

Colonial Statutes and the Market

The common law rules governing economic activity were extensive in this period, but the common law did not occupy the field. All colonial legislatures passed many statutes that regulated, encouraged, and facilitated such activity. Indeed, over time statutes became more important than the common law. That colonial legislatures, not courts, were the active agents of change and innovation was a distinctively British North American aspect of the relation between law and the economy in the earlier nineteenth century, and that trend continued after mid-century. The British model exerted much less influence on legislation than it did on the common law, leaving colonial legislatures free to adapt policies to local conditions. The principal value underlying such legislation, Upper Canada's leading historian of law and economy has argued, was 'the facilitation and encouragement of private initiative.'[22] The decades before and after mid-century in particular were ones that, in Upper Canada in particular, manifested extensive growth and the creation of capital. Legislation was used everywhere to such ends. Legislation was wide-ranging and too prevalent to document extensively, but a few examples can be given. Some statutes provided public financial support for infrastructure projects, which, as we will see, was an area where many corporations were created.[23] Others provided money to promote particular kinds of economic activity. Granting bounties on the development of certain crops was common.[24] A bounty was also employed to promote locally produced chocolate for the sweet-toothed of Nova Scotia.[25] Financial support also came from grants-in-aid – to develop manufacturing processes, to promote agriculture generally, or to encourage the introduction of better breeds of livestock.[26]

New forms of economic activity were also promoted through patent legislation. Upper Canada's Act, passed in 1826, gave the lieutenant governor power to grant fourteen-year patents to any resident of the colony who had invented 'any new or useful Art, Machine, Manufacture, or Composition of Matter.' The time limit indicated a compromise between encouraging innovation and permitting competition, as did a clause providing that those who made improvements to something for which a patent had been obtained could also receive a patent for the improvement but could not use the original process. Not surprisingly the requirements for certification did not involve experts; an oath of originality sworn by the applicant accompanied by drawings and descriptions were all that was required. New Brunswick's Act, passed eight years later, was nearly identical, except for limiting patents to just ten years. Nova Scotia also passed a patent Act and on occasion conferred patents on non-resident individuals by private Act, including one to Henry Bessemer, inventor of the famous steel-making process.[27]

Legislative intervention in the economy went well beyond financial and legal support for private activity and extended to regulation of various activities. Usury laws regulated money lending practices – the maximum interest rate was 6 per cent, as in England. Usury legislation, from which banks and loan companies were exempted, was a controversial and oft-debated topic in the Canadas, with the major issue being that if more than the legal rate was charged the entire agreement was unenforceable. After many attempts this aspect was changed in 1853, and henceforth loan agreements were unenforceable only for the excess over 6 per cent. That change was effectively a reduction in the penalty faced by a usurious lender, and a triumph for advocates of an unrestricted market. A few years later the law was repealed in its entirety. Usury laws exemplified the debates about morality and economics discussed later in this chapter and the next. Their supporters thought high interest immoral and restrictions necessary to protect farmers and small businessmen. Opponents stressed an individual's right to make choices about economic affairs and also assumed that interest rates reflected, and were best decided by, the market.[28]

Other kinds of regulatory legislation included hunting seasons for some animals and conservation-oriented limits for others. They were joined, conversely, by Acts to encourage the extermination of some animals.[29] For certain commodities, especially bread, prices and weights were controlled, while for many others product standards were established and inspection regimes set up.[30] Some statutes were permissive, allowing people to do things normally prohibited by the common law. These included a licence to a transatlantic telegraph company incorporated in Newfoundland to 'enter upon and touch any part of this Province [Nova Scotia] or the coast thereof ... with any telegraphic cable' so that Nova Scotia could be connected to the wider network.[31] Other regulatory measures imposed safety rules, seeking to avoid injuries, such as an Upper Canadian Act requiring guard rails around all machinery, because 'many fatal accidents have occurred' from unguarded machinery.[32] The common law provided few remedies for this, and the legislature preferred to avoid injury rather than impose liability. Legislative intervention in the economy was most obvious and far-reaching in the area to which we now turn – the rise of the corporation.

The Emergence and Growth of Corporations to 1850

During a debate in the Canada assembly over an 1849 bill that would make it easier to create corporations in many sectors of the economy, Robert Baldwin, who opposed the bill, asserted that 'unless a stop were put to it, there would be nothing but corporations from one end of the country to the other.'[33] Baldwin was indulging in a flight of rhetorical fancy, but he had a valid point. One of the most striking changes to the landscape of legal forms in British North America was the growth of corporations. They operated in a wide variety of fields. Some were municipal corporations, some educational institutions, some benevolent societies or social groups, horticultural societies, and the like. The corporations this chapter is concerned with were economic entities, of two principal kinds. One kind we term 'infrastructure corporations' – corporations created to pool capital to build a local harbour, bridge, or the like, to supply municipal services, to build a canal or a railway. In some instances the job was done when the harbour or bridge was built, in others, such as canals and railways, it was not, for the corporation would then look to run the transportation network at a profit. The other principal kind of corporation we term 'business corporations' – bodies created for resource exploitation, manufacturing, or trading, and in this category we also include the provision of financial services.

A corporation is a legal person. It can hold property, make contracts, sue and be sued, just like a natural person, distinct from the natural persons who own the corporation by owning shares in it.[34] These features made it different from the joint stock company, an unincorporated association of merchants pooling capital by buying stock. Many joint-stock companies were also corporations, but in and of itself a joint stock company does not have a separate legal personhood. It was this personhood feature that made the corporation attractive to business people. It provided 'an enduring form for litigation, ownership of property and other rights, and commercial transactions.'[35] Historically corporations derived their corporate status from the Crown, but Parliament could also pass legislation establishing a corporation.[36] Crown and Parliament in Britain had created corporations for centuries, using this legal form for boroughs, guilds, churches, schools, and the like, as well as imperial ventures, such as the East India Company and the Hudson's Bay Company. But the corporation became something of a pariah after the speculative crash colloquially known as the South Sea Bubble, which produced the *Bubble Act* of 1720.[37] The Act effectively prohibited the creation of corporations other than by royal charter. It was extended to the colonies in 1740 and not repealed until 1825, although long before then it was increasingly ignored in Britain. During the century it was in force businessmen in both Britain and its colonies used various unincorporated forms of business organization, especially joint stock companies. Corporations began to be used in the United States around 1780, and in the Canadian colonies a little later. Presumably because of the *Bubble Act* the earliest corporations were created by royal charter, as was the first corporation in British North America, the city of Saint John, given a royal charter and corporate status by letters patent from Lieutenant Governor Carleton in 1785. Many other early corporations were religious or educational bodies.[38]

Colonial assemblies began to confer corporate status on bodies organized for commercial purposes from the very late eighteenth century. The first such corporation in this period was the Halifax Steam Boat Company, founded in 1815 to operate a ferry across Halifax harbour from Dartmouth. In Upper Canada and New Brunswick banks were first – the Bank of Kingston, founded in 1819, and the Bank of New Brunswick, created in 1820. These very early corporations often used the same method that had been earlier employed for Saint John – the statute conferred on the lieutenant governor the authority to issue letters patent to create the corporation.[39] But presumably because the *Bubble Act* was repealed in 1825, incorporation in British North America from the mid-1820s was carried out almost wholly by special Act of the legislature, with no royal charter or reference to letters patent required. In this the British North American colonies employed the same process as the American states had used slightly earlier.[40] No Anglo-North American jurisdiction legislated general incorporation by registration – permitting a group of persons to incorporate by complying with certain procedures and simply registering their businesses – until the second half of the nineteenth century.

Table 1 summarizes the growth of these infrastructure and business incorporations. It distinguishes Upper from Lower Canada, even though there was a unified legislature from 1841. The vast majority of corporations established by legislative act between 1841 and 1850 can be designated as operating in one section or the other by their stated purposes. There were five corporations that cannot be categorized as exclusively Upper or Lower Canadian, and they have been given a separate entry as 'Province of Canada.'

Between 1830 and 1850 the number of special Act corporations increased tenfold; only 30 had been established by 1830, 128 more in the 1830s, and a further 168 in the 1840s. We are not suggesting that the increase in the number of corporations can be used as a measure of economic activity; most businesses in this period were unincorporated bodies, individual businessmen or people acting in partnerships, none of which required legislation for their formation. Rather the table is simply what it says it is, an indication of the increase in the use of a particular legal form. Having said that, the fact that incorporation grew to this extent between 1830 and 1850 is relevant to economic history as well; when Baldwin spoke in 1849 the corporation was on its way to becoming the principal form of large-scale economic organization in British North America.

The standard mode of proceeding was for groups of businessmen wishing to incorporate to persuade assembly members to sponsor their bills. The legislation, which tended to be much longer than most colonial statutes, laid out the names of the directors, the type of business the corporation would be engaged in, the amount of capital subscribed, the number and nature of shares, the number and powers of directors, etc.[41] Special Act incorporations were not uncontroversial. They did not generally excite much debate in the assembly, but a substantial majority

Table 1. Private Act Incorporations before 1850

Jurisdiction	Before 1830	1830–1840	1841–1850	Total
Upper Canada	9	47	63	119
Lower Canada	10	12	32	54
Province of Canada	–	–	5	5
Nova Scotia	7	24	23	54
New Brunswick	4	43	43	90
Newfoundland & Prince Edward Island	0	2	7	9
Total	30	128	173	331

of bills did not pass the first time they were presented. In Upper Canada about three-quarters of the bills passed eventually, some after amendment and many on a second attempt, so the legislative process was far from a rubber stamp. There was regional variation in success rates, for in Nova Scotia 'the vast majority' of acts introduced were passed.[42]

Not surprisingly, given the close links between politics and economic activity in all colonies, figures prominent in politics and in other aspects of governance, including the judiciary, were among the investors in, and directors of, corporations. Two examples must suffice. Two of the first three Upper Canadian corporations were the Welland Canal Company and the Bank of Upper Canada, and both companies numbered among their directors both Solicitor General Henry John Boulton and Attorney General John Beverley Robinson. In both companies also members of the legislative council held a majority of the directorships.[43] The similar example of Lewis Thomas Drummond, from Lower Canada, and a later era, the 1840s and 1850s, can also be cited. Best known as a lawyer, politician, and judge, he is described by his biographer as an 'enthusiastic advocate of commerce and industry'; he was a director of the Montreal City and District Savings Bank, a shareholder in the St Lawrence and Atlantic Railroad, one of the founders of the Garden River Mining Company, president of the Stanstead, Shefford and Chambly Railroad, and an incorporator of the Transmundane Telegraph Company.[44]

The earliest corporations were banks, insurance companies (some for marine insurance only, others more general), and various forms of transportation operations, from canals to roads to steamship lines. Municipal services were also supplied by corporations. Between 1819 and 1825 the Banks of Upper Canada, New Brunswick, Montreal, Quebec, and (Lower) Canada were incorporated, as well as the regional banks of

Kingston and Charlotte County, New Brunswick. The Bank of Nova Scotia was twice denied incorporation, in 1819 and 1825, because of fears of it becoming a monopoly, and operated instead as a partnership under the name of the Halifax Banking Company. A bank also called the Bank of Nova Scotia with a new set of incorporators was finally incorporated in 1832, ironically because the partnership had indeed become a monopoly by default, run by members of the council.[45]

The largest single category of incorporation activity in the 1820s and early to mid-1830s in Upper Canada was transportation networks – canals, roads, and railroads – as well as infrastructure such as bridges, harbours, and piers. Corporate growth thus reflected the principal objective of development in the Canadas in this period, the enhancement of the water transport system based on the St Lawrence and the Great Lakes. One of these enterprises involved William Hamilton Merritt, the driving force behind the Welland Canal, and the Six Nations of the Grand River. Members of the latter promised funds for a project, not to build a canal, but to 'canalize' the Grand River, to add dams and locks and cuts and other works, to make it fully navigable from the Welland Canal to Brantford. Merritt got an Act passed incorporating the Grand River Navigation Company, although no Indigenous people were listed among the incorporators, and the whole venture turned out to be exploitative. The legislation explicitly sanctioned trespasses on reserve land and granted the Six Nations 'free and uninterrupted navigation of the ... Grand River, with their Canoes, for them and their posterity.' No approval of the project was given by those empowered to speak for the Confederacy, indeed they protested the incorporation. The corporation was run by settler trustees, with no direct representation of any member of the Six Nations, although they owned 80 per cent of the stock, and their agent, David Thorburn, was eventually named to the board. Land was expropriated under the statute, but in many cases the arbitration award was not paid. All the band's funds had been invested in 3 per cent bonds in England which were very safe, but they were diverted to this highly speculative investment, presumably through the influence of John Dunn, one of the trustees of the Six Nations funds and also a friend of Merritt. In 1841 the government mandated that two of its own appointees be on the board to guard against exploitation. The corporation operated for many years but went bankrupt in 1861.[46]

In the Maritime colonies, roads were paid for from public funds and built in part by statute labour, and when infrastructure corporations were created it was to operate other kinds of communication networks – stage coaches, ferries, and steamship companies.[47] The establishment of corporations to build transportation networks and public utilities was 'a delegation of public power to private organisations to undertake functions that the state would not, or could not, undertake.' Public utility corporations were literally granted public power – the power to expropriate land provided compensation was paid.[48]

In all regions, the number and type of corporations created fluctuated with the economic cycle and, not surprisingly, mirrored the local bases of the economy. The dominance of the lumber industry in New Brunswick was reflected in a number of 'boom' companies – formed to erect and run floating artificial harbours, where timber propelled down the river was collected. Their purpose was to stop lumber moving about freely on the river and interfering with navigation. In that colony also the mid-1830s lumber boom resulted in twenty incorporations in 1836 alone, almost half of the forty-three created during the entire decade. Eight were for new mill companies, most of the rest for businesses serving the industry.[49] Since one of the benefits of incorporation was the ability to pool capital, a capital-poor colony was likely to use the corporate form a good deal. In New Brunswick this tendency was exemplified by one 1836 statute, *An Act to Incorporate the Tobique Mill Company*, which asserted that 'the extensive erection of mills at the River Tobique for the manufacture of lumber will be of public utility,' but also that 'the amount of capital invested in such a speculation renders it essential that the Company engaged therein should be incorporated.' The Tobique Mill Company principals included at least one American, enabling American money to be invested in buying land, something barred by common law.[50] In both New Brunswick and Nova Scotia there were a substantial number of insurance company incorporations, some formed specifically to provide marine insurance for the maritime trade.

Perhaps surprisingly New Brunswick had considerably more corporations than both Lower Canada and Nova Scotia in the 1830s and 1840s, despite the fact that it had the smallest population of the four principal colonies. Not surprisingly Upper Canada had the largest number, 110 in all created in the 1830s and 1840s, reflecting in part the fact that by mid-century its population had, for the first time, outstripped that of Lower Canada. As many manufacturing corporations were established in Upper Canada before 1850 as in the rest of British North America. During the 1840s the kinds of activities for which corporations were established in Upper Canada changed somewhat from earlier decades. Railroads began to appear in considerable numbers, and mining started to become predominant from the mid-1840s.

Perhaps the most striking feature of table 1 is that Lower Canada, the most populous colony until the late 1840s, had by far the fewest corporations, both in absolute terms and relative to population. Only twelve were established in the 1830s, half of Nova Scotia's total and a quarter of those created in Upper Canada. Things changed a little in the 1840s, with Lower Canada overtaking Nova Scotia, but it still had fewer than New Brunswick and only half of Upper Canada's total. Given that Montreal was very much the economic engine of the Canadas in this period, and that lawyers were an integral part of commercial development, one would have expected the numbers to be higher. Part of the reason for the lower numbers was that the civil law permitted the creation of limited partnerships, not possible in Upper Canada until 1849. In addition, or perhaps as a result of this, the considerable prosperity of Montreal's anglophone commercial class resided in family-based enterprises. A study of Montreal's leading commercial law firm at mid-century, for example, demonstrates that it mostly served or managed such operations. The numbers may also reflect the fact that corporations excluded from the count because they do not appear to be business corporations were actively involved in the economy, especially religious organizations. But it also highlights the overwhelmingly agricultural nature of the economy outside of Montreal. Not until the 1850s can we say that Lower Canada was transitioning from a pre-modern economy to one based on industrial capitalism. Lower Canadians also employed the corporate form for non-commercial purposes; it was often used to organize use of the common lands of seigneuries.[51]

A special Act incorporation amounted to a kind of mini-constitution for each corporation, and perhaps for that reason most such legislation was lengthy; incorporations took up a disproportionate amount of the statute book. The colonies also passed some general legislation pertaining to all corporations. New Brunswick did so in 1836, Upper Canada in various statutes of the 1830s. One simply stated a corporation could be served with a civil action in the same way as a natural person, another made directors of insurance companies personally liable for the corporation's debts if they improperly declared dividends, and the *Interpretation Act* of 1837 legislated some general terms, including the powers of directors to make regulations to administer the corporation. In addition to these general regulatory statutes, specific regulations were occasionally passed, as exemplified by an 1836 Upper Canadian

Act prohibiting corporations from extending their operations onto Crown land without permission, and a Nova Scotia statute barring corporations from issuing their own paper money.[52] From the 1840s colonial governments also required some corporations to submit annual reports to the assembly.[53]

Before concluding this section on the rise of the corporation, five additional points need to be made. First, the establishment of special Act incorporations was only part of the legislative activity surrounding them. Many special Acts were amended; in Upper Canada during the Union period there were some 300 amending statutes, concerned largely with expansion of purposes, increases in capital, and the timing of beginning or finishing projects.[54] Second, the corporation existed alongside other forms of enterprise and other methods of financing and indeed was invariably outnumbered by them. As Beamish Murdoch, who devoted only a few pages of his four-volume analysis of Nova Scotia law to corporations, put it, 'In this Province incorporations are few in number and of recent origin.'[55] Joint stock companies that were not incorporated, individual proprietors, and partnerships abounded. As one author has noted with reference to Nova Scotia, incorporation was not a feature of the activities that 'really drove the economy.' There were none organized to pursue agricultural ventures, and few for either fishing or shipbuilding.[56]

Third, and a related point, selling stock subscriptions was only one method of raising capital. Many businesses received grants of public money. Thomas Stewart and others petitioned in 1827 for money to build a bridge over the Otonabee River at Monoghan, Upper Canada, for example, their petition resulting in legislation authorizing the payment of £100 for this purpose, to be used along with the £300 that the petitioners had already raised. A few years earlier a much larger sum of money was allowed to be raised by debentures for a canal between Burlington Bay and Lake Ontario. The Welland Canal received substantial government support as well.[57] Fourth, a significant number of infrastructural projects, from the Rideau Canal to the wharf in Charlottetown, were not the responsibility of incorporated enterprises, but public works.[58]

Fifth, and finally, there was no necessary connection between corporations and monopolies. Some corporations were given a monopoly, especially in Upper Canada in the 1820s and 1830s, but so too were some non-incorporated businesses. Indeed there is evidence that many in British North America's legislatures distrusted monopolies – what

Nova Scotia Assemblyman William Lawson called 'odious things.'[59] Whether a monopoly was granted tended to depend on the type of business or service being provided, not on the legal form of the enterprise, and even then there was inconsistency. The corporation supplying Halifax with fresh water had a monopoly, as did one Chauncey Beadle, who received one to run 'a line of Public Stages between the Village of Ancaster in the Gore District, and the Town of Sandwich in the Western District.'[60] Yet the Saint John Stage Coach Company did not.[61] The only body of case law about monopolies concerned ferries, by no means all of them corporations, some being given a franchise by legislation. Upper Canadian courts generally assumed they were exclusive, whether or not the legislation said so.[62]

The 1850s and 1860s: Corporate Growth and Sectoral Incorporation

This section examines both the considerable growth in the number of incorporations in the 1850s and 1860s, particularly in Upper Canada, as well as significant legal changes, especially in the same jurisdiction, that streamlined the incorporation process. We begin with the latter, because appreciating the legal changes helps to understand the numbers. After Confederation all provinces and the federal jurisdiction introduced incorporation by registration. General companies Acts laid out a procedure by which people could form a corporation and apply to a government office for it to be registered. No individual statute was required. Between incorporation by private Act and incorporation by registration lay a hybrid system – incorporation by registration for companies operating in certain sectors of the economy, which we term 'sectoral incorporation.'[63] Incorporation of a company in the specified areas did not need a special Act, only the assent of a certain number of persons, the subscription of enough money, and registration of some kind. Businesses outside the scope of those statutes still had to use the special Act procedure.

Before the late 1840s sectoral incorporation by registration was but a small part of the landscape. The first such Acts in the Canadas were for fire insurance companies, passed in 1834 in Lower Canada and 1836 in Upper Canada.[64] Both provided that in order to establish a fire insurance company, any ten freeholders in any district could call a meeting of freeholders. If the meeting agreed to form a company, and sixty (Lower Canada) or forty (Upper Canada) people subscribed, and the total raised was £10,000 (Upper Canada) or £15,000 (Lower Canada), then those people, and any who joined thereafter, were 'ordained, constituted and declared to be a body corporate.' After the union four more sectoral incorporation statutes were passed for Upper Canada and three for Lower Canada. There were statutes for building societies in both sections in 1846 and 1849, and similarly for toll roads, and one for banks, only for Upper Canada, the 'free banking' legislation, in 1850.[65] Some of these Acts were based on New York statutes and laid down similar but slightly different requirements in each case.[66]

The most important sectoral Act, because of the breadth of its terms, was one pertaining to businesses formed to operate in the manufacturing, mining, mechanical, shipbuilding, or chemical sectors, passed for Upper Canada in 1850.[67] Thus it was possible for a wide range of businesses to incorporate by registration. It provided that the declaration of intent to form a company had to be signed by at least five persons, to state the company name and objects, and the total number of shares and their nominal value. The declaration of intent, equivalent to articles of incorporation, had to be filed with the registrar of the county in which the company planned to do business, and the provincial secretary. Publication of a notice by the provincial secretary was conclusive evidence of the other requirements having been met. Although the Act was broad, some types of enterprises, especially railways, were deliberately withheld from it, because of their significance to the economy and the consequent desire that the legislature continue to supervise the rate of creation. An assembly committee report of 1851, which recommended that railroads not be given incorporation by registration powers, cited concerns about untrammelled competition and 'the great powers' of railroads.[68] One result was that special Act incorporations of railroads made up more than one-third of all special Act incorporations after 1850. Another five sectoral incorporation statutes were passed in Canada in the 1850s: for telegraph companies, for harbours, for gas and water services, for river improvements, and for savings banks.[69] In addition the 1850 statute was extended to other kinds operations, some non-commercial, in 1860 and 1864, and in 1864 the statute was extended to operate in Lower Canada also.[70]

Table 2 shows the number of individual incorporation Acts passed between 1851 and Confederation.[71] The advent of sectoral incorporation by registration in Upper Canada obviously means that from mid-century private Acts cease to be an accurate measure of corporation numbers for that jurisdiction, and also, to a much lesser extent, for

Table 2. Private Act Incorporations, 1851–1866

Jurisdiction	1851–1860	1861–1866	Total
Upper Canada	110	48	158
Lower Canada	50	72	122
Province of Canada	4	2	6
Nova Scotia	70	71	141
New Brunswick	72	33	105
Newfoundland & Prince Edward Island	16	15	31
Total	322	241	563

Lower Canada. Nonetheless the table is useful in showing how much the corporate form was embraced everywhere. Over 550 corporations were established by private Act, more than 220 more than in the years before 1850. The increase occurred in every jurisdiction; even in Newfoundland and Prince Edward Island, the colonies with the smallest populations and least diversified economies, the number of corporations almost quadrupled from 9 by 1850 to 31 in this period. As many special Act incorporations were passed in Nova Scotia in the six years between 1861 and 1866 as in the ten years from 1851 to 1860.

We do not know precisely how many more were formed under the various sectoral incorporation statutes, but the number is probably around 300 for Upper Canada.[72] Thus from mid-century many more incorporations were created by registration than by private Act in that jurisdiction. We also speculate that the numbers for incorporations in Lower Canada are higher than the private Act figures; as we have seen, incorporation by registration was also available in Lower Canada, although the broad sectoral incorporation statute did not apply there until 1864.

Sectoral incorporation statutes were not as important a feature of other colonies' corporate law as in the Canadas, and came later. New Brunswick's legislation, passed in 1862, allowed any five persons to form a company for 'mining or manufacturing purposes' and to register with the provincial secretary. This might not seem broad, but the only specific exclusions were banks and insurance companies, not firms engaged in 'ordinary mercantile or commercial business.'[73] The number of special Act incorporations in the colony, however, did not change much; there were seven a year in the 1850s and five to six a year between 1861 and 1866. Newfoundland passed a broad sectoral incorporation statute in 1856, very similar to the Upper Canadian 1850 Act.[74] Nova Scotia passed only one sectoral incorporation Act, in 1851, allowing incorporation by registration of land companies that wanted to grant land and establish settlement along the line of the contemplated Halifax to Quebec railway.[75] The colony also passed what seems by its title to have been a general incorporation statute in 1862 – *An Act for the Incorporation and Winding Up of Joint Stock Companies*. This allowed any five or more people who wished to incorporate to do so by filing with the provincial secretary. But its title is misleading, for it was really legislation to facilitate the incorporation of gold-mining companies, which sprang up after the discovery of gold at Mooseland, Halifax County, in 1860.[76] The Act did not include banks and insurance companies, or firms engaged in 'ordinary mercantile or commercial business.' This broad exclusion was in part the result of a distrust of limited liability, discussed in the next section; as one rural member of the legislative council declaimed in debate on the bill, limited liability had caused 'ruin to hundreds and thousands' in Britain.[77]

Sectoral incorporation streamlined the process of corporate formation. So too did legislation specifying standard clauses in all special Act corporations, notably railway incorporations. An 1851 Canada statute included a list of powers to be granted to every railroad corporation, plan and survey requirements, rules about assessing compensation for expropriated land, and procedures for stockholder meetings. Corporations operating in other sectors were similarly legislated for. A wide range of regulations were included as part of the mining, manufacturing, etc. sectoral statute passed in 1850, then made applicable to all corporations except railroads in 1861. The terms legislated in 1861 included the power to acquire land, minimum and maximum numbers of board members, procedures for the election of directors and the powers they could wield, by-law making procedures, record-keeping requirements, and much else. The statute, and a similar one enacted in Nova Scotia, allowed for the more efficient use of legislative time and created uniformity in particular sectors.[78]

After mid-century there was a considerable increase in the number of manufacturing and, especially, mining corporations in the Maritime colonies. Twenty-three manufacturing corporations and seventeen for mining were created in New Brunswick, compared to five and two respectively in the previous decade. Emblematic of the change was the creation in 1854 of the Sunbury Steam Factory Company for the manufacture of agricultural and other implements, and two years later of the Hopewell chemical manufacturing company.[79] Nova Scotia saw rather fewer manufacturing corporations, eight, but forty-four for mining. Twenty-one and thirty-one special Act mining corporations were also established in Upper and Lower Canada respectively, reflective of the mining boom of the 1850s and 1860s.[80]

The most significant change after 1850 was in the number of railroad corporations, which still required a private Act to incorporate in Upper Canada. Fifty-five such entities were established there between 1851 and 1866. In all over one hundred were created in British North America in this period; by the end of the 1850s the colonies had over 2,000 miles of track. Only twenty-nine of these were Maritime corporations, because most major railways there, including the main line between Halifax and New Brunswick and various branch lines, were public works.[81] Examples of private railroads include a corporation to construct a railway to operate only in Queen's County, Nova Scotia, and one to build short railway slips to facilitate shipbuilding and repairs.[82] It is a commonplace of Canadian economic history that the 1850s was a period of considerable commercial development, and that railways were at the centre of the economic expansion of the decade. Railways were the abiding passion of Sir Alan MacNab, sometime leader of the Conservative party in Upper Canada and a land speculator, banker, and railroad promoter, who famously said, 'All my politics are railroads.'[83] The railroad corporations were, like their earlier predecessors for canals and other works, given extensive powers of expropriation, although compensation was specified in the 1851 clauses consolidation Act noted above.

Limited Liability and the Morality of the Corporation

The rise of the corporation was accompanied by debates over whether this increasingly important legal institution was a clear benefit to society, a necessary evil, or essentially harmful. Those debates involved a variety of themes – the concentration of economic power, the need to pool capital for the more effective development of colonial economies, and, most of all, the benefits or otherwise of limited liability. We associate the corporate form with limited liability, and the common law took the view that it was a right that automatically came with incorporation.[84] The key feature of limited liability is that only the assets of the corporation are available to be used to pay the debts of the corporation, not the personal assets of shareholders. The corporation's assets include its paid up share capital, so to that extent a shareholder's assets could be taken to pay debts. But unless the statute law of the jurisdiction provided for it, other property of the individuals who owned shares was not available to satisfy corporate debts. Limited liability was controversial in Britain and the United States in the first half of the nineteenth century; for its critics it was a doctrine that allowed directors of corporations to incur debts, and then to largely escape the obligation to repay them, and thus raised basic issues of commercial morality and responsibility. In British North America there was an inconsistent approach to liability, with differences between colonies, between whether both directors and shareholders could avail themselves of it, across time, and according to the kind of enterprise involved.

In all colonies other than Nova Scotia the vast majority of corporations were granted limited liability for shareholders and directors in this period. In Canada most private Acts were silent on the question of liability, and thus limited liability, the common law position, was given by default. This was confirmed in the 1849 *Interpretation Act* and in judicial decisions.[85] There were often objections voiced to limited liability, but they came from minority voices. When the major sectoral incorporation statute was debated in 1850, for example, Robert Baldwin opposed it, as we saw in the introduction to this chapter, and Malcolm Cameron, member for Kent, also opposed it, because the idea that debts could be incurred for which contracting parties were not fully liable was 'dangerous in principle.'[86]

There were exceptions to limited liability in individual statutes, but these were rare and display no particular pattern, except that in 1854 three mining company incorporations for Lower Canada imposed personal liability on shareholders for unpaid wages.[87] Conversely, limited liability was extended to business enterprises that were not corporations in Canada, New Brunswick, and in Newfoundland at mid-century; statutes of 1849, 1854, and 1856 respectively permitted limited partnerships, except in banking and insurance.[88] At least one partner had to make his entire estate liable for the debts of the partnership; the other partners were liable only for the money they invested in the partnership. The Canadian Act does not seem to have led to many partnerships, and produced one immediate, spectacular, and scandalous failure.[89] Nova Scotia also gave some partners limited liability, legislating a class of 'sleeping partners' not responsible for the debts of the partnership beyond what they had invested.[90]

In New Brunswick most corporations had complete limited liability, but a few had double liability – shareholders liable for the stock they held in the company and a further equivalent sum. These occasional double liability provisions appeared only in the 1850s, likely the result of the hard economic times of the early years of the decade.[91] In Canada exceptions to limited liability were made for directors of companies who transgressed the rules in some way. Under the 1850 statute for sectoral incorporation, for example, the directors were jointly and severally liable if they paid dividends while the company was insolvent, or if the payment of those dividends made it insolvent.[92] The principal exceptions to limited liability applied to banks and insurance companies. After 1836 double liability was imposed on shareholders, not just directors, of Upper Canadian banks.[93] This and future such provisions were an imposition of the Colonial Office, which would not otherwise assent to the legislation.[94] Similarly, directors, but not shareholders, of banks incorporated in Lower Canada were made personally responsible for the excess if the bank gave out loans worth more than three times the capital stock paid in.[95] In 1833 the directors of the City Bank in Montreal were made jointly and severally liable 'for all claims and demands of any nature whatsoever due' if the value of notes in circulation exceeded the amount fixed in the Act.[96] New Brunswick also had special rules for directors of banks, which were invariably included in incorporation statutes from the 1820s through the 1850s. They were personally liable if the banks loaned more than twice the capital stock.[97] The special insurance company provisions varied from place to place and time to time, but there was always some kind of particular stricture on their directors. In 1836, for example, directors of insurance companies in Upper Canada were made personally liable if they improperly declared dividends. In New Brunswick directors of insurance companies were made personally liable for policies issued after the corporation had incurred losses equal to the paid up capital.[98]

The most inconsistent approach to liability across time, and the least support for limited liability, was found in Nova Scotia. As the province's chief justice, Sir William Young, observed in 1874 when summarizing what had taken place in the past, 'In the Charters which the Legislature have ... granted, no uniform policy has been observed.' The colony's few corporations established before 1830 had complete limited liability, but in the 1830s only two-thirds of them did so, with most of the rest having unlimited liability.[99] In the 1840s the number was reversed, with 65 per cent having unlimited liability, a quarter having limited liability, and fewer than 10 per cent having double liability.[100] Much more so than in Upper Canada, the colony's legislators responded to the increase in the number of corporations after 1830 by evincing a concomitant concern about corporations not paying all debts incurred. When a bill to incorporate with limited liability was debated in 1846, for example, 'several members ... expressed their determination to oppose the Bill in every stage if the requisite guards and checks were not imposed for the protection of the public.' The *Novascotian* wholeheartedly approved, averring that incorporation legislation was 'unsound' if it 'does not give the public every security from loss by reckless or unskillful speculators,' and the general corporations statute in the 1851 revised statutes made personal liability the default position, unless the relevant special Act changed that.[101]

The distrust of limited liability continued to find expression in the 1850s, although often manifested in double liability clauses. In that decade half of the private Act incorporations contained such clauses. The remaining statutes were more likely to impose unlimited liability (about a third) than limited liability (fewer than 20 per cent). While there was a clear overall preference for double liability compared to previous decades in Nova Scotia and to other colonies generally, there is no obvious rhyme or reason for which companies were legislated which form of liability. One assumes that the influence that proprietors or their sponsoring assembly members could bring to bear was what counted. One of the consistent objectors whenever a limited liability clause was included in the initial bill was Attorney General and later Chief Justice William Young, who dispiritedly lamented after he was on the losing side of a debate about whether the Acadian Marble Company should have limited liability, 'I take it for granted the question is now settled, as applicable to all companies.'[102] It was far from settled. Although three companies were incorporated that year with liability limited to the stock invested, the most in any year in the 1850s, only one such company received that privilege in 1856 and one again in 1858, whereas nine companies had double liability in 1856 to 1858 inclusive. Those who disliked limited liability got their way most decisively in an 1862 Act that imposed double liability on all corporations and also extended liability for six months after a shareholder had sold his or her shares. The bill's sponsor, Solicitor General Jonathan McCully, argued that general double liability better protected creditors than the private Acts, in which the nature of liability fluctuated.[103]

Despite its general prevalence, limited liability was always controversial. It offended a bedrock principle of commercial morality – debts should be paid.[104] Upper Canadian reform principal Francis Hincks argued that the corporate form, and limited liability in particular, gave a corporation an unfair advantage over the individual businessman. He thought it unfair that people with capital should compete with small manufacturing concerns when the former had limited liability and the latter had none. For Hincks 'capitalists should not be allowed to come into the Province,... and enter into competition with mechanics; when, at the same time they are not responsible under the act of incorporation, for the payment of their debts.'[105]

Against this simple if compelling argument, proponents of limited liability offered utilitarian justifications. Public utilities such as canals, bridges, and toll roads should be given limited liability in recognition of their usefulness to all. The British North American colonies lacked capital, and limited liability was necessary to encourage investment; people would not invest if they risked losing all. As Adams George Archibald put it in an 1855 debate in the Nova Scotia Assembly over the Acadian Marble Company, 'Capital was necessary to develop the resources of the country,' and all reasonable means should be taken to attract it. Men were willing to invest £1,000 in the colony, 'but they do not wish to risk another £1,000 which they have not invested.'[106] Moreover, since most American states gave limited liability, the terms of investment in British North America had to be equally advantageous, both to attract capital investment from outside, something all colonies wanted, and to prevent capital flight. Writing two decades earlier, Beamish Murdoch also thought limited liability was needed to attract investment, although as we have seen local legislators disagreed with him in the 1840s.[107] Murdoch's argument was repeated twenty years later in strong and rhetorical language by Benjamin Weir in the above-mentioned debate over the Acadian Marble Company. Contrasting Nova Scotia with New Brunswick, where limited liability was well accepted, he urged his assembly colleagues to 'sweep away these old restrictions and absurd clogs on the industry and enterprise of the people.' The United States and New Brunswick had prospered because their corporations were not hampered by a restriction like double liability, and 'it was high time such absurd laws were swept away.' George-Étienne Cartier took a slightly different tack in the debate over Upper Canada's major sectoral statute in 1850. Limited liability was not a threat to creditors, because the public were protected by knowing how much paid up capital an enterprise had: 'He thought that offered the public far better security than it had from any private partnership whose capital the public has no means of ascertaining.'[108]

Not only limited liability in particular but corporations in general were at times controversial. For some they were inimical to public interest, because they wielded excessive power and influence. Speaking very early in our period, Nova Scotia lawyer William H.O. Haliburton took the view that 'corporations should be looked on with jealousy,' although he was as much concerned with monopoly as with corporations as such.[109] William Lyon Mackenzie was their fiercest Upper Canadian critic but not the only one. Mackenzie's draft constitution of 1837 stated, 'There shall never be created within this State any incorporated trading companies, or incorporated companies with banking powers. Labour is the only means of creating wealth.'[110] On the other side of this issue were arguments that corporations permitted the aggregation of capital necessary to create and operate large-scale projects. Cartier stated it simply in 1850: 'In a new country, like ours, where there is not a super-abundance of capital, it is desirable to encourage companies.' In the same debate Canada West's commissioner of public works, William Hamilton Merritt, expressed his 'hearty support' for the 1850 sectoral incorporation bill, because 'laws of the kind desired had been of the very greatest use in developing the manufacturing resources of the United States.' He was committed to laissez-faire, and 'the public were sufficiently able to look after themselves.'[111]

32

Law and the Economy II: Debtor-Creditor Law

Debt was an ever-present reality of the lives of many thousands of British North America's inhabitants. As one Upper Canadian newspaper put it in 1831, 'Debtors comprise nearly the whole community.' Colonial economies relied heavily on credit in an era when capital was lacking or not liquid, specie in short supply, and the margin between economic success and failure narrow. As the same newspaper article stressed, 'He who is a creditor in one case is a debtor in another.'[1] One result was that many creditors did not press for repayment, accepting a default rate of 20 per cent as the price of doing business.[2] But of course forbearance was nowhere near total, and creditors could, and frequently did, use the courts to collect what was owed to them. The remedies available to judgment creditors included being able to seize land in execution, something not possible in Britain. In addition, and frequently a controversial remedy, creditors could also have their debtors imprisoned until debts were paid or compromised. This had long been a central feature of the common law's arsenal of remedies, and, as we have seen, it was also available in Lower Canada. We do not know how widely imprisonment for debt was used, but available figures for Upper Canada indicate that the numbers could be substantial. In 1836 some 48 per cent of those in prison were debtors, over 2,300 people.[3]

Imprisonment for debt was common throughout the decades prior to Confederation and was also widely criticized as inhumane and ineffective. The law changed in various ways, but imprisonment for debt was not abolished in any colony. For every critic who deprecated the practice, there was somebody else who was certain that paying one's debts was a moral necessity, and people should not be allowed to escape their obligations. One newspaper article on the subject captured this sentiment admirably, being entitled 'The Religion of Paying Debts.'[4] Not doing so was tantamount to fraud, even, in some peoples' eyes, to something very close to theft. The fact of indebtedness combined with a distrust of debt relief engendered considerable legal debate in this period, as each colony tried to negotiate the space between the two extremes of imprisonment and acceptance of whatever caused indebtedness – fraudulent behaviour, recklessness, misfortune, or some combination of all three.

Imprisonment for Debt

Imprisonment of the debtor was available to the creditor both before and after judgment. A creditor could imprison before trial with a writ *capias ad respondeum* (*capias*), obtained by swearing that a debt was overdue and that the debtor was about to abscond or to conceal property. This fear of evasion was no fiction, certainly not in Upper Canada from whence hundreds of people a year decamped to the United States. *Capias* gave the sheriff authority to seize and imprison the debtor – this was called *mesne* process. In Lower Canada the debt had to be worth ten pounds, but elsewhere there was a much smaller restriction; in Upper Canada from 1811 the debt had to be at least two pounds.[5] Although it will not be dealt with here, all colonies provided for imprisonment for debtors who were likely to abscond, outside of *mesne* process. If the debtor had already absconded, his or her property could be attached and sold with a court order. If a creditor believed that a debtor was about to leave the colony to avoid paying, or was hiding within it, he or she could apply to a judge for an arrest warrant.[6] Such actions could be taken in chancery also, as James Marchinton, son of the prominent and very wealthy Halifax merchant Philip Marchinton, discovered in 1823 when his sister, Mary Welsford, had him committed to prison on a writ from chancery. The two were embroiled in a dispute over their father's estate, and Welsford swore that she believed her brother was about to leave the colony.[7]

After receiving judgment, creditors had two options. They could obtain a writ of *fieri facias* ordering the sheriff to seize and sell by public auction enough of the debtor's property, including land, to satisfy the debt. Or they could either commit the debtor to prison, or keep him or her there, on a writ *capias ad satisfaciendum* until the debt was paid or in some way compromised to the satisfaction of the creditor. Again, a fear that the debtor would abscond, or that he or she was concealing or had transferred assets, had to be sworn to.[8] This was imprisonment on final process, as opposed to *mesne* process. Lower Canada was exceptional in this last regard. As explained in part 3, imprisonment on final process was available only to merchants, and to merchants' creditors if the debt was a commercial one. The only people who could not be imprisoned for their debts in this period were Indigenous people living on reserves in Upper Canada after 1850, because they could not be held responsible for their debts in any event, and, in some jurisdictions as discussed below, women. The legislation that brought in the former exemption was enacted 'for the protection of Indians in Upper Canada from imposition,' a form of paternalistic protectionism. In practice the people of the Grand River reserve received credit from local merchants before and after 1850, and twice in the 1850s the chiefs agreed to pay the outstanding sums from the interest on their annuities, something the statute explicitly prohibited. Thus the Indigenous people themselves saw it as only right that they live up to their obligations.[9]

Imprisonment for debt was always controversial, for it pitted those who believed that the harsh sanction was the only way to ensure commercial honesty against arguments that it was both cruel and ineffective. Its opponents advocated a broad range of reforms in the first half of the nineteenth century, from outright abolition, to abolition in certain contexts, to amelioration of the conditions under which imprisoned debtors were held. No colony entirely abolished imprisonment for debt, but all colonies changed the common law in some way, including, from the 1840s, passing statutes that established some variant of an alternative legal regime, that of bankruptcy. We will first delineate how laws relating to imprisonment for debt were changed, then examine the rise of bankruptcy regimes, and conclude with looking at the competing ideologies underlying debates over the remedy of imprisonment.

The least controversial measures were statutes to provide for the support of imprisoned debtors. The state did not feed imprisoned debtors as it did accused persons awaiting trial or convicts serving short sentences. The debtor, through family and/or friends, was required to support himself or herself, but if that was not possible the creditor was responsible. All colonies passed legislation to enforce this obligation, and differences between jurisdictions were small and unimportant. New Brunswick's regime can be used to illustrate the general thrust of the legislation. If an imprisoned debtor owed less than £200, raised to any amount in 1822, and was unable to support himself or herself, an application could be made after fourteen days' confinement to a judge of the court (or to any two JPs after 1833) that had issued the process for a 'weekly support and maintenance.' If the debtor was found to be 'utterly unable' to support himself or herself the creditor could be ordered to do so, according to a fixed monetary scale. From 1830 a debtor who received such support for a year would then be released, and a debtor would also be released if the creditor failed to make the payments. The statutes imposed various procedures on a debtor seeking maintenance, such as requiring the judge to be sure that the confined person did not defraud the creditor by hiding assets.[10]

Another set of ameliorative provisions was legislation allowing debtors a certain degree of freedom while they remained theoretically in debtors' prison. JPs could define the 'gaol limits' as including an area well outside the jail itself, thereby allowing a debtor 'to go about and have his liberty within the limits of the gaol so designated,... in as ample and full a manner' as if walls enclosed the limits. These words are from a New Brunswick statute of 1823, which also required those limits to be no less than forty rods (220 yards) from the prison walls and no more than eighty. In 1836 this latter number was increased to 160 rods, and over the decades jail limits were widened for a number of specific communities in the colony.[11] Legislation in other colonies similarly extended jail limits, although Nova Scotia did not do so until the mid-1830s. Upper Canada from 1822 allowed debtors to be bailed to an area not more than six acres around the jail, for example, increased to sixteen in 1830 and increased again in 1834. In 1847 Canada extended the limits to the whole of the district served by a district jail.[12]

More significant than support or jail limits legislation were proposals to abolish imprisonment for debt in whole or in part, and other initiatives aimed at providing mechanisms for some debtors to be released, or spared from confinement entirely, even if their debts went unpaid. All proposals for outright abolition, which began in the 1820s, failed. Less ambitious measures sometimes passed, and sometimes failed. An 1828 Nova Scotia bill, for example, would have abolished imprisonment for all debts under twenty pounds. It declared imprisonment for debt to be 'generally useless and often barbarous and inhuman.' It passed the council but was defeated in the assembly. Conversely, reform bills in Lower Canada invariably failed in the legislative council, which represented the interests of, and on this matter did the bidding of, the merchants of Montreal and Quebec. These bills and Acts can be broadly categorized into two groups – insolvent debtor relief legislation and bankruptcy legislation. The former is discussed here, the latter in the next section. It should be noted that it was also possible to have a private Act passed by the assembly to relieve individual debtors. An average of only one debtor a year was liberated in this way in Nova Scotia between 1820 and 1846.[13]

Insolvent debtor relief legislation appeared frequently on the statute books of every colony. The details varied. Some statutes simply provided that creditors could consent to their debtors being freed without losing the benefit of the judgments they had obtained. Others provided that if the debtor assigned all of his or her property, except some personal effects, to the creditor, and swore an oath before either a superior court or other judge, or a JP, that he or she had not concealed any property, the debtor was released. In different places at different times this remedy was available only to those with debts under a certain amount. We know little about how the process operated, but it could keep judges reasonably busy. NSSC Judge James Stewart told a colleague in the late 1820s that he was 'fairly at leisure,' although he was 'often called upon for the examination of witnesses, the relief of Insolvent Debtors, and other matters.'[14] A successful application under these relief Acts did not extinguish debts, but the debtor could not be imprisoned again for the same ones. These Acts were not as generous to imprisoned debtors as they seemed, for they also often included provisions allowing creditors to resist or delay release. In Nova Scotia, for example, the creditor could prevent or delay release by showing 'good and sufficient reason' for continued detention. Remands to show such reason were only for three months, although further remands could be obtained, but only to a maximum of two years. The legislation establishing this scheme was repealed in toto in 1819, as 'tending to encourage Debtors to defraud their Creditors,' and for some years no general relief was available. Relief for debtors was legislated again in 1832, with a similar requirement of assigning all property, but again a creditor could resist release by showing good cause. Substantial discretion was given to JPs in this respect; if they believed that 'any circumstances in respect of [the] Debt, or the delay in payment thereof' justified a continued remand, they could order one they thought 'proper under all the circumstances of the case.'[15]

As the leading historian of imprisonment for debt in Upper Canada has pointed out, a legal regime that relied on distinguishing mere insolvency from an attempt to defraud creditors by pretended inability to pay 'posed an epistemological problem as much as moral or economic one.' That problem arose with attempts to relieve debtors, and it arose again after bankruptcy regimes, discussed below, were introduced. Unfortunately we have no statistical evidence about what percentage of relief applications were denied on this basis. We do know, however, that judges and JPs were often vexed with this question, and particularly with how the correct answer could be obtained when the parties themselves were not competent witnesses at common law, on grounds of interest. It was the difficulty of finding a satisfactory answer to these vexing questions that in part explains why imprisonment for debt was never abolished, only reformed. Ultimately imprisonment was a device that was believed to test whether, in the words of Charles Richardson, a creditor from Niagara, a debtor 'wants the inclination ... [or] the means of liquidating ... my claim against him.'[16]

The two major pieces of relief legislation in the Canadas were an Upper Canada Act of 1835, the *Mitigation Act*, and Lower Canadian legislation of the same year that allowed many debtors to avoid imprisonment altogether.[17] The former's preamble suggested some dissatisfaction with imprisonment in itself; it was 'not otherwise justifiable than as a means of compelling such persons to apply whatever monies or property they may be possessed of ... to the satisfaction of their creditors.' Nonetheless imprisonment for debt would stay on the books until more 'suitable Laws' had been passed. The Act abolished imprisonment for small debts up to £10, and for debts between £10 and £20 debtors were allowed to apply to a court for release after three months in gaol, or twelve if on the limits. If the debt was more than £20 but less than £100, debtors could similarly apply after six months, and if more than £100 was owed after twelve. Debtors had to swear to not having committed 'fraud, deceit or dishonest practices,' and that they had no more than £5 of property in addition to their clothing and bedding. Creditors owed £20 or more could file affidavits against release, and in such cases the court was allowed to release the debtor only if the creditor 'shows no reasonable ground whatever ... for expecting benefit from further detention.' The Lower Canadian Act of 1835 went further. It permitted any debtor arrested on a writ of *capias* to stay at large in the district if security was given. Debtors also had to file with the court a statement of all real and personal property they owned or which was to come to them, such as rents. Creditors were allowed to challenge such statements, but if they could not do so the debtor was free within the bounds of the district.

Upper Canada's *Mitigation Act* was passed a year after the most generous to debtors relief legislation in British North America, that of Newfoundland. It was similar to elsewhere in requiring debtors in prison to surrender all their property to creditors, and it did not release the debt. But it applied to all non-fraudulent debtors, irrespective of the amount owed, had no waiting period before an application for release from prison could be made, and contained no provisions for creditors to object. The Act also abolished imprisonment for debt for women, the first British North American jurisdiction to do so.[18]

The *Mitigation Act* operated for nearly a decade and was superseded in 1843 by legislation very substantially reducing the availability of imprisonment for debt, despite its misleading title – *An Act to Abolish Imprisonment in Execution for Debt*. It boldly asserted that imprisonment for debt 'where fraud is not imputable to the debtor' was 'as detrimental to the true interests of the Creditor' as it was 'inconsistent with that forbearance and humane regard to the misfortunes of others which should always characterize the Legislation of every Christian country.' It went on to exempt from imprisonment all women, and any person who had contracted debts in a foreign jurisdiction that did not permit imprisonment for debt, or who had contracted debts worth less than ten pounds. Even those who owed ten pounds or more could not be arrested unless the creditor swore an affidavit attesting to the debt and to the fact that he or she had good reason to believe that the debtor was likely to flee the jurisdiction. Later legislation continued to pick away at imprisonment. In 1847 the creditor's power to imprison was restricted to debtors who had property worth five pounds or more. In addition, imprisonment could be transformed into confinement to a district if he or she could find sureties. A decade later, imprisonment could only be obtained if a judge was actually satisfied that the debtor was about to flee the jurisdiction.[19]

Other kinds of ameliorative statutes were passed elsewhere. Lower Canada exempted debtors over seventy and provided, in a series of temporary relief statutes, that debtors on final process could have freedom within the city if they found special bail. By 1849 a series of ameliorating statutes meant that the only imprisoned debtors were those who could not find anybody to stand bail for them. An 1849 Act was passed 'to relieve this poorest and most vulnerable category of debtors'; it released them provided they gave up their property for the benefit of their creditors. In Nova Scotia, legislation of 1846 removed the debt ceiling for obtaining relief, provided for commissioners to administer the Act in each county, and generally made it much easier to obtain a discharge from prison. In 1851 the maximum period of imprisonment was set at one year, even for fraudulent debtors, and imprisonment for debt for women was abolished. New Brunswick followed the same pattern of amelioration but not abolition. The law reform commission of 1854 bluntly stated that 'imprisonment for debt must finally be abolished' but went on to lament that 'we do not think the country prepared for so great a change.' As a result, when the statutes were consolidated that same year any debtor could be released at the discretion of a Supreme Court judge if the debtor had been in prison for six months and had no property. There was no debt ceiling, and clothing and tools of the debtor's trade were exempted from what counted as property.[20] But despite all these ameliorative measures, imprisonment for debt was not entirely abolished anywhere until after Confederation.

Bankruptcy Laws

Insolvent debtor relief was also legislated via bankruptcy laws. Bankruptcy statutes were first passed in England in the sixteenth century, and then and now they interfered with ordinary debtor-creditor relations in two very significant ways. First, they provided for an equitable division of the debtors' assets to creditors on a pro rata basis. At common law, courts had no power to interfere with the distribution of assets. The first creditor to sue and receive judgment would be the first, and perhaps only, creditor to be able to have the debtor's property seized and sold to meet his or her demands. Second, and more importantly for current purposes, bankruptcy law gave the debtor a discharge from debts, a release from obligations, and a 'fresh start.' At common law the only thing that could extinguish a debt was its payment or forgiveness by the creditor(s). Britain had long had such legislation, but it applied only to merchants or traders until 1861. The United States had a federal bankruptcy law briefly in the early 1840s, and thereafter some American states had bankruptcy legislation, without limitation to classes of persons, which also allowed debtors to initiate the process.[21]

The English bankruptcy statutes were one of two aspects of English law specifically not received by Upper Canada's 1792 reception statute. Although no other colony had such a limitation, we must assume that bankruptcy statutes were generally not received because they were considered 'unsuitable' for colonial conditions. Hence bankruptcy laws had to be passed by local assemblies. They were introduced but were consistently defeated in British North America in the 1820s and 1830s. Five bills failed in Nova Scotia, for example, between 1827 and 1842. At times Lower Canada also saw fierce debates over bankruptcy bills in the 1820s and 1830s, all of which failed.[22] Some derided the lack of a bankruptcy law as inhumane, for it kept debtors in prison, and according to the *Montreal Gazette* was 'at variance with the principles of common justice and the dictates of humanity.' It 'substitut[ed] the punishment due to crimes for those due only to accident or misfortune.'

The first bankruptcy legislation in British North America was passed in Lower Canada during the rule of the special council, in 1839. The bankruptcy ordinance applied only to merchants and traders and thus satisfied the powerful English merchant community. It provided for a distribution of assets and, if a commissioner was satisfied that the bankrupt had fully complied with the Act, for him or her to be 'absolutely and wholly discharged from all ... debts.' The bankruptcy principle was extended throughout the province of Canada in 1843. The preamble of the statute succinctly stated the two purposes of bankruptcy: 'the discovery and securing of the estates and effects of bankrupts, for the benefit of their creditors,' and 'the relief of such traders as shall, without any fraud or gross misconduct, have become unable to pay all their debts in full.' The statute applied only to 'traders' but defined that term as including a wide range of commercial and artisanal callings; specifically excluded were 'farmers, graziers, common labourers or workmen for hire.' It allowed the creditors of a trader to start the process if the trader had committed one of a number of 'acts of bankruptcy,' which meant essentially that he or she was unable to pay debts. The process involved the creditor taking his or her complaint to a judge or commissioner, who would then summon and examine the alleged bankrupt. The assets then had to be gathered in and distributed among the creditors. If the debtor had indeed disclosed all assets and given them up for this process, a judge or a commissioner appointed under the statute could grant a discharge.[23]

The Act was for only two years' duration, but in 1846 it was amended and continued for another year. The amendments toughened up the procedural requirements but did not make any substantive change. An attempt by government to continue it again in 1849 failed in the assembly, although it was continued for proceedings that had begun but had not been concluded. The following year the courts were given the power to discharge a bankrupt who had been declared bankrupt under the 1843 Act but had not been discharged. These two latter acts – the one continuing the bankrupt Act only for proceedings begun but not completed, and the 1850 Act on undischarged bankrupts – were continued again at least until 1856.[24] But no new bankruptcy proceedings could be begun in either Upper or Lower Canada after 1849.

Debtors in Upper Canada, although not Lower Canada, could still invoke a process very similar to bankruptcy. In 1845, while the bankruptcy regime enacted in 1843 was still in place, an *Insolvency Act* applicable only to Upper Canada was passed.[25] It applied to debtors who were not traders and thus not able to invoke the 1843 Act. It gave the debtor the power to initiate proceedings for a distribution of assets among creditors and gave a district court judge the power to then grant the debtor immunity from imprisonment, although not a discharge. The judge was to appoint an official assignee who would take ownership of all the debtor's assets and arrange for a distribution of them. Although the debtor was not immune from process while the proceedings were going on, once the judge was satisfied that the debts had not been fraudulently contracted, he could make a 'final order ... for the protection of the person of the petitioner from all process.' This *Insolvency Act* was to last only two years but was later continued. In 1856 it was amended and became in effect a bankruptcy Act because traders who successfully invoked it could now obtain a discharge as well as immunity from imprisonment. But the amended statute stayed in force for only a year before repeal; this volte-face has been attributed to the fact that assembly members did not understand what had been passed in 1856 and voted overwhelmingly for repeal. Bills were introduced to restore full bankruptcy to Upper Canada in 1859 and 1861 but failed.[26]

The 1843 *Insolvency Act* never applied to Lower Canada, which after 1849 had no bankruptcy legislation other than for the limited purposes noted above – to continue the legislation for bankruptcy proceedings started but not completed and to grant discharges to those who had fulfilled the requirements of the 1843 Act. Having a different law for each section of the colony was consistent with one theme in legislative debates – Lower Canada members frequently adverted to the fact that whatever anybody else thought, 'Lower Canadians were opposed to Bankruptcy laws,' especially ones modelled on English legislation.[27] In fact many Upper Canadians were also opposed; John Rolph, who had been a leader of the campaign against imprisonment for debt in 1820s, refused to countenance bankruptcy legislation.[28] The situation was not resolved until 1864, when the *Insolvency Act* was replaced by a new Act of the same name that applied to both the Canadas.[29] The 1864 regime was not called a bankruptcy Act, but it effectively was one, because it did allow for a discharge, called a 'deed of composition and discharge,' if a majority of creditors agreed. It applied in Lower Canada only to traders, but in Upper Canada to all persons. It permitted a debtor to make a voluntary assignment of assets, after calling a meeting of all creditors and showing them a sworn account of his position. The creditors could then appoint an assignee to receive all the debtor's assets. It also mandated compulsory liquidation of the estates of absconding debtors and debtors who performed a series of other acts intended to defraud some or all creditors.

In the Maritimes, Nova Scotia never enacted bankruptcy legislation, but New Brunswick did, in 1842. The Act gave the executive power to appoint a commissioner of the estates of bankrupt persons in each of five counties, and more could be added if applied for. The commissioners had to be barristers of five years' standing and resident in the county to which they were appointed. Creditors, or any one of them, could petition any debtor owing at least £500 into bankruptcy, the formal petition to invoke the process going to the master of the rolls. If the bankrupt 'had in all things conformed himself to the provisions' of the Act he would be 'discharged from all debts due by him' at the time. Newfoundland did not provide for bankruptcy until 1862 and as elsewhere still used the term *insolvency* even though the relevant legislation provided for a discharge of debts and a pro rata distribution. Either the debtor or one of his creditors could petition for a declaration of insolvency, and if granted, trustees would be appointed to gather all assets and distribute them. Stiff prison sentences were to be meted out to those who made fraudulent conveyances (defined as made two months or less before the application) or concealed assets.[30]

Insolvency: A Clash of Ideologies

Colonial lawmakers were willing to ameliorate the rigours of imprisonment for debt but never to actually abolish the practice, because it engendered sharply divergent moral arguments. For opponents of reform, paying one's debts was a moral necessity, as it was for those who were suspicious of limited liability, and nobody should be allowed to escape their obligations. For many the duty was rooted in their Christian beliefs. A Nova Scotia Methodist newspaper, the *Wesleyan*, thundered against such dereliction in an article suitably titled 'The Religion of Paying Debts':

> Men may sophisticate as they please; they can never make it right, for them not to pay their debts. There is a sin in this neglect, as clear and as deserving church discipline, as in stealing or false swearing. He who violates his promise to pay, or withholds the payment of a debt when it is in his power to meet his engagement, ought to be made to feel that in the sight of all honest men he is a swindler.[31]

According to this world view, debtors were not simply unfortunate, they were at least partly, if not entirely, responsible for their plight. One did not have to be actively fraudulent to bear responsibility, recklessness was almost as bad, as was poor judgment – the effect on the creditor was the same in all cases. It was no accident that imprisonment was the remedy provided by law, the same remedy meted out to convicted criminals. Debtors who defaulted should be punished. Upper Canadian notables like John Beverley Robinson resisted the idea that only misfortune led to insolvency, and his sentiments were echoed by Solicitor General Hagerman, who argued that 'it is sometimes a crime for a person to get into debt,' and that 'there is something dishonest in a person incurring debts which he does not expect to pay.'[32] John Sandfield MacDonald, solicitor general for Upper Canada, also thought the issue a simple one: a debtor 'is confined … not because he is in debt, but because he will not pay his debts when he has the means at his disposal.'[33] In Lower Canada the anglophone merchants of Montreal and Quebec, consistent opponents of a change in the law, had an additional local cause of complaint – the matrimonial property regime of community of property. Debtors who knew that half the family property was beyond the reach of creditors because it was part of the marital community would, without the fear of imprisonment, be more inclined to contract debts they could not pay.[34]

Supporters of reform offered both humanitarian and pragmatic arguments. One of the principal campaigners against debtors' prison in the 1820s and 1830s was Halifax lawyer and legal author, and assembly member, Beamish Murdoch. Murdoch's father had spent seven years in prison for debt in Halifax, and he campaigned hard for reform motivated by this experience. He wrote an *Essay on the Mischievous Tendency of Imprisonment for Debt* in 1827 and had it privately printed and circulated to assembly members. The pamphlet made three principal arguments. First, that imprisonment for debt placed too much power in the hands of creditors. Second, that even if some debtors were extravagant and reckless, so also at fault as equally reckless were their creditors for advancing them credit. Third, that imprisonment was ineffective anyway. It did not cure debtor recklessness, and being put in gaol did not allow the debtor to work to repay the debt – indeed it made it harder to pay. A better recourse could be had by attaching wages and choses in action.[35] Not infrequently Murdoch and other reformers also argued that it was wrong to confine debtors with accused or convicted criminals in local jails. As we saw in an earlier chapter, prison reformers also stressed segregation of different classes of inmates, and this was substantially achieved from the 1830s. The change was not universal. When Newfoundland provided for a penitentiary in St John's in 1851 it was explicitly stated that both convicted criminals and debtors would be housed there.[36]

Murdoch's first objection found an echo a few years later in the *British Colonial Argus*, an Upper Canadian newspaper, which rhetorically asked why 'should a hard-hearted and relentless creditor be invested with the power of life and death, and ... be allowed to seize his unfortunate fellow-being, and by the King's authority, drag an unoffending subject to a loathsome and iron-grated den and lock him in for life.' Fifteen years later complaints were still being voiced about 'vindictive creditors' and the lack of procedural protections for debtors. Criminals had to be found guilty by a jury, but creditors were the judges in their own cause. The link between debt and criminal punishment so deprecated by Murdoch was echoed by critics in Upper Canada. Marshall Spring Bidwell, a leading Upper Canadian reformer, insisted that it was not a crime to be in debt, thus it was wrong for him 'to suffer the punishment which is due only to the foulest crime.' Bidwell was also a prison reformer and linked the two campaigns when he stated that debtors ought not to be housed with criminals and 'contaminated' by them. The most extreme rhetorical flourish was uttered by George Boulton, a legislative councillor for the province of Canada, who claimed that 'a creditor cannot commit greater inhumanity than attaches to slavery.'[37]

The leading historian of insolvency in Upper Canada not only comprehensively demonstrates the widespread use of such linkages, but goes further to argue that they demonstrate a new 'culture of sensibility' in public debate. The campaign against imprisonment for debt, he argues, can be fully understood only if we appreciate the power of this sensibility 'to overcome indifference to the fate of others.' Thus legal change in this area, like reform of physical punishments in the criminal law, was driven by much more than pragmatism and purely rational argument. Nor were such sentiments limited to Upper Canada. Leading Lower Canadian politician George-Étienne Cartier argued in 1849 that 'the debtor was in a worse position than the robber,' because while the latter 'could only be imprisoned for two or three years,... the debtor might continue incarcerated for life.' The theme of barbarism and inhumanity was taken up by many critics. A.P. Ross, of Pictou County, Nova Scotia, called imprisonment for debt 'a remnant of barbarous ages.' One Lower Canadian critic took a nationalist stance, complaining that the introduction of imprisonment for debt in that colony meant that legislators had 'lost sight of the humane and Christian fundamental principles of the French code' and had grafted onto the civil law 'the abominable system of imprisonment for debt.' Others in Lower Canada decried the inhumanity of imprisoning debtors with criminals, the prison conditions, and the cruelty of some creditors who kept their debtors inside for long periods over relatively small sums, and thereby deprived women and children of the family breadwinner. They also railed against the pointlessness of imprisoning honest debtors, both for their creditors and for society.[38]

Both opponents of imprisonment and reformers accepted that there was a distinction between dishonest and merely unfortunate debtors. In Lower Canada, for example, sympathy for imprisoned debtors applied only to honest debtors, a point succinctly made by legislative councillor James Ferrier in 1858, when he demanded that 'the honest but unfortunate' should be 'spared the 'humiliation and barbarism' of imprisonment.[39] But it was often pointed out that none could conceive of a law that could make the distinction.[40] Thus the need to maintain a harsh sanction for those who did not pay their debts was paramount, and for those who took this view in Upper Canada frauds perpetrated by some married couples following the passage in 1859 of the first married women's property act, discussed in chapter 34, only reinforced their scepticism about dishonest debtors.[41] Insolvency reform statutes were based on general assumptions about human nature not borne out by experience. There were good and bad debtors, and the law allowed creditors, who presumably were in the best position to know, to distinguish between them. By this reasoning individual relief bills were acceptable because legislators were judging individual cases. Alexander Stewart of Nova Scotia made this point in 1827: '[A] private bill for individual relief is acceptable, but not a bill for general relief.' Coupled with this attitude was a belief that creditors were fair and reasonable, indulgent to honest debtors, and, as Stewart put it in the same debate, the legislation in place was a 'mild, moderate, temperate law.'[42]

To a considerable degree pragmatic arguments about whether imprisonment was the right policy were irrelevant; as one historian succinctly argues, 'Insolvency law was an ideological system to be judged less by its efficiency than the moral and political lessons it taught,' and as a result prior to the union 'no satisfactory balance was struck between relief of the honest insolvent and punishment of the wrongdoer.'[43] The debate on the 1858 Upper Canada bill, which greatly reduced imprisonment, exemplifies the complexity of the considerations involved. Speakers adopted every position mentioned here. Creditors generally acted in good faith, but some were vindictive; many debtors were honest and unfortunate, some were neither; debtors could too easily abscond over the nearby border.[44]

The debates over bankruptcy laws engendered many of the same arguments, for bankruptcy involved, although it was not limited to, avoiding imprisonment. Many argued that most bankrupts were merely unfortunate and should be treated humanely. Against this, morals-based objections similar to those that had been raised in the 1820s and 1830s were voiced – bankruptcy allowed people to evade their just debts.[45] The editor of the *Novascotian*, commenting on a failed 1842 bankruptcy bill, worried that it 'would hold out temptation to speculate, and to evad[e] just demands.'[46] Although the initial scheme for the Canadas legislated in 1843 sparked little controversy, the renewal bills of 1846 and 1849 gave rise to considerable argument. For some the problem with renewing the legislation was simple – debts should be paid. The same opponents of bankruptcy saw it as also oppressive to creditors. Lower Canadians espoused similar views when the provincial legislature passed the 1856 Act applicable only to Upper Canada. Lawyer, investor in many corporations, and sometime Attorney General Lewis Thomas Drummond opposed any bankruptcy act. He asserted that 'Bankruptcy Laws were inimical to common morality' and that 'the present law produced a large amount of fraud and perjury ... [and] caused more demoralization ... in the last ten years than any other thing in the world.'[47] Three years later he beat the same drum: 'The law we used to have in Canada could ruin an honest man,... while it would aid rogues in enriching themselves at the expense of creditors.' Another assemblymen and lawyer, Thomas-Jean-Jacques Loranger, thought that 'the point of view of morality ... is that until a debt has been paid, the debtor remains under the obligation to pay.' When the 1856 bill was repealed a year later, the liberal, modernist, and mildly anticlerical Antoine-Aimé Dorion espoused traditional values on this issue, insisting that while it was 'just' that a person could be freed from prison, it was 'unjust and immoral' that he could also be relieved of his debts.[48]

Supporters of bankruptcy referred to its necessity in a modern commercial society.[49] But they made no headway against the belief, espoused by Thomas Ferguson, the member for Simcoe South, that 'the most barefaced perjury would be committed in the Bankrupt Courts,' the establishment of which would open 'a perfect flood-gate of fraud.' Lewis Thomas Drummond similarly insisted that the purpose of any bankruptcy legislation 'was to enable dishonest men to cheat their creditors.'[50] Opposition to bankruptcy was also fuelled by the experience of the United States, where bankruptcy laws at both the federal and state levels favoured defaulting debtors much more so than English law.[51] A question common to the issues discussed here was what form of modernization the law of debtor-creditor relations should take. As pragmatic solutions became increasingly voiced, and to some extent legislated, they met a rear-guard action that reflected an older moral compass. For some it was always wrong to avoid the payment of debts incurred, whether through limits on the scope of imprisonment for debt or through the forgiveness regime that sat at the heart of bankruptcy.

33

Less Favoured by Law I: Blacks and Workers

The law served many purposes in British North America, including the creation and reinforcement of the gender, racial, and class differences that permeated all societies. It could hardly be otherwise, for legal history shows us that law is not separable from the society that created it, used it, and adapted it over time to achieve ends that had their origin in extra-legal ideologies. This chapter deals with the law relating to two groups – Blacks and workers – whose lives were lived on the margins of a British North American world defined by white, propertied males. The following chapter looks at the status of women. In part this chapter examines the ways in which the law actively placed some individuals in a disadvantageous position compared to others. The most obvious example is master and servant legislation, which treated workers and employers unequally by imposing different legal sanctions for breaches of employment contracts. A related theme in this chapter is the failure of legal institutions and actors to effectively enforce laws that would have benefited marginalized groups had they been applied with rigour. The most glaring example was the experience of British North America's Black residents. The law promised freedom and equality to Blacks. It mostly delivered the former, but very rarely the latter. Blacks were permitted by law to vote in many places and times but were sometimes prevented from doing so by white violence. They could own land but received poor land in very limited amounts and, for some, without the same legal guarantees that white settlers enjoyed. Thus this chapter is about the silence and ineffectiveness of law. Law too often expressed in general terms the best of society's aspirations but failed to deliver. It may be doubted that the law could ever prevent people acting out their beliefs that some people were racially, culturally, or socially inferior, and less deserving of the benefits of progress and prosperity. But whether it was or was not possible, extra-legal actions by some better positioned in society were ignored, tolerated, and unmitigated by law.

Blacks and the Law: Not Slaves, but Not Equal

As we saw in chapter 11, slavery existed in the eighteenth- and very early nineteenth-century colonies but had been effectively abolished, by judicial rather than legislative action, by the early nineteenth century. Legislation formally abolishing slavery had to wait until Britain banned it throughout the empire in 1833, but it had been a dead letter in British North America long before then, aside from Indigenous slavery on the west coast. The absence of slavery did not, however, mean the presence of substantive freedom, and African-descended people faced social and economic discrimination and resulting hardship in many areas. The attitudes of whites towards Black populations remained shaped by the legacy of slavery for decades. Economically Blacks scrabbled a mean living on poor land, lived in impoverished conditions in towns and cities, were denied meaningful employment and education, and were considered inferior in intelligence, industry, and character by a great many inhabitants. As a leading historian of the Black experience aptly states, 'Blacks in Canada lived in a state of paradox, caught between formal legal equality and deeply entrenched social and economic inequality.' The same sentiment was expressed in a different way in 1863 by John Lindsay, a former Tennessee slave who escaped and made his way to St Catharines. He became one of the wealthiest businessmen in the town and influential in local politics through effective control of the Black vote. He was also a vocal Loyalist. Yet he never felt accepted. 'I find the prejudice here the same as in the States. I don't find any difference at all,' he stated in 1863.[1]

What role was played by law and legal institutions in bringing about, or exacerbating, Blacks' second-class status? With a few exceptions, discussed shortly, Blacks were not subject to overt legal discrimination in the form of 'Jim Crow' laws. No statutes required them to live in segregated areas, or attend segregated schools, or barred them from voting or holding office. Indeed, as noted above in the case of John Lindsay, they could and did vote in some locations. When they were prevented from voting, it was by extra-legal means – intimidation – or, in New Brunswick, by the lieutenant governor's fiat. Blacks also appeared on juries in Halifax and probably other locations. And judges and others often proclaimed the colour-blindness of British law and justice, invariably making invidious comparisons to the southern American states. The absence of racially based legislation was considered important by one former slave, John Moore. 'There is prejudice here among the low class of people,' he wrote, but he also believed that such people 'have not got the power to carry it out here that they have in the States. The law here is stronger than the mob – it is not so there.'[2]

Yet there was no legal regime to assist Blacks in a positive way in their search for equality, and white society was largely free to discriminate. Blacks encountered discrimination and unequal treatment in many aspects of the application of the law, and even more so in the administration of government policies. The franchise provides but one example. Nova Scotia's Black population was not legally disqualified from voting, but when in the 1830s some sought to do so, they complained that they could not vote 'without being at every Election questioned, browbeaten and sworn' at.[3] Incidents such as this have led one historian of the Black experience to argue that British North America had its own Jim Crow past. While in the United States legal support for Jim Crow was as strong as its social underpinning, north of the border the latter was much more to the fore than the law, which 'passively supported' discrimination.[4] Before we consider in more detail the extent to which this characterization reflects Blacks' experience with the law, it is necessary to provide a brief survey of the size and location of the Black population.

Although Black people were present in every British North American colony, they were a substantial presence in two particular areas, and it is those areas that will be discussed in detail here.[5] As chapter 11 demonstrated, the Black presence in Nova Scotia went back to the mid-eighteenth century, and a further wave of Black immigration came during and after the War of 1812, usually dubbed the 'Black refugees,' comprising Blacks who had fought on the British side in return for promises of freedom and settlement. Over 2,000 came to Nova Scotia, and another smaller group to New Brunswick. There were no substantial migrations after ca 1815, at which time the Nova Scotia Black population probably numbered some 4,000, situated in Halifax, in communities close to the capital where the War of 1812 immigrants had been granted land (about which more below), and in and around every community where Loyalists had settled earlier, particularly Shelburne and Annapolis.[6] The other principal area of concentration was modern-day southwestern Ontario, the 'terminus' of the 'underground railroad' for escaped slaves. Although there were Black slaves brought by Loyalists to both the Canadas, their numbers were small compared to those who came into Upper Canada from the 1820s.

Nova Scotia's nineteenth-century Black immigrants enjoyed a fate only marginally better than those who had arrived earlier, featuring a disheartening repetition of the experiences of the Black Loyalists three decades earlier. There, and in New Brunswick, they encountered discrimination in three particular areas: in the allocation of land, in the administration of the criminal law, and in official policies aimed at both encouraging them to leave the colony and preventing more from entering. The Black refugees who came after the War of 1812 were granted land but received very different treatment from white settlers. While the standard size of grant in this period when free grants were still operative was 100 acres, and could be more, depending on the size of families and military service, the Black refugees got 10 acres per family, despite the fact that many had indeed served in the army. Moreover, what they got was physically and legally inferior. It was poor, rocky, and swamp-ridden, unproductive land, in what became the new community at Hammonds Plains and the existing Black community at Preston, both just outside Halifax. Local white settlers acknowledged the problem: 'These lands are sterile and unproductive in the extraim [*sic*] ... it would be impossible for any persons to support families on them.'[7] Housing was makeshift and insecure, a situation that could not be ameliorated by people too poor to improve matters. Blacks' legal tenure was also tenuous; they were not given fee simple grants but tickets of location. Providing a ticket of location initially to a new settler was standard practice, but these were quickly converted for whites by the issuance of a patent for fee simple tenure when one had been applied for and the fees paid. The differential treatment of Blacks was the result of the government viewing them as a permanent cheap labour pool. The Black refugees were very much aware of the second-class treatment afforded them and campaigned for better terms. As one petition of 1841 stated, proper tenure mattered: 'Holding under Tickets of location, we cannot sell to advantage, we are tied to the land without being able to live upon it.'[8] The government did finally accede, after a number of years of petitioning, and granted the land in fee simple in 1842. New Brunswick's small group of Black refugees received much the same treatment, not receiving proper title to their land until 1836.[9]

The negative consequences of land allocation policies were long-lived. Black inhabitants lived on land too poor to earn them a decent livelihood and too unproductive to permit moving to other areas. They were effectively segregated, an impoverished underclass living on the fringes of society and the economy. Fringes is a particularly apt description of what became a staple of the subsistence economy of Blacks living near Halifax. They harvested wild fruits and berries, walked the fifteen kilometres or so to the Halifax market overnight on roads that were little more than rock-strewn tracks so as to be there early in the morning, and walked back that same evening.

In such circumstances law did nothing to assist Nova Scotia's Blacks. Nor did it do anything to alter white perceptions of Black people as indolent, liable to commit crime, and unsuited to both the climate and the society of British North America. As a motion in the assembly in 1815 asserted, 'The introduction of more [Blacks] must tend to the ... establishment of a separate and marked class of people, unfitted by nature to this climate, or an association with the rest of His Majesty's Colonists.'[10] A decade later attitudes had not only not become more tolerant, but one Halifax newspaper opined that 'the introduction of so great a number of coloured persons into this province' was a 'matter of deep and universal regret,' including apparently the regret of the Blacks themselves who 'would have been in much less distressing circumstances, had they continued in their previous condition.'[11] In 1851 Richard Nugent, the reform-minded editor of the *Halifax Sun*, used the example of Blacks, who could vote because they were freeholders on their tiny patches of land, as an argument for why the electoral franchise should be extended to white labourers. The latter could not vote, but 'illiterate, negro beggars, hundreds of them hardly raised in intellectual capacity above the inferior order of the animal creation,' could do so.[12]

Officials and assembly members also worked to limit the numbers of Blacks in the colony as much as possible. The starkest illustration was a statute passed by the assembly in 1834 'to prevent the Clandestine Landing, of Liberated Slaves ... from Vessels arriving in this Province.' It was prompted by the freeing of slaves throughout the empire and the consequent possibility that residents of the British Caribbean would seek to migrate elsewhere in the Americas. Although given royal assent locally, the statute was disallowed by London in 1835. A more sustained effort to limit numbers had come more than ten years previously, when in 1820 the government offered incentives to the War of 1812 refugees to move to Trinidad. Fewer than 100 took up the offer, the vast majority fearing they would be re-enslaved.[13]

The criminal law was also used against Black residents, its application to them being consistently harsh when those who ran the system – prosecutors, juries, and judges – made the discretionary decisions that permeated the operation of the criminal law. Here we must rely on anecdotal evidence rather than statistical studies, but that evidence is nonetheless quite compelling. When Laban Powell, a Black resident of Cornwallis, Kings County, got into an argument with a fellow resident of a boarding house in 1826 and killed him, the jury took no time to convict when the Supreme Court circuit came around to Horton in that county a few months later. More importantly, practically no consideration was given to whether he should be pardoned or executed, either by the trial judge or the council. As Chief Justice Blowers told Lieutenant Governor Sir James Kempt, 'The sooner the sentence is carried into execution the more striking will be the example' set. Not surprisingly the council rapidly concluded that it could not recommend mercy. A white perpetrator may have ultimately suffered the same fate, but much more would have been said before that conclusion was arrived at.[14]

In this respect Blacks in Nova Scotia fared worse than they did in Lower Canada. The criminal justice system in Lower Canada seems to have had an essentially even-handed approach to racial difference, convicting and punishing Blacks in numbers proportionate to their demographic presence. Blacks in Montreal also used the courts to seek both civil and criminal justice against those who wronged them. Differential treatment across regions was probably the result of different numbers; where Blacks were very few, as they were in Montreal, they posed no threat to white supremacy or chauvinism. That a person tried or convicted was Black was rarely recorded in Montreal or Quebec City's arrest statistics, whereas race was always a feature of crime reporting in Halifax.[15]

When we turn our attention to Upper Canada, the everyday story of the Black experience is different in details from Nova Scotia but not in broad outline. The 20,000 to 25,000 Blacks in Upper Canada by ca 1860 were mostly former American slaves or their descendants who escaped bondage in the United States, often through the help of the 'underground railroad,' through which white anti-slavery activists helped escaped slaves make it to freedom on British soil.[16] The underground railroad has long been a symbol of Canadian distinctiveness from the United States in race relations. But as many historians of the Black experience in Upper Canada have argued, Blacks in the region were, as in Nova Scotia, no longer slaves but by no means welcome, respected, and equal citizens. They settled in the southwestern region of the colony, in Kent and Essex Counties, some on the land and others in the towns and cities of the area, principally Chatham. No apartheid-style laws restricted them to particular districts, but a combination of their poverty and social ostracism effectively limited them to what one visitor in 1848 described as the 'least valuable corners of the towns.' Attitudes to Blacks were harshest in the areas where they were the most numerous. In 1853, for example, it was a group of Chatham residents who petitioned the government to block further Black immigration. Four years earlier Edwin Larwill, a local politician and the editor of the *Chatham Journal*, made his opposition to Blacks abundantly clear: 'The negro is a distinct species of the human family ... far inferior to the European ... [Integration] is as disgusting to the eye, as it is immoral in its tendencies and all good men will discountenance it.'[17]

In the operation of the criminal law, prosecuting authorities were more willing to pursue charges or to levy more serious charges against Blacks than whites, juries more likely to convict, and judges to hand down harsher prison sentences for comparable crimes.[18] Officially, of course, the law always dealt equally and fairly with all citizens. Indeed the ideology of the law was often to the fore in high-profile cases involving Blacks, commentators extolling the virtue of 'British justice.' Hence judges' benchbooks from the 1840s and 1850s show very few references to racial epithets or even racialized descriptions of defendants, even though other evidence reveals that defendants were Black. A much more detailed analysis of crime in Hamilton in the early 1850s shows lawyers and judges clearly aware of race but no evidence of overt use of racial stereotyping. At the same time, some jury verdicts seem to have been racially motivated. Other research has shown that the legal system often produced biased results, but it has also shown that the record is a complex one, with Blacks receiving leniency on occasion. Perhaps nothing displays with greater force the two-sided nature of social and legal attitudes towards Black people than commutations of death sentence decisions that were based on the assumption that all Blacks operated with diminished responsibility.

Segregated Schools

The closest Upper Canada came to legal segregation was in schooling, an 1850 statute permitting and encouraging it, emblematic of a legal system that did not overtly discriminate but covertly permitted it to happen.[19] The 1843 *Common Schools Act* made public schooling at government expense mandatory for all inhabitants, providing also that there were to be no segregated schools. Section 7 stated that 'it shall not be lawful for such [School] Trustees, or ... [any others] to exclude from any Common School or from the benefit of education therein, the children of any class or description of persons resident within the school district.'[20] Despite this, parents and teachers worked hard in many communities to exclude Black children, or if they were allowed in to segregate them in the classroom. Missionary societies and Black community groups responded by establishing schools open to Black children. In 1850 this informal segregation gave way to the quasi-formal, the *Common Schools Act* being amended to require any local government to 'authorise the establishment of one, or more, Separate schools for Protestants, Roman Catholics or Coloured People' if twelve or more 'resident heads of families' applied for such a school.[21]

Many Black communities did apply under the new law, sparking an at-times heated debate among historians about whether Blacks wanted segregated schools. In many respects this argument seems beside the point. It is clear that applications came from Black parents, but applications also came from white parents – the 1850 statute allowed white parents to apply for the establishment of a separate school for Blacks. There is also much evidence that Black leaders protested the law, including going to court to no avail, and demanded the right to attend common schools. In addition, where there were no segregated schools, the existing practices of denying admission to common schools and/or segregating Black children within them continued. One of the cases that reached the courts exemplifies this. The white trustees of school section 14 in Charlotteville Township prevented Solomon Washington, a local Black boy, from attending, even though his family resided on a fifty-acre farm within the district and no separate school had been established. When Washington's father took the trustees to court their principal argument was that the family did not live in the district, an assertion based on the fact that the trustees had unilaterally declared the boundary of their district to go around the Washington farm, including his neighbours but excluding him. Chief Justice Robinson found against the trustees, who had acted 'very unfairly,' and went further in noting that the separate schools legislation was the product of 'prejudices' in 'the minds of the white inhabitants.' He could do nothing about such prejudice but insisted that the Act did not allow the trustees to 'shut them [Blacks] out from the only public schools that do exist.'[22]

Overall the attitude of many Blacks, faced with people like these trustees, was that a segregated school was wrong in principle, but it was better than no schooling being provided, even if segregated schools were starved of adequate money and resources. As one historian aptly concludes, 'While there is little doubt that some elements in the black population in Canada West had little choice but to accept school segregation, there is no evidence that any blacks … ever endorsed' it. The 1850 statute provides a classic example of the law not discriminating directly but allowing discrimination to occur. The 1854 case of *Hill v Camden and Zone School Board* shows precisely this. Heard in the same year that Solomon Washington won his case, and decided by the same judge, Robinson, the Court of Queen's Bench ruled that if a separate school had been established, 'it was intended by the Legislature … that … the children of people of colour … should be educated within such separate school.'[23] The court had no choice in the matter. Remarkably, the 1850 amendment to the *Common Schools Act* remained on the statute book until 1964. Segregated schools were also the norm in Nova Scotia, without the need for a statute. No public schools legislation ever required schools not to be segregated, and the vast majority of Black children, if they had a school to go to, attended schools established for Blacks, in large part because Blacks in Nova Scotia lived in Black communities, communities either within cities such as Halifax or outside them. The assembly also encouraged separate schools by voting small sums of money for them.[24]

Fugitive Former Slaves and Extradition

The most high-profile legal issue involving Blacks in Upper Canada, albeit one that came up rarely, was the extradition to the United States of fugitive slaves.[25] As we saw in chapter 28, extradition was not governed by any treaty prior to 1842, and by the Webster-Ashburton Treaty between Britain and the United States thereafter. From 1833 Upper Canada did have local legislation on extradition, the *Fugitive Offenders Act* of that year, which conferred authority on the lieutenant governor to send a fugitive out of the colony for trial elsewhere. The statute also confirmed the power granted in a similar much earlier Act to refuse removal 'if for any reason' it was considered 'inexpedient so to do.'[26] In the 1830s and early 1840s a small number of high-profile cases involving former slaves engendered much debate. The cases were precipitated by American requests for extradition of fugitive slaves so that they could be tried for criminal offences, invariably offences committed to aid escapes. Escaped slaves stole horses to speed their flight, or money or food to keep themselves alive. In the most famous case, that of John Anderson in 1860–1, the fugitive had forcibly resisted recapture with the result that a white man was killed.

When fugitive slave cases arose they brought into conflict a number of interest groups and legal issues in Upper Canada. Always resisting extradition was the Black community itself, which mobilized around the notion that slavery was an irredeemable evil and that nothing that a slave did to escape servitude could bring criminal liability. The leaders of this Black opposition to extradition were mostly members of the relatively affluent, well-educated, and articulate Toronto Black community.[27] One of their most consistently used arguments was an appeal to their loyalty to the Crown, of which past service was a tangible reminder. William Lyon Mackenzie disliked the fact that this meant support for the established hierarchy in Upper Canada and called Blacks 'extravagantly loyal.'[28] Blacks were invariably joined in their protests by the coterie of evangelicals from a variety of low Protestant groups who had involved themselves in the underground railroad and also in the British anti-slavery movement prior to 1833. After 1833 they turned their attention south of the border. The anti-slavery movement went into decline for some years but had revived by mid-century. George Brown, publisher of the *Globe*, was the moving force behind the Anti-Slavery Society of Canada, formed after the passage of the American *Fugitive Slave Act* of 1850. The anti-slavery movement could rally substantial numbers to its cause when necessary.

On the other side of the fugitive slave question were conservatives who were not necessarily in favour of slavery but feared an influx of free Blacks into the colony. Often caught in the middle of contentious public debates were officials on both sides of the Atlantic. British politicians wanted to maintain good relations with the United States, both generally and with regard to extradition, before and after the signing of the 1842 treaty. Yet those same politicians knew that public opinion was strongly opposed to extraditing fugitive slaves. On more than one occasion in the 1820s and 1830s the United States tried to have slaves included as a class in any formal extradition agreements that were negotiated, but Britain always refused. In 1828 British Foreign Secretary Lord Aberdeen told an American diplomat, 'British public opinion would not permit it.'[29] It bears emphasis that fugitive slaves were not infrequently an issue of contention between Britain and the United States before 1860, whether or not British North America was involved. In the famous 1842 case of the *Creole*, for example, American slaves being taken to New Orleans rebelled, took over the ship, and brought her to Nassau in the Bahamas. Britain refused to give up either the slaves or the mutineers.[30]

Officials in the colony, who had the discretion to agree to or refuse an extradition request, faced the same pressure to maintain good relations with the Americans and to placate considerable public outcry whenever a fugitive slave case arose. The fact that they did arise, and indeed that on two occasions, discussed below, extradition requests were granted, meant that the threat of extradition was an ever-present reality for the Black population. Black residents and their white allies consistently lobbied to have extradition of fugitive slaves prohibited, arguing that British justice and the tradition of a free British people required it, as did their loyalty. The latter argument was often used in the years surrounding the 1837–8 rebellions. Blacks never got the 'protected refugee status' they wanted; as the leading historian of extradition puts it, the arguments for a protected zone did not prevail over what were seen as the benefits of extradition generally, combined with 'a deep fear of escaping slaves.'[31]

The always complex and often inconsistent attitudes held by the majority white population on this question are revealed by four high-profile cases in the 1830s and early 1840s.[32] Extradition was refused in the cases of Thornton and Lucie Blackburn in 1833 and Jesse Happy in 1837, but the local government agreed to send back Solomon Moseby in 1837 and Nelson Hackett in 1842. In the event only Hackett was returned. Moseby escaped during a violent protest by local Black residents at the Niagara jail where he was being held, which forcibly prevented the sheriff from carrying out his orders. The imbroglio over Moseby caused the local government to refer the Happy case to London, which advised refusal of the extradition request. The rationale for not returning Happy was that he had left the horse he had stolen on the American side of the border, and hence had no criminal intent to steal. Happy thus did not remain free because he was privileged to do so as a fugitive ex-slave, although he and his supporters claimed such an exemption based on

British law and justice. A petition in his case, signed by nearly one hundred Black residents, noted that they had 'received the protection of the British Government and been admitted to the Privileges of British Subjects'; such privileges included, of course, freedom from enslavement. Praising Britain and its institutions was a standard trope for Black leaders in Upper Canada. As perhaps the most prominent of those leaders, Samuel Ringgold Ward, stated in his *Autobiography*, 'There is no country in the world so much hated by slaveholders, as Canada; nor is there any country so much beloved and sought for, by the slaves ... [because] it is a free country.' Petitions not only invoked Black loyalty and praised British justice, they also suggested that American justice could not be trusted. Accusations of theft contained manufactured evidence designed to get the person back across the border and re-enslave him or her.

These were all powerful arguments, but they encountered others, based on what has been termed 'the pervasive underlying anxieties about crystallizing refugee status in law for escaped slaves.' Governor Sir Charles Bagot captured these anxieties when he warned that a blanket exemption for escaped slaves would make Upper Canada 'an asylum for the very worst characters, provided only they had been slaves before arriving here.' Officials also employed legal arguments, countering the British justice claims of pro-Black lobbyists by insisting that under British law all races were treated equally; it would thus be wrong to provide a special status for former slaves. Chief Justice Robinson exemplified both the legalistic approach – extradition required reciprocity to work properly – and the pragmatic view that did not see anti-slavery as something that concerned British North America to any great degree. If extradition requests were not granted 'on both sides' they would 'soon cease to be acted upon on either side.' The fact that slavery was concerned did not overturn this principle. It may have been 'a great evil,' but it was legal in many countries, including the United States.

Only one fugitive slave case arose under the Webster-Ashburton Treaty, the best-known such case in Canadian legal history.[33] John Anderson escaped from his owner's plantation in Missouri in 1853 and shortly afterwards killed a white man, Seneca Digges, who was trying to apprehend him. He made his way to Upper Canada where, six years later, he was arrested, the story having become widely known. A hearing took place before Brantford JP William Mathews, following which Anderson was committed to jail to await the governor's order to return him to Missouri.[34] Anderson's Hamilton lawyer, Samuel Freeman, after corresponding with a sympathetic but publicly silent attorney general, John A. Macdonald, brought a habeas corpus application before the Court of Queen's Bench. Nothing in the treaty required this – it was Macdonald's political decision to approve or not Anderson's removal – but he preferred to avoid responsibility by making the court decide. As it turned out three courts would hear the case, two in Upper Canada and one in London, before it was decided on a technicality.

Abolitionists in Britain and Upper Canada vigorously denounced the idea of sending someone back into slavery and certain execution, given Missouri law and attitudes towards Blacks. Prominent among the defenders of Anderson was Reform party leader George Brown, who seized on the issue as a stick with which to beat the Macdonald-Cartier coalition. The British government did not want to offend an increasingly bellicose and expansionist United States, but also knew that public opinion would not stomach Anderson's extradition. For its part the American federal government was insistent that the treaty be respected. Against this background Anderson appeared before the three judges of Queen's Bench – Chief Justice Robinson and puisne judges Archibald McLean and Robert Easton Burns – in November 1860.

Freeman represented Anderson, relying on the lack of double criminality, the principle, contained in the treaty, that the act for which extradition was sought had to be a criminal act in both jurisdictions. Murder, of course, was a local crime, but Freeman's argument was that any act committed by a slave to aid escape was one of self-defence and could not be a crime in a jurisdiction in which slavery was not legal. This argument, 'based on expansive notions of both domestic and transnational natural law,' was, in effect, one for an exemption for slaves fleeing to freedom, the exemption that anti-slavery activists had argued for before the treaty. But though superficially similar to earlier claims, it was grounded quite differently. It did not simply rely on 'territorially bounded and historically based notions of British justice,' although it did invoke them. The emphasis was on natural rights and universal ideas about human freedom. Anderson had rights that derived from his status as a human being. It was a strategy designed to try to win the court battle, but if that failed Freeman would have laid the ground for a mobilization of public support that would exert substantial pressure on the executive to refuse extradition. The debates in Upper Canada over the earlier cases had shown that many in the assembly favoured a blanket asylum for escaped slaves, based on 'the same notions of the natural rights of man invoked by Freeman.'[35]

Robert Harrison, principal counsel for the Crown, argued that the issue was murder, not slavery. Digges was lawfully attempting to arrest Anderson under Missouri law and was prevented from doing so by an illegal act. When the court ruled on the case on 15 December 1860, it was just five days before South Carolina seceded from the Union, the first act in the civil war. Robinson and Burns ruled for the Crown. Robinson's judgment was straightforward, stressing the fact that Missouri law allowed any white man to detain a fugitive slave, and Digges had thus acted with legal authority, which Anderson had resisted with deadly force. Anderson thus came within the terms of the treaty, which contained no exemptions for fugitive slaves. Law could not assist him, only executive discretion.

The most remarkable judgment of the three was McLean's dissent. A veteran of the War of 1812 and a militia colonel who had participated actively in putting down the 1837 rebellion, McLean had been a Conservative member of the assembly and a member of the Family Compact, except for his Presbyterianism. His stature and connections won him appointment to King's Bench when it was expanded from three to five judges in 1837. In only one respect did he differ from his colleagues in the Toronto establishment – his religiously based fervent abolitionism.[36] McLean addressed procedural irregularities in the warrant of commitment, and the evidence presented by Missouri authorities. Most importantly, he attacked slavery and in doing so made Anderson's actions self-defence. Digges had gone after Anderson 'for the unholy purpose of riveting his chains more securely,' and in such circumstances Anderson 'was justified in using any degree of necessary force to prevent what to him must inevitably have proved a most fearful evil.' In Upper Canada resistance to enslavement was self-defence, and so it was in Missouri. His judgment, echoing the natural law arguments of Freeman, rejected the acceptance of any slave state laws in court: 'In administering the laws of a British province, I can never feel bound to recognise as law any enactment which can convert into chattels a very large number of the human race.'[37]

Anderson's case had been watched closely in England by the colonial secretary and the anti-slavery lobby, and the news of the court decision brought an outcry in the press and other circles. Acting Governor Sir William Fenwick Williams was ordered not to complete the extradition process, but the Anti-Slavery Society, not knowing what the government had done and not trusting them, applied for a writ of habeas corpus to the Court of Queen's Bench in London. There is not space here to discuss how this was possible, but habeas corpus was granted and Anderson ordered to appear before the court in London.[38] A further imbroglio ensued over British interference in colonial internal matters, which proved an embarrassment to many before Freeman and Sir William Draper, chief justice of Common Pleas, combined on a solution. In February 1861 Freeman asked for, and Draper granted, another writ of habeas corpus, meaning there would be another hearing in Toronto, this time in the Court of Common Pleas. It will be recalled from chapter 22 that Queen's Bench and Common Pleas were both common law courts and had concurrent jurisdiction.

Anderson's case was thus heard by three different judges, two of whom, William Buell Richards and John Hagarty, were relatively young and had been Liberals in their political careers. Even more importantly, Draper, the de facto leader of the Conservatives in the 1840s, had argued in 1842 in the legislative debate over Nelson Hackett's extradition that it was not clear to him that a slave could ever be held criminally liable for an act committed while escaping. When the habeas corpus case was heard in Toronto, Freeman had a co-counsel, Conservative assembly member John Hillyard Cameron.[39] They argued, as they had before Queen's Bench, that slavery was inconsistent with natural law and thus that acts done in escaping to freedom could not bring criminal liability. The common pleas judges were both ambivalent about, but in the end very wary of, such an argument. Draper feared the consequences of a blanket asylum, but at the same time was reluctant to surrender a slave who 'as his sole means of obtaining liberty, has shed the blood of the merciless taskmaster who held him in bondage.' Hagarty was similarly unwilling to endorse a broad amnesty, but he thought the Crown's argument that slave status was irrelevant could 'readily be pushed to extravagant results.' He used the example of a woman violently resisting rape by a white man in a jurisdiction where rape of a slave was legal. Ultimately the common pleas judges accepted none of Freeman's and Cameron's arguments, but released Anderson because of errors in magistrate Mathews's arrest warrant; in particular, it did not say 'murder' but used the word 'kill.' The judges thus found a way to release Anderson and assuage public opinion, and to some extent their consciences, while not conceding either that natural law trumped the words of a treaty or that all fugitive slaves were immune from any prosecution once they reached free territory.[40] Anderson was paraded through the Toronto streets in triumph, left shortly afterwards for a lecture tour in England, and eventually relocated to Liberia. In many respects the Anderson case typified the attitudes towards Blacks of mid-nineteenth-century white British North Americans. There was much rejoicing that he was not extradited, but, as we have seen, a much more tempered approach to other aspects of the Black experience. As one historian has succinctly summarized attitudes expressed in Upper Canada newspapers at mid-century, they demonstrated 'a hatred of slavery, ... pathos-driven sympathy for the slave, a casual and hegemonic racism, and indifference to the legal status of African Americans who were not slaves.'[41]

Labour and the Law

In most of British North America the law governing employment relations was the law of contract, albeit a law of contracts whose terms varied according to the type of worker and relied on penal sanctions to enforce contractual terms against employees but not employers.[42] This made the law different, in theory if not that much in practice, to U.S. law, where the employment relationship was 'at-will' – employer and employee could both terminate it at any time for any reason. The law of the employment contract – or, as it was still known for most of this period by its eighteenth-century name, master and servant law – was an amalgam of common law and statute. Broadly speaking, the former fixed the rights and obligations and provided some remedies, and the latter provided additional remedies. The principal rights and obligations were that the servant provided faithful service and obeyed instructions, and the employer provided wages. The principal common law remedy was a civil suit for breach of contract, which meant unpaid wages or desertion or wrongful dismissal, and the successful party would obtain a damages award. The common law would not order an employment contract to be specifically performed – actually carried out – at the behest of either party. The principal statutory remedy was provided by master and servant Acts. They provided that the employee could take the employer before a JP for mistreatment or lack of pay or wrongful dismissal, and the employer could prosecute the employee for failure to work. Remedies under the Acts were broader than at common law. Workers who were found to have been mistreated could obtain a release from their contractual obligations. Employers were given a more powerful weapon. The Acts made breach of contract by an employee a criminal offence, punishable by fine or imprisonment. In effect this meant specific performance, because magistrates typically gave servants the option of avoiding these sanctions by returning to work. The fact that criminal sanctions were available to masters highlighted in stark terms the fact that 'the employment contract was one between unequals.'[43]

The master and servant legislation of the Maritimes, discussed in the previous part, stayed in force through the first half of the nineteenth century. It provided for imprisonment for workers who refused to honour their contracts, but in practice this was ancillary to the main purpose of achieving specific performance. A New Brunswick statute of 1826 was an exception; it specified jail as the 'routine punishment' for worker breaches. Master and servant legislation was complemented by vagrancy Acts, which provided for the imprisonment of 'refractory' or 'runaway' apprentices, and by merchant seamen Acts, which similarly prescribed prison terms.[44] Indeed some 85 per cent of the employment-related cases before the Halifax Police Court between 1846 and 1858 involved merchant seamen, not surprisingly, given the city's status as a major international seaport. Local legislation on seamen permitted these cases to be heard in lower courts rather than the Court of Vice Admiralty. The preponderance of sailor and apprentice cases in the courts was reflected in the fact that when the colony's statutes were revised in 1851, the old master and servant Act was repealed and replaced by one dealing only with apprentices and other minors, merchant seamen being covered in other legislation.[45] The leading historian of master and servant argues that legislation in the Maritime colonies reflected its eighteenth-century origins in its 'reliance on performance remedies' and on 'the enforcement of long-term and long-distance bargains.' Coercive laws were not used against land-based workers; 'the whip of hunger was a more important enforcer of employment bargains than the justice of the peace.'[46]

Lower Canada was an anomaly among the colonies in not having master and servant legislation.[47] Employment contracts were among the many types of contracts drawn up frequently by notaries, and the fact that notaries kept these contracts meant that there was a kind of registry of them, which offered an additional source of protection for both parties. Employment law fell between the civil law of obligations, and criminal law, and as a result the assembly could not agree on general legislation, even though some public regulation was passed, including provisions permitting the imprisonment of workers. An Act of 1802 allowed the quarter sessions in each of the three principal districts to make regulations governing apprentices, domestic servants, and employees, provided fines did not exceed ten pounds or imprisonment of two months. The Montreal JPs did so and regularly amended them, and the regulations stayed in force after local government by sessions was replaced by an elected council in 1833. Different rules were made for country parishes in the 1820s and 1830s. Over time the urban regulations became more punitive, with the mandatory penalty for most kinds of indiscipline imprisonment and a fine, while the rules in the countryside were much more lenient. Yet even in the cities enforcement was lax; the JPs generally ordered the worker to return to work. There was a greater tendency, however, to sentence to prison terms two groups of workers who had their own legislation dating from the late eighteenth century – seamen and voyageurs – probably because their contract performance could not be monitored by a court.[48] On the other side of the equation, employees were more often than not successful in suits for unpaid wages.

In the first half of the nineteenth century some Upper Canadian lawyers assumed that the English master and servant Acts were in force in that colony by virtue of the general reception statute of 1792. The principal proponent of this view was William Conway Keele, author of the first local JP manual for the colony.[49] Yet only five reported cases mention the English Acts, and collectively they are equivocal about a wholesale reception of the English law, although they do suggest that some parts of some English statutes were in force. Research has unearthed only one reported case of a prosecution in Upper Canada under those statutes. The issue was never clearly resolved, but in 1846, in *Shea v Choat*, Chief Justice Robinson came very close to declaring English statutes not to have been received, on the ground that they were 'inapplicable to this province.'[50] That decision prompted the legislature to pass a local master and servant Act in 1847. It made written contracts for employment of any duration, and oral contracts of up to a year, binding on both parties. Employees who refused orders, or quit their jobs, or damaged an employer's property, could be arrested and brought before a JP, who would conduct a summary hearing and impose either a fine of up to five pounds or a sentence of up to a month in prison. Employers who violated the law by 'misusage, refusal of necessary provisions, cruelty ill-treatment or non-payment of wages' could be summoned to appear before a JP, not arrested, and issued orders to pay unpaid wages and see their servants released from their employment contract. They could not be imprisoned or fined, although they could have their property seized to meet their monetary obligations.[51] Ironically the Act followed English legislation very closely, despite Robinson's belief that the latter was 'inapplicable.'

A further near identical statute of 1851 was passed for apprentices, and an amending statute of 1855 confirmed that the 1847 Act applied to skilled tradesmen.[52] The 1847 Act, although it did not specify any particular occupations, was aimed primarily at two groups of workers – domestic servants and those in the lumber industry. It was these two groups who 'epitomised the interrelated difficulties of supply and discipline that constituted the "labour problem" of the mid-nineteenth century.'[53] The limited numbers of domestic servants, the high wages they were able to demand as a result, and their 'insubordinate' attitudes, their lack of appropriate deference, were constant complaints by the propertied, who also saw how easy it was for many immigrant workers to move on to the United States. This concern was why many supported the Wakefieldian colonization schemes discussed in chapter 30, one of their objects being the creation of a permanent and quiescent labour force of British origin. The other group of workers whose refractory behaviour worried the respectable middle classes were the Irishmen who toiled in the Ottawa valley lumber industry and on the canal-building projects of the 1830s and 1840s. Internecine disputes among these groups, and between them and their employers and local communities, often led to violent clashes and inspired 1845 legislation 'for the better preservation of the Peace, and the prevention of Riots.'[54] Indeed it was principally to help employers in this sector that the 1847 legislation was enacted.

The 1847 Act was quite frequently used, both by employers in desertion cases and by workers suing for unpaid wages, discussed immediately below. In both towns and rural areas master and servant cases comprised a little under 10 per cent of all matters dealt with summarily by magistrates, with over a third of such cases being for desertion. Almost 90 per cent of workers prosecuted were convicted, although a fine rather than imprisonment was much the preferred sentence (84 per cent of those convicted). The overall result was that workers who breached the Act represented fewer than 1 per cent of all those in jail in the twenty years prior to Confederation. If we add to that the fact that many charges were settled or withdrawn before actually being heard by a JP, it is clear that imprisonment was little used in everyday employment relations.[55] As important as the volume of cases, however, was the symbolism of the law. The master and servant Act took legal principles originating in early modern England and declared them still applicable in the mid-nineteenth century in the most populous and most economically advanced region of British North America. It was, according to its principal historian, an 'act of policy' rooted in 'ambivalence about wage labour' in a society only slowly transitioning from an employment relationship tied to family, community, and status to one reflecting the values of an industrializing economy. The paradox of harsh statutory law – imprisonment of refractory workers – and rare and mild enforcement suggests strongly that the master and servant Acts were as much symbolic as they were of practical utility.[56]

The criminal sanction available for punishing workers who broke their contracts was the most dramatic part of the law, but the law governing recovery of unpaid wages was also important. In most colonies there were no tailor-made remedies available; unpaid wages were simply debts, recoverable through the same process as any other debt. Thus the monetary limits that determined the jurisdiction of superior and lower courts prescribed whether a worker could go to a JP or other inferior tribunal for a cheap and expeditious remedy, or whether the higher courts were the venue. Until 1834 workers in Lower Canada had to take claims to either the superior or inferior terms of King's Bench, depending on whether the suit was over ten pounds, and from that year wage claims outside of the major cities could be taken to a commissioners' (small claims) court for summary adjudication, albeit only up to a smaller amount.[57] But workers in Montreal, Quebec City, and Trois Rivières never had this facility available to them. Upper Canada's 1847 master and servant Act made summary process for wages available in that colony. As noted immediately above, over 60 per cent of cases brought before JPs were brought by workers for unpaid wages. Some 90 per cent of such claims were successful, in the sense that employers settled the claim or were ordered to pay. But they were invariably given time to pay, and sometimes absconded, with the result that the actual wage recovery rate was very considerably lower.

Seamen's experiences of the law were different. In the early decades of this period they came within the purview of courts of vice admiralty. In 1836 Lower Canada allowed disputes of up to twenty pounds to be taken before two JPs, and New Brunswick and Nova Scotia enacted similar reforms in the 1830s and 1840s.[58] Magistrates' courts in the principal ports in the Maritimes also handled desertion cases involving seamen and convicted five-sixths of those charged. Imprisonment until the ship was ready to sail was a common punishment.[59]

A different law governed labour relations in the HBC territories.[60] The English master and servant Acts were notionally in force, but it was HBC policies that governed locally. Those policies, contained in company circulars that listed offences, included imprisonment for employees in breach. But desertion was hardly a viable option for European employees in such remote locations, and employee discontent was more often manifested by drunkenness and insolence. Factor's responses varied from fines to suspension of privileges to whippings, although imprisonment within the fort was resorted to at times. On the Pacific coast the 1858 reception statute, discussed in chapter 26, made the British master and servant Acts in force.

Turning from individual to collective action, the number of unions grew slowly in the first few decades of the nineteenth century, often facing aggressive and recalcitrant employers when workers combined to demand higher wages.[61] They also faced legal opposition. Although it remains unclear how widespread the view was accepted, there were judges in Britain and in British North America who believed that combinations of workers were a criminal conspiracy to restrain trade.[62] Yet prosecutions for such conspiracies were relatively rare, often resulted in acquittals or, if the workers were convicted, modest fines. The uncertainty about the common law legality of unions persisted until just after Confederation, when the federal Parliament emphatically legislated their legality. Before then serious legal restraints were enacted in some colonial statutes, especially an 1864 Nova Scotia Act 'relating to the combination of workmen,' which barred unions from trying to raise wages or reduce hours not just by violent means but also by 'in any way obstructing' an employer.[63] The Act was passed in response to a hard fought strike by Sydney coal miners; it does not seem to have been employed in practice but does reveal clear distrust of unions.

34

Less Favoured by Law II: Women and the Law

Little changed in the non-statutory – common, civil, and Indigenous – law determining the status and rights of women during most of this period. The common law of property, for example, treated single women formally as near-juridical equals to men but not married women, and that began to change, incrementally, only in the 1850s. The case of Mary Whibby of St John's, Newfoundland, perfectly illustrates the common law. In 1853 Mary and her four children were abandoned by her husband, James, and for the fifteen remaining years of her life she took in washing and scrimped and saved to make ends meet. She even saved a nest egg of some $1,000, which was personal, not real property. Thus when she died in 1868 James Whibby came back and claimed the money. Since the common law gave married women no independent entitlement to personal property, the claims of a son to it as her heir were unavailing. Chief Justice Sir Hugh William Hoyles thought the common law rule harsh in such a case, but it was the law, and James Whibby got his ex-wife's earnings.[1] To similar effect, but involving land, was the case of Hannah Nolan, whose father, John Snider, gave her a life estate in fifty acres of land when she married Henry Nolan of Colchester, Upper Canada, in 1824. Since this was real property, it did not become her husband's at common law, but he did get the right to manage it and take the income from it. He soon abandoned his wife but continued to take the profits for thirty years until he died. Hannah stayed in the area, 'dependent more or less on the charities of those ... acquainted with her.'[2]

Women, and men, other than Indigenous men and women, also had very limited access to divorce, and settler husbands had complete control over custody of children when a marriage ended through divorce or separation.[3] Married women had minimal rights to property owned by their husbands, whether acquired before or after marriage, and even the death of her husband who owned land left a married woman with a dower right only. Even if women were lucky enough to escape a bad marriage with the mutual consent of their husbands, any agreement they might make was fragile, not enforceable, because the common law did not recognize contracts between husband and wife. Married couples who separated could enter valid separation agreements regarding property and living arrangements, but any subsequent reconciliation voided the agreement. In addition, any provisions purporting to interfere with the father's right to custody were unenforceable. This chapter will examine each of the issues raised here, and others, beginning with the common law of married women's property. There follow sections on the common law affecting unmarried mothers and divorce, and on the civil law, both generally and as it also dealt with unmarried parents.

Common Law Married Women's Property: Equity and Statutory Change

We saw in chapter 22 that courts of equity in eighteenth-century England and in the Maritime colonies permitted property to be conveyed to trustees for the 'separate use' of a wife, and the introduction of the Court of Chancery in Upper Canada made trusts creating a woman's separate estate available in that jurisdiction also. Before 1837 any trusts for women probably had to rely on voluntary compliance or ad hoc arbitration.[4] But in practical terms chancery was generally, although not exclusively, available only to women from wealthy families. Thus Simon Bradstreet Robie, Nova Scotia's master of the rolls from 1826 to 1834, and a man who would therefore have known what he was doing, left £400 to his married daughter in his will, with a direction to his trustee 'to dispose of it for her own use.' His trustee happened to be his wife's father, the colony's chief justice, Brenton Halliburton. Another judge, Jonathan McCully of the NSSC, set up a testamentary trust for the 'separate use' of his married daughter.[5] Aside from being a useful tool for the rich, trusts were also used by widows who had assets from a former marriage or from their period of widowhood that they wished to preserve on remarriage, and by women whose husbands' occupations included plasterer, truckman, and bookkeeper. But judging by the amount of litigation over them, they were used sparingly.[6] The vast majority of women, who did not own land or enjoy trust funds set up for them by their fathers, had no right to their personal property, even if it was in the form of wages earned from employment, as was the case with Mary Whibby. Moreover, trusts for separate use appear to have been employed in a more conservative way than in England or the United States. In those jurisdictions the role of the trustee had become largely symbolic by the nineteenth century, and married women exercised effective control over their separate property. Not so in Upper Canada, where trustees retained their managerial powers. In every case, reported and unreported, one study has shown, settlements involved active trustees.[7]

The Upper Canadian Court of Chancery could also grant judicial separation and alimony awards to women.[8] This was a jurisdiction exercised in England by the ecclesiastical courts, which could grant divorces *a mensa et thoro*, literally 'from bed and board.' It effectively meant separation but without the right to remarry. There were no ecclesiastical courts in British North America, but from 1837 chancery in Upper Canada could grant alimony awards, because the statute that created the court gave it jurisdiction over 'all cases of claim for alimony that is exercised ... by any Ecclesiastical or other Court in England.'[9] The local chancery court could have refused to make alimony awards, as the ecclesiastical courts gave alimony only as an adjunct to separation, and the statute did not allow for divorces *a mensa et thoro*. But the chancellors exercised the alimony jurisdiction where there had been an informal separation. Their power to do so was explicitly challenged in an 1851 case in which the husband's lawyer did not contest evidence of physical abuse that made it impossible for the wife to live with him, but argued that the court had no jurisdiction to grant alimony. Chancellor Blake rejected that argument, while also commenting that 'the state of the law' on the court's power was 'highly unsatisfactory.'[10] Blake was trying to push the legislature into action, which was eventually forthcoming in 1859, a statute explicitly providing that if a wife proved adultery, cruelty, or desertion she could claim alimony from the court.[11] As with trusts creating separate estates, alimony suits involved only women from relatively wealthy backgrounds. Suing for alimony was time-consuming and costly, and worth doing only if the husband had resources to pay and a wife took the risk that he would actually do so. On the other hand, the chancellors sided with the women plaintiffs in nearly every case that actually made it to trial.

Moving beyond equity, English law on married women's property did not change until the 1870s and 1880s, but in North America legislation altered the common law to some degree, starting in the 1840s in some of the United States and getting underway the following decade in British North America. This legislation served one or both of two purposes, neither of them being the granting of equal civil status and full autonomy to women within marriage. Legislation doing that would not come until after Confederation. Rather the pre-1867 legislation protected women and their children from the deleterious consequences of desertion or of the financial disaster that could result from a husband's commercial failure or his drunkenness, recklessness, or general profligacy. Such faults in the husband could lead both to his being unable to provide for the family and to his incurring debts that would impoverish the family when creditors seized his assets.[12]

The first such piece of reforming legislation in British North America was a New Brunswick statute of 1851, which responded to both forms of family crisis.[13] Section 1 of the Act provided that a married woman's property, whether acquired before or after marriage, was her 'separate property' and could not be seized to pay her husband's debts. Nor could it be 'conveyed, mortgaged, encumbered, or disposed of without her full consent.' The section did not confer dispositive powers on the woman alone, but she did need to consent to a conveyance or mortgage. The statute thus created a kind of common law separate estate for all women, one that protected family property and allowed women to use property they had brought into a marriage or earned or been given during the marriage to maintain their families, but not to alienate it nor to see it alienated by others. Not included in the exempt property was 'any property received by any married woman from her husband during coverture.' This exception was presumably designed to avoid fraudulent transfers made to evade debts.

The same statute enacted provisions pertaining to married women only 'in case of desertion or abandonment by her husband.' In such circumstances a married woman became juridically much closer to an unmarried one. She could 'sue for, recover and receive from any person or persons ... indebted to her in her separate capacity, for debts due and owing to her.' At common law she could not do so, because the debts would not be owing to her, but to her husband. Moreover, any release of such debts given by her husband after the desertion or abandonment would be ineffectual. Section 5 of the short, five-section statute completed the differentiation between most married women and married women whose husbands had deserted them or who were 'compelled to support' themselves. The latter, if they acquired money or other property by their own 'labour and exertions,' owned it absolutely. Such property was not liable for the debts of the husband, nor could it be controlled or interfered with in any way by the husband. It would be 'at her own sole disposal, free and clear of her ... husband.'

Over the next decade and a half all other jurisdictions enacted either a provision like the 'separate estate' one in New Brunswick, or one that was similar to that applying to 'deserted or abandoned' women, or both. Upper Canada passed legislation in 1859 that was somewhat confusing, but its bottom line was that a married woman's fully independent control over her property applied only if she obtained an order of protection from a court. Such protection orders could be granted in the event of a husband's lunacy, imprisonment, habitual drunkenness, or desertion. More wide-ranging changes had been in the original bill, but amendments pressed by Attorney General John A. Macdonald and Oliver Mowat made the final version more protective and less 'liberating.'[14] Prince Edward Island enacted a statute the following year, 1860, that was very similar to New Brunswick's 1851 Act. Vancouver Island passed legislation in 1862 that protected the earnings of a deserted wife from her husband or his creditors. Nova Scotia passed a similar statute in 1866, more radical bills having failed five times between 1855 and 1865. Newfoundland was the last jurisdiction to pass a protection Act, allowing a wife deserted by her husband to apply for a protection order to shield her property from her husband or his creditors. Unlike in the other colonies, only a wife whose husband had deserted her 'without reasonable cause' and who 'is maintaining herself by her own industry' was eligible to apply for an order.[15]

As one historian has aptly concluded, the goal of all this legislation was 'never ... to endow women with the right to financial autonomy.' It was 'far more limited – to provide temporary relief for families in crisis.'[16] But that still leaves us having to account for the timing, because families in crisis were hardly a new phenomenon in the 1850s and 1860s. Economic factors undoubtedly played a role. American historians have attributed the first wave of married women's property law reform in the 1840s to the nationwide depression that set in in 1837.[17] Similarly, the years immediately prior to 1851 were a period of an economic crisis in New Brunswick caused by the ending of the British tariff preference for colonial timber. The economic downturn led to other radical measures in the colony, including, as we have seen, an attempt to slash judicial salaries.[18] The years 1857 and 1858 witnessed a financial crisis in Canada West, while the 1862 Vancouver Island legislation followed immediately after the boom and bust of the Fraser River gold rush. The island's population swelled to 20,000 in the late 1850s and then plummeted to 3,000. Although much of the population increase derived from an influx of single males, always the case with frontier and resource communities, the exodus included many male heads of households. Indeed the island statute's very title – *An Act to Protect the Property of a Wife Deserted by Her Husband* – made its motivation abundantly clear. It was followed just four years later by the *Homestead Ordinance* of 1866, which protected the family unit by making homes exempt from seizure by creditors.[19]

The trade cycle, however, does not wholly account for all this legislation. It derived in part from the efforts of the small and generally marginal women's movement of the second quarter of the nineteenth century. A series of petitions from women were presented to the province of Canada assembly between 1852 and 1857, for example. One complained that on marriage 'a woman ... is instantly deprived of all civil rights' and asserted that it was wrong to give husbands such 'absolute power.'[20] The women's campaign for change in the 1850s may not have been extensive, but it did represent 'the first organized effort of women ... to improve their ... status.'[21] Reform demands were couched in language similar to that used in other areas such as criminal punishment and imprisonment for debt. The common law was 'too much tinctured with the old doctrine of the feudal ages.'[22] Women's demands reached their crescendo in 1857, with a petition of 1,300 married women to the legislative council. The assembly had passed a version of the bill that eventually became law, but it ran out of time in the upper house.

The fact that the 1850s and 1860s were decades of law and legal system reform in many areas, discussed elsewhere in this part, was doubtless also significant. Lawmakers and their confreres in the middle and professional classes were willing to try new approaches through legislation in areas ranging from court procedure to sectoral incorporation to insolvency to policing, and much more. Lawyers were to the fore among the men supporting change. Married women's property law was no exception to this upsurge in the demand for legal change. It is also important to bear in mind that these reforms represented a way to protect what many, including probably many women, saw as the bulwark of the social order, the family, in times of profound change. The protection of the family unit, through preserving the family assets, was the major goal, and as some historians have pointed out, this fact may well show that women and men were not that unhappy with the common law, provided it operated properly. What was in one sense a highly patriarchal regime also viewed the husband as a person with responsibilities as well as rights, and the family as a community, as 'an economic unit.' What to modern eyes was liberating change was 'a potential threat to the common familial interest.'[23]

The chief sponsors and principal proponents of law reform in this area were elite men concerned to protect families, including those of their own children, from economies and husbands gone wrong. The first proposal for reform in Nova Scotia, for example, came in the form of a bill introduced in the legislative council in 1855, a decade before legislation was passed, by the aforementioned Jonathan McCully, a man who made a trust settlement for his married daughter. His bill would have created separate family property for all women and given those deserted by or not adequately supported by their husbands a right to carry on business and sue and be sued in their own name. McCully was a strong temperance advocate and appealed to other men who might have seen members of their extended family suffer from a drunkard's excess. He also made it clear that he was 'no defender of what are sometimes called the rights of women.' He saw law reform as necessary to help any woman who was 'satisfied with the social position which God and nature designed for her,' which was 'retired from the noise and warfare of society, in which men engage.'[24] To similar effect Malcolm Cameron, the principal advocate for reform in Canada West and an ardent temperance campaigner, bluntly stated, 'The object was to relieve married women from imposition and injustice on the part of their worthless, drunken husbands.'[25] The preamble to Upper Canada's statute proclaimed that married women's property law 'is frequently productive of great injustice' and that it was 'highly desirable' to amend it 'for the better protection of' women.[26]

Included in the group of advantaged men intent on protecting families were, of course, superior court judges, and they tended to support the legislation with generous and purposive interpretations. A suit launched by Mrs Abell of Saint John provides an excellent case in point. Her husband had become insane after a series of setbacks and was confined in the provincial lunatic asylum. Left destitute, she supported herself and her three children by running a boarding house. In 1867 one of her boarders refused to pay, and she sued him in her own name. He argued that she could not do so: the 1851 statute permitted this only when there had been desertion or abandonment, and technically that had not happened. The defendant had a point, but not one that Chief Justice William Johnstone Ritchie, later one of the first judges appointed to the new Supreme Court of Canada, was prepared to agree with. If he did so he would place Mrs Abell in 'a helpless position' and 'entirely frustrate the humane intention of the Legislature.'[27]

Ritchie was prepared to interpret legislation liberally when doing so enhanced its protective aims, and most judges supported it only to this extent. They did not resolve ambiguity in favour of women's autonomy. A prime example is provided by Common Pleas Chief Justice William Draper of Upper Canada. In a case decided just a year after the legislation had been passed, he interpreted the Act as not altering the common law rule that marriage brought about 'an absolute gift in law to the husband, of all the goods and chattels and personal property of the wife.' The section made that property exempt only from seizure for his debts and not available for him to dispose of; marriage still put the property 'in the hands, and under the protection, of the husband.'[28] This interpretation has been called one that went against 'the clear wording of the statute.'[29] But the statute was not that clearly worded, and Draper's interpretation was defensible and, more importantly, in line with seeing the statute as essentially protective, not liberating, for women. Indeed the fact that the legislation represented the state deciding that it should intervene to protect women as defenders of the family unit, and in the process the family itself, did represent 'a significant break with traditional notions of male authority.'[30] Married women's property law reform was a complex, multifaceted matter.

Given that, it is perhaps suitable to end with more complexity, the much less reasonable and clear undermining of the purpose of the legislation, by Draper in an 1865 case, *Lett v Commercial Bank of Canada*. Fanny Lett's father had given her a farm and the rents and profits it generated, 'for her separate use.' Her husband managed the farm, fell into debt, and the bank seized livestock and farming equipment. Mrs Lett's lawyer argued that this was improper, because the seized assets had been bought with farm income and should as a result be protected from paying off the husband's debts under the statute. Draper rejected this argument, concluding that the assets were the husband's. In a judgment showing his fear that 'protection' could widen into a wife in control of the farm and, indirectly, of the husband, he wrote, 'The evidence shews the farm is worked by the husband, and without any evidence he is to be deemed the head of the establishment.... I am not inclined to hold that because the wife has a separate estate, we are to treat the husband as her agent, clerk or farm bailiff, having the interest of a servant or employee, nor ... that he is a mere dependent on her bounty, and owns none of the property which he or those working on the place use in its cultivation.'[31] On the whole, judges, whether sitting in common law or chancery courts, interpreted the legislation of the 1850s and 1860s as protective, not as fundamentally changing women's status. In doing so they showed themselves to be conservative about change, but not greatly more so than the legislators. Judges and legislators alike were also concerned that more liberalising legislation might be used by married couples to collude to defraud creditors, something that did happen later when further reforms were enacted in the 1870s.[32]

The Common Law: Unmarried Parents

The law was also of little help to woman who found themselves the subject of another form of misfortune, unmarried motherhood. The only change to the eighteenth-century system occurred in Newfoundland, where a local statute allowed an unmarried mother to enforce an order for support to the tune of twenty pounds; the Act was motivated by a desire to avoid the child becoming 'chargeable to the Colony.' It was passed in the same session as another statute, which sought to enforce the responsibility that all parents had to support their children and all husbands had to support their wives.[33] Unmarried mothers in all common law colonies did have recourse to the tort of seduction.[34] Seduction was an action taken by the father of an unwed mother against her paramour for the loss of 'services' of the daughter who was pregnant or who had given birth. At common law the plaintiff father had to prove that the defendant had had sexual intercourse with his daughter, that she became pregnant and gave birth as a result, and as a result of that pregnancy the father was deprived of her services and had to pay the expenses of childbirth and childcare. On the surface, therefore, it was not a tort designed to punish either the man or the woman for their immorality, or to ensure that a child was supported by the father. It reflected a father's right to enjoy the labour of his daughters, something akin to a property right in the daughter. This interpretation is reinforced by the fact that the action was also available to masters for the seduction of their female servants. At the same time, a seduction action did bring a degree of moral opprobrium to the father of the child, and moral vindication to the plaintiff and his family, and it did function, indirectly, as a form of child support, assuming that householders did indeed support their daughters' offspring by expending financial resources they might not otherwise have.

Although the tort of seduction in its English origins was concerned principally with loss of services, over time in British North America it came to be seen as being more about avenging and recompensing family dishonour. Plaintiffs increasingly made brief, pro forma allegations about services and highlighted the emotional distress of dishonour stemming from loss of chastity. This shift was exemplified by the 1837 Upper Canada *Seduction Act*, which made the tort action available to a parent 'notwithstanding such unmarried female [daughter] was at the time of her seduction serving or residing with any other person.' The Act also dispensed with the need to prove that services had been provided by the daughter to the parents; that fact was to be 'in all cases presumed, and no proof shall be received to the contrary.'[35] The second half of the Act's title – 'to Render the Fathers of Illegitimate Children Liable for Their Support' – reveals a second motive. Section 4 declared its intention to place constraints on 'the unfeeling conduct of persons who refuse to make provision for the support of their illegitimate children.' The section went on to provide that anybody who provided necessaries for an illegitimate child could sue the father for their value.

The *Seduction Act*, not repealed until 1978, was unique among common law jurisdictions in enacting this change to the common law and reflected the growing reality that more and more young women worked for wages as well as contributing domestic labour at home. Queen's Bench Judge Jonas Jones was in no doubt that 'the great mischief ... relieved against by the statute' was 'the seduction of unmarried females by their masters.'[36] He and others thus saw it as an indirect method of redressing sexual exploitation. The Act also attracted praise from an English traveller of 1838, Anna Jameson, who approved making fathers responsible for illegitimate children just a few years after the United Kingdom had substantially removed such responsibility.[37] Jones and others also stressed the Act's egalitarian nature, giving a remedy to labouring parents whose children had to work outside the home, a somewhat ironic stance in that the tort remained fundamentally rooted in a daughter's status as quasi-chattel through the fact that the parent had to bring the action, and the presumption that parents were entitled to, and did receive, services from their daughters. Jones and others were not wrong; a substantial preponderance of seduction suits involved female servants.[38] Although no other colony passed a similar statute, in 1852 Prince Edward Island went even further, legislating a fundamental change – the woman seduced could bring an action herself. Its effect was largely nullified two years later, however, by a perverse ruling by highly conservative Supreme Court Judge James Horsfield Peters. He held that before a woman could sue in her own name, she had to establish that at the time of the seduction she had a parent, guardian, or master who could have sued successfully at common law.[39]

Seduction actions were launched in every colony and numbered in the hundreds.[40] They were most numerous in Upper Canada, in part because of its greater population and in part because of the *Seduction Act*. Plaintiffs came from the working and middle classes, and awards were often substantial, averaging around £100 in the first half of the nineteenth century and $400 in the second. The men from artisanal, mercantile, and farming backgrounds on civil trial juries who determined whether a seduction had taken place and what the damages should be tended to find for plaintiffs, and this must have encouraged the use of the action.

The tort was regularly employed despite the fact that judges, who had to decide points of law, tended to make narrow rulings that went against plaintiffs, as Peters did. Judges did so because they thought the seduction action encouraged female immorality and dishonesty. William Draper, chief justice of Upper Canada's Queen's Bench, put it this way: 'I am not inclined to extend the operation of the Seduction Act by what may be deemed a large and liberal construction. My own observation as a judge has by no means led me to think that it has had a favourable influence on female morals.' Women succumbed too easily, not just to male blandishments but also to the 'probable prospect of recovering large damages.'[41] Thus, despite the apparently plain words of the statute, a number of cases held that the need to prove loss of services remained.[42] Damages for injury to family honour were available but only if loss of services was established. Yet for all this, the action remained 'remarkably popular,' a conclusion derived from a survey of not just reported cases but archival records from a number of Upper Canadian counties.[43] The *Seduction Act* did indeed make the action much more viable than elsewhere, whatever judges wrote for the law reports.

Divorce

Women in all settler societies looked in vain to the law for help if their marriages did not work out as they had planned or their husbands subjected them to financial hardship.[44] The law on divorce changed very little from the eighteenth century. As we saw in chapter 19, in 1815 divorce was difficult to obtain in Nova Scotia and New Brunswick, nearly impossible anywhere else. In Upper Canada, and also in Nova Scotia, it was possible to obtain a divorce through a private Act of the assembly, although such acts were extremely rare. The first legislative divorce was not granted in Upper Canada until 1841, only three more followed before Confederation, and no woman got one until 1877.[45] The only two changes to divorce law were, first, that Prince Edward Island legislated judicial divorce in 1833, although the Act ran into trouble in London and was not law until resubmitted and approved in 1835. The island statute was almost identical to New Brunswick's 1791 Act, permitting divorce on the grounds of adultery, impotence, consanguinity, and 'frigidity.'[46] Second, when the Pacific coast colonies were established they received the law of England, which after 1857 meant the *Matrimonial Causes Act* of that year. It permitted judicial divorce but employed a double standard. Husbands could divorce wives on the ground of adultery alone, but a wife had to prove adultery and some other aggravating cause, such as incest or bigamy.[47] Beyond these changes, there was no alteration of the existing divorce laws. The one attempt to widen the grounds for divorce, by the Nova Scotia Assembly in 1834, was thwarted by the council. The bill would have widened the definition of cruelty to include 'willful and continued desertion and absence of the husband from the Province and his withholding necessary maintenance ... for ... Seven Years.'[48]

Even though judicial divorce was available in the Maritime and Pacific colonies, it was rarely sought and even more rarely granted. Both men and women sued for divorce, in roughly equal but very small numbers. In Nova Scotia, for example, it is likely that only one divorce petition per year was filed in this period, and they were not all successful.[49] Nova Scotia also saw one parliamentary divorce.[50] In New Brunswick there were about the same number of divorce petitions, but the spottiness of the records leaves unclear how many were granted.[51] On Prince Edward Island only two were definitely granted before 1867, although the lack of records does not necessarily mean those were the only two.[52] Women's inability to escape marriages they no longer wanted was seriously impaired by the law and practice of divorce. Not only did they have to prove a 'ground' – mere incompatibility was never enough – judges tended to find that a husband's adultery was not sufficient grounds by itself, even if the law formally said that it was. Women were most likely to succeed when they alleged, and were able to prove, significant physical violence. Of twenty-two cases with female petitioners, only four alleged adultery alone, the others always found some way to work in a claim of cruelty to aggravate the offence.[53] This is not to say that violence towards wives was not largely tolerated. Studies of divorce petitions, somewhat ironically, are one of our best sources for evidence of such indifference to domestic violence. Also revealing is the response of James Stephen Junior, the principal Colonial Office official of the 1830s and 1840s, when he received a petition that Newfoundland Supreme Court Judge John Bourne should be dismissed. Among his many faults was that he beat his wife, and while Stephen thought such behaviour 'disgraceful,' he also minuted that wife-beating 'can hardly be said to disqualify a man from being a Judge.'[54]

The Civil Law: Married Women's Property

The civil law treated married women in some ways similarly to – and in some respects differently from – the common law. While strongly committed to marital authority, it took the wife's role as an economic partner in marriage more seriously than did the common law, leading Bettina Bradbury to make a distinction between the 'collaborative patriarchy' of the civil law and the 'liberal patriarchy' of the common law's respective marital property regimes.[55] Divorce, available only by private Act, as in Upper Canada, was virtually unknown in Lower Canada: only four were granted between 1852 and 1886.[56] Marital authority remained a key legal concept disempowering wives and was codified in articles 175–84 of the *Civil Code* of 1866. Escaping from a violent or troubled marriage was not easy and voluntary separation was not authorized by law; parties nonetheless entered such agreements, but they would have been unenforceable if brought before a court. As noted in chapter 9, judicial separation was available but hardly used prior to 1815. Thereafter it was sought a little more frequently, but not until the 1850s were there even three applications per year in the judicial district of Montreal, which had a population of perhaps 150,000.[57] Nonetheless, a study of some 253 cases identified in that district between 1795 and 1879 allows some general patterns to emerge.

The causes permitting separation from bed and board were the same as under the French regime – essentially severe physical abuse, desertion, or adultery by the wife (but not the husband).[58] The sexual double standard remained in place throughout this period. Thus, when Jane B. sought a separation from her husband, Thomas K., in 1856 on the basis of both his violence and his having fathered two children by their servant, she failed. While the sexual misconduct was proven, Jane could not produce satisfactory evidence of physical maltreatment, and the adultery alone would not suffice. Had these events occurred ten years later she would have succeeded (assuming the servant lived in the marital home). Article 188 of the 1866 code created a new cause of separation from bed and board for male adultery where (but only where) the husband had introduced his 'concubine' into the marital home.

The gendered pattern of who commenced such actions continued. In 95 per cent of the cases the wife started the action, and she succeeded 80 per cent of the time. The class background of plaintiffs was varied and even showed a strong representation from the labouring and artisanal classes. Physical abuse was alleged in 80 per cent of the cases, and in 17 per cent the husband had already been convicted of domestic violence. Alcohol abuse was also a common complaint, either because it resulted in violence or wasting of the family's resources, or both. As for ethnicity, almost one-third of the actions involved couples where one or both spouses were anglophone, but this figure does not suggest over-representation by them. By mid-century a majority of the inhabitants of the city of Montreal were English-speaking, although this was not the case in the peri-urban and rural parts of the judicial district. The main distinction was rural-urban rather than ethnic: rural wives (mostly Canadiennes) were less likely to seek separation than their urban sisters, whether anglophone or francophone.

Wives in Lower Canada who instituted separation suits benefited from some advantages denied their counterparts in common law provinces as the result of differing matrimonial property laws. Nearly three-quarters of the couples involved were married in community of property. A successful action thus entailed dissolution of the community of property between the spouses, which gave the wife back her private property, half the community assets (that is, assets acquired during the marriage), and allowed her to claim any advantages she had been promised in the marriage contract. Prior to 1866 the separated wife still had to obtain her husband's consent to the alienation of her immoveables, but article 210 of the code now required her to obtain the authorization of a judge instead. These advantages could be illusory: in one-third of the cases where the couple was married in community of property, the wife renounced the community, presumably because the husband was insolvent. Compared to wives in common law jurisdictions, however, where a woman who had no assets in her own name could claim nothing upon separation except prospective alimony, the wife married in community property had some advantages. Perhaps even more importantly, she could count on retaining custody of any minor children should she be successful, as the successful party was almost always awarded custody. Children of the age of twelve could testify in separation cases and did so in favour of the mother 90 per cent of the time. Only very exceptionally did a successful wife not retain custody of her children. It was the fear of losing their children that compelled many wives in the common law colonies to remain with unsuitable or abusive husbands.

While an agreement to separate was invalid in theory, one feature of the action in separation from bed and board allowed couples to achieve the same end if they wished. If the husband did not respond to the action, it was granted, and this occurred in nearly half of the cases studied. As long as the husband was prepared to suffer the dissolution of the community and lose custody of any minor children, his simply not showing up in court would permit the couple to achieve a mutually agreed separation if that was their goal.

Even if the law was somewhat solicitous of women whose marriages were in crisis, these cases touched only a very small number of them. Much more important were changes in the law of dower that occurred during this period.[59] Dower under the civil law was more generous than the common law, as we saw in chapter 9. Customary dower was a matter of status under the Custom of Paris, arising on marriage without the necessity of any contract, although a marriage contract could stipulate for a different form of dower, often an annuity or a lump sum. Insofar as customary dower created rights in a widow to land owned by her husband on marriage or inherited by him during marriage (his private property or 'propres'), it was more relevant in rural society than in urban society where a landless working class was emerging. Nonetheless, it could be highly valuable to the widow of a smallholder as well as to the more generously propertied. Dower was tenacious in that it attached to any private property of the husband, could not be barred on the sale of such land, and was accompanied by a hypothec or charge upon all his property for its satisfaction; it also ranked ahead of claims of the husband's creditors.

The main theme of change in this period was the gradual diminution of dower rights, following the classic nineteenth-century trajectory 'from status to contract.' Dower did not disappear entirely, but it became a creature of contract and thus more a matter of choice on the husband's part. Dower was undermined by a variety of factors that came to a head around the time of the rebellions. The British inhabitants had never liked it, identifying it with what they saw as the illiberal and 'feudal' tendencies of the civil law (even though a similar form of dower had long been part of the common law). The Canadien political class, formerly united around the preservation of dower, began to fracture on the issue: the bourgeois and professional classes, some of whom had become quite successful speculating in immoveable property, began to advocate for the abolition or reform of dower. In this they were joined by the Patriotes, who also began to support the idea of registry offices and the abolition of female suffrage, in a transformation of the 'politico-sexual order.'[60]

Dower and the issue of registry offices were always discussed together because one of the 'problems' with dower was thought to be the 'secret hypothec' that accompanied it, while registry offices were thought to be the solution. If dower could be made a registrable charge and all charges had to be registered, then the maxim *caveat emptor* would settle the issue: the buyer who did not inspect the register had only himself to blame if he purchased subject to a dower interest. In 1841 the special council adopted an ordinance that set up a registry system and also curtailed dower in important ways. The ordinance was a curious mix of post-revolutionary French law, English Acts setting up registry offices in some counties, the English *Dower Act 1833*, and North American common law practices. It put an obligation on husbands to register dower, failing which it would not rank ahead of creditors on his death. Wives were enabled to bar dower by signing the conveyance, as in the common law colonies, but dower was now to attach only to property owned by the husband at his death. The *Civil Code* of 1866 did not abolish customary dower but imposed onerous registration requirements; it would be another twenty years before such dower rights were finally cut off.[61] Married couples continued to stipulate for dower in their marriage contracts, but this gave the propertied party, usually the husband, more control over what obligations he wanted to assume than had previously been the case.

On the issue of dower, Lower Canada moved in the opposite direction from the other British North American colonies. After some debate, they all moved to extending dower rather than restricting it, although the provision for wives barring their dower in those jurisdictions removed the irritant that had most exercised opponents of customary dower in Lower Canada.[62] On the whole, though, the choice of matrimonial regimes in Lower Canada afforded married women somewhat more security than their sisters in the common law jurisdictions, albeit mostly if they survived their husbands. Community of property gave a widow a right to half the property the couple had acquired during marriage, a benefit that had no parallel in the common law. The almost invariable appointment of a widow as tutor to her minor children also spoke to a certain confidence in her as a manager, whereas under the common law the husband could appoint by will any guardian he chose.

The Civil Law: Unmarried Parents

The legal position of unmarried mothers in the civil law was never enviable, but the ancien droit had been somewhat protective of them and their children. In eighteenth-century France, a woman could make a déclaration de grossesse (declaration of pregnancy) before a local notable in which she named the putative father, as a way of obtaining child support from him. Something similar seems to have existed in Lower Canada. In 1826, for example, a young woman of Châteauguay made a declaration before a notary that the father of her unborn child, now about to marry another woman, had promised to marry her first. She thus opposed the marriage, waiving her opposition only when the father made a financial settlement with her.[63]

The Revolution did not take long to abolish déclarations de grossesse, and its masculinist thrust continued with the notorious article 340 of the *Code Napoléon*, which declared that 'La recherche de la paternité est interdite' – paternity searches are forbidden.[64] Unmarried mothers in France thus had no way of enforcing support obligations against the fathers of their children after 1804. The 1866 *Civil Code* did not adopt this provision, leaving the ancien droit in place. It had allowed a type of seduction action, by which an unmarried woman could sue her paramour for lying-in expenses and for damage to her reputation if she had engaged in sexual relations with the defendant on the basis of fraud or deceit, provided she had been of previously chaste character.[65] The fact that a statute of 1843 providing for small claims courts (commissioners' courts) saw fit to exclude actions relating to 'Paternity,... or for Seduction, or Lying-in expenses' from the courts' jurisdiction suggests that they were not rare.[66]

The exact nature of the action(s) available to an unmarried mother was not clear before or after the code. An 1863 case described the woman's claim thus: 'The causes of the demand are seduction, breach of promise of marriage, paternity of the child, expenses of its birth and maintenance,' and there seemed to be no problem in joining together all these different claims. In a case of the previous year a woman obtained personal damages, a declaration of paternity against the defendant, and support for her child, all in the same proceeding. The 'breach of promise of marriage' allegation seemed to be treated as an element of the claim for seduction, rather than a distinct action, as in the common law. The contrast between these two cases shows the way in which the law could be used to police moral regulation. In both cases the plaintiff was of the age of majority and sued in her own name. In *Bonneau v Coupal*, the plaintiff was found to have been inveigled into losing her virginity with the defendant as a result of his 'artifices et fausses promesses.'[67] The trial judge awarded her the princely sum of £500 for unspecified, presumably reputational, harms suffered by her, in addition to support for her child; the Court of Appeal reduced this to £100, still a substantial amount. In *Poissant v Barrette*, by contrast, the plaintiff sought $8,000 general damages and the trial judge awarded her $1,000 (£250), but the Court of Appeal overturned the award after its withering scrutiny of the plaintiff's moral character. Her lawyer was unwise enough to state in the pleadings that the defendant had stated he would marry the plaintiff if she proved her virginity to him by sleeping with him. She carried out her part of the bargain, but they continued to sleep together, even though he did not carry out his. In addition, she was shown to have had companions of dubious moral character, which, in the judges' view, justified the defendant in not carrying out his promise. Justice Badgley, always quick to see things in contractual terms, had no difficulty in declaring this to be an immoral contract that would not be upheld by the law. In general, however, he had no problem with awarding substantial damages to a properly virtuous plaintiff. 'In a case of deliberate seduction,' he observed, 'money can be no compensation to the unfortunate sufferer for the gratification of mere lust and temporary appetite obtained by the seducer, and heavy damages in such cases are rarely, and very properly, not interfered with.'[68]

In spite of the differing moral judgments made about them, both plaintiffs were awarded declarations of paternity and substantial amounts for lying-in expenses and for child support: Mlle Barrette was to receive $60 per annum for her daughter to age seven, and then $120 per annum until age fourteen, payable monthly, with liberty to apply for further support when the child reached that age. Mlle Bonneau was awarded a quarterly pension for her child, with a similar right to apply for renewed support when the child reached the age of fourteen. The reduction of the trial judge's award in general damages in *Bonneau* was justified by the fact that there was nothing particularly aggravating about the defendant's conduct, and he was not wealthy – suggesting that ability to pay was a legitimate factor to take into account. Both these women would have found their actions more difficult to prosecute after the enactment of the *Civil Code* of 1866, however. While continuing to permit paternity suits, it threw up two new procedural hurdles. First, it imposed a new evidentiary requirement: there now had to be a 'commencement of proof in writing' in order to render oral testimony admissible, whereas formerly oral testimony and circumstantial evidence alone were sufficient (article 232). And the unwed mother could no longer bring the action in her own name but had to bring it in the name of the child; thus, she had to have herself named tutor to the child, a process that would entail some time and expense. These new requirements seem to have led to lowered success rates after 1866.[69]

Whether the father of a minor who found herself an unwed mother could sue for loss of services or harm to familial honour remained somewhat unclear. In 1865 Justice Taschereau allowed such a claim by a father who claimed that his minor daughter had been 'violently debauched' by his married neighbour, awarding him $100 for unspecified harms. His one-sentence judgment provided little in the way of reasoning and was overturned by the Court of Appeal, but its judges provided no reasons either.[70]

While in the end the results of the common law and the civil law for unwed mothers may not have been that different, their theoretical foundations were quite distinct. The civil law was more open to compensating harms to family honour and reputation than the common law (although, as noted above, the tort of seduction moved in this direction over the course of the nineteenth century). It also considered the claims of the woman herself directly, rather than through the proxy of a parent's lost services. Finally, the future of the child was highlighted much more in the civil law cases. Its focus on the needs of children, even illegitimate ones, was largely absent in the common law cases and reflected the more 'familial' orientation of the civil law. Still, unwed mothers suffered both social and legal disadvantage. Both men and women could expect a searching probe of their moral character in these cases, but for the men it was only their finances, not their reputations and future social prospects, that were in jeopardy.

35

Law and Legal Institutions on the Eve of Confederation: The British North American Legacy

In every aspect of its social, political, economic, and cultural life British North America was transformed between 1815 and Confederation, and law and legal institutions were no exception. The transformation is perhaps most obviously evident in the basic legal structures constituting how law was made, and how and by whom it was used, applied, and interpreted. By the 1860s the power to make law rested very largely in elected assemblies, bodies that had played much less significant roles in 1815. The law those assemblies made through statutes had grown exponentially over the previous half century, in innumerable ways supplanting and/or modifying the inherited common law. The task of applying and interpreting those laws was performed by a higher judiciary shorn of its formal institutional relationships to the executive and legislature, even if connections between law and politics were still manifest in the judicial appointment process. And from uncertain and tentative beginnings the region's legal professions had carved out a place for themselves, as independent practitioners serving communities on a wide variety of matters and as influential advocates on myriad social and economic policies.

The ascendancy of this model of law-making and law-applying was not achieved through a linear process, nor was it accomplished at the same time in all areas of British North America. The history of law, like all histories, is not reducible to simple narratives or explanations; it invariably combines large doses of continuity coexisting with change and is often marked by dichotomies if not outright contradictions. The transformation described above, for example, included the crisis of the rebellion period, which demonstrated that the rule of law could easily be ignored or subverted when fundamental challenges presented themselves. Similarly, judicial independence may have been inaugurated in the Canadas and Nova Scotia, at different times, but judges did not benefit from this formal guarantee in New Brunswick, PEI, Newfoundland, or British Columbia. Judges may have stopped being legislators in eastern and central Canada, but the establishment of new colonies on the Pacific coast in the 1850s and 1860s meant continuity with the past, the establishment of constitutions redolent of eighteenth-century British North America, complete with judges acting in legislative and executive capacities. We might see responsible government as the victory of local democracy over imperial control, but it did not mean that political power now resided with 'the people,' for excluded from voting were tens of thousands of the poorest members of colonial society, almost all Indigenous people, and millions of women.

Examining this period through another lens, we can also see it as one in which the pillars of the eighteenth-century legal system became less important and had to share centre stage with emerging institutions. As assemblies wrested power from the executive, they were made to concede authority to municipal governments in some colonies. Superior courts and their judges arguably diminished in influence, replaced by a plethora of lesser courts closer to the local communities they served. The common law and the civil law remained important sources of legal rules, but in a host of areas, from criminal sanctions to rules regulating who could hold property, they were supplanted or modified by statute law fashioned through the legislative process. Also somewhat diminished in this period was the influence of inherited traditions, the laws, legal institutions, and constitutional underpinnings of Britain and France. In the former case, British rules on land-holding and the franchise were altered in the colonies or abrogated by being ignored. In the latter case, the initiative came from France, which abandoned its pre-revolutionary law and replaced it with the *Code Napoléon*, effectively severing Lower Canada from any traditional mooring.

The legal legacy of the British North American period also includes two developments relating to legal pluralism. French-derived law and legal institutions survived various assimilationist initiatives from the 1820s through to the early 1840s and emerged stronger than ever before. French law was strengthened in part because in crucial areas, such as the seigneurial system and the *Civil Code*, its principal defenders embraced new liberalizing trends in what might be termed a defensive adaptation. More generally, Lower Canada maintained its legislative independence in a wide variety of areas. Nothing says more about the failure of Britain's post-rebellion policy of assimilation than the fact that when the province of Canada brought out a consolidation of its laws in 1859 and 1861, it was divided into three volumes – one each for Upper and Lower Canada, and one for statutes applicable to both sections. Lower Canadians enjoyed a form of 'provincial' self-government in some areas of jurisdiction substantially similar to what Quebec had from 1867.

The same cannot be said of the other pillar of the legal pluralism that had been a dominant feature of the legal landscape in 1815, the continuing independence of Indigenous communities in the central regions of British North America. The massive erosion of Indigenous peoples' land base in eastern regions, especially Upper Canada, altered the constitutional balance between them and the settler populations profoundly and permanently. Indigenous people continued to be largely self-governing on land reserved to them, although ominous clouds were gathering, in the form of the civilization policy, to threaten even that degree of autonomy. Some Indigenous communities, notably those at Kahnawake and in the Six Nations territories, responded to external pressure by adapting to and using settler legal institutions and ideas that were new to them, but that adaptation, unlike the refashioning of the Lower Canadian civil law, could not hold back the winds of change. Tellingly, the Indigenous peoples of the Pacific coast experienced the effects of European settlement and resource exploitation much more quickly than had their eastern counterparts. Depopulation caused by disease, warfare disguised as criminal law, as well as loss of land, led to the rapid marginalization of the coastal Indigenous people who came into intensive contact with Europeans.

To say that European law became the dominant form of law in British North America in this period is to pose questions of what values that law represented and whose interests it served. In chapter 21 we identified two very broad themes that would run through the chapters to follow. One was the notion of state formation, and we have seen myriad areas in which the power and influence of that cluster of legal ideas and institutions known as 'the state' was profoundly augmented during this period. Public and private resources combined to build economic infrastructure, with banks and other corporations increasingly to the fore.

The nineteenth century was an era marked by faith in material progress, which in British North America was driven by the twin imperatives of liberalism – faith in the individual – and the power of the community to work towards the common good, and both were facilitated by law. Commercial and, especially, corporate law grew exponentially in importance and complexity, the latter fuelled by a belief that the corporate form was necessary to strengthening infrastructure and enhancing material wealth. Other new legal institutions – prisons, police forces, municipalities – funnelled the power of the state to more effectively regulate peoples' lives. Linking all of these developments was the rise of statute law itself; statutes became the predominant legal device through which colonial societies remade their material and intellectual worlds through the law and legal institutions.

A second broad theme identified in chapter 21 was the cluster of values summarized by the notion of reform, within which could be subsumed a wide variety of imperatives – enlightenment, modernization, rationalization, and liberalization. Reform writ large and its constituent parts pervaded discussions over criminal punishment, the criminal trial, policing, imprisonment for debt, family law, the separation of powers, and much else. In the criminal law, for example, enlightened 'humanitarian' reform fuelled the move away from punishment of the body and towards the remaking of the individual through incarceration. In debtor-creditor law advocates of legal change constantly invoked the need for rational and enlightened policies to supplant the archaism of inherited practice. The very methods of recording and preserving and making accessible the law also changed, with the rise of law reporting, the writing of legal treatises, codification, and changes to the ways in which statutes were organized and presented.

Yet reform and modernization were both contested values and not applicable to all persons and legal contexts. The corporate form may have been the most important legal innovation in the economic sphere, but its principal concomitant legal idea, limited liability, was resisted by those committed to an older moral compass centred on paying one's debts. That same moral compass made reform of debtor-creditor law a long, drawn-out, indeed incomplete, process, reminding us that general trends, especially when viewed from the perspective of hindsight and the victory of a certain vision, can conceal the contingent and uncertain nature of legal historical transformation. Moreover, the 'economic law' that perhaps mattered most to the still largely rural societies of British North America, land law, was also the site of competing values.

Lower Canadian advocates of progress may have preferred registration of landed property over the older system of customary rights, and the reform of seigneuralism, but many in Prince Edward Island wanted those who worked the land to prevail over those who had inherited it. Conversely, while the supporters of escheat on the island may not have prevailed in this period, those who made similar arguments based on the idea that possession and labour should bring rights did largely get their way on Cape Breton Island.

It is perhaps appropriate to conclude this summary of a definitive half-century in the history of the law in Canada with where the section itself concludes, a reminder that a consistent theme throughout this period is the many ways in which the law treated a variety of social groups adversely compared to others. There are no women or Blacks, and few Indigenous people, in the early chapters on judges, lawyers, and the sources of law. Women and Blacks make only cameo appearances in the chapters on the Constitution and politics, and Indigenous peoples' roles, and those of the least well-off settlers, in those chapters are confined largely to those of losers, the excluded, and the disadvantaged. Those same social groups play a similar part when we play out the drama of criminal justice – the policed, the tried, and the punished. When we do put the focus directly on these groups, in chapters 33 and 34, we see the many and varied ways in which the law contributed, directly or indirectly, to their subordination.

Abbreviations

Statutes

CSC	Consolidated Statutes of Canada
CSUC	Consolidated Statutes of Upper Canada
OQ	Ordinances of Quebec
OSC	Ordinances of the Special Council (Lower Canada)
RSNB	Revised Statutes of New Brunswick
RSNS	Revised Statutes of Nova Scotia
SLC	Statutes of Lower Canada
SN	Statutes of Newfoundland
SNB	Statutes of New Brunswick
SNS	Statutes of Nova Scotia
SPC	Statutes of the Province of Canada
SPEI	Statutes of Prince Edward Island
SQ	Statutes of Quebec
SUC	Statutes of Upper Canada
SVI	Statutes of Vancouver Island

Legislative Journals and Debates

LC Journals	Journals of the Legislative Assembly of Lower Canada
NB Journals	Journals of the Legislative Assembly of New Brunswick
Nfld Journals	Journals of the Legislative Assembly of Newfoundland

NS Journals	Journals of the Legislative Assembly of Nova Scotia
PC Debates	*Debates of the Legislative Assembly of United Canada 1841–1867*. Edited by Elizabeth Nish. Montreal: Presses de l'École des hautes études commerciales, 1970 et seq. Although its title states that the series was intended to go to 1867, publication was stopped after 1857.
PC Journals	Journals of the Legislative Assembly of the Province of Canada
PEI Journals	Journals of the Legislative Assembly of Prince Edward Island
UC Journals	Journals of the Legislative Assembly of Upper Canada

Case Reports and Courts

BR	Banc du roi or Banc de la reine [King's or Queen's Bench]
GCR	Grant's Chancery Reports (Upper Canada)
LCJ	Lower Canada Jurist
LCR	Lower Canada Reports
NBR	New Brunswick Reports
NBSC	New Brunswick Supreme Court
Nfld LR	Newfoundland Law Reports
NSR	Nova Scotia Reports
NSSC	Nova Scotia Supreme Court
PEIR	Prince Edward Island Reports
SCR	Supreme Court Reports
UCCP	Upper Canada Common Pleas (Court and Reports)
UCQB	Upper Canada Queen's Bench (Court and Reports)

Archival References

AO	Archives of Ontario
LAC	Library and Archives Canada
NSARM	Nova Scotia Archives and Records Management
PANB	Provincial Archives of New Brunswick
PRO	Public Records Office

Published Documents and Collections of Documents

Canada Committee Report	*Report from the Select Committee on the Civil Government of Canada*, British Parliamentary Papers, Cd. no. 569, 1828.

DCNY	*Documents Relative to the Colonial History of New York*. Edited by E.B. O'Callaghan. 15 vols. Albany, NY: Weed, Parsons, 1853–87.
Durham Report	*Report on the Affairs of British North America, from the Earl of Durham*, with annotations by C.P. Lucas. London, 1839.
Documents 1759–91	*Documents Relating to the Constitutional History of Canada, 1759–1791*. Edited by Adam Shortt and Arthur G. Doughty. Ottawa: J de L Taché, 1918.
EO	*Édits, ordonnances royaux, déclarations et arrêts du Conseil d'État du roi concernant le Canada*. 2 vols. Quebec: E.R. Fréchette, 1854–6.
JDCS	*Jugements et déliberations du Conseil souverain de la Nouvelle-France*, 4 vols. Quebec: A. Coté, 1885–8.

Secondary Sources

CLI	*Canada's Legal Inheritances*. Edited by W. Wesley Pue and DeLloyd J. Guth. Winnipeg: University of Manitoba, 2001.
CST	*Canadian State Trials*. Volumes 1 and 2, edited by F. Murray Greenwood and J. Barry Wright. Volume 3 edited by J. Barry Wright and Susan Binnie. Toronto: Osgoode Society for Canadian Legal History and University of Toronto Press, 1996, 2002, and 2009.
DCB	*Dictionary of Canada Biography*. On line at www.biographi.ca
EHCL	*Essays in the History of Canadian Law*. Volumes 1–11. Toronto: Osgoode Society for Canadian Legal History and University of Toronto Press.
Epitome	Beamish Murdoch, *Epitome of the Laws of Nova-Scotia*. 4 vols. Halifax: Joseph Howe, 1832–3.
SCNS	*The Supreme Court of Nova Scotia, 1754–2004: From Imperial Bastion to Provincial Oracle*. Edited by Philip Girard, Jim Phillips, and Barry Cahill. Toronto: Osgoode Society for Canadian Legal History and University of Toronto Press, 2004.

Notes

1. Introduction

1 Hamar Foster, 'One Good Thing: Law and Elevator Etiquette in the Indian Territories,' in Myra Rutherdale, Kerry Abel, and P. Whitney Lackenbauer, eds, *Roots of Entanglement: Essays in the History of Native-Newcomer Relations* (Toronto: University of Toronto Press, 2018), 299. In *Tsilhqot'in Nation v British Columbia*, [2014] 2 SCR 257, the Supreme Court of Canada for the first time declared that Aboriginal title existed over a broad area claimed by the plaintiffs.

2 Katherine A. Hermes, 'The Law of Native Americans, to 1815,' in Michael Grossberg and Christopher Tomlins, eds, *The Cambridge History of Law in America*, 3 vols (New York: Cambridge University Press, 2008), vol. 1. H. Patrick Glenn, *Legal Traditions of the World: Sustainable Diversity in Law*, 5th ed. (Oxford: Oxford University Press, 2014), applies to law the idea of chthonic peoples (those who live in harmony with the earth) put forward by Edward Goldsmith, *The Way: An Ecological World View* (London: Rider, 1992). We think these terms may inadvertently suggest that Indigenous law is on a plane different from common law or civil law. Hence we will refer simply to Indigenous law(s) or legal tradition(s). For the views of early Europeans who asserted the existence of Indigenous law, see chap. 2.

3 Val Napoleon and Hadley Friedland, 'Indigenous Legal Traditions: Roots to Renaissance,' in Markus D. Dubber and Tatjana Hörnle, eds, *Oxford Handbook of Criminal Law* (Oxford: Oxford University Press, 2014), 227.

4 Susan M. Hill, *The Clay We Are Made Of: Haudenosaunee Land Tenure on the Grand River* (Winnipeg: University of Manitoba Press, 2017), 16.
5 Sarah Noël Morales, '*Snuw'uyulh*: Fostering an Understanding of the Hul'qumi'num Legal Tradition' (PhD thesis, University of Victoria, 2014), 16–17.
6 See, e.g., J.A. Clarence Smith and Jean Kerby, *Private Law in Canada: A Comparative Study* (Ottawa: University of Ottawa Press, 1975); Louis Baudouin, *Le Droit civil de la Province de Québec: Modèle vivant de Droit comparé* (Montreal: Wilson & Lafleur, 1953).
7 See, for example, John Borrows, *Recovering Canada: The Resurgence of Indigenous Law* (Toronto: University of Toronto Press, 2002).
8 Alex Castles, *An Australian Legal History* (Sydney: Law Book, 1982). See, however, Bruce Kercher, *An Unruly Child: A History of Law in Australia* (St Leonards, NSW: Allen & Unwin, 1995), which improves considerably upon Castles in this respect.
9 Peter Spiller, Jeremy Finn, and Richard P. Boast, *A New Zealand Legal History* (Wellington, NZ: Brooker's, 1995).
10 Lawrence M. Friedman, *A History of American Law*, 3d ed. (New York: Simon & Schuster, 2005).
11 Christopher Tomlins, *Freedom Bound: Law, Labor, and Civic Identity in Colonizing English America, 1580–1865* (New York: Cambridge University Press, 2010).
12 Anyopeuh Simon Munzu, 'Cameroon's Search for a Uniform Legal System: The Example of Criminal Justice,' *African Journal of International and Comparative Law* 1 (1989): 46.
13 Grossberg and Tomlins, *Cambridge History of Law in America*, vols 2 and 3.
14 See chaps 3 and 4; on later forms of legal pluralism, see Harry Arthurs, *Without the Law: Administrative Justice and Legal Pluralism in Nineteenth-Century England* (Toronto: University of Toronto Press, 1995).
15 Richard J. Ross and Philip J. Stern, 'Reconstructing Early Modern Notions of Legal Pluralism,' in Lauren Benton and Richard J. Ross, eds, *Legal Pluralism and Empires, 1500–1850* (New York: New York University Press, 2013).
16 On the Huron-Wendat Confederacy, see Georges E. Sioui, *Huron-Wendat: The Heritage of the Circle*, rev. ed., trans. Jane E. Brierley (Vancouver: UBC Press 1999), 129–33; on the Six Nations, Hill, *Clay We Are Made Of*.
17 Paul Halliday, 'Law's Histories: Pluralisms, Pluralities, Diversity,' in Benton and Ross, *Legal Pluralism and Empires*, 271.

18 Lauren Benton, *Law and Colonial Cultures: Legal Regimes in World History, 1400–1900* (New York: Cambridge University Press, 2002), 2–3.

19 An 1887 Order in Council outlining this policy remained in force until the *Indian Act* of 1951 revoked it by requiring formal marriages for the transmission of Indian status; Sarah Carter, *The Importance of Being Monogamous: Marriage and Nation Building in Western Canada to 1915* (Edmonton: University of Alberta Press, 2008), 160–3.

20 Michel Morin, 'La perception de l'ancien droit et du nouveau droit français au Bas-Canada, 1774–1866,' in H. Patrick Glenn, ed., *Droit québécois et droit français: communauté, autonomie, concordance* (Cowansville, QC: Yvon Blais, 1993). See also John E.C. Brierley and Roderick A. Macdonald, *Quebec Civil Law* (Toronto: Emond Montgomery, 1993).

21 Jean-Maurice Brisson and Nicholas Kasirer, 'The Married Woman in Ascendance, the Mother Country in Retreat: From Legal Colonialism to Legal Nationalism in Quebec Matrimonial Property Law Reform, 1866–1991' in *CLI*.

22 Philip Girard, 'British Justice, English Law, and Canadian Legal Culture,' in Phillip Buckner, ed., *Canada and the British Empire* (New York: Oxford University Press, 2008).

23 G. Blaine Baker, 'The Reconstitution of Upper Canadian Legal Thought in the Late-Victorian Empire,' *Law and History Review* 3 (1985): 219.

24 H. Patrick Glenn refers to this phenomenon as 'reception as alliance': 'Persuasive Authority,' *McGill Law Journal* 32 (1987): 261.

25 One of the few such papers, perhaps the only one, is that by Paul Williams and Curtis Nelson, 'Kaswentha,' archived at http://data2.archives.ca/rcap/pdf/rcap-185.pdf.

26 See, e.g., Val Napoleon, 'Ayook: Gitksan Legal Order, Law, and Legal Theory' (PhD diss., University of Victoria, 2009). The work of the Indigenous Law Research Unit (ILRU) at the University of Victoria, British Columbia, deserves mention here, as the epicentre of research on the recovery and revitalization of Indigenous law. In 2012 the ILRU partnered with the Indigenous Bar Association and the Truth and Reconciliation Commission to launch the Accessing Justice and Reconciliation project (AJR), which also has a strong focus on revitalizing Indigenous law.

27 Napoleon and Friedland, 'Indigenous Legal Traditions,' 226.

28 For an account of the first written code of law by the Mississaugas of the New Credit, see Mark D. Walters, 'How to Read Aboriginal Legal Texts from Upper Canada,' *Journal of the Canadian Historical Association* 14

(2003): 93. Hill, *Clay We Are Made Of*, discusses change in Haudenosaunee legal traditions at Grand River, Upper Canada, although her main focus is on continuity. In their very thorough book *Secwépemc People, Land, and Laws* (Montreal and Kingston: McGill-Queen's University Press, 2017), Marianne Ignace and Ronald Ignace also focus on the continuity of traditional law, although there is some discussion of adaptation during the colonial period.

29 Sylvia McAdam (Saysewahum), *Nationhood Interrupted: Revitalizing Nêhiyaw Legal Systems* (Saskatoon: Purich Publishing, 2015), 81. For an example of how to use present-day oral tradition to establish Indigenous legal tradition, see Napoleon, 'Ayook.'

30 McAdam (Saysewahum), *Nationhood Interrupted*, 22, referring to Cree (*nêhiyaw*) traditions in this regard.

31 Cited in Jarich Oosten, Frédéric Laugrand, and William Rasing, eds, *Interviewing Inuit Elders: Perspectives on Traditional Law*, 2 vols (Iqaluit: Nunavut Arctic College 1999), 2:14.

32 See generally John Borrows, 'Listening for a Change: The Courts and Oral Tradition,' *Osgoode Hall Law Journal* 39 (2001): 1 at 22.

33 Linda Tuhiwai Smith, *Decolonizing Methodogies: Research and Indigenous Peoples* (Auckland, NZ: Zed Books 1999).

34 Hill, *Clay We Are Made Of*, 7.

35 Ibid., 55.

36 Joseph-François Lafitau, *Customs of the American Indians Compared with the Customs of Primitive Times*, 2 vols (Toronto: Champlain Society, 1974) [trans. by William N. Fenton and Elizabeth L. Moore of original French edition of 1724], 1:310.

37 John Borrows, *Drawing Out the Law: A Spirit's Guide* (Toronto: University of Toronto Press, 2010), 38–47.

38 See, for example, Heidi Bohaker, 'Reading Anishnaabe Identities: Meaning & Metaphor in *Nindoodem* Pictographs,' *Ethnohistory* 57 (2010): 11.

39 A mix of antiquarianism and anthropological curiosity is evident in the work of jurist Beamish Murdoch in the 1840s–1860s, for example; see Philip Girard, *Lawyers and Legal Culture in British North America: Beamish Murdoch of Halifax* (Toronto: Osgoode Society for Canadian Legal History and University of Toronto Press, 2011), 176–81 (creation of Mi'kmaq-English dictionary and Mi'kmaw grammar). The best-known work by a nineteenth-century lawyer-anthropologist is Lewis Morgan's *League of the Ho-de-no-sau-nee, or Iroquois* (New York: M.H. Newman, 1851), though

it has been subject to extensive critique by both Indigenous and non-Indigenous scholars.

40 Walters, 'How to Read Aboriginal Legal Texts'; on the first attempt to write a code of Mohawk law at Kahnawake, see Daniel Rueck, 'Enclosing the Mohawk Commons: A History of Use-Rights, Land Ownership, and Boundary-Making in Kahnawá:ke Mohawk Territory' (PhD diss., McGill University, 2013), 100–4; see also chap. 17.

41 Rita Joe, *Song of Eskasoni* (Charlottetown, PEI: Ragweed, 1988). Joe (1932–2007) attended the residential school for Mi'kmaq at Shubenacadie, Nova Scotia.

42 Deborah Doxtator, 'What Happened to the Iroquois Clans? A Study of Clans in Three Nineteenth-Century Rotinonhsyonni Communities' (PhD thesis, University of Western Ontario, 1996), 51. *Rotinonhsyonni* is a variant spelling of *Haudenosaunee*. Doxtator expands on Indigenous notions of time in 'Inclusive and Exclusive Perceptions of Difference: Native and Euro-Based Concepts of Time, History and Change,' in Germaine Warkentin and Carolyn Podruchny, eds, *Decentring the Renaissance: Canada and the Renaissance in Multidisciplinary Perspective* (Toronto: University of Toronto Press, 2001). See also Sioui, *Huron-Wendat*, 50–1.

43 Hill, *Clay We Are Made Of*, discusses the origins of the Great Law of Peace and reviews the various written versions of it at 27–35. As to dating, see Olive P. Dickason with David T. McNab, *Canada's First Nations: A History of Founding Peoples from Earliest Times*, 4th ed. (Don Mills, ON: Oxford University Press 2009), 50; and the work of Tuscarora historian David Cusick, *Sketches of Ancient History of the Six Nations* (Lockport, NY: Turner & McCollum, 1848), discussed in Doxtator, 'Inclusive and Exclusive Perceptions.'

44 Philip Girard, 'Liberty, Order, and Pluralism: The Canadian Experience,' in Jack P. Greene, ed., *Exclusionary Empire: English Liberty Overseas, 1600 to 1900* (New York: Cambridge University Press, 2009).

45 As to French views of the Acadians' penchant for liberty, see John Mack Faragher, *A Great and Noble Scheme: The Tragic Story of the Expulsion of the French Acadians from Their American Homeland* (New York: W.W. Norton, 2005), 58.

46 W.L. Morton, 'The Relevance of Canadian History,' presidential address to the Canadian Historical Association, 11 June 1960, http://www.cha-shc.ca/download.php?id=1641.

47 Indigenous views of the Royal Proclamation and its relationship to the 1764 Treaty of Niagara are explored in chapter 11.

48 Elizabeth Mancke, 'Another British America: A Canadian Model for the Early Modern British Empire,' *Journal of Imperial and Commonwealth History* 25 (1997): 1.

49 Michel Ducharme, *Le concept de liberté au Canada à l'époque des Révolutions atlantiques, 1776–1838* (Montreal and Kingston: McGill-Queen's University Press, 2010), and in English translation, *The Idea of Liberty in Canada during the Age of Atlantic Revolutions, 1776–1838*, trans. Peter Feldstein (Montreal and Kingston: McGill-Queen's University Press, 2014); though of course, there also emerged a strong demand for reform within the existing constitutional order, based on modern liberty within a parliamentary system, as opposed to natural rights, dealt with in chap. 25.

50 J.R. Miller, *Compact, Contract, Covenant: Aboriginal Treaty-Making in Canada* (Toronto: University of Toronto Press, 2009).

51 See chap. 29.

52 See chap. 6.

53 See chap. 19. Allan Greer, *Property and Dispossession: Natives, Empires and Land in Early Modern North America* (New York: Cambridge University Press, 2018), argues that the importance of the colonial 'commons' (especially allowing livestock to run free on 'waste' land) and their impact on Indigenous commons has been underestimated in the New England context; these traditions were less widespread in the later-settled colonies of British North America, however, and where they existed, made less of an impact on Indigenous societies that were mostly not dependent on agriculture.

54 See chaps 30 and 31.

55 See Bradley Miller, *Borderline Crime: Fugitive Criminals and the Challenge of the Border, 1819–1914* (Toronto: Osgoode Society for Canadian Legal History and University of Toronto Press, 2016); Greer, *Property and Dispossession*.

56 This work has some similarities in this respect to Peter Russell's *Canadian Odyssey: A Country Based on Incomplete Conquests* (Toronto: University of Toronto Press, 2017), but his focus is on politics, not law.

57 See, however, J.P.S. McLaren, 'In the Northern Archives Something Stirred: The Discovery of Canadian Legal History,' *Australian Journal of Legal History* 7 (2003): 73; K.J.M. Smith and J.P.S. McLaren, 'History's Living Legacy: An Outline of "Modern" Historiography of the Common Law,' *Legal Studies* 21 (2001): 251. There does not appear to be any overall modern survey of the law of New France, although the work of John

Dickinson, taken as a whole, achieves this goal: see chaps 6, 8, and 9. As for Quebec law post-1760, see the overview by G. Blaine Baker in his introduction to *EHCL*, vol. 11. And as noted elsewhere, the work on Indigenous law tends to proceed on a nation-by-nation basis, making generalization difficult.

58 Guth and Pue, *CLI*. Although published in 2001, the research for most of the chapters was conducted in the early to mid-1990s.

59 Among many others, see W.P.M. Kennedy, *The Constitution of Canada: An Introduction to Its Development and Law* (Don Mills, ON: Oxford University Press, 2014) [reprint of 1922 edition with introduction by Martin Friedland]; Edmond Lareau, *Histoire du droit canadien: depuis les origines de la colonie jusqu'à nos jours*, 2 vols (Montreal: A. Périard, 1888–9); Hilda Neatby, *The Administration of Justice under the Quebec Act* (London: Oxford University Press, 1937); and the hundreds of works by the indefatigable William Renwick Riddell (1852–1945).

60 For a complete listing of Osgoode Society publications, see www.osgoodesociety.ca. The Law and Society series of UBC Press also contains many works of Canadian legal history; see www.ubcpress.ca.

61 By way of example only, see Benton, *Law and Colonial Cultures*; Lisa Ford, *Settler Sovereignty: Jurisdiction and Indigenous Peoples in America and Australia, 1788–1836* (Cambridge, MA: Harvard University Press, 2010); Saliha Belmessous, ed., *Native Claims: Indigenous Law against Empire, 1500–1920* (New York: Oxford University Press, 2012); Saliha Belmessous, ed., *Empire by Treaty: Negotiating European Expansion, 1600–1900* (New York: Oxford University Press, 2014); Gilles Havard and Mickaël Augeron, *Un continent en partage: cinq siècles de rencontres entre Amérindiens et français* (Paris: Les Indes Savantes, 2013).

62 Volume 1 ends at 1815 rather than the expected 1789 (with the adoption of the federal constitution), but volume 2 recapitulates by designating the 'long nineteenth century' as 1789–1920.

63 John Reid, Maurice Basque, Elizabeth Mancke, Barry Moody, Geoffrey Plank, and William Wicken, *The 'Conquest' of Acadia, 1710: Imperial, Colonial and Aboriginal Constructions* (Toronto: University of Toronto Press, 2004).

64 Jean Lunn, 'The Illegal Fur Trade out of New France, 1713–60,' *Report of the Annual Meeting of the Canadian Historical Association* 18 (1939): 61.

65 Gerhard J. Ens, 'The Battle of Seven Oaks and the Articulation of a Metis National Tradition, 1811–1849,' in Nicole St-Onge, Carolyn Podruchny, and Brenda Macdougall, eds, *Contours of a People: Metis*

Family, Mobility, and History (Norman, OK: University of Oklahoma Press, 2012).

66 Earlier courts of appeal featured a mix of professional judges and members of the executive council; see chap. 22.

67 SPC 1857, c 26.

68 (1867) 11 LCJ 197, affd (1869) 1 *Revue légale* 253.

2. Roots: Indigenous Legal Traditions

1 John Borrows provides an overview of the interaction of the three legal traditions in Canada, stressing commonalities as well as differences, in 'Indigenous Legal Traditions in Canada,' *Washington University Journal of Law & Policy* 19 (2005): 167.

2 Olive P. Dickason with David T. McNab, *Canada's First Nations: A History of Founding Peoples from Earliest Times*, 4th ed. (Don Mills, ON: Oxford University Press 2009), 7.

3 'Hatzic Rock,' http://www.sfu.museum/time/en/panoramas/long-back/hatzic-rock. The recent discovery of 13,000-year-old footprints on Calvert Island, British Columbia, pushes this timeline back even further: 'Scientists Find 13,000-Year-Old Footprints on B.C. Island, the Earliest Known in North America,' *[Toronto] Star*, 28 March 2018.

4 H. Patrick Glenn, *Legal Traditions of the World: Sustainable Diversity in Law*, 5th ed. (New York: Oxford University Press, 2014), 62. Glenn's chapter on 'chthonic' legal tradition includes all Indigenous peoples around the world, not just those in North America.

5 Dickason with McNab, *Canada's First Nations*, viii, 5.

6 Glenn, *Legal Traditions*, 73. See also Susan M. Hill, whose observations about the unicity of the Indigenous knowledge base are quoted in chapter 1; *The Clay We Are Made Of: Haudenosaunee Land Tenure on the Grand River* (Winnipeg: University of Manitoba Press, 2017).

7 Richard Overstall, with Val Napoleon and Katie Ludwig, 'The Law Is Opened: The Constitutional Role of Tangible and Intangible Property in Gitanyow,' in Catherine Bell and Val Napoleon, eds, *First Nations Cultural Heritage and Law: Case Studies, Voices, and Perspectives* (Vancouver: UBC Press, 2008), 95.

8 The 'no law' conclusions of various early explorers are catalogued by Desmond H. Brown in '"They Punish Murderers, Thieves, Traitors and Sorcerers": Aboriginal Criminal Justice as Reported by Early French Observers,' *Histoire sociale/Social History* 35 (2003): 363 at 364–5.

9 Borrows, 'Indigenous Legal Traditions,' 190. Borrows goes on to observe that the common law and civil law also have a strong foundation in customary law, as will be explored in the next two chapters.
10 Joseph François Lafitau, *Customs of the American Indians Compared with the Customs of Primitive Times*, 2 vols (Toronto: Champlain Society, 1974) [trans. by William N. Fenton and Elizabeth L. Moore of original French edition of 1724], 1:28.
11 Ibid., 1:292–3.
12 Louis-Armand de Lom d'Arce de Lahontan, *New Voyages to America*, 2 vols (London: J. and J. Boswicke, 1735) [English translation of 1703 French edition].
13 Hill, *Clay We Are Made Of*, 3. See also Tuma Young, 'L'nuwitasi'mk: A Foundational Worldview for a L'nuwey Justice System,' *Indigenous Law Journal* 13 (2016): 75. According to Young, *L'nu* is the original word for Mi'kmaq, and *L'nuwey* is the adjectival form.
14 Hill, *Clay We Are Made Of*, 30–3.
15 Heidi Bohaker, '"Nindoodemag": The Significance of Algonquian Kinship Networks in the Eastern Great Lakes Region, 1600–1701,' *William and Mary Quarterly*, 3d ser. 63 (2003): 23 at 30. See also notes 37 and 38 in chap. 1.
16 Richard Overstall, 'Encountering the Spirit in the Land: "Property" in a Kinship-Based Legal Order,' in John McLaren, A.R. Buck, and Nancy E. Wright, eds, *Despotic Dominion: Property Rights in British Settler Societies* (Vancouver: UBC Press, 2005), 25. See also Neal McLeod, *Cree Narrative Memory* (Saskatoon, SK: Purich 2007).
17 Reuben Thwaites, ed., *Jesuit Relations and Allied Documents*, 73 vols (Cleveland, OH: Burrows Bros, 1896–1901), 9:227–33.
18 Lafitau, *Customs of the American Indians*, 1:297.
19 Brown, '"They Punish Murderers,"' 380.
20 E. Adamson Hoebel, *Law of Primitive Man: A Study in Comparative Legal Dynamics* (Cambridge, MA: Harvard University Press, 1954), 93–8; Norbert Rouland, 'Les modes juridiques de solution des conflits chez les Inuit,' supplement, *Études Inuit Studies* no. S3 (1979): S7 at S80–S101.
21 Lafitau, *Customs of the American Indians*, 1:295–7.
22 Lafitau, *Customs of the American Indians*, 1:297.
23 Borrows, 'Indigenous Legal Traditions,' makes this point in a more general way at 195–6.
24 Lafitau, *Customs of the American Indians*, notes this practice among the Mohawk: 1:294–5.

25 William N. Fenton, 'Joseph-François Lafitau,' *DCB*. In fact, Morgan generalized his work with the Seneca to all nations of the Confederacy: Hill, *Clay We Are Made Of*, 17.

26 See the remarks of Hill, *Clay We Are Made Of*, in chapter 1.

27 Lafitau, *Customs of the American Indians*, 1:299.

28 On the interface between 'common' and 'individual' property in Indigenous property regimes, see Allan Greer, *Property and Dispossession: Natives, Empires and Land in Early Modern North America* (New York: Cambridge University Press, 2018).

29 Lafitau, *Customs of the American Indians*, 1:299.

30 John Borrows, *Freedom and Indigenous Constitutionalism* (Toronto: University of Toronto Press, 2016), 158–9.

31 John Borrows summarizes a variety of Indigenous constitutional traditions in 'Indigenous Constitutionalism,' in Peter Oliver, Patrick Macklem and Nathalie Desrosiers, eds, *Oxford Handbook of the Canadian Constitution* (New York: Oxford University Press, 2017).

32 Marianne Ignace and Ronald Ignace, *Secwépemc People, Land, and Laws* (Montreal and Kingston: McGill-Queen's University Press, 2017), 320. Ronald Ignace is chief of the Skeetchestn Band of the Secwépemc people, formerly known as Shuswap.

33 As cited in Overstall, 'Encountering the Spirit,' 25.

34 James Youngblood Henderson, 'Mikmaw Tenure in Atlantic Canada,' *Dalhousie Law Journal* 18 (1995): 196 at 230.

35 Deborah Doxtator, 'What Happened to the Iroquois Clans? A Study of Clans in Three Nineteenth-Century Rotinonhsyonni Communities' (PhD thesis, University of Western Ontario, 1996), 72. *Rotinonhsyonni* is a variant spelling of *Haudenosaunee*.

36 Overstall, with Napoleon and Ludwig, 'The Law Is Opened,' 94.

37 John R. Swanton, 'Social Organization of the Haida,' in Tom McFeat, ed., *Indians of the North Pacific Coast* (Montreal and Kingston: McGill-Queen's University Press, 2002), 50–2.

38 T.F. McIlwraith, 'The Ancestral Family of the Bella Coola,' in McFeat, *Indians of the North Pacific Coast*, 60.

39 Dickason and McNab, *Canada's First Nations*, 50.

40 Doxtator, 'What Happened to the Clans?,' chap. 3, provides more detail on the clan system and its evolution in time and space.

41 Overstall, 'Encountering the Spirit,' 35.

42 For example, the possible succession of Edward III of England to the throne of France in 1328 as the son of the sister of the late (and childless) King Charles IV helped launch the Hundred Years' War; the French

decided that only descent through males was permissible, leading them to crown a cousin of Charles IV in the male line, Philip VI. The War of the Spanish Succession (1702–13) likewise resulted from a possible union of the French and Spanish Crowns that many European nations feared.

43 Overstall, 'Encountering the Spirit,' 42.

44 Olive P. Dickason, *Canada's First Nations: A History of Founding Peoples from Earliest Times*, 2nd ed. (Don Mills, ON: Oxford University Press 2002), 49.

45 Brett Rushforth, *Bonds of Alliance: Indigenous and Atlantic Slaveries in New France* (Chapel Hill, NC: University of North Carolina Press, 2012).

46 Carol Cooper, 'Native Women of the Northwest Pacific Coast: An Historical Perspective, 1830–1900,' *Journal of Canadian Studies* 27, no. 4 (1992): 57.

47 Philip Drucker, 'Rank, Wealth and Kinship in Northwest Coast Society,' in McFeat, *Indians of the Northwest Pacific Coast*.

48 Cooper, 'Native Women,' 57.

49 J.A. Frisch, 'Eunice Williams,' *DCB*; John Demos, *The Unredeemed Captive: A Family Story from Early America* (New York: Knopf, 1994).

50 Peter Cook, 'Onontio Gives Birth: How the French in Canada Became Fathers to Their Indigenous Allies, 1645–1673,' *Canadian Historical Review* 96 (2015): 166.

51 Arthur Ray, *An Illustrated History of Canada's Native People: I Have Lived Here since the World Began*, 4th ed. (Montreal and Kingston: McGill-Queen's University Press, 2016), 239.

52 Lafitau, *Customs of the American Indians*, 1:337.

53 Kalervo Obert, 'Crime and Punishment in Tlingit Society,' in McFeat, *Indians of the North Pacific Coast*.

54 Cooper, 'Native Women,' 55–6 (support to separated women); Jean Barman, *The West beyond the West: A History of British Columbia*, 3d ed. (Toronto: University of Toronto Press, 2007), 18 (custody).

55 Hamar Foster, 'One Good Thing: Law and Elevator Etiquette in the Indian Territories,' in Myra Rutherdale, Kerry Abel, and P. Whitney Lackenbauer, eds, *Roots of Entanglement: Essays in the History of Native-Newcomer Relations* (Toronto: University of Toronto Press, 2018), 295. Such principles were common across North America: see John Phillip Reid, *Patterns of Vengeance: Crosscultural Homicide in the North American Fur Trade* (Pasadena, CA: Ninth Judicial Circuit Historical Society, 1999).

56 Brown, '"They Punish Murderers,"' 378–9.

57 Knut Rasmussen, *Across Arctic America* (New York: G.P. Putman's, 1927), 175.
58 Lafitau, *Customs of the American Indians*, 1:305.
59 Thwaites, *Jesuit Relations*, 33:243.
60 Lafitau, *Customs of the American Indians*, 1:301.
61 Knud Rasmussen, *The Netsilik Eskimos: Social Life and Spiritual Culture*, trans. W.E. Calvert (Copenhagen: Gyldendal, 1931), 138, 140.
62 Ibid., 140. More recent scholarship has confirmed the existence of very high male-female ratios among Inuit children in the early twentieth century, and identified infanticide as the most likely cause, though the motivation behind it is debated: Eric Alden Smith and S. Abigail Smith, 'Inuit Sex-Ratio Variation: Population Control, Ethnographic Error, or Parental Manipulation?,' *Current Anthropology* 35 (1994): 595.
63 Lafitau, *Customs of the American Indians*, 1:305.
64 On what follows, see Brown, '"They Punish Murderers,"' 387–90.
65 For the successful invocation of such beliefs in modern times as relevant to self-defence in the context of a trial for manslaughter, see *R v Jacko*, [1997] OJ no. 2472. There is an extensive anthropological and legal literature on the wendigo phenomenon; for an overview from the post-contact period see Sidney L. Harring, *White Man's Law: Native People in Nineteenth-Century Canadian Jurisprudence* (Toronto: Osgoode Society for Canadian Legal History and University of Toronto Press, 1996), 218–38. Val Napoleon and Hadley Friedland examine the normative foundations of the response to the wendigo in 'Indigenous Legal Traditions: Roots to Renaissance,' in Markus D. Dubber and Tatjana Hörnle, eds, *Oxford Handbook of Criminal Law* (Oxford: Oxford University Press, 2014).
66 Johnson to Lords of Trade, 30 Oct. 1764, in E.B. O'Callaghan, ed., *DCNY*, 7:672.
67 Henderson, 'Mikmaw Tenure,' 233.
68 Brian Noble, in consultation with Reg Crowshoe and in discussion with the Knut-sum-atak Society, '*Poomaksin*: Skinnipiikani-Nitsiitapii Law, Transfers, and Making Relatives: Practices and Principles for Cultural Protection, Repatriation, Redress, and Heritage Law Making with Canada,' in Bell and Napoleon, *First Nations Cultural Heritage*.
69 Doxtator, 'What Happened to the Iroquois Clans?,' 51.
70 Representative works include John Borrows, *Drawing Out Law: A Spirit's Guide* (Toronto: University of Toronto Press, 2010); Val Napoleon, 'Ayook:

Gitksan Legal Order, Law, and Legal Theory' (PhD diss., University of Victoria, 2009); Gordon Christie, 'Indigenous Legal Theory: Some Initial Considerations,' in Benjamin J. Richardson, Shin Imai, and Kent McNeil, eds, *Indigenous Peoples and the Law: Comparative and Critical Perspectives* (Oxford: Hart, 2009); Val Napoleon and Hadley Friedland, 'An Inside Job: Engaging with Indigenous Legal Traditions through Stories,' *McGill Law Journal* 61 (2016): 725.

3. Roots: French Legal Traditions

1 H. Patrick Glenn, *Legal Traditions of the World: Sustainable Diversity in Law*, 5th ed. (New York: Oxford University Press, 2014), 134.
2 The text of the Twelve Tables can be found at http://avalon.law.yale.edu/ancient/twelve_tables.asp.
3 A modern edition in Latin and English is *The Digest of Justinian*, 4 vols (Philadelphia, PA: University of Pennsylvania Press, 1985).
4 A modern edition in Latin and English is *The Institutes of Gaius* (London: Duckworth, 1988).
5 Tony Honoré, 'Justinian's Codification,' in Simon Hornblower and Antony Spawforth, eds, *The Oxford Classical Dictionary*, 4th ed. (Oxford: Oxford University Press, 2012).
6 John P. Dawson, *The Oracles of the Law* (Westport, CT: Greenwood, 1978), 266–73.
7 Michel Morin, *Introduction au droit romain, au droit français et au droit anglais* (Montreal: Éditions Thémis, 2004), 157–9. Recent scholarship has suggested that the notion of each custom as being confined to a particular geographic space is inexact and that there was substantial borrowing across custumal lines; Ada-Maria Kuskowski, 'Inventing Legal Space: From Regional Custom to Common Law in the *Coutumiers* of Medieval France,' in Meredith Cohen and Fanny Madeline, eds, *Space in the Medieval West: Places, Territories, and Imagined Geographies* (Farnham, UK: Ashgate, 2014).
8 Glenn, *Legal Traditions of the World*, 143.
9 H.P. Glenn, 'The Capture, Reconstruction and Marginalization of "Custom,"' *American Journal of Comparative Law* 45 (1997): 613.
10 See chaps 9, 18.
11 Jean-Marie Carbasse, *Introduction historique au droit pénal* (Paris: Presses Universitaires de France, 1990), 105–6.
12 Morin, *Introduction historique*, 153.
13 Dawson, *Oracles of the Law*, 267–9.

14 The thirteenth-century Sainte Chappelle, which still stands, was built as the chapel for the Palais de la Cité. From the mid-fourteenth century the king moved to new palaces, the Louvre, the Tuileries, and eventually Versailles.
15 However, a 'powerful' site on Baffin Island where Inuit justice was traditionally administered features a circle of megaliths. Norman Hallendy, 'The Last Known Traditional Inuit Trial on Southwest Baffin Island in the Canadian Arctic [1924]' (1991), Norman Hallendy Fonds, McMichael Canadian Art Collection Archives. Very similar structures have been found in northern Labrador and in Nunavik (northern Quebec); see sources cited in John L. Joy, 'Caubvik and Captain George Cartwright's Legal Regimes: A Comparative Study of Traditional Aboriginal and Settler Justice in 18th-Century Labrador,' in Melvin Baker, Christopher Curran, and Derek Green, eds, *Discourse and Discovery: 1615–2015 and Beyond* (St John's, NL: Law Society of Newfoundland and Labrador 2017), 56–7.
16 Morin, *Introduction historique*, 156.
17 J.H. Baker, *An Introduction to English Legal History*, 4th ed (Oxford: Oxford University Press 2002), 5. See generally Richard Bartlett, *Trial by Fire and Water* (Oxford: Clarendon, 1986).
18 Dawson, *Oracles of the Law*, 287. An echo of this in the English context was the long-standing practice that decisions of the Judicial Committee of the Privy Council, which likewise grew out of the monarch's council, could not feature dissents; also, judicial decisions of the House of Lords were not made public until near the end of the eighteenth century.
19 Dawson, *Oracles of the Law*, 282–6.
20 Ibid., 314.
21 Ibid., 290–305.
22 See chap. 6. The meaning of the French term *police* in these regulations is a broad one, including almost any measure relating to public welfare, and not just those relating to peace officers.
23 Morin, *Introduction historique*, 151–2.
24 See chap. 6.
25 Dawson, *Oracles of the Law*, 370.
26 Vida Azimi, 'L'exhérédation politique de la femme par la Révolution,' *Revue historique de droit français et étranger* 69 (1991): 177.
27 On this struggle and its aftermath, see Harold Berman, *Law and Revolution: The Formation of the Western Legal Tradition* (Cambridge, MA: Harvard University Press, 1983).

28 Michael Burrage, *Revolution and the Making of the Contemporary Legal Profession: England, France, and the United States* (Oxford: Oxford University Press, 2006), 49–52.
29 Ibid., 61. On the office of procureur, see Claire Dolan, 'Les procureurs, intermédiaires entre la justice et les familles,' in Claire Dolan, ed., *Entre justice et justiciables: Les auxiliaires de justice du Moyen Âge au XXe siècle* (Quebec: Presses de l'Université Laval, 2005).
30 Alain Moreau, *Les métamorphoses du scribe: Histoire du notariat français* (Perpignan: Socapress, 1989).
31 See chap. 6.
32 *Corps et Compilation de Tous les Commentateurs Anciens et Modernes sur la Coutume de Paris*, 3 vols (Paris: chez Denys Thierry, 1685–92), 1:i ('there are few truths in jurisprudence that cannot be controverted').
33 *Le Droit Commun de la France et la Coutume de Paris Réduits en Principe* (Paris, 1747).
34 Jacques Vanderlinden, *Le lieutenant civil et criminel: Mathieu de Goutin en Acadie française, 1688–1710* (Moncton, NB: Centre d'études acadiennes [CEA], Université de Moncton, 2004), has a helpful discussion of these at 184–7.
35 J.F. Bosher, 'French Protestant Families in Canadian Trade, 1740–1760,' *Histoire sociale/Social History* 7 (1974): 179.
36 Gaston Tisdel, 'Esther Brandeau,' *DCB*.
37 Moreau, *Métamorphoses du scribe*, 94.
38 Sue Peabody, *There Are No Slaves in France: The Political Culture of Race and Slavery in the Ancien Régime* (New York: Oxford University Press, 2002).

4. Roots: British Legal Traditions

1 Bora Laskin, *The British Tradition in Canadian Law* (London: Stevens & Sons, 1969).
2 Through a *Declaratory Act* of 1719, the British House of Lords was authorized to overrule decisions of the Irish House of Lords. The Act was repealed in 1782 as part of new constitutional arrangements for Ireland, but the British House of Lords became the final court of appeal for Ireland again in 1800 after the *Act of Union* abolished the Irish House of Lords; James Kelly, 'The Politics of Civil and Political Rights in Eighteenth-Century Ireland,' in Jack P. Greene, ed., *Exclusionary Empire: English Liberty Overseas, 1600–1900* (New York: Cambridge University Press, 2010), 100.

3 Lisi Oliver, *The Beginnings of English Law* (Toronto: University of Toronto Press, 2002), provides a transcription, translation, and extended analysis of the laws of Aethelberht.
4 Patrick Wormald, *The Making of English Law: King Alfred to the Twelfth Century* (Oxford: Blackwell, 1999).
5 *Moot* or *gemot* was the Old English word for 'meeting.' Hence the council of the Anglo-Saxon kings was known as the *witenagemot*, *witan* being 'royal advisers.'
6 J.H. Baker, *An Introduction to English Legal History*, 4th ed. (London: Butterworths, 2002), 3–9.
7 Paul Brand, *The Origins of the English Legal Profession* (Oxford: Blackwell, 1992), 5–15.
8 *Tractatus de legibus et consuetudinibus regni Angliae*, thought to be composed 1187–9. For a modern translation, see G.D.G. Hall, ed., *The Treatise on the Laws and Customs of England Commonly Called Glanvill* (Oxford: Clarendon, 1993).
9 Brand, *Origins*, 29–32.
10 Douglas Hay, 'Origins: The Courts of Westminster Hall in the Eighteenth Century,' in *SCNS*, 16.
11 On what follows, see J.H. Baker, 'The Three Languages of the Common Law,' *McGill Law Journal* 43 (1998): 5.
12 4 Geo II, c 26.
13 Roger D. Groot, 'The Early-Thirteenth-Century Criminal Jury,' in J.S. Cockburn and Thomas A. Green, eds, *Twelve Good Men and True: The Criminal Trial Jury in England, 1200–1800* (Princeton, NJ: Princeton University Press, 1988).
14 Baker, *Introduction*, 75–6.
15 John P. Dawson, *The Oracles of the Law* (Westport, CT: Greenwood, 1968), 11.
16 Paul Brand, *The Making of the Common Law* (London: Hambledon, 1992), 96.
17 Cited in Baker, *Introduction*, 57.
18 Baker, *Introduction*, explains how it worked at 302.
19 Philip Girard, 'History and Development of Equity,' in Mark R. Gillen and Faye Woodman, eds, *Trusts: A Contextual Approach*, 3d ed. (Toronto: Emond Montgomery, 2015).
20 David Crystal, *The Cambridge Encyclopedia of the English Language* (Cambridge: Cambridge University Press, 1995), 41.
21 Baker, *Introduction*, 21.
22 Ibid., 24.

23 Thomas Skyrme, *History of the Justices of the Peace*, 3 vols (Chichester, UK: Barry Rose, 1991).
24 Brand, *Origins*, 16. Plea rolls existed before 1195 but were made only for the parties, hence few have survived. After 1195 a copy of record was kept in the Treasury, and these survive in an almost unbroken sequence. Digitized copies of some can be viewed at http://aalt.law.uh.edu.
25 Dawson, *Oracles of the Law*, 10–12, 50–6.
26 Ibid., 80.
27 Ibid., 88–94.
28 Publication of the debates of either house was long forbidden, and the House of Lords did not see why the prohibition should not extend to its judicial work.
29 Robert Stevens, *Law and Politics: The House of Lords as a Judicial Body, 1800–1976* (Chapel Hill: University of North Carolina Press, 1978).
30 Joseph Henry Smith, *Appeals to the Privy Council from the American Plantations* (New York: Columbia University Press, 1950), 658.
31 3 & 4 Will IV, c 41.
32 Brand, *Origins*, 43–69.
33 G.D. Squibb, *Doctors' Commons: A History of the College of Advocates and Doctors of Law* (Oxford: Clarendon, 1977).
34 Recent scholarship has suggested Islamic influences on the emergence of the inns of court, based on contacts developed by the Knights Templar during the Crusades; it is summarized by H. Patrick Glenn, *Legal Traditions of the World: Sustainable Diversity in Law*, 5th ed. (New York: Oxford University Press, 2014), 241–2.
35 Michael Burrage, *Revolution and the Making of the Contemporary Legal Profession: England, France, and the United States* (Oxford: Oxford University Press, 2006), 393.
36 Wilfrid R. Prest, *The Inns of Court under Elizabeth I and the Early Stuarts, 1590–1640* (Totawa, NJ: Rowman and Littlefield, 1972), 117.
37 Ibid., 54–5, 131–6.
38 Burrage, *Revolution and the Legal Profession*, 497–500.
39 J.H. Baker, 'The Judges as Visitors to the Inns of Court,' in *Collected Papers on English Legal History*, 3 vols (Cambridge: Cambridge University Press 2013), 1:238.
40 On what follows, see Burrage, *Revolution and the Legal Profession*, 386, 406–7, 437, 463–4, 509–11.
41 James Muir, *Law, Debt, and Merchant Power: The Civil Courts of Eighteenth-Century Halifax* (Toronto: Osgoode Society for Canadian Legal History and University of Toronto Press, 2016), 91.

42 Wilfrid Prest, 'Sir William Blackstone,' *Oxford Dictionary of National Biography* online.
43 Baker, *Introduction*, 208–12.
44 18 Edw I, c 1. The statute prevented anyone but the king from sub-infeudating, that is, from creating subordinate lordships when conveying property. Henceforth, all land transfers would result in the transferee standing in the shoes of the transferor.
45 Baker, *Introduction*, 205.
46 See the History of Parliament, http://www.historyofparliamentonline.org/volume/1690-1715/parliament/1705.
47 Baker, *Introduction*, 207.
48 Francis Bacon, *Essays Moral, Economical, and Political* (1625; London: T. Payne, 1800), 254.
49 Burrage, *Revolution and the Legal Profession*, 412–15; Donald Veall, *The Popular Movement for Law Reform, 1640–1660* (Oxford: Clarendon, 1970).
50 6 & 7 Will & Mar, c 2 (1694); 1 Geo I St 2, c 38 (1716); the Bill of Rights 1689 can be found at Yale Law School, http://avalon.law.yale.edu/17th_century/england.asp.
51 This provision was not a panacea for judicial independence, however; David Lemmings, *Professors of the Law: Barristers and English Legal Culture in the Eighteenth Century* (Don Mills, ON: Oxford University Press 2000), 271–88, examines the techniques used by successive British governments to ensure that compliant judges were appointed and remained so.
52 See chap. 22.
53 Greg Marquis, 'In Defence of Liberty: 17th Century England and 19th Century Maritime Political Culture,' *University of New Brunswick Law Journal* 42 (1993): 69. The establishment of both Rupert's Land and Newfoundland predated the Glorious Revolution, but neither was considered a colony of settlement; see chaps 7 and 14.
54 See chap. 22.
55 As cited in J.H. Baker, *The Reinvention of Magna Carta, 1216–1616* (Cambridge: Cambridge University Press, 2017), 32. The charter was written as one continuous text; the separation into numbered clauses was a convention adopted by later writers. What follows on the fate of clause 29 is derived from Baker.
56 Baker, *Reinvention*, 33.
57 Ibid., 168.
58 Philip Girard, 'British Justice, English Law, and Canadian Legal Culture,' in Phillip Buckner, ed., *Canada and the British Empire* (New York: Oxford University Press, 2008).

59 Kevin Costello, 'Habeas Corpus and Military and Naval Impressment, 1756–1812,' *Journal of Legal History* 29 (2008): 215.
60 *Somerset v Stewart* (1772) 98 ER 499.
61 Douglas Hay and Paul Craven, 'Introduction' to their *Masters, Servants, and Magistrates in Britain & the Empire, 1562–1955* (Chapel Hill: University of North Carolina Press, 2004).
62 Paul Craven, 'Canada, 1670–1935: Symbolic and Instrumental Enforcement in Loyalist North America,' in Hay and Craven, *Masters, Servants, and Magistrates.*
63 Maeve Doggett, *Marriage, Wife-Beating and the Law in Victorian England* (London: Weidenfeld & Nicolson, 1992), notes that the power of confinement and chastisement was finally disavowed in *R v Jackson*, [1891] 1 QB 671.

5. Early Contacts, Early Charters

1 The following relies on Gilles Havard, *The Great Peace of Montreal of 1701: French-Native diplomacy in the Seventeenth Century*, trans. Phyllis Aronoff and Howard Scott (Montreal and Kingston: McGill-Queen's University Press, 2001), chapter 7.
2 Ibid., 135–6.
3 Cited by Havard, ibid., 139–40.
4 Ibid., 185–7.
5 The treaty, referred to as a 'deed,' is reproduced at *DCNY*, 4:908–11.
6 England would declare war on France in May 1702.
7 On the kaswentha and the Nanfan Treaty, see Paul Williams and Curtis Nelson, *Kaswentha*, research report prepared for the Royal Commission on Aboriginal Peoples, archived at http://data2.archives.ca/rcap/pdf/rcap-185.pdf; and Susan M. Hill, *The Clay We Are Made Of: Haudenosaunee Land Tenure on the Grand River* (Winnipeg: University of Manitoba Press, 2017), 84–95. The treaty of 1701 was considered valid and acted upon in *R v Ireland* (1990), 1 OR (3d) 577 (Gen Div), where it provided a defence to two Oneida hunters found to be hunting out of season.
8 See chap. 11.
9 James A. Tuck and Robert Grenier, *Red Bay, Labrador: World Whaling Capital A.D. 1550–1600* (St John's, NL: Atlantic Archaeology, 1989).
10 H.P. Biggar, *The Voyages of Jacques Cartier: Published from the Originals, with Translations, Notes and Appendices* (Ottawa: Public Archives of Canada, 1924), 21.

11 See chap. 7.
12 Peter Pope, *Fish into Wine: the Newfoundland Plantation in the Seventeenth Century* (Chapel Hill: University of North Carolina Press for the Omohundro Institute of Early American History and Culture, 2004), 14, 20.
13 Reproduced in H.P. Biggar, *A Collection of Documents relating to Jacques Cartier and the Sieur de Roberval* (Ottawa: Public Archives of Canada, 1930), 178–85. Jacques Cartier was acting under royal authority, but no copy of his commission has come to light; Brian Slattery, 'French Claims in North America, 1500–1559,' *Canadian Historical Review* 79 (1978): 140.
14 Helen Dewar, '"Y establir nostre auctorité": Assertions of Imperial Sovereignty through Proprietorships and Chartered Companies in New France, 1598–1663' (PhD diss., University of Toronto, 2012).
15 Cited in Anthony Pagden, *Lords of All the World: Ideologies of Empire in Spain, Britain and France, c. 1500–c.1800* (New Haven, CT: Yale University Press 1995), 32.
16 Biggar, *Collection of Documents*, 180 (authors' translation).
17 Cited in Ken MacMillan and Jenifer Abeles, eds, *John Dee: The Limits of the British Empire* (Westport, CT: Praeger, 2004), 19.
18 Ken MacMillan, *Sovereignty and Possession in the English New World: The Legal Foundations of Empire* (Cambridge: Cambridge University Press 2006), chap. 2.
19 MacMillan, *Sovereignty and Possession*, 30–1.
20 Cited at ibid., 33.
21 R.J. Knecht, *The French Wars of Religion, 1559–1598*, 3d ed. (Harlow: Longmans, 2010).
22 Olive Dickason, *The Myth of the Savage and the Beginnings of French Colonialism in the Americas* (Edmonton: University of Alberta Press, 1984), 181–202.
23 The commission is known from other sources; no copy is known to have survived.
24 *Commissions dv roy & de monseigneur l'Admiral, au Sieur de Monts, pour l'habitation és terres de Lacadie Canada, & autres endroits en la nouuelle France …* (Paris: Philippe Patisson, 1605).
25 Dickason, *Myth of the Savage*, 190, citing Léry, *Histoire d'un voyage fait en la terre du Brésil* (1580).
26 Christopher Tomlins, *Freedom Bound: Law, Labor, and Civic Identity in Colonizing English America, 1580–1865* (New York: Cambridge University Press, 2010), 183–5; in spite of the title of his chapter, Brian Slattery also takes the European charters seriously in 'Paper Empires:

The Legal Dimensions of French and English Ventures in North America,' in John McLaren, A.R. Buck, and Nancy E. Wright, eds, *Despotic Dominion: Property Rights in British Settler Societies* (Vancouver: UBC Press, 2005).

27 Slattery, 'Paper Empires,' 64–5. See also on these early charters and their treatment of native peoples Michel Morin, 'La dimension juridique des relations entre Samuel de Champlain et les Autochtones de la Nouvelle-France,' *Revue juridique Thémis* 38 (2004): 389.

6. Law and Governance in the French Possessions: Public Law and the Growth of Institutions

1 David Hackett Fischer, *Champlain's Dream* (New York: Knopf Canada, 2008), 126, 132–4. The quotation is from Champlain's account of the event.

2 Louis de Buade de Frontenac to M. de Seignelay, 12 Nov. 1690, in Ernest Myrand, *Sir William Phips devant Québec: histoire d'un siège* (Quebec: s.n., 1893), 10, 17.

3 Following convention, we use the label *Abenaki* for the Indigenous people who inhabited what is now western Maine and the Beauce region of Quebec, and the *Wabanaki Confederacy* to describe the larger alliance in which they were joined by the Wulstukwiuk, Mi'kmaq, and Huron-Wendat peoples; see Thomas Peace, 'Two Conquests: Aboriginal Experiences of the Fall of New France and Acadia' (PhD diss., York University, 2011), 34.

4 John Dickinson and Jane Grabowski, 'Les populations amérindiennes de la vallée laurentienne, 1608–1765,' *Annales de Démographie Historique* (1993): 51. Note that this figure does not include Indigenous populations on the north shore of the St Lawrence or in the Gaspé. The estimates for Acadie are those of John G. Reid, '1686–1720: Imperial Intrusions,' in Phillip A. Buckner and John G. Reid, *The Atlantic Region to Confederation: A History* (Toronto: University of Toronto Press, 1994), 79.

5 *Commissions dv roy & de monseigneur l'Admiral, au Sieur de Monts, pour l'habitation és terres de Lacadie Canada, & autres endroits en la nouuelle France* ... (Paris: Philippe Patisson, 1605).

6 The king's edict is reproduced in Jacques Vanderlinden, *Le lieutenant civil et criminel: Mathieu de Goutin en Acadie française, 1688–1710* (Moncton, NB: Centre d'études acadiennes, Université de Moncton, 2004), 368–9, and its effects discussed at 133–45.

7 The charter is reproduced at *EO*, 1:6–12.

8 John A. Dickinson, *Justice et justiciables: la procédure civile à la Prévôté de Québec, 1667–1759* (Quebec: Presses de l'Université Laval, 1977), 35.
9 Marcel Trudel, *La seigneurie de la compagnie des indes occidentales, 1663–1674* (Montreal: Fides, 1997), 115, attests to land grants being made by the intendant in the King's name while New France was in theory governed by the CWI.
10 *Édit de création du conseil souverain de Québec*, April 1663, *EO*, 1:37. The editor has titled this document 'Édit de création du conseil supérieur,' but that is in error; the document itself uses the title 'conseil souverain.'
11 *EO*, June 1675, 1:83.
12 *EO*, 2:66–73.
13 Gregory Kennedy, *Something of a Peasant Paradise? Comparing Rural Societies in Acadie and the Loudonais, 1604–1755* (Montreal and Kingston: McGill-Queen's University Press, 2014), 66.
14 André Vachon, *L'administration de la Nouvelle-France* (Quebec: Presses de l'Université Laval, 1975); an abbreviated version in English can be found as 'The Administration of New France,' in *DCB*, vol. 2 (Toronto: University of Toronto Press, 1966).
15 See below in this chapter, section on notaries.
16 Dickinson, *Justice et justiciables*, 75.
17 André Lachance, *Crimes et criminels en Nouvelle-France* (Montreal: Boréal Express, 1984), 18.
18 See below, 'Criminal and Civil Procedure in the Royal Courts.'
19 Dickinson, *Justice et justiciables*, 198.
20 Ibid., 72–6.
21 Ibid., 76–98.
22 Michel Duquet, 'L'infrajudiciaire et les notaires de Québec, 1650–1784' (PhD diss., Université d'Ottawa, 2008).
23 Arnaud Decroix, David Gilles, and Michel Morin, *Les Tribunaux et l'arbitrage en Nouvelle-France et au Québec de 1740 à 1784* (Montreal: Éditions Thémis, 2012), 109–51.
24 Ibid., 76–7, 80–2.
25 Lachance, *Crimes et criminels*, 20.
26 Cited in Raymond Cahall, *The Sovereign Council of New France* (New York: AMS, 1967), 18.
27 Jean-Philippe Garneau, 'Rendre justice en Nouvelle France: les voies et les limites de l'obéissance,' *Bulletin d'histoire politique* 18 (2009): 87.
28 Vanderlinden, *Le lieutenant civil et criminel: Mathieu de Goutin*, 126; the man accused of witchcraft was acquitted.
29 Kennedy, *Something of a Peasant Paradise*, 155–61.

30 Ibid., 38–9.
31 Louise Dechêne, *Habitants and Merchants in Seventeenth-Century Montreal*, trans. L. Vardi (Montreal and Kingston: McGill-Queen's University Press, 1992), 209.
32 Jean-Baptiste de Saint-Vallier, *Rituel du diocèse de Québec* (Paris: Chez Simon Langlois, 1703), 30–1. Saint-Vallier was the second bishop of Quebec; the *Rituel* contained pastoral letters of his predecessor as well as his own.
33 Ibid., 289. The 1683 prohibition was still being cited by some parish priests in the 1830s to try to quell charivaris: Allan Greer, *The Patriots and the People: The Rebellion of 1837 in Rural Lower Canada* (Toronto: University of Toronto Press, 1996).
34 On the different forms of royal legislation, see chap. 3.
35 Jean-Maurice Brisson, *La formation d'un droit mixte: l'évolution de la procédure civile de 1774 à 1867* (Montreal: Thémis 1986), 34–9; in particular, the Privy Council decided that registration of French ordinances was required before they could enter into force in New France: *Symes v Cuvillier*, [1880] 5 AC 138.
36 *EO*, 1:255–6.
37 Ibid., 185–6.
38 Colin Coates, 'Les cabales coloniales: La présence des élites dans le discours politique de la Nouvelle-France sous Louis XIV,' in Thierry Nootens and Jean-René Thuot, *Les figures du pouvoir à travers le temps: formes, pratiques et intérêts des groupes élitaires au Québec, XVIIe–XXe siècles* (Quebec: Presses de l'Université Laval, 2012), 40.
39 Louise Dechêne, *Habitants et marchands de Montréal au XVIIe siècle* (Paris: Plon, 1974), 241. Clearly royal authority preceded seigneurial authority, but Dechêne is presumably referring here to the creation of institutional structures rather than authority more generally.
40 Allan Greer, *Property and Dispossession: Natives, Empires and Land in Early Modern North America* (New York: Cambridge University Press, 2018), 158.
41 In principle, the lands beyond the Ottawa valley were to be reserved for trade, and thus not to be granted as seigneuries, but there were three exceptions: land around Fort Frontenac (Kingston) was granted as a seigneury in 1675 but later reabsorbed into the Domaine du Roi, or king's demesne; Fort Pontchartrain (Détroit) was also erected as a seigneury when founded in 1701, but one where the censitaires held directly of the king without any intermediary; and near the end of the French régime, in 1750, a seigneury was created around what is now Sault-Ste-Marie, Ontario.

42 Socage tenure was the main freehold tenure in England; it involved no services or payments to any feudal superior.

43 Guillaume Teasdale, 'Des destinées distinctes: Les Français de la région de la rivière Détroit et leurs voisins amérindiens, 1763–1815,' *Recherches amérindiennes au Québec* 39 (2009): 23.

44 For a suggestive case study, see J.I. Little, *Patrician Liberal: The Public and Private Life of Sir Henri-Gustave Joly de Lotbinière, 1829–1908* (Toronto: University of Toronto Press, 2013).

45 Benoît Grenier, '"Le dernier endroit dans l'univers": À propos de l'extinction des rentes seigneuriales au Québec, 1854–1971,' *Revue d'histoire de l'Amérique française* 64 (2010): 75.

46 The characterization of royal authority in France as 'absolute' needs to be considerably nuanced. Absolutism as an ideal coexisted with the reality of constant negotiation between the king's government and regional and local institutions; see James B. Collins, *The State in Early Modern France* (Cambridge: Cambridge University Press 2009).

47 On what follows, see Jean-François Niort, 'Aspects juridiques du régime seigneurial en Nouvelle-France,' *Revue générale de droit* 32 (2002): 443 at 500. There were twenty sols in a French livre (often called the livre tournois), and the sol was itself divided into twelve deniers. On the seigneurial regime in general, the best introduction is Benoît Grenier, *Brève histoire du régime seigneurial* (Montreal: Boréal, 2012).

48 The CNF largely fulfilled these obligations: it brought 7,300 migrants to New France between 1628 and 1662, and promoted alliances with and conversion of Indigenous peoples; Kennedy, *Something of a Peasant Paradise*, 136.

49 See chap. 17 for the aftermath of this transaction.

50 These transactions are reviewed in Isabelle Bouchard, 'Les chefs autochtones comme "seigneurs": gestion des terres et de leurs revenus, 1760–1820,' and David Gilles, 'La souplesse et les limites du régime juridique seigneurial colonial: les concessions aux Abénaquis durant le Régime français,' both in Benoît Grenier and Michel Morissette, eds, *Nouveaux regards en histoire seigneuriale au Québec* (Quebec: Septentrion, 2015).

51 See chaps 8, 17, and 23.

52 Succession is dealt with in more detail in chap. 9.

53 Grenier, *Brève histoire*, 58. For examples, see Vanderlinden, *Le lieutenant civil et criminel: Mathieu de Goutin*, 85 (Acadie); Benoît Grenier, *Marie-Catherine Peuvret: Veuve et seigneuresse en Nouvelle-France 1667–1739* (Sillery, QC: Septentrion, 2005), 49 (Canada).

54 Grenier, *Brève histoire*, 71, 75–6.
55 See J. Mathieu and A. Laberge, eds, *L'occupation des terres dans la vallée du Saint-Laurent: les aveux et dénombrements 1723–1745* (Sillery, QC: Septentrion, 1991).
56 The seigneur could not charge for the land itself, but the censitaire was normally expected to pay the surveying and legal costs, the latter being charged by the notary for preparing the original concession deed, which he retained, and a copy each for the seigneur and the censitaire; Greer, *Property and Dispossession*, 171–2.
57 Louise Dechêne, 'L'évolution du régime seigneurial au Canada: le cas de Montréal aux XVIIe et XVIIIe siècles,' *Recherches sociographiques* 12 (1971): 158 at 172.
58 What follows relies on Niort, 'Aspects juridiques du régime seigneurial'; and Vanderlinden, *Le lieutenant civil et criminel: Mathieu de Goutin*, chap. 4.
59 Kennedy, *Something of a Peasant Paradise*, has a useful comparison of the role of these assemblies in France and Acadie in chap. 5.
60 On the parish, see Donald Fyson, 'La paroisse et l'administration étatique sous le Régime britannique (1764–1840),' in Serge Courville and Normand Séguin, eds, *Atlas historique du Québec: La paroisse* (Sainte-Foy, QC: Presses de l'Université Laval, 2001), which, in spite of the title, discusses the parish under the French regime as well as the British.
61 The 1711 Edits de Marly, discussed in chap. 9, provided a formal mechanism by which censitaires could be deprived of their lands after a year's failure to reside there, in which case the censive would be reunited to the domain of the seigneur and could be regranted; *EO*, 1:326.
62 Cited in Kennedy, *Something of a Peasant Paradise*, 148 (authors' translation).
63 Ibid. A capon is a castrated rooster, fattened for consumption on special occasions.
64 R. Cole Harris, *The Seigneurial System in Early Canada: A Geographical Study* (Madison, WI: University of Wisconsin Press, 1966), 64–5, gives examples of the intervention of the intendant.
65 Dechêne, *Habitants and Merchants*, 138.
66 Niort, *Aspects juridiques*, 513, speculates that the custom originated in the Custom of Normandy, which recognized such a right. For an example, see *EO*, 2:438.
67 Grenier, *Brève histoire*, 86–7.
68 *EO*, 1:105–6 (royal ordinance of 12 May 1678 on hunting); Greer, *Property and Dispossession*, 179–80 (Indigenous hunting). On the slightly different pattern in Acadie, see Kennedy, *Something of a Peasant Paradise*, 151.

69 Greer, *Property and Dispossession*, 78–80. The Jesuits held themselves out as protectors of Indigenous peoples, but the regime they attempted to impose on the Innu when they settled near Quebec was so severe that they all departed.
70 For an example, see Grenier, *Marie-Catherine Peuvret*, 145–6, 154–7.
71 *EO*, 2:444–6.
72 Donald Fyson, 'Judicial Auxiliaries across Legal Regimes: From New France to Lower Canada,' in Claire Dolan, ed., *Entre Justice et Justiciables: Les auxiliaires de la justice du Moyen Âge au XXe siècle* (Sainte-Foy, QC: Presses de l'Université Laval, 2005), 387.
73 Technically, it was granted as allodial land and then regranted as a seigneury in 1651; see Greer, *Property and Dispossession*, 163–5.
74 The survival of seigneurial court records has been spotty, especially for the seventeenth century, but see John A. Dickinson, 'La justice seigneuriale en Nouvelle-France: le cas de Notre-Dame-des-Anges,' *Revue d'histoire de l'Amérique française* 28 (1974): 323; Dechêne, 'L'évolution du régime seigneurial'; Sylvie Dépatie, M. Lancelette, and C. Dessureault, *Contributions à l'étude du régime seigneurial canadien* (Lasalle, QC: Hurtubise, 1987). On the Séminaire de Québec as seigneur, see Jean-Philippe Garneau, 'Droit, famille et pratique successorale: les usages du droit d'une communauté rurale au XVIIIe siècle canadien' (PhD diss., Université du Québec à Montréal, 2003), chap. 4.
75 Grenier, *Marie-Catherine Peuvret*, 146–8. Unhappy censitaires of Michel LeNeuf de la Vallière of Beaubassin in Acadie managed to bring him before the Conseil souverain in 1682. They alleged he had no right to extract corvée from them, but the results of the proceedings are not clear; Kennedy, *Something of a Peasant Paradise*, 154.
76 Jacques Vanderlinden notes a possible exercise of the death penalty by a seigneur in Acadie in 1670, but this may have been done in a gubernatorial rather than seigneurial capacity; *Le lieutenant civil et criminel: Mathieu de Goutin*, 125.
77 Dickinson, 'La justice seigneuriale en Nouvelle-France,' 338.
78 As to these, see chap. 13.
79 André Vachon, 'Le notaire en Nouvelle-France,' *Revue de l'Université Laval* 10 (1955): 235.
80 It is often stated that the will was annulled by the Parlement of Paris, but the contrary is persuasively argued in Lucien Campeau, 'Le testament de Champlain,' *Les Cahiers des dix* 42 (1979): 49.
81 Alexandra Havrylyshyn, 'Barristers, Attorneys, and Legal Practitioners in Early Canada: A Guide,' in Lyndsay Campbell and Ted McCoy, eds,

Canada's Legal Past: Looking Forward, Looking Back (Calgary: University of Calgary Press, 2018).

82 For overviews of the history of the notarial profession, see André Vachon, *L'histoire du notariat canadien, 1621–1960* (Quebec: Presses de l'Université Laval, 1962); J.-Edmond Roy, *L'histoire du notariat au Canada depuis la fondation de la colonie jusqu'à nos jours*, 3 vols (Lévis, QC: Revue du notariat, 1899–1902); F.G. Marchand, *Manuel et formulaire général et complet du notariat de la Province de Québec* (Montreal: A. Périard, 1892). Michel Duquet, 'L'infrajudiciaire et les notaires de Québec, 1650–1784' (PhD thesis, Université d'Ottawa, 2008), adds important corrections and qualifications to Vachon's work.

83 Vanderlinden, *Le lieutenant civil et criminel: Mathieu de Goutin*, 73–8.

84 André Vachon, 'Guillaume Audouart dit Saint-Germain,' *DCB*.

85 Vachon, *Histoire du notariat canadien*, 39.

86 Alain Moreau, *Les métamorphoses du scribe: histoire du notariat français* (Perpignan: Socapress, 1989), 57–8.

87 J.-Edmond Roy, 'La cartographie et l'arpentage sous le régime français,' *Bulletin des recherches historiques* 1 (1895): 17–29, 33–40, 49–56.

88 André Vachon, 'Pierre Duquet de la Chesnaye,' *DCB*.

89 Vachon, *Histoire du notariat canadien*, 39–40.

90 Louis Lavallée, 'La vie et la pratique d'un notaire rural sous le régime français: le cas de Guillaume Barette, notaire à La Prairie entre 1709–1744,' *Revue d'histoire de l'Amérique française* 47 (1994): 499.

91 This conclusion is based on a random survey of documents contained in the Parchemin database of notarial documents, available at the various locations of Bibliothèque et archives nationales du Québec.

92 *Édit du Roi pour les Taxes des Officiers de Justice*, 12 May 1678, *EO*, 1:99–102.

93 *EO*, 1:609. Vachon, *Histoire du notariat canadien*, 44.

94 Vachon, *Histoire du notariat canadien*, 20–1.

95 Ordinance of 30 Apr. 1722, *EO*, 2:297.

96 Duquet, 'Les notaires de Québec,' 66–71.

97 Claude de Ferrière, *La science parfaite des notaires, ou le parfait notaire*, 2 vols (Paris: chez Durand, 1771), 1:48–9.

98 David Gilles, 'Le notariat canadien face à la Conquête anglaise: l'exemple des Panet,' in Vincent Bernaudeau, Jean-Pierre Nandrin, Bénédicte Rochet, Xavier Rousseaux, and Axel Tixhon, eds, *Les practiciens du droit du Moyen Âge à l'époque contemporaine* (Rennes: Presses Universitaires de Rennes, 2008), 191.

99 This paragraph relies on Havrylyshyn, 'Barristers, Attorneys,' and her 'Troublesome Trials in New France: The Itinerary of an Ancien Régime Legal Practitioner, 1740–1743' (MA thesis, McGill University, 2011).

100 J-E Roy, 'La justice seigneuriale de Notre-Dame-des-Anges,' *Revue canadienne* (3d ser) 11, no. 3 (1890): 594, 604–5; France Parent and Geneviève Postolec, 'Quand Thémis rencontre Clio: les femmes et le droit en Nouvelle-France,' *Cahiers de droit* 36 (1995): 293; *JDCS*, 5:873, 875–6 (Conseil supérieur, 1708).

101 Michel Morin, *Introduction historique au droit romain, au droit français et au droit anglais* (Montreal: Les Éditions Thémis, 2004), 163.

102 The entire ordinance with the introductory note and the Conseil's marginal notes is at *EO*, 1:106–230. Future references will be to title and article number only.

103 'ayant égard à la pauvreté des habitans de ce pays, à l'état d'icelui, à la difficulte qu'il y a de faire des voyages dans toutes les saisons, au peu d'expérience de la plupart des juges, au peu de capacité des huissiers et pour éviter aux frais qui arriveroient en beaucoup de rencontres par l'ignorance des habitans qui entreprennent des procès quelquefois sans y pouvoir réfléchir et sans pouvoir prendre conseil, ne se trouvant en ce pays avocats, procureurs ni practiciens, étant même de l'avantage de la colonie de n'en pas recevoir.' *EO*, 1:106–7.

104 *EO*, 1:236–8. Brisson, *Formation d'un droit mixte*, argues at 34–9 that only the remonstrances of the Conseil were registered, as opposed to the ordinance itself, but observes that its provisions were clearly followed with or without registration.

105 Title 17. See generally on what follows Dickinson, *Justice et justiciables*.

106 Dickinson, *Justice et justiciables*, 60–1.

107 Ibid., 62–9.

108 Ibid., 71.

109 Ibid., 74.

110 Ibid., chap. 5. See also Bruce Mann, *Neighbors and Strangers: Law and Community in Early Connecticut* (Chapel Hill: University of North Carolina Press, 1987); and James Muir, *Law, Debt and Merchant Power: The Civil Courts of Eighteenth-Century Halifax* (Toronto: Osgoode Society for Canadian Legal History and University of Toronto Press, 2016), for similar arguments in those jurisdictions.

111 See generally Peter Moogk, 'The Crime of Lèse-Majesté in New France: Defence of the Secular and Religious Order' in *CST*, 1:55–71; Arnaud Bessière, 'La justice étatique mise à mal: l'exemple de la police des domestiques au Canada au XVIIe siècle,' in Pascal Bastien, Donald Fyson, Jean-Philippe Garneau, and Thierry Nootens, eds, *Justice et espaces publics en Occident, du Moyen Âge à nos jours* (Quebec: Presses de l'Université du Québec, 2014), 61–70.

112 This was not stated explicitly in the edict creating the Conseil souverain in 1663, although it could be inferred; the ordinance of 1670, tit. 26, arts 1 and 6, stated that no such sentence could be executed until reviewed by the court of final appeal for that jurisdiction. The ordinance can be found in François-André Isambert, ed., *Recueil générale des anciennes lois françaises*, 29 vols (Paris: Belin-Leprieur, 1829), 18:370.
113 The following incident is known only from the works of Champlain himself, although his account seems to be corroborated by other evidence: *The Works of Samuel de Champlain*, 6 vols, trans. and ed. H.P. Biggar (Toronto: Champlain Society, 1922), 2:25–34.
114 Fischer, *Champlain's Dream*, 248–9.
115 See chap. 16.
116 On the application of the 1670 ordinance in New France, see André Lachance, *La justice criminelle du roi au Canada au XVIIIe siècle* (Quebec: Presses de l'Université Laval, 1978); Lachance, *Crime et criminels*.
117 Lachance, *La justice criminelle du roi*, 79–80. Prosecutors requested the use of la question eight times in the eighteenth century, but the Conseil souverain approved its use in only three. The total numbers of criminal cases are from Lachance, *Crimes et criminels*, 129–30.
118 Morin, *Introduction historique*, 184–5.
119 *JDCS*, 4:109–11.
120 André Morel, 'L'imposition et le contrôle des peines au Bailliage de Montréal (1666–1693),' in *Études juridiques en hommage à Monsieur le juge Bernard Bissonnette* (Montreal: Presses de l'Université de Montréal 1963), 425.
121 Lachance, *Justice criminelle du roi*, 90–1.
122 *JDCS*, 1:746.
123 Peter Moogk, 'The Liturgy of Humiliation, Pain, and Death: The Execution of Criminals in New France,' *Canadian Historical Review* 88 (2007): 89.
124 *JDCS*, 1:686–7.
125 Ibid., 1:649.
126 Ibid., 1:660.
127 Ibid., 1:763–5.
128 Ibid., 957.
129 Ibid., 155.
130 Cited at Lachance, *Crime et criminels*, 56.
131 *JDCS*, 1:642–3.
132 Lachance, *Crimes et criminels*, 63.

133 Jonathan Pearl, 'Witchcraft in Seventeenth-Century New France,' *Historical Reflections* 4, no. 2 (1977): 191; Alison Games, *Witchcraft in Early North America* (Lanham, MD: Rowman & Littlefield, 2010), 36–8.

134 Ordinance of 1670, art. 6, tit. 26.

135 Lachance, *La justice criminelle du roi*, 95–6. Votes were not recorded, so it is impossible to know how often the councillors split on sentence appeals. After 1675 there were eleven councillors, so if all were present, seven votes would be needed for the most severe penalty.

136 Denys Delâge, *Bitter Feast: Amerindians and Europeans in Northeastern North America, 1600–1664*, trans. Jane Brierley (Vancouver: UBC Press, 1993), 250–7.

7. Law and Governance in the English Possessions

1 The following relies on Philip Girard, 'Imperial Legacies: Chartered Enterprises in Northern British America,' in Shaunnagh Dorsett and John McLaren, eds, *Legal Histories of the British Empire: Laws, Engagements, and Legacies* (London: Routledge, 2014).

2 On Plaisance, see Nicolas Landry, *Plaisance (Terre-Neuve) 1650–1713: une colonie française en Amérique* (Quebec: Septentrion, 2008).

3 Peter Pope, *Fish into Wine: The Newfoundland Plantation in the Seventeenth Century* (Chapel Hill: University of North Carolina Press, 2004), 11–15.

4 For the text of the charter and the patents mentioned in this section, see Keith Matthews, *Collection and Commentary on the Constitutional Laws of Newfoundland* (St John's, NL: Maritime History Group, Memorial University of Newfoundland, 1975). On the disputes leading up to its issuance, see Ken MacMillan, *The Atlantic Imperial Constitution: Center and Periphery in the English Atlantic World* (New York: Palgrave Macmillan, 2011), 126–7. On the experience of the early chartered colonies, see Gillian T. Cell, *English Enterprise in Newfoundland, 1577–1660* (Toronto: University of Toronto Press, 1969); Cell, ed., *Newfoundland Discovered: English Attempts at Colonisation, 1610–1630* (London: Hakluyt Society, 1981).

5 Christopher English, 'The Development of the Newfoundland Legal System to 1815,' *Acadiensis* 20 (1990): 89 at 97.

6 Sean T. Cadigan, *Newfoundland and Labrador: A History* (Toronto: University of Toronto Press, 2009), chaps 2 and 3. Debate continues as to whether the Mi'kmaq began to have contracts with the island of Newfoundland in the sixteenth century.

7 Helen Dewar, '"Y establir nostre auctorité": Assertions of Imperial Sovereignty through Proprietorships and Chartered Companies in New France, 1598–1663' (PhD diss., University of Toronto, 2012).
8 For extensive historical and archaeological information on Ferryland, see Colony of Avalon, www.colonyofavalon.ca.
9 Pope, *Fish into Wine*, follows the flip-flopping on this issue, at 194–5.
10 John S. Moir, 'Sir David Kirke,' *DCB*.
11 C.M. Rowe, 'Sir John Berry,' *DCB*.
12 Jerry Bannister, *Rule of the Admirals: Law, Custom and Naval Government in Newfoundland, 1699–1832* (Toronto: Osgoode Society for Canadian Legal History and University of Toronto Press, 2003), 42–3.
13 See chap. 14 for later developments on this topic.
14 Bannister, *Rule of the Admirals*, explores the system of naval governance as it developed after King William's Act of 1699, but Pope, *Fish into Wine*, 309–10, provides some evidence of its origins in the 1680s.
15 For a similar process, see David Allen, *In English Ways: The Movement of Societies and the Transferral of English Local Law and Custom to Massachusetts Bay in the Seventeenth Century* (Chapel Hill: University of North Carolina Press, 1981).
16 The only study of the Act's passage is Alan Cass, 'Mr Nisbet's Legacy, or the Passing of King William's Act in 1699,' *Newfoundland & Labrador Studies* 22 (2007): 505.
17 These ideas are elaborated upon in Philip Girard, 'Newfoundland's Constitution from Contact to *King William's Act*,' in Melvin Baker, Christopher Curran, and J. Derek Green, eds, *Discourse and Discovery: Sir Richard Whitbourne Quatercentennial Symposium, 1615–2015* (St John's, NL: Law Society of Newfoundland and Labrador 2017).
18 The Charter can be found in *Charters, Statutes, Orders in Council Etc. Relating to the Hudson's Bay Company* (London: Hudson's Bay Company, 1960). The grant of the soil was sometimes attacked as void, given the vagueness with which its boundaries were described, but the law officers of the Crown twice opined (1777 and 1803) that it was valid, and no court was ever called upon to settle the question: Hamar Foster, 'Long Distance Justice: The Criminal Jurisdiction of Canadian Courts West of the Canadas,' *American Journal of Legal History* 34 (1990): 1.
19 HBC to John Bridgar, 15 May 1682, as cited in J.R. Miller, *Compact, Contract, Covenant: Aboriginal Treaty-Making in Canada* (Toronto: University of Toronto Press, 2009), 13.

20 Elizabeth Mancke, *Company of Businessmen: The Hudson's Bay Company and Long-Distance Trade, 1670–1730* (Winnipeg: Rupert's Land Research Centre, 1988), 17–18.

21 Heather Rollason Driscoll, '"A Most Important Chain of Connection": Marriage in the Hudson's Bay Company,' in Theodore Binnema, Gerhard J. Ens, and R.C. Macleod, eds, *From Rupert's Land to Canada* (Edmonton: University of Alberta Press, 2001), 81.

22 Driscoll, 'Most Important Chain of Connection,' 91. See also Sylvia Van Kirk, *'Many Tender Ties': Women in Fur-Trade Society, 1670–1870* (Norman: University of Oklahoma Press, 1980); Jennifer S.H. Brown, *Strangers in Blood: Fur Trade Families in Indian Country* (Vancouver: UBC Press, 1980). The gap between official policy and local reality is also demonstrated by the long-standing policy of local governors permitting free treatment to employees suffering from venereal disease, a benefit that began to be rolled back in 1738: K.G. Davies, ed., *Letters from Hudson's Bay, 1703–40* (London: Hudson's Bay Record Society, 1965), 247, 261.

23 Edward Cavanagh, 'A Company with Sovereignty and Subjects of Its Own? The Case of the Hudson's Bay Company, 1670–1763,' *Canadian Journal of Law & Society* 26 (2011): 25 at 29.

24 2 Will & Mar, c 23 (1690). On the events in this paragraph, see E.E. Rich, *The History of the Hudson's Bay Company*, 2 vols (London: Hudson's Bay Record Society 1958–9), 1:266–7.

25 6 Anne, c 37, s XXIII (1707).

8. The Interface of European and Indigenous Law

1 Bruce G. Trigger and William R. Swagerty, 'Entertaining Strangers: North America in the Sixteenth Century,' in Bruce G. Trigger and Wilcomb E. Washburn, eds, *The Cambridge History of the Native Peoples of the Americas*, vol. 1: *North America* (New York: Cambridge University Press, 1996), 378.

2 Thomas Peace, 'Two Conquests: Aboriginal Experiences of the Fall of New France and Acadia' (PhD diss., York University, 2011), argues that the relationship of the French with the Abenaki was actually closer and more important than that with the Mi'kmaq in the seventeenth century. The French wanted the territory of Wabanakia (modern-day Maine) to serve as a buffer state with New England, while the Abenaki needed allies to fight British settler encroachment from that quarter.

3 Edward Cavanagh, 'Possession and Dispossession in Corporate New France, 1600–1663: Debunking a "Juridical History" and Revisiting "Terra Nullius,"' *Law and History Review* 32 (2014): 97.
4 John Dickinson and Brian Young, *A Short History of Quebec*, 4th ed. (Montreal and Kingston: McGill-Queen's University Press, 2008), 18. These figures presumably represent the St Lawrence valley as far as Lake Ontario but do not include the Indigenous populations of the north shore or the Gaspé, home to Algonquin, Innu, and Mi'kmaq, which were outside the zone of European settlement. Earlier work by Dickinson and Jane Grabowksi suggests an Indigenous population as low as a few hundred for the seigneurial zone in the first half of the seventeenth century: 'Les populations amérindiennes de la vallée laurentienne, 1608–1765,' *Annales de démographie historique* (1993): 51 at 61, with significant population recovery thereafter.
5 Allan Greer, *Property and Dispossession: Natives, Empires and Land in Early Modern North America* (New York: Cambridge University Press, 2018), both quotations at 146.
6 See, generally, Michel Morin, 'Propriétés et territoires autochtones en Nouvelle-France I: Contrôle territorial et reconnaissance de territoires nationaux,' *Recherches amérindiennes au Quebec* 43 (2013): 43; Greer, *Property and Dispossession*.
7 Michel Morin, *L'usurpation de la souveraineté autochtone* (Montreal: Boréal 1997), 73.
8 Heidi Bohaker, '"Nindoodemag": The Significance of Algonquian Kinship Networks in the Eastern Great Lakes Region, 1600–1701,' *William and Mary Quarterly*, 3d ser. 63 (2006): 23.
9 Peter Cook, 'Onontio Gives Birth: How the French in Canada Became Fathers to Their Indigenous Allies, 1645–1673,' *Canadian Historical Review* 96 (2015): 166; Michel Morin, 'Fraternité, souveraineté et autonomie des autochtones en Nouvelle-France,' *Revue générale de droit* 43 (2013): 531.
10 Morin, *L'usurpation*, chap. 2.
11 Some scholars, such as Michel Morin in the works cited earlier, take the position that international law could be said to have governed the relations between Native peoples and European nations. In light of the emergent nature of international law itself in the seventeenth century, we prefer to view these relationships as based on a vernacular body of intercultural law specific to North America, while conceding that the relationship between these two positions is a matter for future research.

12 Gilles Havard, '"Les forcer à devenir Cytoyens": État, Sauvages et citoyenneté en Nouvelle-France (XVIIe–XVIIIe siècle),' *Annales: histoire, sciences sociales* 64, no. 5 (2009): 985 at 1010–11.
13 Reuben Thwaites, *The Jesuit Relations and Allied Documents*, 73 vols (Cleveland, OH: Burrows Bros, 1896–1901), 16: 135.
14 Denys Delâge, *Bitter Feast: Amerindians and Europeans in Northeastern North America, 1600–1664*, trans. Jane Brierley (Vancouver: UBC Press, 1993), 218.
15 Daniel K. Richter, 'Iroquois versus Iroquois: Jesuit Mission and Christianity in Village Politics, 1642–1686,' *Ethnohistory* 32 (1985): 1–16.
16 The term *domicilié* is widely used in the French-language literature to describe the Indigenous communities that developed around these missions. It conveys the aspirations of the colonial regime that these groups would become settled ('domiciled') agriculturalists who would adopt French ways, rather than the more complex reality of the situation. Some collective term is needed to distinguish these communities from traditional Indigenous villages, and we will use the term *mission villages* or *mission communities*. At some point (the timing is debated), the seven mission communities united in a loose confederacy known as the Sept Feux or Seven Fires. This term will be used in later chapters. We thank Daniel Ruëck for advice on this point. It should be noted that most of the groups who settled in these communities had some prior contacts with the St Lawrence valley; see Greer, *Property and Dispossession*, 152.
17 Kathryn Magee Labelle, *Dispersed but Not Destroyed: A History of the Seventeenth-Century Wendat People* (Vancouver: UBC Press, 2013).
18 Allan Greer, *Mohawk Saint: Catherine Tekakwitha and the Jesuits* (New York: Oxford University Press, 2005). Tekakwitha's mother was an Algonquin from the St Lawrence valley who had been captured by the Mohawks on one of their periodic raids and adopted into their village of Gandouagué (near Albany, New York), where Tekakwitha was born.
19 Edict establishing the Compagnie des Indes Occidentales, 11 July 1664, art. 34, *EO*, 1: 46.
20 Michel Morin, 'Des nations libres sans territoires? Les Autochtones et la colonisation de l'Amérique française du XVIe au XVIIIe siècle,' *Journal of the History of International Law* 12 (2010): 1 at 25–7.
21 Greer, *Property and Dispossession*, 153.
22 John A. Dickinson, 'Native Sovereignty and French Justice in Early Canada,' in *EHCL*, 5:19.
23 This and other early cases are analysed in detail in Michel Morin, 'La dimension juridique des relations entre Samuel de Champlain et les

Autochtones de la Nouvelle-France,' *Revue juridique Thémis* (n.s.) 38 (2004): 389.

24 *JDCS*, 13 Mar. 1664, 1:129–30 ('whether it was appropriate to subject the natives to French laws').

25 Ibid., 20 Apr. 1664, 1:174.

26 Jan Grabowski, 'The Common Ground: Settled Natives and French in Montreal 1667–1760' (PhD diss., Université de Montréal, 1993), 114.

27 Ibid., chap. 4.

28 *JDCS*, 11 May 1664, 1:188–9.

29 Ibid., 17 Apr. 1664, 1:170–1.

30 Letter from the king to the Marquis de Vaudreuil et Bégon, 19 Mar. 1714, cited in Grabowski, 'Common Ground,' at 110.

31 Camille de Rochmonteix, ed., *Relations par lettres de l'Amérique Septentrionalle (années 1709 et 1710)* (Paris: Letouzey et Ané, 1904), 61–2.

32 Peace, 'Two Conquests,' 255.

33 This is not to say that a *pax gallica* reigned everywhere after the Great Peace of 1701. In the western Great Lakes, some nations such as the Sioux were not part of the settlement, and the French and their allies engaged in a long war with the Fox Nation from 1712 to 1738; Gilles Havard, *The Great Peace of Montreal of 1701: French-Native Diplomacy in the Seventeenth Century*, trans. Phyllis Aronoff and Howard Scott (Montreal and Kingston: McGill-Queen's University Press, 2001), 173–8.

34 On what follows, see Brett Rushforth, *Bonds of Alliance: Indigenous and Atlantic Slaveries in New France* (Chapel Hill: University of North Carolina Press, 2012).

35 Ibid., 143.

36 Claude-Charles Bacqueville de la Potherie, *Histoire de l'Amérique septentrionale*, 4 vols (Paris: Jean-Luc Nion and François Didot, 1722), 4: 209–10.

37 Marcel Trudel, *Canada's Forgotten Slaves: Two Hundred Years of Bondage*, trans. George Tombs (Montreal: Véhicule, 2013) (translation of the author's *L'Esclavage au Canada Français* [1960]), 24–5.

38 Rushforth, *Bonds of Alliance*, 93.

39 Trudel, *Canada's Forgotten Slaves*, 35.

9. French Private Law

1 Michel Morin, *Introduction historique au droit romain, au droit français et au droit anglais* (Montreal: Éditions Thémis, 2004), 157–8.

2 In examining Acadian marriage contracts of the seventeenth and early eighteenth centuries, Jacques Vanderlinden has detected such influences: *Se marier en Acadie française, XVIIe et XVIIIe siècles* (Moncton, NB: Éditions d'Acadie, 1998).

3 Earlier commentators tended to present the Custom of Paris as a set of rigid rules: see Yves Zoltvany, 'Esquisse de la coutume de Paris,' *Revue d'histoire de l'Amérique française* 25 (1971): 365–4. More recent scholarship emphasizes the flexibility and creative ambiguity of the Custom: see Bettina Bradbury, Peter Gossage, Evelyn Kolish, and Alan Stuart, 'Property and Marriage: The Law and the Practice in Early Nineteenth-Century Montreal,' *Histoire sociale/Social History* 26 (1993): 9; and for a later period, Bradbury's *Wife to Widow: Lives, Laws, and Politics in Nineteenth-Century Montreal* (Vancouver: UBC Press, 2011).

4 Ernest Lareau, *Histoire du droit canadien*, 2 vols (Montreal: A. Périard 1888), 1:142–3. The French text of the Custom as well as an unofficial English translation can be found in Nicolas-Benjamin Doucet, *Fundamental Principles of the Laws of Canada as They Existed under the Natives, as They Were Changed under the French Kings, and as They Were Modified and Altered under the Domination of England* (Montreal: John Lovell, 1841–7).

5 Louise Dechêne, *Habitants and Merchants in Seventeenth-Century Montreal*, trans. L. Vardi (Montreal and Kingston: McGill-Queen's University Press, 1992), 217.

6 Cornelius Jaenen, *The Role of the Church in New France* (Toronto: McGraw-Hill Ryerson, 1976), 85.

7 Henry Des Rivières Beaubien, *Traité sur les lois civiles du Canada*, 3 vols (Montreal: Ludger Duvernay, 1832–3), 1:9–11. Those subject to banishment and to capital punishment also suffered civil death.

8 Vanderlinden, *Se marier en Acadie*, 44–5.

9 Ibid., 18–24. See generally on the law of marriage Paul Leclerc, 'Le mariage sous le régime français,' *Revue d'histoire de l'Amérique française* 13 (1959): 240–345, 374–401, 525–54; and 14 (1960): 34–60; 226–45.

10 Leclerc, 'Le mariage,' 374–8.

11 Benoît Grenier, *Marie-Catherine Peuvret: Veuve et seigneuresse en Nouvelle-France, 1667–1739* (Sillery, QC: Septentrion, 2005), 163–74. Late in the French regime the Conseil supérieur began to declare that marriages without parental consent were void, as the parlements of France had begun to do in the seventeenth century; Leclerc, 'Le mariage,' cites the arrêt of 12 June 1741 wherein the Conseil declared invalid the

marriage of the twenty-one-year-old René-Ovide Hertel de Rouville to the thirty-two-year-old Louise André de Leigne because it occurred without the consent of the husband's widowed mother: *EO*, 2:206–11. The parties later married with the consent of both families: Pierre Tousignant and Madeleine Dionne-Tousignant, 'René-Ovide Hertel de Rouville,' *DCB*.

12 See generally Leslie Tuttle, *Conceiving the Old Regime: Pronatalism and the Politics of Reproduction in Early Modern France* (New York: Oxford University Press, 2010), chap. 4; the arrêt is at *EO*, 1:67.

13 Vanderlinden, *Se marier en Acadie*, 41–2.

14 Most of the seventeenth-century notarial registers from Acadie have been lost, such that it is impossible to know if there was such uniformity in that colony. In Canada/Quebec, one study found 70 per cent of couples entering a marriage contract between 1680 and 1780, while another found the rate at Montreal to be 96 per cent between 1750 and 1770; see respectively Geneviève Postolec, 'Le mariage dans la Coutume de Paris: normes et pratiques à Neuville aux XVIIe et XVIIIe siècles,' in Sylvie Dépatie, ed., *Vingt ans après Habitants et marchands* (Montreal and Kingston: McGill-Queen's University Press, 1998); Dechêne, *Habitants and Merchants*, 240.

15 *Traité abrégé des anciennes lois, coutumes et usages de la colonie du Canada* (London: Guillaume Brown, 1775).

16 Des Rivières Beaubien, *Traité sur les lois civiles*. Beaubien does not give sources for his propositions of law. Cugnet cites articles of the Custom of Paris but then rearranges the whole for his own purposes.

17 Ibid., 1:36–7.

18 Sylvie Savoie, 'La rupture du couple en Nouvelle-France: les demandes de séparation au XVIIe et XVIIIe siècles,' *Canadian Woman Studies/Les cahiers de la femme* 7, no. 4 (1986): 58. Spouses, almost invariably women, could also ask for separation of property without asking for separation from bed and board. These are studied by Savoie in 'Women's Marital Difficulties: Requests of Separation in New France,' *History of the Family* 3, no. 4 (1998): 473.

19 Jean-Baptiste de Saint-Vallier, *Rituel du diocèse de Québec* (Paris: Chez Simon Langlois, 1703), 297–8.

20 Savoie, 'Women's Marital Difficulties,' 482.

21 Claude de Ferrière, *Nouveau commentaire sur la Coutume de la prévoté et vicomté de Paris*, 2 vols (Paris: Chez les Libraires Associés, 1770), 2:28. For a study of the functioning of community property in the eighteenth century, see Josette Brun, *Vie et mort du couple en Nouvelle-France: Québec*

et Louisbourg au XVIIIe siècle (Montreal and Kingston: McGill-Queen's University Press, 2006).

22 Savoie, 'Women's Marital Difficulties,' 475–6.

23 David Gilles, 'Être "demanderesse" en Justice: Permanences civilistes dans la Province de Québec, de la Juridiction royale de Montréal (1740–1760) à la Cour des plaids communs de Montréal (1760–1791),' in *EHCL*, 11:335.

24 Des Rivières Beaubien, *Traité sur les lois civiles*, 1:49-50.

25 France Parent, *Entre le juridique et le social: le pouvoir des femmes à Québec au XVIIe siècle* (Quebec: Cahiers de recherché du GREMF, 1991) (study of all cases before prévôté de Québec in 1686); Catherine Ferland and Benoît Grenier, 'Les procuratrices à Québec au XVIIIe siècle: résultats préliminaires d'une enquête sur le pouvoir des femmes en Nouvelle-France,' in Catherine Ferland and Benoît Grenier, eds, *Femmes, culture et pouvoir: relectures de l'histoire au féminin XVe–XXe siècles* (Quebec: Presses de l'Université Laval, 2010).

26 Brian Young, 'Getting around Legal Incapacity: The Legal Status of Married Women in Trade in Mid-Nineteenth-Century Lower Canada,' in Peter Baskerville, ed, *Canadian Papers in Business History* (Victoria, BC: Public History Group, 1989), 1:6 (regarding consent); Des Rivières Beaubien, *Traité sur les lois civiles*, 1:51 (parties to litigation).

27 Under certain circumstances a male minor could withdraw from paternal control by establishing a home of his own. Female minors could be emancipated only by marriage.

28 Edith Deleury, Michèle Rivet, and Jean-Marc Neault, 'De la puissance paternelle à l'autorité parentale: Une institution en voie de trouver sa vraie finalité,' *Cahiers de droit* 15 (1974): 779 at 814–20.

29 Des Rivières Beaubien, *Traité sur les lois civiles*, 1:38–9.

30 See generally on what follows, Zoltvany, 'Coutume de Paris'; Bradbury et al., 'Property and Marriage.'

31 The Custom of Paris distinguished between properties in Paris and elsewhere in article 227. Both Cugnet and Des Rivières Beaubien treat this article as in effect in Quebec, but both refer simply to 'city' property, leaving it unclear whether the term was meant to include Montreal and Quebec; *Traite abrégé*, 1:90, 92; *Traité sur les lois civiles*, 1:54–5.

32 Dechêne, *Habitants and Merchants*, 241.

33 The law in the early nineteenth century remained virtually the same as in the seventeenth century, although the use made of it by married couples began to shift somewhat, as will be considered in the next part.

34 Cugnet, *Traité abrégé*, 53–60.
35 Arts 15, 16, and 25 of the Custom of Paris, discussed by François-Joseph Cugnet, *Traité de la loi des fiefs: Qui a toujours été suivie en Canada* (Quebec: Guillaume Brown, 1775), 23–9.
36 Dechêne, *Habitants and Merchants*, 244.
37 Jean-Philippe Garneau, 'Droit, famille et pratique successorale: les usages du droit d'une communauté rurale au XVIIIe siècle canadien' (PhD diss., Université du Québec à Montréal, 2003), 134–7.
38 Geneviève Postolec, 'L'exclusion de la succession par exhérédation ou par substitution au Canada aux XVIIe et XVIIIe siècles,' in Gérard Bouchard, John A. Dickinson, and Joseph Goy, eds, *Les exclus de la terre en France et au Québec XVIIe–XXe siècles* (Sillery, QC: Septentrion 1998); on the life of Marie Brazeau, see Patricia Simpson and Louise Pothier, *Notre-Dame-de-Bon-Secours: Une chapelle et son quartier* (Anjou, QC: Fides, 2001), 52–3.
39 The debate is reviewed in Sylvie Dépatie, 'La transmission du patrimoine au Canada (XVIIe–XVIIIe siècle): qui sont les défavorisés?' *Revue d'histoire de l'Amérique française* 54 (2001): 558.
40 See, generally, Garneau, 'Droit, famille et pratique successorale,' especially chap. 3; and his 'Droit et "affaires de famille" sur la Côte-de-Beaupré: histoire d'une rencontre en amont et en aval de la Conquête britannique,' *Revue juridique Thémis* 34 (2000): 515.
41 Vanderlinden, *Se marier en Acadie*, 22; Lyne Paquette and Réal Bates, 'Les naissances illégitimes sur les rives du Saint-Laurent avant 1730,' *Revue d'histoire de l'Amérique française* 40 (1986): 239.
42 Savoie, 'Women's Marital Difficulties,' notes how evidence of marital mistreatment in actions for separation from bed and board tended to come from neighbours and community members.
43 The discussion here will be limited to Canada. While the Company of One Hundred Associates did recruit engagés for Acadie in the early 1630s, the leading men of the colony were successful thereafter in encouraging the migration of families from France, lessening dependence on engagés; Gregory Kennedy, *Something of a Peasant Paradise? Comparing Rural Societies in Acadie and the Loudonais, 1604–1755* (Montreal and Kingston: McGill-Queen's University Press, 2014), 137–8.
44 What follows relies principally on Dechêne, *Habitants and Merchants*, 20–36; G. Debien, 'Engagés pour le Canada au XVIIe siècle vus de La Rochelle,' *Revue d'histoire de l'Amérique française* 6 (1952): 177. Single women very seldom came as engagées; mostly they arrived subsidized by the French Crown, to provide brides for the men of the colony.
45 Cited in Dechêne, *Habitants and Merchants*, 27.

46 It is also not clear by what authority the Conseil imposed such penalties, the arrêt of 5 December 1663 having provided only that fugitive servants would have to pay their masters four pounds for each day of service lost; *EO*, 2:13; the Quebec City police regulations of 1676 specified the pillory for a first desertion and corporal punishment and branding for a second: *JDCS*, 2:63.

47 Peter Moogk, 'Apprenticeship Indentures: A Key to Artisan Life in New France,' Canadian Historical Association, *Historical Papers 1971*, 65.

48 David Gilles, *Essais d'histoire du droit: de la Nouvelle France à la Province de Québec* (Sherbrooke, QC: Éditions Revue de Droit de l'Université de Sherbooke, 2014), 581–635.

49 Eric Reiter, 'Translating the Untranslatable: Historical Aspects of the Protection of Honour and Other Extrapatrimonial Interests in Quebec Civil Law,' in Alexandra Popovici, Lionel Smith, and Régine Tremblay, eds, *Les intraduisibles en droit civil* (Montreal: Éditions Thémis 2014), 160–4. A French treatise on the law of defamation emerged in the eighteenth century: François Dareau, *Traité des injures dans l'ordre judiciaire* (Paris, 1775), as well as discrete works on other forms of delictual liability: Jean-François Tournel, *Traité de l'adultère, considéré dans l'ordre judiciaire* (Paris: Jean-François Bastien, 1778); and his *Traité de la séduction, considérée dans l'ordre judiciaire* (Paris: Demonville, 1781).

10. The Early Modern Legacy

1 Yasuhide Kawashima, *Puritan Justice and the Indian: White Man's Law in Massachusetts, 1630–1763* (Middletown, CT: Wesleyan University Press, 1986).

2 'English Settlement and Local Governance,' in Michael Grossberg and Christopher Tomlins, eds, *The Cambridge History of Law in America*, 3 vols (New York: Cambridge University Press, 2011), 1:72.

11. Constitutional Law in the Long Eighteenth Century

1 The following section is lightly footnoted, as the events referred to are well known and treated in the standard historical works. A good overview can be found in Robert Bothwell, *Your Country, My Country: A Unified History of the United States and Canada* (New York: Oxford University Press, 2015); and John Dickinson and Brian Young, *A Short*

History of Quebec, 4th ed. (Montreal and Kingston: McGill-Queen's University Press, 2008). The multiplicity of Indigenous viewpoints means that there is no single overview of this period, but a number of relevant works are cited later in the chapter, including Thomas Peace, 'Two Conquests: Aboriginal Experiences of the Fall of New France and Acadia' (PhD diss., York University, 2011); and John Borrows, 'Wampum at Niagara: The Royal Proclamation, Canadian Legal History, and Self-Government,' in Michael Asch, ed., *Aboriginal and Treaty Rights in Canada* (Vancouver: UBC Press 1997), that deserve special mention.

2 On the Jay Treaty, see Bradford Perkins, *The First Rapprochement: England and the United States, 1795–1805* (Berkeley: University of California Press 1967). Article 3 of this treaty provided that 'Indians dwelling on either side of the said Boundary Line [could] freely … pass and repass by Land, or Inland Navigation, into the respective Territories and Countries of the Two Parties on the Continent of America.' This provision was traditionally respected by the United States with respect to Canadian-born Indigenous people, and legislatively recognized in 1928 in U.S. immigration law: see Gerald F. Reid, 'Illegal Alien? The Immigration Case of Mohawk Ironworker Paul K. Diabo,' *Proceedings of the American Philosophical Association* 151 (2007): 61. However, according to the Canadian Senate Standing Committee on Aboriginal Peoples report, *Border Crossing Issues and the Jay Treaty* (2016), it has no effect on the Canadian side, either because Britain considered the treaty to have been abrogated by the War of 1812, or because the provision was never incorporated by statute into Canadian law.

3 John Borrows has noted the similarity between traditional descriptions of the British constitution and Indigenous law, both possessing a strong 'unwritten' component, in 'Indigenous Legal Traditions in Canada,' *Washington University Journal of Law & Policy* 19 (2005): 167 at 182–3.

4 Linda Colley, 'Empires of Writing: Britain, America and Constitutions, 1776–1848,' *Law and History Review* 32 (2014): 237 at 242–3.

5 Along with the American Constitution and the short-lived French and Polish constitutions of 1791, the *Constitutional Act* of 1791 is one of the earliest written constitutions in the Western world, although it is typically overlooked in constitutional catalogues because the Canadas were not yet independent nations; see Zachary Elkins, Tom Ginsburg, and James Melton, *The Endurance of National Constitutions* (New York: Cambridge University Press, 2009).

6 On the fall of Port Royal, see John Reid, Maurice Basque, Elizabeth Mancke, Barry Moody, Geoffrey Plank, and William Wicken, *The*

'Conquest' of Acadia, 1710: Imperial, Colonial, and Aboriginal Constructions (Toronto: University of Toronto Press, 2004).

7 Gerald S. Graham, 'Sir Hovenden Walker,' *DCB*.

8 The ultimately inconclusive boundary negotiations are examined in Jeffers Lennox, 'Nova Scotia Lost and Found: The Acadian Boundary Negotiation and Imperial Envisioning, 1750–1755,' *Acadiensis* 40 (2011): 3.

9 Cited in John G. Reid with Emerson W. Baker, *Essays on Northeastern North America: Seventeenth and Eighteenth Centuries* (Toronto: University of Toronto Press, 2008), 136.

10 William Wicken, *Mi'kmaq Treaties on Trial: History, Land and Donald Marshall Junior* (Toronto: University of Toronto Press, 2002).

11 A.J.B. Johnston, *Endgame 1758: The Promise, the Glory, and the Despair of Louisbourg's Last Decade* (Lincoln: University of Nebraska Press, 2007).

12 Fred Anderson, *Crucible of War: The Seven Years' War and the Fate of Empire in British North America, 1754–1766* (New York: A.A. Knopf, 2000).

13 Richard Middleton, *Pontiac's War: Its Causes, Course and Consequences* (New York: Routledge, 2007).

14 For the text of the proclamation, see http://www.solon.org/Constitutions/Canada/English/PreConfederation/rp_1763.html.

15 Knox's advice to Lord Shelburne was contained in a document reproduced in Thomas Barrow, ed., 'A Plan for Imperial Reform: "Hints Respecting the Settlement of Our American Provinces," 1763,' *William & Mary Quarterly*, 3rd ser., 24 (1967): 108.

16 J.R. Miller, *Compact, Contract, Covenant: Aboriginal Treaty-Making in Canada* (Toronto: University of Toronto Press, 2009), 66.

17 By the Treaty of Fort Stanwix in 1768, negotiated by Johnson, the Six Nations had already accepted a westward shifting of the Proclamation Line of 1763.

18 Alain Beaulieu, '"An Equitable Right to Be Compensated": The Dispossession of the Aboriginal Peoples of Quebec and the Emergence of a New Legal Rationale (1760–1860),' *Canadian Historical Review* 94 (2013): 1 at 10–11.

19 The Act, 14 Geo III, c 45, abrogated the royal charter of Massachusetts and substituted a governing council appointed by the king for the elective one provided for under the charter. It also forbade all town meetings without the consent of the governor.

20 Its legal aftermath is examined in Jim Phillips and Ernest Clarke, '"The Course of Law Cannot Be Stopped": The Aftermath of the Cumberland Rebellion in the Civil Courts of Nova Scotia,' *Dalhousie Law Journal* 21 (1998): 440.

21 28 Geo III, c 12.
22 *Epitome*, 1:108; 31 Geo III, c 31, ss XLVI, XLVII.
23 Maya Jasanoff, *Liberty's Exiles: American Loyalists in the Revolutionary World* (New York: Knopf, 2011).
24 98 ER 1045 (KB).
25 Gerald M. Craig, *Upper Canada: The Formative Years, 1784–1841* (Toronto: McClelland & Stewart, 1963), 114–15. The imperial statute is 14 Geo II, c 7.
26 Board of Trade to King George, 8 Sept. 1721, in *DCNY*, 5:628. The Crown began to buy out the proprietors of South Carolina at this time, but the first royal governor was not appointed until 1729; J.P. Greene, *The Quest for Power: The Lower Houses of Assembly in the Southern Royal Colonies, 1689–1776* (Chapel Hill: University of North Carolina Press, 1963), 36. Georgia was granted charter government in 1732, but only for twenty-one years, after which a royal government was put in place.
27 Mary Lou Lustig, *The Imperial Executive in America: Sir Edmund Andros, 1637–1714* (Madison, WI: Fairleigh Dickinson University Press, 2002). Craig Yirush, *Settlers, Liberty and Empire: The Roots of Early American Political Theory, 1675–1775* (Cambridge: Cambridge University Press, 2011).
28 Board of Trade to King George, 8 Sept. 1721, in *DCNY*, 5:629.
29 Georgia would be given a very similar constitution in 1754 after its initial 1732 charter was surrendered, and the two colonies were fondly looked upon in London as the way of the future: Edward J. Cashin, *Governor Henry Ellis and the Transformation of British North America* (Athens: University of Georgia Press, 1994). Ellis was the second royal governor of Georgia and later named governor of Nova Scotia but did not take up the position as the result of ill health.
30 John Stewart, *An Account of Prince Edward Island in the Gulph of St Lawrence, North America* (London, 1806), 267–8.
31 98 ER 1045 (KB). The case involved a challenge to a tax imposed by the Crown on Grenada after it had been promised an assembly in the Royal Proclamation of 1763, but before the assembly had actually been called. The court held that the timing made no difference: the tax was still unlawful.
32 Elizabeth Mancke, 'Colonial and Imperial Contexts,' in *SCNS*.
33 D.G. Bell, 'Maritime Legal Institutions under the Ancien Régime, 1710–1850,' *Manitoba Law Journal* 23 (1995): 103.
34 J.G. Simcoe to Phineas Bond, 7 May 1792, in E.A. Cruikshank, *The Correspondence of Lieutenant-Governor Simcoe* (Toronto: Ontario Historical Society, 1923), 152.

35 On what follows, see Philip Girard, 'Rearguard or Vanguard? A New Look at the *Constitutional Act* of 1791' (unpublished, 2017).

36 Governors' instructions were still issued to flesh out their commissions, but their ambit was restricted to matters not dealt with in the *Constitutional Act*.

37 Knox, 'Hints respecting the Settlement'; see also his 'Considerations on the Great Question, What Is Fit to Be done with America?,' part 1 of which was edited by Jack P. Greene as 'William Knox's Explanation for the American Revolution,' *William & Mary Quarterly*, 3d ser., 30 (1973): 293. Part 2 is found in the Sackville Germain Papers, vol. 17, William Clements Library, University of Michigan.

38 The bill was drafted in the late summer and fall of 1789, just as the French Revolution was starting, but not debated in Parliament until the spring of 1791. The revolution did not take a more violent turn until the next year, with the declaration of war on Austria in April 1792 and the deposition of the king in the fall; Peter Jupp, *Lord Grenville, 1759–1834* (Oxford: Clarendon, 1985), 93–5.

39 Grenville to Dorchester, 20 October 1789, in *Documents 1759–1791*, 969 at 982.

40 *Parliamentary Register* 29:365.

41 Kentucky, New Hampshire, and Vermont. In the Canadas, the property qualification in rural areas was land held in freehold or roture (the most widespread form of French land tenure) worth forty shillings annually, while in towns tenants paying an annual rental of ten pounds sterling were also eligible.

42 John Garner, *The Franchise and Politics in British North America, 1755–1867* (Toronto: University of Toronto Press, 1969), 60 (Hurons). Daniel Rueck, 'Enclosing the Mohawk Commons: A History of Use-Rights, Land Ownership, and Boundary-Making in Kahnawá:ke Mohawk Territory' (PhD diss., McGill University, 2013), 118 (Mohawks voting prior to 1810).

43 Frank Mackey, *Done with Slavery: The Black Fact in Montreal, 1760–1840* (Montreal and Kingston: McGill-Queen's University Press, 2010), 218–23.

44 Nathalie Picard, 'Les femmes et le vote au Bas-Canada, 1792–1849' (MA thesis, Université de Montréal, 1992). There were instances of propertied women voting in the 1793 and 1806 elections in Nova Scotia but not, apparently, in the other Maritime colonies prior to 1815; Brian Cuthbertson, *Johnny Bluenose at the Polls* (Halifax: Formac, 1994), 9. In both cases the House of Assembly was asked to rule on the validity of the votes but declined to do so, with the result that they were counted.

45 John Hare, *Aux origines du parlementarisme québécois, 1791–1793* (Sillery, QC: Septentrion, 1993), 85–107.

46 Arguably common law habeas corpus should have continued to be available from the institution of civilian government in 1764, even if habeas corpus under the Act of 1679 came and went under various ordinances: see generally Paul D. Halliday, *Habeas Corpus from England to Empire* (Cambridge, MA: Belknap, 2010), 274–81.

47 F. Murray Greenwood and Barry Wright, 'Introduction: State Trials, the Rule of Law, and Executive Powers in Early Canada' in *CST*, vol. 1.

48 Michel Ducharme, *Le concept de liberté au Canada à l'époque des Révolutions atlantiques, 1776–1838* (Montreal and Kingston: McGill-Queen's University Press, 2010), and in English translation *The Idea of Liberty in Canada during the Age of Atlantic Revolutions, 1776–1838*, trans. Peter Feldstein (Montreal and Kingston: McGill-Queen's University Press, 2014).

49 Elizabeth Mancke, *The Fault Lines of Empire: Political Differentiation in Massachusetts and Nova Scotia, ca 1760–1830* (New York: Routledge 2005), 5; and her 'Another British America: A Canadian Model for the Early Modern British Empire,' *Journal of Imperial and Commonwealth History* 25 (1997): 1; and 'Early Modern Imperial Governance and the Origins of Canadian Political Culture,' *Canadian Journal of Political Science* 32 (1999): 3.

50 Philip Girard, 'Liberty, Order, and Pluralism: The Canadian Experience,' in Jack P. Greene, ed., *Exclusionary Empire: English Liberty Overseas, 1600 to 1900* (New York: Cambridge University Press, 2009).

51 While the insanity of George III and the debauchery of George IV made them less than ideal monarchs, this state of affairs began to change with the accession of Victoria in 1837; initially, her youth and marriage, and later, her frequent child-bearing, rendered her a seemingly accessible and authentic figure, much more so than her predecessors.

52 9 Anne, c 17 (1710) reserved all white pine in America over twenty-four inches in diameter for the Royal Navy.

53 5 Geo II, c 7 (1732). This Act made land in America subject to seizure for debts on the same basis as chattels, contrary to the law in England, where landed debtors benefited from various immunities and privileges.

54 The royal charter granted to Saint John, New Brunswick, in 1785, providing for incorporation of the city and an elected council, was an exception. On the development of elective municipal government, see chapter 27.

55 Jean-Marie Fecteau and Douglas Hay, '"Government by Will and Pleasure Instead of Law": Military Justice and the Legal System in Quebec, 1775–83,' in *CST*, vol. 1.

56 F. Murray Greenwood, *Legacies of Fear: Law and Politics in Quebec in the Era of the French Revolution* (Toronto: Osgoode Society, 1993), 164; and see generally Greenwood, 'Judges and Treason Law in Lower Canada, England, and the United States during the French Revolution, 1794–1800,' in *CST*, vol. 1.

57 In fact, the *Act of Settlement* was not a panacea for judicial independence in Britain itself; David Lemmings has explored how the executive managed to influence the judiciary throughout the eighteenth century via inducements such as pensions (not guaranteed by the 1701 Act) and patronage appointments offered to judicial kin; *Professors of the Law: Barristers and English Legal Culture in the Eighteenth Century* (Oxford: Oxford University Press, 2000).

58 John McLaren, *Dewigged, Bothered and Bewildered: British Colonial Judges on Trial, 1800–1900* (Toronto: Osgoode Society for Canadian Legal History and University of Toronto Press, 2011); Jim Phillips, 'Judicial Independence in British North America: Constitutional Principles, Colonial Finances, and the Perils of Democracy, 1825–1867,' *Law and History Review* 34 (2016): 689 at 690–2.

59 On Nova Scotia, see Jim Phillips, 'The Impeachment of the Judges of the Nova Scotia Supreme Court, 1787–1793,' *Dalhousie Law Journal* 34 (2011): 165; on Quebec, Evelyn Kolish and James Lambert, 'The Attempted Impeachment of the Lower Canadian Chief Justices, 1814–15,' in *CST*, vol. 1.

60 These events can be followed through the subjects' *DCB* entries, and in McLaren, *Dewigged, Bothered and Bewildered.*

61 Board of Trade to King George, 8 Sept. 1721, in *DCNY*, 5:626.

62 Ibid.

63 Ibid., 626.

64 Ibid., 625.

65 Cited in Mark D. Walters, 'The Continuity of Aboriginal Customs and Government under British Imperial Constitutional Law as Applied in Colonial Canada, 1760-1860' (DPhil diss., Oxford University, 1995), 123.

66 Paul Williams, 'The Chain' (LLM thesis, York University, 1982), 69.

67 Borrows, 'Wampum at Niagara.' Similar arguments seem to have been made first by Williams in *The Chain*, chapter 4. For recent scholarship on the Proclamation, see Terry Fenge and Jim Aldridge, eds., *Keeping Promises: The Royal Proclamation of 1763, Aboriginal Rights, and Treaties*

in Canada (Montreal and Kingston: McGill-Queen's University Press, 2015).

68 Cited in Williams, *Chain*, 82.

69 Mark Walters, 'Rights and Remedies within Common Law and Indigenous Legal Traditions: Can the Covenant Chain Be Judicially Enforced Today?' in John Borrows and Michael Coyle, eds, *The Right Relationship: Reimagining the Implementation of Historical Treaties* (Toronto: University of Toronto Press, 2017) 191.

70 William Johnson to Thomas Gage, 19 Feb. 1764, in *The Papers of Sir William Johnson*, 14 vols (Albany: University of the State of New York, 1921–65), 4:328.

71 Williams, *Chain*, 110.

72 Jack M. Sosin, *Whitehall and the Wilderness: The Middle West in British Colonial Policy, 1760–1775* (Lincoln: University of Nebraska Press, 1961), 73–8.

73 See, generally, Walters, 'Continuity of Aboriginal Customs,' quotation at 110.

74 Here and throughout the rest of this book we use the term *Black* for African-Canadians, which is the current practice. See, for example, Barrington Walker, ed., *The African Canadian Legal Odyssey* (Toronto: Osgoode Society for Canadian Legal History and University of Toronto Press, 2012), which obviously employs the latter in the title and then, on the first page of the Introduction, uses *Black* eight times.

75 Kenneth Donovan, 'Slaves and Their Owners in Île Royale, 1713–1760,' *Acadiensis* 25 (1995): 3 at 26; Donovan discusses Roma's slaves at 10.

76 Differing interpretations of this event are provided in Afua Cooper, *The Hanging of Angélique* (Toronto: HarperCollins, 2006); and Denyse Beaugrand-Champagne, *Le procès de Marie-Josephe-Angélique* (Montreal: Libre Expression, 2004).

77 F.H. Severance, *An Old Frontier of France: The Niagara Region and Adjacent Lakes under French Control*, 2 vols (New York: Dodd Mead, 1917), 1:288–90.

78 W.R. Riddell, 'The Slave in Upper Canada,' *Journal of Negro History* 4 (1919): 372, 377–82; Maureen Elgersman, *Unyielding Spirits: Black Women and Slavery in Early Canada and Jamaica* (New York: Garland, 1999), 27–8; Afua Cooper, 'Acts of Resistance: Black Men and Women Engage Slavery in Upper Canada, 1793–1803,' in Lara Campbell, Tamara Myers, and Adele Perry, eds, *Rethinking Canada: The Promise of Women's History*, 7th ed. (Don Mills, ON: Oxford University Press, 2016).

79 Mackey, *Done with Slavery*, 96.

80 T.W. Smith, 'The Slave in Canada,' *Collections* of the Nova Scotia Historical Society 10 (1899): 14 at 40. Charles Field cautioned the public not to harbour 'my Indian slave Sal' in an advertisement in the *Niagara Herald* in 1802, cited by Smith at 48.

81 J.W. Walker, *The Black Loyalists: The Search for a Promised Land in Nova Scotia and Sierra Leone* (Toronto: University of Toronto Press, 1992), 41.

82 David Gilles, 'La norme esclavagiste, entre pratique coutumière et norme étatique: les esclaves panis et leur statut juridique au Canada (XVIIe–XVIIIe s.),' *Ottawa Law Review* 40 (2009): 73; Brett Rushforth, *Bonds of Alliance: Indigenous and Atlantic Slaveries in New France* (Chapel Hill: University of North Carolina Press, 2012). Statutes in Upper Canada and Prince Edward Island are discussed below. On the origins of Panis slavery, see part 2. An overview of slavery in French and British Canada can be found in Barrington Walker's introduction to his edited collection, *African-Canadian Legal Odyssey*.

83 Marcel Trudel, *Canada's Forgotten Slaves: Two Centuries of Bondage*, trans. George Tombs (Montreal: Véhicule, 2013), 53. Trudel identified 4,185 slaves during this period but concluded there must have been more who do not appear in the records. Mackey, *Done with Slavery*, chap. 3, points out problems of over-counting and under-counting in Trudel's slave census, but does not challenge the conclusion that about two-thirds were Panis.

84 *EO*, 2:271–2.

85 See above, chap. 3.

86 *EO*, 2:271.

87 Trudel, *Canada's Forgotten Slaves*, 52.

88 Beaugrand-Champagne, *Le procès de Marie-Josephe-Angélique*, 249.

89 Trudel, *Canada's Forgotten Slaves*, 50; Gilles, 'La norme esclavagiste.'

90 *EO*, 2:371.

91 Trudel, *Canada's Forgotten Slaves*, 179–91.

92 Rushforth, *Bonds of Alliance*, 181.

93 The argument that a slave should be freed by baptism had already been rejected in 1733 with regard to a Comanche slave known as Pierre, but in a suit by Pierre's former owner, not by the slave himself; Michel Paquin, 'Pierre,' *DCB*. See also Paquin's *DCB* entry on Radisson dite Duplessis.

94 On the trial, see Alexandra Havrylyshyn, 'Troublesome Trials in New France: The Itinerary of an Ancien Regime Legal Practitioner, 1740–1743' (MA thesis, McGill University, 2011), 34–43; Signa Daum Shanks, 'A Story of Marguerite: A Tale about Panis, Case Comment and Social History,' *Native Studies Review* 22 (2014): 113.

95 Cited in Trudel, *Canada's Forgotten Slaves*, 57.
96 Ibid., 256.
97 Mackey, *Done with Slavery*, 40–6. Mackey, chap. 2, has the most extensive coverage of the demise of slavery in Lower Canada and is relied upon in this paragraph and the next.
98 Robin W. Winks, *The Blacks in Canada* (Montreal and Kingston: McGill-Queen's University Press, 1997), 100.
99 As reported in *Cours du Temps/The Times*, 20 Oct. 1794, 93.
100 Trudel, *Forgotten Slaves*, 242, misidentifies William Osgoode, chief justice of the Court of King's Bench at Quebec, as the author of these decisions.
101 Donald Fyson, 'Minority Groups and the Law in Quebec, 1760–1840,' in *EHCL*, 11:291–2.
102 *LC Journals 1799*, 122, 126.
103 Mackey, *Done with Slavery*, 55 (sale), 46 (advertisement). As will be seen below, under the Northwest Ordinance of 1787 slaves were supposed to gain their freedom upon being brought into the Northwest Territory, which included Michigan, but Mackey at 56 suggests that the law was 'easily skirted.'
104 LAC, Blowers to Ward Chipman, Apr. 1800, Ward Chipman Papers, MG 23/4/D1, 141–3.
105 SPEI 1781, c 15. The Act was repealed in 1825: SPEI 1825 (2nd sess), c 7.
106 *Morison's Dictionary of Decisions* 14545 (1778).
107 D.G. Bell, J. Barry Cahill, and H. Amani Whitfield, 'Slavery and Slave Law in the Maritimes,' in Walker, *African Canadian Legal Odyssey*, 399.
108 Blowers to Ward Chipman, 1799, reproduced in J.W. Lawrence, *The Judges of New Brunswick and Their Times* (Saint John, NB: n.p., 1907), 73. On the cases of the 1780s, see Julian Gwyn, 'Female Litigants before the Civil Courts of Nova Scotia, 1749–1801,' *Histoire sociale/Social History* 36 (2003): 311 at 340–3.
109 Harvey Amani Whitfield, *North to Bondage: Loyalist Slavery in the Maritimes* (Vancouver: UBC Press, 2016), 107. Bell, Cahill, and Whitfield, 'Slavery and Slave Law,' locates the roots of the judges' views on slavery in their need to restore the social hierarchy they felt had been upended by the Revolution.
110 SUC 1793, c 7.
111 Smith, 'Slave in Canada,' 44–6.
112 Gregory Wigmore, 'From Slavery to Freedom in the Canadian-American Borderland,' *Journal of American History* 98 (2011): 437.
113 Henry Scadding, *Toronto of Old* (Toronto: Adam, Stevenson, 1873), 212–14. The slave was acquitted both times. When charged with grand larceny

in 1815 he was banished from the province but was now described as a 'former slave' of William Jarvis; we thank Patrick Connor for sharing research on this point.

114 W.R. Riddell, 'Notes on Slavery,' *Journal of Negro History* 4 (1919): 396, 396–7.

115 Barry Gough, *Gunboat Frontier: British Maritime Authority and Northwest Coast Indians, 1846–90* (Vancouver: UBC Press, 1984), at 85.

116 James Douglas, 'Diary of a Trip to the Northwest Coast, April 22–October 2, 1840,' as cited in R.S. Mackie, *Trading beyond the Mountains: The British Fur Trade on the Pacific, 1793–1843* (Vancouver: UBC Press, 1997), 302.

117 Gough, *Gunboat Frontier*, 86–9.

118 Peter Skene Ogden, *Traits of American-Indian Life and Character* (London: Smith, Elder, 1853), 67; the passage in question was written in 1838. The author, identified only as 'a fur trader,' is assumed to be Ogden. Born in Montreal and originally an NWC employee, in 1817 Ogden ordered the killing in cold blood of an Indigenous man who persisted in trading with the HBC. He was indicted for murder in Lower Canada but evaded justice by fleeing west of the Rockies. Post-merger he joined the HBC after an initial period of blacklisting; Glyndwyr Williams, 'Peter Skene Ogden,' *DCB*.

119 Although the possibility of manumission meant free Blacks could exist in theory in Canada pre-1760, their presence has not been studied and they are not considered here.

120 Lawrence Hill, *The Book of Negroes* (Toronto: HarperCollins, 2007); a CBC TV mini-series based on the book ran in 2015. There were two versions of the original *Book of Negroes*: one is in the National Archives in the United Kingdom, while the American version was published as Graham Russell Hodges, ed., *The Black Loyalist Directory: African Americans in Exile after the American Revolution* (New York: Garland 1996). Although the *Book of Negroes* contains 3,000 names, Hodges's tables show that 336 of them were actually slaves of loyalists.

121 Walker, *Black Loyalists*, 32 (3,550 figure); Bell, Cahill, and Whitfield, 'Slavery and Slave Law,' 365 (5,000 figure).

122 On these proclamations, see StG Walker, *Black Loyalists*, 1–3. Much of what follows relies on this source.

123 Walker, *Black Loyalists*, 137 (1792 figure); Winks, *Blacks in Canada*, 115 (1812 figure).

124 Walker, *Black Loyalists*, 55.

125 The accounts are cited in the authors' respective *DCB* entries. King's focuses almost entirely on his religious life and does not mention the

riot of 1784, noted later; George's mentions the riot, the pulling down of his house, and some other difficulties, but as bare facts, without any commentary.

126 Walker, *Black Loyalists*, 57.

127 Ibid., 24–7.

128 D.C. Harvey, ed., *The Diary of Simeon Perkins* (Toronto: Champlain Society, 1948–78), 36:238.

129 Winks, *Blacks in Canada*, 39; Walker, *Black Loyalists*, 49.

130 All examples from Marion Robertson, *King's Bounty: A History of Early Shelburne, Nova Scotia* (Halifax: Nova Scotia Museum, 1983), 96–7.

131 Cole Bricker, 'Freedom Denied: An Assessment of the Judicial Treatment of "Free" Blacks in Shelburne, Nova Scotia, 1783–1792' (unpublished, 2016).

132 Paul Craven, 'Canada 1670–1935: Symbolic and Instrumental Enforcement in Loyalist North America,' in Douglas Hay and Paul Craven, eds, *Masters, Servants, and Magistrates in Britain & the Empire, 1562–1955* (Chapel Hill: University of North Carolina Press, 2004), 181n32.

133 Cited in Whitfield, *North to Bondage*, 16.

134 Cited in Walker, *Black Loyalists*, 55.

135 Mackey, *Done with Slavery*, chap. 9, quote at 260.

136 Two Black slaves were sentenced capitally in 1773 and 1795, but both were pardoned on condition of banishment. The 1773 convict appears to have returned and reoffended, but while sentenced to death in 1778, there is no record of his actual execution; ibid., 248.

137 Mackey, *Done with Slavery*, 302 (1,000 figure); Donald Fyson, *Magistrates, Police, and People: Everyday Criminal Justice in Quebec and Lower Canada, 1764–1837* (Toronto: Osgoode Society for Canadian Legal History and University of Toronto Press, 2006), 303 (1 per cent figure).

138 William Renwick Riddell, 'The First Legal Execution from Crime in Upper Canada,' *Ontario Historical Society Papers and Records* 27 (1931): 514. Of the six capital convictions in Upper Canada, three involved Black slaves. Aside from Cutten, one escaped from prison before his execution, while the fate of the third is not known: Robert Lochiel Fraser, 'Mary Osborn' and 'Jack York,' both in *DCB*.

12. New France/Quebec/Lower Canada: Political Institutions, Courts, and Relations with Indigenous Peoples

1 Raymond Du Bois Cahall, *The Sovereign Council of New France: A Study in Canadian Constitutional History* (1915; New York: AMS), 196, 201.

2 Ibid., 204.
3 Cited by A.J.B. Johnston, *Control and Order in French Colonial Louisbourg, 1713–1758* (East Lansing, MI: Michigan State University Press, 2001), 28. This and the following paragraph also rely on this source.
4 See, generally, D.C. Harvey, *The French Regime in Prince Edward Island* (New Haven, CT: Yale University Press, 1926).
5 Margaret Coleman, 'Jean-Pierre Roma,' *DCB*.
6 Johnston, *Control and Order*, 241.
7 The text of the Capitulations of Quebec and Montreal can be found in *Documents 1759–91*, 3–29.
8 Armand Decroix, David Gilles, and Michel Morin, *Les tribunaux et l'arbitrage en Nouvelle-France et au Québec de 1740 à 1784* (Montreal: Éditions Thémis, 2012), 231–22.
9 Governor Murray's proclamation of 8 October 1760, setting up military tribunals within the district of Quebec, concludes, 'We interdict all other courts and jurisdictions which may have been established, as well in the town, as in the suburbs and the country.' 'Interdict' suggests that these courts were prohibited from acting indefinitely, not that they were necessarily abolished; *Documents 1759–1791*, 36.
10 'Report upon the Laws and Courts of Judicature in the Province of Quebec' (15 Sept. 1769), reproduced in W.P.M. Kennedy and Gustave Lanctot, eds, *Reports on the Laws of Quebec 1767–1770* (Ottawa: F.A. Acland, 1931), 66.
11 Decroix, Gilles, and Morin, *Les tribunaux et l'arbitrage*, 247–64; Arnaud Decroix, 'La controverse sur la nature du droit applicable après la conquête,' *McGill Law Journal* 56 (2011): 488.
12 Donald Fyson, 'The Conquered and the Conqueror: The Mutual Adaptation of the *Canadiens* and the British in Quebec, 1759–1775,' in Phillip Buckner and John G. Reid, eds, *Revisiting 1759: The Conquest of Canada in Historical Perspective* (Toronto: University of Toronto Press, 2012).
13 The literature on the Act is enormous; the classic work is Hilda Neatby, *The Administration of Justice under the Quebec Act* (Minneapolis: University of Minnesota Press, 1937); see also Philip Lawson, *The Imperial Challenge: Quebec and Britain in the Age of the American Revolution* (Montreal and Kingston: McGill-Queen's University Press, 1989); David Milobar, 'Conservative Ideology, Metropolitan Government, and the Reform of Quebec, 1782–1791,' *International History Review* 12 (1990): 44; Maurice Séguin, *Les Canadiens après la Conquête* (Montreal: Fides, 1969); Stephen Conway, 'The Consequences of the Conquest: Quebec and British Politics,

1760–1774'; and Heather Welland, 'Commercial Interest and Political Allegiance: The Origins of the Quebec Act,' both in Buckner and Reid, *Revisiting 1759*.

14 Georges-Étienne Proulx, 'Les Canadiens ont-ils payé la dîme entre 1760 et 1775?' *Revue d'histoire de l'Amérique française* 11 (1958): 533.

15 Donald Fyson, *Magistrates, Police, and People: Everyday Criminal Justice in Quebec and Lower Canada, 1764–1837* (Toronto: Osgoode Society for Canadian Legal History and University of Toronto Press, 2006), 85.

16 For details, see André Morel, *Les limites de la liberté testamentaire dans le droit civil de la province de Québec* (Paris: R. Pichon, 1960).

17 Cited in G.P. Browne, 'James Murray,' *DCB*.

18 This was, however, far from the end of the tangled tale of the Jesuit estates, which will be taken up in volume 2; J.R. Miller, *Equal Rights: The Jesuits' Estates Act Controversy* (Montreal and Kingston: McGill-Queen's University Press, 1979).

19 Michel Morin, 'Les revendications des nouveaux sujets, francophones et catholiques, de la Province de Québec, 1764–1774,' in *EHCL*, vol. 11. An adapted version can be found in English as 'The Discovery and Assimilation of British Constitutional Law Principles in Quebec, 1764–1774,' *Dalhousie Law Journal* 36 (2013): 581.

20 Decroix, Gilles, and Morin, *Les tribunaux et l'arbitrage*, 291–310, 355–90.

21 Marianne Constable, *The Law of the Other: The Mixed Jury and Changing Conceptions of Citizenship, Law, and Knowledge* (Chicago: University of Chicago Press, 1994), appears to be the only study of the institution in English, but it does not refer to Quebec.

22 An overview of the development of the courts in Quebec, on which this section relies, can be found on the website of Professor Donald Fyson of Université Laval, http://www.profs.hst.ulaval.ca/Dfyson/Courtstr/contents.htm.

23 Fyson, *Magistrates, Police and People*, 32–48.

24 See chap. 18 below.

25 Denys Delâge and Jean-Pierre Sawaya, *Les traités des Sept-Feux avec les Britanniques: droits et pièges d'un héritage colonial au Québec* (Sillery, QC: Septentrion, 2001).

26 Thomas Peace, 'Two Conquests: Aboriginal Experiences of the Fall of New France and Acadia' (PhD diss., York University, 2011), 284–300.

27 On what follows, see Alain Beaulieu, '"An Equitable Right to Be Compensated": The Dispossession of the Aboriginal Peoples of Quebec and the Emergence of a New Legal Rationale, 1760–1860,' *Canadian Historical Review* 94 (2013): 1.

28 Alain Beaulieu, 'Les garanties d'un traité disparu: le traité d'Oswegatchie, 30 août 1760,' *Revue juridique Thémis* 34 (2000): 369. No written text of this treaty has survived, but Beaulieu has reconstructed its terms from Indigenous oral tradition and colonial correspondence.

29 *Report of the Canadian Archives for the Year 1904* (Ottawa: S.B. Dawson 1905), 237 (emphasis added).

30 Cited in Beaulieu, 'Equitable Right,' 15.

31 Michel Morin, 'Des nations libres sans territoire? Les Autochtones et la colonisation de l'Amérique française du XVIe au XVIIIe siècle,' *Journal of the History of International Law* 12 (2012): 1.

13. The British Colonies of Settlement: Political Institutions, Courts, and Relations with Indigenous Peoples

1 Thomas G. Barnes, '"Twelve Apostles" or a Dozen Traitors? Acadian Collaborators during King George's War, 1744–48,' in *CST*, vol. 1.

2 Caulfeild to Board of Trade, 1 Nov. 1715, cited in Barnes, 'Twelve Apostles,' 11.

3 Board of Trade to King George, 1721, in *DCNY*, 5:592.

4 Micheline D. Johnson, 'Charles de La Goudalie,' *DCB*.

5 For what follows, see Thomas G. Barnes, '"The Dayly Cry for Justice": The Juridical Failure of the Annapolis Royal Regime, 1713–1749,' in *EHCL*, vol. 3.

6 Gregory Kennedy, *Something of a Peasant Paradise? Comparing Rural Societies in Acadie and the Loudonais, 1604–1755* (Montreal and Kingston: McGill-Queen's University Press, 2014), 78–9, 142.

7 Barnes, '"The Dayly Cry for Justice,"' 25–6.

8 Ibid., 3:31.

9 *A History of Nova Scotia, or Acadie*, 3 vols (Halifax: James Barnes, 1865–7), 1:409.

10 This paragraph relies on Ronnie-Gilles LeBlanc, ed., *Du Grand Dérangement à la Déportation, nouvelles perspectives historiques* (Moncton: Université de Moncton, 2005); Earle Lockerby, 'The Deportation of the Acadians from Île St-Jean, 1758,' *Acadiensis* 27 (1998): 45; A.J.B. Johnston, 'The Acadian Deportation in a Comparative Context: An Introduction,' *Journal of the Royal Nova Scotia Historical Society* 10 (2007): 114. Contrary to popular belief, the British did not deport the Acadians to Louisiana, as they did not wish to strengthen another French colony; a number of

Acadians went there voluntarily after the territory was ceded by France to Spain in 1763.

11 Maurice Basque, 'Prudent Robichaud,' *Oxford Companion to Canadian History* online. Robichaud's omission from the *DCB* is an important oversight.

12 A.J.B. Johnston, 'Borderland Worries: Loyalty Oaths in *Acadie*/Nova Scotia, 1654–1755,' *French Colonial History* 4 (2003): 31 at 40.

13 Reproduced in translation in N.E.S. Griffiths, *The Acadian Deportation: Deliberate Perfidy or Cruel Necessity?* (Toronto: Copp Clark, 1969), 82–3.

14 A.J.B. Johnston, 'French Attitudes toward the Acadians,' in LeBlanc, *Du Grand Dérangement*, 150–1.

15 The opinion is reproduced in French translation and in English as 'L'avis du juge en chef de la Nouvelle-Écosse concernant la déportation des Acadiens,' introduced by Hon. Michel Bastarache, at *Revue de droit d'Ottawa* 42 (2010): 253.

16 1 Geo I, c 13, s 26, mistakenly referred to in council as 1 Geo II, c 13; the minutes of the council meeting of 4 July 1755, at which Belcher was present, are reproduced in T.B. Akins, ed., *Selections from the Public Documents of the Province of Nova Scotia* (Halifax: Charles Annand, 1869), 255–6.

17 1 Geo I, c 13, s 26.

18 John Mack Faragher, *A Great and Noble Scheme: The Tragic Story of the Expulsion of the Acadians from Their American Homeland* (New York: W.W. Norton, 2005), 321 wrongly assumes that the statute in question relates only to office-holders.

19 A point made by Emmanuel Klimis and Jacques Vanderlinden, 'Deux juristes face à un évènement historique, ou du bon usage du droit face aux faits,' in LeBlanc, *Du Grand Dérangement*. As Geoffrey Plank, 'King George II and the Acadian Removal,' observes at 98 of the same collection, this legal concern may explain why only the adult males were rounded up, and the women and children were told to 'follow their [male kin] voluntarily.'

20 SNS 1759, c 3.

21 *NS Journals*, 25 Nov. 1763, cited in Barry Cahill and Jim Phillips, 'The Supreme Court of Nova Scotia: Origins to Confederation,' in *SCNS*, 58.

22 Ibid., 65, citing Monk, 'Observations on the Courts of Law' at 138, 140, and 'Observations on the Circuit Courts,' at 142–3.

23 SNS 1809, c 15 forbade the judges from holding any 'Office, Post, Place, Appointment or Situation' other than that of councillor, but there was some doubt as to whether it applied to elected positions such as members

of the assembly. When the member for Halifax, Charles Rufus Fairbanks, was named master of the rolls in 1834 and refused to resign his seat, the assembly passed a law declaring it vacant.

24 D.G. Bell, 'Maritime Legal Institutions under the *Ancien Régime*, 1710–1850,' *Manitoba Law Journal* 23 (1995): 103, quotation at 120.

25 See, generally, Arthur Stone, 'The Admiralty Court in Colonial Nova Scotia,' *Dalhousie Law Journal* 17 (1994): 363.

26 Bell, 'Maritime Legal Institutions,' at 112.

27 Brian Cuthbertson, 'Richard John Uniacke,' *DCB*. Mount Uniacke, built in 1813–15, was donated to the province by Uniacke's descendants and is today part of the Nova Scotia Museum complex.

28 See the discussion of the *nisi prius* system in chap. 4.

29 See below, chap. 16.

30 For example, SNS 1764, c 7, requiring the freeholders in each township to elect overseers of the poor annually, who were to set rates sufficient for their support and appoint collectors. The fullest study of 'low law' in British North America is Paul Craven, *Petty Justice: Low Law and the Sessions System in Charlotte County, New Brunswick, 1785–1867* (Toronto: Osgoode Society for Canadian Legal History and University of Toronto Press, 2014).

31 See, generally, *Epitome*, 1:123–9.

32 SNS 1778, c 2. The legislation on sheriffs was consolidated in SNS 1795, c 1. For the complaints, see the assembly's report on 'Inconveniences Arising from the Want of Sheriffs in Each County,' 23 June 1770, NSARM, RG5, series A, vol. 16, no. 31. The provost marshal was pensioned off, and the office disappeared thereafter in Nova Scotia. The position of provost marshal was also created in early Prince Edward Island, but in 1786 the office of high sheriff was created by statute 'to bring this Government, as near as may be, to resemble the envied and happy Constitution of our Mother Country'; SPEI 1786, c 15, s 1.

33 SNS 1783, c 1.

34 J.B. Brebner, 'Nova Scotia's Remedy for the American Revolution,' *Canadian Historical Review* 15 (1934): 171.

35 Keith Mercer, 'Northern Exposure: Resistance to Naval Impressment in British North America, 1775–1815,' *Canadian Historical Review* 91 (2010): 199 at 208n19.

36 Ibid., 218.

37 Margaret McCallum, 'The Sacred Rights of Property: Title, Entitlement, and the Land Question in Nineteenth-Century Prince Edward Island,' in *EHCL*, 8:360.

38 J.M. Bumsted, *Land, Settlement, and Politics on Eighteenth-Century Prince Edward Island* (Montreal and Kingston: McGill-Queen's University Press, 1987), 71.
39 Bell, 'Maritime Legal Institutions,' 115.
40 Bell, 'Maritime Legal Institutions.'
41 Ann Gorman Condon, *The Loyalist Dream for New Brunswick: The Envy of the American States* (Fredericton: New Ireland, 1984) at 44, 52, 69, 86; Robert Wesley Sloan, 'New Ireland: Loyalists in Eastern Maine during the American Revolution' (PhD diss., University of Michigan, 1971); Joseph Williamson, 'The Proposed Province of New Ireland,' *Collections of the Maine Historical Society* 9 (1904): 147.
42 Marion Gilroy, 'The Partition of Nova Scotia, 1784,' *Canadian Historical Review* 14 (1933): 375.
43 D.G. Bell, *Early Loyalist Saint John: The Origins of New Brunswick Politics, 1783–1786* (Fredericton: New Ireland, 1983), 64–5.
44 SNB 1802, c 5; Bell, 'Maritime Legal Institutions,' at 114.
45 While the exclusion of American vessels from the West Indies trade was lifted by the Jay Treaty in 1794, a combination of British and American actions later reinstituted a quasi-monopoly on the West Indies trade for merchants in the Maritime provinces: W.S. MacNutt, *The Atlantic Provinces: The Emergence of Colonial Society, 1712–1857* (Toronto: McClelland & Stewart, 1965), 131–6.
46 Ibid., 109–10.
47 For example, Anglicans held a monopoly on higher education, and also on incorporation, a privilege denied to dissenting churches.
48 Terrence Murphy, 'The Emergence of Maritime Catholicism, 1781–1830,' *Acadiensis* 13 (1984): 29; John Garner, 'The Enfranchisement of Roman Catholics in the Maritimes,' *Canadian Historical Review* 34 (1953): 203.
49 Brian Cuthbertson, *The First Bishop: A Biography of Charles Inglis* (Halifax: Waegwoltic, 1987).
50 Cited in Judith Fingard, *The Anglican Design in Loyalist Nova Scotia, 1783–1816* (London: SPCK, 1972), 115.
51 Ibid., 120–1.
52 Thomas Peace, 'Two Conquests: Aboriginal Experiences of the Fall of New France and Acadia' (PhD diss., York University, 2011), 191–200.
53 On this and what follows, see especially William Wicken, *Mi'kmaq Treaties on Trial: History, Land and Donald Marshall Junior* (Toronto: University of Toronto Press, 2002).
54 The treaty text is reproduced in Wicken, *Treaties on Trial*, 61–2.
55 Ibid., 219.

56 Beamish Murdoch, *History of Nova-Scotia or Acadie*, 3 vols (Halifax: James Barnes, 1865–7), 2:163.

57 J.M. Beck, 'Edward Cornwallis,' *DCB*. Beck refers to the 'depredations' of the Mi'kmaq at Canso and Halifax without noting that they considered these attacks to be retaliation for the killing of twenty Mi'kmaw women and children at Canso by New Englanders who had come upon the encampment while the men were away hunting; see Geoffrey Plank, *An Unsettled Conquest: The British Campaign against the Peoples of Acadia* (Philadelphia: University of Philadelphia Press, 2001), 127–8.

58 Michael Francklin, 'General Heads to Explain,' 26 May 1768, PRO, CO 217/22:211v (LAC and NSARM).

59 Brian Cuthbertson, *Stubborn Resistance: New Brunswick Maliseet and Mi'kmaq in Defence of Their Lands* (Halifax: Nimbus, 2015), 6–8, 22–3, 198–9.

60 Wicken, *Treaties on Trial*, 222.

61 Julian Gwyn, 'The Mi'kmaq, Poor Settlers, and the Nova Scotia Fur Trade, 1783–1853,' *Journal of the Canadian Historical Association* 14 (2003): 65.

62 SNS 1794, c 4; SNS 1816, c 5.

63 L.F.S. Upton, *Micmacs and Colonists: Indian-White Relations in the Maritimes, 1713–1867* (Vancouver: UBC Press, 1979), 87.

64 According to Donald B. Smith, 'The Dispossession of the Mississauga Indians: A Missing Chapter in the Early History of Upper Canada,' in J.K. Johnson and Bruce G. Wilson, eds, *Historical Essays on Upper Canada: New Perspectives* (Ottawa: Carleton University Press, 1989), the 'Mississauga' were actually Anishnaabe from northwest of Lake Huron, who had driven out the Haudenosaunee from southern Ontario in the 1690s, forty years after the latter had driven out the Huron nation. For reasons that are still debated, the French and later the British bestowed the name 'Mississauga' on these people.

65 Donald B. Smith, 'Wabakinine,' *DCB*.

66 Capt. W.R. Crawford to Haldimand, 9 Oct. 1783, cited in J.R. Miller, *Compact, Contract, Covenant: Aboriginal Treaty-Making in Canada* (Toronto: University of Toronto Press, 2009), 82.

67 *Indian Treaties and Surrenders, from 1680 to 1890* (Ottawa: B. Chamberlin, 1891), 1:5–6.

68 Ibid., 1:1–2.

69 Maclean to Sir Frederick Haldimand, 18 May 1783, in Charles M. Johnston, *The Valley of the Six Nations: A Collection of Documents on the*

Indian Lands of the Grand River (Toronto: University of Toronto Press, 1964), 36.

70 Susan M. Hill, *The Clay We Are Made Of: Haudenosaunee Land Tenure on the Grand River* (Winnipeg: University of Manitoba Press, 2017), 128–9.

71 These nations had fled warfare in the middle Atlantic colonies and been sheltered by the Haudenosaunee in the mid-eighteenth century; Hill, *Clay We Are Made Of*, 112. The Tuscarora, although accepted into the Confederacy as the Sixth Nation in 1722, were not given independent representation on the grand council; they were hosted by the Oneida: ibid., 267.

72 Hill, *Clay We Are Made Of*, 154–5.

73 On what follows, see, generally, Paul Romney, 'Upper Canada (Ontario): The Administration of Justice, 1784–1850,' in *CLI*.

74 This and the next paragraph rely on Margaret Banks, 'The Evolution of Ontario Courts 1788–1981,' in *EHCL*, vol. 2; William N.T. Wylie, 'Arbiters of Commerce, Instruments of Power: A Study of the see Civil Courts in Midland District, Upper Canada, 1789–1812' (PhD diss., Queen's University, 1980).

75 J.H. Aitchison, 'The Courts of Requests in Upper Canada,' in J.K. Johnson, ed., *Historical Essays on Upper Canada* (Toronto: McClelland & Stewart, 1975).

76 Russell Smandych, 'William Osgoode, John Graves Simcoe, and the Exclusion of the Poor Law from Upper Canada,' in Louis A. Knafla and Susan W.S. Binnie, eds, *Law, Society and the State: Essays in Modern Legal History* (Toronto: University of Toronto Press, 1995); Russell Smandych, 'Colonial Welfare Laws and Practices: Coping without an English Poor Law in Upper Canada, 1792–1837,' *Manitoba Law Journal* 23 (1995): 214; David Murray, *Colonial Justice: Justice, Morality, and Crime in the Niagara District, 1791–1849* (Toronto: Osgoode Society for Canadian Legal History and University of Toronto Press, 2002).

77 Nova Scotia's legal culture also had a significant Anglo-Irish strand in the eighteenth and early nineteenth centuries, due to the presence of a number of such men holding positions of influence, including the long-serving attorney general, Richard John Uniacke (1797–1830); Philip Girard, *Lawyers and Legal Culture in British North America: Beamish Murdoch of Halifax* (Toronto: Osgoode Society for Canadian Legal History and University of Toronto Press, 2011), 32–7.

14. The British Commercial Territories: Newfoundland and Rupert's Land

1 The classic works are Harold Innis's *The Cod Fisheries: The History of an International Economy* (Toronto: University of Toronto Press, 1954), and his *The Fur Trade in Canada: An Introduction to Canadian Economic History* (New Haven, CT: Yale University Press 1930).

2 King William's Act was essentially re-enacted in Palliser's Act of 1775, 15 Geo III, c 31.

3 Board of Trade to King George, 1721, in *DCNY*, 5:591.

4 Grenville to Lord Fitzgibbon, 2 Dec. 1789, cited in A.H. McLintock, *The Establishment of Constitutional Government in Newfoundland, 1783–1832* (London: Longmans, Green, 1941), 24; see also Jeff Webb, 'William Knox and the 18th-Century Newfoundland Fishery,' *Acadiensis* 44 (2015): 112. The home secretary had responsibility for colonial affairs at the time. The HBC charter itself declared the watershed of Hudson Bay to be 'henceforth reputed and declared as one of our Plantations or Colonies in America, called Rupert's Land.'

5 J.M. Bumsted, '1763–1783: Resettlement and Rebellion,' in Phillip A. Buckner and John G. Reid, eds, *The Atlantic Region to Confederation: A History* (Toronto: University of Toronto Press, 1994), 160–1.

6 Graeme Wynn, '1800–1810: Turning the Century,' in Buckner and Reid, *Atlantic Region*, 221–2; population figure for Newfoundland in 1815 (38,500) from Christopher English, 'The Development of the Newfoundland Legal System to 1815,' *Acadiensis* 20 (1990): 89 at 90. On the death of the migratory fishery and its impact, see Shannon Ryan, 'Fishery to Colony: A Newfoundland Watershed, 1793–1815,' in Phillip A. Buckner and David Frank, eds, *Atlantic Canada before Confederation* (Fredericton: Acadiensis, 1990).

7 See, generally, J.M. Bumsted, *Lord Selkirk: A Life* (East Lansing, MI: Michigan State University Press, 2009).

8 Ann M. Carlos and Frank D. Lewis, *Commerce by a Frozen Sea: Native Americans and the European Fur Trade* (Philadelphia: University of Pennsylvania Press, 2010), 7.

9 Hamar Foster, 'Long-Distance Justice: The Criminal Jurisdiction of Canadian Courts West of the Canadas, 1763-1859' *American Journal of Legal History* 34 (1990): 1 at 12–14.

10 *The British Empire in America*, 2 vols (London, 1708), 1:11.

11 Peter Pope described Newfoundland as having a 'vernacular' economy, one growing organically out of local conditions, and we draw on that

concept here: *Fish into Wine: The Newfoundland Plantation in the Seventeenth Century* (Chapel Hill: University of North Carolina Press, 2004).

12 PRO, CO 194/7, 22, cited in Jerry Bannister, *The Rule of the Admirals: Law, Custom, and Naval Government in Newfoundland, 1699–1832* (Toronto: Osgoode Society for Canadian Legal History and University of Toronto Press, 2003), 44; Keith Matthews, 'William Keen,' *DCB*.

13 PRO, CO 194/2, 132, cited in Bannister, *Rule of the Admirals*, 33.

14 'Sir N. Trevanion's Orders and Fishery Scheme,' reproduced in D.W. Prowse, *History of Newfoundland* (London: Macmillan, 1895), 272.

15 Jeff A. Webb, 'Leaving the State of Nature: A Locke-Inspired Political Community in St John's, Newfoundland, 1723,' *Acadiensis* 21 (1994): 154 at 155.

16 Bannister, *Rule of the Admirals*, 46; we rely on this source, along with English, 'Newfoundland Legal System,' and English, 'From Fishing Schooner to Colony: The Legal Development of Newfoundland, 1791–1832,' in Louis A. Knafla and Susan W.S. Binnie, eds, *Law, Society, and the State: Essays in Modern Legal History* (Toronto: University of Toronto Press, 1995), for much of what follows.

17 Matthews, 'William Keen,' *DCB*.

18 Bannister, *Rule of the Admirals*.

19 Ibid., 172–3.

20 32 Geo III, c 46, s 1 (1792); English, 'Newfoundland Legal System,' and his *A Cautious Beginning: The Court of Civil Jurisdiction, 1791* (St John's: Jesperson, 1991).

21 In addition to their entries in both the *DCB* and the *Oxford Dictionary of National Biography*, see G. Blaine Baker, 'Musings and Silences of Chief Justice William Osgoode: Digest Marginalia about the Reception of Imperial Law,' *Osgoode Hall Law Journal* 54 (2017): 741; Mark Warren Bailey, 'John Reeves, Esq., Newfoundland's First Chief Justice: English Law and Politics in the Eighteenth Century,' *Newfoundland Studies* 14 (1998): 28. Osgoode (1754–1824) was the son of a hosier, who managed nonetheless to leave his son a substantial inheritance, while the occupation of the father of Reeves (1752–1829) is unknown.

22 A detailed examination of the business of the sessions and surrogate courts in the Burin District can be found in David Brown, 'Flakes, Protests and Privateers: A Glimpse into Outport Justice through the Records of the Burin, Newfoundland, Court of Sessions (1811–1815),' in Melvin Baker, Christopher Curran, and Derek Green, eds, *Discourse and Discovery: 1615–2015 and Beyond* (St John's, NL: Law Society of Newfoundland and Labrador, 2017).

23 Edward Cavanagh, 'A Company with Sovereignty and Subjects of Its Own? The Case of the Hudson's Bay Company, 1670–1763,' *Canadian Journal of Law and Society* 26 (2011): 25.
24 The Charter can be found in *Charters, Statutes, Orders in Council etc. relating to the Hudson's Bay Company* (London: Hudson's Bay Company, 1960).
25 Robert Baker, 'Law Transplanted, Justice Invented: Sources of Law for the Hudson's Bay Company in Rupert's Land, 1670–1870' (MA thesis, University of Manitoba, 1996), 43–52.
26 Cited by Paul C. Nigol, 'Discipline and Discretion in the Mid-Eighteenth-Century Hudson's Bay Company Private Justice System,' in Louis A. Knafla and Jonathan Swainger, eds, *Laws and Societies in the Canadian Prairie West, 1670–1940* (Vancouver: UBC Press, 2005) at 159; see also Russell Smandych and Rick Linden, 'Administering Justice without the State: A Study of the Private Justice System of the Hudson's Bay Company to 1800,' *Canadian Journal of Law & Society* 11 (1996): 21.
27 Bannister, *Rule of the Admirals*, 245, reports that in Trinity, servants initiated three-quarters of the total actions begun between 1765 and 1790, and won up to half of them.
28 Joseph Robson, *An Account of Six Years Residence in Hudson Bay* (London: T. Jeffreys, 1752), 17.
29 See, generally, Edith L. Burley, *Servants of the Honourable Company: Work, Discipline, and Conflict in the Hudson's Bay Company, 1770–1879* (Don Mills, ON: Oxford University Press, 1997).
30 Glyndwyr Williams, ed., *Andrew Graham's Observations on Hudson's Bay 1767–91* (London: Hudson's Bay Record Society, 1969), 27:158.
31 Jennifer S.H. Brown, *Strangers in Blood: Fur Trade Company Families in Indian Country* (Vancouver: UBC Press, 1980), 63–7; Sylvia van Kirk, *Many Tender Ties: Women in Fur Trader Society 1670–1870* (Winnipeg: Watson & Dwyer, 1980).
32 See the discussion of *Connolly v Woolrich* in chap. 23.
33 Cavanagh, 'Company with Sovereignty,' at 46–7; Arthur J. Ray, 'Periodic Shortages, Native Welfare, and the Hudson's Bay Company 1670–1930,' in Shepherd Krech, III, ed., *The Subarctic Fur Trade: Native Social and Economic Adaptations* (Vancouver: UBC Press, 1984).
34 Unlike Cumberland House, built in 1774 as the HBC's first full-service interior trading post, Henley House was a sort of 'loss leader' with a few supplies, whose main role was to convince Indigenous trappers to bring their furs to Albany Fort itself.
35 George E. Thorman, 'Wappisis,' *DCB*.

36 Foster, 'Long-Distance Justice,' at 8.
37 Sewell to Lieutenant Governor Sir Robert Shore Milnes, 23 Oct. 1802, reproduced in 'Courts of Justice for the Indian Country,' note E to *Report of the Archives, Canada, Sessional Papers*, No. 7A (1893), 141–2. Free to resume his fur-trading activities, Lamothe later returned to Montreal where, as captain of a group of Indigenous warriors, he helped repel American troops at the battle of Chateauguay during the war of 1812; Douglas Leighton, 'Joseph-Maurice Lamothe,' *DCB*.
38 43 Geo III, c 138.
39 Macdonell had issued notices to quit to the factors of NWC posts on HBC territory, which Lord Selkirk advised Macdonell to accomplish 'in the manner pointed out in Burns's Justice – Article Distress – Tenant holding over – considering them as tenants at will – This should be done in writing, & verbally also, before enough of witnesses to prevent any question as to the Notice being received.' These formalities were meant to prevent the prescription period from running, but the NWC interpreted them as an attempted ouster and responded in kind; Bumsted, *Lord Selkirk*, 239.
40 Roy C. Dalton, 'William Coltman,' *DCB*. See also Foster, 'Long Distance Justice,' 29–30.
41 Public Archives of Manitoba, HBC Archives, fonds E8/8, ff 116–68.
42 1 & 2 Geo. IV, c. 66.

15. The Legal Professions

1 Rupert Bartlett, 'The Legal Profession in Newfoundland,' in J.R. Smallwood, ed., *The Book of Newfoundland* (St John's, NL: Newfoundland Book Publishers, 1967).
2 Rules of court on these topics were not adopted until 1825 in Newfoundland, pursuant to authority granted under the *Royal Charter for Establishing the Supreme and Circuit Courts of Newfoundland* of that year. For the Charter and rules, see Newfoundland Law Reform Commission, *A History of the Newfoundland Judicature Act, 1791–1984* (St John's, NL: NLRC, 1989); Edward M Archibald, ed., *Digest of the Laws of Newfoundland* (St John's, NL: Henry Winton, 1847).
3 John Dickinson, *Justice et justiciables: la procédure civile à la Prévoté de Québec, 1667–1759* (Quebec: Presses de l'Université Laval, 1982), 85n28.
4 André Vachon, *Histoire du notariat canadien, 1621–1960* (Quebec: Presses de l'Université Laval, 1962), 26–8.

5 The three declarations are found at *EO*, 1:536–44.

6 On what follows, see Claude Vachon, 'Louis-Guillaume Verrier,' *DCB*; E. Fabre-Surveyer, 'Louis-Guillaume Verrier,' *Revue d'histoire de l'Amérique française* 6 (1952–3): 159; J.-Edmond Roy, *Histoire du notariat depuis la fondation de la colonie jusqu'à nos jours*, 4 vols (Lévis 1899-1902), 1:382–6.

7 Louis Lavallée, 'La vie et la pratique d'un notaire rural sous le régime français: le cas de Guillaume Barette, notaire à La Prairie entre 1709–1744,' *Revue d'histoire de l'Amérique française* 47 (1994): 499 at 510–11.

8 Michel Duquet, 'L'infrajudiciaire et les notaires de Québec, 1650–1784' (PhD diss., Université d'Ottawa, 2008), chap. 2.

9 Armand Decroix, David Gilles, and Michel Morin, *Les tribunaux et l'arbitrage en Nouvelle-France et au Québec de 1740 à 1784* (Montreal: Éditions Thémis, 2012), 398.

10 Ibid., 393 (authors' translation).

11 Ibid., 405.

12 Vachon, *Histoire du notariat*, 70–4; Jean-Philippe Garneau, 'Une culture de l'amalgame au prétoire: les avocats de Québec et l'élaboration d'un langage juridique commun au tournant des XVIIIe et XIXe siècles,' *Canadian Historical Review* 88 (2007): 113 at 129–33; David Roberts, 'Alexandre Dumas,' *DCB*. The ordinance itself can be found in *Ordinances Made and Passed by the Governor and Legislative Council of the Province of Quebec, and Now in Force in the Province of Lower-Canada* (Quebec: William Vondenvelden, 1795), 97–104.

13 Vachon, *Histoire du notariat*, 67.

14 Garneau, 'Une culture de l'amalgame.'

15 De Tocqueville witnessed court proceedings in Montreal in the early 1830s and left a vivid account of the bilingual proceedings; *Regards sur le Canada* (Montreal: Éditions Typo, 2003), 163–5, reproduced in Garneau, 'Culture de l'amalgame,' 137.

16 SUC 1794, c 4.

17 SUC 1797, c 13.

18 G. Blaine Baker, 'Legal Education in Upper Canada 1785–1889: The Law Society as Educator,' in *EHCL*, vol. 2; Christopher Moore, *The Law Society of Upper Canada and Ontario's Lawyers, 1797–1997* (Toronto: University of Toronto Press, 1997).

19 Philip Girard, *Lawyers and Legal Culture in British North America: Beamish Murdoch of Halifax* (Toronto: Osgoode Society for Canadian Legal History and University of Toronto Press, 2011), 48; H.T. Holman, 'The Bar of Prince Edward Island, 1769–1852,' *University of New Brunswick Law Journal* 41 (1992): 197.

20 D.G. Bell, *Legal Education in New Brunswick: A History* (Fredericton: University of New Brunswick, 1992), 14. College graduates needed to serve four years only.

21 SNS 1811, c 3.
22 Fernand Ouellet, 'Pierre-Stanislas Bédard,' *DCB*.

16. Criminal Law and Criminal Justice

1 Donald Fyson, *Magistrates, Police, and People: Everyday Criminal Justice in Quebec and Lower Canada, 1764–1837* (Toronto: Osgoode Society for Canadian Legal History and University of Toronto Press, 2006).
2 We do not discuss in detail patterns of offending. Those are more about social history than legal history, and the emphasis here is on the law and the operation of legal institutions. For patterns of offending in the eighteenth century, see Jim Phillips and Allyson N. May, 'Homicide in Nova Scotia, 1749–1815,' *Canadian Historical Review* 82 (2001): 625; Jim Phillips, 'Women, Crime and Criminal Justice in Early Halifax, 1750–1800,' in *EHCL*, vol. 5; Patrick Connor, 'The Purest of Gifts: Royal Clemency, Patronage, and the Politics of Identity in Upper Canada, 1791–1841' (PhD diss., York University, 2012).
3 For this decision see the discussion below. It is examined in detail in John Ll. J. Edwards, 'The Advent of English Criminal Law and Procedure into Canada: A Close Call in 1774,' *Criminal Law Quarterly* 26 (1984): 464.
4 What follows is based on an extensive English literature, with the standard work still being John M. Beattie, *Crime and the Courts in England, 1660–1800* (Princeton: Princeton University Press, 1986). See also Douglas Hay, 'Property, Authority and the Criminal Law,' in Douglas Hay, Peter Linebaugh, John G. Rule, E.P. Thompson, and Cal Winslow, eds, *Albion's Fatal Tree: Crime and Society in Eighteenth Century England* (London: Allen Lane, 1975); John M. Beattie, *Policing and Punishment in London 1660–1750: Urban Crime and the Limits of Terror* (Oxford: Oxford University Press, 2001); Victor Gatrell, *The Hanging Tree: Execution and the English People* (Oxford: Oxford University Press, 1994); Peter King, *Crime and the Law in England, 1750–1840: Remaking Justice from the Margins* (Cambridge: Cambridge University Press, 2006).
5 Beattie, *Crime and the Courts*, 141.
6 Usually cited for the figure of 200 is Leon Radzinowicz, *A History of Criminal Law and Its Administration from 1750* (London: Stevens, 1948), 1:4.
7 For Nova Scotia, see Jim Phillips, 'Securing Obedience to Necessary Laws: The Criminal Law in Eighteenth-Century Nova Scotia,' *Nova Scotia*

Historical Review 12 (1992): 87. English criminal law was partially in effect in Nova Scotia in the 'Annapolis period': see Thomas G. Barnes, 'The Dayly Cry for Justice: The Juridical Failure of the Annapolis Regime, 1713–1749,' in *EHCL*, vol. 3.

8 See Jerry Bannister, *The Rule of the Admirals: Law, Custom and Naval Government in Newfoundland, 1699–1832* (Toronto: Osgoode Society for Canadian Legal History and University of Toronto Press, 2003), chap. 6.

9 On reception in New Brunswick, see chap. 19, below. Some local statutes were passed in the late 1780s and early 1790s, but they were nowhere close to a comprehensive code.

10 For the former, see SNB 1791, c 7. For the latter, SNB 1789, c 7.

11 English criminal law had been introduced with the conquest, and this decision was confirmed in the 1774 *Quebec Act*.

12 SUC 1800, c 1. The Act's preamble stated that 'divers amendments and improvements' had been made to English law since 1774, and it was 'expedient' to introduce those changes to the colony. This did not mean a 'milder' code; capital offences had been added in England since the 1770s. Romney is wrong to state that Upper Canada kept the law as of the *Quebec Act* and introduced only the civil law in 1792; Paul Romney, *Mr Attorney: The Attorney-General for Ontario in Court, Cabinet and Legislature, 1791–1899* (Toronto: Osgoode Society for Canadian Legal History and University of Toronto Press, 1986), 16.

13 SUC 1800, ss 3 and 5. The courts were empowered to substitute fines or whipping for branding in the cases of those who had received their clergy. The Act prescribed death for those caught returning from banishment.

14 SUC 1792, c 2.

15 Belcher's Sentencing Speech, in NSARM, Belcher Papers, MG1, vol. 1738, no. 111, cited in Phillips, 'Securing Obedience,' at 109. Cesare Beccaria's landmark treatise *On Crimes and Punishments* was published in 1764 and advocated elimination of the death penalty and punishments proportional to the crime, among other things. Belcher did not refer to Beccaria, but his reference is pointedly about Beccaria's arguments.

16 The leading account of Quebec in this period is now Fyson, *Magistrates, Police and People*. Still useful are older surveys by André Morel, 'The Reception of English Criminal Law in Quebec, 1760–1892,' *Revue juridique Thémis* 13 (1978): 449; and Claude Désaulniers, 'La Peine de Mort dans la Législation Criminelle de 1760 à 1892,' *Revue Générale de Droit* 8 (1977): 141.

17 Cited in Edwards, 'Advent of English Criminal Law,' at 465.

18 Cited in Douglas Hay, 'The Meanings of the Criminal Law in Quebec, 1764–1774,' in Louis A. Knafla, ed., *Crime and Criminal Justice in Europe and Canada* (Waterloo, ON: Wilfrid Laurier University Press, 1981), 83.

19 SNS 1758, c 13. For a full discussion of this legislation, see Phillips, 'Securing Obedience,' at 114–16.

20 SPEI 1792, c 1.

21 For Lower Canada, see Fyson, *Magistrates, Police and People*, 21, and for Nova Scotia, see Phillips, 'Securing Obedience,' at 122. Nova Scotia added five offences to the lists of those capital, including that of looting at the scene of a fire in Halifax: SNS 1766, c 1. This was later extended to Liverpool, Dartmouth, and Pictou. The Lower Canadian assembly passed at least seven statutes prior to 1815 making offences felonies capital, including one making the forging or counterfeiting army bills capital: SLC 1814, c 3, s 6.

22 Jim Hornby, *In the Shadow of the Gallows: Criminal Law and Capital Punishment in Prince Edward Island* (Charlottetown: Institute of Island Studies, 1998), 2.

23 Nobody has properly calculated this figure for New Brunswick, but an index to the case files of the New Brunswick Supreme Court shows that fewer than two dozen people were tried for a capital crime between 1784 and 1814, meaning that the numbers of those capitally sentenced and executed must have been even smaller: see PANB, RS 42, Supreme Court Case Files, Index Volume. See also PANB, RS 30B, Crown Causes, no. 2, a listing of all cases tried in the Supreme Court at Fredericton 1802–20. In the ten-year period 1805–15 only twenty-four people went before the grand jury and were indicted. Only nine of those faced a capital charge, of whom seven were found not guilty.

24 The most reliable source for execution figures in Upper Canada is Connor, 'Purest of Gifts.' We thank Dr Connor for sharing these statistics and other unpublished work cited in this chapter with us. Slightly less reliable is Peter Oliver, *A Terror to Evil Doers: Prisons and Punishment in Nineteenth-Century Ontario* (Toronto: Osgoode Society for Canadian Legal History and University of Toronto Press, 1998), 14–15, table 1.1, who gives a total of thirty people capitally sentenced but does not say how many were executed. For an account of the first execution, carried out at what is now Sandwich, Ontario, of a Black slave for burglary, see William Renwick Riddell, 'The First Legal Execution from Crime in Upper Canada,' *Ontario Historical Society Papers and Records* 27 (1931): 514. For those executed for treason, see Paul Romney and Barry Wright, 'State

Trials and Security Proceedings in Upper Canada during the War of 1812,' in *CST*, 1.

25 See Bannister, *Rule of the Admirals*, at 190, table 6.1.

26 See Jim Phillips, 'The Administration of the Royal Pardon in Nova Scotia, 1749–1815,' *University of Toronto Law Journal* 42 (1992): 1. For reasons discussed in that article, this number cannot be said to be a definitive count of all executions, but it represents the vast majority of them.

27 Phillips, 'Administration of the Royal Pardon,' especially at 424.

28 These numbers were kindly supplied by Dr Patrick Connor.

29 Bannister, *Rule of the Admirals*, 189.

30 The figures for ca 1778–90 are in Donald Fyson, 'The Canadiens and the Bloody Code: Criminal Defence Strategies in Quebec after the British Conquest, 1760–1841,' *Quaderni Storici* 47 (2012): 771. Numbers for the periods before and after that were kindly supplied by Professor Fyson.

31 Fyson, 'Canadiens and the Bloody Code,' 789, shows that Canadiens were slightly less likely to be pardoned than British subjects between 1764 and 1791. His principal concern, however, is to show that many more people were pardoned under the English criminal law in Quebec than had been the case in New France.

32 To illustrate the point about chance, two people were pardoned in Prince Edward Island because nobody could be found to act as hangman! Hornby, *In the Shadow of the Gallows*, 25–9.

33 See Connor, 'Purest of Gifts,' 135, showing that the pillory was used for counterfeiting and forgery cases, as well as attempted rapes, keepers of houses of ill fame, and fraud.

34 Lieutenant Governor Campbell to Provost Marshall, 24 Mar. 1770, NSARM, RG 1, vol. 170, 31.

35 A 1758 statute provided that the penalty for counterfeiting or debasing foreign coins that were legal tender in the colony was that the offender was to be 'set in the pillory' and that 'one of the ears of such offender shall be nailed thereto': SNS 1758, c 20, s 6; SNS 1774, c 10, s 1, explicitly stated that the intention was always that the ear was to be removed first before being nailed up.

36 NSARM, RG 60, vol. 20, no. 20.3.

37 Beattie, *Crime and the Courts*, 466–8.

38 Fyson, *Magistrates, Police and People*, 259. Neither our own research nor that of Patrick Connor has turned up similar examples of extreme crowd behaviour towards the convicted person: see Connor, 'Purest of Gifts,' 135.

39 For the conviction and other related documents, see NSARM, RG 39, series J, vol. 117; RG 1, vol. 163 [3] at 145, 166; Memorial of Robert Sanderson, n.d. [1760], CO 217, vol. 18, 73–6.

40 NSARM, MG 100, vol. 239, no. 7.

41 Minutes of Council, 16 Feb. 1751, in T.B. Akins, ed., *Selections from the Public Documents of the Province of Nova Scotia* (Halifax: C. Annand, 1869), 639.

42 *Upper Canada Gazette*, 1 Dec. 1798, quoted in Oliver, *Terror to Evil Doers*, 21n45.

43 Fyson, *Magistrates, Police and People*, 260. For other references to quarter sessions handing out sentences of public whipping, see David Murray, *Colonial Justice: Justice, Morality and Crime in the Niagara District, 1791–1849* (Toronto: Osgoode Society for Canadian Legal History and University of Toronto Press, 2002); Marion Robertson, *King's Bounty: A History of Early Shelburne, Nova Scotia* (Halifax: Nova Scotia Museum, 1983).

44 See Bannister, *Rule of the Admirals*, chap. 7. See also chapter 11 above for the excessive use of corporal punishment on Blacks in Shelburne, Nova Scotia.

45 For the prevalence of assault prosecutions, see Connor, 'Purest of Gifts,' table at 48; NSARM, RG 60, Halifax, for the 1750s to the 1770s; and RG 34-312, ser. P, vol. 1, Proceedings Book of the Halifax Quarter Sessions for the 1790s. The last of these sources shows that between 1791 and 1793, inclusive, 102 prosecutions were conducted at quarter sessions, 78 of them for assault.

46 Fyson, *Magistrates, Police and People*, 259; Connor, 'Purest of Gifts,' table at 133; NSARM, RG 34-312, ser. P, vol. 1.

47 For this and the following paragraphs on transportation and banishment, see, in addition to the specific sources cited, Jim Phillips, 'Exile for Offenders: Banishment and Transportation from British North America, 1750–1850,' paper presented to a Symposium in Honour of Douglas Hay, York University, May 2016. Everything said here applies only to civilian convicts. Military offenders convicted by courts martial could be transported from North America, to Britain, Australia, or elsewhere, under the authority of Britain's annual *Mutiny Act*; see the Colonial Office 'Circular,' 2 Mar. 1835, NSARM, MG 1, vol. 334, no. 32.

48 Nova Scotia's second governor, Thomas Hopson, refused to receive transports in 1753: Board of Trade to Hopson, 28 Mar. 1753, CO 218, vol. 4, 449.

49 For the Nova Scotia proposal, see James Lodge to Secretary of State Grenville, 27 May 1791, CO 217, vol. 63, 111–15.

50 For transportation to and from Newfoundland, see Bannister, *Rule of the Admirals*, chap. 6; Jerry Bannister, 'Irish Transportation in 1789 and Government in Newfoundland' (unpublished, 1979); and Ged Martin, 'Convict Transportation to Newfoundland in 1789,' *Acadiensis* 5 (1975): 88.

51 Board of Trade to Lawrence, 29 October 1754, NSARM, CO 218, vol. 5, at 34. For a general account of these events, see J. Barry Cahill, 'The Hoffman Rebellion (1753) and Hoffman's Trial (1754): Constructive High Treason and Seditious Conspiracy in Nova Scotia under the Stratocracy,' in *CST*, 1.

52 NSARM, RG 39, ser. J, vol. 2, 87.

53 Romney and Wright, 'State Trials and Security Proceedings.'

54 See the case of Felix Cannew, convicted of a capital larceny in the Halifax Supreme Court in 1761, at NSARM, RG 1, vol. 165, 146–7.

55 See Hornby, *In the Shadow of the Gallows*, at 23. One of these, Jupiter Wise, is further dealt with by Jim Hornby, *Black Islanders: Prince Edward Island's Historical Black Community* (Charlottetown: Institute of Island Studies, 1991).

56 See the cases of William Lambert, given two months to procure transport after his conviction for rape and pardon in 1772, and of John Peters, burglary, 1782, given six months to leave: Pardons for Lambert and Sloper, NSARM, RG 1, vol. 168, 185, and vol. 170, 325.

57 NSARM, RG 1, vol. 251, 145.

58 SUC 1800, c 1, s 5.

59 These figures are from Connor, 'Purest of Gifts,' 133, table 2.5, and information provided by him. By contrast, in no case prior to 1815 did a Quebec/Lower Canadian court sentence a person to transportation or banishment (thanks to Donald Fyson for this information).

60 Typical was a statute passed in the first session of the Upper Canadian Assembly in 1792, which directed that a gaol be built in every district: SUC 1792, c 8. In early New Brunswick the sole jail was located in Saint John; SNB 1787, c 10. Over the ensuing years the Assembly sanctioned the building of jails in other counties: SNB 1801, c 6 (Westmorland); SNB 1807, c 11 (York); SNB 1812, c 9 (Northumberland); SNB 1812, c 10 (Charlotte).

61 Fyson, *Magistrates, Police and People*, 259.

62 Accounts of late eighteenth- and early nineteenth-century Upper Canadian gaols can be found in Oliver, *Terror to Evil Doers*, 4–12; Rainer Baehre, 'Origins of the Penitentiary System in Upper Canada,' *Ontario History* 69 (1977): 185; and Charles K. Talbot, *Justice in Early*

Ontario 1791–1840 (Ottawa: Crimcare, 1983), 233–78. For other colonies, see Rainer Baehre, 'From Bridewell to Federal Penitentiary: Prisons and Punishment in Nova Scotia before 1880,' in *EHCL*, vol. 3; Fyson, *Magistrates, Police and People, passim.*

63 For JPs see Fyson, *Magistrates, Police and People, passim*; Connor, 'Purest of Gifts,' 87ff; Susan Lewthwaite, 'Law and Authority in Upper Canada: The Justices of the Peace in the Newcastle District, 1802–1840' (PhD diss., University of Toronto, 2000). For a detailed investigation of the JP's role in pre-trial investigations and depositions, see Susan Lewthwaite, 'Pre-Trial Examination in Upper Canada,' in Greg Smith, Allyson May, and Simon Devereaux, eds, *Criminal Justice in the Old World and the New: Essays in Honour of John M. Beattie* (Toronto: University of Toronto Press and Centre of Criminology, 1998).

64 In addition to the specific sources cited below, see, for the operations of constables, Murray, *Colonial Justice*, 64–72; Fyson, *Magistrates, Police and People*, chap. 4; Connor, 'Purest of Gifts,' 27ff.

65 Council Minutes, 18 July 1749 and 14 January 1751, in Akins, ed., *Selections*, 571, 639; SNS 1765, c 1.

66 See SNB 1786, c 28, empowering the justices in General Sessions 'to appoint two or more as they shall see convenient to be constables in said town or parish.' See also *An Act to Authorise the Common Council of the City of Saint John, to Appoint Constables for Such Wards of the City as Shall Omit to Choose the Same*, SNB 1812, c 11.

67 The Quebec system is fully detailed in Fyson, *Magistrates, Police and People*, chapter 4.

68 Six men were chosen annually for the three positions by vote of local householders, and the lists were sent to the central government, which selected three of them: see Fyson, *Magistrates, Police and People*, 141.

69 This account is from depositions taken before a JP, the indictment and the jury verdict in the case file at NSARM, RG 39, ser. C, vol. 79. The case is also in the Proceedings Book for the Supreme Court, NSARM, RG 39, ser. J, vol. 2, 184. For a similar description of how policing operated in early Upper Canada, see Connor, 'Purest of Gifts,' 27ff.

70 See Allan E. Marble, 'The Career of Michael Head in Eighteenth-Century Nova Scotia,' *Nova Scotia Historical Review* 8,no. 2 (1988): 40.

71 The statutes were 1 & 2 P&M, c 13 (1554), and 2 & 3 P&M, c 10 (1555). They are discussed in detail in Beattie, *Crime and the Courts*, 268–88.

72 For his service as a constable, see the constable lists for 1798 and 1799 at NSARM, RG 39, ser. C, vols 80 and 81. For his occupation, see the 1792 and 1793 poll tax rolls, at NSARM, RG 1, vol. 444.

73 See NSARM, Halifax Quarter Sessions Proceedings, 21 June 1798, RG 34-312, ser. P, vol. 1.
74 See NSARM, RG 39, ser. J, vol. 2, 189.
75 Fyson, *Magistrates, Police and People*, reviews the historiography, especially in chapter 4, 'The Police before the Police.' The best account of how the English system actually worked, one that shows much practical innovation, is that of John Beattie in *Crime and the Courts*, chapter 2; see also his *Policing and Punishment in London*, part 1; and his *The First English Detectives: The Bow Street Runners and the Policing of London, 1750–1840* (Oxford: Oxford University Press, 2012).
76 Fyson, *Magistrates, Police and People*, chap. 4; quotation at 143.
77 For the substitute system in Quebec/Lower Canada, see Fyson, *Magistrates, Police and People*, 151ff, figures from the table at 153.
78 NSARM, Quarter Sessions Proceedings, 15 Dec. 1794, RG 34-312, ser. P, vol. 1. For substitution generally, see the Constable Lists for the 1790s, which show consistent repeat service, at NSARM, RG 39, ser. C, vols 76, 78, 80, and 81.
79 York (Toronto) did not establish a police office until 1826: Connor, 'Purest of Gifts,' 28.
80 SNS 1792, c 14. This seems to have been a statutory version of the device of adjournment used by English JPs from the late eighteenth century to allow them to meet as often and for as many days as seemed necessary: see Beattie, *Crime and the Courts*, at 310. The Act expired and was renewed a few times in the succeeding two decades: see SNS 1801, c 15; 1803, c 1; 1804, c 3; 1811, c 5; 1812, c 5; and 1814, c 11. This last renewal measure stipulated that the JPs were to be chosen by rotation from among those who in the opinion of the town's magistrates 'are best qualified, and will be most likely punctually to attend the duties of said Court.'
81 SNS 1815, c 9. See, generally, Philip Girard, 'The Rise and Fall of Urban Justice in Halifax, 1815–1886,' *Nova Scotia Historical Review* 8, no. 2 (1988): 57 at 59–60.
82 *NS Journals*, 6 Mar. 1815. The report stated that 'a Peace Officer should attend the sitting Magistrate daily and be paid … for his attendance and services': Joint Assembly – Council Report, 6 Mar. 1815, at NSARM, RG 1, vol. 305, no. 21.
83 For the theatricality of the proceedings in England, see Beatttie, *Crime and the Courts*, 316–18, and Hay, 'Property, Authority and the Criminal Law,' 26–31.
84 D.G. Bell, 'Maritime Legal Institutions under the *Ancien Régime*, 1710–1850,' *Manitoba Law Journal* 23 (1995): 103 at 110.

85 For the circuit system in general and for circuit travel, see Jim Phillips and Philip Girard, 'Courts, Communities and Communication: The Nova Scotia Supreme Court on Circuit, 1816–50,' in Hamar Foster, Benjamin L. Berger, and A.R. Buck, eds, *The Grand Experiment: Law and Legal Culture in British Settler Societies* (Vancouver: Osgoode Society for Canadian Legal History and UBC Press, 2008). For the formalities of court term opening days, see Jim Phillips and James Muir, 'Michaelmas Term 1754: The Supreme Court's First Session,' in *SCNS*.

86 This summary of trial process is based principally on Jim Phillips, 'The Criminal Trial in Nova Scotia, 1749–1815,' in *EHCL*, vol. 8. For grand juries, see also Jim Phillips, 'Halifax Juries in the Eighteenth Century,' in Smith, May, and Devereaux, *Criminal Justice in the Old World and the New*. For a discussion of English grand juries, see Beattie, *Crime and the Courts*, 318–33. At 326 Beattie notes that the number twenty-three was given formal sanction by a King's Bench ruling of 1761.

87 For analyses of the socio-economic composition of grand juries, and of repeat service, see Phillips, 'Halifax Juries'; Talbot, *Justice in Early Ontario*, 44; Connor, 'Purest of Gifts,' 117–18; and Donald Fyson, 'Jurys, participation civique et représentation au Québec et au Bas-Canada: les grand jurys du district de Montréal, 1764–1832,' *Revue d'histoire de l'Amérique française* 55 (2001): 85.

88 This limitation was justified in English law by Blackstone and others by the fact that the decision on the indictment was only an accusation, not part of the process of deciding guilt: see Beattie, *Crime and the Courts*, 319.

89 Upper Canadian Assize grand juries indicted 85.5 per cent in the 1791–1840 period. See Phillips, 'Halifax Juries,' at 168; and Connor, 'Purest of Gifts,' 114. Connor gives the figure of ignoramus verdicts as 9.6 per cent but includes cases where the result was unknown; the figures have been recalculated so as not to include those cases.

90 Phillips, 'Halifax Juries'; Talbot, *Justice in Early Ontario*, 45–6; and Fyson, 'Jurys, participation civique.'

91 This section on the eighteenth-century English criminal trial is based on three principal sources: Beattie, *Crime and the Courts*, chap. 7; John M. Beattie, 'Scales of Justice: Defence Counsel and the English Criminal Trial in the Eighteenth and Nineteenth Centuries,' *Law and History Review* 9 (1991): 221; and J.H. Langbein, *The Origins of Adversary Trial* (Oxford: Oxford University Press, 2005).

92 This restriction was not removed until 1893 in Canada, 1898 in England. See Ronald D. Noble, 'The Struggle to Make the Accused Competent in England and in Canada,' *Osgoode Hall Law Journal* 8 (1970): 249.

93 Quotations from Beattie, *Crime and the Courts*, 345.
94 Ibid., 390.
95 Ibid., 360–1.
96 Ibid., 341.
97 The literature on the eighteenth-century trial in British North America is not large. The only general survey is Phillips, 'Criminal Trial in Nova Scotia,' from which the Nova Scotia evidence presented here is taken. The role of the attorney general in prosecution in Upper Canada is well covered in Romney, *Mr Attorney*. Trial juries and the trial process in general in Upper Canada are usefully analysed in Connor, 'Purest of Gifts,' 109ff.
98 What is said here about Quebec/Lower Canada is derived from two particular sources: Hay, 'Meanings of the Criminal Law in Quebec'; and Fyson, 'Canadiens and the Bloody Code.' The arguments contained in the former about the initial cultural incomprehensibility of the English system and the values underlying it remain valid and well worth reading, but Fyson's work shows that in practice Canadiens adapted to the new system quickly and effectively.
99 In both Britain and British North America indictment was in fact just one of three methods by which a person could be brought to court to face trial. The other two were coroner's inquisition and ex officio information by the attorney general. The former was employed routinely in murder cases in the eighteenth century but fell out of use in the nineteenth and was abolished in the 1892 *Criminal Code*. The latter was available for misdemeanours, not felonies, and was used in 'political' cases, such as prosecutions for sedition. It was last used in 1819. For a still useful general account, see William Renwick Riddell, 'The Information Ex Officio in Upper Canada,' *Canadian Law Times* 41 (1921): 4 and 87.
100 Stewart also left us with a detailed pamphlet account of the trial, *The Trials of George Frederick Boutelier and John Boutelier, for the Murder of Frederick Eminaud, before a Special Court of Oyer and Terminr and General Gaol Delivery, Held at Lunenburg … in the Province of Nova Scotia … 1791* (Halifax: Stewart, 1792).
101 For an account of this case see Phillips, 'Criminal Trial in Nova Scotia' at 472–5.
102 Examples from the 1790s can be found in Proceedings Book of the Halifax Quarter Sessions for the 1790s, at NSARM, RG 34-312, ser. P, vol. 1.
103 Hay, 'Meanings of the Criminal Law in Quebec,' at 84.
104 The Crown law officers' salaries were always low. New Brunswick's attorney general had a salary of £150 a year, that of Upper Canada £300

a year, and of Nova Scotia £100 in the late 1750s and over £200 by the end of the century. Upper Canada's solicitor general got only £100 a year. Attorneys general augmented their salaries with fees for prosecutions and for many other official duties, such as issuing commissions and deeds to lands. All Crown law officers had the freedom to practise privately as well, but some still complained. In 1798 John White of Upper Canada complained in a letter to London that he was so poor he had to dig his own potatoes and cut his own firewood. See variously, Romney, *Mr Attorney*, 37–41, 51; NSARM, Council Minutes, 13 July 1799, RG 1, vol. 191, 8; RG 1, vol. 398, Public Accounts; Lois Kernaghan, 'William Nesbitt,' *DCB*.

105 Romney, *Mr Attorney*, 47.

106 Ibid., 47–8, 122–3, 125.

107 Fyson, 'Canadiens and the Bloody Code,' at 772.

108 Ibid., 783; Connor, 'Purest of Gifts,' 119.

109 For these figures, see Phillips, 'Criminal Trial in Nova Scotia,' at 482; Trial Minutes, Fredericton, PANB, RS 30B, no. 2.

110 Fyson, 'Canadiens and the Bloody Code,' at 782.

111 For these cases, see Trial Minutes, Fredericton, PANB, RS 30B, no. 2; and for Peters, see Phillip Buckner and Burton Glendenning, 'Charles Jeffery Peters,' *DCB*.

112 Fyson, 'Canadiens and the Bloody Code,' at 780–1.

113 Trial Minutes, Fredericton, PANB, RS 30B, no. 2.

114 See the Proceedings Book of the Halifax Quarter Sessions for the 1790s, at NSARM, RG 34-312, ser. P, vol. 1. For the lack of defence lawyers in Upper Canada's quarter sessions courts, see Connor, 'Purest of Gifts,' 100ff.

115 The only comprehensive examination of defence lawyers is in Phillips, 'Criminal Trial in Nova Scotia.' They are also discussed briefly in Fyson, 'Canadiens and the Bloody Code,' at 783ff. Their presence is also noted in the 1815 trial of Jacob Overholser in Upper Canada: Robert Fraser, 'Jacob Overholser,' *DCB*.

116 Cited in Phillips, 'Criminal Trial in Nova Scotia,' at 475.

117 Ibid., 495; Fyson, 'Canadiens and the Bloody Code,' at 782–3.

118 Trial Minutes, Fredericton, PANB, RS 30B, no. 2.

119 See Talbot, *Justice in Early Ontario*, 45–6.

120 This paragraph is derived from Phillips, 'Criminal Trial in Nova Scotia,' *passim*; Fyson, '*Canadiens* and the Bloody Code'; Trial Minutes, Fredericton, PANB, RS 30B, no. 2; Connor, 'Purest of Gifts,' 119–24.

121 For jury composition and service, see especially Phillips, 'Halifax Juries.'

122 See *The Trials of George Boutelier*, cited in Phillips, 'Criminal Trial in Nova Scotia,' at 492–3.

123 Hay, 'Meanings of the Criminal Law in Quebec.'

124 Ibid., 86–7.

125 Fyson, 'Canadiens and the Bloody Code,' at 776. See the same source generally for the other examples of Canadien participation in and acceptance of the English criminal justice system discussed in this paragraph.

126 For these figures, see Phillips, 'Criminal Trial in Nova Scotia,' at 498 and notes.

127 Fyson, 'Canadiens and the Bloody Code,' at 777.

128 See the table in Connor, 'Purest of Gifts,' 114. The table is for the entire 1791–1840 period, so it is possible that rates were different up to 1815. I have also recalculated Connor's percentages to make them equivalent to those given here for other colonies, principally by excluding cases turned back at the grand jury stage and cases where the result in unknown.

129 Trial Minutes, Fredericton, PANB, RS 30B, no. 2. This figure is based only on cases where the result is known.

17. Indigenous Law

1 For accounts of the interaction of Indigenous and European law in the Hudson Bay watershed, see the work of Janna Promislow, in particular 'Towards a Legal History of the Fur Trade: Looking for Law at York Factory, 1714–1763' (LLM thesis, York University, 2004); and Promislow, '"I smoothed him up with fair words": Intersocietal Law, from Fur Trade to Treaty' (PhD diss., York University, 2013). The dynamic in the north was quite different from that described for the southern communities in this chapter, given that the HBC had to adapt to Indigenous ways if it wished to carry on its trade.

2 Respectively, Thomas Peace, 'Two Conquests: Aboriginal Experiences of the Fall of New France and Acadia' (PhD diss., York University, 2011); Daniel Rueck, 'Enclosing the Mohawk Commons: A History of Use-Rights, Land Ownership, and Boundary-Making in Kahnawá:ke Mohawk Territory' (PhD diss., McGill University, 2013); Isabelle Bouchard, 'Des systèmes politiques en quête de légitimité: terres, pouvoirs et enjeux locaux dans les communautés autochtones de la vallée du Saint-Laurent' (PhD diss., Université du Québec à Montréal, 2017). Bouchard considers both Kahnawake and Odanak.

3 Richard White, *The Middle Ground: Indians, Empires and Republics in the Great Lakes Region, 1650–1815* (Cambridge: Cambridge University Press, 2011). This work, originally published in 1991, is much cited but has been subject to critique by Canadian historians for its tendency to consider only the portion of its titular region within the modern United States; see Allan Greer, 'National, Transnational and Hypernational Historiographies: New France Meets Early American History,' *Canadian Historical Review* 91 (2010): 695.

4 Jan Grabowski, 'The Common Ground: Settled Natives and French in Montreal 1667–1760' (PhD diss., Université de Montréal, 1993).

5 Peace, 'Two Conquests.'

6 Deborah Doxtator, 'What Happened to the Iroquois Clans? A Study of Clans in Three Nineteenth-Century Rotinonhsyonni Communities' (PhD thesis, University of Western Ontario, 1996), 51.

7 Rueck, 'Enclosing the Mohawk Commons,' 49.

8 Denys Delâge and Jean Sawaya, *Les traités des Sept-Feux avec les Britanniques: droits et pièges d'un héritage colonial au Québec* (Sillery, QC: Septentrion, 2001); Jean Sawaya, *La Fédération des Sept Feux de la Vallée du Saint-Laurent, XVII–XIXe siècle* (Sillery, QC: Septentrion, 1998). The seven communities were Wendaké (Jeune-Lorette), Odanak, Wôlinak, Pointe-du-Lac, Kahnawake, Kanesatake, and Akwesasne. Wendaké should not be confused with the original Wendaké, the homeland of the Huron-Wendat near Georgian Bay.

9 Susan M. Hill, *The Clay We Are Made Of: Haudenosaunee Land Tenure on the Grand River* (Winnipeg: University of Manitoba Press, 2017), 110–13. Hill argues at 172–3 that the interior layout of Mohawk homes nonetheless demonstrated continuity with earlier living arrangements.

10 Ibid., 46–52.

11 The residents of Kahnawake did not refer to themselves as Mohawk until the early twentieth century; in their language, residents of Kahnawake were Kahnawakehro:non, while in French they usually referred to themselves as the Nation Iroquoise; Matthieu Sossoyan, 'The Kahnawake Iroquois and the Lower-Canadian Rebellions, 1837–38' (MA thesis, McGill University, 1999), 18. At the risk of anachronism, the term *Mohawk* will be used here.

12 Rueck, 'Enclosing the Mohawk Commons,' 41–2.

13 The current area of Kahnawake is about one-quarter of the original concession.

14 Rueck, 'Enclosing the Mohawk Commons,' 82. Akwesasne is near present-day Cornwall, Ontario, and straddles Ontario, Quebec, and New York state.

15 Joseph François Lafitau, *Customs of the American Indians Compared with the Customs of Primitive Times*, 2 vols (Toronto: Champlain Society 1974–7) [trans. by William N. Fenton and Elizabeth L. Moore of original French edition of 1724]. Page numbers will be to the English translation.
16 See above, chap. 2.
17 Lafitau, *Customs of the American Indians*, 1:292–3.
18 Hill, *Clay We Are Made Of*, 30. *Royaner* is usually translated as 'chief' in English; collectively the royaner are referred to as Rotiyanehson. Hill provides more detail on the role of 'faithkeeper' at 59–60. The fiftieth royaner had a role similar to chair or speaker.
19 The Confederacy Council was abandoned by the Haudenosaunee in the United States after the Revolution but reproduced in full at the Six Nations settlement at Grand River; see below, chap. 23.
20 Lafitau, *Customs of the American Indians*, 1:294.
21 Hill, *Clay We Are Made Of*, 55.
22 Lafitau, *Customs of the American Indians*, 1:299.
23 Ibid.
24 Ibid. By 'code of law,' Lafitau meant a European-style code. He was adamant that the Mohawk did have a legal order and criticized those Europeans who held the contrary: ibid., 1:28.
25 Deborah Doxtator elaborates on the division of labour and geographic space in Haudenosaunee culture, with the 'clearings' being the domain of women and principally concerned with the interior life of the community, and the 'forest' being male space, associated with hunting, war, and external relations; 'What Happened to the Iroquois Clans?'
26 Johnson to Lords of Trade, 30 Oct. 1764, *DCNY*, 7:672.
27 Lewis H. Morgan, *League of the Ho-dé-no-sau-nee, or Iroquois* (New York: M.H. Herman, 1851), 317.
28 Hill, *The Clay We Are Made Of*, 60.
29 'Resolutions of a Six Nations' Council at the Onondaga Village, March 1, 1809,' in Charles M. Johnston, *The Valley of the Six Nations: A Collection of Documents on the Indian Lands of the Grand River* (Toronto: University of Toronto Press, 1964), 111.
30 Guy Johnson to Hector Cramahé, 16 July 1771, *The Papers of Sir William Johnson*, 14 vols (Albany: University of the State of New York, 1921–65), 8:188–9.
31 Similar issues arose on the Grand River. The council invited some non-Indigenous Loyalists to settle among them, but individual Mohawk also purported to sell land to settlers without council approval, leading to many problems in later years; Sidney L. Harring, 'The Six Nations

Confederacy, Aboriginal Sovereignty and Ontario Aboriginal Law: 1790–1860,' in David T. McNab, ed., *Earth, Water, Air and Fire: Studies in Canadian Ethnohistory* (Waterloo, ON: Wilfrid Laurier University Press, 1998).

32 Denys Delâge and Étienne Gilbert, 'La justice coloniale britannique et les Amérindiens au Québec 1760–1820, I, En terres amérindiennes,' *Recherches amérindiennes au Québec* 32 (2002): 63.

33 *Travels through the States of North America and the Provinces of Upper and Lower Canada during the years 1795, 1796 and 1797* (London: John Stockdale, 1799), 170.

34 Ibid., 171.

35 Rueck, 'Enclosing the Mohawk Commons,' 88–9.

36 The cases that follow are reviewed in Delâge and Gilbert, 'La justice coloniale britannique I,' 65; Rueck, 'Enclosing the Mohawk Commons,' 91–2; and Bouchard, 'Systèmes politiques,' 219ff.

37 Bouchard, 'Systèmes politiques,' discusses the court's reasoning at 220–2.

38 *Dictionnaire des parlementaires du Québec, 1792–1992* (Sainte-Foy, QC: Presses de l'Université Laval, 1993), 289.

39 Cited in Delâge and Gilbert, 'La justice coloniale britannique I,' 65.

40 Rueck, 'Enclosing the Mohawk Commons,' 99; Bouchard, 'Systèmes politiques,' 220.

41 They are reproduced in Rueck, 'Enclosing the Mohawk Commons,' 100–4.

42 Bouchard, 'Systemes politiques,' 233.

43 Rueck, 'Enclosing the Mohawk Commons,' 105 (revocation of 1801 code); Bouchard, 'Systemes politiques,' 234 (status of 1804 code).

44 Bouchard, 'Systemes politiques,' 233–4.

45 The interaction of Indigenous people with the seigneurial system, formerly a closed book, has been the subject of much recent research. In addition to the theses cited in note 1, see Benoît Grenier, *Brève histoire du régime seigneurial* (Montreal: Boréal, 2012), chap. 3; Isabelle Bouchard, 'Les chefs autochtones comme "seigneurs": gestion des terres et de leurs revenus, 1760–1820,' in Benoît Grenier and Michel Morissette, eds, *Nouveaux regards en histoire seigneuriale au Québec* (Quebec: Septentrion, 2015).

46 On what follows, see Peace, 'Two Conquests,' 229–83.

47 When the Huron-Wendat left Sillery, the Jesuits tried to reclaim it for themselves. The Huron-Wendat have continued to assert their claim to the present day; see Michel Lavoie, *'C'est ma seigneurie que je réclame': la lutte des Hurons de Lorette pour la seigneurie de Sillery, 1650–1900* (Montreal: Boréal, 2010). On the presence of the Innu in early Sillery, see Allan Greer,

Property and Dispossession: Natives, Empires and Land in Early Modern North America (New York: Cambridge University Press, 2018).

48 Jean Tanguay, 'La liberté d'errer et de vaquer: Les Hurons de Lorette et l'occupation du territoire, XVIIe–XIXe siècles' (MA thesis, Université Laval, 1998). On the domaine du roi, see Michel Lavoie, *Le domaine du roi 1652–1859: souveraineté, contrôle, mainmise, propriété, possession, exploitation* (Quebec: Septentrion, 2010).

49 Serge Goudreau, 'Le village huron de Lorette: une crêche pour les enfants canadiens du XVIIIe siècle,' *Mémoires de la Société généalogique canadienne-française* 51 (Spring 2000): 7.

50 Arnaud Decroix, 'Le conflit juridique entre les Jésuites et les Iroquois au sujet de la seigneurie du Sault Saint-Louis: analyse de la décision de Thomas Gage (1762),' *Revue juridique Thémis* 41 (2007): 279. Gage based his decision on Crown title on the clause in the 1680 concession, stating that if the Mohawk ever left the territory, it would revert to the Crown.

51 Bouchard, 'Les chefs autochtones comme "seigneurs,"' 188–98.

52 *Antill v Lemaître Duhaime*, King's Bench Trois-Rivières 1795, cited in Bouchard, 'Systèmes politiques,' 197.

53 *Seigneurs Propriétaires et possesseurs de la seigneurie appellée la Concession des Iroquois du Sault v Camiré*, Montreal Court of King's Bench 1820, discussed by Bouchard, 'Systemes politiques,' at 200–2.

54 The creation of schools by the Jesuits for the Huron-Wendat contributed to this phenomenon. The literacy rates here refer to the French language, but the Jesuits created a system of orthography for the Huron language, and some Huron-Wendat may also have been literate in their own language. See Peace, 'Two Conquests,' 364–5.

18. Private Law: The Civil Law

1 André Morel, 'Mathieu Collet,' *DCB*.

2 Edmond Lareau, *Histoire du droit canadien*, 2 vols (Montreal: A. Périard, 1888–9), 1:261–2. There is a large literature on eighteenth-century seigneurialism, but much of it is concerned with its impact on agricultural productivity and questions of homogeneity or inequality among the peasantry, not on the legal aspects.

3 Pierre-Georges Roy, *Inventaire des jugements et déliberations du Conseil supérieur de la Nouvelle-France de 1717 à 1760*, 7 vols (Beauceville, QC: L'Éclaireur, 1932–5), preface to vol. I.

4 BanQ(M), Bailliage de Montréal, TL2, 1971-00-000/11695, 'Ordonnances 1653–83.' Collet wished to have all the important laws of New France reproduced and digested in a Code that could be easily circulated, but Versailles did not approve of this innovation; Morel, 'Mathieu Collet.'

5 H. Leander d'Entremont, 'Father Jean Mandé Sigogne, 1799–1844,' Nova Scotia Historical Society *Collections* 23 (1936): 105. On the survival of Acadian legal culture after the Deportation, see Jacques Vanderlinden, 'À la rencontre de l'histoire du droit en Acadie,' *Revue de l'Université de Moncton* 28 (1994): 47. Population figure from J.M. Bumsted, '1763–83: Resettlement and Rebellion,' in Phillip A. Buckner and John G. Reid, *The Atlantic Region to Confederation: A History* (Toronto: University of Toronto Press, 1994), 165.

6 14 Geo III, c 83.

7 Donald Fyson, 'The Conquered and the Conqueror: The Mutual Adaptation of the *Canadiens* and the British in Quebec, 1759–1775,' in Phillip Buckner and John G. Reid, eds, *Revisiting 1759: The Conquest of Canada in Historical Perspective* (Toronto: University of Toronto Press, 2012).

8 (Quebec: Guillaume Brown, 1785) [repr. Toronto, Société bibliographique du Canada, 1951], 9.

9 The literature on the interaction of British and French law in the wake of the conquest is immense, and only some of the major works are cited here: Hilda Neatby, *The Administration of Justice under the Quebec Act* (Minneapolis: University of Minnesota Press, 1937); F. Murray Greenwood, *Legacies of Fear: Law and Politics in Quebec in the Era of the French Revolution* (Toronto: Osgoode Society for Canadian Legal History, 1993); Evelyn Kolish, *Nationalismes et conflits de droits: Le débat du droit privé au Québec 1760-1840* (Montreal: Hurtubise, 1994).

10 Evelyn Kolish, 'Imprisonment for Debt in Lower Canada, 1791–1840,' *McGill Law Journal* 32 (1987): 603 at 606–7.

11 Henry Des Rivières Beaubien, *Traité sur les lois civiles du Bas-Canada*, 3 vols (Montreal: L. Duvernay 1832-33), 3:264ff.

12 F. Murray Greenwood, 'Lower Canada (Quebec): Transformation of Civil Law, from Higher Morality to Autonomous Will, 1774–1866,' in *CLI* at 141–2. On the bicultural nature of the post-1760 legal professions, see Jean-Philippe Garneau, 'Une culture de l'amalgame au prétoire: les avocats de Québec et l'élaboration d'un langage juridique commun au tournant des XVIIIe et XIXe siècles,' *Canadian Historical Review* 88 (2007): 113.

13 Kolish, *Nationalismes et conflits de droits*, 217–44.

14 On Cugnet, see Sylvio Normand, 'François-Joseph Cugnet et la reconstitution du droit de la Nouvelle-France,' *Cahiers aixois des droits de l'outre-mer français* 1 (2002): 127; and on Quebec legal literature more generally, see Normand, 'Les débuts de la littérature juridique québécois, 1767–1840,' in *EHCL*, vol. 11. Pierre Tousignant and Madeleine Dionne-Tousignant, 'François-Joseph Cugnet,' *DCB*.

15 Marine Leland, 'François-Joseph Cugnet 1720–1789 – XI,' *Revue de l'Université Laval* 18 (1963): 339; Michel Morin, 'Blackstone and the Birth of Quebec's Distinct Legal Culture, 1765–1867,' in Wilfrid Prest, ed., *Reinterpreting Blackstone's Commentaries: A Seminal Text in National and International Contexts* (Oxford: Hart, 2014); and in French as 'Le bijuridisme québécois de la Proclamation royale de 1763 au Code civil du Bas-Canada,' in Stéphane Rousseau, ed., *Juriste sans frontières: Mélanges Ejan Mackaay* (Montreal: Éditions Thémis, 2015).

16 Masères to Richard Sutton, 14 Aug. 1768, in W. Stewart Wallace, ed., *The Maseres Letters, 1766–1768* (Toronto: University of Toronto Library, 1919), 103.

17 Ibid.

18 *Traité de la loi des fiefs* (Quebec: Guillaume Brown, 1775); *Traité abrégé des ancienes Loix, Coutumes et usages de la colonie du Canada* (Quebec: Guillaume Brown, 1775); *Traité de la police* (Quebec: Guillaume Brown, 1775); *Extraits des Édits, Ordonnances, Déclarations, Ordonnances et Règlemens de Sa Majesté Très Chrétienne* (Quebec: Guillaume Brown, 1775). The Assembly would later order the publication of two collections of original sources from the French regime: *Édits, ordonnances royaux, déclarations et arrêts du Conseil d'État du roi, concernant le Canada* (Quebec: P.E. Desbarats, 1803); and *Ordonnances des intendants et arrêts portant règlement du Conseil supérieur du Québec* (Quebec: P.E. Desbarats, 1806); these were preludes to the more all-encompassing collections published in the 1850s: *EO*, vols 1 and 2.

19 Imprisonment (contrainte par corps) as a remedy in civil matters was available only on a restricted basis under French law, as in certain types of fraud. It was not available for debts.

20 See, generally, Jean-Maurice Brisson, *La formation d'un droit mixte: l'évolution de la procédure civile de 1774 à 1867* (Montreal: Les Éditions Thémis, 1986).

21 See above, chap. 11.

22 See chap. 23.

23 Monk to Dundas, 6 June 1794, in A.G. Doughty and D.A. McArthur, eds, *Documents relating to the Constitutional History of Canada 1791–1818* (Ottawa: C.H. Parmelee, 1914), 119–20.

24 Kolish, *Nationalismes et conflits de droits*, 239.
25 *An Act for Settling the Law Covering Lands Held in Free and Common Soccage in Lower Canada*, SC 1857, c 45; J.E.C. Brierley, 'The Co-Existence of Legal Systems in Quebec: "Free and Common Soccage" in Canada's "pays de droit civil,"' *Cahiers de Droit* 20 (1979): 277; Brian Young, *The Politics of Codification: The Lower Canadian Civil Code of 1866* (Montreal and Kingston: McGill-Queen's University Press, 1994), 22–4.
26 On what follows, see John Hare, *Aux origines du parlementarisme québécois, 1791–1793* (Sillery, QC: Septentrion, 1993), 86–107.
27 SLC 1801, c 7.
28 André Morel, 'Les réactions des Canadiens devant l'administration de la justice, 1764–1774: Une forme de résistance passive,' *Revue du barreau* 20 (1960): 53.
29 'Report upon the Laws and Courts of Judicature in the Province of Quebec,' in W.P.M. Kennedy and Gustave Lanctot, *Report on the Laws of Quebec 1767–1770* (Ottawa: F.A. Acland, 1931), 65.
30 Jean-Philippe Garneau, 'Droit et "affaires de famille" sur la Côte-de-Beaupré: histoire d'une rencontre en amont et en aval de la Conquête britannique,' *Revue juridique Thémis* 34 (2000): 515.
31 Armand Decroix, David Gilles, and Michel Morin, *Les tribunaux et l'arbitrage en Nouvelle-France et au Québec de 1740 à 1784* (Montreal: Éditions Thémis, 2012), 391–428.
32 This, confusingly, happened twice. An ordinance of 1764 proclaimed the age of majority as twenty-one effective 1 January 1765. The *Quebec Act* abrogated all prior ordinances of the British regime, which by default restored the previous age of majority of twenty-five. The legislative council returned the age of majority to twenty-one by an ordinance of February 1782.
33 Michel Morin, 'La perception de l'ancien droit et du nouveau droit français au Bas-Canada 1774–1866,' in H.P. Glenn, ed., *Droit québécois et droit français: communauté, autonomie, concordance* (Cowansville, QC: Yvon Blais, 1993), 15 ('the published case law does not give the impression of an invasion by the common law' – translation of the authors).
34 Kolish, 'Imprisonment for Debt.'
35 This process also occurred with regard to the criminal law, as shown by the work of Donald Fyson, *Magistrates, Police and People: Everyday Criminal Justice in Quebec and Lower Canada, 1764–1837* (Toronto: University of Toronto Press, 2006).
36 Garneau, 'Culture de l'amalgame.'

19. Private Law: The Common Law

1 *Commentaries*, 1:107.
2 John Stewart, *An Account of Prince Edward Island in the Gulph of St Lawrence, North America* (London, 1806), 272–3.
3 In the unreported case *Norris v Carter and Morrison* (1821), cited by Bruce Kercher and Jodie Young, 'Formal and Informal Law in Two New Lands: Land Law in Newfoundland and New South Wales under Francis Forbes,' in *EHCL*, 9:153. See generally Thomas G. Barnes, '"As Near as May Be Agreeable to the Laws of This Kingdom": Legal Birthright and Legal Baggage at Chebucto, 1749,' *Dalhousie Law Journal* 8 (1984): 1 at 7–8.
4 *Property and Civil Rights Act*, SUC 1792, c 1; now RSO 1990, c P.29.
5 SUC 1800, c 1.
6 The rules on reception did not affect the imperial Parliament's power to pass legislation affecting the empire or a particular colony's constitution or foreign relations.
7 J. Côté, 'The Reception of English Law,' *Alberta Law Review* 15 (1977): 29.
8 Margaret McCallum, 'Problems in Determining the Date of Reception in Prince Edward Island,' *University of New Brunswick Law Journal* 55 (2006): 3.
9 The report is cited in D.G. Bell, 'A Note on the Reception of Statutes in New Brunswick,' *University of New Brunswick Law Journal* 28 (1979): 195 at 198.
10 Reproduced in D.G. Bell, 'The Reception Question and the Constitutional Crisis of the 1790's in New Brunswick,' *University of New Brunswick Law Journal* 29 (1980): 157 at 161.
11 *Scott v Scott* (1970) 2 NBR (2d) 849.
12 Cited in Jim Phillips, '"Securing Obedience to Necessary Laws": The Criminal Law in Eighteenth-Century Nova Scotia,' *Nova Scotia Historical Review* 12 (1992): 87 at 101.
13 Cited in J. Barry Cahill, '"How far English laws are in force here": Nova Scotia's First Century of Reception Law Jurisprudence,' *University of New Brunswick Law Journal* 42 (1993): 113 at 121–2.
14 For such efforts with regard to statutes relating to the criminal law, see chapter 16.
15 Amalia Kessler, *Inventing American Exceptionalism: The Origins of American Adversarial Legal Culture, 1800–1877* (New Haven, CT: Yale University Press, 2017).
16 G.E. Mingay, *English Landed Society in the Eighteenth Century* (London: Routledge & Kegan Paul, 1963), 26. Mingay estimated that 2 per cent of the population owned 70–85 per cent of the land.

17 12 Chas II, c 24 (1672).

18 The first reigning monarch to visit the former Rupert's Land and receive this tribute was George VI in 1939, although his brother the Prince of Wales (the future Edward VIII) had received the same when he visited Winnipeg in 1927. Queen Elizabeth II went through the same ritual when visiting Winnipeg in 1959 and 1970, but the charter was amended thereafter to remove the obligation.

19 J.M. Bumsted, *Land, Settlement and Politics on Eighteenth-Century Prince Edward Island* (Montreal and Kingston: McGill-Queen's University Press, 1987) (proprietors seldom paying quitrents, government reluctant to escheat their lands for non-payment); regarding Nova Scotia, Beamish Murdoch observed in his *Epitome*, 2:79, that the initial quitrents reserved had been abandoned since 1774, and 'the attempt to revive the claim has in 1812 and 1830, been met by strong remonstrances on the ground of expediency and length of discontinuance.'

20 These remain the basic principles of the law of real property in common law Canada; see Bruce Ziff, *Principles of Property Law*, 6th ed. (Toronto: Carswell, 2014).

21 Catharine Anne Wilson, *Tenants in Time: Family Strategies, Land, and Liberalism in Upper Canada, 1799–1871* (Montreal and Kingston: McGill-Queen's University Press, 2009), chaps 6 and 7.

22 Kercher and Young, 'Formal and Informal Law'; Trudi Johnson, 'Defining Property for Inheritance: The Chattels Real Act of 1834,' in *EHCL*, vol. 9.

23 10 & 11 Wm III, c 25.

24 *R v Kough* (1819) 1 *Newfoundland Reports* 172, 175.

25 *R v Thomas Row* (1818) 1 *Newfoundland Reports* 126, 128.

26 51 Geo III, c 45, s 1 (U.K.).

27 NSARM, Kempt to Gordon, 11 Feb. 1825, CO 217, Nova Scotia A series, vol. 166 (reel 13895). See also to the same effect *Epitome*, 2:80–1, 244.

28 William N.T. Wylie, 'Arbiters of Commerce, Instruments of Power: A Study of the Civil Courts in Midland District, Upper Canada, 1789–1812' (PhD diss., Queen's University, 1980), 300–8; Lillian F. Gates, 'The Heir and Devisee Commission of Upper Canada, 1797–1805,' *Canadian Historical Review* 38 (1957): 29.

29 Jason Hall, 'High Freshets and Low-Lying Farms: Property Law and St John River Flooding in Colonial New Brunswick,' *Dalhousie Law Journal* 39 (2016): 195.

30 See, generally, Philip Girard, 'Land Law, Liberalism, and the Agrarian Ideal: British North America, 1750–1920,' in John McLaren, A.R. Buck,

and Nancy E. Wright, eds, *Despotic Dominion: Property Rights in British Settler Societies* (Vancouver: UBC Press, 2005).

31 David Sugarman and Ronnie Warrington, 'Land Law, Citizenship, and the Invention of "Englishness": The Strange World of the Equity of Redemption,' in John Brewer and Susan Staves, eds, *Early Modern Conceptions of Property* (London: Routledge, 1995).

32 J.S. Anderson, *Lawyers and the Making of English Land Law* (Oxford: Oxford University Press, 1992).

33 5 Geo II, c 7 (U.K.).

34 Girard, 'Land Law, Liberalism, and the Agrarian Ideal.'

35 Wylie, 'Arbiters of Commerce, Instruments of Power,' 217–18.

36 Philip Girard, 'At the Crossroads of Fusion: British North America-Canada, 1750–2000,' in John Goldberg, Henry Smith, and P.G. Turner, eds, *Equity and Law: Fusion and Fission* (Cambridge: Cambridge University Press, 2018).

37 Philip Girard, 'Taking Litigation Seriously: The Market Wharf Controversy at Halifax, 1785–1820,' in *EHCL*, vol. 8; David Bulger, '*Bowley v Cambridge*: A Colonial *Jarndyce and Jarndyce*,' in *EHCL*, vol. 9 (Prince Edward Island Chancery suit plus Privy Council appeals lasting from 1794 to 1841).

38 Philip Girard, 'The Making of the Canadian Legal Profession: A Hybrid Heritage,' *International Journal of the Legal Profession* 21 (2014): 145, 153–4.

39 J. Hamawi, *Family Law* (London: Stevens, 1953); Christine Davies, *Family Law in Canada* (Toronto: Carswell, 1984). See, generally, Philip Girard, 'Why Canada Has No Family Policy: Lessons from France and Italy,' *Osgoode Hall Law Journal* 32 (1994): 579.

40 The terms come from law French and hence reflect the older spelling of the word now spelled as *femme*.

41 Lori Chambers, *Married Women and Property Law in Victorian Ontario* (Toronto: Osgoode Society for Canadian Legal History and University of Toronto Press, 1997).

42 Relations by affinity (that is, through marriage) also fell within the incest ban; thus a man could not marry his deceased wife's sister, or a woman her deceased husband's brother. The campaign for statutory reform in this area will be treated in volume 2.

43 12 Chas II, c 24 (U.K.).

44 *Commentaries*, 1:441.

45 16 & 17 Geo V, c 60 (U.K.).

46 Michael Grossberg, *Governing the Hearth: Law and the Family in Nineteenth-Century America* (Chapel Hill: University of North Carolina Press, 1985).

47 Roderick Phillips, *Putting Asunder: A History of Divorce in Western Society* (Cambridge: Cambridge University Press, 1988), 134–40, 241–56; Nancy Cott, 'Divorce and the Changing Status of Women in Eighteenth-Century Massachusetts,' *William & Mary Quarterly*, 3d ser., 33 (1976): 586.
48 SNS 1761, c 8.
49 SNB 1791, c 5.
50 Wendy Owen and J.M. Bumsted, 'Divorce in a Small Province: A History of Divorce on Prince Edward Island from 1833,' *Acadiensis* 20 (1990): 86.
51 Constance Backhouse, 'Pure Patriarchy: Nineteenth-Century Canadian Marriage,' *McGill Law Journal* 31 (1986): 264.
52 L.W. Labaree, *Royal Instructions to British Colonial Governors 1670–1776*, 2 vols (New York: Octagon Books1967), 1:155.
53 Kimberley Smith Maynard, 'Divorce in Nova Scotia, 1750–1890,' in *EHCL*, vol. 3.
54 Julian Gwyn, 'Female Litigants before the Civil Courts of Nova Scotia, 1749–1801,' *Histoire sociale/Social History* 37 (2003): 311.
55 James Muir, *Law, Debt and Merchant Power: The Civil Courts of 18th-Century Halifax* (Toronto: Osgoode Society for Canadian Legal History and University of Toronto Press, 2016), 30.
56 *De Conty and Gravina v William Magee et al*, PANS, RG 36, ser. A, no. 8; discussed in Philip Girard, 'Children, Church, Migration and Money: Three Tales of Child Custody in Nova Scotia,' in Hilary Thompson, ed., *Children's Voices in Atlantic Literature and Culture* (Guelph, ON: Canadian Children's Press, 1995).
57 The case is discussed in Jim Phillips, 'The Impeachment of the Judges of the Nova Scotia Supreme Court, 1787–1793,' *Dalhousie Law Journal* 34 (2011): 265.
58 Krista L. Simon, 'Women in the Courts of Placentia District, 1757–1823,' in *EHCL*, vol. 9. On the narrowing of exceptions to coverture, see Karen Pearlston, 'Married Women Bankrupts in the Age of Coverture,' *Law & Social Inquiry* 34 (2009): 265.
59 Girard, 'Three Tales of Child Custody,' 12–14.
60 Constance Backhouse, 'Shifting Patterns in Nineteenth-Century Canadian Custody Law,' in *EHCL*, vol. 1; Susan B. Boyd, *Child Custody, Law, and Women's Work* (Don Mills, ON: Oxford University Press, 2002).
61 Grossberg, *Governing the Hearth*, 237–40.
62 Ibid., 200–15.
63 SO 1921, c 53.
64 Dennis Guest, *The Emergence of Social Security in Canada* (Vancouver: UBC Press, 1997), 11–14. In Newfoundland and Prince Edward Island,

responsibility for poor relief lay at the provincial level, supplemented by occasional disaster relief from the imperial government.

65 Russell Smandych, 'Colonial Welfare Laws and Practices: Coping without an English Poor Law in Upper Canada, 1792–1837,' in *CLI*, 224. See also Lori Chambers, *Misconceptions: Unmarried Motherhood and the Ontario Children of Unmarried Parents Act, 1921–1969* (Toronto: Osgoode Society for Canadian Legal History and University of Toronto Press, 2007), chap. 1.

66 SUC 1799, c 2.

67 Cited in Smandych, 'Coping without an English Poor Law,' 225.

68 The disability went back to the 1542 *Statute in Explanation of the Statute of Wills*, 34 & 35 Hen VIII, c 5. Married women could, however, make wills regarding any property held to their separate use, as Elizabeth de Conty tried to do.

69 22 & 23 Car II, c 10 (U.K.).

70 Carole Shammas, Marylynn Salmon, and Michel Dahlin, *Inheritance in America: From Colonial Times to the Present* (New Brunswick, NJ: Rutgers University Press, 1987).

71 SNS 1758, c 11; SPEI 1781, c 2; SNB 1786, c 11; the eldest son's double share was removed by SNS 1842, c 22; SNB 1858, c 26, and SPEI 1873, c 23.

72 Andrew Buck, '"This Remnant of Feudalism": Primogeniture and Political Culture in Colonial New South Wales, with Some Canadian Comparisons,' in McLaren, Buck, and Wright, *Despotic Dominion*.

73 Barry Moody, 'Growing Up in Granville Township,' in Margaret Conrad, ed., *Intimate Relations: Family and Community in Planter Nova Scotia, 1759–1800* (Fredericton, NB: Acadiensis, 1995), 91–5.

74 Ibid., 94.

75 Historians have come to opposing conclusions about the motivations of testators regarding their widows and female kin: compare Nanciellen Davis, '"Patriarchy from the Grave": Family Relations in 19th-Century New Brunswick Wills,' *Acadiensis* 13 (1984): 91; and Michelle Stairs, '"The Duty of Every Man": Intestacy Law and Family-Inheritance Practice in Prince Edward Island, 1828–1905,' in *EHCL*, vol. 9. Both are based on nineteenth-century evidence.

76 On what follows, see Girard, 'Land Law, Liberalism and the Agrarian Ideal,' 122–7.

77 Susan Staves, *Married Women's Separate Property in England, 1660–1833* (Cambridge, MA: Harvard University Press, 1990); Girard, 'Land Law, Liberalism and the Agrarian Ideal.'

78 Cited in Barry Moody, 'Land, Kinship and Inheritance in Granville Township, 1760–1800,' in Margaret Conrad, ed., *Making Adjustments: Change and Continuity in Planter Nova Scotia, 1759–1800* (Fredericton, NB: Acadiensis, 1991), 176.

79 Ibid., 177.

80 Stephen Waddams, 'Nineteenth-Century Treatises on English Contract Law,' in Angela Fernandez and Markus D. Dubber, eds., *Law Books in Action: Essays on the Anglo-American Legal Treatise* (Oxford: Hart, 2012); A.W.B. Simpson, 'Innovation in Nineteenth-Century English Contract Law,' *Law Quarterly Review* 91 (1975): 247.

81 Muir, *Law, Debt and Merchant Power: The Civil Courts of Eighteenth-Century Halifax* (Toronto: Osgoode Society for Canadian Legal History and University of Toronto Press, 2016), 4. What follows relies principally on this source. On Quebec, see the work by Dickinson cited above in chapter 6.

82 Wylie, 'Arbiters of Commerce,' 295.

83 Muir, *Law, Debt and Merchant Power*, 92–3.

84 A similar phenomenon appeared in the criminal context: see Jim Phillips, 'Halifax Juries in the Eighteenth Century,' in Greg Smith, Allyson May, and Simon Devereaux, eds, *Criminal Justice in the Old World and the New: Essays in Honour of John Beattie* (Toronto: University of Toronto Centre of Criminology, 1998).

85 RG 39, ser. J, vol. 141 at 1, cited in Cahill, 'Richard Gibbons Review,' 49n49.

86 SUC 1797, c 4; SUC 1801, c 9.

87 For examples, see Julian Gwyn, 'Capitalists, Merchants and Manufacturers in Early Nova Scotia, 1767–1791: The Tangled Affairs of John Avery, James Creighton, John Albro and Joseph Fairbanks,' in Conrad, ed., *Intimate Relations*.

20. The Early Modern Legacy

1 Susan M. Hill, *The Clay We Are Made Of: Haudenosaunee Land Tenure on the Grand River* (Winnipeg: University of Manitoba Press, 2017), 7.

2 William C. Wicken, *Mi'kmaq Treaties on Trial: History, Land, and Donald Marshall, Junior* (Toronto: Osgoode Society for Canadian Legal History and University of Toronto Press, 2002).

3 G. Blaine Baker, 'Musings and Silences of Chief Justice William Osgoode: Digest Marginalia about the Reception of Imperial Law,' *Osgoode Hall Law Journal* 54 (2017): 741 at 752–5.

4 Jack P. Greene, '"By Their Laws Shall Ye Know Them": Law and Identity in Colonial British America,' *Journal of Interdisciplinary History* 33 (2002): 247 at 251.
5 The terms are those of Bettina Bradbury, *From Wife to Widow: Lives, Laws and Politics in Nineteenth-Century Montreal* (Vancouver: UBC Press, 2011).

21. Law in British North America, 1815–1866: Introduction

1 Seven, if one includes Cape Breton Island, which disappeared as an independent entity in 1820 on re-annexation to Nova Scotia.
2 *Censuses of Canada 1665–1871*, online at statcan.gc.ca. The mid-1860s figure does not include Vancouver Island or Assiniboia, which would add some 21,000 people to the total.
3 The phrase is notably employed as the interpretive motif for Allan Greer and Ian Radforth, eds, *Colonial Leviathan: State Formation in Mid-Nineteenth-Century Canada* (Toronto: University of Toronto Press, 1992). See also the recent short but useful volume, Elsbeth Heaman, *A Short History of the State in Canada* (Toronto: University of Toronto Press, 2015).

22. Court Systems and Judicial Personnel

1 *Superior court judges* refers to the common law courts of inherent jurisdiction, and Chancery, which means the jurisdiction of the courts of Westminster Hall – King's Bench, Common Pleas, Exchequer, and Chancery. The common law courts were named Supreme Courts throughout the British North American period in the Maritime colonies, Newfoundland, and British Columbia. In Upper Canada it was solely the Court of King's, later Queen's, Bench until 1849, when it was joined by the Court of Common Pleas. In Lower Canada it was also solely the Court of King's/Queen's Bench until 1849, when the Superior Court was established for civil cases; Queen's Bench continued for criminal cases. Superior courts also includes all separate chancery courts where they existed.
2 The affair can be followed in W. Stewart MacNutt, 'Sir James Carter,' *DCB*.
3 See Alan Wilson, 'John Walpole Willis,' and John D. Blackwell, 'Robert Sympson Jameson,' both in *DCB*. There is also an extensive literature on Willis because of the controversy over his dismissal in 1828: see John P.S.

McLaren, *Dewigged, Bothered and Bewildered: British Colonial Judges on Trial, 1800–1900* (Toronto: Osgoode Society for Canadian Legal History and University of Toronto Press, 2011), 74ff.

4 For Robinson see Patrick Brode, *Sir John Beverley Robinson: Bone and Sinew of the Compact* (Toronto: Osgoode Society for Canadian Legal History and University of Toronto Press, 1984), which should be read with the articles on Upper Canada in *CST*, vol. 2, and Paul Romney, *Mr Attorney: The Attorney-General for Ontario in Court, Cabinet and Legislature, 1791–1899* (Toronto: Osgoode Society for Canadian Legal History and University of Toronto Press, 1986).

5 See Resolutions 76–8, in *LC Journals*, 1834, appendix.

6 James Lambert, 'Sir James Monk,' *DCB*; and Evelyn Kolish and James Lambert, 'The Attempted Impeachment of the Lower Canadian Chief Justices, 1814–15,' in *CST*, vol. 1.

7 For what follows, see Evelyn Kolish, *Nationalismes et conflits de droits: le débat du droit privé au Québec 1760–1840* (LaSalle, QC: Hurtubise, 1994), 153–5; and Augustin-Norbert Morin, *Lettre à l'honorable Edward Bowen, Écuyer, Un des Juges de la Cour du Banc du Roi ... pour le district de Québec* (Montreal: James Lane, 1825). Bowen's biographer reports that he 'had a good knowledge of French and of French laws': Jean-Pierre Wallot, 'Edward Bowen,' *DCB*.

8 Robie to Peleg Wiswall, 14 Mar. 1833, NSARM, Wiswall Papers, MG 1, vol. 980, no. 170. For the lobbying, see Phyllis Blakeley, 'Sir Brenton Halliburton'; J. Murray Beck, 'Samuel George William Archibald'; and Brian Cuthbertson, 'Richard John Uniacke,' all in *DCB*.

9 Quotation from Robert Fraser, 'Christopher Alexander Hagerman,' *DCB*.

10 See J. Murray Beck, 'Samuel George William Archibald'; and Ian Robertson, 'Sir Robert Hodgson,' both in *DCB*. For the Island judiciary generally, see Charles McQuaid, *Without Benefit of Clergy: The Colonial Chief Justices and the Temper of Their Times* (Charlottetown: self-pub., 1987).

11 The island's nineteenth-century judges included Ceasar Colclough, discussed above in chapter 13. Colclough's immediate successors, Francis Forbes and Richard Tucker, were Englishmen trained at the inns of court, as was Boulton's successor, John Gervase Hutchinson Bourne. *DCB*.

12 For Cameron, see William R. Sampson, 'David Cameron'; and for Begbie, see David R. Williams, 'Sir Matthew Baillie Begbie,' both in *DCB*. See also David R. Williams, *The Man for a New Country: Sir Matthew Baillie*

Begbie (Sidney, BC: Gray's Publishing, 1977); Hamar Foster, 'British Columbia: Legal Institutions in the Far West, from Contact to 1871,' in *CLI*; and Foster, 'The Kamloops Outlaws and Commissions of Assize in Nineteenth-Century British Columbia,' in *EHCL*, vol. 2.

13 See generally McLaren, *Dewigged*. For the particular example of Newfoundland, see John McLaren, 'The Joys and Sorrows of British Colonial Judges in 19th-Century Newfoundland: Comparing Chief Justices Francis Forbes and Henry John Boulton and Their Tenure,' in Melvin Baker, Christopher Curran, and J. Derek Green, eds, *Discourse and Discovery: Sir Richard Whitbourne Quartercentennial Symposium, 1615–2015 and Beyond* (St John's: Law Society of Newfoundland and Labrador, 2017).

14 Kempt to Sir George Murray, 3 Jan. 1830, in *Copy or Extracts of the Answers of the Governors*, House of Commons Parliamentary Papers, 1830, no. 574, 3–4. The two executive councillors were Sewell and Kerr.

15 The quotation is from Greenwood and Lambert, 'Jonathan Sewell,' *DCB*. For a more generous treatment stressing his bilingualism and bi-juralism, see Brian Young, *The Politics of Codification: The Lower Canadian Civil Code of 1866* (Toronto: Osgoode Society for Canadian Legal History and University of Toronto Press, 1994), esp. at 27–8.

16 *Novascotian*, 7 Feb. 1833, cited in J. Murray Beck, *Joseph Howe*, vol. 1, *Conservative Reformer 1804–1848* (Montreal and Kingston: McGill-Queen's University Press, 1982), 115.

17 Quotations in this paragraph from *Canada Committee Report*, Minutes of Evidence, 230, and William Blowers Bliss to Henry Bliss, 5 Feb. 1831, NSARM, MG1, vol. 1598, no. 286.

18 *Canada Committee Report*, 8.

19 See Robert Fraser, 'Jonas Jones,' and John Blackwell, 'Robert Sympson Jameson,' both in *DCB*; SPC 1843, c 65. We have referred here to the constituent parts of the Province of Canada as Upper and Lower Canada, not Canada West and East, and will do so throughout this part. In 1849 the *Interpretation Act*, SPC 1849, c 10, s 5 made Upper and Lower Canada the official designations. See generally on this question Margaret Banks, 'Upper and Lower Canada or Canada West and East, 1841–1867,' *Canadian Historical Review* 54 (1973): 473.

20 For the separation of powers, see, generally, Jim Phillips, 'Judicial Independence in British North America: Constitutional Principles, Colonial Finances, and the Perils of Democracy,' *Law and History Review* 34 (2016): 689. See also Christopher English, 'The Legal Development of Newfoundland, 1791–1832,' in Louis Knafla and Susan Binnie, eds, *Law,*

Society and the State: Essays in Modern Legal History (Toronto: Carswell, 1995), 89.

21 *Novascotian*, 16 Feb. 1837.

22 See below, chapter 26.

23 David Williams, 'Sir Matthew Baillie Begbie,' *DCB*; and Foster, 'British Columbia.'

24 For a survey of the judicial appointment process, see Luc Huppé, *Histoire des institutions judiciaries au Canada* (Montreal and Kingston: McGill-Queen's University Press, 2007).

25 This and the next paragraph are based on Phillips, 'Judicial Independence'; and McLaren, *Dewigged*.

26 SNB 1838, c 8, s 1.

27 SNB 1867, c 10.

28 For the details in this paragraph, see SNS 1822, c 33; *UC Journals*, 1835, appendix 21, 56–7; SUC 1839, c 4; SPC 1849, c 63, s 5; Christopher Moore, *The Court of Appeal for Ontario: Defining the Right of Appeal, 1792–2013* (Toronto: Osgoode Society for Canadian Legal History and University of Toronto Press, 2014), 32–3.

29 David Lemmings, 'The Independence of the Judiciary in the Eighteenth Century,' in Peter Birks, ed., *The Life of the Law: Proceedings of the Tenth British Legal History Conference* (London: Hambledon, 1993).

30 Information in this paragraph from *UC Journals*, 1835, appendix A-21, *passim*; SPC 1849, c 63, s 6, and 1866, c 40; SN 1858, c 22, and 1865, c 17.

31 For this paragraph, see Jim Phillips and Bradley Miller, 'Too Many Courts and Too Much Law: The Politics of Judicial Reform in Nova Scotia, 1830–1841,' *Law and History Review* 30 (2012): 89 at 96–114.

32 SN 1855, c 8. For this paragraph generally, see Phillips, 'Judicial Independence,' 732–41.

33 Donald Fyson, with the assistance of Evelyn Kolish and Virginia Schweitzer, *The Court Structure of Quebec and Lower Canada, 1764–1860* (Montreal: Montreal History Group, 1994, regularly revised and available on line at www.profs.hst.ulaval.ca/Dfyson/Courtstr/).

34 This discussion of circuits in Upper Canada is drawn from Donald J. McMahon, 'Law and Public Authority: Sir John Beverley Robinson and the Purposes of the Criminal Law,' *University of Toronto Faculty of Law Review* 46 (1988): 390; and Patrick Connor, 'The Purest of Gifts: Royal Clemency, Patronage, and the Politics of Identity in Upper Canada, 1791–1841' (PhD diss., York University, 2012), *passim*.

35 For examples of such requests, see *UC Journals*, 1833–4, appendices.

36 Robert Fraser, 'Christopher Alexander Hagerman,' *DCB*.

37 RSNS 1851, c 126, s 4. The system is outlined in Jim Phillips and Philip Girard, 'Courts, Communities and Communication: The Nova Scotia Supreme Court on Circuit,' in Hamar Foster, Andrew Buck, and Benjamin Berger, eds, *The Grand Experiment: Law and Legal Culture in British Settler Societies* (Vancouver: Osgoode Society for Canadian Legal History and UBC Press, 2008), 117–18.

38 Prince Edward Island judges did not do circuits until 1835: David Bell, 'Maritime Legal Institutions under the Ancien Régime, 1710–1850,' *CLI*, 109.

39 The best accounts of a Newfoundland circuit are Nina Goudie, *Down North on the Labrador Circuit: The Court of Civil Jurisdiction, 1826–1833* (St John's: Law Society of Newfoundland and Labrador, 2005); and Goudie, 'The Supreme Court on Circuit: Northern District, Newfoundland, 1826–1833,' in *EHCL*, vol. 9. See also Jerry Bannister, *The Rule of the Admirals: Law, Custom and Naval Government in Newfoundland, 1699–1832* (Toronto: Osgoode Society for Canadian Legal History and University of Toronto Press, 2003), 263; and SN 1839, c 12.

40 See Phillips and Girard, 'Courts, Communities,' 129–31, for judges' complaints, and 127–9 for their evasion of the rule. For the circuit expense question, see Bell, 'Maritime Legal Institutions,' 109–10.

41 Moore, *Court of Appeal*, 30–1.

42 Goudie, 'Supreme Court on Circuit,' 119; and Philip Buckner, 'John Gervais Bourne,' *DCB*. For resentment about jury service, see R. Blake Brown, 'Storms, Roads, and Harvest Time: Criticisms of Jury Service in Pre-Confederation Nova Scotia,' *Acadiensis* 36 (2006): 93.

43 For admiralty courts, see Bannister, *Rule of the Admirals*, *passim*; and Arthur Stone, 'The Admiralty Court in Colonial Nova Scotia,' *Dalhousie Law Journal* 17 (1994): 363. For courts of marriage and divorce, see below, chap. 34.

44 For chancery courts, see Philip Girard, 'At the Crossroads of Fusion: British North America/Canada, 1750–2000,' in John Goldberg, Henry E. Smith, and P.G. Turner, eds, *Equity and Law: Fusion and Fission* (Cambridge: Cambridge University Press, 2018); *Judicature Act 1824*, cited in English, 'Legal Development of Newfoundland,' 84; *New South Wales Act*, 4 Geo IV, c 96 (U.K.).

45 See Jim Cruikshank, 'The Chancery Court of Nova Scotia: Jurisdiction and Procedure 1751–1855,' *Dalhousie Journal of Legal Studies* 1 (1992): 27; and William Wylie, 'The Majestic Equality of the Law: Diverging Views on the Reform of the Civil Law and Courts in Upper Canada, 1841–1857,' unpublished, 2016, n44.

46 See SNS 1826, c 11; SNB 1838, c 8; and SPEI 1848, c 6.

47 Quotations from *NS Journals*, 14 Feb. 1826; and *NB Journals*, 22 Jan. and 13 Feb. 1838. For the increased caseload, see Cruikshank, 'Chancery Court,' 31.

48 Quotations in this paragraph from *Novascotian*, 22 Feb. 1826; and J. Murray Beck, 'Simon Bradstreet Robie,' *DCB*.

49 SNB 1852, c 42, and 1854, c 18. The commissioners' recommendations are in Second Report of the Commissioners, printed in the 'Introduction' to RSNB 1854; quotations at viii.

50 For Nova Scotia's abolition, see SNS 1855, c 23; Philip Girard, 'Married Women's Property, Chancery Abolition, and Insolvency Law: Law Reform in Nova Scotia 1820-1867,' in *EHCL*, 3:106–3; *NS Journals*, 1852, appendices 19 and 73, and 1853, appendix 16.

51 This is a simplified version of a complicated process, but the analysis offered here is the most persuasive account of both the lack of equity until the 1830s and its creation in 1837. It is from John Weaver, 'While Equity Slumbered: Creditor Advantage, a Capitalist Land Market, and Upper Canada's Missing Court,' *Osgoode Hall Law Journal* 28 (1990): 871. The Act is at SUC 1837, c 2.

52 For the following account of chancery after 1837, see, especially, Elizabeth Brown, 'Equitable Jurisdiction and the Court of Chancery in Upper Canada,' *Osgoode Hall Law Journal* 21 (1983): 275. See also John D. Blackwell, 'William Hume Blake and the Judicature Acts of 1849,' in *EHCL*, vol. 1; and Wylie, 'Majestic Equality.'

53 For the two commissions discussed here, see *PC Journals*, 1841, appendixes JJ and P.

54 *Globe*, 29 June 1851, cited in Brown, 'Equitable Jurisdiction,' 297.

55 SPC 1852, c 119, and 1857, c 56.

56 SPC 1857, c 44.

57 SN 1866, c 13. Judges of this court were to be 'some person or persons of judicial knowledge and habits, and some person or persons of Nautical skill and experience.'

58 For JPs and/or sessions courts, see, inter alia, Donald Fyson, *Magistrates, Police and People: Everyday Criminal Justice in Quebec and Lower Canada, 1764–1837* (Toronto: Osgoode Society for Canadian Legal History and University of Toronto Press, 2006); Paul Craven, *Petty Justice: Low Law and the Sessions System in Charlotte County, New Brunswick, 1784–1867* (Toronto: Osgoode Society for Canadian Legal History and University of Toronto Press, 2014); Susan Lewthwaite, 'Law and Authority in Upper Canada: The Justices of the Peace in the Newcastle District, 1802–1840,' (PhD thesis, University of Toronto, 2000); David Murray, *Colonial Justice:*

Justice, Morality and Crime in the Niagara District, 1791–1849 (Toronto: Osgoode Society for Canadian Legal History and University of Toronto Press, 2002).

59 This section on lower civil courts in Upper Canada is based principally on Wylie, 'Majestic Equality'; and Jim Phillips, 'Small Claims Courts in Upper Canada, 1792–1866,' unpublished paper, 2017.

60 *UC Journals*, 17 Feb. 1830.

61 SPC 1841, c 3 and 8. The tangled history of the district and county courts is well recounted in Spyros D. Loukidelis, 'Some Aspects of the Development of the County Courts of Ontario and the Evolution of the Office of County Court Judge, 1792–1881' (MA thesis, Laurentian University, 1978).

62 Quotations from *PC Debates*, 1, 234–6.

63 For these various points, see SPC 1845, c 13, s 2; SPC 1846, c 36, ss 1–2; 1849, c 78, esp. s 3; 1850, c 52, s 1; 1856, c 90, s 20; and 1853, c 176.

64 SNS 1823, c 36 and SNS 1824, c 38. For Marshall, see Jim Phillips, 'A Low Law Counter Treatise? "Absentees" to "Wreck" in British North America's First Justice of the Peace Manual,' in Angela Fernandez and Markus Dubber, eds, *Law Books in Action: Essays on the Anglo-American Legal Treatise* (Oxford: Hart Publishing, 2012).

65 SNS 1841, c 3. See generally Phillips and Miller, 'Too Many Courts,' 122–32.

66 SNB 1867, c 10.

67 Fyson, *Court Structure.*

68 See above, chapter 13; and Fyson, *Magistrates, Police and People*, 42–3. For St John's and other Newfoundland communities, see the annual *Appropriations Acts*. For Nova Scotia, see Philip Girard, 'The Rise and Fall of Urban Justice in Halifax, 1815–1866,' *Nova Scotia Historical Review* 8 (1988): 57; Greg Marquis, 'The Contours of Canadian Urban Justice,' *Urban History Review* 15 (1987): 21. For Toronto, where the story is more complicated, see Paul Craven, 'Law and Ideology: The Toronto Police Court, 1850–1880,' in *EHCL*, vol. 2.

69 SPC 1848, c 81, s 70.

70 SNS 1864, c 15.

71 The history of the Red River colony has been discussed in chapter 14, above. For Thom, see Kathryn Bindon, 'Hudson's Bay Company Law: Adam Thom and the Institution of Order in Rupert's Land, 1839–1854,' in *ECHL*, 1; and Bindon, 'Adam Thom,' *DCB*. The most recent and fullest account is in Dale Gibson, *Law, Life and Government at Red River*, vol. 1, *Settlement and Governance, 1812–1872* (Montreal and Kingston: Osgoode

Society for Canadian Legal History and McGill-Queen's University Press, 2015).

72 SUC 1834, c 22, ss 78–86; SNS 1841, c 55, ss 53–4.

73 SPC 1845, c 59; SPC 1851, c 128.

74 *Epitome*, 4:22. For the other points made here, see SNS 1807, c 12; 1837, c 60; 1817, c 11; Girard, 'Urban Justice,' 60; and Philip Girard, *Lawyers and Legal Culture in British North America: Beamish Murdoch of Halifax* (Toronto: Osgoode Society for Canadian Legal History and University of Toronto Press, 2011), esp. chap. 6.

75 SPC 1821, c 2, and 1843, c 19. These commissioners' courts were retained in the reorganization of 1849, which established the Superior Court as the highest civil tribunal.

76 See Greg Marquis, 'Anti-Lawyer Sentiment in Mid-Victorian New Brunswick,' *University of New Brunswick Law Journal* 36 (1987): 163; and Girard, *Lawyers and Legal Culture.*

77 SNS 1832, c 53. For small claims courts and summary jurisdiction elsewhere, see Fyson, *Court Structure;* Craven, *Petty Justice;* SPEI 1836, c 4, and 1837, c 11.

78 See Fyson, *Court Structure;* SPC 1857, c 44, and 1858, c 58.

79 For this paragraph, see, especially, Moore, *Court of Appeal,* chap. 1; Blackwell, 'Judicature Acts'; and Margaret Banks, 'The Evolution of the Ontario Courts 1788–1981,' both in *EHCL,* vol. 1; SPC 1849, c 63 and 64; SPC 1853, c 175, s 2.

80 Quoted in Moore, *Court of Appeal,* 11.

81 SPC 1843, c 18; SPC 1849, c 37. The origins of Lower Canada's Court of Appeal are discussed in Yves-Marie Morissette, 'Aspects historiques et analytiques de l'appel en matière civile,' *McGill Law Journal* 59 (2014): 481.

82 James McGregor, *Historical and Descriptive Sketches of the Maritime Colonies of British America* (London, 1828), 127. For civil procedure in nineteenth-century British North America, see the brief discussion in R.C.B. Risk, 'The Law and the Economy in Mid-Nineteenth-Century Ontario: A Perspective,' in *EHCL,* 1:93–4.

83 *Epitome,* 3:65–6. Chapter 2 of Murdoch's third volume, *Of Actions,* went from 65 to 90 and successively discussed personal actions (66–72) and actions connected with real estate (72–90). Chapters 5–8, 105–69, dealt with various stages of civil process.

84 Both quotations from Risk, 'Law and Economy,' 93.

85 William Blowers Bliss to Henry Bliss, 5 Feb. 1831, NSARM, MG 1, vol. 1598, no. 286.

86 Risk, 'Law and Economy,' 92.
87 2 Will IV, c 39 (1832); and 15 & 16 Vic, c 76 (1852).
88 For the Nova Scotia commission, see SNS 1832, c 42. The New Brunswick Commission is referred to in the report of the one established under this statute, which is at *NS Journals*, 1834, appendix 59.
89 William Blowers Bliss to Henry Bliss, 18 July 1835, and 19 Aug. 1836, NSARM, MG 1, vol. 1599, nos 25 and 31.
90 SUC 1837, c 3.
91 SNS 1841, c 3, quotations from ss 42 and 43.
92 The rules can be found at *PC Journals*, 1842, appendix Q, and in a volume published at the end of the century, *Rules of Court, 1831–1895* (Toronto, 1896).
93 Report of the Commissioners of Judicial Inquiry, 1842, in *NB Journals*, 1842, cxxix–clv.
94 SNS 1848, c 41.
95 SNS 1853, c 4. For the law reform commission report, see *NS Journals* 1853, appendix 16. The writ of replevin was taken out to recover personal property from another when the other had wrongfully taken or detained the property.
96 *Presbyterian Witness*, 2 Apr. 1853, cited in Girard, 'Law Reform,' 80.
97 SPC 1856, c 43 and 175. Little has been written on procedure for Upper Canada. The fullest account is in Wylie, 'Majestic Equality.'
98 *Toronto Examiner*, 12 Dec. 1849, cited in ibid., n74.
99 Third Report of the Law Commissioners, 24 Jan. 1854, in *NB Journals*, 1854, appendix, 26–35.
100 SN 1864, c 9 and 10.

23. Sources of Law and Law Reform

1 The quotations in this paragraph are from *Tarrat v Sawyer*, (1835) 1 NSR 46 at 52; *Hamilton v Niagara Harbour and Dock*, (1842) 6 UCQB 174; *Marshall v The School Trustees of Kitley*, (1855) 4 UCCP 373; and (1848), 6 NBR 213 at 215. Some of these cases, and others used in this section, are also cited in Bernard Hibbitts, 'Her Majesty's Yankees: American Authority in the Supreme Court of Victorian Nova Scotia, 1837–1901,' in *SCNS*; and R.C.B. Risk, 'The Law and the Economy in Mid-Nineteenth-Century Ontario: A Perspective,' in *EHCL*, vol. 1.
2 Contemporary scholars of Indigenous law are exploring the possibility that the stories forming part of oral tradition can themselves be understood as a form of case law; Val Napoleon and Hadley Friedland,

'An Inside Job: Engaging with Indigenous Legal Traditions through Stories,' *McGill Law Journal* 61 (2016): 725.

3 Between 1850 and 1855, for example, Robinson and Macaulay wrote a judgment in virtually every case, and wrote the judgment of the court in 75 per cent of cases: Risk, 'Law and Economy,' 92. For what follows, in addition to case citations, see the same source, and Peter George and Philip Sworden, 'John Beverley Robinson and the Commercial Empire of the St Lawrence,' *Research in Economic History* 11 (1988): 217; Peter Karsten, *Between Law and Custom: 'High' and 'Low' Legal Cultures in the Lands of the British Diaspora – The United States, Canada, Australia and New Zealand, 1600–1900* (Cambridge: Cambridge University Press, 2002). Also useful for the Upper Canada Court of Error and Appeal is Christopher Moore, *The Court of Appeal for Ontario: Defining the Right of Appeal, 1792–2013* (Toronto: Osgoode Society for Canadian Legal History and University of Toronto Press, 2014), chap. 1.

4 *Stalker v Weir* (1854) 2 NSR 248 at 254, and *Fairbanks v Union Marine Insurance Co* (1856) 3 NSR 68 at 72.

5 *J & R Bine v M. Meehan* (1817) 1 Nfld R 5 at 7. See also an 1831 case, *Brehaut & Sheppard v Trustees of LeMessurier's Estate* (1831) 2 Nfld R 27, in which it was said at 32 that the current chief justice of Newfoundland was 'very high authority.'

6 3 NBR at x; James, 'Preface,' 2 NSR vi; *Haliburton v De Wolfe* (1867) 7 NSR 12 at 15.

7 (1838) 2 NBR 442 at 444.

8 *Tarrat v Sawyer*, 52. See also *Murison v Murison* (1840), 1 NSR 131 at 133, in which Halliburton said that while he was 'not bound by the decisions of the tribunals in the United States as we are by those in the mother country,' he found the 'opinions of the learned judges who preside' in American courts gave him 'much assistance.'

9 *Gaudin v M'Killigan* (1852), 7 NBR 392 at 402.

10 (1835) 1 NSR 9; quotation below at 11. See also Halliburton's approach to an adverse possession case in 1841, in which he insisted both that local conditions were dissimilar to England and that they were more like the United States: *Lessess of Lawson v Whitman* (1851), 1 NSR 208.

11 (1826) 1 NBR 37, at 38 and 39, emphasis in original; (1842), 3 NBR 595 at 627.

12 *Kenny v Halifax Marine Insurance Co*, (1840), 1 NSR 141 at 154; *Dimock and another v The New Brunswick Marine Assurance Company* (1848), 5 NBR 654 at 659.

13 (1854) 4 GCR 231 at 241; *Bank of British North America v Ross*, (1844) 1 UCQB 199 at 210. See also to similar effect R.C.B. Risk, 'The Golden Age: The Law about the Market in Nineteenth-Century Ontario,' *University of Toronto Law Journal* 26 (1976): 307 at 339.

14 For this paragraph, see, especially, Moore, *Court of Appeal*, 34–5. The cases referred to include *Shiriff v Holcomb* and *Harvey v Smyth* (1864) 3 E & A 156 and 480.

15 The major work dealing more with the sources of law than its content is G. Blaine Baker, 'The Reconstitution of Upper Canadian Legal Thought in the Late Victorian Empire,' *Law and History Review* 3 (1985): 219; quotations at 234 and 239.

16 Oliver Mowat, 'Observations on the Use and Value of American Reports in Reference to Canadian Jurisprudence,' 1857, cited in ibid., 248.

17 What follows is based on two accounts of Murdoch and his *Epitome* by Philip Girard: *Lawyers and Legal Culture in British North America: Beamish Murdoch of Halifax* (Toronto: Osgoode Society for Canadian Legal History and University of Toronto Press, 2011), esp. chap. 9; and 'Themes and Variations in Early Canadian Legal Culture: Beamish Murdoch and his *Epitome of the Laws of Nova-Scotia*,' *Law and History Review* 11 (1993): 101. Quotation below from the *Epitome*, 1:33.

18 'De la codification des lois du Canada,' *Revue de législation et de jurisprudence* 1 (1846): 337.

19 John E.C. Brierley, 'Quebec's Civil Law Codification Viewed and Reviewed,' *McGill Law Journal* 14 (1968): 521 at 547–52.

20 *Fundamental Principles of the Laws of Canada as They Existed under the Natives, as They Were Changed under the French Kings, and as They Were Modified and Altered under the Domination of England* (Montreal: John Lovell, 1841–7).

21 Brierley, 'Civil Law Codification,' 539.

22 Sylvio Normand, 'L'histoire de l'imprimé juridique: un champ de recherché inexploré,' *McGill Law Journal* 38 (1993): 130 at 141–2.

23 Michel Morin, 'La perception de l'ancien droit et du nouveau droit français au Bas-Canada, 1774–1866,' in H. Patrick Glenn, ed., *Droit québécois et droit français: communauté, autonomie, concordance* (Cowansville, QC: Yvon Blais, 1993), 12; Justice Charles Dewey Day treated the question at length in *Monk v Morris* (1853) 3 LCR 1 at 29–31.

24 SPC 1843, c 16, s 7. Jean-Maurice Brisson, *La formation d'un droit mixte: l'évolution de la procédure civile de 1774 à 1867* (Montreal: Éditions Thémis 1986), 74–5. The parlements in pre-revolutionary France were forbidden

from giving reasons, and only the revolutionary law of 16 August 1790 obliged the courts to do so.

25 Brian Young, *The Politics of Codification: The Lower Canadian Civil Code of 1866* (Toronto: Osgoode Society for Canadian Legal History and University of Toronto Press, 1994), both quotations at 31.

26 The seventeen decisions reported in Pyke's *Reports of Cases Heard and Determined in the Court of King's Bench for the District of Quebec* (Montreal: n.p., 1811), were all written by Sewell, with a few brief concurring decisions by Kerr and Williams.

27 Jonathan Sewell, *An Essay on the Juridical History of France, so Far as It Relates to the Law of the Province of Lower-Canada* (Quebec: T. Cary, 1824), 34.

28 Morin, 'La perception de l'ancien droit,' 18.

29 François-Maximilien Bibaud, 'Observations sur le Projet de Code canadien,' in Bibaud's *Exégèse de jurisprudence* (n.d., n.p.), 12 (authors' translation). While the work is undated, its reference to the draft *Civil Code* places it in the 1860s. See also Young, *Politics of Codification*, 11.

30 See, for example, *Kennedy v Smith* (1856) 6 LCR 260 at 266 (BR) (art. 1793 of *Code Napoléon* overturning ancient droit on a point of contract law; ancien droit still in force in Lower Canada); Morin, 'La perception de l'ancien droit,' 24.

31 'De la codification des lois,' 337.

32 Ibid., 340–1 (authors' translation).

33 Some have speculated that the author was George-Étienne Cartier, but his identity has never been proven conclusively.

34 G. Blaine Baker, 'Law Practice and Statecraft in Mid-Nineteenth-Century Montreal: The Torrance-Morris Firm, 1848–1868,' in *EHCL*, 4:64–6.

35 *Les lois criminelles anglaises, traduites et compilées de Blackstone ...* (Montreal: Fréchette, 1842).

36 John E.C. Brierley and Roderick A. Macdonald, *Quebec Civil Law: An Introduction to Quebec Private Law* (Toronto: Emond Montgomery, 1993), 34–5.

37 *Civil Code of Lower Canada, First Report* (1861), 55.

38 Eric Reiter, 'Imported Books, Imported Ideas: Reading European Jurisprudence in Nineteenth-Century Quebec,' *Law and History Review* 22 (2004): 445 at 470.

39 Brierley, 'Civil Law Codification,' 564.

40 SPC 1857, c 45.

41 These two aspects are well covered by Brierley, 'Civil Law Codification'; and Young, *Politics of Codification*, respectively. The most recent survey of

the field is the introduction to John W. Cairns, *Codification, Transplants and History: Law Reform in Louisiana (1808) and Quebec (1866)* (Talbot, NJ: Clark Publishing, 2015).

42 SPC 1857, c 43.

43 These figures relate only to the *Civil Code*; the minute book for the work on the *Code of Civil Procedure* has been lost. Its work extended over the years 1865–6.

44 Brierley, 'Civil Law Codification,' 537–8.

45 Ibid., 547–53. Ramsay published his research for the commission as *Notes sur la Coutume de Paris* (Montreal: La Minerve, 1863).

46 Sylvio Normand and Donald Fyson, 'Le droit romain comme source du *Code civil du Bas-Canada*,' *Revue du notariat* 103 (2001): 87 at 112. They note at 105 that of the three commissioners Charles Dewey Day made by far the most frequent references to Roman law.

47 Young, *Politics of Codification*, 109–12.

48 On what follows, see ibid., chap. 9.

49 'Secret hypothecs' referred to the practice that notarial deeds constituting debts carried a tacit general security interest over the debtor's property.

50 Cairns, *Codification*, 342 and 419.

51 F. Murray Greenwood, 'Lower Canada (Quebec): Transformation of Civil Law, from Higher Morality to Autonomous Will, 1774–1866,' in *CLI*, 135. Greenwood notes that lesion seems not to have been commonly invoked, as it is not mentioned in Henry Des Rivières Beaubien's *Traité sur les lois civiles du Bas-Canada* (1832–3), Nicolas-Benjamin Doucet's *Fundamental laws of Canada …* (1841–7), or Jacques Crémazie's *Manuel des notions utiles sur les droits politiques, le droit civil, la loi criminelle* (1852). See also *Civil Code of Lower Canada (First Report)*, 13.

52 Young, *Politics of Codification*, 151.

53 SPC 1862, c 66, s 19. The provision thus also allowed minors to deposit money without parental consent, as noted in art. 243 of the CCLC.

54 Young, *Politics of Codification*, 151.

55 Edith Deleury, Michèle Rivet, and Jean-Marc Neault, 'De la puissance paternelle à l'autorité parentale: Une institution en voie de trouver sa vraie finalité,' *Cahiers de droit* 15 (1974): 779 at 817–20.

56 The sole exception was the right of the survivor of a couple married in community of property to enjoy a usufruct over any property coming to minor children as their share of the deceased spouse's half of the community, to the age of eighteen (arts 1426–34 CCLC).

57 André Morel, 'La codification devant l'opinion publique de l'époque,' in Jacques Boucher and André Morel, eds, *Livre du centenaire du Code civil* (Montreal: Presses de l'Université de Montreal, 1970), 43.
58 SPC 1866, c 25. The *Civil Code* had been enacted by SPC 1865, c 41.
59 *Eighth Report of the Commissioners Appointed to Codify the Laws of Lower Canada* (Ottawa: G.E. Desbarats, 1866). The *Tenth Report* contained the draft *Code of Civil Procedure* itself.
60 Much of what follows, including a discussion of these ordinances, relies on Brisson, *La formation d'un droit mixte.*
61 SQ 1965, c 80.
62 By the time of Blackstone, English law held that judges could be challenged only for holding a pecuniary or proprietary interest in the outcome of litigation before them. Some U.S. states added family relationship as a cause of challenge after the Revolution; Anon., 'Disqualification of Judges for Prejudice or Bias-Common Law Evolution, Current Status, and the Oregon Experience,' *Oregon Law Review* 48 (1969): 311.
63 SPC 1855, c 105. The 1667 ordinance is at *EO*, 1:106, the provisions on recusal at Title XXIV.
64 *Orders and Rules of Practice, in the Court of King's Bench, for the District of Quebec, Lower Canada* (Quebec 1809); *Rules and Orders of Practice for the Court of King's Bench, District of Montreal, February Term, 1811* (Montreal, 1811).
65 Brisson, *La Formation d'un droit mixte*, 130, 132.
66 Doucet, *Fundamental Principles.* On the *Extrait des Messieurs*, see chap. 18.
67 *Les lois de la procédure civile*, 2 vols (Montreal: Eusèbe Sénécal Imprimeur 1867-69), II, quotations at vi.
68 SQ 1897, c 48.
69 (1867), 11 LCJ 197.
70 Called Suzanne Pas-de-nom in Justice Monk's reasons, scholars have established that she was known as Suzanne Bellefeuille and as Miyo Nipay: Adele Perry, *Colonial Relations: The Douglas-Connolly Family and the Nineteenth-Century Imperial World* (Cambridge: Cambridge University Press, 2015), 33.
71 *Connolly v Woolrich*, 234.
72 Perry, *Colonial Relations*, 104.
73 (1869) 1 *Revue légale* 253–400.

74 Philip Girard with Jim Phillips, 'Rethinking "the Nation" in National Legal History: A Canadian Perspective,' *Law and History Review* 29 (2011): 607.
75 SNB 1816, c 2, 4, 8, 9, 13, 14, 16, and 26.
76 SLC 1830, c 1, 5, 18, and 27.
77 See, generally, W. Thomas Matthews, 'Local Government and the Regulation of the Public Market in Upper Canada, 1800–1860: The Moral Economy of the Poor?,' *Ontario History* 79 (1978): 297.
78 Risk, 'Law and Economy,' 101.
79 G. Blaine Baker, 'Strategic Benthamism: Rehabilitating United Canada's Bar through Criminal Law Codification, 1847–1854,' in *EHCL*, vol. 10.
80 (Halifax: Howe, 1805).
81 They covered the years 1805–16, 1817–26, and 1827–35, and were all published by Howe.
82 The Upper Canada consolidations are listed in Margaret Banks, 'An Annotated Biography of Statutes and Related Publications: Upper Canada, the Province of Canada, and Ontario 1792–1980,' in *EHCL*, vol. 1. For New Brunswick, see *The Acts of the General Assembly* (Fredericton: John Simpson, 1838). For Prince Edward Island, see *Acts of the General Assembly ...* (Charlottetown: James D. Haszard, 1834); *Acts of the General Assembly of Prince Edward Island 1773 to ... 1844, Inclusive* (Charlottetown: James D. Haszard, 1844).
83 *Acts of the General Assembly* (Charlottetown: James D. Haszard, 1852); *The Acts of the General Assembly* (Charlottetown: Royal Gazette, 1862); *Acts of the General Assembly* (Charlottetown: Royal Gazette, 1868.)
84 *Acts of the General Assembly of Newfoundland* (St John's: Ryan and Withers, 1833–); *A Collection of the Public General Statutes of the Colony of Vancouver Island* (Victoria: British Colonist Office, 1866); *Ordinances Passed by the Legislative Council of British Columbia* (New Westminster: Government Printing Office, 1864–71).
85 For Upper Canada, see Banks, 'Annotated Bibliography.' For the 1838 New Brunswick consolidation, see *NB Journals*, 23 Jan. and 7, 8, 13, 17, 18, and 23 Feb. 1837.
86 What follows is drawn from a variety of accounts of law reform and codification in Britain and the United States. See in particular Charles M. Cook, *The Codification Movement: A Study of Antebellum Legal Reform* (Westport, CT: Greenwood, 1981); Lawrence Friedman, 'Law Reform in Historical Perspective,' *St Louis Law Journal* 13 (1969): 351; Maxwell Bloomfield, 'William Sampson and the Codifiers: The Roots of American Legal Realism,' *American Journal of Legal History* 11 (1997): 234; A.H.

Manchester, 'Simplifying the Sources of the Law: An Essay on Law Reform, *Anglo-American Law Review* 2 (1973): 395.

87 For law reform in nineteenth-century British North America, see Philip Girard, 'Married Women's Property, Chancery Abolition, and Insolvency Law: Law Reform in Nova Scotia 1820–1867,' *EHCL*, vol. 3; see also Girard, *Lawyers and Legal Culture*, chap. 4. An excellent discussion of the phenomenon, albeit in the context of a failed law reform effort, is Baker, 'Strategic Benthamism.' For Lower Canada, see Evelyn Kolish, 'The Impact of the Change in Legal Metropolis in the Development of Lower Canada's Legal System,' *Canadian Journal of Law and Society* 3 (1988): 1; and for Upper Canada, John D. Blackwell, 'William Hume Blake and the Judicature Acts of 1849,' in *EHCL*, vol. 2.

88 For the statute establishing the commission, see SNS 1832, c 42. The report is at *NS Journals*, 1834, appendix 59.

89 See *The Statutes of Upper Canada*, 2 vols (Toronto: Robert Stanton, 1843). The quotations are taken from the commissioners' brief *Report*, which appears at the beginning of volume 1. Both this and the Lower Canadian revision noted immediately below are discussed in Banks, 'Annotated Bibliography,' which also lists other collections of statutes not germane to this survey.

90 *The Revised Acts and Ordinances of Lower Canada* (Montreal: Derbishire & Desbarats, 1845).

91 The commissioners produced three short reports between 1843 and 1845, all of which are included in the *Revised Acts*, iii–xiii. The first two of them are also in appendix OO of the *PC Journals* for 1844. The quotations here are from iv and ix of the *Revised Acts*.

92 *NS Journals*, 30 Jan. and 6 and 7 Feb. 1849. For what follows, see *NS Journals*, 1849, *passim*.

93 For all of this see ibid., 1850, appendix 15.

94 SNB 1852, c 42, and First Report of the Commissioners, in *NB Journals*, 26 Mar. 1853.

95 The brief report of the 1859 commissioners is in the first few pages of the *Revised Statutes*. It noted that since 1851 many amendments had been made to the statutes, but other than changes to take account of this, they had 'endeavored to make as few alterations' as possible, and had 'carefully abstained from making any alteration in the laws themselves.'

96 Three sets of *Consolidated Statutes* were published, for Upper Canada (1859), for Lower Canada (1861), and for the Province of Canada (1859).

97 The quotations are from Reports of the Commissioners for the Revision of the Statutes of Upper Canada, in *PC Journals*, 1859, appendix 9. It also discusses the Lower Canadian consolidation. For Badgley and his unsuccessful Codes, see Baker, 'Strategic Benthamism.'

24. Indigenous Law in British North America

1 Duane Thomson and Marianne Ignace, '"They Made Themselves Our Guests": Power Relationships in the Interior Plateau Region of the Cordillera in the Fur Trade Era,' *BC Studies* 146 (2005): 3 at 35.
2 Tina Loo, 'The Road from Bute Inlet: Crime and Colonial Identity in British Columbia,' in *EHCL*, vol. 5. Seventeen workers building a road across the territory of the Tsilhqot'in without their consent were killed in two related incidents, along with one settler. Eight Tsilhqot'in men surrendered themselves and were tried, of whom five were hanged. The government of Canada issued an apology for the actions of the colonial government and absolved the accused of any wrongdoing on 26 March 2018: John Paul Tasker, '"We Are Truly Sorry": Trudeau Exonerates Tsilhqot'in Chiefs Hanged in 1864,' CBC News, 26 Mar. 2018, http://www.cbc.ca/news/politics/pm-trudeau-exonerate-tsilhqotin-chiefs-1.4593445.
3 Cited in Jean Barman, *The West beyond the West: A History of British Columbia*, 3d ed. (Toronto: University of Toronto Press, 2007), 163.
4 Cited in Dale Gibson, *Law, Life, and Government at Red River*, 2 vols (Montreal and Kingston: Osgoode Society for Canadian Legal History and McGill-Queen's University Press, 2015), 2:24. The trial in question was that of Capenesseweet, to be considered below.
5 On Metis constitutionalism, see John Borrows, 'Indigenous Constitutionalism,' in Peter Oliver, Patrick Macklem, and Nathalie Des Rosiers, eds, *The Oxford Handbook of the Canadian Constitution* (New York: Oxford University Press, 2017), 17–18.
6 What follows is based on the very full account given by Gibson, *Red River*, 2:16–27. Gibson also absolves the court of the charge of carrying out the execution without legal authority, a point he says has been misunderstood by previous historians, including Kathryn Bindon, 'Adam Thom,' *DCB*.
7 Population figures given by Jean Sawaya, *La Fédération des Sept Feux de la Vallée du Saint-Laurent, XVIIe–XIXe siècle* (Sillery, QC: Septentrion, 1998), 30, show 3,000–3,500 Indigenous inhabitants of the Seven Fires communities between 1823 and 1854. Kahnawake and Grand River

also share the common experience of having legal claims arising from the colonial period still under negotiation with provincial and federal authorities.

8 Sally Weaver, 'The Iroquois: The Consolidation of the Grand River Reserve in the Mid-Nineteenth Century, 1847–1875,' in Edward S. Rogers and Donald B. Smith, eds, *Aboriginal Ontario: Historical Perspectives on the First Nations* (Toronto: Dundurn, 1994), 196.

9 Sharon O'Brien, *American Indian Tribal Governments* (Norman: University Oklahoma Press, 1989), 104. The 1848 Seneca constitution proclaimed universal adult male suffrage and thereby disenfranchised Seneca women, a pattern similar to that seen in settler British North America with the shift to responsible government.

10 Isabelle Bouchard, 'Des systèmes politiques en quête de légitimité: terres, pouvoirs et enjeux locaux dans les communautés autochtones de la vallée du Saint-Laurent' (PhD diss., Université du Québec à Montréal, 2017), 327. Bouchard is referring to Lower Canada, but the same was true elsewhere in British North America.

11 Cited in E.J. Devine, *Historic Caughnawaga* (Montreal: Messenger, 1922), 393.

12 On what follows, see Mark D. Walters, 'The Continuity of Aboriginal Customs and Government under British Imperial Constitutional Law as Applied in Colonial Canada, 1760–1860' (DPhil diss., Oxford University, 1995), 234–7, quotation at 235. On the Credit River Mississauga, see Mark Walters, 'How to Read Aboriginal Legal Texts from Upper Canada,' *Journal of the Canadian Historical Association* 14 (2003): 93.

13 Bouchard, 'Systemes politiques,' 99.

14 Douglas C. Harris concludes that Indigenous fishers on the west coast 'continued much as they had done' before Confederation, without significant settler interference, though that would change afterwards with the development of new canning technology: *Landing Native Fisheries: Indian Reserves & Fishing Rights in British Columbia, 1849–1925* (Vancouver: UBC Press, 2008), 35.

15 What follows relies on Matthieu Sossoyan, 'The Kahnawake Iroquois and the Lower-Canadian Rebellions, 1837–38' (MA thesis, McGill University, 1999), 20–1; and Bouchard, 'Systèmes politiques,' 91–8. The seven clans were Turtle, Wolf, Old Bear (Big Bear), Great Bear, Snipe, Stone, and Deer, the first four being Mohawk, the latter three being Onondaga and Oneida. Bouchard reports at 97 that the seventh clan and enlargement of the council to seven chiefs dates from about 1840.

16 On the Seven Fires, see chapter 17, above.
17 Bouchard, 'Systèmes politiques,' 101.
18 Deborah Doxtator, 'What Happened to the Iroquois Clans? A Study of Clans in Three Nineteenth-Century Rotinonhysonni Communities' (PhD diss., University of Western Ontario, 1996), 220–1.
19 Sally Weaver, 'Consolidation of the Grand River Reserve,' 189.
20 On these, see chapter 17, above.
21 Doxtator, 'What Happened to the Clans?,' 80.
22 Susan M. Hill, *The Clay We Are Made Of: Haudenosaunee Land Tenure on the Grand River* (Winnipeg: University of Manitoba Press, 2017), 174.
23 Gibson, *Red River*, 1:111.
24 B.E. Hill, 'The Grand River Navigation Company and the Six Nations Indians,' *Ontario History* 63 (1971): 31.
25 Weaver, 'Consolidation of the Grand River Reserve,' 202. See also chapter 31, below, on the Grand River Navigation Co. investment.
26 On what follows, see Bouchard, 'Systèmes politiques,' 370–5, quotations at 370 and 373.
27 Daniel Rueck, 'Enclosing the Mohawk Commons: A History of Use-Rights, Land Ownership, and Boundary-Making in Kahnawá:ke Mohawk Territory' (PhD diss., McGill University, 2013), 155–8.
28 Bouchard, 'Systèmes politiques,' 237; see also Donald Fyson, *Magistrates, Police and People: Everyday Criminal Justice in Quebec and Lower Canada, 1764–1840* (Toronto: Osgoode Society for Canadian Legal History and University of Toronto Press, 2006), 303.
29 SPC 1843, c 20.
30 Bouchard, 'Systèmes politiques,' makes this argument throughout her thesis.
31 Another development that weakened those Indigenous communities in Lower Canada that acted as seigneurs was the abolition of the seigneurial system in 1854, treated in chapter 30. Indigenous communities were subject to special provisions in the abolition legislation but were supposed to be compensated for their loss of seigneurial dues, just as other seigneurs were. The loss of those rights at Kahnawake was estimated at $100,000 in 1860, but the matter remains an outstanding claim against the provincial government; Rueck, 'Enclosing the Mohawk Commons,' 144.
32 It was at least implicit in the long litigation in *Mohegan Indians v Connecticut*, finally decided by the Privy Council in 1772, that 'Indian nations' in North America possessed some kind of legal personality under the common law; see Mark D. Walters, '*Mohegan Indians v*

Connecticut (1705–1773) and the Legal Status of Aboriginal Customary Laws and Government in British North America,' *Osgoode Hall Law Journal* 33 (1995): 785. Paul McHugh, *Aboriginal Societies and the Common Law: A History of Sovereignty, Status, and Self-Determination* (Oxford: Oxford University Press, 2004), also treats this issue at 153–7.

33 Brian Young, *In Its Corporate Capacity: The Seminary of Montreal as a Business Institution, 1816–1876* (Montreal and Kingston: McGill-Queen's University Press, 1986). And on the role of corporations in general, see chapter 31.

34 Michel Lavoie, *C'est ma seigneurie je réclame: La lutte des Hurons de Lorette pour la seigneurie de Sillery, 1650–1900* (Montreal: Boréal, 2010), 276–8. When the Hurons petitioned for incorporation in 1835, they were denied: Bouchard, 'Systèmes politiques,' 342.

35 Bouchard, 'Systemes politiques,' 257.

36 Ibid., 343.

37 SPC 1850, c 42.

38 Jean-Marie Fecteau discusses the 'véritable mystique' of the corporate form in 'État et associationisme au XIXe siècle Québécois: éléments pour une problématique des rapports État/société dans la transition au capitalisme,' in Allan Greer and Ian Radforth, eds, *Colonial Leviathan: State Formation in Mid-Nineteenth-Century Canada* (Toronto: University of Toronto Press, 1992).

39 (1851), 9 UCKB 105 at 123.

40 (1835), 4 UCKB 142 at 150.

41 (1851), 9 UCKB 105. Quotation from Sidney L. Harring, *White Man's Law: Native People in Nineteenth-Century Canadian Jurisprudence* (Toronto: Osgoode Society for Canadian Legal History and University of Toronto Press, 1996), 72.

42 The statute was SUC 1819, c 12.

43 (1851), 9 UCKB 105 at 123.

44 Ibid., 135–6.

45 Harring, *White Man's Law*, especially chaps 2, 3, and 4.

46 Hill, *Clay We Are Made Of*, reviews the events leading up to the 1847 resettlement at 180–2. The decisions denying legal personality to Indigenous polities did not prevent their leaders from speaking and advocating on behalf of their people or engaging in acts short of actual contracts or property dispositions. Nor has the possibility of creative avoidance of the legal personality problem by both settlers and Indigenous peoples been explored.

47 Weaver, 'Consolidation of the Grand River Reserve,' 204–5.

48 On the shift from 'seigneury' to 'reserve' at Kahnawake, for example, see Rueck, 'Enclosing the Mohawk Commons,' chapter 4.
49 Hill, *Clay We Are Made Of*, 207–10.
50 Sossoyan, 'Kahnawake Iroquois,' 20. The extent of fencing at Grand River is not clear. Bouchard, 'Systèmes politiques,' perhaps too readily assumes that the recording of transfers of individual plots between Mohawks at Kahnawake in notarial registers means that they were treated in all respects as private property by the parties. Thomas Peace, 'Two Conquests: Aboriginal Experiences of the Fall of New France and Acadia' (PhD diss., York University, 2011), 268–76, notes that settler legal forms can disguise Indigenous patterns of land use.
51 Rueck, 'Enclosing the Mohawk Commons,' 159.
52 Hill, *Clay We Are Made Of*, 208.
53 Bouchard, 'Systèmes politiques,' 353–4.
54 Sossoyan, 'Kahnawake Iroquois,' 92–5 and 23.
55 Rueck, 'Enclosing the Mohawk Commons,' 132.
56 John Masiewicz, *Gervase Macomber and His 26 Children in Kahnawake (Caughnawaga)* (self-pub., 2016).
57 SPC 1850, c 42, s 5.
58 Reproduced in Rueck, 'Enclosing the Mohawk Commons,' 156.
59 Audra Simpson, 'To the Reserve and Back Again: Kahnawake Mohawk Narratives of Self, Home and Nation' (PhD diss., McGill University, 2003), 92–3; and Simpson, *Mohawk Interruptus: Political Life across the Borders of Settler States* (Durham, NC: Duke University Press, 2014). Doxtator, 'What Happened to the Iroquois Clans?' makes a similar argument regarding the emergence of patrilineality at Grand River at this time at 217–18.
60 What follows relies on Hill, 'Grand River Navigation.' On the earlier practice, see Walters, 'Continuity of Aboriginal Customs,' 241–2.
61 SUC 1832, c 13.
62 Gerald R. Alfred, *Heeding the Voices of Our Ancestors: Kahnawake Mohawk Politics and the Rise of Native Nationalism* (New York: Oxford University Press, 1995), 52.
63 SPC 1847, c 120; SPC 1850, c 112; SPC 1852, c 46. The merged railway was renamed the Montreal and New York Rail-road in the 1850 statute.
64 Arnaud Decroix, 'Le conflit juridique entre les Jésuites et les Iroquois au sujet de la seigneurie du Sault Saint-Louis: analyse de la décision de Thomas Gage (1762),' *Revue juridique Thémis* 41 (2007): 279 at 294, notes that a cadastral survey of 1860 showed the Mohawk as having 'full and entire ownership of these lands,' but that only seven years later, the lands

were recorded as owned by the Queen, with the Mohawks having only a right of use until the last of them died.

65 Devine, *Historic Cauhnawaga*, 392, refers to a negotiated settlement with the chiefs, but only in passing. Hill, 'Grand River Navigation,' refers to several arbitration awards respecting the Grand River lands. While the Acts in both Canadas stated that the proceeds of arbitration awards should be held by the Indian Department on trust, they were silent on who was to conduct negotiations prior to any arbitration (departmental officials? chiefs?) and what should happen to the proceeds of a negotiated settlement.

66 Sawaya, *Fédération des Sept Feux*, 13.

67 Rueck, 'Enclosing the Mohawk Commons,' 165.

68 Hill, *Clay We Are Made Of*, 189.

25. The Legal Professions

1 In Nova Scotia, the first to provide a listing of lawyers was *Ward's Almanack [for] Nova Scotia … for the Year 1820* (Halifax, 1819).

2 Michael Burrage, *Revolution and the Making of the Contemporary Legal Profession: England, France, and the United States* (New York: Oxford University Press, 2006), 22–3.

3 *Colonial Advocate*, 29 July 1830, cited in R.D. Gidney and W.P.J. Millar, *Professional Gentlemen: The Professions in Nineteenth-Century Ontario* (Toronto: University of Toronto Press, 1994), 32. See generally on these trends Philip Girard, *Lawyers and Legal Culture in British North America: Beamish Murdoch of Halifax* (Toronto: Osgoode Society for Canadian Legal History and University of Toronto Press, 2011), chap. 4, esp. 71–4.

4 SPC 1857, c 63, obliged all clerks apprenticed to attorneys to pass a Law Society exam before they could apply to a judge for permission to practise.

5 David G. Bell, *Legal Education in New Brunswick: A History* (Fredericton: University of New Brunswick 1992), 21–2.

6 Burrage, *Revolution*, 257–61.

7 W. Wesley Pue, 'Guild Training vs Professional Education: The Committee on Legal Education and the Law Department of Queen's College, Birmingham, in the 1850s,' *American Journal of Legal History* 33 (1989): 241.

8 André Vachon, *Histoire du notariat canadien 1621–1960* (Quebec: Presses de l'Université Laval, 1962), 83; Bell, *Legal Education in New Brunswick*, 34;

G. Blaine Baker, 'Legal Education in Upper Canada 1785–1889: The Law Society as Educator,' in *EHCL*, 2:57.

9 Gidney and Millar, *Professional Gentlemen*, chap. 4; see also, Baker, 'Legal Education,' 52: legal education demonstrating a 'striking continuity of goals, forms and personalities.'

10 Vachon, *Histoire du notariat*, 82–95.

11 Christine Veilleux, *Aux origines du barreau québécois 1779–1849* (Sillery, QC: Septentrion, 1997), 45–9; Evelyn Kolish, 'Sir James Stuart,' *DCB*.

12 Julien S. Mackay, *Notaires et Patriotes 1837–1838* (Sillery, QC: Septentrion, 2006).

13 SPC 1847, c 21; SPC 1849, c 46.

14 Bell, *Legal Education*, 41–2; Girard, *Lawyers and Legal Culture*, 58–62.

15 Alfred Watts, *History of the Law Society of British Columbia, 1869–1973* (n.p., n.d.), 4–5, 28.

16 Dale Gibson, *Law, Life, and Government at Red River*, vol. 1, *Settlement and Governance, 1812–1872* (Montreal and Kingston: Osgoode Society for Canadian Legal History and McGill-Queen's University Press, 2015), 346.

17 Cited in Rupert Bartlett, 'The Legal Profession in Newfoundland,' in Joseph Smallwood, ed., *The Book of Newfoundland*, 6 vols (St John's: Newfoundland Book Publishers 1967), 3:522.

18 The text of the Charter may be found in Newfoundland Law Reform Commission, *Legislative History of the Judicature Act 1791–1988* (St John's: Commission, 1989), 39–46.

19 Bartlett, 'Legal Profession,' 524; John McLaren, *Dewigged, Bothered and Bewildered: British Colonial Judges on Trial, 1800–1900* (Toronto: Osgoode Society for Canadian Legal History and University of Toronto Press, 2011), 109; SN 1834, 1st Sess, c 6.

20 Denis Vaugeois, 'Aaron Ezekiel Hart,' and Peter E. Paul Dembski, 'Solomon White,' both in *DCB*; Deidre Rowe Brown, 'Robert Sutherland: Celebrating the Legacy,' *Queen's Law Journal* 35 (2010): 401. John Connolly, son of HBC trader William Connolly and his Cree wife Suzanne Pas-de-Nom, also became a lawyer in mid-century Montreal, but it is not clear that he identified as Métis or Indigenous.

21 Philip Girard, 'The Making of the Canadian Legal Profession: A Hybrid Heritage,' *International Journal of the Legal Profession* 21 (2014): 145.

22 See the essays in *EHCL*, vol. 7.

23 Alice Terry Marion, 'Harry King's Courtship Letters, 1829–1831' (MA thesis, Acadia University, 1986), 283, cited in Girard, *Lawyers and Legal Culture*, 68.

24 The phrase *law offices* is used here in preference to *law firms* to indicate the loose form of organization that prevailed during these years. This paragraph and the next rely on G. Blaine Baker, who considers mainly anglophone law offices in 'Ordering the Urban Canadian Law Office and Its Entrepreneurial Hinterland, 1825–1875,' *University of Toronto Law Journal* 48 (1998): 175. For francophone lawyers with similar career paths, see Brian Young, *George-Étienne Cartier, Montreal Bourgeois* (Montreal and Kingston: McGill-Queen's University Press, 1981), 12–20; and Young, 'Dimensions of a Law Practice: Brokerage and Ideology in the Career of George-Etienne Cartier,' in *EHCL*, vol. 7.

25 Rande Kostal, *Law and English Railway Capitalism 1825–1875* (Oxford: Clarendon, 1994), 335–40.

26 On what follows, see Sylvio Normand, 'La transformation de la profession d'avocat au Québec, 1840–1900,' in Claire Dolan, ed., *Entre justice et justiciables: les auxiliaires de la justice du Moyen Âge au XXe siècle* (Laval, QC: Presses de l'Université Laval, 2005). See also Jean-Roch Rioux, 'Gonzalve Doutre,' *DCB*.

27 M. Mollot, *Règles de la profession d'avocat*, 2nd ed. (Paris: Durand, 1866).

28 Burrage, *Revolution*, 165.

29 'The Great Western Railway Company,' *Upper Canada Law Journal* 4 (1859): 223; Jamie Benidickson, 'Aemilius Irving: Solicitor to the Great Western Railway, 1855–1872,' in *EHCL*, vol. 7.

30 Baker, 'Urban Canadian Law Office,' 209.

31 Hugh C. Macgill and R. Kent Newmyer, 'Legal Education and Legal Thought, 1790–1920,' in Michael Grossberg and Christopher Tomlins, eds, *The Cambridge History of Law in America*, vol. 2, *The Long Nineteenth Century 1789–1920* (New York: Cambridge University Press, 2008). An early form of collective legal education in the United States, the proprietary law school that grew out of a lawyer's taking on numerous apprentices was not possible in British North America because there were restrictions in every colony on taking more than two or three apprentices at a time: Baker, 'Legal Education,' 80–1.

32 Daniel R. Coquillette and Bruce A. Kimball, *On the Battlefield of Merit: Harvard Law School, the First Century* (Cambridge, MA: Harvard University Press, 2015), 191–5, 211–23.

33 Bell, *Legal Education*, 44.

34 Baker, 'Legal Education.'

35 SPC 1849, c 46, s 27; SPC 1847, c 21, s 17; Sylvio Normand, *Le droit comme discipline universitaire: Une histoire de la faculté de droit de l'Université Laval* (Ste-Foy, QC: Presses de l'Université Laval, 2005), 57.

36 Stanley Frost, *McGill University, for the Advancement of Learning, 1801–1895* (Montreal and Kingston: McGill-Queen's University Press, 1980), 105; Ian Pilarczyk, *A Noble Roster: One Hundred and Fifty Years of Law at McGill* (Montreal: McGill Faculty of Law, 1999), 5. What follows on McGill's law school is from this latter source.
37 Carman Miller, 'John Joseph Caldwell Abbott,' *DCB*.
38 Normand, *Le droit comme discipline*, 20. 'Our judges are fine for bringing honour [to the faculty], but we will need others to do the work.'
39 SPC 1853, c 130; the same Act also created a fourth section to the Barreau, separating St-François-Sherbrooke from Trois-Rivières.
40 Normand, *Le droit comme discipline*, 24–31 and 39. At Laval, a larger number of students were allowed to attend on a non-degree basis, as were local practitioners and judges.
41 André Morel and Yvan Lamonde, 'François-Maximilien Bibaud,' *DCB*.
42 Philip Girard, 'The Roots of a Professional Renaissance: Lawyers in Nova Scotia 1850–1910,' *Manitoba Law Journal* 20 (1991): 148.
43 *EHCL*, vol. 4.
44 Jim Phillips, 'A Low Law Counter Treatise? "Absentees" to "Wreck" in British North America's First Justice of the Peace Manual,' in Angela Fernandez and Markus D. Dubber, eds, *Law Books in Action: Essays on the Anglo-American Legal Treatise* (Oxford: Hart, 2012), 210.
45 Philip Girard, 'Themes and Variations in Early Canadian Legal Culture: Beamish Murdoch and his Epitome of the Laws of Nova Scotia,' *Law and History Review* 11 (1993): 101 at 131.
46 *Epitome*, vol. 1, preface; quotation below at 23.
47 See especially various works by William Conway Keele for Upper Canada, principally *The Provincial justice, or, Magistrate's Manual ...* (Toronto: Gazette, 1845). See also by the same author *A Brief View of the Laws of Upper Canada up to the Present Time: Including a Treatise on the Law of Executors and Wills, and the Law Relative to Landlord and Tenant, Distress for Rent, Constables, Assessors, Collectors, and Township Meetings, Innkeepers, Surveyors, [etc.] with Some Useful and Approved Conveyancing Forms* (Toronto, 1838) and *Brief View of the Township Laws up to the Present Time; with a Treatise on the Law and Office of Constable, the Law Relative to Landlord and Tenant, Distress for Rent, Innkeepers* (Toronto, 1835). The first local JP manual for Quebec was H. Taylor, *Manual of the Office, Duties and Liabilities of a Justice of the Peace* (Montreal: Armour, 1843). A more modest book was P. Stubs, *The New Brunswick Manual* (1841).
48 André Morel and Yvan Lamonde, 'François-Maximilien Bibaud,' *DCB*.

49 *Le juge à paix et officier de paroisse, pour la province de Québec* (Montreal: Fleury Mesplet. 1789).

50 *Les premiers rudimens de la constitution britannique: traduits de l'anglais de M. Brooke: précédés d'un précis historique, et suivis d'observations sur la constitution du Bas-Canada ... principalement destiné à l'instruction politique de la jeunesse canadienne* (Montreal: James Lane, 1827); *Les lois criminelles anglaises, traduites et compilées de Blackstone, Chitty, Russell et autres criminalistes anglais, et telles que suivies en Canada, arrangées selon les dispositions introduites dans le Code criminel de cette province par les statuts provinciaux 4 & 5 Victoria* (Quebec: Fréchette & Cie, 1842); quotations below at 75–8 and v–vi.

51 Doucet, *Fundamental Principles,* frontispiece. For Doucet, see Jacques Boucher, 'Nicolas-Benjamin Doucet,' *DCB*. See also François-Maximilien Bibaud, *Biographie des sagamos illustres de l'Amérique Septentrionale* (Montreal: Lovell et Gibson, 1848), but it too was an account of the history of the native peoples of North America, rather than a study of their laws.

52 *Digest of the Laws of Newfoundland: Comprehending the Judicature Act and Royal Charter, and Various Acts of the Local Legislature in Amendment of the Same* (St John's: H. Winton, 1847).

53 For example, T.W. Taylor, *Orders of the Court of Chancery for Upper Canada, with Notes* (Toronto: H. Rowsell, 1860); Richard Snelling and Frederick T. Jones, *The General Orders, and Statutes, relating to the Practice, Pleading, and Jurisdiction of the Court of Chancery for Upper Canada* (Toronto: H. Rowsell, 1863).

54 The history of law journals in Quebec, along with law reporting, is dealt with by Raymonde Crête, Sylvio Normand, and Thomas Copeland, 'Law Reporting in Nineteenth-Century Quebec,' *Journal of Legal History* 16 (1995): 147.

55 *NS Journals*, 18 Mar. 1843, and appendix 85.

56 This section is based, in addition to the sources cited below, on the limited literature on law reporting in British North America. See Jennifer Nedelsky and Dorothy Long, *Law Reporting in the Maritime Provinces: History and Development* (Ottawa: Canadian Law Information Council 1981); G. Howell, *A Slice of Canadian Legal History: 156 Years of Law Reporting in Ontario* (Ottawa: Canadian Law Information Council, 1979); Anne Matthewman, 'Volumes of History: The Legal Profession and the Development of Law Reporting in Ontario,' *Canadian Law Libraries* 21 (1996): 7; William Renwick Riddell, *The Legal Profession in Upper Canada in Its Early Periods* (Toronto: Law Society of Upper Canada, 1916), chaps

19–22; Eric Whan, Tamara Myers, and Peter Gossage, 'Stating the Case: Law Reporting in Nineteenth-Century Quebec,' in Donald Fyson, Colin M. Coates, and Kathryn Harvey, eds, *Class, Gender and the Law in Eighteenth- and Nineteenth-Century Quebec: Sources and Perspectives* (Montreal: Montreal History Group, 1993); Crête et al., 'Law Reporting.'

57 This survey does not include Prince Edward Island, which did not begin reporting until 1872.

58 Publications of this sort included a pamphlet on the 1819 murder trial of Richard Uniacke, son of the attorney general of the same name: see *Acadian Recorder*, 7 Aug. 1819. Other examples are given in the notes to chapter 29 below, on the criminal trial.

59 See *Reports of Cases Decided in the Court of King's Bench, of Upper Canada; … 1823–1827* (Toronto, ca 1827). For the statute, see SUC 1823, c 3.

60 A much more specialized series, *Patrick's Contested Elections*, started publishing in 1824: see A. Patrick, *Digest of Precedents or Decisions by Select Committees to Try the Merits of Upper Canada Contested Elections, 1824–49* (1851).

61 See SUC 1840, c 2.

62 Matthewman, 'Volumes of History,' 8. An example of the rules is an 1849 rule passed by the Law Society, *A Rule for the Better Regulation of the Duties of the Office of Reporter to the Court of Chancery*. These were given force by SPC 1850, c 51.

63 Also begun in the 1840s were *Harrison and Hodgins' Municipal Reports*, from 1845; the *Upper Canada Chambers Reports*, from 1846; the *Upper Canada Jurist*, begun in 1846, although it reported its earliest case from 1830; the *Practice Reports*, from 1848; and the *Upper Canada Common Pleas Reports*, from 1850, the year after the establishment of the Court of Common Pleas.

64 *Select Cases from the Records of the Supreme Court of Newfoundland* (St John's, 1829); *Decisions of the Supreme Court of Newfoundland*, E.P. Morris, ed (St John's, 1828).

65 *Pyke's Reports of Cases Argued and Determined in the Court of King's Bench for the District of Quebec* (Montreal: s.n., 1811); *Reports of Cases Argued and Determined in the Courts of King's Bench and in the Provincial Court of Appeals of Lower Canada: With a Few of the More Important Cases in the Court of Vice Admiralty and on Appeals from Lower Canada before the Lords of the Privy Council* (Quebec: Neilson & Cowan, 1834).

66 David Bell, 'George Frederick Street Berton,' *DCB*. See also SNB 1836, c 14. Berton's collected pamphlets were published as *Reports of*

Cases Adjudged in the Supreme Court of the Province of New Brunswick, Commencing in Hilary Term, 1835 (Fredericton, 1839).

67 His maternal grandfather was Samuel Denny Street, one of the colony's first lawyers, and on his father's side he was related to the Ludlow family. He articled and then entered practice with his uncle, George Frederick Street, who later became a Supreme Court judge.

68 The quotation is from (1835–1839) 2 *NBR* v. In 1840 David Kerr, discussed immediately below, published a retrospective volume covering 1825–35, from the notes kept at the time by Chief Justice Ward Chipman. This was titled volume 1 of the *NBR*.

69 (1839–1842) 3 *NBR* vii and x.

70 See the annual *Appropriations Acts* for New Brunswick, statute volumes 1841–9.

71 SPC 1851, c 37. The statute effected a broader reform by which the various justice officers were to be put on salary and their right to keep the fees they levied for their own use abolished. They were to continue to collect the fees but they would be put in a special fund out of which their salaries would be paid and the balance kept by the government. Advocates, but not notaries, were obliged to pay the levy to support court reporting.

72 (1857) 1 LCJ vi–viii.

73 Thomas Chandler Haliburton, *A Historical and Statistical Account of Nova Scotia*, 2 vols (Halifax: Howe, 1829), 3:333–4. Haliburton noted that 'the decisions of the courts are not easily known for want of reports,' which was unfortunate because there were 'a great variety of questions constantly arising upon our provincial statutes.' Accurate reports would produce 'a uniformity of decision.'

74 See *Epitome*, 3:177 and 183, reporting decisions of the NSSC from 1832 (*Roast v Laffin*) and 1823 (*Wallace v Jenkins*). On another occasion he apologized that 'my notes of *McDonald* v. *Kidston* are too imperfect to introduce' (235).

75 For what follows, see J. Barry Cahill and Jim Phillips, 'Origins to Confederation,' in *SCNS*, the preface to 2 *NSR*, and the following correspondence: Alexander James to Lieutenant Governor Falkland, 31 Dec. 1844; Alexander James to attorney general, 30 Jan. 1852; James Thomson to provincial secretary, 27 Oct. 1852; Alexander James to Joseph Howe, 5 Apr. 1853; Alexander James to Lieutenant Governor, 27 July 1854; at NSARM, RG 1, vol. 255, no. 138; vol. 261, no. 37; vol. 262, no. 7; vol. 263, no. 33; vol. 265, no. 2. See also *NS Journals*, 18, 20, and 25 Mar.

1843; 4 Feb. 1845; 21 and 24 Jan., 14, and 19 Mar. 1850; 11 Feb. 1852; 28 Jan. and 2 Apr. 1853; 26 and 28 Mar. 1855.

76 Committee Report, 31 Mar. 1853, in *NS Journals*, 1853, appendix 64.

77 Alexander James to Joseph Howe, 8 Apr. 1856, NSARM, RG 1, vol. 266, no. 11.5.

78 *NS Journals*, 9 Apr. 1856.

79 Ibid., 5 Apr. 1856; 15 Apr. 1857; 27 Apr. 1858; 5 Apr. 1859; 29 Mar. 1860.

26. Constitutional Developments I: European-Indigenous Relations, the Old Colonial System, and the Rebellions, 1815–ca 1839

1 J.R. Miller, *Skyscrapers Hide the Heavens: A History of Indian-White Relations in Canada* (Toronto: University of Toronto Press, 1990), title of chapter 5.

2 The principal general works on which section is based are J.R. Miller, *Compact, Contract, Covenant: Aboriginal Treaty-Making in Canada* (Toronto: University of Toronto Press, 2009), chap. 4; and Miller, *Skyscrapers*, chap. 5; L.F.S. Upton, *Micmacs and Colonists: Indian-White Relations in the Maritimes, 1713–1867* (Vancouver: UBC Press, 1979); Sidney Harring, *White Man's Law: Native People in Nineteenth-Century Canadian Jurisprudence* (Toronto: Osgoode Society for Canadian Legal History and University of Toronto Press, 1998); Peter Russell, *Canada's Odyssey: A Country Based on Incomplete Conquests* (Toronto: University of Toronto Press, 2017).

3 See especially Mark Walters, 'Rights and Remedies within Common Law and Indigenous Legal Traditions: Can the Covenant Chain Be Judicially Enforced Today?' in John Borrows and Michael Coyle, eds, *The Right Relationship: Reimagining the Implementation of Historical Treaties* (Toronto: University of Toronto Press, 2017).

4 Cited in Russell, *Canada's Odyssey*, 83.

5 Paul McHugh, *Aboriginal Societies and the Common Law: A History of Sovereignty, Status and Self-Determination* (Oxford: Oxford University Press, 2004), 127.

6 Miller, *Skyscrapers*, 83.

7 Upper Canada land cessions before 1815 are discussed in the previous part. For the period after ca 1815 see, in addition to the sources already cited, Canada, *Indian Treaties and Surrenders*, 3 vols (Ottawa: Queen's Printer, 1891; Toronto: Coles, 1971); Robert J. Surtees, *Indian Land Surrenders in Ontario, 1763–1867* (Ottawa: Indian and Northern Affairs, 1984); Surtees, 'Indian Land Cessions in Upper Canada, 1815–1830,' in

I. Getty and A.S. Lussiter, eds, *As Long as the Sun Shines and the Water Flows* (Vancouver: UBC Press, 1983); and Surtees, 'Land Cessions 1763–1830,' in Edward S. Rogers and Donald B. Smith, eds, *Aboriginal Ontario: Historical Perspectives on the First Nations* (Toronto: Dundurn, 1994).

8 Dalhousie to Huskinson, 22 Nov. 1827, cited in Harring, *White Man's Law*, 3.

9 Miller, *Compact, Contract, Covenant*, 95. The total figure is approximate, because in many areas an initial surrender was followed within not many years by a further surrender of part of what had been reserved.

10 These six were: the Lake Simcoe Treaty, 1815, 250,000 acres between Lake Simcoe and Penetanguishene; the Rice Lake Treaty, 1818, 1.951 million acres in the Kawartha Lakes region; the Lake Simcoe–Nottawasaga Purchase, 1818, 1.592 million acres to the west and south of Lake Simcoe; the Ajetance Purchase, 1818, 648,000 acres south of the Lake Simcoe–Nottawasaga purchase; the Long Woods Purchase and Treaty, 1819 and 1822, involving 552,190 acres along the Thames River; and the Rideau Purchase, 1822, 2.748 million acres in eastern Upper Canada.

11 The Huron Tract Purchase, 1827, ceded 2.182 million acres, from the shoreline of Lake Huron to the American border. Two major surrenders took place in 1836. One was the Bond Head/Manitoulin Island Purchase, acreage unspecified, which ceded all the 23,000 islands that made up Manitoulin Island; the other was the Saugeen Purchase, 1.5 million acres south of the Saugeen-Bruce Peninsula.

12 Miller, *Skyscrapers*, 91.

13 For the nineteenth-century debate over the validity of Indigenous dispossession in Lower Canada, see especially Alain Beaulieu, 'An Equitable Right to Be Compensated: The Dispossession of the Aboriginal Peoples of Quebec and the Emergence of a New Legal Rationale, 1760–1860,' *Canadian Historical Review* 94 (2013): 1. See also Michel Morin, *L'Usurpation de la souveraineté autochtone* (Montreal: Boréal, 1997).

14 Alain Beaulieu, 'The Acquisition of Aboriginal Land in Canada: The Genealogy of an Ambivalent System, 1600–1867,' in Saliha Belmessous, ed., *Empire by Treaty: The History of Treaty-Making in the Appropriation of Indigenous Lands* (London: Oxford University Press, 2014), 17.

15 For the Atlantic region see, in addition to sources already cited, Robert Hamilton, 'They Promised to Leave Us Some of Our Land: Aboriginal Title in Canada's Maritime Provinces' (LLM thesis, Osgoode Hall Law

School, 2015); Richard Bartlett, *Indian Reserves in the Atlantic Provinces* (Saskatoon: Native Law Centre, 1986), esp. 3–20; and Gary P. Gould and Alan J. Semple, *Our Land the Maritimes: The Basis of the Indian Claim in the Maritime Provinces of Canada* (Fredericton: Saint Anne's Point, 1980).

16 Here we draw on Harring's typology of three 'distinct sets of inquiry' in the writing of Indigenous legal history: *White Man's Law*, 9–10. The second is 'the interaction of two legal orders, Indian and European,' which seems the most useful approach to this period.

17 For much more on this case see Mark Walters, 'The Extension of Colonial Criminal Jurisdiction over the Aboriginal Peoples of Upper Canada: Reconsidering the Shawanakiskie Case, 1822–1826,' *University of Toronto Law Journal* 46 (1996): 273. Walters also notes other cases, in note 2, 273–4, where the matter of jurisdiction was argued over in both Upper and Lower Canada.

18 For this case see Anna Jarvis, 'Colonial Criminal Justice and the Mi'kmaq: The Case of Tom Williams, Prince Edward Island, 1839,' unpublished paper, 2017.

19 Upton, *Micmacs and Colonists*, 144–5.

20 Ibid., 143. See also David G. Bell, 'Maritime Legal Institutions under the Ancien Régime, 1710–1850,' in *CLI*, noting at 103 that 'the British had no real interest in attempting to regulate the Natives' internal criminal and civil affairs,' and as a result Aboriginal peoples in the Maritimes 'continued largely outside the practicalities of the colonizing power's legal system.'

21 18 UCQB 131, cited in Walters, 'Extension,' 286.

22 This section is based principally on standard political histories of the period; quotations and specific sources on particular issues are given in the notes that follow. Most of the standard histories deal with just a colony or with regions. A few works consider the politics and constitutional developments of British North America as a whole. The best remains Phillip Buckner, *The Transition to Responsible Government: British Policy in British North America* (Westport, CT: Greenwood, 1985). Also very useful are the many *DCB* entries for leading colonial politicians.

23 This statement does not include various administrators of colonies, who held the office temporarily in the absence of a lieutenant governor. The first civilian lieutenant governor of New Brunswick was Sir Edmund Walker Head, who took office in 1848. The first in the Canadas was Lord Durham, appointed in 1838.

24 The account of the electoral franchise given here is based principally on John Garner, *The Franchise and Politics in British North America, 1775–1867* (Toronto: University of Toronto Press, 1969); and Colin Grittner, 'Privilege at the Polls: Culture, Citizenship and the Electoral Franchise in Mid-Nineteenth-Century British North America' (PhD thesis, McGill University, 2015). See also the statutory references given below. As noted in chapter 11, some Indigenous males voted in Lower Canada.
25 See generally Joan Sangster, *One Hundred Years of Struggle: The History of Women and the Vote in Canada* (Vancouver: UBC Press, 2018), chap. 1. See also Brian Cuthbertson, *Johnny Bluenose at the Polls: Epic Nova Scotian Election Battles, 1758–1848* (Halifax: Formac Publishing, 1994), 9.
26 Bettina Bradbury, *Wife to Widow: Lives, Laws and Politics in Nineteenth-Century Montreal* (Vancouver: UBC Press, 2011), 396.
27 In addition to the specific sources noted below, see generally Terrence Murphy and Gerald Stortz, eds, *Creed and Culture: The Place of English-Speaking Catholics in Canadian Society, 1750–1930* (Montreal and Kingston: McGill-Queen's University Press, 1993); see especially in that collection J.R. Miller, 'Anti-Catholicism in Canada'; Garner, *Franchise and Politics*; and the Garner, 'The Enfranchisement of Roman Catholics in the Maritimes,' *Canadian Historical Review* 30 (1953): 203.
28 The English Act is 10 Geo IV, c 7 (1829). The island's emancipation bill, and those of the other two Maritime colonies, passed the next year: SPEI 1830, c 9; SNB 1830, c 33; SNS 1830, c 1.
29 James Lambert, 'Joseph-Octave Plessis,' *DCB*.
30 *NS Journals*, 3 Apr. 1823; Robert J. Morgan, 'Lawrence Kavanagh,' *DCB*; and Morgan, *Rise Again: The Story of Cape Breton Island* (Sydney, NS: Breton Books 2008), 96.
31 See the examples given from Antigonish and Cape Breton Island in Thomas Skyrme, *History of Justices of the Peace* (Chichester: Barry Rose, 1994), 1098.
32 Terrence Murphy, 'The Emergence of Maritime Catholicism, 1781–1830,' *Acadiensis* 13 (1984): 29.
33 SPC 1851, c 175.
34 SLC 1831, c 57 (see also 1846, c 96); Denis Vaugeois, 'Aaron Ezekiel Hart,' *DCB*.
35 SUC 1833, c 13; quotation from s. 4.
36 Those permitted to affirm were 'Quakers, Menonists, Tunkers and Moravians': SUC 1829, c 1. Five years later the first three named groups were exempted from militia service, provided they paid a small sum:

SUC 1834, c 13. Tunkers were a Baptist sect that practised baptism by immersion.

37 SUC 1835, c 44; SUC 1836, c 36; SUC 1839, c 20.

38 Philip Girard, '"I will not pin my faith to his sleeve": Beamish Murdoch, Joseph Howe, and Responsible Government Revisited,' *Journal of the Royal Nova Scotia Historical Society* 4 (2001): 47 at 51

39 Buckner, *Transition*, 65–6.

40 For an excellent discussion of this point, see Jeffrey McNairn, *The Capacity to Judge: Public Opinion and Deliberative Democracy in Upper Canada, 1791–1854* (Toronto: University of Toronto Press, 2000), introduction.

41 *LC Journals*, 1834, appendix.

42 Speech in the Assembly, 5 Dec. 1836, in Joseph Chisholm, ed., *The Speeches and Public Letters of Joseph Howe*, 2 vols (Halifax: Chronicle Publishing, 1909), 1:104. The quotation below from Howe is from the same source.

43 *Durham Report*, 73.

44 *Canada Committee Report*, Minutes of Evidence, Denis-Benjamin Viger, 7 June 1828, 134.

45 *UC Journals*, 14 Mar. 1829.

46 This section on colonial government financing is drawn from Peter Burroughs, *The Canadian Crisis and British Colonial Policy, 1828–1841* (London: Edward Arnold, 1972), and Burroughs, 'The Search for Economy: Imperial Administration of Nova Scotia in the 1830s,' *Canadian Historical Review* 49 (1968): 24. See also Helen T. Manning, 'The Civil List of Lower Canada,' *Canadian Historical Review* 24 (1943): 24; Donald Creighton, 'The Struggle for Financial Control in Lower Canada,' *Canadian Historical Review* 12 (1931): 120; D.C. Harvey, 'The Civil List and Responsible Government in Nova Scotia,' *Canadian Historical Review* 28 (1947): 365.

47 For this paragraph, see SUC 1831, c 6; SNB 1837, c 1. See William G. Ormsby, 'The Civil List Question in the Province of Canada,' *Canadian Historical Review* 35 (1954): 93; SNS 1849, c 1; Jim Phillips and Bradley Miller, 'Too Many Courts and Too Much Law: The Politics of Judicial Reform in Nova Scotia, 1830–1841,' *Law and History Review* 30 (2012): 89 at 105–14; Jim Phillips, 'Judges and Coal Miners: Colonial Fiscal Policy, the Fees Crisis, and the Unpaid Judges of the Nova Scotia Supreme Court,' unpublished paper, 2011. For Prince Edward Island civil list legislation, see SPEI 1850, c 2.

48 Paul Romney, 'From the Types Riot to the Rebellion: Elite Ideology, Anti-Legal Sentiment, Political Violence, and the Rule of Law in Upper Canada,' *Ontario History* 79 (1987): 113.

49 There is a large literature on the rebellions, the best of which includes Allan Greer, *The Patriots and the People: The Rebellion of 1837 in Rural Lower Canada* (Toronto: University of Toronto Press, 1993); and Greer, '1837–1838: Rebellion Reconsidered,' *Canadian Historical Review* 76 (1995): 1; Colin Read and Ronald Stagg, *The Rebellion of 1837 in Upper Canada* (Ottawa: Carleton University Press, 1985); Colin Read, *The Rising in Western Upper Canada, 1837–8: The Duncombe Revolt and After* (Toronto: University of Toronto Press, 1982); Matthieu Sossoyan, 'The Kahnawake Iroquois and the Lower-Canadian Rebellions, 1837–38' (MA thesis, McGill University, 1999).

50 This account of legal strategies and proceedings following the rebellions is very largely drawn from the excellent and comprehensive accounts in *CST*, vol. 2. Other sources and specific chapters in that volume are separately referenced when needed.

51 SUC 1838, c 1, 2, and 3.

52 'Robinson's Remarks upon Certain Acts Passed,' cited in Rainer Baehre, 'Trying the Rebels: Emergency Legislation and the Colonial Executive's Overall Legal Strategy in the Upper Canadian Rebellion,' in *CST*, 2:45.

53 SUC 1838, c 9, 10, and 11. The other two statutes indemnified people who had opposed the rebellion and provided for compensation for loyal citizens who had lost property as a result of it: see SUC 1838, c 12 and 13.

54 Discussed in Baehre, 'Trying the Rebels,' 49ff.

55 For the Toronto trials, see Paul Romney and Barry Wright, 'The Toronto Treason Trials, March–May 1838,' in *CST*, vol. 2; quotation below at 88.

56 For these proceedings, see Colin Read, 'The Treason Trials of 1838 in Western Upper Canada'; Barry Wright, 'The Kingston and London Courts Martial'; and Murray Greenwood, 'The Prince Affair: "Gallant Colonel" or "The Windsor Butcher,"' all in *CST*, vol. 2.

57 See Sherwood's correspondence, in Wright, 'Kingston and London Courts-Martial,' 148.

58 For a detailed discussion, see Greenwood, 'Prince Affair.'

59 OSC 1838, 1st Session, c 15. The other four ordinances are listed in appendix D, Supporting Documents, of *CST*, 2:477–8.

60 See Murray Greenwood, 'The Chartrand Murder Trial: Rebellion and Repression in Lower Canada, 1837–1839,' *Criminal Justice History* 5 (1984): 129.

61 For the tangled history of transportation from the British North American colonies in the 1820s and 1830s see chapter 28 below. For the Bermuda

Ordinance and the resulting legal imbroglio, see Jarrett Henderson, 'Banishment to Bermuda: Gender, Race, Empire, Independence and the Struggle to Abolish Irresponsible Government in Lower Canada,' *Histoire sociale/Social History* 46 (2013): 321; and Thomas Gunn, 'Convicts to Bermuda: A Reassessment of Earl Durham's 1838 Bermudan Ordinance,' *Australasian Canadian Studies* 25 (2007): 7.

62 OSC 1838, 2nd Sess, c 1.

63 Jean-Marie Fecteau, 'This Ultimate Resource: Martial Law and State Repression in Lower Canada, 1837–1838,' in *CST*, 2:225.

64 For the Chartrand trial, see Greenwood, 'Chartrand Murder Trial'; and Elizabeth Nish, 'Charles-Elzéar Mondelet,' *DCB*.

65 See Murray Greenwood and Barry Wright, 'Introduction,' 29; and Greenwood, 'The General Court Martial at Montreal, 1838–9: Operation and the Irish Comparison,' both in *CST*, vol. 2, quotations at 29 and 279. For the General Court Martial, see also Greenwood: 'The Montreal Court-Martial 1838–9: Legal and Constitutional Reflections,' in *CST*, vol. 2.

66 For this discussion of martial law, see especially Fecteau, 'This Ultimate Resource'; quotation below at 212.

67 The Martial Law Ordinance is at OSC 1838, 3rd Sess., c 3. The other ten ordinances are listed in appendix D, Supporting Documents, of *CST*, 2:477–8. Colborne was in command because Durham left Lower Canada on 1 Dec. 1838, two days before the second rebellion began.

68 Greenwood, 'General Court-Martial,' 282; quotation below at 312.

27. Constitutional Developments II: The Act of Union, Responsible Government, and the Origins of Acculturation Policy, ca 1840–1866

1 *Durham Report*, 296.

2 Although always known by this title, its proper title is the *British North America Act, 1840*, 3 & 4 Vict, c 35 (1840).

3 *Durham Report*, 77. Quotations from the *Durham Report* in this and the next two paragraphs are at 79 and 277–8.

4 SPC 1841, c 11; W.P.M. Kennedy, *The Constitution of Canada: An Introduction to Its Development and Law* (New York: Oxford University Press, 1922), 198.

5 SPC 1849, c 27. See, generally, Jacques Monet, *The Last Cannon Shot: A Study of French Canadian Nationalism, 1837–1850* (Toronto: University of Toronto Press, 1969).

6 For these measures and for the remainder of this paragraph and the next paragraph see Colin Grittner, 'Privilege at the Polls: Culture, Citizenship and the Electoral Franchise in Mid-Nineteenth-Century British North America' (PhD thesis, McGill University, 2015); and John Garner, *The Franchise and Politics in British North America, 1755–1867* (Toronto: University of Toronto Press, 1969), 79–93.

7 See Jeffrey McNairn, *The Capacity to Judge: Public Opinion and Deliberative Democracy in Upper Canada, 1791–1854* (Toronto: University of Toronto Press, 2000), 289 and 306.

8 This section is, like the discussion of the old colonial system in the previous chapter, based principally on the standard political histories of the period. Particularly useful is the region-wide account in Phillip Buckner, *The Transition to Responsible Government: British Policy in British North America* (Westport, CT: Greenwood, 1985), esp. chaps 7 and 8. See also the *DCB* entries for leading political figures of the Union period; and Peter Russell, *Canada's Odyssey: A Country Based on Incomplete Conquests* (Toronto: University of Toronto Press, 2017), 113ff.

9 For both these documents, see Buckner, *Transition*, 261–2.

10 Quotations from Phillip Buckner, 'Charles Edward Poulett Thomson,' *DCB*. For Sydenham and the establishment of party government in the Canadas see also Ian Radforth, 'Sydenham and Utilitarian Reform,' in Allan Greer and Ian Radforth, eds, *Colonial Leviathan: State Formation in Mid-Nineteenth-Century Canada* (Toronto: University of Toronto Press, 1992).

11 New Brunswick politics in the 1840s was the least ideological among the British North American colonies. Assemblymen still fundamentally saw themselves as ensuring that their districts received their fair share of money voted by the assembly. See W. Stewart MacNutt, *New Brunswick: A History 1784–1837* (Toronto: Macmillan, 1984). For Prince Edward Island, see below, this chapter.

12 Grey to Harvey, 17 Dec. 1846, cited in Buckner, *Transition*, 298.

13 See generally Buckner, *Transition*, 306–9; and Greg Marquis, 'Contesting Prohibition and the Constitution in 1850s New Brunswick,' in Hamar Foster, Benjamin Berger, and A.R. Buck, eds, *The Grand Experiment: Law and Legal Culture in British Settler Societies* (Vancouver: Osgoode Society for Canadian Legal History and UBC Press, 2008).

14 SPC 1849, c 58. For the rebellion losses bill see Ged Martin, 'The Canadian Rebellions Losses Bill of 1849 in British Politics,' *Journal of Imperial and Commonwealth History* 6 (1977): 3.

15 Cited in Buckner, *Transition*, 315.

16 Grey to Elgin, 23 June 1849, cited in ibid., 316.
17 Grey to Bannerman, 30 Dec. 1850, cited in ibid., 320. For Prince Edward Island generally see W. Ross Livingston, *Responsible Government in Prince Edward Island: A Triumph of Self-Government under the Crown* (Iowa City: University of Iowa Press, 1931).
18 What follows in this paragraph is based principally on Gertrude Gunn, *The Political History of Newfoundland, 1832–1864* (Toronto: University of Toronto Press, 1966); Jerry Bannister, 'The Campaign for Responsible Government in Newfoundland,' *Journal of the Canadian Historical Association* 2 (1991): 17; Hereward Senior and Elinor Senior, 'Henry John Boulton,' *DCB*; 5 & 6 Vict, c 120 (1842).
19 Philip Girard, 'The Supreme Court of Nova Scotia: Responsible Government and the Quest for Legitimacy, 1850–1920,' *Dalhousie Law Journal* 17 (1994): 430.
20 Grittner, 'Privilege at the Polls' for much of what follows; quotations in the paragraphs that follow are at 4 and 113. Also still useful is Garner, *Franchise and Politics.*
21 Quotation from SNS 1854, c 6, s 3. For the other legislation noted here, see SNS 1851, c 2; and 1863, c 28.
22 SPEI 1853, c 9.
23 CSC 1859, c 6, s 4.
24 For women voting and the civil law, see part 3. For the nineteenth century, see Bettina Bradbury, 'Widows at the Hustings: Gender, Citizenship, and the Montreal By-elections of 1832,' in Rudolph M. Bell and Virginia Yans, eds, *Women on Their Own: Interdisciplinary Perspectives on Being Single* (New Brunswick, NJ: Rutgers University Press, 2008). For common law jurisdictions see above, chapter 26.
25 The paragraphs that follow on local government are from G.P. de T. Glazebrook, 'The Origins of Local Government'; and C.F.J. Whebell, 'Robert Baldwin and Decentralization, 1841–9,' both in F.H. Armstrong, ed., *Aspects of Nineteenth-Century Ontario* (Toronto: University of Toronto Press, 1974); J.M. Beck, *The Evolution of Municipal Government in Nova Scotia, 1749–1973* (Halifax: Government Printer, 1973); Donald Fyson, 'La paroisse et l'administration étatique sous le Régime britannique,' in Serge Courville and Normand Séguin, eds, *Atlas historique du Québec: La paroisse* (Sainte-Foy: Presses de l'Université Laval, 2001); J.H. Aitchison, 'The Municipal Corporations Act of 1849,' *Canadian Historical Review* 30 (1949): 107, and Aitchison, 'The Development of Local Government in Upper Canada, 1783–1850,'

(PhD thesis, University of Toronto, 1953); Warren Magnusson and Andrew Sancton, eds, *City Politics in Canada* (Toronto: University of Toronto Press, 1983). For municipalities in Upper Canada, see also especially Mary Stokes, 'Law, Autonomy, and Local Government: A Legal History of Municipal Corporations in Canada West/Ontario, 1850–1880,' (PhD thesis, York University, 2018).

26 For the legislation, see SNS 1855, c 49; and 1856, c 12.

27 For the origin of these elected councils, see, in addition to the sources cited above, Radforth, 'Sydenham and Utilitarian Reform,' quotation below at 83.

28 SPC 1849, c 81. For Lower Canadian legislation, see SPC 1845, c 31; and 1847, c 7.

29 The only areas excluded from the Act were those parts of the colony not included in any district in 1849. A different structure was established for these 'unorganised tracts' by SPC 1853, c 176, which, confusingly, called the regions 'districts.'

30 See, generally, for this paragraph, Sally Weaver, 'The Iroquois: The Consolidation of the Grand River Reserve in the Mid-Nineteenth Century, 1847–1875,' in Edward S. Rogers and Donald B. Smith, eds, *Aboriginal Ontario: Historical Perspectives on the First Nations* (Toronto: Dundurn, 1994).

31 17 & 18 Vict, c 118 (1854 U.K.); SPC 1856, c 140. For what follows, see Grittner, 'Privilege at the Polls,' chap. 5, which also summarizes the historiography; quotation below at 325.

32 *Parliamentary Debates on the Subject of the Confederation of the British North American Provinces, 3rd Session, 8th Provincial Parliament of Canada* (Quebec: Hunter, Rose, 1865), 89–90.

33 SPEI 1863, c 18.

34 Robert J. Surtees, *Indian Land Surrenders in Ontario, 1763–1867* (Ottawa: Indian and Northern Affairs, 1984); and Surtees, *The Robinson Treaties* (Ottawa: Indian and Northern Affairs, 1986).

35 Quotation from J.R. Miller, *Compact, Contract, Covenant: Aboriginal Treaty-Making in Canada* (Toronto: University of Toronto Press, 2009), 115. See, generally, Janet Chute, *The Legacy of Shingwaukonse: A Century of Native Leadership* (Toronto: University of Toronto Press, 1998); and Janet Chute and Alan Knight, 'In the Shadow of the Thumping Drum: The Sault Metis – The People in Between,' in Karl Hele, ed., *Lines Drawn upon the Water: First Nations and the Great Lakes Borders and Borderlands* (Waterloo, ON: Wilfrid Laurier University Press, 2008).

36 J.R. Miller, *Skyscrapers Hide the Heavens: A History of Indian-White Relations in Canada* (Toronto: University of Toronto Press, 1989), 96. For accounts of the origins of 'civilization,' see Judith Fingard, 'English Humanitarianism and the Colonial Mind: Walter Bromley in Nova Scotia, 1813–1825,' *Canadian Historical Review* 54 (1973): 123; and D.B. Smith, *Sacred Feathers: The Reverend Peter Jones and the Mississauga Indians* (Toronto: University of Toronto Press, 1987). What follows is based largely on John L. Tobias, 'Protection, Civilization, Assimilation: An Outline History of Canada's Indian Policy,' in J.R. Miller, ed., *Sweet Promises: A Reader on Indian-White Relations in Canada* (Toronto: University of Toronto Press, 1991); and L.F.S. Upton, 'The Origins of Canadian Indian Policy,' *Journal of Canadian Studies* 34 (1973): 51.

37 Sir George Murray to Sir James Kempt, 25 Jan. 1830, cited in Miller, ed., *Skyscrapers*, 95.

38 Bond Head-Manitoulin Island Purchase, no. 45, in Canada, *Indian Treaties and Surrenders*, 3 vols (Ottawa: Queen's Printer, 1891; Toronto: Coles, 1971), 1:112.

39 For the Bagot Commission, see also John Leslie, 'The Bagot Commission: Developing a Corporate Memory for the Indian Department,' *Historical Papers* 17 (1983): 31. The report is *Report on the Affairs of the Indians in Canada, PC Journals*, 1844–5, appendix EEE, parts 1 and 2, and 1847, appendix T, part 3.

40 Report of the Special Commissioners Appointed ... to Investigate Indian Affairs in Canada, *PC Journals*, 1858, appendix 21.

41 SPC 1850, c 42 and 74.

42 SPC 1857, c 26.

43 *NS Journals*, 1852, appendix 32.

44 SNS 1842, c 16.

45 RSNS 1859, c 58, s 7.

46 SNB 1844, c 47.

47 *NS Journals*, 1853, appendix 30.

48 *Globe*, 16 May 1857.

49 References to many such one-off grants are scattered throughout the *Journals* of every colony and also appear in various departmental reports contained in the appendixes to those same *Journals*.

50 What follows is a necessarily greatly simplified account of the Red River settlement and the District of Assiniboia. The literature on these aspects of western Canadian history in the nineteenth century prior to Confederation is large. For Red River, see especially Jack Bumsted,

Fur Trade Wars: The Founding of Western Canada (Winnipeg: Great Plains Research Centre, 1999); and Bumsted, *Trials and Tribulations: The Red River Settlement and the Emergence of Manitoba, 1811–1870* (Winnipeg: Great Plains Research Centre, 2003); Gerald Friesen, *The Canadian Prairies: A History* (Toronto: University of Toronto Press, 1987), chaps 5 and 6; John S. Galbraith, 'Sir George Simpson,' *DCB*; and the latest detailed account, Dale Gibson, *Law, Life and Government at Red River*, vol. 1, *Settlement and Governance 1812–1872* (Montreal and Kingston: Osgoode Society for Canadian Legal History and McGill-Queen's University Press, 2015), esp. chap. 1. This chapter does not cover the court system in Red River, for which see chapter 22.

51 Sayer was convicted but recommended to mercy by the jury and claimed the verdict as a victory when the HBC authorities released him. Thereafter the HBC stopped trying to enforce its monopoly and instead competed with the Métis and other free traders. For this episode, and for Sayer, see Morton, 'Pierre-Guillame Sayer,' *DCB*.

52 Gibson, *Red River*, 20.

53 After the merger of the two companies in 1821 there were two departments of the HBC territory, northern and southern, each with its own governor. However, Sir George Simpson was effectively the governor of both from 1826, and officially so from 1839.

54 Many such regulations are reproduced in E.H. Oliver, ed., *The Canadian North-West: Its Early Development and Legislative Records*, 2 vols (Ottawa: Government Printer, 1914). They are referred to throughout Gibson, *Red River*.

55 This section on British Columbia is based primarily on Hamar Foster, 'British Columbia: Legal Institutions in the Far West, from Contact to 1871,' *CLI*; and Tina Loo, *Making Law, Order and Authority in British Columbia, 1821–1871* (Toronto: University of Toronto Press, 1994), chaps 2 and 3. For the court system in British Columbia, see chapter 22.

56 The ethnic description was widely used by Douglas's contemporaries: see William Ormsby, 'Sir James Douglas,' *DCB*; and Adele Perry, *Colonial Relations: The Douglas-Connolly Family and the Nineteenth-Century Imperial World* (Cambridge: Cambridge University Press, 2016).

57 Blanshard's commission, very similar to Douglas's, gave him and his council 'full power and authority to make and enact all such Laws and Ordinances as may from time to time be required': cited in Foster, 'British Columbia: Legal Institutions,' 316. See the same source at 296 for the quotation below.

58 Petition to Richard Blanshard, n.d., cited in Loo, *Making Law, Order and Authority*, 37.

59 Douglas to Labouchere, 7 June 1856, cited in Foster, 'British Columbia: Legal Institutions,' 317. The £300 franchise was Douglas's idea, his translation of his commission's requirement that voters hold twenty acres.

60 The Douglas 'treaties' were New Zealand land conveyances from the Indigenous Maori people to the Crown. In some early instances the documents had not arrived, so the Indigenous parties 'signed' blank pieces of paper with an X, and the terms were added later. See, in addition to the sources cited above, Hamar Foster, 'The Saanatchinen Bay Marina Case: Imperial Law, Colonial History and Competing Theories of Aboriginal Title,' *UBC Law Review* 23 (1969): 629; and Foster, 'Letting Go the Bone: The Idea of Indian Title in British Columbia, 1849–1927,' in *EHCL*, vol. 6. The fullest and most recent account is Neil Vallance, 'Sharing the Land: The Formation of the Vancouver Island (or 'Douglas') Treaties of 1850–1854 in Historical, Legal and Comparative Context' (PhD thesis, University of Victoria, 2016).

61 21 & 22 Vict, c 99 (1858).

62 See, inter alia, Tina Loo, 'The Road from Bute Inlet: Crime and Colonial Identity in British Columbia,' in *EHCL*, vol. 5.

28. Criminal Justice I: Criminal Law, Punishment, and Policing

1 New Brunswick repealed the capital punishment section of one English statute that was also the law of the colony: SNB 1816, c 5. The Lower Canadian Assembly was much more active than that of any other colony in this regard, in 1824 passing local versions of the English reform legislation of 1823: SLC 1824, c 4, 5, and 6.

2 See SNB 1829, c 21; and SNB 1831, c 14 and 15. Left as capital were eight offences: treason, murder, rape, statutory rape, buggery, robbery, burglary, procuring a miscarriage, and arson of a ship or a building. The numbers given here for capital offences in each colony are somewhat subjective and on occasion differ from those given in Desmond Brown, *The Genesis of the Canadian Criminal Code of 1892* (Toronto: Osgoode Society for Canadian Legal History and University of Toronto Press, 1989), appendix. For New Brunswick, for example, we have counted arson as one offence, despite the fact that arson was

capital if it was arson of a ship or building, and might be considered as two, as Brown does.

3 SUC 1833, c 4, left as capital the same offences as in New Brunswick, as well as rescuing a person convicted of murder and refusing to disperse after the reading of the *Riot Act*. For the Act see John Blackwell, 'Crime in the London District: 1828–1837: A Case Study of the Effect of the 1833 Reform in Upper Canadian Penal Law,' *Queen's Law Journal* 6 (1981): 528.

4 SPEI 1836, c 21 and 22. Again the list of capital offences was very similar to elsewhere but also included attempted murder, showing lights to wreck a vessel, and destroying ships. See, generally, Jim Hornby, *In the Shadow of the Gallows: Criminal Law and Capital Punishment in Prince Edward Island* (Charlottetown: Institute of Island Studies, 1998), 16.

5 SN 1837, c 4.

6 SNS 1841, c 5, 6, and 7. The eight were murder, treason, rape, statutory rape, attempted murder, robbery, burglary, and arson. Some people were executed for piracy and/or murder on the high seas following trials held in Halifax and Quebec City, but these were offences under English law and obviously did not involve events that took place in the colony. Nor were trials held before domestic courts, but in specially constituted Courts of Admiralty Sessions. Such courts are further discussed in Jim Phillips, '"Securing Obedience to Necessary Laws": The Criminal Law in Eighteenth-Century Nova Scotia,' *Nova Scotia Historical Review* 12 (1992): 87.

7 SPC 1841, c 25, 26, and 27.

8 *Novascotian*, 4 Feb. 1850.

9 SNB 1842, c 32, 34, and 35; SNB 1842, c 35; SNB 1849, c 29; RSNB 1854, c 149–51.

10 SPC 1865, 13; SPEI 1861, c 27; RSNS 1851, c 155 and 162. The law of Assiniboia was also the English law, and the only offences tried as capital were murder and rape: see Dale Gibson, *Law, Life and Government at Red River*, vol. 1, *Settlement and Governance, 1812–1872* (Montreal and Kingston: Osgoode Society for Canadian Legal History and McGill-Queen's University Press, 2015), 356.

11 For examples of clergy and the pillory, see *Acadian Recorder*, 1 June 1817 and 21 Apr. 1821; *Novascotian*, 27 July 1825 and 2 Sept. 1829 (reporting a New Brunswick case); *Philanthropist*, 14 Oct. and 11 Nov. 1824; Patrick Connor, 'The Purest of Gifts: Royal Clemency, Patronage, and the Politics

of Identity in Upper Canada, 1791–1841' (PhD diss., York University, 2012).

12 SNS 1841, c 8; SPC 1841, c 24, s 31; SNB 1842, c 31, s 7.

13 SPEI 1861, c 27, s 2. For the other Maritime colonies, see SNS 1841, c 8; SNB 1842, c 31.

14 SN 1863, c 12.

15 The figures given for the Canadas do not include executions following the rebellions. The Upper Canada figure is an estimate, because nobody has calculated the exact figure. The best source is Connor, 'Purest of Gifts,' esp. at 216, but his study goes only to 1841. The Lower Canada number is much more accurate, the product of the comprehensive research of Donald Fyson. See 'La peine capitale au Québec, 1759–1869: modèle européen ou spécificité coloniale?,' in Eric Wenzel and Eric de Mari, eds, *Adapter le droit et rendre la justice aux colonies, 16e–19e siècles* (Dijon: Éditions universitaires de Dijon, 2015); and Fyson, 'The Spectacle of State Violence: Executions in Quebec, 1759–1872,' in Elizabeth Mancke, Jerry Bannister, Denis McKim, and Scott W. See, eds, *Violence, Order, and Unrest: A History of British North America, 1749–1876* (Toronto: University of Toronto Press, forthcoming 2019); and Fyson, 'Executions in Quebec, 1841–1919' (unpublished paper, 2018). We are also grateful to Professor Fyson for sharing his research data with us. The Nova Scotia figure is drawn from the unpublished research of Jim Phillips. For Prince Edward Island, see Hornby, *Shadow of the Gallows*, 2; and for Assiniboia, Gibson, *Red River*, 356. The New Brunswick figure is courtesy of Michael Boudreau, personal communication, who is researching executions in that province. None of these figures include soldiers and sailors executed for desertion.

16 For Lee, see *Novascotian*, 15 Jan. and 5 Feb. 1834. Other exceptions include the 1828 New Brunswick case of Patrick Burgan, a servant, hanged for burglary in 1828. On the island the only two men executed in this period were James Cash, for rape, and James Christie, for burglary. In Upper Canada as late as 1837 William Brass and Patrick Fitzgerald were convicted of rape and executed. For all this see Joseph Berkovits, 'Criminal Law Reform in New Brunswick' (unpublished paper, 2000), 11; Hornby, *Shadow of the Gallows*, 51–3; William Teatero, 'William Brass,' *DCB*. For Lower Canada, see Claude Désaulniers, 'La Peine de Mort dans la législation criminelle de 1760 À 1892,' *Revue générale de droit* 8 (1977): 141, esp. at 153–7.

17 For the use of the ultimate punishment against the Indigenous population of the Pacific northwest coast, see Hamar Foster, 'The

Queen's Law Is Better Than Yours: International Homicide in Early British Columbia'; and Tina Loo, 'The Road from Bute Inlet: Crime and Colonial Identity in British Columbia,' both in *EHCL*, vol. 5; Tina Loo, 'Savage Mercy: Native Culture and the Modification of Capital Punishment in Nineteenth-Century British Columbia,' in Carolyn Strange, ed., *Qualities of Mercy: Justice, Punishment and Discretion* (Vancouver: UBC Press, 1996).

18 The evidence for relatively 'low' serious crime rates is partly statistical and partly anecdotal, and we acknowledge that whether crime rates were 'high' or 'low' is always a value judgment. The fullest study of the statistics of prosecuted crime in the high courts is Connor, 'Purest of Gifts,' chap. 1, who shows that overall Upper Canadians were not exercised about the crime rate or worried about the existence of a dangerous criminal class. The more limited statistical evidence for Nova Scotia also suggests that serious crime was not a concern. When gathering statistics as part of debates about court reform in the 1830s, an assembly committee found that only sixty criminal trials had taken place in the Supreme Court in the entire colony between 1835 and 1839: *NS Journals*, 1841, appendix 22. See also court statistics collected by Jim Phillips for 1811–28 and 1843–58 (unpublished). For anecdotal evidence see, inter alia, *Novascotian*, 11 Jan. 1826; *City Gazette* (Saint John), 24 Dec. 1828, cited in Berkovits, 'Criminal Law Reform,' 8; John M. Beattie, *Attitudes towards Crime and Punishment in Upper Canada, 1830–1850: A Documentary Study* (Toronto: Centre of Criminology, 1977); and John C. Weaver, *Crime, Constables and Courts: Order and Transgression in a Canadian City, 1816–1970* (Montreal and Kingston: McGill-Queen's University Press, 1995).

19 For Upper Canada, see Connor, 'Purest of Gifts.' The Nova Scotia figure is based on the unpublished research of Jim Phillips. Lower Canada had a similar pardon rate in this period, around 80 per cent: see Donald Fyson, 'Penal Justice and State Violence in Quebec, 1760–1960' (unpublished paper, 2014), 4.

20 In Upper Canada, for example, London's assent was required for all pardons before 1837 but was always given when the local executive recommended pardon. In 1837 Upper Canadian governors were allowed to commute any death sentence other than for murder and treason: see SUC 1837, c 6, s 3. After the Union in 1841 London was not required to be consulted in any case: Connor, 'Purest of Gifts,' 216–17.

21 Order, 7 Nov. 1821, NSARM, RG1, vol. 174, 8; *NS Council Minutes*, 20 Feb. and 27 Oct. 1826, ibid., vol. 214.5B.

22 See the case of Samuel Sherwin, who had been sentenced to a term in the Halifax penitentiary and was released early in 1866 'on condition that he leave the province and never return': pardon issued to Samuel Sherwin, Feb. 1866, NSARM, OS ser., no. 432.

23 See Reginald Good, 'Admissibility of Testimony from Non-Christian Indians in the Colonial Municipal Courts of Upper Canada/Canada West,' *Windsor Yearbook of Access to Justice* 23 (2005): 55 at 74, summarizing a wide range of sources.

24 The legal story is complicated and too detailed to recount here. It is laid out in Jim Phillips, 'Exile for Offenders: Banishment and Transportation from British North America, 1750–1850' (unpublished paper presented to a Symposium in Honour of Douglas Hay, York University, May 2016). The evidence in that paper has been augmented by information provided by Donald Fyson and Patrick Connor. For the legislation in the Canadas, see SUC, 1833, c 4, s 25; SUC 1837, c 7; and SLC 1835, c 1. An 1831 New Brunswick statute also permitted transportation of offenders convicted of a capital offence and pardoned (SNB 1831, c 14, s 31), but we have no evidence that this was ever employed. For the rebellion transportees see Beverley Boissery, *A Deep Sense of Wrong: The Treason Trials and Transportation to New South Wales of Lower Canadian Rebels after the 1838 Rebellion* (Toronto: Osgoode Society for Canadian Legal History and Dundurn, 1995). For transportation otherwise see the examples given in Donald Fyson, 'Prison Reform and Prison Society: The Quebec Gaol, 1812–1867,' in Louisa Blair, Patrick Donovan, and Donald Fyson, *From Iron Bars to Bookshelves: A History of the Morrin Centre* (Montreal: Baraka Books, 2016).

25 Jerry Bannister, *The Rule of the Admirals: Laws, Custom and Naval Government in Newfoundland, 1699–1832* (Toronto: Osgoode Society for Canadian Legal History and University of Toronto Press, 2003), esp. chap. 7. For the other evidence in this paragraph, see *Novascotian*, 14 Dec. 1825; Fyson, 'Penal Justice and State Violence,' 10; Peter Oliver, *Terror to Evil Doers: Prisons and Punishments in Nineteenth-Century Ontario* (Toronto: Osgoode Society for Canadian Legal History and University of Toronto Press, 1998), 14, 17, and 20ff.

26 For two such suggestions more than twenty years apart, see *Acadian Recorder*, 10 Oct. 1818; and *British Colonist*, 18 Oct. 1840.

27 Quotations in this paragraph from John George Marshall, *The Justice of the Peace and County and Township Officer in the Province of Nova Scotia* (Halifax: Gossip and Coade, 1837), vi–vii; Report of a Select

Committee on the Expediency of Erecting a Penitentiary, *UC Journals*, 1831, appendix, 211–12; Charge to the Home District Grand Jury, 17 Oct. 1831, cited in Donald J. McMahon, 'Law and Public Authority: Sir John Beverley Robinson and the Purposes of the Criminal Law,' *University of Toronto Faculty of Law Review* 46 (1988): 390 at 403; and *Novascotian*, 11 Feb. 1841.

28 *Novascotian*, 23 July 1835 and 4 Feb. 1850.

29 There is a large literature on English criminal law reform. See particularly K.J.M. Smith, *Lawyers, Legislators and Theorists: Developments in English Criminal Jurisprudence, 1800–1957* (London: Oxford University Press, 1998); and V.A.C. Gattrell, *The Hanging Tree: Execution and the English People, 1770–1868* (Oxford: Oxford University Press, 1994). Still useful for charting the legislative story is Leon Radzinowicz, *A History of Criminal Law and Its Administration from 1750*, vol. 1 (London: Stevens, 1948).

30 See, inter alia, Katherine Preyer, 'Crime, the Criminal Law and Reform in post-Revolutionary Virginia,' *Law and History Review* 1 (1983): 52; Stuart Banner, *The Death Penalty: An American History* (Cambridge, MA: Harvard University Press, 2002).

31 For the references in this paragraph, see Phillip Buckner, 'Ward Chipman Junior,' *DCB; Courier* (Fredericton), 19 Mar. 1831; *NB Journals*, 4 Apr. 1842.

32 Quotations in this paragraph from *Novascotian*, 5 July 1827 (emphasis added) and 6 Apr. 1837; *Report of the Committee Appointed by the Legislative Council of Nova Scotia to Reduce the Criminal Laws into a System as Near That of England as Circumstances Admit* (Halifax, 1840).

33 For the quotations in this paragraph, see *Novascotian*, 4 Sept. 1839; *Colonial Pearl*, 4 Jan. 1839; Robert Fraser, 'Jonas Jones,' *DCB*; SUC 1833, c 3, preamble; Marshall, *Justice of the Peace*, vi–vii. See generally also Blackwell, 'Crime in the London District'; Beattie, *Attitudes*; and Berkovits, 'Criminal Law Reform.'

34 See SUC 1833, c 4, s 19. The prescribed punishment was to be hanged, although not for long enough that the convict died, then to be taken down still alive and have his bowels removed and burned in front of him, and then beheaded. To our knowledge this method of execution was never used in nineteenth-century British North America.

35 Quotations in this paragraph are from Gregory T. Smith, 'Civilised People Do Not Want to See That Kind of Thing: The Decline of Physical Punishment in London, 1760–1840,' in Strange, *Qualities of Mercy; Colonial Pearl*, 11 Mar. 1839; Halifax Sheriff Sawyer to provincial secretary, 1 Feb. 1834, NSARM, RG 1, vol. 240, no. 89; *Novascotian*, 4 Feb. 1850.

36 New Brunswick provides an instructive example. The first colony to legislate reductions in capital punishment, at the same time it provided for the building of county houses of correction to which to send those sentenced to the new alternative prison terms. Yet those terms were relatively short – a maximum of two years imprisonment for all non-capital offences. A decade later, in 1842, the principal house of correction in Saint John was renamed the Provincial Penitentiary, and the prison terms legislated in 1829 and 1831 were raised to seven years, with a discretionary life sentence for non-capital robbery: SNB 1842, c 31.

37 See variously F. Murray Greenwood, 'The General Court Martial at Montreal, 1838–9: Operation and the Irish Comparison,' in *CST*, vol. 2; Ronald Stagg, 'Samuel Lount,' *DCB;* Blackwell, 'Crime in the London District,' 552; Fyson, 'Spectacle of State Violence,' 8; Robert Lanning, 'Launched into Eternity: Sympathetic Interaction as a Response to Public Executions in Canada West, 1847–1869,' *Journal of Historical Sociology* 13 (2000): 365; *Novascotian*, 3 Sept. 1840.

38 For the location of executions in Lower Canada, see Fyson, 'Spectacle of State Violence,' 14. For executions elsewhere taking place at or near the place of the crime and the trial see, inter alia, Blackwell, 'Crime in the London District,' 552–3; John Weaver, *Crimes, Constables and Courts: Order and Transgression in a Canadian City, 1816–1970* (Kingston and Montreal: McGill-Queen's University Press, 1995), 23–4; *NS Council Minutes*, 2 Oct. 1838, RG 1, vol. 214.5D; Bernadine Dodge, 'Dissonant Voices in a Victorian Court Room: The Murder Trial of Dr William King, Cobourg, 1858–1859,' *Ontario History* 95 (2003): 136 at 157.

39 Figures in this paragraph are from Oliver, *Terror to Evil Doers*, 12ff; SNS 1816, c 9; Petition of the Halifax Magistrates to the Assembly, 28 Feb. 1823, RG 1, vol. 411, no. 107; *Acadian Recorder*, 14 Feb. 1818; Halifax Grand Jury Report, 15 Dec. 1829, in NSARM, RG 34-312, vol. 13; Criminal Statistics, 1830s, in RG 1, vol. 240, no. 89; Rainer Baehre, 'From Bridewell to Federal Penitentiary: Prisons and Punishment in Nova Scotia before 1880,' in *EHCL*, vol. 3; Donald Fyson, 'Experiencing Howard from Within: Prison Reform and Everyday Life in Quebec's City's Common Gaol, 1760–1867,' in Jenneke Christiaens, ed., *Experiencing Justice: Researching Citizens' Contacts with Judicial Practices* (New York: Springer, forthcoming 2019). See also generally Connor, 'Purest of Gifts'; Fyson, 'Prison Reform and Prison Society'; and Donald Fyson, *Magistrates, Police and People: Everyday Criminal Justice in Quebec and Lower Canada, 1764–1837* (Toronto: Osgoode Society for Canadian Legal History and University of Toronto Press, 2006),

passim; Jean-Marie Fecteau, *The Pauper's Freedom: Crime and Poverty in Nineteenth-Century Quebec*, trans. Peter Feldstein (Montreal and Kingston: McGill-Queen's University Press, 2017).

40 SN 1834, 2nd Sess, c 5; and 1865, c 9; SPEI 1840, c 16, s 1.

41 These figures are from Connor, 'Purest of Gifts,' 133, table 2.5, augmented from further statistics kindly provided to us by Dr Connor. See also Weaver, *Crimes, Constables and Courts*, 61; and Report of the Select Committee on the Expediency of Erecting a Penitentiary, *UC Journals*, 1831, appendix.

42 Quotation from Fyson, 'Experiencing Howard from Within,' 9 (typescript). For local jails, see also Oliver, *Terror to Evil Doers*, chaps 1 and 2; Weaver, *Crimes, Constables and Courts*, esp. 59–60; Baehre, 'From Bridewell to Federal Penitentiary'; and Rainer Baehre, 'Prison as Factory, Convict as Worker: A Study of the Mid-Victorian Saint John Penitentiary, 1841–1880,' in *EHCL*, vol. 5; Terry Carlson, 'Dealing with Offenders: An Historical Perspective on Corrections in Newfoundland,' in Gale Burford, ed., *Ties That Bind: An Anthology of Social Work and Social Welfare in Newfoundland and Labrador* (St John's: Jesperson Publishing, 1997).

43 SPEI 1835, c 2, and 1838, c 12; SN 1834, c 5, s 4.

44 Baehre, 'From Bridewell to Federal Penitentiary.'

45 The most comprehensive account is Oliver, *Terror to Evil-Doers*, chap. 3. Other useful studies include John M. Beattie, *Attitudes towards Crime and Punishment in Upper Canada, 1830–1850: A Documentary Study* (Toronto: Centre of Criminology, 1977); and Rainer Baehre, 'Origins of the Penitentiary System in Upper Canada,' *Ontario History* 69 (1977): 185.

46 For these international developments see, inter alia, Michael Meranze, *Laboratories of Virtue: Punishment, Revolution and Authority in Philadelphia, 1760–1835* (Chapel Hill: University of North Carolina Press, 1996); Adam J. Hirsch, *The Rise of the Penitentiary: Prisons and Punishment in Early America* (New Haven, CT: Yale University Press, 1992); R.M. MacLennan, *The Crisis of Imprisonment: Protest, Politics and the Making of the American Penal State, 1776–1941* (Cambridge: Cambridge University Press, 2008); Norval Morris and David Rothman, eds, *The Oxford History of the Prison: The Practice of Punishment in Western Society* (New York: Oxford University Press, 1998); Michael Ignatieff, *A Just Measure of Pain: The Penitentiary in the Industrial Revolution, 1750–1850* (London: Penguin, 1978).

47 Report of the Penitentiary Inspectors, *UC Journals*, 1836–7, appendix; *Reports of Commissioners Appointed to Inquire into the Conduct, Discipline and Management of the Provincial Penitentiary* (Montreal, 1849).

48 See Baehre, 'Prison as Factory'; and Baehre, 'From Bridewell to Federal Penitentiary'; SNB 1842, c 25; *NS Journals*, 1838, appendix 18; SNS 1840, c 41; *Novascotian*, 11 Feb. 1841.

49 SPC 1843, c 69. See generally Fyson, 'Experiencing Howard from Within'; Fyson, 'Prison Reform and Prison Society'; Luc Noppen, 'La Prison du Pied-au-Courant à Montréal: une étape dans l'évolution de l'architecture pénitentiare au Bas-Canada et au Québec,' *Canadian Art Review* 3 (1976): 36.

50 SN 1851, c 8; Carlson, 'Dealing with Offenders.'

51 For a very useful discussion of the distinction between doing police history by form and function, see the aptly named chapter 4 of Fyson, *Magistrates, Police and People*: 'The Police before the Police.'

52 This paragraph on largely pre-1840s policing is based on a variety of sources. The best account is for Lower Canada, in Fyson, *Magistrates, Police and People*. Also very useful is the same author's 'La police au Québec, 1760–1878: des modèles impériaux dans une colonie nord-américaine,' in Vincent Denis and Catherine Denys, eds, *Polices d'empires, XVIIIe–XIXe siècles* (Rennes: Presses universitaires de Rennes, 2012). A good general survey can be found in Greg Marquis, *Policing Canada's Century: A History of the Canadian Association of Chiefs of Police* (Toronto: Osgoode Society for Canadian Legal History and University of Toronto Press, 1993), chap. 1. Other local and regional studies include Greg Marquis, 'State, Community and Petty Justice in Halifax, Nova Scotia, 1815–1867,' in Louis A. Knafla, ed., *Violent Crime in North America* (Westport, CT: Praeger, 2003); T.W. Acheson, *Saint John: The Making of a Colonial Urban Community* (Toronto: University of Toronto Press, 1985); Weaver, *Crime, Constables and Courts;* Paul Craven, 'Law and Ideology: The Toronto Police Court 1850–1880,' in *EHCL*, 2:253–4.

53 SN 1839, c 12; Gibson, *Red River*, 39–40 and 186–7.

54 From 1815 Saint John had a permanent watch paid for from public funds: see Acheson, *Saint John*, 216. Paid night watches were established in the major Lower Canadian towns in 1818: Fyson, *Magistrates, Police and People*, 137.

55 See, for example, the night watch established in Halifax in 1817 following a panic about increased crime. Volunteers came forward and prominent citizens, such as merchants Samuel Cunard and John Tremain, as well as publisher John Howe, were appointed as ward leaders. The 1829 regulations for the night watch required that members not be 'House Servants, Daily Labourers or people of Color': V. Mitchell, 'History of

the Halifax Police Force,' typescript in NSARM, MG 100, vol. 156, no. 28, 4–6 and 7. Even in Saint John, which had a permanent night watch, an emergency could bring out middle-class volunteers. After the great fire of 1839 devastated the central business district and left much merchandise open to looters and the elements, the mayor gathered 128 men from leading families and swore them in as special constables: Acheson, *Saint John*, 218.

56 See generally Marquis, *Policing Canada's Century*, chap. 1. Local studies include Nicholas Rogers, 'Serving Toronto the Good: The Development of the City Police Force, 1834–1880,' in Victor Russell, ed., *Forging a Consensus: Historical Essays on Toronto* (Toronto: University of Toronto Press, 1984); and Weaver, *Crime, Constables and Courts*.

57 SNS 1841, c 55. See s. 52 for the city marshall. For the force's strength see Mitchell, 'History.'

58 For an excellent examination of this phenomenon, see Rogers, 'Serving Toronto the Good.' See also Fecteau, *Pauper's Freedom*.

59 Cited in Acheson, *Saint John*, 219.

60 For this paragraph, see principally Helen Boritch, 'Conflict, Compromise and Administrative Convenience: The Police Organisation in Nineteenth-Century Toronto,' *Canadian Journal of Law and Society* 3 (1988): 141; quotations at 145. For the Orange Order and Toronto politics in this period, see Gregory S. Kealey, 'Orangemen and the Corporation,' in Russell, *Forging a Consensus*. For religious riots in Lower Canada and New Brunswick see Donald Fyson, 'The Trials and Tribulations of Riot Prosecutions: Collective Violence, State Authority and Criminal Justice in Quebec, 1841–1892,' in *CST*, vol. 3, and Scott W. See, *Riots in New Brunswick: Orange Nativism and Social Violence in the 1840s* (Toronto: University of Toronto Press, 1993).

61 Our knowledge of rural policing tends to be episodic and anecdotal. One of the best accounts is Susan Lewthwaite, 'Violence, Law and Community in Rural Upper Canada,' in *EHCL*, vol. 5.

62 Allan Greer, 'The Birth of the Police in Lower Canada,' in Greer and Ian Radforth, eds, *Colonial Leviathan: State Formation in Mid-Nineteenth-Century Canada* (Toronto: University of Toronto Press, 1992).

63 Colborne to Silas Jenison, 23 Mar. 1839, cited in Bradley Miller, *Borderline Crime: Fugitive Criminals and the Challenge of the Border, 1819–1914* (Toronto: Osgoode Society for Canadian Legal History and University of Toronto Press, 2016), 97. This paragraph is taken from this book, especially chapters 3 and 4.

29. Criminal Justice II: The Criminal Trial

1 Allyson May, *The Bar and the Old Bailey, 1750–1850* (Chapel Hill: University of North Carolina Press, 2003), 3. For the evolution of the trial in England, see also John M. Beattie, 'Scales of Justice: Defence Counsel and the English Criminal Trial in the Eighteenth and Nineteenth Centuries,' *Law and History Review* 9 (1991): 221.

2 For the class composition of grand and trial juries, see Patrick Connor, 'The Criminal Courts of Upper Canada, 1791–1841' (unpublished paper, 2015); R. Blake Brown, *A Trying Question: The Jury in Nineteenth-Century Canada* (Toronto: Osgoode Society for Canadian Legal History and University of Toronto Press, 2009), *passim*; Donald Fyson, 'Jurys, participation civique et représentation au Québec et au Bas-Canada: les grand jurys du district de Montréal, 1764–1832,' *Revue d'histoire de l'Amérique française* 55 (2001): 85; John Weaver, *Crimes, Constables and Courts: Order and Transgression in a Canadian City, 1816–1970* (Montreal and Kingston: McGill-Queen's University Press, 1995), 35.

3 SPC 1851, c 96.

4 For a Black foreman of a jury, see *Novascotian*, 9 June 1845.

5 SPC 1850, c 55; SNS 1854, c 11 and 22. For jury-packing, see especially Paul Romney, 'From Constitutionalism to Legalism: Trial by Jury, Responsible Government, and the Rule of Law in Canadian Political Culture,' *Law and History Review* 7 (1989): 121; and Romney, *Mr Attorney: The Attorney-General for Ontario in Court, Cabinet and Legislature, 1791–1899* (Toronto: Osgoode Society for Canadian Legal History and University of Toronto Press, 1986), 154–5; Brown, *Trying Question*, esp. chaps 4–6.

6 R. Blake Brown, 'Storms, Roads, and Harvest Time: Criticisms of Jury Service in Pre-Confederation Nova Scotia,' *Acadiensis* 36 (2006): 93.

7 For the quotations in this paragraph, see *The Queen vs George Preeper: An Indictment for Manslaughter, Tried at Halifax before Mr Justice Wilkins* (Halifax: James Bowes & Sons, 1859); *Novascotian*, 1 Dec. 1842; *Globe*, 6 Nov. 1856; William Marsden, *Report of the Trial and Acquittal of Thomas Burke, for the Manslaughter of William Lawson* (Montreal: John Lovell, 1852), 4; Weaver, *Crime, Constables and Courts*, 36. For two Lower Canadian cases in which the jury reached a decision without retiring, see *Quebec Mercury*, 23 Sept. 1841; and Marsden, *Report*. For juries in Upper Canada invariably retiring but often for a 'brief consultation' or being 'absent but a short time,' see *An Interesting Account of ... the Celebrated Horde of Robbers Known*

as the Markham Gang; with the Trials of the Most Noted of the Criminals ... (Toronto: Scobie and Balfour, 1846).

8 For the quotations in this paragraph, see Robert Fraser, 'Christopher Hagerman,' *DCB*; Trial Report, NSARM, RG 1, vol. 254, no. 82; Bernadine Dodge, 'Dissonant Voices in a Victorian Court Room: The Murder Trial of Dr William King, Cobourg, 1858–1859,' *Ontario History* 95 (2003): 136 at 152. For other evidence of intrusive judges, see Weaver, *Crimes, Constables and Courts*, 37, summarizing evidence from judges' benchbooks.

9 For the quotations in this paragraph, see *Acadian Recorder*, 31 Jan. 1818; *City Gazette*, 19 Jan. 1831; *The Queen vs Preeper*, 47–9.

10 For the examples in this paragraph, see *Novascotian*, 23 July 1829, 14 Feb. 1828, 28 Oct. 1830, and 30 Apr. 1834; Marsden, *Report*, 19.

11 *Upper Canada Herald*, 12 Aug. 1835, cited in Connor, 'Criminal Courts,' 24. Connor provides other examples, 25–6.

12 Nineteenth-century English developments in review of jury verdicts are well summarized in Benjamin Berger, 'Criminal Appeals as Jury Control: An Anglo-Canadian Historical Perspective on the Rise of Criminal Appeals,' *Canadian Criminal Law Review* 10 (2005): 1.

13 SPC 1849, c 63; 1857, c 61, s 1, and c 44, s 21; SNS 1862, c 6; SN 1852, c 15. See generally Christopher Moore, *The Court of Appeal for Ontario: Defining the Right of Appeal, 1792–2013* (Toronto: Osgoode Society for Canadian Legal History and University of Toronto Press, 2014).

14 See Constance Backhouse, 'Nineteenth-Century Canadian Rape Law, 1800–1892,' in *EHCL*, vol. 2, esp. at 214–17 and 221–3; and Backhouse, *Petticoats and Prejudice: Women and Law in Nineteenth-Century Canada* (Toronto: Osgoode Society for Canadian Legal History and Women's Press, 1991), 81–101.

15 Quotation from (1860) UCQB 196 at 197. For a comprehensive analysis, see Reginald Good, 'The Admissibility of Testimony from Non-Christian Indians in the Colonial Municipal Courts of Upper Canada/Canada West,' *Windsor Yearbook of Access to Justice* 23 (2005): 55. Trial reports generally provide little commentary on evidentiary issues, although one case from the 1840s in Upper Canada saw Archibald MacLean warn the jury about the dangers of uncorroborated accomplice evidence: see *Interesting Account*, 10.

16 Ronald D. Noble, 'The Struggle to Make the Accused Competent in England and in Canada,' *Osgoode Hall Law Journal* 8 (1970): 249.

17 *Novascotian*, 23 July 1829; *City Gazette*, 19 Jan. 1831; Thomas Handcock, *The Trial of Isaac Jones and James Jones for the Alleged Murder of Louis Marcoux, at ... Montreal* (Montreal, 1835), 7.

18 SPC 1846, c 3; and 1849, c 21. See to similar effect SPC 1849, c 20.

19 CSUC 1859, c 99.

20 Public supervision of and intervention in the prosecutorial process was not begun until 1879, and even then was limited. The director of public prosecutions created in that year was given no more than six assistants and was to intervene only in exceptional cases. See Romney, *Mr Attorney*.

21 For Upper Canada, see Romney, *Mr Attorney*; and Paul Romney, 'Upper Canada in the 1820s: Criminal Prosecution and the Case of Francis Collins,' in *CST*, vol. 1. For New Brunswick, see Phillip Buckner, 'Thomas Wetmore,' *DCB*.

22 See *CST*, vol. 2, chaps 3 and 4.

23 For both quotations, see Romney, *Mr Attorney*, 17. For Robinson largely confining himself to the Home District, see *UC Journals*, 1826–7, appendix, Public Accounts; and Romney, 'Upper Canada in the 1820s.' The presence of the attorneys general can generally be followed through the biographical portraits of Upper Canadian accuseds in the *DCB*.

24 For other instances, see *L'Ami du Peuple, de l'ordre et des lois*, 4 Sept. 1839; *Canadian Spectator*, 13 and 27 Nov. 1822; Handcock, *Trial of Isaac Jones*.

25 See PANB, RS 13, attorney general, no. 18D; PANB, RS 30B, nos. 1–3, Crown Cause Ledgers, 1802–40; Phillip Buckner, 'Thomas Wetmore' and Phillip Buckner and Burton Glendinning, 'Charles Peters,' both in *DCB*; *Mercury*, 27 May 1828; *New Brunswick Royal Gazette*, 12 May 1828; *City Gazette*, 19 Jan. 1831; *Head Quarters*, 11 Feb. and 29 Nov. 1846, and 11 Nov. 1857; solicitor general to Lieutenant Governor Colebrooke, 13 Feb. 1853, in *NB Journals*, 23 Feb. 1853.

26 C.M. Wallace, 'Charles Fisher,' *DCB*.

27 For Halifax see NSARM, RG 39, Halifax, ser. J, vol. 131; *Novascotian*, 23 Dec. 1844; *The Queen vs Preeper*. See also William Laurence, 'No Sinecure: William Young as Attorney-General of Nova Scotia, 1854–1857,' *Dalhousie Law Journal* 34 (2011): 333.

28 *Islander*, 18 Dec. 1844.

29 See Brian Cuthbertson, *The Old Attorney-General: A Biography of Richard John Uniacke* (Halifax: Nimbus, 1980), 105; and Cuthbertson, 'Richard John Uniacke,' *DCB*.

30 This summary is based on two kinds of evidence. First, public accounts always show fees paid to prosecuting lawyers: see, for example, *UC Journals*, 1826–7, appendix, Public Accounts; and 1839, appendix, 341–3, Public Accounts. Second, various *DCB* entries for lawyers and defendants indicate prosecutions conducted by lawyers other than the law officers:

see, inter alia, Robert Fraser, 'Cornelius Burley' and 'George Powlis,' and William Teatero, 'William Brass.'

31 The organization of prosecution on circuit can, as in Upper Canada, be traced through financial records and other sources. For the former, see *NS Journals*, 1845, appendix 13; 1846, appendix 13; and 1848, appendix 12. See also *NS Journals*, 8 Mar. 1824, recording a vote of thirty-five pounds to Archibald, for 'his services in prosecuting Criminal Offenders in the Supreme Court in the District of Pictou, and the County of Cumberland, during the Eastern Circuit in June last; the same being certified by the Circuit Judges.' Circuit judges were also allowed to make ad hoc appointments of prosecutors whenever one was lacking: see SNS 1828, c 13.

32 *Novascotian*, 21 Oct. 1844.

33 In 1817 Lieutenant Governor Dalhousie made William H.O. Haliburton and Samuel Archibald the first two Nova Scotian KCs. Thereafter government regularly gave the designation of King's/Queen's Counsel to other lawyers, with the understanding that it was for circuit prosecution work: King's and Queen's Counsel Appointments, 1817–1914, NSARM, MG 100, vol. 212, no. 4. For New Brunswick, see Sir John Harvey to Sir Colin Campbell, 27 Sept. 1838, New Brunswick Museum, Harvey Correspondence, A154, 65–6, noting the appointment of four QCs 'ready to act in conducting Crown Prosecutions upon occasions where it may happen to be inconvenient or impossible for the Attorney & Solicitor General to attend.' For Upper Canada, see Romney, *Mr Attorney*, 180.

34 Phillip Buckner, 'Thomas Wetmore,' *DCB*.

35 Quoted in Philip Stenning, *Appearing for the Crown: A Legal and Historical Review of Criminal Prosecutorial Authority in Canada* (Cowansville, QC: Brown Legal Publications, 1986), 64. For the developments in the Union period generally, see Romney, *Mr Attorney*, 168ff.

36 Marsden, *Report*, 15. For the role of QCs, see *Quebec Mercury*, 25 Sept. 1841; *Le Journal de Quebec*, 11 Mar. 1843;

37 *Interesting Account, passim;* Hereward and Elinor Senior, 'Henry John Boulton,' *DCB*.

38 *Globe*, 10 Mar. 1857, cited in Romney, *Mr Attorney*, 221. This account of the coming of county attorneys to Canada West is principally from ibid., 214–22. See also Marvin Bloos, 'The Public Prosecutions Model from Upper Canada,' *Criminal Law Quarterly* 32 (1989–90): 69; and Stenning, *Appearing for the Crown*, 63ff.

39 See *PC Journals*, 1850, appendix BB.

40 For Gowan, see principally Desmond Brown, 'James Robert Gowan,' *DCB*.
41 SPC 1857, c 59. Quotations in this paragraph are from this statute.
42 Dodge, 'Trial of Dr William King,' 148. The provision for central appointment was criticized by some as a patronage device, but defended by Macdonald, who argued that the attorney general needed to retain the discretion to appoint special prosecutors where circumstances warranted: see Romney, *Mr Attorney*, 221–2.
43 Brown, 'James Robert Gowan,' *DCB*.
44 For continued controversy over public prosecutions, see Romney, *Mr Attorney*, 124–41; Stenning, *Appearing for the Crown*, 121ff; and Kimberley Alexander, 'Getting It Right: Debates over the County Attorneys Act, 1857–1900' (unpublished paper, 2000).
45 *Interesting Account*, 5 and 21.
46 Quotations in this paragraph from *New Brunswick Royal Gazette*, 12 May 1828; *Novascotian*, 23 July 1829; *Islander*, 18 Dec. 1844.
47 For these examples, see *City Gazette*, 27 Feb. 1822; Robert Fraser, 'Angelique Pilotte,' *DCB*; *Canadian Spectator*, 13 Nov. 1822 and 5 Mar. 1824; *Novascotian*, 23 July 1829; *Scribbler*, 18 Mar. 1824; *L'Ami du Peuple, de l'ordre et des lois*, 4 Sept. 1839. Both Mondelet and O'Sullivan were sufficiently prominent to merit entries in the *DCB*. For other examples, see PANB, RS 30B, RS 30B, nos. 1–3, Crown Cause Ledgers, 1802–40; Weaver, *Crime, Constables and Courts*, 33; and Romney, *Mr Attorney*, 208.
48 See Connor, 'Criminal Courts,' 39.
49 Ibid., 38; and Patrick Connor, 'The Purest of Gifts: Royal Clemency, Patronage, and the Politics of Identity in Upper Canada, 1791–1841' (PhD diss., York University, 2012), 119.
50 Petition of Moise Plante to Chief Justice Bowen, 23 July 1856, in *PC Journals* 1857, appendix FFF.
51 *Acadian Recorder*, 30 Jan. 1819; RG 39, Series J, vol. 131 (1848).
52 *Novascotian*, 24 May 1837.
53 Ibid., 23 July 1829
54 *La Minerve*, 8 Sept. 1836. For Duvernay, see Jean-Marie Lebel, 'Ludger Duvernay,' *DCB*.
55 *Novascotian*, 28 Oct. 1830. For other examples of effective defence counsel, see Connor, 'Purest of Gifts,' 120; and Connor, 'Criminal Courts,' 38–9.
56 *Quebec Mercury*, 25 Sept. 1841. Aylwin later became solicitor general in the Baldwin-La Fontaine administration: see André Garon, 'Thomas Cushing Aylwin,' *DCB*. See also his leading role in the murder trial the same

year of Josephine Taché, discussed in Céline Cyr, 'Joséphine-Éléonore D'Estimauville,' *DCB*.

57 NSARM, RG 39, Series J, vol. 131 (1847 and 1848).

58 *Novascotian*, 21 July 1845.

59 For Howe's much-written-about case see, inter alia, Lyndsay Campbell, 'A Licence to Publish: Joseph Howe's Contribution to Libel Law in Nova Scotia,' *Dalhousie Law Journal* 29 (2006): 79. For Hooper see the report in *City Gazette*, 19 Jan. 1831.

60 *New Brunswick Courier*, 22 Feb. 1834, cited in Joseph Berkovits, 'The Awful Sentence of the Law' (unpublished paper, 2002), 44.

61 *Novascotian*, 3 Nov. 1830. Quotations in the next paragraph at ibid., 13 Apr. 1825 and 10 Oct. 1832.

62 The best account of the coming of the English legislation is May, *Bar and the Old Bailey*, esp. chap. 7. See also Beattie, 'Scales of Justice.'

63 SLC 1835, c 1, reserved for London's approval, which was not forthcoming until 1836; SUC 1836, c 48; SPEI 1836, c 21, s 19; SNB 1840, c 40; SNS 1840, c 9; SPC 1841, c 24, ss 9 and 11–13.

64 The failed bills can be traced through each colony's *Journals*. See also Lijliana Stanic, 'Two Penny Trespass and Half Penny Cake: The Felons Counsel Bill in Upper Canada' (unpublished paper, 2014); and Romney, *Mr Attorney*, 201–8. For an example of elite lawyers being opposed, see the fact that in 1826 the Upper Canada Assembly passed 'Bidwell's bill' 27:4, with the four dissentient voices including John Beverley Robinson and two other members who later became judges – Jonas Jones and Archibald MacLean: see *UC Journals*, 8, 12, and 15 Dec. 1826.

65 Quotations in this paragraph from *Kingston Chronicle*, 11 Feb. 1825; *Montreal Gazette*, 30 Jan. 1834; *Novascotian*, 5 July 1827.

66 Quotations in this paragraph from *Kingston Chronicle*, 29 Dec. 1826; and *LC Journals*, 3 Mar. 1835.

67 Quotations from William Hawkins, *A Treatise of the Pleas of the Crown*, 2 vols (London, 1721), 2:400, and *Novascotian*, 6 Aug. 1834.

68 Case of Thomas Burns, reported in *Novascotian*, 1 Dec. 1845.

69 *Novascotian*, 20 Apr. 1846; *Head Quarters*, 11 Feb. 1846; *Quebec Mercury*, 23 Sept. 1841.

70 *Novascotian*, 5 May 1845; *Globe*, 6 Nov. 1856.

71 For this case, see *Islander*, 6 and 18 Dec. 1844; and Jim Hornby, *In the Shadow of the Gallows: Criminal Law and Capital Punishment in Prince Edward Island* (Charlottetown: Institute of Island Studies, 1998).

72 There is not space here to consider the operations of the lower courts in any detail. The fullest accounts of JPs' work, on which this section

is based, are contained in Donald Fyson, *Magistrates, Police and People: Everyday Criminal Justice in Quebec and Lower Canada, 1764–1837* (Toronto: Osgoode Society for Canadian Legal History and University of Toronto Press, 2006); David Murray, *Colonial Justice: Justice, Morality and Crime in the Niagara District, 1791–1849* (Toronto: Osgoode Society for Canadian Legal History and University of Toronto Press, 2002); Paul Craven, *Petty Justice: Low Law and the Sessions System in Charlotte County, New Brunswick, 1784–1867* (Toronto: Osgoode Society for Canadian Legal History and University of Toronto Press, 2014); and Craven, 'Law and Ideology: The Toronto Police Court, 1850–1880,' in *EHCL*, vol. 2; Connor, 'Purest of Gifts,' chap. 2; Susan Lewthwaite, 'Law and Authority in Upper Canada: The Justices of the Peace in the Newcastle District, 1802–1840' (PhD thesis, University of Toronto, 2000).

73 Connor, 'Purest of Gifts,' esp. at 99–100.

74 Lewthwaite, 'Law and Authority,' 97; *British Colonist*, 18 Dec. 1860.

75 *Novascotian*, 9 June 1845. For another report of an assault case involving defence lawyers, see *Novascotian*, 27 Sept. 1838.

76 Craven, 'Toronto Police Court.'

30. Land Law and Policy: Titles, Tenure, Squatters, Indigenous Dispossession, and the Rights and Obligations of Ownership

1 As one historian has put it for Upper Canada, by the 1840s 'all of the issues of policy and administration for the nineteenth century had been raised, and none had been settled': R.C.B. Risk, 'The Last Golden Age: Property and the Allocation of Losses in Ontario in the Nineteenth Century,' *University of Toronto Law Journal* 27 (1977): 199 at 201

2 For the Heir and Devisee Commissions, see generally Lillian Gates, *Land Policies of Upper Canada* (Toronto: University of Toronto Press, 1968), and H.P. Gundy, 'The Family Compact at Work: The Second Heir and Devisee Commission of Upper Canada, 1805–1841,' *Ontario History* 66 (1974): 129.

3 The meaning of *Protestant* was contentious. From the beginning Governor Simcoe insisted that *Protestant* meant Church of England, but in 1823 the law officers of the Crown decided that Church of Scotland clergy were included. The classic account of the clergy reserves is Alan Wilson, *The Clergy Reserves of Upper Canada: A Canadian Mortmain* (Toronto: University of Toronto Press, 1968).

This has been supplanted by the much more nuanced account of Catharine Wilson, *Tenants in Time: Family Strategies, Land and Liberalism in Upper Canada* (Montreal and Kingston: McGill-Queen's University Press, 2009). Still useful are Curtis Fahey, *In His Name: The Anglican Experience in Upper Canada, 1791–1854* (Ottawa: Carleton University Press, 1991); and John Richards, 'Lands and Policies: Attitudes and Controls in the Alienation of Lands in Ontario during the First Century of Settlement,' *Ontario History* 50 (1958): 193 at 196. Quotations in this paragraph from Fahey, *In His Name*, 91; *Canada Committee Report*, 9; Wilson, *Tenants in Time*, 81.

4 3–4 Vic, c 78 (1841); SPC 1854, c 2.

5 What follows on the alien controversy and land is based principally on Paul Romney, *Mr Attorney: The Attorney-General for Ontario in Court, Cabinet and Legislature, 1791–1899* (Toronto: Osgoode Society for Canadian Legal History and University of Toronto Press, 1986); and Romney, 'Re-inventing Upper Canada: American Immigrants, Upper Canadian History, English Law and the Alien Question,' in Roger Hall, William Westfall, and Laurel Sefton McDowell, eds, *Patterns of the Past: Interpreting Ontario's History* (Toronto: Dundurn, 1998).

6 A 1740 British statute, 13 Geo II, c 7, allowed naturalization only of people born outside the king's allegiance.

7 SUC 1828, c 21; SPC 1849, c 197.

8 This is the conclusion reached by the leading study of the question, John E.C. Brierley, 'The Co-existence of Legal Systems in Quebec: Free and Common Socage in Canada's "pays de droit civil,"' *Les cahiers de droit* 20 (1979): 277. What follows is principally from this source.

9 6 Geo IV, c 59 (1825); SPC 1857, c 45.

10 What follows on registration and dower is drawn principally from Bettina Bradbury, *Wife to Widow: Lives, Laws and Politics in Nineteenth-Century Montreal* (Vancouver: UBC Press, 2011), 131–8. See also Bradbury, 'Debating Dower: Patriarchy, Capitalism and Widows' Rights in Lower Canada,' in Tamara Myers, Kate Boyer, Mary Anne Poutanen, and Steven Watt, eds, *Power, Place and Identity: Historical Studies of Social and Legal Regulation in Quebec* (Montreal: Montreal History Group, 1988). Also useful is Bradbury, Peter Gossage, Evelyn Kolish, and Alan Stewart, 'Property and Marriage: The Law and the Practice in Early Nineteenth-Century Montreal,' *Histoire sociale/Social History* 26 (1993): 9.

11 OSC 1841, c 30.

12 The account that follows is based principally on a small selection of sources. See Tom Johnson, 'In a Manner of Speaking: Towards a

Re-constitution of Property in Mid-Nineteenth-Century Quebec,' *McGill Law Journal* 32 (1987): 636; and Johnson, 'Perceptions of Property: The Social and Historical Imagination of Quebec's Legal Elite, 1836–1856' (PhD thesis, University of Wisconsin, 1989); Brian Young, *The Politics of Codification: The Lower Canadian Civil Code of 1866* (Toronto: Osgoode Society for Canadian Legal History and University of Toronto Press, 1994), 54–60; Benoît Grenier, *Brêve histoire du régime seigneurial* (Montreal: Boréal, 2012); and Grenier, '"Le dernier endroit dans l'univers": À propos de l'extinction des rentes seigneuriales au Québec, 1854–1974,' *Revue d'histoire de l'Amérique française* 64 (2010): 75.

13 An evocative description of life on Papineau's seigneury is contained in Cole Harris, 'Of Poverty and Helplessness in Petite-Nation,' *Canadian Historical Review* 52 (1971): 23.

14 The resolutions are numbers 56–63 in *LC Journals*, 1834, appendix. The 1836 committee and its report are discussed in Johnson, 'In a Manner of Speaking,' 638ff.

15 Johnson, 'Perceptions of Property,' 24.

16 See Young, *Politics of Codification*, 57; and Brian Young, *George-Étienne Cartier: Montreal Bourgeois* (Montreal and Kingston: McGill-Queen's University Press, 1981), 98–106.

17 Cited in Johnson, 'Perceptions of Property,' 1.

18 Extensively discussed in Johnson, 'In a Manner of Speaking.' The commission reports and documents, including cases relevant to the seigneurial system, are in Report of the Commissioners Appointed to Inquire into the State of the Laws and Other Circumstances Connected with the Seignioral Tenure, *PC Journals*, 1843, appendix F.

19 Quotations from Young, *Politics of Codification*, 56, and 1843 Report, cited in Johnson, 'In a Manner of Speaking,' 639. Doucet was a notary and legal writer who authored works on both the civil and the common law. Vanfelson was a lawyer and a moderate Patriote. See Jacques Boucher, 'Nicolas-Benjamin Doucet,' and Claude Vachon, 'George Vanfelson,' both in *DCB*.

20 SPC 1854, c 3.

21 Michel Morissette, 'L'argent et la propriété seigneuriale de 1854 à 1940: qui sont les gagnants du processus d'abolition?,' in Benoît Grenier and Michel Morissette, eds, *Nouveaux regards en histoire seigneuriale au Québec* (Quebec: Septentrion, 2016). The proceedings of the court were published in a special edition of the *Lower Canada Reports*.

22 The best single account of the Prince Edward Island land question is Margaret McCallum, 'The Sacred Rights of Property: Title,

Entitlement, and the Land Question in Nineteenth-Century Prince Edward Island,' *EHCL*, vol. 8. Other principal sources on which this section is based are Rusty Bittermann, *Rural Protest on Prince Edward Island: From British Colonisation to the Escheat Movement* (Toronto: University of Toronto Press, 2008); Ian Robertson, *The Tenant League of Prince Edward Island: Leasehold Tenure in the New World, 1864–1867* (Toronto: University of Toronto Press, 1996); and Robertson, 'The Tenant League and the Law,' in *CST*, vol. 3; Rusty Bittermann and Margaret McCallum, 'Upholding the Land Legislation of a "Communistic and Socialist Assembly": The Benefits of Confederation for Prince Edward Island,' *Canadian Historical Review* 87 (2006): 1; and Bittermann and McCallum, 'When Private Rights Become Public Wrongs: Property and the State in Prince Edward Island in the 1830s,' in John McLaren, A.R. Buck, and Nancy Wright, eds, *Despotic Dominion: Property Rights in British Settler Societies* (Vancouver: UBC Press, 2005).

23 For tenancy in Upper Canada see Wilson, *Tenants in Time,* and Catharine Wilson, *A New Lease on Life: Landlords, Tenants and Immigrants in Ireland in Canada* (Montreal and Kingston: McGill-Queen's University Press, 1994).

24 Quotation from Bittermann and McCallum, 'When Private Rights,' 146. Leader of this radical group was Assemblyman William Cooper, a former sea captain who for some years worked as Lord Townshend's land agent on Prince Edward Island. By about 1830 he underwent 'a change of heart amounting almost to a religious conversion' on the land question and became 'the lifelong implacable foe of the absentee proprietors.' For his career and the quotations here, see Harry Baglole, 'William Cooper,' *DCB*; and Rusty Bittermann, *Sailor's Hope: The Life and Times of William Cooper: Agrarian Radical in an Age of Revolutions* (Montreal and Kingston: McGill-Queen's University Press, 2010).

25 McCallum, 'Sacred Rights of Property,' 367.

26 See *PEI Journals*, 13 Mar. 1832. The legislation was SPEI 1832, c 9.

27 SPEI 1853, c 18.

28 An edited version of the commission's work is Ian Robertson, ed., *The Prince Edward Island Land Commission of 1860* (Fredericton: Acadiensis Press, 1988). The full report is in *PEI Journals*, 1875, appendix E.

29 SPEI 1874, c 3.

30 *Kelly v Sulivan, Stewart and Fane* (1876), 2 PEIR 34; *Prince Edward Island (Commissioner of Public Lands) v Sulivan* (1877), 1 SCR 3.

31 See, for example, John Weaver, *The Great Land Rush and the Making of the Modern World, 1650–1900* (Montreal and Kingston: McGill-Queen's University Press, 2003).
32 See, especially, for Lower Canada, J.I. Little, 'Contested Land: Squatters and Agents in the Eastern Townships of Lower Canada,' *Canadian Historical Review* 80 (1999): 381, who states at 381 that squatting in the Eastern Townships was 'widespread.' For Upper Canada, see John Clarke, *Land, Power and Economics on the Frontier of Upper Canada* (Montreal and Kingston: McGill-Queen's University Press, 2001), 158–62; Gates, *Land Policies, passim*; and Risk, 'Last Golden Age,' 202–3.
33 For Cape Breton immigration and settlement in the nineteenth century, see principally Robert J. Morgan, *Rise Again! The Story of Cape Breton Island* (Sydney, CB: Breton Books, 2008); Stephen Hornsby, 'Scottish Emigration and Settlement in Early Nineteenth-Century Cape Breton,' in Kenneth Donovan, ed., *The Island: New Perspectives on Cape Breton History, 1713–1990* (Fredericton: Acadiensis, 1990), and Hornsby, *Nineteenth-Century Cape Breton: A Historical Geography* (Montreal and Kingston: McGill-Queen's University Press, 1992). There is also much useful information in an older volume, Richard Brown, *A History of the Island of Cape Breton with Some Account of the Discovery and Settlement of Canada, Nova Scotia and Newfoundland* (London, 1869; reissue Belleville: Mika, 1979).
34 Cited in Brown, *Cape Breton*, 445.
35 The history of the Mire Grant, as it was known, is recounted in the preamble to SNS 1839, c 33.
36 For much of what follows, see Peter Burroughs, 'The Administration of Crown Lands in Nova Scotia, 1827–1848,' *Collections of the Nova Scotia Historical Society* 35 (1966): 80, and Burroughs, *The Colonial Reformers and Canada 1830–1849* (Montreal and Kingston: McGill-Queen's University Press, 1969). There is also discussion of the land sales policy in the *Durham Report*.
37 Report of the Committee on Crown Lands, 14 Mar. 1842, in *NS Journals*, 1842, appendix 82. For studies noting the prevalence of squatting, see Burroughs, 'Administration of Crown Lands,' 97–8; and Danny Samson, *The Spirit of Industry and Improvement: Liberal Government and Rural-Industrial Society, Nova Scotia, 1790–1862* (Montreal and Kingston: McGill-Queen's University Press, 2008), at 188–93.
38 For the combining of the two offices, see SNS 1847, c 48. The gross government take from land sales in the 1827 to 1841 period was approximately £12,700 from the mainland and £6,800 from

Cape Breton, for a total of almost £19,500. But salaries and expenses topped out at £16,661.11s.10d, leaving a net profit of £2,820.11s.6d over the fourteen-year period: see Report of the Assembly Committee on Crown Lands, 14 Mar. 1842, in *NS Journals*, 1842, appendix 82. Land sales and revenue figures generally are in the annual Reports of the Commissioner of Crown Lands, in the appendices to the *NS Journals*.

39 Kempt to Gordon, 11 Feb. 1825, CO 217, vol. 166, 19.

40 SNS 1850, c 11 and c 41.

41 SNS 1840, c 12, preamble.

42 Samson, *Spirit of Industry*, 192–3; *Durham Report*, appendix B, 13.

43 *Smyth v McDonald* (1863), 5 NSR 274 at 279.

44 Quotations from Reports in *NS Journals*, 1847, appendix 19; 1858, appendix 7; 1859, appendix 7; and 1863, appendix 14. Complaints about surveys and proposed remedies appear in almost every such annual report.

45 SNS 1839, c 33, and 1843, c 10.

46 Report of Crown Lands Commissioner, *NS Journals*, 1854, appendix 19.

47 SNS 1854, c 43.

48 SNS 1866, c 40. This paragraph is again based on the annual reports of the Commissioner of Crown Lands, in *NS Journals*, *passim*.

49 Much of what follows on New Brunswick is from W.S. MacNutt, *New Brunswick: A History, 1784–1837* (Toronto: Macmillan, 1984); and Graeme Wynn, *Timber Colony: A Historical Geography of Early Nineteenth-Century New Brunswick* (Toronto: University of Toronto Press, 1981).

50 Campbell to Glenelg, 23 Dec. 1836, in *NB Journals*, 3 Jan. 1837.

51 *NB Journals*, 7 Jan. 1837; Glenelg to Harvey, 2 Mar. 1837, 6 July 1837; Baillie to Lieutenant Governor Colebrooke, 5 Jan. 1843, 10 Feb. 1843.

52 Quotations from Select Committee on Illegal Occupation of Lands, Second Report, in ibid., 29 Mar. 1843, and Speech of Lieutenant Governor Sir Edmund Walker Head to Assembly, in ibid., 6 Feb. 1851. The statute is at SNB 1849, c 3.

53 What follows is based principally on Bruce Kercher and Jodie Young, 'Formal and Informal Law in Two New Lands: Land Law in Newfoundland and New South Wales under Francis Forbes,' quotations below at 162–3; and Trudi Johnson, 'Defining Property for Inheritance: The Chattels Real Act of 1834,' both in *EHCL*, vol. 9. For Francis Forbes, see also Patrick O'Flaherty, 'Sir Francis Forbes,' *DCB*.

54 *R v Thomas Row* (1818) 1 Nfld LR 126 at 128. See also *R v Keough* (1819) 1 Nfld LR 172.

55 (1818) 1 Nfld LR 103. Chattels real in English law means principally leaseholds, and on intestacy they descended by the rules governing chattels – equal inheritance among the next of kin. For this issue, see generally Johnson, 'Defining Property for Inheritance.'

56 The legislation discussed here is at SN 1834, c 18; 1837, c 5; and 1844, c 1. See also Statement of Land Surveyed of Persons in Possession of Land Prior to the Passing of the Crown Lands Bill, *Nfld Journals*, 1848, 174ff.

57 See L.F.S. Upton, 'The Extermination of the Beothuks,' *Canadian Historical Review* 58 (1977): 133.

58 L.F.S. Upton, *Micmacs and Colonists: Indian-White Relations in the Maritimes, 1713–1867* (Vancouver: UBC Press, 1979). What follows on reserves in the Maritimes relies extensively on this source.

59 SNB 1844, c 47. Emphasis added.

60 RSNB 1854, c 85.

61 SNS 1842, c 16.

62 Report of the Commissioner of Indian Affairs, 25 Jan. 1843, *NS Journals* 1842, appendix 1.

63 Copies of Communications Addressed by the Commissioners of Crown Lands for Nova Scotia Proper and Cape Breton to the Provincial Secretary, ibid., 847, appendix 19.

64 Report of H.W. Crawley, 1 Feb. 1849, ibid., 1849, appendix 45. Crawley was proved prescient by a case from 1885 involving squatters who had been on the Whycocomagh reserve since the early 1860s. For decades they defied demands that they leave, and when in the 1880s their principal, David McLean, was fined and jailed he sued the Indian commissioner for Cape Breton, Donald McIsaac, for assault, false imprisonment, and trespass. The trial judge ordered the jury to find for McIsaac, but the jury defied him and gave damages to McLean. McIsaac did win on appeal: see *McLean v McIsaac*, (1885) 18 NSR 304.

65 RSNS 1851, c 58. For squatter resistance, see, in addition to the examples given here, Upton, *Micmacs and Colonists*, 90–7; and L.F.S. Upton, 'Indian Policy in Colonial Nova Scotia, 1783–1871,' *Acadiensis* 5 (1975): 3.

66 RSNS 1851, c 28, s 5; SNS 1851, c 4, s 11; RSNS 1859, c 58; RSNS 1864, c 57.

67 Sidney Harring, *White Man's Law: Native People in Nineteenth-Century Canadian Jurisprudence* (Toronto: Osgoode Society for Canadian Legal History and University of Toronto Press, 1998), 31.

68 UCQB 4 (1835) 142.

69 See Sally Weaver, 'The Iroquois: The Consolidation of the Grand River Reserve in the Mid-Nineteenth Century, 1847–1875,' in Edward S. Rogers

and Donald B. Smith, eds, *Aboriginal Ontario: Historical Perspectives on the First Nations* (Toronto: Dundurn, 1994).

70 Peter Karsten, *Between Law and Custom: High and Low Legal Cultures in the Lands of the British Diaspora, 1600–1900* (Cambridge: Cambridge University Press, 2002), 108.

71 SUC 1839, c 15; SPC 1850, c 74. See also an earlier statute protecting the hunting and fishing rights of the Credit River Mississauga, SUC 1829, c 3.

72 OSC 1840, c 44; SPC 1850, c 42.

73 SPC 1851, c 59 and 106. See Gérard Fortin and Jacques Frenette, 'L'acte de 1851 et la création de nouvelles réserves indiennes au Bas-Canada en 1853,' *Recherches amérindiennes au Québec* 19 (1989): 31.

74 See Harring, *White Man's Law*, chaps 1 and 2.

75 See above, chapter 12.

76 Alain Bealieu, 'An Equitable Right To Be Compensated: The Dispossession of the Aboriginal Peoples of Quebec and the Emergence of a New Legal Rationale, 1760–1860,' *Canadian Historical Review* 94 (2013): 1.

77 Report on Indian Affairs in Canada, in *PC Journals*, 1847, appendix T; SPC 1850, c 42.

78 Report on the Affairs of the Indians in Canada, *PC Journals*, 1844–5, appendix EEE.

79 For what follows see principally Cole Harris, *Making Native Space: Colonialism, Resistance and Reserves in British Columbia* (Vancouver: UBC Press, 2002), esp. chaps 2 and 3. See also Hamar Foster, 'Letting Go the Bone: The Idea of Indian Title in British Columbia, 1849–1927,' in *EHCL*, vol. 6; quotation below at 57.

80 For much of what follows, see David Bell, 'Was Aboriginal Dispossession Lawful? The Response of 19th-Century Maritime Intellectuals,' *Dalhousie Law Journal* 23 (2000): 168. The quotations below are at 171, 172, 176, 178.

81 Bromley served in the British army in Nova Scotia 1810–12, then returned in 1813 as agent for the British and Foreign School Society. He developed a deep interest in the condition of Indigenous peoples and publicized their poor economic and social conditions in both New Brunswick and Nova Scotia. See Judith Fingard, 'English Humanitarianism and the Colonial Mind: Walter Bromley in Nova Scotia, 1813–1825,' *Canadian Historical Review* 54 (1973): 123.

82 For Perley, see W.A. Spray, 'Moses Perley,' *DCB*.

83 For Murdoch's later views, see Philip Girard, *Lawyers and Legal Culture in British North America: Beamish Murdoch of Halifax* (Toronto: Osgoode Society for Canadian Legal History and University of Toronto Press, 2011), 176–82.

84 Philip Girard, 'Land Law, Liberalism and the Agrarian Ideal: British North America, 1750–1920,' in McLaren, Buck, and Wright, *Despotic Dominion*, 120. What follows in this section relies largely on this source.
85 SNB 1858, c 26; SPEI 1873, c 23.
86 Philip Girard, 'At the Crossroads of Fusion: British North America/ Canada, 1750–2000,' in John Goldberg, Henry E. Smith, and P.G. Turner, eds, *Equity and Law: Fusion and Fission* (Cambridge: Cambridge University Press, 2018).
87 Girard, 'Land Law, Liberalism,' 121, and, for details on mortgage law, 131–8.
88 The statute is at SPC 1851, c 6. The discussion here and in the following paragraph is largely based on Jeffrey McNairn, *The Capacity to Judge: Public Opinion and Deliberative Democracy in Upper Canada, 1791–1854* (Toronto: University of Toronto Press, 2000), chap. 8; Andrew Buck, 'This Remnant of Feudalism: Primogeniture and Political Culture in Colonial New South Wales, with Some Canadian Comparisons,' in McLaren, Buck, and Wright, *Despotic Dominion*, quotations at 179; Hereward Senior, 'Ogle Robert Gowan'; and Robert Fraser, 'Christopher Hagerman,' *DCB*.
89 This section on dower in the nineteenth century is taken principally from Girard, 'Land Law, Liberalism,' 122–9; and Douglas Brooker, 'The Invisible Relic: Ontario's Dower History Part 1: Upper Canada, 1792–1840' (unpublished paper, 1992); SUC 1834, c 1, s 13; SUC 1833, c 10, and 1839, c 6.
90 Bills to this effect were introduced in 1847, 1849, 1858, and 1860: see *PC Journals, passim*. See also *PC Debates*, vol. 6, 1847, 361–5; and vol. 8, pt 1, 1849, 615. The later attempts are also discussed in Lori Chambers, *Married Women and Property Law in Victorian Ontario* (Toronto: Osgoode Society for Canadian Legal History and University of Toronto Press, 1997), 19–21.
91 The Law of Dower, in *Upper Canada Law Journal*, Nov. 1857, cited in Chambers, *Married Women and Property Law in Victorian Ontario*, 19–20. The other quotations given here, and the discussion generally, are from the same source.

31. Law and the Economy I: Common Law, Statutes, and the Emergence of the Corporation

1 *PC Debates*, 9:464, 10 June 1850.
2 There is not space here to summarize the international literature on this subject. Suffice it to say here that for more than half a century

American legal historians have debated what role judges played in shaping common law doctrines to facilitate economic development. Among the principal works in this debate are J. Willard Hurst, *Law and the Conditions of Freedom in the Nineteenth-Century United States* (Madison: University of Wisconsin Press, 1956); and Hurst, *Law and Economic Growth: The Legal History of the Lumber Industry in Wisconsin, 1836–1915* (Cambridge, MA: Harvard University Press, 1964); Lawrence Friedman, *A History of American Law* (New York: Simon & Schuster, 1973); Morton Horwitz, *The Transformation of American Law, 1780–1860* (Cambridge, MA: Harvard University Press, 1977); Peter Karsten, *Heart v. Mind, Heart v. Head: Judge Made Law in Nineteenth-Century America* (Chapel Hill: University of North Carolina Press, 1977); Tony Freyer, 'Legal Innovation and Market Capitalism,' in Michael Grossberg and Christopher Tomlins, eds, *The Cambridge History of Law in America*, vol. 2 (New York: Cambridge University Press, 2008). A similar, though less intense and ideological historiography exists for the United Kingdom. It is summarized along with the case law developments in Stuart Anderson and Michael Lobban, *The Oxford History of the Laws of England*, vol. 12, *1820–1914 Private Law* (Oxford: University Press, 2010).

3 Risk's work is 'The Last Golden Age: Property and the Allocation of Losses in Ontario in the Nineteenth Century,' *University of Toronto Law Journal* 27 (1977): 119; 'The Golden Age: The Law about the Market in Nineteenth-Century Ontario,' *University of Toronto Law Journal* 26 (1976): 307; and 'The Law and the Economy in Mid-Nineteenth-Century Ontario: A Perspective,' in *EHCL*, vol. 1. Many of the cases cited below are derived from one or more of Risk's articles. The other historians who have also offered relevant contributions on Upper Canada are principally Bernard Hibbitts, 'Progress and Principle: The Legal Thought of Sir John Beverley Robinson,' *McGill Law Journal* 34 (1989): 454; Peter George and Philip Sworden, 'The Courts and the Development of Trade in Upper Canada, 1830–1860,' *Business History Review* 60 (1986): 258; and George and Sworden, 'John Beverley Robinson and the Commercial Empire of the St Lawrence,' *Research in Economic History* 11 (1988): 217. Peter Karsten, *Between Law and Custom: 'High' and 'Low' Legal Cultures in the Lands of the British Diaspora – The United States, Canada, Australia and New Zealand, 1600–1900* (Cambridge: Cambridge University Press, 2002), contains much useful information but suffers from ranging too widely. Robinson's biographer also discusses his commercial law decisions but does not add materially to

Risk's conclusions: Patrick Brode, *Sir John Beverley Robinson: Bone and Sinew of the Compact* (Toronto: Osgoode Society for Canadian Legal History and University of Toronto Press, 1984).

4 Risk, 'Law and Economy,' 95–6; quotation below at 113.

5 *Bryson v Clandinan* (1850) 7 UCQB 198 at 200; *Brunskill v Rigney* (1857) 6 UCCP 509 at 511.

6 (1847) 3 UCQB 358 at 359.

7 *Marshall v The School Trustees, Township of Kitley* (1854) 4 UCCP 373.

8 Hibbitts, 'Progress and Principle'; George and Sworden, 'Courts and Trade,' 279–80; Karsten, *Between Law and Custom*, 195–6 and 263–4.

9 See Paul Craven, 'The Law of Master and Servant in Mid-Nineteenth Century,' in *EHCL*, 1:185.

10 (1854) 4 GCR 231 at 241. See also the discussion of Blake more generally in Risk, 'Law and Economy,' 115–17.

11 (1849) 1 GCR 34 at 42–3.

12 See, in particular, *Chisholm v Sheldon* (1850) 1 GCR 318; and generally Risk, 'Law and Economy,' 117; and Karsten, *Between Law and Custom*, 127–9. Waste governed what a possessor of land could do with the land by balancing the possessor's rights against those with a future interest in the land – tenants and owners, life estate holders and those with the remainder, even fee tail holders and reversioners.

13 See variously *Greenshields v Barnhart* (1851) 3 GCR; *Holmes v Matthews* (1852) 3 GCR 379; and *La Targe v De Tuyll* (1852) 3 GCR.

14 (1850) 2 GCR 95 at 98–9.

15 *Rector of Hampton v Titus*, (1849) 6 NBR 278 at 314.

16 *Lessess of Lawson v Whitman*, (1851) 1 NSR 208. See generally for Nova Scotia Bernard Hibbitts, 'Her Majesty's Yankees: American Authority in the Supreme Court of Victorian Nova Scotia, 1837–1901,' in *SCNS*.

17 (1835) 1 NSR 9 at 9 and 11.

18 *Wheelock v McKown*, (1835) 1 NSR 41. See also to similar effect *Miller v Lanty*, (1840) 1 NSR 161.

19 (1826) 1 NBR 37; quotations below at 38 and 39.

20 See the case of *Hennessy v Myers*, (1832) 2 UCKB 458, discussed, with other cases, in George and Sworden, 'Courts and Trade,' 272–3.

21 For this paragraph see Bruce Kercher and Jodie Young, 'Formal and Informal Law in Two New Lands: Land Law in Newfoundland and New South Wales under Francis Forbes,' in *EHCL*, vol. 9; Bruce Ziff, 'Warm Reception in a Cold Climate: English Property Law and the Suppression of the Canadian Legal Identity,' in John McLaren, A.R. Buck, and Nancy Wright, eds, *Despotic Dominion: Property Rights in*

British Settler Societies (Vancouver: UBC Press, 2005), and the cases cited therein.

22 Risk, 'Law and Economy,' 103.

23 Examples from just Lower Canada in one year include SLC 1825, c 28, 30 and 35.

24 SUC 1816, c 34; SNS 1834, c 51.

25 SNS 1837, c 9.

26 SUC 1826, c 24; SLC 1825, c 13; SNS 1832, c 44.

27 SNS 1857, c 72. Bessemer was a prolific inventor but is best known for his revolutionary steel-making process, which greatly reduced the cost of making steel. For other colonies' patent acts see SUC 1826, c 5; SNB 1834, c 27; SPEI 1837, c 21; SNS 1833, c 45.

28 For Upper Canada and province of Canada usury legislation, see SUC 1811, c 9; SPC 1853, c 80, and 1858, c 85. See generally Risk, 'Golden Age,' 319–23. For Newfoundland, see SN 1834, 2nd Sess., c 12.

29 For the former, see SUC 1821, c 17; SUC 1823, c 37; SUC 1833, c 30; SUC 1836, c 15; SPEI 1832, c 11; SPEI 1833, c 18; SNS 1824, c 26 and c 27. For the latter see SUC 1830, c 17; SNS 1833, c 70.

30 For bread regulations see, inter alia, SUC 1825, c 6; SPEI 1833, c 21; SLC 1825, c 17; SNS 1830, c 6. For commodity standards and inspection see SUC 1835, c 7, and generally Risk, 'Golden Age,' 314–15.

31 SNS 1857, c 11. See also SNB 1834, c 6 and 10.

32 SUC 1838, c 18.

33 Quoted in R.C.B. Risk, 'The Nineteenth-Century Foundations of the Business Corporation in Ontario,' *University of Toronto Law Journal* 23 (1973): 270. A good deal of what follows draws on this article, supplemented by a modest literature on the corporation in Canada: A.W. Currie, 'The First Dominion Companies Act,' *Canadian Journal of Economics and Political Science* 28 (1962): 387; Barbara Patton, 'From State Action to Private Profit: The Emergence of the Business Corporation in Nova Scotia, 1796–1833,' *Nova Scotia Historical Review* 21 (1996): 16; F.W. Labrie and E.E. Palmer, 'The Pre-Confederation History of Corporations in Canada,' in Jacob S. Ziegel, ed., *Studies in Canadian Company Law* (Toronto: Butterworths, 1967); Jonathan H. Davidson, 'Industry and the Development of Company Law in Nineteenth-Century Nova Scotia,' *Nova Scotia Historical Review* 15 (1995): 88. A broader approach to the corporate form is taken by Jean-Marie Fecteau, 'État et associationisme au XIXe siècle québécois: éléments pour une problématique des rapports État/société dans la transition au capitalisme,' in Allan Greer and Ian Radforth, eds, *Colonial Leviathan: State Formation in Mid-Nineteenth-*

Century Canada (Toronto: University of Toronto Press, 1992); and Fecteau, 'Les "petites républiques": les compagnies et la mise en place du droit corporatif moderne au Québec au milieu du XIXe siècle,' *Histoire sociale/Social History* 25 (1992): 35.

34 See chapter 24, above, for a discussion of corporate status and Indigenous people.

35 Risk, 'Nineteenth-Century Foundations,' 301.

36 The English history is usefully reviewed in ibid., 270–1, and in Patton, 'State Action to Private Profit,' 21ff. For fuller accounts, see Armand B. Dubois, *The English Business Company after the Bubble Act, 1720–1800* (New York: Commonwealth Fund, 1938); and Bishop C. Hunt, *The Development of the Business Corporation in England, 1800–1867* (Cambridge, MA: Harvard University Press, 1936).

37 7 Geo. 1, c 18 (1720).

38 The Saint John Charter is reproduced as an appendix to vol. 1, 1786, of SNB. For legislative confirmation of the city's status, see SNB 1786, c 46. The Parish of Saint John was similarly separately incorporated in 1789: SNB 1789, c 1. For examples of educational institutions, see SNB 1805, c 12, which established and incorporated 'the Public Grammar School in the City of Saint John.' See also SNB 1805, c 15; SNS 1820, c 39; SUC 1815, c 18. For religious incorporations see, inter alia, SNB 1826, c 17.

39 For the corporations mentioned here, see SNS 1796, c 7, 1815, c 19, and 1817, c 15; SUC 1819, c 15; SNB 1820, c 13.

40 J. Willard Hurst, *The Legitimacy of the Business Corporation in the Law of the United States, 1780–1970* (Charlottesville: University of Virginia Press, 1970).

41 See, for example, SUC 1827, c 12; and SNB 1833, c 12. For a general discussion of these Acts in Upper Canada, see Risk, 'Nineteenth-Century Foundations,' 283ff.

42 Risk, 'Nineteenth-Century Foundations,' *passim*; Patton, 'State Action to Private Profit,' 43. For the point about multiple attempts we are grateful to Jeff McNairn.

43 See Labrie and Palmer, 'Pre-Confederation History,' 52. For many other examples see the entries for politicians from all colonies in *DCB, passim.*

44 J.I. Little, 'Lewis Thomas Drummond,' *DCB*.

45 See Patton, 'State Action to Private Profit,' 38–9; and SNS 1832, c 50. For the other entities noted here, see SUC 1819, c 24 and c 35; SNB 1820, c 13; SNB 1825, c 13; SLC 1821, c 25, c 26, and c 27.

46 SUC 1832, c 13; SPC 1841, c 74; Charles M. Johnston, 'The Six Nations in the Grand River Valley, 1784–1847,' in Edward S. Rogers and Donald B.

Smith, eds, *Aboriginal Ontario: Historical Perspectives on the First Nations* (Toronto: Dundurn, 1994); B.E. Hill, 'The Grand River Navigation Company and the Six Nations Indians,' *Ontario History* 63 (1971): 32.

47 See, for example, SNS 1815, c 19; SNB 1836, c 62, c 63, and c 64; SNS 1836, c 90.

48 Quotation from Risk, 'Nineteenth-Century Foundations,' 272–3. Examples of Upper Canadian statutes that granted corporations a power to expropriate include three in 1829: SUC 1829, c 11, c 12, and c 15. For a New Brunswick example, see SNB 1834, c 39.

49 For the mid-1830s boom, see Graeme Wynn, *Timber Colony: A Historical Geography of Early Nineteenth-Century New Brunswick* (Toronto: University of Toronto Press, 1981), 102. For examples of 'boom' corporations see SNB 1844, c 34; SNB 1845, c 46; SNB 1849, c 67.

50 SNB 1836, c 6. For the background see W.S. MacNutt, *New Brunswick: A History, 1784–1867* (Toronto: Macmillan, 1984), 244. This venture did not pan out. The money was to be paid into the company and the land paid for in instalments, but the large number of U.S. bank failures in the mid-1830s meant no capital for continued payments, and the land escheated back to the Crown.

51 See Currie, 'First Dominion Act,' 390. For seigneuries, see SLC 1822, c 10; SLC 1823, c 18; SLC 1825, c 34; SLC 1826, c 10; SLC 1831, c 31. For economic activity and religion see Brian Young, *In Its Corporate Capacity: The Seminary of Montreal as a Business Institution, 1816–1876* (Montreal and Kingston: McGill-Queen's University Press, 1986). For lawyers and business in general see the essays in *EHCL*, vol. 7; and for Montreal, see G. Blaine Baker, 'Ordering the Urban Canadian Law Office and Its Entreprenurial Hinterland, 1825–1875,' *University of Toronto Law Journal* 48 (1998): 175; and G. Blaine Baker, 'Law Practice and Statecraft in Mid-Nineteenth Century Montreal: The Torrance-Morris Firm, 1848–1868,' in *EHCL*, vol. 4.

52 For all this legislation, see SNB 1836, c 33; SNS 1818, c 27; SUC 1833, c 5 and c 8; SUC 1836, c 3 and c 18; SUC 1837, c 14.

53 See, for example, *NB Journals*, appendix p. A-iii.

54 Risk, 'Nineteenth-Century Foundations,' 280.

55 *Epitome*, 2:50.

56 Patton, 'State Action to Private Profit,' 34.

57 SUC 1823, c 8; SUC 1827, c 2 and c 23; SUC 1830, c 30.

58 See, for example, SUC 1827, c 1; SPEI 1833, c 16; SLC 1825, c 19.

59 *Novascotian*, 13 Feb. 1832, cited in Patton, 'State Action to Private Profit,' 39.

60 SNS 1817, c 15; and SUC 1827, c 16.
61 SNB 1825, c 17; SLC 1836, c 18; SNB 1836, c 62.
62 Risk, 'Law and Economy,' 124.
63 Risk, 'Nineteenth-Century Foundations,' 273, calls these 'general incorporation statutes,' but it seems to us that this is a confusing term. They were more 'general' than special Acts, but they were limited to sectors, albeit in one case, the 1850 Province of Canada statute, to a number of broadly defined sectors.
64 SLC 1834, c 33; SUC 1836, c 18.
65 SPC 1850, c 21. See, generally, Roeliff Morton Breckenridge, *The History of Banking in Canada* (Washington: Government Printer, 1910). This authorized as few as five people to set up a bank, and there was no minimum requirement of paid up capital, although the amount of capital stock had to be filed with the local county court. For the other areas mentioned, see SPC 1846, c 90; SPC 1849, c 56, c 57, and c 84.
66 Risk, 'Nineteenth-Century Foundations,' 277.
67 SPC 1850, c 28. While the title did not mention ship-building, the Act itself included it with the other four categories. The Act has been described as 'the beginning of Canadian company law': Labrie and Palmer, 'Pre-Confederation History,' 59.
68 Report of the Committee on Railroads, *PC Journals* 1851, appendix UU.
69 See respectively SPC 1852, c 10; SPC 1853, c 124, c 173, and c 191; SPC 1855, c 96.
70 SPC 1860, c 30, c 31, and c 32; SPC 1864, c 23.
71 For why six corporations are included under 'Province of Canada,' see the text accompanying table 1.
72 About 160 corporations were created under the manufacturing, mining, mechanical statute of 1850 prior to Confederation, and some seventy road corporations were created in the first two years after the 1849 sectoral Act: Risk, 'Nineteenth-Century Foundations,' 274, 277–9, and 304. Risk used the provincial secretary's correspondence for his analysis. We have taken the total given here, 230, as a minimum and assumed that 70 more were established under the road and other sectoral statutes.
73 SNB 1862, c 28.
74 SN 1856, c 18.
75 SNS 1851, 2nd Sess, c 5.
76 See J. Hartlen, 'Nova Scotia's Four Great Gold Rushes,' *Collections of the Nova Scotia Historical Society* 42 (1982): 65.

77 Cited in Davidson, 'Industry and Company Law,' 101. The statute is SNS 1862, c 2. Britain had legislated limited liability as an automatic right for those incorporating in 1855.
78 SPC 1851, c 51; SPC 1861, c 18; RSNS 1851, c 87; SNS 1855, c 47.
79 SNB 1854, c 65; SNB 1856, c 9.
80 See Jeremy Mouat, *Metal Mining in Canada, 1840–1950* (Ottawa: National Museum of Science and Technology, 2000).
81 SNS 1854, c 1.
82 SNS 1856, c 72; SNS 1860, c 67.
83 For MacNab, see Peter Baskerville, 'Sir Allan Napier MacNab,' *DCB*.
84 Patton, 'State Action to Private Profit,' 46.
85 Section 5 of the *Interpretation Act*, SPC 1849, c 10, stated, 'Words making any association or numbers of persons a Corporation ... shall be construed ... to exempt the individual members of the Corporation from personal liability for its debts, provided they do not contravene the provisions of the Act incorporating them.' The most important judicial decisions were *Emerson v Flint*, (1858) 7 UCCP 161; and *Harris v The Dry Dock Company*, (1859) 7 *GCR* 450, both cited in Risk, 'Nineteenth-Century Foundations,' 296.
86 *PC Debates*, 9:464, 10 June 1850.
87 SPC 1854, c 47, s 18; SPC 1854, c 49, s 18; SPC 1854, c 50, s 18. The Upper Canada exceptions are briefly summarized in Risk, 'Nineteenth-Century Foundations,' 297. Only one exception was made in Lower Canada, in OSC 1840, c 34.
88 SPC 1849, c 75; RSNB 1854, c 121; SN 1856, c 16.
89 Eighty-two people set up a partnership in 1849 to own and operate steamships. In 1853 the manager fled to escape creditors. The firm was bankrupt because the manager had used £4,000 of its funds for his own purposes and had not paid his own subscription of £6,000. See Currie, 'First Dominion Act,' 390.
90 RSNS 1851, c 79, ss 12–15.
91 For an example, see SNB 1853, c 66, s 11.
92 SPC 1850, c 28, s 11.
93 See, for example, SUC 1836, c 34, s 27, and 1841, c 96, s 34.
94 Risk, 'Nineteenth-Century Foundations,' 296.
95 See the three banks established in 1821, above. See also OSC 1838, c 14, s 9; SPC 1841, c 96, s 9; SPC 1846, c 115, s 9; SPC 1847, c 113, s 32; SPC 1855, c 201, s 30, and c 202, c 202, s 27, and c 206, s 27.
96 SLC 1833, c 32, s 15.

97 For examples, see SNB 1820, c 13, s 21; SNB 1825, c 13, s 21; SNB 1834, c 44, s 21; SNB 1836, c 56, s 32. For exceptions, all local banks, see SNB 1836, c 32; SNB 1854, c 1, s 21; SNB 1856, c 66, s 21.
98 SUC 1836, c 18; SNB 1831, c 39, s 20; SNB 1836, c 35, s 23; SNB 1841, c 32, s 23; SNB 1845, c 48, s 23; SNB 1854, c 63, s 20.
99 The figures here and below on limited liability in Nova Scotia are from Patton, 'State Action to Private Profit,' 46–7, and a review of the statutes.
100 *Re Nash Brick and Pottery Manufacturing Company*, (1874) 9 NSR 254 at 255.
101 Report of debate and editorial in *Novascotian*, 23 Mar. 1846. For the bill 'to incorporate the Londonderry Mining Company,' see *NS Journals*, 26 Feb. and 18 Mar. 1846. It was amended in committee to provide for unlimited liability and then dropped by its sponsor, John Ross, member for Colchester County. For the default position, see RSNS 1851, c 87, s 13.
102 *NS Debates*, 28 Mar. 1855. For the Act, which gave limited liability, see SNS 1855, c 69.
103 Davidson, 'Industry and Company Law,' 102. For the Act, see SNS 1862, c 2. Section 6 stated, 'Every stockholder shall be liable in his person and separate estate, during membership, to an amount equal to double the stock held by him.'
104 Risk, 'Nineteenth-Century Foundations,' 298.
105 Currie, 'First Dominion Act,' 392. See also the comments of Malcolm Cameron, who opposed the 1850 bill. Allowing some people to band together would mean that 'the interests of individuals engaged in similar pursuits were injured, and debts incurred which the parties were not liable for beyond the amount paid in.' The bill was 'apparently liberal but really dangerous in principle': *PC Debates*, 9:464, 10 June 1850.
106 *NS Debates*, 28 Mar. 1855. The quotation below from the same debate is from the same source.
107 *Epitome*, 2:63.
108 *PC Debates*, 9:464, 10 June 1850.
109 Said in the House of Assembly, reported in the *Acadian Recorder*, 17 Apr. 1819, and cited in Patton, 'From State Action to Private Profit,' 39.
110 Cited in Labrie and Palmer, 'Pre-Confederation History,' 52. For extended treatments of Mackenzie's views, see Lillian Gates, 'The Decided Policy of W.L. Mackenzie,' *Canadian Historical Review* 40 (1959): 185; and W. Mackay, 'The Political Ideas of W.L. Mackenzie,' *Canadian Journal of Economics and Political Science* 3 (1937): 1.
111 *PC Debates*, 9:464, 10 June 1850.

32. Law and the Economy II: Debtor-Creditor Law

1 *Western Mercury*, 24 Feb. 1831, cited in Jeffrey McNairn, 'A Just and Obvious Distinction: The Meaning of Imprisonment for Debt and the Criminal Law in Upper Canada's Age of Reform,' in *EHCL*, 11:192. The leading articles on insolvency and imprisonment for debt in British North America are McNairn, cited above, and McNairn, 'The Common Sympathies of Our Nature: Moral Sentiments, Emotional Economies, and Imprisonment for Debt in Upper Canada,' *Histoire sociale/Social History* 49 (2016): 49; Evelyn Kolish, 'Imprisonment for Debt in Lower Canada, 1791–1840,' *McGill Law Journal* 32 (1987): 603; and Philip Girard, 'Married Women's Property, Chancery Abolition, and Insolvency Law: Law Reform in Nova Scotia 1820–1867,' in *EHCL*, vol. 3. See also McNairn, 'Modes of Ascertaining the Truth: Knowing Fraud and Insolvency in Upper Canada, 1794–1843' (unpublished, 2018).

2 See, for example, Douglas McCalla, 'Rural Credit and Rural Development in Upper Canada, 1790–1850,' in Roger Hall, William Westfall, and Laurel Sefton MacDowell, eds, *Patterns of the Past: Interpreting Ontario's History* (Toronto: Dundurn 1988), 40.

3 Peter Oliver, *Terror to Evil Doers: Prisons and Punishment in Nineteenth-Century Ontario* (Toronto: Osgoode Society for Canadian Legal History and University of Toronto Press, 1998), 48.

4 *Wesleyan*, 27 Sept. 1851, cited in Girard, 'Law Reform,' 100.

5 Kolish, 'Imprisonment for Debt,' 606; SUC 1811, c 9.

6 For the New Brunswick legislation, for example, which dates from the first assembly, see SNB 1786, c 13; 1788, c 2; 1823, c 14; 1834, c 36. For other colonies see SUC 1829, c 2; Kolish, 'Imprisonment for Debt,' 606–7; SN 1835, 2nd Sess., c 2.

7 *Novascotian*, 25 Oct. 1823.

8 For descriptions of the process see Girard, 'Law Reform,' 93–4; and McNairn, 'Just and Obvious Distinction,' 194–5.

9 SPC 1850, c 74, s 3. For the practice see Sally Weaver, 'The Iroquois: The Consolidation of the Grand River Reserve in the Mid-Nineteenth Century, 1847–1875,' in Edward S. Rogers and Donald B. Smith, eds, *Aboriginal Ontario: Historical Perspectives on the First Nations* (Toronto: Dundurn, 1994), 196.

10 Initially a debtor had to wait fourteen days before applying for support, but in 1833 this was changed to allow the application to be made immediately. For the legislation see SNB 1819, c 12; 1822, c 15; 1826, c 13; 1828, c 16; 1830, c 30; and 833, c 18.

11 The 1823 statute quoted is SNB 1823, c 10. For later New Brunswick legislation, see SNB 1826, c 13; 1829, c 7; 1829, c 26; 1830 c 30; 1831, c 31; 1832, c 2; and 1836, c 41. For specific communities see, inter alia, SNB 1837, c 31; 1843, c 15; and 1845, c 93.
12 McNairn, 'Just and Obvious Distinction,' 196–7; SUC 1822, c 6; 1827, c 9; 1829, c 2; 1834, c 10; SPC 1847, c 15, s 1.
13 This paragraph on unsuccessful legislation is derived from reading the *Journals* of each colonial assembly; from Kolish, 'Imprisonment for Debt'; and Girard, 'Law Reform.' Abolition bills were introduced every year in Lower Canada between 1830 and 1835 and in Upper Canada from 1825 to 1840. For individual relief Acts, see SNS 1834, c 59.
14 James Stewart to Peleg Wiswall, 28 Apr. 1828, in NSARM, MG 1, Wiswall Papers, vol. 980, no. 132.
15 SNS 1819, c 22; 1832, c 58.
16 For this paragraph, see McNairn, 'Knowing Fraud and Insolvency.'
17 SUC 1835, c 3; and SLC 1835, c 3.
18 SN 1834, 2nd Sess., c 11. Ten years later the Act was amended to somewhat widen the definition of fraud: SN 1844, c 2.
19 SPC 1843, c 31; 1847, c 15; 1858, c 96.
20 For this paragraph see Kolish, 'Imprisonment for Debt,' 613–14; Girard, 'Law Reform,' 95; SNS 1846, c 12 and 1849, c 49; RSNS 1851, c 131 and 137; SPC 1849, c 42; Third Report of the Law Commissioners, 24 Jan. 1854, in *NB Journals*, 1854, appendix, 33; RSNB 1854, c 124 and c 125.
21 For this paragraph see R.C.B. Risk, 'The Golden Age: The Law about the Market in Nineteenth-Century Ontario,' *University of Toronto Law Journal* 26 (1976): 307 at 342ff; and Thomas Telfer, *Ruin and Redemption: The Struggle for a Canadian Bankruptcy Law, 1867–1919* (Toronto: Osgoode Society for Canadian Legal History and University of Toronto Press, 2014).
22 See Girard, 'Law Reform,' 97–8; and Evelyn Kolish, 'L'introduction de la faillite au Bas-Canada: conflit social ou national,' *Revue d'histoire de l'Amérique française* 40 (1986): 215; quotation below at 609.
23 OSC 1839, c 36; quotation from s 9; SPC 1843, c 10. See also Kolish, 'Imprisonment for Debt,' 613.
24 SPC 1846, c 30; 1849, c 18; 1850, c 20; 1854–5, c 85, s 2.
25 SPC 1845, c 48. Quotation below from s 4.
26 For all this, see SPC 1848, c 3, s 2; 1851, c 68, s 1; 1852–3, c 151, s 1; 1854–5, c 85, s 1; 1856, c 93; and 1857, c 1; Risk, 'Golden Age,' 344–5; *Globe*, 3 Mar. 1859, and 6 and 21 May 1861.
27 *Globe*, 21 May 1861.

28 We owe this reference to Jeffrey McNairn.
29 SPC 1864, c 17.
30 SNB 1842, c 43, revised by 1843, c 4.
31 *Wesleyan*, 27 Sept. 1851, cited in Girard, 'Law Reform,' 100.
32 Cited in McNairn, 'Just and Obvious Distinction,' 211. See for similar comments, Risk, 'Golden Age,' 343; and *PC Debates* 5:1081–93, and 6:1133–5.
33 *Globe*, 15 June 1850.
34 Kolish, 'Imprisonment for Debt,' 611.
35 Girard, 'Law Reform,' 96. A chose in action is a form of intangible personal property, such as a right to bring an action in court to recover chattels, money, or debt.
36 SN 1851, c 8.
37 Quotations in this paragraph from *British Colonial Argus*, 6 Aug. 1833, cited in McNairn, 'Just and Obvious Distinction,' 222; ibid., 200–1 and 210; *Globe*, 15 June 1850.
38 Quotations in this paragraph from McNairn, 'Common Sympathies,' 50; *Globe*, 10 Mar. 1849; *Colonial Patriot*, 27 Feb. 1830; *Scribbler*, 7 Sept. 1826.
39 *Le Courrier du Canada*, 5 Mar. 1858 (original in French, authors' translation). See also generally, Kolish, 'Imprisonment for Debt,' 609.
40 See the quotations in McNairn, 'Just and Obvious Distinction,' 210–11. See also Girard, 'Law Reform,' 99.
41 Lori Chambers, 'Married Women's Property Law Reform, Couples, and Fraud in Canada West/Ontario, 1859–1900,' in *EHCL*, vol. 11.
42 *Novascotian*, 8 Mar. 1827.
43 McNairn, 'Just and Obvious Distinction,' 197 and 210.
44 See the extensive reports in *Globe*, 17 Apr. 1858.
45 See Risk, 'Golden Age,' 343–4; and Girard, 'Law Reform,' 101.
46 *Novascotian*, 10 Feb. 1842.
47 *PC Debates*, 5:1082, 1 May 1846.
48 Quotations from *La Minerve*, 15 Apr. 1856 and 11 Mar. 1857 (originals in French).
49 Kolish, 'Imprisonment for Debt,' 610–11; and Risk, 'Golden Age,' 343; *PC Debates*, 5:1081–93, and 6:1133–5.
50 *Globe*, 6 and 21 May 1861.
51 Tony Freyer, 'Legal Innovation and Market Capitalism,' in Michael Grossberg and Christopher Tomlins, eds, *The Cambridge History of Law in America* (New York: Cambridge University Press, 2008), 2:452. The United States had a federal bankruptcy law for a few years in the early nineteenth century, and then again from 1841 to 1843, but not again

until 1867. See, inter alia, David A. Skeel, *Debt's Dominion: A History of Bankruptcy Law in America* (Princeton: Princeton University Press, 2001).

33. Less Favoured by Law I: Blacks and Workers

1 Quotations from Barrington Walker, *Race on Trial: Black Defendants in Ontario's Criminal Courts, 1858–1958* (Toronto: Osgoode Society for Canadian Legal History and University of Toronto Press, 2010), 3; and Dann J. Broyld, 'Justice Was Refused Me, I Resolved to Free Myself: John W. Lindsay. Finding Elements of American Freedoms in British Canada, 1805–1876,' *Ontario History* 109 (2017): 27 at 55.

2 For Blacks voting see below, this chapter, and Frank Mackey, *Done with Slavery: The Black Fact in Montreal, 1760–1840* (Montreal and Kingston: McGill-Queen's University Press, 2010), chap. 8. For jury service, see R. Blake Brown, *A Trying Question: The Jury in Nineteenth-Century Canada* (Toronto: Osgoode Society for Canadian Legal History and University of Toronto Press, 2009). Generally see the examples given in Walker, *Race on Trial, passim;* and an exploration of the phenomenon of 'British justice' and race in Lyndsay Campbell, 'Race, Upper Canadian Constitutionalism and "British Justice,"' *Law and History Review* 33 (2015): 41; quotation at 51.

3 Robin Winks, *The Blacks in Canada: A History*, 2nd ed. (Montreal and Kingston: McGill-Queen's University Press, 1997).

4 Barrington Walker, 'From a Property Right to Citizenship Rights,' in Walker, ed., *The African Canadian Legal Odyssey* (Toronto: Osgoode Society for Canadian Legal History and University of Toronto Press, 2012), 28.

5 There is a reasonably large literature on the history of Blacks in British North America, and this discussion of the origins and growth of the Black population is based principally on the following works, which also deal in various ways with the legal history. Winks, *Blacks in Canada*; Harvey Amani Whitfield, *From American Slaves to Nova Scotian Subjects: The Case of the Black Refugees, 1813–1840* (Toronto: Pearson Prentice Hall, 2005); and Whitfield, *Blacks on the Border: The Black Refugees in British North America, 1815–1860* (Burlington: University of Vermont Press, 2006); Walker, 'Property Right to Citizenship Rights'; James St.G. Walker, 'The Establishment of a Free Black Community in Nova Scotia, 1783–1840," in Martin L. Kilson and Robert I. Rotberg, eds, *The African Diaspora: Interpretive Essays* (Cambridge, MA: Harvard University Press, 1976); John Grant, *Immigration and*

Settlement of Black Refugees of the War of 1812 in Nova Scotia and New Brunswick (Hantsport, NS: Lancelot, 1990); Alan Stouffer, *The Light of Nature and the Law of God: Antislavery in Ontario, 1833–1877* (Montreal and Kingston: McGill-Queen's University Press, 1992); Mackey, *Done with Slavery.*

6 On the surface, these do not seem to be large numbers, but as of a census of 1817 the Nova Scotian population was some 81,000, so if the Black population was 4,000 it represented 5 per cent of the total.

7 Memorial of John Chamberlain et al., 8 June 1838, cited in Whitfield, *From American Slaves*, 39.

8 Petition of Coloured People at Preston, 1841, cited ibid., 75.

9 See W.A. Spray, *The Blacks in New Brunswick* (Fredericton: Brunswick, 1972), 47–9.

10 *NS Journals*, 1 Apr. 1815, cited in Whitfield, *From American Slaves*, 111.

11 *Acadian Recorder*, 21 Feb. 1824, cited ibid., 115.

12 *Halifax Sun*, 26 Feb. 1851, cited in Colin Grittner, 'Privilege at the Polls: Culture, Citizenship and the Electoral Franchise in Mid-Nineteenth-Century British North America' (PhD thesis, McGill University, 2015), 134.

13 See SNS 1834, c 68. See also Minute of the Privy Council, 4 Mar. 1835, in *NS Journals*, 1836, appendix 13. The minute stated, 'This Act prohibits the access to the Province of a class of your Majesty's Subjects who have, by a recent Act of Parliament, been relieved from the Disabilities formerly affecting them, and to whom it is not fitting that new disabilities … should be extended.' For perhaps consequent efforts to relocate Blacks living at Hammonds Plains to the Caribbean, see *NS Journals*, 1837, appendix 9.

14 For this case see *Novascotian*, 25 Jan. 1826; Brenton Halliburton and Lewis Wilkins to Sir Rupert George, 9 June 1826, NSARM, RG 1, vol. 233, 5; Sampson Salter Blowers to Lieutenant Governor Kempt, 18 June 1826; *NS Council Minutes*, 23 June 1826, RG 1, vol. 214.5B.

15 Donald Fyson, 'Minority Groups and the Law in Quebec, 1760–1867,' in *EHCL*, 11:294–5. The statement about Halifax is from unpublished research by Jim Phillips.

16 This is a much written about the topic. See, inter alia, Karolyn Frost, *I've Got a Home in Glory Land: A Lost Tale of the Underground Railroad* (Toronto: Thomas Allen, 2007); David Murray, *Colonial Justice: Justice, Morality and Crime in the Niagara District, 1791–1849* (Toronto: Osgoode Society for Canadian Legal History and University of Toronto Press, 2002), 198–216; Jason Silverman, *Unwelcome Guests: Canada West's Response to Fugitive*

American Slaves, 1800–1865 (Millwood, NY: Associated Faculty, 1985). The population figure, somewhat lower than nineteenth-century estimates, is from Michael Wayne, 'The Black Population of Canada West on the Eve of the American Civil War: A Reassessment Based on the Manuscript Census of 1861,' *Histoire sociale/Social History* 28 (1995): 465.

17 Winks, *Blacks in Canada*, 148–9; Kristin McLaren, 'We Had No Desire to Be Set Apart: Forced Segregation of Black Students in Canada West's Public Schools and the Myth of British Egalitarianism,' *Histoire sociale/Social History* 37 (2004): 27 at 32.

18 This paragraph is derived from a variety of sources, particularly Walker, *Race on Trial*; Campbell, 'Race and British Justice,' 70ff; and Lyndsay Campbell, 'The Disorderly Conduct of a Few: Crime and Hamilton's Racial Geography in the Early 1850s,' *Queen's Law Journal* 37 (2012): 477.

19 The best succinct account of the segregated schools issue is McLaren, 'Forced Segregation,' from which all quotations in this section are taken unless otherwise specified. See also Robin Winks, 'Negro School Segregation in Ontario and Nova Scotia,' *Canadian Historical Review* 50 (1969): 164.

20 SPC 1843, c 44, s 7.

21 SPC 1850, c 48, s 19.

22 *Washington v Charlottesville Township School No 14* (1854) 11 UCQB 569 at 573.

23 (1854) 11 UCQB 573 at 576.

24 Winks, 'Negro School Segregation'; and Winks, *Blacks in Canada*, 135–7. In New Brunswick and Prince Edward Island, Blacks attended both common schools and segregated ones, depending on the location.

25 For what follows, here and below, on fugitive slaves and extradition the best accounts are Bradley Miller, *Borderline Crime: Fugitive Criminals and the Challenge of the Border, 1819-1914* (Toronto: Osgoode Society for Canadian Legal History and University of Toronto Press, 2016); and Miller, 'British Rights and Liberal Law in Canada's Fugitive Slave Debate, 1833–1843,' in Tony Freyer and Lyndsay Campbell, eds, *Freedom's Conditions in the US-Canadian Borderlands in the Age of Emancipation* (Durham, NC: Carolina Academic Press, 2011). Also useful is Alexander Murray, 'The Extradition of Fugitive Slaves from Canada: A Reevaluation,' *Canadian Historical Review* 43 (1962): 298. Sources relevant to particular cases are given where appropriate.

26 SUC 1833, c 7. The earlier statute, which applied only to other areas of British North America, was SUC 1797, c 15.

27 See Dan Hill, 'Negroes in Toronto: 1793–1865,' *Ontario History* 55 (1963): 76.
28 Cited in Campbell, 'Race and British Justice,' 48. See also Miller, 'British Rights and Liberal Law,' 152.
29 Cited in Miller, *Borderline Crime*, 31.
30 Miller, 'British Rights and Liberal Law,' 146.
31 Miller, *Borderline Crime*, 118.
32 For these cases see also Murray, *Colonial Justice*, chap. 10; David Murray, 'Hands across the Border: The Abortive Extradition of Solomon Moseby,' *Canadian Review of American Studies* 30 (2000): 187; Murray, 'Extradition of Fugitive Slaves'; Roman J. Zorn, 'Criminal Extradition Menaces the Canadian Haven for Fugitive Slaves, 1841–1861,' *Canadian Historical Review* 38 (1957): 284; J. Mackenzie Leask, 'Jesse Happy, a Fugitive Save from Kentucky,' *Ontario History* 54 (1962): 87. The quotations used in this and the next paragraph are from Miller, *Borderline Crime*, 119, 123, and 125.
33 The Anderson case has spawned a large literature. It is summarized in Miller, *Borderline Crime*, 127ff. We have relied here principally on this source and Patrick Brode, *The Odyssey of John Anderson* (Toronto: Osgoode Society for Canadian Legal History and University of Toronto Press, 1989). The case reports are *In the Matter of John Anderson* (1860) 20 UCQB 124; and *In Re Anderson*, (1861) 11 UCCP 54. There is also much material available in *PC Journals*, 1861, appendix 22.
34 The procedures to be followed in an extradition case were enacted in SPC 1849, c 19.
35 For an excellent discussion of the arguments see Miller, *Borderline Crime*, 128ff; quotations above at 128 and 133.
36 Bruce Hodgins, 'Archibald Maclean,' *DCB*.
37 Quotations from Brode, *Odyssey*, 60 and 61.
38 This case is discussed in Paul Halliday, *Habeas Corpus: From England to Empire* (Cambridge, MA: Harvard University Press, 2012), which argues that the London court did have jurisdiction.
39 See Donald Swainson, 'John Hillyard Cameron,' *DCB*.
40 For the quotations from the Common Pleas judgments, see Miller, *Borderline Crime*, 138 and 139.
41 Campbell, 'Race and British Justice,' 53.
42 The principal source for this section is Paul Craven, 'Canada, 1670–1935: Symbolic and Instrumental Enforcement in Loyalist North America,' in Douglas Hay and Paul Craven, eds, *Masters, Servants and Magistrates in Britain and the Empire, 1562–1955* (Chapel Hill: University of North Carolina Press, 2004).

43 Paul Craven, 'The Law of Master and Servant in Mid-Nineteenth-Century Ontario,' in *EHCL*, 1:176.
44 SNS 1815, c 9; SNB 1826, c 5.
45 RSNS 1851, c 125. The legislation was reproduced in the subsequent statutory revision. There was a separate statute dealing with merchant seamen: RSNS 1851, c 76. The New Brunswick story was essentially the same: RSNB 1854, c 134.
46 Quotations and figures in this paragraph are from Craven, 'Canada 1670–1935,' 182–3 and 185.
47 For Lower Canada see, in addition to the sources already noted, Ian C. Pilarczyk, '"Too Well Used by His Master": Judicial Enforcement of Servants' Rights in Montreal, 1830–1845,' *McGill Law Journal* 46 (2001): 491, quotation below at 501; and G.L. Hogg and G. Shulman, 'Wage Disputes and the Courts in Montreal,' in Donald Fyson, Colin Coates, and Kathryn Harvey, eds, *Class, Gender and the Law in Eighteenth- and Nineteenth-Century Quebec: Sources and Perspectives* (Montreal: Montreal History Group, 1993).
48 For this legislation see Craven, 'Canada 1670–1935,' 188–9; SLC 1824, c 33; SLC 1836, c 27.
49 William Conway Keele, *The Provincial Justice* (Toronto: 1839).
50 (1845) 2 UCQB 211 at 221.
51 SPC 1847, c 23.
52 SPC 1851, c 11; and 1855, c 136.
53 Craven, 'Master and Servant,' 191.
54 SPC 1845, c 6; see also SPC 1851, c 76. For detailed studies of conflict in both industries see Michael S. Cross, 'The Shiners War: Social Violence in the Ottawa Valley in the 1830s,' *Canadian Historical Review* 54 (1873): 1; Ruth Bleasdale, *Rough Work: Labourers on the Public Works of British North America, 1841–1882* (Toronto: University of Toronto Press, 2018).
55 This summarizes the detailed and extensive analysis in Craven, 'Canada 1670–1935,' 196–203. The data on wage recovery below are from the same source.
56 Ibid., 175; and Craven, 'Master and Servant,' 205.
57 SLC 1834, c 2.
58 SLC 1836, c 28; SNB 1836, c 44; SNS 1841, c 50.
59 For seamen see Craven, 'Canada 1670–1935,' 183–5; and Judith Fingard, *Jack in Port: Sailortowns of Eastern Canada* (Toronto: University of Toronto Press, 1981).
60 This paragraph is based on Craven, 'Canada 1670–1935,' 203ff.

61 We are not concerned here to tell the history of unions and strikes, but it is necessary background and can be located in Eugene Forsey, *Trade Unions in Canada, 1812–1902* (Toronto: University of Toronto Press, 1982).

62 For an excellent discussion of the issue see Paul Craven, 'Labour Conspiracies in Toronto,' *Labour/Le Travail* 14 (1984): 49. See also, for the view that unions were conspiracies to restrain trade, Mark Chartrand, 'The First Canadian Trade Union Legislation: An Historical Perspective,' *Ottawa Law Review* 16 (1984): 267.

63 SNS 1864, c 11.

34. Less Favoured by Law II: Women and the Law

1 *Whibby v Walbank* (1869) 5 Nfld LR 286, cited in Constance Backhouse, 'Married Women's Property Law in Nineteenth-Century Canada,' *Law and History Review* 6 (1988): 211 at 213.

2 *Nolan v Fox* (1865) 15 UCCP 565 at 576, cited in ibid., 216–17.

3 Custody rights began to change only in the mid- to late 1860s and will be dealt with in volume 2. For custody law see Constance Backhouse, 'Shifting Patterns in Nineteenth-Century Canadian Custody Law,' in *EHCL*, vol. 2.

4 Backhouse, 'Married Women's Property Law,' 215. The most extensive discussion of equity and separate estates in British North America is in Lori Chambers, *Married Women and Property Law in Victorian Ontario* (Toronto: Osgoode Society for Canadian Legal History and University of Toronto Press, 1997), chap. 3, but it deals only with Upper Canada.

5 These examples are in Philip Girard, 'Married Women's Property, Chancery Abolition, and Insolvency Law: Law Reform in Nova Scotia 1820–1867,' in *EHCL*, 3:118.

6 See *Pemberton v O'Neill* (1851) 2 GCR 263; and *Fenton v Cross* (1858), 7 GCR 20, both cited in Backhouse, 'Married Women's Property Law,' 245, n35. For the occupations see Philip Girard and Rebecca Veinott, 'Married Women's Property Law in Nova Scotia, 1850–1910,' in Janet Guildford and Suzanne Morton, eds, *Separate Spheres: Women's Worlds in the Nineteenth-Century Maritimes* (Fredericton: Acadiensis, 1994), esp. 72–3. For a study using all reported and unreported (case files in the chancery records) cases, see Chambers, *Married Women*, chap. 3.

7 Chambers, *Married Women*, 58.

8 This section on alimony is from ibid., 17–18 and chap. 2.

9 SUC 1837, c 2, s 3.

10 *Soules v Soules* (1851) 2 GCR 299; and *Severn v Severn* (1852) 3 GCR 431, quotation at 432, both cited in Chambers, *Married Women*, 30.
11 SPC 1859, c 12, s 29.
12 This section on the early married women's property acts is based on Backhouse, 'Married Women's Property Law,' 217–30; Girard, 'Law Reform,' 83–92; Girard and Veinott, 'Married Women's Property Law'; Chambers, *Married Women*, chap. 4.
13 SNB 1851, c 24.
14 SPC 1859, c 34.
15 SPEI 1860, c 35; SVI 1859–63, c 51; SNS 1866, c 33; SN 1867, c 10, quotations from s. 2. For the failures in Nova Scotia, see Girard and Veinott, 'Married Women's Property Law,' 73–5.
16 Backhouse, 'Married Women's Property Law,' 219.
17 See, in particular, Norma Basch, *In the Eyes of the Law: Women, Marriage and Property in Nineteenth-Century New York* (Ithaca: Cornell University Press, 1982); and Richard Chused, 'Married Women's Property Law 1800–1850,' *Georgetown Law Review* 71 (1983): 1359.
18 See chapter 27 above.
19 SVI 1866, c 6. For a detailed discussion of the origins of the Vancouver Island statutes, see Chris Clarkson, *Domestic Reforms: Political Visions and Family Regulation in British Columbia, 1862–1940* (Vancouver: UBC Press, 2007), chap. 1.
20 These quotations are from Backhouse, 'Married Women's Property Law,' 223, citing the research of Mary Jane Mossman. See also for a more extensive treatment of the campaign Chambers, *Married Women*, 73ff.
21 Chambers, *Married Women*, 70.
22 *Globe*, 26 Dec. 1856, cited ibid., 71.
23 Girard and Veinott, 'Married Women's Property Law,' 68–9.
24 Quotations cited in Girard, 'Law Reform,' 86.
25 *Globe*, 10 Mar. 1859, cited in Backhouse, 'Married Women's Property Law,' 223.
26 SPC 1859, c 34, preamble.
27 *Abell v Light*, (1867) 12 NBR 97 at 100, cited in Backhouse, 'Married Women's Property Law,' 219
28 *Kraemer v Gless* (1860) 10 UCCP 470 at 472 and 475, cited ibid., 225–6.
29 Backhouse, 'Married Women's Property Law,' 225
30 Girard and Veinott, 'Married Women's Property Law,' 77.
31 (1865) 24 UCQB 552 at 559, cited in Backhouse, 'Married Women's Property Law,' 226. For other rulings, before and immediately after Confederation, see ibid., 227–30.

32 Lori Chambers, 'Married Women's Property Law Reform, Couples, and Fraud in Canada West/Ontario, 1859–1900,' in *EHCL*, vol. 11.

33 SN 1834, 2nd Sess., c 7 and 8.

34 This discussion of the tort of seduction draws on Constance Backhouse, 'The Tort of Seduction: Fathers and Daughters in Nineteenth-Century Canada,' *Dalhousie Law Journal* 10 (1986): 45; and Backhouse, *Petticoats and Prejudice: Women and Law in Nineteenth-Century Canada* (Toronto: Osgoode Society for Canadian Legal History and Women's Press, 1991), chap. 2; Patrick Brode, *Courted and Abandoned: Seduction in Canadian Law* (Toronto: Osgoode Society for Canadian Legal History and University of Toronto Press, 2002); Martha Bailey, 'Servant Girls and Upper Canada's Seduction Act, 1837–1946,' in Russell Smandych, Gordon Dodds, and Alvin Esau, eds, *Dimensions of Childhood: Essays on the History of Children and Youth in Canada* (Winnipeg: Legal Research Institute, 1991); and Bailey, 'Servant Girls and Masters: The Tort of Seduction and the Support of Bastards,' *Canadian Journal of Family Law* 10 (1991): 137; Sarah Boulby, 'Force and Fair Promise: Litigating Seduction in Nineteenth-Century Ontario' (unpublished paper, 1991).

35 SUC 1837, c 8, ss 1 and 2.

36 *Biggs v Burnham*, (1843) 1 UCQB 328 at 335–6, cited in Backhouse, 'Seduction,' 52.

37 Anna Jameson, *Winter Studies and Rambles in Upper Canada* (London, 1839), 1:154–6, cited in Bailey, 'Servant Girls and Masters,' 150. The reference to English law is to the *Poor Law Amendment Act*, 4 & 5 Will IV, c 76 (1834), which placed responsibility principally on the mother. Under the poor law in the Maritimes, fathers of illegitimate children continued to be liable for their support.

38 Boulby, 'Litigating Seduction,' esp. at 12.

39 See SPEI 1852, c 23; *McInnis v McCallum* (1854) Peter's PEI Reports 72; Backhouse, 'Seduction,' 54–5; Ian Robertson, 'James Horsfield Peters,' *DCB*.

40 Three studies do some counting and calculations of awards. Brode, *Courted and Abandoned*, appendix A, 211, found thirty-five cases between 1823 and 1849, using law reports, judges' benchbooks, and newspapers. Boulby counted trial cases by using the assize minute books of five Upper Canadian and Ontario judges between 1859 and 1879. She found sixty-seven cases in the period 1859–69 and thirty in the 1870s: Boulby, 'Litigating Seduction.' See also Backhouse, 'Seduction,' 46 and 79.

41 *Hicks v Ross* (1865), 25 UCQB 50 at 53, cited in Backhouse, 'Seduction,' 63.

42 For a number of cases stating this, see Backhouse, 'Seduction,' 64–7; and Bailey, 'Servant Girls and Masters,' 158–60.

43 See especially Boulby, 'Litigating Seduction.' See also Brode, *Courted and Abandoned*, appendix A, 211; and Backhouse, 'Seduction,' 73ff.

44 See generally Constance Backhouse, 'Pure Patriarchy: Nineteenth-Century Canadian Marriage,' *McGill Law Journal* 31 (1986): 264.

45 Chambers, *Married Women*, 18. The 1839 Act was *An Act for the Relief of John Stuart*, SPC 1841, c 72. For parliamentary divorce before and after Confederation, see John Alexander Gemmill, *The Practice of the Parliament of Canada upon Bills of Divorce* (Toronto: Carswell, 1889). As noted above in part 3, in 1773 Britain had instructed the local colonial governments not to permit private bills granting divorces, but the objection must either have been forgotten or dropped at some point.

46 SPEI 1833, c 22; SPEI 1835, c 10; Wendy Owen and Jack Bumsted, 'Divorce in a Small Province: A History of Divorce on Prince Edward Island from 1833,' *Acadiensis* 20 (1991): 86.

47 20 & 21 Vict, c 85 (1857).

48 Kim Smith-Maynard, 'Divorce in Nova Scotia, 1754–1890,' in *EHCL*, vol. 3; quotation above at 237. There were procedural changes. Courts of marriage and divorce were staffed partially with judges, thus ending the monopoly over divorce cases previously enjoyed by the lieutenant governors and councils. Nova Scotia's new arrangements were put in place in 1841, New Brunswick's in 1834. From its establishment in 1833 the Prince Edward Island court was to be presided over by the lieutenant governor or a Supreme Court judge. See SNS 1841, c 13; SNB 1834, c 30; SPEI 1833, c 22. Councillors remained involved in Nova Scotia, supplying the two additional members needed to constitute a quorum of three, until 1866 when the judge in Equity was made the sole judge of a newly named Court for Divorce and Matrimonial Causes: SNS 1866, c 13, s 2.

49 Nova Scotia divorce is discussed in Smith-Maynard, 'Divorce in Nova Scotia.' The figure given here is an estimate because of incomplete records.

50 SNS 1834, c 44.

51 There are no New Brunswick case files for the years before 1847. The one study of New Brunswick divorce found 50 cases between 1847 and 1883, an average of 1.4 cases per year, but we do not know how many of these cases were in the period prior to 1867. The incompleteness of the files also leaves it unclear how many led to successful divorces. See generally Dawn Bourque, 'Speaking of Cruelty: Women's Petitions for Divorce in Nineteenth-Century New Brunswick' (unpublished paper, ca 1995).

52 For these figures see Smith-Maynard, 'Divorce in Nova Scotia,' 259n2; Bourque, 'Speaking of Cruelty,' 4; Owen and Bumsted, 'Divorce in a Small Province,' 90–4.
53 Bourque, 'Speaking of Cruelty,' 9 and *passim*.
54 Phillip A. Buckner, 'John Gervais Bourne,' *DCB*.
55 Bettina Bradbury, *From Wife to Widow: Lives, Laws, and Politics in Nineteenth-Century Montreal* (Vancouver: UBC Press, 2011), 392–3.
56 Joseph Frémont, *Le divorce et la séparation de corps* (Quebec: A. Côté, 1886).
57 On this and what follows see Marie-Aimée Cliche, 'Les procès en séparation de corps dans la région de Montréal, 1795–1879,' *Revue d'histoire de l'Amérique française* 49 (1995): 3. The population for the Montreal judicial district is an estimate based on a population of 210,403 in 1871.
58 Separation from bed and board was dealt with in arts 186–217 CCLC.
59 On what follows see Bradbury, *Wife to Widow*, chap. 4.
60 Allan Greer, *The Patriots and the People: The Rebellion of 1837 in Rural Lower Canada* (Toronto: University of Toronto Press, 1993), 131.
61 Art 2116 CCLC. On the subsequent fate of customary dower see Bradbury, *Wife to Widow*, 138. She notes that dower created in properly drawn contracts was respected by the courts.
62 Philip Girard, 'Land Law, Liberalism and the Agrarian Ideal: British North America, 1750–1920,' in John McLaren, A.R. Buck, and Nancy E Wright, eds, *Despotic Dominion: Property Rights in British Settler Societies* (Vancouver: UBC Press, 2005).
63 Serge Gagnon, *Mariage et famille au temps de Papineau* (Sainte-Foy, QC: Presses de l'Université Laval, 1993), 109. We thank Eric Reiter for sharing the research upon which this section is based.
64 Rachel G. Fuchs, 'Seduction, Paternity and the Law in Fin de Siècle France,' *Journal of Modern History* 72 (2000): 944 at 951. Fathers might voluntarily recognize their illegitimate children but could not be forced to do so.
65 Jean-François Fournel, *Traité de la séduction, considérée dans l'ordre judiciaire* (Paris: Demonville 1781). For the law in practice see James R. Farr, *Authority and Sexuality in Early Modern Burgundy, 1550-1730* (New York: Oxford University Press 1995), chap. 4.
66 SPC 1843, c 19. Marie-Aimée Cliche found thirty-two such actions in the Quebec Superior Court between 1850 and 1859: 'Les filles-mères devant les tribunaux de Québec, 1850–1969,' *Recherches sociographiques* 32 (1991): 9.
67 (1863) 10 LCJ 177 (Sup Ct and QB).

68 (1862), 15 LCR 51 (Sup Ct and QB), quotation at 53. Justice Mondelet, dissenting, thought no damages were payable to a woman of full age.

69 Cliche, 'Les filles-mères,' 16, 21–5. Also periodic payments were notoriously difficult to enforce; it should not be assumed that the women in these cases were able to collect the child support they were awarded.

70 *Neill v Taylor* (1865) 15 LCR 102 (Sup Ct). Curiously the decision of the Court of Appeal was not reported for over twenty years. In (1887) 13 *Quebec Law Reports* 195 under the title *Taylor v Neill*, the editor noted, 'As the reversed judgment in this case is the only one reported, and still appears as settled jurisprudence, we have been requested to report this note of the judgment of the Court of Appeals, showing its reversal.'

Illustration Credits

Page 86: Reproduced courtesy of Archives nationales d'outre-mer, Aix-en-Provence. Image provided by Library and Archives Canada.
Page 87: Reproduced from Thomas Pownall, *The Administration of the Colonies* (1765).
Page 180: *History of the Canadian Peoples: Beginnings to 1867* by Margaret Conrad and Alvin Finkel (2002), Map 7.1, page 110. Reprinted with permission by Pearson Canada Inc.
Page 181: Reprinted with permission of the Publisher from *The Reluctant Land* by Cole Harris. Cartographer: Eric Leinberger. Copyright University of British Columbia Press 2008. All rights reserved by the Publisher.
Page 200: McCord Museum, Montreal.
Page 209: *Nova Scotia Gazette*, 1 September 1772.
Page 323: Fonds Marguerite Aubé, 500-1-6, Centre d'études acadiennes Anselme-Chiasson, Université de Moncton.
Page 328: Published in Benjamin Sulte, *Histoire des Canadiens-français*, vol. III (1882). Image provided courtesy of Bibliothèque et Archives nationales du Québec.
Page 459: Archives of Ontario.
Page 530: *History of the Canadian Peoples: Beginnings to 1867* by Margaret Conrad and Alvin Finkel (2002), Map 23.2, page 416. Reprinted with permission by Pearson Canada Inc.

Pages 540 and 541: Image I-68330/I-68331 courtesy of the Royal BC Museum and Archives.

Page 599: *The Tenant League of Prince Edward Island, 1864–1867: Leasehold Tenure in the New World* by Ian Ross Robertson (University of Toronto Press, 1996), page 46.

Statutory and Proclamation Index

Name Index

Topical Index

PUBLICATIONS OF THE OSGOODE SOCIETY FOR CANADIAN LEGAL HISTORY

2018 Philip Girard, Jim Phillips, and R. Blake Brown, *A History of Law in Canada, Volume One: Beginnings to 1866*
Suzanne Chiodo, *The Class Actions Controversy: The Origins and Development of the Ontario Class Proceedings Act*

2017 Constance Backhouse, *Claire L'Heureux-Dubé: A Life*
Dennis G. Molinaro, *An Exceptional Law: Section 98 and the Emergency State, 1919–1936*

2016 Lori Chambers, *A Legal History of Adoption in Ontario, 1921–2015*
Bradley Miller, *Borderline Crime: Fugitive Criminals and the Challenge of the Border, 1819–1914*
James Muir, *Law, Debt, and Merchant Power: The Civil Courts of Eighteenth-Century Halifax*

2015 Barry Wright, Eric Tucker, and Susan Binnie, eds., *Canadian State Trials, Volume IV: Security, Dissent, and the Limits of Toleration in War and Peace, 1914–1939*
David Fraser, *"Honorary Protestants": The Jewish School Question in Montreal, 1867–1997*
C. Ian Kyer, *A Thirty Years War: The Failed Public/Private Partnership that Spurred the Creation of the Toronto Transit Commission, 1891–1921*
Dale Gibson, *Law, Life, and Government at Red River: Settlement and Governance, 1812–1872*

2014 Christopher Moore, *The Court of Appeal for Ontario: Defining the Right of Appeal, 1792–2013*
Paul Craven, *Petty Justice: Low Law and the Sessions System in Charlotte County, New Brunswick, 1785–1867*
Thomas GW Telfer, *Ruin and Redemption: The Struggle for a Canadian Bankruptcy Law, 1867–1919*
Dominique Clément, *Equality Deferred: Sex Discrimination and British Columbia's Human Rights State, 1953–1984*

2013 Roy McMurtry, *Memoirs and Reflections*
Charlotte Gray, *The Massey Murder: A Maid, Her Master, and the Trial that Shocked a Nation*
C. Ian Kyer, *Lawyers, Families, and Businesses: The Shaping of a Bay Street Law Firm, Faskens 1863–1963*
G. Blaine Baker and Donald Fyson, eds., *Essays in the History of Canadian Law, Volume XI: Quebec and the Canadas*

2012 R. Blake Brown, *Arming and Disarming: A History of Gun Control in Canada*
Eric Tucker, James Muir, and Bruce Ziff, eds., *Property on Trial: Canadian Cases in Context*

Shelley Gavigan, *Hunger, Horses, and Government Men: Criminal Law on the Aboriginal Plains, 1870–1905*
Barrington Walker, ed., *The African Canadian Legal Odyssey: Historical Essays*

2011 Robert J. Sharpe, *The Lazier Murder: Prince Edward County, 1884*
Philip Girard, *Lawyers and Legal Culture in British North America: Beamish Murdoch of Halifax*
John McLaren, *Dewigged, Bothered, and Bewildered: British Colonial Judges on Trial, 1800–1900*
Lesley Erickson, *Westward Bound: Sex, Violence, the Law, and the Making of a Settler Society*

2010 Judy Fudge and Eric Tucker, eds., *Work on Trial: Canadian Labour Law Struggles*
Christopher Moore, *The British Columbia Court of Appeal: The First Hundred Years*
Frederick Vaughan, *Viscount Haldane: 'The Wicked Step-father of the Canadian Constitution'*
Barrington Walker, *Race on Trial: Black Defendants in Ontario's Criminal Courts, 1858–1958*

2009 William Kaplan, *Canadian Maverick: The Life and Times of Ivan C. Rand*
R. Blake Brown, *A Trying Question: The Jury in Nineteenth-Century Canada*
Barry Wright and Susan Binnie, eds., *Canadian State Trials, Volume III: Political Trials and Security Measures, 1840–1914*
Robert J. Sharpe, *The Last Day, the Last Hour: The Currie Libel Trial* (paperback edition with a new preface)

2008 Constance Backhouse, *Carnal Crimes: Sexual Assault Law in Canada, 1900–1975*
Jim Phillips, R. Roy McMurtry, and John T. Saywell, eds., *Essays in the History of Canadian Law, Volume X: A Tribute to Peter N. Oliver*
Greg Taylor, *The Law of the Land: The Advent of the Torrens System in Canada*
Hamar Foster, Benjamin Berger, and A.R. Buck, eds., *The Grand Experiment: Law and Legal Culture in British Settler Societies*

2007 Robert Sharpe and Patricia McMahon, *The Persons Case: The Origins and Legacy of the Fight for Legal Personhood*
Lori Chambers, *Misconceptions: Unmarried Motherhood and the Ontario Children of Unmarried Parents Act, 1921–1969*
Jonathan Swainger, ed., *A History of the Supreme Court of Alberta*
Martin Friedland, *My Life in Crime and Other Academic Adventures*

2006 Donald Fyson, *Magistrates, Police, and People: Everyday Criminal Justice in Quebec and Lower Canada, 1764–1837*
Dale Brawn, *The Court of Queen's Bench of Manitoba, 1870–1950: A Biographical History*
R.C.B. Risk, *A History of Canadian Legal Thought: Collected Essays*, edited and introduced by G. Blaine Baker and Jim Phillips
2005 Philip Girard, *Bora Laskin: Bringing Law to Life*
Christopher English, ed., *Essays in the History of Canadian Law: Volume IX – Two Islands: Newfoundland and Prince Edward Island*
Fred Kaufman, *Searching for Justice: An Autobiography*
2004 Philip Girard, Jim Phillips, and Barry Cahill, eds., *The Supreme Court of Nova Scotia, 1754–2004: From Imperial Bastion to Provincial Oracle*
Frederick Vaughan, *Aggressive in Pursuit: The Life of Justice Emmett Hall*
John D. Honsberger, *Osgoode Hall: An Illustrated History*
Constance Backhouse and Nancy Backhouse, *The Heiress versus the Establishment: Mrs Campbell's Campaign for Legal Justice*
2003 Robert Sharpe and Kent Roach, *Brian Dickson: A Judge's Journey*
Jerry Bannister, *The Rule of the Admirals: Law, Custom, and Naval Government in Newfoundland, 1699–1832*
George Finlayson, *John J. Robinette, Peerless Mentor: An Appreciation*
Peter Oliver, *The Conventional Man: The Diaries of Ontario Chief Justice Robert A. Harrison, 1856–1878*
2002 John T. Saywell, *The Lawmakers: Judicial Power and the Shaping of Canadian Federalism*
Patrick Brode, *Courted and Abandoned: Seduction in Canadian Law*
David Murray, *Colonial Justice: Justice, Morality, and Crime in the Niagara District, 1791–1849*
F. Murray Greenwood and Barry Wright, eds., *Canadian State Trials, Volume II: Rebellion and Invasion in the Canadas, 1837–1839*
2001 Ellen Anderson, *Judging Bertha Wilson: Law as Large as Life*
Judy Fudge and Eric Tucker, *Labour before the Law: The Regulation of Workers' Collective Action in Canada, 1900–1948*
Laurel Sefton MacDowell, *Renegade Lawyer: The Life of J.L. Cohen*
2000 Barry Cahill, *'The Thousandth Man': A Biography of James McGregor Stewart*
A.B. McKillop, *The Spinster and the Prophet: Florence Deeks, H.G. Wells, and the Mystery of the Purloined Past*
Beverley Boissery and F. Murray Greenwood, *Uncertain Justice: Canadian Women and Capital Punishment*
Bruce Ziff, *Unforeseen Legacies: Reuben Wells Leonard and the Leonard Foundation Trust*

1999 Constance Backhouse, *Colour-Coded: A Legal History of Racism in Canada, 1900–1950*

G. Blaine Baker and Jim Phillips, eds., *Essays in the History of Canadian Law: Volume VIII – In Honour of R.C.B. Risk*

Richard W. Pound, *Chief Justice W.R. Jackett: By the Law of the Land*

David Vanek, *Fulfilment: Memoirs of a Criminal Court Judge*

1998 Sidney Harring, *White Man's Law: Native People in Nineteenth-Century Canadian Jurisprudence*

Peter Oliver, *'Terror to Evil-Doers': Prisons and Punishments in Nineteenth-Century Ontario*

1997 James W.St.G. Walker, *'Race,' Rights and the Law in the Supreme Court of Canada: Historical Case Studies*

Lori Chambers, *Married Women and Property Law in Victorian Ontario*

Patrick Brode, *Casual Slaughters and Accidental Judgments: Canadian War Crimes and Prosecutions, 1944–1948*

Ian Bushnell, *The Federal Court of Canada: A History, 1875–1992*

1996 Carol Wilton, ed., *Essays in the History of Canadian Law: Volume VII – Inside the Law: Canadian Law Firms in Historical Perspective*

William Kaplan, *Bad Judgment: The Case of Mr Justice Leo A. Landreville*

Murray Greenwood and Barry Wright, eds., *Canadian State Trials: Volume I – Law, Politics, and Security Measures, 1608–1837*

1995 David Williams, *Just Lawyers: Seven Portraits*

Hamar Foster and John McLaren, eds., *Essays in the History of Canadian Law: Volume VI – British Columbia and the Yukon*

W.H. Morrow, ed., *Northern Justice: The Memoirs of Mr Justice William G. Morrow*

Beverley Boissery, *A Deep Sense of Wrong: The Treason, Trials, and Transportation to New South Wales of Lower Canadian Rebels after the 1838 Rebellion*

1994 Patrick Boyer, *A Passion for Justice: The Legacy of James Chalmers McRuer*

Charles Pullen, *The Life and Times of Arthur Maloney: The Last of the Tribunes*

Jim Phillips, Tina Loo, and Susan Lewthwaite, eds., *Essays in the History of Canadian Law: Volume V – Crime and Criminal Justice*

Brian Young, *The Politics of Codification: The Lower Canadian Civil Code of 1866*

1993 Greg Marquis, *Policing Canada's Century: A History of the Canadian Association of Chiefs of Police*

Murray Greenwood, *Legacies of Fear: Law and Politics in Quebec in the Era of the French Revolution*

1992 Brendan O'Brien, *Speedy Justice: The Tragic Last Voyage of His Majesty's Vessel Speedy*
Robert Fraser, ed., *Provincial Justice: Upper Canadian Legal Portraits from the Dictionary of Canadian Biography*

1991 Constance Backhouse, *Petticoats and Prejudice: Women and Law in Nineteenth-Century Canada*

1990 Philip Girard and Jim Phillips, eds., *Essays in the History of Canadian Law: Volume III – Nova Scotia*
Carol Wilton, ed., *Essays in the History of Canadian Law: Volume IV – Beyond the Law: Lawyers and Business in Canada, 1830–1930*

1989 Desmond Brown, *The Genesis of the Canadian Criminal Code of 1892*
Patrick Brode, *The Odyssey of John Anderson*

1988 Robert Sharpe, *The Last Day, the Last Hour: The Currie Libel Trial*
John D. Arnup, *Middleton: The Beloved Judge*

1987 C. Ian Kyer and Jerome Bickenbach, *The Fiercest Debate: Cecil A. Wright, the Benchers, and Legal Education in Ontario, 1923–1957*

1986 Paul Romney, *Mr Attorney: The Attorney General for Ontario in Court, Cabinet, and Legislature, 1791–1899*
Martin Friedland, *The Case of Valentine Shortis: A True Story of Crime and Politics in Canada*

1985 James Snell and Frederick Vaughan, *The Supreme Court of Canada: History of the Institution*

1984 Patrick Brode, *Sir John Beverley Robinson: Bone and Sinew of the Compact*
David Williams, *Duff: A Life in the Law*

1983 David H. Flaherty, ed., *Essays in the History of Canadian Law: Volume II*

1982 Marion MacRae and Anthony Adamson, *Cornerstones of Order: Courthouses and Town Halls of Ontario, 1784–1914*

1981 David H. Flaherty, ed., *Essays in the History of Canadian Law: Volume I*

www.ingramcontent.com/pod-product-compliance
Lightning Source LLC
LaVergne TN
LVHW020434080826
844660LV00033B/1282

9781487547462